Mark Chaves

THE GOSPEL OF JOHN

The Gospel of John

A COMMENTARY

by Rudolf Bultmann

TRANSLATED BY

G. R. Beasley-Murray, General Editor
R. W. N. Hoare and J. K. Riches

THE WESTMINSTER PRESS • Philadelphia

Translated from the 1964 printing of *Das Evangelium des Johannes* (with the Supplement of 1966) by permission of Vandenhoeck & Ruprecht, Göttingen

ISBN 0-664-20893-2

Library of Congress Catalog Card No. 70-125197

Published by The Westminster Press®
Philadelphia, Pennsylvania

9 8 7 6 5

Den alten Marburger Freunden

Contents

Sections of the Commentary
(in the order of the Gospel text)

Publisher's Note

The translation of a large and outstanding work of scholarship which has attained international reputation is a formidable undertaking. It demands not only close familiarity with and belief in the work itself but also a wide knowledge of the subject with which the work deals. We have been fortunate to get the assistance of two young scholars, John Riches and Rupert Hoare, well versed in the original language and in the subject matter. They have willingly worked under the supervision of Dr. G. R. Beasley-Murray, Principal of Spurgeon's College, London, who not only translated a considerable part of the text himself but has co-ordinated the work of his younger colleagues. To all three the publisher is deeply indebted. He would also like to thank Professor D. M. Mackinnon, who revived the publisher's enthusiasm for the project when translation difficulties seemed insuperable.

INTRODUCTION

Introduction

The German original of the present commentary does not possess any Introduction. The following Introduction was written for the English edition by Walter Schmithals. It brings together the literary and historical results of the Commentary. The questions that arise can be more intensively pursued by consulting the indices II (Literary and Historico-Critical Questions) and IV (Religio-historical Relations).

1. *The Characteristics of the Gospel of John in comparison with the Synoptic Gospels*

The Gospel of John exhibits the same literary form as the Synoptic Gospels. It covers the period from the Baptist's appearance, includes the beginning of the activity of Jesus, and extends to his death and resurrection. Galilee and Jerusalem are the scenes of the work of Jesus, as in the Synoptics. Most of the names of places and persons in John are also met with in the Synoptic tradition. The material of John, as in the Synoptic Gospels, consists of miracle stories and traditions of sayings and narratives. Not a few elements of the Synoptic tradition also appear in John. Above all mention should be made of the passion story, the account of John the Baptist (1.19–34), individual Logia (2.19; 4.44; 12.25f.; 13.16, 20; 15.20 etc.), miracle stories (4.46–54; 6.1–13) and narratives (2.13–22; 6.66–71).

Nevertheless, along with these agreements there are considerable differences.

The *style* of John manifests a more markedly Semitic character than most parts of the Synoptic tradition. Certainly that ought not to lead to the conclusion that John has been translated from an originally Aramaic composition into the Greek language, for in the editorial sections of the Gospel no translation errors can be established. The Gospel of John was undoubtedly written in Greek. But the author's Greek is dyed with a Semitic colour. Perhaps he himself was a Semite and lived in a bi-lingual area. The possibility must be taken into account that one of his sources was originally composed in Aramaic (see below).

The polemical situation manifests a considerable change from that presupposed in the Synoptic Gospels. Admittedly in John, as in them, the Jews are in continual opposition to Jesus. But they no longer appear in the concrete distinctions of Palestinian relations, but always are described simply as "the Jews," in contrast to whom Jesus and his disciples appear as non-Jews (8.17; 10.34). In the Gospel of John the Jews represent the unbelieving world generally, and in the relations of the Jews to Jesus the relations of all unbelievers to the Christian Church and its message are mirrored.

Especially noteworthy are the differences that emerge on form-critical considerations.

The collections of sayings in the Synoptic Gospels consist preponderately of isolated logia, frequently brought together, of course, to form sermonic compositions and parables. John's Gospel, on the contrary, contains continuous sermons, in which occasionally individual and originally independent logia may be found, firmly entrenched. Parables are altogether absent. Even the characteristically Johannine I-words, which often announce the theme of a great parabolic discourse (ch. 10, the Good Shepherd; ch. 15, the Vine), are not parables, but must be understood as direct statements: Jesus does not act *like* a good shepherd, and is not *like* the real Vine etc.; he is *himself* the Shepherd, the Way, the Resurrection, as he is Truth and Life.

The conversations of the Synoptic Gospels follow more or less closely the rule of rabbinic discussion or debate, the point of which forms a single saying of Jesus. John's Gospel, on the contrary, does not contain the thrust and counter-thrust of genuine discussions. These conversations are frequently developed through misunderstandings, which are sparked off by concepts or utterances of Jesus that have a double meaning (3.3ff., on being born anew; 6.27ff., the Bread of Life; 7.34, Jesus' departure)—a technique which is almost entirely foreign to the Synoptic Gospels.

The miracle stories of John are relatively closely related to those of the Synoptic Gospels, though undoubtedly they exhibit an increase in the miraculous element. Above all they have lost their formal independence; they are closely bound up with the addresses and discussions, which on their part take their motives from the miracle stories.

The narrative material, especially the passion story and the accounts of John the Baptist, has the closest contact of all with the corresponding elements in the Synoptic tradition. But even in these respects the author has more or less strongly interposed, transformed and completed them in accordance with his theological views.

In the Synoptic Gospels the editorial framework can be removed from the elements of the tradition with comparative ease. It fulfils the function chiefly of conjoining the earlier isolated elements of tradition into a chronologically and geographically ordered life-story.

In John, by contrast, the editorial comments that provide the structure are closely bound up with the narrative- and sayings-material, and in general they cannot be loosed from this structure. They no longer serve the purpose of adding together individual items of tradition, but rather support the artistic composition of the Gospel in accordance with a dominating theme.

Most striking are the differences of a theological kind. The formal peculiarities that have been enumerated are often merely the outward expression of essential differences. The individual items handed down in the Synoptic tradition, viz. the separate logia, miracle-stories, apophthegms, parables, etc., contain definite themes: they yield declarations about the sovereignty of God, the Son of man, the time of the end, the validity of the Law, the right of forgiveness of sins, ethical behaviour, missionary service, order in the community, the right sort of prayer, the use of sacraments, and many another subject. In most cases the Synoptic evangelists preserve these utterances wholly or essentially in accordance with their subject matter. They give expression to their theological aims in that they interpret the material of their tradition through selection and arrangement, abbreviation and enlargement and reformulation in the sense of their redactional theology. Tradition and redaction often stand clearly alongside each other, and in this manner the tradition, i.e. the detail of the Gospel as a whole, retains the greater importance. In contrast to this the Gospel of John fundamentally contains but a single theme: the Person of Jesus. The entire Gospel is concerned with the fact of his presence, the nature of his claim, whence he comes and whither he goes, and how men relate themselves to him. The miracles supply information about Jesus himself; the speeches are concerned with the speaker; the discussions devolve about the person of Jesus. The stories of healings on the sabbath, for example (chs. 5 and 9) do not, as in the Synoptics, demonstrate the Christian understanding of the sabbath command, but serve as occasions for discussions about the person of the miracle worker. In John the detail no longer possesses worth on its own account, but it can be understood only from the leading theme of the whole.

The formal distinctions between this Gospel and the Synoptics follow from this reorganisation and concentration of the Gospel's content—not vice versa. Because of his specific theme John leaves aside most of the Synoptic material; he treats with particularly great freedom the material of the tradition; he unhesitatingly takes over traditions that have come from outside Christianity, and carries out his redactional reconstructions on a much grander scale than the Synoptists.

The question of tradition and redaction in the Gospel of John, accordingly, must be faced, and above all the question about the sources.

2. *The Sources*

How is the relationship between the Gospel of John and the Synoptic Gospels to be explained? Did the author know one or more of the Synoptic Gospels? Did he use the traditions that lay behind the Synoptics? Or do both possibilities hold good? The question arouses sharp division. It requires a fresh investigation on the basis of modern methods and results of the research into redactional criticism.

Since Mark created the literary type of Gospel, to which John's writing also belongs, a direct or indirect acquaintance with the Gospel of Mark must surely be accepted. Such an acquaintance would also presuppose the use of the Synoptic tradition, as is particularly clear from the Passion story, but also by reason of other narratives and the sayings-tradition. That a continuous account of the Passion lay before the author must be considered as certain, for in his representation of the Passion he merely reproduces numerous accounts without making use of them for his theological ideas, e.g. the story of Peter's denial. At the same time, however, in many passages of the Passion story the Evangelist's additions can be removed on stylistic and objective grounds.

Now the author could have taken over the Passion narrative as a free, pre-Markan tradition, for it is generally acknowledged that such a narrative lay before Mark as an independent and continuous tradition; in that case one would have to presume that the same held good of the other elements that link John with the Synoptic Gospels. However that may be, no reason or possibility whatever exists for tracing the Gospel of John back to a complete Gospel writing, independent of the Synoptics and only edited by the author. But the fact that the Gospel "type" was already in existence prior to John does not prejudice the recognition that the plan and composition of the book reveals a work of the Evangelist, to whose hand also the Gospel's unified linguistic form seen in its entirety goes back.

This unity of language naturally does not exclude the use of traditions, as the material from the Synoptic tradition material, taken up by John, shows.

To these traditions, a *miracle-source* could have belonged. John recounts seven miracles of Jesus. Some of these miracles have no parallels in the Synoptic tradition, e.g. the miracle of the wine at Cana and the raising of Lazarus. In 2.11 and 4.54 the changing of the wine and the healing at Capernaum are reported as the first and second miracles, although the Evangelist in 2.23 (cp. 4.45) already speaks of various miraculous deeds of Jesus. The possibility lies to hand, therefore, of ascribing this precise enumeration to a source of (seven) miracle-stories taken over by John. This source, from which the concluding expression in 20.30 could also have been taken, is related to the Synoptic tradition, but it is recognizable by the previously mentioned heightening of the miraculous. Frequently additions of the Evangelist are clearly separable from the sections taken out of this source (cp. e.g. 4.48; 6.4, 6, 14f.).

Along with the miracle-source the author of this Gospel probably used a *source for his discourses*. The discourses of John often show in their individual sentences a peculiar poetic form, e.g.:

> He who believes on him will not be judged;
> He who does not believe is already judged (3.18).

In this typical sentence from the Johannine discourses there appears, along with the apodictic form, the antithetic parallelism, with the surprising expression "is already judged" instead of "will be judged" in the second member.

In the discourses a pattern can be more or less plainly discerned that advances in three motifs. First the Revealer presents himself and his significance; then follows the invitation to come to him; lastly the consequence of the acceptance or rejection of the Revealer is made known in promise and threat. The style and pattern of these discourses have close parallels in Gnostic revelatory writings. The Prologue most plainly of all enables us to see how the Evangelist has taken up an already existing composition and commented on it by his additions. Admittedly it is not a revelatory address that lies behind the Prologue, but a hymn. Nevertheless in the revelatory addresses comments added by the Evangelist can often be removed from his source.

The supposition lies to hand therefore that the author used a source of revelation discourses, on the basis of which he fashioned the speeches and discussions of his Gospel. The limits of this source admittedly cannot be defined with certainty. Often the question must remain open to what extent the author reproduces a source with comments, or to what extent he himself conceives the words of Jesus in accordance with the pattern of the discourses presumed for this source.

3. *The Relationship to Gnosticism*

An analysis of the discourses of John, their content, style and their sources, leads into the area of early Gnosticism and introduces the problem of the relationship in which the Gospel of John and Gnosticism stand to each other.

The Gnostic view of the world starts out from a strict cosmic dualism. Life and death, truth and falsehood, salvation and ruin of human life are anchored in the cosmos. In it the divine world of light and the demonic power of darkness stand over against one another. In the primeval time a part of the light fell into the power of the darkness. In order to be able to maintain their hold on the light, the evil powers created the world and human bodies. They divided the imprisoned being of light into mere sparks of light, and banned these parts of life to the physical world. In order to redeem and bring home this lost creature of the light, the good God of life sends the saving knowledge (Gnosis) into the world. By illuminating man as to his true origin and his true being, this knowledge bestows on him the power to return to the heavenly homeland after he puts off his body. In this connection the figure of a Redeemer is often met with, who is sent by the Father, mostly in the primeval time, to impart the knowledge. Under his word men separate themselves into the children of light, who are from above, and the children of darkness, who do not bear any soul of light in themselves. After his completed work of redemption the Redeemer ascends again and so makes a way for the elements of light that follow him.

The relationship of John's Gospel to this Gnostic view of the world is twofold.

On the one hand John manifests close contacts with the Gnostic conception of the world. The source of the discourses, which John takes over or to which he adheres, is Gnostic in outlook. It has its closest parallels in the Mandaean writings, the oldest strata of whose traditions go back to the time of primitive Christianity and to the region of Syrian Palestine. In these Mandaean revelatory addresses are also to be found parabolic sayings that characterise the Revealer as the good Shepherd, the real Vine, etc. Moreover, the Gnostic Odes of Solomon are especially closely related to the discourses of John, as are the Letters of Ignatius of Antioch, whose Christology shows itself strongly influenced by a Syrian Gnosticism. In John Jesus descends from heaven, like the Gnostic Redeemer, to bring to men the saving message, and he returns to the Father after completing his work. In face of his word light and darkness separate themselves; before him life and death are decided. He who is of the truth hears his voice; to the blind, however, the messenger of life remains hidden.

The stylistic form of the misunderstanding and the ambiguous address, that John likes to use, offers a formal correspondence to this Gnostic dualism; for the Redeemer and his word must necessarily remain incomprehensible and unrecognisable to mere men of flesh. Naturally the antithetic reasoning of the Gospel of John also goes back to the dualistic thinking of Gnosticism, and often directly to Gnostic terminology.

The influence of pre-Christian Gnosticism can also be discerned in Philo of Alexandria, and particularly in speculations of late Judaism, e.g. the wisdom myth, as well as in the Qumran writings. Notable contacts between these complexes of tradition and the Gospel of John are therefore discernible. Nevertheless one should not fall into the error of attributing the Gnosticising tendencies of John's Gospel to the influences of Alexandrian religious philosophy or the sects of late Judaism. John is directly dependent on Gnostic traditions, and he uses these traditions in far greater measure than Philo and the other late Jewish writers.

The second characteristic relationship of the Gospel of John to Gnosticism consists in the fact that in his Gnostic form a pointed anti-Gnostic theology is expressed. John knows no cosmic dualism. Therefore in John man is not seen dualistically. Flesh and spirit do not stand opposed as substances of the demonic and divine realms. Rather it is stressed, with all sharpness, that the Redeemer has become *flesh*, and shows his glory precisely as the One made flesh. Man's lostness in the world is not the lost condition of a heavenly substance in the power of darkness, but the sinful turning of the creature from the Creator. In place of cosmic dualism steps a dualism of decision: life and death are not determined from all time on natural grounds, but depend on the decision of faith and of unbelief. The Redeemer therefore does not bring a knowledge that illuminates men as to their true nature; rather he reveals to man his sin, and sets him before the decision to live on the basis of the created world or from the Creator.

John thus uses the language current in Gnostic circles to give expression to the Christian understanding of faith. The conclusion perhaps could be drawn from this that he lays worth on convincing adherents of Gnostic circles as to the truth of the Gospel.

4. *The Relationship to Paul*

Paul also shows himself influenced by the language and conceptual world of Gnosticism. His Christology is strongly influenced by the Gnostic Redeemer-myth. Like John he finds himself in debate with adherents of Gnosticism. The relationship of John and Paul thereby suggested goes beyond the limits imposed by the common sphere of Hellenistic Christianity.

Admittedly the essential theological agreement is still more comprehensive. John and Paul interpret the coming of Jesus as eschatological event, and therefore they understand their time as the period of salvation. For both salvation consists in the fact that in Christ God has given to sinful men the possibility of living from God instead of from the world, and thereby for them to make a decision for life. Both oppose Gnostic dualism with faith in the Creator, and both replace the Gnostic ideas of substance with the historical dialectic of judgment and grace.

Now these common features do not rest on the dependence of John on Paul, as has often been imagined. In John no discussion about the Law is to be found. The concept of the "righteousness of God" is lacking in him. In his Gospel the Jews are not the representatives of Jewish orthodoxy, as they are in the Synoptic Gospels and Paul, but representatives of the unbelieving world. Paul's scheme of salvation history will be sought for in vain in John; proof from Scripture occurs seldom; the pair of contrasts "flesh-spirit" falls into the background; the apocalyptic expectation of the future, to which Paul holds fast, has been excluded by John.

In reality Paul and John, independently of one another and in their respective concrete situations, give clear expression to the early Christian understanding of time and existence that in its essentials was already in existence before both.

5. *The Integrity of the Gospel*

Problems of textual criticism significant for the exposition of the Gospel of John are to be found relatively seldom (cp. e.g. on 1.13, 18, 41; 3.34; 6.69; 7.53–8.11; 14.3). In contrast to this there are reasons for doubting whether the Gospel itself has found entrance into the ecclesiastical tradition in the form intended by the author. Two problems require discussion.

The thesis has been represented, occasionally even in very early times but strongly from the beginning of this century, that the original order of the text has been disturbed, through an interchange of leaves or by some other means. For example Jn. 6.1 reports a journey of Jesus to the other bank of Lake Gennesaret, although chapter 5 is set in Jerusalem: 7.15–24 harks back directly to the sabbath healing that lies far off in chapter 5. 14.30f. leads on directly to the Passion story in ch. 18, while the discourse continues in ch. 15. From these and many other examples it must be presumed that the present order of our Gospel is not derived from the author. The thesis that the author himself extended and edited his Gospel in various ways, but did not bring to completion the last edition, has to take account of too many improbabilities. Attempts to restore an original order admittedly remain hypothetical, but they are necessary. How the present (lack of) order came about cannot be determined with certainty. It is not enough to reckon with a simple exchange of the pages of a loose codex, for the sections that appear to demand a change of position are of unequal length. The assumption lies closest to hand that the Gospel of John was edited from the author's literary remains on the basis of separate manuscript pages, left without order. In any case the present form of our Gospel is due to the work of a redactor.

With this observation the second problem emerges: Are we to attribute not only the present order but also particular sections of the Gospel to the hand of the redactor? The question must be answered in the affirmative. Precisely such a redaction of John's Gospel is convincingly demonstrated by ch. 21; for the original Gospel concluded with 20.30.f, and it was subsequently extended by ch. 21, which exhibits in its details many differences from chs. 1–20, as the exposition will show.

If ch. 21 betrays the redactional influence, the further question must be raised whether other parts of the Gospel are due to the redactor. This question also must be answered in the affirmative. An example is the passages that relate to the Lord's Supper and baptism, i.e. 6.51b–58 and 19.34b–35. Sentences which express an apocalyptic expectation of the future are also due to the redactor, i.e. 5.28f.; 6.39, 40, 44; (12.48). And lastly, individual explanatory glosses that clearly break into the context should be viewed as editorial, e.g. 3.24; 4.2; 18.9, 32.

The exposition will go into all these passages more fully. The tendency of the redaction referred to shows features that heighten ecclesiastical interests. Since the redaction additions are current in all manuscripts, it may be assumed that the redactor and the editor of the Gospel, to whom we owe its present order, are identical.

6. *Authorship, Time and Place of Composition*

We are not in a position to say anything definite about the author or about the redactor. The Gospel does not name either person, and the superscription of the Gospel comes from a later time. From 21.24f. (cp. 19.35) we gather that the redactor holds the author to be an eye-witness of the life of Jesus. He identifies him with the enigmatic figure of the Beloved Disciple, mentioned in 13.23, 19.26f., 20.2–10 (hardly in 18.15f.), and in the redactional appendix 21. 20–23 it is assumed that the disciple has died. But the Gospel itself does not mention this identification (see on 13.30).

Later the Beloved Disciple was equated with John, the son of Zebedee and brother of James, a member of the circle of the Twelve, and it was claimed that he died in advanced age in Ephesus. The first clear testimony to this tradition is offered by Irenaeus III, 1.2. But John the son of Zebedee must have been killed by the Jews very early, as Mk. 10.39 shows, and as is indicated by several witnesses of the ancient Church. Moreover the Gospel itself makes no claim to have been written by an eye-witness. And in no way does it give occasion to presume that an eye-witness lies behind it, rather it completely contradicts such an assumption.

Now the much discussed testimony of Papias (in Eusebius, H.E.III, 39.3f.) refers not only to John the son of Zebedee but also to the Presbyter John, who may have written the Book of Revelation. Probably Irenaeus and the whole later tradition confused the Ephesian Presbyter with the son of Zebedee of the same name. Prior to Irenaeus, then, the Presbyter John could have been regarded as the author of the Fourth Gospel, and possibly this was already the view of the redactor of the Gospel. But this assumption, of course, is quite uncertain, and it is no longer possible to demonstrate the correctness of such an opinion. The author remains unknown to us.

Before Irenaeus there is no certain attestation for the use of John's Gospel by any author belonging to the Church; for it is improbable that Papias and Justin knew it, and without question Ignatius did not make use of it. Admittedly in the papyrus P. 52 we possess a testimony to the fact that our Gospel was known in Egypt in the first half of the second century. We cannot therefore put the composition and redaction beyond about 120 A.D., and we should define the period for the composition and redactional edition of the Gospel as about 80–120 A.D.—the processes could have been relatively distant from one another.

The Semitic style of the author and the relationship of the Gospel to the Gnostic revelation discourses, the letters of Ignatius of Antioch and the Odes of Solomon, strongly supports the supposition that the author of the Fourth Gospel originated from the area of Syria. Above all it must be said that nothing in the Gospel points to its origin in Egypt or Asia Minor.

1. 1-18: The Prologue

1. *A preliminary glance* tells us that 1.1–18 forms a whole, and has been placed at the beginning of the Gospel as a kind of introduction. A remarkable introduction, certainly! For the Prologue is no introduction or foreword in the usual sense of the words. There is no indication in it of the content or structure of what follows; nor are we told why the author has set himself his task, as we are, for instance, in the preface to the Gospel of Luke. On the contrary the section forms a whole, and is complete in itself; it is not necessary for anything to follow.[1] And does this introduction give the reader the key for the understanding of the Gospel? It is far more a mystery itself, and is fully comprehensible only to the man who knows the whole Gospel. It is only when the circle is complete, and the "Son" has returned to the δόξα which the love of the "Father" has prepared for him πρὸ καταβολῆς κόσμου (17.24), only when the reader has been led back out of the temporal sphere into the eternal, that he can judge conclusively in what sense the Prologue leads out of the eternal into the temporal.

And yet the Prologue is an introduction—in the sense of being an *overture*,[2] leading the reader out of the commonplace into a new and strange world of sounds and figures, and singling out particular motifs from the action that is now to be unfolded. He cannot yet fully understand them, but because they are half comprehensible, half mysterious, they arouse the tension, and awaken the *question* which is essential if he is to understand what is going to be said. The concepts ζωή and φῶς, δόξα and ἀλήθεια are the kind of motifs for which the reader brings with him a certain prior understanding; but he still has to learn how to understand them authentically. The antithesis φῶς-σκότος, the negatives οὐ κατέλαβεν, οὐκ ἔγνω, οὐ παρέλαβον are the kind of motifs, which together with their opposites ὅσοι δε ἔλαβον,

---

[1] This impression is itself a motive for the attempts to dispute that the Prologue was originally part of the Gospel (Ad. Harnack ZThK 2 (1892), 189–231; so too British scholars, (see Carpenter 290). That it was so is denied mainly on the grounds that the concept of the Logos only occurs in the Prologue, and is not used elsewhere in the Gospel as a title of Jesus, and that the Logos doctrine of the Prologue is foreign to the rest of the Gospel. This conclusion fails to recognize: 1) the fact that the Prologue is not itself a literary whole, but clearly betrays the editorial hand of the Evangelist; 2) that the Logos concept of the Prologue does not have its origin in the philosophical tradition of Hellenism, but in mythology; 3) that the "Logos doctrine" of the Prologue gives expression to the idea of revelation which dominates the whole Gospel; 4) that the language of the Prologue is the same as that of the discourses of the Gospel itself. On each point, see below.

[2] Thus Htm.; so too Cl. R. Bowen (JBL 49, 1930, 298), who not only sees the Prologue in a loose sense as an overture, but regards it strictly as such, because he understands the whole Gospel as a kind of drama.

ἐθεασάμεθα and ἐλάβομεν, at once give the reader an intimation of their meaning, but this has still to grow to full clarity of vision.[1]

2. *The literary character of the Prologue.* At first sight one would call the Prologue *myth*, judging by its subject-matter. For it speaks of a divine being, his life and his destiny. But the myth is not presented in narrative or speculative form; for then the identity of the speaker, which is in fact so clearly expressed in the ἐν ἡμῖν, ἐθεασάμεθα, ἐλάβομεν, would be without importance. And the listener? He is not addressed at all. Who is it who is being addressed? In one sense, no one. There is no differentiation between author and reader, as is the case in I John 1.1–4; rather, just as there the distinction is withdrawn in a first person plural that embraces speaker and listener, so here from the beginning everything stands under this all-embracing "We". It is the community that is speaking! And in what way? In its form the Prologue is a piece of *cultic-liturgical poetry*, oscillating between the language of revelation and confession. On the one side, as a revelation-discourse, the Naassene Hymn provides a parallel[2]; it too starts with the very beginning of all things, and recounts the fate of the soul in the world, and then describes how Jesus asks the Father to send him down in order to bring the Gnosis to the soul. On the other hand, in the style of a confession, the 7th Ode of Solomon sings of how the son of God became man, and took human nature, in order to be a bearer of revelation; and this the singer extols as the grace which he has experienced, and finally calls upon the choir of the community to praise him who "allows himself to be seen". In hymnic form the 12th Ode praises the "Word": it goes forth from the Highest, holds sway through the whole Cosmos, and has taken its dwelling in men; and the song concludes, that those are blessed

> "who by means thereof [i.e. of the Word] have understood everything and have known the Lord in his truth."[3]

Rather differently again in 33rd Ode, which also describes the "descent" of "Grace"; but here the description of grace turns into its proclamation, in which the hearer is promised:

---

[1] Hosk. 137. "The Prologue ... is not so much a preface to the Gospel as a summary of it". Clavier: R. H. Ph. rel. (1955) "le Prologue est la clé de l'évangile ou, si l'on veut, la génératrice du mouvement."

[2] Hippol. El. V 10, 2 p. 102, 23ff. Wendl.

[3] The double theme,—revelation and believing community,—determines the arrangement of a number of the Od. Sal., with differing variations. The 6th Ode (after the introduction, vv. 1–5) consists of: a) a confession of the community (vv. 6–7), b) a figurative portrayal of the revelation (vv. 8–12), c) a declaration of the blessedness of the community (vv. 13–18). The 7th Ode (after the introduction vv. 1–2): a) a portrayal of the revelation (vv. 3–17); b) the calling of the community to worship; (vv. 18–25). The 12th Ode (after the introduction vv. 1–3): a) portrayal of the revelation (vv. 4–12), b) a declaration of the blessedness of the community v. 13, cp. Ode 24 where the mythological portrayal of the revelation in verses 1–13 is followed in verse 14 by the brief characterisation of the community as "those who have known him ..." (cp. John 1.12). Similarly, Ode 30: vv. 1–6, invitation to the source of the water of life; v. 7, declaration of the blessedness of the believers. (English version by Rendel Harris: The Odes and Psalms of Solomon, Cambridge 1909).

"And I will enter in to you,
and will bring you forth from perdition."

The parallels show that, taken as a whole, the Prologue is the hymn of a community which gratefully reveres the secret of the revelation that has been given to it.

The *form* of the Prologue is not loose or haphazard, but rigid and even minor details are governed by strict rules.[1] The construction is similar to that of the Odes of Solomon; each couplet is made up of two short sentences. Sometimes both parts of the couplet express one thought (vv. 9, 12, 14b); sometimes the second completes and develops the first (vv. 1, 4, 14a, 16); sometimes the two parts stand together in parallelism (v. 3), or in antithesis (vv. 5, 10, 11). This form is not foreign to semitic poetry,[2] and recurs often in the discourses of the Gospel; but in the Prologue it is developed further by means of a special artistic device. In each sentence two words normally carry the emphasis, and the second of these stressed words often recurs as the first word emphasised in the next sentence. This is not only the case with the two parts of a couplet; as occasion offers, single verses are also joined together in this way,[3] and the result is a kind of chain-locking of the sentences, e.g.:

V.1 ἐν ἀρχῇ ἦν ὁ λόγος
καὶ ὁ λόγος ἦν πρὸς τὸν θεόν.
καὶ θεὸς ἦν ὁ λόγος.
. . . . .

Vv.4f.: ἐν αὐτῷ ζωὴ ἦν,
καὶ ἡ ζωὴ ἦν τὸ φῶς τῶν ἀνθρώπων.
καὶ τὸ φῶς ἐν τῇ σκοτίᾳ φαίνει
καὶ ἡ σκοτία αὐτὸ οὐ κατέλαβεν.

In the same way verses 9 and 10 are joined together by the key-word κόσμος, v. 11a and b by the concept ἴδιος, vv. 11 and 12 by the concept λαμβάνειν, v. 14a and b by δόξα, vv. 14b and 16 by πλήρης.[4] Now admittedly this pattern does not hold good throughout the Prologue without alteration; if one tries to read it, with the verse rhythm set out above in mind, verses 6–8, 13, 15, stand out as interruptions. But these verses also conflict with the character of the whole, as a hymn of the community praising the revelation; they are partly prose narrative with a clearly polemical purpose, (vv. 6–8, 15), and partly

---

[1] The attempt by N. W. Lund (AThR 13 (1931), 41–46) to expound the structure of the Prologue (leaving out v. 6–8, 15) by means of the principle of Chiasmus, is not convincing.

[2] The synonymous and synthetic Par. membr., so characteristic of semitic poetry, is missing: it often occurs in the Od.Sal., although it is seldom dominant there, (as in Od. 14. 16).

[3] This artistic form occurs occasionally in the Psalms of the O.T. (29.5; 93.3; 96.13; in particular, 121; cp. Burney 42); it is esp. developed in the Mandaean poetry, where the second half-verse frequently appears as the first section of the following verse. Cp. Ed. Schweizer, 45; Kundsin, Char. u. Urspr. 259; also M. Dibelius, Der Brief des Jakobus (Meyers Komm.) 92f.; Becker 34.

[4] With regard to v. 3/4 see below.

have the character of a dogmatic definition (v. 13). This brings us to the critical analysis.

3. *Literary-critical analysis.*[1] The problem raised by the Prologue's textual structure leads us to undertake a critical analysis of it. Since verse 14 reports the incarnation of the Logos, the subject of what has preceded must be the pre-existing Logos. But can it be said of the latter that εἰς τὰ ἴδια ἦλθεν (v. 11)? This gave rise to the old dispute of the exegetes: how far does the Prologue speak of the pre-existent Logos, and from which verse does it begin to speak of his appearance in the flesh?[2] The question is quickly answered when one sees that there lies at the basis of the Prologue a source document to which the Evangelist has added his own comments.[3] In the first place vv. 6–8, 15, which treat of the Baptist, belong to these comments. According to the order of the text as we have it, the Baptist who speaks in v. 15, is still speaking in v. 16; he cannot strictly do this, because the ἡμεῖς of v. 16 must be those of v. 14.[4] V. 15 breaks the continuity and separates the connecting words πλήρης and ἐκ τοῦ πληρώματος: it has been inserted. The same is true of vv. 6–8. V. 9 must follow v. 5.[5] If vv. 6–8 were originally in the text, vv. 9–13 would have to refer to them in such a way as to state that in spite of this witness the Logos found no faith. What is said however is: Although the world was made by the Logos, and belonged to him ...; i.e. reference is made to v. 3f.[6]

These insertions are not to be eliminated as interpolations: they are the Evangelist's own comments (the ancient world has no knowledge of notes

---

[1] Cp. Eucharist. II 3. The analysis given there is developed further here. Particular points will be further substantiated in what follows. Wik. and Schlier take this view. I am as little able to regard Goodwin's scepticism over a division of sources in the 4th Gospel as justified, as I can Barrett's argumentation against it.

[2] Sp., Zn. and L. take v. 4 as the beginning of the ref. to the incarnate Logos: B. Weiss, v. 5. According to Htm., v. 9 tells of the coming of the Logos into the world, and vv. 10f. portray the tragic side of the life of Jesus. So also Bd. and Bl.; undecided, Ho., Harnack, Br.—Cp. Eucharist. II 4f. and cp. Howard, Christianity 44ff. 51f.

[3] One has to suppose that in oral recitation the "comments" would be distinguishable by the tone of the speaker.

[4] This difficulty caused Priestley—as early as 1769—to move v. 15 and place it in front of v. 19 (Carpenter 333, 2). D. H. Müller, SAWien 1909, 2 wants to place v. 15 and 16 before v. 19.

[5] Thus Chr. H. Weise, already: Die Evangelienfrage 1856, 113. Cp. Wellh. 8. in vv. 6–8 the Baptist "is mentioned ad vocem τὸ φῶς—because he is in fact not the light." Wdt. I, 109 correctly stresses the offence given by mentioning the name of the Baptist, before that of Jesus.

[6] It will become evident, apart from this, (see below) that in v. 9 τὸ φῶς is not subject but predicate; the subject of ἦν τὸ φῶς is to be taken from vv. 1–5 (Wellh.; Goguel, J.-B. 77). Another way of producing a uniform movement of thought is to place vv. 6–8, together with v. 15, in front of v. 19 (cp. Carpenter 333, 2)—or, (Hirsch) without v. 15. This breaks down because vv. 6–8 were clearly intended to provide an antithesis to the section vv. 4ff and 9. Sp.'s opinion that vv. 6–8 form the beginning of the original Gospel is fantastic; cp. G.A. v.d. Bergh van Eysinga, NthT 23 (1934), 105–123.—The attempt to save the original unity of the text by appeal to a confusion possible in a mystic (Ed. Meyer I, 314ff.; H. Leisegang, Pneuma Hagion 1922, 55ff.) shows false ideas about the logic of mystical thinking —quite apart from the question whether the Evangelist is a mystic.

placed under the text), as is confirmed by the way he works throughout the Gospel.[1] *It goes without saying that the exegesis must expound the complete text*, and the critical analysis is the servant of this exposition. The case is only otherwise where glosses of a secondary redaction occur.[2]

V. 12c (τοῖς πιστεύουσιν κτλ.) also belongs to the exegetical comments of the author, as also v. 13, an interpretation of the notion τέκνα θεοῦ (v. 12b) which disturbs the rhythm of the hymn.[3] So does v. 17 (an exegetical gloss on v. 16), which mentions the name Ἰησοῦς Χριστός, suppressed until now, abruptly and without any introduction[4] and makes use of the (Pauline) antithesis νόμος-χάρις, which is otherwise foreign to the Gospel. Finally v. 18 is probably to be regarded as an addition of the author's—on stylistic grounds (see below). One must, of course, reckon with the possibility of other small corrections.

It is concluded, therefore, that the Evangelist has made a cultic community hymn the basis for the Prologue, and has developed it with his own comments.[5] It is further clear that in vv. 1–5, 9–12 *the source* spoke of the pre-existent Logos, and in vv. 5, 11f. it described his fruitless or almost fruitless effect as Revealer in this form, before going on to tell of his incarnation in v. 14. It is also clear, however, that *the Evangelist* wants to regard the text from v. 5 onwards as referring to the Incarnate Logos. For it is only because he found in the words τὸ φῶς ἐν τῇ σκοτίᾳ φαίνει κτλ. an expression of the revelation given by the historical Jesus, that he is able to introduce the Baptist at this point as the witness to the light.[6]

The *motive* for the insertion of vv. 6–8, 15 is clear from their polemical character. For their purpose is not only the positive one of proclaiming the Baptist as witness for Jesus; it is also polemical: to dispute the claim that the Baptist has the authority of Revealer.[7] This authority must therefore have

[1] Cp. also my analysis of I Joh. in Festg. Ad. Jül. 138–158. Omodeo is particularly sensitive to the changes of style within the Prologue, but nevertheless rejects a lit.-crit. analysis into different sources, and explains the changes of style in terms of the dramatic structure of the liturgy, in which lyrical and didactic parts are intertwined (Mistica 50ff.).

[2] The grounds for holding that the Gospel in its present state is not as the Evangelist wrote it, but is the product of a redaction, are: 1) that disorders occur in the text; 2) that ch. 21 is an appendix of the editor (or editors). Some glosses of this edition can be established here and there with more or less certainty.—D. H. Müller (op. cit. 2) leaves it open whether the "historical glosses (vv. 6–8 and 15–16) originate from the author himself", or are later.

[3] Cp. Edg. Hennecke, Congrés d'Histoire du Christianisme I, 1928, 209.

[4] 17.3 is also an exegetical gloss;—the only other place in the Gospel where the phrase 'I. Χρ. occurs.

[5] It will become evident that this procedure of the Evangelist is not limited to the Prologue; the underlying source there stems rather from a collection of "Revelation-discourses", which are to be thought of as similar to the Od. Sal., and which the Evangelist has made the basis of the Jesus-discourses in the Gospel. Similarly, Grant 209, 220f., who supposes, that the song is a composition of the Evangelist himself, from his pre-Christian period.—Schlier too (275f) believes that a hymn to the Logos (a cultic-liturgical composition) lies at the basis of the Prologue.

[6] Dodd wants to take vv. 5, 9–12 as referring in the first place to the pre-existent Logos; but he admits that vv. 9–12 can be understood of the incarnate Logos.

[7] So correctly, W. Baldensperger, Der Prolog des vierten Evgs., 1898.

been attributed by the Baptist sect to their master[1]; they saw in him the φῶς, and thus also the pre-existent Logos become flesh. This suggests that the source-text was *a hymn of the Baptist-Community*. By referring it to Jesus, the Evangelist would then have been acting in a way similar to that of the Church Fathers, who saw a prophecy of Jesus Christ in the 4th Eclogue of Vergil. There is no difficulty in this conjecture, if one may suppose that the Evangelist once belonged to the Baptist community, until his eyes were opened to perceive that not John, but Jesus was the Revealer sent by God. For without doubt the narrative I. 35–51 bears witness to the fact that one section of the disciples of the Baptist went over to the Christian community; and must we not therefore assume that Baptist tradition was taken over by the Christians?[2]

The hypothesis, advocated primarily by Burney, that the Johannine Gospel is a work translated in its entirety *from Aramaic into Greek*,[3] can only be maintained, in my opinion, in respect of the source underlying the Prologue and the Jesus-discourses in the Gospel.[4] It will be necessary to consider this question at the appropriate places in the exegesis that follows.[5]

---

[1] The rivalry between the disciples of Jesus and those of the Baptist is already reflected in the synoptic tradition (cp. Gesch. d. Synopt. Tr. 2nd ed. 22. 177–179. 261f.=Hist. of the Syn. Trad. 19, 164–66, 246), and is attested by Acts 18.25f.; 19. 1–7. Cp. M. Dibelius, Die urchristliche Überlieferung von Joh. d. Täufer 1911; M. Goguel, Jean-Baptiste 1928; P. Guemin, Y-a-t-il un conflit entre Jean-Baptiste et Jésus? 1933. Rud. Meyer, Der Prophet aus Galiläa 1940, 96; D. Cullmann, Coniect. Neotest. XI (1947) 26–32.—The traces that the disciples of John the Baptist held their master to be the Messiah, and—at what point?—to be the pre-existent and incarnate Logos, have almost disappeared. They are found (Lk. 3.15?) in the Ps. Clem. Rec. I. 54. 60, in Ephraem ev. exp. ed. Moes. 288, to which Baldensperger (op. cit. 138) has already called attention, and in the medieval heresy-documents (Ign. Döllinger, Beitr. zur Sektengesch. des Mittelalters I 1890, 154. 169. 190; in addition the relevant Documents: II 34. 65. 90. 155. 267. 283. 294. 325. 375.). The Johannine parts of the Mandaean writings are also a witness to this, even if they belong to a later stage.—Cp. R. Reitzenstein, Das mand. Buch des Herrn der Grösse (S. A. Heidelberg 1919, 62, 2;); Das iran. Erlösungsmyst. 1921, 125, ZNTW 26 (1927) 48, 64; Die Vorgeschichte der christl. Taufe 1929, 60; M. Goguel, J.-B. 105ff.—It is not surprising, in the sphere of syncretistic Baptist-belief, that the Baptist sect assimilated Gnostic speculations about the heavenly redeemer become man. Schlatter too (Der Evglist Joh. 13) finds it conceivable that Gnostic piety was attracted to the Baptist.—Cp. Br., additional note on 1.7.

[2] This was moreover without doubt the case; the history of the Baptist's birth in Lk. I (and also the history of his death, Mk. 6.14–29), certainly stems from Baptist tradition. Cp. Geschicht. der Synopt. Tr. 2nd ed. 320f., 328f.=Hist. of the Syn. Trad., 294f., 301f.; Goguel, J.-B. 69–75. For further discussion see on 1.6–8 (48f.), on 35–51 (97f.), on 3.29 (173f.).

[3] C. F. Burney: The Aramaic Origin of the Fourth Gospel, 1922; cp. R. Bultmann: Die christl. Welt 41 (1927), 570f., and the full investigation by M. Goguel, Rev. H. Ph. rel. 3 (1923), 373–382. The question whether the Joh. Gospel has been tr. from Aramaic is answered in the negative by J. Bonsirven, Biblica 30 (1949), 405–432, and by W. F. Albright, The Archeology of Palestine, 1949 (238–248) and in The Background of the N.T. and its Eschatology (Festschr. for C. H. Dodd) 1956, 154f. On the other side, Black regards it as probable that an Aramaic source has been used in the Jesus-discourses (as also in the words of the Baptist in ch. 3).

[4] See page 21, note 1: cp. also Black: page 43 and passim.

[5] See particularly, on 1.9.

A.1. 1–4: The Pre-temporal Existence of the Logos

a) His Relation to God: 1.1–2

ἐν ἀρχῇ ἦν ὁ Λόγος
καὶ ὁ Λόγος ἦν πρὸς τὸν θεόν.
καὶ θεὸς ἦν ὁ Λόγος
οὗτος ἦν ἐν ἀρχῇ πρὸς τὸν θεόν.[1]

Four statements are made about the Logos in the solemn tones of the hymn. They presuppose that the figure of the Logos is well known. No prior statement has to be made that a Logos exists at all,[2] nor is the term defined by any attribute. It is regarded as self-explanatory within the bounds of the community from which the hymn originates; and that is also true for the Evangelist who takes it over. For us, of course, the identity of the Logos will become clear only in the light of what is said about him. And the first thing we see is that he is a divine figure, at once Creator and Revealer. But it is here that the mystery lies! For is he not thereby designated as God himself? For he was ἐν ἀρχῇ. And in fact it is said of him: θεὸς ἦν ὁ λόγος! And yet he is not God himself; for it is also said of him: ἦν πρὸς τὸν θεόν! He is spoken of as a person, in the language of mythology. But is he really to be thought of as a real person? Or has the myth become a picture, and is the Λόγος a personification of the power of God? The Being of God personified, with regard to its activity in the world? The comprehensive term, as it were, for the divine powers that are active in the world? Does not the name Λόγος, borne by this mysterious figure, require some such interpretation? Can the term "Word" or "Reason" denote anything other than a mode of divine manifestation, or a divine law?[3] Furthermore the σὰρξ ἐγένετο would not stand in the way of this: for it would make good sense to

---

[1] For the structure of the verse see page 15. In the first three half-verses the emphasis is carried by a pair of words, the second of which recurs as the first stressed word of the following half-verse. For v. 2, see below.

[2] How differently, e.g. C. Herm. 1.9; 12.1!

[3] Heraclitus had spoken of the λόγος in this way—(H. Diels, Die Fragmente der Vorsokratiker I. 5th ed., 1934, 150f., Fr. 1 and 2), without doubt influenced by mythology, even if the mythological language is greatly weakened by him. Ed. Norden, Antike Kunstprosa, 2nd ed. 1909, II 473, 1, wanted originally to trace the Joh. prologue back to the beginning of the work of Heraclitus, but then came to see in Agnostos Theos 1913, 348 f. "the formal language of Hellenistic mysticism" as the source, under the influence of Reitzenstein.—In any case one cannot simply say with Schl.: "The comparison of the Word with things or powers is foreign to the passage; for it speaks of God." This only obscures the problem; for the question is exactly this: In what way does it speak of God?

say that the fullness of the divine being achieved tangible form in a historical person.

And yet "Consider well that line, the first you see,
That your pen may not write too hastily."[1]

The intention of the text cannot be unravelled by guessing or by a Faustian speculation. Two things are needed for the interpretation: firstly, a view of the whole, and secondly, knowledge of the tradition out of which the assertions of the text have grown.[2] And the exegesis has as its first task to discover what *possible forms of expression were open to the author; the possibilities being those he has inherited with the tradition in which he stands*. What the author intends to say here and now, is of course not simply to be deduced from these possibilities: but they have given a particular direction to what he intends to say, and have imposed particular limits; thus a review of the tradition must be the preliminary for understanding the text.

It would be hard for the Evangelist to begin his work with ἐν ἀρχῇ, without thinking of the בְּרֵאשִׁית of Gen. 1.1. Although there is no mention of the Word of God as a substantive in Gen. 1, the creation is attributed to God's word by means of the declaration, "And God said". Is the Logos therefore to be understood in terms of the *O.T. tradition of the Word of God*?

In the O.T. the Word of God is his Word of power, which, in being uttered, is active as event. God's word is God's deed, and his deed is his word; that is, he acts through his word, and he speaks in his action, and it is man whom he addresses. His word is 1) his sovereign rule in nature and history, in so far as it is comprehensible to man and "speaks" to him, that is, demands something of him; and in truth it demands, in the first place, that he become aware of his humanity before God the Creator, place his trust in God as Creator, and praise him.[3] God's Word in nature and history is not therefore the essence of a system of cosmic laws, such as the Stoic Logos—the meaning of which can be understood by itself, and which serves as a principle for comprehending the unity of the cosmic process. God's Word is 2) his authoritative command, uttered by men (priests and prophets) to men, telling

---

[1] Faust: Goethe: I. l. 1230–1231 tr. George Madison Priest. Great Books of the Western World. No. 47.: Encycl. Britann. Inc. 1952.

[2] In my "Untersuchungen zum Johannes Evangelium" in ZNTW I intend to treat of the Λόγος (among other subjects); I refer provisionally to my article "Der Begriff des Wortes Gottes im N.T." in Gl. und Verstehen I 268–293. As regards the O.T. there, see pages 268ff. Further: O. Grether: Name und Wort Gottes im A.T. 1934; Moore I. 415f.; Lor. Dürr, die Wertung des göttl. Wortes im A. T. und im antiken Orient (Mitteil. d. vorderasiat.—äg. Ges. 42, 1) 1938; R. Asting, Die Verkündigung des Wortes im Urchristentum 1939, 15ff.

[3] Cp. e.g. Ps. 29; 33; 145; 147; Is. 40.8; 55.11.

man what he should do.[1] Here again it is not the essence of ethical demands, to be understood rationally in the light of a principle as a uniform law of morality. In both cases God's Word is not the essence of something that has timeless significance, but is address, which takes place; it is a temporal event, and as such the revelation of God as Creator and Lord.

The Λόγος of Jn. 1.1 cannot therefore be understood on the basis of the O.T.: for the Λόγος here is not an event recurring within the temporal world, but is eternal being, existent with God from the very beginning. This being so, the only thing that could be designated simply his "Word" would be God's revelatory will, in so far as it stands behind, and works in, all the individual "words" of God. Even if our view of the Gospel as a whole could corroborate this interpretation, what remains inexplicable in terms of the O.T., is the fact that the Prologue does not refer to "the Word of God", but speaks simply of the *Word*[2]; it takes the proper name or title ὁ Λόγος as given.

Furthermore, what is said about the working of the Logos before his incarnation cannot be understood in the O.T. sense of a summary of the divine work of revelation, such as is given in the reviews of the history of the nation (e.g. in Ps. 78; Ps. 106; Neh. 9. 6–31; II. Esdras 3. 4–28; Acts 7. 2–47).[3] Two motifs are necessary for such a review: 1) the description of the alternation of divine mercy with judgment, and corresponding to this, of the people's apostasy with their repentance; 2) the conception of history as directed to a goal. Neither motif is present in the Prologue, or elsewhere in the Gospel. And there is the related fact, that the idea of the election of the nation, and of the covenant of God with it, does not occur at all either[4], and nowhere in the Gospel does the Israelite-Jewish nation appear to be raised decisively above the rest of the world.[5] The Prologue does not speak of the relation of the chosen people to the Word of God, but of the relation of the world to the "Word". Finally, the ὁ Λόγος σὰρξ ἐγένετο is hard to understand on the basis of O.T. presuppositions; for in the O.T. to designate a man the bearer of revelation is only conceivable in terms of the category of inspiration[6]; and Jesus is not thought of as bearer of the divine spirit, either in the Prologue or elsewhere in the Gospel.

If the absolute use of the concept ὁ Λόγος shows how far the Prologue is from the O.T. the same holds good of its relation to *Judaism*.[7] For here, too, the Word of God has not become a "hypostasis" existing for itself as a

---

[1] Man is "told" what is right (Micah 6.8). God's commands are his "words" (II Chron. 29.15) etc.

[2] Cp., immediately below, the "Word" in Judaism.

[3] Acts 7.2–47, probably with the appropriation of a Jewish source; the same kind of review also occurs in Acts 13. 17–25, in a shortened form.

[4] Contrast Paul's view of history!

[5] This holds good, in spite of 4.22; 5.39ff. and certain other passages, as will be shown in the exposition. For the Gospel as a whole, the Jews are the representatives of the "world" as such.

[6] Cp. on 5.19f.

[7] Cp. Gl. u. Verst. I 271f.

divine being, nor has the "Word" come to be used absolutely as a proper name or title.[1] Furthermore the paraphrased designation of God as מֵימְרָא דיי the Word of Jahweh, or Adonai,[2] which one meets in the Targumim, does not mean a cosmic potency, a "hypostasis",[3] but is God's mighty Word, his manifestation, he himself as *numen praesens*.[4] It is in accordance with this, that the Memra is never spoken of absolutely, as the Λόγος is here; there is always a genitive with it![5] Therefore here too, God's Word is his powerful action that recurs within time.

On the other hand, the figure of Wisdom, which is found in Judaism, and also in the O.T. itself, does seem to be related to the Logos-figure in the Johannine Prologue. She is spoken of in mythological language as a divine figure, and has a myth, of which tradition has preserved at least fragments.[6] She is pre-existent, and is God's partner at the creation.[7] She seeks a dwelling on earth among men, but is rejected: she comes to her own possession, but her own do not accept her. So she returns to the heavenly world, and sojourns there, hidden. She is indeed sought at the present time, but no one finds the way to her.[8] She reveals herself only to individual religious men, and makes them friends of God and prophets.[9] It is in accordance with the independence of this figure that she is simply designated "Wisdom".[10]—There can be no doubt, in fact, that a connection exists between the Judaic Wisdom myth and the Johannine Prologue.[11] But the two cannot be connected in the sense

---

[1] See Moore 1. 147–149.

[2] "The Word of Adonai" was the spoken form; see Str.—B. II 302, and cp. generally the whole extended note on the Memra Jahveh, pp. 302–333.

[3] So, correctly, Str.-B.; on the other hand wrongly, in saying that מימרא דיי is only the abbreviation for the formula: "He spoke and it came to pass." Cp. V. Hamp, Der Begriff "Wort" in den aram. Bibelübersetzungen 1938.

[4] This is shown by the parallelism of מימרא with גְּבוּרָה, רְעוּתָא and esp. שְׁכִינָה; it corresponds to the parallelism of דָּבָר and רוּחַ in the O.T., while in Targum the מימרא more frequently takes the place of the O.T. רוּחַ.

[5] The Memra of Jahveh, or Adonai, or "my Memra". Philo himself, whose Logos stems largely from hellenistic tradition (see below), through the influence of the Judaic manner of speech never speaks absolutely of ὁ λόγος, but always of ὁ θεῖος λόγος, etc.; cp. Rev. 19.13.

[6] Cp. my article "Der religionsgeschichtliche Hintergrund des Prologs zum Johannes—Evangelium", Eucharist. II 3–26; W. Schencke, Die Chokma (Sophia) in der jüdischen Hypostasenspekulation (Videnskapsselskapets Skriften II. Hist.—Filos. Kl. 1912, * Nr. 6) 1913; W. Staerk, ZNW 35 (1936), 236f., 257f.; by the same author: Erlösererw. 71–85; W. L. Knox, St. Paul and the Church of the Gentiles 1939, 55–89; cp. also Percy, 297, note 43.

[7] Prov. 8.22–30; Ecclus. 1.1–9; 24.3f., 9; Wisdom 8.3; 9.4, 9; Philo ebriet. 30; leg. all. II, 49; virt. II, 62; for the rabbinic literature Str.-B. II, 356f. (as transferred to the law, see below).

[8] Prov. 1.20–32, Job 28, Ecclus. 24.7; Bar 3.10–13, 29–36; Eth. Enoch 42.1–3; Mt. 23.37–39 and parallels. (cp. Gesch. der synopt. Trad. 120f.=Hist. of the Syn. Trad., 114f.).

[9] Wis. 7.14, 27f.; Ecclus. 1.15 (acc. to Smend).

[10] Prov. 8.1; Ecclus. 1.6; 24.1: Wis. 7.22; Bar. 3.20 etc.

[11] H. Windisch, Neutest. Studien für Heinrici 1914, 220–234, has pointed out the connexion between Pauline Christology and the Wisdom—speculation. So also Dupont 36f.

that the Judaic speculation is the source of the Prologue.[1] Quite apart from the fact that the title Logos would then require a special explanation in the Prologue, the Wisdom myth was not as such a living force in Judaism: it was only a mythological and poetic decking-out of the doctrine of the law. Everything that the myth related of Wisdom was transferred to the Torah: the Torah is pre-existent; she was God's plan of creation and instrument of creation; Wisdom, being in some sense incarnate in the law, has found in Israel a dwelling, prepared for her by God.[2] But the Wisdom myth does not have its origin in the O.T. or in Israel at all; it can only spring from pagan mythology; the Israelite Wisdom poetry took over the myth and de-mythologised it.[3] The Wisdom myth is however only a variant on the *Revealer-myth*, which is developed in Hellenistic and Gnostic literature; and the kinship of the Johannine Prologue to the Judaic Wisdom speculation is due to the fact that both go back to the same tradition for their source.[4]

---

[1] Thus, J. Rendel Harris, The origin of the Prologue of St. John's Gospel 1917; the same in The Bull. of the John Ryland Library 7 (1922) 1–17. Howard—Christianity 51—supposes that a hymn to Wisdom "in her later aspect as the Torah" forms the basis of the Prologue.—According to P. Winter, Ztschr. f. Religions.- und Geistesgesch. 5 (1953), 355 note 53, the Wisdom myth has been divested of its cosmological significance in Rabbinic teaching, in that Wisdom has, so to speak, been split into the מימרא and the תורה.—The Wisdom myth does not seem to occur in the Qumran texts, nor is there any other figure there that corresponds to the Logos in the Johannine Gospel. DSD 11.11 is only a formal parallel to Jn. 1.3. K. G. Kuhn Z. Th. K 47 (1950), 192–211, and F. M. Braun R. B. 62 (1955), 5–44, have shown provisionally that a form of Judaism (clearly Essenism) appears in these texts, that in other respects belongs to the religio—historical presuppositions of the Joh. Gospel. The Gnosticising character of this type of Judaism is not pronounced in all the Qumran texts; very clear however in DSD 3.13–4.26. On this, K. G. Kuhn Z. Th. K 49 (1952), 296–316. Cp. too R. Marcus JBL 73 (1954), 157–161, 'Pharisees, Essenes and Gnostics'; L. Mowry, 'The Dead Sea Scrolls and the Background for the Gospel of John', The Biblical Archaeologist 17 (1954) 78–97.

[2] Ecclus. 24.8, 23; Bar. 3.37; 4.1. (Rabbinic literature) Str.-B. II 353–357. This explains why K. Bornhäuser, Das Johannes-Evangelium, eine Missionsschrift für Israel, 1928 5ff., wants to explain the Johannine Prologue by means of the "Toralogy", that is to say, by maintaining that what was said of the Torah in Judaism has been transferred here to Jesus. But the genealogy cannot be:

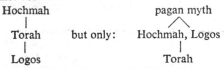

Hochmah
|
Torah
|
Logos

but only:

pagan myth
/\
Hochmah, Logos
|
Torah

[3] Just as the Israelite Wisdom literature itself is only comprehensible within the context of the international Wisdom literature of the ancient orient; cp. W. Baumgartner, Israelit. und altoriental. Weisheit 1933, and his review of research in this field, Th. R, NF 5 (1933), 259–288.—The attempt to trace the myth back to a particular origin, has not yet been successful. Cp. Baumgartner (op. cit. 286f.); P. Humbert R. G. G. 2nd ed. V 1800f.

[4] These two variants (the speculation on the σοφία and that on the λόγος) collided in Alexandrian Judaism, the former clearly from Judaic, the latter from Hellenistic tradition. The Wisdom of Sol., where λόγος and σοφία once occur in parallel (9.1f.), follows the σοφία tradition, but endows the σοφία with the attributes of the λόγος (see Grill I 154ff.). In Philo λόγος and σοφία compete with each other, with the effect that the latter is to a large extent displaced by the former. It appears, moreover, that the oriental figure of σοφία has been transformed through the Isis theology here (Bréhier 115ff.; Bousset, Rel. des Jdt. 345,

This tradition has many ramifications, and the fact that it is combined with different types of mythological and philosophical thinking makes it hard to unravel. But we do not need to analyse the whole tradition, or trace it back to its origin in order to understand the Johannine Prologue; it is enough to recognise that the mythological figure of the Logos has its home in a particular understanding of the world, namely, the Gnostic.

The Greek philosophical tradition, in which the Logos is first encountered as a cosmic-divine potency in Heraclitus, and then achieves its historically most important role in *Stoicism*, is not relevant to our purpose.[1] The Logos is not a mythological figure there,[2] but is the regularity of what happens in the κόσμος, the κοινὸς νόμος τῆς φύσεως, which is at the same time the τονικὴ δύναμις, immanent in the κόσμος, uniting it and holding sway throughout it. As λόγος ὀρθός this cosmic regularity is at the same time the law that guides the thought and action of the individual, whose particular λόγος is identical with the world-Logos. The only thing that the Logos of the Johannine Prologue has in common with this immanent world-law is that both are of fundamental significance for the world; but because the understanding of the world is so totally different in each case, and with it the understanding of the relation of the Logos to the world (in the former transcendence, in the latter immanence), only the name remains the same; and this is only an apparent identity, because the Stoics use the word λόγος as a concept, and not as a proper noun.

Further the Stoic Logos does not assume mythical form, in virtue of the fact that Stoic allegorising sees the Logos in the figure of Hermes,[3] or in other divine figures like the Egyptian Tot.[4] But a *quite different Logos-figure* does appear in certain cosmological speculations of Hellenism of a religious and philosophical nature. These are in the first place the originally dualist systems of what is called *Gnosticism*; here the Greek tradition, in so far as it has been assimilated, provides a secondary element, and has been put to the service of the conceptual development of Gnosticism in the Greek world.

Pascher, Königsweg 60ff.). Plotinus, too, appears to be familiar with the Wisdom myth when he designates the ζωὴ as the σοφία, described as ἡ πρώτη καὶ οὐκ ἀπ' ἄλλης, which is the πάρεδρος of the νοῦς, whose size and might is discernible in this, ὅτι μετ' αὐτῆς ἔχει καὶ πεποίηκε τὰ ὄντα πάντα . . . Enn. V 8, 4, p. 236, 21ff. Volkm.—It is remarkable that in the Odes of Sol. too, where normally the "Word" embodies the Revelation, in Ode 33 the "pure virgin", which is identical with the Sophia, stands alongside the Word (G. Bornkamm, Mythos und Legende 93).

[1] Cf. M. Heinze, Die Lehre vom Logos in der griech. Philosophie 1872; A. Aall, Geschichte der Logosidee in der griech. Philosophie (Der Logos I) 1896; K. Prümm, Der christl. Glaube und die altheidnische Welt 1935, I, 227–252; J. A. Thomsen, The Art of the Logos 1935; Asting, op. cit. 39ff; Ad. Dyroff, in Pisciculi (Festschr. f. F. J. Dölger) 1939, 86ff.—For the connexion between the philosophical concept λόγος and the original Greek concept of Word, cp. Gl. u. Verst. 274ff.

[2] Of course ὁ λόγος is used absolutely, but not as a proper-name or title; it is a general concept here. The Stoic λόγος was identified with the Christian πνεῦμα, not with Jesus Christ; J. Howard. Christianity 34.

[3] Kornutos, Theol. gr. 16. Plato once interpreted Hermes as λόγος and ἑρμηνεύς (Krat 407e), just as the Orphic tradition (Fr. 297a Kem) conceived him as the ἑρμηνεύς.

[4] Cf. Bousset, Kyrios, 2nd ed. 309–312; J. Schniewind, Euangelion 219.

But there are also in the Greek tradition the systems of *Neo-pythagoreanism, Neo-platonism,* and related phenomena[1]; and these modify the Greek idea of the unity of the world to a greater and greater extent until they are forced to abandon it; in this they are not only influenced by the Gnostic understanding of the world as a whole, but themselves take over a more or less Gnostic mythology and adapt it to the terminology of the Greek tradition.

The figure of the Λόγος is encountered in both groups *as an intermediary* between God and the world,[2] whose purpose is to explain how the step from the transcendent divinity to the formation of the world was possible. Here the chief interest lies in the question of man; he feels his being-in-the-world to be a being in exile, and believes that he belonged originally to the divine sphere. The Logos has a *soteriological* as well as a *cosmological* function here; for it is not only the reason for the existence of human souls in the world, but is also the means of their emancipation from it. Whatever its disguise may be, the Logos is in fact the σωτήρ. In so far as we can say that the Stoic λόγος has a soteriological function, as λόγος ὀρθός, the distinction between the Stoic view and these others is plain: the Stoic Logos demands that the individual understand himself to be incorporated into the cosmos, which is his home. On the other hand, in the "dualist" systems the individual, by turning to the Logos, frees himself from the κόσμος, in order to attain to his supra-cosmic home. Thus in the Gnostic systems an eschatology corresponds to the cosmogony; that is to say, the process of the formation of the world, in which the spheres of the divine and anti-divine have joined themselves together, must be annulled by the separation of the elements.[3] And since the Logos initiated the formation of the world, by losing himself as it were to it, through its destruction he returns to himself; he is redeemed, by redeeming himself.

As redeemer the Logos betook himself to the lower world in human form. He disguised himself in a human body, in order to deceive the demonic powers of darkness, and at the same time not to alarm those who are to be saved. This specifically Gnostic motif could not of course be taken over by the philosophical systems.[4] In Christian Gnosticism, the redeemer who

---

[1] Philo belongs here too; but since his doctrine of the Logos is only indirectly connected with that of the Prologue, it does not need to be set out fully here; cp. Aall, op. cit. 184–231; Bréhier, op. cit. 83–111; Bousset, Kyr. 308–316; Pascher, Königsweg, passim; Br., addit. note to the Prologue.

[2] For evidence for all that follows see above, page 20, n. 2; cp. Bousset, Kyrios 304–316 and Br., addit. note to Jn. 1.1–18.

[3] This of course has nothing to do with the Stoic ἐκπύρωσις. In the sphere of philosophical thought, the universal-cosmic eschatology has been displaced by the individual eschatology of the ascent of the soul, and this too has been stripped of its originally cosmic character (the journey of the soul to heaven) and re-interpreted in spiritual terms (Philo, C. Herm. 1 and 13, Plotinus). Or the universal-cosmic eschatology has become the principle used to explain the continuing world-process, (Plotinus' doctrine of the ἐπιστροφή); cp. H. Jonas, Gnosis I 260.

[4] In Poimandres (C. Herm 1) this motif is reduced in the following way: the teaching that mediates the γνῶσις, is attributed to the revelation by the Νοῦς, appearing in the form of the Shepherd; similarly in other Hermetic writings, to a Revelation-divinity, who takes over the roll of the mystagogue. In C. Herm. IV God sent the revelation (the Νοῦς) down as the κρατήρ, accompanied by a κήρυγμα.

becomes man was held to be Jesus. That is not to say that the idea of the incarnation of the redeemer has in some way penetrated Gnosticism from Christianity; it is itself originally Gnostic,[1] and was taken over at a very early stage by Christianity, and made fruitful for Christology.[2]

This figure appears *under different names* and is presented in varying ways, but remains essentially the same. It is called δεύτερος θεός, υἱὸς θεοῦ, μονογενής, εἰκὼν τοῦ θεοῦ, occasionally δημιουργός, and is also termed Ἄνθρωπος, "archetypal man".[3] But almost without exception it carries the title or proper-name Λόγος, although, particularly in the philosophical authors, this is often replaced by the title Νοῦς, which has the same meaning for the Greeks. This figure appears as a mythological person in Gnosticism proper, although it is sometimes weakened to a δύναμις here as well. In the sphere of the Greek philosophical tradition, it is often only the conception of the world-process and the picture-language that recall its mythological origin, and here the figure of the Λόγος or Νοῦς has itself become a cosmic potency, and is often thought of in a platonizing fashion, as the essence of the κόσμος νοητός.[4] In genuine Gnosticism the figure is often attenuated[5] or divided,[6] in accordance with the Gnostic tendency to split up the process of the world-formation into an increasing number of stages, each with its gradual transition to the next.[7] But even where the Λόγος (or Νοῦς or Ἄνθρωπος) has become an apparently secondary figure in the systematic ranks of aeons, its original significance can be seen quite clearly. Furthermore, where the creation of the real sublunar world is attributed to the figure of a demiourge, which has been

---

[1] Cp. Bousset, Hauptpr. 238–260; Bultmann ZNTW 24 (1925), 106f., 119ff.; Schlier, Relg. Unters. 5–17; G. Bornkamm, Mythos und Legende in den apokr. Thomas-Akten 1933, 10; Jonas, Gnosis, I 122ff. 275.—cp. The Hymn of the Soul, Act. Thom. 109, p. 221, 4; Od. Sal. 7.3ff.; Ginza 112, 14ff. Further, see on Jn. 1.14.—E. Percy concludes differently; with ref. to this, see my discussion in Orient. Lit.-Ztg. 1940, 150ff.

[2] Cp. I Cor 2.7f. (see Lietzmann, Hdb. zum N. T.); Phil. 2.6–11. (see Dibelius, ibidem; E. Lohmeyer, Kyrios Jesus, SAHeidelb. 1927/28, 4); Barn. 5.10 (see Windisch, Hdb. zum N. T.); Ign. Eph. 19.1 (see Schlier: prev. note); Asc. Jes. 10–11.—In the Jewish Wisdom-speculation the idea has been taken over in the modified form, by which Wisdom reveals herself in the prophets (cp. Eucharist. 15–19), or is incarnate in the law (ibid. 6f.). For the Gnosticising-Jewish Christendom, cp. the Adam doctrine of the Pseudo-Clementines (ibid 19; Bousset, Hauptpr. 171ff.; L. Troje AΔAM und ZΩH (SAHeidelb. 1916, 17), 23ff.).

[3] The title Ἄνθρωπος clearly has its origin in the Macrocosmos-Microcosmos idea, which uses a human analogy to explain the construction of the universe. This idea has clearly been taken over by the Greek world from the Orient; cp Reitzenst., Studien 69ff.; see below.

[4] Philo, Plutarch, Plotinus; Damaskios (de princ. 125, p. 321f. Ruelle).

[5] The Aeons (=Sygynies) of Simon, of the Barbelo-Gnostics and the Valentinians, of Markos and Basilides, are basically only an attenuation of the Logos figure, or its secondary combination with other mythological figures of importance.

[6] The most remarkable case of a splitting off from the Logos in Christian Gnosticism is that of the Demiourge. The different kind of division, into the λόγος that is to be redeemed, and the redeeming λόγος, is grounded in the same basic conception.

[7] Cp. H. Jonas, Gnosis I, 260. 359 etc. The same procedure can be seen with regard to the figure of Σοφία; cp. the Jewish doctrine of Wisdom with the Valentinian Sophia-speculation.

split off from the Logos, it is the latter that remains the decisive figure, from which the impetus for the formation of the world emanated. Similarly it is only a secondary division, when the Redeemer, who has become man (in Jesus), is distinguished from the cosmic Logos.[1]

Even if the reconstruction of this kind of thinking has to be carried out in the main from sources which are later than John, nevertheless its *greater age* remains firmly established. It is proved in the first place by the appearance of parallel forms of the basic ideas in both the religio-philosophical literature of Hellenism from the first century onwards and in the Christian Gnostic sources. In addition there is the witness of Ignatius and of the Odes of Solomon and of the Mandaean writings. The harmony all these works exhibit, and their presentation of the basic Gnostic view-point in a modified and embellished form, subject to variation, and the frequent reduction of the mythology more or less to a symbol, all show that the basic conception itself reaches back to the pre-christian era. Two further points confirm this view: firstly, the pre-christian Judaic Sophia speculation is a variant of the myth, on the basis of the O.T. faith in God the Creator[2]; and secondly, both Philo, and the Pauline and deutero-Pauline literature presuppose the myth.[3] There can be no doubt that the syncretistic Apocalyptic of Judaism stands under the influence of Gnostic mythology.[4]

But it is most probably the case that decisive ideas of the Gnostic myth —and in particular the idea of the intermediary, that mediates divine powers to the world—are *of pre-gnostic origin*; that is to say, that there was originally a cosmogony, without an eschatology corresponding to it, unrelated to the idea of soteriology, and designed merely to explain the permanence and structure of the world.[5] This could follow from the fact that in some authors, the figure of the Mediator is the κόσμος itself conceived as a person, and contrasted with its own parts as an independent whole; this is a view that can

---

[1] That the Logos (or the Νοῦς) is the incarnate redeemer, is shown by the "Hymn of the Soul" and the Od. Sal., by the doctrine of the Sethians (Hipp. V 19, 20f.), of Simon (Ir. I 23, 3; Hipp. VI 18, 3 and 19, 4), of Markos (Ir. I 15, 3 or Hipp. VI 51), and of Basilides (Ir. I 24, 4).

[2] It appears that Judaism took over this motif, by identifying the Spirit of God mentioned in Gen. 1.2 with the Logos or Wisdom. For the Jewish (Jewish-Christian?) tradition provides almost the only possible explanation of the fact that in Herm. sim. V 6, 5 the πνεῦμα τὸ ἅγιον τὸ προὸν, τὸ κτίσαν πᾶσαν τὴν κτίσιν appears instead of the Logos; cp. IX 12, 2: ὁ μὲν υἱὸς τοῦ θεοῦ (acc. to IX 1, 1, the πνεῦμα) πάσης τῆς κτίσεως αὐτοῦ προγενέστερός ἐστιν, ὥστε σύμβουλον αὐτὸν γενέσθαι τῷ πατρὶ τῆς κτίσεως αὐτοῦ. Cp. II Klem 9.5; 14.4; Pistis Sophia 120 (Kopt.-Gnost. Schriften I 78, 1ff.).

[3] For Philo, cp. esp., Reitzenstein's work, passim. So also for Paul and the Deutero-Paul. Literature; further see J. Weiss, Der erste Korintherbrief, 1910, 225ff.; Bousset, Kyrios 126. 133f. 136f. 140ff.; cp. the commentaries in the Hdb zum NT, e.g. on 1 Cor. 15.45, Col. 1.17; E. Käsemann, Leib und Leib Christi 1933; H. Schlier, Christus und die Kirche in Epheserbrief 1930.

[4] Cp. the figure of the "Son of man"; cp. G. Hölscher, Geschichte der israelitischen und jüdischen Religion 2nd Ed. 19 § 84; Rev. d'hist et de phil. rel. 1929, 101–114.

[5] Cp. esp., Reitzenstein, Studien 69–103.

be traced back to Plato in the Greek world,[1] and which recurs in the pantheistic parts of the Corpus Hermeticum.[2] The supposition that this mythology was taken up and transformed by the dualistic understanding of the world in Gnosticism, accounts for the fact that the Gnostic dualism is developed in varying shades,[3] and also that in some systems which are in fact Gnostic, the creation as such does not appear as a fall. In these systems the creation of worlds is allowed within the sphere of the Pleroma[4]; it is only below this that it implies apostasy.

The *Johannine Prologue*, or its source, speaks in the language of Gnostic mythology, and its Λόγος is the intermediary, the figure that is of both cosmological and soteriological significance; it is the divine being that, while existing from the very beginning with the Father, became man for the salvation of men. This proposition will be confirmed by the Evangelist's presentation of the figure and work of Jesus in the terminology of gnostic mythology as the Gospel develops. The Evangelist was not the first to make use of this mythology for Christian proclamation and theology. *Paul* had preceded him, with his frequent exposition of the eschatological and soteriological meaning of Christ in the terminology of the Anthropos myth, even if he does not use the title Λόγος himself.[5] The Gnostic mythology was put to the service of Christology and soteriology to a greater extent in the *deutero-Pauline* literature (Col. and Eph.). The express identification of Christ with the Logos was carried out by Ignatius, independently of John.[6]

It remains still to ask to which *type of Gnosticism* the source used by the Evangelist belongs.[7]

---

[1] Plato describes the relation of the creating God to the κόσμος in Tim. 37c: ὡς δὲ κινηθὲν αὐτὸ καὶ ζῶν ἐνόησεν τῶν ἀϊδίων θεῶν γεγονὸς ἄγαλμα (that is, the κόσμος) ὁ γεννήσας πατήρ, ἠγάσθη τε καὶ εὐφρανθεὶς. . . . He had described the κόσμος as ζῶον ἔμψυχον ἔννουν τε, as εὐδαίμων θεός, as εἰκὼν τοῦ νοητοῦ θεὸς αἰσθητός (Tim. 30b. 34b. 92c.) (cp. p. 72 (71n.2) f.). For Philo, cp. esp. Pascher's demonstration of the duality of the Logosfigure: the cosmic and the supra-cosmic Logos.

[2] With ref. to Plut. and the Hermetic writings, cp. M. Dibelius Hdb. zum NT, on Col. 1.17; see further J. Kroll, Herm. Trism. 155ff.; ThWB II 386f.

[3] Cp. H. Jonas, Gnosis I 257, and the following analyses of the Gnostic systems.

[4] Just as in Plotinus, within the intelligible world.

[5] Rom. 5.12ff. I Cor. 15.45f. etc.; cp. the literature mentioned on page 27, note 3.

[6] Cp. H. Schlier, Relg. Unters.—Other traces are found in Heb. 1.3 and Rev. 19.13—(here, of course, under the influence of the O.T. linguistic usage, which also affects the Christian reception of the concept of the Logos elsewhere, for the absolute Λόγος has become the λόγος τοῦ θεοῦ). Acc. to Clem. Al. Strom. I 29, 182; II 15, 68; Ecl. proph. 58 the Kerygma of Peter described Jesus as νόμος and λόγος; the designation also occurs in the quotation in Clem. Al. Strom VI 5, 39 where the text is unfortunately doubtful. The Logos of the Apologists is mostly derived from the Stoic tradition, although, e.g. in Tatian ch. 5, the Gnostic figure is also visible. With reference to the Gnostic Logos in the apocryphal Acts of the Apostles, cp. Bousset, Kyrios, 306, 4; on this Act. Joa. 8, p. 156, 7f.; 98, p. 200, 5ff.; Act. Petri c Sim. 20, p. 68, 11ff. and the calls to prayer Act. Joa. 94.96. 109, p. 197, 19; 199, 2; 207, 9ff.

[7] On the question of the type of Gnosticism, cp. R. M. Grant's verdict: "The environment in which he (the Evangelist) lives is no longer that of Judaism, but of a kind of Gnosticism not unlike that of Ignatius and the Odes of Solomon" (JBL 69 –1950–, 322).

1. It belongs to the sphere of early oriental Gnosticism. For the tendency to include *the origin of the sphere that is hostile to God* within the process of the divine self-development is foreign to the source, while being characteristic of the Syrian-Egyptian type.[1] There is no reflection on the origin of darkness in a primeval fall,[2] and even if later in the Gospel traces of the "Iranian" type occur,[3] in which the darkness achieves the role of an active power hostile to God,[4] the mythology has been pushed back so far—as in the Odes of Solomon—that the early oriental type is in fact present in a modified form. And as in the Odes of Solomon, this particular form will be due to the influence of the O.T. belief in God.

2. *The figure of the Logos* stands alone between God and the world. And here the peculiar duality of the historical setting shows itself again; on the one hand the attachment to an early form, in so far as there is no speculative endeavour, such as is characteristic of later Gnosticism, to present "the way of being" in a multiplicity of stages[5]; on the other hand, it is a developed form, in which the mythology, again as in the Odes of Solomon under O.T. influence, has been pushed into the background.[6] The same thing can be seen in that while there is no attempt to expound the procession of the Son from the Father[7] (a characteristic both of the western and of the later oriental systems) the conceptual meaning which the proper-name "Logos" originally had, i.e. "word", is no longer clearly discernible.[8]

---

[1] Cp. H. Jonas, Gnosis I 279.

[2] The same is true of one section of the Mandaean writings; cp. Jonas op. cit. 267. 268f. 283.

[3] Joh. 8.44; 12.31; 14.30; 16.11.

[4] Cp. Jonas op. cit. 267. 280ff. 288ff.

[5] Cp. Jonas op. cit. 260. The parts of the Mandaean writings to be compared are those in which a monotheism is apparent, which has no connexion with the idea of emanation (the type B in Jonas op. cit. 262ff.).

[6] Clearly, it is the speculative doctrine of the development of being in stages, not the conception of a multiplicity within the divine being—consisting of the Pleroma and the Aeons—that represents a later stage. The latter view is attested by the Od. Sal. and Ignatius, both of whom belong to the sphere from which the Prologue's source comes; for the Od. Sal. cp. e.g. 7.11, where the πλήρωμα is characterized by "the fullness of the Aeons and their Father", just as the "way of the Gnosis" leads to שומליא, i.e., to the πλήρωμα (7.13). For Ign. cp. e.g. Eph. 8.1; 19.2 (cp. Schlier Relg. Unters. 28); Trall. 5,2; Smyrn. 6,1. In the Johannine Gospel, apart from terminological allusion (see on 1.16), only the figures of the angels (1.51) and of the Paraclete, and the heavenly "dwellings" (14.2) remind us that the divine world has a greater multiplicity than is disclosed in the Prologue.

[7] Whether it be thought of as a natural process (Mandaeans), or as an Act of reflection (Valentinians).

[8] Many signs show that the Gnostic Λόγος originally had the conceptual meaning of the spoken word (spoken by the Father). In Markos the theogony and cosmogony have their origin in a primordial speaking about the Πατήρ (Iren. I 14, 1; Hipp. El. VI 42, 4ff.) and the Ἄνθρωπος is designated as πηγὴ παντὸς λόγου καὶ ἀρχὴ πάσης φωνῆς καὶ παντὸς ἀρρήτου ῥῆσις καὶ τῆς σιωπωμένης Σιγῆς στόμα (Iren. I 14, 3; cp. 14, 5; Hipp. El. VI 44, 3; cp. 46, 2). Origen attacks this primitive view in Jo. I 24, 151, p. 29, 21ff. Cp. C. Schmidt. Kopt.-Gnost. Schriften 1905, 338, 5ff. For the Mandaeans, cp. Schlier, Relg. Unters. 36f. This view is most clearly expressed in the Od. Sal., cp. e.g. 12 (esp. v. 8), and then 8, where the Logos himself speaks, or 42, 6 where he speaks in the redeemed.—The following also

3. *Neither the origin of the world*, nor that specifically of man, appears as a tragic event. It is at this point that the distance from almost every form of Gnosticism is at its greatest. That the origin of the world and man goes back to a tragic development within the world of light is admittedly only the doctrine of a particular direction of Gnosticism, represented above all in the West; in the "Iranian" type, the world and man are attributed to the creation by the Divinity, but in such a way that this act of creation is seen as a struggle against the darkness.[1] The disappearance of this motif of struggle in the Prologue is in accordance with the severe limitation of the role of darkness as an independent power (see above, under 1). Clearly the influence of the O.T. is at work here; in the Judaic Wisdom speculation the case is the same. This is also true of the Odes of Solomon (as in the Hymn of the Soul—Act. Thom. 108–113), where the dualism only determines the soteriology,[2] not the cosmology, and where the world is understood rather as the creation of God, or of his word.[3] The figure of the demiurge, split off from the Logos, which in the Mandaean literature does at least still belong to the world of light,[4] does not of course appear in the Prologue's source, or in the Odes of Solomon. The Gnostic conception of the pre-existence of the souls of men, and of their belonging to the unity of a Being of light (the archetypal man), plays no part in the Prologue. It does however emerge, as it seems, in a later part of the source-document used there.[5] But since the Evangelist has given this conception up, it is not possible to judge with certainty on this point.

The result of this enquiry is that the Prologue's source belongs to the sphere of a relatively early oriental Gnosticism, which has been developed under the influence of the O.T. faith in the Creator-God. This development has taken the following direction: the mythology has been severely pushed into the background; the Gnostic cosmology has been repressed and has given way to the belief in Creation; and the concern for the relation of man to the revelation of God, that is to say the soteriological concern, has become

---

testifies to the same fact: 1) In the Gnostic use of language, "word" and "voice", just as "word" and "(spoken) name" are interchangeable. Cp. for φωνή, Schlier, Relg. Unters. 37, 1; Iren. I 14, 3.5 (see below); for ὄνομα, Karl Müller, Beiträge zum Verständnis der valentinian. Gnosis, Nachr. der Gött. Ges. der Wiss., Phil.-hist. Kl. 1920, 180f; Od. Sal. 28.17f.; C.Schmidt op. cit. 337, 35f. 2) The Σιγή corresponds to the Λόγος; it was only later that the former was hypostatized as a divine being; originally it only meant the silence of the very beginning; cp. Schlier, Relg. Unters. 38f.; Iren. I 14, 3 (see below); Exc. ex Th. 29; Od. Sal. 12.8; above all Ign. Mg. 8.2: ὅτι εἷς θεός ἐστιν, ὁ φανερώσας ἑαυτὸν διὰ I. Χρ. τοῦ υἱοῦ αὐτοῦ, ὅς ἐστιν αὐτοῦ λόγος ἀπὸ σιγῆς προελθών (cp. Rom 8. 2). On this, Simon Mag. in Eus. eccl. theol. II 9.—For the σιγή in pagan Gnosticism, cp. W. Kroll, de Oraculis Chaldaicis, Bresl. Phil. Abh. 7, 1 (1894), 16. In the Hermetic writings, the conception of the primordial silence of the Divinity is also of importance, in that silence is the mystical state of union with the Divinity.

[1] Cp. Jonas op. cit. 270.—Cp. also, however, how in the syncretist. text of the "Eighth Book of Moses" (Preisendanz, Pap. Graec. Mag. II, 86–131) lines 138–206, 443–564 (Preisend. p. 93–97, 104–114) the creation of the Cosmos is attributed to the highest God.

[2] Cp. the outline in Jonas op. cit. 327f.

[3] Esp. Od. Sal. 12 and 16; in addition e.g. 4.14f.; 7.9.

[4] Cp. Jonas op. cit. 272.

[5] Cp. on 3.4.

dominant. The Odes of Solomon prove to be the most closely related.—The figure of the Logos, as Creator and Revealer, is to be understood in terms of this Gnosticism, on the basis of a characteristically modified dualism, which sees not the world's origin, but rather its actual condition at the moment as the reason why it stands over against God as the darkness. This further explains why there is no talk of a history of revelation in the O.T. sense (see above, page 21). But the figure of the Logos cannot be subjected to further interpretation in advance. In particular, the question whether the Logos was conceived of personally in his pre-temporal existence or not, can be decided only in the exposition of the text itself; the previous history of the concept offers both possibilities.[1]

The first statement about the Logos is that he was ἐν ἀρχῇ, in the very beginning, before all worlds; cp. the description in 2 Esdras 6. 1ff.;

> "In the beginning of the world,
> before the doors of heaven stood,
> or ever the blasts of the winds blew,
> before the voices of the thunder sounded,
> or ever the lightning flashes shone ..."

There is more intended here than in the בְּרֵאשִׁית of Gen. 1.1; for it is not said of the Logos that he ἐκτίσθη, or ἐγένετο, but that he ἦν.[2] The ἀρχὴ is not therefore the first member of a temporal succession, but lies before all time, and therefore before all worlds.[3] Thus the Logos does not belong to the world—not even in the sense of being the key for explaining how the world and time began. It does not say ἀρχὴ ἦν ὁ Λόγος, as if his being were the answer to the Greek or Gnostic question

---

[1] For the understanding of the whole Gospel on the basis of Christendom's dispute with Gnosticism, see the excellent exposition by Ad. Omodeo, La Mistica Giovannea 1930.

[2] Cp. Aall, op. cit. II 110: "The ἦν forces the conception, wherever possible, one step further back. For us, the result is the purely negative concept of Pretemporality".—Otherwise in Prov. 8.22f. of "Wisdom":

> "The Lord possessed me in the beginning of his way,
> Before his works of old.
> I was set up from everlasting, from the beginning,
> Or ever the earth was". (tr.: R.V.)

The LXX, which follows the Heb. text in the ἔκτισέν με ἀρχὴν ὁδῶν αὐτοῦ seeks to go beyond it in the πρὸ τοῦ αἰῶνος ἐθεμελίωσέν με ἐν ἀρχῇ; so too in Ecclus. 24.9: πρὸ τοῦ αἰῶνος ἀπ' ἀρχῆς ἔκτισέν με (the Heb. is lacking).

[3] Cp. 17.24: ὅτι ἠγάπησάς με πρὸ καταβολῆς κόσμου. Acc. to Od. Sal. 41.14, the Logos was "from time immemorial (=ἀπ'ἀρχῆς) in the Father", and "was known before the foundation of the world"; cp. G. Lindeskog, Studien zum Neutest. Schöpfungsgedanken I 1952, 204–207.

about the origin of things.[1] The first clause expresses his absolute otherness; and this is precisely its intention: not to teach anything about the origin of the world, but to designate the Logos in a manner that takes him away from the sphere of the world. This designation is in the first instance wholly *negative*. For nothing positive can be said about that which is before all worlds—unless the ἀρχή is in fact to be brought down to the time sequence of the world. And yet it does have a *positive* significance: for the statement is made with reference to the one who, in his incarnate form, is the bringer of the revelation.[2] The hymn that forms the basis of the Prologue praises the Logos as the Revealer; and the Evangelist's aim is to show that the Logos has become flesh in Jesus of Nazareth. That is to say: in the person and word of Jesus one does not encounter anything that has its origin in the world or in time; the encounter is with the reality that lies beyond the world and time. Jesus and his word not only bring release from the world and from time, they are also the means whereby the world and time are judged: the first words of the Prologue at once prepare us for this.

The first clause presses on to the second; for if ἀρχή is used in its radical sense, the movement of thought must be directed to God himself: in what relation does the Logos stand to God, who is really the only one who can be thought of as being ἐν ἀρχῇ? The answer is given in mythological language; καὶ ὁ Λόγος ἦν πρὸς τὸν θεόν. This answer regards it as self-evident that in the beginning God was: but he was not alone; the Logos was with him.[3] The πρός θεόν excludes all speculation about an

[1] In Greek Gnosticism there is continual talk of the ἀρχή as the origin; cp. e.g. Hipp. El. VI 9, 3 p. 136, 11ff.; the πῦρ as τῶν ὅλων ἀρχή in Simon VI 29, 2 p. 155, 22; the ἀρχὴ τῶν πάντων in Valentinus, and esp. its characteristic ἀγέννητος, as the ἀρχὴ τῶν ὅλων καὶ ῥίζα καὶ βάθος καὶ βυθός VI 30, 7 p. 158, 4f., and generally the synonymity of ἀρχή and ῥίζα, πηγή and σπέρμα in Gnosticism. Cp. with ref. to the second god that has emanated from the highest god, Jambl. de myst. 8, 2 p. 262, 3ff. Parthey: ἀρχὴ γὰρ οὗτος καὶ θεός θεῶν, μονὰς ἐκ τοῦ ἑνός, προούσιος καὶ ἀρχή τῆς οὐσίας. In Philo, the λόγος in conf. ling. 146 is called ἀρχή, and in leg. all. I 19 ἀρχὴ γενέσεως; cp. Pascher, Königsweg 118ff.—If the intention of the Prologue were speculative, the text would not begin with a statement about the Logos (as the second stage of the divine being) but with one about God himself; cp. the beginning of the Naassene Hymn (Hipp. V 10, 2 p. 102, 23 W.): νόμος ἦν γενικὸς τοῦ παντὸς ὁ πρωτότοκος νοός.

[2] This is correctly stressed by Ed. Thurneysen, ZwZ 3 (1925), 18ff. L. Köhler (Ehrfurcht vor dem Leben, Festschr, f. Alb. Schweitzer 1954, 71f.) rightly states that the stress is laid on the ἐν ἀρχῇ and not on the ὁ λόγος.

[3] Εἶναι πρός plus the acc., answering the question where?, here as in Mk 6.3; 9.19; I Thess. 3.4; that is to say like παρά with the dat. (cp. 17.5 Prov 8.30); BlD. §239,1; Raderm. 2nd Ed. 140: 142. 146. Even if the mixing of prepositions like πρός and παρά and the mixing of their constructions (acc. and dat.)—occurs frequently in the Koine (Raderm. 2nd ed. 137–143; Moulton, Einl. 173), in the papyri πρός with the dat. is retained in answer to the question Where?. Πρός with the acc. in answer to the question Where? must be understood as a Semitism; πρός renders לְוָת, which means 1) παρά with the dat., and 2) πρός

archetypal generation in the divine sphere; it excludes every conception of an unfolding of the Diety, or of an emanation, every idea of the archetypal Diety becoming objective to itself. There is no attempt to go back beyond the ὁ Λόγος ἦν πρὸς τὸν θεόν; it was so ἐν ἀρχῇ, and no Σιγή preceded the Λόγος. But is the intention really to express the mythological idea of the existence in the beginning of two divine persons, either alongside each other, or the one subordinate to the other? In any case, not alongside each other: for the relation is not clarified by turning the sentence round, so that it stated: καὶ ὁ θεὸς ἦν πρὸς τὸν Λόγον. Rather: καὶ θεὸς ἦν ὁ Λόγος. There is therefore no talk of subordination; the status of the Λογος is one of equality with God: he was God.[1] For it cannot be taken as meaning: he was a god, a divine being,[2] as if θεός were a generic concept such as ἄνθρωπος or *animal,* so that there could be two divine beings, either in the naive polytheistic sense,[3] or in the sense of the Gnostic idea of emanation.[4] This is clearly out of the question, because in the phrase ἦν πρὸς τὸν θεόν, which both precedes and follows καὶ θεὸς ἦν ὁ Λόγος, the word θεός is intended in its strict monotheistic sense; furthermore, what comes afterwards shows that all polytheistic conceptions and emanationist theories are foreign to the text. And one can hardly translate "of divine being", "of the divine species"[5]; for in that case, *why was not* θεῖος *used?*[6] And if the answer is that the text was a translation of a semitic original, in which there was no concept θεῖος, then this answer itself brings us back in the end to

---

with the acc. That this points to a written source, follows as little in the present case as in I Thess. 3.4; cp. Goguel, RHPhrel. 3 (1923), 374f. against Burney 28f. On εἶναι πρός cp. Dodd 279f.

[1] So correctly, Lagr., Dillersb. and Schlier. Of course, and this is shown at once by the distribution of the article—the subject is not God, but the Logos, as is the case throughout this passage.

[2] The lack of the article in front of θεός does not somehow (contra Origen) necessitate such a translation; it is lacking, because θεός is the predicate.

[3] As in the O.T., in the question asked in Deut 3.24: "For what god is there in heaven or in earth, that can do according to thy mighty works?" Cp. Ez. 28.2, 6, 9. Otherwise in Is. 45.22: "For I am God, and there is none else", where LXX correctly has ὁ θεός; cp. Is. 45.14; 46.9. So also Is. 31.3: "Now the Egyptians are men and not God". On the other hand, polytheistic thought is apparent in the אֱלֹהִים of Ps. 82.1, 6; 86.8; 95.3; 97.9; 136.2, where LXX has θεοί ,and Ps. 8.6; 97.7; 138.1, where LXX has ἄγγελοι. It is of course something quite different, when in Ex. 4.16 Moses takes the place of God over against Aaron, and when according to rabbinic exegetical theory a man (Moses, Jacob) is designated God (Str.-B. II 352).

[4] Thus the δημιουργός is a δεύτερος θεός in Numenius (Aall op. cit. I 236f.); cp. C. Herm. 8, 1.5; hermet. Fr. in Lact. div. inst. IV 6, 4 (Scott Hermetica I 298); Ascl. 8, 29ff. (ebd. 298/300; 348, 8ff.). In the same way the λόγος in Philo is called δεύτερος θεός leg. all. II 86; cp. somn. I 229f. Cp. Kroll, Herm. Trism. 55ff.

[5] So too B. Weiss, Zn., Bl., just as Ho., Htm., Br.

[6] θεῖος in the N.T.: Acts 17.29; II Pet. 1.3f.; θειότης: Rom. 1.20.

the meaning "a God-being". But coming between these two clauses, which express the ἦν πρὸς τὸν θεόν, the θεός cannot possibly mean anything other than God. The Logos is therefore given the same status as God,[1] just as faith confesses the Son, who has been raised again to the glory that he had had before, (17.5), to be ὁ κύριός μου καὶ ὁ θεός μου (20.28).

Of course, the placing of the phrase θεὸς ἦν ὁ Λόγος between these two clauses also shows that no simple identification is intended. A *paradoxical* state of affairs is to be expressed which is inherent in the *concept of revelation*, and which will be developed further in what follows: the paradox that in the Revealer God is really encountered, and yet that God is not directly encountered, but only in the Revealer.[2] Whereas the statement ὁ Λόγος ἦν πρὸς τὸν θεόν could have made us think that we were concerned with the communion of two divine persons, the statement is pushed to its opposite extreme: θεὸς ἦν ὁ Λόγος. But this, too, is at once protected from any misunderstanding by, as it were, revoking what has just been said and repeating the πρὸς τὸν θεόν: **(v.2)** οὗτος ἦν ἐν ἀρχῇ πρὸς τὸν θεόν.[3]

The οὗτος is stressed: *this one*, of whom it has just been said that he was God.[4] The truth to be expressed lies between the alternating and apparently contradictory ways in which the Logos is defined: for it cannot be adequately expounded in the language of the myth; it has rather to be grasped from the succession of contradictory propositions. But this is the same contradiction that pervades the whole of the Gospel: certainly the Father and the Son are one (10.30), and yet the Father is

[1] It is not the case that the ἦν contradicts the equality of status, "because the identity of the Logos with ὁ θεός, if it was ever asserted, could not at the same time be limited to a past that is in some way marked off, by holding on to the ἦν, as is done here" (Zahn). The ἦν does not limit the identity to the past at all; it simply states from the standpoint of the speaker how it was ἐν ἀρχῇ, without inferring thereby, that it was once otherwise. With ref. to ἦν as the appropriate mode of speaking of the eternal being, cf. (after Thomas) Dillersberger 45f.

[2] The relation of the Λόγος to God is analogous to the relation of the "Name" (שֵׁם) of God to God in certain O.T. passages, in which the name of God stands alongside God, as a separate power, without in fact being anything separate. Rather it describes God, in so far as he acts, reveals himself (Ex. 23.21; Isa. 30.27; Ps. 8.2, 10; 20.2 etc.). Cp. O. Grether, Name und Wort Gottes im A.T. 1934, 28ff. 44ff. Cp. also I Jn. 1.2: (ἡ ζωή) ἥτις ἦν πρὸς τὸν πατέρα.

[3] Cp. the quite different statement in Philo de somn. I 65: ὁ πρὸ τοῦ λόγου θεός, and on this see Jonas, Gnosis II 1, p. 75.

[4] The οὗτος is not stressed for the sake of polemical antithesis to other divine figures, of whom it could be asserted that they were with God. Nor does the significance of v. 2 lie in its forming a transition to what follows (Ho.), as if the previous sentence were not suited to this purpose. Why should it not be?—The division: θεός ἦν. ὁ λόγος οὗτος ἦν κτλ., which acc. to Ambrstr. (quaest. 91; cp. Augustine, de doctr. christ. III 2, 3; cp. Nestle, ZNTW 8—1907—78ff.) Photinus had read, and which Jannaris defends (ZNTW 2—1901—24), is not only absurd, but contradicts the structure of the verse.

greater than the Son (14.28). Certainly the Son carries out the Father's will obediently (5.30; 6.38), and yet the Son has the same power as the Father; he bestows life and claims the same honour as the Father (5.21–27), and whoever sees the Son, sees the Father (14.9). God is there only in his revelation, and whoever encounters the revelation, really encounters *God*: θεὸς ἦν ὁ Λόγος. But again, the sense is not such as to suggest that by looking at the revelation and understanding it, one could make God one's own. God is only encountered in the revelation, when it is understood that it is his *revelation*: ὁ Λόγος ἦν πρὸς τὸν θεόν. It is as in the O.T.: there, the belief that God works in the historical event, and yet is not limited to this event, not identical with it, but stands beyond it as God, can be expressed by the juxtaposition of God and his name;[1] so here the Logos stands beside God, so that God must be understood from the outset as the "one who speaks,"[2] the God who reveals himself. And yet this kind of language, taken over from Gnosticism, is more strongly mythological than that found in the O.T. because it has to express still more: the revelation that the community has received in its historical Revealer, has its origin before time. The cosmic and saving event is grounded in the eternity and unity of the divine will: the Logos is not an act of revelation by God, limited to the temporal order, but is pre-existent. For this reason the ἐν ἀρχῇ is repeated here.[3]

The *idea of God* is therefore determined from the outset by the *idea of revelation*. To speak of God, means: to speak of his revelation; and to speak of his revelation, means: to speak of God. And revelation is not here intended in any general sense; it is rather the saving will of God that can be experienced in the incarnate Revealer. God was always the God that was made known in the historical revelation, and he was this alone. As such, however, he is the God beyond the world and time, who is never identical with his revelation in the way he would be, were he immanent in the world and time. Should anyone ask: How can one talk of revelation, whilst there was as yet no creation?—he would be misunderstanding the ἐν ἀρχῇ, and would be thinking of God and the Logos as two beings existing in time, whereas for man ἐν ἀρχῇ by itself is purely negative in meaning; it can only be given positive significance when the sentence continues: ἐν ἀρχῇ ἦν ὁ Λόγος. That is to say, the world and time will not be understood by reference to themselves, but

---

[1] Cp. p. 34, n. 2.

[2] Schl., on v. 1.

[3] This interpretation would receive corroboration, if v. 2 were the work of the Evangelist; in that case it would have displaced a (more strongly mythological?) sentence of the source that would have gone with the καὶ θεὸς ἦν ὁ λόγος, as the second part of the couplet. This suggestion is further substantiated, in that v. 2 has three stressed words, in contrast to the sentences of v. 1, which have only two stressed concepts.

by reference to the God who speaks in the revelation. Thus the philosopher's question, "Why is there not nothing?"[1] would also be answered by the sentence: ἐν ἀρχῇ ἦν ὁ Λόγος.

If Logos is to be translated, the translation can only be "*Word*", the meaning already given to it through the Gnostic myth.[2] It is nevertheless the appropriate translation—however much the conceptual meaning of the term Λόγος has disappeared[3]—in so far as the authentic function of the Λόγος is that of Revealer; that is to say, in so far as the Logos makes God known.[4] Of course Faust finds "it is impossible the *Word* so high to prize",[5] because his is in the first place a speculative question, concerned with the intelligible beginning of things, in the sense of the Greek ἀρχή, a question that makes him consider translating by thought (*Sinn*) or power (*Kraft*). But by discarding both these, and confidently writing deed (*Tat*), he simultaneously discards this formulation of the question and approaches the actual meaning of the text, in so far as he grasped the element of *judgment* in ἐν ἀρχῇ ἦν ὁ Λόγος correctly: how the world and time came to be, is not to be deduced from the timeless; their existence became event through the divine act ("Tat").

b) His Relation to the World: 1.3–4

3 πάντα δι' αὐτοῦ ἐγένετο,
καὶ χωρὶς αὐτοῦ ἐγένετο οὐδὲ ἕν.[6]
4 ὃ γέγονεν, ἐν αὐτῷ ζωὴ ἦν,
καὶ ἡ ζωὴ ἦν τὸ φῶς τῶν ἀνθρώπων.

Here again, the pattern is the same: the preceding statement has already indicated the direction this one will take: for if there is to be talk of God in a sense meaningful to men, there must also be at this point talk of the world, as the sphere in which men find themselves. Thus in v.3, in two parallel sections, the world is defined negatively and positively as the creation of the Logos. The concept κόσμος, of course, which first appears in v.10, is here represented by πάντα—

---

[1] M. Heidegger, Was ist Metaphysik? 1929, 29.
[2] Cp. p. 27 n. 2.
[3] The ἦν πρὸς shows at once the complete absence of the conceptual meaning; cp. further esp. the ἐθεασάμεθα in v. 14.
[4] Cp. v. 4f (φῶς), v. 14 and esp. v. 18.
[5] Tr.: Faust: Goethe: I. ll. 1224–1237. Tr. George Madison Priest.
[6] Instead of οὐδὲ ἕν, ℵ*D, some Min.s and Gnostics read οὐδέν. Acc. to Zn. this would be a correction, because when the ὅ γέγονεν was (falsely) connected to what follows, the οὐδὲ ἕν would have been intolerable. This reasoning is false, see below.

everything that there is—whereby no account is taken of the fact that this can be summarized as τὰ πάντα (τὸ πᾶν), whether it be as a whole over against God,[1] or as the unity of the divine cosmos in itself.[2] But the choice of πάντα rather than ὁ κόσμος[3] is a matter of liturgical style, which likes using parts of the word πᾶς, to arouse a feeling for the fullness of that which has its origin in God.[4] The addition of the negative statement to the positive is also made for liturgical reasons: everything by the Logos, nothing without him.[5]

It is thus stated as strongly as possible that everything without exception[6] has been made by the Logos: on the question of *how* or *when* there is no reflection. The ἐγένετο is the pure expression of the idea of creation[7]; it excludes both the idea of emanation, and the

---

[1] Rom. 11.36; I Cor. 8.6; Col. 1.16f.; Heb. 2.10. For Judaic thought, cp. Schl.,on this verse. There is no playing with prepositions in John, such as is loved by Paul, and stems from the Greek tradition.

[2] For the Greek, specifically Stoic tradition, cp. Ed. Norden, Agnostos Theos 1913, 240–250; for the Hermetic trad., Kroll, Herm. Trism. 43–50. Cp. also Lietzmann, Hdb. zum N.T. on Rom. 11.36.

[3] "The all" and "the World" are also used as equivalents by the Rabbis; Schl., Spr. und H. 17.

[4] Cp. note 2.

[5] For the oriental tradition, cp. J. Hempel, Gott und Mensch im A.T. 2nd ed. 1936, 205; J. Begrich, ZATW 46 (1928) 232. Example in DSD 11,11;

"And everything arises through his knowledge (בדעתו),
And everything that there is, he directs according to his plan (במחשבתו),
And without him nothing can be done".
(from the G. tr. by H. Bardtke).—Cp. IQH Pl. X2.

Cp. A. Ungnad, Die Religion der Babylonier und Assyrer 1921, 204f.
For the Greek-Latin tradition, Ed. Norden op. cit. 157, 3. 159, 1. 349f. 391f. Example in Lucr., de rer. nat. 1, 1ff.:

(4) . . . per te quoniam genus omne animantum
concipitur visitque exortum lumina solis.
. . .
(22) nec sine te quicquam dias in luminis oras
exoritur . . .

Cp. further example: Diog. v. Apoll. Fr. B5.
Cp. Deichgräber, Rhein. Mus. 87, 6.
Only by misunderstanding the style and construction of the verse is it possible to refer the two halves to different classes of the created world. It is the same kind of misunderstanding which finds polemic against other doctrines of the creation in v. 3b (O. Pfleiderer, Urchristentum 2nd ed. II 1902, 337), or indeed which discovers a sideglance at the Baptist in the οὐδὲ ἕν (Bldsp. 8). But Schl.'s interpretation is also impossible: the χωρίς does not exclude gradations in the participation of the divine word in the course of history.

[6] The emphatic ending οὐδὲ ἕν (see on v. 4) is a favourite way of ending a sentence, because of its effect. Cp. examples from comedy in Ed. Schwartz, Ap. IV 534, 3; in addit., Epict., Diss. II 18, 26; Ench. 1, 3 (οὐ μέμψῃ οὐδένα, οὐκ ἐγκαλέσεις τινί, ἄκων πράξεις οὐδὲ ἕν); Philonides, in Stob. Anth. III 35, 6 (III 688 Hense); Epigr. 646, 5f. Analogously, the οὐδε εἷς in Bel 18 (Thdtn.); I Macc. 7.46; Jos., ant. VI 266; Rom. 3.10, (12) (following Ps. 13.1; 52.4).

[7] Cp. Od. Sal. 16, 10ff.

conception of an original duality of light and darkness, according to which the world was formed by a tragic collision of both these powers. The Greek view, that wants to understand the world as a correlation of form and matter, is also excluded: the creation is not the arrangement of a chaotic stuff, but is the καταβολὴ κόσμου (17.24), creatio ex nihilo.[1]

But there is no consideration either of the question as to what belongs to the πάντα, what beings are included in the world. There is no mention either of other cosmic powers, or of the Devil, although he does play a part in the Gospel.[2] Of course he belongs to the created world as a possibility, and v. 5 will show that he belongs to the fallen world as a reality. On the other hand, it is clear that mankind belongs to the πάντα, and mankind alone is the subject of what follows. The fact that in v. 10 both the πάντα of v. 3 and the ἄνθρωποι of v. 5 are taken up again in ὁ κόσμος, shows that men are not just beings who like others happen to be found in the κόσμος, but that it is they who make the κόσμος a κόσμος.

The question what God was doing, while the Logos was creating, is illegitimate, after vv. 1f. The Logos is as little separated from God by his relation to the world, as he is afterwards by becoming incarnate (10. 30); otherwise he would not be the Logos of vv. 1f. He is not, as Philo's Logos, or the Nous of Plotinus, a mediator between the world and the transcendent Divinity; he is God himself in so far as he reveals himself.[3] The world is God's creation, and as such God's revelation; this is the sense of v. 3, and both these aspects are developed in v. 4.

If v. 3 had considered the "when" of the creation, the result would have been the necessity of distinguishing between the making of the world and its conservation, even if it were only in the primitive sense of Gen 1.11, 22, 28.[4] The radical nature of the idea of creation is evident at this point: in the beginning the world did not, so to speak, receive

---

[1] Philo, spec. leg. IV 187, attempts to interpret the idea of creation in a Greek manner: τὰ γὰρ μὴ ὄντα ἐκάλεσεν (God) εἰς τὸ εἶναι, τάξιν ἐξ ἀταξίας καὶ ἐξ ἀποίων ποιότητας καὶ ἐξ ἀνομοίων ὁμοιότητας καὶ ἐξ ἑτεροιοτήτων ταυτότητας καὶ ἐξ ἀκοινωνήτων καὶ ἀναρμόστων κοινωνίας καὶ ἁρμονίας καὶ ἐκ μὲν ἀνισότητος ἰσότητα ἐκ δὲ σκότους φῶς ἐργασάμενος· ἀεὶ γάρ ἐστιν ἐπιμελὲς αὐτῷ καὶ ταῖς εὐεργέτισιν αὐτοῦ δυνάμεσι τὸ πλημμελὲς τῆς χείρονος οὐσίας μεταποιεῖν καὶ μεθαρμόζεσθαι πρὸς τὴν ἀμείνω. For the Hermetic view cp. the fragments collected in Scott, Herm. I 544 to 548: 29.30. 33. 35. esp. 27: ὁ γὰρ λόγος αὐτοῦ (τ. θεοῦ) προελθών, παντέλειος ὢν καὶ γόνιμος καὶ δημιουργ-<ικ>ός, ἐν γονίμῳ φύσει πεσών . . . ἔγκυον τὸ ὕδωρ ἐποίησε.

[2] 8.44; 12.31; 13.2; 14.30; 16.11.

[3] Dillersberger (54ff.) finds in the δι' αὐτοῦ (not perchance, ἐξ αὐτοῦ) a hint that God himself stands in the background as the "first Creator"!

[4] The plants carry seeds; animals and men are to be fruitful and multiply. Philo, opif. m. 43f., has expanded the naïve idea by reflection along Stoic lines: the fruits of the plants are παρασκευαὶ πρὸς τὴν τῶν ὁμοίων ἀεὶ γένεσιν, τὰς σπερματικὰς οὐσίας περιέχοντες, ἐν αἷς ἄδηλοι καὶ ἀφανεῖς οἱ λόγοι τῶν ὅλων εἰσί, δῆλοι καὶ φανεροὶ γινόμενοι

as its own that which it then maintains by itself; both its beginning and its continuing existence are attributed to the Logos.[1] Precisely this is the meaning of **v. 4a**: ὃ γέγονεν, ἐν αὐτῷ ζωὴ ἦν:[2] the vitality of the whole creation has its origin in the Logos; he is the power which creates life.[3] And it does not matter here, whether one understands the text as: "What has come to be—in him (the Logos) was the life (for it)"; or as: "What has come to be—in it he (the Logos) was the life".[4] In both cases

---

καιρῶν περιόδοις. ἐβουλήθη γὰρ ὁ θεὸς δολιχεύειν (to run round in circles) τὴν φύσιν, ἀπαθανατίζων τὰ γένη καὶ μεταδιδοὺς αὐτοῖς αἰδιότητος.
Cf. W. W. Graf Baudissin, Kyrios III 458.

[1] This is correctly stressed by Calvin: simplex enim sensus est, sermonem dei non modo fontem vitae fuisse creaturis omnibus, ut esse inciperent, quae nondum erant, sed vivifica eius virtute fieri, ut in statu suo maneant.

[2] More recent exegesis (since the end of the fourth cent.) has usually preferred to take ὃ γέγονεν with the preceding οὐδὲ ἕν (and yet one would expect ὧν γεγ.!), and this has become normal practice since Chrys., in the interest of the struggle against the heretics (cp. Addit. Note I in Zn and E. Nestle, ZNTW 10, 1909, 262-264; also G. D. Kilpatrick, JTS 46 (1945) 191f.). But it not only contradicted the linguistic sensitivity of the older Greeks; it is in fact impossible; for it contradicts the rhythm of the verse, while on the other hand the artistic form of the Prologue is maintained, if the verse starts with ὃ γέγονεν, thereby picking up the ἐγένετο οὐδὲ ἕν, with which the previous sentence ended (v. p. 15f.). Cp. E. Hennecke, Congrès d'Histoire du Christianisme I 212f.; M. d'Asbeck, ebenda 220ff; Ad. Omodeo, Saggio 14f.—The correct division of the verses also in Grant 220; Wik., Dupont (35, 2) and Schlier. Otherwise, J. Rendel Harris, The Bull. of the John Rylands Library 6 (1922), 11. The elimination of ὃ γεγ. (Htm., Br., Hirsch) destroys the rhythm of the verse. With ref. to the variant ἐστιν, see below p. 40 n. 1.

[3] Ζωή, asserted with ref. to the Logos or Jesus, is not vitality itself, but the power that creates this vitality. The ζωή which he "has", consists (as is the case with the Father) in his making alive (5.21, 26). He gives the world its life (6.33); he gives his own the ζωὴ αἰώνιος (10.28). In this sense he "is" the ζωή (11.25; 14.6) as the ἄρτος τ. ζωῆς (6.35, 48), as the φῶς τ. ζωῆς (8.12). He bestows the ὕδωρ ζῶν (4.10; 7.38), the ἄρτος ζῶν (6.51). Because his words make alive, they are πνεῦμα καὶ ζωή (6.63), they are ῥήματα ζωῆς αἰωνίου (6. 68).

[4] The following is determinative for the interpretation: 1. The sentences of the Prologue, all the way through, are to characterise the Logos; v. 4a therefore may not interrupt the continuity, by being a characterisation of what is created. 2. The passage must speak of the ζωή as that power of the Logos that creates life (i.e. that which makes alive), not as the vitality itself (i.e. that which is alive); for the ζωή is immediately to be designated the φῶς, which stands over against what is created; therefore it cannot be the vitality that belongs to what is created. To understand it as follows is then impossible: "In it (what is created) was life". If ἐν αὐτῷ refers to what is created (in which case ἐν τούτῳ would be better, but is not essential), ζωή can only be the predic. and the subj. must be the "he" contained in the ἦν. This could be maintained on analogy with vv. 4b/5a; just as in v. 4b φῶς is the predic., and is then picked up again in v. 5a as the subj., so ζωή would be the predic. in v. 4a, in order to be picked up again in v. 5a as the subj. On the other hand, one is inclined to understand the ἐν αὐτῷ of the Logos, since the δι' αὐτοῦ and χωρὶς αὐτοῦ referred to him in v. 3 (thus Omodeo, Saggio 14f.).—Another punctuation is frequently preferred: ὃ γέγονεν ἐν αὐτῷ, ζωὴ ἦν. On no account may one then read it as: "That which came into being in him (in the Logos), was life"—as if this were the assertion of the ideal (pre-) existence in the Logos of all that has been created. This would come in the end to the idea that is expressed in a variety of ways by Philo (the λόγος as the κόσμος νοητός opif. m. 25 etc.), by Plotinus (the individual Ideas are contained in the δυάς that follows the ἕν:... ἦν δὲ καὶ νοῦς καὶ ζωὴ ἐν αὐτῷ VI 7, 8 p. 435, 9f. Volkm.), and in the Hermetic writings

it is stated that life was not inherent in creatures as creatures. This was the case from the very first—it is not as though it was once otherwise! But the ἦν (like that which follows) is spoken with the words οὐ κατέλαβεν (v. 5), οὐκ ἔγνω (v. 10), or with the incarnation in view: the possibility of revelation was given from the first.[1]

Verse 4b affirms that revelation is possible because the world is the creation of the Logos: καὶ ἡ ζωὴ ἦν τὸ φῶς τῶν ἀνθρώπων. This vitalising power,[2] it is stated, that gave permanency to the creation, was the light of men, i.e. the light for men.[3]

That φῶς is not spoken of figuratively is indicated by the article attached to it. The ζωή of the Logos is not *compared* with the light; it is the light.[4] That is to say, it signifies for men, in a way that is conclusive and final, everything that each individual, momentary light attempts to signify.[5] And what is the significance of the light? By making the world bright, it makes it possible for men to see. But sight is not only significant in that it enables man to orientate himself in respect of objects; sight is at the same time the means whereby man understands himself in his world, the reason he does not "grope in the dark", but sees his

---

(the κόσμος, hypostatized as a unity, is God's υἱός and εἰκών and is the πλήρωμα τῆς ζωῆς, 12.15); it may also be present in Col. 1.16f. This speculative idea contradicts the δι' αὐτοῦ ἐγένετο of v. 3.—In relating ἐν αὐτῷ to ὃ γέγονεν, it would be necessary to understand the ἐν instrumentally: "That which came into being through him, was life". In that case, why would the δι' αὐτοῦ of v. 3 not have been used again? For it is not credible that the ἐν αὐτῷ should be a false translation of an underlying בֵּיהּ (Burney, Burrows); for why should the translator have translated correctly in v. 3, and falsely in v. 4?! But both the possibilities that arise by connecting ἐν αὐτῷ with ὃ γέγονεν are excluded by the fact that they would grant the ζωή to the creation instead of to the Creator, and thus not fit in with what follows; both would have to understand ζωή as the vitality itself, and not as the power that creates life. To assume textual corruption (Htm., Br.) seems unnecessary to me.—With ref. to the Valentinian interpretation cp. W. von Loewenich, Das Johannes-Verständnis im 2 Jahrh. 1932, 77. 84.

Both Schaeder (in R. Reitzenstein and H. H. Schaeder, Studien zum antiken Synkretismus 1926, 312) and Black (56f.) in different ways take the ὃ γέγονεν ἐν αὐτῷ ζωή ἦν as a false rendering of the Aramaic text, which simply meant: "For in him was (the) life".—Wik. and Schlier also take the ἐν αὐτῷ to ref. to the λόγος.—The notion that Philo and Plotinus expound goes back to Plato's Timaeus.

[1] The ἐστιν, which ℵ D it syr^c , Valentinians and Iren. I 8, 5 read instead of ἦν, is an obvious correction, which overlooks the context, and is at once shown to be false by the ἦν of the following sentence.

[2] The art. is used by anaphora, or demonstratively, not generically.

[3] This is of course the sense of the Gen. τ. ἀνθρ.; elsewhere the Dat. is used in the same sense: cp. examples in Br.

[4] For this reason the Rabbinic passages, in which the Torah is compared with a light (Str.-B. II 357, cp. I 237f.), are without value for the interpretation. Cp. esp.: Siphre Dt. 33, 2 §349 a b in Bonsirven, Exègése Rabbinique, etc. 1939, 237; Megillah 16 b in P. Winter op. cit. (see on p. 23 n. 1) 359, note 53.

[5] In the same way, water and bread are not spoken of in ch. 4 and ch. 6 in a "figurative" sense; the significance of water and bread is only to be grasped in respect of what they do for men; see on the respective passages; so too on ch. 10 and ch. 15.

"way". In its original sense light is not an apparatus for illumination, that makes things perceptible, but is the *brightness* itself in which I find myself here and now; in it I can find my way about, I feel myself at home, and have no anxiety. Brightness itself is not therefore an outward phenomenon, but is the illumined condition of existence, of my own existence.[1] Such brightness is necessary for life; so that from the first, and throughout the ancient world, light and life, darkness and death are seen as belonging together.[2] And since man in the first place finds himself in the outside world and finds his way about there, light generally means the brightness of the day, i.e. the sunlight.[3] And from this light comes to be used frequently in a figurative sense, to denote the power which enables man to find his way about in life at all, whether it be the power of thought,[4] or the guiding norm,[5] or personal

---

[1] This is evident in the concept of "Augenlicht" (English: "Eyesight", tr.) which the German has as well as the Greek (Pind. Nem. 10, 40). "Light" can mean "eye" (Eur. Kykl. 633). Cp. Verg. Aen. 11, 819. In Aristoph. Thesm. 17, the ὀφθαλμός is seen as the ἀντίμιμος ἡλίου τροχῷ.—The deliverer, the bearer of salvation, can be described as "eye" (Pind. Ol. 2, 10; 6, 16; Pyth. 5, 56; Aesch. Pers. 168f., 980; Soph. Tr. 203; Oed. r. 987; Eur. Andr. 406; ὀφθαλμός βίου), just as well as "light" (Hom. Il. 16.39; 17.615; 18.102; Pind. Isthm. 2.17; Aesch. Pers. 300). Cp. Matt. 6.23 and parallels: ὁ λύχνος τοῦ σώματός ἐστιν ὁ ὀφθαλμός κτλ. (here the σῶμα φωτεινόν clearly does not mean the body that is "lit up", but the body or man that is "in the light", that can see, just as in Eph. 1.18 the πεφωτισμένοι ὀφθαλμοὶ τῆς καρδίας are the eyes that can see). Cp. Philo leg. all. III 171ff., where the λόγος is first described as κόρη (apple of the eye) and then as φῶς; Hipp. El. X 11, 5, p. 271, 10f. W.: ἡ κόρη τοῦ ὀφθαλμοῦ ... φωτίζεται. H. Usener, Götternamen 1896, 177ff., 331f.; R. Bultmann Philolog. 97 (1948), 1–35 (cp. this also on what follows).

[2] The concept of the "light of life" is familiar to Greek thought. "To be in the light" means "to live" (Soph. Phil. 415; 1212; Eur. Hec. 707), "to see the light" (Hom. Od. 4. 540, 833, etc.) means the same. Hades is dark. In line with this, death is considered in Semitic thought to be dark, cp. L. Dürr: Die Wertung des Lebens im A.T. und im antiken Orient 1926, 33, 35, 38; cp. Ps. 88.7, 13; 134.4; Job 10.21f.; 17.13. On "to see the light" for "to live", see Ps. 36.10; 49.20; Job 3.16; on "light of life", see Ps. 56.14; Job 33.30; on "light" = "life" see Job 3.20. With ref. to Judaism, see too A. Marmorstein ZNW 32 (1933), 36.

[3] Cp. the hymns to Shamash, A. Ungnad, Die Religion der Bab. und Ass. 1921, 185ff.; Altoriental. Texte zum A.T. 2nd ed. 1926, 242ff., in which the significance of light for life comes out very clearly.

[4] So especially in Greek thought, which developed the notion of ὄμμα τῆς ψυχῆς in this sense. Cp. J. Stenzel, Die Antike I (1925), 256ff.; II (1926), 235ff. Above all, cp. Plato's exposition of the idea of the ἀγαθόν as the φῶς—Resp. VI p. 507e–509b. Cp. P. Friedländer: Platon I 2nd ed. 1954, 70, 74. Hellenistic Judaism took over this way of talking. Just as in Wis. 7.10 the σοφία is called the φῶς, so Philo describes σοφία and ἐπιστήμη as φῶς διανοίας (spec. leg. I 288; migr. Abr. 39f.); so too νοῦς (post. Caini 57f.) and παιδεία (leg. all. III 167) are called φῶς, and ἀγνοία is considered blindness (ebr. 154ff.). Philo, of course, speaks of the ὄμμα τῆς ψυχῆς as well (migr. Abr. 39 etc.).

[5] So especially in O.T.; Ps. 19.9; 119.105; Prov. 6.23; Bar. 4.2 etc.; for the ancient Orient in general cp. H. Gressmann, Messias, 1929, 290–292. For Rabbinic Judaism, cp. Odeberg 140–144; see also 286; in addit. see Dupont 67f., 77ff., and esp. Sverre Aalen, Die Begriffe Licht und Finsternis im A.T., im Spätjudentum, und im Rabbinismus, 1951 esp. 178ff., 272ff. Str.-B. II 427f. ibidem 357 for the comparison of the Torah with a light.—

integrity.[1] Alongside this, the original sense of "light" as the illumined quality of existence is preserved by its use to designate happiness and salvation;[2] thus the word comes to describe the divine sphere in general;[3] and its original meaning is preserved above all by the description of salvation itself, in its "eschatological" sense, as "the light".[4] Thus τὸ φῶς comes to mean exactly the same as the eschatological ζωή, and is used as an alternative to it, or combined with it.[5]

But Greek thought too originally connects "the notion of sin and the image of darkness, and the notion of a redemption and salvation from evil and the image of the light", (Stenzel op. cit. I 256); in the same way for Plato (see previous note) the idea of the ἀγαθόν is that which, as the φῶς, makes the world intelligible.—For Hellenistic Judaism, cp. Wis. 5.6 (τὸ τῆς δικαιοσύνης φῶς); 18.4 (τὸ ἄφθαρτον τοῦ νόμου φῶς); Test. Levi 14.4 (τὸ φῶς τοῦ νόμου). Philo speaks of the φῶς of the Logos as an ἀρετή (leg. all. I 18) and calls the conscience a φῶς (deus imm. 135; Jos. 68); similarly of the νόμοι decal. 49. For the N.T. cp. Rom. 13. 12; I Thess. 5.4ff.; Eph. 5.8ff.—To a certain extent the Iranian linguistic usage has worked its way in (esp. in the Test. Patr.), whereby truth and light, deceit and darkness belong together; cp. Bousset, Rel. des Jdt. 3rd ed. 334. 515f.; see Kuhn ZThK 47 (1950), 206f.; 49 (1952), 308f.

[1] Cp. Str.-B. II 427 on Jn. 3.19.

[2] On the Greek usage, see p. 41 n. 1; for the O.T. usage cp. Amos 5.18; Job 22.28; Ps. 27.1. The king, as bringer of salvation, is described in ancient oriental idiom as the "Sun" and so on; L. Dürr, Ursprung und Ausbau der israelit.-jüd. Heilandserwartung 1925, 106ff. Cp. T. Boman, Das hebräische Denken im Vergleich mit dem Griechischen 112f.

[3] Naturally the sphere of the divine, which is full of undisturbed life, and of happiness and joy, is conceived everywhere as the sphere of light and splendour. God is clothed in light (Ps. 104.2; Isa. 60.19f. etc.; cp. Eth. Enoch 14.15ff.; I Tim. 6.16); and beside him sun and moon themselves appear black as the Moors (Apc. Mos. 35f.). Heavenly figures are numinously bright (II Macc. 15.13; Mk. 9.3; 16.5; Lk. 24.4 etc.), while the Devil is black (II Cor. 6.14; Bar. 4.10; 20.1; cp. J. Dölger, Die Sonne der Gerechtigkeit und der Schwarze 1918). Cp. too Staerk, Erlöserw. 11; Aalen (see p. 41 n. 5). Corresponding to this, in the divine world as conceived by the Greeks κάλλος λαμπρόν, αὐγὴ καθαρά (Plato Phaidr. 250bc) are dominant ideas; cp. Plat. Alc. I 134de: εἰς τὸ θεῖον καὶ λαμπρὸν ὁρῶντες —εἰς τὸ ἄθεον καὶ σκοτεινὸν βλέποντες. Cp. Dodd 201ff. In Philo too, Jos. 14.5, the heavenly world is seen as φως εἰλικρινέστατον καὶ καθαρώτατον. With ref. to Gnosticism, examples are unnecessary; cp. H. Jonas, Gnosis und spätantiker Geist 1934, 103, and Hipp. El. VIII 9.3, p. 228 7f. W.; C. Herm. 1.21; 7.2; 10.4, 6. On the Mandaeans see Helm. Kittel, Die Herrlichkeit Gottes 1934, 115–124.—Cp. p. 43 note 1. Cp. Percy 23ff., 51ff.

[4] In the O.T. cp. Isa. 9.1; 60.1–3, 19f.; Zech. 14.7; Dan. 12.3 etc. In Judaism cp. Str.-B. II 428; cp. too Staerk Erlösererw. 23; Dupont 82ff. The eschatological existence of the Christians is characterised by φῶς: II Cor. 4.6; Rom. 13.12; I Thess. 5.5; Coll. 1.12 etc. Examples in Gnosticism, according to which the emancipated soul returns to the world of light, are superfluous; but cp. Od. Sal. 11.19; 21.3, 6; 38.1.—The transference into the eschatological existence can be described as a "being illumined" or a "becoming light", cp. C. Herm. 13.18f., 21; Od. Sal. 11.14; 25.7; 36.3; 41.6 etc. Acc. to Philo (vit. Mos. II 288) Moses is transformed εἰς νοῦν ἡλιοειδέστατον; cp. C. Herm. 10.6; Plotin. Enn. VI 9,9, p. 522, 15ff. Cp. G. P. Wetter: Phos 61ff.; J. Dölger Sol. salutis 1920.

[5] Esp. in Gnosticism; cp. C. Herm. 1.9, 12, 21; 13.9, 18; Λόγος τέλειος (Scott, Herm. I 374; Reitzenst., HMR 3rd ed. 286). Od. Sal. 10.1ff.; 38.1ff. With ref. to Judaism, see Bousset, Relg. des Jdt. 3rd ed. 277. Cp. II Tim. 1.10: φωτίσαντος δὲ ζωὴν καὶ ἀφθαρσίαν. Of course ἀθανασία etc. can take the place of ζωή—cp. C. Herm. 1.28; 10.4; Od. Sal. 11.11f.; Act. Thom. 12, p. 118.9f.

For just as "life" necessarily includes the definitive understanding of the self, that knows no further question or mystery, so the "light" for which man longs as this definitive state of enlightenment, necessarily includes freedom from death, from the fate that makes existence sheerly unintelligible.[1] But the more completely φῶς is regarded as something eschatological, the stronger grows the conviction that the definitive illumination of existence does not lie within human possibilities, but can only be divine gift. Thus φῶς comes to mean revelation.[2] And where one speaks of a Revealer, one can describe him as the "Light" or as the Giver of light.[3]

---

[1] By being combined with ζωή (ἀθανασία), φῶς often comes to mean a divine power. Indeed, the essential nature of the Divinity is seen as φῶς: and by coupling together the concepts of light and fire, the conception of the divinity as the radiating archetypal light becomes particularly significant, where the relation between God and the world is conceived in terms of emanation. The result is a metaphysic of light, where the divine light, as the νοητὸν φῶς etc. (see p. 53 note 2 on v. 9) is contrasted with the perceptible light. Cp. Cl. Baeumker, Witelo (Beitr. zur Geschichte der Philosophie des Mittelalters III 2) 1908, 357–421. Cp. also Kroll, Herm. Trism. 21ff. In line with this, in cultic piety φῶς comes to mean a power-substance of magical efficacy, or the power of immortality (for this cp. esp. G. P. Wetter, Phos 1915; Pascher, Königsweg 177ff.). So too in the language used in the Mysteries; here the deifying act of consecration is carried out with the aid of light effects, and the consecration itself is described as φωτισμός, φωτισθῆναι; this is also used to describe Christian baptism (cp. besides Wetter: G. Wobbermin, Religionsgeschichtl. Studien 1896 154ff.; Bousset Kyr. 2nd ed. 172ff.; Reitzenst. HMR 3rd ed. passim). So too in magic, where φῶς is synon. with other designations of the divine power, such as πνεῦμα and δόξα (Wetter op. cit.). At the same time φῶς continues to mean the illumination of the self-understanding (see following note).

[2] Φῶς becomes synonymous with γνῶσις (on this concept see ThWB I 693, 18ff.), cp. C. Herm. 1.32; 7.2; C. Herm. 10.21 speaks of τὸ τῆς γνώσεως φῶς; Λόγος τέλειος (Scott. Herm. I 374); one can talk of the illumination of the γνῶσις (C. Herm. 13.18) or of the νοῦς (C. Herm. 13.21). Cp. the association of ζωή with ψυχή and of φῶς with νοῦς in C. Herm. 1.17. For φῶς γνώσεως as designation of the eschatological salvation see Test. Levi 4.3; 18.3. Philo too describes φῶς as the divine revelation; ebr. 44; Abr. 70, 119. So too Porphyr. ad Marc. 13.20 p. 282, 22ff.; 287, 18ff.; Nauck. In the Od. Sal. the "light" is the revelation proclaimed in the Word: 6.17; 10.1, 6; 11.11; 12.5, 7; 29.7ff.; 32.1ff.; and just as light and word can be combined, so can light and truth; 18.6; 25.7, 10.—This involves in Gnosticism the clear statement that the knowledge given in the revelation is self-knowledge; cp. ThWB I 694, 26ff., esp. C. Herm. 1.19–21; Od. Sal. 6.18: "For they all came to know themselves in the Lord"; 7.12; 13.—Furthermore, light retains its fundamental meaning—the illumination of existence—where the mystic gaze beholds the divine light, in which all duality disappears, and nothing more that is individual can be recognised, and in which consciousness of the self finally fades away. For what is dominant here is the longing for definitive self-understanding, which the duality, the separation of subject and object, is felt to destroy. It can only be said to have been reached, when I see myself in the "All", and that means ultimately as the All. Cp. the descriptions in Phil. opif. m. 71; ebr. 44; C. Herm. 10.4–6; Plot., Enn. V 8, 10; VI 9.9. Since in such a vision every opposite ceases to exist (cp. P. Friedländer Platon I 1928, 93–95), it is understandable that the light can turn into darkness. The first instance of this seems to be Dionys. Areop. de myst. theol. 1 and 2; ep. 1 and 5; since then it has occurred both in medieval and modern mysticism (Novalis and Rilke).

[3] The Logos is light acc. to Phil. leg. all. III 171 (cp. opif. m. 31). Just as the Νοῦς

Jesus is the φῶς in this eschatological sense in John; he is the Revealer, who gives man that particular understanding of himself in which he has the "life". The Prologue, however, affirms that the significance that the Logos has in his incarnate state has been his from the beginning: ἦν τὸ φῶς τῶν ἀνθρώπων. And to say that he was the light as the Creator, as the ζωή, is to say that the possibility of the *illumination* of existence (the salvation that consists in the definitive understanding of existence itself) was inherent in its very *origin*. Creation is at the same time revelation, inasmuch as it was possible for the creature to know of his Creator, and thus to understand himself. Thus the self-understanding that would have been decisive for man, would have been knowledge of his creatureliness;[1] only with such knowledge would he have been "in the light", and thus have had life in the sense in which created man (in contrast to the Creator) can have it.[2] It is self-evident, and in line with the synonymity of φῶς and ζωή in their eschatological sense (see page 41f.), that the Revealer, by being the "light", gives the "life". Equally the significance of his coming is expressed by saying that he is "the light of the world",[3] that he "has come into the world as the light"

C. Herm. 1.6 is φῶς (Or ζωὴ καὶ φῶς 9, 12, 21), so his son is the φωτεινὸς λόγος springing up out of him, Od. Sal. 41.14:

> "And light dawned from the Word,
> That was beforetime in him (the Father)".

Od. Sal. 12.7 (of the Logos),

> "For as its work, so is its end,
> For it is light and the dawning of thought".

GR 91.11ff.

> "A beloved son comes ...
> He comes with the illumination of life".

[1] This is also the sense of the revelation in Od. Sal. 7.14:

> "He has given himself
> To be revealed to them that are his,
> In order that they may recognise him that made them,
> And that they might not suppose that they came of themselves".

[2] That the ζωή was the φῶς, is not therefore to be interpreted in the sense that there have always been expressions of "spiritual" life in the world, such as morality or culture, that is to say, something that testifies to divine life. Nor is there any reference to OT revelation; this is excluded by the τῶν ἀνθρώπων. Rather the thought is the same as in Rom. 1.18–21 (cp. Wis. 13.1f.; and see C. Herm. 5.2): the world is originally intelligible, as creation, and so too is God's claim on man as his creature, the claim being that man should honour God. Of course man's knowledge of his creatureliness is neither a theory nor "an emotion of creatureliness", grounded in some kind of "numinous" experience; it is, rather, existential self-understanding, whatever the thoughts or feelings may be in which it becomes explicit.—Correctly, against the view that sees sporadic "acts" of the Logos in the pre-Christian era, W. Lütgert, Die Joh. Christologie, 2nd ed., 1916, 82ff.

[3] 8.12; 9.5; cp. 3.19–21; 12.35f.

(12.46), and that he has come to give the world "life";[1] and in the same way it can be said that man receives the φῶς τῆς ζωῆς from him (8.12). The integral connection between light and life is grounded in the fact that life achieves its authenticity in the proper understanding of itself.

For this reason Catholic exegesis (Tillm., Dillersb.) is right in not wanting to take the ζωή of v. 4 in any sense other than that of the ζωή which the incarnate Jesus has, and in the power of which he "makes alive"[2]. For clearly the ζωή of v. 4 is, in the first place, the life-creating force that calls the creation into existence; but this existence is not bare living vitality in the most general sense; it is—because the ζωή is the φῶς—that life that carries within itself the necessity and the possibility of illumined existence. The ζωή bestowed by Jesus is not *another* ζωή different from that bestowed by the pre-existent Logos; Jesus gives man the possibility, realized through faith in him, of understanding himself in the ζωή. The saving revelation brings back the lost possibility of revelation in creation[3]; and we can leave out of account for the moment the fact that this possibility, as it has been restored to men, is different from what it was, before it had been lost originally.

The statement that the ζωή of the Logos was the φῶς for men, includes the conviction that it *alone* was the φῶς. This kind of statement can only be made if one sees men as beings who need light, who as men live in the possibility of erring, of going wrong; the possibility of darkness corresponds to the possibility of light. Thus the way is prepared for v. 5.

B. 1.5–18: The Logos as the Revealer in History

a) *Preliminary Description:* 1.5–13

5 καὶ τὸ φῶς ἐν τῇ σκοτίᾳ φαίνει,
καὶ ἡ σκοτία αὐτὸ οὐ κατέλαβεν.

Whereas up till now the imperfect tense has been used to speak of the Logos, with φαίνει there is a change to the present.[4] For it is the present revelation which is being discussed here. But in what sense?

---

[1] 6.33; 10.10; I Jn. 4.9; cp. 4.10f.; 6.35, 48, 51, 63, 68; 7.38; 11.25; 14.6. Thus Wisdom (see pp. 22f.), which corresponds to the Logos, promises life to the man who listens to her, while he who lacks her has death (Prov. 8.35).

[2] See page 39 n. 3.

[3] See on verse 5.

[4] The source, in which all statements before v. 14 referred to the pre-existent Logos (see p. 15f.), must have had the imperfect, or alternatively, if it was written in Aram. (or Syr.) a participle with imperf. sense (Burney and Burrows translate back to מְנַהַר. However φαίνει is not a mistranslation but has been deliberately altered.

One might be tempted to take the pres. φαίνει to indicate a timeless presence, so that it would refer to the pre-temporal Logos. Yet the οὐ κατέλαβεν which follows cannot have any other meaning than that of the οὐκ ἔγνω and the οὐ παρέλαβον of vv. 10f., i.e. of the rejection of the incarnate Revealer; φαίνει must then refer to *his* revelation, in the same sense as the τὸ φῶς ... ἤδη φαίνει of I Jn. 2.8. Yet it does not, or rather it does not only, refer to his earthly work, which for the Evangelist lies in the past, but to the revelation which has been given to the world through this work and now lives on in the community.[1]

At first sight the sentence is a riddle; for it is not till v. 14 that the miracle is named by virtue of which it is possible to say: τὸ φῶς ἐν τῇ σκοτίᾳ φαίνει. The miracle however is already hinted at in vv. 9–13. Yet v. 5a anticipates the consequence of this miracle and so states, as it were, the theme of the Gospel, which can be fully understood only on the basis of what has been said in vv. 1–4: it is the light of the eternal Logos, which shone in creation, which has now become present. Here already, therefore, we can clearly hear the claim which is made in v. 14 by the identification of the Logos with the man Jesus: that in Jesus there shone a light which was none other than that which had always shone in creation. Thus the understanding of himself which man gains in the saving revelation is in no way different from that which he should have already derived from the revelation in creation.[2] There is continuity between creation and redemption.

Yet it is assumed in this statement that the φῶς shone in vain in creation[3]; and this assumption is brought out by ἐν τῇ σκοτίᾳ: The men for whom the light now shines in the saving revelation were previously without light! They were in darkness; not *although* as creatures they had the possibility of light; but on the contrary, just *because* they had this possibility. For just as light is the illumined state of existence, so darkness is that constitution of existence in which it does not understand itself, is lost, does not know its way (12.35), is blind (Chap. 9) and dead,

---

[1] This is confirmed by the introduction in vv. 6–8 of the Baptist as witness, and of course as a witness to Jesus as the incarnate Revealer, as vv. 15, 19 ff. show; see p. 15f.—In the source, in which the sentence referred to the pre-temporal Logos (see p. 45 n. 4), it had much the same sense as Wis 7.27f.:

> μία δὲ οὖσα πάντα δύναται (sc. ἡ σοφία),
> καὶ μένουσα ἐν αὐτῇ τὰ πάντα καινίζει,
> καὶ κατὰ γενεὰς εἰς ψυχὰς ὁσίας μεταβαίνουσα
> φίλους θεοῦ καὶ προφήτας κατεργάζεται.

Cp. on v. 12.—By recognising exceptions to the massa perditionis even before the revelation in the Incarnate, the source has not abandoned the fundamental understanding of φῶς.

[2] Basically what is assumed are the ideas expressed in vv. 5.9–11, as understood by the source.

[3] Cp. Od. Sal. 7.12 see p.44 n. 1.

for to the real life belongs the illumined state of the self-understanding. To answer the question how existence can go astray, or whence the σκοτία has come into the creation, with mythological speculation would be to misunderstand the notion of creation in the Prologue, for it has abandoned every kind of mythology. The σκοτία is not an autonomous power existing alongside the φῶς, but it is only because of the light that there is darkness at all; and this is because the φῶς has its basis in the ζωή of the Creator, because men are creatures who can find the proper understanding of themselves only by returning to their origin. It is because the φῶς is not a mysterious substance which can be possessed when present, but is the light of self-understanding which man is challenged to embrace, for which he is always seeking, because he is sought of it. It is the light of the self-understanding, which does not consist simply in knowing about the self as a neutral phenomenon, but is the knowing choice of one's self, which lies at the root of every particular act. If it is man's part to understand himself—and it is, if the ζωή which called him into existence is for him the φῶς— then this means that he also has the possibility of σκοτία, the possibility that instead of being illumined by his knowledge of his creatureliness, he should be darkened by turning away from his Creator and by the folly of imagining that he has his origins in himself. Of course the Prologue gives no explanation of why men seized upon the possibility of σκοτία instead of φῶς; indeed such an explanation may not even be attempted, if the basic meaning of φῶς and σκοτία as possibilities of human self-understanding is not to be surrendered.

Yet the ζωή of the Logos does not cease to be the φῶς of men just because men have chosen the possibility of darkness. Rather it is only because the Logos is constantly present as the light of men that the world of men can be σκοτία at all. For darkness is neither a substance nor the sheer power of fate; it is nothing other than the revolt against the light. The interpretation in the Gospel of the darkness of the world as the constant revolt and hostility against God has found its expression in the mythological figure of the devil, of the ἄρχων τοῦ κόσμου τούτου. He is the murderer and the liar (8.44) because he represents the deliberate blindness of the world, which excludes everyone who belongs to it from the true knowledge of himself and thus robs him of the proper life.[1]

V. 5a states that the light of the saving revelation shines in this world of darkness and v. 5b adds that the same process has been repeated: καὶ ἡ σκοτία αὐτὸ οὐ κατέλαβεν, that is to say that the darkness

---

[1] For further discussion cp. on κόσμος v. 10.

has not understood it.[1] The thematic character of v. 5 thus comes to full expression. The two sentences summarise the content of the Gospel under one aspect, and indeed under that aspect that is presented and developed above all in the first part, chaps. 3–12. That the rejection of the revelation runs parallel to its acceptance by the believers will be said in vv. 12f., which thus formulates the other side of the theme as it is presented and developed in the second part of the Gospel (chaps. 13–17). The statement of only one side of the theme first, as if the other did not exist, brings out immediately the character of the revelation as critical of this world, its nature as offence, and so it shows the particular relation to the world which is chosen by those who open themselves to the revelation. The terrifying nature of the fact which is stated in v. 5 is again especially stressed by the continued liturgical style, where all the sentences are linked by a simple καί, and by the absence here also of an adversative particle. These solemnly objective tones lend to the verse the character, as it were, of a divine judgement.[2]

At this point the Evangelist leaves his source, which he will take up again in vv. 9–13, when he turns to the preliminary exposition of his theme, to insert in **vv. 6–8** a note on the *witness of the Baptist to the Light*.[3] In so doing he anticipates another theme which will be heard at

[1] Since the οὐ κατέλαβεν has its parallels in οὐκ ἔγνω, οὐ παρέλαβον vv. 10f., καταλαμβάνειν cannot have the meaning of "attack" (cp. on 12.35), "seize" in a hostile sense, "overwhelm", although Orig. and the majority of Gk. exegetes took it in this sense, but can only mean "grasp" = to make one's own, as in Rom. 9.30, I Cor. 9.24, Phil. 3.12; Plat. Phaed. 250d etc. Cp. Mand. Lit. 131: "The worlds do not know thy (sc. Manda d'Haije) name, do not understand thy light"; esp. Od. Sal. 42.3f.:

"I am hidden to them who do not 'grasp' me,
But I come to those who love me."

"Grasp" here translates אחד (Heb. אחז), and Schaeder (Studien 312f. 339) suggests that this is also true of the source of the Prologue. "Grasp" here does not mean a simple "understanding", (which is not uncommon for καταλαμβ. v. Br.), but the comprehension of faith (vv. 7 12).—Omodeo (Saggio 16f.) wants to find two meanings in κατελ.: to seize in a hostile way, and thereby to see through and to understand. Wik. and Schlier take κατελ. as "grasp". Hoskyns (143) and Barrett see both meanings.—Burney's suggestion of a mistranslation (according to Ball): "The darkness did not darken it", is totally unnecessary and is rejected by Burrows, Torrey, Schaeder, Colwell (108f.) and Black (10).—According to Dodd 156–160 the οὐ κατέλαβεν, or alternatively the οὐκ ἔγνω (v. 10), goes back to OT prophetic tradition.—According to Mowry, who takes καταλ. as "overwhelm", it is the victory of the pre-existent Logos over the darkness which is stated in v. 5. But this breaks down as soon as we look at the double νῦν in 12.31.

[2] This style can be traced throughout the whole Gosp. (1.10f.; 3.11, 19; 7.34; 10.25 etc.); in itself it is permissible in Gk.; for Gk. knows καί in the sense of "and yet" (Br. and Colwell 86f.). Yet this is irrelevant here, for what we have is the simple καί of liturgical style.

[3] I have set out the grounds for taking vv. 6–8 as a note inserted by the Evanglist into his source, on pp. 15f. In the first place the insertion is characterised by its wholly prosaic style, which contrasts strongly with the style of the source. Further it exhibits

frequent intervals in the first half of the Gospel.[1] Its insertion here shows how important this witness is for him; indeed the more one sees how loosely this insertion is related to the main line of thought of the Prologue (and it is no more than a note), the more apparent it becomes that the Evangelist includes it here for a special personal reason. For he is concerned here to oppose those who also proclaim the φῶς of the Logos, and its appearance in a historical figure, but who venerate none other than the Baptist as the incarnate Logos.[2]

---

the characteristic style of the Evangelist. This may be summarised in the following way: 1) in his imitation of OT forms of speech, which are foreign to his source; 2) in peculiarities of linguistic usage which are typical of Rabbinic style (cf. Schl.'s study of this question. It is significant that the parallels he finds, in so far as they are parallels at all, only apply to the passages written by the Evangelist himself, and not to those which have been taken from the "Revelation discourses", as is the case with the Prologue); 3) in peculiarities of usage characteristic of the Evangelist himself.—Ad 1. ἐγένετο ἄνθρωπος corresponds to אֶחָד וַיְהִי אִישׁ Judg. 13.2; 19.1; 1 Sam. 1.1 (cp. Mk. 1.4; Lk. 1.5); it is a Hebraism and not (as one would expect from the source) an Aramaism or Syriacism (in Syriac והוא occurs only as a Hebraism, Nöldeke, Syr. Gramm. para. 338C). ὄνομα αὐτῷ Ἰ. is equally an O.T. figure of speech, cp. Judg. 13.2; 17.1; 1 Sam. 1.1; 9.1f. etc.; so also in Rev. 6.8; 9.11 (no proof of course of the Aramaic source, as Burney 30–32 suggests; Colwell 34–36 rightly takes the opposite view: the phrase also occurs in Greek).—Ad 2. ἦλθεν εἰς μαρτυρίαν corresponds to בָּא לְ (most often with inf. see Schl. on Mt. 2.2; sometimes however with subst., see Schl. on Jn. 1.29; Schl., Spr. und H. compares εἰς μαρτυρίαν with the rabbinic לְעֵדוּת); Greek would normally have ἦλθεν μαρτυρήσων; εἰς μαρτυρίαν κληθῆναι Plat. leg. XI p. 937a is in no way analogous.—Ad. 3. οὗτος ἦλθεν εἰς μ. is qualified by a ἵνα clause, cp. 11.4 and similar cases where a demonstrative is qualified by a ἵνα clause, such as 6.29, 40.; 15.8, 12f.; for this see Festg. Ad. Jül. 142 and also Schweizer 89. The Evangelist favours the exepeget. ἵνα clause (e.g. 4.34), which in the Koine suppresses the inf. (Bl-D. para. 392; Raderm. 2. ed. 190–193). The explanation of the demonstrative often follows the pattern found in v. 8, where that which is asserted in the explanatory clause is preceded by a negation of its opposite: cp. 1.31; 2.25; 3.17; 6.46; 7.22; 10.18; 11.4; 15.15; 17.9; Festg. für Jül. 143. Emphasised in this way ἐκεῖνος occurs throughout the Gospel; cp. v. 18 etc.; also p. 79 n. 3. (It is not a Semitism, as αὐτός often is in LXX and in the Synoptics, Bl.-D. para. 277, 3).—Under 2 and 3 we must also include the ellipsis ἀλλ' ἵνα v. 8, which is characteristic both of rabbinic usage (Schl., Spr. und H.) and of the Evangelist (1.31; 9.3; 13.18; 14.31; 15.25; 1 Jn. 2.19). Of course such ellipses are also possible in Greek (Bl.-D. §448, 7; Raderm. 2 ed. 170). Burney's suggestion that ἵνα is a mistranslation of ד (ὅς) is somewhat arbitrary (Goguel, RevHPh. 3, 1923, 375; Colwell 96–99, who further shows that ἵνα in Hellenistic Greek can occur in the sense of ὅς. Cp. too Black 59f.; A.W. Argyle, JThSt.NS V(1954), 210; E. Ullendorf, NtSt II (1955), 50f.).

[1] Not only in the extended account of the witness of the Baptist, 1. 19–34, but also 1.35f.; 3.22ff.; 5.31ff.; 10.41.

[2] Cp. pp. 16f.—Schaeder (Studien 325f.) claims that v. 6a also belongs to the source. He argues that ἄνθρωπος is not, as Burney suggests, a translation of גַּבְרָא but goes back to אֱנָשׁ or אֱנוֹשׁ. The translator mistook this for an appellative (which is found in the Hebrew and in the Nabataean inscriptions), whereas it is in fact the proper noun "Man", found in the Mandaeans writings. The sense would then be: "Enosh was sent by God". But 1. It is hard to believe that the translator, who was otherwise well acquainted with the figure of the "Man", would have been capable of this mistake; we would have to say that

In his account of the *appearance of John*, the Evangelist falls into the style of Old Testament narrative[1]; it is clear to any Christian reader that, as is shown in 1.19ff., it is the Baptist whom the Evangelist has in mind. Evidently he assumes that his readers will know whom he is referring to; no attempt is made, by way of introduction, to chronicle his activity, as in the Synoptics (Mk. 1.6 & par; Lk. 3.1f.); all interest is concentrated on his μαρτυρία. Accordingly neither here nor elsewhere are we told anything about the content of his preaching; he is not the "forerunner", but merely a witness; even his ministry of baptism, which is not so much as mentioned here, serves only his calling as a witness (1.19ff.; 3.22ff.). This is why his authorisation as a witness is immediately brought out by ἀπεσταλμένος παρὰ θεοῦ.[2] He came[3] to bear witness to the light[4]; and this means, as is clearly shown in 1.19–34, to *Jesus* as the Revealer, and not to the divine revelation (the pre-existent Logos) in general. His witness[5] consists in his confession that Jesus is

---

he had consciously altered the sense; 2. ἐγένετο ἄνθρωπος does not correspond to the style of the source; 3. on this understanding, the structure of the source becomes unintelligible; it is not possible that the appearance of the heavenly emissary should be mentioned there before v. 14, cp. pp. 15f. For the argument against Schaeder see Ch.H Kraeling, Anthropos and Son of Man 1927, 170–174.

[1] See p. 48 n. 3. It is therefore not permissible to take ἀπεσταλμένος together with ἐγένετο = ἀπεστάλη, even if Greek exegesis on occasions understood it in this way (Br.).

[2] ἀποστέλλειν (in contrast to πέμπειν), indicates primarily the task and authorisation of the emissary (Rengstorf, ThWB I 397ff.). It should be noticed that John always uses ἀποστ. in the same sense, cp. 1, 19.22; 5, 36f; 20, 21 and C. C. Tarelli, JThSt. 47 (1946), 175. It is therefore frequently used of a mission with a divine task and a divine authorisation, both in the LXX and in Judaism, as well as in the Cynics (Rengstorf, loc. cit.). The characterisation of the Revealer or the revelation as "having been sent" by God is particularly striking in Gnosticism; cp. Br. on 3.17; G. P. Wetter, Der Sohn Gottes 26ff.; Bultmann ZNTW 24 (1925), 105f.; G. Bornkamm, Mythos und Leg. 9f. See C. Herm. 4.4 (the Κρατήρ of the divine revelation); act. Jo. 96 p. 198, 13 (the word of the mysteries).—The place to which the emissary is sent may be indicated (Ex. 3.10–15; Mt. 15.24; etc. Epict. III 22, 23.46; IV 8.31), but need not necessarily be so, as it is perfectly clear when the emissary is sent from God (Is. 6.8; Jer. 14.14; Mt. 10. 40; Rom. 10.15; 1 Cor. 1.17; etc.; Epict. I 14, 6); this is the case here.

[3] His coming corresponds to his mission; this is not the normal OT expression for the appearance of the divine emissaries (prophets), but it is frequently used in the NT for the appearance of Jesus (John usually adds εἰς τὸν κόσμον). Where the coming of the emissary corresponds to his mission, it is not possible to trace the usage back to cultic language, in which the coming of the Godhead is its epiphany, or to eschatological language (as it occurs frequently in OT and NT). For an analogous usage and for the roots of this usage, we must look rather to Gnostic language, which corresponds to the notion of revelation; cp. J. Schneider, ThWB II 662ff.; G. P. Wetter 82ff.; Bultmann, Gesch, der synopt. Trad. 2 ed. 164ff. = Hist. of the synopt. Trad. 152ff.; ZNTW 24 (1925), 106f.; Schlier, Rel. Unters. 34ff.; Jonas, Gnosis I 123.

[4] For a discussion of the style see p. 48 n. 3,

[5] Μαρτυρέω (μαρτυρία, μάρτυς) ordinarily has the (legal) meaning of testifying in a statement to the reality (or unreality) of a *state of affairs* which has been questioned. The testimony is based on *knowledge*, particularly on the account of an eye-witness (Pollux 4.36: μαρτυρία δὲ καλεῖται ὅταν τις αὐτὸς ἰδὼν μαρτυρῇ; cp. Jn. 1.32, 34; 3.11, 32; 15.27;

the "Son of God" (v. 34). The Evangelist leaves the discussion of the content of the μαρτυρία till later; here he simply stresses its purpose: ἵνα πάντες πιστεύσωσιν δι' αὐτοῦ. Πιστεύειν[1] should not be taken here merely in the sense of "being (or becoming) a Christian",[2] but in the full sense of 20.31: ἵνα πιστεύητε ὅτι Ἰησοῦς ἐστιν ὁ Χριστὸς ὁ υἱὸς τοῦ θεοῦ[3]. Thus for the first time the word "believe" is mentioned, which is for man the appropriate answer to the revelation, and the meaning of which will be developed in what follows. The fact that *all* men are to be brought to faith by the Baptist, shows that the Evangelist was not thinking of the historical situation of the Baptist's preaching, but that he was referring to his witness as it was constantly re-presented through the tradition and which in this way retains its actuality.

The positive statement of v. 7 is now repeated antithetically in v. 8: he, the Baptist, was not the light! This is a clear rebuttal of those who regarded the Baptist as the Revealer.[4] Yet it is characteristic of the Evangelist that he does not see the Baptist as a pseudo-Messiah or an emissary of the Devil, as one who "comes in his own name" (5.43);

I Jn. 1.2; 4.14). It is made before a *tribunal* which has to give judgement on the matter, and this judgement *must* be based on the statement of the witness; on the other hand the witness is in *duty bound* to make his statement, and in so doing commits himself to what he says. Witness is given either *for or against* the person (or state of affairs) awaiting judgement. Any one of the elements which make up the concept μαρτ. may recede into the background, or may equally become dominant. Similarly the Hebrew עוד (עֵד ,עֵדָת); except that here the forensic element is stressed so strongly that "witness" may be identical with "accusation" (cp. Mk. 6.11; etc.); on the other hand the binding character of the witness is dominant, so that הֵעִיד comes to mean: affirm solemnly, protest, adjure, either in the sense of admonish or warn; here the personal commitment of the witness may be stressed. In the latter case the LXX regularly has διαμαρτύρεσθαι (originally like μαρτύρεσθαι: to call as witness; then also—less frequently for the simple μαρτύρεσθαι—to adjure). διαμαρτυρεσθαι is used with the same meaning in the NT (I Th. 4.6; Lk. 16.28 etc.), as is the simple μαρτύρεσθαι (Gal. 5.3; I Th. 2.12 etc.), and in Rev. μαρτυρεῖν (1.2; 22.18, etc.). (δια) μαρτύρεσθαι does not occur in Joh. and μαρτυρεῖν and μαρτυρία have the original forensic meaning, which may however be used paradoxically (see on 3.11). Here the sense of bearing witness *for* something is most often stressed, with the result that μαρτυρεῖν almost takes on the meaning of "confessing" (von Campenhausen, Die Idee des Martyriums in der alten Kirche 1936, 37f.). It is only in the constant stress on the binding character of the witness that the Joh. usage resembles the usage of the OT and the rest of the NT.

[1] ἵνα πάντες κτλ. is not parallel to ἵνα μαρτυρήσῃ κτλ. but rather subordinate to it. Burney's suggestion that δι' αὐτοῦ is a mistranslation of בֵּיה, which should properly have been translated as εἰς αὐτόν, is purely arbitrary. Elsewhere the Evangelist rightly understood הימין ב as πιστεύειν εἰς! (Burrows).

[2] So e.g. often in Acts 2.44; 4.4, 32; 8.13 etc.

[3] In John πιστεύειν used absolutely has throughout the same value as πιστεύειν εἰς τὸ ὄνομα αὐτοῦ (1.12 etc.), εἰς αὐτόν (2.11 etc.), εἰς τὸν υἱόν (3.26), πιστεύειν ὅτι . . . (6.69 etc.) and similar expressions. Cp. the change in 3.18; 4.39–41; 11.40–42; 12.37–39; 16.30f. See Dodd 182–186.

[4] See above pp. 16f. and p. 48.—On the style of the sentence see p. 48 n.3.

rather he not only accepts the witness of the Baptist, but expressly lays claim to it—and in this he agrees with the rest of the Christian tradition, which sees the Baptist as the "Forerunner".[1]

The Evangelist now returns to the text of his source, and so to the initial description of the revelation-event, whose detailed portrayal will form the contents of the Gospel. The negative side, which was stated thematically in v. 5, is now described in **vv. 9–11** in such a way that vv. 10 and 11, like v. 5, characterise the revelation-event and its rejection by the world in antithetical phrases, while v. 9 brings out the terrifying nature of this happening by once again calling attention to the importance of the Revealer:

> 9 ἦν τὸ φῶς τὸ ἀληθινόν
> ὃ φωτίζει πάντα [ἄνθρωπον] ἐρχόμενον εἰς τὸν κόσμον

Just as in v. 4 it was said that the ζωή of the Logos was the light of men, so too here the Logos is himself called the φῶς[2], indeed the light which has appeared in history, and for whom the Baptist bears witness. He is the *proper*, *authentic* light, who alone can fulfil the claim to give existence the proper understanding of itself. In this it is assumed that human existence searches for the light, i.e. that it searches for an understanding of itself, and that in this very search it can err, can mistake a false light for the true light, that it can misunderstand its own

---

[1] See on 3.29.

[2] The argument of the passage in itself suggests that the subject of ἦν is "he", the Logos, while τὸ φῶς is the predicate (it must have the article, since the concept of the φῶς ἀλ. must necessarily be qualified). Masson and Wik. 300 also take the Logos as the subject of ἦν and τὸ φῶς as predicate. For a different view see Dodd (268) and Barrett. This becomes clear when it is seen that the subject must be the same as for ἦν in v. 10 and for ἦλθεν in v. 11; but this, as αὐτόν vv. 11f. shows, is the Logos (as Hirsch rightly sees). The assumption of an Aram. (or Syr.) original is convincing here: ἦν would then be a rendering of הוא (thus Burney and Burrows) and there is no need to suppose that the Evangelist misunderstood this as הֲוָא; following on vv. 6–8 he could not begin οὗτος ἦν.

—This also shows that, as earlier exegesis rightly saw, ἦν is not to be taken with ἐρχόμενον, for which 2.6 and 18.18 provide no analogy (for nowhere else do we find a relative clause between a modal verb and its participle!), and which would be contrary to the verse structure; it would finally give no tolerable sense to the passage, as is clearly shown by the embarrassment of the commentators. The only ground for wrongly taking the two words together is the feeling that ἐρχ. εἰς τ. κόσμ. alongside ἄνθρ. is superfluous. In fact ἄνθρ. is an explanatory gloss (of the translator) on πάντα ἐρχ. εἰς τ. κ.; for this is a common paraphrase in Semitic languages for "every man" (Str.-B. II 358; Schl. ad loc.). Thus it should be taken not as a descriptive attribute placed *after* "man", but as used *instead* of "man". It is clear then that ἄνθρ. is an explanatory addition. (So too C. H. Kraeling op. cit. 172; for the contrary view cf. Sickenberger, Theol. u. Glaube 1941, 129–134). Once it is removed v. 9b is seen to have the required length. It is at this point that the hypothesis of an Aram. (or Syr.) original seems to me to receive the strongest confirmation.—Schaeder (see p. 49 n.2) suggests: "He was the light of the Kušta, which illuminates all men, Enos, who comes into the world"; arguments similar to those put forward in the discussion of v. 6 could be brought against this rendering.

significance. And it is claimed that only in the revelation which occurred in Jesus can man receive the proper understanding of his existence which he constantly seeks and fails to find. The "proper" light is also the divine light, the light which shines in the revelation. It is the φῶς τῆς ζωῆς (8.12); for life in its authenticity is possible only in the clarity of the self-understanding which is given through the revelation[1]. Originally (that is, in the source) the contrast of the φῶς ἀλ. was seen in the earthly light of day;[2] but when the notion is incorporated into the context of the Evangelist's thought we can detect, as v. 8 shows, the further contrast with alleged revelation and would-be revealers. Barrett and Dupont (99ff.) rightly say that the contrast to the φῶς αλ. can be seen in the Baptist. But it would be wrong to restrict it to him. The exclusiveness of the revelation which occurred in Jesus is further brought out by the relative clause ὃ φωτίζει κτλ: he and only he is the Revealer for all men.[3]

The meaning of the present tense φωτίζει is no different from that of φαίνει v. 5; it states that the incarnate Logos is the Revealer, without considering the question whether or to what extent men open themselves to his revelation.[4] In him and in him alone the possibility is given to man to see himself as he is before God; but this also means that man has

---

[1] In the context ἀληθινός has the original formal meaning of "proper, authentic". It is however in line with the Joh. and Hellenistic use of ἀλήθεια, which not only has the formal sense of "truth" and "reality" but also takes on the meaning of "divine reality" (ThWB I 254, 23ff.), to catch in τὸ φῶς τὸ ἀληθινόν the further meaning of "the divine light", in the sense of Luther's "the eternal light enters in" (Luther's Christmas hymn: Gelobet seist du, Jesu Christ. v. 4). The same meaning attaches to φῶς τῆς ζωῆς 8.12; cp. the parallel between ἄρτος τῆς ζωῆς (6.35, 48) and ἄμπελος ἀληθινή (15.1) and cp. ThWB I 251, 18ff. Hirsch strikes out τὸ ἀλ. and thus destroys the rhythm.—It should further be noticed that φωτίζειν does not of course mean "light up" but "enlighten", i.e. to give the possibility of sight. Cp. Ps. 18.9; Eph. 1.18; 3.9; C. Herm. 1.32 (see n. 86 in Nock-Festugière I 28), and in relation to baptism Hebr. 6.4; 10.32; Justin, Apol. I 61, 12; 65, 1. In the terminology of the mystery religions it means "to turn into light", i.e. to divinise; see Reitzenst., H.M.R. 264. 292.

[2] The earthly light of day is contrasted with the φῶς νοητόν in Phil. opif. m. 30f.; Abrah. 119; Plot. Enn. VI 9.9 p. 522, 15; the νοερὸν φῶς Exc. ex Theod. 12; the φῶς ψυχικόν Phil. leg. all. III 171; the φῶς αἴδιον Wis. 7.26; the φῶς αἰώνιον Act. Thom. 34 p. 151, 5f.; the γνήσιον φῶς Phil. mut. nom. 4f.; the ἀληθινὸν φῶς Plot. Enn. VI 9.4 p. 513, 12; the vera lux Sen. ep. 93.5. In Phil. quis. rer. div. her. 263f. we find the θεῖον φῶς contrated with the light of the νοῦς.—On the antithesis between the divine sphere as authentic and the eartly sphere as the sphere of appearance, see on 4.10; cp. too Omodeo, Mistica 55ff.

[3] Thus the "Wisdom" which corresponds to the Logos calls (see p. 22f.): "Come to me, all you who desire me!" (Ecclus. 24.19).

[4] Cp. Test. Levi 14.4: τὸ φῶς τοῦ νόμου τὸ δοθέν εἰς φωτισμὸν παντὸς ἀνθρώπου. Also analogous expressions in Christian hymns, for example Luther's "The light eternal enters in and gives a new appearance to the *world*", and Paul Gerhardt's "Thou art the comfort and the light of *all* the heathen".—The invocation, Pap. Gr. mag. IV 990ff., of the μέγιστος θεός as τὸν τὰ πάντα φωτίζοντα και διαυγάζοντα τῇ ἰδίᾳ δυνάμει τὸν σύμπαντα κόσμον is different, for it is pantheistic.

the possibility—in unfaith—of losing himself irrevocably.[1] The φωτίζειν of the Revealer is an act which also impinges on the unbelievers; but only in the sense that as a result they become completely "blind". For just as there can only be *sight* where there is light, so too it is with *blindness*; this paradox is expressly drawn out by the Evangelist in 9.39–41.

10 [ἐν τῷ κόσμῳ ἦν καὶ] ὁ κόσμος δι' αυτοῦ ἐγένετο,
καὶ ὁ κόσμος αὐτὸν οὐκ ἔγνω.

Against the background of v. 9, **v. 10** gives us the first antithetical description of the fate of the revelation, and so developes the theme of v. 5: he, the Logos, was (as the Incarnate) in the world (cf. v. 11), and although he was the Creator of the world, the world did not know him.[2] The power and the claim of the historical Revealer are grounded, that is to say, in the fact that he is the Logos, the Creator. For if the proper self-understanding of man consists in understanding himself in relation to his origin, the illumination of his existence can only come from his origin, from his Creator.

The place and the object of revelation are here stated to be the κόσμος instead of the ἄνθρωποι. The κόσμος is seen not as the σύστημα ἐκ θεῶν καὶ ἀνθρώπων καὶ ἐκ τῶν ἕνεκα τούτων γεγονότων[3] but as the world of men. Yet the latter is considered as a whole, viz. as the κόσμος, in as much as it stands over against God and confronts him with hostility; the κόσμος then is the σκοτία (v. 5), which constitutes itself as such by turning away from the revelation.[4] As the κόσμος which stands over

---

[1] In the source, where vv. 9–12 refer to the pre-temporal Logos, the understanding of φωτίζει (for which in Semit. a partic. would have stood, see p. 45 n. 4, is fundamentally the same; i.e. it refers to the possibility of the revelation (as understood in the Od. Sal.), not to the participation in the Logos, in the Reason of the world (as understood in the Stoa and Philo, opif. m. 146; leg. all. III 171–176; plant. 18 etc., and the Apologists, Just. ap. 28.46. p. 71c, 83c).—On φωτίζω as a technical term for the Mysteries and Revelation cp. C. Herm. 1.32; 13.18f., 21; Hipp. El. VII 26, 5f., 7f., p. 204, 23.26; 205, 3.14 W. (Od. Sal. 11.14); Clem. Al. Paed. I 25, 1 (ἐφωτίσθημεν γάρ· τὸ δὲ ἔστιν ἐπιγνῶναι τὸν θεόν); 27, 3; Eph. 1.18; 3.9; Hebr. 6.4; 10.32. Cp. Reitzenst., HMR. 3 ed. 263 f.; Wetter, Phos 61ff.

[2] The first line has one foot too many. We may suspect that the source, which is here still speaking of the pre-existent Logos, and thus solely of the revelation in Creation, contained only ὁ κόσμ. δι' ἀυτ. ἐγ., and that the Evangelist, who has been concerned with the revelation of salvation since v. 5, added ἐν τ.κ. ἦν, which gave the sentence in the source the meaning: "And although ...". Even if ἐν τ.κ. ἦν was contained in the source (where it would have referred to the eternal presence of the Logos in Creation), it could only have been the first part of a couplet, whose second part was omitted by the Evangelist.

[3] Chrysipp fr. 527 in v. Arnim, Stoic. vet. fr. II 168; cp. Plat. Gorg. 507e.

[4] Cp. on v. 5.—Of course it would be wrong to try and draw a distinction between κόσμος as the whole of creation (cp. esp. 17.24). and as the world of men. Admittedly κόσμος is often used of the world of men without any reference to the rest of creation; this is so here: ὁ κ. αὐτὸν οὐκ ἔγνω, and in passages where the κ. is the object of the divine act of salvation (3.16f.; 4.42; 6.33 etc.) or the subject of actions directed against God (15.19; 16.20 etc.). But κόσμος can also be the whole of creation, although even here the world of

against God, it has made itself independent of him; because it refuses to see itself in relation to God as creation, it can only seek its understanding of itself in itself. This is the basis of the Johannine "dualism" of God and world, of light and darkness.[1] The κόσμος is not, therefore, the πλήρωμα τῆς κακίας (C. Herm. 6.4) as understood by radical Gnosticism,[2] where creation and the existence of the world are evil in their very origins—which means that evil must be understood not as sin but as an inherent quality. Rather men are κόσμος and σκοτία *by virtue* of their being God's creation and the place and object of the saving revelation; they are κόσμος and σκοτία because they have made themselves independent of God, and correspondingly the σκοτία is the darkness of lies and sin.[3] For this very reason the κόσμος can be described both as the object of God's love (3.16) and receiver of the revelation (4.42; 6.33; 12.47), and also as the deceitful power which revolts against God (14.30; 16.11) and is rejected (12.31; 17.9). Both elements go to make up the concept of κόσμος, and it is wrong to try to distinguish two separate concepts of κόσμος in John.[4]

The κόσμος did not "know" the Revealer, i.e. it failed to believe in Jesus as the Revealer (v. 11) and so to accept the possibility of illumination which was offered to it (v. 5). For such knowledge is not a theoretical perception of truths, but recognition.[5] It could only occur in the act of abandoning one's own chosen, false self-understanding and in receiving the gift of a proper understanding of oneself in relation to the Creator. The sin of the world, which makes it the "world", is that it rejects this gift; this is unbelief (16.9).[6]

---

men is seen as the essential factor in the world; so here: ὁ κ.δι'αὐτοῦ ἐγενετο, and for example in passages which speak of the mission or the coming into the world (3.17, 19; 9.39; 10.36; 16.28 etc.); see n. 4.

[1] Cp. GuV 135ff.; Gaugler 53: "The Joh. Dualism is not cosmological but historical." Faulhaber 28f.; Howard, Christianity 83.

[2] Examples in Br., Note on 1.10. It is interesting to note that "world" in DSD is not used in this sense; cp. F.-M. Braun RB 62 (1955), 21.

[3] That ψεῦδος and ἁμαρτία describe the character of the world is clear from 8.30–40, 41–47; for ἁμαρτία cp. too 8.21–29; 9.39–41; 15.21–25; 16.8–11.

[4] The fact that the κόσμος, because it is God's creation, may be seen in different ways (as a whole or as the world of men, as at enmity with God or as object of His love) has its parallels in systems of thought which contain a religious understanding of the world, i.e. in the Rabbinic literature, in the Hermetic writings, in the Mandaeans, and particularly in the Od. Sal.; cf. on this Odeberg 115–130. Cp. also Omodeo, Saggio 13f.

[5] Br. is right in his definition: "To recognise someone as that to which he lays or has claim." Only we should be careful to notice that such γινώσκειν "signifies" nothing else than γινώσκειν = "know, perceive." For it certainly refers to an act of cognition, but to one which if it is to be complete must issue in recognition. An objective and neutral apprehension of the matter (which would then be followed by an "evaluation" or the taking of a "personal attitude") would be no apprehension at all of what we are concerned with here.

[6] In the context γινώσκειν has precisely the same meaning as πιστεύειν, vv. 7, 13. It is of course possible to distinguish between the two; see on 6.69.

[11] εἰς τὰ ἴδια ἦλθεν
καὶ οἱ ἴδιοι αὐτὸν οὐ παρέλαβον.

V. 11 is exactly parallel to v. 10, and each verse explains the other: εἰς τὰ ἴδια ἦλθεν corresponds to ἐν τῷ κόσμῳ ἦν as οἱ ἴδιοι αὐτὸν οὐ παρέλαβον corresponds to ὁ κόσμος αὐτὸν οὐκ ἔγνω. Τὰ ἴδια refers therefore to the world of men, which belongs to the Logos as its Creator, and the ἴδιοι equally are men.[1] Thus the same idea, which was expressed in v. 10 by ὁ κόσμος δι' αὐτοῦ ἐγένετο, is here contained in the notion of ἴδιον. Equally the rejection of the revelation, which was expressed by οὐκ ἔγνω in v. 10, is now affirmed by οὐ παρέλαβον, an expression which becomes clearer by its reference to the efforts of the historical Revealer to win men to him.[2] "To receive" him, would of course mean to believe him.[3] In the saving revelation the ἴδιοι are asked if they are willing to recognise themselves as belonging to their Creator. If they refuse, then in so doing they assign to themselves another origin; they deliver themselves into the hands of the world (15.19); the Devil is now their Father (8.44). Accordingly only those who believe in him can be counted as ἴδιοι (10.3f.; 13.1). That such a division takes place when men are confronted with the revelation is said in **v. 12**:

---

[1] τὰ ἴδια cannot here mean "home, homeland" as in 16.32; 19.27 Acts 21.6 (and elsewhere often, see Br.), but only "property, possession," (often with this meaning in Pap. and Inscr., see Br. ad loc. and Br. Lex. 616 = E.T.370.) The ἴδιοι are "his own", who belong to him as their creator, as in Od. Sal. 7.12 (see p. 44, n. 1). This also provides us with a basis for understanding the dualistic gnostic sense of the concept, according to which ἴδιον means that which shares in a common nature; cp. on the one hand 8.44; 15.19; on the other hand 10.3 f.; 13.1 and on this C. Herm. 1.31; Iren. I, 21, 5; Hipp. El. V 6, 7; 8. 12.17; 19, 16; 21, 8 p. 78, 18; 91, 11; 19, 13; 120, 4; 124, 7; Act. Thom. 124 p. 233, 14; Od. Sal. 26, 1 (דילה); Mand. Lit. 114, 4f.—It is impossible in the Prologue, which treats of the ἄνθρωποι and the κόσμος, to take τὰ ἴδια (or οἱ ἴδιοι) to mean Israel or the Jewish people, which is, according to Ex. 19.5; Dt. 7.6; 14.2; 26.18; Ps. 135.4 God's "own people," or a people as God's "possession" (סְגֻלָּה or עַם סְגֻלָּה = LXX λαὸς περιούσιος not ἴδιος). For even if Merx is mistaken in supposing John to be the most anti-Jewish book in the world, he is least right when he says: "The sentence, He came into his own ... may mean what it will; but one thing it cannot mean, namely: he came to the Jews ..." (p. 5). There is however a parallel in the Wisdom myth (see p. 22), where peoples and nations as well as earth and sea are seen as the possession of Wisdom (Ecclus. 24.6), just as in the Wisdom myth there is a parallel to the οὐ παρέλαβον (Prov. 1.24–31; Bar. 3.12f.; Eth. Enoch 42.1f.; cf. Eucharist. II 6–11). Wik. and Schlier have interpreted τὰ ἴδια correctly, while Barr. wants to take it as God's "own people".—The alternation between τὰ ἴδια and οἱ ἴδιοι should probably be traced back to the translator; Aram. (or Syr.) would in both cases have had דִּילֵיהּ; cf. Od. Sal. 7.12; 26.1.

[2] Bl. considers it remarkable that the cross is not mentioned here. Yet of course it could not have been named in the source which is the basis of the passage.

[3] Παραλαμβάνειν is used in this sense only here in John (a use also found in Jambl. Myst. 88.2); λαμβάνειν is used in exactly the same sense in 1.12 (which see), 5.43, and has, as vv. 11 and 12, and also 5.43 and 44, taken together show, the meaning of πιστεύειν.

[12] ὅσοι δὲ ἔλαβον αὐτόν,
ἔδωκεν αὐτοῖς [ἐξουσίαν] τέκνα θεοῦ γενέσθαι,
[τοῖς πιστεύουσιν εἰς τὸ ὄνομα αὐτοῦ].

There are, that is to say, exceptions in the *massa perditionis;* there are those[1] who "received" him.[2] ὅσοι in itself, however, tells us nothing about how great or small their number is. But it must be small; for the general picture is conveyed by v. 11: οἱ ἴδιοι αὐτὸν οὐ παρέλαβον.[3] This is the constant complaint whenever we hear of a message which calls men to salvation, to themselves and to God.[4] Yet to these few—and one can already grasp the implication that they are the "we" referred to in vv. 14, 16—the Revealer has given authority[5] to become the children

[1] The relative clause which qualifies the indirect object of the main clause (αὐτοῖς) has been placed first in the sentence, this being a not uncommon rhetorical device which is by no means specifically Semitic; Colwell quotes p. 39 BGU I 19 (135 B.C.) col. II 1.4f.: ὅσα προσήναντο πα[τρι]κῶν περὶ τὸν προκείμενον ἀπὸ τῆς εὐ[δ]αιμονίδος διαθήκης ... ταῦτα μετεῖναι τοῖς ἐκείνου τέκνοις. This is somewhat different from the device, much favoured by the Evangelist, of placing the subject or the direct object at the beginning of a sentence as a casus pendens; see on 1.18; 6.39.

[2] The use of λαμβάνειν as interchangeable with παραλαμβ. (cf. Rom. 15.4; II Cor. 5.3 and Br.) is not normal Greek use (one would expect δέχεσθαι; cp. C. Herm. 4.4); it is a Semitism (Aram. קַבֵּל, Schl., Spr. und H. 20f.); see on v. 16.

[3] The idea that the few are predestined by virtue of their heavenly nature (Omodeo 50) is foreign to the text.

[4] The ἐξιστάμενος τῶν ἀμθρωπίνων σπουδασμάτων καὶ πρὸς τῷ θείῳ γιγνόμενος is called mad by the πολλοί, Plat. Phaedr. 249d. Cp. the lamentations of Epict. diss. I 3, 3f.; 16, 19 (ἐπεὶ οἱ πολλοὶ αποτετύφλωσθε); Isai. 10.22; C. Herm. 9.4; Ascl. 18 p. 320, 16ff. Scott; esp. C. Herm. 4.4f.; ὅσοι μὲν οὖν συνῆκαν τοῦ κηρύγματος κτλ.: Similarly for the Mandaeans the elect are only very few in number, see Br., and Mand. Lit. 203:

"They noticed me not, recognised me not
and concerned themselves not about me.
...
The man who saw and recognised me
receives his way to the place of life."

Further Ginza 387, 34f.; 389, 7f.

[5] Ἐξουσία in John is always used in the normal Greek sense of "right", "authority" (1.12; 5.27; 10.18; 17.2; 19.10f., which are all from the Evangelist), and not in the sense developed in Gnosticism and magic, where the emphasis is placed not on the element of right but of power (here the freedom from other powers may also be stressed), and according to which ἐξουσία, related as it is to δύναμις, refers to the power of the spiritual man. Cp. C. Herm, 1.15, 32; 16.14; Reitzenst. HMR. 3 ed 301f., 363; Th. Schermann, Griech. Zauberpap. und das Gemeinde- und Dankgebet im I. Klemens-Briefe 1909, 45f.; L. Bieler, Θεῖος Ἀνήρ I 1935, 80ff. So too I Cor. 8.9 Mk. 3.15; 6.7; Lk. 4.36; 10.19;—For a similar use to John see C. Herm. 1.28: τί ἑαυτοὺς ... εἰς θάνατον ἐκδεδώκατε, ἔχοντες ἐξουσίαν τῆς ἀθανασίας μεταλαβεῖν. Διδόναι ἐξουσίαν in some ways corresponds to the Aram. נְתַן רְשׁוּת (to give permission, to do something); cp. Schl. on Mt. 9.8; 28.18; Foerster, ThWB II 562, 22ff. Yet probably the Evangelist inserted the word in his source for the sake of clarity; in Semitic נתן (διδόναι) can be used by itself in the sense of "give permission", "delegate authority", cp. 5.26; often in Rev. with the inf. 2.7; 3.21 etc.; with ἵνα 6.4; 9.5; 19.8; used absolutely 11.3; at the same time ἐξουσίαν διδόναι 2.26; 6.8 etc. There is no

of God. The significance of this gift of adoption by God will be drawn out in 3.1–21. But it is already clear from this passage that it is a description of salvation, of the eschatological existence.

The idea of God as Father and man as his child is found throughout the history of religion from the primitive stages onwards.[1] Variations within the notion depend in the first place on which of the main elements in the notion of fatherhood is most strongly stressed—the natural element (the procreator), the legal (the master), or the personal (the provider), or on how these various elements are played off against one another;[2] but they also depend on whether the fact of man's being a child of God is seen as something perfectly obvious,[3] as simply given, or whether it is seen as by no means obvious, but as a relationship which is shared only by particularly favoured men,[4] or which is given by God only on special conditions.[5] Above all the notion that men are related to God as his children develops into an "eschatological" concept, both in Judaism and in the Mystery religions:[6] man becomes God's child (or son) only when he has been transferred into a new existence, whether it be at the end of the present aeon, when God renews the world, or whether it occurs in the present, when a man is made the son of God by initiation into the Mysteries, and thus is "begotten" anew or "born" anew. It is clear that in John τέκνα θεοῦ γενέσθαι is intended in such an "eschatological" sense. Moreover the fact that this notion is derived from the Mystery religions, and not from Jewish eschatology is shown

Semitic equivalent to ἐξουσία in the sense of "authority"; see Bonsirven Bibl. 30 (1949) 416.—Διδόναι is characteristic of the Revealer: 4.14; 6.27, 33f., 51f.; 10.28; 14.27; 17.2, 7, 22. See further on 3.27.

[1] Cp. for example N. Söderblom, Das Werden des Gottesglaubens, 2.ed. 1926, 146ff. 192; Fr. Heiler, Das Gebet, 2.ed. 1920, 89–93; Seeger, RGG 2.ed. V 1442–1445; G.v.d. Leeuw, Phänomenologie der Religion 1933, 161–166, 492f. W. Twisselmann, Die Gotteskindschaft der Christen im NT. 1939.

[2] For the OT cp. R. Gyllenberg, Gott der Vater im AT und in der Predigt Jesu, Studia Orientalia I 1925, 51–60; Baudissin, Kyrios III 146f. 309ff. 391f.; for Judaism cp. Bousset, Rel. des Judent. 3. ed. 377f.; Str.-B. I 392–396 etc. H. Gödan, Das Bild von Gott dem Vater im rabb. Judentum, Diss. Leipzig (1941?).—In the OT, as indeed throughout the ancient world, the notion of father and ruler are closely connected.

[3] In Greek Zeus is accepted unquestioningly as the Father of the Gods and of men. In the Stoa the principle that men were related to God as his children gained particular importance: it gives man his nobility and his sense of obligation as well as his confidence in the divine πρόνοια; cp. esp. Epict. Diss. I 3 and 9. For the cosmolog. meaning of the description of God as Father (since Plat. Timaeus 28c) cp. Dupont, Gnosis 1949, 340f.

[4] Just as Israel knows itself to be the Son of God by contrast with other peoples, so too the king is in a particular sense the Son of God (e.g. II Sam. 7.13ff.; Ps. 2). The idea that the king is the Son of God is widespread in the East and in ancient Greece; cp. v.d. Leeuw, op. cit. 102f. and the numerous studies of the Hellenistic and Roman cult of the rulers.

[5] The pious know themselves to be the children of God in distinction from the godless, Wis. 2.13, 16, 18; the phrase υἱοὶ θεοῦ (cp. Gal. 3.26) is avoided by John (Gosp. and Epist.).

[6] For Judaism: Ps. Sal. 17.30; Jubil. 1.34f.; Mt. 5.9; Lk. 20.36. For the Mystery religions, Albr. Dietrich, Eine Mythrasliturgie 2. ed., 1910, 134–156. See below p. 90 n. 3.

clearly by ἄνωθεν γεννηθῆναι 3.3ff.[1] It is equally clear that the transference into this new mode of existence is given only to the man who believes in the revelation with which he is confronted in Jesus; further that the new existence is characterised by the illumination which comes from understanding oneself in relation to God: the τέκνα θεοῦ are the υἱοὶ τοῦ φωτός (12.36).

That this gift can be received only by those who believe is brought out again by the Evangelist through his addition of τοῖς πιστ. κτλ.[2] These are the men who, as **v. 13**[3] further explains, by virtue of their faith[4] are God's children, God's offspring.[5] In order to underline the

---

[1] Cp. as well I Jn. 2.29; 3.9; 5.18. In this respect there is no difference between the source and the Evangelist.

[2] πιστεύειν εἰς τὸ ὄνομα αὐτοῦ has precisely the same meaning as πιστεύειν εἰς αὐτόν; see p.51 n. 3. (Cp. the Jewish formula "to believe in the Name of God", Schl.). Only the phrase πιστ. εἰς τὸ ὄν. brings out more clearly that "believing in him" is the recognition of that which is signified by his person, i.e. that he is the "son" etc. (3.18; 20.31 etc.); cp. W. Heitmüller, Im Namen Jesu 1903, 114, 3.—The thesis that the words are an addition of the Evangelist finds support when we consider the form of the source (the words break the rhythm of the line), and the content of the source (it is not possible that the source should speak of the incarnate Logos before v. 14). In v. 12 the source spoke of the few individuals who had received the revelation and who thus were exceptions within the different generations. Cp. esp. Wis. 7.28 of the σοφία (see p. 46 n. 1). Also Ecclus. 1.15 (acc. to Smend). Cp. Eucharist. II 15–19; for the idea that the Gnostic Redeemer "wanders through history in changing form" see Jonas, Gnosis I 125f. 278f. 311f.

[3] V. 13 is the Evangelist's explanatory addition. It noticeably disturbs the rhythm of the verse. Even if one supposed with Burrows that in the first line the predicate (יְלִידִין) had been omitted by the translator, the difficulty remains that the first section is much too long, while in the second the subject is missing. Moreover v. 13 explains τοῖς πιστ. v. 12, which is itself an addition of the Evangelist.

[4] Naturally procreation by God is not the "root and presupposition" of faith, as H. J. Holtzmann, Lehrbuch der neutest. Theol. II 2. ed. 1911, 534f. thinks possible; that it is not, is shown clearly by v. 12.

[5] Naturally οἱ ἐγενν. explains τέκνα θεοῦ and not πιστ.—ὃς ἐγεννήθη is again defended by M.-E. Boismard, RB 57 (1950), 401–408; F.-M. Braun, Aux sources de la tradition Chrétienne (Festschr. f. M. Goguel) 1950, 11–31. The opposite view is rightly held by Dodd (260, 1), Wik., Barr. and Schlier. The context of the passage makes it impossible that the original text should have contained the reading attested in many Latin additions: qui natus est (see Br., Lagr. and Note II in Zn). If modern exegetes argue for the originality of (ὃς) ἐγεννήθη (Zn., Burney, Bl. and others), then this is simply wishful thinking. No one will credit Tertullian's assertion that the plur. is a correction of the Valentinians, who wished to introduce semen illud arcanum electorum et spiritualium, quod sibi imbuunt, if only for the reason that the Valentinians also consider the ψυχικοί as πιστεύοντες (see v. Loewenich 81f.).—If the description in v. 13 is applied to Jesus as the Logos, then it makes very peculiar sense after what has been said in vv. 1–5 and 9–11. But if the sentence in the singular is taken to refer not to Jesus' eternal generation but to the virgin birth (as for example, the epist. apost. 3, p. 6. Duensing), then it stands in complete contradiction to the Fourth Gospel, which not only does not contain the idea of the virgin birth, but (like Paul) excludes it; cp. on v. 14. If, as seems likely, the singular form of the text first occurred in a Latin text, then it is possible that it goes back to a translation from the Syriac; for in Syriac a plural ending may be elided, and אתיליד of the syr^{cur} can be taken either as sing. or plur. (Burrows). Yet the more probable explanation is that the copyist involuntarily related the

miraculous nature of man's relation to God[1] as his child, the divine act of procreation which establishes the relation is sharply contrasted with man's origins in the human sphere.[2] A contradiction of the Evangelist's notion of Creation will be found in this antithesis only if one has misunderstood his statement about ζωή in v. 4. For the activity of the divine ζωή as the φῶς of the Creation does not issue from the vital processes of natural life. Whatever Creation produces by its own efforts remains in its own sphere; eschatological existence is the gift of God.

b) The Logos in the Flesh: 1.14–18

14 καὶ ὁ Λόγος σὰρξ ἐγένετο
καὶ ἐσκήνωσεν ἐν ἡμῖν.

Just as the *et incarnatus* est marks a turning point in the Mass, so too here the character of the Prologue changes.[3] This is most noticeable

---

qui to the preceding eius.—Cp. further A. v. Harnack, SABerlin 1915, 542–552, alternatively Studien zur Gesch. des NTs und der alten Kirche 1931, 115–127; Cadbury, Expositor 9 (1924), 436f.—It is instructive to consider the relation of the doctrine of the Virgin Birth to the Redeemer myth in Ignatius; for this see Schlier, Relig. Unters. 42f. Further literature: M. Dibelius, Jungfrauensohn und Krippenkind, SAHeidelberg 1932, 19, 2; now in Botschaft u. Geschichte I, 1953, 1–78.

[1] Γεννᾶσθαι can mean to "be conceived" or to "be born"; ἐκ here is said of the mother (v. Br. Lex.). If in 3.3ff. the meaning "to be born" is dominant, then I Jn. 3.9 shows that γεννᾶσθαι ἐκ can also be used of begetting by the Father. The more specific meaning has obviously been suppressed by the more general, "to receive one's origin".

[2] The human sphere is designated by concepts which, taken together, give a uniform description of that which is human as opposed to divine. In Semitic thought σάρξ and αἷμα are traditional descriptions of that which is human and earthly (I Cor. 15.50; Gal. 1.16; Mt. 16.17, etc.). Yet the phrase here cannot be traced back to such a formula, but is original. To understand the unusual plural ἐξ αἱμάτων we must look not to Semitic but to Greek, where at least Eurip. Ion 693 provides a proper parallel: ἄλλων τραφεὶς ἐξ αἱμάτων = a son sprung from strange blood. Otherwise the plur. of blood is only used of drops or streams of spilt blood (Lev. 12 and 15 passim and the Tragedians, cf. Liddell and Scott, or in the Pap. Amh. II 141, quoted by Br.). Here the plur. is only used to refer to the "sphere" of the blood. For attempts to explain the plur. by means of the physiology of conception, see Cadbury, Expositor 9 (1924), 430–436. Hoskyns' explanation is very forced: the Evangelist could not use the sing. because the believers themselves are in fact born of the blood (sing.), namely the blood of Jesus (acc. to 19.34).—ἐκ θελήματος σαρκός also describes the human sphere, and one may point (Br.) to Pap. mag. IV 1430, 1521, 1533, where θέλημα is used in the sense of sexual desire. In any case σάρξ is not used here in the sense of a principle which is at enmity with God. Cf. also on v. 14.—Without drawing an undue distinction, as B. Weiss wished, between the foregoing and the following, it is not surprising that the human initiative can also be described by the phrase ἐκ θελήματος ἀνδρός, for it was an unquestioned assumption of the ancient world that the man played the leading part. —The fact that in the antithesis the θέλημα of God is not named is to be explained partly by the fact that "to be born of God" is a typical expression of the Evangelist, and partly by the fact that in the context θέλημα refers to a natural movement of the will which could not be attributed to God.

[3] Schlier sees the change as the transition from a revelation discourse to a confession.

in the source, which till now had only spoken of the revelation in creation; but there is also a change in the style of the Evangelist, who from v. 5 onwards has spoken indirectly, only hinting at what is to come. Now the riddle is solved, the miracle is proclaimed: the Logos became flesh!

It is the *language of mythology* that is here employed. Just as the ancient world and the Orient tell of gods and divine beings who appear in human form, so too the central theme of the gnostic Redeemer-myth is that a divine being, the Son of the Highest, assumed human form, put on human flesh and blood, in order to bring revelation and redemption.[1] In this mythology the concept of revelation receives a definite form; it affirms 1) that revelation is an event with an other-worldly origin; 2) but that this event, if it is to have any significance for men, must take place in the human sphere. And indeed, man knows what revelation *means,* in the same way as he knows what light means, and in the same way as he can speak of the bread or water of life.[2] For this reason the Evangelist can make use of the mythological language of Gnosticism. In the *notion* of revelation, man possesses a prior knowledge of revelation, and this consists in a knowledge of one's own situation which leads one to seek constantly for its true meaning. In such prior knowledge man in no way possesses the revelation—the ἀληθινόν[3]; indeed it can lead him to destruction, if he attempts to derive from it the criteria

---

[1] For a list of individual examples see Br. and Bultmann, ZNTW 24 (1925), 104ff.; cp. H. Gressmann, Messias 373.—In Gnosticism the Redeemer clothes himself in human form principally for the purpose of disguise; the Redeemer must not be recognised by the demonic powers of this world; cp. Iren. I 24, 6; Asc. Is. 10f.; 1 Cor. 2.7f.; Ign. Eph. 19.1 etc.; cp. H. Schlier, Relg. Unters. 6–17; G. Bornkamm, Mythos und Legende 10. The other motive is give most clearly in Od. Sal. 7.3ff.:

> "He revealed himself to me richly in his truthfulness,
> for his kindness made his greatness small.
> He became equal to me, that I might take hold of him,
> in form he appeared like unto me, that I might put him on.
> I did not start back when I saw him,
> because he had pity on me.
> He became like my nature, that I might comprehend him,
> and like my form, that I should not flee from him."

So, too, Exc. ex Theod. 4; Ginza 112, 16ff.; Barn. 5.10 etc.; cp. H. Windisch on Barn. 5.10. Erich Auerbach, Sermo humilis in Roman. Forschungen 64 (1952), 326f. who also draws attention to Tert. Adv. Marc. 2, 27.—On the attempts to explain Jn. 1.14 without mythology (Loofs, Jannaris) cp. Carpenter 326f. A further proof of the thoroughly unjewish character of the verse is given by Leop. Cohn's protest (Judaica, Festschr zu H. Cohens 70. Geburtstag 1912, 330f.) against Ed. Schwartz's attempt to interpret the verse in the light of Jewish presuppositions.

[2] Cp. on 4.10 and Bultmann, Der Begriff der Offenbarung im NT 1929, 'The Concept of Revelation in the New Testament', in Existence and Faith, 1961.

[3] See p. 53 n. 1.

by which to judge how God must confront him and how the revelation must become reality. For it becomes reality only as an event which passes all understanding. Our prior knowledge is a negative knowledge: the knowledge of man's limitations and his estrangement from God, combined with the knowledge that man must look to God for his salvation; the knowledge that God does not confront me in my world, and yet that he must confront me if my life is to be a true life.

Yet on the basis of this negative prior knowledge man constructs out of his longings and desires a positive but illusory knowledge. The decisive question is therefore whether man, when confronted by the event of the revelation, will remain true to his genuine prior knowledge of the revelation, whereby he sees it as an other-worldly event which passes judgement on him and his world; or whether he will make his own illusory ideas the criterion by which to judge the revelation, i.e. whether he will choose to judge the revelation only by these worldly standards and human values. The event of the revelation is a question, is an offence. This and nothing else is what is meant by ὁ λόγος σὰρξ ἐγένετο.

Σάρξ in John refers to the sphere of the human and the worldly as opposed to the divine, i.e. the sphere of the πνεῦμα,[1] 3.6; 6.63, (cp. above v. 13);[2] but whereas σκότος refers to the worldly sphere in its enmity towards God, σάρξ stresses its transitoriness, helplessness and vanity (3.6; 6.63); κόσμος on the other hand can be used in both senses.[3] Thus the Evangelist, following the usage of the OT, can refer to humanity as πᾶσα σάρξ (17.2). It is the realm of first appearances, of that which is immediately to hand, and it exerts on those who belong to it a corrupting power, with the result that they judge things κατὰ σάρκα (8.15), i.e. κατὰ ὄψιν (7.24). It possesses an illusory form of life (3.6; 6.63) which man at first takes for real life. It is in this sphere that the Logos appears, i.e. the Revealer is nothing but a man.[4] And the men who meet

[1] On πνεῦμα see on 3.5.

[2] In this respect there is no difference between the view of the Evangelist and that of his source. 1.13; 6.63; 8.15; 17.2 may be attributed to the Evangelist; 1.14; 3.6 to the source (6.51–56 to the editor).—This corresponds to the fact that both in Gnosticism and the OT "flesh" is used to refer to the wordly sphere which is at odds with God. This can also be seen in Ignatius' notion of σάρξ, cp. Schlier, Relg. Unters. 131.

[3] See above on v. 10.

[4] This makes superfluous all questions about the way in which the ἐγένετο took place or about the time at which the Logos united itself with the man Jesus. The man Jesus is, as the Revealer, the Logos. The notion that the Logos descended into Jesus at his Baptism will not do, simply for the reason that 1.32f. does not speak of the descent of the Logos but of the πνεῦμα; but above all because the Logos is not someone or other, but God, in so far as he reveals himself. To see the ἐγένετο as a miraculous process, that is as a physiological miracle, is to do violence to the main theme of the Gospel, that the Revealer is a man. Moreover 1.45; 6.42; 7.27f., show that the Evangelist knew or wished to know nothing of the

him take him for a man,[1] as is seen most clearly in the ἰδοὺ ὁ ἄνθρωπος (19.5). For they know his father and mother (6.42; 7.27f.; 1.45) and therefore take offence at his claim to be the Revealer (10.33); they cannot tolerate the "man" who tells them the truth (8.40). It is therefore perfectly appropriate for the title Logos to play no further part in the rest of the Gospel. The Logos is now present as the Incarnate, and indeed it is only as the Incarnate that it is present at all.

Thus the *offence* of the gospel is brought out as strongly as possible by ὁ λόγος σὰρξ ἐγένετο. For however much man may await and long for the event of the revelation in the human sphere, he also quite clearly expects—and this shows the peculiar self-contradiction of man's existence—that the Revelation will somehow have to give proof of itself, that it will in some way be recognisable. The Revealer—although of course he must appear in human form—must also in some way appear as a shining, mysterious, fascinating figure, as a hero or θεῖος ἄνθρωπος, as a miracle worker or mystagogue. His humanity must be no more than a disguise; it must be transparent. Men want to look away from the humanity, and see or sense the divinity, they want to penetrate the disguise—or they will expect the humanity to be no more than the visualisation or the "form" of the divine.

All such desires are cut short by the statement: the Word became flesh.[2] It is in his sheer humanity that he is the Revealer. True, his own also see his δόξα (v. 14b); indeed if it were not to be seen, there would be no grounds for speaking of revelation. But this is the paradox[3] which runs through the whole gospel: the δόξα is not to be seen *alongside* the σάρξ, nor *through* the σάρξ as through a window; it is to be seen in the σάρξ and nowhere else. If man wishes to see the δόξα, then it is on the σάρξ that he must concentrate his attention, without allowing himself to fall a victim to appearances. The revelation is present in a peculiar *hiddenness*.

---

legend of the Virgin Birth. The error of the Jews (6.42; 7.27) is not so much that they are misinformed, but rather that they put their questions about Jesus' origin κατὰ σάρκα, when what they should be doing is listening to his words. They are perfectly well informed; yet it is precisely here that we see the paradox, namely, that while their judgements κατὰ σάρκα are here as elsewhere perfectly *correct* (as Jesus 7.28 expressly admits), nevertheless *in these judgements* they cut themselves off from the revelation, which cannot be grasped by the questions of the worldly sphere.—Moreover the assumption that the ἐγένετο is a physiological miracle rests on a misunderstanding of σάρξ and πνεῦμα; they do not refer to a particular thing or substance, but to the way in which something exists, to a sphere. Cp. Goodenough, 170f.

[1] Cp. 4.29; (5.12); 7.46, 51; 9.16; 11.47, 50; 18.14, 17, 29.

[2] It is not clear in what sense the Gnostics, who are under attack in I Jn. 4.1–3 and II Jn. 7, challenged the notion of the ἐληλυθέναι ἐν σαρκί of the Revealer; but it is clear that for the author the ἐν σαρκί is decisive.

[3] The paradox of the joh. Christology has been developed by H. Clavier, Rev H. Phrel. 35 (1955), 174–195.

Yet in this hiddenness God's revelation is really present among men: for the first time since v. 1 the Logos is again mentioned by name.[1] This means that we are to look to the Revealer for nothing else than that which was given from all time in the eternal Λόγος: the light which he as Creator signified and by which man should understand himself. Nothing else—hence the Revealer does not come to fulfil the desire and longings which stir in the man who has failed to come to a true understanding of himself. Whether man can overcome the offence of the σάρξ will depend on whether in his search for revelation he is really looking for *God*, on whether he is prepared to abandon his claim to self-glorification. Nothing else—therefore nothing less than everything that brings man to himself and to God.

The manner of the coming of the Logos in the Incarnate and its dwelling among men will be developed in the Gospel, whose theme—as was hinted in v. 5a—is stated in the ὁ λόγος σὰρξ ἐγένετο. For the moment all one can do is to exclude certain misconceptions. In *speculative Gnosticism*, the coming of the Redeemer in the form of a man is not seen as a revelation, in the sense of an event which challenges and illumines man, but rather as a cosmic process. Redemption is brought about by the Redeemer in his human form, who gathers and leads up the souls of men, the particles of light scattered from the figure of light, which in the very beginning was snatched away by darkness; in so doing the Redeemer frees his second self, the figure of light which fell at the beginning of all things. By their φύσις the pre-existent souls are predestined for salvation, and the whole process of redemption consists in the disentangling of the unnaturally confused φύσεις of the divine and the demonic powers of darkness.[2] The individual is involved in this process, so far as he is a cosmic being and stands within the sphere of this cosmic event. For what is meant here by soul,[3] body and redemption is not indeed *my* particular soul, *my* body and *my* redemption, but the soul, the body and the redemption *in general*. The redemption is a great natural process which, as it were, passes me by; it cannot in any sense

[1] Zahn is right when he says that the Logos does not cease to be the Logos at the Incarnation. But it is absurd that he should maintain that the Logos ceases to be θεός at the Incarnation, although not in every respect. In how many respects is it possible to be θεός? This is to conceive divinity and humanity according to the category of substance. If the Incarnate is the Logos, then he is also θεός.

[2] For this basic theme of Gnosticism see Jonas, Gnosis. On redemption as the gathering up of the scattered particles of light, e.g. Iren. I 30, 14; Exc. ex Theod. 36; Bultmann, ZNTW 24 (1925), 118f. 131f.; Schlier, Relg. Unters. 88ff.; esp. 100ff.; Christus und die Kirche im Epheserbrief 27ff.; E. Käsemann, Leib und Leib Christi, 1933, 65ff.—The image of the redeemer as the magnet drawing the men of spirit to him is given in Jonas, op. cit. 341.— Φύσει σωζόμενος Exc. ex Theod. 56; Clem. Al. str. IV 13, 89; Iren. I, 6, 1.

[3] By soul I do not of course mean the ψυχή, which as the vital life-force is considered to be of little worth, but the spiritual ego or self of the Gnostic.

be understood as an event in the history of my own life. Equally the Redeemer is in truth no specific historical figure, but primal man (*Urmensch*). He wears not *his* body and *his* flesh, but body and flesh *in general*. Thus the place and time of his appearance are in effect of no importance; the myth can attach itself to any saviour figure, and let the historical tradition be submerged.

It is easy to see that in John revelation (and redemption) is not understood as a cosmic process; one has only to consider the fact that the idea of the pre-existence of souls, which has a central role in the Gnostic myth—as we can see from the Od. Sal.—finds no place here.[1] Equally there is no speculation whatever on the destiny of the soul, or on its heavenly journey. Rather the destiny of the soul is determined by faith or unbelief, not by its φύσις—a concept which never occurs in John. And just as unbelief is seen as sin (9.14 etc.), so too the notion of sin receives a meaning which goes beyond the significance it has in Gnosticism. It should not be necessary to produce further arguments to show that a distinction similar to the one we have drawn between the Johannine and the Gnostic view of revelation could also be drawn between the Johannine view and any doctrine of revelation and redemption which takes no account of the particularity of individual men.

Of course in Gnosticism there is a "revelation", connected with the process of redemption set in motion by the advent of the Redeemer in human form, inasmuch as the Redeemer also brings the γνῶσις which the individual must acquire if he is to enter into this process of redemption; in this way such knowledge can actually be described as the redemption.[2] In the γνῶσις man achieves knowledge of himself and his origins, the knowledge that in this earthly world he is an exile, and the knowledge of the way back to his heavenly home.[3] Yet apart from the fact that such teaching instructs him about man in general without helping him to understand his own concrete existence, when the Redeemer does bring him such revelation, his incarnation is only a *means* to the revelation which he brings and not the revelation *itself*. The Revealer, once he has become man, assumes the role of the mystagogue; and the Gnostic no longer needs him as the Incarnate, once he has himself acquired the γνῶσις. In John, however, the encounter with the Incarnate is the encounter with the Revealer himself; and the latter does not bring

---

[1] Cp. ZNTW 24 (1925), 140.

[2] Cp. Jonas, op. cit. 347f.

[3] Exc. ex Theod. 78: . . . ἡ γνῶσις, τίνες ἦμεν, τί γεγόναμεν· ποῦ ἦμεν, ποῦ ἐνεβλήθημεν· ποῦ σπεύδομεν, πόθεν λυτρούμεθα· τί γέννησις, τί ἀναγέννησις. Cp. ThWB I 694, n. 24; also the formula used for the sacrament administered at death by the Marcosians, Iren. I 21, 5: ἐγὼ οἶδα ἐμαυτὸν καὶ γινώσκω ὅθεν εἰμί. Further Schlier, Relg. Unters. 141f.; Bornkamm, Mythos und Legende 13f.; Jonas, Gnosis 206.261.

a teaching which renders his own presence superfluous; rather *as* the Incarnate he sets each man before the decisive question whether he will accept or reject *him.* So too the Gospel presents us with the peculiar dilemma, that it does not offer a real "teaching" of Jesus.[1]—Of course it must be realised that the imparting of doctrine in Gnosticism is not simply the imparting of information about man's situation. It is also a challenge which, by demanding that men should live out the understanding of existence which it expounds, faces them with a decision; in this way the teaching can be accompanied by the call to repentance.[2] Yet because the understanding of existence demanded in this teaching is developed speculatively, it comes to be understood as something which is in principle universally possible and accessible; the confrontation with the teacher is only the *occasion* for reflexion on the situation of man, and does not itself create a *new* situation. In John, on the other hand, the confrontation with the Incarnate Revealer is the decisive, eschatological situation.

Finally there is in Gnosticism the danger of what one might call a *pietistic misunderstanding* of the Revealer; it occurs when his humanity is seen, not as an offence and a paradox, but as an act of condescension which makes the Revealer visible, removing all fear from the man who encounters him, and enabling the latter to enter into a merely human and personal relationship with the Revealer.[3] Thus the significance of the Revealer's humanity is that it makes him visible, arousing in us trust and confidence and even emotion. But it is only the man who is visible, not the Logos; my knowledge that this man is the Logos is something that must come from elsewhere. This means, however, that on such a view the incarnation is not understood as the decisive revelation-event. Accordingly in the Johannine portrayal of the incarnate Revealer there is no attempt to present him as a visible figure;[4] to encounter the Revealer is not to be presented with a persuasive set of answers but only to be faced with a question.

V. 14b explains the miracle of the incarnation of the Logos: "He dwelt among us";[5] that is, he stayed among us men as a man,[6] and he

[1] Cp. ZNTW 24 (1925), 102; see on 3.11 etc.

[2] C. Herm. 1.27–29; 4; 7. Mand. J-B. II 87.5ff.; 92.27ff.; 101.15ff.; 225.6ff.; Ginza 180.20ff.; 391.23ff.; 585.1ff. etc.

[3] See p. 61 n. 1.

[4] In particular W. Wrede has brought out this unrecognisability (Charakter und Tendenz des Johannes-Evangeliums. 2. ed. 1933).

[5] It makes no difference whether one regards the aor. ἐσκήν. as ingressive, ("he came to dwell") which would correspond to the parallelism to σάρξ ἐγένετο, or complexive (Bl.-D. para. 332, 1), casting a general glance back over the course of Jesus' life on this earth.

[6] It fits into the parallelism of v. 14a if we take ἐν ἡμῖν to refer to mankind in general: cf. 12.35 and Bar. 3.38 on σοφία: μετὰ τοῦτο ἐπὶ τῆς γῆς ὤφθη καὶ ἐν τοῖς ἀνθρώποις

did so—for this is what is implied, even if the emphasis is on the positive content of the statement—as a guest who took his leave again.[1] The real paradox of the revelation, however, is brought out in the following couplet:

καὶ ἐθεασάμεθα τὴν δόξαν αὐτοῦ,
δόξαν ὡς μονογενοῦς παρὰ πατρός.

It is the confession of those who, having overcome the offence, have perceived the divine glory in the man Jesus.[2] Yet how can God's

---

συνεστράφη. There can be no question of ἐν ἡμῖν referring to the indwelling of the Logos in the soul of the Gnostic (Act. Thom. 88.148, p. 203, 7f.; 258. 19) or of the mystic (H. Leisegang, Pneuma Hagion 1922, pp. 55–58), for v. 14 states the theme which will be developed by the Gospel itself. For the extreme opposite of this view see Spitta: Jesus lived in a tent among the disciples of John in the desert! Schlier sees the meaning of ἐσκήν. ἐν ἡμῖν as: he entrusted himself to the Church!

[1] Σκηνοῦν means not only to "live in a tent" but also to "dwell", in a general sense, and is used especially in the sense of "taking up quarters" (Herm. sim. V 6, 5 has κατοικεῖν in a similar context, and in para. 7 uses κατασκήνωσις for "dwelling"). It seems possible that the expression was chosen as a play on the common use in the Orient of the "dwelling" of the Godhead, to refer to its salutary presence among men (in a town, a temple, etc.); cp. Streck, Assurbanipal II (Vorderasiat. Bibl. VII 2) 1916, 230f., 248.262f., 266f.; Textb. zur Religionsgesch. 2. ed. p. 302. In the OT: Ex. 25.8; 29.45, etc. L. Goppelt, Typos 1939, 218f. attempts a typological interpretation of ἐσκήν. and δόξα: in the time of Moses God's δόξα descended into the σκηνή (Ex. 33.9, 22; Num. 12.5). But the idea of a "time of salvation in the past" is quite foreign to John. The Hebr. שָׁכַן is frequently translated by κατασκηνοῦν in the LXX Ps. 77.60; Joel 3. (4), 17; Zach. 2.20 (14). For Judaism see Ps. Sal. 7.5: ἐν τῷ κατασκηνοῦν τὸ ὄνομά σου ἐν μέσῳ ἡμῶν ἐλεηθησόμεθα. Ecclus. 24.8. κατασκ. of "Wisdom". Jos. ant. III 202; VIII 106 on the κατασκηνοῦν of God in the temple. In Rabbinic literature שְׁכִינָה has become a technical term for the divine presence, for the numen praesens; cf. Bousset, Rel. des Jdts. 315, 346f.; Str.-B. I 794; II 314f.; A. Marmorstein, The old Rabbinic doctrine of God I 1927, 103f.; ZNTW 26 (1927), 239f.; Schl. ad loc. Moore I 419f.434ff. It would then be possible to translate, "He manifested himself among us"; but this unlikely as a continuation of the σὰρξ ἐγένετο (see below on δόξα). Burney wants to translate back to וְאַשְׁרִי שְׁכִינְתֵּיהּ בֵּינָנָא = "he made his Shekhina dwell among us"; however Burrows is right to suggest simply ישכן בנא. Did. 10.2 comes close to Jewish usage: (τοῦ ὀνόματός σοῦ) οὗ κατεσκήνωσας ἐν ταῖς καρδίαις ἡμῶν, cp. also II Cor. 12.9 and Act. Thom. 52, p. 168, 19: in the invocation of the divine δύναμις: ἐλθὲ καὶ σκήνωσον ἐν τοῖς ὕδασι τούτοις. Cp. also W. Michaelis, 'Zelt und Hütte im bibl. Denken', ZevTh 14 (1954), 24–49. O. Cullmann (JBL 74 [1955] 222) sees here a polemic against the temple, in which, according to Jewish thought, the Shekhina dwells.—It is however in the Wisdom myth that we find actual parallels: Eth. En. 42.2: "Wisdom went out to seek a dwelling among the children of men", Ecclus. 24.4: "I established my dwelling in the height"; 8, "And he who made me, set up my tabernacle and said to me: In Jacob shalt thou dwell (LXX κατασκήνωσον) and take possession in Israel." Bar. 3.28, see previous note. Above all cf. Ginza 454.15f.; 575.10ff.; 592.17ff.—It would be wrong to try to explain ἐσκήνωσεν on the basis of the dualistic usage of σκῆνος for the transitory body of flesh (Wis. 9.15; II Cor. 5.1, 4; II Pet. 1.13f.; Windisch on II Cor. 5.1; H. Leisegang, Pneuma Hagion 30f.); for then instead of ἐν ἡμῖν we would expect ἐν σώματι φθαρτῷ (Wis. 9.15), or something similar.

[2] Δόξα in the LXX, the NT and in the literature of magic, the mysteries and related Hellenistic literature, refers to the epiphany and the manifestation of the Godhead. The

glory be manifested in the σὰρξ γενόμενος?[1] The claim that it was so is the subject of the Gospel; its aim is to show how this is possible. But here the paradoxical tone of the statement should alert us: the revelation clearly does not occur, as some might naively wish to imagine, in a divine demonstration, visible to the natural eye of the body or the soul and with the power to fascinate and convince the natural man; equally the θεᾶσθαι is not an act of perception which is given to the natural man. Indeed we can already see from the context that the beholding of the δόξα takes place within the process indicated by the διδόναι of the Revealer (v. 12) and the λαμβάνειν of the believer (v. 16); that is to say, that the notion of the vision of the glory has been historicized (see p. 44, i). The δόξα (of the Revealer) consists in what he is as *Revealer* for men, and he possesses the δόξα *really*—as becomes

origin of this meaning, which is divergent from the normal Greek meaning of δόξα (1. opinion, 2. honour), is disputed and need not bother us here (Reitzenst., HMR 3. ed. 289, 315, 344, 355, 358ff.; Joh. Schneider, Doxa 1932; ThWB II 238, 20ff.; 255, 22ff.; Helm. Kittel, Die Herrlichkeit Gottes 1934, Percy 24; Dodd 206–208; Dupont 235–293. Further lit. in Bauer, Wörterb.s.v. and on 2.11). In any case the Hellenistic δόξα corresponds to the כָּבוֹד of the OT and Rabbinic literature (the Targums have יְקָרָא), so far as this refers to the manifestation of God; also to the Iranian concept of glory (Schaeder in Reitzenst., Studien 321).—Even though the δόξα is conceived as a shining light or substance, it nevertheless describes not so much the mode of *being* (the φύσις), the What of the Godhead, as its mode of *operation*, its active power, its how, so that δόξα and δύναμις come to have a related or identical meaning (Philo, spec. leg. I 45; Preis. Zaub. IV 1616ff.; XIII 511ff. 554; Mk. 13.26; Rev. 15.8; cf. Rom. 6.4 with I Cor. 6.14; II Cor. 13.4. Cp. G. P. Wetter, Die Verherrlichung im Joh-Evg. = Beitr. zur Rel. wiss. II 1914, 32ff.); thus in Act. Jo. 93, p. 196, 19 δόξα simply means "miracle".—In the context of an eschatological faith δόξα refers to the eschatological epiphany (Mk. 8.38; Rom. 8.18, etc.; cf. A. v. Gall, Βασιλεία τοῦ θεοῦ 1926, 332ff.); the same is true in the LXX, where δόξα corresponds to כָּבוֹד: God shows forth his "glory" or "glorifies" himself in the eschatological event; inasmuch as this is accomplished within the processes of history (Ez. 39.13, 21ff.; Isai. 40.5; 59.19, etc.; cp. also Ex. 14.4, 17f.; Isai. 26.15; 2 Macc. 2.8, etc.). the concept of the (eschatological) glory is historicized. This happens most radically in Paul in II Cor. 3.7ff. he sees the manifestation of the δόξα as taking place in the preaching of the gospel and understands faith as gazing on the δόξα of the κύριος. In the same way the concept of the eschatological δόξα is historicized in John cp. Faulhaber 22f.—If ἐσκήνωσεν is a play on the notion of the שְׁכִינָה (see p. 67 n. 1) v. 14 contains two terms referring to the divine manifestation, which Dalman (Worte Jesu I 189) would refer back to Rabbinical tradition, Schaeder (Reitzenst., Studien 318ff.) to Iranian tradition. In any case it would be wrong to take the concept of the Logos in v. 14 as a third expression for the divine manifestation, as if λόγος = מֵימְרָא; for the λόγος is here not a manifestation, but the one who manifests himself.

[1] Cp. Ginza 318.29ff.:

"I am the Jokabar-Kušta
who went out from the house of my father and came hither.
I came with concealed glory
and with light without end." Cf. Ginza 455.17ff.

Ginza 353.18, 25; 355.13, where the "disciples" are characterised as those who have "seen" the "glory" of the emissary.

clear towards the end of the Gospel (12.28; 13.31f; 17.1ff.)—when that which he himself is has been *actualised* in the believer. Correspondingly it is those who, as believers, allow him to be for themselves what he *is*, who see his glory.[1] The vision of faith takes place in the process of the upturning of all man's natural aims in life, a process which is described in v. 12 as τέκνα θεοῦ γενέσθαι. Those who speak the ἐθεασάμεθα are the believers. The old dispute whether the speakers in v. 14 are eye-witnesses or those who see in a "spiritual" sense, is based on a false alternative, inasmuch as the precise character of "spiritual" sight is not defined. For on the one side it is clear that the specifically Johannine "seeing"[2] is not concerned with eye-witnessing in an historical or a legal sense. For in this sense the "Jews" were also eye-witnesses, and yet they saw nothing (9.39–41). On the other hand such "seeing" has nothing to do with the "spiritual" sight, found in the Greek contemplation of Ideas or in mysticism. The Revealer is not an Idea of Christ, nor a symbolic figure, but the Logos as the σὰρξ γενόμενος; and the object of such "seeing" is no less than the σὰρξ γενόμενος.[3] This "seeing" is neither sensory nor spiritual, but it is the sight of *faith*.[4] What faith sees—briefly summarised

[1] According to Dupont (278–280) the δόξα which is the object of the θεᾶσθαι is the miracles of Jesus, according to Schlier (282) it is the love of the Father resting on the Son. The sight is therefore the sight of faith (see note 4.)

[2] The verbs of seeing (John uses ὁρᾶν, ἰδεῖν, ὄψεσθαι, βλέπειν, θεᾶσθαι and θεωρεῖν interchangeably;—see Tarelli, JThSt 47 (1946), 175f.) are used in a three-fold sense: 1. of the perception of earthly things and happenings accessible to all men (1.38, 47; 9.8 etc.); 2. of the perception of supernatural things and events accessible only to a limited number of men (1.32, 33, 34; 20.12, 14, etc.). Whereas in both these cases what is referred to is perception with one's physical eyes, "seeing" is used 3. of the perception of matters not visible to the organs of sight. The object of such "seeing" is the revelation-event, or alternatively the person of Jesus as the Revealer. Thus 1.14; 6.40, 62; 12.45; 14.7, 17; I Jn. 1.1f.; 4.14 etc. Also 9.37; 14.9; except that here there is a play on the meaning in 1., and in 11.40; 14.19; 16.10, 16f., 19, a play on the meaning in 2. βλέπειν in 9.39–41 is used absolutely in this sense. This is the specifically joh. usage. (Apart, that is, from traditional usage in 4.19; 7.52; 8.56; 11.19 and in fixed expressions as in 3.3, 36; 8.51). The relation of the Revealer to the Father is also referred to as "seeing" of this kind (3.11, 32, 38; 6.46); see n. 4 and cp. Faulhaber 35f.

[3] Cp. the polemic against docetism I Jn. 4.2f.—Torm, ZNTW 30 (1931), 125f. rightly objects to any attempt to spiritualise θεᾶσθαι.

[4] That the seeing here is the sight of faith is shown by 6.40 and 12.44f. where θεωρεῖν and πιστεύειν are used together or in parallel to each other. Equally in 5.24 ἀκούειν and πιστεύειν are also used together while in 8.45–47; 10.26f.; 12.46f. they alternate. On the other hand ὁρᾶν and ἀκούειν are either used (3.32; 5.37; I Jn. 1.1, 3.) together or alternatively (8.38). And just as the relation of the Son to the Father can be described as "seeing" (see n. 2), so too it can be described as "hearing" (5.30; 8.26, 40; 15.15). It is also true of "hearing", as well as of "seeing", that it is not limited to contemporaries (5.24; 10.3, 16; 12.47; 18.37), equally as the hearing of the unbelieving contemporaries was no "hearing" (8.43, 47).—"Seeing" and "hearing" refer, that is, to faith, although admittedly a fulfilled faith, in which the "knowledge" at which it aims has already been realised. For this reason "seeing" and "knowing" can alternate (14.7, 9) or be combined (14.17; I Jn. 3.6); thus the

in I Jn. 4.14: ὅτι ὁ πατὴρ ἀπέσταλκεν τὸν υἱὸν σωτῆρα κόσμου—has never been perceived as an empirical event by any man. Faith sees it constantly, and yet it sees it only by directing its attention towards the σὰρξ γενόμενος. Such sight is not limited to the contemporaries of the Revealer, but it is passed on by them to all the succeeding generations; indeed it can be passed on *only* by them, for it is not the contemplation of a timeless eternal truth but of ὁ λόγος σὰρξ ἐγένετο. The ἐθεασάμεθα is not spoken by a limited number of "eye-witnesses,"[1] any more than θεωρεῖν 6.40; 12.45 and ὁρᾶν 14.9 are limited to "eye-witnesses". But because there were once believing eye-witnesses, it is spoken by all believers; in the same way the Evangelist desires to pass on the θεᾶσθαι[2] through his Gospel. Just as the ἐθεασάμεθα 1.14 could not have been spoken only by "eye-witnesses", so too it could not have been spoken outside the history which is founded on the believing eye-witnesses and the tradition passed on by them. The community which speaks it is not constituted by an idea and by eternal norms, but by a concrete history and its tradition. The sight of faith cannot be loosed from this tradition if it is not to be lost in the contemplation of the Divine as a timeless universal, which would equally involve the loss of the revelation of God.

The "eye-witnesses" as such are considered not as those who stand guarantee for some later generation for the truth of the revelation, but as those who confront every generation anew with the offence that the δόξα must be seen in the one who became σάρξ. Precisely those witnesses who seem to *take away* the offence for coming generations, because they pass on the σὰρξ γενόμενος together with their own interpretation of it, *are* themselves the σκάνδαλον for later generations. For one cannot by-pass them to gain the immediate vision of the δόξα of the Revealer; one is tied to them. Thus every generation is tied to the previous one, in whose proclamation the offence of the σὰρξ γενέσθαι is renewed, because this proclamation does not pass on a timeless idea but transmits an historical event. So too the ἐθεασάμεθα, in which the offence is overcome, is renewed again and again.[3]

"Jews" have neither seen God (5.37) nor have they known him (8.55); and as Jesus has seen the Father (6.46 etc.), so too he has known (17.25) and knows him (8.55; 10.15). On the other hand πιστεύειν is not said of Jesus, because faith cannot be thought of solely with regard to the moment of its fulfilment (see on 6.69). The fulfilment of faith may also be described by λαμβάνειν; see on v. 16.

[1] On the eye-witnesses see O. Cullmann, Aux sources de la trad. Chrét. 54.

[2] H. von Campenhausen, Die Idee des Martyriums 37.2 takes the correct view when he describes the "we" here as a pluralis ecclesiasticus.—The problem is discussed by Robert Browning in the speech of the dying John ("A Death in the Desert" in "Dramatis personae" 1864).

[3] The matter was most clearly seen by Kierkegaard who developed it above all in the "Philosophical Fragments" (E.T. 1936) under the headings "The Contemporary Disciple" (pp. 44–58) and "The Disciple at Second hand" (pp. 74–93). Cp. p. 57, the "immediate

The characterisation of the δόξα of the Incarnate as the δόξα of the μονογενὴς παρὰ πατρός[1] confirms that his glory consists in nothing other than in being the Revealer. For this characterisation, in which for the first time the Revealer is spoken of as the Son and God as the Father, designates him precisely as the Revealer,[2] and it contains the main

---

contemporaneousness" (of the "eye-witnesses") can become the *occasion* of their "seeing the glory with the eyes of faith". "Yet such a man is not an eye-witness (in the direct sense), but in the autopsy of faith it is because he is a believer that he is a contemporary. In this autopsy every non-contemporary (in the direct sense) is the contemporary."—The extraordinary way in which every new generation enters again into the situation of Jesus' contemporaries is shown in I John. Cp. Iren. V 1.1 where Irenaeus accounts himself one of the magistrum nostrum videntes et per auditum nostrum vocem eius percipientes.—The sort of semi-pietistic, semi-liberal interpretation such as is given by Zahn, who describes the θεᾶσθαι 1.14 as seeing "the glory which shone forth from the bodily appearance of the incarnate Logos, and which presented itself to all men's senses in his visible actions, audible words and majestic countenance" is scorned by Kierkegaard (p. 52) "And when in the strength of his omnipotent resolve. . . . God makes himself the equal of the humblest, let no innkeeper or professor of philosophy imagine that he is a shrewd enough fellow to detect anything unless God gives the condition."

[1] παρά may denote either the descent (6.46; 7.29; 9.16, 33; although here it is always preceded by εἶναι) or even the origin (cp. 15.26; 16.27; 17.8; although here it is with ἐκπορεύεσθαι and ἐξέρχεσθαι, and with γίγνεσθαι e.g. Plato Symp. 179b); more probably, however, it is doing duty here for a simple gen., as μονογενοῦς πατρός would be ambiguous. —The ὡς can hardly be intended simply as a comparison, but means "in accordance with the fact that" (cp. Ps. Sal. 18.4 and Chrys. in Lagr.). The omission of the art. before πατρ. must be a sort of assimilation to μονογ. (Bl.-D. para. 257, 3); this does not need to take the art. because it has the character of a predicative nominative (scil. ὄντος. Cp. Aall II 120: "The absence of the art. throws the weight of the argument on the particular content of the term.").

[2] Μονογενής (cp. Büchsel ThWB s.v.; P. Winter op. cit. (see p. 23 n. 1), 335–365; D. Moody JBL 72 (1953) 213–219) is understood as "unique in its γένος" (Parm. fr. 8, 4; I Clem 25.2 of the phoenix) or "uniform in its manner" (H. Diels, Doxogr. Gr. 278, a 17, b 13; 279, a 7, b 4 (syn. ἁπλοῦς)), or as "only begotten". Occasionally it is understood as "descended from a single begetter" (Hippol. El. VI 31, 4, p. 159, 4 W.; cp. Eur. Hel. 1685: ἀδελφὴ μονογενοῦς ἀφ' αἵματος), or even as "making one unique" (Pluto, de fac. in orbe lunae 28, 5 p. 943b). From Hes. op. 376 (μονογ. παῖς); Herod. VII 221 onwards it is used in the third sense for the only child. So often in LXX: Judg. 11.34; Tob. 3.15; 8.17; in Jos. ant. V 264; XX 20; in the NT: Lk. 7.12; 8.42; 9.38; Hebr. 11.17. It is used to translate יָחִיד Judg. 11.34 which is also often translated by μονογ. elsewhere, but in the sense of "lonely", "deserted" (Ps. 21.21; 24.16; 34.17; Ps. 67.7 has instead μονότροπος), while יחיד in the sense of "only son" is frequently rendered by ἀγαπητός (Gen. 22.2, 12, 16; Jer. 6.26; Am. 8.10; Zach. 12.10; ἀγαπώμενος Prov. 4.3). The parallelism of its use with ἀγαπητός shows that in such cases μονογ. also ascribes value to that of which it is predicated, which is completely proved by the combination of "only (son)" and "first-born" Ps. Sal. 18.4; II Esr. 6.58; as does the fact that Israel is described as the "only son" (see ad loc.). The μονογενὴς (προφήτης) Test. Benj. 9.2 is probably a Christian addition. So too, P. Winter, op. cit. 344ff. This ought to give us the key to Jn. 3.16, 18; I Jn. 4.9, as well as to 1.18, if it is right to read μονογ. υἱός (see below). Μονογ. in this sense, does not occur elsewhere in the NT as a characterisation of Jesus (later Mart. Pol 20.2 in the final doxology and in credal formulae up till Symbol. Rom.; examples in Lietzmann ZNTW 22 (1923), 277f.; also Geschichte der alten Kirche II 108; Ad. v. Harnack, 'Die Bezeichnung Jesu als „Knecht" Gottes und ihre Gesch. in der alten Kirche', SABerlin 1926 XXVIII; E. Boecklen, Theol. Stud. und Krit. 101 (1929), 55–90), it corresponds roughly to the ἀγαπητός Mk. 1.11 parr.;

themes which run through the Gospel, and which are stated cogently towards the end: he is the only way to the Father (14.6); but whoever sees him, truly sees the Father (14.9).

9.7 alt. Mt. 17.5; cp. Mt. 12.18. Since however Jn. 1.14 comes from the source (only here is μονογ. found without υἱός), whereas the other references are the Evangelist's own, μονογ. 1.14 must be taken in a different sense.

Μονογ. occurs not infrequently as the attribute of divinities of the occult or the underworld; for Hecate from Hes., Op. 426.448; in "Orphic" literature for Core, Persephone and Demeter, admittedly attested only in later literature but probably on the basis of old tradition (refs. in G. Wobbermin, Religionsgeschichtl. Studien 1896, 118f.; further for Persephone Plut. de fac. in orbe lunae 28.5, p. 943b. None of these refs. is given in Kern, Orph. Fr., where we only find the description of Moses as μονογ. Fr. 247, 23). The characterisation of Athene as μονογ. is certainly very late, Hymn. Orph. 32.1 and here the attribute is clearly used to mean "begotten by one (father) alone (without the assistance of the mother)" (see below); Rendel Harris wants to trace the ascription of μονογ. to the Logos back to this use ('Athena, Sophia and the Logos', Bulletin of the John Ryland's Library VII 1, 1922). Here μονογ. is in every case the attribute of female divinities. (It is extremely doubtful whether it is in accordance with old tradition for the Orphic Phanes, who is usually characterised as πρωτόγονος, on one occasion to receive the attribute μονογ. (K. Buresch, Klaros 1889, 116)). In every case the meaning should be taken as "unique," and the designation has became a formula; this is most clearly seen in the invocations of magicians (Pap. Gr. mag. IV 1586; Wünsch, Antike Fluchtafeln 4, 36 in Kl. Texte 20; as attribute of the ἅγιον πνεῦμα Pap. Gr. mag. XII 174), where it is no longer referred to any one particular divinity.

There is no question of this "Orphic" usage in any way conditioning the use in Jn. 1.14, except very indirectly, if there is a connection between it and the use of μονογ. as a *cosmological attribute*. This use of μονογ. occurs first in Parm. fr. 8, 4 as a characterisation of being in its unity and totality (Plut. and Procl. read οὐλομελές; cf. μονοειδές for the Universe in Empedocl. A 32); then in Plat. Tim. 31b. 92c. as attribute of οὐρανός i.e. of the uniform, closed κόσμος. In any case Plato is dependent on mytholog. tradition; the κόσμος is thought of as having been created by the demi-urge, by its father as the θεὸς αἰσθητός, who is the εἰκὼν τοῦ νοητοῦ (Tim. 37c. 92c.; see p. 28 n. 1). Cp. also Plut. de def. orac. 23, p. 423a: Πλάτων ... αὐτῷ δή φησι δοκεῖν ἕνα τοῦτον (sc. τὸν κόσμον) εἶναι μονογενῆ τῷ θεῷ καὶ ἀγαπητόν. Does the attribute μονογ. also come from this tradition? Naturally it has lost its mythological meaning when later it is used by Cornutus theol. gr. 27 to describe the κόσμος as εἷς καὶ μονογ. Yet the use which we find in the realm of Gnosticism points back to an originally mythological meaning; μονογ. seems here to be one of a series of terms υἱός, ἄνθρωπος, εἰκὼν τοῦ πατρός, λόγος (νοῦς), which all denote the second stage in the unfolding of the Godhead, and thus sometimes refer pantheistically to the κόσμος, sometimes dualistically to the spiritual world in its unity, and thus also to the Revealer. The Neo-Platonist Damascios, in his recounting of the Babylon. cosmogony (acc. to Eudemos of Rhodes) de princ. 125 (p. 321f. Ruelle), declares that the Mummu, who is the μονογενὴς παῖς of Tiâmat and Apsû, is the κόσμος νοητός. In Suidas (J. Kroll, Herm. Trism. 56) we find the invocation: ὁρκίζω σε, οὐρανέ, θεοῦ μεγάλου σοφὸν ἔργον, ὁρκίζω σε, φωνὴν πατρός, ἣν ἐφθέγξατο πρώτην ἡνίκα τὸν πάντα κόσμον ἐστηρίξατο, ὁρκίζω σε κατὰ τοῦ μονογενοῦς αὐτοῦ λόγου. In the C. Herm. the κοσμος is often seen as the υἱός θεοῦ; admittedly μονογ. is not predicated of him, and in the rendering of the characterisation of Plato's Tim. (in the fr. in Lact. div. inst., IV 6, 4. in Scott I 298) he is called πρῶτὸς καὶ μόνος καὶ εἷς (see on v. 14c). This in substance is the same; we find too a similar state of affairs in Philo, who has no use of the pred. μονογ. but who, in a passage which is certainly influenced by the Gnostic myth, ebr. 30 (God the Father and the ἐπιστήμη as the Mother), refers to the κόσμος as the μόνος καὶ ἀγαπητὸς υἱὸς (in Wis. 7.22 the cosmic σοφία is described as the πνεῦμα μονογ., a passage which is admittedly strongly influenced by Stoic terminology). According to Clem. Al. str. V 74, 3 Basileides referred to the κόσμος as μονογ.; and when Clement speaks in str. VII 16, 6 of the τῷ ὄντι μονογ. he clearly has in mind the contrast to

Finally in **v. 14e** the Incarnate as the Revealer is characterised as

πλήρης χάριτος καὶ ἀληθείας.[1]

For χάρις and ἀλήθεια describe God's being; not "in itself", but as it is open to man (in his receptivity) and in its activity towards man: they refer, that is, to the benefits in which God (or the Revealer) abounds,[2] and which he bestows on the believer. Χάρις and ἀλήθεια are here a hendiadys, since χάρις has the formal meaning of "giving grace" and

---

the false μονογ. of the Gnostics (a similar contrast seems also to be suggested in Act. Phil 43 p. 19, 37, where it is said of Jesus: αὐτός ἐστι μόνος μονογενὴς ὁ τοῦ ἐπουρανίου θεοῦ υἱός). According to Clem. Exc. ex Th. 6 (cp 7), the Valentinians referred to the ἀρχή as the Μονογενής and Νοῦς (which was artificially distinguished from the Λόγος) and this is confirmed by Iren. I 1, 1 (in Iren. I 1.2 a second Μονογ. appears at the end of the Dekad; this appears otherwise only in Hippol. El. VI 30, 4). In the Ptolemaic system the Βυθός stands at the beginning, and to him are ascribed two σύζυγοι, Ἔννοια and Θέλησις whose προβολή is the Μονογ., who is also called Νοῦς (Hipp. El. VI 38, 6). In the "Docetics" μονογενὴς παῖς or υἱός is the name given to the σωτὴρ πάντων, who is begotten by the three aeons, who is like the original σπέρμα and who becomes man in Jesus (Hipp. El VIII 9, 2f.; 10, 3.9; in the recapitulation X 16, 6 he is called instead the μονογ. δύναμις). In Exc. ex Th. 7.10 the μονογενής, brought forth from the ἄγνωστος πατήρ and the ἐνθύμησις, is expressly characterised as the Revealer; similarly in Iren. I 2 (1.)5. The Μονογ. is also involved in the tortuous mythology of the "unknown Gnostic work" (C. Schmidt, Kopt.-gnost. Schriften I 1905), and so much is clear that he is a primary cosmological figure (esp. 342, 9ff.; 343, 10ff.); he is also characterised as the Revealer (346, 31ff.) It is, however, hardly possible to trace the Gnostic usage back to John, even if the Gnostics themselves made fruitful use of the Gospel of John.—The Mand. writings also know the "only son", the "great, just Single one, who went forth out of the great just Single One, who created life by His word (Ginza p. 236, 7ff.); he is then portrayed not only as the Revealer, but also as the one who orders the world 237, 35ff.; cp. 251, 20ff.; 91, 11ff.). Gnostic terminology must also lie behind the invocation in Act. Thom. 48 p. 164, 14f.: ὁ πολύμορφος, ὁ μονογενὴς ὑπάρχων, and behind the characterisation in Act. Thom, 143 p. 250, 3: υἱὸς βάθους μονογενής. The phrase "The Christ is *one* in truth" Od. Sal. 41, 15 is shown to be Gnostic by its continuation, "and was known before the foundation of the world," as well as by the preceding verses, which contain the title "Son of the Highest" and "Logos" (cp. too H. Schlier, Relg. Unters, 78f.). Böcklen op. cit. tries to show why it is probable that μονογ. in this tradition has the meaning "begotten by a single person (i.e. without a mother)".—It can hardly have anything to do with this tradition if, according to Epiph. haer.51, 22, 11, p. 287, 1f. Holl, the Arabian God Dusares, the son of Kore, is called μονογ. τοῦ δεσπότου, or if—perhaps—the Syrian Adonis was referred to as the "Only (Son)" (W. W. Graf. Baudissin, Adonis und Esmun 1911, 89ff., acc. to Philo Bybl. in Eus. Praep. evang. I 10, 30, p. 48 Heinichen).

[1] The line seems to overrun; yet neither this nor the previous line should be taken as additions of the Evangelist. V. 14d is linked to v. 14c by the keyword δόξα (see p. 16f. and cp. n. 2); and v. 14e is clearly presupposed in v. 16. If one rejects the thesis that the Evangelist has omitted a line (containing, for example the concept εἰκών, which he clearly always avoids), then it would seem resonable to take v. 14e with v. 16 (as does Burney) and to suggest that the original text read as follows:

‹ἦν› πλήρης χάριτος καὶ ἀληθείας,
καὶ ἐκ τοῦ πληρώματος αὐτοῦ ἡμεῖς πάντες ἐλάβομεν

[2] πλήρης is clearly not predicated of δόξα (for it is the Revealer who is being described); it is either "related to the dominating term ὁ λόγος" (Schl.; this is surely right if

"gracious gift",[1] while ἀλήθεια denotes the content of the gift, the divine reality revealing itself.[2] Moreover each of these expressions can denote both the content and the form: in the χάρις as the *divine* gift, the ἀλήθεια is included (v. 16), just as the ἀλήθεια is the *gift* which one receives from the Revealer (8.32; 14.6).—But before the argument in v. 14 is resumed in v. 16, the Evangelist again inserts a note:[3] it relates to the witness of

---

v. 14e and v. 16 originally belong together, see n. 1), or else it is to be taken with αὐτοῦ and is used without inflection, as is not uncommon in Koine Greek (Bl.-D. para. 137, 1; Raderm. 60; Moulton, Einl. 73f.; Deissmann, L.v.O. 99f.)—The characterisation as πλήρης κτλ. seems to be a traditional description of the Son of God (when understood as κόσμος or as the Revealer). This is found as early as Plat. Tim. 92b, (see p. 72 n.): θνητὰ γὰρ καὶ ἀθάνατα ζῷα λαβὼν καὶ ξυμπληρωθεὶς ὅδε ὁ κόσμος . . .; similarly this is echoed in the description of the κόσμος in the Hermetic writings as πληρέστατος πάντων τῶν ἀγαθῶν (Scott I 298, see p. 000). In Philo, too, the κόσμος is: τελειότατον δὲ καὶ πληρέστατον (Abr. 2; cp. plant. 128); God also is characterised by him as πλήρης (used absolutely: sacr. Ab. et C.9; det. pot. ins. 54; rer. div. her. 187; πλ. ἑαυτοῦ leg. all. I 44; mut. nom. 27; πλ. ἀγαθῶν τελείων spec. leg. II 53), and the Logos as πληρέστατος (somn. I 75; πλ. ἑαυτοῦ rer. div. her. 188, ad. loc.; κόλλα γάρ καὶ δεσμὸς οὗτος πάντα τῆς οὐσίας ἐκπεπληρωκώς); he is πλήρης τοῦ σοφίας νάματος (somn. II 245), and his διαθήκη is πλήρης χαρίτων (somn, II 223). Cp. Grill I 363ff. Among the Peratae the ἀληθινός ὄφις is ὁ τέλειος, ὁ πλήρης τῶν πληρῶν Hipp. El. V. 16, 7 p. 112, 11f. W. Further discussion, see on v. 16.

[1] Originally χάρις is the act or conduct which brings joy and happiness, the *demonstration* of goodness; yet this may be seen not only from the point of view of the agent but also of the recipient, of the one who enjoys the χάρις, so that it can equally well mean goodness and kindness or gift, present, (and finally also thanks). Cp. esp. Arist. rhet. B 7 p. 1385a 15-b10; O. Loew, Χάρις, Diss. Marb. 1908. The use of χάρις for the grace or the demonstration of the grace of God is to be found in Greek before the LXX. In the latter χάρις usually renders חֵן although this may sometimes be translated by ἔλεος.—The context determines whether it is to be taken as "gracious deed", "gracious gift" or "gracious attitude"; it gains the further meaning in Hellenism of "the (gracious, salutary) power of God", so that χάρις can be synon. with δόξα, πνεῦμα, δύναμις and νίκη; cp. G. P. Wetter, Charis 1913. —χάρις occurs in John only in 1. 14,16f. and in the formula of greeting II Jn. 3. In 1.14 and 16 the meaning is clearly that of the demonstration of grace, seen in v. 14 more from the point of view of the agent, in v. 16 more from the point of view of the receiver. For further discussion see on v. 16,17. A. Lang, Christentum und Wissenschaft 8 (1932), 408–414 is inadequate. Hoskyns' distinction χάρις = the miracles, ἀλήθεια = the teaching is impossible.

[2] In Hellenism ἀλήθεια received over and above the formal meaning of truth, reality (and truthfulness) the meaning of "divine reality", with the connotation that this divine reality *reveals* itself (ThWB I 240, 26ff.) The joh. usage is based on this (ThWB I 245, 23ff.). In view of the pervading sense of ἀλ. in John, it is not possible to take ἀλ. 1.14 in the sense of "faithfulness" as in the LXX (for אֱמֶת) and to see in πληρ. χαρ. κ. ἀλ. a reference to Ex. 34.6, where God is described as רַב־חֶסֶד וֶאֱמֶת (Zn.), and where the LXX, which normally translates חסד as ἔλεος has πολυέλεος καὶ ἀληθινός. Dodd (175f. 272) and Barr. see Χάρ. καὶ ἀλ. as a reproduction of the OT חֶסֶד וֶאֱמֶת.—What is here described is the gift and not the "experiences which confer happiness" (Gulin 29.1; G. P. Wetter, Charis, 1913, 154).

[3] See p. 15. The style of v. 15 also betrays it as the work of the Evangelist; the saying of the Baptist is one of the typical identification statements; cp. 1.33; 4.42; 6.14; 7.25f., 40f.; 21.24, etc., I Jn. 2.22; 5.6, 20; II Jn. 7,9. Λέγειν τινα = to say something about someone, is also typical for the Evangelist (see p. 75 n. 3). Finally the occurrence of rabbinical expressions is also characteristic for him (see p. 75 nn. 4, 5). Cp. Thomas op. cit. 106f.123f., 130, he

the Baptist, as to an inspired[1] witness, confessing and testifying[2] of the Incarnate one that this is he who was promised and expected, because he is the pre-existent one. Such is the force of the οὗτος ἦν κτλ. The Baptist refers back[3] to one of his own sayings (as in v. 30), which the Evangelist assumes to be well known; it is the saying which we know from the synoptic tradition (Mk. 1.7f. parr.), expressed admittedly in a typically Johannine way, full of associations and paradoxes: the ὀπίσω μου refers, as in the Synoptic version (metaphorically expressed in spatial terms), to the chronological order of the appearance of the Revealer;[4] but the ἔμπρ. μου γέγ., which we have here instead of the Synoptic ἰσχυρότερός μου κτλ., refers to his status (though still using the same metaphor).[5] However, the Synoptic account is taken further, in that a justification of these claims is added: ὅτι πρῶτός μου ἦν,[6] which

---

rightly finds that there is here a reference to the polemic between the communities of Jesus and John. So too O. Cullmann, Coniect. Neotest. 1947, 26–32 and JBL 74 (1955), 218.

[1] Κράζειν (cry aloud) is used with a special sense for inspired speech, as for the speech of Jesus 7.28; 12.44; elsewhere of cries in the Spirit, Lk. 1.41f. Rom. 8.15; Gal. 4.6; Ign. Phld. 7.1. For the cries of demoniacs Mk. 3.11; 5.5, 7; 9.26, etc. For the cry of the prophet Rom. 9.27 corresponding to the Rabbinic use of צוח (Str.-B.III 275; II 135f.; Schl. ad. loc.). For the Eleusinian hierophants Hipp. El. V 8, 40, p. 96, 17 W.: βοᾷ καὶ κέκραγε λεγών, for the Pythia Plut., de orac. def. 438b. Cp. H. Leisegang, Pneuma Hagion 1922, 23, 4; Schlier, Relg. Unters. 144; E. Peterson, Εἷς θεός 1926, 191, 3.—Dodd (382, 1) points out that κράζειν in LXX translates the OT קרא alternatively with κηρύσσειν; whereas the latter word in the Synopt. and elsewhere in the NT means "proclaim", Dodd maintains that John instead uses κράζειν in this sense. For the combination of μαρτυρεῖν and κράζειν cp. H. Almquist, Plutarch und das NT 1946, 71f.—Cp. also Jos. Bonsirven, Exégèse Rabbinique, etc., 1939, 32.

[2] The present tense μαρτυρεῖ is used because of the continuing actuality of the witness of the Baptist. That is to say, it is not an historical report; cp. on vv. 6–8. κέκραγεν also describes the cry as one which, after it has died away, is still there, cp. Bl.-D. para. 341.

[3] "Ον εἶπον = ὑπὲρ οὗ εἶπον (as also 6.71; 8.27, 54; 10.36) is perfectly good Greek (see Br.). On the other hand the reading ὁ εἰπών of BC is meaningless; the intention probably was to remove the difficulty, which was felt because the saying of the Baptist had not yet been quoted. The same effect is achieved by the omission of ὃν εἶπον and the insertion of ὅς after ἐρχόμενος in א. Instead of ἦν one expects ἐστίν, as in v. 30; the ἦν is probably an attraction to εἶπον and is to be explained psychologically: "This is the man whom I meant when I said ..."

[4] "To come behind someone" is a common Rabbinical expression for chronological order; cp. Schl. on Mt. 3.11 (p. 78). Burney who takes γέγ. as a mistranslation of an Aram. participle, suggests that it means "he anticipates me", or "he will anticipate me". This is completely unnecessary and only serves to destroy the paradox. Black (108, 1) suspects that ἔρχεσθαι ὀπίσω has the same sense as ἀκολουθεῖν, meaning the following (discipleship) of a pupil. Then the meaning of the Aram. saying which here lies behind the text would be: "My pupil is superior to me."

[5] Ἔμπροσθεν is commonly used of time and rank. The basis of the use here is probably the Rabbinic "to precede" = to have the greater dignity; Siphre Deut. 11, 10 para. 37 (76a) in Str.-B. III 256. Schlier suggests as the meaning of ἔμπρ. μου γεγ.: "he existed before me", which can scarcely be correct.

[6] πρῶτος = προτέρος, as is common in the Koine, because of the appended μου; see Bl.-D para. 62; Raderm. 70; Colwell 77f.; Br.—Burney rejects μου as a translator's error and thus again destroys the paradox.

again must be taken in a temporal sense. Thus the contradiction between πρῶτός μου and ὀπίσω μου poses a riddle which remains unsolved. And yet it is precisely this which gives the grounds for the ἔμπρ. μου, because the πρῶτός μου refers to his pre-existence.[1] Thus the meaning of the Baptist's saying is that in Jesus as the incarnate, eternal Logos all the Jewish messianic expectations and all the Gnostic hopes of a Redeemer are fulfilled; it finds its rightful place here because v. 14 has already given the essential characterisation of the Incarnate.

After this note the Evangelist again returns to the text and argument of the source;[2] to the first confession of the congregation (ἐθεασάμεθα v. 14) is now added the second:

v. 16: ἐκ τοῦ πληρώματος αὐτοῦ ἡμεῖς πάντες ἐλάβομεν,[3]
καὶ χάριν ἀντὶ χάριτος.[4]

The vision of the δόξα of the Revealer is realised in the acceptance of his gift;[5] he allows man to share in the fulness of his divine

---

[1] The full significance of the concept of pre-existence is brought out in the body of the Gospel, so far, that is, as it has not already emerged from the Prologue as a whole. In its terminology it follows the Gnost. notion of Pre-existence; on the πρῶτός μου ἦν, cp. Od. Sal. 28, 17f.:

> "They sought my death, but could not find it,
> for I was older than their name.
> In vain they threatened me
> who came into being after me.
> In vain they sought to root out
> the name of him who was before them!"

For the joh. concept of pre-existence see v. 30 and 6.62; 8.58; 17.5, 24.

[2] See p. 73, n. 1.

[3] It is unlikely that a conclusion can be reached on the question whether the sentence originally began with ὅτι (א BC*DL 33) or with καί. καί would suit the style of the source better; but the Evangelist could have changed it to ὅτι, if, that is, the ὅτι is not an early correction, due to a view widely held in early exegesis (see Zn. 5. ed., p. 90, n. 2) that in vv. 16ff. it is the Baptist who is speaking, considering himself as one of the righteous of the OT.—Against Burney, who sees ὅτι as a mistranslation (instead of οὗ), see Colwell, 101–103, and cp. on 9. 17; for Burney cp. Black 56. Hirsch sees ὅτι as part of the editor's insertion in v. 15.

[4] If v. 16a originally belongs to v. 14e (see p. 73, n. 1), then v. 16b would overrun its proper length. This could be due to an addition of the Evangelist's; on the other hand it is not unusual for the last line of a hymn to overrun its length. cp. Od. Sal. 3.11; 4.15; 16.20; 18.16; 41.16; esp. 21.9; 22.12c; 23.22c. Cp. also Phil. 2.11; I Pet. 3.22.

[5] As far as the argument of the passage is concerned, it makes no difference whether v. 16 is connected to v. 14 by καί, or whether it is thought of as giving the grounds for v. 14 (see n. 3). Just as "beholding" denotes the reception of the revelation in faith, so too does λαμβάνειν; yet there are subtle differences in the use, which correspond to the various shades of meaning of λαμβ. It has the meaning "grasp", "lay hold of", when its obj. is τὴν μαρτυρίαν or τὰ ῥήματά μου (3.11, 32f.; or 12.48; 17.8), and in this case it denotes the act of turning towards someone in faith. It is used in relation to faith, in the sense of "receive (a gift)", both in 1.16 and 14.17, and so corresponds to a divine διδόναι (see on v. 12, p. 57, n. 5); here it sees faith as fulfilled, as having come to its goal (see p. 69, n. 4),

Being.[1] Whereas elsewhere this gift of the Revealer is mostly referred to as ζωὴ (αἰώνιος) (3.15f; 6.33, 40; 10.10, 28; 17.2 etc.), here, following

---

and is thus connected in 14.17 with θεωρεῖν and γινώσκειν. Finally it is used in the non-Greek sense of "to welcome, receive" (1.12; 5.43; 13.20; see p. 57, n. 2), and then also means to turn towards someone in faith. It is not possible to decide whether in v. 16 ἐλαβ. has as its object in the first place ἐκ τοῦ πληρ αὐτ. (for ἐκ with verbs of taking, enjoying, etc. see Bl.-D. para. 169, 2; Raderm. 137ff.), and then receives a second accusative obj. in χάρ. ἀντὶ χάρ. which is separated from it by καί = "namely" (Bl.-D. para. 442, 9); or whether it is used absolutely and must then be supplied again before the καὶ χάρ. κτλ. As far as the meaning is concerned it makes no difference.

[1] Like πλήρης (see p. 73, n. 2) πλήρωμα is also a traditional characterisation of the divine sphere. In Greek Gnosticism πλ. is used absolutely as the name of the divine kingdom of the aeons, and can also denote the sphere of the individual aeons (K. Müller, Nachr. der Gött. Ges. der Wiss.; phil.-hist. Kl. 1920, 179). Originally πλ. did not have the Gnostic dualistic meaning, but denoted the fulness of the world which (as the second degree of being) is developed from the original Godhead. The κόσμος (of the υἱὸς τοῦ θεοῦ or his εἰκών) is described in a pantheistic sense as πλήρωμα τῆς ζωῆς C. Herm. 9, 7 (cp. the anti-Gnostic polemic 9.4); 12.15f. (cp. 16.3; Ascl. 29, Nock-Festugière, Hermes Trismes. 337.11; Ascl. 26.32 N.F. 331, 18; 340.2). Elsewhere, too, in pantheistic mystic speculation the "Full" or the "Fulness" appear as characterisations of the divinity, cf. R. Otto, West.-östl. Mystik 1926, 31f. 75f. In Neo-Platonism the character of πλ. is naturally ascribed to the νοητὸς κόσμος. In Plotinus the concept of πλήρωμα naturally does not occur (it is replaced by the concept of the κόρος); but cp. Enn. III 8, 11 p. 346, 15 Volkm. of the νοητὸς κόσμος as the παῖς of the Highest and as νοῦς and κόρος: πλήρωσιν δὲ ἀληθινὴν καὶ νόησιν ἔχει. Further Jambl. myst. I 8 p. 28, 18 Parthey: τὰ δ'ἐπὶ γῆς ἐν τοῖς πληρώμασι τῶν θεῶν ἔχοντα τὸ εἶναι; Damasc., inst. Plat. c. 85, p. 160, Kopp: ἕτερον δὲ λέγεται Ὂν τὸ ὁλοφυές πλήρωμα τῶν γενῶν ὃ παρουσίαν ἰδίως καλοῦμεν ὡς ὁ Πλωτῖνος. The concept of the πλ. is presupposed by Philo, when he says of the Logos: ὃν ἐκπεπλήρωκεν ὅλον δι' ὅλων ἀσωμάτοις δυνάμεσιν αὐτὸς ὁ θεός (somn. I 62; cp. the ψυχή as πλήρωμα ἀρετῶν praem. et poen. 65), and when he characterises the ark as the ἀντίμιμον γῆς ἀπάσης because of its πλήρωμα: ἐν ἑαυτῷ φέρον τὰ ζῴων γένη Vit. Mos. II 62. (The frequent statements that God fills the universe and that the universe is filled by him are of a different nature; cp. Isai. 6.3). This usage is also at the basis of Col. 1.9, 19; 2.9; Eph. 1.23; 3.19. The concept of the divine πλ. is also presupposed when it is said in C. Herm. 6.4, in a dualistic sense: ὁ γὰρ κόσμος (the world of coming into being and passing away) πλήρωμά ἐστι τῆς κακίας. Cp. Dibelius on Col. 1.19 in Hdb. zum NT.

In the Od. Sal. the pleroma is the heavenly world. There are echoes of the cosmological usage when the Logos 7.11 is described as the "pleroma of the aeons and their father", and when the Revealer is called the "Highest in all his pleroma" (17.7), to whom the pleroma belongs from the height of heaven to its very edge (26.7). However pleroma is used essentially in a religious sense, so that it is synonymous with "eternal life" (9.4). The way of "Gnosis" leads to the pleroma (7.13). The singer prays God not to take it away from him (18.5 cp. 8); he refreshes himself from the Lord's gracious gift and pleroma (35.6), and sings of God's pleroma and glory (36.2; not with the division suggested by Gressmann!) as one who has been anointed with the pleroma (36.6). Above all it is said of the Son that he has appeared with the pleroma of the Father (41.14). In all this I have assumed that שומליא is to be understood throughout, and not merely occasionally (as Gressmann), as πλήρωμα. This is however confirmed by the use of the verb מלא. In Paradise "everything" is "full of thy fruits" (11. 23!). The Revealer "fills" the believer with his love or with the word of truth (11.2; 12.1); the Gnosis "fills" everything (6.10; cp. 23.4), and man is to "fill" himself from the spring of life of the Lord (30.1). Cp. J. B. Lightfoot, St. Paul's Epistles to the Colossians and to Ph. 1882, 257–273; J. A. Robinson, St. Paul's Epistle to the Ephesians. 1903, 255–259. M. Dibelius, on Col 1. 19 (Hdb.z.NT); W. L. Knox, St. Paul and the Church of the Gentiles 1939, 163ff.; J. Dupont, Gnosis 1949, 421–427 (–453), 453–476; Festugière in Hermes Trismeg. I 76, 17; II 238, 12.

on v. 14, χάρις is used[1]. This denotes the character of the revelation as pure gift; the formulation is appropriate in this context because, in contrast with the ζωή-sayings which are spoken by the Revealer, the recipients of the gift themselves are here speaking, and v. 16 is their confession of thanks. The same is true of the χάριν ἀντὶ χάριτος,[2] which praises the inexhaustible bounty of his gift. "We *all* received", confesses the congregation; it is not the number of the πάντες that is thereby reflected on, but the inexhaustibility of the gift which is brought out.[3]

With this confession of thanks the hymn reaches its proper conclusion; what follows are the Evangelist's own additions, antithetical statements put in to bring out more clearly the meaning of what has been said and to guard it against error.

V. 17 stresses the absoluteness of the revelation in Jesus by contrasting it with the νόμος, or to put it in Jewish Christian language, with the Torah, or indeed with the OT as a whole (Dupont 39 suggests that this is directed against Jewish speculation on the Torah). The question whether there is perhaps also a positive relationship between the OT

---

[1] On χάρις see p. 74, n. 1. The description of the revelation as the reception of χάρις has its parallels. In a sacramental sense Iren. I 13.3 on the consecration of the Marcosian prophets: λάμβανε πρῶτον ἀπ' ἐμοῦ καὶ δι' ἐμοῦ τὴν χάριν ... ἰδοὺ ἡ χάρις κατῆλθεν ἐπὶ σέ (viz. in the mystery of the νυμφών); cp. 13.3, the invocation of the χάρις on the chalice of the sacrament. Cp. Ginza 273.18. In an eschatological sense in the prayer Did. 10.6; ἐλθέτω χάρις καὶ παρελθέτω ὁ κόσμος οὗτος; cp. Ginza 274, 20. C. Herm. 1.32 about Gnosis: τῆς χάριτος ταύτης φωτίσω τοὺς ἐν ἀγνοίᾳ τοῦ γένους ...; the grace which grants the γνῶσις Ascl. 41 (Scott I 374): τη γὰρ σῇ μόνον χάριτι τὸ φῶς τῆς γνώσεώς σου εἰλήχαμεν. More generally Phil. ebr. 149: παμπόλλη γε παρρησία τῆς ψυχῆς, ἡ τῶν χαρίτων τοῦ θεοῦ πεπλήρωται; somn. II 183 on the Logos: ὃς τὰς τῶν ἀεννάων χαρίτων λαβὼν προπόσεις ἀντεκτίνει, πλῆρες ὅλον τὸ σπονδεῖον ἀκράτου μεθύσματος ἐπιχέων, ἑαυτόν; somn. II 223 (see p. 73, n. 2).

[2] Ἀντί means "instead of". Yet neither for the source nor for the Evangelist (v. 17), can the meaning be that the χάρις given by the Revealer takes the place of an earlier OT grace (thus since Chrysost., both old and new exegetes like Baldensp., Ed. Schwarz, Loisy). It can only mean the χάρις of the Revealer, whose inexhaustibility is unfolded in its ever changing variety (thus Schl., who sees in this the radical rejection of a theology of rewards.) In a similar sense Phil. post Caini 145, admittedly in a scholastic interest regarding God: διὸ τὰς πρώτας αἰεὶ χάριτας, πρὶν κορεσθέντας ἐξυβρίσαι τοὺς λαχόντας, ἐπισχὼν καὶ ταμιευσάμενος εἰσαῦθις ἑτέρας ἀντ' ἐκείνων καὶ τρίτας ἀντὶ τῶν δευτέρων καὶ ἀιεὶ νέας ἀντὶ παλαιοτέρων ... ἐπιδίδωσι (so also ἀντί leg. alleg. III 82). The meaning of χάρις ἐπὶ χάριτι Ecclus. 26.15 (cp. Ez 7.26; Phil. 2.27) or ἐλπίσιν ἐξ ἐλπίδων (Bl.-D. para 208, 2) is not noticeably different. P. Joüon, Recherch. de Science Rel. 22 (1932), 206 wants to take ἀντί in the sense of כְּנֶגֶד (Gen. 2.18, 20): "une grâce répondant à sa grâce"; similarly Bernard and others. Black (JThSt 1941, 69f.) raises the question of a possible translator's error.

[3] Cp. C. F. Meyer's poem "All": "No place was empty, and none might go without". "He alone was the giver, and they were all only recipients" (Zn) hardly seems to catch the meaning of the verse. According to Schl. the πάντες suggests that all the different gifts of the congregation are gifts from Jesus, and he deduces from this that the Evangelist too refuses to recognise an independent Paulinism!

and the revelation in Jesus is not raised here (cf. on 5.39–47); the Evangelist is only concerned with the contrast between the two, which is shown as the contrast between their origins,[1] between *Moses* and *Jesus Christ*. Following v. 14 the new revelation is called ἡ χάρις καὶ ἡ ἀλήθεια and thus the contrast between νόμος and χάρις is introduced; the contrast is otherwise foreign to John and comes from the Pauline school; moreover vv. 14 and 16 in no way lead us to expect it here.[2]

V. 18 is likewise a note inserted by the Evangelist[3] to stress the absoluteness of the revelation in Jesus; it is not directed in particular against the Jews' claim to possess the revelation in the νόμος but against any claim to enjoy the vision of God; indeed—since ὁρᾶν must not be restricted simply to visual perception[4]—against any striving after or imagining that one can gain or possess knowledge of God outside the revelation given in the incarnate Son of God. Thus although the Jews are certainly included in this polemic (5.37; 7.28; 8.19, 55) the verse is certainly not directed against them alone; the Evangelist will unquestionably also have had the Gnostics in mind,[5] who were for their part quite capable of speaking in this way.[6] However the Evangelist's chief concern is not with his contemporaries but with the basic truth of the gospel.

---

[1] Διδόναι νόμον is not Greek and corresponds to the Rabbinic נָתַן תּוֹרָה (Schl.); similarly ἐγένετο corresponds to נַעֲשָׂה (Schl.), which again is characteristic of the Evangelist's usage, as is also the name 'Ιησοῦς Χρ., which otherwise only occurs in the egexetical gloss 17.3 and in I and II Jn. (see p. 17). Further it should be noticed that the antithesis in v. 17 is of a quite different kind to the antitheses of the source vv. 5, 10f., since in the latter the second sentence always repeats antithetically a term from the preceding sentence.

[2] The meaning of χάρις in vv. 14 and 16 corresponds more nearly to the Pauline πνεῦμα, which is normally contrasted with σάρξ; indeed outside the doctrine of justification (where νόμος and χάρις are contrasted with each other) Paul himself also uses χάρις in a Hellenistic sense, so that it is related to πνεῦμα, I Cor. 15.10; II Cor. 1.12; 12.9.—It is hard to think that any significance attaches to the alternation of δοθῆναι and γενέσθαι. Διδόναι is elsewhere used of the revelation, and in v. 16 is presupposed in correlation with λαμβάνειν. On διδόναι see p. 57, n. 5; cp. Rom. 12.3, 6; Gal. 2.9 etc.—Subtle distinctions in Ho., Zn. and others.

[3] The style of v. 18 shows it to have come from the Evangelist. The antithesis is of the same type as the one in v. 17 (see n. 1); moreover the second sentence is too long to fit the rhythm of the verse, and the insertion of the appositional ὁ ὢν κτλ. and the repetition of the subject by ἐκεῖνος are thoroughly prosaic. Finally the use of this pronoun to repeat a subj. or obj. is characteristic for the Evangelist (ἐκεῖνος: 1.33; 5.11, 43; 9.37; 10.1; 12.28; 14.21, 26; 15.26; similarly οὗτος 3.26, 32; 5.38; 6.46; 7.18; 8.26; 15.5), and this is yet another indication of the Rabbinic character of his style (Schl. on 1.18). The antithesis here, by which the argument is carried forward, corresponds to countless sentences of the Evangelist's, where an idea is developed by preceding it with a negation, see on v. 8, p. 48 n. 3 and cp. esp. 6.46. Finally see on the use of μονογενής.

[4] See p. 69, n.2 on ἐθεασάμεθα v. 14.

[5] Carpenter 329f.; v. 18 is directed against the Mystery religions. Delafosse 14f. sees only the contrast with the OT.

[6] Iren. I 2, 1: τὸν μὲν οὖν Προπάτορα αὐτῶν γινώσκεσθαι μόνῳ λέγουσι τῷ ἐξ αὐτοῦ γεγονότι, Μονογενεῖ τουτέστι τῷ Νῷ (of the Valentinians).

The sentence θεὸν οὐδεὶς ἑώρακεν[1] πώποτε denies that God is directly accessible to men. At the same time it assumes that it is natural for man to wish to see God and to be able to approach him, as is expressed in Philip's prayer (14.8): δεῖξον ἡμῖν τὸν πατέρα, καὶ ἀρκεῖ ἡμῖν. Man's efforts to gain access to God are nothing but the expression of his yearning to have "life" in the "light" of a definitive understanding of himself, and thus to be in the "truth" in order that he may truly *be*. Jesus is the Revealer because he is the "truth" and the "life" (14. 6) and the "light" of the world (8.12). And yet, it is only in his revelation that God may be approached—formerly in the revelation in creation, in which the Logos as the light was at the same time the life (1.4); now, when the world has turned to darkness (1.5), the revelation is given in Jesus as the incarnate Logos, who is the sole "way" to God (14.6). The assertion, however, that God is not directly accessible has nothing to do with the Greek idea that God is a being of such a kind that he cannot be grasped by the senses, but only by the νοῦς;[2] for the Evangelist it is not the νοῦς but πίστις which sees him, and then only πίστις which is directed towards the Revealer. Equally the thought is far from the Gnostic idea of the ἄγνωστος θεός, according to which God as the Irrational is sheerly incomprehensible to men. Of course the idea of the ἄγνωστος θεός in Gnosticism is linked with the idea of revelation; yet even here God is conceived as a being among others, who can become the object of possible knowledge, and for whose comprehension we simply lack the necessary faculties. Here again, his being is conceived after the pattern of substantial, natural being, so that the man who would see God must first be transformed into the divine nature. In such a view the revelation is the mysterious doctrine and discipline which prepares man for this transformation. The transformation itself is experienced in the ecstasy which is the direct vision of God.[3] Similarly for Philo the θεῖος λόγος accompanies the soul as her guide only to the point where she is completely prepared; thereafter the soul becomes independent of her guide and journeys on to God alone.[4] John knows neither an ecstasy where man receives the direct vision of God, nor a time when the soul becomes independent of the Revealer: only he who sees *him*, sees the Father (14.9). For this reason the idea of the direct inaccessibility of God

[1] On the popular perfect form of ἑώρακα which is used consistently in the Pap. see Bl.-D. para. 68. On the perfect instead of the aorist, which would here have been better with πώποτε, see Moulton, Proleg. 144. Cp. Pap. Gr. Mag. V 101f. σὺ εἶ Ὀσοροννωφρις, ὃν οὐδεὶς εἶδε πώποτε.

[2] Cf. R. Bultmann, ZNTW 29 (1930), 169ff.; also the criticism there of W. Graf Baudissin, ARW 18 (1915), 173–239; E. Fascher, Deus invisibilis (Marburger theol. Studien I) 1930.

[3] Cp. op. cit. 173ff.

[4] Phil., migr. Abr. 174f. and see on 14.6.

is not founded on a concept of God as a being of a particular kind, nor on the notion of the inadequacy of the human faculties to perceive him; there is no attempt whatever to raise ontological and epistemological questions about God. This does mean, however, that the Evangelist rejects any concept of God by means of which God can be thought of as the object of human or suprahuman knowledge. God ceases to be God, if he is thought of as an object. Correspondingly in John man is seen as God's creature, at God's mercy, standing under the claim of God: for man to abandon the path ordained for him by God, and to attempt to make God into the direct object of his vision, is to lose the true idea of God. That God is inaccessible, means that he lies beyond man's control. This freedom from man's control, however, is not the accidental property of an unreachable being; at the same time it also points to man's inability to master himself. The desire to see God, when it becomes the desire to turn God into an object of our knowledge, inevitably leads man into a radically false self-understanding; for it wrongly assumes that man could in some way be free, or be made free by God, to undertake such a task, and that he could find the ποῦ στῶ from which to enjoy such a vision. We have here in a radical form the oriental and OT idea of the sovereignty and absoluteness of God.[1]

The sentence is not directed against those who seek God, knowing their own blindness, but to the blind who think that they can see (9.39), to the poor who imagine that they are rich. In this way it shows that the idea of the invisibility of God is by no means so obvious as one might assume. It directs man back into his own sphere, and by pointing to the Incarnate as the Revealer, corrects man's *desire* to see God, inasmuch as such desire is always guided by the wish to gain control over oneself and over God. Those who harbour such desires necessarily fail to understand why they can never be fulfilled; they misunderstand the invisibility of God after the manner of the Greeks or the Gnostics. The very fact that God is invisible can be properly understood only in the light of the revelation, because through the latter man comes to understand anew his own humanity. For if in the desire to see God there was anywhere present a true readiness to accept God, then this must give proof of itself in the fact that God's revelation, *this* revelation finds faith. Yet in faith the idea of God's invisibility has become not a negative, but a positive concept; it has become the expression of man's true knowledge of himself.

V. 18b describes the Revealer as the μονογενὴς υἱός,[2] that is to say,

---

[1] Cp. ZNTW 29 (1930), 176ff.

[2] Μονογενὴς θεός is read by ℵBC*, and Greek texts up to and even later than the 3rd century (cf. Lagr., Zn. Excursus III; cp. also v. Loewenich 77, 1); μονογ. υἱός is read by most MSS, the Greek from the 4th century on, Latin, and syr^{c}. Even though θεός may

with the title taken from the confession in v. 14. However, the title is used in a manner characteristic of the Evangelist, with the result that μονογενής is the attribute and υἱός the actual characterisation. In this way the μονογενής receives the sense commonly found in the LXX of an ascription of value,[1] in which sense it is also clearly used in 3.16, 18; I Jn. 4.9. Its use here on the one hand brings out the character of the revelation as an event which springs out of the divine love (3.16; I Jn. 4.9), and on the other hand it stresses the absoluteness and sufficiency of the revelation, because the Revealer as the Son of the divine love stands in perfect communion with the Father. It is this communion which is stressed by the appositional phrase: ὁ ὢν εἰς τὸν κόλπον τοῦ πατρός.[2] This characterisation is set by the Evangelist in place of what one might otherwise have expected, following the line of the Gnostic concept of revelation, namely that the Son is εἰκών of the Father.[3] Here as elsewhere he avoids this term, heavy as it is with cosmological associations.[4] The general sense of the characterisation[5]—itself admittedly expressed in highly mythological language–is clear, even if there is some doubt about the precise meaning of ὤν. Does it refer to the pre-existent one, who was in the bosom of the Father, or to the post-existent one, who is now with the Father again?[6] In any case the purpose of the phrase is to describe

be considered better attested, and even if the predication of θεός of the Revealer is not in itself impossible for John (1.1; 20.28; I Jn. 5.20), nevertheless θεός cannot be defended here, for it neither fits in with the preceding θεὸν κτλ., nor can it take the appositional phrase ὁ ὢν κτλ. The latter must have υἱός, which is what the Evangelist always writes (3.16, 18; I Jn. 4.9). θεός is most likely the result of an error in dictation. Against Burney's suggestion that μονογ. θεός should be regarded as original, but that it is a mistranslation of μονογενὴς θεοῦ, it can be argued that the correct reading and translation would have been the most obvious. There remains only the suggestion that θεός and υἱός are both later additions to μονογ., which originally stood by itself (Lagr.; Bousset, Kurios 247, 1; Hirsch).—The art. is missing because it is intended in the sense of "one who is the only begotten son"; that the Evangelist thought of μονογ. υἱός as qualified is shown by the apposition which follows.

[1] See p. 71, n. 2.

[2] Εἰς stands for ἐν (like πρός with acc. in v. 1 for παρά with dat.), see Bl.-D. paras. 205.218 and Br. ad loc.; on the other hand Schl. thinks that εἰς "suggests the position of two people lying next to each other at table and turning towards each other."—The expression εἰς τ. κολπ. (in its proper sense in 13.23; Lk. 16.23, etc.). occurs elsewhere in Greek and Latin in a figurative sense, indicating close fellowship, cp. Wetstein and Br. ad loc. For its interpretation cp. Calvin: sedes consilii pectus est. ergo filium ab intimis secretis patris fuisse docet, ut sciamus in evangelio nos habere quasi apertum Dei pectus.

[3] On εἰκών cf. M. Dibelius. Note on Col. 1.17 (Hdb.z.NT).

[4] In 14.9 εἰκών is also avoided.

[5] On this mythology cp. on 5.19.

[6] It is possible that ὤν stands in place of the missing preterite participle. This would agree with the statements that Jesus bears witness to what he has seen with the Father and what he has heard from him 3.11, 32; 8.26, 38 etc. It is more probable, however, that ὤν is to be taken as a true present, and that it is therefore said of the Revealer who has returned to the Father. This would thus introduce the idea, which is so important for the Gospel that the work of the Revealer is bounded by his "coming" and by his "return", 6.61f.;

the unity of the Father and the Son, which is central to the Johannine concept of revelation.[1] His function as Revealer is denoted by ἐξηγεῖσθαι—this being the only time it occurs in John—a word which from earliest times was used in a technical sense for the interpretation of the will of the gods by professional diviners, priests and soothsayers, but which can also be used of God himself when he makes known his will.[2] This, then, is the final characterisation of the Revealer, that he "has brought knowledge of God",[3] and in this the Evangelist shows that it is in his *word* that he is the Revealer. At the same time the unity of the incarnate and the pre-existent one is suggested, for the latter as the "word" was in the beginning with God. Thus the argument has come full circle; and so again we are told not to see in Jesus as the Revealer a kind of hierophant or mystagogue, who fades into obscurity beside his word. For Jesus speaks the word, in that at the same time he *is* the word; and in what is to come the Evangelist gives us not the teaching of Jesus, but his life and teaching as a unity.[4]

8.14; 16.28.—It is hardly probable that ὤν denotes the continuing timeless existence of the Revealer with the Father; see on 3.13 and cp. H. Windisch, ZNTW 30 (1931), 221–223.

[1] Cp. on 5.19f.; 10.30 etc.

[2] Examples in Wetstein; see E. Rohde, Psyche, Index s.v. Exegeten; ἐξηγητής is closely related to προφήτης, see E. Fascher, Προφήτης 1927, 22.29, 1.40—ThWB II 910, 21ff. Similarly Philo calls the Logos ἑρμηνεύς, προφήτης, ὑποφήτης leg. all. III 207; quod deus imm. 138; mut. nom. 18.—It is possible that the Evangelist had a saying like Ecclus. 43.31 (35) in mind: τίς ἑόρακεν ἀυτὸν (Κύριον) καὶ ἐκδιηγήσεται; (no extant Hebr. text).

[3] 'Εξηγ. stands without the obj., for the verb as such can mean: to give divine knowledge, divine instructions; cp. Aesch., Choep. 118; Plat., resp. 427c.

[4] It is not possible to find parallels in any and every divine figure who gives a revelation, for they only illustrate mythological thinking in general. So, for example, Apollos in Aesch., Eum. 19: Διὸς προφήτης δ' ἐστὶ Λοξίας πατρός, on which the scholiast comments: δοκεῖ γὰρ ὁ 'Απόλλων παρὰ Διὸς λαμβάνειν τοὺς χρησμούς (cp. Fr. Blass, Die Eumeniden des Aischylos 1907, 69); Verg., Aen. III 251:

> Quae Phoebo pater omnipotens, mihi Phoebus Apollo
> Praedixit, vobis Furiarum ego maxima pando.

A more likely parallel is the mediator figure of Gnosticism (and so too in Philo's Logos), in whom the cosmological and soteriological functions are united (see p. 25). There is a very close parallel here, in that not only the teaching of this figure but also its fate is of decisive importance for its soteriological role. On the other hand the fundamental difference lies in the fact that the redemption in Gnosticism is understood as a cosmological process (see p. 64).

1.19-51: The Μαρτυρία of the Baptist

The expectation raised in v. 14, that the narrative that follows would tell of the δόξα of the incarnate Logos, will not be fulfilled till chap.2. The preceding section therefore is an introduction, whose heading presents it as a commentary on the statements in 1.6-8,15 about the Baptist's role as witness. It falls into two parts: 1) 1.19-34: 2) 1.35-51. The first part, which would be headed specifically "the witness of the Baptist", develops the positive and negative sides of the theme announced in v. 8; and here, moreover, the μαρτυρία is addressed specifically to the Jews. The second part, "the calling of the first disciples", illustrates the ἵνα πάντες πιστεύσωσιν δι' αὐτοῦ of v. 7, but while doing this at the same time it also comments on the οὐκ ἦν ἐκεῖνος τὸ φῶς of v. 8: it is the Baptist's disciples themselves who leave their master to follow Jesus; here then the μαρτυρία is directed specifically to the Baptist's disciples. In addition the importance of 1.35-51 is that it leads over into the following chapter, not merely outwardly, in that Jesus' accompaniment by his disciples is the necessary condition of 2.1-11, but also inwardly, in that the expectation which had been raised by v. 14 (-18) is again brought to life by the crowning verses of the narrative 1.50f.[1]

A. 1.19–34: The Witness of the Baptist

1.19–34 is not an original unit.[2] In the first place vv. 22–24 stand out clearly from the rest of the section and break the continuity between v. 21 and v. 25. The question is whether they have been inserted by the Evangelist in a source which he was using, or whether they are the later interpolation of an editor. The latter must be the case, for the basis of the text clearly comes from the Evangelist. The dominant thought that the Baptist is μάρτυς, and only μάρτυς, is the Evangelist's idea. It is characteristic for him that Jesus is the "prophet" (6.14; cf. 4.19, 44; 7.52; 9.17), and that the titles ὁ προφήτης and ὁ Χριστός are coordinated (7.40f.); his hand is also betrayed by the style (see below). Finally it would be impossible to explain how the Evangelist could

[1] Bowen, JBL 49 (1930), 298–302, gives a description of 1.19–28, 29–34, 35–39, (40–42,) 43–51 as dramatic scenes. Muilenburg JBL 51 (1932), 42–53 gives an analysis of 1.19–28, 29–34, 35–42, 43–51.

[2] Wellh., Spitta, Goguel (J.-B.80) think of the combination of variants, Schw., Hirsch of interpolations.

have inserted into his source the characterisation of the Baptist in vv. 22f., which cannot be brought into any clear relation to his statements in v. 21. It is however understandable that an editor should have inserted the characterisation of the Baptist on the basis of Isa. 40.3 (Mk. 1.2?; Mt. 3.3; Lk. 3.4; cf. Justin Dial. 88,7) which was traditional in the community. Thus we may conclude that we have here the first case in which it becomes evident that the Gospel owes its present form to an ecclesiastical redaction.

Further traces of the redaction are also to be found in what follows. For v. 26 should clearly be followed by v. 31; only when vv. 26 and 31 are taken together do they give the answer to the question in v. 25. V. 27 is again an additional comment from the Synoptic tradition (Mk. 1.7 par.); v. 28 on the other hand is the original conclusion of the section[1] and originally came after v. 34. Vv. 29–30 are connected with v. 28. The misplacing of vv. 28–30 can be attributed only to the disorder of the text which the editor had before him. The new start in v. 32 and the repetition of the κἀγὼ κτλ. in v. 33 are surprising. Clearly v. 32, which alongside v. 33b is quite superfluous, is an insertion from the Synoptic tradition, after which the editor takes up the κἀγὼ again, in order to establish the connection with what follows. Naturally this originally began (after v. 31) not with ἀλλά, but with καί or γάρ. Finally the editor has added in v. 26 the ἐγὼ βαπτίζω ἐν ὕδατι, and in vv. 31 and 33 the ἐν ὕδατι, and has in v. 33 appended ὁ βαπτίζων ἐν πνεύμ. ἁγ., in order to bring the account into line with that of the Synoptists, which is based on the contrast between baptism by water and by the spirit.

Thus the original text of the Gospel reads: (19) καὶ αὕτη ἐστὶν ἡ μαρτυρία τοῦ Ἰωάνου, ὅτε ἀπέστειλαν πρὸς αὐτὸν οἱ Ἰουδαῖοι ἐξ Ἱεροσολύμων ἱερεῖς καὶ Λευείτας ἵνα ἐρωτήσωσιν αὐτόν· σὺ τίς εἶ; (20) καὶ ὡμολόγησεν καὶ οὐκ ἠρνήσατο, καὶ ὡμολόγησεν ὅτι ἐγὼ οὐκ εἰμὶ ὁ Χριστός. (21) καὶ ἠρώτησαν αὐτόν· τί οὖν σύ; Ἠλίας εἶ; καὶ λέγει· οὐκ εἰμί. ὁ προφήτης εἶ σύ; καὶ ἀπεκρίθη· οὔ. (25) καὶ ἠρώτησαν αὐτὸν καὶ εἶπαν αὐτῷ· τί οὖν βαπτίζεις εἰ σὺ οὐκ εἶ ὁ Χριστὸς οὐδὲ Ἠλίας οὐδὲ ὁ προφήτης; (26) ἀπεκρίθη αὐτοῖς ὁ Ἰωάνης λέγων· μέσος ὑμῶν στήκει ὃν ὑμεῖς οὐκ οἴδατε. (31) κἀγὼ οὐκ ᾔδειν αὐτόν, ἀλλ' ἵνα φανερωθῇ τῷ Ἰσραήλ, διὰ τοῦτο ἦλθον ἐγὼ βαπτίζων. (33) καὶ ὁ πέμψας με βαπτίζειν, ἐκεῖνός μοι εἶπεν· ἐφ' ὃν ἂν ἴδῃς τὸ πνεῦμα καταβαῖνον καὶ μένον ἐπ' αὐτόν, οὗτός ἐστιν. (34) κἀγὼ ἑώρακα καὶ μεμαρτύρηκα ὅτι οὗτός ἐστιν ὁ υἱὸς τοῦ θεοῦ. (28) ταῦτα δὲ ἐν Β. ἐγένετο πέραν τοῦ Ἰορδάνου, ὅπου ἦν Ἰωάνης βαπτίζων. (There follow vv. 29–30).

V. 19 is the *heading*[2] which announces the theme, the Witness of John,[3] and at the same time states the occasion on which he made his

---

[1] Cp. the conclusions 6.59; 8.20; 12.36.

[2] The sentence has the form typical of the Evangelist's explanatory comments: an important concept in the preceding passage is picked out by the demonstrative and commented on, cp. 3.19; 6.39; 17.3; Festg. Ad. Jul. 142; cp. Muilenberg JBL 51 (1932), 43.—Thus the καί does not simply lead on to what follows as in 2.13; 4.46; 9.1 etc. (Schl), but points to v. 15 (Lagr.) and means "and indeed", as in I Jn. 1.5; 2.25 etc., cp. δέ 3.19 etc.

[3] On μαρτυρία cp. p. 50, n.5.

witness.[1] This however is not an historical note, but is intended to bring out the official character, as it were, of the witness, by naming the forum which demanded it and before which it was given. The forum are the "Jews"; just as in the rest of the Gospel they appear as the opponents of Jesus, here they appear as the opponents of his witness. This, then, is the prelude to the struggle which runs through the whole of the life of Jesus: it is a struggle between Christian faith and the world, represented by Judaism, a struggle which is continually portrayed as a trial, in which the "Jews" are under the illusion that they are the judges, whereas in fact they are the accused before the forum of God; it is a struggle which reaches its conclusion in the κέκριται 16.11 and the ἐγὼ νενίκηκα τὸν κόσμον 16.33.

The term οἱ Ἰουδαῖοι, characteristic of the Evangelist, gives an over-all portrayal of the Jews, viewed from the standpoint of Christian faith, as the representatives of unbelief (and thereby, as will appear, of the unbelieving "world" in general). The Jews are spoken of as an alien people,[2] not merely from the point of view of the Greek readers, but also, and indeed only properly, from the stand-point of faith; for Jesus himself speaks to them as a stranger and correspondingly, those in whom the stirrings of faith or of the search for Jesus are to be found are distinguished from the "Jews", even if they are themselves Jews.[3] In this connection therefore even the Baptist does not appear to belong to the "Jews".[4] This usage leads to the recession or to the complete disappearance of the distinctions made in the Synoptics between different elements in the Jewish people;[5] Jesus stands over against the Jews. Only the distinction between the mass of the people and its spokesmen[6]

[1] Since the comment here is given by the whole of the following narrative, it is not possible to take καὶ αὕτη—τ. Ἰωάνου as a complete sentence by itself, and then to see v. 20 as a concluding sentence to the ὅτε κτλ. of v. 19; rather the ὅτε-clause determines the καὶ αὕτη κτλ. The heading, then, runs over into the narrative.

[2] As when he speaks of the customs and feasts of the Jews, 2.6, 13; 5.1; 6.4; 7.2; 19.40. This corresponds to the usage of Mt. 15.2, 9, of Acts and also of Paul, who practically only ever speaks of Ἰουδαῖοι when it is a question of distinguishing them from the Ἕλληνες (Rom. 1.16; 2.9 etc.). Correspondingly the Rabbis say "Israel", "when they speak to the community or about it", but "Jews", when they introduce strangers in a speech. (Schl. on 1.47 and Spr. und H. 43f.; Str.-B. on Rom. 2.17; ThWB III.360–366; 372, 14ff; 378, 26ff.).

[3] 8.17: "in your law"; so too 10.34; cp. 7.19,22 (ὑμῖν) and contrast 7.51 in the mouth of Nicodemus: "our law".

[4] 5.15; 7.13—Thus this usage does not tell us one way or the other whether the Evangelist was of Jewish descent.

[5] The different types of rich and poor, tax-gatherers and prostitutes, the sick seeking to be healed and the questioners eager for knowledge, have disappeared. Only where the material used by the Evangelist demands it, do we meet individual people.

[6] For this the Evangelist can choose the traditional terms, as οἱ ἀρχιερεῖς, οἱ Φαρισαῖοι (in which case the Φαρ. are seen as an authoritative body 7.45, 47f., 11.47, 57; cp. on v. 24) or else the colourless term οἱ ἄρχοντες (3.1; 7.26, 48; 12.42).

occasionally proves to be necessary for the Evangelist's presentation of his theme; but this, characteristically, is often drawn in such a way that the 'Ιουδαῖοι, who are distinguished from the ὄχλος, appear as an authoritative body set over the Jewish people.[1] 'Οι 'Ιουδαῖοι does not relate to the empirical state of the Jewish people, but to its very nature.[2]

So too in 1.19 the 'Ιουδαῖοι are seen as an authority which, from its seat in Jerusalem,[3] sends out learned men to conduct an enquiry;[4] it is as such that the priests and Levites are named, for it is a question of baptism, of purification.[5] Their question, σὺ τίς εἶ; is indeed put in an extremely general form, but its intention (as v. 25 confirms) is to enquire into the authorization of the Baptist's action;[6] thereby it is assumed that the reader knows that this action is his baptism. Indeed there is a wider assumption that the reader is acquainted with the Christian tradition about John. He is not introduced and characterised as in the Synoptics (cp. Mk. 1.2ff. parr.). He is not described as ὁ βαπτιστής or ὁ βαπτίζων; indeed it is not till v. 25 that it emerges at all that he baptises. Nor is any motive suggested for the mission of the "Jews". It might, for example, have been suggested that from a report on his activity they had formed the idea that he wanted to be the Messiah (cp. Lk. 3.15; Justin, Dial. 88.7). Correspondingly the scene has only a formal conclusion (v. 28), and no record is given of what impressions the delegates received, or of what they reported in Jerusalem. The messengers simply disappear; for the only purpose of the questioning is to inform the reader of the μαρτυρία of the Baptist.

The cumbrous introduction to the Baptist's answer (**v. 20**) corresponds to its preparation in v. 19; it has the full weight of the solemn

---

[1] 5.15; 7.13; 9.22; 18.12. On the other hand it is used in the normal way to describe the members of the Jewish people, or indeed the people itself, in 4.9 (22), in the Passion narrative and in the places listed in p. 86 n. 2; see ThWB III 378ff.

[2] The view of Lütgert (Neutest. Studien für G. Heinrici 1914, 147–154) and Bornhäuser (Das Johannesevg. 19–23), according to which the 'Ιουδαῖοι form the part of the Jewish people which adheres strictly to the law, can be reduced to this formula.—Gutbrod, ThWB III 380, 44ff. is right, although he has not put it clearly or forcibly enough.—According to J. Jocz, Judaica, 9 (1953), 129–142 the 'Ιουδαῖοι in John are "the unbelievers of the house of Israel".

[3] 'Ιεροσόλυμα is the Hellenised form of יְרוּשָׁלַםִ which is used throughout John (Lk and Acts mostly have 'Ιερουσαλήμ; Paul also has it in most cases, while Rev. has only 'Ιερουσαλήμ), and indeed frequently with the art. 2.23; 5.2; 10.22; 11.18, which is not otherwise instanced in the NT, but cp. II Macc. 11.8; 12.9.

[4] The uncertainty of πρὸς αὐτόν whose position varies, and which is altogether missing from many of the texts, does not affect the meaning.

[5] It is because they are learned in questions about purification that the Levites are mentioned here (and only here) as well as the priests.

[6] The formulation of the question corresponds to Jewish and also to Greek usage, cp. Schl. and Br.

testimony of a witness in a trial.[1] The answer itself, ἐγὼ οὐκ εἰμὶ ὁ Χριστός, points us clearly to the contemporary background. Debate[2] centres on the question whether John or Jesus is the Messiah, and the Christian community in its struggle with the disciples of John can appeal to a ὁμολογία of John himself, that he did not wish to be the Messiah. But before the positive content of this statement is given, further distinctions are made to exclude any form of rivalry between him and Jesus. Thus the messengers, dissatisfied with the merely negative reply, ask further[3] whether he is Elijah, and when he denies this, whether he is the "prophet", which he equally denies (**v. 21**). These questions presume certain possibilities: if John were Elijah or the "prophet", then there would be a reason for his baptising. This rests on a double assumption: I. that baptism is considered a messianic act; 2. that Elijah and the "prophet" are messianic figures.

That baptism was considered a *messianic act*, i.e. a purification (an "eschatological sacrament") which qualified the baptised for participation in the messianic salvation (endowed them with an "eschatological" character), is shown by the Synoptic tradition concerning the Baptist, as well as by the early Christian understanding of baptism. The same is shown by the Jewish and Jewish-Christian, as well as by the gnostic Baptist sects, whose originally messianic character cannot be doubted.[4]

---

[1] The first ὡμολ. is used absolutely as is οὐκ ἠρν.; the second ὡμολ. is qualified by the ὅτι- clause. The first two appearances of καί in v. 20 mean "and", and the third means "and indeed". Whereas in v. 19 the question was put in the subordinate clause, in v. 20 the narrative of the scene in which John made his μαρτυρία comes to the forefront· The fact that καὶ οὐκ ἠρν. καὶ ὡμολ. looks like "an emphatic addition" (Hirsch), is no reason for striking it out; for the Evangelist wants to lend emphasis to the statement here, while the conjunction of the positive and negative statements (see p. 48 n. 3) is in accordance with his style, even if this is the only instance where he uses the form of the litotes. For examples of the combination of positive and negative statements in Mandaean lit. see Ed. Schweizer, EGO EIMI, 45 n. 244. Ὁμολογεῖν does not of course refer here to the confession of faith, but is used like ἀρνεῖσθαι as a juridical term. Ὁμολ. and ἀρν. occur together elsewhere used in this sense; Thuc. VI 60; Jos. ant. VI 151 (cp. Eur. El. 1057; Aelian, Nat. an. II 43); correspondingly הוֹדָה and כִּפֵּר in Rabbinic lit., Schl. ad loc. and on Mt. 10.33.

[2] See pp. 17f. and 49 (on 1.6–8). The stressed ἐγώ, which is missing in the following answers, is used to bring to the fore that there is another person who is the Christ! It is evident that in the question ὁ Χριστός is used as a title (the "Messiah").

[3] The way the question is put varies; in some authorities(ℵL) τί οὖν; stands alone, in others it is preceded by σύ (B), in others the σύ comes afterwards (C*33); other authorities have the σύ after Ἠλείας εἶ. The variants may best be explained from the original τί οὖν σύ;. The position of σύ after τί οὖν here is not a Semitism (as is supported by Burney 82; the opp. view is held by Lagr. CXIV; Colwell 25); yet the primitive character of the dialogue is reminiscent of the Rabbinic way of retelling conversations (cp. Schl. on v. 21), which is again characteristic of the Evangelist's style.

[4] See Jos. Thomas. op. cit. On Jewish soil prophetic warnings and predictions will have contributed to this, even if the "washing" of which they spoke was only intended metaphorically; cp. Is. 1.16 (Wash yourselves; make yourselves clean!), 18; 4.4; Ezek. 36.25, 29, 33; 37.23.

Equally well attested is the expectation in Judaism that at the onset of the time of salvation *Elijah would return*. The messenger who, according to Mal. 3.1–3, is to precede the judgement of God, is interpreted in 3.23 by an interpolator as Elijah. In Ecclus. 48.10f. he is also seen as the forerunner, as well as in Rabbinic lit.,[1] as is shown by Justin, Dial. 8.4; 49. If a Messiah was expected, then Elijah naturally had to become his forerunner, which is assumed in Mk. 9.11–13; for this reason the Christian tradition,[2] which saw John as Jesus' forerunner, in the main recognised in him the returned Elijah (Mk. 9.11–13; Mt. 11.14).

It is not possible to determine with certainty who is meant by the *figure of the "prophet"*. For the general expectation of a prophet who can announce the will of God in a time of doubt and perplexity has nothing to do with this (I Macc. 4.46; 9.27; 14.41); it must refer to a particular messianic figure such as Elijah, and the expectation of such a figure is also clearly presupposed in 6.14 and 7.40, where the figure is of equal importance with the Messiah.[3] Now the prophecy in Deut. 18.15, 18, that God will always send a prophet when his people have need of one, is referred in Acts 3.22; 7.37 to the Messiah himself; yet this must be a specifically Christian interpretation.[4] In Judaism the expectation of the "prophet" is not attested.[5] Since however for Judaism Moses is the prophet above all others,[6] and since, on the other hand, the

---

[1] Cp. Bousset, Rel. des Jdt.s 232f.; Str.-B. IV 2, p. 779–798; P. Volz, Die Eschatologie der jüd. Gemeinde 1934, 195ff.

[2] Luke, who omits Mk. 9.11–13; Mt. 11.14 seems, like John, to have rejected this interpretation; the phrasing of Lk. 1.17 modifies and limits the idea of a return.

[3] Torrey's (p. 343) explanation of ὁ προφ. in 1.21 and also 7.40 as a mistranslation of a simple נָבִיא is sheerly arbitrary. Nor is it right to say that for John προφ. and ὁ προφ. are synonymous (E. Fascher, Προφήτης 1927, 179). Thus it is of little value to point out that the possibility was discussed that John (Mt. 11.9 par.; 14.5) and Jesus (Mk. 6.15; 8.28; 11.32; Lk. 7.16, 39; cf. Mt. 21.11, 46; Lk. 24.19) were prophets (this is the general direction of Jn. 7.52; 9.17). Nor therefore to point to the general expectation that in the age of salvation prophets would again make their appearance (cp. Str.-B. II 479f.; Fascher op. cit. 162f.; see esp. Rud. Meyer, Der Prophet aus Galiläa 1940, 97f.; W. Staerk, Erlösererw. 99ff.).

[4] In Rabbinic literature Deut. 18.15 is taken either to refer generally to the appearance of prophets or to refer to Jeremiah (Str.-B. II 626); in the latter case however Jeremiah is not understood as the "forerunner" (Str.-B. I 730). The expectation of the prophet of Deut. 18.15 is also found in a Qumran fragment; see J. T. Milik, Discoveries in the Judaean Desert I (1955), 121. In DSD 9.11 it is anticipated that a prophet and the anointed ones (Messiahs) of Aaron and Israel will come. F. M. Braun (RB 62 [1955] 22) is of the opinion: "Il est clair que l'attente du prophète, entretenue dans la secte, doit être interprétée en un sens messianique". So too Brownlee in the notes to DSD.—See further H. J. Schoeps, Geschichte u. Theologie des Judenchristentums 1949, 90.3.

[5] Admittedly A. v. Gall. Βασιλεία τοῦ Θεοῦ 1926, 381f. believes that he can produce evidence for this hope in Judaism, though he thinks that it originated in Iranian eschatology. Similarly W. Staerk, Soter I 1933, 64. According to J. Jeremias the interpretation of Deut. 18.15,18 with reference to the Messiah probably existed in Judaism; however the term "the prophet" is not attested (ThWB IV 863, 1ff.).

[6] For Philo cf. Fascher op. cit. 152f.; for Jos. Schl. ad. loc.

return of Moses was also expected in the time of salvation,[1] it is possible that the expectation of the "prophet" is, in fact, the expectation of Moses.[2]

On the other hand what is perhaps referred to is a figure which, although not attested in orthodox Judaism, does occur in heretical and syncretistic circles, namely, the figure of the Revealer who, throughout the generations (or aeons), embodies himself in different forms as the "prophet".[3] Nor is it impossible that the question: ὁ προφ. εἶ σύ is motivated by the fact that at the time of the Evangelist the Baptist sect referred to their master as the "prophet" in this sense.[4]

In any case, these three titles, which the Baptist rejects as being inapplicable to himself, denote the eschatological bringer of salvation.[5] And this is what John in no way wishes to be.[6] In that case, then, his baptism can have no saving significance! So in **v. 25** the delegates quite logically ask what the meaning of his baptism can be.[7] The answer

---

[1] Cp. Bousset, Rel. des Jdts. 232f.; Schl. on Mt. 17. 3; Volz. op. cit. 194f.; B. Murmelstein, Wiener Zeitschr. für die Kunde des Morgenlandes 36 (1929), 51f. The evidence for the expectation of the return of Moses is admittedly relatively late; the expectation that the Messiah will be a second Moses (whereby the eschatological redemption is thought of as parallel to the Exodus) is clearly earlier; cp. Str.-B. II 481; Volz op. cit. 370; R. Eisler, ZNTW 24 (1925), 178, Staerk. Erlösererw. 50ff. This expectation is presupposed in Jn. 6.31. —The expectation that Moses and Elijah will return as the "forerunners", is not attested till late (circa 900?) according to Str.-B. I 756; where the return of Moses is expected, he is not, like Elijah, thought of as the "forerunner". According to J. Jeremias (ThWB IV 860, 30ff.) in the earlier Jewish lit. the idea is nowhere to be found that the returning Moses will be the Messiah. On the other hand H. J. Schoeps op. cit. (see p. 89 n. 4) 87–98, believes that he can show that there existed in (perhaps Essene) Judaism the idea of the Messiah as the "novus Moses", which was also taken over by early Christianity. Cp. also O. Cullmann, Le problème littéraire et historique du roman Pseudo-Clémentin 1930, 120f.

[2] This is perhaps confirmed by 6.31; see previous note. It is hardly likely that Jeremiah was intended, see Str.-B. I 730.

[3] The idea is attested in the Ps. Clem. writings and elsewhere in Gnosticism, but also in Wis. 7.27f.; cp. Eucharisterion II 14–19; Br., extended note on Jn. 1.21; Wetter, Sohn Gottes, 21ff.; Fascher op. cit. 195f.; R. Eisler, Ἰησοῦς βασιλεύς II 1930, 356f.; Percy 297, n. 43; Staerk, Erlösererw. 40ff. and ZNW 35 (1936), 232ff.; Thomas 169.—Dodd (239f) is sceptical about the explanation of Jn. 1.21 in terms of this idea, which admittedly does not give a sharply defined explanation.

[4] Cf. Bldsp. 134. Cp. Goguel's (J.-B, 78, 3) tour de force in tracing v. 20 back to an editor on the basis of the insight that the Messiah and the "prophet" were rival figures.

[5] The number three here is not connected with any system in which the three figures have a particular position or rank, such that, if John was not the first, he might be the second or the third. It is possible to find some such relation between the Messiah and Elijah (as his forerunner) but not for the "prophet", who is a rival of the Messiah. If this is the case then we will also have to view Elijah (as the forerunner of God) as a rival figure. Thus the three possibilities rejected by the Baptist correspond to the expectations of different messianic circles, and so the artificial construction of the conversation becomes clear.

[6] It is not correct to say that with the denial that the Baptist was Elijah "the whole complex of Jewish expectations for the future" is specifically rejected (Hirsch). What is under debate is not the conception of salvation, but the question whether it is John or Jesus who is the bringer of salvation.

[7] The editor has, by the insertion of vv. 22–23, introduced the Synoptic characterisation of the Baptist based on Is. 40.3 (see p. 85) and by the addition of v. 24, has succeeded

vv. 26, 31 says that its only meaning is to make known the unknown one who is already present; and it is understood by all that this unknown one is the awaited bringer of salvation.[1] He is already there,[2] although no one knows him. This first statement, which contains an allusion to a messianic dogma,[3] introduces a motif which will be heard again and again throughout the Gospel: the "Jews" are blind; they look for the one who stands among them, without recognising him as the one they are looking for.[4] Admittedly no one can recognise him before the

---

in introducing the Pharisees, the typical opponents in the Synoptics, alongside the priests. (The sentence does not report a second deputation to John but is a parenthetical note. This does not imply that the delegates belonged to the Pharisees, which was obviously understood by the later scribes who insert the art. before ἀπεστ, but that the messengers, who have just been mentioned, were sent by the Pharisees, that is to say that the latter are behind the Ἰουδαῖοι of v. 19). The brachylogy in v. 22. (ἵνα κτλ. scil. "Tell us!" cp. 9.36 and Bl.-D. para. 483) is nothing unusual; nor is ἀπόκρισιν διδόναι (Br. Lexic.), so that there is no particular significance in Rabbinic parallels (Schl.). The quotation in v. 23 is taken, as in the Synoptics, from the LXX; yet here the last line has been omitted and ἑτοιμάσατε changed into εὐθύνατε.—It is not possible to discern whether the editor reflected on the relation of the answer given in v. 23 to the statements made by John in vv. 20f.; in any case the relation is not clear; for the view of the Baptist as the φωνή of Is. 40.3 can be very easily reconciled to an interpretation of him as Elijah, as is shown by Mt. and Mk. Since however the editor will hardly have taken the κύριος of the quotation to refer to God (Schl.) but to Jesus (which is alien to the Evangelist, see on 4.1), he may well have taken the quotation in the context to give a characterisation of the Baptist as the witness.

[1] The ἐγὼ βαπτίζω ἐν ὕδατι in v. 26 must be an addition of the editor. For 1) this statement has no relation whatsoever to the following μέσος ὑμῶν κτλ.; "I baptise . . ." would have to be followed by "but *he* . . ." (cp. Mk. 1.8 parr.) and at least a μὲν-δέ would be indispensible, which the Evangelist does use elsewhere (10.41; 16.9, 22; 19.32f.; 20.3; while 7.12; 11.6 contain at least a μέν) although admittedly infrequently. The ἐγὼ κτλ., as understood by the editor, is contrasted with v. 27, which is again inserted by the editor. 2) The ἐν ὕδατι in vv. 31, 33 is without doubt an insertion which disturbs the sense. The editor is attempting to assimilate the Gospel to the synoptic tradition.

[2] The μέσος στήκει does not of course mean that Jesus is present in person.

[3] Cp. 7.27; Justin, Dial. 8.4: Χριστὸς δὲ, εἰ καὶ γεγένηται καὶ ἔστι που, ἄγνωστός ἐστι καὶ ὀυδὲ αὐτός πω ἑαυτὸν ἐπίσταται οὐδὲ ἔχει δύναμίν τινα, μέχρις ἂν ἐλθὼν Ἠλίας χρίσῃ αὐτὸν καὶ φανερὸν πᾶσι ποιήσῃ, cp. 49,1. For further discussion see Schürer II 260; Bousset, Rel. des Jdt.s 320; Volz, Eschatologie 208; Str.-B. IV 797f. Moore II 360; E. Stauffer, The Background of the New Testament and its Eschatology, 1956, 281–299.—Probably what is alluded to here is the Judaised form of the Gnostic motif of the hiddenness of the revealer, cp. ZNTW 24 (1925), 119–123; Schlier, Rel. Unters. 14ff.; cp. also Justin, Dial. 110,1.

[4] The editor inserted v. 27 in accordance with the Synoptic tradition; it is the only case in John where the relative is taken up by a pronoun (at the most one could compare 13.26); cp. Wellh. 135; Burney 84f. takes a different view, which is opposed by Colwell 46–48. Since the sentence comes from an early tradition, the construction here should be taken as a Semitism, even if similar constructions occur in the Koine (Br. ad loc.; Bl.-D. para. 297; Raderm. 217). The same is true of the ἵνα-clause, which follows ἄξιος instead of the inf. (Bl.-D. para. 379).—In the form of the words v. 27 partly resembles Mt. 3.11 (ὁ . . . ἐρχόμενος), partly Mk. 1.7 or alternatively Lk. 3.16 (λῦσαι τὸν ἱμάντα). In the relative clause v. 27 agrees with the three Synoptics, except that it has ἄξιος instead of ἱκανός and a ἵνα-clause instead of the inf. Since this clause is linked to the previous one as a conjunctive participle, the ἰσχυρότερος of the Synoptics had to drop out.

witness to him has been made; but for this reason John came to bear witness to him. Even he did not recognise him of his own accord,[1] but along with his commission to baptise he received the ability to recognise and to make known the expected one. This is the purpose of his baptism, as stated in v. 31.[2] **V. 33** then comments on this: God who had sent him,[3] had also told him the sign by which he should recognise the Christ.[4] The sign has occurred (**v. 34**), and so John has given his witness.[5] God has said to him, "This is he!"—meaning of course, the bringer of salvation, who has been under discussion since v. 19; and that means that Jesus is in his person all that the Baptist has denied of himself—the Messiah, Elijah, the prophet. John bears witness to this by surpassing all the titles mentioned in vv. 20f.: "This is the Son of God!".[6] This

---

[1] There can be no doubt that the sentence ὃν ὑμεῖς οὐκ οἴδατε· κἀγὼ οὐκ ᾔδειν αὐτόν corresponds to the antithesis ὑμεῖς οὐκ οἴδατε· ἐγὼ οἶδα in 7.28f.; cp. 8.14, 55. Only Jesus enjoys original knowledge; the Baptist has secondary knowledge.

[2] V. 31 shows the style of the Evangelist 1) in the οὐκ . . . ἀλλ' (cp. on 1.8 p. 48 n.3). 2) in the elliptical ἀλλ' ἵνα (cp. ad loc.), 3) in the explanatory διὰ τοῦτο (cp. 5.16,18; 6.65; 7.22; 8.47; 9.23; 10.17; 12.18, 27, 39; 13.11; 15.19; 16.15; 19.11; I Jn. 3.1; 4.5; III Jn. 10).—The ἐν ὕδατι is a clumsy addition (see p. 85); for the question is why John *baptises* at all; it is the *meaning* of his baptism which has to be explained, not its inferiority. Equally the ἐν ὕδατι in v. 33 is an unskilful addition, and this means that the ὁ βαπτ. ἐν πν. ἁγ. v. 33 must also be discarded. For not only is the οὗτός ἐστιν perfectly adequate as an answer, it is indeed more emphatic without the addition, which anyway introduces a motive foreign to the Gospel.

[3] Ἦλθον v. 31 and ὁ πέμψας με v. 33 correspond to the formulation in 1.6f.

[4] It is not important on what occasion or in what situation this occurred; on the motive of the sign cp. Lk. 1.18, 36f.; 2.12 etc. (Gesch. der synopt. Trad. 321=Hist of the Syn. Trad. 295). V. 33 of course assumes knowledge of the Synoptic baptismal narrative. In v. 32 the editor comments unnecessarily on the short ἐφ' ὃν κτλ. by giving a more detailed account of the coming of the Spirit on the lines of the Synoptics, and he takes away the force of ἑώρακα in v. 34 by the insertion of τεθέαμαι; of course the seeing ought to be related first, once the sign by which he was to be recognised has been given (ἐφ' ὃν ἂν ἴδῃς κτλ.). It is interesting to notice the καὶ μένον ἐπ' αὐτόν in v. 33 (on ἐπί with the acc. in answer to the question where? See Bl.-D. para. 233,1), which has been added to καταβαῖνον and which has probably been taken from a traditional formulation (cf. Gospel acc. to Hebrews: in Jerome on Is. 11.2; Mand Lit. 208, 247; Ginza 7.5; 487.25 Justin. Dial. 87, 3 p. 314c.).—The Evangelist has clearly not thought out the relation between the Spirit which Jesus receives in his baptism and his character as the Logos; in the rest of the Gospel Jesus appears not as the bearer but as the giver of the Spirit. The imparting of the Spirit to Jesus is taken from the tradition and has, in the Evangelist's interpretation, no longer any importance for Jesus; it is significant only for the Baptist as a sign of recognition, see below p. 94 n.3.

[5] Vv. 33f show the style of the Evangelist 1) in the ἐκεῖνος (cp. on 1.18 p. 79 n.3) 2) in the pair of verbs introduced by καί (=and so) and linked by καί (=and) (cp. 6.69; 8.56; 15.24). The μεμαρτύρηκα shows that this scene does not record the first occasion on which John made his witness.

[6] As well as ὁ υἱὸς τ.θ., ὁ ἐκλεκτὸς τ.θ. is also well attested (ℵ syr^sc and Latin Mss). It is hardly likely that they are both expansions of an original simple οὗτός ἐστιν; for although this accords well with v. 33, it hardly fits into a verse which summarises the μαρτυρία of the Baptist. Rather, what we would expect here is the title which throughout John is ascribed to the Incarnate Logos, that is ὁ υἱὸς τ.θ. (Bousset, Kyrios, 2. ed. 156); whereas ὁ

phrase suggests that the μαρτυρία of the Baptist, even if it is addressed in the first place specifically to the Jews, is nevertheless directed beyond them to the whole world. For the whole world shares the expectation and knows of the glorification of sons of God.[1]

V. 28[2] is the original conclusion of the scene.[3] Yet apart from this

---

ἐκλεκτός, which occurs nowhere else in John, must be a correction (dating from as early as the redaction?), based on a baptism narrative of the Synoptic type (ἀγαπητός Mk. 1.11 is equivalent to ἐκλεκτός; cp. Lk. 9.35 parr.; Bousset, Kyrios 2. ed. 57.2); in any case it is a traditional title (Lk. 23.35), which shortly afterwards fell out of general use. Cp. A. v. Harnack, SA Berlin 1915, 552–556 or Studien zur Gesch. des NTs und der alten Kirche 1931, 127–132, who supports ἐκλ.

[1] The title "Son of God" (cp. v. 49; 11.27) was already present at the time of the Evangelist in the Christian tradition, where it is particularly connected with the baptismal confession (G. Bornkamm ThBl 21 (1942), 58, 8). The history of the origins of the title goes back to the OT and Judaism, where it was used as the title of the (messianic) king (H. Gressmann, Der Messias, 1929, 9f. et passim; G. Dalman, Worte Jesu I 219ff.; Str.-B. III 15f. 17ff.; Bousset, Rel. des Jdt.s 227f.; Volz, Eschatologie 174; Bousset, Kyrios, 52ff.; Jesus der Herr 4f.), but it also has its roots in Hellenism, where it is used to denote the θεῖος, ἄνθρωπος, the Revealer (G. P. Wetter, Der Sohn Gottes 1916; L. Bieler, Θεῖος Ἀνήρ 1935, 134ff.; Br., extended note on Jn. 1. 34), as well as the Emperor (Deissmann, L. v. O. 294f.). The common feature to all these uses is that they refer to the bringer of salvation, whereas the precise meaning of the title varies in accordance with the individual world-view and the particular understanding of "salvation." There can be no doubt that the Evangelist intends the title to outdo the messianic titles listed in vv. 20f. It is characteristic of him that he should stress the relation to the Father which is expressed by the title "Son of God" (cp. already 1.14, 18); thus what is important for him in the title is that it contains the idea that Jesus is the Revealer, in whom God encounters man. Cp. E. Gaugler 46ff.; Faulhaber 24f.

[2] The ἦν should be taken together with βαπτίζων. Εἶναι with the pres. part. (periphrastic conjugation) occurs frequently in John; the ἦν however often has a certain independence (2.6? 11.1; 13.23; see Bl.-D. para. 353,1). This is the case here: "where John was staying while baptising" cp. 3.23; 10.40.

[3] Neither the question of the textual variants nor that of the precise location intended by the Evangelist is of any interest in the exposition of the text. As far as the different readings are concerned, which Torrey (343) would trace back to a copyist's error, both variants were known to Orig. (VI 40, 204ff.): Βηθανίᾳ (ℵ*B lat al) and Βηθαβαρᾷ (syr^{sc} al). His decision in favour of Βηθαβ., because he knew of no Bethany east of the lower Jordan, is valueless, for the simple reason that there is no need to assume that John baptised in the lower Jordan. Since in v. 28 it is not the Jordan, but only the land east of Jordan which is mentioned, it is conceivable that the place of the baptism was at some stream which flows into the Jordan. The attempts to identify a Bethany or a Bethabara east of the Jordan have not led to any definitive conclusion; cp. Dalman, Orte und Wege Jesu 3. ed. 1924, 95–102; D. Buzy, Rech. de Science rel. 21 (1931), 444–462; M. Goguel, (J.-B.) 82–85; Carl H. Kraeling, John the Baptist 1951, 8f.—P. Parker (JBL 74 [1955] 257–261) avoids the difficulty of trying to find a Bethany east of the Jordan, by taking πέραν not as "on the other side" but as "over against", and is thus able to identify the Bethany of 1.28 with the Bethany of 11.1 etc.—Hirsch (II 4) infers from Jn. 10.40 that there was originally no precise indication of the place in 1.28; probably there stood τῇ Ἀραβίᾳ, which a copyist must have changed into Βηθαραβᾷ (ℵ² syr^{hmg}). The other two readings were then attempts to turn this into a possible place name. N. Kruger (ZNW 45 [1954], 121–123) also considers that the indication of the place in 1.28 is not genuine.—The Evangelist, as 10.40–42 shows, was interested in the location of the events. Perhaps he thought that Jesus himself had baptised there (3.22), "for the remark that John was at that time baptising elsewhere (3.23), seems to assume that

formal purpose which it has, it is also intended to stress the importance of what has been reported, as are 6.59; 8.20; 12.36). The witness of the Baptist is an established fact; no "Jew" can play off the Baptist against Jesus (cp. 3.22–30; 5.33–35) and this means that his μαρτυρία is turned into an accusation against the "Jews".[1] In composing 1.19–34 the Evangelist worked over the tradition freely. Whereas the Synoptics had taken up the figure of the Baptist into the "Gospel" as the forerunner and preparer of the way,[2] and in doing so had also taken up his eschatological message and interpreted it as a foretelling of the coming of Jesus, John no longer speaks of the forerunner and preparer of the way; the Baptist is seen only as the witness to Jesus. Thus we learn nothing of his preaching, and his mission of baptism is only hinted at. Even the baptism of Jesus himself by John is not related as such. It is only referred to as the event which was for the Baptist the sign by which he should recognise the Saviour; it is subordinated to the main theme of his witness, in the same way as the disciples of the Baptist in 3.26 say to their master, not ὃν σὺ ἐβάπτισας, but ᾧ σὺ μεμαρτύρηκας. Yet it would be wrong to conclude from this that Jesus' baptism was an embarrassment for the Evangelist, so that he passes over it as quickly as possible.[3] On the contrary he clearly refers to it without misgivings. Yet he does not give an account of it, firstly because he can assume that his readers are acquainted with the story, and secondly, because for him the mere historical fact is of no significance by comparison with the witness of the Baptist which is based on it. Nor is the significance of this witness solely to point to Jesus as the Revealer and to demand faith in him, for at the same time it teaches us the proper understanding of the figure of the Baptist himself: οὐκ ἦν ἐκεῖνος τὸ φῶς, ἀλλ' ἵνα μαρτυρήσῃ περὶ τοῦ φωτός.

There now follows in **vv. 29-30** a second, shorter scene, which abandons altogether the realm of historical narrative, with its attention to vivid portrayal of dates and facts, and—like an old stylised picture,

---

Jesus had taken his place" (Dalman 96). This would make K. Kundsin's suggestion convincing (Topol. Überlieferungsstoffe im Joh-Evg. 1925, 20f.), that the place is mentioned because at the time of the Evangelist it was the home of a Christian congregation which had gone over from the Baptist to Jesus.

[1] See p. 50 n.5.

[2] Cp. the kerygmatic formulations in Acts 10.37f.; 13.23–25.

[3] It would only have raised difficulties for the Evangelist if he had conceived Jesus' character as the Logos and also as the πνεῦμα under the category of the Greek concept of φύσις. Since however he thinks in the category of revelation, he could take over the tradition of the coming of the Spirit on Jesus at his baptism without further reflection, even if for him to say that Jesus was filled with the Spirit is not an adequate expression of his conception of the Revealer; see above p. 92 n.4. Much too contrived is H. Windisch, Amicitiae Corolla (Festschr. für Rendell Harris) 1933, 303–318. In Syrian Gnostic Christianity no importance could be attached to Jesus' baptism as far as his own person was concerned, see Schlier, Relg. Unters. 43ff.

which omits all superfluous detail—shows the reader the man to whom the μαρτυρία has been born. Just as vv. 19ff. are an explanation of vv. 6-8, so too vv. 29f. comment on v. 15. The delegates from Jerusalem have disappeared; there is no mention of any public present; John alone stands there, pointing to Jesus, and Jesus comes walking towards him; the reader knows neither whence nor why he comes, and may not even ask.[1] Jesus appears, only so that John may point to him. Nor do the words by which he points Jesus out have any immediate consequences. It would have been easy for the Evangelist to have made the two disciples of v. 35 into witnesses straightaway, and to have continued with vv. 37ff. But the Evangelist is interested solely to show this one picture, and so at the same time to bring the saying of the Baptist, which he has already given in a note in v. 15, within the framework of a narrative.

The saying of the Baptist, by which he points to Jesus, is an oracular utterance: "Behold the Lamb of God, who takes away the sin of the world!"[2] The definite form ὁ ἀμνὸς τ.θ. shows that the phrase refers to a particular figure, whom the Evangelist assumes to be known to his readers. The general sense is immediately clear, inasmuch as the title, which occurs only here in the NT[3] (v. 29 and 36), proclaims the decisive eschatological significance of its bearer as the bringer of salvation. It is as a result of this title that afterwards (v. 37) the two disciples of the Baptist follow him and recognise in him the Messiah (v. 41). The Evangelist most probably took the title from the saying of the Baptist v. 36, which he found in the source he used in vv. 35–50. He has brought out the meaning of the title[4] by the attribute: ὁ αἴρων τὴν ἁμαρτίαν

---

[1] Naturally Jesus does not come to be baptised himself (Orig.); equally there are no grounds for saying that he has come from the desert after the temptation (Chrys., who takes τῇ ἐπαύριον to mean the day after the forty days in the desert). Other suggestions, such as that Jesus came to take his leave of the Baptist or to win disciples are sheerly a waste of time (Loisy).

[2] On the typically Semitic expression ἴδε see Schl., Spr. und H. 28.

[3] The quotation of Is. 53.7 in Acts 8.32 is comparable but not identical; so too I Pet. 1.19. It can hardly be correct to identify the ἀμνὸς τ.θ with the ἀρνίον of Rev. (anyway never as ἀρνίον τοῦ θεοῦ!). For the rest the ἀρνίον is not a uniform figure; on the one hand it is the "slain" lamb, which has bought the redeemeds' freedom with its blood, on the other it is the messianic ruler; and further it is indiscriminately made to bear all sorts of messianic functions. The original sense is not clear. Cp. Lohmeyer (Hdb. zum NT) and Hadorn (Theol. Handkomm. zum NT) on Rev 5.6. Bousset (Meyers Komm. on Rev. p. 259) suspects that behind the ἀρνίον lies a pagan myth.—Fr. Spitta (Streitfragen zur Geschichte Jesu 1907, 172–224) tries to show that the image of the Messiah as a horned ἀρνίον or ἀμνός was known to Jewish apocalyptic. Against this K. F. Feigel, Der Einfluss des Weissagungs-bewieses etc. 1910, 30–32.

[4] Spitta's and Lohmeyer's suggestion (see previous note) that "lamb" had already come into use as a messianic title in Judaism, can hardly be maintained on the basis of Eth. En. 89, where the people of Israel is admittedly depicted as a herd of lambs, without however the messianic ruler being specifically designated by the word "lamb". In the vision in Test. Jos. 19 the lamb, (ἀμνός) who is born of the virgin and overcomes the wild beasts, is certainly intended as the Messiah; but the passage is not free from suspicion of Christian interpolation.—Dodd (230–238) also takes ἀμνὸς τ.θ. as a messianic title.

τοῦ κόσμου: Jesus is the bringer of salvation, because it is he who takes away the sin of the world[1]. As elsewhere in the early Christian tradition, this clearly refers to the power of Jesus' death to expiate sin; that is, the lamb is thought of as the sacrificial lamb.[2] It is not, however, of particular importance here whether the title was chosen with Isa. 53.7 in mind,[3] or—more probably—the paschal lamb,[4] or the lambs[5] sacrificed in Israel, perhaps specifically the two lambs sacrificed daily in the temple. For the Evangelist the title must have seemed specifically Old Testament and Jewish, for he does not use it again. The death of Jesus is only rarely seen by him from the point of view of

---

[1] Αἴρων is an atemporal descriptive pres. Αἴρειν means "lift up (with the purpose of getting rid of)" or "get rid of", "carry away". Occasionally it is assimilated to φέρειν= "carry", "take upon oneself" (see ThWB I 184f.), but elsewhere in John αἴρειν is always used in the sense of "get rid of", "carry away" (2.16; 5.8ff.; 10.18 etc.). The same is true here; just as the ἵνα τὰς ἁμαρτίας ἄρῃ of I Jn. 3.5, when seen in the light of 1.7, 9, must clearly also bear this sense. Dodd (237), on the basis of Test. Levi 18.9; Ps. Sal. 17.29. Apc Bar. 63, 1–4, wants to take ὁ αἴρων κτλ. as referring to the office of the Messiah who is to rid the world of sin.

[2] Cp. I Jn. 1.7, 9; 2.2; 3.5; 4.10 whose meaning is clearly determined by the terms καθαρίζειν, αἷμα, ἱλασμός. The view of the ἀμνὸς τ.θ. as the sacrifice for sin is defended by P. Joüon (NRTh 72 [1940], 318–321) against Prat's view, that the lamb is the symbol of innocence.

[3] It is improbable that the Evangelist was thinking of Is. 53.7. For there the "servant of God", who as a substitute bears the sins, i.e. the penalties of the sins of others, is compared to the patient lamb. Even if one disregards the fact that the lamb is not intended to depict the bearing of sins, but silence under punishment, it still remains clear that Is. 53.7 is concerned with the servant's taking the punishment upon himself, and not with the removal of the debt of sin. The LXX then translates both נָשָׂא and סָבַל of the Hebr. text by φέρειν (and ἀναφέρειν)="take upon onself". Since however αἴρων κτλ. Jn. 1.29 may be an explanatory addition of the Evangelist's, it would still be possible for the title "Lamb of God" to come from Is. 53.7, just as the λέων ὁ ἐκ τῆς φυλῆς Ἰουδᾶ and the ῥίζα Δαυρίδ in Rev. 5.5 come from Gen. 49.9 and Is. 11.10. This view is taken by Strathm. I do not find convincing the suggestion, made by Lohmeyer (on Rev. 5.6) and J. Jeremias (ThWB I 343 and ZNTW 34 [1935], 117–123), following Ball and Burney, that ἀμνός is a translation of the Aram. טַלְיָא (=boy, servant, and =lamb) and that the title originally referred to the servant of God of Deutero-Isaiah. For טַלְיָא primarily and most frequently means "boy", and the Aram. עַבְדָּא, which is used by the Targum of the Prophets, suggests itself more obviously for the translation of עֶבֶד יהוה (cp. C. H. Dodd, Journ. of Theol. Studies 34. [1933] 285). Furthermore there is no reason to assume an Aram. original for Jn. 1.29, 36 The thesis that ἀμνός is a mistranslation of טַלְיָא has again been advanced by H. W. Wolff, Jesaia 53 im Urchristentum 1942, 70–73; according to Wolff the title originally referred to the servant. Against this view see esp. Dodd 235f.—The gen. τοῦ θεοῦ is in itself no reason for resorting to the עֶבֶד יהוה; the gen. indicates that the lamb was given by God himself. For the Evangelist the τοῦ θεοῦ has the same meaning as elsewhere ἀληθινός 1.9; 6.32; 15.1.

[4] I Cor. 5.7 shows that the interpretation of Christ as the paschal lamb is of an early date, and 19.36 clearly refers to such an interpretation. Even if the Passover in later Judaism was not seen as a sacrifice of expiation (Dalman, Jesus-Jeschua 114f., 152f.) such a function nevertheless was attached to the blood of the lambs slain at the Exodus from Egypt (J. Jeremias, Die Abendmahlsworte Jesu 1935, 81). Dodd, who rejects the interpretation of ἀμνός as the paschal lamb, rightly points out that in the LXX the paschal lamb is never

sacrifice, and in any case he nowhere else attaches the gift of the forgiveness of sins specifically to Jesus' death, but understands it as the effect of his Word (8.31f.). The title must come from the Jewish-Christian tradition, perhaps from its liturgical vocabulary,[1] in which it was used as the title of the Messiah without further reflection on its original meaning, while at the same same time it gave room to gather further associations.

The acclamation of Jesus is followed by the saying quoted in v. 15,[2] and it is done in such a way that the Baptist can now declare that Jesus is the one to whom his saying had referred. Naturally this relates, not to the saying in v.15, which is quoted without reference to its situation, but to a scene which the Evangelist has not described, but has assumed as known. The reference, of course, is to the parallel saying in the Synoptic tradition, which the editor has inserted at v. 27. Thus what is naively suggested by the Synoptic tradition, when it refers the prophecy of the Baptist to Jesus, is worked out deliberately by the Fourth Evangelist. In Jesus the proclamation of the Baptist has found its fulfilment (cp. 10.41). The Baptist is the μάρτυς.

B. 1.35–51: The Calling of the First Disciples

The account is essentially uniform. The movement of the narrative is only interrupted by minor additions; these however must be traced back to the Evangelist and not to the editor, so we must assume that the Evangelist is here using a literary source. The link with the preceding section in v. 35: τῇ ἐπαύριον πάλιν,[3] assuredly comes from his pen, and certainly the chronological

---

referred to as ἀμνός except in Ex. 12.5 v. 1.—The interpretation of ἀμνός as the paschal lamb is supported by Wik. and Barr.; the latter admittedly assumes that it is also connected with the ideas of Is. 53; so too in NTSt 1 (1954/55), 210–218, where he enlarges this thesis to take in Dodd's view (see p. 96 n. 1).

[5] So Schl. ad loc.; Hoskyns 169.176; cp. on the sacrifice of Tamid: Schürer II 345ff.; Str.-B. III 696ff. and passim; Moore III 153.—O. Schmitz, Die Opferanschauungen des späteren Judentums 1910, 237–240, draws a general distinction between the "Lamb of God" and the lambs sacrificed in Israel. In any case the essential thing is the positive content of the saying namely that the sacrifice really takes away the sin of the world. There is no particular reason to suppose that the saying is directed specifically against the sacrificial cult (Hirsch); nowhere else in John do we find such an attack, for it was not a subject which any longer directly concerned the Evangelist. H. v. Campenhausen (Die Idee des Martyriums 1936, 67) rightly points out that it is no mere chance that the idea of an objective expiation recedes into the background in John, "since there is a certain tension between this and the dialectical character of the saving encounter with the 'Word'."

[1] So Br.

[2] The ἦν of v. 15 must now become ἐστίν; for the rest the form varies, in that the phrase ὁ . . . ἐρχόμενος (under the influence of Mk 1.7; Lk 3.16?) has now become a main clause, so that ἀνήρ has had to be inserted, and the main clause of v. 15 has had to become a subordinate clause.

[3] There is no reason for assuming that the saying of the Baptist v. 36 goes back to the Evangelist's redaction; on the contrary, it is this saying which must have prompted him to compose his own saying in v. 29, see p. 95.

scheme in v. 43, for it makes the account obscure.[1] In the first place it is surprising that at the end of v. 43 ὁ Ἰησοῦς is expressly named as the subject, although Jesus was the subject in the preceding sentence.[2] Further it is strange that Jesus himself should find Philip; for this 1) runs contrary to the idea, that is evidently consciously worked into rest of the account, that one disciple brings the next disciple to Jesus, and 2) it accords ill with the εὑρήκαμεν, spoken by Philip in v. 45. Further there would then be no reason for the πρῶτον or πρῶτος, which is said of Andrew in v. 41.[3] Indeed, would it be possible to imagine the situation at all? In v. 43 Jesus sets out on his journey; thus the εὑρίσκει must mean that he meets him on the way. How then would Philip have the opportunity of finding Nathanael, speaking to him, and bringing him to Jesus (vv. 45f.)? All becomes clear if the subject of εὑρίσκει in v. 43 was originally one of the disciples who had already been called, either Andrew, who first finds Simon and then Philip, or else the disciple called at the same time as Andrew, who then finds Philip. Thus v. 43 has been altered by the Evangelist—perhaps simply in order to prepare the transition to the next section by ἠθέλησεν ἐξελθεῖν εἰς τ. Γαλ., but perhaps in order to suppress the name of the disciple called with Andrew, if he was originally the subject of εὑρίσκει in v. 43.[4] Finally vv. 50f. come from the Evangelist and limit in a peculiar manner the importance of the miracle which has just been told.[5]

The accounts falls clearly into sections: 1) vv. 35–37, the acclamation by the Baptist; 2) vv. 38–39, the meeting of the first two disciples with Jesus; 3) vv. 40–42, the calling of Simon; 4) vv. 43–44, the calling of Philip; 5) vv. 45–51, the calling of Nathanael. The style of the narrative is throughout Semitic in tone.[6]

---

[1] As has been rightly seen by Wellh., Schw. and Spitta.

[2] For this reason Pesch. puts ὁ Ἰησ. at the beginning, in front of ἠθέλησεν.

[3] On the variants, see on v. 41.

[4] It is not possible to say with certainty how far the Evangelist's alterations extend in v. 43. Just as it is not possible to decide whether the subj. of εὑρίσκει was originally Andrew or (as appears more probable to me) his companion, nor to decide whether the τῇ ἐπάυριον was already in the source or whether it was included by the Evangelist in the interests of his dating of the days (see on 2.1). Naturally v. 43 must take place a day later than vv. 35–39 on account of the παρ' αὐτῷ ἐμ. τ. ἡμ. ἐκ. v. 39. Yet for this reason the events told in vv. 40–42 must also have taken place a day later than v. 39. Yet since v. 41 does not start with the date (assuming that πρωί is not to be read instead of πρῶτον, see on v. 41), then it is probable that v. 43 also contained no date (syr^{s} expressly dates vv. 41f. on the same day as vv. 35–39). If one were to take v. 39b as an addition of the Evangelist's, then all the events recorded in vv. 35–50 would take place on *one* day; but there is no reason for this assumption; only the indication, that it was at the 10th hour, will have been added by the Evangelist.

[5] Cp. the materially and formally related sentence 20.29; on μείζονα τούτων cp. the Evangelist's addition in 5.20b and his formulation 14.12.—It is not possible to say whether the translation of the Aram. words in vv. 38, 41, 42 come from the Evangelist or the editor. —Noack (154) sees in vv. 50/51 the combination of "two originally independent elements"; acc. to him v. 51 has been joined to v. 50 by the key-word (ὄψῃ-ὄψεσθε).

[6] In almost every case the verb stands at the beginning of the sentence, while the passage is comprised almost entirely of asyndeta (καί in v. 37 and δέ in v. 38 should probably be omitted as in א* al); for a more detailed account see Schl. Yet this is clearly not a translation

1) **Vv. 35f.** show the Baptist with two of his disciples.[1] He sees Jesus walking along,[2] and calls his disciples' attention to him. Again this is told without any attention to historical detail. Neither the place[3] nor the situation is described. The fact that the Baptist had disciples is not recorded, but merely assumed; nor does the narrator raise the question whether the two disciples had heard the μαρτυρία of the Baptist on the previous day. Nor, in the last place, are we told whence and why Jesus comes.[4]

The Baptist's acclamation consists in the oracular saying: ἴδε ὁ ἀμνὸς τοῦ θεοῦ. This is sufficient indication for the disciples; they understand that they must leave their master (**V. 37**) and follow Jesus.[5] There is no attempt to give a psychological explanation of how it was that they could understand and why they were immediately convinced. The narrative is not concerned with historical or psychological matters; rather it attempts to give a symbolic portrayal of that which in 3.30 is represented as a law of history, namely that the Baptist must surrender his disciples to Jesus.

2) Nor is it possible to look for the psychological motivation in **vv. 38f.** Jesus turns round,[6] sees the two following him, and asks what they want. It is not as if he, who sees into all men's hearts (vv. 42, 47), did not know what they were looking for. But his question provides an

---

from the Aram.; for a Greek translator would certainly have linked up the sentences; nor are there any mistakes in translation. The source was therefore probably written in Greek by a Greek-speaking Semite. For further discussion of this source, see on 2.1–12.

[1] If in this story there is preserved an old tradition about the conversion of the first two disciples of the Baptist to Jesus, then one would expect the names of the two to be given. This was indeed perhaps the case in the source (see p. 98 n. 4), and I consider this more likely than the suggestion that vv. 35f. have been constructed as a counterpart to the story in Lk. 7.19 of the two disciples sent by the Baptist to Jesus (Windisch, Jesus und die Synopt. 112f.; Hirsch).

[2] ἐμβλέπειν (v. 35) refers simply to the perception which is the occasion of the saying, whereas in v. 42 it means to "look straight at s.o."

[3] In the context this is unnecessary after v. 28; but the indication of the place in v. 28 did not of course come in the source.

[4] The Baptist omits any account of Jesus' temptation, as he does of his baptism. Yet just as it would be wrong to say that he tries to suppress the baptism story (see p. 94 n. 3), so too it would be wrong to suggest that he omitted the temptation story because it was offensive to him. That no one can convict the Son of God of sin (8.46), does not mean that he could not have encountered Satan as the tempter. Yet the Evangelist is as little interested in the story of the temptation as he is in the story of the baptism. For him all Jesus' activity is a struggle against Satan; cp. 12.31.

[5] ἠκολ. in the first place means only "they went after him". Yet the repetition of the word (vv. 38, 40, 43) already shows that this is meant to depict their "discipleship"; cp. 8.12; 10.4f., 27; 12.26; 13.36f.; 21.19f., 22. The description of their discipleship as "following" is taken over from Rabbinic terminology (Str.-B. I 187f. 528f.; G. Kittel, ThWB I 213f.).

[6] στραφεὶς is often used as a sort of formula in Lk. The δὲ should be omitted with ℵ[c]pc. Asyndeta are characteristic of the style of the narrative.

occasion for them to speak. They want to know where he is staying.[1] They are invited: "Come and you shall see".[2] They accept the invitation, see where he is staying, and spend the day with him—all, apparently, facts of no particular importance; and yet the essential meaning of the narrative is hidden behind these events.[3] Why do they want to know where he lives?[4] They do not say what they really want. They only address him as "Rabbi", so that outwardly no more seems to be recorded than the following of two enthusiastic pupils after a teacher.[5] What they find in him is not recorded. Naturally they find confirmation of the Baptist's acclamation and recognise him as the Messiah (v. 41). But all that has, as it were, till now been hidden under a veil, and it would be an absurd mistake to think that any real interest attaches to the external details.[6] If the original narrative intended to say more than it actually expresses, this is certainly the case with the Evangelist: τί ζητεῖτε; are the first words that Jesus speaks in the Gospel.[7] It is clearly the first question which must be addressed to anyone who comes to Jesus, the first thing about which he must be clear. And it is essential to know where Jesus "lives"; for in the place where Jesus is at home the disciple will also receive his dwelling (14.2). So too the hour of the day[8]—inserted perhaps by the Evangelist—probably has a particular significance: the tenth hour is the hour of fulfilment.[9]

---

[1] μένειν = "stay at an inn", as in Mk. 6.10; Lk. 19.5 and often; also in Pap. (Preisigke, Wörterb.); similarly the Aram. שְׁרָא, Schl. ad loc.

[2] A common phrase in Semitic languages (Schl. ad loc.). In spite of Str.-B. the καί should be taken consecutively (Bl.-D. para. 442, 2; Burney 95f.).

[3] Cp. Omodeo, Mistica 70.

[4] Loisy holds that the question about where he is staying can be explained from the Rabbinic custom, whereby the rabbi taught sitting down and not walking about. This may be the external reason. But why then are we told only that they saw where he lived, but nothing of the questions and the teaching in his dwelling?

[5] The mode of address is in no way intended as disrespectful, and thus as betraying a still imperfect understanding. It is a formula, so that even when Nathanael recognises Jesus as the Son of God, he addresses him as "Rabbi" (v. 49). The disciples use the same form in 4.31; 9.2; 11.8. The form of address brings out the paradox that the Son of God appears as a Jewish Rabbi.

[6] Or else why is not the name of the place given where the inn was which this is all about? Equally, no consideration is given to the question where the two went in the evening. Yet the main point of the story, that the disciples of the Baptist henceforth became disciples of Jesus, is only made indirectly!

[7] Rightly stressed by Cl. R. Bowen, JBL 49 (1930), 300; Hosk. 171

[8] In accordance with the Semitic character of the story we shall have to reckon the hours of the day after the Babylonian Jewish system (as in 4.6), so that the 10th hour = 4.00 p.m.

[9] The number ten has particular significance in the OT and Judaism, for the Pythagoreans and in Gnosticism; for Philo it is the τέλειος ἀριθμός, vit. Mos. I 96 etc., see Hauck, ThWB II 35f.; Carpenter 238f.; Er. Frank, Plato und die sog. Pythagoreer 1923, 251f., 309ff. The explanation is often given, pointing to 11.9; I Jn. 2.8, that the twelve hour day signifies the time of the world, and that the 10th hour therefore refers to the beginning of

in Mk, Simon + Andrew are together the first disciples – in Jn, Andrew explicitly given primacy over Peter.

3) **Vv. 40–42** give a report about one of the two disciples, Andrew,[1] who is identified as the brother of Simon Peter (the latter, it is assumed, being known to the readers). Andrew finds—again we are not to ask where and how, at any rate on some later day[2]—his brother Simon,[3] and he tells him, "We have found[4] the Messiah", and brings him to Jesus. What will Jesus say? What impression will Simon receive? Jesus looks at him and calls him by his name! That is to say, he knows him, although he has never seen him before! And more, he adds the prophecy that Simon will some day bear another name,[5] the name "the Rock".[6] Thus—in Hellenistic terms—Jesus shows himself to be

---

the working of Jesus, or of the "Christian era" (Ho.). Yet the "day" 11.9 is a figure of the time of the earthly working of Jesus (cp. 9.4f.; 12.35). H. Huber (Der Begriff der Offenbarung im Joh.-Evg. 1934) 49, 1 thinks (following J. Jeremias, Das Ev. nach Joh. 1931, 90) that the 10th hour refers to a sacramental meal, which Jesus celebrated with the disciples at the time of the Mincha sacrifice. Fantastic!

[1] Ἀνδρέας, a Greek name also used by the Jews, Str.-B. I 535.—In John, Andrew appears again in 6.8; 12.22.

[2] See p. 98 n. 4; on the reading πρωί, see the following note.

[3] In v. 41 ℵ^c AB etc. read πρῶτον, ℵ*L al πρῶτος. It is not possible to decide between the two readings because the original text of v. 43 is no longer extant, see p. 98 n. 4. If in v. 43 Andrew was the subj. of εὑρίσκει, then πρῶτον is demanded in v. 41; if it was Andrew's companion, then we must read πρῶτος. In any case either reading must be understood in the light of what follows in the story. If we read πρῶτος, then this exludes the hypothesis that the "other one", as a second person (i.e. after Andrew), must also have found his brother (there is no need at all to stress τὸν ἴδιον, v. 41; for like suus it can be used in a weakened sense, see Bl.-D. para. 286, 1 and esp. Br. ad loc.) and that therefore the "other" was one of the second pair of brothers among the twelve, namely one of the sons of Zebedee. Rather, if we read πρῶτος, then it follows that the second one, the "other one", found Philip. (For the rest the sons of Zebedee are not mentioned in John, and they do not appear till 21.2, in the chapter added by the editor.) The arbitrary suggestion that the "other one" must be the Evangelist is purely wishful thinking. A. B. Hulen's suggestion (JBL 67 [1948], 153–157), that the unnamed disciple was Philip, is not convincing.—Bd. wants to read πρωί in v. 41 with b e (r) which would improve the chronological scheme, but is too poorly attested.

[4] In vv. 41, 43, 45 εὑρίσκει refers to an unintentional finding, while εὑρήκαμεν vv. 41, 45 refers to the finding of those who have sought. Μεσσίας occurs in the NT only here and in 4. 25; it is a transliteration of מָשִׁיחַ or alternatively of the Aram. מְשִׁיחָא; on its spelling see Schl. ad loc.

[5] Of course this does not mean that Simon receives a new name from Jesus *now*. For this reason 1.42 cannot be taken as the Johannine form of the tradition found in Mk. 1.16–18 or 3.16 (Windisch, Joh. und die Synopt. 91). Rather Jn. 1.42 *foretells* such a scene, which however the Evangelist did not need to retell afterwards, because he could assume that it was well known. Nor is it in any way "assumed that Peter has, prior to this, in some way confessed the Messiahship of Jesus, i.e. that he has indicated that he endorses the confession of his brother in 1.41" (Windisch, loc. cit.).

[6] Σίμων is the Greek name which is used for the apostle throughout the NT instead of Συμεών (שִׁמְעוֹן); see Deissmann, Bibelstudien 184, 1; Str.-B. I 530. His father is referred to as Ἰωάνης (יוֹחָנָן) as in 21.15–17, whereas in Mt. 16.17 he is called Ἰωνᾶς (יוֹנָה or יוֹנָא). On Κηφᾶς (כֵּיפָא) see Str.-B. I 530–535. The Synoptists use only Πέτρος, while Paul mostly has Κηφᾶς.

make the other one Peter or too same – then Jn explicitly makes Peter secondary

the θεῖος ἄνθρωπος, who recognises and sees into the hearts of the strangers whom he meets.[1] The impression made on Peter is not recorded; but the reader realises that Peter is won over by the revelation. However the narrator does not describe the result of the revelation, but reserves this for a second case, which is even more astounding.

4) **Vv. 43–44** briefly record the calling of Philip. Jesus wants to leave for Galilee[2] and finds Philip[3]—again it is not possible to know whether

---

[1] The same motif occurs in vv. 47f.; 2.24f.; 4.17–19. The idea is widespread in pagan and Christian Hellenism; the ability to recognise and to read the thoughts of those whom one meets characterises the θεῖος ἄνθρωπος cp. Reizenst., HMR. 238f. Hist. Mon. et hist. Laus. 90f.; G. P. Wetter, Der Sohn Gottes 69–72; W. Bousset, Apophthegmata 1923, 85f.; E. Fascher, Προφήτης 1927, 194–196; L. Bieler, Θειος 'Ανήρ I 1935, 89–94; for Islam: R. Otto, Reich Gottes und Menschensohn 1934, 302–306 = E.T. The Kingdom of God and the Son of Man, 1943, 351–356. Just as Apollonius of Tyana can divine the thoughts of men, so too acc. to Apul. met. XI 15 the priest of Isis "recognised in the spirit the experiences and thoughts of Apuleius when he came to him and told them to him, just as the astrologist Horus does with Propertius (IV 1) when he meets him" (Reitzenst., HMR. 238). Cp. Pap. Graec. Mag. V 286ff.—I Sam 9.19f. shows that such figures were known in ancient Israel, but they gave place to the prophets and do not occur in Judaism. Yet here the idea occasionally occurs, as is shown by the story in T. Pes. 1. 27f. (157) where a rabbi knows the man whom he meets, although he has never seen him before (Str.-B. I 528). This ability is naturally not attributed here to the divine quality of the rabbi, but to the Holy Spirit. So too Paul knows (I Cor. 14.25) that the Holy Spirit gives men the ability to see into the hearts of others, which is otherwise the privilege of God alone (Str.-B. II 412). The gift of seeing into the future is somewhat different; this was given to the OT prophets by God and was still claimed by the Essene prophets (Schl. on 1.47). The Johannine Jesus is not however portrayed as a prophet, but in his omniscience he is more like the θεῖος ἄνθρωπος (he knows events which occur at a distance 11.4, 11–14; he knows his own future destiny in advance 2.19, 21; 3.14; 6.64, 70; 13.1, 38; 18.4; 19.28, as well as the fate of others 13.36; 16.2), whose miraculous knowledge is not based on a gift of God which has to be constantly renewed, but on his own personal divinity.—However the θεῖος-ἄνθρ.-motif, which undoubtedly is found in 1.42, 47f.; 4.17–19; 11.11–14, is not the decisive element in the Gospel; for Jesus' omniscience is not based on any particular talents which enhance his humanity, but on his unity with God, which he enjoys in his full humanity, just as the confession νῦν οἴδαμεν, ὅτι οἶδας πάντα 16.30 is called forth not by a display of supernatural knowledge, but by the totality of the self-revelation of the Son of God. Thus the idea of omniscience belongs to the mythological elaboration of the idea of revelation, while the task of the θεῖος- ἄνθρ. motif is to help portray the idea of omniscience (see the text above). The close connection between the omniscience of the Revealer, grounded in his unity with God, and his task of revelation can already be seen in Gnosticism. "Wisdom" is the companion of God; God loved her; for she is μύστις τῆς τοῦ θεοῦ ἐπιστήμης (Wis. 8.4; cp. 9.9 and p. 22). The messenger of the Mandaeans, before he is sent out, is instructed in all the cosmic mysteries (Ginza 381.7ff.); he too "knows men's hearts and sees into their minds" (Ginza 194.14ff.; M. Lit. 67, 258). Equally the metatron of Jewish Gnosticism has been initiated into all mysteries and knows the hearts of all men (Odeberg 43–47). On the other hand it is questionable whether Philo's characterisation of the Logos goes back to this tradition: leg. all. III 171 ... οὕτως καὶ ὁ θεῖος λόγος ὀξυδερκέστατός ἐστιν, ὡς πάντα ἐφορᾶν εἶναι ἱκανός.—As in John, so too in Ign. Eph. 15.3 the notion is transferred to Christ (Schlier, Relg. Unters. 58).

[2] 'Εξελθεῖν: out of the house or the area.

[3] The name Φιλ. is found elsewhere of Jews, Str.-B. I 535.—Phil., mentioned in the Synoptics only in the list of the apostles, appears again in Jn. 6.5ff.; 12.21f. (on both occasions together with Andrew); 14.8f. It hardly is possible to say what sort of tradition this is taken from.

this happens before he crosses the Jordan, or when he has already reached Galilee. His brief injunction; "Follow me",[1] makes Philip into his disciple,[2] as is shown by v. 45. Philip is described in terms of his home town Bethsaida, and of the relation that he consequently has with Peter and Andrew.[3]

5) Vv. 43f. are only the prelude to the more splendid event in **vv. 45–49**, which repeats the motif of v. 42 in a more elevated form and provides the climax of the section. Philip—again without any indication of the particular circumstances—finds Nathanael,[4] and announces to him, as Andrew did to Simon: εὑρήκαμεν! But here the "Messiah" of v. 41 is paraphrased: "Him of whom Moses in the law and also the prophets wrote"; i.e. the one who was promised.[5] It is "Jesus, the Son of Joseph, from Nazareth".[6] The reason for this being said here (and not in v. 41) is that it is used to link up with what follows. It seems incredible to Nathanael that obscure Nazareth could be the home of the promised one.[7] But—as the reader must learn—God's action

---

[1] On ἀκολ. see v. 37; the imperative as in Mk. 2.14 parr.; Mt. 8.22. The phrase, which in itself is not uncommon (see Schl.), has of course a particular ring on the lips of Jesus.

[2] On the view that in the source it was Andrew (or the disciple called at the same time as A.) who brought Phil. to Jesus, see p. 97.

[3] The remark in v. 44 probably belongs to the source, since it is analogous to the remark in v. 40. Within the context of the source it is intended to stress that it was Philip, and none other, who was found. Again there is reflected in the report the fact that it was a group of people from a particular district, formerly disciples of the Baptist, who had gone over to Jesus.—On Bethsaida (= Julias) on the east bank of the Jordan, before it flows into Lake Genesareth, see Schürer II 208f.; Str.-B. I 605; Dalman. Orte und Wege, 4th ed. 173–180; see also on 12.21.—ἀπό and ἐκ are used interchangeably in the NT as in the LXX and Pap. to describe a person's origins, Bl.-D. para. 209.3, "That Beths. is named after a person living there is in accordance with a well-established Rabbinic usage", Schl. Spr. und H. 31).

[4] Ναθ. = נְתַנְאֵל (in Greek it would be Θεόδωρος). He is mentioned again in the editor's addition 21.2; there it is said that he comes from Cana. Otherwise nothing is known of him. Since the Middle Ages he has been readily identified with the Bartholomew mentioned in Mk. 3.18. Others believe that he is identical with Matthew, who is not mentioned in John, because their names both mean the same (מַתַּי = gift of Jahweh). Cp. Br., ext. note after 1.51. R. Eisler, Das Rätsel des Johannes-Evangeliums 1936, 475–485 identifies Nathanael with Dositheus, "Simon's predecessor among the leaders of the Baptists."

[5] It is not possible to say whether this refers to particular passages. It was a well established usage that the law and the prophets together referred to the whole of the OT., see Lk 16.6, 29; Rom. 3.21; Str.-B. I 240.

[6] Ἰησοῦς = יֵשׁוּעַ, the shortened form of יְהוֹשֻׁעַ Str.-B. I 63f. Ἰωσήφ = יוֹסֵף. Nazareth is attested neither in the OT nor in Jos., nor in other contemporary Jewish or pagan sources. For a late Rabbinic attestation see Str.-B. I 92; G. Dalman, Orte und Wege Jesu 3. ed. 65f.; this is based on early (perhaps as early as the 3rd cent. B.C.) tradition, see S. Klein, Beiträge zur Geschichte und Geographie Galiläas; Jos. Klausner, Jesus von Nazareth 1930, 311f.

[7] It makes no difference whether one takes the sentence as a question or an ironic

is surprising and incredible; and the offence of the Messiah's coming from Nazareth belongs, as the Evangelist understands it, to the offence of the incarnation of the Logos.[1] No attempt is made to give a rational defence.[2] Nathanael is simply told: "Come and see!"[3]

Again Jesus shows himself to be the θεῖος ἄνθρωπος; this time not because he knows the name, but because he knows the character of the man he meets. He is a true Israelite,[4] in whom there is no guile.[5] Jesus' words provoke the surprised question of Nathanael, who feels that he has been seen through and through. This question again serves to make Jesus' miraculous knowledge evident: Jesus has seen him before with far-seeing gaze under the fig-tree.[6] This proof of Jesus' miraculous power overwhelms Nathanael, and he confesses the Rabbi as the Son of God and the King of Israel.[7] But faith based on miracle has only a

---

statement.—There is no need to suppose that Nazareth had a bad reputation; it is enough that it was an insignificant village.

[1] Neither is Joseph's fatherhood disputed (see on 1.14 p. 62 n. 4) nor is the statement of Jesus' origins in Nazareth modified by the assertion that he was born in Bethlehem (see 7.42). Cf. Ph.-H. Menoud, Revue de Theol. et Phil. 1930, 276ff.

[2] By attempting for example to produce a proof text as in Mt. 2.23.

[3] Bengel: optimum remedium contra opiniones praeconceptas.—The phrase is common (Str.-B. ad loc.) and the καί is consecutive as in v. 39.

[4] Ἴδε weakened with Nom. see Bl.-D. para. 144. Ἰσρ. as distinct from Ἰουδαῖος, is the name used in the saving history, cp. Rom. 9.4; 11.1; II Cor. 11.22; see p. 86 n. 2. Ἀληθῶς is attributive, with much the same force as ἀληθινός, i.e. "one who is worthy of the name of Israel". Cp. Ruth 3.12; Ign. Rom. 4.2 and Plato, leg. 642 D: ἀληθῶς καὶ οὔ τι πλαστῶς εἰσὶν ἀγαθοί.

[5] On ἐν ᾧ δόλος κτλ. cp. Ps. 31.2 μακάριος ἀνὴρ ... οὐδέ ἐστιν ἐν τῷ στόματι αὐτοῦ δόλος (Rev. 14.5); Is. 53.9; but also Theogn. 416: πιστὸν ἑταῖρον, ὅτῳ μή τις ἔνεστι δόλος. The description scarcely refers to the fact the Nath. v. 46 has spoken out openly—for why then should he have kept anything back from Philip?! Rather one would think that Nath. shows himself to be without δόλος in what follows. But since the statement, which is intended to show Jesus' knowledge of men's hearts, is shown to be correct by Nath.'s question in v. 48, it must have referred to a state of affairs already in existence; this is perhaps hinted at in v. 48, see below. See C. Edlund, En räth Israelit 1949.

[6] On the fig-tree, cp. C. F. D. Moule, JTS 5 (1954), 210f. Maldonatus warns us: quaerere quid Nath. sub ficu egerit, nescio an satis moderati sit ingenii, and in fact we cannot guess quid egerit. It is questionable whether there is in the background here a legend according to which Nathanael under the fig-tree exhibited those qualities for which Jesus called him an "Israelite without guile" (Dibelius, Formgeschichte. 2. ed. 114 = From Trad. to Gospel, 117). If we are to assume that there is a connection between this description and Nath.'s behaviour under the fig-tree (see previous note), then perhaps it is enough to point out that the Rabbis favoured a place under a tree for study and teaching. Nath. would then show himself to be a true Israelite by searching the Scriptures (5.39) and to be without δόλος by coming to Jesus—as opposed to the Jews who study the Scriptures but do not believe them (5.39, 46f.!). This would at least correspond to the Evangelist's intention, for to him Nath. is a symbolic figure (regardless of the fact that he occurs in the tradition); cp. Hirsch I 116f.—It is too much to suppose that Nath. had been studying the story of Jacob's dream under the fig-tree (Str.), or even that this was how the Evangelist understood it, although he wrote v. 51.

[7] It is possible that σὺ εἶ ὁ υἱὸς τοῦ θεοῦ was first added by the Evangelist; in the context of the source the title could only have the same meaning as βασιλεὺς τοῦ Ἰσρ. (see

relative value as a stepping stone to true faith, which once awakened will see "something greater" than such miracles (v. 50).[1]

The Evangelist gives an indication of how this is meant by making Jesus take up the point again (**v. 51**)[2] and repeat the promise of fresh miracles—a promise now addressed to all disciples (ὑμῖν)—in a figurative saying reminiscent of the story of Jacob.[3] The Evangelist understands the angels ascending and descending upon the "Son of Man" as a

---

p. 93 n. 1). And this means essentially the same as Μεσσίας v. 41; cp. on this 6.15; 12.13; Ps. Sol. 17.23 etc.; Volz Eschatologie 173ff.; W. Staerk, Soter I 1933, 48ff.; Dodd 229f.

[1] Vv. 50f. an addition of the Evangelist's, see p. 97-8. It makes no difference whether one takes πιστεύεις as a question or a statement. Either way the meaning is: "If at this point you already believe, you will see still greater things." For a discussion of the theological content see on 2.23; 4.48; 20.16f., 29.

[2] V. 51 an addition of the Evangelist's, see p. 98.—The emphatic ἀμήν is doubled, as occurs frequently in the OT (in the LXX usually γένοιτο), whereas in the Synoptic sayings of Jesus the single ἀμήν is found. (The double "Amen" is also found in the responses in DSD 1.20; 2.10, 18.) In contrast with the OT, where the formula comes at the end of a speech, it comes in John and the Synoptics at the beginning (and is here only found on the lips of Jesus). In Rabbinic usage "Amen" is used to indicate assent to the speech of another, whereby the speaker makes the opinion of the other his own, as it were by an oath; see Dalman, W. J. I 185–187; Str.-B. I 242–244. II Cor. 1.20; Rev 1.7 show that Amen could be used simply as an emphatic Yes.—The emphatic λέγω (ὑμῖν) is Rabbinic (Schl. Spr. und H.40 on 3.3).—The ἀπ' ἄρτι which in K it syr precedes ὄψεσθε must be taken from Mt. 26.64.

[3] There can be no doubt that there is an allusion here to Jacob's dream, Gen. 28.10–17, where the unusual order ἀνα- and καταβαίνειν is found. In the Rabb. tradition the בּוֹ (Gen. 28.12) is sometimes correctly taken to refer to the ladder on which the angels ascended and descended (so too the LXX ἐπ' αὐτῆς), sometimes incorrectly to refer to Jacob (see Burney 116, note). The latter interpretation, which appears to be assumed in the ἐπὶ τ. υἱὸν τ. ἀνθρ. here, is connected with a mystical interpretation of the passage as a whole in Gen R. 68.18, which interprets the ascending and descending of the angels as the communication between the earthly Jacob (= Israel) and his heavenly archetype (εἰκών). Odeberg suspects (33–42), probably rightly, that it **is** this interpretation which lies behind Jn. 1.51, and that further behind this interpretation lies the Gnostic idea of relation of the earthly person to its heavenly archetype. According to Ginza 68.13ff.; 296.32ff. 316.28ff. the communion between the messenger on earth and his heavenly home is mediated by helping spirits. (See also Black 85, who takes ἐπί as "unto" or "towards", while Torrey (The four gospels 318) wants to take it as "in the service of the Son of Man".) On the basis of this understanding, Odeberg attempts an explanation of the title of the Son of Man, which occurs here for the first time in John; he suggests that it denotes the earthly man as distinct from his archetype which dwells in heavenly δόξα. In the Gnostic and in the Johannine view the "Son of Man" must be "glorified" (i.e. in Gnostic terms: be united with its heavenly archetype); cp. 3.14; 6.62; 12.23, 34; 13.31. This is also most probably correct, but it is not correct to suggest that the title "Son of Man" has here an "inclusive" meaning, according to which the believers belong, together with the Revealer, to the one "man", which would mean that the believers themselves received here the promise of the communication with their heavenly archetypes. For even though John has taken over the Gnostic idea of the original community between the believers and the Revealer (see below), he has reserved the title of the "Son of Man" for Jesus; the believers are not here promised communion with the divine world, but the vision of the communion which is enjoyed by Jesus. Str. (op. cit. 10), following Odeberg's interpretation, takes v. 51 to mean that Jesus is the ladder between heaven and earth, by which God's power and love is mediated to men.

mythological picture of the uninterrupted communion between Jesus and the Father (cp. 8.16, 29; 10.30; 16.32); there is no account of angelophanies in what follows. Thus the vision which is promised to the disciples is not conceived as the vision of heavenly beings, but as the vision in faith of his δόξα (1.14), as the vision which sees in him the Father (14.9f.). It is the promise of the vision of the δόξα in all that Jesus does; and inasmuch as this includes the working of particular miracles, the latter are to be thought of as a manifestation of the communion between Jesus and the Father (5.19f.).[1]

In this way the Evangelist indicates also how he would have us understand 1.35-51. *The source* showed Jesus as the θεῖος ἄνθρωπος, whose miraculous knowledge overwhelms those who meet him. It depicts these events in a remarkably dry narrative style, by which it creates an impression of mystery; as soon as Jesus appears there are at work in everyday life higher powers which, from time to time, break through into the open. And when the source tells how one disciple brings the next to Jesus, it allows us to feel the almost magical power of attraction of his person.[2]—It is easy to see how *the Evangelist* could use this narrative not only as an indirect μαρτυρία of the Baptist, but also as an illustration of the paradox of the δόξα of the Incarnate; for it is a narrative which at once portrays the right way of seeking Jesus,[3] the power of the word which acclaims him, and the right way of hearing this word—in the "following" of discipleship. Equally the demonstration of Jesus'

Dodd (241–246), like Odeberg, takes the Son of Man to be the true Israel of God, as the epitome of the new humanity.

By contrast with Odeberg, H. Windisch (ZNTW 30 (1931), 215–35; similarly E. Gaugler 45) finds in Jn. 1.51 a traditional "Son of Man-saying", a fragment of a Son of Man tradition in which the idea of the eschatological appearance of the Son of Man surrounded by angels (Mk. 8.38; 14.62) is historicized, i.e. transferred to the Son of Man who is active on earth; it is a "fragment", because the ὄψεσθε refers to visible angelophanies, which are not however actually recorded in the rest of the Gospel! On the other hand Goguel (J.-B. 189f.; 219f.) believes Jn. 1.51 to be a fragment of a baptismal narrative, which was originally an Easter narrative; against this view Windisch ZNTW 31 (1932), 199–203.—J. Jeremias, Angelos 3 (1928), 2–5 suggests that Jn. 1.51 should be understood on the basis of the Jewish mythology of the stone of Bethel, according to which the stone of Bethel is the rock on which the creation was begun, the place of the presence of God, above which the gate of heaven is situated. Yet the stone is not even mentioned.

[1] Wik. and Barr. also take the ascending and the descending of the angels on the Son of Man as a symbolic description of the communion or unity between Jesus and the Father. Clavier (Rev. Phil. rel. 31 [1951], 289f.) and Dodd (294) also take it as a symbolic description; the former however as a symbol of the new relationship between God and men, the latter (see p. 105 n. 3) of the continual communion between God and the new people of God. As opposed to this H.v.d. Busche (NRevTheol. 75 [1953], 1101f.) takes the phrase to refer to the exaltation of Jesus.

[2] The fairy-tale motive of "Swan, join on!" is transposed into a higher sphere.

[3] See p. 100.

omniscience has a meaning which goes beyond the outward miracle. Jesus shows himself to be the Revealer because he knows the people who meet him; he knows his "own" (10.14) and in his word reveals to them what they are and what they will be; in this way he compels them to confess and follow him (cp. 4.16-19, 29). Thus faith in him is grounded in the fact that in the encounter with him the believer's own existence is uncovered.[1]

Finally we may ask whether *the titles* which Jesus receives in this passage are not intended to bring out his importance in a particular way.[2] The source contains the titles ὁ ἀμνὸς τοῦ θεοῦ (v.36), "Messiah" (v. 41), "King of Israel" (v. 49), and perhaps "Son of God" (v. 49), which would then have the same meaning as the previous title. Thus for the source Jesus is the messianic king in whom the Old Testament prophecies find their fulfilment, as v. 45 expressly emphasises. The Evangelist was able to take over this idea (5.46); but he gave it a new meaning by the (interpretation or) addition of "Son of God" and, in any case, by the title of the "Son of Man" in v. 51. In the earthly presence of the Son of God the promise is fulfilled.[3] Jesus is the Son of Man, not, as understood by Jewish and early Christian apocalyptic, as he who one day will come on the clouds of heaven, but in his earthly presence; for in this earthly presence, in which he enjoys continual communion with the Father, he shows to faith the miracle of his δόξα. Thus in the Evangelist's view the passage already reflects the truth that Jesus' coming is the judgement of the world (3.19), and that it is in the present time, when his word calls us to faith, that the decision between life and death is made (5. 25).

The difference between the narrative 1.35–51 and the Synoptic account of the calling of the first disciples Mk. 1.16–20 parr. is evident. The only similarity is that in both accounts the two brothers Peter and Andrew are among those first called. Admittedly in John they are both said to come from Bethsaida, whereas in Mk. 1.29 Peter is said to live in Capernaum. In John there is no mention of the sons of Zebedee, while Mk. does not have the unknown companion of Andrew, Philip and Nathanael. Moreover the situation is

---

[1] Cp. Ad. Schlatter, Der Glaube im NT 4. ed. 1927, 193.

[2] Windisch (ZNTW 30 [1931], 218), who takes 1.19–51 as a single unit, counts eight titles; apart from those mentioned above in the text: ὁ βαπτίζων ἐν πν. ἁγ. v. 33, ὁ ἐκλεκτὸς τ. θ v. 34, which he considers to be original, and ὃν ἔγραψεν κτλ. v. 45.—Hirsch (Das vierte Evangelium 119) counts seven titles in 1.19–51; apart from those mentioned in the text: ὁ ἐκλεκτὸς τ. θ and ῥαββί: "Jesus is the fulfilment of the ultimate, hidden truth which lives in the search for God of the Israel. religion. But he is the fulfilment which breaks Judaism and the law asunder."—On the messianic titles in John see also Dodd 228ff.—According to E. L. Allen (JBL 74 [1955], 89) Nathanael and his confession represent Jewish Christianity, which as Jesus shows, must be raised to a higher plane.

[3] See p. 104 n. 7.

completely different. In John the first disciples come from the Baptist's following, and he it is who directs them to Jesus;[1] whereas in Mk. (1.14) the calling of the disciples does not take place till after the arrest or the death of the Baptist, and then it occurs on Lake Genesareth, where those who have been called give up their trade as fishermen. Principally the difference lies in the basic idea of the call-narrative in Mk., that the disciples are suddenly called away from their normal occupations in every day life.[2] Further in Mk. the first disciples are called to be apostles, whereas in John there is no mention of their apostleship.

The two narratives cannot be harmonised as historical accounts; indeed any attempt to do so destroys the specific intention of each narrative. Yet since the two scenes related in Mk. 1.16–20 are not historical accounts,[3] it is possible that the Johannine narrative contains reliable historical tradition, namely, the fact that there were erstwhile disciples of the Baptist among Jesus' first disciples, who perhaps joined him when he broke away from the Baptist.[4] This however is uncertain, whereas it may be taken as certain that there is in the account a reflection of the fact that, in general, a part of the Baptist's following went over to the Christian community.[5] It is probable that the Evangelist himself was among these disciples; for this would explain the way in which he deals with the Baptist tradition.[6]

---

[1] Because 1.19–34 and 1.35–51 have been put together, the place is πέραν τοῦ Ἰορδάνου; but of course this need not have been the case in the source on which 1.35–51 is based.

[2] See Bultmann, Gesch. der synopt. Trad. 2. ed. 27 = Hist. of the Syn. Trad. 28.

[3] See Gesch. der synopt. Trad. 2. ed. 27 = Hist. of the Syn. Trad. 28; M. Dibelius, Formgesch. 2. ed. 108f. = From Trad. to Gospel, 111f.

[4] The historically indisputable fact that Jesus had himself been baptised by the Baptist, proves that Jesus belonged for a time to the disciples of the Baptist.

[5] The less 1.35–37 can be viewed as historical event, the more certain it is that such an account could only be formed if it was known that the way to Jesus for many had in fact lain via the Baptist. Moreover we have in Acts 19.1–7 an historical account of this fact. Cp. too p. 17 n. 1 and Kundsin, Topolog. Überlieferungsstoffe 20f.

[6] See p. 16—1.35–51 would then provide evidence for the conversion of the Evangelist by such disciples of the Baptist as had become believers in Jesus before him; the source which he uses here is part of the propaganda made by such disciples for the Christian faith.

CHAPTERS 2-12
THE REVELATION OF THE ΔΌΞΑ TO THE WORLD

GLORY

Chapters 2-12
The Revelation of the ΔΌΞΑ to the World

Chapter 2, as we had been led to expect by ch. 1, and as is confirmed by 2.11, sees the beginning of the *revelation of the* δόξα *of Jesus.* It is easy to discern the basic structure of the Gospel: chs. 3–12 portray the revelation of the δόξα to the world, or the struggle between light and darkness, in such a way that they illustrate 1.5, 9–11,[1] while in chs. 13–17 (or alternatively -20[2]) is portrayed the revelation of the δόξα to the believers, or the victory of the light, whereby 1.12–18 is illustrated.[3] The first part may be summarised by the word κρίσις; for the struggle of the revelation is portrayed as κρίσις, in the double sense of "judgement" and "division": 3.19; 5.22ff.; 8.15, 26; 9.39; 12.31, 46ff.[4]; while at the same time this division in the "world" has a debased analogon in the σχίσμα which is called forth by the word of Jesus: 7.43; 9.16; 10.19.

The more precise division of the Gospel is, however, open to question, for the original order of the Gospel has in many places been disturbed. Admittedly it is clear that 6.59 marks the conclusion of one section and 7.1ff. the beginning of another. Thus one must regard chs. 3–6 and chs. 7–12 as the main divisions of the first part, with the exception of 6.60–71, which has been displaced and should come at the conclusion of the public ministry of Jesus (see below pp. 285f., 420). Within chs. 3–6, apart from minor alterations, 6.1–59 should come between chs. 4 and 5. Thus we can reconstruct the main divisions of chs. 3–6 as follows: *ch. 3* (for which the introduction is provided by 2.23–25) *and chap. 4 should be taken together*; in each of the two chs. (and only there) the central feature is provided by Jesus' conversation with a single person, with the διδάσκαλος τοῦ Ἰσραήλ and with the γυνὴ Σαμαρεῖτις, with the man and the woman, with the official orthodoxy and with heresy. Moreover the structure of the two chs. is similar, inasmuch as in both cases the main section, which contains the revelation of Jesus (3.1–21 and 4.1–30), is followed by a section which deals with the relation of the witness of others

---

[1] The τὸ φῶς ἐν τῇ σκοτίᾳ φαίνει of 1.5 is heard again and again: 3.19; 8.12; 9.5, 39; 11.9f.; 12.35f., 46. Equally the οὐ κατέλαβεν, οὐκ ἔγνω, οὐ παρέλαβον of 1.5, 10f. in 3.19, 32; 5.39f.; 6.66; chs. 7 and 8; 10.31ff.; 11.45ff., 12.37ff. and elsewhere.

[2] The passion narrative chs. 18–20 is portrayed by the Evangelist as the revelation of the δόξα of Jesus, and therefore forms a single unit together with chs. 13–17, in which Jesus reveals himself to his own as the δοξασθείς.

[3] See p. 48.

[4] The "division" is specifically portrayed in the scene in 6.66ff.

to the revelation (3.22–30, the witness of the one who represents the time *before* the revelation; 4.31–42, the witness of those who represent the time *after* the revelation).

Equally *chs. 6 and 5 should clearly be taken together.* Both are introduced by a σημεῖον,[1] which provides the starting point and the subject for the ensuing discussion or discourse. In 6.1–59 the revelation is portrayed as the κρίσις of the natural, human desire for life, in ch. 5 as the κρίσις of religion. The introduction to chs. 6 and 5 seems to be provided by 4.43–54. Since the point of the story is contained in 4.48: ἐὰν μὴ σημεῖα καὶ τέρατα ἴδητε, οὐ μὴ πιστεύετε, and since ch. 6 and ch. 5 open with σημεῖα, one might be tempted to contrast chs. 3–4 and chs. 6–5 under the headings: "πίστις and the word" and "πίστις and the σημεῖον". However, according to 2.23–25; 3.2, Nicodemus was also led to Jesus by σημεῖα, and Jesus' demonstration of his omniscience 4.16–18 has also the character of a σημεῖον. And on the other hand in 5.24, 47 it is precisely through his λόγοι or ῥήματα that Jesus reveals himself. Thus we can say no more than that we find in chs. 3 and 4 a portrayal of the confrontation of the most diverse individuals with the revelation, and in chs. 6 and 5 a portrayal of the conflict of the revelation with the questions of natural life and religion.

This leaves ch. 2, which is unusual in that it describes two events, neither of which is followed by a discourse.[2] Clearly they form a *prelude* or a diptych, which represents Jesus' ministry symbolically: the miracle of the wine in 2.1–11 is expressly designated the ἀρχὴ τῶν σημείων (v. 11), and the cleansing of the temple 2.13–22 symbolises the end—the death and the resurrection of Jesus. This is made all the more clear by the fact that the miracle of the changing of the wine is an epiphany miracle, and that the Evangelist has taken the story of the cleansing of the temple, which in the old tradition, represented by the Synoptics, was placed at the end of Jesus' ministry, and he has put it at the beginning, alongside the epiphany miracle.[3]

---

[1] Ch. 6 should not be taken as two σημεῖα; for in the tradition the miracle of the walking on the water and the feeding of the multitude were given as a unit. It is equally wrong to wish to annex 4.43–54 to ch. 5 to provide two σημεῖα as an introduction for the chapter (Htm); for no reference is made to 4.43–54 in Jesus' discourse in ch. 5; on the contrary, 4.43–54 must have an independent meaning of its own (see above). Nor can one take 2.1–12 and 2.13–22 as the two σημεῖα which precede the conversations in chs. 3 and 4 (Htm); for the σημεῖα in ch. 2 (even if one were to take the cleansing of the temple as such) do not provide the themes for chs. 3 and 4.

[2] 2.13–22 does indeed contain a discussion; yet, because of its brevity—a single exchange of words—it cannot be compared with the other discussions, not even those in ch. 11.

[3] What I have said above shows that I cannot accept E. Lohmeyer's attempt to divide the Gospel as a whole and in its individual sections by the number seven (ZNTW 27 [1928], 11–36). To do so he has to combine sections of unequal value, to split up sections which should be taken together (e.g. 2.1–12 and 2.13–22) and to obscure important dividing lines (e.g. 18.1).—Nor is E. Hirsch's division of the Gospel into seven "rings" (Das vierte Evg. 1936) any more convincing, if for no other reason than that it does not recognise the displacement of chs. 6, 8, 17.—I can find no trace of the importance of the number seven for John. One can, of course, count seven miracles, but only by including in the number the miracle in 6.16–21, which is of no importance within the context of the Gospel and belongs

Prelude: Chapter 2

A. 2.1–12: The Miracle of the Epiphany

There can be no doubt that the Evangelist has again taken a story from the tradition as the basis of his account here. Manifestly he has taken it from a source which contains a collection of miracles, and which he uses for the following miracle stories. It is the *σημεῖα-source*, which in its style is clearly distinguishable from the language of the Evangelist or of the discourse-source, which is the basis of the Prologue and the following discourses; it is equally clearly distinguishable from the miracle stories of the Synoptic tradition. The similarity of the style with 1.35–50[1] makes it likely that 1.35–50 was the introduction of the σημεῖα-source, and in fact the content and also the conclusion of 1.35–50 would be admirably suited for this. Obviously in the source the miracles were numbered; for the fact that 2.11 (in its basic outlines) comes from the source and is not an addition of the Evangelist's is shown by 4.54, where the reported miracle is described as Jesus' δεύτερον σημεῖον, thus contradicting 2.23; 4.45. It is clear that the conclusion of the Gospel 20.30f. also comes from this source, of which it originally was the conclusion.[2]

Now if the Evangelist dared to use this ending as the conclusion of his book, it shows not only that the σημεῖον is of fundamental importance for him, but at the same time—if he can subsume Jesus' activity, as he portrays

---

to the narrative of the feeding of the multitude, and by overlooking the different degrees of importance which the individual miracles have within the structure of the Gospel; only the miracles in chs. 5, 6, 9, 11 are roughly parallel. Anyway such obvious doublets as chs. 3/4, chs. 6/5 undermine the principle of division by seven.—Fr. Quiévreux (RevHPhrel 33 [1953], 123–165) attempts to discover Pythagorean number symbolism in the structure of John.—Dodd (297) believes that 2.1–4.42 should be taken as a unit and headed "The new Beginning".

[1] 2.1–12 also shows the positioning of the verb at the beginning of the sentence and numerous asyndeta; admittedly the text has been more heavily edited (see below).

[2] For the argument for the σημεῖα source see A. Faure, ZNTW 21 (1922), 107–112, who considers, probably rightly, that 12.37 also belonged to the source. Wellh., Schw. and Spitta, as well as Ed. Meyer (Urspr. und Anf. des Christentums I. 337) also recognised the original connection between 2.1–12 and 4.46–56.—Were the miracles of the OT chronologically ordered and numbered in Judaism? Cp. Joma 29a (Str.-B II 409f.): "R. Asi (c. 300) said: Esther is the last of all the (OT) miracles."—A. T. Olmstead, Jesus in the Light of History 1942, believes that the narrative material in John was composed before A.D. 40 in Aramaic; similarly Albright, "The Background etc." (see on p. 18), with the difference that he dates it between 60 and 70 and thinks that it existed only in the form of oral tradition.

it, under the concept of σημεῖον!—that this concept is more complex than that of the naive miracle story. Rather it is clear—and it will be made perfectly clear by the exegesis—that the concepts σημεῖα and ῥήματα (λόγοι) both qualify each other: σημεῖον is not a mere demonstration, but a spoken directive, a symbol;[1] ῥῆμα is not teaching in the sense of the communication of a set of ideas, but is the occurrence of the Word, the event of the address. 2.1–11 therefore can immediately be seen to be a symbol. Yet this raises the question how far the Evangelist has put a new interpretation on the traditional material, and whether he has brought this out by editing his source.[2]

The *Evangelist's redaction* in 2.1–12 may perhaps be responsible for the date in v. 1,[3] but not for v. 12, which must have been in the source, since it does not link up with the following section.[4] The fact that some authorities omit the μαθηταί in v. 12, while others mention them *before* the ἀδελφοί,[5] shows that they were not originally mentioned in the text; they were added later, since they were missed after (v. 2 and) v. 11. Indeed it is likely that they were not even mentioned in v. 2, but that they have replaced here the ἀδελφοί, who originally were mentioned[6] alone. For the rest, v. 9b. (καὶ οὐκ ᾔδει—τὸ

[1] Σημεῖον = "miracle", in John as elsewhere in the NT; in the LXX for אוֹת; with this meaning also in Hellenism, see Br. on 2.11 and Wörterbuch s.v.; the Greek word was borrowed by the Rabbis (סִימָן, סִימָנָא) for "miracle" "miraculous sign" (Str.-B. II 409).

For John the original meaning of "sign" is uppermost, see on 6.26. Fr. W. Young (ZNW 46 [1955] 224) believes that John is dependent on Is. 53.13 in his use of σημεῖον.

[2] For the division between the redaction and the tradition in Jn. 2.1–12 cp. K. L. Schmidt, Harnack-Ehrung 1921, 32–43; of course I cannot agree that 2.1–12 contains only "the torso of a short-story".

[3] The dating is perhaps only intended to bring out the sequence of events, as in 1.29, 35, 43; naturally the time which has elapsed must now be rather longer because of the journey. Whether the dating "on the third day", i.e. "two days later", is determined by a clear idea of the length of the journey is not known, since neither the scene of 1.19–51 nor the Cana mentioned in 2.1 can be identified for certain (see p. 93 n.3). Dodd (300) sees in τ. ἡμέρᾳ τ. τρίτῃ an allusion to the date of the resurrection.—It is possible that the Evangelist has simply added up all the previous dates, although this is quite uncertain because of the obscurity of 1.40–42 (see p. 98 n.4). If this were the case, then naturally he would not have done so in order to date 2.1–12 historically (which is in any case impossible, as the terminus a quo 1.19 is not dated), but in order to emphasise the importance of the day on which the events in 2.1–12 happened. If one counts 1.19ff. as the first day, and includes, apart from the times mentioned (1.29, 35, 43) an extra day for vv. 40–42, then one arrives at the conclusion that 2.1–12 occurred on the seventh day, i.e. on the Lord's day, the day of the epiphany (Htm., Omodeo, Hirsch).—B. W. Bacon (HThR 8 [1915], 94-120) puts 2.1ff. on the sixth day and sees in this a conscious contrast to the Dionysius epiphany, which is also put on the sixth day.—Bd., who accepts the seventh day as probable, thinks that 1.35–39 occurs on the Sabbath, so that 2.1ff. falls on a Wednesday, which according to the Talmudic prescriptions (see Str.-B. II 398f.) was the day laid down for the marriage of virgins.—Quiévreux loc. cit. (see p. 112 n.3), 131, argues that the seven days correspond to the seven days of the Creation in Gen. 1.

[4] V. 12 probably led on to 4.46–54, q.v.

[5] καὶ οἱ μαθ. αὐτοῦ is omitted by ℵ abe ff^2 al. It comes before οἱ ἀδ. H δ 371 = 1241 al. In W the order is μαθηταί, μήτηρ, ἀδελφοί.

[6] Thus Wellh. Perhaps one may quote Epist. Apost. ch. 5 (Schmidt p. 29f.) in support of this: "Then there was a marriage in Cana in Galilee. And he was invited with his mother and his brothers."—Of course the correction of "brothers" by "disciples" might well

ὕδωρ) should probably be ascribed to the Evangelist, as should the end of v. 11 (καὶ ἐφανέρωσεν), on which see below.[1]

As far as the form is concerned we have here a typical *miracle story*. Vv. 1–2 give the setting, vv. 3–5 the preparation of the miracle, told, as is proper to the genre, so as to create a certain tension; vv. 6–8 contain the miracle itself, related only indirectly, without describing the actual miraculous process, which is again true to the genre; the same applies to vv. 9–10, which form the conclusion and emphasise the παράδοξον of the miracle.

2.1-2: *The Setting.* The scene is Cana in Galilee, a place which is also frequently mentioned in Josephus.[2] Here a wedding is taking place,[3] at which Jesus' mother also is among the guests. Whether she is thought of as being temporarily or permanently resident in Cana does not matter;[4] but she must be mentioned explicitly by name, because of the role which she will presently have to play. Jesus and his disciples[5] have also been invited to the feast, but there is no need to give any particular explanation of this.[6]

---

have occurred in the σημεῖα-source, if the miracles there were linked together to form a continuous narrative.

[1] Might not οἱ μαθ. αὐτοῦ in v. 11 also be an editorial addition? Then the rest of v. 11 could be assigned to the source.

[2] Cp. Br.—Acc. to Eus., On. 116.4 there were several places of the same name in Galilee. Perhaps the addition τῆς Γαλ. is intended to distinguish this Cana from one outside Galilee. It is not of importance for the exegesis which Cana is intended; cf. Dalman, Orte und Wege 3. ed. 108–114; Str.-B. II 400; Kundsin, Topol. Überl. 15.22–25.—It is pointless to try and guess which way he went from 1.43 to 2.1; and it is amusing to read reflections on the speed of Jesus and his disciples walking, see below, n. 6.—For the question whether the location of the narrative in Cana can be explained from the history of the Christian community there, see Kundsin, loc. cit.

[3] On the Jewish marriage customs, see Str.-B. II 372–399.—Doubtless no one will any longer want to try and guess who the bridegroom was, whether Σιμὼν ὁ Κανανaῖος of Mk. 3.18 or even the Evangelist himself, the "virginal" John, who straight after the marriage left his wife. Nor is it permissible to suggest that the people at the wedding were poor people.

[4] The phrase "she was there" is common in Rabbinic usage and simply refers to her presence, see Schl.; see also on v. 12.

[5] If one takes the combination of the narratives seriously, then this refers only to the five disciples called in 1.35–51. Yet there can be no doubt that in the rest of the Gospel, where the μαθηταί are given as Jesus' followers, it refers to the traditional twelve, even though the Evangelist does not record their calling; yet in 6.67ff.; 20.24 he assumes that it has taken place. Thus it is the twelve who must be referred to here; see Cl. R. Bowen, JBL 49 (1930), 303.—The Evangelist also uses μαθ. in a wider sense, cp. 6.60, 61, 66.

[6] καλεῖν = "invite" is common, as is קָרָא. The marriage feast usually lasted seven days (Str.-B. I 517); whereas the bridal party had to last out the whole week, new guests could come and go (op. cit. 506). One cannot deduce from ἐκλήθη v. 1 that Jesus and his disciples were only invited later when the feast had already begun and that their arrival was not noticed (B. Weiss, Zn.). It is grotesque to suggest that the wine ran out earlier than had been planned, because of the "unexpected increase" in guests and because the newly arrived guests, as a result of the haste in which they had accomplished their long journey (see n. 2), were particularly thirsty (B. Weiss). Acc. to Lagrange it was Nathanael, who came from Cana (21.2), who had arranged the invitation.

2.3-5: *The Preparation of the Miracle.* When the wine runs out,[1] Jesus' mother brings it to his notice; of course she does this with the aim of getting him to perform a miracle, as can be seen from Jesus' answer v. 4, and as was also to be expected from the style of the miracle story, in which everything is related with an eye on the main point of the story and must be understood in relation to this point.[2] The purpose of the preparation is precisely to bring out the character of the miracle as παράδοξον by raising the tension. This is done here, as elsewhere,[3] by making Jesus at first refuse the request, but in such a way as to keep the expectation alive. The refusal is a rough one: "Woman, what have I to do with you?"[4] What is surprising here is the form of address, γύναι, where one expects "Mother". Even though it is not disrespectful or scornful,[5] it sets a peculiar distance between Jesus and his mother.

---

[1] ὑστερεῖν in the sense of "to be lacking" is common in late Greek; for Pap. see Preisigke, Wörterb.—However the gen. abs. ὑστερήσαντος οἴνου is undoubtedly a smoothing over of the clumsy original text (א it syr^hmg) οἶνον οὐκ εἶχον, ὅτι συνετελέσθη ὁ οἶνος τοῦ γάμου. εἶτα ... On the wine consumption at Jewish weddings, see Str.-B. II 400.

[2] There is no room here for psychological interpretations, as for example, that Mary (whose name is anyway never mentioned in John) was in the habit of sharing her difficulties and worries with her son, in the expectation that he would know what to do; how they might, for instance, be able to get new supplies from the neighbourhood (B. Weiss, Zn.), for she was embarrassed that the supplies of wine had run out so quickly as a result of the arrival of Jesus and his disciples (Zn.). But this is not so grotesque as the view that Mary was telling Jesus that they ought to go; but he replied that the hour was not yet come!—The question why it is Mary in particular who asks Jesus, can best be answered, not by wondering what particular position Mary had in the marriage-feast, but by pointing out that the narrative probably comes from circles in which a certain authority was already ascribed to the mother of the Lord as a matter of course; this is already suggested by the absence of any reference to Jesus' father. (This is true, even if the story really contains an attack on the veneration of Mary.) Thus we must dismiss the question how it could have occurred to Mary that Jesus might be able to help with a miracle.

[3] Cp. Mk. 7.27; Mt. 8.7 (to be read as a question, refusing the centurion); similarly the drawing out of the action in Jn. 4.48; Mk. 9.19ff.

[4] τί ἐμοὶ καὶ σοί; (Bl.-D. para. 299.3) is a popular formula, in the LXX frequently used for מַה־לִּי וָלָךְ, occurring often in the NT. It does not mean that one completely refuses to have anything to do with someone, but refers only to the case in question. A. Karfess (ZNTW 44 [1952/53], 257) tries to give an interpretation of τί ἐμοὶ καὶ σοί; (= Don't worry yourself about my affairs) by taking the οὔπω ἥκει ἡ ὥρα μου as a question (after H. Seeman). Most improbable!

[5] Odysseus in disguise addresses Penelope as (ὦ) γύναι (Od. 19.221), just as Oedipus addresses Jocasta (Soph. Oed. tyr. 642, 800, 1054). Further examples in Wetst. and Br., cf. Jac. Wackernagel, Über einige antike Anredeformen 1912. According to Str.-B. II 401 "Woman" (אִשָּׁה) also occurs as a form of address in Rabbinic lit.; but this is questioned by Dalman, Jesus—Jesch. 182f. The examples of ὦ γύναι in Jos. (Schl. on Mt. 15.28) are not sufficient evidence to decide the question.—It is a gross exaggeration to say that Jesus disowns his mother with this form of address (Delafosse 9–13); but it is true that this rough refusal cannot be watered down by an allegorical interpretation of Mary as the Synagogue or by any other artificial means.—According to Zahn, the "harmless remark" of the mother is a temptation for Jesus to enter upon his ministry too early and on his own initiative, which temptation he rejects with horror; Zn.'s interpretation is individualistic

Human ties and obligations in no way influence Jesus' action; the miracle worker is bound to his own law and must listen to another voice: οὔπω ἥκει ἡ ὥρα μου.[1] The preparation is concluded by v. 5: the mother has understood her son; all she can do now is to await the commands of the miracle worker. So she directs the servants to do whatever Jesus tells them.[2]

2.6-8: The Miracle. A description of the scene is necessary for what is to come. Six large water jars of enormous capacity are standing ready.[3] Since this would seem strange to anyone unfamiliar with Jewish customs, it is added that they are there for the Jewish purification rites.[4] Jesus has the jars filled up to the brim; this is done, and followed by the command: "Take it to the steward of the feast".[5] The reader knows, without being told in so many words, that the water—and in such

---

and moralistic.—All one can find is the general idea that the θεῖος ἄνθρωπος is not influenced by human motives; for otherwise it would be impossible to see why, in spite of this, Jesus so shortly afterwards in fact performs the miracle; do we suppose that 2 hours later, or even 24 hours later, it was no longer a temptation? And why not? Hosk.'s remarks (188) are apposite here.

[1] Cp. Eunapius, Vita Jambl. p. 459 Didot (Weinreich, Antike Heilungswunder 46.4): Aidesios and others want to see great miracles, ὁ δὲ πρὸς αὐτούς· ἀλλ' οὐκ ἐπ' ἐμοί γε τοῦτο, ἔλεγε, ἀλλ' ὅταν καιρὸς ᾖ (cp. Jn. 7.6). In astrological belief and magic "the hour" plays an important part, cp. Juvenal, 6.597: ad primum lapidem hora sumitur ex libro. Cp. also Frz. Boll, Aus der Offenbarung Johannis 24f. With regard to the miracle the apostle Act. Thom. 73 p. 188.12ff. prays: τί ἑστήκαμεν ἀργεῖς; Ἰησοῦ κύριε, ἡ ὥρα πάρεστιν· τί ἀπαιτεῖ γενέσθαι; κέλευσον οὖν ἐκπληρωθῆναι ὃ δὴ γενέσθαι ὀφείλει. The hour of a vision is determined precisely in Herm. vis. III 1.2, 4.—The examples given by Str.-B. II 401–405, Schl. and Odeberg 271.273ff. for the belief in particular hours, have a somewhat different meaning. In the cases where it is not simply the belief in some particular time laid down by the law, it is the belief in the hour determined by God (or sometimes by the stars) for the destiny of a man. Cp. the texts quoted by G. Kittel, Probleme des paläst. Spätjudent. 169–178. This is indeed the key to the understanding of Jn. 7.30; 8.20; 12.23; 13.1; 16.21; 17.1 as well as Mk. 14.41, but not of Jn. 2.4—or at least only in the sense given to the narrative by the Evangelist himself; on this see below.—A further type of belief in hours in Hes. Theog. 754.

[2] There is of course no point in wondering how Mary comes to be giving orders to the servants in a strange house (see p. 116 n.2); rather one should admire the economy of the miracle story in its giving an indirect characterisation of Mary's attitude by this command and at the same time introducing the servants necessary for the ensuing action.

[3] Each jar contains 2–3 μετρηταί; μετρ. (in the NT only here, often in Pap.) is the name for the Attic measure which corresponds to the Hebrew בַּת. The measure is equal to nearly 40 (to be exact 39.39) litres, so that the total volume would come to 480–700 litres; see Str.-B. II 405–407.

[4] On the ἦσαν . . . κείμεναι see Bl.-D. para. 353, 1; yet in the light of א al we should probably omit κείμεναι. κατὰ κτλ. hardly refers to the purpose of the jars (although this is admittedly possible, Br.), for then τῶν Ἰουδ. would not have been put in; rather κατά here means "according to". Καθαρισμός for the Jewish purification rites as in Lk. 2.22; 5.14; The purification is the ritual washing of the hands before and after meals; see Schürer II 560–565; Str.-B. I 695–704; W. Brandt, Die jüd. Baptismen 1912.

[5] On ἀρχιτρίκλινος (steward of the feast, master of ceremonies) see Br. Wörterb.

quantities![1]—has been changed into wine. It is in accordance with the style of the miracle stories that the miraculous process itself is not described; the divine action remains a mystery.[2]

2.9-10: The Conclusion. As in other miracle stories, the greatness of what has happened is emphasised by a demonstration or acclamation by the public.[3] Yet there the παράδοξον is not brought out by a generalised phrase, but by a concrete scene: the water has been turned into the most excellent wine! The steward of the feast, who tastes the wine, asks the bridegroom why he has kept the best wine back till the guests can no longer appreciate it![4] This saying marks the end of the narrative proper: any further words would only detract from the effect.[5]

The *source* counted this as the first miracle.[6] It is easy to see why it put it at the beginning of its collection; for it is an epiphany miracle. There are no analogies with it in the old tradition of Jesus-stories, and in comparison with them it appears strange and alien to us.[7] There can be no doubt that the story has been taken over from heathen legend and ascribed to Jesus. In fact the motif of the story, the changing of the

---

[1] The enormous amount of wine is of special significance in the miracle story. Act. Thom. 120 p. 230.16ff. also speaks of μετρηταὶ οἴνου, in order to stress that it is a large quantity. The attempts to reduce the quantity (for instance that only a part of the water, as much as was necessary, was changed into wine) are simply comical, as is the assurance that Jesus would by his presence have ensured that the wine was not misused.

[2] Cp. Gesch. der synopt. Trad. 2. ed. 237, 239 = Hist. of the Syn. Trad. 221, 223; Dibelius, Formgesch. 2.ed. 88.91 = From Trad. to Gospel, 101f. Thus it would be wrong to say that the story lacks the typical vividness of miracle stories (K. L. Schmidt, op. cit. 35).

[3] Cp. Die Gesch. der synopt. Trad. 2.ed. 240f. = Hist. of the Syn. Trad. 224f.

[4] The rule spoken by the ἀρχιτρ. in v. 10 is contradictory to both modern and ancient custom. Windisch, who devoted his great learning to the subject of the "Johannine wine rule" in ZNTW 14 (1913), 248–257 could nevertheless reach no more of a conclusion than Wetst. before him, namely that poor hosts or dishonest publicans will give drunken guests bad wine. It is possible that the ἀρχιτρ. is making a rough joke about such practices; it is equally possible that the rule "has been formulated ad hoc for the purposes of the miracle" (Br.). It is too subtle to suggest that this contains a polemic against Lk. 5.39 (Omodeo, Saggio 58).

[5] The sentence καὶ οὐκ ᾔδει—ὕδωρ in v. 9 interrupts the construction; for it is not possible to take the ὡς (δὲ ἐγεύσατο) temporally in relation to ἐγεύσατο and then causally in relation to οὐκ ᾔδει. Admittedly as understood by the story the sentence may be intended to give a reason for the steward's remark and to point to the servants as impeccable witnesses. But Faure and K. L. Schmidt are probably right in taking it as an addition of the Evangelist's; the πόθεν reflects too clearly the question that will again and again be raised in respect of Jesus (7.27f.; 8.14; 9.29f.; 19.9), and the antithesis between knowing and not knowing sounds Johannine.

[6] See p. 113. ἀρχὴν is here predicative (Bl.-D. para. 292) as in Isocr. Paneg. ch. 10.38: ἀλλ' ἀρχὴν μὲν ταύτην ἐποιήσατο τῶν εὐεργεσιῶν, τροφὴν τοῖς δεομένοις εὑρεῖν (Br.).—As understood by the source the reference to the place where the miracle took place is intended to strengthen the credibility of the account; see Lohmeyer, ZNTW 27 (1928), 17f.—On the notion of σημεῖον see on 6.26.

[7] On this strange and alien quality of the story see Dibelius, Formgesch. 2.ed. 98f. = From Trad. to Gospel, 101f.; Carpenter 377 and others.

water into wine, is a typical motif of the Dionysus legend. In the legend this miracle is the miracle of the epiphany of the God, and was therefore dated on the day of the Dionysus Feast, that is on the night of the 5th to 6th of January. This relationship was still understood in the Early Church, which saw the Feast of Christ's Baptism as his epiphany and celebrated it on the 6th of January. Equally it held that the 6th of January was the date of the marriage at Cana.[1]

For the Evangelist the meaning of the story is not contained simply in the miraculous event;[2] this, or rather the narrative, is the symbol of something which occurs throughout the whole of Jesus' ministry, that is, the revelation of the δόξα of Jesus.[3] As understood by the Evangelist this is not the power of the miracle worker, but the divinity of Jesus as the Revealer, and it becomes visible for faith in the reception of χάρις and ἀλήθεια;[4] his revelation of his δόξα is nothing more nor less than his revelation of the ὄνομα of the Father (17.6). Of this the epiphany story can provide only a picture; and equally the ἐπίστευσαν εἰς αὐτὸν (οἱ μαθηταὶ αὐτοῦ), in the Evangelist's view can be no more than a symbolic representation of the faith which the Revealer arouses by his Word.[5]

The question arises how far one can carry this basic understanding

[1] Every year on the day of the Dionysus feast the temple springs in Andros and Teos were said to have poured out wine instead of water. In Elis on the eve of the feast three empty jars were set up in the temple, which were then found full of wine on the next morning.—As well as Br. ext. note on 2.12 see Arn. Meyer, Das Weihnachstfest 1913, 12ff.; Bousset, Kurios Chr. 2.ed. 62, 270–274; J. Grill II 1923, 107–119; P. Saintyves, Essai sur folklore biblique 1922, 205–229; K. Holl, Der Ursprung dcs Epiphanienfestes, SA Berlin 1917, XXIX, or in Ges. Aufs. II 1927, 123ff.; Dibelius, Formg. 2. ed. 98f. 277ff.; Carpenter 379f., C. Bonner, Amer. Journ, of Archaeol. 36 (1929), 368–375; M. P. Nilsson, Geschichte der griech. Religion I (Handb. d. Altertumswiss. V 2.1, 1941), 556f.; O. Eissfeldt, AO 40, (1941), 24.—In later Christian legend the miracle of the wine is frequently dated on Christmas night or New Year's night; cp. as well as Santyves, K. Müllenhof, Sagen, Märchen und Lieder der Herzogtümer Schleswig, Holstein und Lauenburg 4. ed. 1845, 169; Kleiner Führer für die Samlandbahn 5. ed. (after "Sagen des Preuss. Samlandes" by R. Reusch, 2. ed. 1863), 16; Joh. Künzig, Schwarzwaldsagen 1930, 211.

[2] The question whether the Evangelist believed the miracle to have been an actual historical occurence may not, it seems to me, be answered so obviously in the affirmative as usually happens; but here we may leave it on one side.

[3] It is very likely that the Evangelist could find support for his interpretation in an earlier tradition. Even according to Philo the Logos (represented by Melchisedek) gives to the souls ἀντὶ ὕδατος οἶνον (leg. all. III 82; but here ἀντί is used as in Joh. 1.16; see H. Lewy, Sobria Ebrietas 1929, 22.3), and is called the οἰνοχόος τοῦ θεοῦ (somn. II 249). See Dodd 298f.

[4] On δόξα see p. 67 n.2.

[5] If the sentence καὶ ἐφανέρωσεν κτλ. really stood in the source (see p. 115 n.1) then δόξα here referred to the power of the miracle worker (see p. 67 n.2), and πιστεύειν had the primitive meaning of belief aroused by external miracles, which it cannot have for the Evangelist if for no other reason than that the sentence, as a description of a single event, is not in any way related to the preceding section (1.35–51) or to the following one (6.68f.); moreover the faith which did not understand the miracle as σημεῖον in the sense of 6.26, would in reality be no faith at all; see also on 7.3f.

over into the interpretation of the individual details of the story. For here, as elsewhere, the Evangelist's figurative language refers not to any particular gift brought by the Saviour Jesus, but to Jesus himself as the Revealer, as is true of the images of the living water, the bread of life and the light, as well as of the shepherd and the vine; equally the wine refers not to any special gift, but to Jesus' gift as a whole, to Jesus himself as the Revealer, as he is finally visible after the completion of his work.[1] And whereas elsewhere the predicate ἀληθινόν is used to contrast Jesus' gift with some other imagined or temporary good (1.9; 6.32; 15.1), here the same contrast is achieved by setting the wine and the water over against each other. This means that it would also be wrong to attempt to give a more specific interpretation of the water; for it stands for everything that is a substitute for the revelation, everything by which man thinks he can live and which yet fails him when put to the test.[2]

---

[1] The *view that the wine specifically refers to Jesus' blood* is unlikely, for the reason that the blood of Jesus has hardly any role to play in John (only in 19.34, which however with its αἷμα καὶ ὕδωρ does not fit in well with the "wine instead of water" of 2.1–11 and I Jn. 1.7—6.51b–58 come from the editor, see ad loc.). And how should such an idea come at the beginning of a ministry which will be portrayed as a whole as a ministry through the word!—R. Eisler also thinks that the wine represents Jesus' blood (Das Rätsel des Joh-Evgs 487f.), and indeed he sees in the story a justification of the (Baptist) circles who partook of the communion with *water* instead of with wine—for which he quotes Iren. I 13,2 (Markos by his epiclesis succeeds in having the water appear as wine in the chalice). This is probably all too subtle.—Similarly Omodeo (Saggio 58) suspects that the wine miracle presupposes a eucharistic rite, in which the chalice contained water. The wine into which the water was changed for the participants was the Spirit. Yet it is not in character with the rest of the Gospel to take the wine as a figure of the *Spirit*, if the latter is understood as a specific gift of Jesus; it is correct, admittedly, inasmuch as according to 6.63 Jesus' ῥήματα are πνεῦμα and ζωή. But then one could just as well say that the wine represents the *life*; in other words we must avoid trying to give a specific interpretation. Wik., Dodd and Barr, also reject a specific interpretation of the wine in terms of the blood of Jesus.—J. Jeremias, Jesus als Weltvollender 1930, 28f., maintains that the wine is the *symbol of the time of salvation*. Yet more proof must be given for this symbolic language than references which speak of the drinking of wine in the time of salvation (Gen. 49.11f., Mk. 14.25; and the reference to Num. 13.23f. is totally inapposite). The wine of the marriage at Cana does not come from the OT expectation of salvation but from the Dionysus cult in Syria (see pp. 118f. and, for the significance of the vine in the Syr. cult: H. Schlier, Relg. Unters. 54f.).—Above all it would be quite improper to seek an interpretation in the Jewish Christian idea of the Messianic banquet or marriage feast (Str.- B. I 517), for no emphasis is put on the marriage as such in 2.1–11, and there is no mention of the guests' enjoyment of the feast, nor of the impression made on them by the miracle.

[2] It would be tempting to take the water of the jars of purification as referring specifically to the Jewish religion; cp. Dodd and Barr., who take the water as referring to Jewish ritualism. But just as the "Jews" represent the world in general for John, so too their religion stands for all false or temporary salvation beliefs; cp. on 4.21. Moreover in John there is hardly any trace of an attack on the Jewish law (see p. 96 n.5) If Loisy was right in suggesting that the 6 jars portray the "nombre imparfait" then Jesus ought to have conjured up another! The same sort of argument could be brought against Carpenter [378] Howard [186f.], and others who see in the 6 jars the 6 days of the week of the world, which is

But the Evangelist will doubtless have attached particular significance to the part of the story where Jesus at first refuses the request that he should perform a miracle, because his action is determined by his "hour". For the Evangelist this "hour" is the hour of the passion,[1] which is however the hour of the δοξασθῆναι of Jesus. The story then will teach us that the help for all man's perplexity is to be found in the miracle of the revelation; but the event of the revelation is independent of human desires and cannot be forcibly brought about by man's supplication;[2] it comes to pass where and how God wills, and then it surpasses all human expectation. Perhaps v. 10 may also be interpreted in this sense, namely, that the divine action runs contrary to all human rules. In any case the Evangelist's addition in v. 9,[3] with its οὐκ ᾔδει πόθεν ἐστίν, represents the blindness of men confronted by the Revealer. The steward of the feast does not know where the wine has come from, just as the Jews do not know where Jesus comes from, even if they imagine that they do (7. 27f.; cp. 8.14); only the servants who drew the water know this, just as only the faith which receives of his fulness knows him.[4]

V. 12 in the source led on to another narrative.[5] It can hardly be that it tells of a change of abode, but simply of a journey made by Jesus and his followers to Capernaum, which seems to have been thought of as his permanent home.[6]

---

followed by the 7th day, (the day of salvation). On the other hand it is clear that he is fighting against Gnosticism. Yet even if this confronts him in the Baptists above all, it would be absurd to see in the Jewish water of purification a representation of the water baptism of John, particularly since the ἐν ὕδατι 1.21, 26, 31 should be ascribed to the editor (see ad loc.).—Hosk. thinks that ἀντλήσατε v. 8 is an allusion to the fact that Jesus is the spring of living water (4.10–15), since ἀντλεῖν (acc. to Westcott) means to draw water from a spring; But cp. Theocr. 10.13: ἀντλ. ἐκ πίθω.

[1] 7.30; 8.20; 12.23, 27; 13.1; 16.31; 17.1. Cf. also on the ἕως ἄρτι v. 10: 10.24; 16.24. Cp. H.v.d. Bussche, NThRev 75 (1953), 1009–1019.

[2] It can hardly be right to take Mary as an alleg. representation of Judaism or of the expectant Jewish community (in 19.26f. she clearly does represent Jewish Christianity); for she does not ask Jesus to give a proof of his authority by the miracle; and if she did, then Jesus would hardly have been able to agree to the request so shortly afterwards.

[3] See above p. 118 n.5.

[4] One may hardly extend the allegory any further, see p. 120 nn. 1, 2 and n. 2 above; Br., Bd., Carpenter 377f.—The parallelism between 2.1–11 and 7.1–10 is obvious: in both Jesus is challenged to show his power, in ch. 2 by his mother, in ch. 7 by his brothers; in both this is rejected with a reference to his ὥρα (2.4) or καιρός (7.6); and in neither case is any explanation given when he afterwards proceeds to comply with the request. Since 7.1–10 shows more signs of having been worked over by the Evangelist it is possible that he introduced this parallelism himself. But it is more likely that in 7.1–10 he used a piece of tradition which was originally the introduction to a miracle story.

[5] See p. 114. The Evangelist has perhaps added the οὐ πολλὰς ἡμέρας (Wellh.), in order to prepare the way for the appearance of Jesus in Jerusalem which is narrated in 2.13ff.

[6] Μετὰ τοῦτο (2.12; 11.7, 11; 19.28) and μετὰ ταῦτα (3.22; 5.1, 14; 6.1; 7.1; 19.38; 21.1) are used interchangeably in John as transitional phrases (cp. 4.43; 20.26). It is pure

B. 2.13–22: The Cleansing of the Temple

The story of the epiphany is now followed by the story which portrays the end and fulfilment of the revelation.[1] Clearly the Evangelist has taken the story of the cleansing of the temple from the tradition, for the same story is also to be found in Mk. 11.15–17 parr. Yet he has not taken it from the Synoptics, nor from oral tradition, but from a literary source,[2] as can be seen from the fact that vv. 21f. are a reflexion of the Evangelist's which he himself has added or inserted; this literary source, however, was almost certainly related to the Synoptic accounts. The narrative used by the Evangelist differed from that of the Synoptics in that a short dispute over the question of Jesus' authority had been added to the act of the cleansing of the temple, based on the motif found in Mk. 13.2; 14.58 etc. of the prophecy of the destruction of the temple. It is easy to see that this saying and the story of the cleansing of the temple would have attracted one another, resulting in the dramatic account we have here.—The editorial introduction in v. 13 is obviously the Evangelist's, as are perhaps some smaller additions in vv. 15f. and certainly the reflection in vv. 20–21; vv. 17 and 22 are the work either of the Evangelist or of the ecclesiastical redaction. There was no need for an editorial conclusion since it is provided for by the transition in vv. 23–25.

The editorial introduction **v. 13** explains the appearance of Jesus in Jerusalem in a way typical of the Evangelist;[3] the occasion for the

---

fantasy for Zn. to suggest that μετὰ τοῦτο = "very shortly afterwards" as opposed to μετὰ ταῦτα = "later". Both expressions simply refer to a certain lapse of time. καταβαίνειν, because of Capernaum's lower position by the lake (see Schl.). Schl. gives Rabbinic parallels for αὐτὸς καὶ . . . καὶ . . .; but of course this is not a specifically Rabbinic usage, but a primitive oriental manner of speech which is also to be found in the OT. On Καφαρναούμ see Dalman, O. und W. 3. ed. 142ff.; Str.-B. I 159f.—ἔμεινεν is perhaps to be preferred to the better attested ἔμειναν.

[1] See p. 113.—R. Eisler, Das Rätsel des JohEvgs 358, believes that the Evangelist put the story of the cleansing of the temple here in order "to obscure the connection between this revolutionary attack on the powers of the temple authorities and Jesus' condemnation by the Romans".

[2] The source is Semitic in tone; cp. beginnings of the sentences v. 14, 18, 19.; typical too the "sitting" of the dealers (see Schl.); that Jesus drives them out with a rope and not with a stick shows a knowledge of the situation; for "sticks and weapons were not carried in the courts of the temple" (Schl.). Above all the question of authority (v. 18) is typically Jewish (see Schl.).

[3] We can see here particularly clearly that the Johannine journeys to the festivals are editorial explanations; for the story is put here only because of its symbolic importance. The note in 6.4 that the Passover was near is only put in for reasons of composition, namely to prepare for Jesus' journey to Jerusalem, which follows shortly afterwards (5.1). Nor can one deny the symbolic significance of the feasts mentioned in 7.2 (σκηνοπηγία); 10.22 (ἐγκαίνια). The Passover in 11.55 is the traditional Passover of the passion (12.1; 13.1). On the disappearance of Galilee as the scene where the greater part of Jesus' ministry took place and the substitution of Jerusalem, see Hosk. 63f. Jerusalem and the Temple represent the power against which the Johannine Jesus fights—as is the case with the OT prophets.

journey up to Jerusalem is a festival,[1] in this case the festival of the Passover,[2] which was mentioned in the tradition as the date of the events in the story. We are not actually told that Jesus was accompanied by his disciples, although they are naturally thought of as witnesses.[3] While the Synoptic account, which clearly did not have non-Jewish readers in mind, only relates Jesus' action in the temple, the source used here first describes the situation, **v. 14:** Jesus finds dealers in animals[4] and money-changers[5] in the temple.[6] No account is given of the impression this made on Jesus, nor are we told explicitly of his judgement on them; rather in **v. 15** we are told what he does, that he makes a whip[7] out of cords and clears the temple of the business which is being conducted there.[8]

While in the Synoptics the saying of Jesus which interprets his action has been given little importance,[9] here a similar reproach is closely bound into the story, **v. 16.** In place of the simple statement of fact (Mk. 11.17 parr.) we have the imperative, "Take these things away! You must not make my Father's house into a house of trade!"—a statement which very much meets the situation, whereas in the Synoptics

---

[1] ἀναβαίνειν is traditionally used of the journey to Jerusalem, see III Macc. 3.16; Mk. 10.32f., Acts 8.5; 11.2; Gal. 2.1 etc., Schl., Spr. und H. 36f. and on Mt. 20.17.

[2] On τὸ π. τῶν Ἰουδ. see p. 86 n. 2. On the feast of the Passover: Str.-B. IV 41–76; G. F. Moore II 41f.; Klostermann on Mk. 14.1 (Handb. zum NT).

[3] They do not appear again till 3.22; for the mention of them in 2.17, 22 is parenthetical, although it also shows that they are presupposed as witnesses.

[4] Instead of πωλοῦντες and ἀγοράζοντες as in Mk. 11.15, in Jn. 2.14 only the πωλοῦντες are mentioned, and their wares are given as oxen, sheep and pigeons, whereas in Mk. only pigeons are mentioned. On the business done in the temple area with sacrificial animals, see Str.-B. I 850–852.

[5] κερματιστής is otherwise not attested; from κέρμα=small coin (v. 15).

[6] Naturally in the outer forecourt; on the topography see Schürer II 342—345; Klostermann on Mk. 11.11 (Hdb. zum NT).

[7] This detail is missing in the Synoptics.—φραγέλλιον is a borrowed Latin word (flagellum) which has also found its way into the Mischna; the verb in Mk. 15.15; Mt. 27.26. Cp. Bl.-D. para 5, 1b; 21, 2.—σχοινίον originally a rope plaited out of reeds, but then often simply=rope, cord, string, see Preisigke, Wörterb.

[8] ἐξέβαλεν as in Mk. 11.15; also in Jn. 6.37; 9.34; 12.31.—τά τε πρόβατα καὶ τοὺς βόας is a poor apposition to πάντας; it is clearly an editorial addition (perhaps wholly secondary), particularly as the correlative τε-καὶ does not occur in the Gospel or the Epistles of John (only a forward pointing τε 4.42; 6.18). This raises the question whether all the rest of v. 15 is not also a secondary addition, based on Mk. 11.15 or Mt. 21.12; the same question can be asked about the dative object τοῖς τὰ περ. πωλοῦσιν at the beinning of v. 16. That this might be the case is suggested by the Synopt. κολλυβισταί in v. 15 instead of the κερματ. of v. 14 (or was this merely to avoid the clash between τῶν κερματιστῶν . . . τὰ κέρματα?); further by the fact that Jesus' saying in v. 16 is directed not only to the pigeon sellers but to the πάντες of v. 15a.—B's, and Origen's reading of τὰ κέρματα instead of the non-Attic τὸ κέρμα of other authorities is perhaps a correction. It is an unimportant variant, as is B's ἀνέστρεψεν instead of ἀνέτρεψεν.

[9] Mk. 11.17 is surely an accretion to the original narrative, see Gesch. der synopt. Trad. 2. ed. 36=Hist. of the Syn. Trad. 36.

Jesus is made like a Scribe to reflect on the Scriptural significance of his action.[1]

The account is interrupted in **v. 17** by a note of the Evangelist or of the editor.[2] Jesus' words remind the disciples of the saying in Ps. 69.10.[3] Clearly what is meant here is the same as in v. 22 and in 12.16: they later realised that this event was the fulfilment of the saying in the psalm. And yet the meaning can scarcely be that Jesus' action was an expression of his consuming zeal (i.e. that καταφάγεσθαι is taken to refer to his consuming emotions).[4] Rather the Evangelist (or the Editor) is looking forward to what is to come—or alternatively at the whole of Jesus' ministry—and he means that Jesus' zeal will lead him to his death.[5]

In reply to Jesus' attack **v. 18** the "Jews" question him about his authority, just as the ἀρχιερεῖς and γραμματεῖς do in Mk. 11.27;[6] thus they make their appearance here as the authorities.[7] They ask for an authorisation which will show the lawfulness of his action.[8] The Evan-

---

[1] From the fact that Jesus' words in John are better adapted to the situation we can only infer that the narrator was skilled at his task, and not that his account is historically more faithful (R. Eisler, Ἰησ. βασ. II 499ff. draws different conclusions).—Instead of ὁ οἶκός μου Mk. 11.17, which is taken from Is. 56.7 (cp. Jer. 7.11), in John we have ὁ οἶκος τοῦ πατρός μου, which need not of course be a Johannine correction; for Jesus does not speak of God as "my Father" for the first time in John (cp. Mt. 7.21; 10.32f.; 11.27; Lk. 2.49 etc.).—It is customary to compare Jn. 2.16 with Zech. 14.21: καὶ οὐκ ἔσται Χαναναῖος (=dealer) ἔτι ἐν τῷ οἴκῳ κυρίου παντοκράτορος ἐν τῇ ἡμέρᾳ ἐκείνῃ. However the text does not itself suggest such an allusion; as v. 17 shows, the Evangelist felt himself reminded of another passage in the OT; if, that is, these verses should not perhaps be ascribed to the redaction, see p. 417 n.5.

[2] V. 18 with its οὖν follows on directly from v. 16, and v. 17 is a reflection, as are v. 22; 12.16, which clearly come from the Evangelist's pen.

[3] The quotation agrees word for word with the LXX. On the Hellen. future φάγομαι see Bl.-D para 74, 2. The variant κατέφαγεν (in John and LXX) is at least for John a correction; if he, in fact, read κατέφαγεν in the LXX, then his turning it into a future is characteristic of the understanding of the Psalms as prophecies.—γεγραμμένον ἐστίν (cp. 6.31, 45; 10.34; 12.14, 16) like γέγραπται (cf. 8.17) corresponds to the Rabbinic (דְּ)כְתִיב see Schl. on Mt. 2.5; Bacher, Die exeg. Terminologie der jüd. Trad.-Lit. II 1905, 90f.

[4] For the use of καταφάγεσθαι to refer to the emotions see Hom. Il. 6, 202: ὃν θυμὸν κατέδων. Aristoph. Vesp. 286f. μηδ' οὕτως σεαυτὸν ἔσθιε μηδ' ἀγανάκτει.

[5] This corresponds to the use of Ps. 69 in the Early Christian proofs from prophecy; cp. Rom. 15.3, where the second half of the verse is quoted.

[6] ἀποκρίνεσθαι as often="make a rejoinder".

[7] Of course the Evangelist will have understood οἱ Ἰουδ. here as elsewhere; but it is unnecessary to suppose that he substituted this subject for another. For in Christianity the "Jews" must have been thought of more and more as a united opposition; cp. the usage of Acts.

[8] The ὅτι is not elliptical, in the sense that one would have to complete: "we ask thus (because you do this)" (Bl.-D. para 456, 2). Rather the ὅτι depends quite correctly on (τί) σημεῖον (δεικνύεις); and the meaning of the question is brought out by the pregnant use of ποιεῖν: "What kind of sign can you show as a proof that you are doing this *lawfully* (or alternatively that you are *allowed* to do this)?" Of course one can give a more general translation of σημεῖον: "sign by which we shall know that...." But there can be no question that a part of the sentence has been suppressed, as in 7.35; 8.22; 11.47.

gelist will certainly have taken the σημεῖον asked for here, as in 6.30, to be a miracle which would prove his authority; as will the source, which makes Jesus answer by the announcement of a miracle—even if it is of a different kind to that expected by the questioners. The question therefore is a parallel to Mk. 8.11; Mt. 12.38=Lk. 11.16,[1] and it is put from a typically Jewish standpoint,[2] which admittedly in this case is also the natural human point of view: unbelief asks for a sign so that it can dare to believe, as is clearly expressed in 6.30.

This question, which was probably put to the historical Jesus more than once and was rejected by him, is also rejected here, but in such a way that the question receives an answer which formally meets its demands. **V. 19**: the destruction of the temple and the building of a new temple will be the σημεῖον, the eschatological catastrophe which brings judgement and salvation—salvation naturally only for those who believe. Jesus' reply means therefore that whoever asks for a σημεῖον will receive a σημεῖον—but not until it is too late.[3] Jesus refuses to give a sign in proof of his authority, such as would enable men to recognise him without risk, without committing themselves to him. Yet the prophecy has a characteristic form; its first part is cast in the ironic imperative of prophetic style,[4] "Destroy this house!"[5] If on the one hand this indirectly implies that the judgement on the temple is the consequence of the failure of the Jews to believe in Jesus, it also looks forward to the future and foretells that the appearance of the eschatological salvation, represented by the new temple, will be nothing more nor less than the final completion and fulfilment of the eschatological event which began with Jesus' mission. "I will (re-)build it in three days!" It is then the

---

[1] While the content of the question is parallel to that of Mk. 11.27, there is, on the other hand, no literary parallel here; thus there is no need to suppose that the narrator had made the connection between Mk. 11.27 and 11.15–17, which is so much favoured by modern exegesis.

[2] Cp. I Cor. 1.22. That a prophet must prove his authority by an אוֹת and מוֹפֵת see Str.-B. II 480; I 726f.

[3] This also seems to be the meaning of the saying about the sign of Jonas in the Lucan version, Lk. 11.29; see Gesch. der synopt. Trad. 2. ed. 124,=Hist. of the Syn. Trad. 118.

[4] Cp. Am. 4.4: "Go to Bethel and transgress!
to Gilgal and multiply transgression!"
Is. 8.9f.: "Gird youselves and be dismayed . . .
Take counsel together—it will come to nought.
Say a word—it will not stand."

Jer. 7.21; Mt. 23.32.—One may hardly say that the imperative here is equal to a concessive clause (Bl.-D. para 387, 2), see J. Jeremias, Jesus als Weltvollender 43, 3; Dodd (302, 1) and Barr.

[5] λύειν (as καταλύειν Mk. 13. 2; 14. 58; 15. 29; Acts 6. 14) is, like ἐγείρειν, often used of the destruction and construction of buildings, see Br. Wörterb. and for ἐγ. Preisigke. Wörterb.

judgement and the onset of the salvation after three days which will be the σημεῖον of his authority.[1]

Whereas in the source this marked the end of the story the Evangelist has added to it in **vv. 20-21** an interpretation of Jesus' saying as a prophecy of his death and resurrection.[2] He leads into this with the

---

[1] Thus the source had linked to the story of the cleansing of the temple the saying, which also occurs in Mk. 13.2 and Acts 6.14 simply as the threat of the *destruction of the temple*, and combined it with the prophecy of the *rebuilding of the temple* in three days Mk. 14.58 (or Mt. 26.61); 15.29. It is scarcely possible now to come to any decision about the original form of the saying, or to decide to what extent it goes back to Jesus himself. In any case it is an old saying, which was early found to be difficult to understand and was subjected to different interpretations. Whereas Mk. (14.58) describes the new temple as ἄλλον ἀχειροποίητον, and clearly takes this to mean the Christian community, Mt. (26.61) has retained the—certainly original—identity of the old and the new temple, but has by his δύναμαι καταλῦσαι . . . καὶ . . . οἰκοδομῆσαι made the prophecy into a mere statement of possibility. John's source (2.19) has also retained the identity τοῦτον τὸν ναὸν . . . αὐτόν, but unlike Mt. has allowed the saying to retain its character as an eschatological prophecy. Thus the form which we have in John ought to be relatively original (cp. A. Chiapelli, Estratti Rivista Bilychensis II Ser., No. 117, Rome 1923 as reported by H. Koch, Theol. Lit-Zeitg. 1924, 538f.) The *age* and perhaps also the *originality* of the saying are confirmed by its intelligibility within the context of the apocalyptic prophecies of Judaism. Just as the destruction of the temple had already been prophesied in Mic. 3.12, Jer. 26.(33) 6, 18, so it seems that similar voices were heard in Jesus' age (cp. jer. Joma 43c in Str.-B. I 1045 and the appearance of Jesus, son of Ananias in the reign of Albinus, Jos. bell. VI 300ff. cp. 295). In any case there were ancient prophecies of the rebuilding of Jerusalem and the temple in the age of salvation (apart from Ezek. 40–44; Hag. 2. 7–9; Zech. 2.5–9; cp. Tobit 13.15f.; 14.5), which were revived before the destruction of Jerusalem in 70 (Str.-B. I 1004f.), and had already begun to rouse men's hopes (Eth. Enoch 90.28f., see Bousset, Rel. des Jdt. 8 239; Str.-B. IV 928f.; A. v. Gall, Βασιλεία τοῦ Θεοῦ 1926, 359f.), even as the prayer of Schemone Esre 14 for the restoration of Jerusalem and the temple has its precursor in Ecclus. 36.18f. (see J. Jeremias, Jesus als Weltvollender, 1930, 38f. who also cites Jos. ant. XVIII 85–87). What is surprising in the saying of Jesus is the mention of the "three days"; it is not found in parallel Jewish prophecies, nor does it belong, as does for example "three and a half" (Dan. 7.25; 12.7; Rev. 11.9, 11 etc.), to the significant apocalyptic dates. Nevertheless the Rabbis, following Hos. 6.2, dated the resurrection of the dead on the third day after the end of the world (Str.-B. I 747), and some such dating must be supposed for the saying of Jesus, unless one wants to take the "three days" as referring generally to a short time. On the other hand, if one assumes that the "three days" originally referred to Jesus' resurrection, then the saying is a Christian vaticinium ex eventu (so G. Hölscher, Theol. Blätter 12 [1933], 193). Then, of course, the old temple could only refer to the Jewish worshipping community, and correspondingly the new temple would refer to the Christian community. However this is most improbable; for we would then expect not ἐν τρισὶ ἡμέραις i.e. "in the course of three days" (so too Mk. 15.29 par.; similarly διὰ τριῶν ἡμ. Mk. 14.58 par.), but μετὰ τρεῖς ἡμ. (Mk. 8.31; 9.31; 10.34; Mt. 27.63) or alternatively τ. τρίτῃ ἡμ. (I Cor. 15.4; Mt. 16.21 etc.). Further it would be hard to understand the embarrassment of the tradition which traces the saying of Mk. 14.57 (Mt. 26.60), as in Acts 6.13f., back to "false witnesses". Moreover Jn. 2.21 shows that the interpretation of the saying to refer to Jesus' death and resurrection is secondary. Cp. on the whole question: Gesch. der synopt. Trad. 2. ed. 126f. = ET.120f.; M. Goguel, La vie de Jésus 1932, 399ff. 491ff.

[2] It is clear that the verses are a secondary interpretation; the temple referred to in v. 19 is the real temple in Jerusalem, as is shown both by the variants of the saying and by the (τὸν ναὸν) τοῦτον. The suggestion that at the word τοῦτον Jesus pointed to his body is an extraordinary way of getting out of the predicament! The attempt to show that τοῦτον

question of the "Jews", who crassly misunderstand what Jesus has said.[1] Judging κατὰ σάρκα, (8.15) they understand the miracle of the rebuilding of the temple as a miracle in the most trivial sense (as is not unknown in fairy tales).[2] The building of the temple lasted 46 years,[3] and Jesus wants to rebuild it in three days.[4] By contrast with this absurd interpretation of the saying, its true meaning is given in v. 21: Jesus spoke of himself, the "temple" refers to his body;[5] that is, the saying is about his death and resurrection.[6] **V. 22** adds that the disciples did not realise that

---

is a word which has strayed from another context, and thus to omit it (Merx: it is missing in syr[s]), is fruitless; for it breaks down over the αὐτόν, which can refer back only to τ. ν. τοῦτον. This interpretation would require an ἄλλον (as in Mk. 14.58) instead of the ἀυτον. Cp. Wendt I 62f.; II 28f.—Not only the use of the device of the misunderstanding (see next note), but also the typical ἐκεῖνος (see p. 48 n.3) and the formula-like (ἐκεῖνος) δὲ ἔλεγεν περί cp. 7.39; 11.13 shows that the interpretation comes from the Evangelist; Ph. Vielhauer, Oikodome (Diss. Heidelberg 1939), 65–67, suspects, probably rightly, that the actual formulation of v. 19, (which comes from the source) is the work of the Evangelist, who has substituted the ambiguous ἐγείρειν for an original οἰκοδομεῖν. M. E. Boismard (RB 57 [1950]) raises the question whether τοῦ ναοῦ is not a secondary gloss.

[1] The device of the misunderstanding occurs again and again throughout the Gospel: 2.20; 3.3f.; 4.10ff., 32f.; 6.32ff.; 7.34ff.; 14.4f., 7ff., 22ff.; 16. 17f.—The device is taken from Hellenistic revelation literature, as it is found for example in C. Herm. 13; Hermas vis. IV 1.4f.; sim. IX 9.2; cp. Reitzenstein, Poimandres 246; Dibelius on Hermas in Handb. zum NT; and earlier still W. Wrede, Das Messiasgeheimnis 1901, 199.—If the peculiar combination of Jewish and Hellenistic pagan motives in John should seem surprising, then at least we have an undeniable analogy in the Shepherd of Hermas.

[2] Cp. for example in "Märchen der Weltliteratur", published by Diederichs, Jena: Neugriechische Märchen 43; Nordische Märchen II 293.

[3] On the temporal dative see Bl.-D. para 201.—According to Jos. ant. XV 380 the building of the temple was begun in the 18th year of Herod's reign, i.e. 20/19 B.C. The final completion of the temple is put at 63 A.D. (Schürer I 369; Str.-B. II 411f.). There is nothing to be gained for the exegesis of Jn. 2.20 by pondering the question whether the Evangelist was not fully informed about the length of time spent on the building of the temple, or whether he regarded a stage reached before 63 as the completion on the building (perhaps because of a pause in construction); nor from the dating of the Passover of 2.23 in the year 27, which is in fact possible (G. Hölscher, SA Heidelberg 1939/40, III 26). It is doubtful whether one can infer from 8.57 that the Evangelist put Jesus' age at 46, and thus concluded that building of the temple lasted 46 years. Even more questionable is the allegorisation of the calculation: Jesus' life corresponds to the seven year-weeks of Dan. 9.24; his three and a half year ministry begins in the second half-week of the 46th year, so that he was nearly 50 when he died (Loisy). On the interpretation of Augustine and others, see Carpenter 370f.

[4] The reply only deals with the ἐν τρ. ἡμ.; so it is reading too much into it to find the sentence characteristic of the Jewish stand-point (Schl.): the Jews, when they thought of the temple, thought more of its splendour and greatness than of God's presence there.

[5] τοῦ σώματος is either an appositional or explicative genitive.

[6] The basis of the interpretation of the saying (cp. Mt. 12.40) is clearly the "three days", which in the early Christian tradition refer to the lapse of time between the death and resurrection of Jesus (on the different formulations cf. e.g. Klostermann on Mk 8.31); also the ambiguous ἐγερῶ (taken by the Evangelist in the sense stressed in 10.17f?). It is possible, too, that the interpretation was made easier by the fact that "temple" and "house" were already in common use as figurative expressions for the "body". On the other hand such metaphors in I Cor. 6.19; II Cor. 6.16; Barn. 16.8 etc., are influenced by the notion

this was[1] the meaning until after the resurrection,[2] with the result that their faith received a double support in the Scriptures and the word of Jesus. In this the Evangelist presupposes the Christian proof from prophecy of the death and resurrection of Jesus, whether he thought of the γραφή as the whole of the OT or as a particular proof-text.[3]

If in the source the combination of the cleansing of the temple with the prophecy had its unity in the notion that the cleansing of the temple, desecrated by the Jews, was a prelude to the reconstruction of the sanctuary, which has been destroyed by the guilt of the Jews, the Evangelist gives the story a new meaning: Jesus is himself the temple which the Jews will destroy, and who will shortly afterwards rise up anew. In this way he gives the old eschatology a new meaning, which will be found throughout the rest of the Gospel. The completion of the eschatological event is not to be awaited at some time in the future; it is taking place even now in the life and destiny of Jesus. And the Jews themselves, in the blindness of their unbelief, have become instruments of the revelation-event. They themselves must carry out the command, "Destroy this Temple!" which brings down judgement on their own persons, just as 8.28 contains the prophecy that they will "exalt" the Son of Man.—The unity between the prophecy and the cleansing of the temple, therefore, is now grounded in a totally different idea. In the narrative of the cleansing of the temple there is no indication that we should equate the temple with Jesus' body; rather Jesus' action is an attack on the "Jews" and their sanctuary. The action of Jesus represents and portrays the struggle between the revelation and the world, and this struggle is subject to the prophecy in v. 19, which in turn is to be understood in the light of v. 21. That is to say, the struggle in the last resort

---

of the body as a dwelling-place (for the indwelling spirit), which is foreign to Jn. 2.21. The Rabbinic practice of referring to the body as a small city quite clearly provides no parallel (Str.-B. II 412). Rather we find parallels in the Mandaean use of "building", "palace", "house" for the human body; see H. Schlier, Christus und die Kirche im Epheserbrief 1930, 50. It is not possible that σῶμα should refer to the community in a Pauline sense (Str.; O. Cullmann, Urchristentum u. Gottesdienst 1944, 46–49), since the object of λύειν and ἐγείρειν must be one and the same.

[1] Burney (108) objects for no good reason to the imperf. ἔλεγεν v. 22, where he thinks a pluperfect (or εἶπεν) is demanded; the Aram. אמר הוא has been mistaken for an imperf. Against this Torrey 328f.; Colwell 107f. Black (254) thinks that the ἔλεγεν should be taken as a pluperf.

[2] V. 22, like v. 17, is an editorial addition; see p. 122. W. Wrede, Das Messiasgeheimnis, 183f. 195 points out that in a saying like this we find a reflection of the awareness of the community that they were only gradually—and only since the resurrection—coming to a specifically Christian knowledge of Jesus. The Evangelist gives the theological justification of this, 14.26; 16.14.

[3] The expression is as general as 20.9 and as κατὰ τὰς γραφάς in I Cor. 15.3. It is not possible to guess what passages the Evangelist may have had in mind. The type of proof from Scripture given in early Christianity can be seen in Acts 2.24ff.; 13.34ff.

revolves about the person of Jesus, who though seemingly vanquished, yet gains the victory.[1]

Thus by setting the picture of the τέλος alongside that of the ἀρχή, the Evangelist gives us a portrayal of the meaning and fate of the revelation, and consequently of the fate of the world: in Jesus God is present, pouring out his fulness on man in his perplexity; and in him faith sees the glory of the Revealer. The world, however, has to face the attack of the revelation. It demonstrates its unbelief by autocratically demanding from the Revealer a proof of his authority. He will indeed prove his authority, but this proof is for the world the judgement which in its blindness it calls down on itself. Thus in these two symbolic narratives motifs are announced which will run through the whole of the Gospel.

[1] For the interpretation of the temple which Jesus will build, see M. Simon, Aux sources de la tradition Chrétienne 1950, 253f.; Dodd 301f.—O. Cullmann, JBL 74 (1955), 222f., suspects that the story contains an attack on the Jewish temple cult.

I. 2.23–4.42: The Encounter with the Revealer

A. 2.23–3.36: Jesus and the Teacher of Israel[1]

a) Introduction: 2.23–25

Although the arrangement of the material in the Gospel has been dictated by the particular theological interests of the Evangelist, he nevertheless gives the Gospel the appearance of an historical narrative. Just as ch. 2 is connected chronologically with ch. 1, so here the actual account of Jesus' revelatory work, which comes after the symbolic prelude, is made to follow the second story of the prelude without any noticeable break. The time and place of 2.13–22 also set the scene for 3.1ff., and this setting is sketched in the connecting verses 2.23–25. It is obvious that these verses are an editorial addition, made by the Evangelist.[3] They indicate a certain openness in Jesus' audience, and are thus designed to bring out clearly the offence of the revelation, for which a reasonable human openness is in no way an adequate preparation. Thus 2.23–25 prepares the way for the paradox of rebirth, which is set out in 3.1ff.

The place and time given in **v. 23** indicate that the situation is still the same as in 2.13ff.; and the allusion to the miracles which Jesus worked during the feast[4] shows that the Evangelist is not intending to

---

[1] Cp. Bertrand Zimolong, Die Nikodemus-Perikope (Jn. 2.23–3.22) nach dem syrosinaitischen Text. Diss. Breslau 1919.

[2] Ch. 3 is connected to 2.25 simply by δέ, and Jesus is not re-introduced or even mentioned by name in 3.1f. (3.2: ἦλθεν πρὸς αὐτόν!).

[3] Editorial additions of this kind are to be found further in 4.43–45; in 7.1–13 (although here the contrast with the traditional material is not so clear); 10.19–21, 40–42; 11.55–57; 12.17–19, (37–)41–43.—Typical of the Evangelist's style is the connecting ὡς δέ, or alternatively ὡς οὖν (4.1, 40; 7.10; 18.6, which admittedly also occurs in the traditional material 6.12, 16; 11.6; on οὖν see Schweizer 89f.), further ἀυτὸς δέ (2.24) and αὐτὸς γάρ (2.25; 4.44; 6.6; αὐτοὶ γάρ 4.42, 45). On πολλοὶ ἐπίστευσαν . . . θεωροῦντες αὐτοῦ τὰ σημεῖα ἃ ἐποίει cf. 11.45: πολλοὶ . . . θεασάμενοι ὃ ἐποίησεν ἐπίστευσαν . . . On καὶ οὐ χρείαν εἶχεν ἵνα cp. 16.30; I Jn. 2.27.—Again the constantly recurring observation that many believed (7.31; 8.30; 10.42; 11.45; 12.42) is typical of the Evangelist, as is the general reference to Jesus' σημεῖα (3.2; 6.2; 7.31; 11.47; 12.37; indirectly 10.41)—'Εν τ. πάσχα, which is superfluous with ἐν τ. ἑορτῇ, might be a gloss of the ecclesiastical redaction.

[4] The impf. ἐποίει suggests that Jesus' activity as a miracle-worker was extensive. 4.45 confirms that this does, in fact, refer to miracles performed during the feast.

give an exhaustive description of the setting. He is only interested in sketching in the background for the following account.[1] The very fact that many people have been brought to faith by the miracles[2] is an indication that such faith is of doubtful value. For in reality faith should not have to rely on miracles (4.48; 20.29). This is not, of course, to say that faith aroused by miracles is false, but that such faith is only the first step towards Jesus; it has not yet seen him in his true significance, and it is therefore not yet fully established. Later the example of the healing of the blind man will be used to show how such a first step towards Jesus, if it turns into trust in him, can issue in true faith (9.35ff.). Here however **v. 24** teaches that such a turning towards Jesus, simply on account of his miracles, is suspect. Jesus does not trust himself to these believers,[3] i.e. he considers them unreliable, for he sees through them all. That this is due to his omniscience is brought out painstakingly in **v. 25.**[4]

b) The Coming of the Revealer as the κρίσις *of the World:* 3.1–21 (+3.31–36)

Ch. 3 falls into two parts of differing length and importance: 3.1–21, Jesus and Nicodemus; 3.22–30, the witness of the Baptist. This is followed by a section which in the present order of the text still belongs to the speech of the Baptist, but which cannot be understood if it is taken as having been spoken by him. On the contrary the sayings in 3.31–36 belong, as is demonstrated by their style and theme, to Jesus' discourse beginning at 3.11. Originally they will most likely have come after v.21.[5] The structure of the ch. as a whole is then quite simple. If for the time being we set 3.22–30 on one side as an appendix in which the μαρτυρία of the Baptist is heard again

---

[1] On πιστ. εἰς τὸ ὄνομα αὐτοῦ see p. 59 n.2.

[2] 4.45 shows that θεωροῦντες has been used instead of the pres. part. of ὁρᾶν, which becomes rare in Koine Greek (Bl.-D §101, p. 60).

[3] πιστεύειν ἑαυτόν τινι = "to trust oneself to someone" is not frequent, but is perfectly correct Greek, see Wetst. and Br.; also in Jos. ant. XII 396.—In fact, according to the best authorities, we shold read not ἑαυτόν but αὑτόν (not αὐτόν as Bl.-D. §64, 1), but this would of course have a reflexive sense. E. Stauffer's suggestion (The Background etc. 281–299) that v. 24a reflects the Messianic secret is fantastic.

[4] See p. 102 n.1.—On χρείαν ἔχειν ἵνα Bl.-D. §393, 5.—τί ἦν instead of τί ἐστιν Bl.-D. §330.—The cumbrous formulation is typical of the Evangelist (see p. 130 n.3); for this reason it is not correct to omit διὰ τὸ κτλ. v. 24 with syr^s. and to start v. 25 with καὶ ὀυ χρείαν εἶχεν or alternatively οὐ γὰρ χρ. εἶχεν (Bl.-D. §402, 1).

[5] So too J. H. Bernard and Wik.—similarly F. Warburton Lewis and J. Moffat, with the difference that they place 3.22–30 after ch. 2. H. G. C. Macgregor places 3.31–36 after 3.13, at the cost of having to place 3.14–15 after 12.32, and 3.16–21 after 12.34. Cp. Howard 125ff. 264. It would seem more reasonable to insert 3.31–36 after 3.16, and for the rest to leave the text as it is. Lagr. leaves 3.31–36 in its present place but separates it from the Baptist's speech as a "réflexion de l'Evangeliste".—Gourbillon wants to place 3.14–21 between 12.31 and 32 (acc. to Wik.).

after the Revealer's witness to himself, then the main section falls into three sub-sections, all of which are related to the theme of the coming of the Revealer as the κρίσις of the world: 1) 3.1–8, the coming of the Revealer is explained by the necessity of rebirth; 2) 3.9–21, the coming of the Revealer as the κρίσις of the world; 3) 3.31–36, the authoritative witness of the Revealer.[1]

The chapter begins with a realistically described *scene*, which, however, is never brought to a conclusion; for the dialogue between Jesus and Nicodemus, which begins in this scene, issues in a discourse by Jesus which is not related to any particular situation at all, and in which, from v. 13 onwards, the Revealer is spoken of in the third person. As far as the content of the composition is concerned, the primary element is the *discourse*. The same appears on a purely literary analysis of the passage. Its close relationship, both in form and content, to the Prologue[2] and to the discourses of the following chapters show that the Evangelist has taken it from the "revelation-discourses"[3] which he uses as a source. This is, moreover, confirmed by the exegesis of the passage which, as in the case of the Prologue, brings out the difference between the source and the explanatory additions of the Evangelist. The latter are more extensive here (as they often are later on), so that the source provides, as it were, the text for the Evangelist's sermon. The Evangelist "historicizes" the revelation-discourses by working them into his portrait of the life of Jesus. In a more primitive form the Synoptics had also woven independent logia of Jesus into their portrait of his life, sometimes by using a traditional story as the framework for such a saying, sometimes by composing a setting of their own. The same technique, in a more developed form, is to be found in John. It seems likely that he composed the Nicodemus scene himself, drawing thereby on the traditional motif of the dialogue as used in the schools, and probably using a traditional Dominical saying as well (see on 3.3). In this he has been visibly influenced by the religious literature of Hellenism, which also knows the dialogue form contained in the revelation-book. The difference between the discourse of 3.1ff. (together with the related farewell discourses) and the Synoptic discourses lies not only in its length, but also in the type of argument used. For even if the latter are in fact literary compositions, they reflect in their form and content the actual conversations of the world in which Jesus, the Rabbis and the primitive Church moved. In John one feels that one has been transported into the world of C. Herm. 13 and the Λόγος τέλειος.[4]

---

[1] P. Winter op. cit. (see p. 23 n.1) 353, 51 wants to trace 3.16, 20f., 31–36 and the basis of 4.4–42 back to the same source, which also lies behind the Prologue. He thinks that this "Israel-source" has been combined with a "Baptist-source", from which 3.23–30 and perhaps also 4.1 are taken. According to him the Evangelist has modified this in 3.26, 28, 29, 30.

[2] Ch. H. Weisse (Die Evangelienfrage 1856, 113ff.) thinks that the sections 1.1–18; 3.13–21; 31–36, 5.19–27 originally belonged together. Similarly Soltau 15; Faure, ZNTW 21 (1922), 115, 1.—The verse form is clearly not as strict as in the hymn which lies behind the Prologue.

[3] See pp. 16f.; see also Kundsin, Charakt. und Urspr. 198f.

[4] See p. 127 n.1. Cp. Wellhausen 16f.: "This is the only discussion in John with a scribe, but even here the subject under discussion is not the law and legal questions, but

The nocturnal setting and the style of the dialogue—above all Nicodemus' misunderstanding and the οὐκ οἶδας; of v. 8—give the whole passage an air of mystery. Moreover the theme of the dialogue is itself a mystery, which is developed in a three-fold sense as the mystery of rebirth, the mystery of the Son of Man, and the mystery of the witness. But above all an air of mystery lies over the whole passage, because Jesus only speaks of the Revealer in the third person and never discloses himself by an ἐγώ εἰμι-saying. His sayings in vv. 3, 5 and 11 are indeed introduced by ἀμὴν ἀμὴν λέγω σοι, which shows that he speaks with authority, but even in vv. 12ff. he does not say that he is speaking about himself. Equally in vv. 31–36 it remains obscure who the ἄνωθεν ἐρχόμενος is, whose witness is under discussion.

1) *The Mystery of Rebirth:* 3.1–8

Vv. 1f. are closely connected with the previous section,[1] and yet it is hardly probable that Nicodemus is intended to represent one of the unreliable "believers" of 2.23f.[2] Jesus' miracles have, it is true, made an impression on him also, but this does not mean that they have moved him to "faith"; they have drawn his attention to Jesus and set him asking questions. Nicodemus himself is otherwise unknown.[3] The description given of him is important, for in him Jesus is confronted by a representative of official Judaism. He is a Pharisee and a ruler[4] and, as is suggested by ὁ διδάσκαλος (v. 10), a scribe (cp. 7.50f.). This then, is the kind of man on whom Jesus' appearance has made an impression, and he comes to him by night.[5]

The words which he addresses to Jesus have the form of a simple statement, but in fact they contain a question, as is shown by Jesus'

---

something which is foreign to the Jews. One can recognise in Nicodemus a shadow of the scribe in Mk. 12.28ff., who is not far from the Kingdom of God and yet does not belong to it . . ."

[1] See p. 130 n.2.

[2] Calvin: nunc in persona Nicodemi spectandum nobis evangelista proponit, quam fluxa et caduca fuerit eorum fides, qui miraculis commoti Christo repente nomen dederant. —But if his coming to Jesus bears witness to his seriousness of purpose, his later conduct (7.50f., 19.39) also bears witness to his faithfulness. Thus it is not correct exegetically to take Nicodemus as the type of the admirer as opposed to the disciple (Kierkegaard, Training in Christianity, 1941, 240ff.).

[3] ἄνθρωπος = τις, as in 1.6; 5.5 etc.; ἐκ τ. Φαρ. (which is the usual way of describing someone's membership of a group or class) is attributive to ἄνθρ. here and should not be taken with ἦν.—On ὄνομα αὐτῷ see p. 48 n.3; ℵ* reads Νικόδημος ὀνόματι—The name, which was common among the Greeks, also occurs frequently of Jews, see Br., Schl., Str.-B. II 413–419. Nicodemus appears in John again in 7.50; 19.39, see previous note.

[4] The title ἄρχων refers here, as in 7.26, 48; 12.42 and in Lk. and Acts, to a member of the Sanhedrin; it is also found in Jos. and other Jewish literature, but it is not always possible to determine the meaning exactly; see Schürer II 251f.; Schl. on Mt. 9.18.

[5] There is no indication that his coming by night was occasioned by his "fear of the Jews" (19.38). It is more likely that this is intended to show his great zeal, in the same way as nocturnal study is recommended to the Rabbis (Str.-B II 420). But above all it allows the Evangelist to fulfil his intention of creating an air of mystery.

reply. It would be wrong to give a psychological or individual interpretation of this question.[1] Nicodemus comes with the *one* question which Judaism, of which he is a "teacher", has to put to Jesus, and must put to him. It is the question of *salvation*. Jesus replies by giving the conditions for entry into the *rule of God*, and in so doing he proceeds on the self-evident assumption that for the Jews the question of salvation is identical with the question of participation in the rule of God.[2] It is typical that Nicodemus should use the form of an indirect question, starting from what is safe ground: οἴδαμεν![3] This much one could say with certainty on the basis of Jesus' miracles: he is an accredited "teacher"[4]—for this is the only title which the Scribes could have given him—and Nicodemus accordingly has addressed him as "Rabbi".

If Nicodemus' question has been based on an understanding of the matter formed in accordance with traditional standards of judgement, Jesus' answer tears him away from his rational considerations and makes him listen to something which he cannot understand. In truth, the dialogue cannot run along the lines expected by the διδάσκαλος, such as he could expect if he were confronted by another διδάσκαλος. He may well consider Jesus, a man accredited by miracles, to be a superior teacher

[1] The sort of guesses made by the exegetes is well illustrated by the note in B. Weiss ad loc.: "The form of address is not merely a polite convention (Wahle). Nor is it convincing to suggest that, in addressing him as he did, he thought of him as the Messiah, and therefore had in mind the conditions for entry into the Messianic kingdom (Hengstenb.) and only refrained from specifically mentioning the question because he cleverly preferred to wait his time (Lange), so that Jesus in his answer anticipated Nic.'s actual question (Meyer); equally unconvincing is the suggestion that N. wanted to find out whether Jesus was perhaps the Messiah (Meyer, Godet, Keil, Schanz), or whether he stood in some other relation to the kingdom proclaimed by the Baptist (Lücke), in particular, whether his miracles were the beginning of the Messianic kingdom (Luther). The suggestion that he came with the hypocritical intention of luring Jesus into making statements which could be used against him (Koppe . . .) is a purely arbitrary insinuation." Admittedly B. Weiss' own view is no better, for he suggests that Jesus had appeared at the feast in Jerus. also as a teacher, and that in the recognition of him as a teacher sent from God there is contained the indirect challenge "to say what new teaching he had to give".

[2] Cp. Mt. 5.3; Mk 10.14f., 23ff. etc.

[3] The plur. οἴδαμεν does not necessarily need to refer back to a subject in the plur. (see 20.2); for a "we" of this sort spoken by a single person corresponds to the Rabbinic, and indeed general Oriental usage, in which the form of speech is determined by the individual's consciousness of belonging to a community (Schl., Torrey 329f.). The "we" in 3.2 however expressly refers to the speaker as a representative of his own group, which here stands in contrast to another "we"; for the contrast between "we" and "you" see v. 7, 11f. and cf. 4.22.

[4] Just as a miracle is considered as a divine sign accrediting the word of a prophet (see p. 125 n.2), so too it is the case with doctrinal decisions of a Rabbi; Str.-B I 127; IV 313f.; P. Fiebig, Jüd. Wundergesch. des neutest. Zeitalters 1911, 31f.—On ὅτι ἀπὸ θεοῦ ἐληλ. see p. 50 n.3; the Gnostic phrase sounds strange in the mouth of a Rabbi. The ἐὰν μὴ ᾖ ὁ θεὸς μετ' αὐτοῦ which follows is, by contrast, good OT Jewish usage (Gen 21.20; Judg 6.13; Acts 10.38).

to him, to whom he, the Φαρισαῖος, the ἄρχων and the διδάσκαλος comes to put questions; the Revealer, however, is not quantitatively, but qualitatively superior to the human teacher, and the criteria which the latter has at his disposal are not capable of providing an adequate basis for understanding him.

The reply in **v. 3**, which is introduced by the emphatic ἀμὴν ἀμὴν λέγω σοι, reads: "Unless a man be born anew,[1] he cannot see God's rule."[2] Thus right at the beginning it is stated uncompromisingly that man, as he is, is excluded from salvation, from the sphere of God; for man as he is, there is no possibility of it. Yet at the same time it is said in such a way that a hint is given that salvation may be a possibility for him, inasmuch as it is possible for him to become another man, a new man. The saying therefore also contains an injunction; not, however, of a moralistic[3] sort, but rather the injunction to put oneself in question.[4]

---

[1] Ἄνωθεν can mean "from above" as well as "anew", and also "from the start", "from the beginning" (see instances in Br.). In 3.31; 19.11, 23 it means "from above", whereas in 3.3, 7 it can only mean "anew" (most exegetes give this translation, see Br., Lagr., but Büchsel ThWB I 378 differs). Nor is "anew" to be taken as a secondary meaning here. The ambiguity of Johannine concepts and statements which lead to misunderstandings does not consist in one word having two meanings, so that the misunderstanding comes as a result of choosing the wrong one; it is rather that there are concepts and statements, which at first sight refer to earthly matters, but properly refer to divine matters. The misunderstanding comes when someone sees the right meaning of the word but mistakenly imagines that its meaning is exhausted by the reference to earthly matters; it is a judgement κατὰ ὄψιν (7.24), κατὰ σάρκα (8.15). L. Cerfaux, Coniect. Neotest. XI (1947), 15–25; O. Cullmann, ThZ 4 (1948), 360–372.

[2] ἡ βασιλεία τοῦ θεοῦ is in the Synoptics by far the most frequent designation of the eschatological salvation. In John it only occurs in 3.3, 5 (18.36 is different). Ἰδεῖν is a common term for participating in salvation (3. 36; Lk. 2.26; Acts 2.27; I Pet. 3.10), corresponding to the use of רָאָה to mean "come to know", "experience," but also not foreign to Gk. usage (Br. Wörterb. 364). εἰσελθεῖν, which replaces it in v. 5, has the same meaning. (Mk. 9.47; 10.15 etc.).

[3] B. Weiss thinks that Jesus' answer is intended to make Nicodemus conscious of his moral inadequacy, which is why, like Mk. 1.15 he starts by demanding μετάνοια! On the contrary, it is significant that the concept of μετάνοια which is open to this kind of moralistic understanding does not occur in John, either in the Gospel or in the Epistles (cp. on the other hand Rev.!).

[4] It is clear that the Evangelist in v. 3 has chosen a traditional dominical saying as a means of leading up to the saying in vv. 5ff. That this is the case is suggested by the concept of βασ. τ. θ., which occurs nowhere else in John, and is confirmed by the occurence of a variant of the saying in Justin apol. I 61,4: ἂν μὴ ἀναγεννηθῆτε, οὐ μὴ εἰσέλθητε εἰς τ. βασ τῶν οὐρανῶν (other variants, which can hardly be independent, are found in Ps. Clem. Hom. XI 26; Rec. VI 9). It is the Hellenistic form of the dominical saying, found in two variants in Mt. 18.3; Mk. 10. 15. (Dodd [304] is right in pointing out that v. 3 is not directly based on Mt. 18.3.). Clem. Al. Protr. IX 82.4 has fused the Hellen. and Synopt. forms of the saying together. Cp. W. Bousset, Die Evangeliencitate Justins des Märt., 1891, 116–118.

The reason for this procedure was most probably that while the revelation-discourse, on which the following passage is based, discusses the theme of ἄνωθεν γεννηθῆναι, the actual phrase does not occur in the sayings which the Evangelist quotes from the source. However a trace is to be found in the γεννηθῆναι ἐκ τοῦ πνεύματος of v. 6. At least one can

This is emphasised and made clear[1] by Nicodemus' misunderstanding in **v. 4**; for the Evangelist chooses this grotesque way of making it abundantly clear that rebirth is in no sense a natural process, an event which can be set in motion by man himself. In the human sphere it is

---

say that the source dealt with the question of the origin of faith in the Spirit. There can, however, be no doubt that the source spoke not of "being born", but of "being conceived", and that—to assume its Semitic origin—the equivalent word for ἄνωθεν had the meaning of "from above" (the corresponding word for ἄνωθεν in Aramaic is מִלְּעֵילָּא, which has only a spatial and not a temporal meaning, Str.-B. II 420). This is shown 1) by the fact that ἐκ θεοῦ γεννηθῆναι, which (equally on the basis of the source) occurs in I Jn. 2.29; 3.9; 4.7; 5.1, 4, 18, is understood as "being begotten by God" (as is shown by 3.9), and that εἶναι ἐκ which, as a way of referring to someone's origin, is analogous to γεννηθῆναι ἐκ, equally refers to the origin in the father (see esp. 8.44); 2) that εἶναι ἐκ τ. θεοῦ can be used as an equivalent for εἶναι ἐκ τῶν ἄνω, which in 8.23, where it is contrasted with ἐκ τῶν κάτω, clearly means "from above". Further proof is given by the fact that in similar expressions ἐκ τ. θεοῦ and ἄνωθεν = "from above" are used synonymously; cp. 3.31 with 8.42; 16.28, and 19.11 with 3.27; 6.65. (On "above" see on 3.31.

Thus we may conclude that the Evangelist has here *transformed the idea of "being begotten from above"*, which was suggested by the source and is elsewhere readily utilised by him (see 1.13), *into the idea of "rebirth"*, and that surely because the latter idea was already common in the Christian tradition (cp. I Pet. 1.3, 23; Tit. 3.5; Justin apol. 61.3; 66.1; dial. 138. Act. Thom. 132 p. 239.10ff.). This need not have made any material difference. Admittedly, as originally understood by the Gnostics, "begetting from above" probably referred to the pre-existent origin of the spiritual ones. They are φύσει σωζόμενοι (Exc. ex Theod. 56; Clem. Al. strom IV 89; Iren. I. 6, 1; see p. 64 n.2), because their φύσις comes from above (ἄνωθεν) Iren. I, 6, 4; Clem. Al. strom IV, 89; Act. Thom. 61 p. 178, 10f.; cp. Hipp. V, 7, 36; 8, 21.41, p. 88, 1; 93, 3; 96, 19ff.: ὅτι ἤλθομεν . . . οἱ πνευματικοὶ ἄνωθεν ἀπὸ τοῦ 'Αδάμαντος; Iren. I 21, 5. But since in practice the spiritual men on earth are only brought back to their origin by the Gnosis, their redemption has the appearance of "being begotten from above" *anew*, or of a "rebirth". The ἀναγεννηθέντες πνευματικοί Hipp. V 8, 23 p. 93, 18 refers to those who have been reborn (cp. V. 8, 10 p. 91, 4f.); the ἀναγέννησις is the ἄνοδος of the archetypal man from his submersion in the earthly body Hipp. V, 8, 18, p. 92, 15 (cp. VI, 47, 3 p. 179, 10). ἀναγέννησις is contrasted as "rebirth" to ποίησις (creation; Hipp. VI, 47, 4, p. 179, 13ff.) and to γέννησις (Exc. ex Theod. 78), as γεννᾶν εἰς θάνατον καὶ εἰς κόσμον is contrasted with ἀναγεννᾶν εἰς ζωήν (loc. cit. 80). Thus C. Herm. 13 (cp. Act. Thom. 15, p. 121, 13: ἵνα πάλιν γένωμαι ὃ ἤμην) can speak specifically of παλιγγενεσία. In the Naassene sermon the ἔσω ἄνθρωπος is said to come from the archetypal man, ἄνωθεν. His γένεσις in the earthly sphere is worked κάτω (downwards), and must be followed by the γένεσις ἄνω (upwards). The Christian version of these ideas interprets them on the basis of Jn. 3.5f. (Hipp. El. V, 7, 35–41 p. 87, 15ff.).—It may be that the general usage of the mystery religions has had an influence on Gnostic terminology. The *source* used by the Evangelist, however, as seems to be indicated by vv. 12f., took the "begetting from above" in its original sense as referring to the pre-existent origin.—For a full discussion of this usage, c.f. A. Dieterich, Eine Mythrasliturgie, 3. ed. 1910, 157–179; Reitzenstein, HMR. passim; Die Vorgeschichte der christlichen Taufe 1929, 103–126; Lagr. 83ff.; Br., ext. note on Jn. 3.3, and on 3.4; Lietzmann, ext. note on Rom. 6.4; Dibelius, ext. note on Tit. 3.5; Windisch, ext. note on I Pet. 2.2 and on I Jn. 3.9 (all in the Handb. zum NT). For a further discussion see Br., Wörterb. on ἀναγεννάω and παλιγγενεσία; Büchsel, ThWB I 667ff. 685ff. For the religious background of the terms see G. v. d. Leeuw, Phänomenologie der Religion 1933, passim, esp. §§ 22, 49, 79; H. Festugière, HThR 31 (1938), 8.42 and 43.

[1] The form of the question, πῶς δύναται ...; is Rabbinic (Schl. on Mt. 12.29), and is one of the Rabbinic turns of expression which are characteristic of the Evangelist's

impossible for there to be anything like a rebirth.[1] For rebirth means—and this is precisely the point made by Nicodemus' misunderstanding—something more than an improvement in man;[2] it means that man receives a new *origin*, and this is manifestly something which he cannot give himself. For everything which it lies within his power to do is determined from the start by his old origin, which was the point of departure for his present life, and by the person he has always been. For it is one of the

---

style (3.9 and the interrogative πῶς, which is intended to point out the absurdity of Jesus' statement, 6.42; 8.33; 12.34). Cp. however the question of the man who is to be initiated C. Herm. 13, 1f.: ἀγνοῶ, ὦ τρισμέγιστε, ἐξ οἵας μήτρας ἄνθρωπος <ἀν>αγεννηθ<εί>η <ἂν>, σπορᾶς δὲ ποίας κτλ. and further αἴνιγμα μοι λέγεις ... see below p. 143 n.2. For C. Herm. 13.1 Nock (N.-Fest., Herm. Trism. II 200, 15f.) following the codices reads: ... ἐξ οἵας μήτρας ἄνθρωπος ἐγεννήθη ... On this he comments: malim ἄνθρωπος ἂν ἀναγεννηθείη.

[1] B. Weiss again attempts an individualistic and psychological interpretation: Nicodemus' inability to understand Jesus is the result of his internal resistance to what Jesus really meant! But Schl. is also wrong when he suggests that Nicodemus rejects the possibility of a new beginning in the sphere of man's inner life on the ground that the miracle of the resurrection will not come to pass till the new aeon, and that there is no place for a divine miracle in the present age.—Nicodemus' remark is not an expression of doubt in God's present activity. His reply is only intended to show the absurdity of the idea of a "rebirth" from a human standpoint. So he makes not a typically Rabbinic, but a specifically human reply. If the figure of Nicodemus had been intended to represent the Rabbinic point of view, his reply would be hard to understand. For the idea that man can can become a "new creature" (בְּרִיָּה חֲדָשָׁה), if God heals him from his sickness, rescues him from his plight, and forgives him his sins, is Rabbinic (Str.-B. II 421f.); equally in Rabbinic Judaism we find the phrase "to be like a new-born child" used as a description of the proselyte (loc. cit. 422f.; Rengstorf ThWB I 644, 30ff.). The school of Hillel spoke of the Tamid sacrifices as making the children of Israel like a year-old child (Str.-B. II 423).—The only way of giving a specifically Rabbinic interpretation of Nicodemus' reply is to take it as a counter-question by means of which he hoped to refute Jesus (see Gesch. der synopt. Trad. 2. ed. 42ff. = Hist. of the Syn. Trad. 41ff.). Yet this method of disputation ill accords with the style of the Johannine dialogues; moreover the rest of the dialogue shows that Nicodemus should be seen not as a skilled debater, but as a man full of amazement and incomprehension. It is possible that in v. 4 we have a typical objection to the insistance on the need for rebirth taught in the (Gnostic) mystery religions (see below). This is suggested by Lidzbarski, J. B. 123 (122, 5), because the objection (admittedly here raised against the chimerical wish for a prolongation of life, J. B. II 122, or for the return of the soul to the body, Ginza 188, 10ff.) is also found in Mandaean literature. On the other hand Justin apol. 61, 5, shows that the idea of v. 4 was also used outside John to interpret the meaning of rebirth, as does C. Herm. 13.1 (see previous note).

[2] Calvin is right here: ... atque hac locutione simul docemur, exsules nos ac prorsus alienos a regno Dei nasci, ac perpetuum nobis cum ipso dissidium esse, donec alios secunda genitura faciat... Porro verbo "renascendi" non partis unius correctionem, sed renovationem totius naturae designat. Unde sequitur nihil esse in nobis nisi vitiosum.—The contrast is well brought out by the saying of the philosopher, who is also acquainted with the longing to become a "new man", M. Aurelius X 8: one should ponder the ὀνόματα: ἀγαθός, αἰδήμων, ἀληθής, ἔμφρων, σώφρων, ὑπέρφρων: ἐὰν οὖν διατηρῇς σεαυτὸν ἐν τούτοις τοῖς ὀνόμασι, μὴ γλιχόμενος τοῦ ὑπ' ἄλλων κατὰ ταῦτα ὀνομάζεσθαι, ἔσῃ ἕτερος, καὶ εἰς βίον εἰσελεύσῃ ἕτερον. τὸ γὰρ ἔτι τοιοῦτον εἶναι, οἷος μέχρι νῦν γέγονας, καὶ ἐν βίῳ τοιούτῳ σπαράσσεσθαι καὶ μολύνεσθαι, λίαν ἐστὶν ἀναισθήτου καὶ φιλοψύχου . .

basic ideas of Johannine anthropology—as was hinted at already in 1.13—that man is determined by his origin, and determined in such a way that, as he now is, he has no control over his life, and that he cannot procure his salvation for himself, in the way that he is able to procure the things of this life.[1] Moreover the goal of man's life corresponds to his origin. If his way is to lead to salvation, it must start from another point, and man must be able to reverse his origin, and to exchange the old origin for a new one. He must be "reborn"!

Nicodemus cannot see that there is such a possibility, and Jesus' reply in **v. 5**, which is made with great emphasis, repeats again the condition for participation in salvation;[2] and yet he repeats it in a slightly different form, which suggests an answer to the riddle. For now γεννηθῆναι ἄνωθεν is replaced by γεννηθῆναι ἐκ πνεύματος.[3] In the first

---

[1] The reason for stating a person's *origin* (i.e. of the Revealer, the believer or the unbeliever) in Gnosticism was originally speculative, but in John it is used to describe a person's *nature* as expressed in his words and actions. A person or thing is ultimately determined by his origin. The origin can be described generally by εἶναι ἐκ (see on 3.31), while for believers γεγεννῆσθαι ἐκ (see p.135 n.4) is also used, for the Revealer (ἐξ)έρχεσθαι (ἐκ) or εἶναι παρά. 8.42 shows that εἶναι ἐκ is synonymous with ἐξέρχεσθαι ἐκ, cp. 8.44. I Jn. 2.29; 4.7 show that it is also synonymous with γεγεννῆσθαι ἐκ, cp. III Jn. 11; further I Jn. 4.1f., cp 5.1; I Jn. 3.8, cp. 3.9.

The believers (or alternatively the unbelievers) are characterised like the Revealer by their εἶναι ἐκ, and the origin of the Revealer and the believer is the same. Like him, the believers are not ἐκ τοῦ κόσμου (8.23, 15.19; 17.14; I Jn. 2.16; 4.4f.); they are ἐκ τοῦ θεοῦ (8.47; I Jn. 4.4, 6; 5.19; ἐκ τοῦ πατρός I Jn. 2.16; ἐκ τῆς ἀληθείας Jn. 18.37), just as he has come ἐκ τοῦ θεοῦ or alternatively ἐκ τοῦ πατρός (8.42; 16.28 or ἄνωθεν 3.31), or as he is ἐκ τῶν ἄνω (8.23), or as his doctrine is ἐκ τοῦ θεοῦ (7.17).

3.31 shows clearly that εἶναι ἐκ describes someone's nature, for here a person's nature and origin are expressly identified; so does I Jn. 2.19, where εἶναι ἐκ is expressly distinguished from an ἐξέρχεσθαι, ἐκ that refers only to one's historical descent. 8.43f., 47; 18.37; I Jn. 3.9; 4.5f.; 5.18 show that the possibilities which are open to a man are determined by his origin; equally 3.31; I Jn. 4.5 say expressly that the εἶναι ἐκ τῆς γῆς (or alternatively ἐκ τοῦ κόσμου) issues in a λαλεῖν ἐκ τῆς γῆς (τοῦ κόσμου). This is important for the understanding of the notion of pre-existence in Johannine Christology, for it means that for John pre-existence refers not to a mythical existence, but to the character of a man's existence.

[2] εἰσελθεῖν is synonymous with ἰδεῖν in v. 3; ℵ* M pc read ἰδεῖν in v. 5 as well. The variant βασ. τῶν οὐρανῶν (ℵ* pc e m and Fathers) must go back to the influence of Mt. 18.3. Instead of γεννηθῇ nearly all the Latin texts read renatus (fuerit).

[3] The originality of the words ὕδατος καί, which link the rebirth with the sacrament of baptism, is at the least very doubtful. Admittedly they are found throughout the tradition (by contrast with v. 8, which is only infrequently found and is certainly an interpolation), but they are, in my opinion, an insertion of the ecclesiastical redaction, which in 6.51b–58 has also forged the link with the Last Supper. The meaning of baptism is not only not mentioned in the following passage, but if mentioned could only confuse the ideas in v. 6 and v. 8. Similarly in ch. 6 and ch. 13 (which see) the Evangelist consciously rejects the sacramentalism of ecclesiastical piety. The relation of spirit and water Ezek. 36.25–27 can hardly be cited in favour of the tradition, which is defended by O. Cullman (Urchristent. u. Gottesdienst 50). Admittedly in the tradition of the Church the event of the rebirth has been tied to baptism; as early as Tit. 3.5 baptism appears as λουτρὸν παλιγγενεσίας, and

place this means that the condition can only be satisfied by a miracle; for πνεῦμα refers to the power of a miraculous event.[1] Secondly, however, it suggests to Nicodemus, and indeed to anyone who is prepared to entertain the possibility of the occurrence of a miraculous event, that such a miracle can come to pass.

---

in Justin apol. I, 66, 1 as εἰς ἀναγέννησιν λουτρόν, cp. Justin apol. I, 61, 3f. 10; dial. 138, 2; Act. Thom. 132, p. 239, 8ff.; Ps. Clem. Hom. XI 26 p. 116, 33ff. Lag.; cp. p. 4, 26f. (Cp. how in Herm. sim. IX, 16 and II Clem. 6.9 the εἰσέρχεσθαι εἰς τ. βασ. τ. θ. is linked with baptism.) In favour of the exclusion of ὕδατος καί can be cited Wendt, Wellh., Merx (who thinks that the words have strayed from another context, because syr^s has them in the reverse order), K. Lake (The influence of textual criticism 1904, 15f.), v. Dobschütz (ZNTW 28 [1929], 166). So too Hirsch, who however excludes vv. 5 and 7 in their entirety as editorial additions, thereby completely destroying the dialogue.—On the other hand Odeberg 48–71 wants to retain the words but in so doing takes ὕδωρ to refer, not to baptism, but to the seed of divine procreation (which view he bases on the idea, found in Jewish and pagan Gnosticism, of the heavenly (spiritual) water), which would mean that ἐξ ὕδ. καὶ πνεύμ. would be equivalent to ἐκ σπέρματος πνευματικῆς. Yet the analogies in the Christian tradition which we have cited make this unlikely.—In C. Herm. 13.3 rebirth (παλιγγενεσία see p. 135 n.4) is described as a γεννηθῆναι ἐν νῷ. Νοῦς should not here be taken in the Classical Greek sense, but in the sense which it has in (Gnostic) dualism of the transcendent divine power, i.e. = πνεῦμα. Cp. esp. C. Herm. 4, where the νοῦς is the gift sent by god, with which man must be baptised in order to achieve the Gnosis. Cp. note 7 on C. Herm. 4.3, in N.-Fest., Herm. Trism. 1, 53; further on the relation of the concepts νοῦς and πνεῦμα (and λόγος) see Reitzenst., H.M.R. 308–333; Dodd 213–227.

[1] πνεῦμα does not mean "spirit" in the sense of the Platonic distinction between ψυχή (or νοῦς) and σῶμα, or of the idealist distinction between spirit and nature. This interpretation was, under the influence of F. C. Baur, widespread among scholars, but was refuted above all by H. Gunkel (Die Wirkungen des heil. Geistes, 3. ed. 1909), whose view was confirmed by the work of Reitzenstein and Leisegang. Both the Greek πνεῦμα and the Hebrew רוּחַ underwent a change in meaning, referring first to something existing in the human sphere (breeze, breath, wind), and then secondly to a suprahuman divine power. Although at first in primitive modes of thought the latter is thought of as a substance, a materialised power ("Mana"), this is not the proper meaning of the concept. Rather such concepts as πνεῦμα and רוּחַ refer in their proper sense to a mode of human existence, inasmuch as the latter is aware that it is at the mercy of the mysterious, of a superior power. Thus both πνεῦμα and רוּחַ refer to the divine power, whereby the latter is conceived not as it is in itself, but as it impinges on human existence. This means to say that there are two constitutive elements in the concept of spirit: 1) the element of the *miraculous*, of that which lies beyond the human sphere. Here the precise object to which the concept pneuma or "pneumatic" refers varies, depending on what limits are set to the sphere of human possibilities. This does not however cause any variation in the *concept* of pneuma itself. 2) An active element; here pneuma is spoken of wherever the miraculous appears within the sphere of human existence as an event worked in man, whether man is thought of as passive or active. Thus πνεῦμα is to be distinguished from δύναμις (leaving aside the Stoic usage). For δύναμις can refer to the divine activity in general, including, that is, his activity in nature. Equally it is to be distinguished from δόξα, which refers to the epiphany of the Godhead, to the self-portraying numen praesens, as opposed to the miraculous events worked in man (see p.67 n.2). Of course there are modulations and combinations of these ideas; in magic all three words (and others as well) may be used synonymously.—Other elements however are *not* constitutive for the concept of pneuma. 1) the moral element, as can be seen from the fact that the daemon can also be called πνεῦμα, and that actions caused by the daemon can be called "pneumatic" (cp. I Jn. 4.1ff., 6; I Cor. 12.2f.).

V. 6, in which the Evangelist quotes from his source, stresses that what is being discussed here is indeed no less than a miracle.

τὸ γεγεννημένον ἐκ τῆς σαρκὸς σάρξ ἐστιν,
καὶ τὸ γεγεννημένον ἐκ τοῦ πνεύματος πνεῦμά ἐστιν.[1]

This antithesis[2] makes it quite clear to Nicodemus—and with him to

---

Yet inasmuch as the moral good is conceived as lying beyond man's possibility, as a miraculous phenomenon (as e.g. in Paul), it is naturally attributed to the pneuma, without this however in any way modifying the *concept* of pneuma itself.
(2) the element of the *psychic* and the *abnormal*, e.g. ecstasy, prophecy, etc. Of course such phenomena—particularly in primitive thought—are ascribed to the pneuma, because they are considered miraculous, yet they are not constitutive of the *concept* of pneuma.—Obviously πνεῦμα can be spoken of apart from its concrete manifestations, as for example, God's nature may be spoken of as πνεῦμα (4.24). But this does not give a metaphysical definition of God as he is in himself, but states how he encounters man (the same is true of ἀγάπη when used of God, I Jn. 4.8, 16).

John speaks relatively infrequently of πνεῦμα. Apart from 1.(32), 33, where, following the tradition of the baptismal narrative, πνεῦμα is spoken of mythologically, πνεῦμα is seen as the divine power which establishes and rules over the being of the believer and the community, in other words as the miraculous manner of Christian being (3.5f., 8). Moreover the combination of πνεῦμα with ἀλήθεια (4.23f.; 14.17; 15.26; 16.13) and ζωή (6.63), and its characterisation as ζωοποιοῦν (6.63), shows that *Christian being is eschatological existence established by the revelation.* This is not characterised by any particular striking phenomena, but is seen as a whole in contradistinction to σάρξ, by which is meant worldly being (3.6; 6.63), so that for the world it remains invisible (14.17). Since the revelation which establishes this existence is Jesus' ῥήματα, which are πνεῦμα and ζωή (6.63), it is not realised by means of a miraculous event or in a mystical experience, but only in the faith which recognises the Revealer (6.69). Christian existence of this sort only comes into being with the fulfilment of the revelation-event (4.23f.; 7.39); and this event establishes such existence because, when it is seen and understood as it really is, it lives in the tradition of the community (14.17, 26; 15.26; 16.13; I Jn. 4.6; 5.6) and determines the character of the life of the community (I Jn. 3.24; 4.13).—20.22, which follows the tradition closely, speaks of πνεῦμα in a mythologising manner, but is of course to be taken in the sense of 14.16f., 26. Similarly the unmythological meaning of πνεῦμα (πνεύματα) in I Jn. 4.1–3 is clear. It does not refer to demons, but to teachers. The figure of the ἀντίχριστος I Jn. 2.18, 22; 4.3; II Jn. 7 is demythologised in a corresponding manner.

[1] The verse has been glossed in 161 syr^c and a number of Latin MSS, the second half has also been glossed by syr^s (see Merx 56ff.). To the first half ὅτι ἐκ τῆς σαρκὸς ἐγεννήθη. has been added; to the second ὅτι ἐκ τοῦ πνεύματός ἐστιν, or alternatively, quia deus spiritus est et ex deo natus est.

[2] The form of the verse is characteristic of the revelation-discourses. 1) It is an apodictic statement, for which no explanation is given. 2) In the antithetic par. membr. the second half is a simple inversion of the first (Festg. Ad. Jül. 141; on the style of the revelation-discourses see H. Becker, Die Reden des Joh.-Evg. und der Stil der gnost. Offenbarungsrede 1956, esp. p. 24).—This form is characteristic of Gnostic (dualistic) revelation literature in general; cp. the Hermet. sayings from Stob. Ecl. I 275f. in Scott, Hermetica I 428, 430 (some also in Reitzenst., HMR 78, 2), e.g.:

οὐδὲν ἀγαθὸν ἐπὶ τῆς γῆς,
οὐδὲν κακὸν ἐν τῷ οὐρανῷ (Scott No. 18).
οὐδεν ἐν οὐρανῷ δοῦλον,
οὐδεν ἐπὶ γῆς ἐλεύθερον (Scott No. 26).
πάντα τὰ ἐν οὐρανῷ ἄμωμα,
πάντα τὰ ἐπὶ γῆς ἐπίμωμα (Scott No. 29).

every reader—what the alternatives are by which he is confronted.[1] The statement assumes a general understanding of σάρξ and πνεῦμα; i.e. that σάρξ refers to the this-wordly, human mode of being, and πνεῦμα to the other-wordly, divine mode. Yet neither σάρξ nor πνεῦμα refers here to a material substance, however much this may have been the case in some cosmological theories. Rather σάρξ refers to the nothingness of man's whole existence; to the fact that man is ultimately a stranger to his fate and to his own acts; that, as he now is, he does not enjoy authentic existence, whether he makes himself aware of the fact or whether he conceals it from himself. Correspondingly πνεῦμα refers to the miracle of a mode of being in which man enjoys authentic existence, in which he understands himself and knows that he is no longer threatened by nothingness.[2]

Behind all such talk of σάρξ and πνεῦμα there also lies the assumption that man stands, as it were, between these two possibilities of existence, in that he knows, or is able to know, that his proper place is in the other-worldly being, whereas in fact he has become entangled in the this-worldly. The statement in v. 6 is intended to make the man, who, like Nicodemus, is searching for salvation, realise that these two possibilities of being are not open possibilities between which he can freely choose; that the alternatives by which man is confronted are not governed by choice, but by destiny. It is intended to make him aware that his goal is determined by his origin,[3] and that his end will be nothingness, because it is in nothingness that he has his origin. He must realise that everything that he can achieve, and everything that can happen within the sphere of life in which he has existed till now, will come to nothing. Nor will the sphere of this-worldly, human life provide him with the miracle he is looking for. If he is to enjoy a miracle at all, his whole being from its very origin must be changed into a miraculous,

---

Further Scott I 380, 5ff.; 408, 12ff., 15ff. (ἐκεῖνα μὲν τὰ σώματα ὡς ἐξ ἀσωμάτου οὐσίας γεγενημένα, ἀθάνατά ἐστι· τὰ δὲ ἡμέτερα διαλυτὰ καὶ θνητά, ὡς τῆς ὕλης ἡμῶν ἐκ σωμάτων συνεστώσης, cp. C. Herm. 13.14); P. Oxy. VIII No. 1081: πᾶν τὸ γε[ινόμε]νον ἀπὸ τῆς [φθορᾶς] ἀπογείνε[ται ὡς ἀπ]ὸ φθορᾶς γεγ[ονός· τὸ] δὲ γεινόμεν[ον ἀπὸ] ἀφθαρσίας [οὐκ ἀπο]γείν[εται], ἀλλ[ὰ μ]έ[νει] ἄφ[θαρ]τον ὡς ἀπὸ ἀφθ[αρσία]ς γεγονός (for the Herm.texts see now Nock-Fest., Herm. Trism. III 54ff.; 2f.; 30). Similar formulations can be found in Ign., see Schlier, Relig. Unters. 132f.

[1] The use of the neuter form instead of the masculine stresses the fundamental and thematic character of the sentence.

[2] On σάρξ see pp. 62f., on πνεῦμα see p. 139 n.2. This understanding of σάρξ and πνεῦμα is typical of Gnostic anthropology, and is taken over by both Paul and John. What is decisive in each case is the radical way in which the nullity of human existence is understood, whether it is more or less limited to the idea of transitoriness and death, or whether it is related to the radical perversity of man's will and of his understanding of the world and himself. Cp. on the concept of φῶς pp. 40ff.

[3] See pp. 136f.

other-worldly being. Once he has understood this, he will no longer be surprised by talk of rebirth (**v. 7**)[1]; for he will then understand that the attainment of authentic existence can for him be only a miracle—just as the "becoming like little children" which, according to the Dominical saying in the Synoptics, is the condition of salvation, cannot be achieved by deliberate action on the part of man, but can only be received by him as a divine gift.

Yet precisely because the power of the πνεῦμα is a miraculous power, the μὴ θαυμάσῃς applies not only negatively, in the statement that salvation is impossible when considered as a human possibility, but also positively, in the statement that it is possible as a divine possibility. This is the force of **v. 8:**

> τὸ πνεῦμα ὅπου θέλει πνεῖ,
> καὶ τὴν φωνὴν αὐτοῦ ἀκούεις,
> ἀλλ' οὐκ οἶδας πόθεν ἔρχεται
> καὶ ποῦ ὑπάγει.[2]

The miraculous operation of the spirit is bound by no discoverable law; its presence is revealed by its effect. Admittedly it is the ambiguity of the term πνεῦμα that makes it possible for us to entertain this idea, as a hidden meaning lying behind the initial sense of the word. For in the first place the sentence is a comparison whose application is expressively given in the clause οὕτως κτλ. Just as the *wind* is incomprehensible,[3] and no one knows whence it comes and whither it goes, its origin and its destination, yet none can deny its reality—τὴν φωνὴν αὐτοῦ ἀκούεις—so it is with him who is born of the *Spirit*.[4] Thus there are such men, or at least such men can exist. And yet it is not within man's possibility to bring this to pass! Their existence, where indeed they exist at all,

---

[1] μὴ θαυμάσῃς is a characteristically Rabbinic turn of speech. (see Schl.; A. Marmorstein, Hebr. Union College Annual VI 1929, 204), which the Evangelist makes his own (5.28 red.; I Jn. 3.13). But it also occurs in Luc. Men. 1; hist. quom. conser. 40; C. Herm. 11.17; cp. οὐ θαῦμα and similar transitional formulae in diatribe (Windisch on II Cor. 11.14).—On the aor. subj. after μή see Bl.-D. para. 337, 3 and Br.

[2] On the pres. ὑπάγει see Bl.-D. para. 323, 3; on ποῦ in the NT and LXX for ποῖ see Bl.-D. para. 103; Raderm. 2. ed. 65f.

[3] The incomprehensibility of the wind is used more than once in the OT and in Jewish literature to provide a comparison for the incomprehensibility of God's ways, Eccles. 11.5; Prov. 30.4; Ecclus. 16.21; II Esd. 4.5–11). Cp. also Xen. Mem. IV 3, 14: καὶ ἄνεμοι αὐτοὶ μὲν οὐχ ὁρῶνται, ἃ δὲ ποιοῦσι φανερὰ ἡμῖν ἐστι, καὶ προσιόντων αὐτῶν αἰσθανόμεθα. An Indian example is given in Grill II 339. It is used directly of God, without the comparison in Soph. Ai. 14ff.: . . . κἂν ἄποπτος ᾖς, ὅμως φώνημ' ἀκούω . . . and in Eur. Hippol. 86: κλύων μὲν αὐδήν, ὄμμα δ' οὐχ ὁρῶν τὸ σόν.

[4] ℵ it syr[sc] add ὕδατος καὶ see p. 138 n.3.

is an enigma to the man "of the flesh", as is the person of the Revealer himself, whose origin and goal are hidden from the eye of the world.[1]

2) *The Mystery of the Son of Man:* 3.9–21

The discourse now moves a step forward. Up to now the man who has asked how he might find salvation has been told that only rebirth will lead to it. Now his attention is directed to the event in which the possibility of such a miracle is grounded, to the revelation and to the Revealer, the "Son of Man". The Evangelist indicates the transition by the short dialogue in **vv. 9f.**

Nicodemus' question: πῶς δύναται ταῦτα γενέσθαι; accurately represents the inadequency of the way in which man puts his questions,[2]

---

[1] It is a fundamental tenet of Gnosticism that the Redeemer is a "stranger" to the world, which does not know his origin or his destination. The ignorance of the world corresponds, however, to his own knowledge. By virtue of their secret relationship with the Redeemer, the same is true of the redeemed, the spiritual men; indeed for them the decisive Gnosis is to know whence they themselves have come and whither they are going. (see Schlier, Relg. Unters. 141f.; the wicked do not know whence they have come: Ginza 374, 4). —John took over the Gnostic view of the Redeemer and applied it to the person of Jesus in an interpretation determined by his idea of revelation (see on 8.14); equally he applied it to the person of the believer, but in this respect he has moved further away from the Gnostic view as a result of rejecting the idea of the pre-existence of souls and of the cosmic relationship between the Redeemer and the redeemed (see p. 65). The believer's knowledge of his origin is the knowledge of his εἶναι (or γεγεννῆσθαι) ἐκ, which here, however, no longer gives a speculative account of man's descent, but a characterisation of his nature (see p. 138 n.1). The believers' knowledge of their destination is stated indirectly in 12.35; I Jn. 2.11, and directly in 14.4; as a result of the Evangelist's abandoning the idea of the heavenly journey of the soul, the concept of knowledge has also been demythologised.—The ignorance of the world about the nature of the believers, which corresponds to this knowledge, is stated in 3.8 and I Jn. 3.1 (the Pauline parallel is I Cor. 2.14f.), and this motif is also dominant in 15.18ff. The sense, therefore, is that those who are born of the Spirit are a mystery to the world; not, that in them the voice of the Spirit is heard (Lagr.).

The formula in 3.8 has remarkable parallels. Firstly in Ign. Phld. 7.1, where the knowledge of the spiritual man corresponding to the ignorance of the world is described: τὸ πνεῦμα οὐ πλανᾶται, ἀπὸ θεοῦ ὄν· οἶδεν γὰρ πόθεν ἔρχεται καὶ ποῦ ὑπάγει; this goes back not to Jn. 3.8 but to Gnostic tradition (Schlier, Relg. Unters. 141f., in spite of Loewenich, 36f.). Then Clem. Al. strom. VI, 6, 45 and Adumbr. in I Pet. 3.19, where with reference to the descent into hell it is said: λέγει ὁ Ἅιδης τῇ Ἀπωλείᾳ· εἶδος μὲν αὐτοῦ οὐκ εἴδομεν, φωνὴν δὲ αὐτοῦ ἠκούσαμεν. This, however, originally applied to the descent of the Redeemer to earth, and was only secondarily taken to refer to the descent into Hell (see ARW 24 [1926] 102; Reitzenst., JEM 112f.; this view is not shared by J. Kroll, Gott und Hölle 1932, 331), while in Hipp. V, 8, 14 p. 91, 22 the saying is made to refer to the descent of the archetypal man into the world: φωνὴν μὲν αὐτοῦ ἠκούσαμεν, εἶδος δὲ αὐτοῦ οὐχ ἑωράκαμεν. Further variants in ZNTW 24 [1925], 121f. It ought then to be clear that Jn. 3.8 goes back to Gnostic tradition.

[2] The πῶς of this question is typical of the "common-sense" point of view, which recognises only that reality which it can master with its reason, and which, in so far as it believes it can recognise a divine reality, subjects also that reality to rational criteria: cp. 6.42, (52); 7.15; 8.33; 12.34; 14.5.—In the context the question is perfectly appropriate and in no sense out of place, as if Nicodemus would not be able to ask this sort of question

and the perplexity of man confronted with the miracle of rebirth.[1] Jesus' answer is not intended to imply that the scribe ought himself to have been able to give the answer, which would mean that one should look for the scriptural references which, in the Evangelist's view, contain the doctrine of rebirth. Rather Jesus' answer makes it clear that the teachers of Israel *can* give no answer. They necessarily fail when they are faced with the decisive questions.[2]

Vv. 11–15 begin to unfold the mystery. V. 11 and v. 12 assert that it can only be spoken of in the language of witness, a witness that is confronted by the world's unbelief. Then in vv. 13–15 the witness is given indirectly: the descent and the exaltation of the Son of Man are the miracle by means of which rebirth can come to pass. Yet clear as this is, it is most difficult to understand it in detail.[3] This is partly because the Evangelist discontinues the dialogue at this point and ceases to relate the discourse to the particular situation[4] (though not to the theme of the previous discussion). Jesus now no longer speaks only to the Jews, as

---

once the rebirth had been described in v. 8 as a mystery (Wellh. and Spitta; Wendt's view is correct, II 81f.). There is then no justification for a critical treatment of the passage, for example by excluding vv. 4–8 (Spitta). The question is also in accordance with the style of revelation literature, cf. Herm. mand. XI 19 and see p. 136 n.1.

[1] Material parallels to the situation of the dialogue (G. P. Wetter, ZNTW 18 [1917/1918], 51 are to be found in C. Herm. 9, 10: ταῦτα σοι . . . ἐννοῦντι <μὲν> ἀληθῆ δόξειεν ἂν, μὴ <ἐν>νοοῦντι δὲ ἄπιστα· τῷ γὰρ νοῆσαι ἕπεται τὸ πιστεῦσαι, τὸ ἀπιστῆσαι δὲ τῷ μὴ νοῆσαι (text in Scott I 184, 25ff.); 11, 21:

ἐὰν δὲ κατακλείσῃς σου τὴν ψυχὴν ἐν τῷ σώματι
    καὶ ταπεινώσῃς αὐτὴν καὶ εἴπῃς·
οὐδὲν νοῶ, οὐδὲν δύναμαι·
    φοβοῦμαί γῆς κ<αὶ> θάλασσαν·
εἰς τὸν οὐρανὸν ἀναβῆναι οὐ δύναμαι
    οὐκ οἶδα τίς ἤμην, οὐκ οἶδα τίς ἔσομαι·
τί σοι καὶ τῷ θεῷ;
οὐδὲν γὰρ δύνασαι τῶν καλῶν καὶ ἀγαθῶν νοῆσαι
    φιλοσώματος ὢν καὶ κακός. (Scott I 220, 32ff.).

[2] The article in front of διδάσκαλος raises a certain difficulty. Zn. and Lagr. want to read: "you are the teacher of both of us". But why then add τοῦ Ἰσρ.? Probably we should understand: "In you I encounter the teachers of Israel; you represent them." Similar expressions are also found elsewhere, see Schl. and Br., Bl.-D. para. 273, 1. τοῦ Ἰσρ. not τῶν Ἰουδαίων, for Israel is used to denote the people of God (ThWB III, 387, 34ff.).

[3] For this reason Hirsch wishes to exclude v. 11 as an editorial gloss. He wants to retain the connection between vv. 10ff. and the situation, but this is impossible.

[4] Spitta's explanation is extraordinary. For Nicodemus, who is reprimanded for his lack of belief in Jesus and the Baptist, "there is nothing left to do but to disappear from the scene and perhaps to exert an improving influence on his colleagues". Hoskyns is good here. The dialogue ends by leaving Nicodemus faced with the final issue of faith and unbelief, and thus by bringing the reader into the same situation. He does not need to know how Nicodemus decided, but must himself come to a decision.

represented by Nicodemus, but to the κόσμος (vv. 16f., 19)[1] and the concept of the βασιλεία τοῦ θεοῦ is replaced by the concept of eternal life. It is also because the Evangelist has here to use an artificial, forced interpretation of the sayings which he takes from his source in order to make them fit into the movement of his argument.

The initial meaning of **v. 11** is that the words of the Revealer are themselves words of *witness*:

ὃ οἴδαμεν λαλοῦμεν καὶ ὃ ἑωράκαμεν μαρτυροῦμεν.

In the first place μαρτυρεῖν has here its normal forensic meaning.[2] The eye-witness, by virtue of his knowledge, can remove all doubt about matters to which others have no access. For this reason what he says has authority. Yet none of the other conditions which a witness is normally expected to fulfil are applicable here: his statements cannot be checked, nor is he known as a reliable witness. More important still: neither here nor elsewhere, where Jesus claims to be speaking of what he has seen and heard with the Father,[3] does he in fact speak of things or events, heard or seen, which he himself has witnessed. In all possible variations he speaks of nothing else than that the Father has sent him, that he has come, that he will go away again, and that he must be raised up. For this he demands faith, and to such faith he promises life. Manifestly the original mythological meaning of such language[4] has been abandoned.[5] Its sole purpose is to bring out the nature of the word of revelation as a word which 1) comes from outside man's sphere to confront man, which cannot be checked and which cannot be arrived at on the basis of man's observation and reasoning, and 2) which is an authoritative word, binding its hearer to obedience. Thus the heavenly provenance of the messenger is not a guarantee which makes belief in his proclamation easier; rather his very proclamation consists in the scandalous claim that his origins are in heaven, and it is this which man is called on to believe. The fate of the μαρτυρία corresponds to its nature:

---

[1] οὐδείς in vv. 13, 32 does not mean "no Jew" but "no man", and πᾶς in v. 15 not "every Jew" but "every man"; cf. v. 19 οἱ ἄνθρωποι. The "Jews" represent the "world"; see Hosk. 49, 138, 173, 284.

[2] Cp. p. 50 n.5.

[3] The Son tells of what he has seen when he was with the Father: 3.(11), 32; 5.19f.; 8.38; and of what he has heard: 3.32; 5.30; 8.26, 28, 40. The same is said of the Spirit 16.13. Cp. further discussion on 5.19.

[4] Cp. on 3.35; 5.19.

[5] This can also be seen from the fact that the expression "speaking of what the Son has seen or heard" is equivalent to the expressions "doing the works with which his Father has charged him", 4.34; 5.36; 9.4; 17.4; "fulfilling the will or the command of the Father", 6.38; 10.18; 12.49; 14.31; 15.10. Further discussion on 5.19.

καὶ τὴν μαρτυρίαν ἡμῶν οὐ λαμβάνετε:[1] the world rejects the word which is alien to it.[2]

The unexpected plural "we . . ." probably goes back to the source, where the speaker was speaking as one of the group of messengers from God.[3] The Evangelist has retained the plural because in a peculiar manner he disguises the person of Jesus and conceals the fact that ultimately Jesus is the only one who speaks from knowledge and who bears witness to what he has seen.[4] He wants the discourse to retain its air of mystery, and he does not yet wish to state clearly that Jesus is the Revealer—witness the fact that in vv. 13–21, 31–36 Jesus *uses only the third person*[5] to refer to the "Son of Man", the "Son", and him "who has come from above". The nature and destiny of the message he brings must first be made clear. The "you", contrasted here with the "we" refers not only to the Jews, but to the unbelievers as a whole. Οὐ λαμβάνετε has the same comprehensive meaning as οὐ κατέλαβεν, οὐκ ἔγνω, οὐ παρέλαβον (1.5, 10f.), and οὐδεὶς λαμβάνει (3.32).

V. 12 gives the reason for the οὐ λαμβάνετε. If what has been said till now has not been believed, how can one expect the witness to the heavenly things to be believed?

---

[1] Λαμβάνειν τὴν μαρτυρίαν 3.11, 32f. seems to be a Semitic expression (קָבֵל עֵדוּת Schl. ad loc.); an analogy to it is probably to be found in λαμβάνειν τὰ ῥήματα, 12.48; 17.8 (or to קָבֵל תּוֹרָה? Schl. on Mt. 13.20). In Greek λαμβ. τ. λόγον means to "enter a discussion" or "to understand, comprehend what has been said", also "to admit sth. to be true", which probably comes closest to the Johannine usage here. Yet the "admitting", or "refusing to dispute" in John is not based on logic, but on the obedience of faith. In Greek we would expect δέχεσθαι instead of λαμβ, see p. 57 n.2.

[2] It is true that v. 11 is unnecessary in the context (Hirsch); yet there is no reason for omitting it as a result. V. 11 in no way alters the meaning of v. 12 (Hirsch), but, together with v. 12, v. 11 prepares the way for the incredible utterances of vv. 13–21.

[3] In the Mand. texts the messenger mostly speaks in the 1st person sing. (Joh.-B. 44ff., 144ff.; Mand. Lit. 196f.; Ginza 57, 33ff.; 455, 24; 503, 10ff. etc.); occasionally, however, he uses "we" to speak of himself along with other divine beings (Ginza 458, 30ff.; 476, 4; 501, 29ff.). Sometimes "I" and "we" alternate (Ginza 59, 39, "we" instead of "I", which is otherwise used throughout in this passage, but here see Schweizer 37, n. 217; Ginza 461, 17ff., where there are frequent changes; there are also changes in 473, 28ff.; similarly 488, 20ff. What in Ginza 537, 21 is said by one messenger is said in 590, 17 by the messengers).

[4] The usual explanation of the plural is that Jesus is speaking of himself as of one of the Christian preachers, and that is correct, inasmuch as v. 11 gives a description of the Christian message as a whole. Cp. Dodd 328, 3: "The 'testimony' of 3.11 is that of Christ, but, as occasionally elsewhere, the evangelist betrays the fact that it is mediated corporately by the Church." According to Barr. "Jesus ... associated with himself his disciples ...".—The view that Jesus sees himself as one of the prophets—of the OT (Bl.), or the Christian prophets (v. Dobschütz, ZNTW 28 [1929] 162)—is based on the mistaken idea that ἑωράκαμεν should be taken realistically to refer to visions. It is odd that B. Weiss and Zn. should take the plural to refer to Jesus and the Baptist. According to Hosk. 204, 215f. the "we" embraces the prophets, the Baptist, Jesus and the Christian witnesses.

[5] See p. 132.

ἐι τὰ ἐπίγεια εἶπον ὑμῖν καὶ οὐ πιστεύετε,
πῶς ἐὰν εἴπω ὑμῖν τὰ ἐπουράνια πιστεύσετε;

It is presupposed that Jesus has already spoken of the ἐπίγεια (the Evangelist, following his source, now returns to the 1st person). If the continuity of the passage is not to be disrupted then ἐπίγεια must be taken to refer to what has been said in vv. 3–8. Yet how can rebirth be seen as ἐπίγειον?[1] The phrase has been taken from the source, where its meaning was unambiguous: ἐπίγεια referred to the

---

[1] The general distinction between *earthly* and *heavenly* is common in Jewish and Christian, as well as in Hellenistic-dualist thought. Cp. Wisd. 9.16:

καὶ μόλις εἰκάζομεν τὰ ἐπὶ γῆς . . .
τὰ δὲ ἐν οὐρανοῖς τίς ἐξιχνίασεν;

II Esd. 4.1–21 (esp. v. 11 and 21); Sanh. 39a (Str.-B. II 425): "What is on earth, thou knowest not; shouldst thou then know what is in heaven?" cp. Schl. ad loc.; Philo leg. all III 168: τούτοις (who see their good in the διάνοια) συμβέβηκε μὴ τοῖς γηΐνοῖς ἀλλὰ τοῖς ἐπουρανίοις τρέφεσθαι. I Cor. 15.40; Phil. 2.10; Ign. Eph. 13.2: οὐδέν ἐστιν ἄμεινον εἰρήνης, ἐν ᾗ πᾶς πόλεμος καταργεῖται ἐπουρανίων καὶ ἐπιγείων; Trall. 5.1f.; 9.1; Polyc. Phil. 2.1. In Jas. 3.15; Herm. mand. IX, 11; XI, 6ff. the distinction between ἄνωθεν-ἐπίγειον.—Cp. the Hermetic sayings quoted on p. 140 n.2 and the Hermetic fragment περὶ ἀληθείας N.-Fest., Herm. Trism. III, 4–12. Some of the examples we have quoted (for others see Br.) show that it is also everywhere taken for granted that man can at the most understand what is earthly, and not what is heavenly. It is only suprahuman knowledge, such as that enjoyed by the "Metraton", which knows both the earthly and the heavenly (Odeberg 46f.). ἐπίγεια here is taken as referring to the realm of earthly, natural things and events (τὰ ἐν χερσίν, Wisd. 9.16), ἐπουράνια as referring to the heavenly mysteries of cosmology, of the divine plan for the world, of the angelic hierarchies and so on, cp. esp. Ign. Trall. 5.1f.

This cannot be the meaning of Jn. 3.12, for on the one hand the ἐπουράνια which Jesus reveals to faith are not the mysteries of cosmology, mythology and speculation (cp. the Farewell Discourses), and secondly what is said in 3.3–8 is not characteristic of the ἐπίγεια in the normal sense of the word. It is easy to see why Odeberg (49) takes what has been said up till this point as ἐπουράνια; but the difficulty then would be to know what the ἐπίγεια were, of which it is said: οὐ πιστεύετε. According to Zn. the distinction is made between the earthly and the heavenly side of God's rule; yet how far does God's rule have an earthly side, and where does Jesus speak of it? Schl. gives the correct explanation of ἐπίγεια as "what happens on earth", but not of the ἐπουράνια, which he takes to refer to heavenly things as understood in the Book of Revelation, for such things lie beyond John's field of vision.

It might seem more likely that we have here something like the Pauline distinction between preaching (μωρία) for the νήπιοι and the teaching (σοφία) for the τέλειοι (I Cor. 1.18–3.3), and that we should assume that the Evangelist wanted to contrast his own work with the gospels of the Synoptic type. Yet it would be hard to see how he could describe them as ἐπίγεια. Moreover this would mean that there would now be no connection whatsoever with the section vv. 3–8. Ho. and L. similarly think that the distinction here is a distinction between different forms of proclamation: ἐπουράνια refers to the order of salvation which is expounded in the following section, and ἐπίγεια refers to the same subject matter, but in the symbolic form in which it is spoken of in vv. 3–8. Yet vv. 3–8, as understood by the Evangelist, are not intended symbolically at all! Moreover οὐ πιστεύετε can only have for its object a material content. Nor can rebirth, water and wind, which Hosk. wants to take as ἐπίγεια, be conceived as the object of πιστεύειν, in so far as they are earthly phenomena. And Jesus does not even speak of them as such.

earthly world as understood in Gnosticism; the Revealer sheds light on its origins and nature, and consequently on the nature of man, who is called on to see the earthly world as alien to himself. ἐπουράνια referred to the heavenly world which, according to the Revealer's teaching, is to be seen as the home of souls, to which he opens the way back.[1] In Gnosticism soteriology is linked to a particular cosmology, and whoever refuses to accept the understanding of the world and man contained in this cosmology will also refuse to believe in the Gnostic doctrine of redemption. The doctrine of ἄνωθεν γεννηθῆναι, i.e. of the pre-existence or heavenly origin of souls, also belongs to the ἐπίγεια, and is the real crux of the cosmology. The central doctrine of the ἐπουράνια[2] is the doctrine of the ascent of the soul, as will immediately be confirmed by v. 13.[3]

---

[1] The Naassene sermon (Hipp. El. V, 8, 39–44 p. 96, 9ff. W) distinguishes the μικρὰ μυστήρια (τῆς Περσεφόνης) from the μεγάλα and ἐπουράνια μυστήρια; the former are the mysteries of the σαρκικὴ γένεσις, the latter of the πνευματικὴ γένεσις. Accordingly the Peratai (Hipp. V, 16, 1 p. 111, 9ff.), say: μόνοι δὲ . . . ἡμεῖς οἱ τὴν ἀνάγκην τῆς γενέσεως ἐγνωκότες καὶ τὰς ὁδούς, δι' ὧν εισελήλυθεν ὁ ἄνθρωπος εἰς τὸν κόσμον, ἀκριβῶς δεδιδαγμένοι διελθεῖν καὶ περᾶσαι τὴν φθορὰν μόνοι δυνάμεθα. Equally two stages of Gnosis are distinguished Hipp. V, 6, 6 p. 78, 14f.: ἀρχὴ τελειώσεως γνῶσις ἀν<θρώπου, θεοῦ δὲ>γνῶσις ἀπηρτισμένη τελείωσις. Cp. also the difference between κρείττονα and ἐχάσσονα μυστήρια in the difficult passage Κόρη Κόσμου, Herm. Trism. IV, 1, 12ff. (on this see p. 23 n. 7), where at least it is clear that the κρείττονα μυστήρ. correspond to the οὐρανός, and the ἐλάσσονα to the lower φύσις. According to the Hermetic fragment N.-Fest. Herm. Trism. III, 58, 2ff., the γνῶσις brings with it the knowledge ὅτι γενητὸς ὁ κόσμος, καὶ ὅτι πάντα κατὰ [πρόνοιαν καὶ] ἀνάγκην γίνεται, εἱμαρμένης πάντων ἀρχούσης (which is of course misunderstood by the wicked man), that is the knowledge of the ἐπίγεια. It is not quite clear how the mysteries of earth and heaven are distinguished in the Mand. J.B. 167–199. The text is uncertain in many places, but the basic idea is clear, viz. that there is a mysterious correspondence between the symbols of earth and heaven; it is necessary to know both. Cp. the conclusion: "The mystery of the elect is the myrtle and the mystery of the body is the rose. For as the myrtle breaks freshly into flower, so too the elect also break into flower; yet as the rose petals fall, so too the bodies fall into decay. The bodies decay and the measure of the world is filled." Here, too, it is assumed that the Gnosis embraces knowledge about the mysteries of the earthly and heavenly realms. The corresponding parts of the Gnosis are described in a kind of catechism in Exc. ex Theod. 78: ... ἡ γνῶσις τίνες ἦμεν, τί γεγόναμεν· ποῦ ἦμεν, [ἢ] ποῦ <ἐν>εβλήθημεν· ποῦ σπεύδομεν, πόθεν λυτρούμεθα· τί γέννησις, τί ἀναγέννησις. The ascending soul of the Gnostic must have learnt to understand both τὰ ἀλλότρια (the earthly things) and τὰ ἴδια (the heavenly things), Iren. I, 21, 5; cp. Act. Andr. 6, p. 40, 26ff. This corresponds to the plan of C. Herm. I, where first the doctrine of the origin of the world and of man (1–23), and then the doctrine of the ἄνοδος (24–26) is expounded.

The same idea lies behind *Philo's* distinction between the small and the great mysteries (sacr. Ab. et C. 62; Abr. 122): the small mysteries give knowledge of the κόσμος, which includes man's self-knowledge, the great mysteries lead to the vision of the supra-mundane God (the reference in Pascher, Königsweg); cp. also the warning, de somn. I 52–60, that the striving for knowledge should not be directed towards the heavenly things (τὰ μετέωρα, ἄχρις οὐρανοῦ, τὰ ὑπέρ σε καὶ ἄνω), before man has examined himself and has thus recognised the οὐδένεια τοῦ γενητοῦ: ὁ δ' ἀπογνοὺς ἑαυτὸν γιγνώσκει τὸν ὄντα.

[2] On the interpretation of ἐπίγεια and ἐπουράνια see H. v. d. Bussche op. cit. (see

Although the Evangelist has abandoned the Gnostic meaning of ἄνωθεν γεννηθῆναι as signifying the heavenly origin of souls, and has reinterpreted it to refer to rebirth, he can still use the statement in v. 12 for his own purposes. The discussion of rebirth belongs to the ἐπίγεια in as much as it records man's judgement on his situation in the world, that being born of the σάρξ, he is σάρξ, that he is lost, that he has failed to reach the destination to which he has striven and that his point of departure has lead him astray. Thus, as in the Gnostic myth, the ἐπίγεια indicate the meaningless situation of man. Only by seeing himself in this way can man gain the prior understanding which is necessary in order to understand the revelation. We can paraphrase as follows: If a man cannot see the *necessity* of rebirth, he will also be unable to see that in Jesus it has become *possible*. 6.61f. provides a parallel to this: If a man cannot surmount the offence of the σκληρὸς λόγος, which questions his previous understanding of himself, he will also be unable to understand the mission of Jesus which brings salvation.[1] For it is the mission of Jesus, his descent from heaven and his return, which is seen here as the ἐπουράνια.[2]

This in turn points the way to the correct understanding of **v. 13**:

καὶ οὐδεὶς ἀναβέβηκεν εἰς τὸν οὐρανόν,
εἰ μὴ ὁ ἐκ τοῦ οὐρανοῦ καταβάς,
ὁ υἱὸς τοῦ ἀνθρώπου.

The meaning of this sentence in the source is clear. Only one whose origins are in heaven[3] can ascend thither; only, that is, the ἄνωθεν γεννηθείς, the pre-existent souls.[4] This is the mystery of the ἐπουράνια,

---

p. 121 n.1) 1013. He takes ἐπίγεια as the doctrine of the new life mediated by the Spirit, and ἐπουράνια as the eschatological event. This is not possible in my view.

[3] Unfortunately Iren. tells us nothing about the content of the teaching when, in I, 7, 3, he records of the Valentinians: πολλὰ δὲ καὶ τὴν μητέρα περὶ τῶν ἀνωτέρω εἰρηκέναι λέγουσιν.

[1] Naturally v. 11 does not mean that Jesus will not speak of the ἐπουράνια (πῶς ἐὰν κτλ. is not an unreal conditional), but that when he speaks of it, he will not find faith.

[2] Hirsch II 50 rightly says: "The heavenly mystery is the revelation-mystery of the incarnation of the word."—But of course we must always hold the incarnation and the exaltation together.

[3] The perf. ἀναβέβηκεν in the source had the force of a present tense.

[4] If ὁ υἱὸς τοῦ ἀνθρώπου was contained in the source, it will have presupposed there the Gnostic idea that it is the totality of the pre-existent souls which make up ὁ υἱὸς τ. ἀνθρώπ., the archetypal man, who in some former age fell from the world of light into darkness, and whose liberation and exaltation can only be accomplished by the redemption of every individual soul. (Cp. H. Schlier, Christus und die Kirche im Epheserbrief 1930, 27ff.; E. Käsemann, Leib und Leib Christi 1933, 65ff.) Yet it may be that ὁ υἱὸς τ. ἀνθρ. has been added by the Evangelist in order to establish the reference of the sentence to Jesus, and to prepare the way for vv. 17–21, according to which Jesus' coming is the judgement; for according to 5.27 it is as the Son of Man that Jesus is the Judge. He uses the title ὁ υἱὸς τ. ἀνθρ. exclusively as a title for Jesus, the divine messenger wandering on the earth

which is incredible to those who reject the proper understanding of the ἐπίγεια.[1]

Manifestly the sentence must have had a quite different meaning for the Evangelist. He does not teach the pre-existence of souls, and for him the "Son of Man" means not the totality of (pre-existent) souls, but it is the Messianic title of Jesus. For him, therefore, the one of whose ascent and descent the passage speaks is Jesus himself. The verse cannot then bear the meaning which is normally attributed to it, that "no one has ever ascended into heaven, in order, that is, to bring back knowledge of the ἐπουράνια, except the one who descended from heaven". For Jesus did not first ascend into heaven to bring such knowledge back to earth again.[2] Rather he first came down from heaven with the message

---

(see p. 105 n.3 and 107). It is not possible to tell with certainty whether the source used the title in the "inclusive" sense suggested by Odeberg (72–100), according to which Son of Man means the totality of the souls in their union with the Redeemer. 1.51; 5.27; 6.62 are the Evangelist's own compositions (6.27b and 6.53 are from the redaction). 8.28; 12.34 have also been given their present form by the Evangelist but here he has used a source text as a basis for the verses. Such a text can be found in 12.23, 13.31 and even though the Evangelist takes ὁ υἱὸς τ. ἀνθρ. in an exclusive sense to refer to Jesus alone, the title could have been used in an inclusive sense in the source.

[1] V. 13 quite clearly contains the Gnostic idea of the κατά- and ἀνάβασις. G. P. Wetter, Der Sohn Gottes 1916, 82ff., 101ff., does not distinguish clearly enough between examples of the occurrence of this idea and other statements about θεῖοι ἄνθρωποι. Mandaean instances in Odeberg 75–88. C. Herm. 10, 25 (cp. M. Dibelius, Die Isisweihe, SA Heidelberg 1917, 53) may perhaps contain an attack on the Gnostic idea: οὐδεὶς μὲν γὰρ τῶν οὐρανίων θεῶν ἐπὶ γῆς κατελεύσεται . . . ὁ δὲ ἄνθρωπος εἰς τὸν οὐρανὸν ἀναβαίνει (that is to say by means of the νοῦς in speculation), where as Jn. 3.13 (as understood by the source) may be an attack on this sort of Greek speculation. It is more likely, however, that it is directed against the various types of (visionary) heavenly journeys, which were commonly expounded in Jewish apocalyptic and in the speculation of Merkaba (Odeberg 94f.). There is no question of a parallel here with general statements about the impossibility of man's ever ascending into heaven (Deut. 30.12; Bar. 3.29; II Esd. 4.8; Prov. 30.4).

[2] This is source of great embarrassment for the exegetes. B. Weiss wants "somewhat violently" to make ἀναβ. refer to Jesus' original existence in heaven.—Zn. paraphrases: "No man has ascended into heaven (and consequently *no man has been in heaven*, before he lived and spoke on this earth), except him who has come down from heaven." But this is not what the text says.—Bl. thinks that ἀναβ. refers to Jesus' times of prayer in which he raised himself above the earth. In that case however we would expect a pres., and the εἰ μὴ κτλ. would be unintelligible. Moreover we cannot give ἀναβαίνειν here a different sense from that which it has in 6.62;20. 17; cp. καταβαίνειν 6.33ff. and p. 152 n.4. Hirsch shares Bl.'s view.—L. and Br. rightly relate ἀναβεβ. to the ascension, but think that it is spoken from the stand-point of the Christian community as it looks back to Jesus' exaltation. Yet it is as the καταβάς that Jesus brings knowledge from above, and not as the ascended Lord. Clearly if the sentence was meant to say that only someone who had ascended could bring knowledge, it would have to read: "No one has ever ascended into heaven and returned thence again (with knowledge)"; cp. Deut. 30.12; Prov. 30.4; Bar. 3.29, and the lament of the Šum Kušta J.B. 59: "My measure is full. Now I will journey forth, but know not who shall lead me, nor (whom I can ask) how far I have to travel. Neither among the good men nor among the wicked is there anyone who has been there and returned, whom I might ask how far I have to travel." As the text stands the ἀναβαίνειν does not precede the καταβαίνειν but rather the reverse. Odeberg has rightly

entrusted to him by the Father and then he ascended again into heaven. The Evangelist cannot have thought of his ascent as a means for him to gain knowledge of the ἐπουράνια. For the ascent is itself one of the unbelievable ἐπουράνια. His exaltation, his δοξασθῆναι, is the fulfilment of the work of salvation, by which he draws his own to himself (12.32). The exaltation, however, presupposes the incredible fact of the σὰρξ ἐγένετο, and belief in the exaltation means also that one should recognise in the man Jesus the "Son of Man" descended from heaven.[1] That this is the meaning of v. 13 is confirmed by vv. 14f. Thus the argument of vv. 12–15 runs as follows: "If you find the σκληρὸς λόγος of rebirth incredible, how much less will you be able to believe when I speak of the descent of the 'Son of Man', his exaltation and the salvation wrought by it! Yet no one has ever ascended into heaven[2] except the 'Son of Man', who came down from heaven, who must be exalted in order that he may mediate eternal life to those who believe in him."[3] The ἐπουράνια which the world refuses to believe are comprehended in the statement that in the man Jesus we are confronted with the one who has come down from heaven and who must again be exalted.

This is now stated explicitly in **vv. 14f.** The event which is necessary

---

seen that v. 13 is not intended as an answer to the question; "Who can bring knowledge from the heavenly world?" but: "Who can enter the heavenly world?"

[1] Cp. Eph. 4.9f.; the καταβαίνειν and the ἀναβαίνειν of the Redeemer are seen as a unity.

[2] The pref. ἀναβ. (see p. 149 n.3) is to be taken as a perf. of the kind used in general statements or fictitious examples (Bl.-D. para. 344; Raderm. 152f.; cp. Rom. 9.19), if one rejects the idea that it was spoken from the point of view of the community as it looked back on the exaltation.

[3] Western and Syrian authorities also add in v. 13: ὁ ὢν ἐν τῷ οὐρανῷ (syr^s: "from heaven", syr^c: "who was in heaven", which is a correction or alternatively an interpretation). It is possible that the source thought of the Son of Man (yet see p. 149 n.4) as still being present in heaven, while at the same time he was dwelling on earth. For he is never "cut off" from the Father and can be above and below at the same time. Cp. Exc. ex Theod. 4, 2: . . . οὐδὲ διεκέκοπτο ἢ ἄνωθεν μετέστη δεῦρο, τόπον ἐκ τόπου ἀμεῖβον, ὡς τὸν μὲν ἐπιλαβεῖν, τὸν δὲ ἀπολιπεῖν· ἀλλ' ἦν τὸ πάντη ὂν καὶ παρὰ τῷ πατρὶ κἀνταῦθα.

Cp. vv.7, 10; M.L. 242: "Who has sent thee, new king, thou who sittest in the realm of the great (life)?" The same idea can also be expressed by saying that the "image" or the heavenly robes of the messenger remain above, while he himself is in the world (Ginza 91, 11f.; the pearl song of Act. Thom. Further discussion in H. Schlier, Relg. Untersuch. 40; cf. also Christus und die Kirche im Epheserbr, 27ff. and Käsemann op. cit.; Odeberg 33–40, 114). The idea is expressed less speculatively in many of the Mand. texts and in the Od. Sal., where it simply describes the indissoluble community between the messenger on earth and God; cp. ZNTW 24 (1925), 108. Similarly Ign. Mg. 7, 1f.: ὥσπερ οὖν ὁ κύριος ἄνευ τοῦ πατρὸς οὐδὲν ἐποίησεν, ἡνωμένος ὤν . . . ἐπὶ ἕνα 'Ιησοῦν Χρ., τὸν ἀφ' ἑνὸς πατρὸς προελθόντα καὶ εἰς ἕνα ὄντα καὶ χωρήσαντα. So too Jn. 8.16, 29; 10.30; 16.32. Yet this idea has no place in the verse (3.12) as understood by the Evangelist. Nor would it be easy to see why he had taken over the sentence from the source. It is more likely that ὁ ὢν κτλ. is an old gloss, which, assuming that ἀναβεβ. refers to the ascension, refers to Jesus' post-existence: "who is now (again) in heaven". Cp. on 1.18; p. 82 n.6.

in order that faith may receive eternal life is the exaltation of the "Son of Man".[1] In other words, the event which makes rebirth possible, and consequently makes it a reality for faith,[2] is the saving event enacted in the mission of the Revealer.[3] V. 14 mentions only the exaltation;[4] this is the fulfilment of the Son's mission, and by this alone is it

---

[1] Vv. 14f. have been composed by the Evangelist himself, for his source was far from being interested in establishing a positive connection with the OT (see on 5.39). It is however probable that vv. 14f. have replaced a sentence in the source, which spoke of the necessity of the exaltation of the Son of Man (cp. 8.28; 12.34). This would, of course, not have spoken of faith in the Son of Man, if by Son of Man the source meant the totality of souls (see p. 149 n.4). The Evangelist was probably acquainted with the typological interpretation which the Christian tradition had given to Num 21.8f., for it also occurs in Barn 12.5–7; Just. Apol. I 60; Dial. 91, 94, 112. This interpretation almost certainly represents a continuation of the Jewish tradition (Wisd. 16.8; Philo leg. all. II 76–81; agric. 95–101; Rabbin. in Str.-B. and Schl. ad loc.; Odeberg, 107–109; T. W. Manson JTS 46 (1945), 129–136.) The account of the teaching of the Peratai given in Hipp. El. V 16, 5ff. (p. 111, 27ff. W), which uses Num 21.8f. to illustrate the nature of the ἀληθινὸς ὄφις as the θεὸς τῆς σωτηρίας, admittedly presupposes the influence of Jn. 3.14f. It is however probable that the use of Num. 21.8f. in Ophitic Gnosticism is older (Odeberg 104f.; cp. too Omodeo, Saggio 71). Yet it is not possible to show that Jn. 3.14f. is dependent on any such Gnostic tradition, for on the one hand John puts no emphasis on the identification of Jesus with the serpent, while in the Ophitic interpretation of Num. 21.8f. no use is made of the ὑψωθῆναι, which is for John the main point of the verse. See on the whole question Odeberg 98–113.—Hirsch wants to omit vv. 14f. as an editorial gloss, on the grounds that they render v. 13 unintelligible, whereas in fact the very opposite is true. Nor is it correct to say that the mention of the exaltation before 8.28ff. would destroy the carefully conceived dramatic composition of the Gospel. For ἀναβαίνειν v. 13; 6.62, ὑπάγειν 7.33; 8.14, 21f., πορεύεσθαι 7.35, all speak of the exaltation.

[2] Βασιλεία τοῦ θεοῦ is replaced here by the concept of ζωὴ αἰώνιος, which occurs here for the first time in John. As far as the actual meaning is concerned this makes no difference; but it does mean that the Evangelist has now left the sphere of specifically Jewish terminology. For although the concept of ζωὴ αἰώνιος is common in the Jewish sphere, where it can be used interchangeably with βασ. τ. θ. to refer to salvation (cp. e.g. Mk. 10.17; Lk. 10.25; with Mt. 25.34; I Cor. 6.9f. and see Bousset, Rel. des Judentums 213ff., 275ff.), its meaning here is not to be gathered from the Jewish sphere (ThWB II 840, n. 56).—Since ζωή is only true life when it is ζωὴ αἰώνιος, ζωή can often stand by itself for ςωὴ αἰώνιος (as in Jn. 3.36; 5.24, 40 etc., also Mk. 9.43, 45; Mt. 19.17 etc.). However a distinction is made, inasmuch as ζωή, when characterised as ἀιώνιος, always refers to the life as a *condition* of man, while ζωή by itself may also refer to the *power* which creates life (see p. 39 n.3). Thus ζωὴ αἰώνιος is never predicated of God or the Revealer, whose ζωή is the power which creates life (1.4; 5.26; 11.25; 14.6). Jesus' words are the ῥήματα ζωῆς αἰων. (6.68) because they create life; as such they are themselves πνεῦμα and ζωή (6.63).—Hirsch (II 51) mistakenly wants in every case to ascribe the concept ζωὴ αἰώνιος to the editor, believing that the Evangelist only used ζωή.

In v. 15 ἐν αὐτῷ (which should be read as in B al as opposed to the variants) should be taken with ἔχῃ κτλ., since πιστεύειν in John always has the construction with εἰς. On ἔχειν ἐν αὐτῷ cp. 20.31; 16.33.

[3] Δεῖ indicates that the saving-event is governed by a divinely ordained necessity, cp. 3.30; 20.9 and esp. 12.34. Cp. the δεῖ of the eschatological statements in Mk. 8.31; 9.11; 13.7 etc. and of the proofs from Scripture in Mt. 26.54; Lk. 22.37; 24.44 etc. Cp. E. Fascher in Neutest. Studien f. R. Bultmann 242–245; J. Bonsirven, Bibl. 30 (1949), 412f.

[4] Dodd 247 finds confirmation in v. 14 of his view of the meaning of Son of Man (see p. 105 n.3): "the character of the inclusive representative of true humanity". Yet the

made effective (cp. 13.31f.), for it is the exalted, glorified Lord who is the object of Christian faith. Yet the necessary condition of his exaltation is his humiliation, as v. 13 has already said. The saving event embraces both these elements. Indeed the real miracle is the humiliation, which is described in v. 16. Vv. 17–21 work out the implications of this miracle by describing the mission, or rather the coming of the Son, as the eschatological event.

V. 15 stated that belief in the exalted Son of Man is crowned with the gift of eternal life.[1] Why? In **v. 16**[2] we have the answer. The event which is brought to fulfilment in the exaltation of the Son of Man is grounded in the love of God which sent him, so that faith might receive eternal life.[3] The real miracle, therefore, is the mission of the Son, which men believe when they believe in the exaltation of the Son of Man. Belief in his mission is belief in his exaltation. For only the man who overcomes the offence of Jesus' humility and who perceives his exaltation in his death, can see in Jesus the Son sent by the Father. The reverse is

---

exalted Lord of v. 14 is also the καταβάς of v. 13, to whom such a description cannot apply. —In the first place ὑψωθῆναι simply means the return of the Revealer from the world to his heavenly home, as in 12.32, 34 and as ἀναβαίνειν v. 13; 6.62; 20.17 (cp. ὑπάγειν 7.33; 8.14, 21f.; 13.3, 33, 36; 14.4f., 28; 16.5, 10, 16f.; and πορεύεσθαι 7.35; 14.2f., 12.28; 16.7, 28). At the same time the ὑψωθῆναι is also the δοξασθῆναι (7.39; 12.16, 23 etc.); yet just as the δοξασθῆναι is ambiguous, in that Jesus' glorification is achieved through the cross, so too is his ὑψωσθῆναι, which can also mean his raising up on to the cross (8.28). The Evangelist intends it to be taken in both senses in 3.14 as well, as is shown by v. 16. Cp. Dodd 147.375, 2.—It is impossible that, as Odeberg (in connection with his "inclusive" understanding of the Son of Man) suggests, ὑψωθῆναι here also refers to the exaltation of the Son of Man which is brought about by the vision of faith (Odeberg 99.112). It is highly unlikely that ὑψωθῆναι has its origins in the acclamation ὕψου (Er. Peterson, Εἷς Θεός 176, also 318).

[1] Vv. 16–21 are the Evangelist's own composition, although he perhaps used parts of the source on which vv. 31–36 are based in v. 18a and vv. 20f. The Evangelist's style can be easily recognised. V. 16 is prose; the οὕτως-ὥστε-sentence is one of his favourite definitions (Festg. Ad. Jül. 142), cf. esp. I Jn. 4.9, 10. V. 17 is also prose and gives the justification for v. 16 in a way typical of the Evangelist, by putting the negative before the positive statement (Festg. Ad. Jül. 143; see on 1.8, p. 48 n.3 and cp. esp. 5.22; 8.42; 12.47; 16.13, and on οὐ γάρ in such explanations also 3.34; 4.9; 7.1, 5, 39; 20.9, 17). μονογενὴς υἱός is also one of the Evangelist's own terms, see p. 71 n.2. In v. 18 the explanatory ὅτι-clause is characteristic of the Evangelist, cp. e.g. 14.17, 19; 15.5; I Jn. 2.11; 4.18; 5.10. αὕτη δέ ἐστιν κτλ. in v. 19 is one of the typical definitions (Festg. Ad. Jül. 142 and see 15.12; 17.3).—Vv. 16–21 also could not have come from the source, for the further reason that in them vv. 12f. are understood in a sense which they first received in the Evangelist's own treatment of them. If 3.31–36 come from the section of the source from which 3.6, 8, 12f. are also taken, then the source must of course have had some discussion of the divinely sent Redeemer, who comes from above (v. 31), in order to achieve the ἀναβαίνειν of the souls who are begotten from above.

[2] The ὅτι read by Chrys. and Nonnos instead of ὥστε is impossible. It can only be explained in a highly artificial way, as is shown by Bl.-D. para. 391, 2; cp. Raderm. 196f.—On οὕτως followed by a consecutive ὥστε with the indicative, see Br.

[3] In v. 16 υἱὸς τ. ἀνθρ. is replaced by the simple υἱός. For the Evangelist the identity

also true, that faith in the exalted Lord (v. 15) involves the affirmation of his humiliation (v. 16).

The mission of the Son, embracing as it does both his humiliation and his exaltation, is of decisive importance, for it is by faith in this mission that man gains life. This means that the mission is the eschatological event, as the present tense ἔχει in v. 15 indicates, and as **vv. 17–21** expressly state. In this event the judgement of the world takes place. For if faith in this event brings life, then it follows that unbelief is excluded from life (cp. Ps. 18.26f.). Moreover if this event is grounded in the love of God, it follows that God's love is the origin of the judgement. It is of course contrary to the intention of God's love, for he wishes not to judge, but to save the world (**v. 17**).[1] Unbelief, by shutting the door on God's love, turns his love into judgement. For this is the meaning of judgement, that man shuts himself off from God's love. There would therefore be no judgement at all were it not for the event of God's love.[2] And with the mission of the Son this judgement has become a present reality **v. 18**:

---

of the two figures is a matter of course. He cannot however speak of the mission of the υἱὸς τ. ἀνθρ., for it is only as a result of his mission that the Son becomes the υἱὸς τ. ἀνθρ. On υἱὸς μονογ. see p. 71 n.2.—This is the only instance where the mission is referred to by ἔδωκεν (used in 14.16 of the mission of the Paraclete), which is to be distinguished from ἀπέστειλεν (v. 17; I Jn. 4.9f., 14 etc.) in that it stresses God's gift in the mission of the Son (see esp. I Jn. 3.1). The Evangelist will also have chosen the expression because he was alluding to God's giving Jesus up into death (thus παραδιδόναι Rom. 4.25; 8.32; Mk. 9.31 etc. and διδόναι or alternatively παραδιδόναι ἑαυτόν Gal. 1.4; 2.20 etc.)—The mission of the Son as the demonstration of God's love, as in I Jn. 4.9f., 14f., 19. ἠγάπησεν (not ἀγαπᾷ!), describes the unique event of the demonstration of God's love. The object of this love is here said to be the κόσμος, which is used in the normal Johannine way here to refer the world which is at enmity with God, and does not imply that the world loved by God consists only of the believers (Br.), cp. p. 54f..—The parallels adduced by Br. for the love of God for the world really apply to v. 35.—'Απόλλυσθαι for the eternal corruption of the world corresponds to the early Christian usage. (Oepke, ThWB I 393ff.); in John cp. 6.39; 10.28; 12.25; 17.12; 18.9; ἀπώλεια 17.12. The opposite is σωθῆναι, see v. 17.

[1] The explanation for the construction οὐ γὰρ . . . ἀλλὰ (see p. 153 n.1) lies in the method peculiar to the Evangelist of explaining his ideas by saying what he does not mean. The occasion for this is provided here by the fact that the mission of the Son, of which the purpose is the σωθῆναι of the κόσμος, in actuality turns into a judgement on the world. The Evangelist is not prompted by the contrary views of the Jews (Loisy), of the Baptist sect (Baldensperger), or of other prophets (Br.). There is certainly no question of the Evangelist defending his own view here against Stoic or Philonic statements, according to which the λόγος can be accredited only with σώζειν and not with βλάπτειν (Br.)—κρίνειν τ. κόσμον is a Jewish expression, see Rom. 3.6 and Schl. ad loc.—σωθῆναι is used here for the first time to refer to the fruits of salvation, as is common in OT-Jewish and Hellenistic usage. It is found relatively infrequently in John: 3.17; 5.34; 10.9; (11.12), 12.47; further σωτήρ 4.42; I Jn. 4.14 (σωτηρία 4.22). On the subject of the κρίσις in John see also Dodd 208–211.

[2] John no more eliminates the idea of God as the judge than does Paul. The message of the love of God does not bring a rationalistic image of God, but brings out the notion of judgement in its full force.

ὁ πιστεύων εἰς αὐτὸν οὐ κρίνεται,
ὁ μὴ πιστεύων ἤδη κέκριται.[1]

Thus the judgement is not a specially contrived sequel to the coming and the departure of the Son. It is not a dramatic cosmic event which is yet to come and which we must still await. Rather the mission of the Son, complete as it is in his descent and exaltation, *is* the judgement.[2] This means that the earlier naive eschatology of Jewish Christianity and Gnosticism has been abandoned, certainly not in favour of a spiritualising of the eschatological process to become a process within man's soul, but in favour of a radical understanding of Jesus' appearance as the eschatological event.[3] This event puts an end to the old course of the world. As from now on there are only believers and unbelievers, so that there are also now only saved and lost, those who have life and those who are in death. This is because the event is grounded in the love of God, that love which gives life to faith, but which must become judgement in the face of unbelief.

---

[1] This antithesis could have been taken from the source, in which case it would have come from the section which is used in vv. 31–36. On the other hand the Evangelist may have composed it himself, using v. 36 as his model. In any case the appended explanatory ὅτι μὴ κτλ. (μή in the ὅτι-clause to avoid the hiatus, see Bl.-D. para. 428, 5; Raderm, 212; on πιστεύειν εἰς τὸ ὄν. see p. 59 n.2) is certainly the work of the Evangelist. The fact that πιστεύειν is contrasted with μὴ πιστ. and not with ἀπιστεῖν may show the influence of Semitic usage (Schl.), but it also accords with the rhetorical character of the antithesis.

[2] It is wrong to paraphrase οὐ κρίνεται as, "He has escaped the judgement to come before it has taken place" (Zn.). This would be the sense of the Mandaean parallels in Ginza 323, 13ff.:

"The true and faithful Nazorites
will ascend and see the place of light
....
They will not be kept back (in the world)
and in the great judgement they will not be called to account.
On them the judgement will not be pronounced
which will be pronounced on all beings."

Cp. Ginza 512, 22ff. (or M.L. 157):

"The worlds gather for judgement,
and they will be judged.
Judgement will be passed on those
who have not done the works of an upright man.
Thou alone, O Elect and Pure One,
....
Thou shalt not come before the court of judgement,
On thee no judgement shall be passed,
....
For thou hast done the works of an upright man."

At the same time this means that faith is not one of man's good works, receiving life as its reward; nor is unbelief seen as an evil deed incurring judgement. Just as faith already possesses life (5.24: 6.47), so too unbelief is already lost (3.36; 9.41). Faith and unbelief are the answer to the question posed by God in the mission of Jesus; they are a new possibility for man which is made open to him only by the saving event (cp. 9.41; 15.24). If faith and unbelief are not the works of man, neither are they spiritual dispositions (διαθέσεις) which can be developed. Rather just as πίστις, so to speak, does not know what it is doing—in as much as it cannot consciously decide to acquire ζωή—so too unbelief is also ignorant of the fact that it is bringing judgement on itself. It is blind.[4] Yet since faith and unbelief are the answer to the question of the divine *love*, they are (notwithstanding the fact that they are not achievements or spiritual dispositions) responsible *deeds*, in which it becomes manifest what man is. This means that John can speak with a peculiar sort of ambiguity about judgement. Thus in 8.15; 12.47, as in 3.17, he can say that the Son does not come to judge and in fact judges no one; and yet in 3.19 he can say that his coming is the judgement, that God has entrusted the judgement to him (5.22, 27).

The Evangelist is aware of the novelty of this conception, and so in **v. 19** he gives a clear statement of his own understanding of judgement.

Cp. Ginza 60, 26ff. and for the self-condemnation of the wicked, Ginza 183, 11f.: "They will be cut down with their own blows, so that I shall not need to strike them down." Cp. Odeberg 135ff. and Br. on 3.18.

The original meaning of such parallels has been radicalised by John, who understands the history of Jesus, the Revealer, as the eschatological event, see 128 and 5.24f.; 8.51; 11.25f.; 12.31; I Jn. 2.8; 3.14 etc.—There can, of course, be no parallels in Rabbinic literature, since it cannot point to an eschatological event. (The reinterpretation of Gehenna, Odeberg 137, is not a genuine parallel). Nor is "the idea that man's decision for or against God's purposes of love is the actual judgement on man, to be found in Rabbinic literature" (Str.-B. II 427). In Rabbinic lit. the righteous can only be said to be exempt from God's דִּין inasmuch as דִּין is generally taken in the specific sense of condemnation (Odeberg 147f.).

[3] Cp. Bultmann GuV I 134–152.—This interpretation of the appearance of Jesus is the same as that attempted by Paul, even if Paul did not interpret so radically as John; cp. Gal. 4.4; II Cor. 5.17; 6.2; see GuV I 145, 1. Cp. also Groos, ThStKr 41 (1868), 244–273; Faulhaber 44f.; Hosk, 123, "The mainspring of Johannine Christology is not eschatology, but epiphany".

[4] Cp. by contrast J.B. 244, 18ff. where the alternative with which the revelation confronts man is clearly formulated, yet without the idea that faith and unbelief *are* as such life or death:

"Everyone who . . . hears and believes me,
For him is a dwelling prepared in the place of light.
Whoever . . . hears me not,
His dwelling will be removed from the place of light,
His name will be excised from my roll,
His figure will become dark and will not be bright."

There can be no mistaking the attack which this statement makes on traditional eschatology, even though the Evangelist does not specifically refer to it. Judgement for him is nothing more nor less than the fact that the "light", the Revealer,[1] has come to the world.[2] This saving event is judgement, for the reason that men—by which he again means men in general[3]—have shut themselves off from the "light".[4] And so the judgement, in the sense of the great division of the world, takes place (the Evangelist making play on the ambiguity of κρίσις). This is described in vv. 20f. as the division between light and darkness.[5]

Vv. 20f.[6] pick up and justify the last sentence of v.19, which in its turn gave the reason why men in general shut themselves off from the

---

[1] On φῶς see p. 40ff. esp. 43 n.3.

[2] The perf. ἐληλ. characterises the event of the coming as valid for all future time.

[3] Cp. on οὐ λαμβάνετε v. 11.

[4] μᾶλλον ἀγαπᾶν means, as in 12.43, "to prefer", "to decide for"; it is a Semitic expression (Schl. ad loc.). 12.43, for example (cp. with 5.44) shows clearly that it is a question of deciding between alternatives.—Philo, spec. leg. I 54 says of the Jews who have fallen away from monotheism: σκότος αἱρούμενοι πρὸ αὐγοειδεστάτου φωτός.

[5] The understanding of the judgement as the division of light and darkness was already to be found in the Gnostic tradition, in which the division is thought of in the first place as a cosmic process. "On the day when the light ascends, the darkness will return to its place." (M. L. 54.97; cp. Bousset, Hauptprobl. 102; H. Jonas, Gnosis 103f., 278; Br. on 3.18 etc.). The division however takes place above all in the world of men. The Redeemer, who "shone in the world" (M. L. 192), is the one "who divides life from death . . . divides light from darkness . . . divides good from evil . . . divides truth from error" (Ginza 56, 14ff., similarly M. L. 128; cp. Ginza 306, 20ff.; 321, 8ff.). Further Gnostic material on the parallel distinctions between light and darkness, life and death, faith and unbelief can be found in ZNTW 24 (1925), 110f.; Odeberg 130–135. In itself the drawing of parallels between life and death, good and evil, and light and darkness is, of course, not only to be found in Gnosticism but is far more widespread (for Judaism cp. Odeberg 138–145, for the Greeks see Wetst. and p. 40f). In Gnosticism however the metaphysic of light has been developed within the framework of a clearly defined cosmology and eschatology, and the terminology which is employed here is the basis of the Johannine usage. On the other hand the Johannine conception of the coming of the Revealer has nothing to do with Philo's (or the Stoics') λόγος τομεύς, or with the σοφία interpreted as κρίσις, Philo de fuga et inv. 196.

[6] The antithesis in vv. 20f. may, like v. 18a, come from the source (from the section used in vv. 31–36?); only the explanatory ἵνα- clauses should be taken as the Evangelist's addition.

On the terminology of vv. 20f.: τὰ φαῦλα πράσσειν is relatively infrequent in Christian usage (5.29; Rom. 9.11; II Cor. 5.10; cp. Jas. 3.16; Tit. 2.8); but φαῦλος is common in Greek thought and in the LXX as an ethical term.—On ἐλέγχειν cp. 8.46; 16.8 and esp. Eph. 5.13, from which it becomes apparent that ἐλεγχθῆναι v. 20 and φανερωθῆναι v. 21 are synonomous.—ποιεῖν τ. ἀλήθειαν goes back to the OT עָשָׂה אֱמֶת, which originally means "to give proof of one's faithfulness" (ZNTW 27 (1928), 115f. 122), but then comes to mean "to act uprightly" (loc. cit. 129.130f.; ThWB I 243, 6ff.); this is the meaning here (and I Jn. 1.6) when it is contrasted with τὰ φαῦλα πρ. However since ἀλήθεια for John refers to the divine reality, the emphasis here in ποιεῖν τ. ἀλ. is clearly less on upright actions, as such, than on the fact that such action is genuine action, which has permanence and which in this sense is referred to as having occurred ἐν θεῷ (cp. its opposite ψεύδεσθαι I Jn. 1.6) cp. also DSD 1, 5: ולעשות אמת וצדקה ומשפט; similarly 5, 3; 8, 2.—ἔργα ἐργάζεσθαι as in

light: their works were evil.[1] Yet this latter explanation seems to rob of its seriousness the question posed to man by the mission of the Son. For does it not mean that the decision has already been made, and that the coming of the Revealer merely reveals what has been decided beforehand?[2] This would then mean that, for those who had done good,

---

6.28; 9.4 is a Semitic expression, see Num. 8.11; Ecclus. 51.30; Mk. 14.6; I Cor. 16.10; but it does also occur in Greek literature.—ἐν θεῷ cannot mean "in the judgement of God"' for in that case we would certainly expect καλῶς or something similar, but it can only mean "in communion with God". The expression is unusual; at most it can be compared with Rom. 16.12 (ἐκοπίασεν ἐν κυρίῳ). It is a Semitism, cp. Ps. 17.30. M. Goguel, l'Eglise primitive 1947, 491, 1 wants to take ἐν θεῷ instrumentally, "par l'action de Dieu".—The ὅτι should not be taken causally but as an explanatory clause after φανερ.

[1] The ἵνα-clauses in vv. 20f. are, of course, final clauses; they do not refer to the subjective and conscious intention of the agent, but to the tendency of their nature, which necessarily determines the content of their action. It does not refer to a bad conscience (Bl.). For this is the really terrifying thing, that a man can love the darkness and still have a good conscience (cp. Plat. Phileb. 65e/66a). The numerous occurrences of the idea that evil is afraid of the light (κλεπτῶν γὰρ ἡ νύξ, τῆς δ' ἀληθείας τὸ φῶς Eur. Iph. Taur. 1026 etc., see Wetst. and Br.), which move on the psychological level, are only parallel in as much as vv. 20f. are formally a general statement which plays on the meaning of φῶς. For material parallels we must rather look to Gnostic statements such as J. B. 203: "The evil are blind and cannot see. I call them to the light, but they bury themselves in the darkness." Ginza. 285, 30ff. speaks of those who "leave the call of life and love the call of darkness". See on 9.40f.; ZNTW 24 (1925), 111 and Br. ad loc. This terminology also lies at the basis of Eph. 5.8–14, but there it has been used in the exhortation, see H. Almquist, Plutarch u. das NT., 1946, 72.

[2] The same is found in Gnosticism which propounds the doctrine of the φύσει σωζόμενος (see p. 136): Od. Sal. 23.2f.:

"Grace belongs to the elect;
  who shall receive it
  but those who trust in it from the very beginning?
Love belongs to the elect;
  who shall receive it,
  but those who possessed it from the very beginning?

Od. Sal. 18.11–14 (the saving event only reveals that which always was):

"Their ignorance was revealed as foam,
  and as the mud of swamps.
The vain men thought themselves important,
  they entered into their own figure and became void.
But those who had knowledge knew them and pondered on this,
  and were not sullied in their thoughts;
For their thoughts remained fixed on the most High,
  and they mocked those who walked in error."

Of course the Gnostic has no criterion in his theory of the φύσις for recognising the σωζόμενοι, but he addresses his proclamation to all men and exhorts them to make the decision of faith. Moreover he does not believe that this decision will make no difference at all to man, he speaks not only of being begotten from above, but also of rebirth, see p. 136. The theory of the predestination of the believers on the basis of their φύσις is, on the one hand, the expression of the Gnostic's certainty of his salvation, and it serves on the other to relieve anxiety caused by the fact that most men do not believe. But even here, behind all

rebirth would no longer be a radically new beginning effected by the exchange of the old origin for a new. If vv. 20f. only meant that immoral men are predestined to ἀπώλεια and moral men to ζωή,[1] then the seriousness of the basic idea of ch. 3 and indeed of the whole Gospel would have been forfeited, and all that would be left would be a mythologically embellished moralism. This is certainly not what is intended. Rather what is meant is that in the decision of faith or unbelief it becomes apparent what man really is and what he always was. But it is revealed in such a way that the decision is made only now. In the encounter with the Revealer man is put in question in such a way that his whole past, which determines his present being, is also put in question. Only so can he be called to rebirth, to the rebirth which is the exchange of his old origin, for a new one. His decision as to his destination at the same time settles his decision on his origin. Before the encounter with the Revealer the life of all men lies in darkness and sin. Yet this sin is not sin, insofar as God, by the sending of his Son, holds the whole past *in suspenso* and so makes the encounter with the Revealer the moment of true decision for men. But for this encounter there would be no sin in the definitive sense of the word (9.41; 15.24). If the encounter leads to faith, the decision is thereby made that the believer is ἐκ τῆς ἀληθείας (18.37); the believer becomes a new man, in that his past too becomes a new past, and his works can be regarded as ἐν θεῷ εἰργασμένα. If the encounter leads to unbelief, then this also decides a man's past. Now sin "remains", the anger of God "remains" (9.41; 3.36). The statement that man in the encounter with the Revealer decides for or against him *on the basis* of his past is only a boldly paradoxical way of saying that in man's decision it becomes apparent what he really is. He does indeed reach his decision on the basis of his past, but in such a way that this decision at the same time gives the past its real meaning, that in unbelief man sets the seal on the worldliness and sinfulness of his character, or that in faith he destroys its worldliness and sinfulness. In the decision man makes when faced with the question put to him by God, it becomes apparent, in his very act of decision, what he really is. Thus the mission of Jesus is the eschatological event in which judgement is made on all man's past. And this mission can be the eschatological event, because in

this, lies the conviction that in the decision for faith or unbelief the real nature of man becomes apparent.

[1] The same view is found in Philo de Somn. I 86; ὁ γὰρ τοῦ θεοῦ λόγος, ὅταν ἐπὶ τὸ γεῶδες ἡμῶν σύστημα ἀφίκηται, τοῖς μὲν ἀρετῆς συγγενέσι καὶ πρὸς αὐτὴν ἀποκλίνουσιν ἀρήγει καὶ βοηθεῖ . . ., τοῖς δὲ ἀντιπάλοις ὄλεθρον καὶ φθορὰν ἀνίατον ἐπιπέμπει. C. Herm. 1, 22f.; παραγίνομαι ἐγὼ ὁ Νοῦς τοῖς ὁσίοις καὶ ἀγαθοῖς . . . καὶ ἡ παρουσία μου γίνεται <αὐτοῖς> βοήθεια . . . τοῖς δὲ ἀνοήτοις καὶ κακοῖς καὶ πονηροῖς . . . πόρρωθέν εἰμι, τῷ τιμωρῷ ἐκχωρήσας δαίμονι.

it God's love restores to man the freedom which he has lost, the freedom to take possession of his own authenticity.[1]

3) *The mystery of the witness:* 3.31–36[2]

3.9–21 dealt with the mystery of the son of Man, the one who is the Son sent by the Father (vv. 16f.), who has come down (v. 13), and whose coming and exaltation are the eschatological event. 3.31–36 also treat of him who has come down from above (v. 31), of the Son (v. 35) whom the Father has sent (v. 34). But now he is spoken of as the one who brings *witness* of what he has seen and heard (v. 32), that is of the ἐπουράνια (v. 12) and as the one who speaks God's *words* (v. 34). Thus it becomes clearer in what sense his coming is the coming of the light (v. 19); he reveals God through his word. It becomes clearer, too, in what sense the judgement is enacted through faith in him or through unbelief (vv. 18f.): faith or unbelief in *him* is the faith which man puts or refuses to put in his *words*. Jesus' coming and exaltation have their place within the scheme of salvation because he is the Revealer who speaks God's word.

Yet everything remains shrouded in mystery; for the word of God

---

[1] Zn. weakens the sense of the words: "These statements would only be wrong, i.e would correspond neither to the reality nor to the teaching of Jesus, if one were to exaggerate them to mean that *all* faith is preceded by and based on a continual doing of the truth . . . as *all* rejection of the revelation brought by Jesus is preceded by and based on a decidedly immoral character and a hatred of the truth." According to him Nathanael is the type of one extreme and the priests of the other, while Nicodemus stands for a type in the middle. This destroys the radical alternative.—Schl. thinks that in vv. 20f. Nicodemus "is told how he should act, and at the same time he is given the charge to act in this way", which is that he should do the work which is done in communion with God, which gives rise to the desire for the light. This does justice to the actual wording of the verses, but in their context they are certainly not intended to indicate a particular course of action, but to explain why men decided against the light.—According to Hirsch "man's relation to the light which relentlessly illuminates him, his relation, that is to Jesus, is determined" by whether he is upright or not. "It is the question of the nature of man in the roots of his being before God", —that is, whether he is upright or not. But what if there are no men who, in the root of their being, are either upright or dishonest? If all men are always both upright and dishonest? On the contrary, it is only in the encounter with the light—in so far as this is really the eschatological event—that the decision is made whether man is upright or not! Hirsch has here, as elsewhere, eliminated John's eschatology. Hosk. sees correctly that ἔργα cannot refer to meritorious deeds, and thinks that they are ἐν θεῷ εἰργασμένα when they are governed by the knowledge that all human action is in itself incomplete and requires the creative act of God for its completion. Such knowledge is faith:—but we can talk of this faith before Jesus' coming? Wik. has the correct answer.

[2] 3.31–36 did not originally belong to the sayings of the Baptist, as can be seen from the fact that as far as their form and content are concerned, they belong to 3.1–21, and from the fact that v. 32b does not fit the situation described in v. 26 (which is why Reitzenstein, Taufe 58, 2, takes v. 32b as a rhetorical question and reads λαμβάνοι, which is impossible). Moreover if it were the witness of the Baptist, then it could hardly speak of the Revealer without saying of Jesus that οὗτος ἐστιν (1.34). Dodd's (308–311) attempt to show that 3.31–36 is the proper continuation of 3.22–30 is highly artificial.

which he speaks is nothing more nor less than the witness *that* he is the Revealer, *that* he speaks God's word! Whereas in the normal way the one who bears witness and the one to whom the witness is borne are two different persons, and while this could appear to be the sense of vv. 11–21, it is made clear that here the two are identical. For the time being the riddle remains. So does the air of mystery of 3.9–21; for Jesus still speaks of the Son in the 3rd person. Of course the reader of the Gospel could already have learnt from Chapters 1 and 2 that the speaker is himself the one of whom he speaks. Yet if he now hears Jesus' words with Nicodemus' ears, and forgets, as it were, what he already knows, then he must see that the kind of knowledge under discussion cannot be directly mediated by reports about the Revealer, but can only be attained by man allowing himself to encounter the word of the Revealer, which at once reveals and conceals him.

V.31: [ὁ ἄνωθεν ἐρχόμενος ἐπάνω πάντων ἐστίν].
ὁ ὢν ἐκ τῆς γῆς ἐκ τῆς γῆς ἐστιν
[καὶ ἐκ τῆς γῆς λαλεῖ.]
ὁ ἐκ τοῦ οὐρανοῦ ἐρχόμενος ἐπάνω πάντων ἐστίν·
V.32: ὁ ἑώρακεν καὶ ἤκουσεν, [τοῦτο] μαρτυρεῖ,
καὶ τὴν μαρτυρίαν αὐτοῦ οὐδεὶς λαμβάνει.[1]

The subject of these verses is the figure who was discussed in vv. 13–21. Just as in v. 13 he was referred to as the ἐκ τοῦ οὐρανοῦ καταβάς so too here he is referred to as the ἄνωθεν ἐρχόμενος,[2] or, in the same verse, as ὁ ἐκ τ. οὐρ. ἐρχ.[3] The messenger from God is first described as ἐπάνω

---

[1] The antithetical style and the terminology of the verses show that they come from the source. Yet clearly the rhythm has been disrupted. It is not really possible to reconstruct the original form of the source, since the text of the Gospel is itself uncertain. ἐπάνω πάντων ἐστιν v. 31d is omitted by ℵ*D al it syr^c; τοῦτο v. 32 by ℵ D al (τοῦτο, which picks up again the preceding object, could very well have been inserted by the Evangelist in the source; if it comes from a copyist, then even so it corresponds to the Johannine style, see p. 79 n.3). Most probably, I would think, v.31a is the Evangelist's own composition which anticipates v. 31d, and equally it is probable that v. 31c is his own addition.

[2] Obviously ἄνωθεν (see p. 135 n.1), contrasted as it is here with ἐκ τ. γῆς, means "from above", cp. 8.23.—The reason for the Revealer's being referred to as ὁ ἐρχ. and not as ὁ ἐληλυθώς is that the pres. part. is used as a timeless description of the messenger, cp. 11.27; II Jn. 7. On "coming" see p. 50 n.3 and esp. Mand. Lit. 125: "Thou hast come, thou comest, apart from thee no one has come."

[3] On the distinction between "heavenly" and "earthly" see p. 147 n.1. The practice of referring to the divine sphere as "above" is wide-spread; for Judaism see Str.-B. and Schl. ad loc. The expression was common in the Greek world, esp. from the time of Plato, who speaks of the ἄνοδος of the ψυχή (P. Friedländer, Platon 2 ed. 1954, I. 69ff. 205) and also in mythological and philosophical Gnosticism, for which we need hardly give examples. —See also M. Dibelius on Jas. 3.17; E. Lqhmeyer on Col. 3.1f. (both in Meyers Kommentar).

above all πάντων, which is to say that he is equal to God in his relation to the world.[1] The contrast with ὁ ὤν εκ τῆς γῆς,[2] similarly implies that he is of divine nature; for the former, as a result of his earthly origin, is of earthly nature.[3] Moreover—and this is the essential point in this context—the man who is of the earth ἐκ τῆς γῆς λαλεῖ. This contrast is used as a foil for the description of the Revealer, and it makes no real difference whether or not the Evangelist was thinking of particular persons who had set themselves up as rivals to Jesus.[4] In any case a word could never come out of the earth comparable to that of the divinely sent Revealer, a word which could demand "faith", whose acceptance or rejection could decide between life and death. Only he who has come from heaven gives the authentic witness; or to put it another way, Jesus' word encounters us as the authoritative word spoken to us from beyond.[5]

Yet, as in 1.11, the very word that comes from beyond is rejected by the world, which loves only what belongs to it (15.19), and for which the language spoken by the Revealer is strange and unfamiliar (8.43). Yet, as in 1.12, there are exceptions.

---

[1] Cp. Rom. 9.5 (ὁ ὢν ἐπὶ πάντων θεός); Eph. 4.6. It is not possible to decide whether πάντων is neuter or masc. (Lagr.).

[2] The article in ὁ ὢν ἐκ τ.γ. must clearly be taken in a general sense (as in 8.47 etc.), in spite of the contrast with the specific ὁ ἄνωθεν ἐρχ. If ὁ ὢν ἐκ τ.γ. in the source, however, was intended to refer to specific individuals, then it would have had the antichrist or Satan in mind. And as the latter, according to I Jn. 2.18–23; 4.1–6 is embodied in the teachers of false doctrines, who ἐκ τοῦ κοσμοῦ εἰσίν and who ἐκ τοῦ κόσμου λαλοῦσιν (I Jn. 4.5), it is possible that the reference here is to them. It is quite impossible, however, that ὢν ἐκ τ.γ. should refer to the Baptist, for he is sent by God (1.6) and commissioned by him to bear witness for Jesus. The Baptist is not even considered in the antithesis in 3.31; his position is exceptional.

[3] On εἶναι ἐκ as referring to someone's origin and consequently to his nature, see p. 135 n.1.—In Greek the phrase εἶναι ἐκ is commonly used to refer to someone's descent; correspondingly the Rabbinic מִן refers to a man's origin (Schl.). For Gnosticism see Iren. I 6, 4: εἶναι ἐξ ἀληθείας or alternatively ἐκ κόσμου. (cp. e.g. Ginza 379, 24f.). In Jn. εἶναι ἐκ θεοῦ 7.17; 8.47; I Jn. 3.10; 4.1, 3, 4, 6, 7; 5.19 (ἐκ. τ. πατρός I Jn. 2.16); ἐκ τῶν ἄνω 8.23; ἐκ τῆς ἀληθείας 18.37; I Jn. 2.21; 3.19; ἐκ τοῦ κόσμου 8.23; 15.19; 17.14, 16; 18.36; I Jn. 2.16; 4.5; ἐκ τῆς γῆς 3.31; ἐκ τῶν κάτω 8.23; ἐκ τοῦ διαβόλου 8.44; I Jn. 3.8 (ἐκ τ. πονηροῦ I Jn. 3.12); ἐξ ἡμῶν I Jn. 2.19.—The reason for the use of γῆ here, and not κόσμος as in I Jn. 4.5, is that ἐκ τ. γῆς suggests itself more naturally as a contrast to ἄνωθεν or ἐκ τ. οὐρ. The comparison of 12.32; 17.4 with 13.1; 8.26, for example, shows that there need not be any difference in meaning. There is, of course, the difference that κόσμος is determined by its use in dualism, and can refer to the power which is at enmity with God (see pp. 54f.), whereas γῆ does not have these associations and can also be used in a neutral sense (6.21; 12.24).—There is no substantial difference between the ὢν ἐκ τ. γ. and the γεγεννημένος ἐκ. τ. σαρκός (v. 6).

[4] See p. 162 n.2.

[5] See pp. 144f. and on 5.19.—Bl.-D para. 342, 2 explains the change from the perf. (ἑώρακεν) to the aor. (ἤκουσεν) by saying that it is to stress the seeing. Yet it is hardly likely that there is any particular significance in the change (so too Acts 22.15; Clem. Hom. 1.9); cp. 5.37; I Jn. 1.1, 3.

V.33: ὁ λαβὼν αὐτοῦ τὴν μαρτυρίαν
ἐσφράγισεν ὅτι ὁ θεὸς ἀληθής ἐστιν.

New and interesting light is cast on the nature of μαρτυρία and πίστις in this verse.[1] It does not describe the faith which accepts the witness, as in 1.12, nor does it say that it "has the life" (3.15f.) but that it confirms the truth of God.[2] Since the μαρτυρία of the Revealer is identical with what it attests, and not complementary to it, it finds confirmation paradoxically not by appealing from the word which bears witness to the truth of that to which it bears witness, but in its acceptance by faith. It is only in faith in the word of witness that man can see what it is to which the word is bearing witness, and consequently can recognise the legitimacy of the witness himself. Thus according to I Jn. 5.10, he who believes in the Son has "the testimony in himself", that is to say, he does not need to look any further for something to confirm the testimony, for he already possesses it in the testimony itself. And so according to 7.17, whoever does the will of God, that is whoever believes, will recognise the truth of Jesus' teaching.

V. 34 explains why in the previous verse it says, "He confirmed that God is true" rather than ". . . that the witness is true".[3]

ὃν γὰρ ἀπέστειλεν ὁ θεός
τὰ ῥήματα τοῦ θεοῦ λαλεῖ.

That is to say, God himself speaks in the words of the God-sent Revealer. Now we can see more clearly why the word of witness and that to which the word bears witness are identical, for what God *says*, simply because it is said by *God*, can be nothing else than God's *action*. Inasmuch as he reveals himself, he is the λόγος.[4] If in Jesus the λόγος became flesh, then God's action is carried out in Jesus' words. The eschatological

---

[1] See p. 146 n.1.

[2] In early usage σφραγίς means a mark which is used as a means of identification, particularly of property, and which is thus a guarantee for the genuineness of sth. or someone's right of ownership (cp. IV Macc. 7.15 Rom. 4.11; I Cor. 9.2); σφραγίζειν (and σφραγίζεσθαι) means "to mark (with a seal) as a means of identification, and thus can mean simply "to confirm"; cp. 6.27; Heitmüller, Neutest. Studien f. Heinrici 45f.; Br. ad loc. and Wörterb.—The Rabbinic חָתַם (to seal or to sign) also seems to occur with the meaning of "to recognise", Str. -B. and Schl. ad loc.

[3] In the context ἀληθής here, as in 8.26, can only mean "truthful"; its opposite is ψεύστης 8.44, 55; I Jn. 1.10 and esp. I Jn. 5.10. It is, however, possible that it also (as in 7.18) has the further meaning of "real". Whoever denies God's truth in his revelation also denies the reality of God, which manifests itself in the revelation, and indeed only in the revelation. He who does not believe in the Revealer denies God, even if he theoretically recognises the "existence" of God. For God does not exist as a theoretically demonstrable being, but only as the Λόγος for the world and men.

[4] See pp. 34f..

event, in which God's love is active (3.16), is realised in the act of the Son's bearing witness to it in his word.

The identity of the words of Jesus with the words of God is underlined by the following sentence: οὐ γὰρ ἐκ μέτρου δίδωσιν.[1] The Father's gift to the Son is not measured out,[2] but given abundantly (πάντα v. 35). That is to say, the revelation which Jesus brings is complete, sufficient and in need of no amplification. And it means that Jesus is the Revealer in the entirety of his person; for if we were to distinguish in his appearance between what is and what is not revelation, we would have reduced the revelation to the level of a determinable quantity; that is to say we would again be looking at it from the point of view of the μέτρον. Now according to John the revelation is neither a complex of statements and thoughts whose completeness would consist in its forming a unified system—nor is it the visible "figure" presented by the appearance of Jesus, whose completeness would consist in its forming an organic whole. The completeness of the revelation is nothing other than the definitive character of the event which comes to pass in him, i.e., nothing other than the fact that he is the eschatological event.

The same point is made in mythological language in v. 35:

ὁ πατὴρ ἀγαπᾷ τὸν υἱὸν
καὶ πάντα δέδωκεν ἐν τῇ χειρὶ αὐτοῦ.

The mythological statement that God, "the Father", loves the Son is always found combined with the idea that God, creatively or redemptively, takes on tangible form in his "Son", becomes visible and active in him. The declaration means that God himself becomes present in his Son—whether he be the Cosmos or the Redeemer—as in

---

[1] The sentence has been added by the Evangelist to the source (cp. the explanatory οὐ γάρ v. 17; 5.22; 8.42), and anticipates the idea expressed in v. 35 (source). Black (op. cit.) wants to put v. 34c (οὐ γὰρ ... δίδωσιν) after v. 35. The subject of δίδωσιν would then, of course, be the πατήρ of v. 35, which is in fact, read by syr^{cur} in v. 34c (syr^{sin} has θεὸς ὁ πατήρ). Dodd (310f.) wonders whether Christ should be taken as subject, as in the *Catenae*. The object τὸ πνεῦμα, which is in the margin in B and omitted by syr, is a completely unjohannine addition (Zn. wants to retain τὸ πν., and moreover to take it as the subject of the sentence). The addition of the subject ὁ θεός in KD al gives the right sense. It is possible that originally the subject was given as ὁ πατήρ, which was then omitted because of the subsequent ὁ πατήρ in v. 35.—Afrahat and Ephr. add the Dative object filio suo, which also gives the correct meaning. For in the context the statement cannot have been intended as a general proposition, that wherever God gives, he always gives without measure, which would in any case be a doubtful proposition; cp. Rom. 12.3, and the Rabbinic theory that God gives the Spirit to the prophets in due proportion (Str.-B. ad loc.). On the present δίδωσιν (cp. 5.20, 30) see on 5.19.

[2] ἐκ μέτρου, which occurs only here, can only mean what is elsewhere expressed by ἐν μέτρῳ: "measured out", "sparingly" (Ezek. 4.10, 16 Judith. 7.21). This is the explanation given by Chrys. hom. 30, 2 t. VIII p. 172: ἀμέτρητον καὶ ὁλόκληρον πᾶσαν τὴν ἐνέργειαν τοῦ πνεύματος. Has it been confused here with ἐκ μέρους (Merx)?

his own image. The second statement in v. 35, that the Father has given over all things to him, carries the same meaning.[1] In Jesus the Father is present; he represents the Father. Whoever is directed to the Son

---

[1] In cosmological speculation the thesis that God the Father brought forth the cosmos as his son, has endowed him with perfect power, and loves him, is found as early as Plato's Timaeus (see p. 28 n. 1). For the Herm. lit.: Ps.-Apul. Ascl. 8 p. 300, 3ff. Scott; Lact. Div. inst. IV 6, 4 (in Scott I 298); C. Herm. 12, 4; cp. J. Kroll, Herm. Trism. 155f. Scott, Hermetica III 48. For Philo: ebr. 30; on this M. Adler in Die Werke Philos von Alex. V 1929, 17, 4 and Leisegang, loc. cit. IV, 78, 2; E. Bréhier, Les Idées phil. et rel. de Philon d'Al. 1907, 74. For Gnosticism: Hipp. El. VII 23, 5f. p. 201, 9ff. W.; C. Herm. 1, 12. This passage expressly emphasises the handing over of the power to the Son (καὶ παρέδωκεν αὐτῷ πάντα τὰ δημιουργήματα [text according to Scott]; cp. 1, 14: ... ἔχων πᾶσαν ἐξουσίαν]. Similarly Orac. Chald. in Psell. 1140c (W. Kroll, 'De orac. Chald.', Bresl. phil. Abh. VII 1895, 14); πάντα γὰρ ἐξετέλεσσε πατὴρ καὶ νῷ παρέδωκε δευτέρῳ.

In Gnosticism this mythology has been transferred from cosmology to soteriology, so that in Hipp. VII 23, 5f. (see above), 26, 2 the υἱός is identified with Christ. Cp. further Iren. I 4, 5 and the parallel text Exc. ex Theod. 43. Cp. above all the Od. Sal. and the Mandaean texts, according to which, as in Jn. 3.34f. the proof of the relationship between the Father and the Son is given in the fact that the Son speaks the words of the Father. In the Od. Sal. the Redeemer is the "Beloved" (of God, or of the Father) 8.22; 38.11, who has appeared with the "fulness" of the Father (41.13, cp. Jn. 1.14, 16; see p. 71 n. 2). He says:

"The Lord guided my mouth through his word,
  and opened my heart by his light.
He made immortal life dwell in me,
  and made me speak of the fruit of his salvation" (10.1f.).

In the Mand. lit. cp. esp.

Ginza 70, 3ff.: "The great (life) has created and commissioned thee,
  has arrayed, commissioned and sent thee,
  and given thee authority over every thing."
Ginza 333, 27ff.: "The great (life) called and commissioned me,
  and laid his wisdom over me.
(He laid over me) the well-guarded form,
  which is kept for me in the hidden places.
He laid over me love,
  which shall be given to my friends.
He laid over me gentle words,
  with which I should speak to my friends.
I am to speak to my friends,
  and redeem them from that which is transitory."

Cp. Ginza 68, 26ff.; 70, 1ff.; 78, 29ff.; 272, 21ff.; 305, 38 (the beloved Son); 316, 9ff.; 343, 21ff.—There is, of course, no point here in considering general parallels for the fact that the inspired prophet speaks the word of God (cp. Br. on 12.49), because the "speech" of the prophet is here seen within the context of a particular myth.—Further mention of the love of the Father for the Son is made in Jn. 5.20; 15.9; 17.23f., 26; 10.17. There are many variations in the Evangelist's way of describing the handing over of power; the Father has "given" the Son: everything 3.35; 13.3; (17.7); his name 17.11; δόξα 17.22, 24; ἐξουσία πάσης σαρκός 17.2; ζωὴν ἔχειν ἐν ἑαυτῷ 5.26; works, or the work 5.36; 17.4; words 17.8; the κρίσις, or the ἐξουσία for the κρίσις 5.22, 27; everything that he asks for 11.22; the believers 6.37, 39; 10.29; 17.2, 6, 9, 12, 24; 18.9.—Cp. M. Dibelius, Festg. für Ad. Deissmann 1927, 173–178: "Love refers here not to the unity of will by virtue of an affective relationship, but the unity of nature by virtue of divine quality" (p. 174). This is right,

can be sure of having for himself the Father who loves his Son, and can be sure of encountering in him the omnipotence of God himself.[1]

Such statements made about the man Jesus of Nazareth bring comfort and strength to those who hear them. There is nothing incomprehensible or mysterious which need frighten men away from Jesus. For the Father's love rests on him, and the power of the Father rests in his hand. Yet only the believer will be able to grasp the real meaning of this verse, for such words on the lips of Jesus are at first an offence to men, which must be overcome in faith. Even then this meaning is only implicit in v. 35, for the ἐγώ εἰμι has yet to be spoken. It is however implied, inasmuch as in **v. 36** the hearer is confronted with the possibility of faith and unbelief, together with their consequences, and so made to face the radical alternative, and also inasmuch as this alternative is the final word of the discourse:

ὁ πιστεύων εἰς τὸν υἱὸν ἔχει ζωὴν αἰώνιον·
ὁ δὲ ἀπειθῶν τῷ υἱῷ οὐκ ὄψεται ζωήν,
ἀλλ' ἡ ὀργὴ τοῦ θεοῦ μένει ἐπ' αὐτόν.[2]

It is the same alternative which we found in v. 18. Because man's eternal destiny is decided in faith or unbelief in him, his coming is the eschatological event. The judgement is accomplished in the way men divide over his person.[3] The ἔχει ζωὴν αἰώνιον (cp. v. 15) corresponds to the οὐ κρίνεται of v. 18, the οὐκ ὄψεται ζωὴν κτλ, to the ἤδη κέκριται.[4] The conclusion is less a promise than a warning. The consequences of unbelief are therefore once more emphasised in a third line, ἀλλ' ἡ ὀργὴ κτλ. The unbeliever always was under God's judgement.[5] Through his unbelief, his decision against God's revelation,[6] he makes this

---

inasmuch as the relationship of the Father to the Son is not thought of as a "moral" relationship; nevertheless this interpretation remains in the sphere of mythology, which John reinterprets in accordance with his idea of revelation; that is, that in Jesus we encounter God himself, his words are God's words.

[1] Διδόναι ἐν τ. χειρί or alternatively εἰς τ. χεῖρας 13.3 is an OT expression, cp. Is. 47.6; Dan. 2.38 and Schl. ad loc. For the interchanging of ἐν and εἰς, see Br. ad loc. and Bl.-D. para. 206, 218.

[2] These sentences also formed the conclusion of a discourse in the source, as is shown by the irregularly long third line (see p. 76 n. 4); there is no reason to take this third line as the Evangelist's addition.

[3] See pp. 153-6 (esp. p. 156 n. 4 and 157 n. 3.

[4] On ὄψεται see p. 135 n. 2 and Is. 26.14; Eccles. 9.9 and cp. 8.51.

[5] The ὀργή of God does not, of course, refer to an emotion or disposition of God, but as in the whole of the NT, corresponding to the OT and Jewish usage, to God's eschatological judgement. At first this is expected as a future event (Mt. 3.7 = Lk. 3.7; 21.23; Rom. 2.5, 8; 3.5; 5.9; I Th. 1.10 etc.); Paul does, however, think of it as something which is already present (Rom. 1.18; 4.15? I Th. 2.16).

[6] ἀπειθεῖν, referring to unbelief, is contrasted here with πιστεύειν, by which the character of faith as obedience is emphasised; this is the only occurrence of this in John,

situation irrevocable[1]. Thus the full weight of the eschatological event is found in Jesus' coming, precisely because by calling men to faith he questions man's entire past, and consequently the ὀργή of God, which threatens sinful man. It is this present moment which is decisive (cp. 9.41; 15.24).[2]

c) *The* Μαρτυρία *of the Baptist:* 3.22–30

The witness of the Revealer (3.1–21, 31–36) is now followed by the μαρτυρία of the Baptist.[3] As in 1.19–51 this discussion of the Baptist's witness has not only the positive purpose of confirming Jesus in his office as the Revealer, but also the negative purpose of excluding any possible rivalry between the Baptist and Jesus. The Baptist is only his witness. The introduction (vv. 22–26) which leads to the μαρτυρία (vv. 27–30) is primarily concerned to make this second point. It shows the rivalry between Jesus and the Baptist in their ministry of Baptism, and shows how the Baptist is defeated in this rivalry, and how this fact is confirmed by the Baptist's disciples.

It ought not to be difficult to see that this scene (vv. 22–26) is a *literary composition*, reflecting the rivalry between the sects of the Baptist and Jesus, nor to see that the Baptist who bears witness to Jesus is a figure from the Christian interpretation of history.[4] The question however remains, whether the scene is a *free composition* of the Evangelist's or whether it is based on some kind of *tradition*.[5]

Taken as a whole 3.22–26 gives the impression of being the Evangelist's own composition,[6] and in any case the utterance of the Baptist's disciples,

---

but it occurs frequently elsewhere (Rom. 11.30f.; 15.31; I Pet. 2.7f.; 3.1; 4.17; Acts 14.2; 17.5; D 19.9, cp. Rom. 10.3, 16; II Th. 1.8; the noun ἀπείθεια Rom. 11.30, 32; Col. 3.6; Eph. 2.2; 5.6; Heb. 4.11).

[1] On ἐπί with the acc. in answer to the question: Where? see Bl.-D. para. 233; Raderm. 142, 146.

[2] See pp. 159f.

[3] On the structure of the passage see p. 114.

[4] See pp. 16f., 94, 107f.

[5] Goguel, J. B. 86–95, particularly, has been at pains to show that the Evangelist in 3.22–4.3 has used a source containing particularly good ancient tradition. He believes that the statement that Jesus baptised (v. 22) and the description of the scene of the action (v. 23), could not have been invented; and as he suspects that the original text of v. 25 read μετὰ Ἰησοῦ, he believes that the source related that Jesus worked for a time alongside the Baptist, sharing his views, and that he baptised in the Jordan district. Further it told how the break between the two had come over their understanding of baptism.

[6] Μετὰ ταῦτα is a favourite transitional phrase of the Evangelist's, see p. 000. On (ἦν δὲ καὶ v. 23, see 2.1; 18.2, 5; 19.19, 39. The link with οὖν (v. 25) is very frequent. The simplicity of the style is like that of other editorial passages of the Evangelist's, 7.1–13; 10.19–21, 40–42; 11.55–57; further the construction of the scene is like 7.1–9. However many of the characteristic marks of the Evangelist's style are missing, and the Semitic type of language can be characteristic of the Evangelist and also of the source. The sequence of the sentences is simple and unsophisticated; in vv. 23, (24), 25 the predicate is placed first in the sentence; ὕδατα πολλά v. 23 is like מַיִם רַבִּים, although the plural ὕδατα is found in Greek (Colwell 82f.; Bl.-D. para. 141, 7); see Schl. on v. 23. Μετὰ Ἰουδαίου without τινός v. 25 is not a Greek construction.

which refers back to 1.19–34, must come from his pen. It is possible that he took the description of the scene of the action (v. 23) from oral tradition, while Jesus' baptising (v. 22) may be his own invention. He wanted to give a pictorial representation of the rivalry between the two Baptist sects by setting Jesus and John alongside each other as Baptists.[1] It is not a very plausible objection to this to say that, since a baptism performed by Jesus could only have been a baptism imparting the Spirit,[2] and that since such baptism was only made possible by his death and resurrection, it would have been impossible for the Evangelist to have invented the figure of Jesus the Baptist.[3] Even if the Evangelist, in his concern with the confrontation between the two Baptists, gave any thought to such questions, he could well have made the reservation which he makes with regard to the whole of Jesus' activity as Revealer, namely that such baptism receives its efficacy proleptically, in that the achievement of his work is already contained in the incarnation of the Logos.

Such arguments do not show that the statements in 3.22 *could* not be based on *tradition*. Nor is it any argument to point out that the Synoptic tradition makes no mention of Jesus' ministry of baptism. For the account of the relationship between Jesus and the Baptist in that tradition is clearly based on a one-sided selection. Yet even if v. 22 really should contain ancient tradition, this would be no proof that 3.22–26 has been taken from a source. This is in any case unlikely as far as v. 22 is concerned, for one would then expect an exact description of the place where Jesus baptised, such as is given for John in v. 23.

The only verse which, in my view, really gives one the impression that a source has been used in 3.22–30 is the puzzling **v. 25**; for it is not clear how the way it is formulated serves the purpose of the narrative. Not only is it entirely superfluous[4] but the story would be made more coherent by its omission. Nor is it possible to see why such a verse should have been interpolated here. The most striking thing about the verse is that the discussion is περὶ καθαρισμοῦ.[5] In the context this can only refer to baptism,[6] which would mean that it was a discussion about the relation of Jesus' and John's baptism. Why then is it not called περὶ βαπτισμοῦ (or βαπτισμῶν, cp. Heb. 6.2)? Περὶ καθ. suggests rather that the discussion was about questions of purification, as in

---

[1] It is possible that in 4.2 the Evangelist himself attempts to correct what he has said in 3.22. Yet there is a strong suspicion that 4.2 is an editorial gloss. Admittedly one would rather have expected an editor who wanted to make a correction here to have done so at 3.22. Cp. Dodd 310.

[2] Following Tert. and Chrys., Lagr. (and many others) defends the view that the dispute was over the question of the continuance of John's baptism of repentance; yet can this really be what the Evangelist meant?

[3] So esp. Goguel, J.-B. 92–94, cp. Rud. Meyer, Der Prophet aus Galiläa 115.—There is no need to bother ourselves here about the question whether 7.39b is the Evangelist's or an editorial gloss.

[4] "One" would be quite sufficient as the subj. of ἦλθον v. 26.

[5] Καθαρισμός refers to cultic or ritual purity, see 2.6.

[6] This is of course possible, see p. 87 n. 5.

Mk. 7.1ff. and parr. (cp. Lk. 11.37ff.; Mt. 23.25 ff.) and P. Oxy. 840 (Kl. Texte 31 [1908].3–9);[1] or perhaps that the Jew raised the question: What is the point of your baptism, when we already have the καθαρισμοί of Moses? Yet there is no reference to any such question in the following verses.[2] It is also striking that the dispute is between the disciples of John and a *Jew*,[3] whereas one would really expect it to be between the disciples of John and *Jesus*, or his disciples (cp. Mk. 2.18). The only way of making sense of it in the context would be to suppose that the disciples of John have met up with a Jew who has been or wants to be baptised by Jesus. Yet why is this not said plainly? Indeed, why is the main point of the discussion not even mentioned?

Thus we must certainly reckon with the possibility that we have in v. 25 a part of an old tradition.[4] The only reason the Evangelist could have had for incorporating it in his own account would have been that there was something in the rest of this traditional narrative which was useful to him. Since vv. 26 and 28, with their reference to 1.19–34, certainly come from the Evangelist's pen, this leaves only v. 27, and at most v. 29a, which could have been taken from the source. These verses would then be based on an apophthegm from the Baptist tradition,[5] which dealt with a dispute over the question of purification rites. In this dispute the Baptist defended his own position (his rite, or rather his criticism of Jewish rites) by appealing to the authority given to him by God; for this would be the sense we should have to attach to v. 27.[6] Also we should have to assume that the Evangelist had made this apophthegm into a μαρτυρία of the Baptist for Jesus—in the same way in which he based the Prologue of the Gospel on a Baptist Logos hymn.

Of course all this does not take us out of the realm of suppositions, which are nevertheless suggested by v. 25. And in fact it is of no real importance for the question of how the Evangelist himself understood 3.22–30.

---

[1] This is the sense in which Lagr. takes it.

[2] According to Schl. the dispute in v. 25 was about baptism; if the Baptist in vv. 27ff. does not mention baptism at all, but speaks only of Jesus, this brings out the fact that baptism, both in what it is and in what it imparts, is completely dependent on Jesus and what he is. "It is because he is the Christ, that baptism is the καθαρισμός." Yet the point which Schl. holds to be the central point here is not even mentioned in the text.

[3] As well as 'Ιουδαίου (ABL syr sin) the tradition also has 'Ιουδαίων (ℵ Ferrar group it syr[cur]), which must be a correction of the unusual sing., for it would be hard to see how the sing. could itself be a correction. One can see why modern exegetes have been led to make conjectures such as: μετὰ τῶν 'Ιησοῦ, μετὰ τοῦ 'Ιησοῦ, μετὰ 'Ιησοῦ. Goguel J. B. 89f. believes the latter to have been the original reading, if not of the Gospel then at least of the source. According to Strathm. the 'Ιουδ. is a Jew who has received baptism at the hands of Jesus.

[4] If 3.25 does come from a collection of (Baptist) controversies, there would have been no need to preface it with a special introduction. On the other hand it is possible that v. 23 is the original introduction.

[5] For the view that the Evangelist also draws elsewhere on Baptist tradition, see p. 18, 108.

[6] This would mean that we had a Baptist parallel to the synoptic account in Mk. 11.27–33. Yet even if the parable in v. 29a has been taken from the tradition, it would be possible to give various accounts of this. Do we perhaps have a parallel here to Mk. 2.19a?

1) *Introduction*: 3.22–26

The passage is connected to the previous section by the typical μετὰ ταῦτα,[1] which cuts short any speculation about what had gone before.[2] The passage of time is, as usual, combined with a change in geographical situation.[3] Jesus goes into the Judaean territory, although we are not told his motive for doing so.[4] He remains there, but we are not told for how long. In contrast with the information which is normally given, we are told here what Jesus did throughout this time: he baptised.[5] We are not given any details about this,[6] nor is it mentioned anywhere again. It is brought in merely to set the scene for what follows. One further piece of information must be given before the scene is fully set for the action which begins in v. 25. In **v. 23**, we are told that John also baptised,[7] and that people came to him,[8] and we are given an exact description of where he baptised together with the reason for his choice.[9] We may not ask why John is still baptising, now that Jesus has appeared and John has borne witness to him, when the only purpose

---

[1] See p. 167 n. 6.

[2] See p. 121 n. 6.

[3] Since the previous action has taken place in Jerusalem, Ἰουδαία γῆ here can mean only the Judaean countryside. Γῆ is then used here as χώρα (11.54f. and elsewhere), which is however permissible in Greek (Aesch. Eum. 993: καὶ γῆν καὶ πόλιν). Ἰουδ is used adjectivally as in Mk. 1.5, with the narrower meaning of "Judaean" (as opposed to Galilean), and not of "Jewish", as in Acts 16.1.

[4] Διατρίβειν in the sense of remaining in a place occurs frequently in Acts, but only here and in 11.54 (which see) in John. Elsewhere John uses μένειν 2.12; 4.40; 7.9; 10.40; 11.6, 54.

[5] Εβάπτ. imperf., referring to the duration of the action.

[6] See p. 168.

[7] On ἦν ... βαπτίζων, see p. 93 n. 2.

[8] Hirsch wants to take καὶ παρεγίνοντο καὶ ἐβαπτίζοντο (by making a strong break after ἐκεῖ) to refer to the flocking of the people to Jesus.

[9] It is very unlikely that the *place name* has been invented simply because of its allegorical meaning. For then, surely, the place where Jesus' baptised v. 22 would have been given in full, too. Nor does the reason given for John's choice support this view (ὅτι ὕδατα κτλ.). It seems probable that the description is based on tradition about the place where John baptised. According to Kundsin (Topol. Überlieferungsstoffe 25–27) Aenon near Salim was "in the Evangelist's time still thought of as a centre, if not *the* centre of the Baptist sect, which was still present in Palestine". It is possible that the Evangelist also had the allegorical meaning of the place name in mind (cp. 9.7). Since Αἰνών = עַיִן, spring (or alternatively the aram. plur. עֵינָוָן, see Lagr.), and Σαλίμ = שָׁלֵם, salvation, the meaning would be "springs near to salvation". It is questionable whether one should try to connect this with the spring (Aina) in the Mandaean baptismal liturgy and with the Mandaean angel of baptism Silmai (Br.).—The uncertain attempts to identify the places named here geographically have no importance for the exegesis of the passage. V. 26 shows only that the scene takes place west of the Jordan; see further Br., Schl., Lagr. ad loc. and Zahn, Neue kirchliche Zeitschr. 1907, 593–608; Dalman, Orte und Wege Jesu, 3. ed. 98f., 250f.; Albright (see on p. 18) The Archaeology 247 or The Background 159. Further see p. 93 n. 3.

of his baptism was to bear witness of Jesus as the Messiah.[1] The Evangelist is only interested in the picture of the two Baptists working alongside each other, and it gives a topographical illustration of the saying in v. 30. If in **v. 24** we are expressly told that John had not yet been arrested which is of course perfectly obvious after v. 23, then it seems that this note must have been inserted to bring this account somewhat closer to the tradition, according to which Jesus only began his ministry after the Baptist's arrest.[2]

The action begins in **v. 25.** A dispute[3] arises between the disciples of John[4] and a Jew[5] περὶ καθαρισμοῦ—in the context that can mean only a dispute about the relation of Jesus' baptism to John's baptism.[6] In **v. 26** John's disciples do not report the actual dispute to their master,[7] but rather inform him of what gave rise to the dispute, namely that Jesus is baptising, and that his success has exceeded that of John: "All are going to him!" Of course we have an echo here of the Baptist sect's jealousy of the sect of Jesus, which was outdoing them. Nevertheless one must not attempt to give a psychological interpretation of the disciples' report to John. At least on the face of it, this report can be and indeed ought to be a joyful piece of news; for if John's disciples refer to

---

[1] The question is raised by Bretschneider, Probabilia 47. (Cp. Justin dial. 51 p. 271**a**: καὶ Χριστὸς ἔτι αὐτοῦ (sc. τοῦ 'Ιωάννου) καθεζομένου ἐπὶ 'Ιορδάνου ποταμοῦ ἐπελθὼν ἔπαυσέ τε αὐτὸν τοῦ προφητεύειν καὶ βαπτίζειν). The Evangelist could reply that his continued ministry of baptism gave the Baptist renewed opportunity to bear witness to Jesus, as is shown in the present narrative.

[2] According to Mk. 1.14 (Mt. 4.12; cp. Lk. 3.19f.) Jesus made his appearance only after the Baptist had been arrested (by Herod Antipas). It is this tradition which Jn. 3.24 clearly has in mind. It is not clear that he wants to correct the tradition. It is more likely that he wants to harmonise his account with the Synoptic tradition, and to make room for the narrative of Jesus' and John's baptising alongside each other, which seems to contradict that tradition. It is even more probable that 3.24 (like 7.39b) is a gloss inserted by the ecclesiastical editor. Elsewhere the Evangelist makes no effort to harmonise his narrative with the Synoptic account, and indeed shows no further interest in the history of the Baptist, who is mentioned again only in 5.33–35; 10.40f. and there again only as a witness to Jesus. Cp. H. Windisch, Joh und die Synoptiker 1926, 62f.

[3] ζήτησις = controversy, disputation, only here in John; elsewhere in the NT, Acts 15.2; I Tim. 1.4; 6.4; II Tim. 2.23; Tit. 3.9. Cp. συζητεῖν = dispute (דְּרַשׁ) and see following note.

[4] The ἐκ after ζήτησις (searching, questioning) introduces the person who does the searching or questioning, as in Herod. V 21; Dionys. Hal. VIII 89, 4; ζήτησις δὴ ... πολλὴ ἐκ πάντων ἐγίνετο (Br.). That is to say, it is not the ἐκ which does duty for the gen. part. (7.40; 16.17; see Bl.-D. para. 164, 2).

[5] See p. 169 n.3.

[6] See pp. 168f.

[7] See pp. 168f.—V. 26 is clearly shown to be the Evangelist's own composition by the reference it contains to 1.19–34. On the carrying forward of relative clauses (ὅς ... ᾧ ...) by οὗτος see p. 79 n. 3. The stressing of οὗτος by ἴδε is specifically Rabbinic; Schl. ad loc.

Jesus as the one to whom their master bore witness,[1] then they must know that the πάντες ἔρχονται πρὸς αὐτόν is precisely what John wants.[2] Yet the Evangelist gives no thought either to the excited joy or to the embittered jealousy of the speakers in v. 26. His only aim is to reach a position from which he can address the words in vv. 27–30 to the Baptist sect of his own day.

2) *The* Μαρτυρία: 3.27–30

V. 27: οὐ δύναται ἄνθρωπος λαμβάνειν οὐδέν,
ἐὰν μὴ ᾖ δεδομένον αὐτῷ ἐκ τοῦ οὐρανοῦ.

The passage starts with a maxim, which provides the main theme for what follows.[3] It is a principle which is set forward as universally valid, and from which the consequences for the present case may be deduced. "No one can take anything, unless it has been given to him by God."[4] Every time, therefore, a man takes something, even if superficially it appears to be an arbitrary, foolish or high-handed action, we must recognise that he is receiving something.[5] The principle says nothing about whether the man who does the taking is in the right or the wrong. Indeed it would still be true of the robber, who could not take his spoils unless God so disposed (cp. 19.11). The statement points beyond the sphere of moral judgement—which has its justification elsewhere; it justifies events, not persons.[6] In this case it is applied

---

[1] μαρτυρεῖν does not, of course, have the special meaning of "giving a good report" of someone, as in Lk. 4.22; Acts 6.3; I Tim. 5.10 etc., but the forensic meaning of 1.34; see p. 50 n. 5.

[2] It is ridiculous to suggest that the disciples of John thought that ᾧ σὺ μεμαρτ. was an expression of the superiority of the Baptist to Jesus, the one bearing witness being superior to the one to whom witness is borne. For the testimony to which they appeal itself referred to Jesus as being superior to John.

[3] It is possible that the sentence comes from the Baptist source, see p. 169; this is supported by the fact that stylistically (5.19; 6.44; 15.4) and in its thought (5.19, 30) it corresponds to sayings taken from the "revelation-discourses". The reflexion on the δύνασθαι is also characteristic of the "revelation-discourses"; as well as 5.19, 30, cp. 5.44; 7.7, 34; 8.21, 43; 9.4; 10.29; 14.17; 16.12.—The οὐ ... ἄνθρ. (= οὐδείς) is a Semitic expression, in spite of Colwell 74, and the position of οὐδέν at the end of the clause is also probably Semitic, see Schl.—For the maxim cp. Hom. Il. 3, 65f.

[4] 'Eκ τ. οὐρ. (synonymous with ἄνωθεν 19.11) in normal usage = from God; cf. Mk. 11.30, Schl. ad loc. and on Mt. 21.25.

[5] It is wrong to translate λαμβ. as "receive" (1.16; see p. 76 n. 5), for the point of the maxim is that every act of taking is a receiving.—God's διδόναι to men: 3.16; 6.32; 14.16; 15.16; 16.23; I Jn. 3.1, (23), 24; 4.13; 5.11.16? 20; to the son: 3.34f.; 5.22, 26f., 36; 6.37, 39; 11.22; 13.3; 17.2ff.; 18.11. On the διδόναι of the Revealer see p. 57 n.5. The essential role played by the concept of διδόναι is shown particularly clearly by 14.27.

[6] Lagr. interprets differently and following Aug., Cyr. Al. wants to relate the statement to the Baptist and read: "It is not fitting that a man should take anything which has not been given to him from heaven."

to the fact that the Christian community is growing, while the community of the Baptist is on the decrease.

While the principle is self-explanatory its application is not expressly stated. But it is reinforced by the appeal in **v. 28** to the earlier μαρτυρία of the Baptist.[1] "You are my witnesses,[2] that I said, I am not the Messiah, but[3] am only a messenger[4] sent before him."[5] Here, too, the conclusion which might be drawn from this in the present situation is left unsaid, for it is perfectly obvious. Lastly in v. 29 we have the parable which describes the subordinate but essential role of the Baptist.[6] He is compared to the "friend of the bridegroom".[7] According to Oriental custom the "friend" has an important role to play, both before and after the marriage, in wooing the bride, arranging the feast, etc.[8] The bridegroom, on the other hand, is described with a certain humour as "he who has the bride," i.e. as the central figure. The happiness and joy of the bridegroom is taken for granted[9] and is reflected in the portrayal of the joy of the friend, who rejoices in the bridegroom's joy.[10] Thus the metaphor shows that the course of events has not reduced the importance of the Baptist, but has rather shown where it really lies.[11] As in the Synoptics, the Baptist is seen here not as a heretic,

---

[1] V. 28, which corresponds to v. 26 and which again refers back to 1.19–34, is of course also the Evangelist's own composition; see also n.5.

[2] Of course, one can also translate: "You must bear witness to me."

[3] On ἀλλ' ὅτι see Bl.-D. para. 470, 1: "ὅτι is omitted before οὐχ, because ὅτι stands before εἶπον; the missing ὅτι is then inserted after ἀλλ'."

[4] There is no need to find any difficulty in the fact that there is no saying of the Baptist in 1.19–34 which precisely corresponds to this one. ὁ ὀπίσω μου ἐρχόμενος 1.15 shows that the Evangelist was acquainted with the Christian interpretation of Mal. 3.1 (Mt. 11.10 = Lk. 7.27; Mk. 1.2).

[5] 'Εκεῖνος, used to refer to Jesus, is a favourite expression of John's (1.18; 2.21; 3.28, 30; (4.25); 5.11; 7.11; 9.12, 28, 37; 19.21), but is also common elsewhere.

[6] In its form v. 29 is not a comparison (ὡς ... οὕτως), but a metaphor (see Gesch. der syn. Trad. 2. ed. 181f. = Hist. of the Syn. Trad. 167ff.), the application of which is linked to it by αὕτη οὖν.

[7] The question has been raised whether ὁ ἔχων τὴν νύμφην is a legal term for the bridegroom (cp. Leo Haefeli, Stilmittel bei Afrahat, Leipzig. Semit. Stud. N.F. IV, 1932, 149). Or is the form here stylistically the same as in 14.21; I Jn. 3.3; 5.12 and elsewhere? (see Schl.).

[8] On the שׁוֹשְׁבִין see Str.-B. I 500–504. Cp. Leonh. Bauer, Volksleben. im Lande der Bibel 1903, 190.

[9] The joy of the bridegroom is proverbial, Is. 62.5; Jer. 7.34; 16.9; 25.10. On the rejoicing at Jewish marriage feasts see Str.-B. I 504–517.

[10] ὁ ἑστηκὼς καὶ ἀκούων is a typically Semitic general description, see Schl.—The dative χαρᾷ with χαίρειν corresponds to the Hebr. inf. abs. as in Is. 66.10 LXX; so too I Thess. 3.9, but the construction is not unknown in Greek, see Bl.-D. para. 198, 6; Raderm. 128f.; Colwell 30f.; admittedly it more usually takes the accusative, as in Mt. 2.10.

[11] This is a genuine metaphor, as in Mk. 2.19a, and not an allegory (as is correctly seen by Lagr.). Neither is Jesus referred to here as the heavenly bridegroom, as in Rev.

but as a God-sent messenger subordinate to Jesus; his disciples should be won over to the Christian faith. We can see the reason and the justice of the picture which the Evangelist gives us of the Baptist and his μαρτυρία, if we assume that the Evangelist himself once belonged to these disciples, that what he learnt there appeared in a new light from the standpoint of faith in Jesus, and that he saw it as a promise which had now received its fulfilment.[1]

The application is given in **vv. 29b, 30.** V. 29b remains close to the metaphor: αὕτη οὖν ἡ χαρὰ ἡ ἐμὴ πεπλήρωται. Here two ideas are drawn together: 1) this joy, i.e. the joy of the "friend", is mine; 2) it has come to fulfilment. Doubtless the way this is formulated contains a play on the χαρὰ πεπληρωμένη which the Revealer promises to his own, when he leaves them and which is at the same time the joy of the Revealer himself.[2] The joy of the Baptist stands in discreet contrast to the joy of Jesus and his disciples; for theirs is the eschatological joy. The saying then—virtually a variant of Mt. 11.11 = Lk. 7.28—contains the idea that the end of the old epoch has now come.[3] This is confirmed by what follows: "He must increase, but I must decrease."[4] This is the law which gives the key to the understanding of the process described in vv. 22–26. These events, that is, only reflect on a small scale what is happening throughout history; the old epoch of the world has run its course, the eschatological age is beginning.[5] Thus there are good reasons for taking

---

19.7, 9, nor is there any reference to the messianic marriage of the eschatological community (Rev. 21.2, 9; II Cor. 11.2). The fact that the Rabbis thought of the community as the bride of God, and that they interpreted the Song of Songs in this way (Schl.) has no bearing on Jn. 3.29. It is quite absurd of G. P. Wetter, Sohn Gottes 54, to take νύμφη as referring to the Spirit which Jesus has.—Br. citing the mystery cry χαῖρε νύμφιε, χαῖρε νέον φῶς (Firmic. Matern. de err. prof. rel. 19, 1), draws attention to the Gnostic myth of the ἱερὸς γάμος of the Redeemer with the σοφία. But in Jn. 3.29 the primary figure in the comparison is the "friend", who plays no part in the Gnostic myth. We might note here that the motif of the ἱερὸς γάμος does not occur in all Gnostic systems; it is not found in the Mandaeans, for example, whereas it does occur (at least as an image) in Od. Sal. 38.11; 42.8.

[1] See pp. 18, 51, 107.

[2] 15.11; 16.24; 17.13; (I Jn. 1.4); see on 17.13.

[3] There is a certain parallel to this idea in the words addressed by Johana to Manda d'Haije, Ginza 193, 16ff. However the Johana sections of the Mandaean literature seem to be late (H. Lietzmann, SA Berlin 1930, 27. Abh.), so that there is unlikely to be any connection.

[4] 'Ελαττοῦσθαι here does not, of course, mean "to be in need", as often in the LXX, but has the usual meaning of "to be diminished", "to decrease"; in this sense it is used specifically of stars in Dio Cass. 45, 17. 'Αυξάνειν is also used in this specific sense, see Frz. Boll, SAHeidelb. 1910, 16. Abh., 44, 2; cp. also Boll, Die Sonne im Glauben und in der Weltansch. der alten Völker 1922, 22; Ed. Norden, Die Geburt des Kindes 1924, 99ff. esp. 107f.; H. Schlier, Christus und die Kirche im Eph.-Brief 1930, 71f. H. Almquist, Plutarch u. das NT 72.

[5] On the δεῖ see p. 152 n. 3.

the words αὐξάνειν and ἐλαττοῦσθαι in the solar sense, as was indeed done by early exegesis:[1] the old star is sinking; the new star rises.

B. 4.1–42: Jesus in Samaria

4.1–3(4) is the editor's introduction. It leads into the geographical setting presupposed in the traditional material which begins with v. 5(4). The fact that the Evangelist has used traditional material in vv. 5(4)ff. is shown by the tension between the main lines of the narrative and the sections containing the Evangelist's characteristic ideas.[2] Vv. 5 to 9 relate the first part of the story of Jesus and the Samaritan woman. Clearly the point of this story originally lay in the question of the relation of the Jews to the Samaritans.

Yet in vv. 10ff. this point is not at first made; indeed vv. 10–15 (the living water), which employ the literary devices of *double-entendre* and misunderstanding, show themselves to be the Evangelist's own composition for which in vv. 13f. he has used the "revelation-discourses". The original continuation of the traditional material used in vv. 5–10 is obviously contained in vv. 16–19, where Jesus gives proof of his authority as προφήτης by his miraculous knowledge. The original conclusion is to be found in vv. 28–30 and 40.[3] However it is possible that this unit of traditional material has also been used as the basis of vv. 20–26, where the motif of vv. 5–9 is repeated, as it were, on a higher level (see below). In their present form vv. 20–26 have, of course, been completely remoulded by the Evangelist to form the climax of the story. He uses the conclusion of the narrative to add two further ideas: 1) vv. 31–38: Jesus and the disciples, or the task of mission. This implies that v. 8 and v. 27 should be attributed to the Evangelist, for the old narrative no more mentions the disciples than do 2.1–12, 13–22 and, for example, Lk. 10.38–42.[4]—2) Vv. 39, 41–42: Jesus and the Samaritans, or first- and second-hand faith. Since this question also belongs to the problem of the mission, the two sections are internally related.

---

[1] Admittedly the exegesis of the early Church takes this interpretation too far, when it tries (from Ambr. and Aug. on) to extract from Jn. 3.30 the dates of the birth of the Baptist (summer solstice) and Jesus (winter solstice); see Norden op. cit. 101.

[2] Cp. the analyses made by Wdt., Schw., Wellh., and Sp.—Wellh. suspects that 4.4ff. originally came after 7.1ff. because Jesus could originally have passed through Samaria only on his way from Galilee to Jerusalem, and because there is no account of his journey after 7.1ff. But this sort of argument arbitrarily supposes a "basic written text" corresponding to the schema of the Synoptics.—The analysis of the composition of 4.1–42 given by L. Schmid ZNTW 28 (1929), 148–158 attempts to show that the whole passage is planned as a unit, but he fails to give a critical analysis of the passage.

[3] V.39 and v. 40 are quite incompatible with each other. Equally v. 39 is quite impossible after v. 30, for it completely ignores the arrival of the Samaritans reported in v. 30. Yet one can hardly omit v. 30 in favour of v. 39, since v. 30 is demanded by v. 29 (δεῦτε ἴδετε); moreover v. 39 betrays the style of the Evangelist. This means that v. 40 was the original continuation of v. 30 and must have run something like: ἐξῆλθον ἐκ τῆς πόλεως καὶ ἠρώτων αὐτὸν μεῖναι παρ' αὐτοῖς κτλ.

[4] Cp. also Gesch. der synopt. Trad. 2. ed. 368f. = Hist. of the Syn. Trad. 343f. Noack 124 argues against the analysis given above.

Thus the rather complex edifice created by the Evangelist can be divided up quite simply: vv. 1–30 Jesus' witness to himself, vv. 31–42 the relation of the believer's witness to Jesus' self-witness. This shows that the construction of 4.1–42 is parallel to that of chapter 3,[1] forming, as it were, the other side of the diptych. Whereas ch. 3 placed Jesus' self-witness alongside the Baptist's μαρτυρία to him, 4.1–42 places it alongside the preaching of the believers, which points back to him.

a) Jesus and the Samaritan woman: 4.1–30

1) *Introduction:*[2] 4.1–4

The reason for Jesus' journey cannot here, as it is elsewhere, be a festival,[3] it must be, rather, the jealousy of the Pharisees,[4] occasioned by the success of his baptising,[5] which makes him take measures for his safety.[6] Jewish traditions about Rabbis' journeying through Samaria and disputing with the Samaritans,[7] may well have influenced the Evangelist, just as they had earlier left their mark on the traditional material he uses here (vv. 5ff). The fact that Galilee is given as the destination to which Jesus is returning once more (πάλιν v. 3, referring to 1.43–2.12), shows the influence of the old tradition, according to which Jesus never purposely chose out Samaria for his ministry. Here, too, he only passes through Samaria because it is the shortest route to Galilee.[8]

---

[1] See p. 111.

[2] As it stands v. 4 belongs to the introduction written by the Evangelist (see p. 175), but he may have used a sentence from the source. μαθητὰς ποιεῖν is characteristic of the Semitising style of the Evangelist (Str.-B., Schl.).—In v. 1 ἔγνω ὁ κύριος ὅτι is a clumsy gloss, which makes the structure of the sentence cumbrous. Prior to ch. 20 Jesus is otherwise referred to as ὁ κύριος only twice, in 6.23; 11.2, and these are also glosses. ὁ Ἰησοῦς ℵ D al is a correction to bring the text in line with Johannine usage.—The parenthetical v. 2 corrects the statement in 3.22, and the καίτοιγε which occurs nowhere else in Joh (nor in the rest of the NT) suggests that it is an editorial gloss, although it is hard to see why the editor did not make the correction at 3.22. Dodd (311, 3) is also inclined to take v. 2 as an editorial addition, but Barr. has his doubts. See p. 168 n.1.

[3] See p. 122 n. 3. The unexpected aor. ἀπῆλθεν v. 3 must be complexive, see Bl.-D. para. 327.

[4] The usual article before Ἰησοῦς is omitted in v. 1, as in 4.47; 6.24, because the ὅτι is recitative here. (Bd.)—The view that the Pharisees were championing the Baptist (Htm.) finds no support in the text (Lagr.).

[5] πλείονας is the object of both μαθ. ποιεῖ and βαπτ.; that is to say, being baptised by the Baptist and becoming his disciple are one and the same! As in 6.60f., 66 μαθ. refers here to a wider circle of followers. It has nothing to do with the Twelve, who are referred to in 4.8, 27ff. and who should be thought of as Jesus' permanent following (see p. 115 n.5)

[6] This motif also occurs in 7.1.

[7] Cp. Dalman, O. u. W. 3. ed. 229.

[8] ἔδει also has this harmless meaning in Jos. vit. 269 (cp. also ant. XX 118).

2) *Jesus and the Samaritan woman:* 4.5–30

i. *Setting the scene*: 4.5–6

Jesus comes into the vicinity of the town of Sychar[1], whose position is described as being close to the field that Jacob gave to Joseph.[2] Since this description would only make sense to someone with knowledge of those parts, the narrative evidently assumes local knowledge in its hearers.[3] This also applies to the statement that Jesus sat down[4] by Jacob's[5] well. For this lies on the main highway running south to north from Jerusalem to Galilee, and is near the place where the main road was joined by the road to West Galilee.[6] The important points for the

---

[1] Sychar, which is not mentioned in the OT, appears to be attested in Rabbinic lit. (Str.-B. II 431f.; Dalman, O. u. W. 226–229; Schl. ad loc.). If it is the same as present-day Askar, it lies at the foot of Ebal. It can only have been a village; the use of πόλις to refer to it here (as in Mt. 2.23 for Nazareth) corresponds to the Palestinian use of עִיר and קִרְיָה for places of every possible size (Schl. on Mt. 2.23).—According to Albright (Archaeol. 247f.; Backgr. 160) we should read Συχέμ with syr^{sin}.

[2] This piece of information presupposes the tradition based on the combination of Gen. 33.19 and 48.22, which is to be found in Josh. 24.32 (Str.-B. II 432f.). The tradition also looks here for Joseph's grave, which is not mentioned by John. Cp. too Joach. Jeremias, Golgotha, 1926, 23, n. 6.

[3] Of course the more precise description of the position of the place, πλησίον κτλ., could also have been added by the Evangelist.

[4] οὕτως can scarcely mean "without further ado" (Br., who bases this view on Cat. p. 216, 21: ὡς ἁπλῶς καὶ ὡς ἔτυχε) but means simply "so" (that is, wearied by his journey), although in this case it would have been better to have placed it before ἐκαθέζετο (cp. Acts 20.11; 27.17; and Br. ad loc.). For the argument against Torrey 343, who wants to take οὕτως as a Semitism, see Colwell 118 to 120.—On ἐπί with the dative (as also in 5.2) instead of the genitive (as in 21.1) see Bl.-D. para. 235, 1.

[5] The omission of the article before πηγή in ἦν δὲ κτλ. might be a Semitism (Torrey 323), cp. Josh. 15.9; I Kings 6.18; II Es. 13.16; in Greek usage the omission of the article could be justified if πηγὴ τοῦ 'I. were felt to be a proper noun (Bl.-D. para. 261, 1).—The reason for referring to the well as πηγή may have been that it was filled by ground-water as well as by rain water. Yet πηγή (v. 6) and φρέαρ (vv. 11f.) are used interchangeably in Gen. 16.7, 14; 24.16, 20; Song. 4.15 (for עַיִן and בְּאֵר), whereas Philo post Cai. 153; vit. Mos. I 255 naturally distinguishes between the two. In John 4 the fact that it is a well and not a spring only becomes significant for the Evangelist at vv. 11f.

[6] This is assuming that the tradition about Jacob's well, which is found neither in the OT nor in Rabbinic lit., and which after John is not found again till the Pilgrim of Bordeau (333), is correct. There are hardly any grounds for doubting (Loisy) that it is, even if the well is 1½ kilometers away from Askar, which makes one wonder why people from Sychar should fetch their water from here, and not from a nearer spring. The reason for this may be that they attributed special power to the water of Jacob's well (Zn., Dalman). On the other hand in the story the well is the central feature, and it would be natural to choose an important well. If he had to mention a "town" as well, the narrator would choose the nearest one without considering whether it was likely that people would go there from the town to fetch water. Dalman (O. u. W. 228) points out that v. 11 gives one the impression that this was the only place in the neighbourhood where it was possible to draw water, which was not in fact the case.—The origins of the story must be sought in the local tradition of the Christian communities of Samaria; cp. Kundsin, Topol. Überl. 27–30.

following narrative are that the scene takes place in Samaria, and that it is set at a well; moreover the fact that it is Jacob's well also enters into the story (v. 12). The situation at the beginning of the scene is that Jesus, tired by his journey, sits down by the well.[1] The mention of the time of day[2] has a like significance: it is mid-day, so one would expect him to be tired and thirsty. The only thing that is not mentioned here is that his disciples are not present, and the Evangelist adds this in v. 8. If this had formed part of the original description of the scene it would have been joined on to v. 6, which is where syr^{s} places it.[3]

ii. *Jesus Asks for Water*: 4.7–9

The action proper begins with the arrival of a woman. In order to bring out the point of the story she is expressly described as a Samaritan woman.[4] The enmity between the Jews and the Samaritans[5] noted by the gloss at the end of v. 9,[6] was common knowledge to the original narrator and his audience, so they would have immediately realised that Jesus' request for water signified an abandonment of the Jewish viewpoint. The problem is brought out by the astonished question of the woman (v. 9): how can Jesus, as a Jew, ask a Samaritan woman for a drink?[7] The narrator here shows no interest in how the woman managed to recognise that Jesus was a Jew.

---

[1] κεκοπιακώς simply provides a reason for what happens in the story. No thought is given here to the paradox which is expressed in Act. Thom. 47, p. 164, 9ff.: Ἰησοῦς ὁ ἐπαναπαυόμενος ἀπὸ τῆς ὁδοπορίας τοῦ καμάτου ὡς ἄνθρωπος καὶ ἐπὶ τοῖς κύμασι περιπατῶν ὡς θεός.
—The narrative portrays a typical scene, cp. the expansion of Ex. 2.15 in Jos. ant. II, 257 which in style reminds one of a short story: εἴς τε πόλιν Μαδιανὴν αφικόμενος (ὁ Μωυσῆς) . . . καθεσθεὶς ἐπὶ τινος φρέατος ἐκ τοῦ κόπου καὶ τῆς ταλαιπωρίας ἠρέμει μεσημβρίας οὔσης οὐ πόρρω τῆς πόλεως . . . 258: παραγίνονται οὖν ἐπὶ τὸ φρέαρ ἑπτὰ παρθένοι ἀδελφαὶ . . . (Kreyenbühl II 397)

[2] No thought is given to the question why the woman should be coming to fetch water at this improbable hour. Hosk. points to Jos. Ant. II 257 where (in his account of Ex. 2.15) he says of Moses: καθεσθεὶς ἐπί τινος φρέατος ἐκ τοῦ κόπου καὶ τῆς ταλαιπορίας ἠρέμει μεσημβρίας οὔσης οὐ πόρρω τῆς πόλεως.

[3] See also p. 175.—The plural τροφαί (as not uncommonly like ὀψώνια, ὕδατα etc. Bl.-D. para. 141, 7) corresponds to both Greek and Jewish usage (Schl.).

[4] Σαμ. v. 7, of course, refers not to the town, but as always in the NT to the country. Ἐκ τῆς Σαμ. must therefore be taken with γυνή (cp. 3.1) and not with ἔρχεται.

[5] On the relation of Jews and Samaritans see Ecclus. 50.25f.; Mt. 10.5; Lk. 9.25ff.; the treatise Kuthim; Schürer II 22f.; Moore I 24–27; Str.-B. I 538–560; Hamburger, Realenzykl. für Bibel und Talmud II 1062–71; M. Gaster, The Samaritans 1925.

[6] The gloss is omitted by ℵ*D and the ancient Latin authorities; if originally it was contained in the text, then of course it comes from the Evangelist.—Both Ἰουδ. and Σαμ. are used in a specific sense (Bl.-D. para. 262, 3). For the dispute itself see previous note. The sentence is still proverbial according to L. Bauer, Volksleben im Lande der Bibel 1903, 226, and is used by the members of different confessions when, for example, they fall out over business transactions, or when one of them disapproves of the dishonest actions of another.

[7] Jesus is a Ἰουδαῖος, even though he is a Galilean, because he belongs to the Jewish

Yet surprisingly the question of the relation of the Jews and the Samaritans, or—to put it in the form in which it was raised for the early community—the relation of Jesus' disciples and the Samaritans is immediately put on one side (vv. 10ff.),[1] despite the fact that it had exercised the early community a great deal in the initial stages, Mt. 10.5; Lk. 9.52ff.; 10.30ff.[2] Its place is taken by the characteristic question of Johannine dualism, whether Jesus' gift is of the earth or of God. Besides this, the question of the Jews and the Samaritans fades into insignificance.[3] Whereas the original narrator would have felt that this cut across the main line of his story, it was not so for the Evangelist; for in vv. 20–26 he again turns to the problem which he had left unanswered in vv. 10ff., and in his own particular terminology states explicitly what had only been hinted at in the rapid transition of v. 10. The old distinction between Jews and Samaritans has lost its force in the light of the revelation which confronts man in Jesus.

It is, of course, not possible to reconstruct the rest of the original story. There was certainly no need to mention that Jesus accepted the drink. But the narrative must have included Jesus' reply to the woman and this has been lost in the Evangelist's rewriting of the story. We can get some idea of what it might have been from a Buddhist parallel, which can be traced in the 2nd or 3rd century A.D. Buddha's favourite disciple Ananda, tired after a long journey, asks a girl of the Candala caste who is drawing water at a well for a drink. When she warns him not to contaminate himself, he replies: "My sister, I do not ask what your caste or your family is; I am only asking you for water, if you can give it to me."[4] In the tradition used by the Evangelist the conversation must have ended with some such saying of Jesus. However this was probably only the first part of the conversation which, was then followed by vv. 16–19, where Jesus reveals himself to be a προφήτης; and this in turn will have prepared the way for the final exchange, which the Evangelist has

prophet

---

national and cultic community.—The view that the question is an unfriendly rejection of Jesus' request (Bl.) has no basis in the text.

[1] The link between vv. 7–9 and v. 10 is clumsy, inasmuch as one must naturally emphasise "*you* would have asked *him*"—yet the contrast which one would expect to this: "not *he* would have asked *you*", makes no sense at all after εἰ ᾔδεις.

[2] In Acts the problem has disappeared, and the Samaritan mission is regarded as a matter of course (1.8; 8.5ff.; 9.31; 15.3). Acts 8.5ff. raises a different problem altogether.

[3] The extent to which this has become insignificant is shown by v. 27; the disciples are not surprised that Jesus is talking to a *Samaritan*, but that he is talking to a *woman*.

[4] G. A. van den Bergh van Eysinga, Indische Einflüsse auf evangelische Erzählungen, 2. ed. 1909, 49–53; G. Faber, Buddhistische und neutest. Erzählungen 1913, 60–62; R. Garbe, Indien und das Christentum 1914, 34f. Winternitz, Gesch. der ind. Lit. II 223f. The end of the story is specifically Buddhist; the girl falls hopelessly in love with Ananda, but is converted by Buddha to his teachings. It is debatable whether there is any genealogical relationship between the Johannine and the Buddhist story and a final answer seems hardly possible.

replaced by vv. 20–26.[1] It is most likely that in this final exchange Jesus revealed himself as the Messiah, which would mean that vv. 25f. are based on old tradition. This view is supported by the original conclusion, vv. 28–30, 40. It would also mean that the traditional material used here was related to that used in 1.35–51, wherein Jesus also shows himself to be the θεῖος ἄνθρωπος, and consequently the Messiah, by his supernatural knowledge of the men he meets. If 1.35–51 is taken from the σημεῖα-source (see p. 113), it would lead us to suspect that it has also been used as the basis of 4.5–42.[2] It would then be possible to see why the Evangelist follows this narrative with the story in 4.46–54, which certainly comes from the σημεῖα-source, and whose position here would otherwise be hard to understand (see below).

iii. *The Living Water:* 4.10–15

Jesus' reply (**v. 10**), in which he corrects the woman's question,[3] is intended to make it clear, more to the reader than to the woman, that the encounter with him means a radical reversal of normal standards: man, for all his possessions, is in truth poor, and Jesus' poverty only conceals the riches of his gift. If men are to recognise his riches two conditions must be fulfilled: 1) εἰ ᾔδεις τὴν δωρεὰν τοῦ θεοῦ.[4] A man must know what it is that he has to receive from God, a knowledge which is at one with the realisation of his own poverty. 2) καὶ τίς ἐστιν ὁ λέγων σοι . . . A man must recognise the Revealer when he encounters him in tangible form. Since, however, the gift of the Father is the Revealer

---

[1] The question in v. 19, beginning as it does with a captatio benev., recalls Mk. 12.14. Was it originally meant to be a trap, which Jesus skilfully avoids? On the question of the source, see also p. 193.

[2] Both linguistically and stylistically the sections 4.5–9, 16–19, 28–30, 40 reveal the same character as the source which is used in 1.35–51. The same simple way of stringing together short sentences without any connecting links (how different are vv. 10–15, 21, 23f.!) and the same habit of putting the verb at the beginning of the sentence, without there being any evidence of a translation from a Semitic original. The expressions in vv. 16f. for which Schl. adduces Semitic analogies can just as easily be Greek; the τοῦτο ἀληθῶς εἴρηκας v. 18 is specifically Greek (see Br.).

[3] Naturally the Evangelist must here say ὕδωρ ζῶν without the article, to make the misunderstanding possible, whereas in analogous cases we find τὸ φῶς, ὁ ἄρτος, ἡ ἄμπελος.

[4] δωρεά in early Christianity and in Philo (see Leisegang, Index) is the usual word for referring to a (the) gift of God. In Acts 2.38; 8.20; 10.45; 11.17; Heb. 6.14 it is the Spirit; in Rom. 5.17 the δικαιοσύνη; in Eph. 3.7; 4.7 salvation in general; in Barn. 9.9 the διδαχή. Rabbinic Judaism speculates about God's "gifts" (מתנות), of which the highest is the Torah (Odeberg 149–151). But the Greeks also speak of God's δωρεά, particularly the gift of Dionysus: Plato leg. II, p. 672a; Athen. XV, p. 693b. It is used of God's revelation in C. Herm. 4.5; ὅσοι δὲ τῆς ἀπὸ τοῦ θεοῦ δωρεᾶς (sc. τοῦ νοός) μετέσχον, οὗτοι . . . ἀθάνατοι ἀντὶ θνητῶν εἰσί. Cp. the Herm. fragment in Scott I 384, 14: ἐὰν ὁ θεὸς τὴν θεοπτικὴν δωρήσηται δύναμιν. Pap. Gr. Mag. XII 92.—According to Arist. Top. IV 4, p. 125a 18 the δωρεά is a δόσις ἀναπόδοτος; according to Philostr. vit. soph. II 10, 4 δῶρον refers to material and δωρεά to ideal gifts.

himself, such knowledge and recognition are intimately connected. Yet the knowledge may precede the recognition, inasmuch as there is a knowledge of God's gift which precedes the actual receipt of the gift, a questioning, waiting knowledge, which contains the prior understanding from which, in the encounter with the Revealer, recognition springs.[1] The nature of this recognition is, however, made clearer by the portrayal of the Revealer as a tired traveller who asks for something for himself. Such recognition is a recognition in spite of appearances; it must overcome the offence of the σάρξ.

The peculiarity of this knowledge and recognition corresponds to the peculiarity of the gift. Here it is referred to as ὕδωρ ζῶν—an ambiguous expression; for "living water," in general oriental usage, means running water, spring water,[2] as is shown by the woman's reply (vv. 11f). But the reader can see without difficulty that something else is meant, viz. the revelation which Jesus brings, as is immediately made clear by what Jesus says in vv. 13f.[3]

Like Nicodemus in 3.4, the woman here misunderstands the ambiguous words of Jesus (**vv. 11f.**) and imagines that he is claiming to be able to get her spring-water, which would be impossible.[4] The point of the misunderstanding is to bring home the fact that the water which men call "living" is not really "living water" at all. The use of ὕδωρ ζῶν to refer to the revelation is based on the peculiar type of "dualism" which we find in John, according to which all earthly goods are only apparent, false goods, and natural life is only inauthentic life. Only what is given by the divine revelation can be said to have the character of the real, the genuine, the ἀληθινόν.[5]

---

[1] See p. 62. This still holds good if, with Schweizer (161, n. 122), one takes the καί as epexegetical.

[2] Gen. 26.19; Lev. 14.5; Jer. 2.13; Zech. 14.8; for Judaism see Str.-B. on 4.11; Schl. on 4.10; for Babylonian usage see P. Karge, Rephaim 1918, 558. The phrase does not appear to be usual in Greek; Latin has aqua viva, fons vivus, etc.

[3] It would (as in 2.1–12, see p. 120) be inappropriate and uncalled for by the text, to take this to refer to any particular gift bestowed by Jesus, as for example the Spirit. The water, like the bread and the light, refer to Jesus' Revelation as a whole, or to him as the Revealer; see also on 6.35.

[4] There are grounds for taking the first clause of the woman's reply v. 11: οὔτε ... βαθύ (on οὔτε-καί see Bl.-D. para. 445, 3; Br., Schl.) as a clumsy gloss (Wendt), since it does not fit in with the dominant contrast drawn in v. 12 between well water and spring water, but asks: "How can *you* draw water from this well?" But perhaps one should translate: "You can't even give me well-water, so how can you give me spring water?!" —On the honour accorded to the "Fathers" by the Samaritans, see Schl.—θρέμματα = "livestock", particularly grazing or fattened cattle; it occurs frequently in Pap., see Preisigke, Wörterbuch.

[5] ὕδωρ ἀληθινόν would have the same denotation as ὕδωρ ζῶν; cp. φῶς ἀλ. 1.9 with τὸ φῶς τῆς ζωῆς 8.12; ἄρτος ἀλ. 6.32 with ἄρτος τῆς ζωῆς 6.35, 48, or ζῶν 6.51; further ἄμπελος ἀλ. 15.1, cp. also 4.23; 8.16. Cp. Omodeo, Mistica 55f.

This mode of speech about "living water", "bread of life", "true light" "true vine" comes from the sphere of Gnostic dualism. For there the view is developed that all earthly things, whether food or clothing, birth or marriage, life or death, are temporary, transitory and false, whereas their heavenly counterparts are true, eternal and final. Yet this contrast of the earthly with the heavenly does not only mean that the former is debased. It is also a consequence of the basic position of Gnostic dualism, according to which man misconstrues his own end if he is set on earthly things, because fundamentally he does not desire these earthly things but their heavenly counterparts. Fundamentally he desires *life.*[1] Thus the fact that in John the revelation is deliberately referred to in terms which denote earthly goods, indicates that there is a positive relationship between natural human life and the revelation. This relationship consists in the fact that whereas human life is false and inauthentic, the revelation bestows true, authentic life. For the false points to the true, the inauthentic to the authentic. The very fact that man mistakes what is inauthentic for what is authentic, what is temporary for what is final, shows that he has some knowledge of what is authentic and final. He knows what the revelation means, inasmuch as he attributes an importance to earthly things which can only properly be attributed to the revelation.[2]

The reason for describing the gift of the Revealer as ὕδωρ ζῶν is that water is sheerly indispensable for natural human life[3]. On the one hand this indispensability is the basis of the *figurative* use of "water" to refer to any good, or to any salvation.[4] On the other hand the experience of water's

---

[1] The correspondence between the temporal and eternal goods is vividly portrayed in act. Thom. 36 and 124.

[2] Hamann saw this connection very clearly; cp. E. Metzke, J. G. Hamanns Stellung in der Philosophie des 18. Jahrh.s 1934, 18f.

[3] Pindar 01.I 1: ἄριστον μὲν ὕδωρ (cp. III 42; fr. 101). The Orient, being short of water, is particularly aware of its blessing. Thus in the OT the rain and the springs are thought of as the gift of God (Ps. 65. 10f.; Job 38.25 etc.; for Egyptian examples see Ad. Ermann, Lit. der Ägypter 1923, 360). Thus the *eschatological hope* also contains the hope that in the end there will be abundance of water Is. 43.19f.; 49.10; Joel 4.18 etc.); a spring will burst forth from Jerusalem (Ezek. 47.1–12; Joel 4.18; Zech. 13.1; 14.8); Rabbinic lit. in Str.-B. II 436; III 854–856; cp. Rev. 7.16f.; 21.6; 22.1f.—On the other hand there is the well attested custom of *giving water for the dead*, cp. P. Karge, Rephaim 1913, 559ff.; Br. Meissner, Babylonien und Assyrien I 1920, 428; II 1925, 147; M. Holmberg, Studia Orientalia I 1925, 73f.; H. Diels, Philothesia für P. Kleinert (1907) 43, 6.—Correspondingly the mythological idea of the *springs in the beyond* which quench thirst, or bring men back to life (or to consciousness); cp. Karge, op. cit. 561f.; A.v.Gall, Βασιλεία θεοῦ 1926, 328f.; E. Rohde, Psyche II 390, 1; A. Dieterich, Nekyia 1893, 90–100; Frz. Cumont, Die oriental. Religionen im röm. Heidentum 3. ed. 1931, 93.250; A. Parrot, Le "Refrigerium" dans l'au-dela. Rev. d'Hist. des Religions 113 (1936), 149–187; 114 (1936) 69–92; 115 (1937), 53–89; G. v. d. Leeuw, Refrigerium, Mnemosyne III 3 (1936), 125–148; G. Sverdrup, Rauschtrank u. Labetrank (Avh. utg. av det Norske Vidensk. Ak. i. Oslo II Hist.-fil. Kl. 1940, No. 5) 1941.

[4] Cp. Ps. 23.2f.; 36.9f.; 42.1f.; Is. 12.3; 55.1 etc.; see Kundsin, Charakter u. Urspr. 231f. God himself is "the spring of living water", Jer. 2.13; 7.13; Eth. En. 96.6; as is "wisdom" Bar. 3.12; Ecclus. 24.21, 30–33 (cp. Odeberg 153); Wisd. 7.25. In Judaism this idea has been vested in the Torah; this is also found as early as Ecclus. 24.23–29. (For further discussion see Str.-B. II 435f.; Odeberg 154f.; 157ff.). The "Spirit" is also thought

life-giving power is the basis for the belief in the *magical "power" of water*,[1] originally of all running water, but later of the "power" and "holiness" of particular springs and waters.[2] This belief in the "power" of water is also connected with cosmological ideas of an archetypal water, which is the origin of all life in the world.[3] As soon as this belief in the magical "power" of

---

of as water, when it is said that God will "pour it out", Is. 44.3; Joel 3.1; Acts 2.17ff.; Tit. 3.6, and in Rabbinic exegesis the "water" of the OT is frequently interpreted as the Spirit (Str.-B. II 434f.). A "spring of life" is said of the fear of God (Prov. 14.27), of wisdom (Prov. 16.22), of the sayings of the righteous and the wise (Prov. 10.11; 13.14; 18.4), of the teacher (Str.-B. II 492f.), whose "water" is drunk by his pupils (Str.-B. II 436).—Philo also compares (the ἐπιστῆμαι fug. et inv. 187 and) the σοφία with water leg. all. II 86f.; post Caini 125; fug. et inv. 175 and calls it πηγή quod det. pot. ins. 117; post Caini 136.138; fug. et inv. 195f.; spec. leg. IV 75. He interprets the φρέαρ of Gen. 24.20 as the σοφία post Caini 151. In somn. II 242ff. it is the πηγή from which the λόγος flows out as a ποταμός, whereas in fug. et inv. 97 the θεῖος λόγος is the πηγή σοφίας. (H. Lewy, Sobria Ebrietas 7, 4; 9, 1; 99, 2). In virt. 79 he speaks of the χαρίτων πηγαί of God and in fug. et inv. 197f., after Jer. 2.13, he calls God himself the ζωῆς αἴτιος, the ἀνωτάτη καὶ ἀρίστη πηγή, which admittedly shows the influence of another usage, as in the Mandaean literature, in which the "water of life" is constantly used as a picture of the salvation which is given by the heavenly world (Odeberg 55–58.160–163), see below.—In the course of time the epitaph δοίη σοι ὁ Ὄσιρις τὸ ψυχρὸν ὕδωρ was also taken figuratively, to express a wish for immortality (Cumont op. cit. 93.205). Outside these systems it may also occasionally be used figuratively, cp. Epict. diss. III 1, 18: Apollo as the πηγὴ τῆς ἀληθείας, M. Aurel. 8, 51: πῶς οὖν πηγὴν ἀέναον ἕξεις; ἂν φυλάσσῃς σεαυτὸν πάσης ὥρας εἰς ἐλευθερίαν κτλ.—On πηγή used to refer to Jesus cp. F. J. Dölger, ΙΧΘΥΣ II 1922, 488f.; 569, 4; to Mary loc. cit. 254f.

[1] The "power" of the water may be appropriated by washing as well as by drinking; for washing not only purifies, but it mediates the salutary "power"; cp. G. v. d. Leeuw, Phänomenologie der Religion 1933, 320ff.; on purification with running water cp. also E. Rohde op. cit. II 405f.; M. Nilsson, Gesch. d. griech. Rel. I, 92ff.; J. Thomas, op. cit. 294ff., 303f., 315.—How close a connection existed between washing and drinking is shown by the custom, which is attested for some Gnostic sects, of drinking the baptismal water, cp. Bousset, Hauptprobleme 293 (for the Mandaeans, the book of Baruch, and the Sethians); L. Fendt, Gnostische Mysterien 1922, 36; the custom, though re-interpreted, is also attested in Od. Sal. 6.11ff.; 11.6.—The importance of the fish as a symbol of life is also based on the belief in the "power" of water, F. J. Dölger op. cit. 180f.; 225f.—This belief is also probably the basis (partly, at least) of the custom of drinking water at communion, instead of wine, see Fendt op. cit. 29ff.; H. Lietzmann, Messe und Herrenmahl 1926, 246ff.

[2] Cp. v. d. Leeuw op. cit. 40f.; J. Hempel, RGG 2. ed. IV 1668; Thomas op. cit. 289ff. 304ff.—For the Babylonian belief in the holiness of springs, see Karge op. cit. 558, for the Iranian belief in the "power" contained in the water: N. Söderblom, Werden des Gottesglaubens 2. ed. 1926, 248, for the belief in the saving power of certain waters, see O. Gruppe, Griech. Mythologie und Religionsgesch. II 888.—The belief in the "power" of running water leads to the mythologising of springs and rivers, cp. L. Preller-C. Robert, Griech. Mythologie I 4. ed. 1894, 546ff.; K. Weinhold, Die Verehrung der Quellen in Deutschland 1898; O. Waser, Flussgötter, in Pauly-Wissowa VI 1909; M. Ninck, Die Bedeutung des Wassers in Kult und Leben der Alten 1921, esp. p. 12ff. (on the fertilising power of water 25ff.); J. R. Smith, Springs and wells in Greek and Roman literature 1922. —It is worth noting the idea that water gives the gift of soothsaying, cp. K. Buresch, Klaros 1889; Ninck op. cit. 47ff.; Reitzenstein, Studien 45; E. Fascher, Προφήτης 1927, 58; Nilsson op. cit. 513, 2; Sverdrup op. cit. 45; cp. II Esd. 14.38ff.

[3] Aug. Wünsche, Die Sagen vom Lebensbaum und Lebenswasser 1905, 71; K. Galling, RGG 2. ed. V 1770; Preller-Robert op. cit. 32ff.; Ninck op. cit. 1ff.; Waser op. cit. 2774f.—On the one hand the idea lives on in the Gnostic speculations, see below; on the other in the fairy-tale idea of the "children's well", Wünsche op. cit. 86f.

water begins to disappear, it is replaced by the mythological notion of miraculous *water of life*, which gives men immortality, and of a *well of youth*, which restores men's vanished youth.[1] And as all natural earthly water gradually comes to be thought of as profane, this gives rise to the idea of *sacramental* water, which receives its life-giving force only after consecration.[2] In the Gnostic baptist sects the idea of the "power" of running water —at least of certain rivers—is fused with the idea of sacramentally consecrated water,[3] and similarly with the mythological idea of a life-creating cosmic archetypal water.[4] True to the dualist character of this kind of thought, the "heavenly" water which is given in the sacrament is distinguished from all earthly water as the true "living water".[5] Nor is the life which is given by this water any longer the natural life-force, but immortality, so that baptism becomes a new birth.[6]

However the idea of "living water", combined with the water of baptism as a divine power, can be used figuratively, or better *symbolically, to refer to the divine revelation, or alternatively to the gift bestowed by the revelation.* This

---

[1] Cp. v. d. Leeuw op. cit. 41; Wünsche op. cit. 71ff.; Ninck op. cit. 32ff.; Karge op. cit. 562; Hempel, RGG 2. ed. IV 1669; H. Gunkel, Genesis 3. ed. 7f.; H. Gressmann, Der Messias 18; v. d. Leeuw, Mnemosyne 140ff.; H. J. Schoeps, Theol. u. Gesch. des Judenchristentums 202–211.—The notion of the water of life has fused with the notion of the thirst-quenching water in the beyond (see p. 182 n.3); cp. E. Rohde op. cit. II 390, 1; Ninck op. cit. 106f.; Karge op. cit. 580f;. cp. Karge 581f. on the refrigerium in the Christian paradise; cp. also Dietrich op. cit. 95ff.; on the Egyptian origin of the term refrigerium see Cumont op. cit. 251f.

[2] Cp. A. Dietrich, Eine Mithrasliturgie 2. ed. 1910, 170ff.; v. d. Leeuw, op. cit. 41, on the epiclesis, by which the "power" is called down on the water, loc. cit. 401f.; P. Drews, RE 3. ed. V 409ff.; Bousset, Hauptpr. 282; Reitzenstein, Vorgesch. der christl. Taufe 191ff.—The old idea of the well of life can be combined with the idea of the baptismal water. The well of life lives on in the history of art as the well of pines (Cantharus or the well of purification), which is found in the fore-court of Byzantine churches and palaces, and also lives on in the baptismal well of Christian churches; cp. K. v. Spiess, Orientalistische Studien für Fr. Hommel 1918, 328–341.

[3] Cp. Bousset, Hauptpr. 278ff. But in the Church, too, value was placed in the beginning on baptism in running water, Did. 7.1f.—For the survival of the terminology of water-belief in the terminology of baptism, cp. Dölger op. cit. passim.

[4] See p. 183 n.3, for Gnosticism see Ps. Clem. Hom. XI 24; Hippol. V 14, 1ff., p. 108 13ff.; V 19, 13ff., p. 118, 25ff; for the Mandaeans see following note. The idea of the cosmic water is used only figuratively in Orac. Chald., where the Godhead is called the πηγὴ τῶν πηγῶν (W. Kroll, Bresl. Phil. Abh. VII, 1 (1894), 19.23f.), and in Philo, see p. 182 n.4. The figurative use lives on in poetry, cp. Goethe, Faust I 459ff. 1201f.

[5] Cp. the distinction between the heavenly and the earthly water made by the Naassenes Hippol. V 9, 18ff., p. 101, 22ff. W.; more clearly in Justin's Book of Baruch, Hippol. V 27, 2f., p. 133, 3ff.; further act. Thom. 52, p. 168, 13ff.—The Mandaeans make a sharp distinction between the water of salvation and the water of perdition, e.g. Ginza R. 285, 27ff.; 307, 24ff.; see Odeberg 56f.163; cp. too Galling, RGG 2. ed. V 1770f. Elsewhere fire and water are contrasted as the two hostile cosmic forces, cp. Schlier, Relg. Unters. 147. O. Cullmann, Le Problème litt. et hist. du roman Ps.-Clem. 214ff.; Thomas op. cit. 150, 179, 181 n.2, 238f.

[6] In the Church, too, baptism was seen as one of the mysteries of rebirth, cp. Tit 3.5 and see p. 138 n.3. On the connection between the idea of rebirth through baptism and the old water-belief, cp. v. d. Leeuw op. cit. 323f.

usage is to be found principally in the Odes of Solomon. "Draw your water from the life-source of the Lord!" cries the singer, (30), and confesses:

> "Speaking water[1] came to my lips
> abundantly from the spring of the Lord.
> I drank and became drunk
> from the spring of immortality;
> Yet my drunkenness was not that of ignorance,
> but I departed from vanity" (11.6–8).

It is this usage[2] which must give us the clue to Jn. 4.10–15. The revelation brought by Jesus gives life, and thus stills the desire which no earthly water can satisfy.[3] The description of the revelation as "water" differs from its description as "light", in that "light" originally refers not to an object or thing, but to the illumined state of existence,[4] whereas water (and bread) originally refers to something which living creatures constantly require. Yet each time man feels this need, it only points him to the fact that he wants to *live*. When he hungers and thirsts, then fundamentally he does not desire this or that thing,

---

[1] Cp. Ign. Rom 7.2: ὕδωρ δὲ ζῶν καὶ λαλοῦν ἐν ἐμοί, ἔσωθέν μοι λέγον· δεῦρο πρὸς τὸν πατέρα. Here "water" is the πνεῦμα (or the Christ, cp. Reitzenstein, Taufe 159, 2) and it is possible that the expression "speaking water" goes back to the idea of mantic inspiration by water (see p. 183 n.2 and Burney 160). Od. Sal. 11.6 refers to the word of revelation, even if the Syrian text goes back to ὕδατα λογικά and not to ὕδ. λαλοῦντα (W. Frankenberg, Das Verständnis der Od. Sal. 1911, 13; H. Lewy op. cit. 84, 1), as in Od. Sal. 12 the "word of truth" is said to pour forth from the mouth of the singer "like a stream of water". Cp. Epiph. haer. 19, 37, p. 221, 4f. Holl: πορεύεσθε δὲ μᾶλλον ἐπὶ τὴν φωνὴν τοῦ ὕδατος. In Mand. Lit. 187 the "voice of living water" is expressly identified as the speech of the Revealer, and in Mand. Lit. 62f. the Revealer is told: "You are the living water"; cp. 77; 107. In Joh.-B. 219 "the speech of the great and the word" is also identified as the "living water". In Act. Joa. 109, p. 208, 6 Jesus is worshipped as ἡ ῥίζα τῆς ἀθανασίας καὶ ἡ πηγὴ τῆς ἀφθαρσίας. In C. Herm. 1, 29 (=Nock.-Fest., Herm. Trism. I 17; see n. 75, p. 26), the prophet says: καὶ ἔσπειρα αὐτοῖς τοὺς τῆς σοφίας λόγους καὶ ἐστράφησαν ἐκ τοῦ ἀμβροσίου ὕδατος. Cp. Reitzenst., JEM 145, 2; Schlier, Relg. Unters. 147, 2; H. Lewy op. cit. 91, 2.

[2] As well as the references given in the previous note, cp. Od. Sal. 6, where the gnosis is represented as a river (v. 11: "All the thirsty of the earth drank therefrom, and their thirst was quenched and stilled", v. 18: "For all knew themselves in the Lord and were redeemed by the eternal immortal water"); also 4.10; 28.15. The Marcionites boast of τὸ μέγεθος τῆς γνώσεως τῆς ἀρρήτου δυνάμεως μόνους καταπεπωκέναι (Iren. I 13, 6); cp. act. Thom. 25 p. 140, 13f.; 148 p. 256, 8f.; further Justin dial. 69. 6; 114, 4; P. Oxy. 840, 43f. (Kl. Texte 31, 5); cp. H. Lewy op. cit. 91f. For the image of the watering of the planting of the faithful, which occurs so frequently in the Mand. lit., see Od. Sal. 38.17f.

[3] That the water of Jn. 4.10–15 is not the water of the Messianic age of salvation (J. Jeremias, Golgotha 1926, 82), but is based on the Gnostic usage, specifically as in Od. Sal., is shown by the parallels and by the fact that the meaning of ὕδωρ ζῶν is governed by the contrast with natural spring-water. Of course in vv. 20-26 the Evangelist relates this to Messianic eschatology (see below), but he does so without using the term ὕδωρ ζῶν again. For further discussion see on 7.37ff.

[4] See p. 40.

but he wants to *live*. The real object of his desire is not water and bread, but something which will give him life and will rescue him from death, something which might therefore be called real water, real bread. Clearly, then, ὕδωρ ζῶν really means "life-giving water", corresponding to the meaning of ζωή which it had when predicated of the Revealer.[1]

In **vv. 13f.**[2] the peculiarly double-sided relationship of the revelation to natural benefits is stated clearly:

> πᾶς ὁ πίνων ἐκ τοῦ ὕδατος τούτου
> διψήσει πάλιν·
> ὃς δ' ἂν πίῃ ἐκ τοῦ ὕδατος οὗ ἐγὼ δώσω αὐτῷ,
> οὐ μὴ διψήσει εἰς τὸν αἰῶνα.[3]

The revelation quenches in a radical way the thirst for life, which makes itself felt in physical thirst,[4] it achieves what no earthly sustenance can achieve, not even the highest and most indispensable of all, which is water. But it can do this only if man ceases to search for natural water in the belief that this will preserve his life, if he ceases to confuse the inauthentic with the authentic, and if he opens himself to the Revealer who confronts him. Of course this would still be compatible with the saying in Ecclus. 24.21, where Wisdom says:

> "Those who eat of me, still hunger for me,
> and those who drink of me, still thirst for me."

The meaning of these apparently contradictory sayings is the same! Once a man has tasted this drink, he will never seek any other means of quenching his thirst; his need is past.[5] For manifestly the Evangelist does not suggest that the believer must not again and again "drink"

---

[1] See p. 39.

[2] It is hardly possible that the water of Jacob's well was thought of as a symbol of the Torah, as Dodd (312) and F.-M. Braun (RB 62 (1955) 24f.) suggest; the latter cites the Zadokite fragment, 6.4–11, where Jacob's well is interpreted as the Torah.

[3] The Evangelist is clearly using a part of the revelation-discourses, which also appears in 7.37f. The style is related to the antithetical style, which is predominant in the source used in I Jn. The actual phrasing has probably been adapted by the Evangelist to fit the situation. —On πίνειν see Raderm. 11.

[4] The formula εἰς τ. αἰῶνα occurs 12 times in Jn; as in I Jn. 2.17; II Jn. 2 (as well as ἐκ τ. αἰῶνος 9.32). It is also found on inscriptions and elsewhere (see Br., C. Lackeit, Aion 1916, 32; E. Peterson, Εἷς Θεός 1926, 168ff.), and in the LXX, where the plural is also found; in the NT the latter is favoured by Paul and Rev. (where it is used throughout), whereas Heb. almost always uses the sing. Jos. has εἰς αἰῶνα, see Schl. on Mt. 21.19. The meaning depends on the particular context: indefinitely, always, for ever; here it means "for ever".

[5] In just the same way in Is. 49.10. "They shall not hunger or thirst", comes in the same verse as, "He will guide them by springs of water". Cp. too act. Thom. 7, p. 110, 18f.· ἔπιον δὲ ἀπὸ τοῦ οἴνου τοῦ μὴ δίψαν αὐτοῖς παρέχοντος καὶ ἐπιθυμίαν.

from the revelation, so surely as the branch must "abide" in the vine (15.4ff.).

This negative description is followed by a positive one:

ἀλλὰ τὸ ὕδωρ ὃ δώσω αὐτῷ
γενήσεται ἐν αὐτῷ πηγὴ ὕδατος ἁλλομένου εἰς ζωὴν αἰώνιον.[1]

This equally expresses the inexhaustibility of the revelation, which is a πηγή for him who receives it; it also tells us that the purpose of the revelation is to give life.

The character of the revelation is once again brought out in **v. 15** by contrasting it with the natural needs of man. The woman still has not understood what Jesus is talking about.[2] The only advance in understanding is that she has now realised that he must be talking about something miraculous. This she imagines to be some kind of magic water, the possession of which would make it unnecessary ever to draw water again. She can only see the miracle as a welcome means of making natural life easier, which is of course a usual misunderstanding of the revelation. However the discussion of this subject is at first cut short. The Evangelist returns to the traditional material he had left in v. 9 and prepares the way for the final section by the dialogue in vv. 16–19.[3]

iv. *The Revelation as the Disclosure of Man's Being:* 4.16–19[4]

There is no point, as far as the traditional material is concerned, in asking when Jesus tells the woman to fetch her husband, or what purpose would be served by his arrival on the scene. For, as is shown in what follows, Jesus' request is only a means of demonstrating his own omniscience. The story represents Jesus as the προφήτης, as the θεῖος ἄνθρωπος who knows the secret things which are hidden from other

[1] εἰς ζωὴν αἰών. should not be taken with γενήσεται but with ἁλλομένου, as is shown by 6.27. Schl. is right when he says that the εἰς does not have a spatial connotation, but certainly not right when he says that like 4.36; 12.25, it refers to the aim and success of an action (i.e. = "for"). Rather, as in 6.27 it is used temporally, and the difficulty of understanding it lies in the fact that on the one hand ἅλλεσθαι suggests something spacial, and on the other hand that εἰς ζ. αἰ. suggests something temporal. The meaning cannot, however, be in doubt. He who has drunk the ὕδωρ ζῶν has in him the life-giving power, which is bestowed by the revelation. In Hippol. El. ὕδωρ ἁλλόμενον occurs more frequently, but almost certainly in every case, where it is not a direct quotation it is an allusion to Jn. 4.14.

[2] I cannot find that her request is "crafty" (Zn.).

[3] Any attempt to reconstruct the line of thought in the conversation is bound to fail. Cp. B. Weiss: "Since what the woman said in v. 15 has shown that she is lacking in spiritual needs, Jesus attempts to arouse these by rousing her feelings of guilt, and so taxes her with the weak point in her life" (similarly Zahn). This approach would have failed hopelessly —quite apart from the fact that the Revealer does not appeal to the "spiritual needs" of man, but to his longing for life.

[4] On the literary character see p. 179.

men, and who knows the strangers whom he meets.[1] This is the impression that he makes on the woman (v. 19), and it is what she tells the people in the town (v. 29). Her exclamation in v. 19 is not an expression of guilt, but simply a cry of amazement. For the Evangelist however, the episode is more than a demonstration of Jesus as the θεῖος ἄνθρωπος: the revelation is for man the disclosure of his own life.[2] Man is made aware of the unrest in his life, which drives him from one supposed satisfaction to another, never letting him attain the final fulfilment until he finds the water of life, of which "one drink for ever stills the thirst". This unrest is portrayed by the woman's disturbed past and her unsatisfied present state.[3] Perhaps one may go as far as to say that the married life of the woman "who reels from desire to pleasure" portrays not only the unrest, but the aberrations of the desire for life.[4] This leads on naturally to the next point. The fact that Jesus has shown the woman the truth of her own situation, leads her to suspect that he is the Revealer. Only by man's becoming aware of his true nature, can the Revealer be recognised. The attainment of the knowledge of God and knowledge of self are part of the same process. This also makes the way clear for taking the actual story a stage further: if Jesus is a prophet he will be able to shed some light for the woman on the old dispute between the Samaritans and the Jews.

---

[1] See p. 101.

[2] See p. 106.—There is no support in the text for Schl.'s explanation, that Jesus condemns her as an adulteress, according to the Mosaic law which applied to her, and that he at the same time forgives her, in that he converses with her in spite of her guilt and offers her his grace (v. 10).

[3] The allegorical interpretation of the woman's five husbands and her present illicit partner is wide-spread. It is customary to interpret the 5 husbands as the 5 Babylonian tribes, which according to II Kings 17.24–34; Jos. ant. IX 288 had settled in the area of the northern kingdom; the present illicit partner is then taken as Jahwe, or even Simon Magus. But in II Kings 17. 30f. not 5 but 7 divinities are mentioned, some of which are female; also the fact that they are all worshipped at the same time does not accord with the fact that the woman had her husbands one after the other (see too Howard 184f. 272, b). And in general the allegory is not suggested by anything that follows; for it can hardly be right to find in ὑμεις προσκυνεῖτε ὅ οὐκ οἴδατε v. 22 a reference to the νῦν ὃν ἔχεις οὐκ ἔστιν σου ἀνήρ v. 18 (Odeberg 185f.). The Evangelist does not use allegorisation, but rather symbolic representation as his main literary device.—It is hardly possible to determine whether the number five has been chosen at random, or whether it is due to its importance in Gnosticism (see Bousset, Hauptprobl. passim; Reitzenst., HMR 162). With reference to the five verses of the cultic hymn of the Arval brotherhood, Ed. Norden (Aus altröm. Priesterbüchern 1939, 240f.) draws attention to the φύλλον πέντε δακτύλου βοτάνης Pap. Gr. Mag. II 40, and to the Pythagorean πεντάγραμμον.

[4] To the Jew, who felt that three marriages was the most that could be allowed (Str.-B. II 437), the married life of the woman itself is a scandal, quite apart from the present illicit relationship, which is even more shocking. (This relationship is referred to by ἔχειν as in I Cor. 5.1; Lucian, Dial. meretr. 8.3. On ἀληθές v. 18, describing her statement = "correct", cp. Br.; on τοῦτο ἀλ. εἰρ. Bl.-D. para. 234.292; on νῦν ὃν ἐχ. Bl.-D. para. 474, 5c; 475, 1.)

v. *The Self-revelation of Jesus:* 4.20–26[1]

Up to now Jesus has determined the course of the conversation. Now the woman takes the initiative, which is an indication that the Revealer, although he certainly demands obedience and sacrifice from men, is also the one who gives answers to men's questions. There is no need to give any particular reason[2] why the woman asks the "prophet" whether Jerusalem or Gerizim is the true place of worship.[3] It is the traditional source of contention between the Samaritans and the Jews,[4] and in the context the only point of the question is that it provides an opportunity for the answer of Jesus in vv. 21–24.

V. 20 puts the alternative: "This mountain" or Jerusalem! Jesus' answer in **v. 21**[5] refuses to accept the alternative as such, but contrasts the present cultic division with the future, in which every local cult, both Jewish and non-Jewish, will have ceased to be of importance. Without any doubt, this is the eschatological age, in which, according also to the Rev. 21.22, there will no longer be any temple. **V. 23**[6] then

---

[1] On the possibility that the section of traditional material used in vv. 5–9, 16–19, 28-30, 40 also forms the basis of vv. 20–26 see p. 180. We can best see why the question μήτι κτλ., v. 29 was asked, if we assume that v. 25f.—or at least its theme—is taken from the source.

[2] Zahn: "She changes the subject away from this embarrassing question to a confessional question about the national cult. She is not without interest in religious questions and not without patriotic feelings. But when she is confronted by this Jew, who from the first has shown himself to be free of the narrow misgivings of other Jews, and who now has shown himself to be a seer of great insight, she no longer feels certain of her inherited cult, which is rejected by the Jews."—J. Horst, Proskynein 1932, 295 rightly objects to this sort of explanation; but his own suggestion that the woman's expression of astonishment v. 19 was combined with the proscynesis, and that she then became embarrassed about her own proscynesis, is quite fantastic. Hoskyns thinks her question is about the proper place of the forgiveness of sins, now that she has been recognised as a sinner.

[3] προσκυνεῖν refers to the cultic worship of God, and is not specifically associated with any particular liturgical gestures; so too 12.20, but 9.38 is different. In classical Greek πρ. takes the accusative; the Koine prefers the dative. The change in vv. 22–24 is of no importance; Bl.-D. para. 151, 2; Horst, op. cit. 33ff.

[4] According to the Massoretic text of Deut. 27.4, Israel is to offer up the first thank- and peace-offering when it has gone up to Mount Ebal, whereas the Samaritan text names Gerizim, and this is taken as a justification for establishing the cult there. (Deut. 11.19; 27.12 refers to Gerizim as the mountain of blessing, and Ebal as the mountain of curses.) The temple of Gerizim was destroyed 128 B.C. by Hyrkan I (Jos. ant. XIII 255f.), but the cult persisted until later (Schürer II 21f.). The question of the legitimate place of worship was discussed between Jews and Samaritans, see Str.-B. I 549–551; Dalman, O.u.W. 229; Br.

[5] It is introduced by the singular πίστευέ μοι, which clearly stands in place of ἀμὴν ἀμ. λέγω σοι (the latter occurs nowhere in ch. 4).

[6] **V. 22** is completely or partially an editorial gloss. The ὅτι ἡ σωτηρία ἐκ τ.'Ιουδ. ἐστίν is impossible in Jn., and that not only because of 8.41ff.; for 1.11 already made it clear that the Evangelist does not regard the Jews as God's chosen and saved people (see p. 56 n.1). And in spite of 4.9 it is hard to see how the Johannine Jesus, who constantly disassociates himself from the Jews (8.17; 10.34; 13.33; and p. 86 n.3) could have made such a

tells us how this eschatological time and its worship of God is to be understood. This time is coming and is already here,[1] and the true worship of God is worship ἐν πνεύματι καὶ ἀληθείᾳ. The two statements are mutually explanatory.[2] For the eschatological hour comes only with the Revealer and his word. 3.19 has already stated that his coming is the eschatological "now", and this will be reiterated at 5.25, as well as here at 4.23.[3] This gives us the clue to the ἐν πνεύματι καὶ ἀληθείᾳ: the cultic worship of God is contrasted, not with a spiritual, inward form of worship, but with the eschatological worship.[4] Correspondingly the terms πνεῦμα and ἀλήθεια are used in John to bring out the fact that the eschatological age has been brought about by the miracle of the revelation in Jesus. The πνεῦμα is God's miraculous dealing with men[5] which takes place in the revelation. Those who worship ἐν πνεύματι are the ἐκ τοῦ πνεύματος γεγεννημένοι of 3.3–8.[6] The ἀλήθεια is the

---

statement (see also W. Grundmann, Jesus der Galiläer u. das Judentum 1940, 229ff.). It is only the first half of v. 22 where there is room for doubt. If ὑμεῖς refers to the Samaritans and ἡμεῖς to the Jews, then this statement is also part of the gloss. For in the light of 5.37; 8.19 it is not possible that the Evangelist should have written it. However if ὑμεῖς refers to the Samaritans and Jews together, who are contrasted with ἡμεῖς referring to Jesus and his followers (cp. 3.11!), then this would be intelligible, and the gloss ὅτι κτλ. would be a false interpretation of ἡμεῖς κτλ. as misunderstood by the editor. This would, however, make it difficult to see why v. 23 should be joined to it by ἀλλά, where we would expect γάρ.

[1] If the coming of the ὥρα is stressed, as in 5.25, as well as its presence, this is done in order to show that the present hour is the eschatological hour. For its "coming", even if it is present, is never a thing of the past. In the same way the Revealer can be referred to as ὁ ἐρχόμενος even after he has come, II Jn. 7. On the Johannine νῦν see Faulhaber 89f.

[2] Thus it is impossible to see why H. Windisch, Amicitiae Corolla (Festschr. f. R. Harris) 1933, 309 should have remarked on this verse: "The verse is a remarkable example of a non-christocentric revelation-discourse."

[3] Cp. also 12.31; 16.11 and p. 128.

[4] Neither Jews nor Greeks were in any need of enlightenment about the superiority of a spiritual form of worship over a cultic form of worship. I Kings 8.27–30; Is. 66.1f.; Mal. 1.11 (cp. Acts 7.48f.) already knew that God was not bound to the place of the cult. For Judaism see Bousset, Rel. d. Judent. 302ff.; Str.-B.II 437.—In the Greek world the idea of spiritual worship had been introduced by the Ionic philosophers, and had long since been popularised by the Stoics and the Sceptics; cp. Br. ; further P. Wendland, Die hellenist.-röm. Kultur 2. ed. 1912, 99ff. Ed. Norden, Agnostos Theos 1913, 130ff.; J. Kroll, Herm. Trism. 90ff.326ff. J. Geffcken, ARW 19 (1916–19) 286ff.; Bodo von Borries, Quid veteres philosophi de idolatria senserint, Diss. Gött. 1918; J. Weiss, Urchristentum 1917, 175ff.; further see the literature in Lietzmann (Hdb. z. NT) on Rom. 1.20. The Hellenistic enlightenment was adopted by the Jews; cp. Schürer III 504ff.; P. Krüger, Philo und Josephus als Apologeten des Judentums 1906 (cp. n. 7 and Acts 17. 24f.).—The argument against a spiritualising interpretation of Jn. 4.23 in Horst op. cit. 301ff.; he says rightly that ἐν πνεύμ. corresponds to the Pauline ἐν Χριστῷ. Hosk., Dodd (174f.) and Wik., all argue very much to the point here. Omodeo, Mistica 75 draws attention to Eph. Cp. also the πνευματικαὶ θυσίαι I Pet. 2.5 (synonymous with the λογικὴ λατρεία Rom. 12.1).—In pagan lit. C. Herm. 5, 10f. seems to come closest to Jn. 4.22–24. On Heracleon's view see v. Loewenich 88.

[5] On πνεῦμα see p. 139 n. 1.

[6] Odeberg 169 sees the parallel between 4.20–25 and 3.1–8, but rather exaggerates it.

reality of God[1] revealed in Jesus, the "Word" of God by which the believers are "sanctified", i.e. are taken out of this wordly existence and set in the eschatological existence (17.17, 19). Thus only the believers, those who are ἐκ τοῦ πνεύματος γεγεννημένοι and sanctified by the ἀλήθεια, are ἀληθινοὶ προσκυνηταί.[2] All other worship is untrue.[3] God demands such worshippers;[4] for worship of this kind is the only worship which accords with his nature; for he is πνεῦμα (**v. 24**). This is not a definition in the Greek sense. It is not, that is, an attempt to define the mode of being proper to God as he is in himself, by referring to it as the mode of being of a phenomenon from the observable world, i.e. the πνεῦμα.[5] It does however "define" the *idea* of God, by saying what God *means*, viz. that for man God is the miraculous being who deals wonderfully with him just as the definition of God as ἀγάπη (I Jn 4.8, 16) refers to him as the one who deals with men out of his love and in his love.[6] The statement here justifies the demand for a προσκυνεῖν ἐν πνεύματι καὶ ἀληθείᾳ, inasmuch as it tells us that every

---

[1] On ἀλήθεια see p. 53 n. 1. There is no parallel here with Ps. 145.18: God is near πᾶσι τοῖς ἐπικαλουμένοις αὐτὸν ἐν ἀληθείᾳ for here ἐν ἀλ. corresponds to בֶּאֱמֶת (Targum בְּקֻשׁוֹט) and means "upright"; similarly Ginza 5, 25f.

[2] The only previously known occurrence of the substantive προσκυνητής (which occurs only here in the Bible) is on a Syrian inscription; see Deissmann, L.v.O. 79f.—'Ἀληθινός naturally means "genuine" (see p. 53 n. 1); the play on words with ἐν ἀλ. is intentional.—Philo quod det. pot. ins. 21 speaks of God who γνησίους θεραπείας ἀσπάζεται . . . τὰς δὲ νόθους ἀποστρέφεται, and for him this is the opposite of a form of worship based purely on an inward spiritual disposition or on sacrifice (see p. 190 n. 4).

[3] This does not of course mean that cultic forms of worship are to be excluded as such, but that any cultic worship is only true worship if the eschatological event is realised in it. O. Cullmann (JBL 74 (1955), 223) and F.-M. Braun (RB 62 (1955), 25f.) find in vv.23f. an attack on the Jerusalem temple-cult and show the relationship with the Qumran-texts (cp. esp. DSD 4.20–22).

[4] τοιούτους . . . τοὺς προσκ. = "such as the (i.e. his) worshippers", Bl.-D. para. 412, 4; Raderm. 115.—In this context, where the conditions of the true cult are laid down, ζητεῖν cannot mean "look for" in the sense of "striving for" (Mk. 3.22 etc.), but only "demand" (Mk. 8.12, etc.). Its meaning in Philostr. Vit. Apoll. VIII 7, p. 320, 24f. Kayser: καὶ οὐκ ἀπεικός, οἶμαι, ἀγαθῶν δεῖσθαι σφᾶς (sc. τοὺς θεούς) ὑπὲρ καθαρῶν θυμάτων is different.—V. 23b etc., is clearly an explanatory comment of the Evangelists, cp. 4.45; I Jn. 2.19 and similar comments. Vv. 23a, 24 are probably taken from the "revelation-discourses".

[5] Thus the Greeks often describe God's nature as νοῦς (Diels, Doxogr. Gr. 301ff.), particularly the Stoics; cp. Stoic. vet. Fr. (v. Arnim) I 40.3ff.: (Zeno) ἔφη μὴ δεῖν θεοῖς οἰκοδομεῖν ἱερά, ἀλλ' ἔχειν τὸ θεῖον ἐν μόνῳ τῷ νῷ, μᾶλλον δὲ θεὸν ἡγεῖσθαι τὸν νοῦν. Also as πνεῦμα: ibid. II 299, 11ff.: ὁρίζονται δὲ τὴν τοῦ θεοῦ οὐσίαν οἱ Στωϊκοὶ οὕτως· πνεῦμα νοερὸν καὶ πυρῶδες . . . Further discussion in Br. on v. 24.—This is also the sense of Justin apol. 6, 2, where he is describing the Christian σέβεσθαι καὶ προσκυνεῖν: λόγῳ καὶ ἀληθείᾳ τιμῶντες. Cp. Origen's attempt c.C. VI 71 to distinguish the Christian meaning of πνεῦμα εἶναι θεόν from the Stoic understanding of the statement. Also see Orig. Comm. on St. John XIII 21.23, to which Dodd 225f. draws attention. Lagr., who takes ἀλ. to mean veracity, defines πνεῦμα as a "disposition humaine".

[6] Schl's view is correct here: "πνεῦμα describes God qua active in the world", just as I Jn. 1.5; 4.8 "describe God's behaviour and activity."—Cp. Is. 31.3.—On the use of πνεῦμα in Jos. see Schlatter, Wie sprach Josephus von Gott 1910, 28. The Rabbinic

cult undertaken by man (which is at best a searching for God) is illicit. Adequate worship can only be given as an answer to God's miraculous promulgation, and as such is itself miraculous. There can be no true relationship between man and God unless it first be grounded in God's dealing with man. Any attempt by man to establish such a relationship remains within the sphere of human works from which God is unattainable; for God is πνεῦμα.

The woman's answer in **v. 25** is correct, inasmuch as she has seen that Jesus is speaking of an eschatological event;[1] but she has not grasped the meaning of the καὶ νῦν ἐστιν, and consequently has also failed to understand what is meant by ἐν πνεύματι καὶ ἀληθείᾳ. For the present she leaves the question open and hopes that the future Messiah will be able to enlighten her.[2] Thus, like the "Jews", she cannot see that the δόξα of the Revealer appears in the σάρξ. For she expects the πνεῦμα to give proof of itself by miraculous and remarkable phenomena, as is shown by her remark in v. 29. Accordingly she is not aware that it is the awaited Revealer who is speaking to her. Even so she is not portrayed as being completely unresponsive to the revelation; her expectation makes it possible for Jesus to reveal himself (**v. 26**). He does this in the simple words: ἐγώ εἰμι, ὁ λαλῶν σοι. The person whom she has been asking after is Jesus; the Messiah for whom men wait is already present. Whoever hears these words spoken by the Revealer is faced with the ultimate decision: the ἐγώ εἰμι lays absolute claim to faith.[3]

vi. *Conclusion:* 4.27–30

The Evangelist is not concerned to round off the narrative as such, but seems content to have covered the essential ground for the

---

references in Str.-B. II 437f. provide no parallel; they speak of God as the soul of the world which, as invisible and imperishable, is contrasted to the world as the human soul is contrasted to the body; it is moreover likely that the passages quoted betray Stoic influence.

[1] On the Messianic expectation of the Samaritans see Schürer II 608; Bousset, Rel. d. Judent. 224f.; Ad. Merx, Der Messias oder Ta'eb der Samaritaner 1910 (discussion of this by P. Kahle, Theol. Lit Ztg. 1911 198); Odeberg 182f. M. Gaster, ZDMG 64 (1910), 445ff. or Stud. and Texts I, 638ff.

[2] The ὁ λεγ. Χρ. gives the impression at first of being an explanatory gloss (of the Evangelist's or the editor's); cp. 1.38, 41f.; 9.7; 11.16; 19.13, 17; 20.16. However one then notices that it is not the borrowed word (cp. 5.2) but the translation which is qualified by λεγόμενον. This is admittedly also the case in 11.16; 20.16 (19.13, 17 is different); λέγεσθαι can therefore have the sense of "to mean" (scil. μεθερμηνευόμενον, see 1.38). Yet the ὁ λεγ. Χρ. is so striking that Odeberg may be right when he suggests (187) that the source read: "Ta'eb, the so-called (by you Jews) Messiah."—The reason for the ὅταν κτλ is that the Samaritan Ta'eb was expected, on the basis of Deut 18.18, to come as a prophet and teacher. Of course ὅταν κτλ. may have been added by the Evangelist.; the ὅταν ἔλθῃ ἐκ. and the ἀναγγελεῖ occurs again in 16.13–(15). Black 183f. wants to trace the reading of syr^{sin} δώσει (instead of ἀναγγελεῖ) back to the dependence of syr^{sin} on extra-canonical tradition.

[3] On ἐγώ εἰμι see on 6.35.

reader. He does not return to the discussion in vv. 10–15; but now the reader knows what is meant by Jesus' gift of living water.[1] Nor does the Evangelist want to make this into a conversion narrative, any more than he did in the story of Nicodemus in ch. 3. He has no special interest in the figure of the woman herself. It is enough that through her conversation with Jesus the reader should be shown what the possibilities of the revelation are; how the revelation, by appealing to man's thirst for life, can make him see himself as he really is in his unrest, can point him to God's miracle and itself confront him as this miracle, the miracle which calls him to the decision of faith. The Evangelist adds only the conclusion of the conversation in his source.[2] The details which he adds about the woman serve only to bring the Samaritans to Jesus, and this in turn sets the situation for the discussion of the theme in 4.31–42. The woman's account of her strange experience rouses the curiosity of the people, as to whether the stranger outside the town may not be the Messiah,[3] and they go out to him (**vv. 28–30**). The Evangelist, however, weaves into this passage the account of the return of the disciples (**v. 27**),[4] in order to lead into what follows. Moreover he does not leave this item till after v. 30, because he wants the disciples to witness the conversation and so to emphasize what is so remarkable about it. They are amazed to find Jesus in conversation with a woman,[5] but they do not dare to question him about it. The Evangelist draws out the fact that the Revealer encounters individual people, whether men or women, often to the surprise of his disciples, who cannot understand why it should be this particular man or woman with whom he speaks; it is however, not permissible to ask why this is so.

b) Jesus and the Messengers of the Revelation: 4.31–42

In spite of its apparent simplicity this account is put together with great skill. The section has two parts, the second of which forms the conclusion for the whole narrative from 4.1ff. In both parts both aspects of the problem of "first and second-hand hearers" are discussed: 1) vv. 31–38: What is the

---

[1] That the woman leaves her jug on the well (v. 28) certainly does not have the allegorical meaning that her thirst for life has been stilled by Jesus' words, so that she no longer needs earthly water, but merely shows her zeal.

[2] See p. 175.

[3] The question (v. 30) (μήτι, although expecting an answer in the affirmative, Bl.-D. para. 427, 2) has been formulated from the point of view of the person addressed; cp. 7.26; Mt. 12.23; Lk. 3.15.

[4] See p. 175 and following note.—'Επὶ τούτῳ = "during this", Raderm. 11.

[5] The fact that Jesus is talking to a Samaritan woman is not, as one would expect after vv. 7–9, really drawn out; this only makes it clearer that the verse does not belong to the traditional material used there.—On the Rabbinic views on conversations with women see Br.; Str.-B. II 438; H. Strathmann, Geschichte der frühchristl. Askese I (1914), 16f.; Moore II 269f.

relation of the proclamation of the Revealer's witnesses to his own work? 2) vv. 39–42: What is the relation of those who are won over by the witnesses to the Revealer himself?

1) *Jesus and the Proclamation of the Witnesses:* 4.31–38[1]

Vv. 31–34 are a prelude whose connection with what follows is not immediately clear. The disciples, having returned meanwhile[2] from the town (see v. 8), tell Jesus to have something to eat (v. 31), which provides an occasion for Jesus to refer to himself as the one who does the will of God.[3] This idea, which is stressed again and again,[4] is intended to describe the revelation as God's action. In himself the Revealer is nothing; he has been "sent",[5] and his life and ministry is service.

---

[1] One might well suspect that this section, with its complicated argument, has been worked over at a later date (Soltau, Schw., Wellh.); on the other hand it is difficult to produce a really convincing analysis and to find a reason for a redaction. Whatever the case, vv. 31–34 in its style (misunderstanding) and thought (see below) is completely Johannine. Odeberg would like to exclude vv. 35–38, but gives no reason why they should have been inserted. Stylistic arguments establish rather than discredit its Johannine origins. The Evangelist often introduces Jesus' questions with οὐχ, see 4.35, 6.70; 7.19; 10.34; 11.40; 14.10; and as in 4.35, the statement which follows in 6.70; 7.19 corrects what has been said in the question ("and yet", "nevertheless"; similarly in questions put by others 6.42; 7.25). Elsewhere, too, Jesus answers his own questions by correcting them in a further sentence, 1.51; 3.11; 6.62; 13.38; 16.20, 32 (here by καὶ ἰδού as in 4.35 by ἰδού).—The ἤδη vv. 35, 36 must be taken with what follows; sentences which begin with ἤδη are also in 7.14; 9.22; 15.3.—If in v. 36 we should read a καί before ὁ σπείρων as in ℵ K D al, then cp. with the καί -καί 12.28; 15.24 (Bl.-D. para. 444, 3).—The ἐν τούτῳ (followed by ὅτι) in v. 37 means "here", "in this case" as in 9.30; similarly 13.35; 16.30 "by this"; cp. 15.8: ἐν τούτῳ ... ἵνα.—Further the language of vv. 35f. has the Rabbinic flavour characteristic of the Evangelist, see Schl. and see below. For the rest it should be noted that the passage is based on proverbial sayings; these account for the terms θερίζειν, σπείρειν, κοπιᾶν, which otherwise do not occur in John.

[2] Μεταξύ is used elsewhere in the NT as a preposition, except in Acts 13.42, where it is an adverb, and means "afterwards". Here "meanwhile", as elsewhere (Bl.-D. para. 215, 3; Br. Wörterb.)

[3] Ποιεῖν τὸ θέλημα τοῦ θεοῦ is an expression common in the OT, in Judaism and in primitive Christianity, see Br. Wörterb. (s.v. θέλημα); Str.-B. I 467; Schl. on Mt. 7.21. In John with reference to Jesus 5.30; 6.38–40, with reference to men 7.17; 9.31 (ποιήσω BCDL al as opposed to ποιῶ ℵA al must be an assimilation to τελειώσω). Τελειοῦν τὸ ἔργον as in 5.36; 17.4 refers to the activity of the Revealer. These passages show firstly that ἔργον is not the work done by God, but the work which he commits to the Revealer, secondly that τελειοῦν does not have to mean bringing something to a finish which has already been begun, but can also mean the execution or completion of something one has been commissioned to do. So here; cp. Act. Thom. 167, 282, 1: ἐτελείωσά σου τὸ πρόσταγμα; see Dalman, Jesus-Jesch. 190 to 192. Ποιεῖν τ. θελ. and τελ. τ. ἔργ. are synonymous with ἐργάζεσθαι τὰ ἔργα τοῦ πέμψαντός με (9.4), Zn.'s and Lagr.'s view that the ἔργον of God which Jesus brings to its conclusion is God's preparation of the woman for the word of Jesus, is untenable.

[4] 5.30; 6.38–40 and elsewhere; see on 5.19.

[5] This is the first occurrence of the expression πέμψας (πατήρ) which occurs in all 24 times.

If this service is referred to here (vv. 32, 34) as his food,[1] it means that he has come not only *for* this service, but indeed *through* this service. The idea is again stressed here by the typical way in which it is misunderstood by the disciples: they do not "know" the food (v. 32) which is his nourishment.[2]

Of course no historical interest attaches to the scene. We are not told whether Jesus did, in fact, eat material food, or why he did not.[3] But what is the importance of vv. 31–34 in the context? Clearly one cannot show any close connection between the motif of the βρῶμα here and that of the ὕδωρ in vv. 10–15. For there the ὕδωρ was a gift which he gives to men; here he himself lives from the βρῶμα.[4] The counterpart to the ὕδωρ is much more the ἄρτος of 6.27ff., nevertheless vv. 31–34 must be connected in some way with what follows. For as in vv. 31–34 Jesus is portrayed as the one sent by God, who of himself and for himself is nothing, but simply carries out the work of the Father, so too according to vv. 35–38 the disciples sent out by him are nothing in their own will and strength; and yet their ministry is the continuation of the eschatological event which has begun in Jesus. Thus the reason for putting vv. 31–34 before vv. 35–38 is to explain the disciples' mission on the analogy of the mission of Jesus.[5]

Moreover just as Jesus' activity is not governed by the laws which

---

[1] Βρῶσις v. 32 (as in 6.27, 55) in the sense of βρῶμα = "food" (v. 34) is common, see Br. Wörterb.—"Food", "nourishment" is that which maintains life, existence; *this* constitutes its essence, and not the fact that in general it is a material substance which is chewed with one's teeth. The use here is therefore not "figurative" (as in Ps. 63.6; Prov. 9.5f.), but it is used in its proper sense. Philo opif. m. 158; sacr. Ab. et C. 86; vit. Mos. II 69 uses τροφή in the same way. Further discussion on 6.27.—A. Schweitzer's view, Die Mystik des Apostels Paulus 1930, 352f. is quite impossible. He suggests that Jesus' food is the food which brings immortality, which is obtained by his surrendering his body unto death and is offered in the eucharist of the believers.

[2] Cp. their lack of knowledge in 3.4; 4.10f. and above all their "not knowing" in 4.22; 7.29; 8.14f., 19,54f.—The Evangelist, like Mk., gives no indication that there was a development in the disciples' understanding. Their ignorance remains constant despite 6.66ff. (9.2; 11.8, 12; 13.33; 14.4ff.); this is shown by the fact that despite 1.41ff.; 6.69 they still address Jesus as Rabbi (9.2; 11.8). Understanding comes to them only after he has left them (14.15ff.; 16.7ff., 25ff., cp. 2.22; 12.16).

[3] Htm. correctly takes this view. Cp. the psychologising in Zn: "Both his thirst and his hunger have left him during his conversation with the Samaritan woman. One can see the tension and excitement aroused in Jesus by this unplanned conversation with the non-Jewish woman." Similarly Lagr., Bl. But Delafosse is equally wrong 29f.: "Ajoutons, que notre régime physiologique lui est étranger",—John does not give the question any thought.

[4] Of course it is not impossible that the Evangelist was influenced in his choice of expression in vv. 31-34 by the fact that the section of the "revelation-discourses" used in vv. 10–15 spoke not only of the living water, but also of the heavenly food. Drink and food (or alternatively eating and drinking) are not infrequently mentioned together to refer to the nourishment which is above the earth cp. Ecclus. 24. 21; C. Herm. 1, 29; Ign. Rom. 7.2f.; Act. Thom. 7, p. 110, 17ff.; cp. also 6.35.

[5] Htm. is right here.

apply to other human activity, so too the activity of those whom he sends is not governed by the laws of earthly harvesting.[1] Their activity, too, has its own law, and it contradicts "good common-sense", for it is the eschatological event. This is the principal idea of what follows (vv. 35f.).

The οὐχ ὑμεῖς λέγετε[2] (**v. 35**), which does not seem to be demanded by the situation as it stands, draws attention to the fact that the sentence ἔτι τετράμηνός ἐστιν καὶ ὁ θερισμὸς ἔρχεται,[3] is either a statement of "good common-sense" à propos of the matter in question (viz. the disciples' "harvesting"), or—more probably—a proverb which expresses such typical common-sense.[4] Since what follows shows that the contrast to this saying is, "The harvest has already come", its meaning must be that there is plenty of time between seed-time and harvest; there is still a good while to go! This means that the saying, like many proverbs, is capable of various applications; it can be used to urge someone to have patience—"More haste, less speed!"—or it can be an expression of indolence—"Tomorrow, tomorrow, but never to-day!" But whatever its intention the application is clear. In earthly work there is a place for waiting, whether it be the result of patience or of indolence. The time is not always ripe for decision. Not every present moment is of equal importance, some only point us forward to the future. By contrast we are told here: ἰδοὺ λέγω ὑμῖν κτλ.;[5] the time of harvest has

---

[1] In Mt. 9.37f. the harvest is the image of the mission; principally it is the traditional image for the eschatological judgement Is. 27.12; Joel 4.13; II Esd. 4.28ff.; syr. Bar. 70.2ff.; Mk. 4.29; 13.28f.; Mt. 3.12; 13.30, 37ff.; Rev. 4.15f.

[2] The expression is probably specifically Rabbinic (see Schl.); λέγειν with reference to what "one" says, also in Lk. 12.54f.

[3] Τετράμηνος sc. χρόνος as in cod. A Judg. 19.2; 20.47; see Bl.D. para. 241, 3.—Admittedly if one disregards the ἔτι, which is omitted by D L al but is nevertheless certainly original, one can read the sentence as an iambic trimeter (Bl.-D. para. 487), but the expressions, although not un-Greek, are typically Semitic (cp. esp. LXX Jer. 28.33; 35.3; Jonah 3.4; ἔτι ... καί), so that one must assume the sentence to be Semitic in origin, particularly as it would not be possible to make sense of the rule here on the basis of the Greek reckoning for seed-time and harvest (Olck in Pauly-Wissowa VI 1,474: the barley-harvest, which is the earliest, begins in the 7th or 8th month after sowing).

[4] The sentence is, of course, not attested as a proverb.—To be exact there are 6 months in Palestine between sowing and harvest, since wheat sowing begins in October/November and the harvest in April (G. Dalman, Arbeit und Sitte in Palästina I 1928, 164ff., 413ff.). Since however the winter sowing, depending on the beginning of the rains, can go on as late as December, the sentence can be given a perfectly good meaning as a proverb; it gives the minimum period of waiting (cp. Str.-B. II 439f.; Schl.).—The idea that the situation is to be dated in December by this sentence is far from the Evangelist's mind. F. M. Braun (RB 62 [1955], 26) argues from DSD 10, 7, and the Gezer calendar which agree with it (to which Lagr. had previously drawn attention), that the Qumran sect reckoned the time between the germination of the seed and the harvest to be four months.—Wik. also assumes that this is a proverb, and correctly explains ἰδοὺ κτλ. as meaning (that Jesus asserts) "that in the time of salvation other laws will apply on God's acre."

[5] There are signs of Semitic or Rabbinic expressions in v.36b as well. On ἰδού

already come. In the work of proclamation, in the service of the revelatory event the decisive moment is always the present moment. It does not belong to some future time, but always to the present, and this because, as is suggested by the reference to this work as θερισμός, and as v. 36 further makes clear, it is an eschatological event. This idea is illustrated by the scene which forms the background of the conversation, viz. the coming of the Samaritans (vv. 30,40). Nevertheless the scene illustrates the idea symbolically; for the conversation has no historical significance, it is the basic conception the Evangelist is concerned to draw out.

The proclamation of Jesus' messengers[1] is an eschatological event, just as much as his own ministry. The "harvest" of missionary work is the eschatological "harvest".[2] This is stressed by **v. 36**: the fruits are even now being[3] gathered in for "eternal life"[4] For, if Jesus' "coming into the world" is the eschatological event, then everything that happens as a consequence of this coming, must also be an eschatological event. The rules of human activity are not applicable to such an event.[5] The joy of sower and reaper,[6] i.e. seedtime and harvest, coincide.[7]

λέγω ὑμῖν see Schl.; ἐπαίρειν τ. ὀφθ. as in Gen. 13.10; Lk. 6.20 etc., cp. Schl. on Mt. 17.8 – Χώρα = field is not uncommon, see Br. Wörterb.; λευκός = 'ripe', see Wetstein and Br., Act. Thom. 147, p. 255,7f.: αἱ ἄρουραί μου ἐλευκάνθησαν· θερισμὸν προσδέχονται probably goes back to Jn. 4.35. Cp. esp. in the eschatological prophecy Virg. Ecl. 4,28: molli paulatim flavescet campus arista. Yet it is usual to speak of corn 'growing white' in Palestine as well, according to G. Dalman, Arbeit und Sitte I 413.

[1] The rule in v. 35 would also be applicable to Jesus' own ministry (see 9.4); but v. 36 shows that the reference here is to the θερίζειν of the disciples. For if Jesus was thought of as the θερίζων, then the sentence would have to read: ἵνα ὁ σπείρων ὁμοῦ καὶ θερίζῃ, unless of course Jesus the reaper were distinguished from God the sower (thus Zn., Tillmann). But v. 38 confirms that it is the disciples who are the reapers. Strathm. thinks that Jesus is himself the θερίζων.

[2] See p. 196 n.1.

[3] It makes no real difference whether ἤδη is the conclusion of the previous sentence or the beginning of a new one, since the meaning of "already now" is contained in both sentences. It is more likely, however, that it is the beginning of the sentence, see p. 194 n.1, and the eschatological ἤδη Mt. 3.10 = Lk. 3.9.

[4] The μισθὸν λαμβ. has no special meaning of its own, but like συνάγει is a way of referring to the end of the harvest, for the point of the story depends on the temporal relation of seed-time and harvest. For this reason εἰς ζωὴν αἰων. should not be taken with μισθόν but with καρπόν (as its place in the sentence shows); συνάγει κτλ. thus shows clearly that the reference is to the eschatological "harvest".

[5] For a similarly paradoxical description of the age of salvation, admittedly referring to seed-time and harvest in their natural sense, see Am. 9.13; p. Ta'an 1, 64a (Str.-B. II 440d). As a fairy-tale motif, in H. Schmidt-P. Kahle, Volkserzählungen aus Palästina II 1930, 9.

[6] Joy at harvest is typical, see Is. 9.2; Ps. 126.5f. The coincidence of the joy of the sower and the reaper in time (ὁμοῦ) is the point of the story, and not the fact that the joy of the sower is the same as the joy of the reaper. Thus there is no connection here with the ancient popular view that the work of sowing is like mourning (Gunkel on Ps. 126.5f. in Gött. Handkomm. z. AT).

[7] ʽΟμοῦ means either "together (in the same place)" or "at the same time", but not "aussi bien que" (Lagr.).

The paradoxical character of this eschatological event is heightened by the fact that sower and reaper are two different persons. This is stated in **v. 37**, which employs a further proverb.[1] In its original meaning the proverb records the tragic truth that in the course of time what is sown by one man is reaped by a second.[2] When applied to the eschatological event this proverb receives its proper sense,[3] for which till now it had had to wait: precisely here, where sower and reaper rejoice together, it is true that the sower and the reaper are two different persons. In the eschatological "time" the tension between present and future is resolved; and yet, for a while at least, the law governing earthly time, viz. that sower and reaper are two different persons, remains in force. But now the sower no longer comes first and then the reaper. Admittedly this is how it appears to be, for the ministry of the disciples follows on the ministry of Jesus—and this viewpoint is brought out by v. 38—yet in truth, as is taught by vv. 35–37, the ministry of Jesus and the disciples, the seed-time and the harvest, take place at the same time.[4] This means, on the one hand, that the ministry of the "historical Jesus" is not something which we may look back on as an organic whole, with its own special importance. The intention of his activity is realised only when it has become a thing of the past, when its ending becomes a new beginning. In earthly time the "coming" of the Revealer and his "going away" are separate events, in eschatological time they are contemporaneous.[5] The Evangelist will make this paradox clear by means of the concept of Jesus' δοξασθῆναι, which took place in his activity in the past, but which comes to fruition only in his death.[6]

On the other hand the contemporaneity of the activity of Jesus and the disciples means that the disciples' activity is in itself powerless and unauthorised. Without him they can do nothing (15.5), and he is glorified in them (17.10). This is brought home to them here, in that their

---

[1] Λόγος = "proverb" is common, see Wetst. and Br.; ἀληθινός (see p. 53) here means the same as ἀληθής, cp. Soph. Ai. 664: ἀλλ' ἔστ' ἀληθὴς ἡ βροτῶν παροιμία (=λογός, cp. Soph. Trach. 1). It has however also the connotation of the Johannine ἀληθινός, see n. 3. Ὅτι here in the sense of "in that", rather than "because".

[2] The saying is not attested anywhere else in this precise form, but the idea itself is common enough in the OT (Deut. 20. 6; 28.30; Mic. 6.15; Job 15.28; LXX 31.8; cp. Philo leg. all. III 227; Mt. 25-24), and in Greek literature (see Br.; e.g. ἄλλοι σπείρουσιν, ἄλλοι δ' ἀμήσονται). Cp. G. W. Freytag, Arabum proverbia I 1838, 570, No. 166: saepe sibi serit, at alius demetit. As an African saying in B. Gemser, De Spreuken van Salomo I 1926, 19.

[3] Thus ἀληθινός (see n. 1) also has the same meaning as in φῶς ἀλ. (1.9), ἄρτος ἀλ. (6.32), ἄμπελος ἀλ. (15.1). The earthly meaning of the λόγος is an improper meaning.

[4] According to Eisler, Rätsel 474 the σπείρων is Jesus, the θερίζων Simon Magus, and the paradox is resolved by the fact that Simon is identical with Jesus. But this eliminates the contemporaneity of seed-time and harvest.

[5] Cp. 3.19 with 12.31.

[6] See on 12.28; 13.31f.

attention is focussed on the earthly sequence of events, yet as vv. 35f. have just taught, it has been made void by the eschatological event. **V. 38**: ἐγὼ ἀπέστειλα ὑμᾶς θερίζειν ὃ οὐχ ὑμεῖς κεκοπιάκατε.[1] The task of the disciples then is only that of harvesting. This means on the one hand that they may not think of their work as a sowing for the future. The preaching of the word is not a human undertaking, where the results may be different from the work which has actually been done, where caution, hesitation and laziness may lead to delay and where it is possible to entertain doubts about the success of the enterprise. In the eschatological event there is no preparation and no development; everything depends on the present moment of decision; what comes after or later does not come into view (v. 35). And yet—and this is the point which is stressed here—so surely as there is no room for hesitation and worry, so too here is no room for looking back to one's past achievements, for pride in the "world-wide effects of Christianity". Even if these do exist, they are not what is referred to by συνάγειν καρπὸν εἰς ζωὴν αἰώνιον. For here no successes can give proof of the purpose and value of one's efforts. What the preacher reaps he owes to the κόπος of others.

And who are these ἄλλοι? One would expect the contrast to be made between the disciples' θερίζειν and Jesus' κοπιᾶν. Yet can Jesus' activity be bracketed with that of another or others, so that the ἄλλοι—among whom Jesus is numbered—would be those who prepared the way for Christian missionary work?[2] These ἄλλοι surely cannot refer to the Father and Jesus, since the Father's work is neither antecedent nor complementary to Jesus' work; rather the Father works through him.[3] Indeed, can Jesus in any sense be included among those who prepare the way for the missionary work, when he himself is active in the work of his disciples? Since however v. 38, unlike vv. 35–37, is not spoken eschatologically but historically, one can certainly say that Jesus belongs to the ἄλλοι as the precursor of the Christian mission; but the others among whom he numbers himself are those who in each case have preceded the missionaries now at work. The ἀπέστειλα, for which there is

---

[1] κοπιᾶν originally means "to become tired", "to *endure* hardships" (as in 4.6), but is then used of tiring *work*, particularly of the countryman's work, see II Tim. 2.6 and v. Harnack, ZNTW 27 (1928), 5.—Cp. Josh. 24, 13: καὶ ἔδωκεν ὑμῖν γῆν, ἐφ' ἣν οὐκ ἐκοπιάσατε ἐπ' αὐτῆς καὶ πόλεις, ἃς οὐκ ᾠκοδομήσατε.

[2] There can be no question here of any reference to the prophets of the OT (as is suggested by Lagr. and the early Church, see Br.); a correlation of Jesus and the prophets would be quite contrary to the Johannine view. There may be a reference to the Baptist and his disciples (Lohmeyer, U.C. I, 26, 3), if v. 38 is an earlier saying used by the Evangelist; such a view must not be attributed to the Evangelist himself. According to O. Cullmann, (JBL 74, [1955], 221) the ἄλλοι are the Hellenists of Acts 8.4ff.

[3] This is also the meaning of 5.17, where God's and Jesus' ἐργάζεσθαι are formally correlated; see ad loc. Nor does the fact described in 6.44 justify the correlation of the work of God and that of Jesus.

no explanation in the preceding narratives,[1] is spoken from the standpoint of later missionary work, where every missionary could look back on some predecessor in his field. They all stand in an historical tradition, which had its beginnings in the historical Jesus.

The eschatological event then is played out in history. The fact that within this historical tradition everyone, through the succession of his predecessors and on, is borne along by the beginning of this history, brings it home to the individual that he is not the creator nor even a helper in the creation of this tradition and independent in it, but that it is in the tradition that the eschatological event is realised. Just as Jesus is only what he is through the Father (vv. 31–34), so too the Christian messengers are only what they are through him. And just as the Baptist's mission was nothing of itself, its only purpose being to bear witness to Jesus (3.22–30), so too the witness of Jesus' messengers is nothing of itself, but finds its meaning only in him.

2) "*First-*" *and* "*Second-hand*" *Hearers:* 4.39–42[2]

The idea worked out in vv. 35–38, namely that Jesus himself is active in the work of his messengers, is straightway put into use, as the theme of Christian proclamation is now considered from the point of view of the hearer. The messenger through whom Jesus works is of decisive importance because he leads others to Jesus. Yet in so doing he renders himself of no importance, and the "second-hand" hearer now hears the message at "first-hand".

In the source **v. 40** followed on v. 30 and recorded a successful visit of Jesus to Samaria.[3] The Evangelist, by adding **vv. 39, 41f.,**[4] has turned this account into a symbolic representation of the problem of those who hear the message at "second-hand".[5] He could hardly have created a scene in which those who heard the word from the messengers

---

[1] John has no knowledge of the sending out of the disciples during Jesus' life-time, as reported by the Synoptists (Mk. 6.7ff. parr.). They first receive their mission from the Risen Lord 20.21.

[2] For the analysis see pp. 175-6.

[3] The reason for its being said that Jesus remains two days may be that the writer of the source had in mind the rule, attested in the Did. 11.5, that a travelling preacher may stay only two days in a particular congregation. It was also necessary to state that he remained only a very short while, if the narrative was not to appear too contradictory to the Synoptic tradition, which makes no mention of Jesus' ministry among the Samaritans. Cp. Br. extended note after 4.42.—'Ερωτᾶν = "to ask" is common in the Koine.

[4] Stylistic characteristics: separation of πολλοί from the genitive τῶν Σαμ. by the finite verb, as in 12.11; 19.20; (cp. 6.60). On ὡς οὖν see p. 204 n.1. On διὰ τ. λόγον τ. γυν. μαρτ. cp. II Jn. 2: διὰ τ. ἀλήθειαν τὴν μένουσαν ἐν ἡμῖν. On οἴδαμεν ὅτι cp. the credal definitions I Jn. 3.2, 14; 5.15, 18–20. σωτὴρ τ. κόσμου as in I Jn. 4.14. 12.47: ἵνα σώσω τ. κόσμον also comes from the Evangelist, as does 3.17.

[5] Cp. Kierkegaard, Philosophical Fragments.

of Jesus come to Jesus himself, since in his scheme the disciples receive their mission only from the risen Lord.[1] Thus the messengers are represented here by the woman. She symbolises mediatory proclamation which brings its hearers to Jesus.[2] This idea is strongly emphasised. For if the woman's witness was for the people the necessary condition of their faith, in itself it is of no importance; rather its importance lies in the fact that it brings people to Jesus, so that faith becomes faith διὰ τὸν λόγον αὐτοῦ, while human witness appears by contrast as λαλιά, as mere words which in themselves do not contain that to which witness is borne.[3] That is to say, the believer may not base his faith on the authority of others, but must himself find the object of faith; he must perceive, through the proclaimed word, the word of the Revealer himself. Thus we are faced with the strange paradox that the proclamation, without which no man can be brought to Jesus, is itself insignificant, in that the hearer who enjoys the knowledge of faith is freed from its tutelage, is free, that is, to criticise the proclamation which brought him himself to faith. This is why it is impossible ever to give a definitive dogmatic statement of the proclamation, because every fixed form of words, in that they are human words, becomes λαλιά. The eschatological word becomes a phenomenon within the history of ideas.

Ὅτι οὗτός ἐστιν ἀληθῶς ὁ σωτὴρ τοῦ κόσμου states *what* it is that the believer knows. The expression is related to the discussion in vv. 20–26. This title applied to the Revealer announces that through his coming the national cultic barriers have been thrown down. Materially this adds nothing to what has already been said by 3.17. But, as in 3.17, the important thing here is not only that the title announces the universal significance of the Revealer, but the fact that this is expressed by an eschatological title.[4] For faith has to learn that the Revealer is the eschatological Saviour.

---

[1] See p. 200 n.1.

[2] One can, of course, say that the conversion of the Samaritans represents the mission to the heathen (Omodeo, Mistica 76); and yet this is not emphasised. The passage is concerned with mission as a whole; the subject of the mission to the heathen is raised specifically in 12.20ff.—Odeberg (178, 189) rightly stresses the difference in the bearing of the Jews and the Samaritans to Jesus; cp. 4.12ff. with 8.53ff. The Samaritans rightly appeal to their fathers 4.12, whereas the Jews do not 5.46f.; 8.38ff., 56. Jesus is upbraided as a Samaritan 8.48.

[3] Λαλιά, in Classical Greek usually "chatter", means "talking", as opposed to the λόγος which refers to a statement of definite content, see Br. Wörterb. (it has a different meaning in 8.43). The fact that in the Rabbinic view women's statements are not considered reliable (Str.-B. II 441) is of no importance here, as is shown by v. 39.—The substitution of μαρτυρίαν for λαλίαν after v. 39 in א* D latt is certainly secondary.

[4] The title σωτὴρ τοῦ κόσμου is taken from Hellenistic eschatology, although there are parallels in Judaism (Str.-B. I 67–70); cp. the many references in Br. ad loc. and Wörterb., discussed by R. Eisler, Ἰησ. βασ. II 616, 4; 635f.; L. Bieler, Θεῖος ἀνήρ I 1935, 120f. K DΘ pl it add ὁ Χριστός.

Then it is clear that such knowledge can be gained only in the eschatological event of an encounter with the Revealer himself, and that therefore the man who bears the message at second-hand is in no sense inferior to the man who hears it at first-hand.[1]

[1] Wik.'s interpretation of vv. 39–42 is very much to the point.—L. Köhler (after K. H. Rengstorf) sees in the clause: ὅτι οὗτός ἐστιν ἀληθῶς ὁ σωτὴρ τοῦ κόσμου an attack on the Asclepios cult (Ehrfurcht vor dem Leben, Festschr. f. Alb. Schweitzer 75).

II. 4.43–6.59; 7.15–24; 8.13–20: The Revelation as Κρίσις

The external course of the narrative runs on without any noticeable break or interruption. As far as the substance of the Gospel is concerned, however, 4.43, just like 2.23, marks the beginning of a new section. The similarity of 2.23–25 and 4.43–45 shows that the latter should be taken as the introduction to a new section running parallel to 2.23–4.45. This new section runs from 4.43–6.59, since 7.1ff. clearly marks the beginning of another section.[1] The main contents of this section are the two miracle stories and the discourses or dialogues which follow them: 6.1–59; 5.1–47 (to which must be added 7.15–24 and 8.13–20[2]). Thus the stories of the feeding of the multitude and the healing of the lame man correspond to the stories of Nicodemus and the Samaritan woman. Jesus' conversations with individuals are followed by his disputes with the people (in Galilee) and with the leaders of the people (in Jerusalem). Whereas chs. 3 and 4 showed the coming of the Revealer as the κρίσις by which the possibility of a new existence and a new form of worship is brought to man, chs. 6 and 5 show how the revelation works as the κρίσις of the natural desire for life (ch. 6) and as the κρίσις of religion (ch. 5).

What is not quite clear is the significance of the preceding account of the healing in 4.46–54;[3] in all probability it owes its position here only to the fact that in the σημεῖα-source, from which it is taken, it happened to be placed here between the story of the Samaritan woman, to whom Jesus shows himself as a προφήτης by his omniscience, and the story of the miraculous feeding of the multitude.[4] Since the story, as adapted by the Evangelist, reaches its climax in v. 48—"Unless you see signs and wonders you will not believe!" —it seems likely that he saw in this saying a particular significance for what followed. The world which asks for signs is given what it asks for; but only in one exceptional case—4.46–54—does this actually result in faith. In general the world responds to these miracles by complete incomprehension (ch. 6) or horrified contradiction (ch. 5). All the same, the motif of πίστις and σημεῖα can only be a secondary motif and not the leading idea of the composition.[5]

---

[1] See p. 111f.

[2] For the order of the text see below.

[3] For the meaning of the healing-story 4.46–54, see Dodd 318, who suggests that what unites the two stories 4.46–54 and 5.1–18 is that "they both tell how the word of Christ gave life to those who were as good as dead", which theme is then further developed in 5.19ff.

[4] See p. 180.

[5] See p. 111. Htm., who takes 4.46–54 with 5.1–18 (see p. 112 n.1), considers that the pair of stories form an introduction to the following section, which portrays Jesus as the

A. 4.43–45: Introduction[1]

As 4.1 led us to expect, Jesus now continues his journey to Galilee (v. 43). V. 44 does not, of course, give an explanation of the journey, for this has already been given in 4.1; rather it is a note added by the Evangelist to remind the reader of a saying spoken by Jesus on another occasion,[2] and which was known to the reader from another tradition.[3] Thus what is meant is not that the truth of the saying about a prophet was the reason for this further journey, but that it here received its confirmation. The assumption is that the saying will now be fulfilled, although v. 45 seems to give it the lie. However, the acclaim which Jesus finds in Galilee is not true recognition, just as the faith of the people of Jerusalem (2.23) was not true faith. 6.26ff. shows that such acclaim, after it has reached its height (6.14f.), soon turns into rejection. V. 44 thus confirms that in the original order ch. 6 followed ch. 4, and this becomes still clearer when we see that Jesus' saying (4.44) is a variant of the traditional saying in Mk. 6.4, and that on the other hand 6.41ff. is the Johannine variant of the scene in Mk. 6.1–6.[4]

B. Prelude: 4.46–54: The Healing of the Son of the βασιλικός

It is obvious that 4.46–54 is based on the same piece of tradition as that found in Mt. 8.5–13=Lk. 7.1–10.[5] The Synoptic ἑκατόνταρχος in Capernaum corresponds to the βασιλικός of Capernaum: in both cases the

mediator of *life*. Thus he sees the point of 4.46–54 in the ζῇ which occurs three times (vv 50, 51, 53). Similarly H. Pribnow, Die joh. Anschauung vom "Leben" 1934, 154f.

[1] 4.43–45 is an editorial composition of the Evangelist's, see p. 130 n.3. In v. 45 he refers back to his own composition in 2.23. The style is "Semitising", particularly if one may read v. 43, following K 33 pm, as ἐξῆλθεν ἐκ. καὶ ἀπῆλθεν (L pc ἦλθεν); cp. Mk. 1.35. Characteristic for the Evangelist αὐτός γάρ v. 44, αὐτοὶ γάρ v. 45, see p. 130 n.3; ὅτε οὖν cp. 2.22; 6.24; 13.12 and ὡς οὖν 4.40.

[2] V. 44 is, as it were, in parenthesis; v. 45 is linked with v. 43 by οὖν .'Εμαρτύρησεν does not introduce Jesus' saying as having just been spoken; in that case there would have to be a λέγων (cp. 1.15, 32, also 13.21). The aorist ἐμαρτ. has a pluperfect meaning, as does ἦλθον v. 45.—This is seen rightly by Bd.

[3] Variants of the saying to be found in Mk. 6.4 par.; Lk. 4.24 Pap. Oxy. I 5.

[4] Πατρίς v. 44 of course means "fatherland" and not "home-town" (see Br.). The attempt (by the early exegetes, and more recently by Wendt, Hosk. and Barr. among others) to make the saying intelligible in this context by taking Jesus' πατρίς as Judaea (or Jerusalem), comes to grief over 1.46; 7.41, 52, where Jesus' home-country is clearly assumed to be Nazareth or Galilee. Nor is there any substance in the much favoured view that v. 44 gives the reason for Jesus' journey, namely, that because he wishes to carry out his ministry unnoticed and undisturbed, he goes to a place where he may expect not to enjoy any great success or τιμή. But apart from the fact that τιμὴν μὴ ἔχειν does not mean "to be undisturbed but rather "not to find recognition", what other object has Jesus in his ministry if

miracle cures the sickness of the son;[1] it is achieved by words which Jesus speaks at a distance; and it happens after the father has sought Jesus out,[2] suffered a rebuff by him, and then persuaded him to fulfil his request. There is also a considerable amount of agreement in detail,[3] which does not of course prove the literary dependence of John on the Synoptics, but must be accounted for by their use of similar traditional material and the conventionality of the narrative style. Moreover the enumeration of the miracle as the second in Galilee (v. 54) shows that the Evangelist has taken the story from the σημεῖα-source.[4]

Against these similarities—apart from a few minor discrepancies—there are certain striking differences. 1) In John the story takes place, not in Capernaum, but in Cana. 2) The father is not portrayed as a heathen, which gives a new meaning to Jesus' initial refusal and subsequent persuasion. Both these points show that the Johannine account is secondary; 1) Clearly by moving the scene of the story to Cana the miracle of healing at a distance has been heightened;[5] 2) Equally clearly, the Synoptic form of the motive behind the refusal and persuasion, with its parallel in Mk. 7.25–30,[6] is original, as is shown by the obscurity of the Johannine dialogue (4.48f.) in its context (as opposed to Mt. 8.7–10). Jesus' reluctance to provide a guarantee for faith in answer to a man's desire for a sign (v. 48) makes no sense after v. 47, since the βασιλικός has in no way asked for a miracle as a proof of Jesus' authority. On the contrary his request proves his faith, and so his reply (v. 49) can only be to repeat his request, which makes it hard to see why this should now persuade Jesus to change his mind.

---

not his recognition, his τιμή (5.23)? B. Weiss, on the other hand, thinks that v. 44 means that Jesus left Samaria where he was held in honour in order to win himself such acclaim in his home-country, which as yet did not recognise him! Loisy thinks that Samaria, because it was part of Palestine, was also Jesus' πατρίς; since he had found honour there, he must now leave on the principle stated in v. 44! Similarly Hirsch (who takes v. 44 as a gloss, as do others): Jesus leaves Samaria so quickly lest it becomes a πατρίς for him.

[5] Cp. P. Wendland, Die urchristl. Literaturformen 275f. (or 209f.)

[1] The δοῦλος in Lk. is secondary to Mt.'s παῖς = "child"; cp. Gesch. der synopt. Tr. 2. ed. 39 = Hist. of the Syn. Trad. 39.

[2] Here too Lk. is secondary to Mt.

[3] Cp. Jn. 4.47: ἀκούσας κτλ. = Lk. 7.2f. ἀκούσας κτλ.
ἤμελλεν κτλ. = ἤμελλεν κτλ.
ἠρώτα κτλ. = ἐρωτῶν κτλ.
4.53: ἐκείνῃ τῇ ὥρᾳ—Mt. 8. 13: ἐν τῇ ὥρα ἐκείνῃ

[4] See p. 113.

[5] Grill (II 134) is over-subtle when he suggests that the story has been reset in Cana, as the place of the Dionysian miracle (2.1ff.), because Jesus appears again as Dionysus, this time as 'Ιατρός or 'Υγιάτης.—Indeed the parallelism which, it has so often been argued, exists between 4.46–54 and 2.1–11 is an illusion. The only similarity is that in both stories Jesus at first refuses to perform a miracle, and then does it after all; but both the reason for the refusal and the reaction of those who ask for the sign are quite different. That in both cases the request is granted in a way which was quite unexpected (Ho.) can at best be said of 4.46–54, inasmuch as Jesus does not accompany the father, but cures the son from a distance; it is just not true of 2.1–11.

[6] See Gesch. der synopt. Trad. 2. ed. 38f. = Hist. of the Syn. Trad. 38f.

The particular characteristics of the Johannine narrative must evidently be attributed to the Evangelist himself, even if it is not always possible to separate his own contribution from the original on which he worked.[1] In the σημεῖα-source the story takes place in Capernaum; for 2.12, which recorded Jesus' journey from Cana to Capernaum, comes from this source[2] and obviously formed the introduction to the "second" sign. This means that the first sentence of v. 46: ἦλθον ... οἶνον must be an editorial addition of the Evangelist's,[3] as can also be seen from the way in which it refers to what has gone before.[4] We should also attribute to him ἐκ τ. 'Ιουδ. εἰς τ. Γαλ. in v. 47, which has become necessary as a result of his own composition, and further καταβῇ καί (which may have replaced an original ἐλθών cp. Mt. 8.7: Lk. 7.3). In v. 52 he has added ἐχθές, which was necessary because of the greater distance between Cana and Capernaum.[5] V. 48 is uncalled for by the story and has no effect on it; it, too, as well as v. 49, must be attributed to the Evangelist; v. 48, however, has suppressed an original dialogue, which must have corresponded to Mt. 8.7–10. By this alteration the Evangelist has destroyed the original point of the story, in order to make it illustrate the motif of "πίστις and σημεῖα". He it is who must also have changed the heathen officer into a Jewish court-official.

V. 46a is an editorial link with the previous passage.[6] It describes the general situation, whereas **v. 46b** leads into the miracle story which follows; vv. 47–50 are the corpus of the story. It begins in **v. 47** with the request of the Herodian court-official,[7] the urgency of which is drawn out by ἤμελλεν γὰρ ἀποθνήσκειν. Jesus' reply in **v. 48** does not really answer the question; for in fact the father has turned to him because he has faith

---

[1] Cp. particularly Wellhausen's and Spitta's analyses.

[2] See p. 114 n.4.

[3] It is quite clear that the Evangelist has a preference for Cana, cp. Kundsin, Topolog. Überlieferung 22ff.

[4] Cp. 1.30; 6.65; 13.33; 15.20; 16.15; 18.9.

[5] Since in their present form vv. 52f. presuppose the distance between Cana and Capernaum, Spitta wants to take the verses as a whole as an editorial addition. However it is sufficient to omit ἐχθές. The concluding phrase καὶ ἐπίστευσεν κτλ. does not sound like the Evangelist, but rather betrays the terminology of missionary stories, cp. Acts 16.31–33; 18.8; also Acts 10.2; 11.14.

[6] Πάλιν does not record the next of a series of events as Mk. 2.13, etc., but refers back to 2.1. The editorial character of the verse (see above) is also shown by the fact that we are told neither the destination of the journey, nor what else happened during the stay in Cana. The Evangelist simply wants to fit in an isolated story at this point.

[7] On the different meanings of βασιλικός see Br. In the Pap. it refers to civil and military officials of the king or state. In Jos. all the relatives and officials of the Herods are called βασιλικοί (Schl.). Since in the NT βασιλεύς is usually used to refer to the Herods and Καῖσαρ to the Emperor (so too Jn. 19.12, 15), the βασιλικός is probably an Herodian court official. The fact that he is a representative of the worldly power (Schl.) seems not to be stressed. It is evident that he is a Jew, since nothing is said to the contrary. Also Jesus' reply in v. 48 in John can have been addressed only to a Jew.—The reading βασιλίσκος = "little king" (D it var) is not to be trusted.—'Ερωτᾶν = "ask", as in v. 40; on ἵνα see Bl.-D. para. 392, 1, cp. Mk. 7.26; καταβαίνειν corresponds to the geographical position of Capernaum.

in his miraculous power—in the sense, of course, in which the Synoptics talk of faith.[1] No other sort of faith had till now been required of him, and so he had not asked for the miracle as a proof of Jesus' authority to claim faith from men.

Of course for the Evangelist the very appearance of Jesus means that men are faced with the challenge to believe in him as the Revealer; and for him it is a misunderstanding if "faith" expects from Jesus a miraculous liberation from physical distress.[2] This is the only way in which any sense can be given to Jesus' refusing the father's request. The Evangelist may have cases in mind where a miracle was demanded as the condition of belief. He may also have been thinking of a missionary practice which sought to arouse faith by appealing to σημεῖα καὶ τέρατα.[3] Clearly by his treatment of the story he wanted to correct the naive faith in miracles, such as is exhibited by the Synoptic tradition, and he has therefore at this point worked into the miracle story itself the motif which rejects miracles as a means of authorisation[4]—a motif which in the synoptics stands *alongside* the miracle tradition. This means that Jesus' refusal no longer has bearing on the situation of the story itself, and it has become a general lament on the weakness of men who ask for a miracle. The miracle is then (as in 20.26ff.) finally granted to them; for there is always the possibility that such a miracle will lead them on further. Thus while the story has lost its organic unity, it has gained in content, so that it provides an example of the recourse from λαλιά to Jesus' λόγος itself (see p. 201).

This means that the progress of the narrative is halted at this point; for the father in his reply (**v. 49**) can hardly take up the question raised in v. 48. An answer like that in Mt. 8.8f. is excluded here, and all that remains is to repeat the request in different words. Of course it now comes to mean: "I do not ask you to give proof of your authority, I come only in my distress and ask your help for my child"; thus the father shows one of the characteristics of true faith, even if his faith is at any early stage. He has come no further than to recognise his own

---

[1] See Gesch. der synopt. Tr. 2. ed. 234f. = Hist. of the Syn. Trad. 219f. Σημεῖα καὶ τέρατα (which occurs only here in John) is a common combination (Acts 2.19, 43 etc., see n. 3); it goes back to the OT אֹתֹת וּמֹפְתִים (Ex. 7.3; Deut. 4.34 etc.) and is also found in Jos. (Schl., Wie sprach Jos. von Gott? 52). The original distinction between the two terms (R. Ch. Trench, Synonyma des NT 218ff.) has ceased to play any role in this traditional combination.—The strong negative οὐ μή is rarely used in Classical Greek and occurs only rarely in the Pap.; it is common in the NT because of the influence of the LXX; see Bl.-D. para. 365; Moulton, Proleg. pp. 187ff.

[2] Cp. Ad. Schlatter, Der Glaube im NT 4. ed. 1927, 197.

[3] Cp. Rom. 15.19; II Cor. 12.12; Heb. 2.4; Acts 4.30; 5.12; 6.8 8.13; 14.3; 15.12; in each case here the combination σημεῖα καὶ τέρατα occurs (see n. 1).

[4] Mk. 8.11f. or Mt. 12.39f. = Lk. 11.16, 29.

need for help. This is enough for his request to be granted. (**v. 50**).[1] 'Επίστευσεν ὁ ἄνθρωπος κτλ. underlines the moral of the story. It does not of course refer to faith in its full sense, for this is not reached till v. 53; but inasmuch as the father believes without seeing (20.29), his faith shows one aspect of true faith, which is then followed by the experience of the miracle.[2] The setting of the story in Cana heightens the power of this faith without sight. The Evangelist is not afraid of being misunderstood; the miracle in an external sense is heightened, while man's desire for miracles is reproved.

Vv. 51–53 form the conclusion of the miracle story as demanded by the genre. It is dominated by the motif of attestation.[3] The reason why the father does not simply confirm the healing on his return home, but has to be told the news of the cure on the way[4] by his servants,[5] is that they cannot know the reason for the cure and are thus beyond suspicion as witnesses.[6] They must even confirm that the cure[7] took place at the same time[8] at which Jesus spoke the decisive word; this too is a favourite motif.[9] That the miracle results in the father and his whole household becoming believers corresponds to the conclusion of other miracle stories which record the impression made by the miracle.[10] This traditional motif has been reshaped under the influence of the

---

[1] Naturally Jesus' word is thought of as having power to work miracles, as is confirmed by v. 53. Since the Synoptic dialogue has been suppressed here, the healing at a distance goes back, not to the father's request, but to Jesus' own initiative.—πορεύου corresponds to the Semitic phrase for dismissing people (see Schl. on Mt. 2.8), which in the Synoptics is often found as ὕπαγε in miracle stories. (Mk. 5.19, 34 etc.). The ὁ υἱός σου ζῇ in I Kings 17.23 comes after the raising from the dead. However the phrase is appropriate here too. for in Semitic usage illness is thought of as a kind of death, and there is no specific word for "to recover"; see Baudissin, Festschr. für Ed. Sachau 1915, 143ff.

[2] So too Wendt I 28.

[3] Gesch. der synopt. Trad. 2. ed. 240 = Hist. of the Syn. Trad. 224.

[4] Αὐτοῦ καταβ ... ὑπήντ. αὐτῷ as in Mk. 5.2 etc., see Bl.D. para. 423.1. Mk. 5.35 par. gives a further case where servants come to meet their master.

[5] ℵ D lat add καὶ ἤγγειλαν before λέγοντες, but this is omitted by BLN. On this and similar variants see Schniewind, ThWB I 60, 28ff. The mss. also have υἱός instead of παῖς, σου instead of αὐτοῦ, but the variants are not uniformly distributed; they are probably both assimilations to v. 50 (in spite of Noack 138).

[6] Wendland, Urchristl. Literaturformen 276 (or 210).

[7] Κομψῶς ἔχειν is found only here in the NT, but is common in Epict., see Br.; ἀφῆκεν αὐτὸν ὁ πυρετός (as Mk. 1.31 parr.) is Semitic, see Str.-B. I 480; II 441; Schl. on Mt. 8.15.

[8] ὥρα in the accusative in reply to the question when? is also Classical (B.-D. para. 161.3; see also Schl. on Mt. 10.19). It makes no difference to the point of the story whether the time was reckoned on the Jewish or the Roman system (Str.-B. II 442), nor whether the distance between Cana and Capernaum (Dalman, O. u. W. 113f.; Lagr.) is large enough to make the times given probable.

[9] Cp. Mt. 8.13; Mk. 7.29f.; Gesch. der synopt, Trad. 2. ed. 240 = Hist. of the Syn. Trad. 224; Str.-B. II 441; P. Fiebig, Jüd. Wundergeschichten 20.

[10] Gesch. der synopt. Trad. 2. ed. 241 = Hist. of the Syn. Trad. 225f.

Christian mission and its terminology.[1] For the Evangelist, however, this ἐπίστευσεν clearly means more than simply that "he became a Christian"; it represents the step which leads from the preliminary stage of faith (v. 50) to faith proper. Thus the miracle to which man has no right, since he may not require the Revealer to give proof of his authority, is nevertheless on occasions granted to man in his weakness so long as man is aware of his own helplessness. For where it is granted it can lead man on beyond the faith that is based on miracles. Admittedly chs. 6 and 5 show that this is an exception.

V. 54 is an editorial conclusion already contained in the σημεῖα-source, which numbers this miracle as the second; the Evangelist has added the ἐλθὼν κτλ. in accordance with his own composition.[2]

C. 6.1–59: The Bread of Life

The present order of chs. 5 and 6 cannot be the original one. Since in 6.1 Jesus goes "to the other side" (πέραν) of the lake, he must have been at the lake-side beforehand; but in ch. 5 he is in Jerusalem.[3] Thus ch. 6 has no connection with ch. 5. On the other hand it would follow on ch. 4 very well. Correspondingly 7.1 assumes that Jesus had been staying in Judaea (Jerusalem) up till then, and ch. 7 would thus link up with ch. 5. So the original order must have been chs. 4, 6, 5, 7.[4] This is confirmed by the fact that this order makes good sense of 4.44, which otherwise makes no sense at all (see p. 204), and also by the fact that 6.2 (σημεῖα ... ἐπὶ τῶν ἀσθενούντων) is now seen to be a reference back to the exemplary story of 4.46–54. It also enables us to see the chronological order which the Evangelist had in mind. The festival which was imminent in 6.4 has started in 5.1. Finally 7.1 states that Jesus left Judaea because the Jews wanted to kill him, which is appropriate only as a reference back to 5.18 provided ch. 5 immediately preceded ch. 7. Moreover the themes which are discussed in chs. 5 and 6 also make the order 6, 5 more

---

[1] See p.206 n.5.—Οἶκος is commonly used to refer to the family or the members of a household. Zahn, with his customary ingenuity, suspects that the conversion must have been important for Galilee; he raises the question whether one should identify the βασιλικός with Chuza, Herod's (Antipas') ἐπίτροπος, whose wife Joanna was one of the women accompanying Jesus in Lk. 8.3, or with Manaen, Herod's σύντροφος in Acts 13.1.

[2] Grammatically it would be possible to take this to mean: "As the second miracle which Jesus performed after his arrival". But this is not possible, because in that case the first miracle would have had to be recorded. V. 54 clearly points back to 2.11, and the enumeration is taken from the source, since it ignores 2.23.—πάλιν is added pleonastically to δεύτερον, see Bl.-D. para. 484.

[3] It is meaningless to refer to a point on the Lake of Galilee as lying "on the other side" from Jerusalem; cp. even Zahn.

[4] Apart from 6.60–71. The suggestion that ch. 6 should be placed after ch. 4 is nothing new; see Howard 126ff., 264. Wik. is also in favour of placing it here, while Strathm. would like to place ch. 5 after 7.13.

probable. Ch. 6 shows that the revelation is the κρίσις of man's natural desire for life, ch. 5 that it is the κρίσις of his religion. In ch. 6 we have the dispute with the people, in ch. 5 with their leaders.—Whereas the Synoptics portray Jesus' ministry by collecting together a large number of small pieces of tradition, which they try to join up into a coherent whole as best they can, John gives his portrayal in a series of large detailed pictures. And even if he fits these pictures into a chronological scheme, the individual sections are still not intended as particular historical scenes, but as representative pictures of the revelation-event. This is also the way in which chs. 6 and 5 are to be understood.

a) The Feeding of the Multitude and the Journey on the Lake: 6.1–26

That the Evangelist in 6.1–26 has again used part of a literary source is shown by his own editorial insertions in v. 4, v. 6, vv. 14f., vv. 23f., and by the not entirely organic relationship of 6.27–59 (which in the main is his own composition) to 6.1–26 (see below). The tradition used here is the same as in Mk. 6.30–51, which also combines the miracles of the feeding of the multitude and the walking on the sea, whereas in Mk. 8.1–10 a variant of the feeding story appears on its own. In fact the agreement between Jn. 6.1–26 and Mk. 6.30–51, both in the construction of the narrative and in matters of detail, is very considerable. Yet even here we find characteristic divergences. In the Johannine account great stress is laid on the fact that Jesus seizes the initiative;[1] Jesus knows what he will do and starts things moving by asking a question to which he well knows the answer. Correspondingly the disciples' dilemma is stressed more strongly (v. 7 and v. 9); the help of two of the disciples, who are mentioned by name, is enlisted[2] and this makes the preparation of the miracle more complicated. Whereas in Mk. 6.37 two hundred denarii worth of bread would suffice, according to John 6.7 it would not be enough; the ὅσον ἤθελον in v. 11 also heightens the effect. Finally the use of direct speech is more frequent than in Mk.[3] Since these divergences should be attributed to the source, rather than to the Evangelist himself, he cannot have used Mk. as his source.[4] This becomes much clearer in the story of the walking on the lake. The source used by John seems to come from an earlier stage of the tradition, since the motifs of the stilling of the storm and of the disciples' lack of understanding (Mk. 6.52) are missing. On the other hand the narrative has been further developed in another direction in that

---

[1] Cp. Mk. 8.1f. as opposed to Mk. 6.35f.; see Gesch. der synopt. Trad. 2. ed. 69f. = Hist. of the Syn. Trad. 65f.

[2] Gesch. der synopt. Trad. 2. ed. 338. = Hist. of the Syn. Trad. 310.

[3] Op. cit. 340f. = 311f. On the whole question cp. P. Wendland, Die urchristl. Literaturformen 237 (303).

[4] Quite certainly he did not use Mt. or Lk. Mt. on the one hand makes no mention of the 200 dinarii, which John has in common with Mk, while on the other hand John does not have the story of Peter's sinking, Mt. 14.28–33. Lk. does not give the story of the walking on the lake.

1) the motif of the miraculous landing has been added (v. 21) and 2) it has been given a conclusion which presents the motif of attestation in an unusual way (vv. 22, 25, see below). The most obvious inference to draw is that the Evangelist has taken the section from the σημεῖα-source.[1]

Vv. 1–4 set the scene for the story which follows:[2] Jesus' crossing of the lake provides the correct geographical setting for the story,[3] and the fact that people are continually coming to him (ἠκολ. imperfect!) explains why they search him out on the other side of the lake. Whereas, by contrast with Mk. 6.31f., no reason is given for Jesus' ἀπελθεῖν (v. 1), his following among the people is explained by the impression made on them by his healing miracles, of which an example has just been given.[4] It is of course implied that the people go on foot round the lake; before they catch up with Jesus he has already sought out a place with his disciples on the hillside.[5] Again no explanation is given and we are told no more than this bare fact. Nor are we told that it is evening (Mk. 6.35 parr.). Evening does not fall till v. 16, where it is required by the events which follow. The account in these first four verses is concise and serves only to introduce what follows. The only thing that goes beyond this is the

---

[1] Stylistically the source shows the same characteristics as the sections which we have already attributed to the σημεῖα-source. The style is a "Semitising" Greek, but it does not seem possible to discern in the story a translation from a literary Semitic source. The passage is characterised by the placing of the verb at the beginning of the sentence; also by the lack (in vv. 7, 8, 10 where K pl have δέ) or very simple form of connection between the sentences (δέ and οὖν). Ποιήσατε (in Greek we would expect κελεύσατε)... ἀναπεσεῖν v. 10 corresponds to the Semitic causative (see Rev. 13.13 and Schl.). The constantly repeated αὐτοῦ also is not Greek (it corresponds to the Semitic suffix) after the different forms of μαθηταί vv. 3, 8, 12, 16; significantly the only case in which it does not occur is in the addition to v. 11 in D. Goodenough (156ff.), who also disputes John's dependence on Mk., believes that they are both dependent on a "ritualistic tradition", which was already present in literary form.

[2] As in 3.22; 5.1 etc., the time which had elapsed is only loosely indicated; see p. 121 n.6.

[3] The reference to the lake (θάλασσα as in Mk. and Mt.) is overlong. D al try to correct this by inserting εἰς τὰ μέρη before τῆς Τιβ. (Hirsch II 58f. interprets this differently). But it can hardly be right to leave out one of the genitives, even though τῆς Γαλ. is omitted by N pc syr[s]. Probably τῆς Τιβ. (which can hardly be adjectival) has been added by the Evangelist or the editor (cp. 21.1) to the name which was commonly given to it in the earlier tradition (this is disputed by Barr.). The custom of describing the lake by reference to Tiberias, which was founded by Herod Antipas c. 26 A.D. (Schürer II 216f.; Dalman, O. u. W. 195f.; Str.-B. II 467–477), must have grown up gradually. As well as 21.1 cp. Jos. bell. III 57: τῆς πρὸς Τιβεριάδα λίμνης (inferior mss: τῆς Τιβεριάδος), IV 456: ἡ Τιβεριέων (λίμνη); Pausanias V 7.3; λίμνην Τιβεριάδα ὀνομαζομένην. In the Synoptics: τῆς Γαλιλαίας (Mk., Mt.) or Γεννησαρέτ (Lk. 5.1); cp. Dalman, O. u. W. 128f.

[4] The reason given must have been added by the Evangelist., see p. 130 n.3.—Instead of the rare imperf. ἑώρων (Bl.-D. paras. 66, 2.101) H D al read ἐθεώρουν, which may be an assimilation to 2.23.

[5] Neither here nor in Mk. 3.13, Mt. 5.1 etc. is any particular hill intended.—The statement in v. 15 contradicts v. 3, but this is probably carelessness on the part of the narrator; the reason can hardly be that v. 3 was modelled on Mt. 15.29 and v. 15 on Mk. 6.46.

mention of the date, which the Evangelist has added in v. 4 to the traditional material[1] for the sake of the unity of his own composition. It prepares the way for 5.1.[2]

In **v. 5** the action begins with Jesus calling Philip's attention to the difficulty raised by the presence of so many people.[3] His question however, as **v. 6** expressly states, is only an apparent one, and its purpose is to make clear the παράδοξον of the miracle.[4] This is also the point of Philip's reply in **v. 7,** which explains to the reader what a large number of people there was to be fed.[5] The same is true of the information supplied by Andrew, for want of anything better to suggest, in **vv. 8f.** and which brings out the helplessness of man.[6] The fact that it does not occur to any of the disciples that Jesus might perform a miracle shows that the story was originally told as a unit complete in itself.

The miracle itself, as usual, is only indirectly related (**vv. 10–11**).

---

[1] The date here given has no bearing on the events which follow; this would be unlikely anyway, as the stories in the early tradition contain no such dates. Certainly the reason for its inclusion cannot be that it is intended to give a further reason for the crowds following Jesus, which had already been explained in v. 2—for instance, that they were a crowd of pilgrims who were going to Jerusalem for the festival. For their way would not take them past the lake, and moreover pilgrims carried supplies of food with them.

[2] Exegetes are fond of pointing out that v. 4. sets the story of the feeding of the multitude, together with Jesus' subsequent discourse, in the context of the Passover, or its replacement, the Eucharist. Yet the subsequent discourse is related to the Eucharist only by the editorial addition 6.56–58 (see below); one would then have to attribute v. 4 to the editor as well. Moreover the discourse refers to the feeding of the Israelites by manna, but not to the Passover meal. Further the Evangelist does not present Jesus' last meal as a Passover meal, nor does he present it from the point of view of the Eucharistic meal.—According to P. Saintyves, Essais de folklore biblique 1923, 299ff. the miracle of the feeding was dated at the time of the Passover because it was originally the cultic legend of the festival of the first-born. As if John could still contain a reference to such an (anyway highly questionable) fact!—Many exegetes leave out the universally attested τὸ πάσχα (cp. Herm. v. Soden, Encycl. Bibl. 803) in an attempt to preserve the harmony of the Synoptic and the Johannine chronology. This is done particularly by Catholic exegetes (cp. H. J. Cladder, Unsere Evangelien I 1919, 207–212).

[3] There is nothing particularly solemn about the expression ἐπάρας τοὺς ὀφθ. in v. 5, any more than there was in 4.35.

[4] V. 6 is clearly a note added by the Evangelist which shows his own typical style. On τοῦτο δὲ ἔλεγεν cp. 7.39; 11.51; 12.33; (21.19); on αὐτὸς γὰρ cp. 2.25; 4.44, further 6.64; 13.11.

[5] Philip's inability to see that Jesus really knows the answer to his own question has nothing to do with Johannine "misunderstandings", but merely shows that he is rather naive. For the Johannine "misunderstandings" have nothing to do with πειράζειν, while on the other hand we miss here the ambiguity which goes with such "misunderstandings".—The ἵνα v. 7 is consecutive, see Raderm. 193.

[6] On v. 9: παιδάριον, which occurs frequently in the LXX and the Pap., = "young boy" or "slave".—Barley bread is generally considered to be an inferior food (see Br., Schl., Str.-B. II 478); yet this is not the point here, nor is it in II Kings 4.42.—ὀψάριον (diminutive of ὄψον) = "something cooked" eaten with bread; it can refer to delicacies (Tob. 2.2 ℵ and elsewhere) and specifically also, as here, to fishes. References to the literature and Pap. in Br.—IV Kings 4.43 (LXX) (τί δῶ τοῦτο ἐνώπιον ἑκατὸν ἀνδρῶν) need not have had any influence on ἀλλὰ ταῦτα κτλ.

Jesus gives a command, as in 2.7f., which must at first seem pointless to the disciples who are assisting him. Then, in order to raise the tension here, we are told at some length that the crowd sat down on the grass, and that there were five thousand men alone.[1] In **v. 11** an account is given quite objectively and without any pathos, about the distribution.[2] Finally **vv. 12–13**, in the proper style of miracle stories, bring home the greatness of the miracle by adding yet another παράδοξον: after all have been satisfied there is more left over than there was at the beginning![3]

Vv. 14f. tell of the consequences of the miracle. The early tradition, as is shown by the miracle stories of the Synoptic Gospels, records the effect which the miracles had on the witnesses, but is not interested in their further consequences, and in this respect the Synoptic writers are virtually the same.[4] In John, however, the miracles are closely related to the history of the Revealer. They are σημεῖα in a special sense (see v. 26), and so compel men to take their stand for or against the Revealer. Vv. 14f. therefore have been added by the Evangelist.[5] Now we see clearly, what had only been hinted at in 2.24: the crowd misunderstand the σημεῖον,[6] as Jesus expressly tells them (v. 26); they want to make Jesus the Messianic king. Admittedly they have at least understood that the miracle worker is the eschatological bringer of salvation;[7] but they

---

[1] Since vv. 2, 5, 22, 24 have ὄχλος and vv. 10a, 14 ἄνθρωποι, οἱ ἄνδρες is without doubt used as in Mt. 14.21; 15.38: χωρὶς γυναικῶν καὶ παιδίων.

[2] Εὐχαριστήσας (cp. Mk. 6.41; 8.6f.) is not intended to present the feeding as a prefiguration of the Eucharist. The prayer of thanksgiving corresponds rather to the Jewish custom (Str.-B. I 685f. IV 621); it is also in accordance with Jewish custom that Jesus as host should distribute the bread (op. cit. IV 621). Temple (75) and Str. (184) stress that v. 11 does not speak in sacramental language, and that it is not said that Jesus "broke" bread. It is clear that the distribution to the crowd had to be delegated to the disciples, as is expressly stated by KD pm b e by the addition after διέδωκεν (or ἔδωκεν ℵ D al it) of τοῖς μαθηταῖς, οἱ δὲ μαθηταί.

[3] Κλασμάτων v. 13 depends on ἐγέμισαν or κοφίνους, Bl.-D. para. 172. It is senseless to ask why it was only the bread which was left over at the end and not the fish too (see Mk. 6.43). According to B. Weiss because the fishes, unlike the bread were not distributed to all, but only to those who asked for them! According to Ho. and L. because only the bread had symbolic significance.—Even if Tert. de cor. 3; Orig. in Ex. hom. 13.3; Const. Ap. VIII 13 relates ἵνα μή τι ἀπόληται v. 12 to the Eucharistic elements, this does not prove that John understood the sentence in this way. The collecting up of what was left over at the end of the meal was a Jewish custom at meals (Str.-B. IV 625f.).

[4] Only Mk. 3.6 (which is Mk.'s own editorial addition) gives any thought to the consequences—and then less to the consequences of the miracle than to those of breaking the Sabbath.

[5] Neither v. 4 nor vv. 14f. have any parallels in the Synoptic feeding narratives. Nor do the events related in vv. 14f. have any consequences for Jesus' meeting with the people on the next day (vv. 25ff.).

[6] There can be no doubt that we should read: ὃ ἐπ. σημεῖον with ℵ ADW etc., and not ἃ ἐπ. σημεῖα with B pc.

[7] V. 15 shows that the "prophet who comes into the world" is not a forerunner of salvation but the bringer of salvation himself, for the people believe that the "prophet" must be king. The "prophet" can hardly be meant to refer to Moses at his second coming (J.

have a false conception of the eschatological salvation. This will be stated more clearly in v. 26, but is is suggested clearly enough here when their intention is given as: ἵνα ποιήσωσιν βασιλέα. Just as in vv. 26, 34 the crowd expect the bringer of salvation to fulfil their natural desires and longings, so too in vv. 14f. they see him as a king whose kingdom is "of this world" (18.36); indeed they themselves want to "make" him king. Jesus resists such pressure.[1] The symbolic character of the scene is clear; for we are not to ask how it is possible to reconcile Jesus' flight with the fact that shortly afterwards he is again standing before the people (v. 25). The Evangelist is concerned to make this protest against the old eschatology.[2]

Of course the Evangelist could have introduced the discussion of vv. 26ff. immediately after the feeding of the multitude. His reasons for not doing so are probably not only the mere fact that the miracles of the feeding and Jesus' walking on the lake at night are closely connected in the tradition,[3] but also that the source immediately afterwards brings Jesus and the people together again, so providing the Evangelist with the situation he required for the subsequent discussion. Perhaps, too, he was moved by considerations of the symbolic significance which he attaches to the second miracle (see below). Dodd (344f.), also finds a symbolic significance in the order of the narrative in ch. 6: the progression in the dialogue from the misunderstanding of Jesus as a second Moses (6.30) to his understanding of himself as the bread of life corresponds to the progression in the sequence of incidents from the crowd's misconception of him as the messianic king (6.14f.) to his ἐγώ εἰμι (6.20). This seems too artificial to me.

V. 16 describes a change in the situation. Evening has come and the disciples go down to the lake.[4] In view of vv. 14f. this cannot be explained as in Mk. 6.45 so that now it is hard to see why they do not wait for Jesus. It is taken for granted that the crowd go home on foot, although it is not actually recorded, but is assumed in vv. 22, 25; it is also assumed

Jeremias, Golgotha 1926, 83); for was he ever expected to return as "king" in Judaism? Cp. pp. 89f. Dodd describes the title of "the coming Prophet" as a "quasi-messianic designation". On the commingling of the figures of the prophet and the messianic king see P. Volz, Die Eschatologie der jüd. Gemeinde 1934, 193f.; W. Staerk, Soter I 1933, 61ff.—H. Windisch, Paulus und Christus 1934, 79 thinks that the judgement of the people is based on the old belief in the magic powers of the king.

[1] On αὐτὸς μόνος v. 15 = "by himself", "alone", see Raderm. 77.

[2] In this the Evangelist uses the motif of Jesus' retreat from the crowd, which also occurs in Mk. 6.45f., but which here of course takes on a quite different meaning. D alone, following Mk. (or Mt. 14.23), adds: κἀκεῖ προσηύχετο.—On the relation of v. 15 to v. 3 see p. 211n.5.

[3] Cp. Mk. 6.30–52; Mt. 14.13–33; Lk. in 9.10–17 gives only the miracle of the feeding.

[4] Perhaps they go down from the ὄρος v. 3; but there is no need to give much thought to the question. In any case it is obvious that one "goes down" to the shore, see Schl.

that the ὄχλος has watched the disciples leave in their boat. **Vv. 17f.** record their destination[1] as Capernaum[2] and give a brief description of their journey in the dark.[3] In contrast with Mk. 6.47f., the journey is described not from Jesus' standpoint as he sees the boat battling with the storm, but from the stand-point of the disciples; and no mention is made of their distress. Thus the motif of danger plays no part in this account.[4] The narrator continues the story from this point of view, for he gives no account of Jesus' crossing of the lake (as in Mk. 6.48) let alone any reason for it. Instead he simply adds without further explanation, καὶ οὔπω ἐληλύθει πρὸς αὐτοὺς ὁ 'I., which neither the disciples nor the uninstructed reader could have expected. The narrator was obviously thinking ahead to what would follow, and the statement shows clearly that for him the real point of the story is the miracle of Jesus' walking on the lake. This is also shown by the mention of the distance which the boat had covered: the boat has already reached the middle of the lake.[5] The disciples then suddenly see Jesus walking towards them[6] on the water and approaching their craft (**v. 19**). They are frightened; and this, although it is not expressly stated, must clearly be taken in the sense of Mk. 6.49; they are awe-struck by the miracle of the manifestation of the divine.[7] That this is the reason for their fear, is confirmed (as in Mk. 6.50) by Jesus' words in **v. 20**: ἐγώ εἰμι, μὴ

---

[1] The πλοῖον had not previously been mentioned (but cp. Mk. 6.32), although it is assumed in v. 1. Εἰς πλοῖον (without the article, BℵL) is probably analogous to εἰς οἶκον lBl.-D. para. 259.1). The imperfect ἤρχοντο denotes, as in 4.30, an uncompleted action.

[2] In Mk. 6.45 their destination is Bethsaida; but the σημειᾶ-source obviously must have said Capernaum. The reason for this preference for Capernaum, according to Kundsin, Topol. Überl. 33f., was that Capernaum was the scene of the conflict in early Christianity between Hellenistic sacramentalism and Judaeo-Christianity.

[3] Instead of καὶ σκοτία ἤδη ἐγεγόνει (B etc.), ℵ D read κατέλαβεν δὲ αὐτοὺς ἡ σκοτία, clearly following 12.34.

[4] Wendland, Die urchristl. Literaturformen 210 (276). Htm. rightly wants to omit v. 18 as a gloss; the stilling of the storm is not recounted later, and stylistically the verse with its genitive absolute is out of place.

[5] 'Εληλακότες should certainly not be taken transitively ("row"), but intrans. ("journey"); according to v. 18 the boat is driven by the wind (yet see previous note). 'Ελ. gives no grounds for supposing that the boat was driven off-course (Zn.).—The 25–30 stadia (=3–3½ miles) are intended to refer to the middle of the lake, which according to Jos. bell. III 506 was 40 stadia (4½ miles) wide, and 6 miles at its widest part (Benzinger, RGG 1. ed. II 1284).—Obviously this is put in here to make the miracle seem as great as possible.

[6] 'Επὶ τῆς θαλ. means of course not "by" but "on" or "across the lake" (see Job 9.5; Rev 10.5). B. Weiss gives a rationalistic explanation. Since the disciples have covered about 25–30 stadia they believe themselves to be in the middle of the lake, whereas in fact they are nearly at the other side, where Jesus is walking on the shore. Naturally then they come into and immediately afterwards. They have been misled by the darkness of the night and their excitement betrays them into thinking that it was a miracle!

[7] Cp. Lk. 1.12; 2.9; Rev. 1.17, etc., Cp. Gesch. der synopt. Trad. 2. ed. 241. = Hist. of the Syn. Trad. 225.

φοβεῖσθε which is the traditional formula of greeting used by the deity in his epiphany.[1] The conclusion (**v. 21**) gives no account of the stilling of the storm,[2] but tells how the disciples desire to take Jesus into the boat,[3] which immediately arrives at its destination. Thus the miracle of the landing is added to the miracle of the walking on the lake.[4]

The continuation, or rather the conclusion of the story in the source, which is here contained in vv. 22–26 in a form modified by the Evangelist, shows however that the real point of the story is the miracle of the walking on the lake.

The ὄχλος of whom we are told in **v. 22** is, according to vv. (24 and) 25, the crowd who had witnessed the feeding on the previous day, and who are thus assumed to have arrived back on the other side of the lake.[5] When it is stated that the crowd is πέραν τῆς θαλάσσης, this clearly is spoken, as is v. 25, from the stand-point of the feeding miracle. Thus the crowd is in Capernaum. Here, to their surprise, they find Jesus (**v. 25**), and they ask in amazement how he has got there. The reason for their amazement over the παράδοξον of Jesus' presence has been given clearly in v. 22: the crowd know[6] that in the place where the feeding

[1] Cp. L. Köhler, Schweizer Theol. Zeitschr. 1919, 1–6.

[2] Even in Mk. 6.45–52 the motif of the stilling of the storm is secondary; it has been imported from Mk. 4.37–41; Gesch. der synopt. Trad. 2. ed. 231.—Hist. of the Syn. Trad. 216.

[3] Should one assume that they carried out their intention? Or should one imagine that "Jesus, going before the ship, drew it to land" (Sp. 142; cp. Chrys. in Br. and Nonnos VI 80ff.)?

[4] On parallels to the miracle of the walking on the lake see Gesch. der synopt. Trad. 2. ed. 251f. = Hist. of the Syn. Trad. 236f.; L. Bieler, Θεῖος Ἀνήρ I 1935, 96f.—On the miraculously rapid landing, cp. Hymn. Hom. II 221ff. (or 399ff.), esp. 255ff. (or 433ff.); also Act. Petr. c. Sim. 5, p. 51, 10ff. As a motif in fairy-tales: Märchen der Weltliteratur, Südseemärchen 1921, 273; Buddhist. Märchen 1921, 45; Plattdeutsche Volksmärchen I 1914, 223. It is also found as a motif in novels, see K. Kerenyi, Die Griech.–Oriental. Romanlit. 1927, 98ff.; Rosa Söder, Die apokr. Apostelgesch. u. die romanhafte Literatur der Antike 1932, 86f.

[5] The narrator gives as little thought to the question how the ὄχλος could get round the lake to Capernaum on foot so quickly as he did in v. 2. In fact there is no problem. For there is time enough at their disposal; v. 21 takes place when it is still night and τῇ ἐπαύριον v. 22 does not have to mean the first light of day.

[6] This is certainly what is meant by εἶδον v. 22. It cannot refer to what they saw at Capernaum, for there would have been more ships there. Anyway it would be pointless to say that the people saw that "on the next day" there was only one ship on the shore near the place where the feeding had occurred. Probably εἶδον is intended to have a pluperfect sense (as ἐμαρτ. 4.44 and ἦλθον 4.45) and ought really to stand in a relative clause. There is no need to alter the text; all that is necessary is to take τῇ ἐπαύριον, which does not logically belong to εἶδον, as governing by anticipation the complete statement of vv. 22, 25 (cp. 13.1). It is possible that εἶδον is the result of a copyist's error for ἰδών, even though ἰδών ΔW, which is favoured by Zn. and Schl., is no more than a conjecture, as is the εἰδώς of e, which is favoured by Bl.-D. para. 330. If the text should go back to a Semitic original, it is possible that ὁ ἑστηκώς is a mistranslation of a finite verb which should have been joined to εἶδον by καί.

took place there was only one boat available,[1] and that the disciples crossed over in it without Jesus. Yet it goes without saying that Jesus did not return on foot with the crowd. How then has he got to Capernaum? The purpose of this account is quite plain: vv. 22, 25 contain the typical motif of the attestation of miracles. Like the unsuspecting, ἀρχιτρίκλινος of 2.9f., or the uninformed servants of 4.51f., so here the ὄχλος which had been elsewhere at the time of the miracle must be called as witnesses to it.[2]

The Evangelist has misunderstood the εἶδον, and has taken the πέραν to refer to the eastern shore of the lake, where the feeding occurred. Thus he has to get the crowd across to the western shore and so adds **vv. 23f.**[3] He introduces a deus ex machina in the form of ships from Tiberias, which come near the place of the feeding[4] and carry the crowd over to Capernaum.[5] Thus by one means or another we get the situation of v. 25 as it was given in the source, and the question πότε ὧδε γέγονας; can now be asked.[6]

It is most unlikely that the account in the source ended with this question. But the Evangelist has left out the original conclusion and replaced it by **v. 26.** Jesus' reply gives no answer to the question, but accuses the crowd of seeking him out because they experienced the miraculous feeding, and—as is obviously implied—because they hope to experience more such miracles from him.[7] The crowd thus have

---

[1] The ἦν has pluperfect sense (Bl.-D. para. 330). ℵ* D al add ἐκεῖνο εἰς ὃ ἐνέβησαν οἱ μαθηταὶ τοῦ ᾿Ι. after εἰ μὴ ἕν, which gives the right sense.

[2] See p. 118 and 208f.; Gesch. der synopt. Trad. 2. ed. 240 = Hist. of the Syn. Trad. 224; Wendland, Die urchristl. Literaturformen 211 (277), 1.

[3] The insertion of vv. 23f. cannot be attributed to the editor (Strathm.) but must be the work of the Evangelist whose ζητεῖτε v. 26 refers back to the ζητοῦντες v. 24 (see also the two following notes). The only thing which might have been added by the editor is εὐχαριστήσαντος τοῦ κυρίου but this phrase is a late gloss (see p. 204f.) whose omission by D 69 pc a e syr$^{\text{s.c.}}$ is manifestly original.—Hirsch also assumes that vv. 22–26 have been worked over by an editor, but he destroys the point of the verses by his omissions.

[4] We should read ἀλλὰ (not ἄλλα) ἦλθεν κτλ. The ἀλλά-clause, where the verb follows immediately after ἀλλά, is typical for the Evangelist., cp. 6.64; 8.37. ℵ tries to smooth out the style.

[5] The Evangelist does not make the connection very well between ὁ ὄχλος . . . εἶδον v. 22 and ὅτε οὖν εἶδεν; for it is not very appropriate after v. 22 to say that the crowd sees that the disciples "are not there". (On ἔστιν see Raderm. 153.156). The clause (ὅτε οὖν) is typical of the Evangelist, see p. 204 n. 1.—ζητοῦντες is also poor after v. 22; how then could they start looking for him! Originally v. 22 was followed by the surprising discovery, v. 25 καὶ εὑρόντες, but the Evangelist needed the key-word ζητεῖν for v. 26.

[6] Γίνεσθαι = παραγίνεσθαι as often, cp. v. 19; Lk. 22.40 etc., see Br.—The perfect γέγονας is really intended to be an aorist, Bl.-D. para. 343, 3.—Since according to v. 59, the scene takes place in the synagogue, which means on the Sabbath, and since ships (v. 23) were not allowed to sail on the Sabbath, Zn. concludes that some days must have passed before they discovered him (v. 25)—which of course removes the point of the question πότε κτλ.

[7] There is no reference back to vv. 14f. The Evangelist no longer needs the motif of vv. 14f. for the following passage.

misunderstood Jesus' action, just as the Samaritan woman (4.15) misunderstood the promise of the ὕδωρ ζῶν—a motif soon to be developed further (vv. 27, 34f.). The people have perceived only the outward miracle, they have not "seen" it as a σημεῖον. The Evangelist plays on the word σημεῖον, which is the traditional way of referring to miracles.[1] In truth the miracle as a sign *says* something, and here "seeing" is used paradoxically instead of "hearing".[2] Thus v. 26 shows that Jesus' σημεῖα, like his words, are ambiguous, and that they can arouse misunderstanding and offence just as easily as faith,[3] his last and greatest σημεῖον similarly brings him to the cross (ch. 11).

b) The Bread of Life: 6.27-59

V. 26 gives the Evangelist the lead into the discussion which follows; it must now be clear in what sense the events in 6.1–25 were σημεῖα. Of course the way v. 26 is related to v. 25 has already shown that the transition to the dialogue is artificial, so that the dialogue has no real bearing on the situation produced by 6.1–25. Indeed the way the Evangelist links vv. 27ff. with the previous events is most awkward, inasmuch as it is difficult to see why, after what has already happened, the crowd in vv. 30f. should ask for a miracle (and that a feeding miracle!) as a proof of his authority, when the feeding miracle which occurred in vv. 14f. would have served that purpose.[4] Clearly the Evangelist ignores the external situation and uses the feeding miracle, which he takes from the source, as a symbolic picture for the main idea of the revelation discourse, namely that Jesus gives the bread of life. If the miracle of the walking on the water had a symbolic meaning for the Evangelist, as well as serving to link up the two scenes,[5] then this can only be complementary to the main idea, since the following discussion makes no reference to the walking on the water. It is possible that this miracle, which shows Jesus' freedom from the laws of nature that bind man, is meant to teach the superiority and otherness of the revelation, as opposed to all forms of earthly natural life.

The argument and structure of 6.27–59 raise great difficulties.[6] In the first place 6.51b (καὶ ὁ ἄρτος δὲ κτλ.)–58b form a marked contrast to the previous course of the discussion. These verses refer without any doubt to the

---

[1] On σημεῖον = "miracle" see p. 114 n.1.

[2] See p. 113f., also p. 69 n.3.

[3] Cp. Kierkegaard, Training in Christianity, 44f.

[4] One may not conclude from the uneasy relationship of 6.27ff. to the previous section that 6.27ff. really belonged to ch. 5 (Wendt I, 70ff.; II, 67f.), particularly since ch. 5 must follow ch. 6.

[5] See above p. 214.

[6] Cp. P. Gächter's attempt, quite regardless of any critical problems, to establish the structure of the verses and strophes of Jesus' "eucharistic" discourse (vv. 35–58). Zeitschr. f. kathol. Theologie 59 (1935), 419–441.

sacramental meal of the Eucharist, where the flesh and blood of the "Son of Man" are consumed, with the result that this food gives "eternal life", in the sense that the participants in the meal can be assured of the future resurrection.[1] Thus the Lord's Supper is here seen as the φάρμακον ἀθανασιάς or τῆς ζωῆς.[2] This not only strikes one as strange in relation to the Evangelist's thought in general, and specifically to his eschatology, but it also stands in contradiction to what has been said just before. For here the bread of life which the Father gives by sending the Son from heaven (vv. 32f.) is the Son himself, the Revealer. He gives (v. 27) and is (vv. 35, 48, 51) the bread of life, in the same way that he gives the water of life (4.10) and is the light of the world (8.12), and as the Revealer gives life to the world (v. 33; cp. 10.28; 17.2)—to those, that is, who "come" to him (v. 35; cp. 3.20f.; 5.40), who believe in him (v. 35; and cp. 3.20f. with 3.18). In all of this there is no need for a sacramental act, by means of which the believer must make the life his own.[3] Furthermore the terminology of 6.51b–58 is taken from a quite different circle of ideas from that of 6.27–51a.[4] Thus we must inevitably conclude that vv. 51b–58 have been added by an ecclesiastical editor;[5] it is the same editor who has added at the end of vv. 39, 40, 44 the refrain: κἀγὼ ἀναστήσω αὐτὸν ἐν τῇ ἐσχάτῃ ἡμέρᾳ. This sentence has its proper place in v. 54; in the other places, particularly in v. 44, it disturbs the line of thought. It has been added in an attempt by the editor to make the whole discourse reflect the views of

---

[1] Lagr.: "L'allusion à l'Eucharistie est évidente, et ne peut être méconnue par personne, sauf pour les protestants à méconnaître la clarté des termes."

[2] Ign. Eph. 20.2; Act. Thom. 135 p. 242, 1.

[3] This explains why many of the earlier exegetes denied that vv. 51b-58 referred to the Eucharist; for the early exegesis, see Br. Lohmeyer, ThR 1937, 304–309. See also J. M. Nielen, Gebet u. Gottesdienst im NT 1937, 223.4 (see also 267f.). According to B. Weiss, Jesus used the image of eating and drinking his flesh and blood to refer to "the acceptance in faith of his human appearance on earth," whereas the Evangelist uses the imagery to refer to the appropriation in faith of the reconciling death of the Christ. Like Kreyenbühl, Odeberg (237, 239, 260) believes that the eating and drinking of Jesus' flesh and blood refers to the appropriation in faith of his teaching, or of his spiritual body, the reality of which is clearly stressed by "flesh" and "blood".

[4] See below p. 224 n.2.

[5] Sp. separates vv. 51–58 from the previous section as part of another source A.; Andersen (ZNW 9 [1908], 163f.); Merx and v. Dobschütz (ZNTW 28 [1929], 163.166) omit vv. 51–56 as an interpolation, as does Carpenter (428) with vv. 51–58, whereas according to Wellhausen vv. 51–59 have been added later (by another hand); similarly Bousset RGG 1. ed. III 616; Ed. Schweizer op. cit. 155ff. This is now disputed by Menoud op. cit. 23ff.; O. Cullmann, Urchristentum u. Gottesdienst 1944, 61ff. The originality of vv. 51b-58b is also defended by J. Schneider (In memoriam Ernst Lohmeyer 1951, 132–142) Ed. Schweizer (ThZ 12 [1952/53], 358–363), J. Jeremias (ZNW 44 [1952/53], 256f.), Dodd (342, 3) and Barr.—Strathm. believes this section to be the real point of the chapter, whereas Wik. points to Lagr.'s view that the Evangelist in vv. 51b–58b has placed sayings of Jesus at this point which Jesus had spoken to the disciples in private on another occasion.—J. Schneider defends the originality of the whole text 6.27–59; he does not however think that it contains a single line of argument, but rather that the Evangelist has composed it from three different meditations, which were originally created at different times; vv. 37–40 and vv. 44–46 are meditations which originally belonged to a different context!

vv. 51b–58.[1] Just as in ch. 3 the editor felt the lack of any reference to baptism, and added it himself,[2] so too he did in ch. 6 with reference to the Eucharist. That the Evangelist adopts a critical position with regard to cultic sacramental piety can also be seen in ch. 13 (see commentary there).

But even when we have made these omissions we have still by no means established a clear line of argument. Rather the present text is in a state of disorder, or at least of very poor order, which I can only explain by suggesting that it is the work of an editor who, having found a text which for external reasons been completely destroyed and so disordered, attempted himself to reconstruct the original order.

When Jesus tells the people to work for the food of eternal life themselves (v. 27), they reply by asking him how they can do the work of God (v. 28), and receive the answer that the work of God consists in believing in him whom he has sent (v. 29). Now this question in v. 28 is unmotivated after Jesus' injunction in v. 27;[3] rather one would expect them to ask, as in fact they do in v. 34 (in the same way that 4.15 follows 4.14): "Give us this bread." V. 30 is connected to v. 29 only in appearance, for v. 30 assumes that Jesus has demanded that they should believe on him, which in fact happens in v. 35. And although in vv. 30–33 the dialogue runs smoothly enough, with the pople asking Jesus to give proof of his authority in vv. 30f. and being refused in vv. 32f., nevertheless v. 34 cannot really be taken as a continuation of vv. 32f. For the request: "Give us this bread always" (cf. 4.15), assumes that the people think of the bread of life as a miraculous bread, and not, as had been stated in vv. 32f. as the one καταβαίνων ἐκ τ. οὐρ.[4] Vv. 34–35, by contrast, form a unit in themselves. To the request in which the nature of the bread has been completely misunderstood, the answer is given that the Revealer is

---

[1] So too Sp., Dibelius (RGG 2. ed. III 356); similarly Bousset, Kyrios 2. ed. 177, 1; Faure, ZNTW 21 (1922), 119f., with the difference that these two want also to omit the statement when it occurs in v. 54.

[2] See p. 138 n.3.

[3] In order to show that there is a connection between v. 28 and v. 27, it would have to be assumed that they understand Jesus' words in v. 27 correctly (even if they only half understand them), and that at the same time they make a clever play on the word ἐργάζεσθαι; for in v. 27 ἐργ. means "to work for, to produce" (Hesiod Op. 42f. βίον ἐργ. etc.), in v. 28 "to do the work" (Herm. mand. II4; IV 1, 1: τὸ ἀγαθὸν or ἁμαρτίαν ἐργ.). While on the one hand this is unlikely, when one thinks of the way in which the other dialogues in John are conducted, it also completely contradicts the subsequent remarks of the people (especially v. 34!) in which they show themselves to have completely misunderstood him.—Odeberg (256) admittedly thinks that the people were able to understand v. 27 and to reply with v. 28, since the Jews were familiar with the identification of the "food which endures" and the "works of God", seeing that they thought of the Torah as spiritual food. Yet why would they then *ask* if the allegorical meaning of Jesus' words was already clear to them? Rather v. 34 shows that they have not understood.

[4] Again it would to some extent help to take ὁ καταβαίνων in v. 33 adjectivally, and not substantivally: "the bread which comes down from heaven". Although this would not contradict vv. 41, 50, 51a (58), v. 32 still makes it impossible to take it in this way. For it would then be a meaningless tautology. The only possible meaning is: the Father gives the true bread from heaven (v. 32), and this bread (which comes down from heaven) is he who comes down from heaven, the Revealer (v. 33).

the bread of life, and that life is promised to faith. Vv. 36–40 again strike one as somewhat strange; for v. 36 upbraids the people for their unbelief. This is uncalled for at the beginning of the discussion, before the question of the believers' assurance of salvation has been discussed in vv. 37–40. But even then vv. 36–40 can hardly be considered the organic and necessary continuation of vv. 34, 35.[1] And in any case v. 41 is quite unmotivated as a direct continuation of vv. 37–40. The Jews' murmuring about Jesus' claim: ἐγώ εἰμι ὁ ἄρτος ὁ καταβ. ἐκ τ. οὐρ. has no bearing on vv. 37–40, but refers back to words such as he speaks in v. 33, or better v. 51a. On the other hand vv. 41–46 again form a closely-knit unit. The Jews' unbelief, which finds expression in their murmuring (vv. 41f.), is traced back to its metaphysical roots: the possibility of faith is given only by God (vv. 43–46). The reference to faith here as "coming to Jesus" gives the theme of "coming" its organic place within the dialogue, and vv. 36–40 would doubtless most appropriately follow on vv. 41–46. Even if vv. 47–51a, which characterise the Revealer as the bread of life, are not impossible where they now stand, they still come post festum; a more suitable place for them would be, for example, after v. 33.

Even if the original order cannot be restored with certainty, we must still make the attempt. This is made all the more difficult by the fact that the Evangelist, as so often, has used a part of the "revelation-discourses" as the basis of his composition; his own work is to be found in the dialogue and the sentences commenting on it, and it is perhaps not always possible to distinguish the Evangelist's comments from the editor's glosses.[2] By taking as my starting-point that v. 27 (by analogy with 4.14) must be the beginning of the dialogue, and that this must be followed by v. 34 (by analogy with 4.15), I arrive at the following order: vv. 27, 34, 35, 30–33, 47–51a, 41–46, 36–40.

This leaves out of account **vv. 28f.**, which is a detached fragment added by the editor after v. 27 by association with the word ἐργάζεσθαι.[3] The style makes it probable that it comes from the Evangelist. The question τί ποιῶμεν κτλ., which is out of place after v. 27, could come from a dialogue whose key-word was the ἔργα τοῦ θεοῦ; and the question has the characteristically

---

[1] Cp. even Lagr.: "Le v. 36 est un peu en dehors du thème."

[2] V. 27b ἦν κτλ. is probably an addition of the editor's (see below).

[3] This may in part give an explanation of the editor's arrangement of the verses. If vv. 28f. were added to v. 27 by association with ἐργ., this would mean that vv. 34f., which originally followed v. 27, could no longer be used here, but that it was now possible to fit in here the question about Jesus' authority and his answer to it vv. 30–33. Vv. 34f. were then appended at this point. Vv. 47–51a, which originally followed on here, were put at the end in order to provide a lead into vv. 51b–58. For the Eucharistic words are, of course, thought of as the solution to the mystery of the bread of life and had to form the conclusion. The reason for vv. 41–45 being placed after vv. 35–40 is possibly that the editor wanted to make the two parts of the discussion, which was split up by the objection of the people, of more or less equal length.—In all this we must remember that the editor did not bring an ordered text into disorder, but was attempting to arrange a number of fragments in their original order. – very hard to imagine how these 'fragments' came to be fragments instead of an ordered text!

Johannine ring of a misunderstanding or failure to understand.[1] It seems that nothing else has been preserved of this dialogue.[2] Jesus' answer corrects the question in two ways. In the first place ἔργα, which characterises the piece-meal nature of man's efforts,[3] is replaced by the single, unified ἔργον. And secondly, belief in the divine messenger is described paradoxically as "work", which thus "resolves" the concept of ἐργάζεσθαι: God's commands[4] are not fulfilled by what man works, but in obedience to what God works. Inasmuch as man's work is not just a series of isolated achievements, but properly speaking the persistent attitude of his true being, one can also say that Jesus' saying gives a radically new meaning to the concept of ἐργάζεσθαι: a man finds his true being not in what he himself achieves, but in submission to what God works; he finds it, that is to say, in what, by faith, he allows to **happen** to himself.

v. 27:

Ἐργάζεσθε μὴ τὴν βρῶσιν τὴν ἀπολλυμένην,
ἀλλὰ τὴν βρῶσιν τὴν μένουσαν εἰς ζωὴν αἰώνιον[5]

This warning is again delivered against the background of Johannine "dualism". It is open for all to understand; for it is addressed, as was the offer of the living water,[6] to man's will for life. It brings home to man that life is not assured by human food; for such food is perishable as is the life which it gives. If man wants eternal life, he must find the food which endures.[7] But what is this *miraculous food*, and where is it to be found?

---

[1] In detail the Evangelist's style can be seen in the τοῦτό ἐστιν . . . ἵνα, cp. (4.34); 6.40; 15.8, 12, (13); I Jn. 3.8, 11 etc.; cp. Festg. Ad. Jül. 142.

[2] It is not impossible that 6.28f. belongs to the fragments of discourse or dialogue which have been given some sort of order in chs. 7 and 8; cp. the key-word ἔργα, or alternatively ἐργάζεσθαι, 8.39, 41 and at the beginning of the miracle story in ch. 9: v. 3f., which originally came before ch. 8. Particularly in the middle sections of the Gospel, the editor must have had a text which was highly disjointed and full of omissions; see p. 312ff.

[3] The plur. "works" is used without further ado both in the OT (cp. Num. 8.11 of the Levites: ἐργάζεσθαι τὰ ἔργα κυρίου) and often in the NT cp. 3.19f.; Mt. 5.16 (καλὰ ἔ.); Eph. 2.10 (ἀγαθὰ ἔ.); Jas. 2.14ff.; part. in the Past. (ἀγαθὰ and καλὰ ἔ.) and in Rev. The idea of the unity of the one work is found especially in Paul (Rom. 2.7; I Cor. 15.58; I Th. 1.3; cp. I Pet. 1.17). Where Jesus is concerned John speaks both in the plur. of his ἔργα (5.20, 36; 9.3f.; 10.25, 32, 37f.; 14.10–12; 15.24), and in the sing. (4.34; 17. 4), which makes the meaning of the plur. unmistakable.—On ἔργα ἐργάζεσθαι see p. 157 n.6.

[4] Τὰ ἔργα τοῦ θεοῦ are, of course, the works which God demands of man, as in Jer. 31 (48), 10; II Esr. 7. 24; cp. τὸ ἔργον τ. κυρίου I Cor. 15.58; τὰ ἔργα μου Rev. 2.26; τὰ ἔργα τοῦ νόμου Rom. 2.15 etc. (the use in Rom. 14.20; I Cor. 16.10; Phil. 2.30 is different).

[5] V. 27 is probably based on a saying taken from the source (the revelation-discourses); it is doubtful whether it is quoted word for word, since the style of the source would lead us to expect a verb in the second half verse as well.

[6] See p. 185.

[7] Μένειν εἰς τὸν αἰῶνα (see Schl. on 8.34) is used of Christ Heb. 7.24; Act. Thom 117 124, 139 p. 227, 20; 234, 1f.; 246, 21f.; of his own I Jn. 2.17; Act. Thom. 117 p. 227, 20f. (cp. Herm. vis. II 3, 2), of the spiritual γάμος Act. Thom. 124 p. 233, 19; παράμονος (with

The idea of such food and man's desire for it are very old and widespread, as also, in its different forms, the promise that the desire will be fulfilled. In primitive faith the life-preserving force of food is thought of as a magic power, and in such faith bread is specifically thought of as containing the concentrated power of fertility.[1] Yet neither bread nor any other type of nourishment ever achieved the degree of importance which was attached to water.[2] The reason for this, at least in part, is that unlike corn the spring and the running water are things which do not require man's labour, and which in the freedom and unpredictability of their movement seem to give direct proof of the operation of divine power. Nevertheless, alongside the living water myth has a place for the *bread of life*, or some type of food which gives eternal life.[3] For it is easy to see that man's imagination leads him to attribute the eternal life enjoyed by the gods and coveted by men to some kind of food which gives in full what earthly food only gives in part. In Homer nectar and ambrosia are the food of the gods; in the Babylonian heaven there is the "food of life";[4] in Judaism we find the heavenly food of the Parnasa, or the heavenly manna, on which the angels feed and which in the Messianic age will be the food of the redeemed;[5] and the wedding guests at the heavenly wedding enjoy the ἀμβροσία βρῶσις.[6]

Naturally man would like to possess this food of life. While in general its enjoyment is thought of as an eschatological gift (as the participation in heavenly meals, or as the gift of the coming age of salvation), man in his longing often dreams of a place somewhere on earth where such food, "the plant of life", is to be found,[7] or where an elixir of life could be produced.[8]

ἀληθινός and βέβαιος) as the attribute of divine things and acts (opp. σωματικός, πρόσκαιρος etc.) Act. Thom. 36.61. 78.124 (130), p. 154, 3; 178, 9; 193, 17; 233, 17; (238, 8f.).—On μένειν see on 15.16.

[1] Cp. the article "Brot" in the Handwörterb. des deutschen Aberglaubens (bread is holy, contains concentrated power and is used for all manner of magic, particularly magic concerned with growth and fertility).

[2] The only food which might be considered of equal importance with water is milk, for which there is evidence that it was used as a sacramental food in some cults (esp. mystery cults). In Gnosticism "milk" then comes to be used to refer to the word of revelation, see Schlier, Relg. Unters., 150, 2; ThWB I 645, 10ff.—On the tree of life see on ch.15. Cp. also ThWB II 841, n. 63.

[3] Water and food of life often occur together, as in the Babylonian Adapa myth B 60ff. (Altoriental. Texte zum OT 1926, 145). Bread and water, which were taken in the Mithras mysteries, were also taken by some Christian groups in the celebration of the Lord's Supper, see A. Harnack, Texte und Unters. VII 2 (1891), 115ff.; A Jülicher, Theol. Abhandl. f. C. Weizsäcker 1892, 217ff.; L. Fendt, Gnost. Mysterien 29ff.

[4] Adapa Myth B 60f, op. cit. 145.

[5] Odeberg 240ff. and see on v. 31. Cp. also the idea of the messianic meal Lk. 14.15; Mk. 14.25; Rev. 3.20 etc., Dalman, W. J. 90–92; P. Volz, Die Eschatologie der jüd. Gemeinde 1934, 367f.; H. Lewy, Sobriaebrietas 99, 1; for the Greeks and Hellenism: E. Rohde, Psyche I 315, 2; A. Dietrich, Nekyia 79f.

[6] Act. Thom. 7. p. 110, 17.

[7] The search for the plant of life is one of the main themes of the Gilgamesh epic; it is wide-spread, and there are many variations of it, particularly in fairy-tales; cp. A. Ungnad-H. Gressmann, Das Gilgamesch-Epos 1911, 147ff.

[8] Cp. the ἄλιμος τροφή of Epimenides, Plut. sap. conv. p. 157d, of Pythagoras, Porphyr.

The *figurative* usage of the terms runs parallel to this, describing God's law or the knowledge of the eternal as spiritual "food".[1] More important still, in the sphere of dualism, there arises, under the influence of the old cultic practices, the idea of a *sacramental meal* at which the initiates into the mysteries are given the food which endows them with eternal life.[2] Again, however, the sacrament can become the *symbol* of the divine revelation and the gifts which it brings.[3] Sacramental faith and faith in the word of revelation are often combined, particularly since the "word" can be thought of as being filled with magic power. For this reason it is often not possible to decide whether the texts are referring to the sacramental food or to the spiritual gifts.[4] Both are contrasted with the κοσμικὴ τροφή as the τροφὴ πνευματική,[5] ἀσώματος and νοερός,[6] ἀμβροσιώδες,[7] τελεία[8] and θεϊκή.[9] In the Christian sphere, Christ who gives such food is called τροφεύς.[10]

Vit. Pyth. 34 p. 35, 11ff. Nauck., also Porphyr. de abst. IV 20, p. 266, 5ff. Cp. further the tradition of the φάρμακον ἀθανασίας ThWB III 24, 6ff.

[1] The soul "feeds" on the καλόν, σοφόν, ἀγαθόν (Plat. Phaedr. p. 246e); it aspires to the "meal" of the gods (loc. cit. 247a). Porphyr. de abst. 20, p. 264, 20ff. N. (yet in Porphyry the language is also influenced by the usage of the Mysteries, see below). Cp. in general the derivative meaning of τρέφειν, τροφή = "educate", "education". Similarly in Judaism the Torah is referred to as "bread", Str.-B. II 483f.; Odeberg 241f. For Philo see on v. 31 (p. 228 n.1). See also H. Lewy op. cit. 99f.

[2] For a general account of sacramental meals see G. v. d. Leeuw, Phänomenologie d. Relig. 335f., 342f. For the Hellenistic mysteries cp. Frz. Cumont, Die oriental. Religionen im röm. Heidentum passim; A. Dieterich, Mithraslit, 100ff.; H. Hepding, Attis, 1903, 184ff.; for Gnosticism L. Fendt, Gnostische Mysterien 1922.—In the Hellenistic mysteries the food taken in the sacred meal is generally considered to be the god himself (cp. Br. ext. note on 6.59). This view, which has also influenced the interpretation of the Christian Eucharist, lies behind Jn. 6. 51b–58, *but not* behind 6. 27–51a. Rather here the background is provided by the quite different conception of the bread of life, which belongs to the same way of thought as the conception of the living water (ch. 4) and of the tree of life (ch. 15). This points to an Iranian tradition. In the Mithras mysteries, where we do not find the idea that it is the godhead who is devoured in the meal, the initiates (as in the Mazdaic mass) take bread and water; Frz. Cumont, Die Mysterien des Mithra 1911, 145f.

[3] See p. 184.

[4] Cp. the references in Schlier, Relg. Unters. 149ff. Ignatius (Rom 7.3) seems to interpret martyrdom as the reception of the Eucharist (Schlier op. cit. 151f.). The sacramental food has been completely turned into a symbol for the word of revelation in the Od. Sal. (see above p. 184), e.g. 4.10; 8.16; 19.1ff.; 20.8; 35.5. It is most strange in Clem. Al. Ecl. Proph. 14, where the τροφὴ θεϊκή is interpreted as πίστις, ἐλπίς, ἀγάπη etc., that the τροφὴ κοσμική is not understood as earthly food, but is reinterpreted as ὁ πρότερος βίος καὶ τὰ ἁμαρτήματα.

[5] Did. 10.3.

[6] Porphyr. de abst. IV 20 p. 265, 11 N. (cp. p. 264, 23f.: ψυχῆς οὖν λογικῆς τροφὴ ἡ τηροῦσα λογικήν.)

[7] Act. Thom. 36 p. 154, 2.

[8] Act. Thom. 120, p. 230, 14.

[9] Clem Al. Ecl. Proph. 14, 3.

[10] Cp. Schlier, Christus und die Kirche im Epheserbrief 1930, 59, 2; G. Bornkamm, Mythos und Legende 13.—Schlier rightly understands the Mandaean title of "guardian" in this sense. If Christ is referred to even as "bread" (Act. Jo. 98, p. 200, 7; for the Manichaens see E. Waldschmidt-W. Lentz, Die Stellung Jesu im Manichäismus [Abh. d. Berl. Akad. 1924, 4] 65), this must be attributed to John's influence.

This circle of ideas and its language provides the background against which we must understand Jn. 6.26ff. In reply to the question about the food which gives eternal life, and in contrast to the answers otherwise given to this question, the Revealer replies: "I am the bread of life!" This reply however, is not given until v. 35, after the people have made their request for the miraculous bread.[1] The people's request, that Jesus should give them this bread always,[2] like the absurd request of the Samaritan woman, shows the lack of understanding on the part of the κόσμος (**v. 34**). Jesus' reply (**v. 35**), expressed by means of the revelatory formula, ἐγώ εἰμι,[3] says that what they are looking for is present in his person:

---

[1] V. 27b ἥν κτλ. is a note. Yet in this present form it can hardly have been written by the Evangelist. Otherwise one would have to assume that the people are able to identify the Son of Man as Jesus without any trouble, which is, in the light of 12.34, most improbable. Moreover the sentence accords ill with the other Son of Man statements in the Gospel; in them Jesus is the Son of Man, inasmuch as he walks this earth as the Revealer, but must also be exalted and as such be the judge of the world. V. 27b however is clearly about the activity of the Exalted Lord (it makes no difference whether one reads δώσει with ABL etc., or the timeless δίδωσιν with ℵD.). The only other verse which agrees with this is v. 53; but this verse, like v. 27b., must be attributed to the editor: Jesus will give "the food which endures" in the Last Supper. This interpretation seems to be confirmed by the explanation which is given: τοῦτον γὰρ κτλ.; for σφραγίζειν here hardly means "confirm", as in 3.33, but "consecrate", "dedicate"; see Br., Wörterb. s.v. σφραγίς and particularly Frz. J. Dölger, Sphragis als Taufbezeichnung 1911, 39ff., 156ff., Antike und Christentum I (1919), 1ff. Schweizer 152, n. 66 takes a different view.—It is possible that the Evangelist wrote ἥν ἐγὼ ὑμῖν δώσω, which would correspond to 4.14. This would then make a better connection with the request in v. 34: δὸς ὑμῖν, as far as the form was concerned.

[2] If the Jews now say ἄρτος instead of βρῶσις, this is of course so that the key-word for the discussion may be mentioned. βρῶσις is interchangeable with ἄρτος as the representative food, just as βρῶσις v. 27 took up ἄρτος, v. 26.

[3] We must distinguish various forms of the ἐγώ-εἰμι formula, although of course there are transitions between them: 1. *The "presentation formula"*, which replies to the question: "Who are you?" By the use of ἐγώ εἰμι the speaker introduces himself as so and so; here ἐγώ is subject. The examples in profane literature are numerous, cp. Aristoph. Plut. 78: ἐγὼ γάρ εἰμι Πλοῦτος, Eur. Tro. 862f.; Hymn. Hom. I 480 = II 302 etc. It is used as a sacred formula in the Orient: the God who appears introduces himself by it, cp. Gen. 17.1: "... the Lord appeared to Abram and said to him, "I am El-Shaddai"; Gen. 28.13; Jub. 24.22; Rev. 1.17. So too in the opening passages of the Isis inscriptions of Ios, Cumae, Andros and Nysa, e.g. Εἶσις ἐγώ εἰμι ἡ τύραννος πάσης χώρας (W. Peek, Der Isis-Hymnos von Andros 1930; Deissmann, L.v.O. 4. ed. 109 ff.; Br., ext. note on 8.12). So too C. Herm 1.2: ἐγὼ μὲν ... εἰμὶ ὁ Ποιμάνδρης, ὁ τῆς αὐθεντίας νοῦς, Ginza 246, 1ff.; 318, 29ff. Equally the phrase "the messenger of light am I" and similar expressions, Ginza 58, 17.23; 59, 1.15; "the treasure am I, the treasure of life" J.B. 202, 28ff.—A derivative form of this is found where the law-giver introduces himself at the beginning of the law with "I am", as does Hammurapi (Altoriental. Texte zum AT 1926, 381) or Jahweh Ex. 20.2. —2. *The "qualificatory formula"*, which answers the question: "What are you?", to which the reply is, "I am that and that", or "I am the sort of man who...". Here too ἐγώ is subject. Profane examples: Epict. diss. IV 8, 15f.: ἐγὼ φιλόσοφός εἰμι ... μουσικός ... χαλκεῦς, I 19, 2; II 19, 29; III 1, 23; Ez. 28.2, 9 (the king of Tyre says, "I am a god"). This is also used in the sacred language of the Orient: Is. 44.6: "I am the first and the last, and apart from me there is no God"; 44.24: "I am Jahweh, who made all things"; 45.5–7; 48.12. Such qualificatory formulae often follow on after presentation formulae, and the speech

ἐγώ εἰμι ὁ ἄρτος τῆς ζωῆς.
ὁ ἐρχόμενος πρὸς ἐμὲ οὐ μὴ πεινάσῃ,
καὶ ὁ πιστεύων εἰς ἐμὲ οὐ μὴ διψήσει πώποτε.[1]

---

then goes on to enumerate the deeds of the godhead (in the first person). This is the case in Deut.-Is., and also in the prayer to Ishtar in A. Ungnad, Die Religion der Babylonier u. Assyrer 1921, 200f., and in the Isis inscriptions. Cp. the qualificatory formulae of the Isis inscriptions of Cumae 41f. ἐγώ εἰμι πολέμου κυρία, ἐγὼ κεραύνου κυρία εἰμί (Peek op. cit. 124). It occurs frequently in Mandaean texts: "A shepherd am I, who loves his sheep" (J. B. 44, 27); ,'A fisherman am I who ..." (J. B. 144, 8; 154, 26). The qualificatory formula is often followed by prayers or hymns in the second person, cp. the prayer to Ishtar; Apul. Met. XI 25 (prayer to Isis); Ginza 271, 22ff.; Ed. Norden, Agnostos Theos 183ff. (In the mouth of men this formula becomes a *confessional formula*, as in Ginza 454ff., where it is the standard opening of the songs: "A mana am I of the great life" and similar expressions, cp. Ginza 251, 15ff.; 273, 1ff. and Lidzbarski, J.B. 43f. Equally in the death formula of the Marcosians, Iren. I 21,5 ἐγὼ υἱὸς ἀπὸ Πατρὸς, ... σκεῦός εἰμι ἔντιμον ...) 3. *The "identification formula"*, in which the speaker identifies himself with another person or object. Here too ἐγώ is subject. Thus the Egyptian god Rê identifies himself with Chepre: "I am he who arose as Chepre" (Altoriental. Texte 1). So too Isis, in the inscription quoted by Plut. de Is. et Os. p. 354c, says: ἐγώ εἰμι πᾶν τὸ γεγονὸς καὶ ὂν καὶ ἐσόμενον. Similar cosmic identification formulae in Ginza 207, 33ff. Modern examples in Stephan George: "I am the one and am both ..." (Der Stern des Bundes 1920, 21); "I am only a spark of the holy fire ..." (Der siebente Ring 1919, 123). The ἐγὼ ὁ θεός εἰμι etc., of the Syrian prophets Orig. c.C. VII 9, p. 161, 6f. K should perhaps be taken as an identification formula (if not as a presentation formula). Such formulae occur especially frequently in magic, which often uses old presentation and qualificatory formulae for the purpose, cp. Pap. Gr. mag. IV 185ff.; V 145ff.; XII 227ff., also Deissmann, L.v.O. 113; Br., Ext. note on Jn. 8.12); cp. esp. ἐγώ εἰμι ἡ ἀλήθεια (Pap. Gr. mag. V 148), ἐγὼ ἡ Πίστις εἰς ἀνθρώπους εὑρεθεῖσα (loc. cit. XII 228). —4. *The "recognition formula"*, which is to be distinguished from the others by the fact that here ἐγώ is the predicate. For it answers the question: "Who is the one who is expected, asked for, spoken to?", to which the reply is: "I am he." (Cp. questions like those in Eur. El. 581: ἐκεῖνος εἶ σύ; Is. 41.4, "Who has performed and done this?"; Mt. 11.3). Thus the Paphlagonian in Aristoph. Equ. 1023 says: ἐγὼ μέν εἰμ' ὁ κύων, namely, the dog who had been announced in the oracle which has just been read out. (In the Greek world ὅδε is usually used in such sentences instead of ἐγώ, Aesch. Cho. 219; Eur. Or. 380 etc.) This formula is also found in sacred language, sometimes in such a way that by the ἐγώ εἰμι something which men are looking at or already know is given a new interpretation; cp. C. Herm 1, 6: τὸ φῶς ἐκεῖνο ... ἐγώ, Νοῦς, ὁ σὸς θεός; Isis inscription of Cumae 7: ἐγώ εἰμι ἡ καρπὸν ἀνθρώποις εὑροῦσα. (I am she who ...") 10: ἐγώ εἰμι ἡ παρὰ γυναιξὶ θεὸς καλουμένη (Peek 122). It is used as a revelation formula proper (i.e. where the speaker, being present, reveals himself by the ἐγώ εἰμι as the one whom people were waiting for or looking for), Ps. Clem. Hom. 2, 24, p. 28, 30ff. Lag., where Dositheos says to Simon: εἰ σὺ εἶ ὁ ἑστώς, καὶ προσκυνῶ σε and he replies: ἐγώ εἰμι. An unusual use is found in Deut.-Is., where God reveals himself in the judgement against the other gods imagined by the poet by his "I am he who ...", Is. 41.4; 43.10f.; 52.6; similarly Deut. 32.39.—In the ἐγώ-εἰμι statements Jn. 6.35, 41, 48, 51; 8.12; 10.7, 9, 11, 14; 15.1, 5 we clearly have recognition formulae, even if in the source they were perhaps intended as presentation or qualificatory formulae. For in the context of the Gospel the ἐγώ is strongly stressed and is always contrasted with false or pretended revelation (cf. 6.49–51; 10.10, 11–13; cp. also 5.43). On the other hand 11.25, and perhaps too 14.6, are probably identification formulae. On 8.24, 28; 13.19 see the relevant passages in the commentary. Elsewhere, as in 4.26; 8.18, 23; 18.5f., 8 the ἐγώ εἰμι is not used as a sacred formula. For the whole question see Schweizer; Kundsin, Char. und Urspr. and Zur Diskussion etc.; H. Becker; W. Manson, JTS 48 (1947), 137–145; G. Widengren, Muhammad, The Apostle of God and his Ascension 1955, 48–54.

[1] This revelation saying is certainly taken from the source, while the following dialogue

The whole paradox of the revelation is contained in this reply. Whoever wants something from him must know that he has to receive Jesus *himself*. Whoever approaches him with the desire for the gift of life must learn that Jesus is *himself* the gift he really wants. Jesus *gives* the bread of life[1] in that he *is* the bread of life. Yet he is the bread of life surely because in his person he is nothing in himself, but is present in the service of the Father[2] for man. Whoever wishes to receive life from him must therefore believe in him—or, as it is figuratively expressed must "come to him".[3]

Yet the world when challenged to believe in him demands a σημεῖον as proof of his authority (**v. 30**); it wants to see in order to be able to believe (see 4.48; 20.29). By asking τί ἐργάζῃ;[4] it shows its folly to the full. For the work of the Revealer is never a τι, a particular ἔργον by which one might recognise him and so believe in him.[5] The Jews demand a miracle, similar to the miracle performed by Moses in feeding the people with manna (**v. 31**). They speak like this because Jesus has promised them the bread of life, and so they show that they have not understood his words, but still vainly imagine that life is given by physical food.[6] The reference to the manna is important also, because according to the Jewish belief the coming Messiah, as the "second Redeemer", must correspond to Moses, the "first Redemeer",[7]

---

vv. 30–32 comes from the Evangelist, who in v. 33 again uses a saying taken from the source. In the source the "I am" probably had the force of a presentation formula (see previous note). The presentation is then followed by the promise as in Ginza 58, 23ff.; 59, 1ff., 15ff.; J. B. 204, 5ff.; cp. Od. Sal 33, 6ff., see on 7.37.

[1] The genitive τῆς ζωῆς is, as is shown by ὁ ἄρτος ὁ ζῶν v. 51a, a qualifying genitive; ζωή means the life-giving force; see p. 39, ὁ ἄρτ. τῆς ζωῆς vv. 35, 48 and ὁ ἀρτ. ὁ ζῶν v. 51a are, of course, synonymous and ζῶν means "making alive, quickening", as it did when predicated of ὕδωρ (see p. 186).

[2] Cp. E. Gaugler op. cit. 55f., who rightly says that the ἐγώ-εἰμι statements may not be taken as statements about Jesus' *being*, i.e. they are not descriptions of Jesus' nature as he is in himself, but of the revelation event.

[3] "Coming" to Jesus, as in vv. 37, 44f., 65; 5.40; 7.37. The expression should be understood neither in terms of Jesus' historical situation, nor of the cultic terminology which is found in Rom. 5.2 (προσαγωγή), Heb. 4.16 (προσέρχεσθαι) and elsewhere (see M. Dibelius, SA Heidelberg 1917, IV, 19f.); for it is a traditional expression in the myth: the revealer "calls" men to him, and those who hear "come" to him; see on 7.37.—In the promise the fulfilment of man's desire for life is split up into the stilling of man's hunger and the stilling of his thirst (cp. Ecclus. 15.4; 24.21 and see p. 223 n.3). This shows clearly the symbolic meaning of ἄρτος, and the identity of the bread of life and the living water.

[4] Blass wants to omit τί ἐργάζῃ following syr[s]; but this is incorrect.

[5] The Jews' question is similar to that in 2.18, but betrays the Evangelist's style by the ἵνα κτλ. On this cp. Mk. 15.32 and the Rabbinic parallels in Schl.—Burney's view (75), that ἵνα is a mistranslation of the relative ὅ, is challenged by Goguel, Rev. H. Ph. rel. 3 (1923), 377.

[6] This shows the artificiality of the connection between vv. 27ff. and the preceding feeding narrative, see p. 218.

[7] See p. 90 n.1; furtherStr.-B. I 68f., 85ff.; IV 798. Cp. also O. Cullmann (see p.90n. 1) 232; Schoeps (Theol. u. Gesch. etc.) 92.

because, that is to say, the miracle of manna must be repeated in the final age.[1] Thus this reference to the manna gives expression to man's folly in imagining that he knows the signs by which the Redeemer is to be recognised, his folly in imagining that he has criteria at his disposal to which the revelation must conform in order to gain recognition; whereas in fact God's revelation destroys every picture which man's desires make of it, so that the real test of man's desire for salvation is to believe even when God encounters him in a totally different way from that which he expected. In the ἀμ. ἀμ. λέγω ὑμῖν (**v. 32**), Jesus rejects the deluded view of the Jews that the bread once given by Moses could be the true "bread of heaven".[2] In the antithesis, which states that only the Father can give the "bread of heaven", the emphatic τὸν ἀληθινόν[3] makes it clear that all earthly goods are mere appearances in relation to the revelation. The general statement in v. 32 is then substantiated in **v. 33**; there is only *one* way in which life is given to the world, and that is God's revelation: the bread of God is the Revealer who comes from heaven and gives life to the world.[4]

This brings the discourse back to the point where it had left off in v. 35 to deal with the objection of the Jews. In **vv. 47f.** man is challenged to believe in terms which suggest the promise which belongs to faith:

[ἀμὴν ἀμὴν λέγω ὑμῖν],
48 ἐγώ εἰμι ὁ ἄρτος τῆς ζωῆς·
47 ὁ πιστεύων (εἰς ἐμὲ) ἔχει ζωὴν αἰώνιον.[5]

---

[1] The miracle of the manna, Ex. 16, played an important role in the OT (Deut. 8.3; Neh 9.15; Ps. 78.24—to which Jn. 6.31 alludes—105.40) and then in the Jewish tradition (Wisd. 16.20; Sibyll. Fr. 3, 466 p. 232 Geffken; syr. Bar. 29.8; I Cor. 10.3; cp. Str.-B. II 481f.; Odeberg 239ff.). The Messiah is expected to repeat this miracle (syr. Bar. 29.8; Str.-B. II 481; IV 890; 954; Schl. ad loc.; J. Jeremias, Golgotha 83, 4; Die Abendmahlsworte Jesu 88, 2; Odeberg 242f.).—Philo interpets the manna in terms of the θεῖος λόγος (or the σοφία) as the οὐράνιος ψυχῆς τροφή leg. all. II 86; III 169–175; det. pot. ins. 118; quis rer. div. her. 79.191; congr. er. gr. 100, 173f.; fug. et inv. 137. Cp. P. Winter (see p. 23 n.1) 360 n. 60.

[2] ἔδωκεν, which BD al read in v. 32 instead of δέδ., must be an assimilation to v. 31. The present tense in syr[sc] is more correct.—ὑμῖν shows the unity which was thought to exist between the generations of the wildernesss and the present.—Young's suggestion (228) that the formulation of v. 33 and v. 38 is dependent on Is. 55.1–11 is not convincing.—Schoeps (Theol. u. Gesch.) 90 finds in 6.32f. (as in 1.17f.; 6.49f.; 9.28f.) "the fourth Gosp.'s violent attack" on the identification of Jesus and Moses.

[3] See p. 53 n.1.

[4] ὁ καταβ. ἐκ τ. οὐρ. should not be taken as the attribute of ὁ ἄρτος τ. θ. but the predicate, see p. 220 n.4.

[5] Vv. 47f. (with the exception of the introductory formula) are taken from the source; yet the Evangelist must have reversed the order of the two lines. The ἐγώ-εἰμι formula must precede the promise. In v. 47 πιστ. must be completed (cp. v. 35); CKD pl do, in fact, read εἰς ἐμέ, but perhaps this is only a correct conjecture. The Evangelist could have omitted the εἰς ἐμ. The εἰς θεόν which is read by syr[sc] is a false conjecture.

V. 32 had stated that only God gives the bread of heaven, and v. 33 had added that the bread of God is the Revealer; vv. 47f. now complete the argument by declaring, "I am he!" What is true in principle has become historical reality in Jesus' person. To this is added the promise given to faith, which is at the same time a challenge of faith—as it was in v. 35, only here the language used is non-figurative, as in 3.15f.

The discourse in **vv. 49–51a**, like the dialogue in vv. 30–33, moves on from the promise of eternal life to make the contrast between the true bread of heaven and the manna.[1] The contrast is first made in general terms. The manna could not give life; the fathers who ate it have all died (v. 49). Only that which gives indestructible life can be called the bread of heaven (v. 50).[2] This is again followed in v. 51a by the word of revelation: "I am the one who fulfils that which is said about the bread of heaven".[3]

The three-fold ἐγώ-εἰμι has held together the first part of the discussion. This has shown Jesus as the true bread of life and confronted man with the decision of faith in the form of a promise. In the *second part* the express theme is the *possibility of faith*; this again is introduced by the "Jews", who fail to understand, and interrupt Jesus, thus drawing from him his words on the possibility of faith (vv. 41–46).

The murmuring of the Jews (**v. 41**)[4] is directed against the decisive ἐγώ εἰμι in v. 51. The claim of revelation provokes the opposition of the world. It takes offence at the fact that the revelation encounters it in history, in the very sphere with which it is familiar and where it feels at home; it is offended by the fact that the man, whose father and mother they know, claims to be the Revealer (**v. 42**).[5] The πῶς νῦν λέγει . . .

---

[1] V. 49 and v. 50 are the Evangelist's own composition; both verses are in prose; v. 50 betrays the Evangelist's style by the οὗτος, which is explained by the ἵνα clause, see next note.

[2] Οὗτος not only refers back to the Revealer (the ἐγώ of vv. 47f.) but forwards to the ἄρτος. This is one of the Evangelist's typical definitions (Festg. Ad. Jül. 142); the οὗτος is explained by ἵνα ("this" i.e. "the bread is of such a sort ..., that"). Goguel rightly challenges Burney's view here, see p. 227 n.5. ὁ ἐκ τ. οὐρ. καταβαίνων here (unlike v. 33) is, of course, attributive.

[3] V. 51a must have καταβάς after the timeless definition καταβαίνων in v. 50, because now (v. 51a) καταβάς refers to an historical event; cp. the development of the ideas from vv. 32f. to vv. 47f.—On ὁ ἄρτος ὁ ζῶν see p. 227 n.1.

[4] Γογγύζειν vv. 41, 43, 61; 7.32 (γογγυσμός 7.12) means at first an inarticulate murmuring, then the suppressed grumbling and mumbling which is a sign of anger or dissatisfaction. In the LXX γογγ. (for לון and רָגַן) often refers to ungrateful obstinacy and doubt in God's faithfulness; so too I Cor. 10.10; Phil 2.14 etc., see Rengstorf, ThWB s.v.; E. Lohmeyer on Phil. 2.14 (Meyer Komm.). In John we have the usual profane usage.

[5] In ℵ b syr^{sc} καὶ τ. μητέρα is omitted, obviously because for later Christians the folly of the Jews could only consist in their belief that they knew the father of Jesus (see Br.). This is, of course, to misunderstand the Evangelist; for the folly of the Jews does not consist in their being mistaken about Jesus' father, but in their refusal to allow that a man might be the Revealer; see p. 62 n.4 on 1.14, and see Menoud see p. 104 n.1.

brings out characteristically[1] the absurdity—in the eyes of the world—of the Revealer's claim. In the opposition of the "Jews" we can see the strange way in which man's knowledge of the revelation is perverted into ignorance.[2] For even the Jews' opposition is based on *knowledge* of the revelation, the knowledge, that is, that the revelation must come to them from God and not from men. But this knowledge is turned to *ignorance*, inasmuch as they conceive the divine nature of the revelation as a suprahuman phenomenon which could be observed as such, instead of as an event which destroys the man who only accepts what he can observe and determine. Thus the Jews with their objection do not see that the divine cannot be contrasted with the human in the confident way in which they say, "How can an ordinary man claim to be the Revealer!" For this is the very absurdity which the event of revelation proclaims; and the condition of its understanding is that man should relinquish the assurance with which he believes he can pass judgement on the human and the divine as objectively determinable phenomena.[3]

The subject of Jesus' origin is developed further in 7.26–28.[4] But at this point the Jews' remarks, in which the Evangelist has reshaped in his own way the tradition preserved in Mk. 6.2f., serve only to demonstrate their unbelief, and lead the Evangelist into the next section of his source. He prefaces this by the μὴ γογγύζετε of **v. 43**. Murmuring and anger are unnecessary; for they have their place only in the cut and thrust of debate between equals, where it is always possible that the one will convince or disprove the other. It is this level of security which man must abandon; as long as he persists in it he remains blind to the revelation (**v. 44**):

οὐδεὶς δύναται ἐλθεῖν πρός με
ἐὰν μὴ ὁ πατὴρ ὁ πέμψας με ἑλκύσῃ αὐτόν.[5]

---

[1] Cp. πῶς 3.4, 9; 7.15; 8.33; 12.34; 14.5, 9, and see p. 136 n. 1. Odeberg (264, 3) considers the question how far Jesus' statement that, although a man, he has come down from heaven, agrees with or contradicts Jewish ideas. He is right to say that the latter is the case; however the important point is not that the Jews have inadequate theories about the possibilities of God's revelation, but that they have theories about it *at all*, and so fail to hear the call of God when it meets them in tangible form. Man may fail to hear even when his theories are much better, Mt.23.29f.

[2] See p. 62.

[3] It is evident that the dogmatic attempts of the early Church to conceive the unity of the human and the divine in Jesus in some of the categories of human and divine "nature" are absolutely contradictory to John.

[4] The origins of the divine messenger are also discussed in heathen and Gnostic Hellenism, cp. ZNTW 24 (1925), 119f.; G. P. Wetter, Der Sohn Gottes 90ff.

[5] On the disrupting editorial addition κἀγὼ κτλ. see p. 219. Of course, it is possible that ὁ πατήρ or ὁ πέμψας με in the second line is the Evangelist's own addition. A's omission of ὁ πατήρ is hardly significant, nor are other variants. H. Becker 69, 1 thinks that ὁ πέμψας με is an addition to the source.

The Jews do not have it in their power to form a judgement about the Revealer; they have indeed already passed judgement, before they began to think about it. For their thinking is itself unbelief because it takes place within the security of human judgement. Moreover their thought, which always remains within the sphere of unbelief, is equally powerless to overcome their unbelief. Only God himself could alter that; only that man "comes" to Jesus,[1] who is "drawn" by the Father.[2]

In **v. 45a** the Evangelist comments[3] on this statement by making an allusion to Is. 54.13.[4] By this he intends to say that the event which makes faith possible is an eschatological event; for the saying of the prophet is an eschatological prophecy which finds its fulfilment for faith.[5] The idea (and the citation from the tradition) is carried on in vv. **45b,**[6] **37b:**

> 45b πᾶς ὁ ἀκούσας παρὰ τοῦ πατρὸς καὶ μαθὼν
> ἔρχεται πρός με,
> 37b καὶ τὸν ἐρχόμενον πρός με
> οὐ μὴ ἐκβάλω ἔξω.

It is now perfectly clear what is meant when it is said that the Father "draws" men to him. The πᾶς already indicates that it does not refer to the selection of a chosen few, but that any man is free to be among those drawn by the Father. V. 44 following on v. 42 leaves no doubt about the matter: faith becomes possible when one abandons hold on one's own security, and to abandon one's security is nothing else than to let oneself be drawn by the Father. Moreover v. 45b shows that this "drawing" is not a magic process, nor is it governed by rigid laws like the laws of nature.[7] It occurs when man abandons his own judgement

---

[1] On ἐλθεῖν, see p. 227 n.3 and on 7.37.

[2] Ἕλκειν in a metaphorical sense in Classical Greek and in the LXX, see Br. ad loc. and Wörterb.; Oepke, ThWB II 500, 21ff. Similarly in Rabbinic Judaism the corresponding: מְשַׁךְ see Schl. ad loc.; Odeberg 266, 1. On the "drawing" of god or the divine in the Gnostic sphere, see Oepke op. cit. 500, 32ff.—Odeberg 266 (n. 3 of p. 264) is right: v. 44 is the correct reply to v. 42; but Br. is also right when he points out that Jesus ignores the objection of the Jews, i.e. that he does not accept the basis for discussion which they offer.

[3] On the formula ἔστιν γεγρ. see p. 124 n.3, and Schl. ad loc.—The appeal to the prophets (plur.) as in Acts (7.42) 13.40. The Evangelist could have had in mind passages like Jer. 24.7; 31.33f. (LXX 38.33f.) Joel 2.27, 29; Hab. 2.14. This hope is also kept alive in the Rabbinic literature: Str.-B. III 634 (on I Th. 4.9) 704; IV 1153f.

[4] Καὶ (sc. θήσω) πάντας τοὺς υἱούς σου διδακτοὺς θεοῦ.

[5] Cp. I Th. 4.9, whereas Bar. 21.6 says in the imperative: γίνεσθε δὲ θεοδίδακτοι ἐκζητοῦντες τί ζητεῖ κύριος ἀφ' ὑμῶν.

[6] H. Becker 69, 2 thinks that καὶ μαθών is an addition to the source.

[7] Cp. Ad. Schlatter, Der Glaube im NT 1927, 205f. 213; W. Herrmann, Ges. Aufsätze 1923, 111; Temple 87f.91; Howard, Christianity 92ff.—On determinism cp. also DSD 3, 15f. 25 and F.-M. Braun, RB 62 (1955), 16.

and "hears" and "learns" from the Father, when he allows God to speak to him.[1] The "drawing" by the Father occurs not, as it were, *behind* man's decision of faith but *in* it. He who comes to Jesus, however, receives the promise, "I will not reject him".

Since hearing and learning from the Father are basically nothing other than faith, i.e., coming to Jesus, the statement is a paradox which makes clear the nature of faith. It means that only he who believes, believes; but this is to say that faith has no support outside itself; it sees what it sees only in faith.[2] Nor, of course, is faith a spiritual disposition which, by reflection on itself, could assure itself of its validity. For faith is related to its object; it is a relationship to that which is believed and as such it has its own security, which can rest only in the object of faith: τὸν ἐρχόμενον πρός με οὐ μὴ ἐκβάλω ἔξω. Faith is sure of itself only as it seizes hold of the promises made to it.

The Evangelist has commented (**v. 46**) on the statement as it was in the source, lest there should be any misunderstanding about the ἀκούειν and μανθάνειν, and in order to bring out their identity with the coming of Jesus.[3] It is not that man has the possibility of a special and direct relationship to God; for this can be said only of the Revealer; any other relationship to God must be mediated by the Revealer.[4]

The continuation of the discourse is to be found in **v. 36**, which has been incorrectly placed by the editor: ἀλλ' εἶπον ὑμῖν κτλ.[5] The hearers had the possibility of enjoying the "sight" which is mediated by the Revealer, but they have not taken advantage of it. Thus what Jesus said at the beginning (v. 26)[6] is confirmed by their behaviour when confronted with his word; they have failed to understand the σημεῖον

---

[1] The ἀκούσας is qualified by μαθών as the true hearer as opposed to the mere casual listener; cp. 5.25 and Polyb. III 32.9: ὅσῳ διαφέρει τὸ μαθεῖν τοῦ μόνον ἀκούειν, τοσούτῳ κτλ.

[2] See p. 163, on 3.33.

[3] We can see the Evangelist's style here clearly. The positive statement is preceded by the negative statement that the opposite is not true, see p. 48 n.3, especially on οὐχ ὅτι 7.22; I Jn. 4.10. On the continuation of the subject by the demonstrative cp. 7.18; 10.25; 15.6; II Jn. 9; on the stressed οὗτος in general see p. 79 n.3.

[4] See p. 80f.—Ὁ ὢν παρὰ τ. πατρ. = who is from the Father, i.e. who has come from the Father; cp. 7.29; 9.16, 33; 17.7 and Bl.-D. para. 237, 1; see p. 298 n.1.

[5] If v. 36 originally came after v. 46, then it is doubly clear that the omission of με after ἑωράκατε in A ℵ pc it syr^{sc} gives the correct reading. This can also be seen by considering the relation of v. 36 to v. 26 (see next note). Moreover the addition of the με robs the sentence of much of its force. For the point here is the contrast which is made between seeing and believing as types of behaviour, just as in 20.29.—On καὶ-καὶ used to connect two opposites (although-nevertheless) see Bl.-D. para. 444, 3 and Br. ad loc.

[6] It seems certain to me that v. 36 refers to v. 26. Wendt (I 73ff. II 67f.) tries to show that v. 36 refers to the discourse in 5.17ff., but this does not seem feasible to me; see p. 218 n.4—Cp. for the rest the Revealer's (Hermes) answer to a question in the Herm. fragment No. 29 Scott I 544: καὶ ἐν τοῖς ἔμπροσθεν εἶπον· σύ δὲ οὐ συνῆκας.

of the feeding. There is a play here on the word "see". In the true sense of seeing, that is of hearing and learning from the Father, they have not "seen". Yet they have seen, in so far as the possibility of true sight is given in the perception of the historical event. Indeed in the σημεῖον this possibility was open to them in an extreme sense. For although the sight of faith really needs no σημεῖον (14.8–10; 20.29), nevertheless in some circumstances a σημεῖον may be granted to man's weakness.[1] But the sign may also—as here—reveal that the demand for it was not inspired by a genuine desire for God; even though the world "sees", it does not believe.

In order to be able to return to the argument of the source the Evangelist now has to repeat the saying contained in vv. 45b and 37b. He does this (**v. 37a**) by varying the first half of the verse in his own typical fashion: πᾶν ὃ δίδωσίν μοι ὁ πατὴρ πρὸς ἐμὲ ἥξει.[2] He then adds the thought, admittedly taken from the source, but also often emphasised by the Evangelist himself (**v. 38**): ὅτι καταβέβηκα ἀπὸ τ. οὐρ. οὐχ ἵνα ποιῶ τὸ θέλημα τὸ ἐμὸν ἀλλὰ τὸ θέλημα τοῦ πέμψαντός με.[3] Having explained v. 37 by the reference to the will of the Father, the Evangelist goes on to describe in his favourite way, in the sense of v. 37, the content of the Father's will (**v. 39**): τοῦτο δέ ἐστιν τὸ θέλημα κτλ.[4] The "will not cast out" now becomes, "will not lose";[5] since Jesus alone is the σωτήρ (3.17; 4.42), his ἐκβάλλειν would mean ἀπώλεια. Just as in 3.17 we have a negative and positive description of the purpose of his mission, so here the negative description of the divine will is followed by the positive description in **v. 40**: ἵνα κτλ.,[6] which characterises the relation of faith to the historical Revealer by the hendiadys θεωρεῖν and πιστεύειν.[7]

---

[1] See p. 209.

[2] The Evangelist is fond of the neuter πᾶν (the use in v. 45a is different), see v. 39; 17.2; I Jn. 2.16 (also I Jn. 5.4?) For the rest the διδόναι of the Father to the Son is characteristic for the source, see pp. 165 n.1, 172 n.5, and esp. 164 n.1.

[3] V. 38 betrays the style of the Evangelist; on the prefatory negative, see 232 n.3 and p. 48 n.3. ἀπο τ. οὐρ. (as in Wisd. 16.4) is synonymous with ἐκ τ. οὐρ. vv. 31–33, 41, 51.—The thought is the same here as in 4.34, see on 5.19.

[4] On the editorial addition ἀλλά ἀναστήσω κτλ., see p. 219f. The definition is characteristic for the Evangelist, see p. 229 n.2 and Fest. Ad. Jül. 142., as is the placing of the nominative absolute at the beginning of the sentence, which is perhaps a semitism (Bl.-D. para. 466, 3; Raderm. 21f.), cp. 8.45; 15.2; 17.2.—As opposed to the timeless present δίδωσιν, v. 37, v. 39 has δέδωκεν, because something must have been given before it can be lost. R. Hermann, Von der Antike zum Christentum 1931, 38f. would like to attach more significance to the change in tense.

[5] This also is a favourite concept with the Evangelist, 3.16; and see esp. 10.28; 17.12; 18.9.

[6] Here too we have a typical definition, as in v. 39; ἔχειν ζωὴν αἰων., as in 3.15f., etc. On the editorial addition καὶ ἀναστήσω κτλ., see p. 219f.

[7] On θεωρεῖν, see p. 69 n.2, on πιστεύειν εἰς, see p. 51 n.3; the two words are also paired together in 12.44, but here in the parallelism of the verses (source!)

Θεωρεῖν, when paired like this with πιστεύειν, is the true sight, which seizes the possibility of ὁρᾶν (v. 36). And the fact that this phrase is used instead of ὃ δίδωσίν (or δέδωκέν) μοι ὁ πατήρ again makes it clear that God's work in man occurs in the act of faith, and does not stand in some mysterious sense behind it.

The Evangelist's exposition of this theme (vv. 38–40) is based on statements taken from the source (vv. 45b, 37b) and forms a kind of homily. It reaffirms that in Jesus God acts, that his history is an event of revelation, that salvation depends on faith in him, and that faith in him is assured of salvation because God himself is active in this faith. Since vv. 45b and 37b seem to be the last part of the source to be used in the discussion, it is likely that this was brought to a conclusion in v. 40. **V. 59** was the original conclusion of the whole scene. This takes place, as we are now told for the first time, in the Synagogue in Capernaum.[1] The men who dispute with Jesus are referred to in v. 41 as the 'Ιουδαῖοι; this is characteristic of the Evangelist,[2] whereas in v. 24 he had adhered to the designation used in the σημεῖα source (vv. 2, 5, 22) and called them the ὄχλος.

The Lord's Supper: 6.51b–58

At this point the editor, employing the style and language of the foregoing discussion, has added or inserted[3] a secondary interpretation of the bread of life in terms of the Lord's Supper. He begins in the first sentence[4] by commenting on the meaning of the bread: καὶ ὁ ἄρτος δὲ ... ἡ σάρξ μού ἐστιν = "and indeed this bread is ... my flesh".[5] If this flesh is described as the

---

[1] This is not the only place where the Evangelist mentions the scene of the action late on in the story: 1.28; 8.20. The concluding phrase ταῦτα εἶπεν is similar to 12.36b, cp. 8.30.—On the omission of the article before συναγ. (as ἐν οἴκῳ and the like) see Bl.-D. para. 255. There is no reason to suppose that συναγ. here refers not to the building but, as in Rev. 2.9; 3.9 to the congregation (Schl. "at the time of the assembly"); συναγ. occurs again in John at 18.20, where it certainly refers to the building. According to Loisy Capernaum was given as the setting of the action instead of Nazareth (although in v. 42 the Evangelist seems to have the scene in Mk. 6.1ff. in mind), because the Evangelist wanted to set this scene in the centre of Jesus' ministry in Galilee, and because he could not get the crowd who were at the feeding to Nazareth. The latter is probably the correct reason.

[2] See p. 85f.

[3] See p. 218f.

[4] From a stylistic point of view the sentence could have been written by the Evangelist, who also liked commenting on terms by a clause introduced by καί (followed by δὲ, as here, I Jn. 1.3; not in Jn. 8.16, 17), see Festg. Ad. Jül. 142. However this does not betray an individual style, but is the style of the exegetical gloss, cp. Mt. 10.18; II Tim. 3.12; Bl. D. para. 447, 9.

[5] The oldest text is certainly that given by BCDL syr[sc] it: καὶ ὁ ἄρτος δὲ ὃν ἐγὼ δώσω ἡ σάρξ μού ἐστιν ὑπὲρ τῆς τοῦ κόσμου ζωῆς, where ὑπὲρ κτλ. is intended as an apposition to σάρξ, which means that one must supply διδομένη (Br. Lagr.). The placing of ὑπερ κτλ. after δώσω ℵ and some other authorities, or the repetition of ἣν ἐγὼ δώσω before ὑπὲρ κτλ. in ℜ, are simply corrections to make the sense easier. One might ask however if ὑπὲρ κτλ. is not an early gloss.

flesh which was given for the life of the world, clearly this has Jesus' submission unto death in mind, which in the early Christian view was a death ὑπὲρ ....[1] Moreover the reason why the passage speaks not of Jesus' ψυχή (=life), which would be specifically Johannine,[2] but of his σάρξ, is that it refers to the eating of his flesh (and the drinking of his blood) in the Lord's Supper, which he instituted by his submission unto death.[3] At the outset this is expressed in a deliberately mysterious way, and the "Jews" react accordingly by taking offence **v. 52:** πῶς δύναται ...[4] In doing so they quite correctly see that a real eating of his flesh is intended, but they regard it as absurd.[5]

Jesus' reply (**v. 53**), cast in solemn terms with the ἀμ. ἀμ. λέγω ὑμ. and with its marked rhythm, unmistakably refers to the Lord's Supper, since now the drinking of the blood is added to the eating of the flesh.[6] What was absurd has now become offensive, since the drinking of blood must be regarded as particularly revolting.[7] It would, however, be wrong to suggest that τοῦ υἱοῦ τ. ἀνθρ., which is used here instead of μου, is intended to heighten the mystery; for since it is used interchangeably with μου (vv. 52, 54–56) its identity with μου was obviously assumed without further thought, and so there can be no question of any particular mystery being attached to it.[8] Its use here is probably occasioned by the occurrence of the phrase in v. 53 in the liturgical language of the community.

Those who do not eat the Lord's Supper are thus denied all claim to life; the Lord's Supper, as v. 54 shows more clearly, is understood as the φάρμακον ἀθανασιάς.[9] This explains why the editor says ἔχειν ἐν ἑαυτοῖς instead of the simple ἔχειν (vv. 40, 47).[10] Those who participate in the sacramental

---

[1] Mk. 14.24; I Cor. 15.3; II Cor. 5.21; Gal. 3.13; Heb. 2.9; etc.; specifically with διδόναι; Gal. 1.4; 2.20; Rom. 8.32; Eph. 5.2; Tit. 2.14; Lk. 22.19.

[2] Cp. 10.15, 17; 15.13; I Jn. 3.16; see also 13.37f.

[3] Cp. Mk. 14.22–25 parr.; I Cor. 11.23–25 etc.—The use of σάρξ and αἷμα in Jn. 6.51b–58 instead of σῶμα and αἷμα to refer to the elements clearly agrees with the Syrian usage attested by Ign. Rom. 7.3; Phld. 4; Smyrn. 7.1; Trall 8.1; see also Justin apol. I 66, 1f. Cp. Carpenter 434; Howard 265f.

[4] Cp. v. 42; 3.4, 9, etc. The editor clearly models himself on the Evangelist's technique; but it is easy to see that it is an imitation. For the misunderstanding here is not based on the Johannine "dualism".—μάχεσθαι assumes that there has been an interchange of differing views but need not mean that the hearers have split into two parties, those for Jesus and those against.

[5] Even though according to B it syr^{sc} αὐτοῦ should be omitted, it still gives the right sense.—The suggestion that the people are horrified by Jesus' exhortation to anthropophagy (Ho.), can hardly be found in the text; the πῶς κτλ. refers to the absurdity of Jesus' words. —R. Eisler ZNTW 24 (1925), 185ff. makes the fantastic suggestion that in the Aramaic original Jesus was asked for meat (בִּשְׂרָא) to which he replied that he brought them the good news (בִּשְׂרָא). Cp. R. Eisler, Das Rätsel des Joh.evg. 498.

[6] Accusative instead of the genitive with φαγεῖν see Bl.D. para. 169, 2; Raderm. 121.

[7] Cp. Lev. 17.10 ff.; Acts 15.20, etc.

[8] As in v. 27, see p. 225 n.1.

[9] See p. 219f.

[10] See on 5.26.

meal bear within them the power which guarantees their resurrection.[1] **V. 54** returns to the style of the discourse and elucidates what has been said so far by explicitly stating the idea presupposed in v. 53: Those who partake of the Lord's Supper "have" life, inasmuch as Jesus will raise them up on the last day.[2] This of course, is quite different from the Johannine view (3.18f.; 5.24f.; 11.25f. etc.). On the other hand the offence is heightened in v. 54 by the substitution of the stronger τρώγειν for φαγεῖν.[3] It is a matter of real eating and not simply of some sort of spiritual participation. Thus there is every indication that **v. 55** should also be taken in this way. It is really so! Jesus' flesh is real food and his blood is real drink![4] However, it is possible that ἀληθής (as is usually the case with ἀληθινός) should be taken in a "dualistic" sense;[5] it would not be the specifically Johannine dualism, but rather the sacramental dualism of the mysteries. All other food can give life only apparently, but not really; the sacrament alone is real, true nourishment, since it gives life.

V. 56 brings out the idea of the sacramental union, which finally makes clear the thought of vv. 53f: whoever eats Jesus' flesh and drinks his blood in the Lord's Supper is united with him in a mysterious way, and this is why he has life in him.[6] The formula employed to describe the union—"he in me and I in him"—is the Johannine formula which elsewhere is used to describe relation of faith to the Revealer.[7] Just as the editor employs this formula to develop his view of the sacrament here, so in **v. 57** he uses the idea of 5.21, 26 to describe the living power of Jesus, which is the basis of the power of the sacrament: "As (i.e. correspondingly as) I have life because of the Father, so too he who eats me will live through me".[8] In **v. 58** we at last have the

---

[1] Cp. the similar idea in Rom. 8.11.

[2] On the Rabbinic conception of the "last day" see Schl. on v. 39; similar formulae occur frequently, see Br. Wörterb, 522.

[3] Τρώγειν, which does not occur in the LXX, and in the NT only 13.18; Mt. 24.38, means to "munch", "chew", see Br., Wörterb. However it is possible that in colloquial usage τρώγειν took on the meaning of "eat"="devour", which it has in modern Greek.

[4] א D al syr^{sc} latt read ἀληθῶς instead of ἀληθής, which in any case gives the right meaning, and is perhaps also the right reading.

[5] Assuming that we should not read ἀληθῶς, see previous note.

[6] On the idea of the sacramental union see A. Dieterich, Mithraslit. 95ff., E. Reuterskiöld, Die Entstehung der Speisesakramente 1912; G. v. d. Leeuw, Phänomenologie der Religion 335f. 342f.; Br., ext. note on 6.59; H. Lietzmann, ext. note on I Cor. 10.20 (Hdb. z. NT.).

[7] 15.4f.; 17.21–23; see there and on 10.14f. In D and a few cod. the text has been expanded as follows: καθὼς ἐν ἐμοὶ ὁ πατὴρ κἀγὼ ἐν τῷ πατρί (after 10.38; 14.11). ἀμὴν ἀμὴν λέγω ὑμῖν, ἐὰν μὴ λάβητε τὸ σῶμα τοῦ υἱοῦ τοῦ ἀνθρώπου ὡς τὸν ἄρτον τῆς ζωῆς, οὐκ ἔχετε ζωὴν ἐν αὐτῷ. The second sentence as well as the λάβητε and the τὸ σῶμα show that this is a gloss on the basis of the Synopt. account of the Lord's Supper, Mk. 14.22; Mt. 26.26.

[8] As is shown by the context διά cannot mean "on account of", "for the sake of", even though ζῆν διά τινα = "to live for the sake of another" is a not uncommon phrase, cp. Wetst. and Br., who also give examples to show that ζῆν διά with the accusative can also mean "to owe one's life to", esp. Plut. Alex. 8, p. 668d, where Alexander, referring to his father and Aristotle, says: δι' ἐκεῖνον μὲν ζῶν, διὰ τοῦτον δὲ καλῶς ζῶν, see Bl.-D. para. 222; Raderm. 142.

conclusion of the discourse and consequently of the whole section, in which the editor restores unity to the whole passage by taking up terms and phrases from the Johannine text. For this reason he takes up again the concept of the "bread which comes down from heaven" from v. 51a (or v. 33, or v. 50), and he assures his readers by the οὗτός ἐστιν that this miraculous bread is indeed the sacrament of the Lord's Supper.[1] The last sentence finally promises the participants in the sacrament eternal life, and takes up again from vv. 31f. and v. 49 the motif of the contrast between the bread of life and the manna.

The editor, in placing 6.60–71 after 6.1–59, obviously understood vv. 51b–58 in terms of vv. 60f, as a σκληρὸς λόγος and σκάνδαλον. For him the σκάνδαλον consisted in the fact that the historical Jesus, while he was still alive, had referred to his flesh and blood as food, which was of course unintelligible to his hearers. On the other hand the idea of the sacrament itself is not as such a σκάνδαλον, and cannot be so. But this has the result of externalising the concept of σκάνδαλον and makes a literary motif out of one of the characteristics of the revelation, which as such—ὁ λόγος σὰρξ ἐγένετο!—always remains a σκάνδαλον. Here it has been reduced to the idea that the hearers cannot understand that Jesus is speaking of the Lord's Supper.

scandal

D. 5.1–47; 7.15–24; 8.13–20: The Judge

In the original order of the Gospel 6.1–59 was followed by ch. 5.[2] Ch. 6 portrayed the revelation, against the background of a miracle story, as the κρίσις of man's natural desire for life; similarly ch. 5, again with a miracle story as the point of departure, portrays it as the κρίσις of religion.[3] It is symbolic of this that the scene of the discussion is now the temple in Jerusalem (5.14ff.), so that at the end of the section comprising chs. 3–6 we have reached the place where all the discussions of the following section, chs. 7–12, are to take place.

As in ch. 6 the Evangelist takes a miracle story as his starting point, in this case a healing story. In many of its characteristics it reminds one of the Synoptic healing stories,[4] although it is not taken from the Synoptic tradition,

---

[1] Οὗτος here does not point forward as in v. 50 but refers back to vv. 51b–57; it does not define but identifies.

[2] See p. 209.

[3] See p. 111f.

[4] The style corresponds to the Synoptic healing stories, inasmuch as there is no attempt to give psychological explanations of peoples' motives. The statement of the length of the illness, v. 5, and the fact that the healed man carries away his bed, vv. 8f., are also true to the style. Yet this latter motif, the original sense of which was to demonstrate that he had been healed, is used here to connect the healing story with the dispute about the Sabbath. That this is secondary can be seen from the way the date in v. 9b (as in 9.14) has been added. Also the fact that Jesus seizes the initiative, v. 6, is a sign of later composition (as 6.5; see p. 210). For further discussion see below, p. 239 n.2. See J. Buse, Jn. 5.8 and Joh.-Marcan Relationships NtSt 1 (1954/55), 134–136.

but was probably derived from the σημεῖα source,[1] as also the section 7.19–24 (see below). At the point where the healing story developed into a controversy the Evangelist has introduced a long discourse, and he has worked over the original text in order to establish the transition from story to discourse. Instead of vv. 16–18 of the present text the source probably had something like: καὶ διὰ τοῦτο ἐζήτουν οἱ Ἰουδαῖοι ἀποκτεῖναι τὸν Ἰησοῦν, ὅτι ταῦτα ἐποίει ἐν σαββάτῳ.[2] The Evangelist has made this one sentence into two (v. 16 and v. 18) and inserted between them Jesus' "reply" (v. 17), so that now the reason for the Jews' wanting to kill him is his claim to be the Revealer, and Jesus can now go on to discuss this claim in vv. 19ff.

The discourse is again based on a text from the "revelation-discourses", with which the comments of the Evangelist form a marked contrast. As in ch. 6 the editor has here added a section designed to harmonise Jesus' bold words with traditional eschatology; for this is the only possible explanation for 5.28f. The continuation of the composition is to be found in 7.15–24. This section cannot possibly have stood in its present place and belongs without doubt to ch. 5. For 7.19–23 refer clearly to the healing on the Sabbath and to the Jews' intention to kill Jesus (5.1–18), while 7.16f. refer to 5.19, 30 and 7.18 to 5.41–44. In addition 7.15 connects up admirably with 5.45–47; this would explain why the Jews are shocked by his appeal to the Scriptures (7.15). Finally, the call to δικαία κρίσις (7.24) manifestly refers back to the starting-point of the discussion; it is directed against the "Jews", who have set themselves up as judges over Jesus (5.9ff).[3] In 7.19–24 the Evangelist has used the original conclusion of the source which he took as the basis of 5.1ff. Jesus' question (7.19), τί με ζητεῖτε ἀποκτεῖναι, originally followed ἐζήτουν ... ἀποκτεῖναι (see above), and then came vv. 21–23, which in their present form of course have been worked over by the Evangelist (see below).

We are still left, however, without a formal conclusion to the scene to correspond to 6.59, or to other conclusions like 8.59; 10.19–21. I suspect that the original conclusion is to be found in 8.13–20.[4] 8.20 is parallel to 6.59; the

---

[1] Stylistically the narrative shows strong similarities with the other sections which probably come from the σημεῖα-source. The Greek is not bad Greek, or translation Greek, but "Semitising" Greek. Typical of this is the placing of the verbs at the beginning of sentences in v. 7 (ἀπεκρίθη), v. 8 (λέγει), v. 12 (ἠρώτησαν), v. 15 (ἀπῆλθον), and the corresponding lack of connecting particles. Ἐν τῇ ἀσθενείᾳ αὐτοῦ, v. 5. is not Greek. Nor can ἦν δὲ σαββ. ἐν ἐκ. τ. ἡμ. really be said to be good Greek. According to Black ἄνθρωπον οὐκ ἔχω (v. 7) is an Aramaism. See also Goodenough, 155f.

[2] It may be that the διὰ τοῦτο should be attributed to the Evangelist. He is especially fond of it; in 5.16 as in 5.18; 8.47; 10.17; 12.18, 39, it is related to the following ὅτι. He is also fond of οὐ μόνον—ἀλλὰ καὶ, in v. 18, cp. 11.52; 12.9; 17.20; I Jn. 2.2; 5.6.

[3] The transposition of 7.15–24 after 5.47 has been suggested by Wendt and a number of English scholars (Howard 264; see also v. Dobschütz, ZNTW 28 (1929), 162f. and Wik.). On the other hand Spitta and Hirsch want to take only 7.19–24 from ch. 7; Spitta then places the verses after 5.18 (and continues with 5.30ff.) while Hirsch inserts them in 5.17 (after ὁ δὲ ἀπεκρ. αὐτ.).

[4] One would hesitate to make such a suggestion, were it not that ch. 8 proves on examination to be a collection of isolated fragments which have been put together without

key-words μαρτυρία and κρίσις of 5.30–47; 7.15–24 appear again in 8.13–19, and the ironic appeal to the law of Moses 5.45–47; 7.19–23 has its climax in the pastiche in 8.17f.[1]

The story used in ch. 5[2] shows a markedly close relationship to the healing story in 9.1–34, which is constructed in a very similar way. There too, after the detailed account of the healing, we have the appended note that it was the Sabbath (9.14), which is then followed by an account of the opponents' action (who in ch. 9 are referred to alternatively as Ἰουδαῖοι and Φαρισαῖοι), and there also they lay hold of the healed man. The account in ch. 9 admittedly is much more detailed than that in ch. 5, and does not lead to a plot on Jesus' life but concludes with the Pharisees "throwing out" the healed man. In ch. 9 also the Evangelist has expanded the source, principally by adding a conversation of Jesus with the healed man (9.35–38), and then by a discourse of Jesus (8.12 etc.), which is connected to the story by a short exchange of words (9.39–41).

Manifestly the two stories in chs. 5 and 9 must be understood against the same historical background. Both reflect the relation of early Christianity to the surrounding hostile (in the first place Jewish) world; in a peculiar way they reflect, too, the methods of its opponents, who directed their attacks against men who did not yet belong to the Christian community, but who had come into contact with it and experienced the power of the miraculous forces at work in it. These men were interrogated, and in this way their opponents attempted to collect evidence against the Christian community. Such stories provided the Evangelist with an external starting-point, and at the same time they were for him illustrations alike of the world's dilemma, as it was faced by the revelation, and of the world's hostility. The world attempts to subject to its own κρίσις the event which is, in fact, the κρίσις of the world; it brings the revelation, as it were, to trial.[3]

---

much plan, so that one is faced with the task of seeking the original position of these fragments. Among these fragments is the section 8.48–50, 54–55 (see below). One might be tempted to find a place for this in ch. 5, since here too we have the theme of δόξα, and because the content of 8.54f. is the same as 5.37; 8.19. However I have tentatively placed it in ch. 7. It is, of course, not possible to achieve certainty in these matters.

[1] If one asks how the editor came to put the isolated fragments in their present positions, then as far as 7.15–24 is concerned we can say that this must have suggested itself as an illustration of the ἐδίδασκεν in 7.14; for in vv. 16f. it treats of Jesus' διδαχή; moreover the key-word ζητεῖν ἀποκτεῖναι (v. 19) seems to recommend its connection with 7.25. It is not possible to discover similarly obvious reasons for the present position of 8.13–20. However it is possible that the objection in 8.13 seemed to be the most likely continuation of the ἐγώ εἰμι 8.12; this is confirmed by the views of present-day exegetes.

[2] A form-critical analysis shows that the story is a secondary composition. In the Synopt. apophthegmata, where a healing miracle leads to a controversy only a brief account is given of the miracle (see Gesch. der synop. Trad. 2. ed. 223 = Hist. of the Syn. Trad. 209), while what has happened here is that a controversy has been attached later to a detailed miracle story. The appended date v. 9b and the obscurity of the situation (vv. 15ff.) are characteristic.—At most one can compare Mk. 2.1–12, which is also a secondary combination of a miracle story and a controversy (Gesch. der synopt. Trad. 2. ed. 12f. = Hist. of the Syn. Trad. 14f.).

[3] Cf. Hosk. 361f.

a) The Healing Story and Controversy: 5.1–18

1) *The Healing of the Lame Man:* 5.1–9a

V. 1 is an editorial addition made by the Evangelist to connect the story with the preceding passage; like 2.13 it explains the reason for Jesus' journey to Jerusalem[1] by reference to a feast.[2] No precise description of the feast is given; but it can only be the feast of the Passover, which was imminent in 6.4 and which is followed some time later by the feast of the Tabernacles (ch. 7).[3] **Vv. 2–5** describe the situation.[4] The scene is a pool in Jerusalem by the Sheep Gate,[5] called in the local language[6] Bethzatha;[7] it is surrounded by five porticos,[8] where invalids

---

[1] See p. 86.

[2] See p. 122 n.3; 123 n.1. It is obvious that the explanation has been added by an editor; for the feast plays no part in what follows.

[3] The readings vary between ἡ ἑορτή (ℵCL) and the simple ἑορτή (BAD Ferrar group, also Orig., contrary to Hautsch's view, Die Evangelienzitate des Orig. 1909, 132). Other readings such as ἡ ἑορτὴ τῶν ἀζύμων (instead of τῶν Ἰουδ. Λ) and ἡ σκηνοπηγία(131) are clearly corrections. Although ἑορτή is better attested, ἡ ἑορτή is to be preferred; for elsewhere the Evangelist always mentions a specific feast; this must also be the case here, but there was no need to mention the name of the feast explicitly, since ἡ ἑορτή referred to the Passover, which had just been mentioned in 6.4. One can easily see why, when the original order had been lost, and with it the reference to 6.4, the ἡ was omitted. (There is no real point in mentioning the fact that in the OT the feast of Tabernacles is sometimes simply referred to as חָג, which the LXX renders as (ἡ) ἑορτή, as in I Kings 8.2A; Ezek. 45.25; Neh. 8.14, 18; II Chron. 7.8, since there can be no question of this referring to the feast of the Tabernacles). Cp. for the rest, esp. Br., Zn.; also J. Blinzler, Bibl. 36 (1955), 20–35, particularly 21.2.

[4] Ἔστιν v. 2 hardly proves that at the time of the narrator the temple had not yet been destroyed (Schl.); nor does ἦν 11.18 prove the contrary.

[5] ἡ ἐπιλεγ. demands that the object to which it refers should have been already mentioned (Bl.-D. para. 412.2); thus we must supply κολυμβήθρα nominative and πύλη for ἐπὶ τῇ προβατικῇ, (Bl.-D. para. 241, 6; Br. The sheep gate is mentioned in Neh. 3.1, 32; 12.39; it lies to the north of the temple). There are a number of variants which have been occasioned by a misunderstanding of the construction; κολ. was taken as a dative (see Tischendorf; thus B. Weiss and Nestle, ZNTW 3 [1902], 172), or ἐπὶ τῇ was omitted so that προβ. became a nominative (ℵ* 554e al. see Br. ad loc.), or an ἐν was substituted for ἐπί (ℵ c ADGL al; here προβ. seems to be taken as a district in the city; cp. in inferiore parte a b ff 2). Instead of ἡ ἐπιλεγ. some authorities, particularly of the W- and C-text have ἡ λεγομένη ℵ* τὸ λεγόμενον (noticed by Tischendorf and Schwarz III 153f.), 1321 ἡ διερμηνευομένη—all of which are corrections with regard to the following Ἑβραϊστί.

[6] Ἑβραϊστί can refer both to OT Hebrew and to the Aramic actually spoken at the time (Str.-B. II 442ff.); here, of course, it refers to the latter.

[7] The name varies considerably in the tradition. Βηθσαιδα (BΨ 0137 sa bo c vg syr[h] Tert. Hieron.) cannot be correct, for it is only a variant of Βηθζαθα. Βηθζαθα is read (disregarding orthographic variants) by ℵ W L 33 D 713 e a b d ff2 1 r Eus. Barhebr. (Nestle, ZNTW 3 [1902], 171). The other authorities have Βηθέσδα. Zn., Merx, Schl., support the latter reading; yet (apart from the fact that it is less well attested) the allegorical meaning of Βηθέσθα (חִסְדָּא or בֵּית חֶסְדָּא = house of mercy) should probably be allowed to count against it. Βηθζαθα is at least a topographically established name; for it is probably identical with Βεζεθα, which is mentioned several times in Josephus (Dalman, O. u. W. 325f.). This is the name of the northern suburb of the city, which was settled later. (The name

lie,[1] who, as the reader immediately understands, are seeking to be cured. V. 7 shows that the cure can only be had at certain times,[2] namely when the water of the pool is disturbed. Clearly what lies behind the story is the idea of a pool fed by an intermittent source.[3] This is developed in detail in v. 4, which is of course only a secondary gloss,[4] inserted into the initial description of the scene; it expresses the popular belief that from time to time an angel troubled the water, and so endowed it with temporary healing powers. V. 5 then introduces the other main character in the story besides Jesus, an invalid,[5] who has already been lying at the pool for 38 years[6] without having found any cure.[7] He himself

---

must then have been given, by way of abbreviation, to the pool.) In the 4th century a double pool near the Sheepgate was shown as the "sheep-pool", and this is perhaps confirmed by excavations (Dalman op. cit.; Meyer II 244; J. Jeremias, Die Wiederentdeckung von Bethesda 1949). It is however doubtful whether the narrator's local knowledge was as good as Kundsin, Topol. Überl. 34ff. supposes. For the narrative assumes the existence of an intermittent source, such as is attested for the pool of Siloam. (Dalman, O. u. W. 327). Thus there may be a confusion here.

[8] In the source the five porticos certainly do not refer allegorically to the Pentateuch; it is also hardly likely that the Evangelist had this in mind, for he attaches little importance to the idea of Jesus as the liberator from the OT; neither can one interpret 5.39f. in this way, see below. Merx even finds a symbolic representation of Jesus the "shepherd" in the Sheepgate and of baptism in the pool. Cp. O. Cullmann, Urchristent. u. Gottesdienst 58ff. According to Grill II 61ff. the 5 porticos refer to the five levels of society: Pharisees, Sadducees, Samaritans, disciples of John and Essenes!—Dodd sees the water of the pool as a symbol of the Torah.

[1] Κατακεῖσθαι of invalids, as in Mk. 1.30, and elsewhere not infrequently, see Br., Wörterb. and Schl. ad loc.—Ξηρός as in Mk. 3.1 = "lame", see Br., Wörterb.; Schl. on Mt. 12.10. On the list see Bl.-D. para. 460, 3; in D a b παραλυτικῶν is added.

[2] The addition attested by the Western text: ἐκδεχομένων τὴν τοῦ ὕδατος κίνησιν is an explanatory gloss.

[3] This is true of the pool of Siloam, see p. 240 n.7; see also Br. ad loc.

[4] V. 4 is omitted by ℵ BC syr^c (syr^s has a lacuna here) and by D 1. The manuscripts which contain the verse (in slightly varying forms) in part add glosses (cp. Nestle, ZNTW 3 (1902), 172, 1) or critical marks. It would be impossible to explain how it had come to be omitted, whereas its insertion can easily be explained on the basis of v. 7.—The *angel* is probably not the angel of water in general (Rev. 16.5; Eth. En. 66.1f. and elsewhere; cp. Boussett, Rel. des Jdt. 323f.; M. Dibelius, Die Geisterwelt im Glauben des Paulus 1909, 80f.; Str.-B. III 818–820), but a special angel for this pool (cp. Str.-B. II 453ff.). The belief that angels or spirits belong to a particular source, or that they endow streams or rivers with healing powers at particular times, is widespread, cp. Br. ad loc., Wellh. Joh. 25, 1; Smith-Stübe, Die Religion der Semiten 1899, 129ff.140f., Thomas 352.—On καταβαίνειν ἐν Bl.-D. para. 218 and Br. ad loc., on κατέχεσθαι νόσῳ Br. ad loc. and Wörterb.

[5] The illness is not described any closer; but vv. 8f. (as compared with Mk. 2.11) make it more probable that it was lameness than blindness, see Br.

[6] τρ. καὶ ὀκτὼ ἔτη ἔχων (cp. v. 6; 8. 57; 11.17) is not impossible in Greek (admittedly the examples which Br. gives are not applicable, because they have the ordinal number), but is made impossible by the following ἐν τῇ ἀσθ. αὐτοῦ. Correct usage would be τρ. καὶ ὀ. ἔτη ὢν ἐν ἀσθ. (without the article and αὐτοῦ!) or ὄγδοον καὶ τριακοστὸν ἔτος ἔχων ἐν ἀσθ.

[7] The indication of the length of the illness is one of the marks of the healing stories, see Gesch. d. synopt. Trad. 236, =Hist. of the Syn. Trad. 220. The view, held by early exegetes, that the angel came only infrequently, or only once a year at the said feast, has

explains the reason for this in v. 7., he can never get to the water at the right time because he has no one to put him in.[1] This information is given in answer to Jesus' question (v. 6)[2], for Jesus it is who seizes the initiative. In reply to the sick man's answer he pronounces the miraculous word[3] (v. 8), the immediate[4] success of which is related in v. 9a.

2) *The Controversy:* 5.9b–18

The narrative is comprised of three scenes: vv. 10–13, v. 14 and vv. 15–18. The appended note v. 9b,[5] to the effect that it was the Sabbath, is followed in **v. 10** by the Jews' attack; yet unlike the attacks in the Synoptic accounts of Sabbath healings, the one here is not directed against Jesus but against the healed man.[6] Thus the object of

---

been read into the text. Nor is there any basis for Loisy's allegorical interpretation, according to which the source represented Judaism, which only (if at all) healed one invalid a year while the others had to wait.—Neither the source nor the Evangelist has in mind an allegorical interpretation of the 38 years, in terms of the 38 years' journey of the Israelites from Kadesh-Barnea to the crossing of the brook Zered (Deut. 2.14), as is rightly seen by Howard 184. Loisy calculates that there are still two years to the Passion so that 38+2= years would symbolise the forty years of the wandering in the desert! Strathm again interprets the 38 years in terms of the wandering of the Israelites.

[1] Ἄνθρωπος need not be taken as "servant" (Lk. 12.36 and elsewhere). Burney 99 wrongly claims the ἄνθρ. οὐκ ἔχω as a Semitism, see Colwell 74. The ἵνα corresponds to an Aramaic relative (=ὅς), but need not necessarily be a mistranslation (Burney 75; against this Goguel, Rev. H. Ph. rel. 3 (1923), 377; Colwell 96ff.; see Bl.-D. para. 379). Βάλλειν = "lay", "bring", as in 10.4; 20.25, 27; Mk. 7.33; Jas. 3.3 and elsewhere; this is good Greek.

[2] This is the only possible meaning of the question. Zn. thinks that θέλεις ὑγιὴς γενέσθαι is a means of strengthening the faltering will of the sick man. The impossibility of such a psychological interpretation is brought out by its consequences. The command to take up his bed (v. 8) fills the soul of the sick man with courage to believe and his limbs with strength. Zn. takes this rationalistic interpretation yet a stage further. It is doubtful if the cure took place immediately (Zn. omits εὐθέως, v. 9, with ℵ D, whereas this omission can only be explained by ἴδε ὑγιὴς γέγονας, v. 14); Jesus left the scene of the healing before the full effects of the healing had become apparent.—Of course, one may not ask why Jesus went to the pool. Γνούς (as in Mk. 2.8, for example) refers to the miraculous knowledge enjoyed by Jesus; it would be quite out of character with the simple story to ask how then Jesus can question the sick man. J. Jeremias (Jerusalem zur Zeit Jesu II A 1924, 34) has let his imagination run away with him when he suggests that the invalids were beggars, and that the conversation probably arose when the sick man asked Jesus for alms.

[3] The formulation is almost precisely the same as Mk. 2.9, 11. However this does not necessarily mean that it is dependent on Mk. It need not surprise us that the κράβατος, vv. 8f. is not mentioned earlier, since it is obvious that invalids must lie on beds.—The asyndetic imperative ἔγειρε ἆρον (Bl.-D. para. 461, 1) is correct Greek; cp. Soph. Trach. 1255; Ant. 534; frequently in Epict. and in Pap., see Colwell 16f. On the popular κράβ. see Br. Wörterb.—On the original meaning of the carrying of the bed as a proof of the miracle, see Gesch. d. synopt. Trad. 240 = Hist. of the Syn. Trad. 224. and cp. particularly Mk. 2.11f. According to Hirsch, for the healed man "to parade publicly before the Jews with the bed on his back" at Jesus' command was a deliberate attack on the Sabbath customs. But this is to strain the meaning of περιπάτει.

[4] On εὐθέως, see n.2.

[5] See p. 239 n.2.

[6] καί v. 10 (="and therefore") need not necessarily be a Semitism, see Burney 68; Colwell 88f.

their attack is not the healing itself, but the fact that the man is carrying his bed.[1] The healed man's answer (**v. 11**)[2] contains no argument whatsoever, but merely appeals to the command of the miracle worker. When the Jews (**v. 12**) want to know who this was,[3] it appears (**v. 13**) that the healed man does not know Jesus, and that Jesus has already left the scene of the healing.[4] The next scene (**v. 14**) takes place in the temple.[5] Here Jesus finds the healed man and speaks to him; he warns him of further sin, which would result in even greater misery.[6] Thus the saying reflects the Jewish idea of retribution, according to which sickness must be attributed to sin.[7] This is most surprising on the lips of the Johannine Jesus, since it makes men accept the principle he had rejected in 9.2f.[8] Moreover the saying bears no relation to the question which was raised in v. 10, and the only point of v. 14 is to prepare the way for the next scene.

The healed man now (**v. 15**) tells[9] the Jews that Jesus is the man they are looking for.[10] The situation is difficult to understand, but obviously one is meant to imagine that everything narrated in vv. 14ff. takes place in the temple, since no other place is mentioned.[11] The imperfect tenses (**vv. 16, 18**), which have no bearing on the situation, show that the narrator is less interested in the details of the story than in portraying the Jews' habitual bearing towards the normal (or repeated) activity of

---

[1] On the law against carrying loads on the Sabbath see Str.-B. II 454–461.

[2] Since δς δὲ (AB) occurs only here in John, we should probably read ὁ δὲ with ℵ C*L al. (D and K have neither.)—The Evangelist must have inserted ἐκεῖνος; see p. 79 n.3.

[3] There is no need to read a pejorative sense into ὁ ἄνθρ.; the Jews obviously want simply to find out what has happened.

[4] 'Εκνεύειν occurs only here in the NT, synonymous with ἀναχωρεῖν (6.15) or ὑποχωρεῖν (Lk. 5.16; 9.10), with which it is used interchangeably in Justin dial. 9.2f. The presence of the ὄχλος is meant to explain the ἐκνεύειν; although quite how it does, it is hard to see (Schanz: fear of a conflict; B. Weiss and Ho.: to avoid a disturbance). It is pointless to ask where the crowd came from.

[5] No interest attaches to the question how much time had elapsed. The temple is probably mentioned as a place where one could expect to find plenty of people. Εὑρίσκει clearly refers to a chance meeting, as in 1.41ff.; 9.35.

[6] Μηκέτι with the imperative as Epict. diss. IV 19, 9; Frg. 23, 19.

[7] Cp. Mk. 2.5, and Klostermann's commentary on this in Hdb. zum NT; Schl. on Jn. 9.2; Bousset, Rel. des Jdt. 411f.; Str.-B. I 495f., II 193–197.

[8] Hirsch allegorises: "By its separation from Jesus (this is how H. takes: μηκέτι ἁμάρτανε!), who wishes to free it from enslavement to the law, Judaism delivers itself up for judgement."

[9] B 𝕶 al: ἀνήγγειλεν, ℵ C al: εἶπεν, D φ 33 al: ἀπήγγ.

[10] There is no point in speculating about how in the meantime he had found out Jesus' name. One would certainly have to assume that his motive for telling the authorities was to free himself from suspicion of having questioned the validity of the Sabbath (Schl.), but that, of course, raises the question how far it is proper to look for his motive at all. The reader is clearly not required to pass judgement on the behaviour of the healed man; all interest in him ceases after v. 15.

[11] See p. 239 n.2.

Jesus.[1] Nevertheless **v. 17** presupposes a definite scene; "Jesus answered them". And this produces the real conflict. For the Jews understand only too well (**v. 18**) the claim which is made by this saying, and this confirms them in their intention to kill Jesus.[2]

The starting point for Jesus' subsequent discourse[3] is provided by the statement in v. 17, which stands out from the rest of the scene:[4] "As my Father is working still, so I am working, too."[5] The Jews rightly understand that Jesus makes himself equal to God in these words, and so for their ears it is an insane blasphemy.[6] The precise nature of this equality is suggested by the title given to God, ὁ πατήρ μου, which is, of course, used in the exceptional sense in which the Johannine Jesus speaks of God as his Father.[7] This, too, the Jews rightly understand. One

---

[1] The Evangelist's ἐδίωκον (v. 16) has naturally been made to agree with the imperfect ἐζήτουν (v. 18, see p. 238) of the source. Καὶ ἐζήτουν αὐτὸν ἀποκτ. in v. 16, which is read by 𝕶 etc., is an addition from v. 18.—The descriptive imperfect in ὅτι ταῦτα ἐποίει ἐν σαββ. includes the particular case which has just been related. Because the story is concerned to describe the Jews' attitude to Jesus, it gives as the reason for their hostility, not, as one might expect from v. 10, his command to the sick man, but his behaviour in general.—There are no grounds for Schl.'s comment: "The haste with which the Jews lay hold of the Sabbath breaker, assumes that they know he is about to flee." Nor for his remark that the proceedings had not progressed far enough for them to be able to forbid Jesus to speak—"They still have to listen to him". It is not the Evangelist's intention here to describe proceedings against Jesus under Jewish law, as can be seen from the fact that no verdict is recorded.

[2] Λύειν, used of breaking the law, is both Jewish (הִתִּיר) and Greek; see Str.-B. I 739–741; Schl. on Mt. 16.19; Br., Wörterb., from which it is clear that λύειν can also mean "to abolish".—According to Methodius v. 17 is a "Wisdom" saying; cp. R. Harris, The Origin of the Prologue to St. John's Gospel 1917, 42.

[3] For the suggestions that 7.19–24 should be inserted in v. 17 or v. 18 see p. 238 n.3.

[4] 'Απεκρίνατο occurs only here and in v. 19, while ἀπεκρίθη occurs over 50 times. Perhaps to show the official character of the reply (Abbot, quoted in Bd.)?

[5] This is, of course, how the Greek paratactical construction should be understood (see Wellh., Joh. 134); it corresponds to ὥσπερ—οὕτως in v. 21, cp., also H. Almquist, Plutarch u. das NT 73.

[6] According to the Jewish view the great blasphemers, Hiram and Nebuchadnezzar, Pharaoh and Joash, made themselves equal to God, Str.-B. II 462–464. According to II Th. 2.4, this is the blasphemy of the Antichrist. According to Philo it is a φίλαυτος καὶ ἄθεος νοῦς which believes: ἴσος εἶναι θεῷ, leg. all. I 49; leg. ad Cai. 118; cp. Jos. ant. XIX 4ff. on Caligula. Neither the fact that Rabbinic exgesis takes אלהים in some passages to refer to men (Str.-B. II 464f.), nor the Greek use of ἰσόθεος as a title of honour for outstanding mortals (Wetst.) has any bearing on the exegesis of Jn. 5.18. The Greeks would also have considered the statement in Jn. 5.17 to be madness, see Dodd 224–228.

[7] It does not matter here whether ἴδιον v. 18 is stressed, or whether it is used in the debased sense of the Koine (Bl.-D. para. 286). The former is possible in John (cp. 5.43; 7.18); it goes without saying that for John, Jesus in speaking of his Father lays claim to a particular relationship to God (whereby ὁ πατήρ and ὁ πατήρ μου are synonymous). In spite of 1.4 God is never referred to as the Father of men or of the faithful, with the exception of 20.17, where this Fatherhood is specifically distinguished from God's Fatherhood of Jesus.—For the discussion of the idea of God's Fatherhood see p. 58f.

thing, however, they do not understand, namely that Jesus' Sonship, and his claim to be equal to God and to work like God, only make sense in that Jesus, as the Son and as the one who works like the Father, *reveals* God,[1] and that precisely because he is the Revealer he must make the claim which sounds so blasphemous to their ears. They can only conceive equality with God as independence from God,[2] whereas for Jesus it means the very opposite, as is brought out immediately in v. 19.[3]

Whereas in the following discourse the question of the observance of the Sabbath is completely disregarded, Jesus' saying in v. 17 answers the charge of Sabbath-breaking; for it contains not only the assertion of the *equality* of Jesus' work with God's work, but this equality, which is described in vv. 19f. with regard to content the work, is regarded in v. 17 in terms of its *constancy*. This is certainly what is meant by ἕως ἄρτι[4] although it is not immediately apparent whether ἕως ἄρτι refers also to the continuation of the work until its expected end.[5] In the context, however, the emphasis is in the first place on its constancy, and in so far as ἕως ἄρτι points to an end of the work, this can only really be the end referred to by 9.4, the night when no one can work (cp. 11.9f.; 12.35f.), i.e. the end of Jesus' work of revelation.[6] Thus there is to be not an interruption in the work of Jesus but its cessation.[7] For the present, however, "as long as it is day" (9.4), he must work; and in this he is no more restricted by the Sabbath than the Father is.

still

---

[1] See on 1.18, p. 82f.

[2] This is how "to make oneself equal to God" is understood in Rabbinic Judaism, see Odeberg 203.

[3] Odeberg 203f. has rightly seen the connection between v. 17 and v 19.

[4] One might ask whether the saying in v. 17 also does not come from the passage of the "revelation-discourses" used in vv. 19ff., and whether the Evangelist has not inserted the ἕως ἄρτι in order to make it relevant to the situation. Or perhaps ἕως ἄρτι is a clumsy translation?

[5] Ἕως ἄρτι = "till now", in the first place indicates the terminus ad quem, but it can be used in a less precise way = "still" (I Jn. 2.9; I Cor. 4.13; 8.7; 15.6), always assuming though, that the behaviour or events in question can, will or ought to come to an end. This assumption need not, of course, be made explicit, so that ἕως ἄρτι is almost equivalent to ἀεί (cp. I Cor. 4.13 with II Cor. 4.11).—O. Cullmann (In memoriam E. Lohmeyer, 127–131) sees in ἕως ἄρτι a reference to the Christian Lord's day, which takes the place of the Jewish Sabbath, and also a reference to Jesus' resurrection and the new creation at the end.

[6] So too Hosk. Clearly it would be wrong to take this to mean, "Now also, even though it is the Sabbath"; for ἕως ἄρτι is spoken, not with an *interruption*, but with a (definitive) *conclusion* to the work in mind.—Nor, of course, can one take it to mean, "Till now the Father worked; from now on I am working"; for then "from now on" would have to be expressed; also this idea would be meaningless in John.—One may, of course, think here of the "world-Sabbath", on which God's activity ceases (G. Stählin, ZNTW 33 (1934), 244f.), but only in the Johannine modification in which God's work, is carried out and ceases *together with* Jesus' work.

[7] Cp. the idea that it is "too late", 7.33f. etc.

The constancy of the divine activity is taken as a self-evident axiom; it is not here that the paradox lies, but in the fact that Jesus makes the same claim for himself. Yet in what sense can the constancy of the divine activity be taken as axiomatic? Obviously it is not based on the Greek view, where the notion of the constancy of divine activity is conceived in terms of law or natural power.[1] God is no more thought of as the origin, power and norm of the κίνησις,[2] than the ζωή, discussed in vv. 21ff., is thought of as the life-force in nature, or the power of κίνησις in the κόσμος. The work of God and the Revealer is conceived as the work of the eschatological Judge, in whose power it lies to give or to refuse the eschatological ζωή. This, clearly, is based on the Jewish idea that although God rested from his work of creation (Gen. 2.2f.; Ex. 20.11; 31.17), he is still constantly at work as the Judge of the world —even if in John there is no longer any trace of the exegetical discussion by which the Rabbis developed the idea.[3] The relationship between the dispute over the Sabbath and Jesus' reference to his work as Judge is now plain: the constancy predicated of the divine activity is also predicable of Jesus' activity, precisely because the work of the Revealer is the work of the Judge.[4]

Thus we can see why the Evangelist has taken the healing story of 5.1–9a as the starting point for Jesus' discourse: as a story of the breaking of the Sabbath it becomes a symbolic portrayal of the constancy of the Revealer's work. The healing itself seems to have no symbolic importance for the discourse—in contrast with the healings in chs. 6 and 9. For there is no suggestion that the health given to the sick man might symbolise the "life" which the Revealer in his function as Judge gives

---

[1] See p. 24f. on the Stoic concept of the Logos.

[2] Cp. Cic. de off. III 28; Max. Tyr. Diss. XV 6, 2 (both in Br.); Plotin Enn. IV 7, 13, p. 141, 10f. Volkm., of the νοῦς: εἴπερ ἀεὶ καὶ αὐτὸς ὢν ἔσται δι' ἐνεργείας ἀπαύστου. Frequently in Pantheistic sections of the C. Herm., e.g. 5.9; 9.9 (καὶ τοῦτό ἐστιν ἡ αἴσθησις καὶ νόησις τοῦ θεοῦ, τὸ τὰ πάντα ἀεὶ κινεῖν); 11.5f. (οὐ γὰρ ἀργὸς ὁ θεός), 12–14, 17; 14.3f.; 16.19. Similarly in Hellenistic Judaism: Philo leg. all. I 5f. παύεται γὰρ οὐδέποτε ποιῶν ὁ θεός κτλ.) 16–18; Cher. 87 (φύσει δραστήριον τὸ τῶν ὅλων αἴτιον παῦλαν οὐδέποτε ἴσχον τοῦ ποιεῖν τὰ κάλλιστα κτλ.); prov. I 6ff. (see W. Bousset, Jüdisch-christl. Schulbetrieb 1915, 144f.) Jos. does not discuss the problem when he retells the story of creation Ant. I 33; nor do his other statements give us any clear picture of his views, see Ad. Schlatter, Wie sprach Josephus von Gott? 49ff. Aristobulus earlier expressed the same ideas as Philo, in Eus. praep. ev. XIII 12, 11.—On Epicurus' polemic against the deus otiosus see A. Fridrichsen, Symb. Osl. 12 (1933), 52–55; cp. also Dodd 320ff.

[3] The Rabbinic exegetes attempted in different ways to bring together the OT statements about God's Sabbath rest and the idea of God's constant activity (see Str.-B. II 461f.), above all by distinguishing his activity as Creator from his activity as Judge; see esp. Odeberg 201f.; E. Sjöberg, Gott u. die Sünder im paläst. Judentum 1938, 4.—Ep. Arist. 210 seems to combine the Greek and the Jewish idea: the pious mind sees ὅτι πάντα διὰ παντὸς ὁ θεὸς ἐνεργεῖ καὶ γινώσκει καὶ οὐθὲν ἂν λάθοι ἄδικον ποιήσας ἢ κακὸν ἐργασάμενος ἄνθρωπος.

[4] Odeberg 202f. draws out the connection well.

to men. Lastly the fact that the passage is concerned with the portrayal of the Revealer's authority (v. 27) is made clear when we see how differently the Sabbath question is treated by the Evangelist, as compared with the synoptists, who are concerned with the question how far the law of the Sabbath is valid for *men* and how far it is limited (by the law of love.) Accordingly the Evangelist does not include here (or in ch. 9) the arguments of the Synoptic Jesus in the Sabbath controversies. For him the only question is whether the law of the Sabbath is binding on the *Revealer*, and his only concern is with the freedom of the Revealer, which is grounded in the constancy of his revealing work.[1] Of course *indirectly*, this also affects man's obligations to the Sabbath; just as the revelation-event is not bound to any religious law, so too the reception of the revelation transcends all laws and rules. The healed man must also break the Sabbath. The revelation-event means the disruption and negation of traditional religious standards, and their protagonists must become enemies of the Revealer.

b) The Judge: 5.19–47; 7.15–24; 8.13–20

The *structure* of the composition is simple. The theme of 5.19–30 is the equality of Jesus' activity as Judge with the activity of God; 5.31–47 and 7.15–24 discuss the rights of such a claim of Jesus, in other words the question of the μαρτυρία; 8.13–20 finally bring the themes of μαρτυρία and κρίσις together. The argument of the first section is as follows. Vv. 19f. give a formal definition of this equality, teaching us to see the equality of Jesus' and God's work as grounded in the absolute dependence of Jesus on God. Vv. 21–23 then describe the work of the eschatological Judge, followed in vv. 24–27 by a description of the eschatological judgement as the judgement which is carried out through Jesus' word. V. 30 looks back to the beginning and gives a summary of the discussion.

1) *The Revealer as the Eschatological Judge:* 5.19–30

The discourse is introduced by the phrase ἀπεκρίνατο . . . καὶ ἔλεγεν which, occurring as it does for the first time in ch. 5, now strikes a solemn note. Similarly the discourse begins by claiming the attention of its hearers with the formula: ἀμὴν ἀμὴν λέγω ὑμῖν. Jesus at first speaks of himself in the third person, although now there is no secret about it as there was in ch. 3; for in v. 24 the first person takes its place, to be

---

[1] It is therefore completely wrong to suggest that v. 17 shows the "true piety" of Jesus (Bl.).

replaced again in v. 25 by the third person, which is yet again followed by the first person.[1] This introduces a strange element of pathos into the discourse. The words of the speaker are not to be taken as the words of one who speaks as a merely human individual. The speaker, who stands before them as a human subject, is at the same time separated from them by an infinite divide. They see the one about whom the words are spoken, and at the same time they do not see him.

v. 19:

οὐ δύναται ὁ υἱὸς ποιεῖν ἀφ' ἑαυτοῦ οὐδέν,
ἂν μή τι βλέπῃ τὸν πατέρα ποιοῦντα.
ἃ γὰρ ἂν ἐκεῖνος ποιῇ,
ταῦτα καὶ ὁ υἱὸς ὁμοίως ποιεῖ.[2]

The Jews had met Jesus' words of v. 17 with the accusation of pride. There now follow what appear to be words of humility. Yet Jesus' words, as the words of the Revealer, transcend the human possibilities of pride and humility. The same claim lies behind v. 19 as was made openly in v. 17; for v. 19, by describing both negatively and positively Jesus' absolute dependence on the Father, is intended to lay bare the ground of the equality of his work with the divine work, and not to show his subordination to the Father. The negative statement, which comes first, shows that what is being propounded is not a cosmological theory, which describes God's activity through a mediator. Clearly the theme of the discourse is the activity of the "Son", which is played out before his hearers in Jesus' activity, and which is addressed to them and confronts them with the decision of faith. The negative formulation attempts to guard against the mistaken view that the Revealer can be understood as a human person apart from his divine commission; or that it is possible to make a distinction, with regard to Jesus' person, between what has the quality of revelation and what does not; or that those aspects of his person which create an impression of greatness or magnificence can be taken as an image or shadow of God's nature.

---

[1] The interchange between first and third person gives no grounds whatsoever for doubting the literary integrity of the text; rather it belongs to the style of the "revelation-discourses"; see M. Dibelius, Die Formgeschichte des Evg. 2. ed. 1933, 284, n.1 = From Trad. to Gospel, 283 n. 1.

[2] The two sentences, joined together by γάρ, consist of two lines each, of which one is a main clause and the other a relative clause. The reversal of the order of main and relative clause in the second sentence allows the two to be joined together by γάρ, whereas otherwise one would have expected an antithesis. Becker 74 takes ἃ γὰρ κτλ. as an addition to the source.—ὁμοίως in the last line does not describe the identity in manner of the ποιεῖν (= "in the same way"), but simply refers to the correspondence between the two (= "similarly", "also") as in 6.11; 21.13.

The idea that the Revealer does not act ἀφ' ἑαυτοῦ runs through the whole Gospel.[1] The origin of his decisions and actions lies outside him; he has been "sent"[2] and acts on behalf of him who sent him. All this is said not in order to provide the basis for a speculative Christology, but because his origin is grounded in *what he means for us*;[3] whoever hears him, hears God, whose words he speaks (3.34; 17.8); whoever sees him, sees God (14.9). Thus the statement about his equality with God refers to the situation of those who hear and see him, and not to his own metaphysical nature.[4]

It would therefore also be wrong to conceive the *unity of Jesus with God* as a moral union, as the conformity between the decisions and actions of Jesus and his Father.[5] For from the moral point of view Jesus would appear to be fundamentally the same as other men, and in so far as one could refer to an act of moral obedience as a μὴ ποιεῖν ἀφ' ἑαυτοῦ, this could be said of all men, when they act morally. Jesus' μὴ ποιεῖν ἀφ' ἑαυτοῦ refers to the authorisation of his mission, which, as the Revealer, he shares with no man. Jesus is not seen as a moral personality in John;[6] indeed, 5.19 seeks to guard against just such a way of looking at him. The μὴ ἀφ' ἑαυτοῦ gives expression, not to his humility, but to his claim as the Revealer. His activity is not considered with regard to what it means for *him*, but with regard to what it means for his *hearers*, with regard to that which happens in the κόσμος through him.[7] In the same way the high priest does not speak ἀφ' ἑαυτοῦ 11.51,

---

[1] He does not act on his own authority 5.19; 8.28, nor does he speak on his own authority 7.17f.; 12.49; 14.10 (the same is said of the πνεῦμα 16.13); he has not come of his own accord 7.28; 8.42 (cp. 5.43), and he does not seek his own will 5.30; 6.38. Stated positively, he does the will of the Father, fulfils his commandments, does his works, see p. 145 n.5—On the phrase ἀφ' ἑαυτοῦ see Schl. ad loc. and on 7.17.

[2] This explains Jesus' continual use of ὁ πέμψας με (about 17 times) or ὁ πέμψας με πατήρ (about 6 times, the mss. sometimes vary in their use of the two titles) to refer to God. Also the phrase that the Father has "sent" him is used about 15 times (ἀποστέλλω see p. 50 n.2).

[3] Cp. the discussion on the meaning of the statements about his pre-existence p. 138 n.1, and see below p. 254f. So too Hosk. 389f. on 10.30.

[4] Cp. Calvin on v. 19: Arius minorem Patre Filium inde colligebat, quia ex se nihil possit: excipiebant Patres, notari tantum his verbis personae distinctionem, ut sciretur Christum a Patre esse, non tamen intrinseca agendi virtute eum privari. Atqui utrinque erratum est. Neque enim de nuda Christi divinitate habetur concio, et quae mox videbimus, in aeternum Dei sermonem per se et simpliciter minime competunt, sed tantum quadrant Dei Filio quatenus in carne manifestatus est. Sit nobis ante oculos Christus, ut a Patre missus est mundo redemptor.

[5] Cp. Harnack, ZThK 2 (1892), 195f.; Bl. ad loc.: "It is merely a question here of the perfection of the religious relationship which a man may enjoy with God"!

[6] Wrede (Vorträge und Studien 206f.) and Htm. (p. 27f.) have rightly seen that to judge the Johannine Jesus according to ethical standards would be to make him into a kind of ghost.

[7] Cp. the moralistic interpretation in B. Weiss: the original meaning of 5.19 (as spoken by the historical Jesus) cannot have been that Jesus was attributing to himself a

when his (humanly speaking) clever words suddenly gain the character of a prophecy.[1] Equally when Moses says in Num. 16.28; ὅτι οὐκ ἀπ' ἐμαυτοῦ (sc. τὰ ἔργα ταῦτα), it refers not to his moral worth, but to his mission, and the same is true of Balaam's words in Num. 24.13 when he says, οὐ δυνήσομαι παραβῆναι τὸ ῥῆμα Κυρίου, ποιῆσαι αὐτὸ πονηρὸν ἢ καλὸν παρ' ἐμαυτοῦ ὅσα ἂν εἴπῃ ὁ θεὸς ταῦτα ἐρῶ.[2]

Thus in a certain sense the unity of the Father and the Son is understood by analogy with *the relationship to God of the Old Testament messengers from God and Prophets*, men who must speak God's word even when they do not want to.[3] The unity does not consist in the particular divine quality which these persons or their words have, taken by themselves (for example by virtue of their ethical content), but in the fact that God works in them, that they act on God's behalf, that their words confront their hearers with a decision over life and death.

Yet, in spite of this, the idea of the unity of Jesus with God in John was not formed under the influence of OT prophecy,—a conclusion confirmed by the fact that the OT nowhere speaks of the equality of the prophet with God[4]. It is not only that Jesus' equality with God is asserted of his actions as well as his words, it is also that Jesus' words of authority are not interpreted in terms of election, vocation and inspiration, but

---

special relationship to God, from which he then deduced his own imitation of the divine action, "for the imitation of the works of the Father is the task of all the children of God (Mt. 5.45) and not a prerogative of the Son of God κατ' ἐξοχήν". The original meaning was that the child of God reaches a kind of activity which no longer recognises the distinction between work and rest, just as God's Sabbath rest in no way excludes his continued activity. For the man to whom the fulfilment of God's command is no longer a burden but a pleasure, and is not toil but refreshment (4.34), the distinction between week-day work and Sabbath rest has ceased to have any meaning." Compared with such banalities M. Dibelius (Festg. Ad. Deissmann 174f.) is right when he takes the unity of Jesus and God "as the unity of natures by virtue of their divine quality". "God does not *give*" the divine nature "to the Son because he loves him, but he *bequeaths* it to him because of the community of their natures." Yet this interpretation still remains within the sphere of the mythology which has been discarded in John. Cp. also Loisy: the community between Father and Son is metaphysical; but the Evangelist describes it not as "métaphysique et éternel", but as "actuel".

[1] On the formal meaning of (μή) ἀφ' ἑαυτοῦ cp. also 18.34.

[2] In Jer. 23.16 it is said of the false prophets that: ἀπὸ καρδιάς αὐτῶν λαλοῦσιν καὶ οὐκ ἀπὸ στόματος κυρίου, similarly Ezek. 13.3. The reverse is found in Jer. 29 (49).14: ἀκοὴν ἤκουσα παρὰ κυρίου, similarly Obad. 1.1; cp. Is. 21.10 (ἀκούσατε ἃ ἤκουσα παρὰ κυρίου); 28.22; Ezek. 33.30 (ἀκούσωμεν τὰ ἐκπορευόμενα παρὰ κυρίου). "Not of one's own accord, but from God" refers, not to the moral submission of the will to God, but to inspiration, to divine compulsion. See Schl. on 7.17.

[3] Cp. Num. 24.13 (see above in the text); Jer. 1.4–10; 20.7–9. See Dodd 254ff., who thinks that the idea of the Son of God has been moulded upon the prophetic model.

[4] Rather the relationship to God is here conceived of in terms of (election) vocation and inspiration, which correspond to the idea of the distance of the prophet as man from God. Heathen antiquity, of course, was also acquainted with the idea of prophetic inspiration, see Br. on 12.49f.

in terms of the Gnostic myth.[1] The latter speaks of the sending of a pre-existent divine being, which in its metaphysical mode of being is equal to God, and was sent by him to carry out his work of revelation, for which he is commissioned and equipped by the Father,[2] and which he achieves in unity with him.[3] Here the revelation is based not on intermittent inspiration but on the permanent identity of being of the divine messenger with God.

John of course frees himself from this mythology, but at the same time he retains its terminology. Jesus' destiny is not an event of cosmic significance which inaugurates the natural process of redemption,[4] nor does he bring miraculous cosmological and soteriological doctrines. His doctrine is the *that* of his mission,[5] the fact that he is the Revealer. More important, *the idea of God's activity in his Revealer has been historicised.* All the expressions which say that the Son does what the Father does, that he carries out the will of the Father, fulfils his commandment, and works his work,[6] that he acts on the authority of the Father (5.27; 17.2), that that which belongs to him belongs to the Father and vice-versa (17.10), that he speaks God's words, or alternatively what he has seen and heard with the Father,[7] that he who sees him, sees God (14.9), that he is one with the Father,[8] he in the Father and the Father in him,[9] that the Father works his works in him (14.10)—all these expressions assert what at the very beginning was asserted by καὶ θεὸς ἦν ὁ λόγος:[10] the Father and the Son may not be considered as two separate persons, whose work is complementary to each other, while the Father—as in the myth—remains in the twilight of that which lies beyond history; nor as two separate persons united in their purpose; rather all these expressions assert that the activity of the Father and the Son is *identical.*[11]

---

[1] See the following note and on v. 20.

[2] Cp. ZNTW 24 (1925), 104–107, 114f.; esp. Joh.-B. 222 (the Father says to the Son): "My son, come, be my messenger, come, be the bearer (of my tasks) ..." 224: "Whereupon I carried out in order the works which my Father gave me to do." Ginza 175, 4f. On the messenger's equipment see op. cit. 109. On this Ginza 70, 3ff.; 333, 27ff.; Od. Sal. 10, 1f., see above p. 165 n.1; and Br. ad loc. In Jewish Gnosticism similar statements are made about the Metatron, see Odeberg 204f.

[3] See on 8.16 and ZNTW 24 (1925), 108; Schlier, Relg. Unters. 39ff. and cp. J.B. 32, 18 (the messenger speaks): "Do not say that I have come to you on my own initiative."

[4] See p. 64f.

[5] See p. 144f.

[6] See p. 145 n.5 and 249 n.1.

[7] See p. 145 n.3 and on this Jn. 3.34; 17.8.

[8] 8.16, 29; 10.30; 16.32; 17.11.

[9] 10.38; 14.10f.; 17.23.

[10] See p. 32f.

[11] Cp. Calvin on ἵνα πάντες τιμῶσιν v. 23: hoc membrum satis confirmat ..., Deum non ita in Christi persona regnare, quasi ipse, ut solent ignavi reges, quiescat in coelo, sed quia in Christi persona potentiam suam declaret seque praesentem exhibeat.

John does not recognise two divine beings in a mythological sense; Jesus' activity is conceived strictly in terms of his revelation. What he says and does is the word and deed of the Father. The "coming" of the Revealer is the appearance of a particular historical person in a particular history, and his exaltation is the historical event of the crucifixion.

Thus the terminology of the myth provides John with a means of describing the person and the word of Jesus in a way which takes him beyond the OT idea of prophecy. The "Word of God" spoken by Jesus, unlike the word of the prophets, does not give man knowledge of what, in the light of God's command, he must do in his particular historical situation. It was this which the idea of vocation and inspiration expressed. Rather the word of Jesus cannot be separated from his person. The revelation has happened once and for all in the total historical appearance of a man, in such a way that on the decision for or against him hangs the decision over life and death for all men and for all time. The consequence is that it is not possible to record individual sayings of Jesus, as the warnings and invocations, the threats and the injunctions of the prophets had been recorded; for his proclamation can only be the proclamation of the single fact of his coming, of the coming which is the eschatological event.[1] The consequence is therefore that whereas one must hear the prophets when they speak, where Jesus is concerned one must "believe" in him.[2]

V. 20 expresses the idea of the revelation in the language of the myth:

---

[1] Cp. P. Humbert, Les Prophètes d'Israel (Rev. H. Ph. rel. 1936), 41.

[2] The peculiar nature of the relationship between the word and person of Jesus, namely, the extraordinary fact that in his person he is the Revealer, and that through his word he bears witness to nothing other than the fact that he is the Revealer, is reflected in the double use of πιστεύειν. To recognise him as the Revealer is called πιστε ύειν εἰς αὐτόν (or εἰς τὸ ὄνομα αὐτοῦ, or simply πιστεύειν see p. 51 n.3). Since, however, as a result of his word one believes "in him", it looks as if the condition for belief "in him" is that one should believe "him"; thus as well as πιστεύειν εἰς αὐτόν, πιστεύειν with the dative can also be used, where πιστ. has the general sense of "putting one's trust in", "believing in the truth (reliability) of". Just as one believes the Scriptures (2.22), or Moses, or alternatively his γράμματα (5.46f.), or the preaching (12.38 after Is. 53.1), so too one believes his words (5.47), one believes "him" (5.38, 46; 8.31, 45f.; 10.37f.; 14.11). All these statements are made, as it were, from the point of view of the hearer (cp. 6.30: ἵνα ἴδωμεν καὶ πιστεύωμεν σοι. Cp. also 10.38: τοῖς ἔργοις). In practice there is no difference, for one must believe "him" when he says that one must believe "in him". The one cannot happen without the other. Thus πιστ. εἰς αὐτόν can be used interchangably with πιστ. αὐτῷ 8.30f., and in I Jn. 5.10 we find πιστεύειν εἰς τ. μαρτυρίαν, while λαμβάνειν τ. μαρτ. (meaning to believe 3.11, 32f.; I Jn. 5.9) or λαμβάνειν τὰ ῥήματα (12.48; 17.8) is synonymous with λαμβ. αὐτόν (1.12; 5.43).—Correspondingly πιστεύειν when used of God can be constructed with εἰς (12.44; 14.1) or with the dative (5.24; I Jn. 5.10).—Cp. J. Huby, Rech. sc. rel. 21 (1931) 404ff. Further ThWB s.v. πίστις.

ὁ γὰρ πατὴρ φιλεῖ τὸν υἱόν,
καὶ πάντα δείκνυσιν αὐτῷ ἃ αὐτὸς ποιεῖ,
[καὶ μείζονα τούτων δείξει αὐτῷ ἔργα, ἵνα ὑμεῖς θαυμάζητε].[1]

The Father "loves" the Son[2] and "shows" him everything that he does. This corresponds to what was said in v. 19, that the Son only does what he sees the Father doing.[3] Thus what in the myth was originally taken literally, is taken by the Evangelist—and also by his source—as an image of the relationship of the Father and the Son. All these different phrases, that the Son does or says what he has seen or heard with the Father, give expression to the same idea, namely, that he is *the Revealer in whom we encounter God himself speaking and acting*.[4] This can be seen above all from the fact that the words spoken by Jesus never actually describe things he has seen or heard in the heavenly

[1] The last sentence of v. 20 must be an addition of the Evangelist's, who thus again relates the discourse to vv. 1–18; cp. 7.21. Becker, 74f. thinks that the end of v. 19 ἃ γὰρ κτλ. and of v. 20 ἃ αὐτὸς ποιεῖ κτλ. are additions to the source. The Jewish parallel adduced by Odeberg 208 (God commands Moses to do greater works than before, in order to astound the people) is purely fortuitous. One would more readily think of the promise of "greater things than these", cp. 1.50; 14.12. There is no need to see in 5.20 a reference to specific events related later in the Gospel, and certainly no cause to suppose that the μείζονα ἔργα refer to Jesus' "life-giving activity as Spirit, which he will carry out in the sacraments" (A.Schweitzer, Die Mystik des Apostels Paulus 1930, 357). According to v.d. Bussche (see on p. 106) 1015 the μείζονα ἔργα refer to Jesus' office as Judge.—The ἵνα can be taken as consecutive, Bl.-D. para. 391, 5. ὑμεῖς is not stressed (Bd.); cp. vv. 38, 39, 44.

[2] See pp. 164f. on 3.35. φιλεῖ 5.20 (D: ἀγαπᾷ) has the same meaning as ἀγαπᾷ 3.35 (17.24); cp. the interchange of the verbs 11.3, 5, 36; 13.23; 19.26; 21.15–17.

[3] On the mythological terminology see p. 165 n.1 and p. 251 n.2. The idea that the "Son" "sees" what the Father does and imitates his works originally has a cosmological meaning (see pp. 27f.). According to Plat. Tim. 37c the demiurge creates the αἰσθητὸς κόσμος, by looking at the νοητὸς κόσμος as its παράδειγμα. Plotinus says the same of the νοῦς: ἕνα νοῦν ... μιμούμενον τὸν πατέρα καθ' ὅσον οἷόν τε αὐτῷ (Enn. II 9, 2); he then applies the same idea to the Ψυχή, which is the second being after the Νοῦς: κοσμεῖν ὀρεγόμενον καθ' ἃ ἐν νῷ εἶδεν . . . ποιεῖν σπεύδει καὶ δημιουργεῖ Enn. IV 7, 13 p. 140, 28ff. Volkm. Philo stands in this tradition conf. ling. 63, of the Logos: τοῦτον μὲν γὰρ πρεσβύτατον υἱὸν ὁ τῶν ὅλων ἀνέτειλε πατήρ, . . . καὶ ὁ γεννηθεὶς μέντοι, μιμούμενος τὰς τοῦ πατρὸς ὁδούς, πρὸς παραδείγματα ἀρχέτυπα βλέπων ἐμόρφου τὰ εἴδη. Similarly in the Hermetic literature: C. Herm. 9, 6 (the κόσμος as ὄργανον τῆς τοῦ θεοῦ βουλήσεως); 12, 15f. (the κόσμος, the μέγας θεὸς καὶ τοῦ μείζονος εἰκών is described as ἡνωμένος ἐκείνῳ καὶ σῴζων τὴν τάξιν κα<τὰ τὴν> βούλησιν τοῦ πατρός); particularly kore kosmu p. 458, 18ff. Scott, of Hermes: ὃς καὶ εἶδε τὰ σύμπαντα καὶ ἰδὼν κατενόησε καὶ κατανοήσας ἴσχυσε δηλῶσαί τε καὶ δεῖξαι κτλ. (This is strangely modified in C. Herm. 1, 12f.; Fr. in Scott I 408–410.—On Jewish Gnosticism see Odeberg 204, also 46f. on the Metatron's knowledge of the heavenly mysteries.

[4] The Son's proclamation is traced back in 1.18; 3.11; 6.46; 8.38 to his "seeing". In the same way that ἀκούειν 5.30 replaces βλέπειν 5.19, so too in 3.32 seeing and hearing are combined, whereas in 8.26, 40; 15.15 hearing stands by itself (as it does in 16.13, where it is used of the Spirit). The change in 8.38 is characteristic: ἃ ἐγὼ ἑώρακα παρὰ τῷ πατρὶ λαλῶ· καὶ ὑμεῖς οὖν ἃ ἠκούσατε παρὰ τοῦ πατρὸς ποιεῖτε, which is immediately followed in 8.40 by ... ὃς τὴν ἀλήθειαν ὑμῖν λελάληκα, ἣν ἤκουσα παρὰ τοῦ θεοῦ. Cp. also the change in 6.45f.

sphere; they do not initiate us into any mysteries.[1] In the same way Jesus does not "show" us any particular thing (10.32; 14.8f.) in the sense of displaying an object or state of affairs to our view. His "showing" consists in his speaking to us and challenging us to believe.

It makes no difference whether the present tense is used, as in 5.19f. (the Son does what he *sees*) and 5.30 (he judges as he *hears*), or whether, as elsewhere, the past tense is used (he speaks what he *has* seen or heard). Similarly we find both πᾶν ὃ δίδωσίν μοι ὁ πατήρ (6.37) and δέδωκεν (10.29) (cp. 5.36; 13.3; 17.2ff.). It is clear that the expressions in the past tense refer to the *pre-existence*, as is shown by 5.36: τὰ ἔργα ἃ δέδωκέν μοι ὁ πατὴρ (namely in the pre-existence) ἵνα τελειώσω αὐτά (namely in the historical ministry), or by 8.26: ἀλλ' ὁ πέμψας με ἀληθής ἐστιν, κἀγὼ ἃ ἤκουσα παρ' αὐτῷ, ταῦτα λαλῶ εἰς τὸν κόσμον, where εἰς τ.κ. shows that the "hearing" has not taken place in the κόσμος. It can also be seen from the fact that the "speaking" corresponds to the appearance of the Revealer, or that the μὴ ἀφ' ἑαυτοῦ λαλεῖν[2] corresponds to his not having come or having been sent of his own accord,[3] and that his having come or having been sent is often combined with his having seen and heard.[4] This is further confirmed by 1.18: the giver of the revelation is the Pre-existent one.[5]

On the other hand the statements in the present tense show that the *pre-existence* is not thought of as some former observable state and that the mission is not conceived as a mythical event. The content of what was seen and heard in the pre-existence is nowhere described,[6] and the Evangelist rejects mythological ideas about Jesus' entry into the world.[7] The point of the statements about pre-existence and mission is not that they describe things which in themselves are important for Jesus, but that they draw out the importance of his person and word.[8] Jesus' words and actions are not the result of human choice but are *determined*, just as the actions of his opponents are determined (8.38, 41) and the word of his community, in which he speaks as the Spirit (16.13). Nor is Jesus' word determined by a momentary decision,

---

1 See p. 144 on 3.11.

2 See p. 249.

3 7.28; 8.42.

4 3.11–13. 31f., 8.26; 12.49f., cp. 5.36; 7.16–18; 14.24.

5 Naturally the fact that the seeing and hearing refer to the pre-existence of the Revealer is simply due to the statements being derived from the tradition of the myth. But in the above discussion we have been concerned with the question how these statements are interpreted in John, and have therefore left this out of account.

6 See p. 144f. and p. 253.

7 2. See p. 62 n.4.

8 Cp. R. Hermann, Von der Antike zum Christentum 1931, 37: "One can see everything that the Father has given into his hands here on earth among men and in the historical circumstances of his life.... Nothing that the Father has given to him remains purely transcendent",—but this means that Jesus' person is portrayed exclusively in terms of the revelation. This is also the reason for the future δείξει (v. 20). For the intention is not to describe a metaphysical relationship, but to draw out the revelatory character of all Jesus' actions So too Hoskyns.

based on the knowledge of a particular situation. On the contrary the Evangelist denies that Jesus' word is based on this sort of personal decision.[1] His word is determined because it is God's word, which, as the eschatological word, does not arise out of the particular historical situation, but qualifies the historical situation anew as the ultimate situation. As such the word is beyond human criticism and assessment, and simply demands belief. It cannot be contemplated; for it addresses man and confronts him with the decision of faith. In this sense Jesus' word does not represent his own personal judgement on the world and men, and still less is it the expression of his inner life, of his piety, but a λαλεῖν εἰς τὸν κόσμον (8.26); his words and his mission are one and the same. Thus the statement about the pre-existence describes in mythological imagery the word which encounters man as a word whose origins are not in this world, and man's situation as one where he must take the decision between life and death.[2] The statements about pre-existence are not intended to make faith easier by tracing Jesus' words back to a reliable source, but they are an offence to men, inasmuch as they portray the character of the claim made by the word.[3]

---

[1] At this point there is agreement with the prophetic word (see p. 249f.). The prophets also do not appeal to their "experience" (whether it be their vocation, or the particular occasion on which they have received a revelation), in order to justify the certainty with which they pass judgement on a particular historical situation, or in order to describe the way in which they have come to a personal decision; rather they appeal to it in order to describe the authority of their word, which does not spring from their personal judgement of the situation, but is also divinely determined. However John, as it were, fills out the prophetic idea with the Gnostic idea by asserting the identity of the Revelation and the Revealer.

[2] See p. 248.—L. Brun, Symb. Osl. V (1927) 1–22 argues that the statements about Jesus' having seen and having heard do not refer to pre-existence, and takes them (as does, for example, W. Lütgert, Die joh. Christologie 2. ed. 1916, 25–36; similarly Bl., p. 15f.) to refer to Jesus' present activity. Jesus always acts on God's initiative, his actions are always based on God's "showing", so that his activity is a continual imitation of the Father. The statements in the past tense mean that Jesus' hearing and seeing always precedes his speaking and acting. Brun wants to interpret these statements by analogy with OT prophecy (cp. especially Is. 21.10). This, however, is only justifiable up to a certain point, see above. He is also partly right to want to exclude the mythological idea of pre-existence from Jesus' statements. For the idea of pre-existence is only an image; it is quite right that the Evangelist did not have in mind that Jesus had at some time in the past seen and heard something; he can also use the present tense (see above), and indeed even the future (5.20c). Yet even if the idea of pre-existence has been demythologised the concept itself has been retained, and the concept of pre-existence may not be eliminated by a psychological interpretation. The analogy of prophetic inspiration (which for the rest should not be interpreted psychologically and isolated from the idea of election and vocation) does not provide an adequate basis for the intepretation of the Johannine statements, for these clearly stand in the tradition of the Gnostic myth. One may not isolate the statements about Jesus' seeing and hearing from those relating to his mission and his coming, and these latter statements cannot be understood in terms of the prophetic mission, since they have their counterparts in the statements about his departure and exaltation. Finally these declarations must be understood within the context of the Johannine view that all speech and action is determined by its origin (see p. 138 n.1).

[3] See p. 144f.

Vv. 21–23 develop this idea by saying that the equality of Jesus' activity with God's activity is to be seen in that *Jesus is the eschatological Judge.* Jesus, that is to say, is the Revealer, inasmuch as he is the Judge who decides between life and death.

V. 21:

ὥσπερ γὰρ ὁ πατὴρ ἐγείρει τοὺς νεκροὺς καὶ ζωοποιεῖ,
οὕτως καὶ ὁ υἱὸς οὓς θέλει ζωοποιεῖ.[1]

If the Son acts like the Father, this means that he does the work which is characteristic of God, that he raises the dead and gives them life, that he fills the office of the eschatological Judge.[2] Does this then mean, as the ὥσπερ-οὕτως seems to suggest, that they both act as Judge? No, for as the Evangelist's comment in **v. 22** explains, the Father has relinquished his office to the Son.[3] In **v. 23** he immediately takes steps to guard against a possible misunderstanding of this statement by adding a note as to the purpose (ἵνα κτλ.) of this relinquishment. According to this, what is asserted in v. 22 is not, as it were, that God has been relieved by another Judge; rather v. 22 asserts the *equality* of the working of the Father and the Son, described in vv. 19f. The Son must be honoured in the *same* way as the Father is honoured. The Father *remains* Judge; as indeed v. 21, with its ὥσπερ-οὕτως, had affirmed that they *both* exercise the office of Judge. But now the meaning of the ambiguous ὥσπερ-οὕτως is made clear; for by referring back to vv. 19f., we can see that it means that God exercises his office as Judge *through* the Son. Moreover any possibility of misunderstanding which may still attach to the mythological formulation of the ἵνα-clause of v. 23, as if there were two divine figures alongside each other, and as if the Son must be treated in an *analogous* way to the Father, is removed by the addition of the principle: ὁ μὴ τιμῶν κτλ. One cannot honour the Father without honouring the Son; the honour of the Father and the Son is *identical;* in the Son we are confronted by the Father and we can approach the Father only through the Son.

---

[1] Becker 75 takes ὥσπερ γὰρ and οὕτως καὶ v. 21 as additions to the source.

[2] Only one aspect of the judge's function, the ζωοποιεῖν, is described (cp. Schemone esre 2: "Thou art a strong Hero, eternal Life, and feedest the living and givest life to the dead. Praise to Thee, Jahweh, who makest the dead to live!"). Of course it is obvious that the counterpart of giving life is killing, or (according to vv. 24f.) allowing men to remain in death, and this is hinted at by οὓς θέλει. θέλει (the subject is the Son and not, as Odeberg maintains, the Father) does not refer to his own decision (= οὓς ἂν θέλῃ); it is intended to stress the congruity of his purpose and his actions (as Zn. rightly sees), so that the sentence gives a description of the ἐξουσία of the Son. There is no explicit indication here of an attack on the claim of the Jews to be the children of Abraham (Schl.).

[3] It makes no difference to the sense of v. 22 whether one reads κρίνει or κρινεῖ. However the present tense is to be preferred in the general statement.

One thing has yet to be expressly stated, although it is clearly implied by 3.19, namely, that the Son's eschatological judgement takes place *in his present activity as the Revealer*. Jewish and early Christian apocalyptic had already given expression to the idea that the Messiah or the "Son of Man" would exercise the office of judgement alongside or in place of God.[1] Yet in John no mention is made of the eschatological drama of the end-time, which was the object of such hopes or fears. Vv. 24–27 correct the ideas of the old eschatology in accordance with 3.19. The truth of the eschatological idea is to be found in what takes place *now*, as the words of Jesus ring out, and this makes it perfectly clear why God has handed over the judgement to him.

The two decisive sentences (v. 24 and v. 25) are introduced by the solemn ἀμ. ἀμ. λέγω ὑμῖν. The newness of what is said here is also stressed by the change in the first sentence from the third person to the first.

V. 24:

ὁ τὸν λόγον μου ἀκούων
    καὶ πιστεύων τῷ πέμψαντί με
ἔχει ζωὴν αἰώνιον
    καὶ εἰς κρίσιν οὐκ ἔρχεται,
ἀλλὰ μεταβέβηκεν
    ἐκ τοῦ θανάτου εἰς τὴν ζωήν.[2]

The situation of being confronted with the *word* is the situation of judgement. Naturally the statement is not to be confined to the external situation and time described in ch. 5. It is true for all time and for all places.[3] Everyone who hears the word of Jesus, wherever or whenever it may be, stands before the decision between life and death. Judgement—the division of 3.18–21—is brought about as the question of faith is put to all who hear the word.[4] The last clause gives unequivocal

[1] Bousset. Rel. d. Jdt. 263f.; Str.-B. I 978 (the idea is not Rabbinic, see loc. cit. IV 1199–1212 also 1103–1105); H. Windisch on II Cor. 5.10 p. 170f. (Meyer Komm.). Further Mt. 25.31ff.; Lk. 21.36; Acts 10.42; 17.31; I Th. 2.19; I Cor. 4.5; II Cor. 5.10; Rom. 14.9 and elsewhere; cp. Br. on v. 22. In Jewish Gnosticism the office of the Judge has been transferred to the Metatron (Odeberg 204).

[2] Becker 71 believes that the conclusion ἀλλὰ μεταβέβηκεν is an addition to the source.

[3] The world is seen as a world in which the Word rings out. In such statements no thought is given to the problem of the "heathen world", which has not yet heard the Word. The world is judged inasmuch as and in so far as the Word is spoken, as a result of which men divide into believers and unbelievers. That part of mankind which has not yet heard the Word remains, as it were, in suspenso.—G. Stählin ZNTW 33 (1934), 229f. rightly distinguishes between the Johannine "now" and the nunc aeternum of mysticism.

[4] See pp. 154–7.—Εἰς κρίσιν οὐκ ἔρχεται = "he has no need to appear before the seat of judgement", and so has the same sense as οὐ κρίνεται 3.18. The expression is just as possible in Greek (see Wetst. and Br.) as it is in the Jewish language . (Schlalscp.p. 155 n.1).

expression to this idea, and to the distinction between this conception of judgement and the traditional eschatology: the believer has already passed over from death to life.[1] Thus here the concepts of *death* and *life* which dominated the old eschatology have been abandoned, at least in the sense which they had there, where "death" referred to the destruction of earthly life in dying, and the awaited eschatological "life" referred to the immortality which is bestowed in the annulment or abolition of physical death. John 5. 24 does not deal with the problem of physical death as such;[2] yet the way for a discussion of the problem is prepared, inasmuch as life and death are discussed here without any mention of physical death. What then is the meaning of the death and life which are spoken of here? If Jesus' promise to the believer is in any sense to be understood by the hearer, then the life that it promises him must be the object which he longs for in all his desires and hopes, however darkly, misguidedly and mistakenly; it is that authenticity of existence, granted in the illumination which proceeds from man's ultimate understanding of himself.[3] It teaches him that if he is to find this authenticity, he must turn away from the common understanding of death and life, and he must know that life is given only in faith in the Revealer, since it is in him that God is encountered and recognised (17.3).

V. 25 stresses with all possible emphasis that the eschatological moment is now present in the word of revelation:

> ἀμ. ἀμ. λέγω ὑμῖν ὅτι
> ἔρχεται ὥρα καὶ νῦν ἐστιν
> ὅτε οἱ νεκροὶ ἀκούσουσιν τῆς φωνῆς τοῦ υἱοῦ τοῦ θεοῦ
> καὶ οἱ ἀκούσαντες ζήσουσιν.[4]

[1] Similarly the believers who see the criterion of faith in love (see 13.34f.) confess: ἡμεῖς οἴδαμεν ὅτι μεταβεβήκαμεν ἐκ τοῦ θανάτου εἰς τὴν ζωὴν, ὅτι ἀγαπῶμεν τοὺς ἀδελφούς, I Jn. 3.14. For the expression and the idea cp. Philo post. Caini 43, where he speaks of those who have escaped from the βίος of πάθη and κακίαι: οὓς γὰρ ὁ θεὸς εὐαρεστήσαντας αὐτῷ μετεβίβασε καὶ μετέθηκεν ἐκ φθαρτῶν εἰς ἀθάνατα γένη, παρὰ τοῖς πολλοῖς οὐκέθ' εὑρίσκονται; cp. vit. contempl. 13. Plotinus Enn. I 4, 4 p. 67, 16ff. Volkm. where the εὐδαίμων is described as: ὅς δὴ καὶ ἐνεργείᾳ (not merely δυνάμει) ἐστὶ τοῦτο (τὸ τέλειον or the τελεία ζωή) καὶ μεταβέβηκε πρὸς τὸ αὐτὸ εἶναι τοῦτο.

[2] See on 11.25f.

[3] See pp. 40–45 and cp. ThWB II 871, 35ff.—It would be wrong to read into this the Hellenistic doctine of immortality (Br. on v. 28). But it would be equally wrong to describe the "life" as a condition of the soul. "The 'life' is not manifested in the motions of our consciousness, or in the effects of our strength ... for what is manifested and experienced in our consciousness in that respect is that we believe and are able to love" (Schlatter, Der Glaube im NT 4. ed., 496f.). Cp. also D. Faulhaber, Das Joh-Evg u. die Kirche, 1938, 20f. Thus John has no knowledge of the crowning manifestation of Gnosticism, in which (in ecstasy) the negation of the this-worldly is transformed into a positive experience of the other-worldly, in which the other-worldly is reduced to the level of a this-worldly phenomenon, and consequently faith is reduced to sight, in such a way that the present moment of this experience would not be considered a moment in the

In the same phraseology and sense as in 4.23,[1] the "coming" eschatological hour, which men had hoped for at the end of time, is declared to be already present, for it is the hour in which the Word of the Revealer is heard. It is the hour of the resurrection of the dead.[2] And this leads us to a clearer grasp of the new understanding of death that is required of us. For the νεκροί, who are here spoken of, are the men of the κόσμος who live a life which lacks authenticity, for they do not know the ἀληθινὸν φῶς (1.9) and the ζωή which it gives.[3]

Like the concepts of death and life, the concept of *hearing* is also redefined, this time by a play on the word. True "hearing" is distinguished from hearing which is no more than a mere perception, and which is attributed here to the "dead": οἱ ἀκούσαντες ζήσουσιν. It is hearing in which mere perception of sound is combined with πιστεύειν (v. 24) or φυλάττειν (12.47); a hearing of which the "Jews" are not capable

---

this-worldly life. The Johannine Revealer does not take the believers out of the world (17.15); and the elimination of the future judgement does not mean the complete elimination of the future in a mystical present.

[4] The rhythm of vv. 24f. is not quite clear; it must have been modified by the translation into Greek (and by the revision of the original?).

[1] See p. 190 n.1.

[2] The formulation is again influenced by the tradition of the Gnostic myth, the main idea of which has been radically historicised. The word of the Mandaean messenger, his "call", his "voice", wakes the dead. "Life rests in his mouth" (Mand. Lit. 134). Cp. Ginza 596, 9ff.: "Thereupon there called a voice of life;
A watchful ear hears.
Many heard and revived;
Many wrapped themselves round and laid themselves down (to sleep)."
272, 23ff.: "Thou art the highest of the Ganzibrās (treasurers),
To whom life gave dominion over every thing.
The dead heard thee and revived,
The sick heard thee and were cured."
275, 19f.: "He who hears the speech of life,
finds room in the Skinā of life" (cf. 257, 18ff.).
Further passages are given in Odeberg 194f., ZNTW 24 (1925), 109f. In the fragment M.311 in F. W. K. Müller, Abh. d. Berl. Ak. 1904, 66f., it is said of Mani: "He revives the dead, illumines the darkness"; cp. M.32, loc. cit. p. 62. Hippol. El. V 14, 1 p. 108, 14W quotes from the manual of the Peratai: ἐγὼ φωνὴ ἐξυπνισμοῦ ἐν τῷ αἰῶνι τῆς νυκτός. Cp. Eph. 5.14 (and on this M. Dibelius in the Hdb. zum NT and Reitzenstein J.E.M. 6.135ff.) and the φωνὴ τῆς ἀναστάσεως of the Alchemist manual quoted in Reitzenstein, op. cit. 6 and H.M.R. 314. Cp. further Od. Sal. 10.1f. (see above p. 165 n.1); 22.8–11; 42.14ff. ("I created the community of the living among his (death's) dead, and spoke to them with living lips.")—Cp. Br. ad loc.; above all H. Jonas, Gnosis I 120ff., 126ff.

[3] Occasionally in Jewish writings one finds unauthentic life referred to as death (see Str.-B. I 489; III 652 on Mt. 8.22; I Tim. 5.6), but the usage was not well-established. In the Greek world it was common from the time of the Orphic σῶμα-σῆμα onwards, and is found particularly in the later Stoics, see ThWB III 12, n. 33 and s.v. νεκρός. Above all however it expresses the basic view of Gnostic dualism; see the previous note, and on this ThWB III 12, 14ff.; Reitzenst. J.E.M. 137; H. Jonas, Gnosis I 103ff.—Philo (see ThWB II 861, 6ff.; III 13, 1ff.) and Plotinus (see ThWB II 839, 20ff.; III 12, 4ff.) also stand in this tradition.

(8.43, 47), because it is only possible for those who are "of the truth" (18.37).

The powerful statements of vv. 24ff. receive their justification in **v. 26:**

ὥσπερ γὰρ ὁ πατὴρ ἔχει ζωὴν ἐν ἑαυτῷ,
οὕτως καὶ τῷ υἱῷ ἔδωκεν ζωὴν ἔχειν ἐν ἑαυτῷ.[1]

This is a new formulation, though related to v. 21, in which the Revealer is identified with God. ζωὴν ἔχειν can, of course, also be said of men who believe; but the latter have life "in him",[2] while God and the Revealer have life "in themselves";[3] i.e. they possess the creative power of life;[4] whereas the ζωή which man can enjoy is the kind of life proper to the creature.[5] In a certain sense v. 26 goes a step further behind the statement in v. 21, and so gives grounds for it: the Son exercises the office of Judge because he shares the divine nature.

V. 27 is another, and indeed unnecessary and clumsy repetition of the statement, which has yet to be justified: καὶ ἐξουσίαν ἔδωκεν αὐτῷ κρίσιν ποιεῖν.[6] It is not given as the consequence of what has gone before, but simply joined to the rest by καί. It can hardly be a further sentence from the source. Probably it was added by the Evangelist or even by the editor who inserted vv. 28f.[7] The suspicion that it is an editor's work is heightened when one looks at the justification which is added:[8] ὅτι υἱὸς ἀνθρώπου ἐστίν[9]—after what has gone before (vv. 19–23,

---

[1] Becker 71f. believes that ὥσπερ γὰρ and οὕτως v. 26 are additions to the source.

[2] 3.16; 20.31, cp. also 16.33: ἵνα ἐν ἐμοὶ εἰρήνην ἔχητε. Just as this εἰρήνη is "his" εἰρήνη (14.27), so too the ζωή of the believer is really "his" ζωή, from which the believer lives.

[3] ἔχειν ζωὴν ἐν ἑαυτοῖς is attributed to the believers (inasmuch as they receive the sacrament) only in the editorial addition 6.53 (see p. 235). Not so in I Jn. 3.15: πᾶς ἀνθρωποκτόνος οὐκ ἔχει ζωὴν αἰώνιον ἐν αὐτῷ μένουσαν, where any misunderstanding is averted by the addition of μένουσαν, lest one should think that it referred to man's own possession.

[4] God's ζωή is of course his power as Creator, which he also wields as Judge. It does not consist in God's "continual contemplation of himself in blessed self-sufficiency" (B. Weiss). Cp. rather Od. Sal. 10.2: "He made immortal life dwell in me etc.", see p. 165 n.1.

[5] See p. 39 n.3.

[6] Κρίσιν ποιεῖν in the context means "to sit in judgement", as in Jud. 15; Gr. En. 1.9 (also Rabbinic, see Schl.), and not, as in Gen. 18.25 "to do right" (עָשָׂה מִשְׁפָּט). On ἐξουσίαν ἔδωκεν see p. 57 n.5.

[7] The first clause of v. 27 could be attributed to the source, if there was a new beginning in the discourse at this point and it led on to v. 30 with a further sentence (now omitted by the Evangelist or the editor); but see H. Schlier, Relg. Unters. 94, 4.

[8] The feeling that the ὅτι-clause is, in the context, an unsatisfactory justification, probably led Chrys., Theod. Mops. and the Pesh. into thinking that it was dependent on the following μὴ θαυμάζετε τοῦτο: but this is a rather desperate solution.

[9] Is the article omitted because υἱὸς τ. ἀνθρ. is treated analogously to θεός, κύριος etc.? cp. 4.25; 10.36; Bl.-D. para. 254.

26) one expects ὅτι υἱός ἐστιν at the most. It is possible that the editor added only ἀνθρώπου to prepare for vv. 28f., i.e., to bring the statement into line with traditional eschatology,[1] according to which Jesus, as the Son of Man, is the eschatological Judge.[2] For to the Evangelist, to whom the title "Son of Man" is the title of the Revealer who walks this earth in human form,[3] Jesus, as the "Son of Man", who is "exalted", is of course also the Judge;[4] but this statement itself would have to be justified, and could not be advanced as an explanation of something else.[5]

In any case vv. 28f.[6] have been added by the editor, in an attempt to reconcile the dangerous statements in vv. 24f. with traditional eschatology.[7] Both the source and the Evangelist see the eschatological event in the present proclamation of the word of Jesus. Yet the popular eschatology, which is so radically swept aside by such a view, is re-instated again in vv. 28f.[8] The editor corrects the Evangelist by this simple addition, so that it is difficult to say how he thought the statements in vv. 24f. could be reconciled with it. Perhaps he thought that the κρίσις which takes place in Jesus' present activity was an anticipation of the last judgement, so that the resurrection of the dead at the end of

---

[1] Wendt I 121; II 76 wants for this reason to omit ἀνθρ. The attempt to remove the difficulty by splitting up ὅτι: κρίσιν ποιεῖν ὅ τι υἱὸς ἀνθρ. ἐστιν (Ch. Bruston, see Bl.-D. p. 308 on para. 300, 1) has only a certain curiosity value.

[2] See p. 257 n.1.

[3] See p. 105 n.3, 149n.4, 225 n.1.

[4] See p. 151f., and esp. 8.28; 12.31–34.

[5] It is quite impossible, in view of the use of υἱὸς τ. ἀνθρ. elsewhere in John, and indeed in the whole of the NT, that υἱὸς τ. ἀνθρ. v. 27 should, as Zn., Bl., Temple suggest, mean "man" in the simple sense (child of man), and that the clause therefore explains why Jesus is the proper judge of men (in the sense of Heb. 4.15). The idea that a man is the proper judge of men is to be found in the late Christian apocryphal writing Test. Abrah. p. 92 James. The remarkable similarity between this passage and Jn. 5.22, 27 should not, in my opinion, be ascribed to the fact that they both share a common source (as Schlier, Relg. Unters. 94, 4 suggests), but to the fact the Test. Abrah. is influenced by Jn. 5.

[6] τοῦτο v. 28 clearly refers not to the following ὅτι, but to the content of v. 21 as a whole; ὅτι here gives the justification for what has been said, it is not explanatory. μὴ θαυμ. must therefore be distinguished from the formulation in 3.7, see p. 142 n.1. (On the view that μὴ θαυμ. is a question see Bl.-D. p. 316 on para. 427, 2). The expressions ἀνάστασις ζωῆς and κρίσεως (genitive of purpose; see Bl.-D. para. 166; for a discussion of the question whether the omission of the article is a Semitism see Torrey 323; Bl.-D. para. 259, but also Colwell 79) occur only here; cp. ἀνάστασις εἰς ζωήν II Macc. 7.14, and see ThWB II 861, n. 214. Κρίσις has a different meaning here from its usual one in John and = "condemnation". On τὰ φαῦλα πράττειν see p. 157 n.6; τὰ ἀγαθὰ ποιεῖν occurs nowhere else in John; τὸ ἀγ. ποιεῖν is common in Christian usage, cp. Mt. 19.16; Rom. 7.19; 13.3 etc.

[7] The motive is made quite clear by passages like II Tim. 2.18; Pol. Phil. 7.1. For further discussion see Lietzmann on I Cor. 15.12 in the Hdb. zum NT.

[8] The fact that vv. 28f. teach a general resurrection of the dead, whereas in vv. 24f. only the "hearers" are called back to life (cp. οὓς θέλει v. 21) also shows that vv. 28f. do not agree with what has gone before. On the other hand it is quite wrong to give a spiritualising interpretation of vv. 28f. in terms of vv. 24f. in spite of Od. Sal. 22.8f.

time would "confirm his Word before all men."[1] This is approximately the understanding found in the Mandaean texts.[2]

V. 30 leads back to vv. 19f., and thus completes the circle for the first section of the discourse:

οὐ δύναμαι ἐγὼ ποιεῖν
    ἀπ' ἐμαυτοῦ οὐδέν·
καθὼς ἀκούω κρίνω,
    καὶ ἡ κρίσις ἡ ἐμὴ δικαία ἐστίν,
ὅτι οὐ ζητῶ τὸ θέλημα τὸ ἐμόν,
    ἀλλὰ τὸ θέλημα τοῦ πέμψαντός με.[3]

The first sentence, which corresponds to v. 19, gives a formal and general description of the Son's dependence on the Father. The second applies this truth to the Son's activity as the Judge, described in vv. 21–27, and draws the conclusion from this that the Son's judgement (i.e. the judgement which he passes[4]) is just. The third sentence gives the grounds for this contention, namely, that the will of the Father is carried out in the activity of the Son.[5] The fact that this concluding verse is again spoken in the first person makes it clear that what has been said applies to the man Jesus of Nazareth, who is now speaking to the hearers.[6] This last formulation leads on into the second part of the discourse, which raises the question of the validity of this enormous claim made by a man.

2) *The Witness for the Revealer:* 5.31–47; 7.15–24

The key-word of 5.31–40 is μαρτυρία, that of 5.41–47; 7.15–24 is δόξα. As in v. 31 Jesus will not bear witness to himself, so too, according to 7.18, he does not seek his own glory; and as v. 34 states that he accepts the witness of no man, so v. 41 declares that he accepts no glory from men. All this is connected together very closely. The man who

---

[1] Thus Bl.; much the same view is held by Br., Lagr. and others; cp. too the defence of the originality of vv. 28f. in H.-D. Wendland, Die Eschatologie des Reiches Gottes bei Jesus 1931, 80–89; G. Stählin, ZNTW 33 (1934), 237ff.; H. Pribnow, Die joh. Anschauung vom Leben 1934, 102ff., esp. Odeberg 196, 209f.—Wendt, Bousset (Kyrios 177, 1), Goguel, Introd. au NT II 1924, 358f.; Faure (ZNTW 21 [1922], 119) and v. Dobschütz (loc. cit. 28 (1929), 163), Schlier (Relg. Unters. 94, 4) and others (see Howard 258ff.) maintain that the verses are a later addition. Schwartz and Wellh. have a complicated view of the matter.

[2] See p. 155 n.2.

[3] Becker 72 believes that the text of the source for the ὅτι-clause read: ὅτι ζητῶ τὸ θέλημα τοῦ πέμψαντός με.

[4] 'Η κρίσις ἡ ἐμή = "the judgement which I have passed" (Schl.).

[5] See p. 249 n.1.

[6] On the present tense καθὼς ἀκούω see p. 253f. It goes without saying that ἀκούω refers to hearing what the Father says, and not to hearing the words of the man who stands before the judgement seat.

himself bears witness on his own behalf, and who dispenses with the witness of others, seems to make himself independent of men. And yet by *bearing witness on his own behalf* he becomes dependent on men, for he submits to their standards, to their judgement in order to gain their recognition, in order "to seek his glory". The Revealer then rejects both courses of action: he neither bears witness to himself, nor is he concerned about his own glory.[1]

i. *The* μαρτυρία: 5.31–40

Vv. 31f.

ἐὰν ἐγὼ μαρτυρῶ περὶ ἐμαυτοῦ,
ἡ μαρτυρία μου οὐκ ἔστιν ἀληθής.
ἄλλος ἐστὶν ὁ μαρτυρῶν περὶ ἐμοῦ,
καὶ οἶδα ὅτι ἀληθής ἐστιν ἡ μαρτυρία,
ἣν μαρτυρεῖ περὶ ἐμοῦ.[2]

It is assumed as self-evident, and in accordance with the way of the world, that the words of 5.19–30 would prompt the question about the authorisation of the one who, speaking as a man to men, makes such claims for himself. Human thought would demand that the man give proof of his authority, that he make his claim credible by appealing to accepted authorities or by producing "testimonials" from other people. Since Jesus refuses to do this the world can only understand him to mean that he "witnesses" to himself,[3] and such a witness would be invalid (8.13). In this verdict the world is right: if he really bore witness to himself,[4] his witness would not be "true".[5] This presupposes that the world thinks of self-witness only in terms of the witness of a man who is concerned with his own glory; it is this sort of self-witness that Jesus rejects.

Yet the world is wrong when it demands that he should produce a witness to support his claim in a manner that it would find acceptable.

---

[1] The parallels to the theme of μαρτυρία which Odeberg 226ff. adduces from Mandaean and Jewish Gnosticism only show the similarity of terminology without being material parallels, since they are not concerned with the authorisation of the Revealer, but with the witness for or against the souls undergoing judgement.

[2] V. 32 contains three lines. Has the Evangelist expanded the two lines of the source by inserting the οἶδα ὅτι? see on 12.50. In I John reference is frequently made to the knowledge of the community (3.2, 5.14; 5.15, 18, 19, 20; see Festg. Ad. Jül. 146).—Becker suggests that the text of the source in v. 32 read: ἄλλος ἐστὶν ὁ μαρτυρῶν περὶ ἐμοῦ, καὶ ἀληθής ἐστιν ἡ μαρτυρία (αὐτοῦ).

[3] In v. 31 the emphasis is not on περὶ ἐμαυτοῦ but on ἐγώ, as is shown by the contrast with ἄλλος in v. 32.

[4] Is μαρτυρῶ in v. 31 indicative (Bl.-D. para. 372, 1a)? The meaning would then be: "If really, as you believe ..."

[5] On the invalidity of self-witness, see Str.-B. II 466, 522 for Rabbinic statements, and Wetst. and Br. ad loc. for Classical parallels.

For his claim is the claim of the Revealer, and to subject this claim to the criteria which man has at his disposal would be to assert the continuity between the human and the divine, and that there is a commensurable relationship between human and divine standards; it would be to draw the revelation into the sphere of human discussion.

Accordingly Jesus can in fact also say that he will dispense with every authorisation and will bear witness to himself, and that his witness is nevertheless true (8.14). Even here, where he rejects self-witness as understood by the world, what he says amounts to the same, for he appeals to the witness of another,[1] and this other who bears witness to him is the Father whom they know not (vv. 36–38; 8.19). The fact that he does not say simply: "and his witness is true", but "*I know* that his witness is true", points to the barrier which separates him, the one who "knows",[2] from the world. Only the direct knowledge of the Revealer, and not the appeal to generally recognised criteria, can guarantee the truth of the witness.[3]

However, before moving on to a more detailed discussion of the Father's witness, the Evangelist in **vv. 33–35** again underlines the importance of the Baptist's witness.[4] He, when questioned by the Jews, bore witness to the truth[5] (v. 33), and this witness has a certain relative importance; indeed fundamentally it too is God's witness, for God has commissioned the Baptist (1.6–8, 33f.). That such importance as it has is only relative is strongly emphasised. The only witness which Jesus can consider[6] cannot be accepted from men. Yet for the sake of the hearers,[7] who in questioning the Baptist have recognised his authority, attention may be drawn to the witness of John (v. 34). One may well ask what good it has done, for in truth no one listened seriously to the

---

[1] On ἄλλος instead of ἕτερος see Bl.-D. para. 306, 3.

[2] See p. 143 n.1. Admittedly it is possible that the Evangelist inserted οἶδα ὅτι himself see p. 263 n.2.

[3] Οἴδατε, which is read by ℵ D codd. it syr[c], is certainly wrong, and owes its origin to the misunderstanding that ἄλλος referred to the Baptist, who is mentioned in v. 33. Zn. prefers οἴδατε, on the grounds that οἶδα contains an appeal to Jesus' own consciousness, which conflicts with v. 31. But then not only should we expect ὑμεῖς οἴδ.—whereas in fact the stressed ὑμεῖς does not occur till v. 33—but above all this sort of argument fails to recognise the paradoxical nature of the self-witness.

[4] Naturally vv. 33–35 (as well as vv. 36, 37a, see below; similarly v. Dobschütz, ZNTW 28 [1929], 163) come from the Evangelist, who after 1.6–8, 15, 19ff.; 3.22ff. could not ignore the μαρτυρία of the Baptist when dealing with the theme of μαρτ. This is shown clearly enough by the reference to 1.19ff.; it is confirmed by the style, which is prosaic, particularly ἀλλὰ ταῦτα λέγω ἵνα ... v. 34 (cp. 11.42; 13.19; 14.29; 15.11; 16.1, 4, 33; 17.13; I Jn. 1.3, 4; 2.1; 5.13); on ἐκεῖνος see p. 48 n.3. The sentence ἐγὼ δὲ οὐ παρὰ ἀνθρ. v. 34 is modelled on v. 41 (source).

[5] Vv. 33–35 look back on the Baptist's activity as a completed and past event; the Evangelist gives no thought to their relationship to 3.22ff.

[6] With the article: τὴν μαρτ.!

[7] ἵνα σωθῆτε should be taken in the sense of ἵνα ... πιστεύσωσιν δι' αὐτοῦ 1. 7.

Baptist. His appearance, which caused something of a sensation, gave them a certain short-lived satisfaction.[1] But they are incapable of making a decision and then abiding by it, in order that the object of their decision may itself *abide* (cp. v. 38a). They have not seen what the Baptist's light was intended to show.[2] Thus it only turns into an accusation against them, if their demands are conceded, and they are granted as a witness an authority which they themselves recognise (v. 35).

Jesus, however, has no need of this witness; the witness which accredits him is a greater than could be given by the Baptist;[3] it is the witness of the Father (**vv. 36, 37a**).[4] In the first place this witness consists in the ἔργα which the Father has "given" him to do.[5] Ἔργα here as elsewhere[6]—in an expression traditional in the myth[7]—refers to the whole of Jesus' activity as the Revealer.[8] Even if an allusion to the σημεῖα may be in view as in 5.1–9, it is clear from 5.19ff. that the real ἔργα are the κρίνειν and the ζωοποιεῖν. To be more precise, Jesus' words and deeds are μαρτυρία, in that they are the κρίνειν and ζωοποιεῖν;

---

[1] E. Lohmeyer, Das Urchristentum I 1932, 29 on Jn. 5.35: "More than probably a scarcely concealed allusion to the fact that John was for them a Messianic figure."

[2] The Baptist is compared with a burning light which illumines men (the article accords with the style of parables, cp. Mk. 4.21 etc. though Bl.-D. para. 273, 1 disagrees); thus his relative importance is recognised: he was not the φῶς (1.8), but a λύχνος. (The comparison of the leader or teacher to a light is obvious and occurs frequently; see Schl. and Str.-B. II 466. The comparison between death and the extinction of a lamp is different, Ginza 254, 12f.; 256, 8f., see Br. Cp. Hölderlin, Empedokl. I 2: "Do they love him? Yes, so long as he flowers and gleams ... they nibble away. But what are they to do with him when he has grown dull and barren?") The ὑμεῖς δὲ κτλ., in which the image is now developed metaphorically, says that the light has not fulfilled its purpose (ἀγαλλ. ἐν τ. φωτὶ αὐτοῦ means "in his light", not in the sense of the place where they rejoiced, but of the object in which they rejoiced, which is a Semitism). To take the first clause of v. 35: ἐκεῖνος κτλ. as a criticism of the Baptist (Schwartz IV 521f.; he wants to take πρὸς ὥραν with καιόμενος καὶ φαίνων cp. Mart. Pol. 11.2) is to contradict both the previous ἀλλὰ ταῦτα λέγω κτλ. and the following ὑμεῖς δὲ κτλ.—Πρὸς ὥραν = "for a limited time", as in II Cor. 7.8; Gal. 2.5; Phm. 15; Mart. Pol. 11.2; it seems to be a specifically Jewish phrase (לְשָׁעָה) see Schl.; Str.-B. II 466f.

[3] Zn.'s view, that it means that Jesus has a stronger witness to his person than the Baptist to his, is grammatically correct but is impossible in the context, in which it can only be a question of the Baptist's witness to Jesus. The correct Greek would be: μείζω ἤ (or τῆς) τοῦ 'I. Bl.-D. para. 185, 1. The abbreviated form is not uncommon in Hebrew and Aramaic; see Black 87.—On the form of μείζω or μείζων (BA) see Bl.-D. paras. 46, 1; 47, 2; both are accusative = μείζονα (D).

[4] Vv. 36, 37a are the Evangelist's own composition; τὰ γὰρ ἔργα κτλ. is prose. On the picking up of the subject which has been placed earlier in v.36 and v.37a, see p. 79 n.3; on v. 36 see particularly 10.25, on the "greater" witness of God I Jn. 5.9.

[5] On the Father's διδόναι to the Son see p. 172 n.5. On τελειοῦν see p. 194 n.3; on ἵνα τελ. Bl.-D. para. 390, 2.4. The appeal to works as a witness to something occurs, of course, elsewhere as well; see Br., Str.-B. ad loc.

[6] 10.25, 32, 37f.; 14.10ff.; 15.24; the singular τὸ ἔργον 4.34; 17.4 has the same force.

[7] See p. 145 n.5, 251 n.2

[8] Wendt II 40f. is essentially right here.

i.e. they are not μαρτυρία as visible demonstrative acts, but only taken together with what they effect, in the same way that faith can be called the attestation of Jesus.[1] Then it becomes clear that the witness which accredits him, i.e. the Father's witness *to* him, and the witness which he *bears* to what he has seen and heard,[2] are identical. Apart from his witness he offers no other proof of his authority which might provide a man with a *means* of believing in that witness. The hearer who asks can be referred only to the very thing whose validity he is questioning, to the object of faith itself. There are no criteria for determining the validity of the claim of the revelation, whether it be the reliable witness of others, or rational or ethical standards, or inner experiences. The object of faith makes itself known only to faith; and this faith is the only means of access to its object.

Not only do the works bear witness but the Father himself also bears witness (v. 37a). How are we to understand this? Fundamentally the Father's witness can be nothing other than the witness of the ἔργα which he has given the Son to do. One might well think that the two witnesses are mentioned together only in order to stress that the Son is not "alone" (8.16), that his actions can never be understood if taken in isolation, but must always be seen in the light of this particular duality, as is stated by 8.16–18. Yet 5.37a reads μεμαρτύρηκεν, and not μαρτυρεῖ as in 8.18. The reference is to a witness which was made in the past by the Father, which however is still valid in the present, namely the witness of the Scripture; for only that can be meant by the λόγος of God in v. 38 (cp. 10.35).[3] Yet in what sense is Scripture a witness? It cannot be a question of proof-texts in the traditional sense; for the Johannine Jesus never uses them; above all, it would completely destroy the idea of v. 36, if the appeal to Scripture was thought of as an appeal to a generally recognised authority, through whose good offices one might be led to accept the word of Jesus. V. 39 will show more clearly what is meant.

The double witness in vv. 36,37a is paralleled by the double reproach in **vv. 37b, 38a**:[4] God is completely hidden from the Jews; they have no access to Him.[5] Thus they cannot understand the witness of

---

[1] Odeberg 221f. is right here; see also p. 163 on 3.33.

[2] See p. 253f.

[3] R. Asting, Die Verkündigung des Wortes im Urchristentum 1939, 679f., believes that the witness is the voice from heaven at Jesus' baptism.

[4] V. 37b is a sentence from the source which originally followed on directly after v. 32. V. 38 is the Evangelist's own composition. Both the source and the Evangelist use the expression μένειν ἐν; it is typical for the latter to speak of the Word abiding in the hearer (5.38; 15.7; I Jn. 2.14, 24), whereas the source says that the Revealer or God abides in the believer (15.5; I Jn. 4.12, 16; for a further discussion see on 15.4). V. 38 is prose; on the picking up of the object by the demonstrative, see p. 79 n.3.

[5] On the idea of the hiddenness of God see p. 80f.—Φωνή and εἶδος, speech and form,

the works, nor do they really allow the word of God which encounters them in the Scripture to speak to them (as is shown by vv. 42 and 44)[1] and so they do not understand the witness of the Scripture. The proof of both these charges[2] lies in the fact that they do not believe in the Revealer sent by God. If the Jews really knew God, if they listened seriously to the word of Scripture, this would be shown clearly enough by their believing when God revealed himself to them. God's revelation is encountered in the works of Jesus; if one fails to believe at this point, then it is a sign that one does not know God. Whoever fails to hear *Jesus'* φωνή shows that he has never heard *God's* φωνή.[3] Thus the Jews' pretended knowledge of God is a lie (cp. 7.28; 8.19, 55; 16.3); not merely an error based on inadequate information, but guilt; for it is the consequence of their shutting the door against God. The following verses make this plain.

Vv. 39f.:

ἐραυνᾶτε τὰς γραφάς
ὅτι ὑμεῖς δοκεῖτε ἐν αὐταῖς ζωὴν αἰώνιον ἔχειν.
[καὶ ἐκεῖναί εἰσιν αἱ μαρτυροῦσαι περὶ ἐμοῦ]
καὶ οὐ θέλετε ἐλθεῖν πρός με
ἵνα ζωὴν ἔχητε.[4]

The world's resistance to God is based on its imagined security, which reaches its highest and most subversive form in religion and thus,

---

constitute a person, in so far as he is perceptible to others (naturally φωνή has nothing to do with בַּת קוֹל, see Odeberg 222f.); cp. Lohmeyer on Rev. 13.11 (Hdb. zum NT).—There is no contradiction between the statement οὔτε φωνὴν αὐτοῦ πώποτε ἀκ. and the fact that God spoke to Israel on Sinai, so there is no need to try and find a way out by suggesting that the Evangelist ascribed the voice on Sinai to the angels (Schl.); for Israel may well have "heard" God's voice—but it has not heard in the true sense (see p. 259). The same could be said with regard to the prophetic words of the OT.

[1] Καί v. 38 is coordinating and not antithetical ("and yet" Br.); see Bl.-D. para. 445, 4. Μένειν in John normally refers not to the future state of that which exists in the present, but to the present state of what is past. The relationship expressed by μένειν ἐν is the relationship of trust, and naturally what is meant here is that the Jews are not faithful to the Scriptures, that they do not listen to it seriously; cp. v. 42.

[2] Ὅτι v. 38 gives the epistemological rather than the ontological ground for the preceding clause; the logic can be seen clearly in 8.19.—Ὑμεῖς is no more stressed than in vv. 39, 44; Chrys. omits it in each of the three verses.

[3] Odeberg 223f. rightly points out the connection between vv. 37f. and vv. 24f.

[4] In vv. 39f. Becker 73 wants to attribute to the source only: ἐρευνᾶτε τὰς γραφὰς καὶ οὐ θέλετε ἐλθεῖν πρός με.
A variant of vv. 39f. is to be found in Pap. Egerton (Bell and Skeat, Fragments of an Unknown Gospel 1955; see also H. J. Bell, ZNW 37 [1938], 10–13):

ἐραυ
‹νατε τ›ας γραφας. εν αις υμεις δο
‹κειτε› ζωην εχειν εκειναι ει‹σ›ιν
‹αι μαρτ›υρουσαι περι εμου.

for the Jews in their pattern of life based on Scripture. Their "searching" in the Scriptures makes them deaf to Jesus' word.[1] Appropriately, seeing that the Jews' began their attack on Jesus by accusing him of breaking the law (5.16), ἐραυνᾶν here refers not to the study of prophecy but to the study of the law, which determined the Jews' attitude to life, as is also shown by the reference to Moses in vv. 45f. Only in this way can one see why they should be reproached for thinking that they "possess eternal life" in the Scriptures.[2] For it is precisely this attitude which lies behind their rejection of Jesus,[3] as was shown by 5.1–18. As understood by the source, this sentence is a rejection of the Jewish religion in toto. The Evangelist has added the parenthesis, (corresponding to vv. 37a, 38a) "and it is they that bear witness to me", thus expanding the source in the same sense as he does in vv. 45–47. In this way the accusation is heightened; for it is in the Scriptures that the λόγος of God speaks, and so through them men had the possibility of being open to the revelation. For in the Scriptures the command of God is heard, and through them man's poverty is revealed to him. The Jews have perverted their meaning and believe that they—the blind—can see (9.41).[4]

ii. *The* δόξα: 5.41–47; 7.15–24

As we might expect from the close relation between the concepts of μαρτυρία and δόξα,[5] the concept of δόξα[6] is now taken as the subject

---

Black 55 suspects that the fragment is independent of John, and that it goes back to an extra-canonical collection of dominical sayings; on his view the texts of the fragment and of Jn. 5.39f. would be different translations of a saying which was originally handed down in Aramaic. M. E. Boismard, RB 55 (1948), 5–34 takes a similar view. Barr. is however sceptical of this. If the analysis which we have given above is correct, then the dependence of the fragment on Jn 5.39f. is proved.

[1] If for no other reason than that it corresponds to καὶ οὐ θέλετε, ἐραυνᾶτε must be taken as indicative and not imperative. This is is howi t is taken by Wik., Dodd (329.1), Barr. and Dupont (206); also by the Zürcher Bibel and the RSV. 'Ερauνᾶν (Hellenistic instead of ἐρευνᾶν Bl.-D. para. 30, 4) also occurs frequently in Philo in this sense, and corresponds to the Rabbinic דָּרַשׁ for the study and expounding of the Scriptures and for the doctrine based on this, see Schl. ad loc. and Str.-B. II 467.

[2] This corresponds to the Rabbinic statements that eternal life is given to Israel in the Torah, see Schl. ad loc. and Str.-B. II 467; III 129ff. Cp. Schlatter, Der Glaube im NT 4. ed. 50 (on Jn. 5.39): "This gives precise expression to the view of Akiba." On the unstressed ὑμεῖς see p. 267 n.2; δοκεῖν of false opinions, as v. 45; 11.13, 31; 13.39; 16.2; 20.15.

[3] On "coming" to Jesus see p. 227 n.3 and on 7.37.

[4] It is fundamentally the same objection that Paul makes to the Jews, Rom. 10.3 (cp. II Cor. 3.14 and Jer. 8.8ff.). John admittedly takes this a stage further, for he will not even allow the Jewish ζῆλος θεοῦ. It is, of course, incorrect to say that the Johannine Jesus accuses the Jews of hypocrisy in the sense of Is. 29.13 or Mk. 7.6f., as is suggested by C. K. Barrett. The latter would like to show that although the OT quotations of the Synoptics have as such disappeared in John, their effect is nevertheless still to be perceived (JTS 48, 1947, 155–169).

[5] See p. 262.

[6] It is obvious that δόξα here means "honour". In effect Jesus' "honour" (his

of the accusation. The men who demand a proof of Jesus' authority reveal their resistance to God by their conception of glory. Jesus expresses his opposition to their attitude in the first sentence:

v. 41: δόξαν παρὰ ἀνθρώπων οὐ λαμβάνω.

To give a proof of his authority would be to receive δόξα from men. In this way he would make himself dependent on them and would enter into their world. The second sentence tells what kind of a world this is:

v. 42: ἀλλὰ ἔγνωκα ὑμᾶς,
ὅτι τὴν ἀγάπην τοῦ θεοῦ οὐκ ἔχετε ἐν ἑαυτοῖς.[1]

Their stand-point is the very opposite of Jesus'—for this is what in the context must be implied by the reproach that they do not have the ἀγάπη τοῦ θεοῦ within them. Moreover since in v. 44 their stand-point is described as one in which the honour given by God appears irrelevant to them, ἀγάπην τ. θ. μὴ ἔχειν must refer to the exclusion of God from their life; they have no interest in him.[2] The reproach runs parallel to that in v. 38. Just as the Jews have not the word of God abiding in them, so too they have not the love of God in them (the possibility of which was opened up to them by the word of Scripture).[3] And as they falsely imagine themselves to be true to the Scriptures, they naturally suppose that they love God. The one however is as much a lie as the other.

Jesus has *seen* this.[4] However this does not refer to the supernatural knowledge of men's souls which Jesus has as the θεῖος ἀνήρ—for the Evangelist this is at most of symbolic importance.[5] Rather what

---

recognition as the Revealer) is no different from the "glory" which is given to him by the Father (see on 8.49f., 54 and esp. on 17.1). However the Evangelist plays on both meanings of the word, and it is not possible to equate the *literal meaning* of δόξα 5.41, 44 with that of 1.14 etc. (see p. 67 n.2), as does D. Faulhaber, Das Joh-Evg und die Kirche 22f.

[1] The formal correspondence between v. 41 and v. 42 is not strong; the Evangelist must have altered the phrasing of the source in v. 42 in order to bring it in line with v. 38.

[2] Thus the genitive τ. θεοῦ must be an objective genitive. This is also suggested by the material parallel in 3.19, where men are said to love the darkness more than the light. Since, however, the "light" is the revelation of God's love to the world (3.16), and since man's love for God corresponds to God's love for man (cp. I Jn. 4.7ff., esp. vv. 10,16), it actually makes no difference whether one takes τ. θεοῦ as an objective or subjective genitive or whether one believes that there is an intentional ambiguity here. It is, however, impermissible to take the subjective genitive to refer to God's love for men, which is active in Jesus and makes him heal the lame man (Zn.), and to take v. 42 as meaning that love of this kind is not present in his hearers. The context does not allow this kind of interpretation.

[3] Ἔχειν ἐν ἑαυτῷ distinguishes serious love of God from mere pretended love of him, cp. v. 38.

[4] Ὅτι v. 42 is explicative. Ὑμᾶς after ἔγνωκα corresponds to Semitic usage, see Schl. on Mt. 25.24.

[5] See p. 104.

is meant here is that man's resistance to God, of which man himself is unaware, is thrown into relief by the light of the revelation, inasmuch as men reject the claim of the Revealer. This is stated in v. 43:

ἐγὼ ἐλήλυθα ἐν τῷ ὀνόματι τοῦ πατρός μου,
καὶ οὐ λαμβάνετέ με·
ἐὰν ἄλλος ἔλθῃ ἐν τῷ ὀνόματι τῷ ἰδίῳ,
ἐκεῖνον λήμψεσθε.

Since they are not open to God they are unable to recognise[1] the one who comes in the "name", i.e. on the behalf of, God.[2] On the other hand they will unhesitatingly accept the man who comes on his own authority. Why? Because in him they hear only themselves speaking! For whoever comes on his own behalf or—which is the same—whoever speaks on his own authority (7.18) seeks his own honour (7.18); but this means that he makes himself dependent on those to whom he speaks. A man like this finds recognition from the world; for the world loves what is its "own" (15.19). Being deaf to the true authority which speaks to it from beyond, the world receives its punishment in its subjection to those leaders (*Führer*) who have no real authority at all, but who give expression only to their own leanings and desires. "To come on one's own behalf", "to speak on one's own authority" is synonymous with ἐκ τῆς γῆς, ἐκ τοῦ κόσμου λαλεῖν (3.31; I Jn. 4.5). This, moreover, is grounded in an εἶναι ἐκ τῆς γῆς, ἐκ τοῦ κόσμου (3.31; I Jn. 4.5), ἐκ τῶν κάτω (8.23). This, however, means that in such alleged authority it is only the world which speaks to itself, it falls a prey to itself. And consequently it becomes the cause of its own destruction; for it is the devil which speaks when the world speaks to itself, the devil whose children the "Jews" are, and whose desires they realise, while the message of Jesus sounds untrustworthy to their ears because it is the truth (8.44f.).

It is very possible that in the source ἄλλος meant the devil (or the Antichrist),[3] and that the Evangelist also refers to him here, as he does expressly in 8.41ff. If this is the case then he clearly thinks of him as embodied in historical personages, in pseudo-messiahs and false teachers.[4]

---

[1] On the untypically Greek use of λαμβάνειν see p. 57 n.2. On "coming" see p. 50 n.3.

[2] Ἐν τ. ὀνόματι originally means "while naming (or calling on) the name" (see W. Heitmüller, Im Namen Jesu 1903), but it can also take on the meaning of "while appealing to", "on behalf of", see Heitmüller op. cit. 85f.; cp. also O. Grether, Name und Wort Gottes im AT 1934, 23f.

[3] As did the Early Church (see Br.) and also Odeberg 226.

[4] Cp. p. 162 n.2 on 3.31.—It is not necessary to assume that the Evangelist was thinking of particular historical personages, and in any case there is certainly no need to assume that he was thinking of Bar-Kochba (his rising 132–135). For the "Unknown Gospel",

The caustic question in **v. 44** states clearly that the reason for the world's unbelief is that it has fallen a prey to itself. By gaining its security through mutual recognition it shuts itself off from God:

> πῶς δύνασθε ὑμεῖς πιστεῦσαι,
> δόξαν παρ' ἀλλήλων λαμβάνοντες
> καὶ τὴν δόξαν τὴν παρὰ τοῦ μόνου θεοῦ οὐ ζητεῖτε;[1]

They cannot "believe"—that is, of course, in him, the Revealer; but to believe in *him* means to believe absolutely; for in him alone is God encountered. They are incapable of this because they receive "honour" from one another; i.e., they accept each other and thus achieve their security by satisfying their need for acceptance, which security, however, is challenged by the Revealer.

The reproach that they spurn the δόξα given by God contains the idea that man is insecure and that by nature he seeks δόξα, recognition. In this he is certainly looking for the right thing, but in attempting, as he does in every sphere,[2] to provide the answers himself, he perverts the truth into a lie. He loses sight of the fact that his *whole* existence—as a creature— is in question, and that the only authority from which he should seek recognition and in which he could find acceptance is the one God himself.[3] To ask for the δόξα which God gives would be to recognise the insecurity of worldly existence and to abandon the attempt to manufacture one's security for oneself. For this reason the question about the δόξα which God gives is also the question about the δόξα which is due to God (cp. 7.18). Only he who accepts God will be accepted of God. This is the double claim made by the revelation in Jesus:

---

whose fragments have been edited from papyri by H. Idris Bell and T. C. Skeat 1935, and above all the fragment of the Fourth Gospel, published by C. H. Roberts in 1935, show that the Gospel must have been known in Egypt about 100.

[1] If in the source v. 44, as seems probable, formed the conclusion of a discourse, this would explain the irregular third line (see p. 76 n.4). Becker however believes that the third line is the Evangelist's own composition. Burney 96 wants to ascribe the incorrect co-ordination of participle and finite verb (Bl.-D. para. 468, 3) to the original Aramaic text.

[2] See pp. 52, 69, 181f., 222, 230.

[3] θεοῦ after μόνου is omitted by B a b sa bo and some of the Fathers, but is indispensable. The omission is perhaps due to a misreading of the spelling ΜΟΝΟΘΥΥΟΥ (Bd.).—The description of God as μόνος is common in the OT and in Judaism (see Br. Schl. ad. loc. and Wie sprach Jos. von Gott? 9.16; for Philo see Leisegang, Index). It was equally common in Primitive Christianity: Rom. 16.27; I Tim. 1.16; 6.15f.; Jude 14.25 I Clem. 43.6; II Clem. 20.5 etc. For Classical antiquity: E. Norden, Agnostos Theos 1913, 245, 1; in Byzantine acclamations: E. Peterson, Εἷς θεός 1928, 134, 196, 256, 3.—This stereotyped use also occurs in Jn. 17.3, but not here, where the contrast to the μόνος is provided, not by the many gods of polytheism but by the παρ' ἀλλήλων. God as the One is contrasted with the multiplicity of human relationships. The one thing that matters is to listen to the voice of the one God, and not to bother oneself about satisfying the many demands made by men, as required by the δόξαν παρ' ἀλλ. λαμβ.

he who honours him, honours the Father (v. 23). He who refuses to abandon his this-worldly security and recognition cannot believe.[1]

For the source, and indeed for the Evangelist in so far as for him the "Jews" represent the "world", δόξαν παρ' ἀλλήλων λαμβάνειν refers to the general disposition of mankind; but in the Jewish sphere the phrase has a particular meaning, in that here the misunderstanding of the law provides man with an opportunity of creating this area of security. Therefore because this security based on Moses leads to the rejection of Jesus' claim, vv. **45–47** demonstrate the falsehood of this security by appeal to Moses.[2] There is no need for Jesus himself to take on the role of the accuser; for even in their own sphere where they believe that they have life (v. 39) there is one who accuses them,[3] and this is Moses, in whom they have put their hope:[4] The attack is all the stronger in that it manifestly refers to the fact that the Jews regarded Moses as their "spokesman", as their paraclete;[5] whereas in truth he is their accuser.[6] They have indeed "hoped" in him, but they have not "believed" him.[7] The evidence for this (vv. 46b, 47) is that they now do not believe the words of Jesus. For Moses "wrote about him", and had they been open to the words of Moses they would also have been open to the words of Jesus.[8]

---

[1] The attack is directed against man's need for recognition and the security which he creates for himself, and not specifically against the sins of ambition. This is only one particular form of that general human disposition. Thus there is no parallel here to the exhortations to humility and the warnings against ambition found in Mk. 10.42–45 parr.; Mt. 23.6–12 etc., and also in Jewish literature (Str.-B. I 192ff., 917f.; II 553). The same view as in Jn. 5.44 of the relation of one's own honour to God's honour is given in Seder Elij R. 14 (65): "If any one increases God's honour, then both God's honour and his own honour will be increased; but if anyone decreases God's honour and increases his own, then God's honour remains as it was and his own honour is diminished."—It would be wrong to draw a sharp contrast between John and the Rabbinic exhortations to honour the learned and their discussions about the limitations of the honour shown to teachers in relation to honour shown to God, and their discussions about whether a teacher might dispense with the honour shown to him (Str.-B. II 553–556). Nor can one draw any strict contrast between John and general exhortations to respect other men's honour. The Johannine idea lies at a deeper level; it is directed against men's acceptance of others' recognition of them, by which the world shuts itself off from God. Modesty can also come under the heading of δόξαν παρ' ἀλλήλων λαμβάνειν.

[2] The Pap. Egerton (see on p. 267) has, immediately after the fragment mentioned in the discussion of vv. 39f., a variant of v. 45 in which ἦλθον κατηγορῆσαι replaces κατηγορήσω and a μου is added to τὸν πατέρα.

[3] Ἔστιν ὁ κατηγ. ὑμ. Μ. = "he who accuses (article!) you is present; it is Moses".—This must, of course, be taken in the sense of vv. 38f.; there is no trace here of the mythological idea that Moses now stands in heaven and accuses them before God.

[4] On ἐλπίζειν εἰς cp. Barn. 16, 1.—Vv. 45–47, like v. 39b (see p. 267), are the result of an expansion of the source by the Evangelist. The source did not appeal to Moses.

[5] Str.-B. II 561.

[6] The concepts κατήγορος and παράκλητος had been taken into Rabbinic Hebrew as borrowed words Str.-B. II 560.

[7] On πιστεύειν with the dative see p. 252 n.2.

[8] It can hardly be that the distinction between γράμματα and ῥήματα is stressed

The idea, then, is the same as in vv. 38f. It would be wrong to think of Moses' writings about Jesus as consisting primarily in the Messianic prophecies; it is much more a question of the characteristically Mosaic writings, the Law.[1] This is also in accordance with the occasion of the discourse, namely the conflict over the Sabbath. For this illustrates just how the "Jews hope" in Moses: the law opens up to them the possibility of δόξαν παρ' ἀλλήλων λαμβ. and thereby makes it possible for them to imagine that they are secure, whereas in reality the law is intended to make them aware of God's command and at the same time of their dependence on the δόξα which God gives. This is shown also by the following dialogue (7.19–24).

The Jews reject this appeal to Moses as presumption (**7.15**).[2] How can Jesus appeal to the Scriptures! He has not made a proper study of them! He does not belong to the guild of the Scribes.[3] Jesus' reply has the same force as his remarks in 5.19, 30:

V. 16

ἡ ἐμὴ διδαχὴ οὐκ ἔστιν ἐμὴ
ἀλλὰ τοῦ πέμψαντός με.[4]

That is to say that they are right. His doctrine is not the result of study; it is not the product of a closed and limited science. But then he is in no sense responsible for his doctrine, for it has been given to him by the Father.[5] In the ears of his audience this must sound like

---

(Schl. ad loc. and Der Glaube im NT 4. ed. 201f.). Indeed perhaps the reason why Jesus' words are called ῥήματα here, and not λόγοι, is to stress what the words of Moses and Jesus have in common. For the νόμοι can be referred to specifically as ῥήματα (R. Hirzel, Ἄγραφος νόμος, Abh. d. Königl. Sächs. Ges. d. Wiss. XX 1, 1900, p. 73,1), cp. the famous epigram on Thermopylae: ὅτι τῇδε κείμεθα τοῖς κείνων ῥήμασι πειθόμενοι.

[1] This is also the view held by Hosk.

[2] Θαυμάζειν here = "to be surprised", cp. 7.21; Mk. 6.6; Eccles. 5.7; Ecclus. 11.21; this is good Greek, see esp. Aesch. Ag. 1399: θαυμάζομέν σου γλῶσσαν, ὡς θρασύστομος.

[3] Γράμματα εἰδέναι (ἐπίστασθαι), according to a wide-spread usage, means to have been educated at school, and refers in the first place to the elementary instruction in reading and writing (see Wetst. and Br.). Since, however, literary texts (in Judaism, the OT) were used in this instruction γραμμ. εἰδ, can refer to education in general, in the same way that ἀγράμματος means not only an illiterate person but an uneducated one as well (Acts 4.13, which is good Greek). Cp. Vit. Aes.: οὗτος ὁ σαπρὸς γράμματα οἶδεν;—Since there is no article the meaning is not: "How can this man understand the Scriptures?" However in Judaism instruction at school is, in effect, instruction in the Scriptures, so that "to be educated" and "to know the Scriptures" come to mean the same thing, in the same way that in Judaism γραμματεύς means one learned in the Scriptures, and not as in Greek usage a writer (secretary).

[4] Jesus' words in vv. 16–18 were most probably taken from the source; if they belonged to the section used in 5.19ff., their original place might have been before δόξαν παρὰ ἀνθρ. κτλ. 5.40.

[5] The motif here is mythological, see p. 165 n.1, and not the idea of the θεῖος ἀνήρ who has knowledge without ever having learnt it (L. Bieler, Θεῖος Ἀνήρ I, 35).

a bald and presumptuous statement; yet there is no other way for the word of revelation to "prove'' its authority; it must risk being misinterpreted as mere presumption. There is only *one* proof of his authority:

V. 17:

ἐάν τις θέλῃ τὸ θέλημα αὐτοῦ ποιεῖν,
γνώσεται περὶ τῆς διδαχῆς,
πότερον ἐκ τοῦ θεοῦ ἐστιν,
ἢ ἐγὼ ἀπ' ἐμαυτοῦ λαλῶ.[1]

Only the man who hears the challenge of the Revealer's word and obeys it, i.e. the believer, will be able to judge[2] whether it is the Word of God or the assertion of an arrogant man.[3] For ποιεῖν τὸ θέλημα αὐτοῦ means no more nor less than believing. There is a popular but nonetheless crude misunderstanding of v. 17 which suggests that it wants to make the way to faith easier by advising that a man should first take seriously the ethical demands, which are universally evident, and that this will lead him on to an understanding of the dogmatic teaching.[4] For John there is no "ethics", no doing of the will of God.[5] which is not primarily the obedience of faith; it is the action demanded by God (cp. 6.29). Admittedly for John there are no "dogmatics" without "ethics"; but the love which is demanded of men grows out of faith and cannot exist without it.[6] The consequence of faith is the work of love, because faith is not abstract speculation (neither of course is it the blind acceptance of dogma), but it is the answer to the challenge which is issued in Jesus' word. This answer is the work demanded of man; and faith receives the promise that its object will disclose itself to faith[7].

---

[1] The saying, with its positive formulation and promissory future (γνώσεται) strikes a note of invitation, like many of the revelation sayings (cp. 7.37; 8.12; Od. Sal. 33.6ff. etc.). It is only in the context here that it gains its polemical character.

[2] On γινώσκειν περί see Bl.-D. para. 229.

[3] Of course διδαχή has the same meaning as λόγος and ῥήματα elsewhere. Admittedly διδαχή occurs only here and in 18.19 (cp. II Jn. 9f.), but there are several references to Jesus' διδάσκειν 6.59; 7.14, 28; 8.20. The word is appropriate here as an answer to the Jewish objection v. 15; for to Jewish ears Jesus' proclamation must sound like διδαχή (cp. 18.19). The source probably had "my word(s)", and the Evangelist then substituted "my teaching" because of the context.

[4] So too Hirsch: "The conscience which lies in his (God's) power creates in us a mute state of preparation for God's will and activity; this is the way to Jesus." Doubtless there is a measure of truth in this, but it is not the meaning of Jn. 7.17. M. Dibelius, Geschichte der urchristl. Lit. I 1926, 77, believes that Jesus' διδαχή contains an allusion to the Sermon on the Mount.—W. Wrede, Messiasgeheimnis 201, 3; Charakter u. Tendenz des Joh-Evg. 3 is right here.

[5] See p. 194. n 3.

[6] See on 13.34f.; 15.1ff.

[7] See p. 163.

Such seeing faith is the "work" to which the Revealer bears witness.[1]

V. 18 returns again to the key-word of 5.41ff., δόξα:

> ὁ ἀφ' ἑαυτοῦ λαλῶν
> τὴν δόξαν τὴν ἰδίαν ζητεῖ.
> ὁ δέ ζητῶν τὴν δόξαν τοῦ πέμψαντος αὐτόν,
> οὗτος ἀληθής ἐστιν
> [καὶ ἀδικία ἐν αὐτῷ οὐκ ἐστιν.][2]

In a series of maxims[3] the man who seeks the δόξα of his master is contrasted with the man who is concerned with his own δόξα. Obviously this is intended to apply to the Revealer. But is v. 18, when taken together with v. 17, intended as an aid to the man who inquires after the truth of Jesus' doctrine, pointing him to the convincing "unselfishness of Jesus and the Christian preachers, as opposed to the obvious thirst for honour of the Jewish teachers"?[4] By no means! For in the first place the "thirst for honour" on the part of the Jewish teachers is not obvious; rather it is the desire for recognition, which is natural to man, which he may well be unaware of, and which becomes apparent only in the light of the revelation.[5] Secondly, it is by no means apparent that the Revealer is "unselfish"; rather he is always giving rise to the misunderstanding that he is seeking his own δόξα. Only faith can overcome this misunderstanding and see that Jesus does not "speak on his own authority" (v. 17).

Admittedly v. 18 gives us the criteria for recognising the Revealer as such. The two statements in v. 18 contain, in antithetical form, a deduction. If it is true that the man who speaks on his own authority seeks his own honour—and all will agree to this—then it must be true that he who seeks the honour of his master does not speak on his own authority, and that his words are true[6]—and all would agree to that too. They would also admit its application to the Revealer, namely, that it shows him to be the sort of man who seeks the honour of the one who sent him. But faith alone can see whether this criterion applies in the particular instance, whether, that is, it applies here to Jesus. In other

---

[1] See p. 266.

[2] Since the Semitic original would have been briefer, the four lines here probably represent a couplet in the source, particularly since οὗτος should be ascribed to the Evangelist (see p. 79 n. 3. The last line (καὶ ἀδ. κτλ.) destroys the rhythm, and is the Evangelist's addition which prepares the way for vv. 19–24. Becker 76 also believes that the last line was added by the Evangelist.

[3] The article in v. 18 is in both cases generic. The way it is phrased leaves open the question whether the principle could, in fact, be applied to others apart from Jesus.

[4] Htm.

[5] See pp. 268., 271 n. 2.

[6] 'Αληθής here, of course, means "true", "veracious".

words v. 18, on the lips of Jesus is simply a challenge to men to accept him as the true Revealer.

The Evangelist adds: καὶ ἀδικία ἐν αὐτῷ οὐκ ἔστιν,[1] and so, by means of the ambiguity of ἀδικία, he manages to link up vv. 15ff. with vv. 19-24. For, when contrasted with ἀληθής, ἀδικία has the specific meaning of "lie, deceit".[2] Yet at the same time it has the general meaning of "wrongdoing". The Revealer is "true", because his words are spoken solely on behalf of him who sent him, and so cannot be influenced by personal motives. Moreover, since his actions are entirely determined by his commission, no one can accuse him of "wrongdoing",[3] as the Jews have done.

7.19–24, as it were, tackle the Jews on their own ground and show that Moses is their accuser, as was said in 5.45–47. Jesus' breaking of the Sabbath was the occasion of their attack on him, and in this they believe that they are acting out of regard for the law. But this is a delusion, for Moses, their acknowledged authority, speaks not for them but rather for Jesus. This idea emerges clearly enough, but the detail of the argument is complicated and obscure. The reason for this is obviously that the Evangelist has here taken and expanded the original conclusion of the healing narrative used in 5.1–18.

The line of the argument in **v. 23** is clear. If the Sabbath may be broken in order to circumcise someone in compliance with the Mosaic law,[4] it is surely entirely in accord with Moses' intention to break it to heal the whole man. This is a typically Rabbinic argument, both with regard to the inference a minori ad maius[5] and to its application to a specific case.[6] It must necessarily be taken together with the statement in the

---

[1] The phrase is typically OT (II Sam. 14.32; Ps. 91.16) and Jewish (Schl.).

[2] Ἄδικος and ἀδικία in the LXX are used frequently (for שֶׁקֶר) in the sense of "liar", "lie", see ThWB I 152, 20.29ff.; 154,13ff.; also in the NT, see Lk. 16.11: ἐν τ. ἀδίκῳ μαμωνᾷ—τὸ ἀληθινόν. The ambiguity is all the easier to understand when one remembers that "lie", as used in the OT and NT, means not only subjective untruthfulness but also objective worthlessness, "deception" in the sense of "appearance". When used in antithesis to this, "truth" comes to mean also what is genuine and right, so that the distinction between ἀλήθεια and ἀδικία is full of subtle differences of meaning, see ThWB I 156, 8ff.: 243, 6ff.; see also on 3.21 p. 157 n. 6.

[3] There is no question here of a moral judgement on the ethical person of Jesus. For the Revealer is above such judgements; see on 8.46.

[4] On λύειν τ. νόμον see p. 244 n. 2.

[5] On the Rabbinic argument קַל וָחוֹמֶר (light and heavy) see Str.-B. III 223–226.

[6] Yoma 85b: "If circumcision, which concerns one of the 248 members of the man, can displace the Sabbath, how much more must the whole body (if his life be in danger) displace the Sabbath!" (in Schl. and Str.-B. ad loc., see also Br., who draws attention to a related form of argument in Justin Dial. 27).

preceding **v. 22**: "Moses gave you circumcision,[1] and (consequently) you circumcise a man on the Sabbath."[2] We should also take with it the question in **v. 19**, which forms a link with the statement from the source[3] found in 5.16–18. The question: τί με ζητεῖτε ἀποκτεῖναι; introduces the argument in a way typical of this style of dispute.[4] Yet the original continuation of this question, which prepared the way for v. 22, is clearly provided by the words in **v. 21**: ἓν ἔργον ἐποίησα καὶ πάντες θαυμάζετε διὰ τοῦτο. For here there is a clear contrast between the "one work" (Jesus' breaking of the Sabbath)[5] and the continual breaking of the Sabbath by circumcision (v. 23). How can the Jews take offence at Jesus' *one* work,[6] when they themselves continually break the Sabbath in order to circumcise people?[7]

This clear line of argument has been confused by the Evangelist's treatment because, as a consequence of 5.45–47, he wants to portray the Jews as transgressors of the Mosaic Law. This explains firstly the rhetorical question in **v. 19**: "Did not Moses give you the law?",[8] which prepares the way for the accusation, "Yet none of you keeps the law!"[9] How then can they want to kill Jesus because he breaks the Sabbath? The enormity of their intention to kill Jesus is underlined by the crowd's remark (**v. 20**), which is of no importance for the argument. The ὄχλος,[10] which is distinguished from the 'Ιουδαῖοι (5.15) and is ignorant of the latter's intention, refuses to believe Jesus' words.[11] Jesus' reply (**v. 21**) ignores this and returns to the subject under discussion,

---

[1] Διδόναι and (v. 23) λαμβάνειν τ. περιτομήν is Rabbinic usage, see Schl.

[2] On the practice of circumcising on the Sabbath see Str.-B. ad loc.

[3] See p. 238.

[4] Cp. Mk. 2.8; 3.4 and Gesch. der synopt. Tr. 42 = Hist. of the Syn. Trad. 41.

[5] Ἔργον refers to Jesus' deed, not as a miraculous deed, but as a "work" which breaks the Sabbath (so rightly Bd.).

[6] On θαυμάζειν see p. 273 n. 2.

[7] Διὰ τοῦτο, with which v. 22 begins (omitted by ℵ*), should probably be taken with the preceding θαυμ. If one takes it with what follows, then we have the elliptical expression, "Therefore I say to you ..." (cp. Hos. 2.14). Hoskyns takes it to mean "For this cause", namely, that the circumcision should be a type and anticipation of Jesus' healing ministry, which equally breaks the Sabbath.

[8] On διδόναι νόμον see p. 79 n. 1.

[9] Τὸν νόμον ποιεῖν corresponds to the Rabbinic עָשָׂה הַתּוֹרָה (Schl.); in Greek we find ποιεῖν τὰ δέοντα, τὰ δίκαια, τὰ τοῖς θεοῖς νομιζόμενα (BGU 1197, 21).—The reproach is clearly intended in a quite general sense, and does not refer specifically to the breach of the Sabbath mentioned in v. 23.

[10] The same distinction is made in 7.12; see p. 86.

[11] Δαιμόνιον ἔχειν refers to possession by spirits (as in 8.48f. 52; 10.20; Mt. 11.18; Lk. 7.33; 8.27; cp. Mk. 3.22, 30; 7.25; Lk. 4.33; 13.11; Acts 8.7; 19.13) and is the Hellenistic expression, whereas Semitic usage constructs the formula with ἐν (ב), cp. Lk. 4.33 with Mk. 1.23; Lk. 8.27 with Mk. 5.2. Mk. 3.22 has both formulae together. Cp. Iren. I 13.3: δαίμονά τινα πάρεδρον ἔχειν.—In Jn. 7.20 the expression has been watered down, "You are mad!". Not so 8.48, which see.

taking up the thread of the argument as it was in the source:[1] How can the Jews condemn Jesus for *one* breach of the Sabbath? Moses ordained circumcision (which is admittedly described in a note[2] as being not really Mosaic)[3] and in complying with it they break the Sabbath. How then dare they condemn Jesus? For this would be superficial (κατ' ὄψιν[4]) judgement, and the men who set themselves up as judges over Jesus need to be told to "judge with right judgement" (v. 24).[5]

There is only one way in which we can attach any meaning to this confused speech, in which the Jews are accused on the one hand of breaking the Mosaic law (v. 19) and on the other of breaking the Sabbath in compliance with the Mosaic law (v. 23). It must mean that the Jews break the Mosaic law, because, even though they act in compliance with the law of circumcision, they fail to ask what Moses' real intention was. Thus the very people who believe that they have security in the law, are made aware of their insecurity. And since in their deluded security they make the wrong decision, Moses becomes their accuser.

3) *Conclusion:* μαρτυρία *and* κρίσις*:* 8.13–20[6]

8.13–20 form the real conclusion to the whole complex of 5.1ff. For here the theme of the μαρτυρία, which dominated the discussion from 5.31 onwards, is combined with the theme of 5.19–30, the theme of κρίσις. And now a final explanation of the paradoxical nature of the Revealer's κρίνειν and μαρτυρεῖν is given, when it is asserted that Jesus does not judge and that his self-witness is true, both of which statements outwardly contradict what has been said before. Thus it is maintained that he judges, and that he does not judge; that he does not bear witness to himself, and that he does bear witness to himself; that he does both and he does neither—depending on how one understands the concepts of judging and bearing witness. The phrasing of the parallel verses 8.14 and 16, "Even if . . .", indicates that it is a question of looking at the matter from the correct point of view.

---

[1] One might almost be led to think that vv. 20, 21a come from the editor, who put 7.15–24 in its present position. V. 22b (ἓν ἔργον ἐποίησα) would certainly follow on better after v. 19.

[2] The note is typical of the Evangelist, see p. 232 n. 3.

[3] The law of circumcision comes, according to Gen. 17.10; 21.4, from the time of the πατέρες, the Patriarchs (see Rom. 9.5 and Schl. ad loc.), even though it appears in the Mosaic law (Lev. 12.3).—The note is clearly of only academic interest, for it is of no importance in this context and only disturbs the line of the argument.

[4] Ὄψις here means not "face" (as in 11.44; Rev. 1.16) but the external appearance, as often; cp. Lysias. or 16, 19 p. 147: ὥστε οὐκ ἄξιον ἀπ' ὄψεως . . . οὔτε φιλεῖν οὔτε μισεῖν οὐδένα, ἀλλ' ἐκ τῶν ἔργων σκοπεῖν.

[5] Cp. Zech 7.9: κρίμα δίκαιον κρίνατε.

[6] See p. 239.

There is a close connection here with what has gone before. The opponents[1] make the formally quite correct statement (**v. 13**) that Jesus bears witness to himself. If we call to mind what was said in 7.16–18, this objection brings out clearly the nature of the word of revelation; it can only be self-witness; for it would no longer be God's Word if it demanded other authorities recognised by men to confirm its authenticity.[2] Its opponents naturally think of it as the word of man, and are therefore bound to contest its veracity.[3]

By contrast Jesus can only insist that his word is true precisely as witness to himself, **v. 14a**:

κἂν ἐγὼ μαρτυρῶ περὶ ἐμαυτοῦ,
ἀληθής ἐστιν ἡ μαρτυρία μου.[4]

Yet although this assertion is in strict accord with the nature of the revelation, so too is the fact that outwardly it is in contradiction to 5.31.[5] Outwardly—for the self-witness there rejected was the self-witness of the man who seeks his own glory, who gives proof of his authority to others, and thus recognises their claim on him. Yet this is just how Jesus does *not* bear witness to himself. He "bears witness to himself" by making his own claim heard; and only in this way is his witness true as the word of the Revealer, which must always incur the risk of being misunderstood by the world.

The justification of this statement is given in peculiarly Johannine terms in **v. 14b**:

ὅτι οἶδα πόθεν ἦλθον καὶ ποῦ ὑπάγω·
ὑμεῖς δὲ οὐκ οἴδατε πόθεν ἔρχομαι ἢ ποῦ ὑπάγω.[6]

---

[1] As distinct from the ὄχλος (7.20; cp. 7.12, 31f., 40, 43, 49) the opponents are referred to indifferently as Ἰουδαῖοι (5.15; 7.13; 9.22) or Φαρισαῖοι (here as in 7.32, 47; 9.13 etc.); cp. esp. 4.1 with 7.1.

[2] Calvin: quod in propria causa quisque suspectus est et legibus cautum est, ne cui in rem suam credatur, id in filio Dei qui supra totum mundum eminet, locum non habere.

[3] See p. 263 n. 5.

[4] V. 14 must come in its entirety from the revelation-discourses, in particular from the section used in 5.19ff. The section of the source used in vv. 14,16,19 may well have followed on directly after the section used in 5.42–44. Becker 78 believes that both vv. 15 and 16 have been added by the Evangelist to the source.

[5] κἂν which refers back to 5.31 is intended in the sense of "Even if from another point of view (namely on another understanding of self-witness) I bear witness to myself."—Zahn's explanation of the outward contradiction, namely that Jesus was only contradicting himself in the same way that any clever and witty person might do in the heat of debate, completely destroys the sense of the contradiction, which springs from the very nature of the revelation. Jesus is speaking neither as privatus quispiam ex communi hominum grege (Calvin), nor as a "clever and witty" person.

[6] On the alternation of καί and ἤ (whereas ℵ al have καί) see Bl.-D. para. 446; ἤ approximates to a copulative meaning.—The second line is missing in Origen, clearly as a result of the homoioteleuton.

The self-witness of the Revealer is true because he knows where he comes from and where he is going. It is entirely in accord with the Gnostic view that it is his knowledge of his origin and destination which justifies this statement, and not his origin itself; for on the Gnostic view it is this knowledge which characterises the Revealer and the Gnostics whom he redeems, while for the rest of mankind the Revealer and his followers are "strangers".[1] The Evangelist can take over this Gnostic characterisation of the Revealer, because in Gnosticism the Gnostic's knowledge—however much it may have been elaborated mythologically and speculatively—was in a decisive sense a form of self-understanding, an understanding of himself both as a stranger in the world and as belonging to the divine world.[2] Thus the Revealer's appeal to his knowledge of his origin and destination is nothing more nor less than an appeal to his unity with the Father, as stated in 5.19ff. and as soon to be repeated in v. 16.

The antithesis might well have been expressed in another way: "*Your* origin and destination you do not know". Yet the way it is expressed here, "*My* origin and destination you do not know", not only indicates that man's decisive self-knowledge is dependent on his knowledge of the Revealer, but above all it shows the Revealer himself in his "estrangement" and distance from the world;[3] and it is for this reason that *his* self-witness, unlike the self-witness of other men, is true. The standards which apply to the Revealer are not the ones which apply to men; and this is true not only with regard to his μαρτυρία but also with regard to his κρίσις. And just as his gigantic claim to be the judge (5.19ff.) led into the theme of his μαρτυρία (5.31ff.), so too now the clarification of his μαρτυρεῖν leads on to a clearer definition of his κρίνειν. There is a further parallel in the argument: the assertion that he does not bear witness to himself (5.31) found its complement in the assertion that, rightly understood, he does bear witness to himself (8.14); similarly the statement that he is the judge (5.22, 27, 30) finds its complement in the statement that he judges no man (**v. 15**): ὑμεῖς κατὰ τὴν σάρκα κρίνετε, ἐγὼ κρίνω οὐδένα.[4]

---

[1] See p. 143 n. 1. References in G. P. Wetter, ZNTW 18 (1917/18), 49–63; Schlier. Relg. Unters. 141f.; Br. ad loc.; ThWB I 694, 23ff.—For the idea that the Revealer and his followers are "strangers" in the world, see ZNTW 24 (1925), 119f.; Schlier. Relg. Unters. 16f.; Jonas, Gnosis 122ff.

E. 179

[2] In Gnosis I, H. Jonas interprets the Gnostic myth as a particular understanding of the world and the self.

[3] See n. 1.

[4] Vv. 15f. seem strange after vv. 13f. (thus leading Wellh. and Sp. to assume that they are an interpolation) only if one fails to see that 8.13–20 belongs to chap. 5. Once this has been seen it is easy to understand why the motive of κρίνειν has been introduced alongside

One would like to complete ἐγὼ κρίνω οὐδένα by κατὰ τὴν σάρκα. Yet it has been purposely omitted in order to stress more clearly the main idea of the passage, namely that just as Jesus' μαρτυρία is by human standards no μαρτυρία at all, so too by human standards his judgement is no judgement. For human judgement is judgement κατὰ τὴν σάρκα. The norm of human judgement is the σάρξ; that is to say on the one hand that it is based on what man can observe and outwardly determine (κατ' ὄψιν 7.24) and on the other hand that precisely for this reason it is restricted in its judgment to the human sphere, and breaks down when applied to anything which puts this sphere in question. This is not the way that the Revealer judges, and so (cp. 3.17; 12.47) he can say that he judges no man.[1] Yet of course in a certain sense he does judge (**v. 16**):

καὶ ἐὰν κρίνω δὲ ἐγώ,
ἡ κρίσις ἡ ἐμὴ ἀληθινή ἐστιν,
ὅτι μόνος οὐκ εἰμί,
ἀλλ' ἐγὼ καὶ ὁ πέμψας με.[2]

Like his μαρτυρία, his κρίνειν is also "true", that is to say, valid.[3] This is because of his unity with the Father,[4] i.e. because his judgement is the event of revelation, as described in 3.17–21; 5.24f.

---

the motive of μαρτυρεῖν.—V. 15 must have been added by the Evangelist to the source, in which κἂν ἐγὼ μαρτυρῶ κτλ. v. 14 and καὶ ἐὰν κρίνω δὲ ἐγὼ κτλ. v. 16 stood immediately alongside each other. This is also shown by the use of the expression κατὰ τὴν σάρκα, which is probably taken from Christian usage. It occurs in the form κατὰ σάρκα (only II Cor. 11.18 perhaps has κατὰ τὴν σάρκα) in the Pauline and Deutero-Pauline literature, and often in Ignatius; also I Clem. 32.2; Diogn. 5.2.

[1] See p. 157.

[2] On the parallel between v. 16 and v. 14 see p. 280 n. 4. καὶ ἐὰν ... δὲ ἐγώ (on the word order see Bl.-D. 475, 2) as opposed to κἂν ἐγώ must be seen as a translator's variation; see following note.

[3] 'Αληθής (ℵ al) as opposed to ἀληθινή (B· D.al) must be an assimilation to v. 14. The change must go back to the translator (see previous note); in v. 16 he is influenced by the LXX (whose influence is also felt in Rev. 16.7; 19.2) in his use of ἀληθινή. In the LXX ἀληθινός is more frequently predicated of κρίσις (Is. 59.4; Dan 3.27; Tob. 3.2, 5; Test. Levi 2,3e) or of κρίμα (Ps. 18.10). The same usage is found in Judaism, see Schl. and Str.-B. ad loc. "True" in this context is equivalent to "just", and so ἀληθινή 8.16 corresponds to δικαία 7.24. Greek does not use ἀληθινός in this way, but prefers ἀληθής; cp. Soph. Oed. Tyr. 501. κρίσις ἀληθής = right judgement, and see Wetst.

[4] See pp. 151 n. 3, 244f., 248f. 5.17, 19f., also pp. 165n. 1, 194n. 3; further on 10.30. The formulation that the Son is not "alone", is not "cut off" from the Father, but is one with him, is typically Gnostic. Cp. J.B. 39, 15f.: "But I have a stay, in that I know that I am not alone"; 40, 1f.; Ginza 296, 37ff. (the "great life" speaks to the messenger):

"Be not anxious and afraid,
And say not, I am alone.
If fear overcomes thee,
We will all be with thee."

In **vv. 17f.** the Evangelist has taken the mythological statement of the unity of the Father and the Son and used it to add[1] a satirical reply which will satisfy the Jew's demand for proof of Jesus' authority. It is written[2] in the Jews' law—the distance between the Johannine Jesus and the "Jews"[3] is sharply illuminated by ἐν τῷ νόμῳ δὲ τῷ ὑμετέρῳ—that the witness of two people, if it agrees, is valid.[4] Well then, the Father's witness, which has already been given in 5.32ff., and Jesus' witness do in fact agree![5] So the Jews have certainly no right to complain indeed on the basis of their law they are really bound to accept Jesus. This idea, which was stated quite generally in 5.39ff., admittedly carries no conviction here, where it is applied to a concrete instance, for the legal requirements are met only in a highly external way, and moreover the Father's witness has itself still to be demonstrated. The sentence is in fact, not an argument at all but an expression of scorn: "The requirements of your law have been satisfied, indeed radically so, for here the two witnesses really are in unity, for the two witnesses *are* one!" This pushes the satirical treatment of Jewish legalism to its extreme. What we are taught by this law, with its rule about the two witnesses, is that God's revelation does not have to answer for itself before men, may not be subjected to man's demand for witnesses to support it; for otherwise the rule about two witnesses would have to be applied, and that is sheerly absurd.

The Jews give proof of their lack of understanding of the unity of the Father and the Son, and consequently of the meaning of the revelation, by their question (**v. 19**) "Where then is your Father?"—so that he can appear as a witness. This leads the Evangelist on to the next saying in the source:

Similarly 316, 32ff.—Further discussion in ZNTW 24 (1925), 108; Schlier. Relg. Unters 39f. Cp. too C. Herm. 12, 1: ὁ νοῦς οὐκ ἔστιν ἀποτετμημένος τῆς οὐσιότητος τοῦ θεοῦ, ἀλλ' ὥσπερ ἡπλωμένος, καθάπερ τὸ τοῦ ἡλίου φῶς cp. loc. cit. 15b; 1, 6; 11, 14. On the relationship of the human νοῦς to the θεία ψυχή Philo quod det. pot. ins. 90; cp. Gig. 23ff.

[1] Becker 78 attributes v. 18 to the source, in which, according to him, it followed on immediately after v. 14.

[2] On the formula γέγραπται cp. the Rabbinic כַּכָּתוּב (καθὼς γέγραπται) Bacher, Die exeget. Terminologie der jüd. Traditionslit. II 1905, 90f. On the lips of strangers, כָּתוּב בְּתוֹרַתְכֶם = γέγραπται ἐν τῷ νόμῳ ὑμῶν, Schl. ad loc. Similarly from the 3rd. cent. B.C. onwards Greek legal language uses the formula ἐν νόμῳ γέγραπται, Deissmann, Bibelstudien 1895, 109f.; O. Michel, Paulus u. seine Bibel 1929, 68ff.; Br. ad loc. and Wörterb. sub γράφω.

[3] See p. 86.

[4] Deut 17.6; 19.15, cp. Str.-B. I 790f. on Mt. 18.16 and Schl. ad loc.

[5] 'Εγώ εἰμι ὁ μαρτ. κτλ. is not, of course, one of the great ἐγώ-εἰμι sayings (see p. 225 n. 3). The sentence (in which ἐγώ is the predicate) is not a revelation saying but part of a discussion. There is no allusion to Is. 43.10 (Bd.).

οὔτε ἐμὲ οἴδατε οὔτε τὸν πατέρα μου·
εἰ ἐμὲ ᾔδειτε, καὶ τὸν πατέρα μου ἂν ᾔδειτε.[1]

Thus, as in 5.37, the claim is made that when men shut themselves off from Jesus' witness, it is a sign that God has shut himself off from them. God can only be approached through his revelation (1.18). To have *knowledge of God* does not mean to have adequate information about him, whether this be gained from the tradition (as is the case with the Jews, or with any form of orthodoxy, including Christian orthodoxy) or whether it be derived from general thoughts and ideas; it means to know him as the one who encounters man in his revelation, who puts man in question and demands his obedience. Thus knowledge of God includes true readiness to hear him when he speaks. If this readiness is absent, if, that is, there is a refusal to accept the Revealer, there is no true knowledge of God. Of course it goes without saying that such acceptance of the Revealer is not the acceptance of a Christological dogma (indeed such dogmas are satirised in 6.42; 7.26f, 41f.); rather it is the hearing of his eschatological word, proclaimed again and again in the νῦν. It is a hearing which entails the surrender of all reassuring dogmas. This readiness is not present in Jesus' opponents, and so he has become their judge.

V. 20 (like 6.59) is the conclusion of the whole complex. The place where the scene takes place shows its importance. It is in the temple that Jesus pronounced the judgement on the Jews, that they have no knowledge of God. In the temple itself they gave proof of their being closed to the Revealer![2] Hereby judgement is passed on the Jewish religion; and at the same time, since the "Jews" represent the world as a whole, it is

---

[1] Ἄν which in B comes before ᾔδειτε and in א after it, should perhaps be omitted with D, since it is often omitted in John, see v. 39; 9.35, Bl.-D. para. 360, 1.—In John εἰδέναι can be synonymous with γινώσκειν; see 14.7—It is unlikely that the Jews' question refers to the supposed illegitimacy of Jesus' birth, as is suggested by Hosk., following Cyril of Alexander.

[2] Presumably ἐν τῷ γαζοφυλακίῳ is intended to underline the particular importance of the scene; however it is not possible to be sure how it is meant. γ may refer to the treasury in the temple, yet according to II Esr. 22.44; Jos. bell. 5, 200; 6, 282 there were several of these. It is possible that one of these was referred to specifically in this way, and that it played a role in the Jewish tradition, cp. I Macc. 14.49 and esp. II Macc. 3.6, 22f. (Heliodor legend); 4.42. If this is the one referred to here, then ἐν τῷ γ. means "by the treasure house". —On another view γ. is the alms chest of Mk.12.41 par. (even then ἐν would still mean "by") and in this case, according to Str.-B. II 37ff. (where ἐν τῷ γ. is admittedly understood as "in the room before the γ."), it would refer to the alms box for free-will offerings,which paid for the burnt-offerings that were the "dessert of the altar".—It is not impossible that ἐν τῷ γ. has come from the Christian tradition, and is intended only to make the scene more vivid; this is the view put forward by Hirsch I 73, who denies the Evangelist any knowledge of the locality.

a judgement on all religion as a sphere which gives man this security and his self-consciousness.[1]

Since the Revealer's judgement on Judaism has been portrayed in the form of a narrative recounting the clash between Jesus and the Jewish authorities, some explanation must be given why the opponents take no action after his attack, and why they do not have him arrested.[2] This is given when we are told that "his hour has not yet come."[3] Thereby it is clearly stated that the Revealer's judgement is not dependent on man's will but on divine necessity.[4]

[1] Cp. p. 189f. on 4.21 and p. 267 on 5.39f.

[2] Whereas in 7.30, 44; 10.39 the statement that they were unable to lay hands on Jesus is prefaced by the statement that they wanted to lay hands on him, here this prefatory declaration is missing. This can hardly provide grounds for an argument against the way we have positioned 8.13–20 above, as if καὶ οὐδεὶς ἐπίασεν αὐτόν required some preceding account of an attempt to seize Jesus. For this is not even the case in the text as we have it. In any case καὶ οὐδεὶς κτλ. is perfectly adequately explained by the whole situation (which begins in 5.16–18), so that καί takes on the adversative sense which it has in 1.5 etc. (see p. 48 n. 2).

[3] On ὥρα see p. 117 n. 1. What is referred to is the hour of the passion, which has come in 12.23; 13.1; 17.1, whereas here as in 7.30 it is still to come.

[4] Similarly 7.30, 44; 10.39, to which correspond materially 10.18; 14.30f.; 18.10f.

III. Chapters 7-10: The Revealer's Struggle with the World

In our exposition of chapter 6 we left 6.60–71 out of account. In seeking the *original position* of 6.60–71 we shall have to consider *three possibilities*: 1) that the correct position of 6.60–71 is after 6.1–59, where it provides the conclusion of that complex; 2) that its correct position is before the complex which begins in 7.1ff., which was originally separated from 6.1–59 by chap. 5 (i.e. 5.1–47; 7.15–24; 8.13–20); 3) that it has been divorced from its original context, which must be sought in another part of the Gospel altogether.

The *first possibility* can be eliminated with reasonable certainty: a) The conclusion of 6.1–59 is to be found in v. 59. b) The assumption in 6.60ff, is that it is the μαθηταί who are listening to Jesus—not the "twelve", but the "disciples" in a more general sense.[1] However these are not in view in 6.1–59; for the μαθηταί who are here mentioned (for the last time in 6.24) are the twelve, and they, in line with the traditional material on which the passage is based, are thought of as Jesus' constant companions in his ministry. c) 6.60–71 clearly marks an important dividing line in Jesus' ministry, namely the separation of the twelve as the true disciples from the mass of untrue disciples. It is hard to see how this passage could have come between chs. 6 and 5, which form a matching pair;[2] moreover the situation in 6.66f., where the disciples make their decision for or against Jesus, suggests that it must have been preceded by a much longer public ministry than could be adequately represented by the single example in 6.1–59.[3]—It could perhaps be argued against these points that 6.65 seems to be a reference to 6.44. However, if this were so, why should 6.44 be quoted so loosely?[4] Moreover according to 6.65, the saying of Jesus there quoted was addressed to the "disciples", whereas in 6.44 it was addressed to the unbelieving multitude.[5]

The *second possibility* seems to be the most likely, for it would then be

---

[1] See pp. 115 n. 5, 176 n. 5.

[2] See pp. 209f.

[3] The description of Jesus' sayings as σκληρὸς λόγος (v. 60), which must have preceded 6.60–71, gives no grounds for arguing that all Jesus' speeches have this character.

[4] Instead of ἐὰν μὴ ὁ πατὴρ ... ἑλκύσῃ αὐτόν (v. 44): ἐὰν μὴ ᾖ δεδομένον αὐτῷ ἐκ τοῦ πατρός (v. 65). The discrepancy is all the more surprising in that διδόναι in 6.37, 39 was used in a different sense (the Father "gives" the Son to the believers). Elsewhere in John Jesus quotes himself much more accurately, cp. 8.24 with 8.21; 13.33 with 7.33f.; 15.20 with 13.16; 16.15 with 16.14 (also 13.11 with 13.10). 14.28 is the only quotation which is not accurate, but this refers not to an individual saying, but to the basic idea of the preceding discourse (14.3f., 18).

[5] On the possible relationship of 6.62 to 6.33, 50f., 38, see the exposition of 6.62.

easy to see why 6.60–71 occupies its present position; the reason is that it was connected with 7.1ff. in the textual tradition. Yet if one accepts this view one must also accept the consequence that there must be a passage missing in front of 6.60–71; for 6.60–71 cannot follow on immediately after the complex 5.1–47; 7.15–24; 8.13–20, because a) the complex in ch. 5 is concluded by 8.20; b) the μαθηταί presupposed by 6.60–71 are also not to be found in this complex; c) in this case also the decisive situation in 6.66f. would still seem to come very early on in the ministry. Thus if one accepts 6.60–71; 7.1ff. as the original order, one will have to assume that a section has been omitted which contained the beginning of the scene whose conclusion is given by 6.60–71. By analogy with the other narratives in John, one would expect this to have begun by giving the setting of the scene (its time and place), and that it be followed by a discourse of Jesus, or a discussion with the "disciples", which reached its climax and conclusion in 6.60–71. As we can see from 7.1, the scene must have taken place in Jerusalem, or at least in Judaea.

Now it is possible that the section, whose conclusion is given by 6.60–71, has become detached from its original context and that it might be possible to discover it elsewhere in the Gospel. In fact, the analysis of ch. 8 leads one to suppose that 8.30–40 is a section which came immediately before 6.60–71 (see below). Yet even this would not completely fill the gap, for 8.30–40 cannot be the beginning of a scene, but only the continuation of one. For the moment we must leave on one side the question whether it is possible to find the beginning. As is indicated by the state of chs. 7 and 8, one must at least reckon with the possibility that parts of the original text have been lost. Thus it would be possible that the Gospel originally contained a whole complex before ch. 7, of which only the conclusion, 8.30–40; 6.60–71, has been preserved. However this assumption is not really to be recommended, since 7.1ff. is closely connected to the complex in ch. 5. For 7.1, 25 speaks of the Jews' intention to kill Jesus, and this is a reference to 5.17–19 (7.19).

There remains, therefore, only the *third possibility*, namely that 6.60–71 is a section which has been divorced from its original context; if so where is this to be found? On the basis of the content of the verses one would be inclined to place it between chs. 12 and 13. Jesus' ministry to the people and its leaders extends to the end of ch. 12. From ch. 13 onwards he is alone with the twelve.[1] If it is the case that the Evangelist, by this ordering of his material (which is quite foreign to the Synoptics), illustrates the κρίσις brought on the world by Jesus' activity, then the best place for the narrative 8.30–40; 6.60–71, wherein the κρίσις is brought about in a concrete symbolic scene, is doubtless between chs. 12 and 13. Admittedly 8.30–40; 6.60–71 cannot simply be added on to the end of ch. 12, nor can they easily be fitted into that chapter. But we shall have to reckon with losses of traditional material in ch. 12 as well, or at least with editorial insertions (see below).

In the light of all this, it seems advisable to expound 8.30–40; 6.60–71 in the context of ch. 12, and to move from the complex 5.1–47; 7.15–24; 8.13–20 immediately to ch. 7.

[1] That is, of course, apart from the actual passion narrative chs. 18–19.

Lastly it is possible to provide an answer to the question how the editor came to place in their present position the dislocated sheets which contained 6.60–71 and 8.30–40. The description of Jesus' discourse as σκληρὸς λόγος (6.60), and equally the statement about πνεῦμα and σάρξ (6.63), fitted in well after the verses 6.51b–58, which he had added to the discourse on the bread of life. This addition provided him with the ideal place for 6.60–71. As far as 8.30–40 is concerned, it is at least clear that there were obvious reasons for taking it with 8.41–47; for in both sections the Jews are upbraided as children of the devil, though in 8.30–40 they are contrasted with the children of Abraham, in 8.41–47 with children of God.

A. 7.1–14, 25–52; 8.48–50, 54–55: The Hiddenness and Contingency of the Revelation

7.1–13 is the introduction to the whole complex; it prepares the way for Jesus' appearance in Jerusalem at the feast of Tabernacles, which is surprising both in its timing and its manner. This introduction is followed quite naturally by 7.14, 25f.[1] The scene which begins in these verses is concluded in 7.30. It is followed by a second scene, which has no conclusion, 7.31–36, and two further scenes, 7.37–44 and 7.45–52. While there is a space of several days between the second and third scenes, the first two appear to take place on the same day, as do the third and fourth scenes. Thus the whole section 7.14–52 seems to be clearly divided into two parts, each of which consists of two sub-sections, and the division is made in such a way that the themes of the first two sub-sections and of the second two sub-sections correspond to each other: 7.14, 25–30 and 7.37–44 the question of Jesus' origin; 7.31–36 and 7.45–52—the attempt of the authorities to have Jesus arrested by the servants sent out by them. Yet however obvious this may seem, it is not the original structure of the section; for 7.31–36 and 7.45–52 must take place on the same day, since the servants sent out in 7.32 would hardly return only after three or four days! 7.37–44 thus disturbs the course of the narrative[2]; probably it originally came after v. 30, for v. 31 is awkward after v. 30, but fits very well after v. 44. In this way the σχίσμα mentioned in v. 43 is portrayed in v. 44 from both points of view. This also removes the difficulty caused by Jesus' continuing to speak in v. 33 as if nothing had happened, in spite of what has been recounted in v. 30; for now some days have passed between v. 30 and v. 33. Moreover the conclusion of the scene 7.31–36 is now provided by 7.45–52.[3]

---

[1] After the transposition of 7.15–24 to ch. 5; see pp. 237f..

[2] Cp. the different attempts made to overcome this difficulty in the analyses given by Wendt, Wellh., Sp. and others.

[3] Joh. Schneider (ZNW 45 [1954], 108–119) wants to take ch. 7 as a single unit, except for vv. 33–36, which are an insertion; the only change in the order which he makes is to put v. 32 between vv. 44 and 45.—Becker (115, 118) wants to place 8.48–50, 54–55 after 5.44. —According to Dodd (345–347) chs. 7 and 8 contain "a collection of miscellaneous material", but he does not attempt himself to give a critical analysis; he thinks that the dialogues are all held together by the motif of conflict.

The original intention must then have been that 7.1–13 and 7.45–52 provide the introduction and conclusion for Jesus' appearance in Jerusalem, the account of which falls into two scenes, 7.14, 25–30 and 7.37–44, 31–36. In this, however, it is noticeable that the first scene is extremely short, and without much incident. It is also hard to see why Jesus' brief words in vv. 28f. should arouse the wrath of his audience to such pitch that they are moved to lay hands on him (v. 30). One would have expected sayings of Jesus here which would have given better grounds for the attempt to arrest him, and which would also have given more force to the scene. In fact, the collection of fragments in ch. 8 does contain a passage which one might well insert here, namely 8.48–50, 54, 55, which has, in its present form, been joined with 8.51–53, 56–59 to form an unconnected block of material.[1] Of course it is impossible to reach any certainty in these matters; but it cannot be denied that 8.48–50, 54–55 fits extremely well between 7.28f. and 7.30, and provides an excellent explanation for 7.30.[2]

a) Introduction: 7.1–13

The introduction is obviously intended on the one hand to prepare the way for Jesus' appearance in Jerusalem, and on the other to make it clear that the motives for this appearance are not worldly ones, that his choice of the καιρός is not based on worldly considerations. This intention is fulfilled by recording how Jesus rejects his brothers' demand that he should reveal himself to the "world" in Jerusalem, but nevertheless shortly afterwards goes up to Jerusalem. This is perfectly clear, and the idea provides a most suitable introduction to what follows. Nevertheless the form in which the idea is expressed raises grave difficulties, for Jesus' actions contradict his own words.[3]

[1] For the analysis of ch. 8 see below.

[2] One might very well be tempted to transpose the fragment 8.21–29 to ch. 7 as well. It may be felt that 7.31–36 is also rather thin, and that it ought to contain a saying of Jesus which would give a better explanation of the servants' remark in v. 46. 8.21–29 would fit in well after 7.31–36; the themes agree: Jesus' departure and man's search for him when it is "too late". Yet it is more probable that 8.21–29 is a part of the discourse on light, beginning in 8.12; see below.

[3] It makes very little difference whether in v. 8 we read οὔπω (as in 2.4) or οὐκ with ℵ D al lat syr[sc]. Οὔπω is probably intended to tone down the categorical οὐκ. But even οὔπω ἀναβ. εἰς τ. ἑορτ. ταύτην can only be a refusal to go to *this* feast, to which he goes all the same. Οὐ φανερῶς ἀλλ' (ὡς) ἐν κρυπτῷ only roughly conceals the contradiction in v. 10. Lagr. thinks that Jesus was refusing to go in the great crowd of pilgrims to Jerusalem and to make a solemn entrance with them, but that can only be read into the text. What Jesus refuses to do and then does is simply ἀναβαίνειν vv. 8, 10. The same can be argued against O. Cullmann, Urchristent. u. Gottesdienst 42f. The idea that Jesus received a divine sign to alter his decision after his brothers had left (B. Weiss, Zn., Bl., Lütgert, Joh. Christ. 103f.) is most odd, in view of the Johannine picture of Jesus. Does Jesus ever say anything but what he has heard from God, and did God alter his decision after three days?—It can hardly be right to resolve the difficulty by assuming that v. 8 is ambiguous, as Br. and Omodeo (Mistica 58f.; and also Ephraem much earlier), Wik. and Barr. would like. According to them the brothers take ἀναβαίνειν κτλ. to mean: "to journey up (to Jerusalem) for this feast"; while Jesus takes it to mean "to ascend up (into heaven) at this

The difficulties are resolved as soon as we see that the Evangelist has used a piece of traditional material in 7.1–13, namely the introduction to a miracle story. This contention is supported by the parallel which has often been noticed between 7.1–13 and 2.1–11.[1] Both deal with the question of the καιρός (or the ὥρα—2.4). This (i.e. the time of the miracle) cannot be determined by man's wishes. To ask why the καιρός was at first not present, and yet arrived a little later, would be pure pedantry in relation to a miracle story; for this sort of story is only interested in the demonstration of God's arbitrary power. It was enough for the Evangelist roughly to conceal the contradiction by οὐ φανερῶς κτλ. (v. 10); he used the introduction because he, too, was interested only in the demonstration of God's power. Accordingly it would be quite wrong to question Jesus' motives.[2] This also explains the other contradiction, namely that the brothers challenge Jesus to continue his ministry in Jerusalem, and even to perform miracles there, as if 2.13–22, 23–25; 4.45; 5.1ff. had never happened.[3]

V. 1 links up the new section with the preceding one, and at the same time gives a general description of the situation: Jesus is staying in

---

feast". In that case Jesus would have deliberately deceived his brothers, who in this situation could not but understand his words in the way they did. In addition to this the Johannine misunderstandings are not caused by the ambiguity of prepositions; see p. 121 n. 2.—Another way of removing the difficulty is by accepting the omission of ἐις τ. ἑορτ. ταύτην in Chrys., min. 69 and q. 'Αναβαίνω then loses its future sense and only refers to the present moment; see Bl.-D. para. 323, 3.—It is oversubtle to suppose that Jesus' refusal to go to the feast of Tabernacles is an expression of the Christian protest against taking over this Jewish feast (Ed. Schwarz, ZNTW. 7 [1906], 22).—Cp. too R. Schütz, ZNTW. 8 (1907), 251f.

[1] See p. 121 n. 4. It should also be noticed that these two passages are the only places in John in which Jesus' brothers appear (in 20.17 the ἀδελφοί are the disciples, and in 21.23 Christians in general). The Lazarus story, ch. 11, contains a third variation on the theme that Jesus does not perform his miracles when they are expected of him, but only later. The identity of theme seems to be fair proof of the fact that all three stories have been taken from the σημεῖα-source. (See p. 113 n. 2.)—If 7.1–13 was originally the introduction to a miracle story, and if, like 2.1–11, it was taken from the σημεῖα-source, one can well wonder if in the source it formed the introduction to the miracle recorded in 5.1ff. This idea is supported by the fact that 7.3 assumes that Jesus has still performed miracles only in Galilee, and that it is now time for him to perform a miracle in Jerusalem.

[2] The analyses of Wellh. and Goguel (Introd. au NT. II 411ff.) are right in so far as they gain the impression that 7.1–13 must be based on earlier tradition, but I can neither find a "basic document" (Wellh.) nor ancient historical tradition (Goguel, who here finds the same tradition as in 10.40–42) at this point.—Sp. was working on the right lines in his attempt to analyse out the Evangelist's redaction from the traditional material, only one must take this a stage further. V. 1 comes, of course, from the Evangelist; it is designed to link ch. 7 with ch. 5. (On μετὰ ταῦτα see p. 121 n. 6; on οὐ γάρ see p. 153 n. 1.) Further in vv. 4–8 the Evangelist has worked over the source, and here vv. 4b, 5, 6b, 8b, are editorial additions proper, while v. 7 is probably a verse taken from the revelation-discourses. Finally vv. 10b, 13 probably come from the Evangelist.

[3] "Jesus is challenged to go to Judaea, because Galilee is only a remote corner of the country; Judaea has till now seen nothing of his ministry. This flatly contradicts what can be read in chs. 1–6" (Wellh.). The view that 7.3 refers not to miracles such as Jesus had already performed, but to the sort of ἔργα which he had only promised in 5.20, 36 (Wendt I 133; II 46f.) is impossible, if only because of εἰ ταῦτα ποιεῖς v. 4 (see below).

Galilee[1] in order to escape the Jews' attempts to have him arrested.[2] Thus it is assumed that he had previously been in Judea (Jerusalem). **V. 2** gives a more precise account of the chronological situation, presupposed in the following narrative: it is just before the feast of Tabernacles[3] of the Jews[4]. In **vv. 3–5** the world's failure to understand the manner of the revelation is shown by the brothers' demand that Jesus go up to Jerusalem for the feast[5] and there reveal himself to the world. For the brothers, as is shown by vv. 6f., are representative of the world, and so the folly of their demands is ascribed to their unbelief (v. 5).[6] According to v. 3 their unbelief is shown, not in their rejection of his person, but in their failure to understand his ἔργα, by which of course, they mean his miracles.[7] As they see it, his miracles are the proof of his authority[8] and so they urge him to provide a similar demonstration in Jerusalem.[9] They justify their demand by appealing to the general truth

---

1 The imperfects περιεπάτει and οὐ ... ἤθελεν denote a period of time of some length, namely the time between the Passover (5.1) and the feast of Tabernacles. The emphasis in the meaning of περιπατεῖν is not on walking around, but it has the meaning, as it often does in context, of "staying, spending some time" (cp. 10.23; Mk. 11.27).

2 "Οτι ἐζήτουν κτλ. refers to 5.17–19 (7.19).—In the same way that Jesus' journeys to the festivals are used to give a schematic explanation of his visits to Jerusalem (see p. 122 n. 3), the motif of his pursuit by the Jews is used here also and in 4.1–3 to explain his visits to Galilee.

3 In the LXX the feast of *Tabernacles* is called ἑορτὴ (τῶν) σκηνῶν (Lev. 23.34; Deut. 16.13 and elsewhere; similarly in Philo spec. leg. I 189) or ἑορτὴ (τῆς) σκηνοπηγίας (Deut. 16.16; 31.10; so too Jos. ant. 4, 209; 8, 100; 13, 241). Jos. frequently has the simple σκηνοπηγία (ant. 13, 372; 15, 50; cp. 8, 123: τὴν σκηνοπηγίαν καλουμένην ἑορτήν).—According to Deut. 16.13, 15; Ezek. 45.25; Jubil. 16.20–31; Jos. ant. 13, 242 the feast lasted seven days, from the 15th to the 21st Tischri (Sept./Oct.). Lev. 23.34–36; II Chron. 7.8f.; II Esr. 18.18; Philo spec. leg. I 189; II 211 add to this a further concluding day, so that in Num. 29.12–39; II Macc. 10.6; Jos. ant. 3, 245 the feast is considered to last eight days. According to a gloss on I Kings 8.65 (based on II Chron. 7.19), which is not included in the LXX, Solomon celebrated the festival for 14 days; Jos. ant. 8, 123 is based on this.—On the celebration of the feast see Str.-B. II 774–812.

4 See p. 86 n. 2.

5 Μετάβηθι (not ἀνάβηθι) v. 3 might refer to a change of abode, rather than a journey to the feast. If this was the meaning in the source, then we would have to ascribe the dating of the narrative to the Evangelist's redaction (as does Wellh.). One must certainly take this possibility into account.

6 The motivation given in v. 5 is typical of the Evangelist, see p. 153 n. 1 and cp. esp. 5.22; 8.42; 20.9. He knew from the tradition (Mk. 3.21, 31–35; 6.6 etc.) that Jesus' brothers did not belong to his followers during his lifetime. As understood by the source the brothers were no more "unbelieving" than Jesus' mother 2.3. A certain parallel is afforded by the Gospel of the Hebrews, where Jesus' mother and brothers urge him to go to John's baptism, see Arn. Meyer, Handb. zu den Neutest. Apokr. 1904, 25.

7 Cp. the usage presupposed in 5.20; 7.21; 9.3, which should be distinguished from the Evangelist's usage (see pp. 264ff.), but which is to be found quite clearly in Mt. 11.2. —If the traditional material on which this passage is based came from the σημεῖα-source, then the brothers are referring to the miracles related in 2.1–11; 4.46–54; 6.1–26.

8 This is the same as the view expressed in 6.14f.; see p. 212f.; cp. also p. 134 n. 4.

9 On ἵνα with the indicative future (which occurs elsewhere in the NT and in inscriptions and papyri) see Bl.-D. para. 369, 2; Raderm. 173.—The subject οἱ μαθηταί σου is

that no man who lays claim to public recognition should continue to work in obscurity.[1] They judge by human standards, according to which the obscure Galilee signifies a mere κρυπτόν, and the capital city by contrast παρρησία. Yet for the Evangelist, the meaning of their words extends far beyond this present situation, as he shows by this addition, v. 4b: εἰ ταῦτα ποιεῖς, φανέρωσον σεαυτὸν τῷ κόσμῳ[2]. Materially it is the same demand which is made of Jesus in 10.24.[3] As if Jesus had not from the beginning revealed himself to the world and spoken publicly—in so far as one can speak of "revealing" at all in his interpretation! As if the κρυπτόν, which is an essential element in this revelation—since it is said; καὶ ὁ λόγος σὰρξ ἐγένετο—were to be attributed to the temporary limitation of his ministry to Galilee!

The world does not see that Jesus' φανεροῦν is always ambiguous, and that therefore, so long as it holds fast to its worldly being, this

---

surprising here. In the context it cannot refer to the disciples who were with him in Galilee and were journeying up to the feast with him; for vv. 3 f. assume that Jesus has already performed miracles in Galilee. Thus it can only refer to the disciples (in a more general sense) which Jesus had made during his earlier activity in Jerusalem (cp. 2.23; 3.26; 4.1); and yet the source cannot have been referring to disciples of this kind, for it assumes that till now Jesus has performed no miracles in Jerusalem at all. And apart from this, why should it only be disciples of this kind who are to see the miracles, and not everyone? We must therefore conclude that οἱ μαθ. has been inserted as the subject of the sentence by the Evangelist in order to establish some sort of harmony with what has been recounted earlier. In fact, however, he has succeeded in "producing the purest nonsense" (Wellh.). Originally the meaning was "so that they (in Jerusalem as well) may see the works which you perform". —Torrey 340 suspects that there may have been an error in translation here; it ought to read, "in order that they may see your disciples and the works which you perform". Yet there is no reason for supposing that the σημεῖα-source was translated from the Semitic.

[1] This claim is denoted by ζητεῖ ... ἐν παρρησίᾳ εἶναι. Παρρησία here does not, of course, mean, as it originally did in Greek, the right or the courage to appear in public, freedom of speech, openness (cp. E. Peterson, Reinh. Seeberg Festschr. 1929, 283–297), but as is common later, it refers to actions performed in public. In this meaning παρ. was taken over into Rabbinic Hebrew as a borrowed word (see Str.-B. and Schl. ad loc.).—In view of the fundamental character of the word it makes no difference whether we read αὐτό (BD*; where the agreement is better) or αὐτός (also read by the Syrians; possibly corrected to agree with the following φαν. σεαυτόν); see Bl.-D. para. 405, 1.

[2] V. 4b comes from the Evangelist, for it is unlikely that the σημεῖα-source spoke of a revelation to the κόσμος. That is the language of the Evangelist and the revelation-discourses, cp. 1.9; 3.17, 19; 8.26; 9.39 etc., also 2.11; 17.6.—Windisch, Theol. Tijdschr. 1918, 230 draws attention to Kore Kosmou Stob. I 403, 18ff., where the elements pray to the Creator: ἀνάτειλον (Scott, Herm. I 486, 37: ἀνάδειξον) ἤδη σεαυτὸν χρή [ματί] ζοντι τῷ κόσμῳ, which cannot be considered to be a material parallel. Nor can Tos. Sota 4, 7 (Schl. ad loc.), where Moses cries to Joseph, who is buried in the Nile (in Schl.'s translation): εἰ φανεροῖς ἡμῖν σεαυτόν, καλόν (similarly in other versions of the legend in G. Kittel. Die Probleme des paläst. Spätjudentums 1926, 169ff.). φανεροῦν σεαυτόν here only means "to show oneself", "to appear", and does not have the meaning "to reveal oneself."—Εἰ ταῦτα ποιεῖς (which is not hypothetical but refers to an actual fact, see Bl.-D. para. 372, 1a) also characterises Jesus' claim. The particular formulation is a result of the link with v. 3: if you perform miracles such as you have performed till now, then this is a demonstration which must be brought out into the open.

[3] In 10.24 παρρησία does, of course, mean openness.

revelation will always remain for it κρυπτόν, because the δόξα is only to be perceived in the incarnate Logos.[1] In precisely that activity which the world considers inadequate, the Revealer fulfils their demand, φανέρωσον σεαυτὸν τῷ κόσμῳ; and in just this way the revelation is made ἐν παρρησίᾳ. This παρρησία is a "public act", not as the world understands it, namely as a demonstrative act which forces itself upon man's attention, but a "public act" in the sense of an undemonstrative everyday occurrence (18.20).

Jesus' answer (**v. 6**) rejects the world's understanding of the matter; "My time is not yet come; your time is always here."[2] The καιρός is the decisive moment, plucked out of the stream of time (χρόνος), which is favourable for a particular action.[3] The world also knows that every important action and event has its καιρός; and in this sense the brothers could well understand why he might reject their suggestion for the present moment and then follow it later. But ὁ καιρὸς ὁ ἐμὸς οὔπω πάρεστιν does not point forward, as the world might think, to a future occasion which would be more propitious; it is a complete rejection of the world's view of the matter. It does not mean, "not now, but later", but asserts that the time (the "now") of the revelation cannot be determined at all from the world's point of view.[4] Similarly the words which follow, ὁ δὲ καιρός ὁ ὑμέτερος κτλ., say that the world is completely ignorant of the moment (the "now") of genuine decision.[5] For if their

---

[1] See p. 62f. and Hosk. ad loc.—It is possible that the Evangelist had in mind heathen attacks on the obscurity of Jesus' ministry, such as are attested in Orig. c. Cels. VI 78, p. 149, 22ff., Koetschau (cp. Acts 26.26). But the sentence expresses an idea which is so fundamental to the Evangelist that there is no need to assume that there is an express reference to such attacks. In any case the sentence is directed every bit as much against a misconceived Christianity.

[2] It is very difficult to decide whether the antithesis in v. 6 comes from the revelation-discourses, as does v. 7, or whether it was composed by the Evangelist. Becker 75 considers it to have come from the source.

[3] In Greek καιρός denotes the decisive, irrevocable time for an action which is offered by fate (or alternatively the cosmic constellation) and determined in this way. Thus in Biblical (or Rabbinic) usage καιρός is used for the moment determined by God, above all for the eschatological moment in time (which is either defined more specifically, as in Lk. 19.44; Rev. 11.18; I Pet. 1.5 etc. or left without such further definition Mk. 13.33; Lk. 21.8; Rev. 1.3; etc.). In Jn. 7.6 καιρός is also the eschatological moment, but this is understood in the way typical of the Evangelist, i.e. in such a way that Jesus' activity is conceived as the eschatological event (see above); for this reason καιρός can also retain its original meaning of the decisive moment for an action.—See also ThWB s.v. καιρός.

[4] Odeberg 270ff. rightly protests against taking Jesus' καιρός to mean the time which is propitious for his activity, as is done, e.g. by Sp. and Bd. It is a question of the "spiritual time" which has been determined for the Redeemer.

[5] Weiss: "For them the time *to show themselves publicly to the world* is always ready." This expansion of the sentence is pedantic, for there is no question whatsoever of them showing themselves publicly to the world. The sentence has a very general sense.—The correct interpretation is given by Odeberg 279f. and D. Faulhaber, Das Joh-Evg. und die Kirche, Diss. Heidelberg 1935, 44.

καιρός is always there, then in reality it is never there, and their actions never decide anything, because everything is decided in advance; for the world is "in death". The world can make a decision only when it is faced with the question whether it wishes to "remain" in death (12.46 etc.), that is, only when man acts not from worldy motives and according to worldly criteria, but when in his action he abandons the world. But this is the way of the Revealer's action; it is eschatological event, and for this reason the world's point of view can have no power over him (v. 4). The revelation is not an unambiguous, demonstrative act made by the world to the world, and so the feast at Jerusalem could not be its καιρός.

V. 7 states that the true καιρός is the moment of decision for or against the world;

ὀυ δύναται ὁ κόσμος μισεῖν ὑμᾶς,
ἐμὲ δὲ μισεῖ,
ὅτι ἐγὼ μαρτυρῶ περὶ αὐτοῦ
ὅτι τὰ ἔργα αὐτοῦ πονηρά ἐστιν.[1]

Whoever recognises the καιρός, which is provided by the encounter with the Revealer, calls down on himself the hatred of the world, because for him the moments which the world thinks important are reduced to insignificance. The fact that the brothers' καιρός is always at hand corresponds to the fact that they are not subject to the hatred of the world. Their actions take place within the sphere of the world; they belong to the world.[2] Jesus, on the other hand, arouses the world's hatred, because his action gives the world the true καιρός, because the revelation questions the security and self-sufficiency of the world.[3] Jesus "bears witness"[4] to the world that its works are evil. Yet he does so not through moral sermons[5] but rather as the Revealer who puts the world in question, who comes to win the world. The world's "works"

---

[1] V. 7 probably comes from the revelation-discourses; but it might have been composed by the Evangelist, on the pattern of that part of the discourses used in 15.18ff.; cp. esp. 15.18f., 22.

[2] Cp. 15.19.—That like attracts like (Ecclus. 13.15), that the evil band together against the righteous (Wisd. 2.12), that moral judgement easily arouses hatred (Rabb. in Str.-B.), are statements which at most illustrate Jn. 7.6, but which do not have the fundamental character of this saying, since they remain within the sphere of experience.

[3] Cp. 3.20; 15.18. The same is true of Jesus' disciples, who by their decision against the world in their turn call the world to decision (15.18f.; 17.14; I Jn. 3.13).

[4] Μαρτυρεῖν here is employed in an entirely forensic sense, and is equivalent to "accuse" (see p. 50 n. 5 and cp. κρίσις and ἐλέγχειν 3.19–21). The forum before which the world stands accused is God; see p. 85f..—This μαρτυρεῖν also becomes part of the disciples' task 15.26f.

[5] Such sermons are not to be found in John at all; nor are the terms μετανοεῖν and μετάνοια.

are not "evil" because they are immoral; they are evil because they are worldly actions, actions, that is, of a world which is incapable of a true decision. The event of revelation is the coming of light into darkness, and the "witness", the accusation, results automatically from the world's reaction to the light.[1]

Vv. 8f. return to the initial situation. Jesus will not go to the feast with his brothers.[2] He remains in Galilee, for his time is not yet "fulfilled"—a phrase which hints at the eschatological character of his actions.[3]

However, after a certain time has passed—we are not told exactly how long—Jesus does in fact make the journey to Jerusalem[4] (**v. 10**). The Evangelist attempts to patch over the contradiction[5] with v. 8 by οὐ φανερῶς ἀλλ' (ὡς) ἐν κρυπτῷ.[6] While admittedly it is impossible strictly to reconcile these two verses, because Jesus does in fact appear publicly (vv. 14, 25f.), it is possible to remove the contradication so far as the Evangelist's understanding of the matter is concerned, since Jesus remains the hidden Revealer, in spite of his public teaching, and his work does not lose the character of the κρυπτόν, as was demanded of him in vv. 3f.

Vv. 11f. introduce a motif which runs through the whole of the following passage. Jesus' previous activity disquiets[7] the crowd at the feast;[8] they raise question and counter-questions about him. Whereas till now (5.16ff.; 6.41f.) Jesus' words had provoked only opposition,

---

[1] See p. 158f.

[2] The antithesis ὑμεῖς-ἐγώ v. 8 is not, of course, a specifically Johannine antithesis, but arises naturally out of the situation.—On the different readings οὐκ and οὔπω see p. 288 n. 3.—On ἀναβαίνειν see p. 123 n. 1 ;ἀναβ εἰς τ. ἑορτήν is in accordance with Jewish usage, see Schl.

[3] Πληροῦν or πληροῦσθαι of the fulfilment or running out of a particular period of time is common in Greek, in the LXX, in Jos. and in primitive Christian literature; see Br. ad loc. and Wörterb.—Properly speaking the object or subject can only be a period of time (χρόνος, ἡμέραι, ἔτος also καιροί plural, e.g. Acts 7.23, 30; 9.23; Lk. 21.24) and not a point in time. καιρός is, however, used improperly as the subj. of πληροῦσθαι Jos. ant. 6, 49; Mk. 1.15; so too here. Naturally the usage here is eschatological, see p. 292 n. 3 and on πληρ. II Esr. 4.35ff., Mk. 1.15; Gal. 4.4.

[4] This also must have been related by the source, and v. 10 may have been taken from it (on ὡς δὲ ... τότε cp. 11.6 from the σημεῖα-source?). But vv. 11–13 is, of course, an editorial section added by the Evangelist; cp. 7.43, 31; 10.19–21. The stressed ἐκεῖνος is typical of his style (see p. 48 n 3.), as is μέντοι after a negative (4.27; 7.13; 20.5; also 21.4; ὅμως μέντοι 12.42; μέντοι occurs otherwise only three times in the NT, and then never after a negative); φόβος τ. 'Ιουδ also in 19.38; 20.19.

[5] See p. 288f.

[6] ὡς is omitted by ℵ D pc it^{var} syr^{sc}.

[7] On γογγυσμός see p. 229 n. 4. Here as in v. 32 it refers not to indignant anger but to something supressed, indefinite, undecided.

[8] 'Εορτή here probably refers not to the feast but to the crowd at the feast, as in Plot. Enn. VI 6, 12, p. 412, 21 Volkm. and perhaps also Mk. 14.2 (Joach. Jeremias, Die Abendmahlsworte Jesu 1935, 35).

they now create σχίσμα, division (7.43; 9.16; 10.19). Yet the fact that no one is prepared to commit himself to Jesus' cause shows that such argumentation[1] is not the true κρίσις that divides the believers from the world; rather it remains within the κόσμος, which loves sensation and excitement,[2] which likes to have something to argue about. (**v. 13**).[3] The crowd are all dominated by the fear of the "Jews", i.e., the authoritative voices of the world. And yet they are all part of the world, and this is expressed symptomatically in the use here of the words ὄχλος and 'Ιουδαῖοι. For on the one hand the ὄχλος (which is of course itself Jewish) can be distinguished as the mass of the people, speaking without authority, from the 'Ιουδαῖοι, who are the authorities (vv. 12, 40, 43, 31f.); and yet on the other hand ὁ ὄχλος and οἱ 'Ιουδαῖοι (vv. 11, 35) can be used interchangeably.[4]

b) The Hiddenness of the Revelation: 7.14, 25–29; 8.48–50, 54–55; 7.30

On the fourth day of the feast[5] Jesus appears in the temple[6] and begins to teach[7] (**v. 14**). This causes considerable surprise among some of the people of Jerusalem[8] (**vv. 25f.**), who know that there had been a

---

[1] The judgement of the first group here, that Jesus is ἀγαθός, chooses a predicate which is as general as possible, by contrast to the judgements passed later on, that he is ὁ Χριστός (vv. 26, 41) and ὁ προφήτης (v. 40). The judgement of the other group πλανᾷ τὸν ὄχλον is clearly typical of Jewish polemics, cp. v. 47; 12.19; Mt. 27.63; Justin dial. 69, 7 (Jesus as μάγος and λαόπλανος); Str.-B. I 1023f.—The text variants (ἐν τ. ὄχλῳ ℵ D, the addition of δὲ after ἄλλοι in many authorities, see Bl.-D. para. 447, 6) are of no importance.

[2] 'Εκεῖνος is certainly not used in a pejorative sense (Chrys., etc., cp. Br.) but is typical of the sensation produced by Jesus. Just as the σχίσμα gives a distorted reflection of the κρίσις, so too ἐκεῖνος on the lips of the Jews gives a broken image of the Christian ἐκεῖνος.

[3] Παρρησία (see p. 291 n. 1) means publicly as opposed to the suppressed nature of the γογγυσμός; materially speaking it has at the same time the sense of open and bold speech.

[4] See p. 86f.

[5] τῆς ἑορτῆς μεσούσης = in the middle of the feast, which is normal Greek usage, with which the LXX, Philo and Jos. were also familiar; see Br. and Schl. ad loc.—The middle of the feast is the fourth day, see p. 290 n. 3.—Dodd (351) thinks that the verse is intended as a fulfilment of the prophecy of Mal. 3.1: "The Lord whom ye seek shall suddenly come to his temple."

[6] "To go up" into the temple is a phrase common with the Rabbis and Jos.; see Schl.

[7] Διδάσκειν is said of Jesus, as in 6.59; 7.28, 35; 8.20, 28; 18.20 (see p. 274 n. 3). It would be incorrect to think that 7.14 refers to a different sort of teaching from that which is referred to in all the other references (namely ethical teaching), as does e.g. Schl., who appeals to Rabbinic usage and is clearly influenced by his misunderstanding of v. 16 (see p. 274).

[8] 'Ιεροσολυμίτης occurs in the NT only here and in Mk. 1.5, a few times in the LXX and Jos., see Br. Wörterb.—The reason why "some" of the Jerusalemites speak in this way is that, according to the account given in 7.20, the crowd as a whole has no knowledge of the authorities' intention.

plot to kill Jesus (5.18), and that he (as one may surely supply) had as a result left Jerusalem (7.1). Yet if he is now speaking publicly,[1] without hindrance from the authorities,[2] it seems as if they must have recognised him as the Messiah.[3] But this absurd idea is immediately rejected (**v. 27**). It is impossible! The origins of the Messiah must be mysterious,[4] and everyone knows where Jesus comes from. That is to say, no one whose origins are generally known[5] can be the one in whom God reveals himself. The origin of the Revealer must be a mystery.

Again we see that the world is certainly in possession of concepts which are appropriate to the revelation, for the origin of the revelation is, in fact, a mystery. Yet again, we see that the world does not understand itself, and that it perverts the meaning of its concepts, rooted as they are in its search for the ultimate, into a quite contrary sense.[6] For what the world calls a mystery is not a true mystery at all. In its foolish mythology it turns its mysterious, transcendent origin into something belonging to this world. It imagines that it has criteria by which it can determine whether and where God's mystery has become visible, with the result that nothing remains mysterious. The recognition of the true mystery presupposes that man has gone astray with respect to normal standards. It is for this reason that the revelation remains hidden to the world, and that the world's knowledge only leads it further into ignorance.

---

[1] On παρρησιά see p. 291 n. 1.

[2] Οὐδὲν αὐτῷ λέγουσιν, according to Schl. ad loc. and on Mt. 21.3, is a "genuinely Palestinian formula". This is the only occurrence in John of μή ποτε (4.29 μήτι).—On ἄρχοντες see p. 133 n. 4.

[3] It is assumed as a matter of course that the whole of Jesus' activity and preaching contains the claim to the Messiahship.

[4] This is based on one of the principles of Messianic dogmatics (see p. 91n. 3 and also H. Gressmann, Der Messias 1929, 449ff.; Str.-B. II 488f.). The idea behind Jn. 7.27 is not that although it is known that the Messiah will be of the house of David, he will spend the time before his appearance in an unknown place (on this also Str.-B. II 339f.); for πόθεν ἐστίν makes it clear that we are concerned here with his origin, and this, according to II Esr. 7.28; 13.22, Syr. Bar. 29.3, is absolutely hidden. It is more than likely that the Gnostic myth has influenced Jewish messianic mythology at this point.—Analogous discussions in the life of real or pretended θεῖοι ἄνθωποι occur in Hellenism on the basis of this myth, if not indeed on the basis of the generally accepted idea of the mysterious origin of the divine as such (G. P. Wetter, Sohn Gottes, 90ff.; cp. L. Bieler Θεῖος 'Ανήρ I 1935, 134f.). When the accused Apollonios of Tyana is accredited by a miracle, the city governor Tigellinus takes him aside and asks him who he is; Apollonios tells him the name of his father and home-town and states only that God is with him; but ἔδοξε τῷ Τιγελλίνῳ ταῦτα δαιμόνιά τ' εἶναι καὶ πρόσω ἀνθρώπου (Philostr. Vit. Ap. IV 44, similarly I 21). By contrast the false prophet Alexander of Abonuteichos claims to be a descendant of Perseus, and the Paphlagonians (εἰδότες αὐτοῦ ἀμφοτέρους τοὺς γονέας ἀφανεῖς καὶ ταπεινούς) are taken in by the fraud (Luc. Alex. 11).

[5] It is of course assumed, as in 6.42, that they are not mistaken in this respect; see pp. 62 n. 4; 229 n. 5.

[6] See pp. 60f., 182f., 186f., 230 esp.

Jesus' words in **vv. 28f.** reply to all this talk as if it had been addressed directly to him.[1] The difficulties of visualising the scene show that this is not really an account of a discussion in Jerusalem; the historical scenery is only a disguise for the real event, which is the conflict between the world and the Revealer before the tribunal of God.[2] Jesus makes reply not to "certain people of Jerusalem" but to the whole world, whose views were expressed in the words of those men. The introduction to his speech ἔκραξεν οὖν ἐν τῷ ἱερῷ διδάσκων already indicates that his words have their origin in a very different sphere.[3]

κἀμὲ οἴδατε καὶ οἴδατε πόθεν εἰμί.
καὶ ἀπ' ἐμαυτοῦ οὐκ ἐλήλυθα
    ἀλλ' ἔστιν ἀληθινὸς ὁ πέμψας με,
ὃν ὑμεῖς οὐκ οἴδατε,
    ἐγὼ οἶδα αὐτόν,
ὅτι παρ' αὐτοῦ εἰμι
    κἀκεῖνός με ἀπέστειλεν.[4]

The irony of Jesus' observation that they know him and his origins does not lie in the suggestion that their knowledge is based on faulty information. No, they are quite right;[5] people know very well who his parents are (6. 42). Yet in a paradoxical way this is at the same time the proof of their ignorance.[6] Their knowledge is unknowing; for they use their knowledge, which in itself is perfectly correct, to conceal the very thing which it is important to know. Their knowledge serves only to prevent them from recognising Jesus; he cannot be the Messiah

---

[1] It is one of the characteristic marks of the Gospel that Jesus often takes up a point that has not been addressed to him directly: 4.34; 6.43, 61; 7.16, 28; 16.19. 7.33 also is one of these instances.

[2] See p. 85f.

[3] On κράζειν = inspired speech see p. 75 n. 1 'Εν τ. ἱερ. διδ. was unnecessary, so the intention must have been to stress the importance of the saying.

[4] Vv. 28f. are most probably quoted from the revelation-discourses, which were edited by the Evangelist. He probably composed the first line himself in order to fit the quotation into the context. In the Semitic text of the source the relative clause (ὅν ὑμεῖς κτλ.) and the explanatory clause (ὅτι παρ' αὐτοῦ εἰμι) will have been main clauses, if they were not in fact added by the Evangelist himself. According to Becker 76f. not only the first line of v. 28 (with the following καί) but also the last two lines of v. 29 should be ascribed to the Evangelist.—In v. 29 some authorities add a δέ after ἐγώ. Instead of παρ' αὐτοῦ ℵ e syr[sc] Tert read παρ' αὐτῷ (syr[s] admittedly also has ἤμην instead of εἰμί), which is accepted by Zn. and Bl.; it must however be a correction, intended to express the idea of the Son's continual presence with the Father (see p. 82 n. 6, 151 n. 3). The variants on ἀπέσταλκεν ℵ D are of no importance.

[5] The καὶ ... καί (both ... and) gives particular ring to the sentence: "Certainly! You know me and know...." Weizsäcker catches the paradoxical tone of the sentence very well: "So? You know me and do you know that ... ?"

[6] καί in κὰι ἀπ' ἐμ. κτλ. has the same adversative sense as in 1.5 etc.; see p. 48 n.2

because they know where he comes from (v. 27)! Thus in truth they do not know him, for they do not know him who sent him.

'Απ' ἐμαυτοῦ οὐκ ἐλήλυθα, which denotes his divine authorisation,[1] is intended in the context to state that any judgement on his origin as understood by the world is senseless. For his origin can be understood only if one recognises his authority, hears his word and disregards his person as it appears to the world. For he has been commissioned to speak by God, ἀλλ' ἔστιν ἀληθινὸς ὁ πέμψας με. He has not authorised himself (cp. 5.43) but he has really been *sent*, and—the two ideas are interwoven in this sentence—he who sent him is *true*.[2] Whoever refuses to believe in him convicts God of lying, just as whoever believes in him recognises God's truth (3.33).

Whereas in 5.37f.; 8. 19 their unbelief, when confronted with Jesus, earns the Jews the reproof that they do not know God, here their ignorance of God serves as a proof that they are ignorant of Jesus' origins. There is, of course, no reference at this point to the sort of knowledge of God which one might enjoy outside a relationship to Jesus. Rather what is assumed here is the idea of 5.37f.; 8.19; the proof of the reality of a man's knowledge of God lies in his recognition of Jesus. If then ignorance of Jesus' origins is grounded in an ignorance of God, this means that it is grounded in a man's refusal to recognise Jesus. Manifestly, then, knowing Jesus' origin does not mean entertaining some kind of mythological or speculative theory about the origin of the Revealer—it is just such theorising which obstructs the Jews' path to Jesus—but it means believing in the divine authorisation of his word.

The Revealer himself bases his claim simply on the fact that he knows God: ἐγὼ οἶδα αὐτόν. Again this knowledge of God does not consist in some kind of mythological or speculative theology,[3] but simply in the knowledge of his commission: ὅτι παρ' αὐτοῦ εἰμι κἀκεῖνός με ἀπέστειλεν.[4] He lays no claim for himself to any kind of metaphysical qualities and makes no appeal to any authority recognised by the Jews, but solely to his knowledge of his mission. It is only as the messenger

---

[1] See p. 249.—For the "coming" of Jesus ἔρχεσθαι abs. 5.43; 7.28; 8.14, 42; 10.10; 12.47; 15.22; ἔρχ. εἰς τ. κόσμον 3.19; 9.39; 11.27; 12.46; 16.28; 18.37; ἐξέρχ. ἐκ (ἀπὸ, παρὰ) τ. θεοῦ (πατρός) 8.42; 13.3; 16.27f., 30; 17.8; καταβαίνειν ἐκ (ἀπὸ) τ. οὐρανοῦ 3.13; 6.34, 38, 41f. (50f., 58). Cp. p. 50 n. 3. For Ign.'s terminology cp. Schlier, Relg. Unters. 35f.

[2] 'Αληθινός here means not "real", as it often does when predicated of God (ThWB I 250, 19ff.), but (as in 3.33 and 8.26) = ἀληθής, "true" (this is also used elsewhere of God, loc. cit. I 250, 14ff.; 249, 41ff. on the interchanging of ἀληθινός and ἀληθής).

[3] See p. 253.

[4] "Οτι of course gives the justification and is not introductory of reported speech. But inasmuch as the Son's relation to God is said to be based on his mission, the mission itself is at the same time declared to be of the essence of the Son's relationship to God (i.e. to be the content of his knowledge).—It makes no material difference whether one takes κἀκεῖνος κτλ. as part of the ὅτι clause or not.—On εἶναι παρά see p. 232 n. 4.

that he lays his claim before his hearers, and only when man recognises him as the messenger does he know who he is and where he comes from.

As the assertion in 5.37f. of the unity of the knowledge of God and the recognition of Jesus was followed in 5.41ff. by the question about Jesus' δόξα, so here again the discussion is continued in 8.48–50, 54f. by the introduction of the theme of δόξα.[1] The Jews[2] understandably take offence at Jesus' words[3] (**8.48**). His words are proof for them that he is a Samaritan,[4] that he is possessed.[5] In his reply (**v. 49**) he brusquely rejects this charge! "I am not possessed, but I honour my Father and you dishonour me."

The Jews' objection arises directly out of his colossal claim that *only* he, an ordinary mortal, whose origin is known to them, knows God, and moreover that he has been *sent* by God. And yet he must make this claim; for it is in this way that he honours the Father, from whom he has received his commission. The Jews, by their cursing, dishonour *him*. The paradoxical nature of the situation is brought out clearly here; for he does not say, as one might expect, that they dishonour God. Of course they do that as well. They make God a liar by refusing to believe in Jesus (I Jn. 5.10). Yet they do this by refusing to honour his Revealer. The Revealer must claim this honour, for his honour and the Father's honour are one (5.23)! Does he then seek his own honour? Once again

[1] On the insertion of 8.48–50, 54f. after 7.29 see p. 287.

[2] See p. 295.

[3] καλῶς λέγειν = "speak correctly, to the point", is common in Greek. Οὐ καλῶς λέγομεν cannot refer to any previous utterance, for Σαμαρ. εἶ σύ has not been said anywhere up till now, and δαιμ. ἔχεις cannot refer to 7.20. The meaning is, "Are we not right when we say...." The meaning is the same as in v. 52. It is however very probable that the Evangelist has put into the Jews' mouths a sentence which is typical of Jewish polemics; see next note. Cp. too C. H. Kraeling, John the Baptist 11.

[4] Σαμαρίτης εἶ σύ perhaps means no more than the accusation made against the Amhaaretz, "He is a Samaritan", i.e. as it were, a heretic (Str.-B. ad loc.). In the context the particular reason for this would be that Jesus had impugned the Jews' knowledge of God (7.28). In any case there is no evidence that Σαμ. was used simply as a term of abuse. It is also possible that Jesus is accused here of being a Samaritan Goet or Gnostic, such as are described by Celsus (Orig. c. Celsus VII 8; cp. Norden, Agnostos Theos 188–190); thus in addition to the judgement on the Amhaaretz, he is also accused of being a *magician*; cp. Merx 215–218. 221–235. The accusation would then be identical with the following δαιμ. ἔχεις (O. Bauernfeind, Die Worte der Dämonen im Mk-Evg. 1927, 1); in v. 49 Jesus, in fact, only replies to the accusation of madness.—Eisler's explanation, Rätsel 455 is fantastic.

[5] Δαιμόνιον ἔχεις here has a more precise meaning than in 7.20. It is used in the same sense as in Mk. 3.22. However the difference between this and the Synoptic tradition (Mk. 3.22; Mt. 12.24 = Lk. 11.15) is characteristic. In John Jesus is not attacked for having worked his miracles with the aid of demonic power, but with being possessed by a demon, to whom his words are attributed. It is the same attack which in Hellenism is made by the unbelievers on the θεῖος ἄνθρωπος, and which is made by the Gnostics on the Christians and vice-versa; cp. Wetter, Sohn Gottes 73–80; for a more general discussion of the mocking of the θεῖος ἄνθρ. see L. Bieler, Θεῖος Ἀνήρ I 132f.

there is a danger of misunderstanding, which Jesus anticipates in vv. **50, 54f.:**

ἐγὼ δὲ οὐ ζητῶ τὴν δόξαν μου·
ἔστιν ὁ ζητῶν καὶ κρίνων.
ἐὰν ἐγὼ δοξάσω ἐμαυτόν,
ἡ δόξα μου οὐδέν ἐστιν.
ἔστιν ὁ πατήρ μου ὁ δοξάζων με,
ὃν ὑμεῖς λέγετε ὅτι θεὸς ἡμῶν ἐστιν,
καὶ οὐκ ἐγνώκατε αὐτόν,
ἐγὼ δὲ οἶδα αὐτόν.
κἂν εἴπω ὅτι οὐκ οἶδα αὐτόν,
ἔσομαι ὅμοιος ὑμῖν ψεύστης.
ἀλλὰ οἶδα αὐτὸν,
καὶ τὸν λόγον αὐτοῦ τηρῶ.[1]

No! He does not seek his own honour. But there is a parallel here with the other paradoxical statements about his judgement and his witness. He does not *judge* (8.15; 12.47), but the Father makes him judge (5.22, 27), and so he does judge (5.30). Similarly he does not bear *witness* to himself (5.31), but points to the Father's witness to him (5.32, 36f.), and so in fact he does bear witness to himself (8.18). In the same way then, he does not seek his *honour*, but the Father seeks it, and intervenes for him in his struggle with the world;[2] and so he too lays claim to his honour by making plain the Father's intervention. All this is true because and in so far as he is the Revealer who acts only on behalf of the Word. For if he sought his δόξα in the way the world understands it, his δόξα would be of no account, just as his witness would be of no value if he bore witness to himself in accordance with the world's understanding (5.31).

But *how* does the Father ensure that he receives δόξα? Whereas it is explicitly stated that he is the judge, inasmuch as he proclaims the *word* which raises the dead (5.24f.), and equally explicitly that the Father bears witness for him through the *works* which he has given him to do

[1] The whole of vv. 50, 54f. probably come from the revelation-discourses. It is however possible that the sentence which comes between the two, οἶδα αὐτόν, has been inserted by the Evangelist. Becker 83 thinks that ὅν ὑμεῖς λέγετε κτλ. in v. 54 and κἂν εἴπω to οἶδα αὐτόν in v. 55 have been added by the Evangelist. Ἡμῶν v. 54 has understandably often been corrected to ὑμῶν (H K pm), but the ὅτι-clause here introduces, as in v. 55, what is really direct speech.

[2] ὁ ζητῶν v. 50 should be completed by τὴν δόξαν μου, as is shown by ὁ δοξάζων με v. 54; cp. also ἄλλος ἐστιν ὁ μαρτυρῶν 5.32. In fact, it makes no material difference to the sense if one takes it absolutely, because of its conjunction with κρίνων (Br.): "He who conducts the inquiry and passes judgement as the judge"; for in either case we must preserve the image of Jesus' law-suit against the world before the tribunal of God (see p. 297), as is shown by κρίνων.

(5.36), there is no explicit statement here of how it happens that the Father gives him honour. Yet this does not need to be stated explicitly, for it is self-evident: just as he carries out his office as judge *in his present activity*, which indeed consists in the works given him by his Father, so too the Father's δοξάζειν takes place in precisely *this activity of the Revealer*, and that means at this very moment, before the eyes of the opponents to whom he is speaking. Of course they are blind to this; they cannot see his δόξα because they do not know his Father, just as they cannot understand the witness of his works because they do not know God.[1] The Revealer's δόξα is hidden. It is not "honour" as the world understands it, but it is the hidden "glory", which belongs to him as the Revealer, as the Son.[2] 12.28 states explicitly[3] that he obtains this glory through his activity as the σὰρξ γενόμενος, and in 1.14 the believing community confesses that it has seen his glory.

Yet when confronted with the world Jesus can only *appeal to his knowledge* (cp. 7.29 and see p. 298). Indeed he must do so, and in doing so cause offence to the world; for if he denied it he would himself be as much a liar as his opponents. Even to keep silence would be to deny it, for his knowledge of God is no more nor less than his knowledge of his own mission.[1] In this way his knowledge of God and his knowledge of his own mission coincide: "But I know him and keep his word."[4]

[1] In 5.37 the impugnment of the Jews' knowledge of God follows Jesus' appeal to the Father's witness, and similarly here it follows his assertion of the Father's δοξάζειν On the charge that the Jews are ignorant of God, see Dodd 156–160.

[2] On the double-meaning of δόζα as "honour" and "glory" see on 17.1. It is wholly mistaken to attempt to take it in every case in the sense of "honour" (Hirsch I 226); predominantly it is used in John to mean "glory", in the sense of the manifestation of the divine (see p. 67 n. 2). In this Faulhaber 22f. is quite right; however she does not see that the Evangelist·on occasions plays with the double meaning of the word, as is shown quite clearly here by the alternation between τιμᾶν, ἀτιμάζειν, ζητεῖν τ. δόξαν.

[3] See also on 13.31; 17.4.

[4] See p. 298.

[5] In the phrase τὸν λόγον τηρεῖν, λόγος refers to the word of command, the commandment, as is shown by the phrase τὰς ἐντολὰς τηρεῖν (14.15, 21; 15.10; I Jn. 2.3f.; 3.22, 24; 5.2f.) with which it is used interchangeably. τ. λόγ. τηρ. here describes Jesus' relation to the Word of God, elsewhere men's relation to Jesus' word (8.51f.; 14.23f.; 15.20; 17.6; I Jn. 2.5). Cp. Jesus' appeal to the ἐντολή which the Father has given him 10.18; 12.49; 15.10; also 14.31.—Τηρεῖν in Greek means not only to guard, to take care of, but also to give heed to, to watch narrowly. It can take as its object words like ὅρκους, τὴν πίστιν, τὸ τρέπον (see Liddell and Scott). Thus in the LXX it is used (as well as φυλάσσειν) to translate נָצַר and especially שָׁמַר, and can here take as its object τοὺς λόγους (I Sam. 15.11), τὰ ῥήματα (Prov. 3.1), ἐντολάς (Ecclus. 29.1). Similarly Jos. ant. 8, 120 (τ. ἐντολάς). 395 and 9, 222 (τὰ νόμιμα); so too τηρεῖν τ. ἐντ. Mt. 19.17; Rev. 12.17; 14.12; cp. τήρησις ἐντολῶν I Cor. 7.19; and for related expressions see Br. Wörterb. τηρεῖν here in every case means to "keep", in the sense of observing and ordering one's life by something. Elsewhere τηρ. can be used in the sense of preserving (διατηρεῖν τὸ ῥῆμα Gen. 37.11 = not to forget; similarly συντηρεῖν Lk. 2.19), or in the sense of taking care of something, as in Jn. 12.7; 17.11f., 15; I Jn. 5.18.—τηρεῖν can be used interchangeably with φυλάττειν, which

Understandably Jesus' words arouse the anger of his hearers (**7.30**), and they seek to lay hold of him. Yet, as in 8.20, it is as if a spell lay on his opponents: no one can lay hands on him,[1] for his hour is not yet come.[2] His fate is not determined by what man wills but by God's governance.[3]

c) *The Contingency of the Revelation:* 7.37–44, 31–36

The section falls into two closely interconnected parts, 7.37–44, 31 and 7.32–36.[4] Jesus' words of invitation, with which the first section begins, do not announce the theme of the section, but provide only an occasion for a σχίσμα among his hearers (v. 43), in which the question of the origin of the Revealer is again at issue. However, this question is not the main theme of the section, and Jesus does not take it up as he did in vv. 28f. The really new element in his words in this section, and consequently the theme of the section, occurs only in the second part; it speaks of his departure, and that means the contingency of the revelation.

1) *The* σχίσμα*:* 7.37–44, 31

The new scene takes place on the "last day of the feast, on the great day" (**v. 37**), which is the third or fourth day after the events just related.[5] It is not said in so many words that the scene of the action is the temple, for that can be taken for granted. The scene is introduced by a saying of Jesus, which as ἔκραξεν (as in v. 28) again suggests, is divinely inspired:

---

also has the double sense of guarding and observing faithfully; in John the first meaning occurs in 12.25; 17.12; I Jn. 5.21; the second in 12.47 (sc. τὰ ῥήματα); cp. Lk. 11.28 (τ. λόγον). Cp. Herm. sim. V 3, 3–5; Dio Chrys. or. 31, 150 p. 333, 27f. de Budé; Inscr. SA Berl 1935, 719.

[1] Πιάζειν as in 8.20 etc.; ἐπιβάλλειν τ. χεῖρα is common; usually the plural is used, as in v. 44, see Br. ad loc.

[2] The ὥρα here as in 8.20 is the hour of the passion.

[3] Zn. gives a rationalistic explanation: "They (the Jerusalemites of v. 15) must have been afraid of the ὄχλος (the pilgrims to the feast)!" This is, of course, an example of a mythical or legendary motif, such as we find in a very debased form in mand. Joh. B. 96. Slav. Jos. Fr. 1, 16 (Kl. Texte 11, 19) is probably dependent on Christian tradition. Cp. K. Zwierzina, Die Legende der Märtyrer vom unzerstörbaren Leben (in Innsbrucker Festgruss 1909, 130–158), and see on 8.59.

[4] On the rearrangement of the two parts see p. 287.

[5] This refers either to the 7th or the 8th day of the feast, depending on whether the final day is included in the seven days of the actual feast or not (see p. 290 n. 3). Nowhere else is either of the two days referred to as "the great day". Since however the actual rites of the feast were no longer performed on the 8th day (among which was the water libation on the altar of burnt-offerings, see below), and since too the 7th day was marked out from the others by particular festivities, it is probably the seventh day which is referred to here; both Str.-B. II 490f.; and Joach. Jeremias, Golgotha 1926, 81 hold this view.

ἐάν τις διψᾷ, ἐρχέσθω [πρός με?[1]]
καὶ πινέτω ὁ πιστεύων εἰς ἐμέ.[2]

Jesus appears before the crowd at the feast as the bringer of salvation, the Revealer, and he calls the thirsty to him.[3] He gives the water which quenches all thirst (4.14), the "water of life".[4] Without any doubt this refers to the gift which he brings as the Revealer no matter what images may be used to describe it on other occasions: it is the revelation, or better, Jesus himself. Admittedly in the Evangelist's note **v. 39**[5] the water which Jesus gives is interpreted in terms of the Spirit

---

[1] πρός με is omitted by ℵ* D be and is perhaps an addition suggested by the context; it gives the correct sense.

[2] Ὁ πιστεύων εἰς ἐμέ is the subject of the preceding πινέτω, and should be taken together with it. The reasons for this are three: a) because if ὁ πιστ. εἰς ἐμέ is taken with what follows it is impossible to find any suitable scriptural quotation; b) because the rhythm of the sentence demands that it should be taken in this way; c) most importantly, because otherwise it would produce the grotesque picture of streams of water flowing out of the body of the man who is drinking to quench his thirst.—In the context there is no question of any man being compared, because he bestows good gifts, with a source (Prov. 18.4; Song 4.14) or with a well (Rabbis in Str.-B. and Schl.).—On the divergency in the views of the Early Church, see Lagr. and Hosk. The view of the division of the clause given above is also shared by Wik. and Dodd (349).

[3] The cry, ἐρχέσθω (πρός με) is typical of the bringer of salvation and the Revealer; see p. 227 n. 3 and cp. the cry of "Wisdom", Prov. 9.4; Ecclus. 24.19; 51.23f. (where the cry is also addressed to the thirsty); further Mt. 11.28; Od. Sal. 30.1ff. (here too men are summoned to the "living spring of the Lord"); 31.6; 33.6; Joh. B. 48, 6ff. (the cry of the shepherd); 87, 6; 154, 8ff.; Ginza 29, 21; 47, 21f.; (here linked with "believe in me"); cp. P. Oxy. XI 1318, 203. H. Lewy, Sobr. ebr. 77, 1 compares with P. Oxy 1, 17ff.—It is, in fact, probable that the saying of Jesus in v. 37 was taken from the revelation-discourses, in particular from the same section as that used in 4.13f. Was it preceded in the source by an ἐγώ-ἐιμι saying? Promises are usually preceded by such sayings; see p. 226 n. 1.

[4] See pp. 181ff. According to Hosk. there is here a typological correspondence with the water from the rock Num. 20 (cp. I Cor. 10.4) as there is between the "bread of life" ch. 6 and the Manna.

[5] There is no reason for omitting **v. 39** as a gloss, inserted by the ecclesiastical editor; rather the latter is responsible for v. 38b, which makes an inadmissible break between Jesus' words in vv. 37.38a and v. 39. Cp. the Evangelist's notes in 2.21f.; 11.13; 12.16, 33. Moreover the fact that the interpretation of the water, given by Jesus in terms of the Spirit, corresponds to the Jewish view of the feast of the Tabernacles (see in text) supports the view that v. 39 comes from the Evangelist. Only v. 39b could possibly be an editorial gloss (see p. 171n. 2), although the view that the community will not receive the Spirit until after Jesus' δοξασθῆναι is also the view of the Farewell discourses (cp. esp. 14.26; 16.7), and also of 20.22.—On the conception of the Spirit in terms of water see p. 182 n. 4.—V. 38b on the other hand, which breaks the continuity between vv. 37, 38a and v. 39 should be ascribed to the ecclesiastical editor. The difficulty of finding the scriptural quotation referred to only really arises if one takes ὁ πιστ. εἰς ἐμέ as part of the quotation. If one takes it with the previous clause (see n.2 above) then although it is not possible to find anything of which ποταμοὶ κτλ. is a direct quotation, it is clear that it refers to eschatological prophecies, according to which a spring will rise in Jerusalem or the temple in the age of salvation (see p. 182 n. 3). The phrase ἐκ τ. κοιλίας αὐτοῦ which does not occur in OT texts, may have been included because the editor had 19.34 in mind (Jeremias, Golg. 82; A. Schweitzer, Die Mystik des Apostel Paulus 347f.). There can be no question of an error in translation, since the editor wrote in Greek (Burney suggests the confusion of מַעְיָן = spring (Joel 3.18) with

which the believers will receive after his glorification.[1] But this does not mean that the Evangelist has limited the gift to a specific object; for as we shall see from the Farewell Discourses, the Evangelist does not see the Spirit as a special gift which gives proof of its presence in the particular phenomena of the Christian life.[2] Rather for him the πνεῦμα is the ἄλλος παράκλητος (14.16), who takes Jesus' place, in whom Jesus himself comes to his own.

Yet why does the Evangelist choose this saying of Jesus, which is thematically unrelated to the following scene, for his starting point in this section? Obviously because this saying becomes particularly significant within the context of the feast of Tabernacles and because, like 4.21–24, it states that the eschatological event which takes place in

---

מַעַיִן = body; this is challenged by Goguel, Rev. H. Ph. rel. 1923, 380; Torrey suggests the confusion of מִתּוֹכָהּ = from her (Jerusalem's) midst, (Zech. 14.8) with מִתּוֹכוֹ = from his stomach. Similarly de Zwaan 165f., who however takes it to mean, "from its (the Scripture's) midst". It would however be a strong Aramaism (as opposed to a mistranslation) if κοιλία corresponded to the Rabbinic גוף (גּוּפָא), which originally means "cavity", but is then used in the sense of "person", or as a substitute for the personal pronoun, so that ἐκ τ. κοιλ. αὐτοῦ would simply mean "from him" (Str.-B. II 492; Jeremias, Golg. 82, so too Strathm.) L. Köhler (Marti-Festschrift 1925, 177; see too "Kleine Lichter" 1945, 39–41) wants to trace the saying back to Is. 58. 11f., more particularly to a text of Isaiah, which in John's time was still undamaged. He suggests that ממך in Is. 58.12 should be inserted after מים v. 11 as מֵעֶיךָ: "May thy body be a place from which the waters spring." Yet a further conjecture is to be found in R. Eisler, Orpheus 1921, 148f.; Ἰησοῦς βασιλεύς II 1930, 101, 249). Ch. Goodwin (JBL 63 (1954), 72f.) suspects that the quotation comes from an apocryphal writing.—If these explanations fail to satisfy, then one can still remember that κοιλία in the LXX, apart from its physiological and anatomical meaning, can also refer to the inner (man), and can be synonymous with καρδία, which is substituted for it in some variants (see Br. ad loc.).—The phrase the "living source of the Lord" was certainly known in Gnostic circles (Od. Sal. 30.1), and the Mandaeans refer to the messenger directly as the "Spring of life" and the "living water" etc. (see p. 185 n. 1). But there is no known instance of the view that the living water comes from the body of the Redeemer. For this one would have to look to cultic images, cp. Bousset, Hauptpr. 280, 2; H. Gressmann, Die oriental. Religionen im hellenist.-röm. Zeitalter 1930, 31; E. Curtius, ges. Abh. II 1894, 127–156; H. Prinz, Altoriental. Symbolik 1915, 81, 87, 137 (table X 7–9; XII 5, 8; XIII 1, 2). Rev. 9.19 shows that such representations can influence the writer's fantasy, as do Herm. vis. 3, 8, 2; 9, 2, 4 and esp. Eus. h.e. V 1, 22; cp. Wetter, Sohn Gottes 55, 1.—Exegetes who take ὁ πιστ. κτλ. as part of the quotation try to attribute a special meaning to ἐκ τ. κοιλ. Zn. on the basis of the physiological meaning of κοιλ. thinks it refers to the organ of propagation: the believer will be a source of the Spirit for others. Leisegang (Pneuma Hagion 1922, 37f.) takes κοιλ. to refer to the whole of the abdomen. He draws attention to the understanding of inspiration in the Hellenistic Mysteries as an impregnation by the Spirit, and sees here a prophecy that the disciples will become ἐγγαστρίμυθοι (prophets). See also H. Rahner, Bibl. 1941, 396f.

[1] Δοξασθῆναι refers here to Jesus' glorification through the cross and exaltation; cp. esp. 12.16 and see on 17.1. Cp. J. Schneider, Doxa 1932, 123; H. Kittel, Die Herrlichkeit Gottes 1934, 246f.

[2] E.g. miraculous deeds, speaking with tongues; see H. Gunkel, Die Wirkungen des hl. Geistes 3. ed. 1909.

Jesus has set an end to the Jewish cult. The libation of the water, typical of the feast of Tabernacles, was seen as a symbolic representation of the blessing of water in the final age, and as an anticipation of the reception of the Spirit in the end time;[1] now its place is taken by Jesus, who comes as the giver of the water of life, the giver of the Spirit. The promise is fulfilled; the age of salvation is present in Jesus.

This provides us with the best approach for understanding the account of the effects of Jesus' word[2] on the crowd (**vv. 40–42**).[3] It raises again the question whether he is the eschatological bringer of salvation. Some think he is "the Prophet", others the Messiah,[4] and lastly others reject these views on the basis of their own messianic doctrine: the Messiah must be a member of the house of David born in Bethlehem,[5] whereas Jesus comes from Nazareth.[6] Again we see

---

[1] Cp. Str.-B. II 799–805 on the water libation at the feast of Tabernacles; Jeremias, Golgotha 60–65; 80–84; W. A. Heidel, Americ. Journ. of Philology 45 (1928), 233f.; Moore II 43–48.—The libation, which was offered at the morning sacrifice on each of the seven days of the feast, seems early to have been connected with the eschatological prophecies of the spring of salvation. Even though the libation water was not drunk, Is. 12.3 was applied to the rite: "With joy you will draw water from the wells of salvation", and the forecourt of the women, which was the place of the festive rejoicing, was called the "place of drawing water". The joy at the feast was attributed to an outpouring of the Spirit. On Messianic significance of the feast of Tabernacles see Har. Riesenfeld, Jésus Transfiguré 1947 24ff., 43ff., 275ff.

Jeremias draws attention to the fact that the altar for burnt offerings, on which the libation was poured out, was thought of in the Jewish tradition (from what date?) as the holy rock, and at the same time as the stone which sealed off the underworld and from which the waters of the final age would stream forth. On the basis of this he argues that Jesus in his saying v. 37 thought of himself as "the holy rock which gives the water of life". So too Staerk, Erlösererw. 493. And yet the holy rock is not so much as mentioned!—It is even more fantastic to try to interpret v. 37 on the basis of the symbolism of the Eleusinian celebrations which occur at the same season as the feast of Tabernacles (Grill II 129, n. 384).

[2] A secondary tradition reads τὸν λόγον (τοῦτον) instead of τῶν λ.τ. If this is not an oversight, then it is a correction, because Jesus has only uttered *one* saying. The plural, which is certainly original, is used not because it refers to all his sayings at the feast (since v. 14), but because v. 37 is thought of as representative of Jesus' proclamation. There hardly seems to be any need to raise the question whether there is a section missing after v. 39.

[3] The style exhibits the characteristic traits of Jewish usage which are typical of the Evangelist:—the question οὐχ ἡ γραφὴ εἶπεν, the use of σπέρμα to refer to posterity (in Greek it is mostly used to refer to individual descendants), the phrase ὁ Χρ. ἔρχεται; see all this Schl. ad loc.—For the rest ἀπὸ Βηθλ. τῆς κώμης κτλ. is perfectly good Greek, Colwell 41f.

[4] There is no more attempt here to give the titles in order of importance than there was in 1.20f. (see p. 90 n. 5); both titles refer to the eschatological bringer of salvation, and the two-fold statement serves only to illustrate the uncertainty of Messianic doctrine.—On ὁ προφ. see pp. 89f., 213 n. 7. Perhaps the Jewish expectation that Moses on his return would repeat the miracle of the spring at Horeb (Jeremias, Golgotha 64) is an indication that "the Prophet" refers to Moses.

[5] According to II Sam. 7.12f.; Is. 11.1; Jer. 23.5 the expected Messiah is to come from the house of David; according to Mic. 5.1 he must be born in Bethlehem; cp. Schürer II 615; Bousset, Rel. des Jdt. 226f.; Str.-B. I 11–13, 82 f.; Volz, Eschatologie 203f.; Staerk,

that doctrine bars the way to Jesus.[1] Nevertheless the Evangelist does not go into this again at this point, but mentions only that there was a σχίσμα in the ὄχλος about Jesus (**v. 43**),[2] a division which he illustrates in **vv. 44, 31.** Some of the people want to lay hold of Jesus, but again it is as if their hands were tied (as in v. 30); however, many of the ὄχλος believe, remembering the many miracles which Jesus has performed.[3] This faith, recorded here schematically as in 8.30; 10.42; 11.45, is based on miracles, like the faith in 2.23; 10.42; and 11.45. It is as little reliable as the faith in 2.23.[4] In the context it is mentioned only to explain the intervention of the authorities, and so to lead on to the saying of Jesus which introduces the real theme of this section.

2) *Too Late!*: 7.32–36

The authorities[5] learn of what has happened (**v. 32**)—the Evangelist is not interested in how they learn this—and they send servants to arrest Jesus.[6] The assumption of v. 45 is that the servants arrive on the scene immediately, although this is not stated in so many words. Indeed the whole account is extremely sparse in such details; the only thing of importance is Jesus' saying (**v. 33**). This refers directly to the authorities'

Soter I 1ff.—There is no need to try and find a reconciliation between this doctrine and the doctrine of the hidden origin of the Messiah (v. 27); it is enough that two principles of Messianic speculation can be advanced against Jesus. If any reconciliation were needed we would have it in v. 27, if the hiddenness did not refer to his origin, see p. 296 n. 4.

[6] This is assumed on the basis of 1.45; (6.42) 7.52. The Jews, of course, are as little mistaken in this as they were in 6.42; 7.27. That is to say the Evangelist knows nothing, or wants to know nothing of the birth in Bethlehem; see W. Wrede, Charakter und Tendenz des Joh-Evg. 2. ed. 1933, 48; Goodenough 171.

[1] See p. 297.

[2] The same motif is to be found in 9.16; 10.19.

[3] Clearly what is assumed here is the view that the *Messiah on his appearance will give proof of his authority by miracles.* This view is not very clearly attested in Jewish literature. But it seems that the miracles which were expected to occur in the age of salvation (cf. e.g. Is. 35.5f. and see p. 228 n. 1) could also be thought of as accrediting miracles for the Messiah. This view is presupposed in Mt. 11.2ff. parr.; Mk. 13.22; II Th. 2.9. Cp. also the demand for a sign in Mk. 8.11; Mt. 12.38 par. and see Volz, Eschatologie 209.

[4] Cp. 2.24f. and see on 8.30.

[5] The subjects in v. 32 are mentioned twice: (ἤκουσαν) οἱ Φαρ. and (ἀπεστ.) οἱ ἀρχιερ. καὶ οἱ Φαρ. This is in all likelihood original, although syr[s] mentions the high priests and the Pharisees right at the beginning, and then continues with a simple "they". Οἱ Φαρ. by itself refers to the persons themselves, and οἱ ἀρχ. καὶ οἱ Φαρ. (as in v. 45; 11.47,57; 18.3) refers to the authorities, the Sanhedrin; see Schürer II 251f. The Pharisees were commonly confused with the Scribes, and thus are often linked with the ἀρχιερεῖς, as are the γραμματεῖς in the Synoptics (though this never happens in John) cp. 7.32, 45, 48; 11.47, 57; 18.3. In 11.46 (12.19, 42) and in ch. 9 the Pharisees also appear as the authorities.

[6] On the "servants" (also 18.3, 12, 18; 19.6), who were half cultic officials and half police, see Schürer II 443.—'Αποστέλλειν is used absolutely in 5.33; 11.3 but even then there is hardly any cause for thinking that ὑπηρέτας has been interpolated here (after v. 45), although its position varies and it is occasionally even omitted.

intention to arrest him (v. 32).[1] Their real intention, of course, is to remove Jesus altogether (according to 5.18). Jesus replies to this in words of terrible irony. His opponents, like the Jews in v. 27, are right. He must be removed! Yet they are as fatally mistaken as those Jews; for they do not even suspect how right they are, and what Jesus' removal will mean.

> ἔτι χρόνον μικρὸν μεθ' ὑμῶν εἰμι
> καὶ ὑπάγω πρὸς τὸν πέμψαντά με.
> ζητήσετέ με καὶ οὐχ εὑρήσετε,
> καὶ ὅπου εἰμὶ ἐγὼ ὑμεῖς οὐ δύνασθε ἐλθεῖν.[2]

It is not Jesus whom they will destroy, when they remove him, but *themselves*. Fundamentally, it will not be *their* work if they kill him, but *his* deed, his return to the Father who sent him.[3] Yet his return to the Father is not seen here in terms of his exaltation and glorification, and of what that means for the believers,[4] but in terms of his departure from the world, and of what that means for the unbelievers, namely that it is too late. His departure from the world means that the world is judged,[5] and this judgement will consist in the very fact that he has gone, and therefore that the time of the revelation is past. Then "they will seek him", they will long for the revelation, but in vain; for then it will be too late; he will no longer be accessible to them.[6]

Thus it is *the historical contingency of the revelation* which throws this terrible weight of responsibility on the hearer of the word. For the revelation is not generally available, but presents itself to man only at a certain limited time of its own choosing.[7] It does not consist in universal truths, which can be grasped at all times and for all times, nor in dogma

---

[1] See p. 297 n. 1.

[2] This is without doubt a quotation from the revelation-discourses, which probably originally belonged to the quotation in 7.28f. The Evangelist uses it again in 13.33.—The idea goes back to the *myth* and was applied in Judaism to "Wisdom" (Prov. 1.23–31; and cp. Eucharisterion II 8ff.); cp. ZNTW 24 (1925), 126–128; Schlier. Relg. Unters. 76f.—According to Gnosticism the return of the Redeemer, who has freed his own by his ascension into heaven, and thereby withdrawn all the particles of light from the world (see on 12.32), is the world's judgement; see ZNTW 24 (1925), 136; Jonas, Gnosis I 278 and cp. esp. Ginza 346, 33ff.; 517, 6ff.; also 529, 30ff.; 530, 25ff.; see below p. 308 n. 2.

[3] 8.14; 13.3 speak of Jesus' ὑπάγειν in relation to his coming; instead of ὑπάγειν 16.28 has πορεύεσθαι, 3.13; 6.62 have ἀναβαίνειν. 'Υπάγειν is used without reference to his coming in 7.33; 8.21f.; 13.33, 36; 14.4f., 28; 16.5, 10, 17; πορεύεσθαι 7.35; 14.12, 28; 16.7, 28; ἀναβαίνειν 20.17. On Ignatius' terminology see Schlier, Relg. Unters. 76.—On the terminology of "coming" see p. 298 n. 1.

[4] 'Υψωθῆναι is seen in this way in 3.14; 12.32 (although it can also be portrayed in relation to the judgement 8.28), δοξασθῆναι in 12.23, 31f.; 17.5.

[5] Cp. on 8.28; 16.8–11. 8.21–24 is an exact parallel.

[6] syr^{sc} read εἰμί as εἶμι; this is certainly incorrect; εἰμί is also used with future meaning in 12.26; 14.3; 17.24.

[7] Ἔτι μικρόν and πάλιν μικρόν 16.16ff. show how in another respect temporality is also of the nature of the revelation event.

which one could invoke at any time, but it confronts man in time, it is in every case the present moment in a personal history. Should one neglect the opportunity, when confronted with the challenge of the Revealer, then the verdict applies: too late!

Of course in this symbolic scene no consideration is given to the fact that the word of Jesus is taken up again by the community, and that the revelation is again and again made present in time. We have to grasp the fundamental meaning of this symbolic account: just as in Jesus the revelation is realised as an historically limited event, so is it again and again in the preaching which proclaims him.[1] The latter is authoritative only because of this event, and not because of its agreement with universal truths or dogmatic systems. Admittedly it is not a question of recreating this event by historical reminiscences of the "life of Jesus", nor can the event be "realised" by pointing out the cultural and intellectual effects of the historical person of Jesus, in an attempt to extrapolate a timeless content from the subsequent course of events by means of a philosophical-historical analysis, and thereby bringing the revelation under man's control again. For in the word of proclamation he is himself made present to the world (as is the case in this Gospel), in the "Now", in the present moment in time. And the threat is always present, "Too late!" For human inquiry and research cannot find the revelation; it is inaccessible.

In this "too late" the judgement is present. For it means that man shares the fear which is described by ζητήσετέ με κτλ.[2] It makes no difference whether this fear breaks out in a despairing search for the Revealer; it is also present in the seemingly fearless "unspiritual" man,[3] where it is only biding its time. The ζητήσετέ με does not describe something which will some day come to pass, but describes something which will determine the very being of the world.[4] For here we can for the moment leave out of account that there is a search which will be rewarded with success.[5]

you will seek me

The world's lack of understanding is characterised by the "Jews'" grotesque misunderstanding in **v. 35.**[6] They think that Jesus wants to

---

[1] See p. 68f.

[2] In the same way the despair of the faithless people of God is portrayed as a hopeless search for God in Hos. 5.6; Am. 8.12. Jn. 7.34 however is based on the Gnostic myth, cp. (Prov. 1.28) Ginza 347, 15ff.; 588, 26ff.; Mand. Lit. 155 and see p. 307 n. 2.

[3] Cp. Kierkegaard, Concept of Dread, 1944, 85f.

[4] It is pointless to ask whether the Evangelist was thinking of a particular situation in the history of the Jewish people (cp. 5.43). It is usual to point to the prophecies in Lk. 17.22; 19.43f.; 21.20–24.

[5] Cp. Deut. 4.29; Is. 55.6; Jer. 29. 13f. etc.

[6] On the technique of the misunderstanding see p. 127 n. 1; see esp. 8.22.—Πρὸς ἑαυτ. = πρὸς ἀλλήλους (as in 4.33), Bl.-D. para. 287; ποῦ = whither, Bl.-D. para. 103. Bl.-D.

leave the country, perhaps in order to instruct[1] the Greeks in the Diaspora.[2] **V. 36** shows the Jews' uncertainty about this, and their perplexity in face of the saying of Jesus[3]; and precisely the emphasis on their perplexity draws our attention to the irony with which their remark in v. 35 was recorded. Like Caiaphas in 11.51f., they become prophets without knowing or willing it. For Jesus' departure will indeed lead to Jesus' preaching to the Greeks.[4] And as a result the "too late" will become effective for the people as a whole, and God's rule will be taken away from the Jews, as Matthew puts it (21.43), and be given to a people which will bear its fruit.

d) Conclusion: 7.45–52

The scene in 7.32–36 needs no special conclusion, like that in vv. 30, 44/31, for its place is taken by 7.45–52. That is to say, the concluding motif has been expanded into a scene on its own, in which again a kind of σχίσμα is recorded. The division which Jesus' appearance causes among the people makes itself felt to some extent also in the circle of the authorities.

The servants sent out in v. 32 return without success to the Sanhedrin and justify themselves (**v. 46**): "No man ever spoke like this man!"[5]

---

prefers not to take ὅτι elliptically but = δι'ὅτι as in 14.22; 9.17 etc. (cp. also para. 299, 4; 456, 2). But perhaps ὅτι should be taken consecutively (as 14.22?), cp. Job 2.6 = Ps. 8.4 etc., see Br. ad loc.

[1] Zn.'s suggestion is quite pointless, namely that the Jews "probably thought it possible that, since he was not the pupil of any of the local Rabbis (7.15), he was alluding thereby (by ὑπάγω κτλ.) to a well-known teacher in the Diaspora, and suggesting that he had been his teacher and that it was he who had sent him". It is equally incorrect to omit καὶ ὑπάγω κτλ. v. 33 as Sp. does, on the grounds that it could not give rise to a misunderstanding.

[2] Διασπορά in the LXX frequently refers to the dispersion of the people among the heathen (Deut. 28.25; 30.4; Jer. 41.17), but also to the dispersed people as a whole (Is. 49.6; Ps. 146.2; II Macc. 1.27; Ps. Sal. 8.34); it is further used, as here, to refer to the place in which the dispersed are found (Judith 5.19). The genitive affixed to this can refer to the people who have been dispersed (διασπ. τοῦ Ἰσραήλ Is. 49.6) or, as here, to the peoples among whom Israel has been dispersed; see Bl.-D. para. 166; Rabbinic lit. in Schl. and Str.-B. Hosk. in line with 11.52 (cp. 10.16; I Pet. 1.1) wants to take διασπ. to refer to the dispersed τέκνα τοῦ θεοῦ. This would mean that the Jews were unwittingly prophesying the fulfilment of Is. 49.1.—The Ἕλληνες are the Greeks (or alternatively sophisticated Orientals), see Windisch, ThWB II 506, 25ff.

[3] The phrase τίς ἐστιν ὁ λόγος οὗτος seems to be typically Rabbinic, see Schl.

[4] See on 12.20ff.

[5] The clause ὡς οὗτος κτλ. is omitted in ℵ c B al probably because of the homoioteleuton.—According to Burney 99 οὐδέποτε . . . ἄνθρωπος is a Semitism; Colwell 74 disagrees.—For the rest 7.45–52 of course betrays the Evangelist's Semitising style, his habit of putting the predicates at the beginning of clauses (vv. 45, 47, 50, 52), and the inadequate way in which he joins up his clauses. On the formulation of the questions διὰ τί v. 45 and μὴ καὶ ὑμεῖς v. 47 cp. Schl. on 6.9 and on Mt. 22.29; on ὁ ὄχλος κτλ. v. 49 see below and on v. 49. On ἐγείρεσθαι Schl. on Mt. 11.11.

Jesus' words, that is, have such power that his would-be arresters dared not lay hold of him.[1]

The reply of the authorities (**vv. 47f.**), who think that the opinion of the official representatives of the people[2] is ground enough for convicting Jesus as a seducer of the people,[3] shows the blindness precisely of men in positions of responsibility, those whom the world has charged with its government. The curse they pronounce on the people[4] who do not know the law (**v. 49**),[5] shows where they, and

---

[1] The motif is the same as in vv. 30, 43; cp. esp. 18.6. Psychological explanation of the conduct of the ὑπηρέται should be avoided. By contrast Plutarch's account of the soldiers who are sent out to arrest Marius for the murder of M. Antonius is psychologically vivid, Marius 44; they surprise him but τοιαύτη δέ τις ἦν, ὡς ἔοικε, τοῦ ἀνδρὸς ἡ τῶν λόγων σειρὴν καὶ χάρις ὥστε ἀρξαμένου λέγειν . . . ἅψασθαι μὲν οὐδεὶς ἐτόλμησεν οὐδὲ ἀντιβλέψαι κτλ. Again the account in Act. Thom. 105 p. 217, 20ff. of the soldiers who are sent out by King Misdai to arrest the Apostle Thomas, though perhaps influenced by John, is very different in character: εἰσελθόντες δὲ οἱ πεμφθέντες ἔσω εὗρον αὐτὸν πλῆθος πολὺ διδάσκοντα . . . θεασάμενοι δὲ τὸν πολὺν ὄχλον περὶ αὐτὸν ἐφοβήθησαν καὶ ἀπῆλθον πρὸς τὸν βασιλέα αὐτῶν καὶ εἶπον· οὐκ ἐτολμήσαμεν εἰπεῖν αὐτῷ τι· ὄχλος γὰρ ἦν πολὺς περὶ αὐτὸν κτλ.—See also on 8.59. According to the account in 7.32–36 the servants only heard *one* saying of Jesus; but this as, in 7.37 is certainly intended to be representative of Jesus' other sayings (see p. 305 n. 2, so that the impression they have received is adequately motivated, which means that there is no need here for a critical treatment of the passage (see p. 218 n. 2). It is in any case extremely difficult to reconstruct the scene 7.32–36 accurately (see p. 306).

[2] The different titles ἄρχοντες (see p. 133 n. 4) and Φαρ. are used to distinguish between the members of the Sanhedrin and the members of the religious group which enjoyed the greatest respect among the people. No great importance can have attached to this distinction, since both groups put their faith in the νόμος.

[3] See p. 295 n. 1.

[4] 'Επάρατος (in the LXX ἐπικατάρατος) is found in Philo and Jos., and is also Greek; see Br. Wörterb.—The indicative clause, as in other Semitic curses and blessings, has the force of an imperative: "May they be cursed!" (Merx ad loc.).—V. 49 is probably not a combination of two sentences (Zn., Br.). But its conjunction with the previous clause (ἀλλά) implies the idea, "What if the ὄχλος does believe in him!"

[5] There can hardly be any doubt that the ὄχλος *which does not know the law* is the Am-haaretz (עַם הָאָרֶץ) of Rabbinic literature, which is frequently described as being ignorant of the law. In the OT Am-haaretz refers in the pre-exilic age to the full citizens who possess land and are liable for military service, in the post-exilic age usually to the foreign or nationally mixed population of the country as opposed to the Gola, the returned exiles (E. Würthwein, Der 'am haarez im AT 1936). In Rabbinic usage Am-haaretz is used exclusively as a religious descriptive term. It is a term of abuse, and refers to those who are lax in their observance of the laws and customs, thereby causing offence to the righteous. (In the 2nd. cent. A.D. a more specific use seems to have been developed, where Am-h. refers to the Galilean peasantry who refusd to pay their tithes.) Since knowledge and practice of the law in Judaism are normally as one, and since education and piety coincide with each other, the Am-h. can be described as a people which knows not the law, as in the well-known saying of Hillel: "An uneducated man (בּוּר) is not afraid of sin and an Am-haaretz is not righteous." This should not, of course, be taken to mean that a specifically academic education is necessary for piety, and that lack of education in the theoretical sense is characteristic of the Am-haaretz. For this reason Am-haaretz is not used to describe a particular group or class (as Str.-B. suggest, although they are refuted by their own material), and it would certainly be quite wrong to imagine that the Am-haaretz was the πτωχοί of Lk.

consequently where the world also, find their security: in the Law. Yet the ὄχλος is made uneasy by Jesus' words, and in the ὄχλος there are believers—however much they may waver—whereas the official authorities, on the whole, remain unshaken; this but serves to illustrate that it is among those who, according to the world's standards, are the most questionable, that we may in the first place expect to find a readiness to receive the word of the Revealer.

Yet Nicodemus'[1] behaviour immediately shows us that there are exceptions. Even among the official authorities a kind of σχίσμα arises, although it is only a single man who contradicts the united front of the others (**vv. 50f.**). For neither are they whom men judge to be questionable, as such believers, nor *need* human rank exclude a readiness to receive the revelation.

Nicodemus' cool objectivity allows us to see that the revelation does not simply contradict the law, but that it is the misuse of the law which makes the world deaf to the Revealer. 5.38f., 45–47 showed that the law becomes the accuser[2] of those who seek in it their own security instead of allowing themselves to be challenged by it, and here we see that such men lose their objectivity and no longer hear what the law says.[3] Nicodemus must needs remind them that according to the law no one may be condemned without first being heard.[4] But their lack of objectivity is shown clearly enough by their reply: for them the matter is already closed! Moreover they can give their judgement an appearance of legality (**v. 52**). They appeal to the Scriptures, and in so doing provide a confirmation of Jesus' charge in 5.39f.[5] They know that no prophet

---

6.20; Mt. 5.3 (Str.-B. I 190). On the contrary Am-haaretz is a term of abuse which is levelled at individuals (priests can also be castigated in this way, Str.-B. II 495), and which can, of course, also be directed at a crowd (ὄχλος) of individuals. It is likely that ἐθνικός Mt. 5.47; 18.17 is a translation of Am-h.—Cp. Schürer II 468f.; Str.-B. I 190–192; II 494–500; J. Abrahams in Montefiore, The Synoptic Gospels II 2. ed. 1927, 647–669; C. G. Montefiore, Rabbinic Literature and Gospel Teachings 1930, 3–15; S. Daiches, JTS 30 (1929), 245–249; Moore II 157–160; also G. Dalman, Jesus-Jeschua 29f.; M. Dibelius, Der Brief des Jakobus 39f.

[1] The description of Nicodemus as ὁ ἐλθὼν κτλ. which is omitted by ℵ* may have found its way in here via 19.39.

[2] See p. 273.

[3] Νόμος is used here as the subject of κρίνειν in the same way as it is in Rom. 3.19, where it is the subject of λέγειν. This corresponds to Rabbinic usage and to Jos.' usage, see Schl. However this usage is also to be found on Greek inscriptions, see Br. On the personification of the νόμος in Greek literature see R. Hirzel, Ἄγραφος νόμος (Abh. der Königl. Sächs. Gesells. der Wissensch., phil.-hist. Kl. XX 1, 1900) 80, 2.

[4] This principle is true both in OT law (Deut. 1.16f.; 17.4; so, too, in Rabbinic Judaism and in Jos., see Schl.) and in Greek law, see Wetstein.

[5] In the context ἐραύνησον certainly refers to the study of the Scriptures, as it did in 5.39, and not to the investigation of the existing circumstances as in 2 Kings 10.23. For ὅτι ... ἐγείρεται cannot denote a present fact, but is a dogmatic principle. If ἐγειρ. were in fact a correction of an original ἐγήγερται, as read by syr^{sc}, then it would indeed have

can come from Galilee.[1] Their study of the Scriptures leads them to a dogmatics which provides them with the security they want, in that it puts at their disposal criteria by which to judge the revelation but which make them deaf to the word of revelation.

Thus the fact that on the one hand the authorities' teaching is in strict accordance with Scripture, and on the other that they allow themselves to be drawn into irregularities with regard to the law, (v. 51) shows that they are interested only in their own security, to which the Scripture is no more than the means. It is not the irregularities in themselves which put them in the wrong. They are but a symptom of their real malady. Ch. 9 will show that their misuses of the law can go hand in hand with the utmost correctness in its observance; for there the members of the Sanhedrin do in fact institute proceedings such as Nicodemus has demanded.

B. 8.41-47, 51-53, 56-59: A fragment. Analysis of Chapter 8[2]

10.19–21 shows clearly enough that, as we have them, chs. 8–10 are not in their original order. For these verses can have been only the conclusion of a complex which contained the narrative of the healing of a blind man and Jesus' subsequent discourse (or discussion). Their present position is quite impossible. For although admittedly the chapter continues in a perfectly acceptable manner with the beginning of a new scene in 10.22ff., the preceding passage 10.1–18 cannot possibly have been the discourse which originally followed the narrative of the healing of the blind man in ch. 9. Furthermore the order of 10.1–18 and 10.22–39 is impossible. 10.22ff. is the introduction to the discourse on the Good Shepherd, of which 10.1–18 forms a part. 10.27ff.

---

to be taken in the sense we have rejected (see next note). But ἐγείρ. must be original; it is the timeless present of dogmatic principles. In any case ἐγήγ., even though it refers to a state of affairs in the past, would also carry the dogmatic sense that it is impossible for a prophet to come from Galilee.

[1] This principle contradicts II Kings 14.25, for the prophet named there, Jona ben Amittai, is a Galilean. Nor does the principle agree with the Rabbinic tradition (see Str.-B. and Schl.), according to which a prophet has come from each of the tribes of Israel. It may be that it was out of consideration for II Kings 14.25 that ἐγείρ. was changed to ἐγήγ. (see previous note). If one will not allow the Evangelist to have overlooked II Kings 14.25, or to have followed another tradition unknown to us, then it might be supposed that one ought to read ὁ προφ. and that the members of the Sanhedrin were denying that it was possible for "the" prophet (in the sense of v. 40) to come from Galilee. It can hardly be right to assume that the Evangelist has "in his mistaken zeal" intentionally made the members of the Sanhedrin err (Ho., B. Weiss).

[2] As the textual tradition shows, 7.53–8.11 belonged neither to the Fourth Gospel in its original form, nor to the ecclesiastical redaction, and it is therefore omitted here. For a detailed discussion cp. Br.

clearly refers to what is said in 10.1ff. and cannot be separated from this, as is the case in the present order, by a gap of several weeks, or even for that matter of a few days.[1] Thus 10.1–18 belongs to the scene which begins in 10.22ff. and should be inserted after 10.26 (see below).

Which, then, is the *complex of which* 10.19–21 *was the original conclusion*? The healing of the blind man to which it refers is related in ch. 9; but 10.19–21 cannot be simply appended to the end of ch. 9,[2] for it presupposes a longer discourse or discussion than the brief exchange in 9.39–41. This we would expect by analogy with the structure of chs. 6 and 5. For there 6.22–27 and above all 5.17–19 lead over from the miracle story to Jesus' discourse (or to the discussion), and similarly 9.39–41 is clearly the *transition from the miracle story to Jesus' discourse on the light*. The beginning of the story (9.4f.) also points forward to a discourse of this kind. The discourse most likely began with 8.12. However, 8.12 is not continued in 8.13–20; this passage cannot have belonged to the discourse on the light, if for no other reason than that it has its own conclusion in v. 20, whereas the conclusion of the discourse on the light is found in 10.19–21. It is much more likely that 8.13–20 is the original conclusion of the complex in ch. 5.[3] However in 12.44–50 we find a passage, divorced from its original context, which is clearly a part of the discourse on the light, and which in fact makes most sense if it is placed after 8.12.[4]

The question, then, is whether the *discourse on the light* contained more than this. In the first place we must see whether the following passage in ch. 8 (8.21–29) might not have formed a part of it. As it stands in its present position there is little reason for supposing it to have been part of the discourse on the light.[5] There is a further factor however to be taken into consideration: ch. 12 contains another displaced fragment of the discourse on the light besides vv. 44–50, namely, vv. 34–36.[6] These verses have been tacked on to the preceding verses because of the key-word ὑψωθῆναι; but in truth, it is very ill-suited to its present position. For 12.34 clearly assumes that Jesus has just been speaking about the exaltation of the Son of Man (in the third person). Yet this is not the case, for in the immediately preceding verses there is no mention whatsoever of the Son of Man.[7] On the other hand 12.34–36 follows admirably on 8.28f.[8] This shows conclusively that 8.21–29; 12.34–36

[1] 10.22ff. takes place at the feast of the Dedication of the Temple, that is in December; the last date to be given was 7.37, that is, Sept/Oct. Between these two dates falls ch.9, which, however, is not dated any more precisely than that. Since the next date is given in 10.22ff., which follows on directly after ch.9, one is inclined to think that the distance between chs. 9 and 10 is probably quite considerable.

[2] The view is held by a number of English scholars, see Howard 264; also by Wik., but not by Dodd (359).

[3] See p. 238f.

[4] Hirsch also inserts 12.44–50 in 8.12ff., but wants to leave 8.13–20 in its present position and to insert 12.44–50 after 8.19.

[5] On the possible position of 8.21–29 after 7.31–36 see p. 288. n. 2.

[6] There is no need to deal here with 12.33, as it is probably a gloss on 12.32.

[7] The last time the Son of Man was mentioned was in 12.23, and there the reference was to his δοξασθῆναι. 12.34 cannot, of course, refer to that.

[8] Hirsch was the first to see that 12.34–36 belonged to 8.28.

was originally a part of the discourse on the light. There is now little reason to look for further material which might have belonged to it; for 10.19–21 forms an appropriate conclusion to the complex which we have so far discovered (9.1–41; 8.12; 12.44–50; 8.21–29; 12.34–36).[1]

This brings us to the further question how we are to assess *the rest of the material in ch. 8.* It is probably best to start at the end, since this is clearly the conclusion of a complex, and so appears to offer a clue by which to find one's way back to the beginning of the chapter. Now it is obvious that 8.48–59 contains two themes, which alternate with each other without being in any way organically related: 1) Jesus' δόξα vv. 48–50, 54–55; 2) Jesus and Abraham vv. 51–53, 56–59. Vv. 54 and 50 are connected, as are vv. 56 and 53. Vv. 48–50 and 51–53 have clearly been placed together because of the key-words δαιμόνιον ἔχεις. The continuation of the first segment fitted in quite well after v. 53, since ἐὰν ἐγὼ δοξάσω ἐμαυτόν (v. 54) seemed appropriate after τίνα σεαυτὸν ποιεῖς (v. 53), whereas the second half of the second segment (vv. 56–59) was then added mechanically. Now 8.51–53, 56–59 obviously form the conclusion of a discussion, into which has been inserted from another context 8.48–50, 54–55. If we remove these last-mentioned verses,[2] the question is whether 8.51–53; 56–59 can be taken as the conclusion of the preceding passage.

It is immediately preceded by 8.30–47; but even this is not a single unit but is made up of two fragments, 8.30–40 and 8.41–47. In vv. 30–40 the Jews appeal to the fact that they are children of Abraham, which Jesus contests; in vv. 41–47 they appeal to the fact that they are children of God, and Jesus rebukes them as children of the Devil. Of course, the themes of the children of Abraham and of God are related, and this is the explanation for the editor's having placed them together. But in the text the two themes are not specifically related; indeed v. 41 follows on very awkwardly, while the theme of ἐλευθερία, which is related to that of the children of Abraham, is missing in vv. 41–47. The contrast here is no longer between ἐλεύθερος and δοῦλος, but between ἀλήθεια and ψεῦδος. Naturally there is a material relationship between ἐλευθερία and ἀλήθεια, as is shown by v. 32. But a material relationship is not adequate proof of an original literary relationship. On the contrary, it is apparent that 8.30–40 is addressed to people who have declared their faith in Jesus (vv. 30f.)—however valueless that faith might be—and that vv. 41–47 are addressed to those who reject his word from the very start. The fact that in vv. 41–47 Jesus expressly calls the "Jews" children of the Devil and denies their claim to be children of Abraham explains why they are unable to believe, whereas in vv. 30–40 these charges are made only indirectly and explain why it is that the Revealer's word leads to freedom. It now seems evident that 8.41–47 originally preceded 8.51–53, 56–59. V. 51 follows excellently after v. 47, and in all these segments we find the same

[1] Wik. also thinks it probable that 12.44–50 is in the wrong place.—On the (hypothetical) discourse on the light, see Becker 114–116; he too places 12.44–50 after 8.12.

[2] 8.48–50, 54–55 should probably be inserted after 7.29; see p. 288.

sharply polemical tone. As opposed to this 8.30–40, to judge by the audience to which it is addressed, should probably be taken with 6.60–71. These two fragments are best placed at the end of ch. 12.[1]

We still, however, have to find *the original beginning of the complex* 8.41–47, 51–53, 56–59. In my view the only solution is that the section whose conclusion is found in 8.41ff. has been lost (with the exception, that is, of this conclusion). This surely will be no surprise to us, in view of the state of the Gospel. For once it is accepted that the original text has been disrupted, then the possibility must also be reckoned with that parts of the text have been lost. The test of this is to collect together the passages of which we can be certain that they are either introductions or conclusions.[2] We then find that in our text there are more conclusions than introductions, which is proof enough that some of the original text has been lost.[3]

8.41–47, 51–53, 56–59 therefore is *a fragment*, and the only thing which remains is to determine its place in the Gospel, or in other words to see where in the Gospel there is a break in the continuity. Since it would obviously be unwise to posit more gaps in the text than we are obliged to by our examination of it, there is no reason to cast doubt on the originality of the sequence of 9.1ff. on 8.59 (nor of the sequence of 10.22ff. on 10.19–21). Thus the break must lie between 7.52 and 8.41.

a) The Jews as children of the Devil: 8.41–47, 51

The section begins with Jesus making a sharp attack on the "Jews",[4] whom he denounces—at first covertly—as children of the Devil, **v. 41**: "You do the works of your father!" There is no point in speculating on the original reference of this attack;[5] but it is clear from the rest of the passage that the "father" of the Jews is the Devil. The reply shows that this subject has not been broached till now. Rather this marks the beginning of its discussion. Jesus' reproof assumes what was common knowledge, namely that the Jews call themselves children of

---

[1] See p. 287.

[2] Introduction 6.1ff. = conclusion 6.59; 5.1ff. = 8.20; 7.1ff. = 7.30; 7.37ff. = 7.43f., 31; 7.32 = 7.52; 9.1ff. = 10.19–21; 10.22ff. = 10.39. This leaves the conclusions 6.71 and 8.59, for which there are no introductions.

[3] In the case that 8.30–40 together with 6.60–71 originally formed part of the scene which begins in 12.20, we would still have to reckon with a loss of part of the text. For it is not possible to fit this materially smoothly into 12.20ff.

[4] The 'Ιουδαῖοι are given as subject in 8.52, 57. They are obviously Jesus' opponents in the discussion in vv. 41ff., for only so would there be any point in the discussion of paternity.

[5] All one can say is that it is possible that the preceding passage was based on the key-word ἔργα. If that were so then 6.28f. might be a fragment of the lost text (see p. 222 n. 2). The work demanded by God, according to 6.29, is to believe in Jesus. The Jews prove that they do the works of the Devil by not "loving" Jesus (8.41f.) or by not believing in him (8.45f.).

God and that they call God their Father.[1] Jesus challenges their right to do so. But if God is only nominally their father, then they are children conceived in adultery,[2] who have a real father as well as their nominal father. This train of thought is echoed in the Jews' reply: "We were not conceived in adultery! We have only *one* Father, even God!"[3]

Jesus replies with a long denunciation (vv. 42–47, 51).[4] He begins **v. 42** by refuting the Jews' reply: if they really were children of God they would furnish proof of this by recognising him[5] (which is the same condition for the true knowledge of God, given in 5.37f; 8.19). For he—and this is again expressly stated[6]—is nothing of himself, but only God's messenger. And since unbelief is the rejection of his word, the reproachful question (**v. 43**) can take the form: "Why do you not understand what I say?"[7] The reason for this is their very unbelief itself: "Because you are unable to hear my word."[8] Thus whoever excuses himself by saying that he is unable to understand the Revelation lays himself open to the reply that his incomprehension is grounded in his unbelief.

---

[1] Bousset, Rel. d. Jdt. 377f.; Str.-B. I 219f., 392–396; Moore II 201–209. Rabbinic literature also discusses the question when the Israelites have the right to call themselves children of God, whether they always have it, or only when they accept his Word and do his will; Str.-B. I 220; Moore II 203.

[2] On ἐκ πορνείας cp. Gen. 38.24: ἐν γαστρὶ ἔχει ἐκ πορνείας; Rabbinic מְנָאוּף Schl. on Mt. 15.19. Hosk. and Barr., following Orig., think that the Jews' reply contains a malicious allusion to Jesus' supposed illegitimate birth, while according to Dodd (260, 1) this is at most a possibility.

[3] Equally one could translate: "God is the only father whom we have."

[4] In this discourse the Evangelist has used a text from the revelation-discourses, and it is on this that vv. 43–46, 51 are based. V. 42 seems to be the Evangelist's own formulation, in which he has used expressions which commonly occur in the revelation-discourses. The only other possibility is that ἐγὼ [γὰρ] ἐκ. τ. θεοῦ ἐξῆλθον καὶ ἥκω is a quotation, and that it was originally part of an antithetical couplet of which the other half was ὑμεῖς ἐκ τοῦ πατρὸς τοῦ διαβόλου ἐστέ v. 44. In any case οὐδὲ γὰρ κτλ. is characteristic of the Evangelist, see p. 290 n. 6; as is the favourite ἐκεῖνος. Cp. the analysis given by Becker 81f.

[5] See p. 267. The recognition of Jesus is referred to here (cp. 3.19) by ἀγαπᾶν—perhaps because he had in mind the idea found in I Jn. 5.1 (cp. also the contrast between ἀγαπᾶν and ἀνθρωποκτόνος I Jn. 3.14f. and see here v.44). Other occurrences of this use of ἀγαπᾶν are in 14.15, 21ff.; φιλεῖν is used in this way in 16.27. It has here the same meaning as πιστεύειν, which takes the place of ἀγ. in vv. 45f.

[6] On Jesus' "coming" see p. 298 n. 1 (ἥκω only 8.42). On "not on my own authority" see p. 249 f.

[7] Λαλία (see p. 201 n. 3) here means "language", as opposed to λόγος = the content of what is said; more strictly it means "dialect", as in Mt. 26.73 and elsewhere. Γινώσκειν is used of understanding a language, as in Acts 21.37 and ἐπιγιν. II Esr. 23.24.—The formulation is taken from the myth, in which the Revealer appears in this world as a "stranger"; see p. 280 n. 1; on this G. Bornkamm, Mythos und Legende 11; and cp. esp. Mand. Lit., 224: "Whence is this stranger, whose speech is not like our speech?"

[8] On ἀκούειν see p. 259. Zahn's misunderstanding is typical. He thinks that ὅτι κτλ. cannot be the answer to the question διὰ τί κτλ., because "being unable to hear the word" can only be the effect and not the cause of "not being able to understand what he says". Thus one should take ὅτι (as in 7.35) to mean: "I ask this because ...". But this is precisely the Jews' logic which Jesus is attacking.

It is impossible to gain a real understanding of what someone is saying unless one has some relationship to the subject matter which he is trying to express, and this applies equally to the word of the Revealer. If the revelation consists in a calling into question of the natural man, then it will be unintelligible to a man who is not aware of his own questionableness. Thus it is impossible for anyone who is convinced of his own security to understand the revelation; and it is equally impossible to understand it by means of a neutral assessment and objective evaluation of its claims. For all man's understanding is conditioned by his understanding of himself, and it is precisely this which is put in question by the revelation. Outside faith it is impossible to understand what the revelation says—however much faith itself is a process of understanding.[1]

If the "Jews" are unable to understand, it is because they are unable truly to hear. They are prepared to hear only what they already know, even though of course they are interested in deepening and enrichening this knowledge; but they are not prepared to hear anything new, and so to surrender all that they knew before, and with it the condition of such knowledge, their own understanding of themselves. They *cannot* hear in this way! To raise the question why they cannot hear would only be to show a lack of understanding that in this sphere being able to do something and willing to do something are one and the same. For the being of the unbeliever is constituted by the will to unbelief. What he *wills* is determined by this *being*, and he *cannot* will any differently. Can he then *be* any different? Yes, for the question of the Revealer puts his very being in question; the Revealer calls on him to decide. But if he makes his decision in unbelief and for unbelief, then we may not ascribe this decision to any cause external to the decision; for in that case the decision would not be a decision with regard to the revelation, nor would it be a decision which determined man's being. For this is what is meant by ὅτι οὐ δύνασθε, namely that the decision of unbelief constitutes man's *being*, that unbelief is the very core of the unbeliever's *being* and that there is no neutral area of being, as it were, behind unbelief.

One can indeed say that in the decision of unbelief the *origin* of the unbeliever is laid bare. But "origin" here is ambiguous. Confronted by the revelation man, by his decision, chooses his origin; and this origin which he chooses is unambiguous: God or the Devil.[2] If one asks what is the ground of the unbeliever's being, then one cannot point to an

---

[1] Cp. M. Scheler on the conditions of understanding in Krieg und Aufbau 1916 393–429: Liebe und Erkenntnis.

[2] See p. 159.

historical origin, but only to a mythical one: the unbelievers are children of the Devil (**v. 44**).

In the Gnostic myth the indication of a man's origin can truly be described as an attempt at a rational aetiology, for here faith is not a decision in the true sense of the word, but a recalling of one's mythical origin. For the Gnostic is a φύσει σωζόμενος,[1] and the unbeliever is lost because of his corrupt φύσις. John, by accepting this mythological language, is only expressing in an extreme form a double fact: 1) that rational, calculable grounds can have no bearing on faith and unbelief (it is not possible to explain why one man believes and another does not, for man realises himself only in faith or unbelief); and 2) that the decision of faith or unbelief deprives man of his ability to calculate his actions; since it is a decision for this or that origin, an origin which completely determines him, so that nothing that he does can ever be done if it be not done in God or the Devil—which means no more nor no less than that man becomes himself only in faith or unbelief. This is what is meant when the Jews in v. 44 are denounced as children of the Devil.

The present text clearly speaks not only of the Devil but also of the father of the Devil. For grammatically ὑμεῖς ἐκ τ. πατρ. τ. διαβ. ἐστέ can mean only: "you come from the father of the Devil." If what was meant was "... from the Devil, your father" then the article before πατρός, which would then be predicative, would have to be omitted. (Bl.–D. para. 268, 2). Even if one were prepared to admit that there was a grammatical error here, the conclusion could still mean only "for his (namely the Devil's) father also is a liar". It is illegitimate to find in the individual ψεύστης a general ψεύστης as the antecedent of αὐτοῦ, so as to produce the meaning: "For he (the Devil) is a liar and the father of every liar." Nor can one extract the concept ψεῦδος from ψεύστης (despite Bl.–D. para. 282, 3), so that αὐτοῦ would refer back to ψεῦδος and the meaning would be: "For he is a liar and the father of lies." Now it is in principle possible that these verses refer to the myth of the Devil and his father;[2] but in fact there is no sense here in referring to the father of the Devil. For it is the Devil himself who is described as ἀνθρωποκτόνος and a liar.[3] He is the Jews' father and they strive to fulfil his desires, just as in I Jn. 3.8 the sinner is described as a child of the Devil.[4] And it would be senseless if the πατήρ in ὑμεῖς ἐκ τοῦ πατρός were different to the πατήρ in τ. ἐπιθυμίας τ. πατρὸς ὑμῶν, namely the father of the Devil. Accordingly, if it is undesirable to go against the grammar in translating the verses, it would

murder

---

[1] See p. 64 n. 2.

[2] Gnosticism frequently speaks of the Devil's father or origin; see Br. and cp. esp. Act. Thom. 32, p. 148, 16ff.; 76, p. 195, 5; Act. Phil. 110, p. 42, 8ff.

[3] In the same way that in Act. Phil. 119, p. 48, 10 the "serpent" is called ἀνθρωποκτόνος.

[4] So too in Act. Verc. 28 p. 77, 4; Mart. Petr. 7 p. 90, 15ff.

seem most reasonable to assume that τοῦ διαβόλου at the beginning is an explanatory gloss which gives the correct sense, or else with K and Orig. to omit τοῦ πατρός (not however ἐκ as well, as do syr^s and Chrys.) as an incorrect addition. This would still leave the father of the Devil at the end and here again one would have to make corrections.

It seems probable to me that the difficulties have arisen because the text as we have it has been translated from the Semitic. In the original text "from the father" at the beginning of the verse must have been qualified by the possessive pronoun, and the correct translation would have been: ἐκ τ. πατρὸς ὑμ. τοῦ διαβ., where τοῦ διαβ. would have been appositional. The conclusion could be explained in the same way. There can be no doubt about the main point of the passage, which is to show that the Jews' unbelief, with its hostility to truth and life, stems from their being children of the Devil. Thus λαλεῖν τὸ ψεῦδος should be said, not of the Devil, but of the child of the Devil, of whom alone it can be said: ψεύστης ἐστὶν καὶ ὁ πατὴρ αὐτοῦ: his father, the Devil, is also a liar. A man like this speaks ἐκ τῶν ἰδίων, i.e. "like the rest of the family, in the way they have learnt from their father".[1] This is also supported by the difference in the tenses, on the one hand ἦν (and ἕστηκεν—see below), on the other λαλεῖ. The different tenses must have different subjects; the preterite (or preterites) refers to the Devil,[2] and the present tense describes (here as in 8.38) the constant behaviour of the child of the Devil. This meaning can easily be gained by correcting ὅταν into ὃς ἄν, as was first suggested by Lachmann.[3] However, it seems to me more probable that there has been an error in translation here; it ought to read: (πᾶς οὖν) ὁ λαλῶν το ψεῦδος ....[4]

If this is the original meaning then we have to admit that it is not to be found in our present text. If this present text comes from the Evangelist, then the only solution seems to be that the Evangelist misunderstood his source and ascribed the Jews' unbelief to their direct descent from the Devil and to their indirect descent from the father of the Devil. For the solution which is often recommended, namely to see Cain as the father of the Jews and the Devil as Cain's father, instead of the devil and the father of the Devil respectively,[5] does not seem viable to me. Apart from the fact that it means one must either omit (Wellh.) τοῦ διαβ. at the beginning, or replace it by Κάϊν (Drachmann,

---

[1] Thus Wellh., who however wrongly contrasts 'like the rest of the family' with ἐκ τ. ἰδ.

[2] Wellh. rightly stresses the difference in the tenses, but is wrong when he thinks that the preterites could not apply to the devil.

[3] Or else by inserting τις after λαλῇ, see Bd.

[4] On the style cp. I Jn. 2.4, 9–11, 29; 3.4, 6–10; 4.7 etc.—On the argument in this paragraph see Black 73f., who has however written to me to say that he finds my explanation convincing.

[5] Thus Wellh., Drachmann, ZNTW 12 (1911), 84f.; Hirsch.—This is how the verse is taken in Corderius-Cat. 238 (πατέρα τῶν 'Ιουδ. καλεῖ τὸν Κάϊν. In the same way Ps. Clem. Hom. 3, 25, p. 43, 5 Lag. says of Cain: φονεὺς γὰρ ἦν καὶ ψεύστης. In Afraat (331 Wright) the Jews are also addressed as sons of Cain. According to Cyriacus' prayer, Cyriacus 8 (ZNTW 20 [1921] 25), the "serpent" deceived Adam and incited Cain to fratricide.

Hirsch), it is highly unlikely that a figure from the OT, and consequently an historical event like Cain's fratricide, would be suggested as the origin of the Jews' unbelief. Only the antithesis: from God—from the Devil corresponds to the antithesis: I—you (cp. from above—from below (8.23)). Vv. 42–44 are directed against the Jews' claim to be children of God, and not against their claim to be children of Abraham, which is dicussed in vv. 30–40 (see pp. 314 ff). This alone corresponds also to I Jn. 3.8.

By their unbelief the "Jews" show that they are children of the Devil.[1] This determines their being; they strive to fulfil the desires of their father,[2] that is, they are out to kill and to lie. For their father was from the beginning a murderer,[3] and had no standing in the truth.[4]

---

[1] On εἶναι ἐκ referring to descent or origin see pp. 135 n. 4, 138 n. 1, 162 n. 3.

[2] This is the only occurrence of ἐπιθυμία in the Fourth Gospel; it also occurs in I Jn. 2.16f. The verb occurs neither in the Gospel nor in the Epistles.—'Επιθυμίαι are characteristic of the devil, cp. Act. Phil 111, p. 43, 12; 44, 1.20. Rom. 7.7ff., where the ἐπιθυμίαι are ascribed to ἁμαρτία, seems also to be based on a myth about the devil, his deception and his intent to kill (v. 11), which Paul has then presented in historical terms.

[3] 'Ανθρωποκτόνος is rare in the NT; it only occurs here and in I Jn. 3.15 (which is also based on a source text, see Festg. Ad. Jül. 149f.). It also occurs in Act. Phil. 119, p. 48, 10 where it is predicated of the "serpent". 'Απ' ἀρχῆς, as in I Jn. 3.8, refers not to an historical event but to an event before the beginning of history, such as are spoken of in the myth in order to explain man's historical situation in terms of his origin in the mythical age before the dawn of history; cp. Act. Phil. 111, p. 44, 20; ἡ γὰρ ἐπιθυμία τοῦ ὄφεώς ἐστιν ἐξ ἀρχῆς.—There is no need to ask whether the source had a particular mythological story in mind. Both in Gnosticism and in Iranian dualism, where the figure of the Devil originated (see Br. extended note ad loc.), it is taken for granted that the Devil is the originator of all murder; cp. Eth. En. 8, 1; Jub. 11, 5. It is possible that the Evangelist had the Paradise story in mind (cp. Rom. 7.11). Judaism had taken over the Iranian idea that the Devil was God's opponent and that through him death had come into the world; cp. Wisd. 1.13; 2.24; Vit. Ad. et Ev.; Bousset, Rel. d. Jdt. 408f.; Str.—B. I 139–149.

[4] Εστηκεν should either be read as ἕστ., and then be taken as the present perfect of ἵστημι (Bl.-D. para. 97, 1): "he does not stand (fast)"; or as ἔστ., when it would be the imperfect of the present στήκω, which is a late form derived from ἕστηκα (Bl.-D. para. 73). In the first case we would then have a statement in the preterite (ἦν) followed by one in the present. Now it is in itself quite possible to refer to the Devil's behaviour in the present tense (I Jn. 3.8: ἀπ' ἀρχῆς ... ἁμαρτάνει). But here we should read the imperfect after ἦν; the statement in the present tense: ὅτι οὐκ ἔστιν κτλ. is clearly intended to explain how it always *was*.—"Standing in" refers to someone's belonging to something in such a way that that to which he belongs completely determines his being; cp. Rom. 5.2; I Cor. 15.1; 16.13; Phil. 4.1 etc. Rabbinic usage is the same (Schl.); cp. Ginza 276, 29; 286, 31: "they stand outside the Kušta (= ἀλήθεια)". Here too there is no need to suppose that there is any allusion to a myth, according to which the Devil once stood within the sphere of truth and then lost his standing. It goes without saying, on the basis of his Iranian origin, that lying is the nature of the Devil; see Br. ext. note, and cp. esp. Act. Thom. 143, p. 250, 15f. of the ἄρχων (τοῦ κόσμου): τὸ ἀληθὲς οὐκ ἔγνω, ἐπειδήπερ ἀληθείας ἐστὶν ἀλλότριος. Porphyr. abst. II 42, p. 171, 22 Nauck of the evil demons: τὸ γὰρ ψεῦδος τούτοις οἰκεῖον. Ginza 22, 22f.: Satan is "completely full of magic, deceit and seduction". In Mand. Lit. 198 the messenger says to Ruha (the demonic spirit of the world): "Your eyes are eyes of lying, my eyes are the eyes of truth. The eyes of lying grow dark and do not see the truth."

The Evangelist's addition, "For truth was not in him",[1] makes it clear that murder and lies are of the very nature of the Devil.

The description of the Devil as a *murderer* and a *liar* must be seen in its unity. Ζωή and ἀλήθεια together are the divine powers which bestow on man the authenticity of his existence.[2] Thus lying and the hostility to life are also closely connected. The mythological form of the discourse shows that the concepts ἀλήθεια and ψεῦδος on the one hand, and ζωή and θάνατος on the other are not related here to the Greek question of the rational knowledge of all existents, but to the question of the reality and authenticity of human existence, of its ζωή. And just as ἀλήθεια does not refer to the "uncoveredness" of all (worldly) existents, but to God's reality, in particular to God's reality as it unveils and reveals itself to man and so brings him to his authenticity, so too ψεῦδος here does not have the formal meaning of the deceptive "coveredness" of existents or of error in general, but refers to the will which is opposed to God, which indeed creates its deceitful reality only by such opposition;[3] that is to say, it refers to nothingness, which in its revolt claims to be something and whose only being lies in this revolt. It is because of this nothingness that the ψεῦδος kills, because it robs the man who imagines it is real of his own authenticity.

It is this hostility to life which constitutes the very nature of the "Jews", and it is from this that their unbelief stems.[4] In view of the universal character of the statement it would be wrong to ask whether there is any more specific reason for the *charge* made against the Jews *of intended murder*. For hostility to the revelation is as such hostility to life. Yet as seen by the Evangelist, this enmity is expressed symbolically in the Jews' intention to kill Jesus; it was first mentioned in 5.18, and referred to again in 7.25, and from then onwards is always lurking darkly in the background (7.30, 44, 32; 8.59; 10.39), until in 11.53 it emerges as the firm determination to put an end to him.

---

[1] On this use of εἶναι ἐν cp. 1.47; 2.25; 7.18 etc.; it is used of ἀλήθεια again in I Jn. 1.8; 2.4. Ἔχειν ἐν ἑαυτῷ 5.26, 42 and μένειν ἐν 5.38; 14.10; I Jn. 2.14 etc. are related to this use. It refers to the determination of a person's being by the thing which "is" or "remains" in him, as do the corresponding expressions which speak of a person's being (10.38; 14.10f., 20; I Jn. 1.7; 2.5; etc.) or remaining (8.31; 12.46; I Jn. 2.6, 10 etc.) in ....—The ὅτι-clause must have been added by the Evangelist to the source.

[2] On ζωή see p. 39ff. and especially 39 n. 3; on ἀλήθεια see pp. 53 n. 1, 74 n. 2, 190f.

[3] See pp. 46f.—Büchsel (Joh. und der hellenistische Synkretismus 1928, 106) and Odeberg (303) are right to maintain that there is no real dualism in John.

[4] There is no question here of the view that Satan can *inspire* men, in order to use them as his tools (cp. Mk. 3.22 etc.). The statement is much more likely to be based on the Gnostic idea that the *origin* of evil is in evil, an idea which is often expressed in a crudely mythological form (being begotten by the Devil or by an evil spirit). Cp. Act. Pt. et Pl. 55, p. 203, 1f.; Iren. I 15,6; Ginza 25, 22ff.; 374, 35 etc. See Br. ad loc. On Heraclean's exegesis, see v. Loewenich 144.

Equally the *accusation of lying,* levelled against the Jews, does not refer to particular lies which they may have told. The λαλεῖν τὸ ψεῦδος which they are (indirectly) charged with refers to their speech in general, insofar as it is motivated by their enmity towards the revelation, i.e., to the truth. The very fact that they can speak τὸ ψεῦδος unwittingly, or even "with a good conscience", shows the uncanny power that the Devil has over his children. Just as the reality of God, which is present in the continuing existence of the world, is perpetually concealed by the "world",[1] so too the λαλεῖν τὸ ψεῦδος occurs continually in the intercourse of men who seek their own honour and receive honour from one another (5.41ff.). It occurs, of course, in the speech which morality calls "lying"; but it also occurs in everything man says when he wants to secure himself against God, whether in the sciences or in art. In an extreme sense it occurs in everything that man says in resistance to the revelation which encounters him; here the "lie" is no more than unbelief coming to expression. This is why it would be wrong to ask in what respect the Jews have "lied" in the present discussion. Their whole conduct is lying; and vv. 45f show us immediately that the ψεύστης is not simply one who "lies", but one who will have nothing to do with the truth.[2]

V. 45: "But because I am the one who tells you the truth, you will not believe me."[3] There is a formal contrast between the ἐγὼ δὲ of this verse and the ὑμεῖς which dominates v. 44. The conclusion to be drawn from this is clear: because he tells them the "truth", they, whose nature it is to be at enmity with the "truth", cannot believe him.[4] Like λαλεῖν τὸ ψεῦδος, τὴν ἀλήθειαν λέγειν is also ambiguous: when it is said of any and every man, it means to tell the truth in a general sense, as a moral imperative; but when it is said of the Revealer it means to reveal the reality of God in the word, and to present it as a challenge to men. Jesus' words play on this double meaning. For when he asks, "Why do you not believe me when I speak the truth?" (**v. 46b**), this makes the Jews' behaviour appear capricious and contrary, because they refuse

---

[1] See pp. 44f., 46f.

[2] This explanation is valid even if, following the Evangelist, we must take the subject of λαλεῖν τὸ ψεῦδος not as the child of the Devil but as the Devil (or even Cain) himself (see pp. 318ff.). For in any case the Evangelist traces the conduct of the unbelieving Jews back to the Devil, and explains thereby that unbelief has its ground in the power which gains its illusory being from its revolt against the truth, and that therefore lying is of the nature of unbelief.

[3] It can hardly be right to read, with two Vulg.-Mss ὅς instead of ὅτι, as is suggested by Black (56).

[4] Burney's suggestion (77) that ὅτι is a mistranslation and should read ὅς (see on 9.17) completely misconstrues the main idea here.—On the position of ἐγώ at the beginning of the sentence see p. 233 n. 4.

to believe a man who tells the truth;[1] but their contrariness has its explanation, for this man, who "tells them the truth", at the same time reveals the "truth", namely God's reality, in such a way that they are quite unable to believe. For they can assert their own being only if they conceal that reality from themselves.

The peculiar ambiguity of τὴν ἀλήθειαν λέγειν is reflected in the question interjected between v. 45 and v. 46b: "Which of you can convict me of sin?" (**v. 46a**).[2] For the question in the first place assumes the general meaning of truth; they ought to believe him because he speaks the truth. But, they might ask, what guarantee have they that he is really speaking the truth? Well, he is trustworthy because he is unimpeachable, for who could convict him of sin?[3] But the question is ambiguous. Is Jesus' claim to speak the "truth" to be made subject to man's judgement on his unimpeachability? For in that case the man challenged by the Revealer would after all have a criterion by which to judge him. No! For just as ἀδικία ἐν αὐτῷ οὐκ ἔστιν in 7.18 stated that Jesus encounters man only as the Revealer, and is nothing in himself,[4] so too the "sinlessness" of Jesus which is asserted in 8.46 means nothing other than that he is "from God", whereas his opponents are of the Devil.[5] Thus the question τίς . . . ἐλέγχει με κτλ. can only really be answered in faith; it does not point the man who is challenged by the Revealer to a criterion by which to judge him, but once again affirms the claim of the Revealer. His "sinlessness" does not describe his "personality", which could be judged by human standards. It is not demonstrable nor can it be confirmed by the charitable observer. It is the character of his word, which, as the word of revelation, forbids all critical questions.[6]

---

[1] For this reason we have οὐ πιστεύετέ μοι, and not εἰς τὸ ὄνομα τοῦ υἱοῦ τ. θεοῦ, εἰς τὸν υἱὸν etc. On the interchangeability of πιστ. with the dative and πιστ. εἰς see p. 252 n. 2. Cp. the reconstruction of the source in Becker 82.

[2] The omission of v. 46 in D pc was occasioned by the homoioteleuton.

[3] 'Ελέγχειν περί = "convict of" is also good Greek, see Br.

[4] See p. 275.

[5] The Gnostic myth also characterises the messenger as sinless. Cp. Ginza 59, 1ff.:

> "I am the true messenger
> In whom there is no lie,
> The true one in whom there is no lie,
> In him there is no failing or fault."

Cp. ZNTW 24 (1925), 113f. and Br. ad loc.

[6] Thus "sinlessness" applies not only to the person of the Revealer but also to the community which proclaims him. For what v. 47 says of the former, I Jn. 4.6 says of the latter: "He who knows God hears us; he who is not of God hears us not."—Thus Luther can dare to say that the preacher qua preacher does not have to pray for the forgiveness of his sins (EA 26, 35; cp. F. Gogarten, Glaube und Wirklichkeit 1928, 52f.).

V. 47 answers the question in v. 46b, and in so doing abandons the ambiguity of the question. Why do they not believe him, when he "speaks the truth"? The "truth" which he speaks is the words of God, and only "he who is of God hears the words of God." Thus they cannot hear because they are not "of God".[1] This brings the discourse back to its starting point. Vv. 43f. asked, Why do you not understand what I say? Because you cannot hear my word! And why is this? Because you come from the Devil! Vv. 46f., repeat the question and answer, Why do you not believe? Because you do not come from God!

In **v. 51** the denunciation reaches its conclusion. In the presence of the "Jews", who as children of the Devil are in death, Jesus issues the solemn promise: (introduced by ἀμὴν ἀμὴν λέγω ὑμῖν) "He who keeps my word,[2] will never see death."[3] Just as in 6.63 his words were described as "spirit and life", so here the promise is made that life will be given to those who believe in his word,[4] a life over which death will no longer have any power.[5] Will the "dead" hear the voice of the Son of God?

---

[1] V. 47b διὰ τοῦτο κτλ. has been added to the source by the Evangelist, see p. 92 n. 2. (The omission of the ὅτι-clause in some authorities is clearly due only to an oversight.) All in all I would like to reconstruct the source as follows:

43 διὰ τί τὴν λαλιὰν τὴν ἐμὴν οὐ γινώσκετε;
ὅτι οὐ δύνασθε ἀκούειν τὸν λόγον τὸν ἐμόν.
42 ἐγὼ [γὰρ] ἐκ τοῦ θεοῦ ἐξῆλθον καὶ ἥκω,
44 ὑμεῖς ἐκ τοῦ πατρὸς ‹ὑμῶν› τοῦ διαβόλου ἐστέ.
ἐκεῖνος ἀνθρωποκτόνος ἦν ἀπ' ἀρχῆς
καὶ ἐν τῇ ἀληθείᾳ οὐκ ἕστηκεν.
ὁ λαλῶν τὸ ψεῦδος ἐκ τῶν ἰδίων λαλεῖ,
ὅτι ψεύστης ἐστὶν καὶ ὁ πατὴρ αὐτοῦ.
46c ὁ ὢν ἐκ τοῦ θεοῦ τὰ ῥήματα τοῦ θεοῦ ἀκούει,
45 ἐγὼ δὲ ὅτι τὴν ἀλήθειαν λέγω, οὐ πιστεύετέ μοι.
46a.b τίς ἐξ ὑμῶν ἐλέγχει με περὶ ἁμαρτίας;
εἰ ἀλήθειαν λέγω, διὰ τί οὐ πιστεύετέ μοι;
51 ἐάν τις τὸν ἐμὸν λόγον τηρήσῃ
θάνατον οὐ μὴ θεωρήσῃ εἰς τὸν αἰῶνα.

Of course the reconstruction is uncertain. I am still not sure whether the last line of v. 44 may not come from the Evangelist (ὅτι ψεύστης κτλ) and whether the source instead may not have had something like: ἐγὼ δὲ τὰ ῥήματα τοῦ θεοῦ λαλῶ.

[2] This translation is not intended to indicate that I favour the reading ὃς ἂν (D sy sa) as opposed to ἐάν τις, which the other authorities read. The actual meaning of the two readings is the same.

[3] Θεωρεῖν like ἰδεῖν 3.3 (see p. 135 n. 2). When the Jews repeat the saying in v. 52 θεωρεῖν is replaced by γεύεσθαι, which is synonymous, see below.

[4] Τὸν λόγον τηρεῖν means obedience to the word, that is faith, see p. 301 n. 5.

[5] Faith is promised ζωὴ (αἰώνιος) in 3.16, 36; 5.24; 6.40, 47, whereas unbelief will not "see" life 3.36. The negative form as here in 8.51 also occurs in 11.25f., where it is coupled with the positive statement.

b) Jesus and Abraham: 8.52–53, 56–59

This last saying of Jesus, his promise, stings the Jews into contradiction (v. 52): Now it is beyond doubt—Jesus is possessed.[1] Their νῦν ἐγνώκαμεν is the counterpart to the ἐγνώκαμεν of the faithful community (6.69; I Jn. 3.16; 4.16). Both types of γινώσκειν are called forth by the word of the Revealer; before him the division between faith and unbelief takes place. Unbelief argues: How can Jesus' word give eternal life,[2] when even Abraham[3] and the prophets are dead? That would mean—and here they have grasped the meaning of v. 53 aright—that Jesus claims to be more than these.[4] Τίνα σεαυτὸν ποιεῖς; does no more than put in the form of a question what had already been stated in the charge in 5.18, namely, that Jesus has made himself equal to God (cp. 10.33; 19.7). And the formulation shows at once why they cannot understand his claim. They mistake it for the claim of a man seeking to establish his own standing; they judge him by themselves, filled as they with a boundless need for recognition and standing.[5] Even as such they are understand the context of his words aright; he does claim to have divine life.[6] And yet they misunderstand him, because they are unable to free themselves from the concepts of life and death which dominate their own sphere.[7] They know only the kind of life which is a struggle for self-preservation, a holding fast to oneself; whereas the life which is opened up when a man abandons this struggle for survival they can only call death.

---

[1] Δαιμόνιον ἔχεις as in 8.48 see p. 299 n. 5. Νῦν shows that they have only just come to this conclusion, cp. 16.29f. This also shows that the combination of vv. 51–53 with vv. 48–50 is secondary.

[2] Instead of θεωρεῖν, as in v. 51, they say γεύεσθαι θανάτου, which also occurs in Mk. 9.1; Job 2.9; II Esr. 6.26 and which is Rabbinic terminology; see Schl. and Str.-B. on Mt. 16.28. However the metaphorical use of γεύεσθαι is also found in Greek authors (ThWB II 674, 31ff.), and there we find γ. θανάτου (Leonidas, Anthol. Pal. VII 662) and ἀθανασίας (C. Herm. 10, 8).—Odeberg 305 thinks that the reason for the change from θεωρεῖν to γεύεσθαι is that the sentence has a different meaning when spoken by Jesus and when spoken by the Jews. This seems oversubtle.

[3] Ὅστις v. 53 has the force of "who *even*" (Bl.-D. para. 293, 2). Ὅτι, which is read by D a instead of ὅστις, is a Semitism according to Burney 77.

[4] Similarly the Samaritan woman 4.12 had realised that Jesus' claim put him above Jacob. On the veneration of Abraham in Judaism see O. Schmitz in Theol. Abh. Ad. Schl. dargebracht 1922, 99ff.; J. Jeremias, ThWB I 7, 30ff. "The fact that Abraham died is the most conclusive proof of the inevitability of death" (Schl. ad loc.; see also Str.-B. ad loc.).—The prophets are grouped with Abraham or the "fathers", cp. Ecclus. 44–49; Zech. 1.5 says that the "fathers" and the prophets have died.—There is a formal similarity in Hom.Il. 21, 107: κάτθανε καὶ Πάτροκλος, ὅς περ σέο πόλλον ἀμείνων. Lucr. III 1042ff.: ipse Epicurus obit decurso lumine vitae, qui genus humanum ingenio superavit ... tu vero dubitabis et indignabere obire?

[5] See p. 271.

[6] In the context it is unlikely that Jesus' words suggested to the Jews that he was claiming to be a man like Enoch or Elias, of whom legend said that they had not died (Str.-B. IV 766; Odeberg 305f.).

[7] See p. 257f.

Jesus' answer shows clearly the inadequacy of Jewish standards of judgement (**v. 56**): I am indeed greater than Abraham! Yet of course the answer is not immediately given as directly as this. It is given in a form which suggests that the important thing about the person of Jesus is not his greatness as a human figure, but his role in the salvation history: "Your father Abraham rejoiced to see my day; he saw it and was glad."[1] The "day" of Jesus is not only the time of his appearance in a merely chronological sense, but at the same time, and chiefly (there is a certain intentional ambiguity here), the eschatological day, the day of the coming of the "Son of Man".[2] That is to say, Abraham knew that he was not himself the fulfilment of the saving will of God, nor the yard-stick for judging the greatness of divine revelation; he looked forward to the fulfilment in the Messiah, and welcomed the day when he himself would be judged by one greater than himself.[3] Thus when the Jews try to play off Jesus against Abraham, they distort the meaning of the promise, in

---

[1] Instead of the infinitive of purpose and consequence (τοῦ ἰδεῖν) we have ἵνα, in accordance with Hellenistic usage. This can only mean: "he desired with delight to see" or "he rejoiced that he should see", Bl.-D. para. 392, 1a; Windisch, ZNTW 26 (1927), 206; according to Barr. ἵνα is explanatory or gives the reason for the rejoicing, and in support of this he points (following Br.) to BGU 1081, 5. Colwell 114 is opposed to the suggestion that there has been a mistake in translation (Burney 111; de Zwaan 164f.) or any textual mistake in the Aramaic original (Torrey 329).—On ἰδεῖν see p. 135 n. 2; it occurs frequently with ἡμέρα when used in the sense of "experience", see Wetst.

[2] The OT speaks of the "day of Jahweh" and the day of the eschatological judgement and salvation (ThWB II 946, 22ff.). This day can also be referred to as the "day of judgement" etc. or simply as "that day", and where the notion of the Messiah has been assimilated by eschatology, as the "day of the chosen one" (Eth. En. 61, 5) and other similar titles (Volz, Eschatologie 208; ThWB II 954, 1ff.). The Rabbinic expression "the day of the Messiah" (Str.-B. IV 816; Schl. ad loc.) is somewhat different, in that it refers to the Messianic epoch of salvation. Lk. 17.24 presupposes the formula "day of the Son of Man", and in Greek Primitive Christianity ἡμέρα τοῦ Κυρίου (I Cor. 1.8; 5.5; II Cor. 1.14 etc.) was automatically taken to refer to the day of the parousia of Jesus Christ, as was the formula ἡμέρα (Ἰησοῦ) Χριστοῦ (Phil. 1.6, 10; 2.16). Dodd (261), Wik., Barr. and Dupont (271) all take the "day" to refer to the eschatological day of the coming of the Messiah.—The fact that ἀγαλλιᾶσθαι is used to denote Abraham's rejoicing also shows the eschatological nature of his joy (ThWB I 19, 40ff. and cp. esp. I Pet. 1.6, 8). See also next note.

[3] In Rabbinic speculation it was self-evident that Abraham's hope was set on the eschatological age of salvation; such speculation had sketched out (above all on the basis of Gen. 15.9ff.) the way in which God had shown Abraham the "coming world" (with many details); cp. Merx 179ff.; Str.-B II 525f.; Schl. ad loc.; Odeberg 306; Lohmeyer, Urchristentum I 132; Staerk, Erlosererw. 48f.; Dodd 261; Barr. In such accounts it is sometimes said that Abraham rejoiced in what he saw (cp. Abraham's joy at the promise Yeb. 14, 21; 15, 17). In spite of this it is not likely that εἶδεν καὶ ἐχάρη v. 56 refers to the joy which Abraham experienced in his vision of the future world, but in accordance with ἠγαλλ. ἵνα to his present joy at the fulfilment of the promise (Odeberg 307 combines them both). So too Test. Levi 18, 14: τότε ἀγαλλιάσεται Ἀβρ. καὶ Ἰσαὰκ καὶ Ἰακώβ, κἀγὼ χαρήσομαι. Jewish speculation also believed that Abraham in his present heavenly existence participated in the fate of his people (Str.-B. Index, s.v. Abr.); it is also presupposed in the prayer in Lk. 16.24. See too on 12.41.—Eisler, Rätsel 474f. thinks that Abraham's joy occurred in Hades, and that 8.56 therefore presupposes Jesus' descent into Hades.

the same way as they distorted the meaning of the law by their appeal to Moses.[1] What they lack is the readiness to wait, a readiness which culminates in the acceptance of faith, when it is confronted with what has been promised. Now the day has come; now the eschatological age is present. But for the Jews it is hidden because they are ensnared in the standards of the world view through which they try to find security. It is hidden, because they are quite unable to comprehend the meaning of God's eschatological action which breaks the world and its standards.

The Jews remain caught in the trammels of their own thought (**v. 57**): How can Jesus, who is not yet 50 years old,[2] have seen Abraham![3] Yet the world's conception of time and age is worthless when it has to deal with God's revelation, as is its conception of life and death (**v. 58**): "Before Abraham was, I am." The Revealer, unlike Abraham, does not belong to the ranks of historical personages.[4] The ἐγώ which Jesus speaks as the Revealer is the "I" of the eternal Logos, which was in the beginning, the "I" of the eternal God himself.[5] Yet the Jews

---

[1] See p. 273.

[2] On ἔχειν used in referring to people's ages, see p. 241 n. 6. It can hardly be that 50 years is intended to give Jesus' approximate age (thus the Presbyter in Iren. II 22, 5), which would strongly contradict the tradition attested in Lk. 3.23 (see p. 127 n.3). The reference is simply to the age of a fully grown man. According to Num. 4.3; 8.24f., the Levites were under obligation to serve till their 50th year According to Hippocrates (in Philo opif. mundi 105) the 50th year is the limit of man's span of life.

[3] Instead of ἑώρακας ℵ* 0124 syr^{s} sa read ἑώρακέν σε, which is accepted by Bd. and Strachan, but which is certainly a correction to conform with v. 56. The change of subject may be accidental; ἔχεις may have prompted an unintentional alteration to ἑώρακας; but it may have been intentional. According to Odeberg (307) the purpose is to make it clear that Abraham not only foresaw Jesus' "day", but that there is an "actual interrelation in the spiritual world". Perhaps, however, the Jews' ἑώρακας is meant to indicate that they misunderstand the manner of seeing, that they think of it in terms of earthly sight, where men observe each other as existent beings, i.e. that they conceive Abraham's sight in crudely mythological terms.

[4] Εἰμί instead of ἤμην, which one might expect (not of course ἐγενόμην on the lips of the Revealer) is admittedly characteristic. But it cannot be original, for the present εἰμί would be stressed. Merx (179, 1) is certainly right when he suggests that ἐγώ εἰμι corresponds to a simple אָנֹכִי (cp. Ps. 89.2: πρὸ τοῦ ὄρη γενηθῆναι ... σὺ εἶ = אַתָּה and even if the text were written in Greek the Semitising Evangelist would have produced a "virtual translation". The being of the Revealer, to which all becoming is alien, cannot really be defined in any temporal sense, and this is the contrast that is being made here. Γενέσθαι cannot be predicated of him; cp. W. Manson, JTS 18 (1947), 141. The contrast between γενέσθαι and εἰμί is stressed by Dodd (261) in particular. According to Bonsirven (Bibl. 30 [1942], 412) the contrast cannot be expressed in Semitic. (Admittedly in D γενέσθαι is omitted, and so πρίν has to be taken prepositionally; see Bl.-D. para. 395. This makes the contrast simpler.)—This sentence has nothing to do with the ἐγώ-εἰμι statements of the revelation-discourses, where the ἐγώ is predicative, and which require a substantive as subject (see p. 225 n. 3).

[5] This formulation is necessary in view of 1.1: καὶ θεὸς ἦν ὁ λόγος (see p. 32f.), i.e. in Jesus' words God speaks the ἐγώ εἰμι. We should, however, reject the view that ἐγώ εἰμι means: "I (Jesus) am God", i.e. that the sentence identifies Jesus with God. This

cannot comprehend that the ἐγώ of eternity is to be heard in an historical person, who is not yet 50 years old, who as a man is one of their equals, whose mother and father they know. They cannot understand, because the notion of the Revealer's "pre-existence" can only be understood in faith; for only then can the meaning of "pre-existence" be grasped, namely, as the eternity of the divine word of revelation.[1] For all speculative notions of pre-existence which conceive of Jesus or the Messiah as a pre-existing being occupying some place or other,[2] consider the Revealer in the same temporal terms as did the Jews in their objection in v. 57, whereas the true meaning of "pre-existence" excludes any such way of thinking.

In the Jews' ears Jesus' saying is blasphemy—and the revelation cannot avoid calling forth this sort of reaction. They attempt to stone him (**v. 59**);[3] but Jesus hides himself and leaves the temple.[4] Again there is a lack of detail and preciseness in the account, which shows that the Revealer is beyond the reach of the world.[5]

---

view rests on the belief that ἐγώ εἰμι renders one of the mysterious Jewish formulas, which were used in order to avoid direct mention of the divine name and which were formed on the one hand out of the letters of the tetragrammaton יהוה or יהוא, and on the other hand from OT sayings. The suggestion is that ἐγώ εἰμι renders אֲנִי הוּא (or alternatively אֲנִי וְהוּ), which came to be used to refer to God because of verses like Deut. 32.39; Is. 41.4; 43.10; 46.4; 48.12 (G. Klein, Der älteste christliche Katechismus und die jüdische Propaganda-Literatur 1909, 44ff.; G. P. Wetter, ThStKr. 88 (1915), 224ff.; cp. Odeberg 308f.). Alternatively, it might be a rendering of אֶהְיֶה, which came into use as a divine title because of Ex. 3.14 (K. Zickendraht, ThStKr 94 [1922], 162ff.; Lagr.; Odeberg 309f.) Jesus' statement would then mean: "I am the 'I-am'". But is it possible to read this out of the simple ἐγώ εἰμι? It would mean that ἐγώ would have to be both subject and predicate! And apart from the question when and in which circles these titles were used (they do not occur in the list of the divine names in A. Marmorstein, The Old Rabbinic Doctrine of God I 1927), this view is not possible in the context; for then the stress would lie on the predicate, whereas in the context after πρὶν Ἀβρ. γενέσθαι the stress must be on the subject ἐγώ, and there is no reason to expect a substantial predicate at all. This is seen rightly by Schweizer 44, n. 241.

[1] See p. 35f. and pp. 253ff.

[2] On the Jewish notions of the pre-existence of the Messiah, see Bousset, Rel. d. dt. 263; Volz. Eschatologie 204ff.; Str.B. II 333–352.

[3] Stoning as a punishment for blasphemy Lev. 24.16; Sanhedr. 5.3ff.; Acts 7.58. On stoning in the temple, see Schl. ad loc. It is superfluous to ask where one would have got the stones from in the temple (Str.-B.; Schl.: because building was constantly in progress). Cp. further Str.-B. I 1008–1019.

[4] Bl.-D. para. 471, 2 raises the question whether the co-ordinated ἐκρύβη καὶ ἐξῆλθεν should be taken as ἐκρῦβη ἐξελθών.—ἐκρύβη also occurs in 12.36. The combination of these passages with the idea of the "hidden Messiah" in R. Eisler, Ἰησοῦς βασιλεύς II 47, 3 is fantastic.

[5] Cp. 7.30, 44; 8.20; 10.39 and see p. 302 n. 3. Cp. further Lk. 4, 30 and the snatching away of the God in the Apollonios legend (Philostr. Vit. Ap VIII 5 p. 300, 26 Kayser). On the miraculous disappearance cp. Lucian, Philops. 36 and Rosa Söder, Die apokryphen Apostelgesch. und die romanhafte Lit. der Antike 1932, 66f.—Zn. again gives a rationalistic explanation: "They must have hesitated for a moment, which provided Jesus with his

C. 9.1-41; 8.12; 12.44-50; 8.21-29; 12.34-36; 10.19-21: The Light of the World

a) Healing narrative, Discussion and Controversy: 9.1–41

As in ch. 5 the new section is introduced by a healing story (9.1–7). The transition to Jesus' discourse for which this story paves the way is afforded by a conversation about the miracle (or rather about the miracle-worker) between the healed man and the Jewish authorities (9.8–34) and between the former and Jesus himself (9.35–38). The narrative is far more detailed than in ch. 5, and is dominated from the start by a mood of excitement and tension. The miracle becomes a source of contention because it was performed on the Sabbath, but this—as in ch. 5—we are told only subsequently (v. 14). Finally, again as in ch. 5, there is a short controversy between Jesus and his opponents (9.39–41), which provides the immediate introduction for the following discourse.[1]

The miracle story and the discussion which follows is taken, as in ch. 5, from a source—we need not hesitate to surmise that it was the σημεῖα-source[2]—and it has been embellished by the Evangelist's additions, which are more extensive than in ch. 5. Vv. 4–5, 22–23, 29f. (-34a) and 39–41 may be attributed to him; and his editors have also left their mark on vv. 16f. and 35–38.[3]

---

chance to slip away unnoticed." Similarly B. Weiss, whereas according to Ho., the Evangelist leaves the reader "to ponder and guess."—Cp. the scene in Lucian, Demon. 11, where the Athenians who want to stone Demonax are dissuaded by his clever speech; see p. 310 n. 1.

[1] For the reconstruction of the whole complex, see p. 312f.

[2] The language, as in all parts of the σημεῖα-source, is a Semitising Greek, but not translation Greek (the view held by Burney, which is rightly challeneged by Colwell). The conjunction of the clauses is primitive throughout (asyndeta, καί, οὖν, δέ without μέν). The predicate often stands at the beginning of a sentence. Αὐτοῦ in vv. 2, 18 is superfluous (assuming that it is not meant to be stressed here), as is ἡμεῖς in v. 24. Ὕπαγε νίψαι v. 7 is also Semitic, see Black 46. The conjunctive participle in vv. 6, 11, 25 is Greek, but not in vv. 2, 19 (ἠρώτησαν λέγοντες is a poor attempt at a more elegant form of ἠρώτησαν καὶ εἶπαν); the conjunctive participle is avoided in the phrase ἀπεκρ. καὶ εἶπ. vv. 20, 30, 34. The position of αὐτοῦ v. 6, of σου v. 10, of ποτε v. 13 (although τὸν πρὶν τυφλ. or τὸν πρὸ τοῦ τυφλ. would have been better) is Greek; ἐκ γενετῆς v. 1 and θεοσεβής v. 31 is also Greek.

[3] Wellh. and Sp. see the change from Φαρ. vv. 13, 16 to Ἰουδ. v. 18, as an indication that vv. 17 (or alternatively 18)—23 have been added to the source by the Evangelist. But it seems to me that one cannot really maintain that in vv. 18–23 the blind man is treated as if he had not previously been questioned (Wellh.). Nor does the fact that the Pharisees in vv. 13–16 (unlike the Jews in vv. 18–23) did not doubt that the man really was blind, provide much of an argument against the originality of vv. 18–23; rather it is a sign of their perplexity that they should now seize on this idea. Nor is it any argument against vv. 18–23 that the parents had not been mentioned till now. This would only be so if, like Sp., one took ἐκ γεν. v. 1 to be an addition, for the sake of which the parents must be introduced later because they are the only people who can testify to the ἐκ γεν.; on this point see below.

1) *The Healing of the Blind Man:* 9.1–7

There is no strict literary dependence of the healing of the blind man in Jn. 9 upon the stories in Mk. 8.22–26; 10.46–52,[1] for the Johannine account produces its own independent variant of the motif in those stories.[2] Stylistically the greatest difference between the Synoptic and the Johannine stories lies in the fulness of the discussion which follows the miracle in the Johannine account. It is a sign of the advanced stage of development of the story that Jesus himself seizes the initiative in performing the miracle,[3] so that the miracle becomes a demonstration of his power; this is particularly underlined by the Evangelist's own verses 4f. Consequently the mention of the sick man's πίστις is omitted, as in 5.6ff.

There is no attempt in the setting of the scene in **v. 1** to link up the narrative with the preceding events. It has more the character of an introduction to what was originally an isolated story.[4] It is automatically assumed that Jesus is accompanied by his disciples,[5] even though this has not been mentioned since ch. 6. The sight of a blind man[6] gives rise to a discussion between Jesus and the disciples. Their question (**v. 2**), whether the cause of a man's blindness is his own sin or that of his parents,[7] assumes certain well-known Jewish views.[8] Whether the question is

---

[1] The motif of the spittle (v.6) need not necessarily have been taken from Mk. 8.23 (this contrary to what I said in Gesch. der syn. Tr. 242 = Hist. of the Syn. Trad. 226).

[2] There is no reason to suppose that a story from another tradition has been attributed to Jesus here. The question of theodicy, occasioned by people who are blind from birth, is dealt with in Jewish legend (two variants in Bin Gorion, Der Born Judas II 206–210, one version in Gaster, Exempla No. 407); but in these cases the blind man's wickedness is every time disclosed and shown to be a proof of God's justice.—On healings of blind men in the Hellenistic miracle tradition see Gesch. der syn. Tr. 248 = Hist. of the Syn. Trad. 233; Br. ext. note after v. 34. Against the assumption of Buddhist influence on John 9, see R. Garbe, Indien und das Christentum 1914, 35ff.

[3] As in 6.5 ff.; 5.6; see p. 210 n. 1, 242.

[4] καὶ παράγων εἶδεν as in Mk. 2.14; cp. Mk. 1.16; 2.23; Mt. 9.27.—παράγειν means not only "to pass by" (= עבר, Schl. on Mt. 9.9) but also "to proceed, go on further" cp. Mt. 9.9, 27.

[5] See p. 115 n. 5.

[6] In Greek usage a man born blind is referred to as τυφλὸς ἐκ γενετῆς (Wetst. and Br.); the Semitic equivalent would be "blind from his mother's womb" (Schl.; cp. Mt. 19.12; Acts 3.2; 14.8, etc.).

[7] Of course one may not ask how the disciples know that he was born blind.—Ἵνα is consecutive, as in I Jn. 1.9, etc., Bl.-D. para. 391, 5.

[8] Illness was thought of as the punishment for a man's own sins, p. 243 n. 7. The idea that parents' guilt was punished in their children was universal in the ancient world (for the OT see Ex. 20.5; Deut. 5.9, etc., for Classical antiquity see Br.) and was developed particularly in Judaism (cp. Tobit 3.3f. and see Str.-B. ad loc.).—The fact that it is hard to see how one can talk about a man's own guilt when he was born blind leads Sp. to omit ἐκ γενετῆς as an addition (see p. 329 n. 3; cp. Dibelius, Formgesch. 89 = From Trad. to God. 92). Rabbinic statements about a child's sinning in its mother's womb in Str.-B. do not occur earlier than the (2nd.) 3rd. century. Schl. (ad loc.) shows that God had also to be praised for his justice with regard to those who were deformed at birth; cp. also n. 1 above.—The

simply prompted by curiosity, or whether it is meant to bring out from the start the absurdity of the Jewish view, it does at least serve to provide occasion for a saying of Jesus (**v. 3**). The saying cuts short the discussion of the question; yet what he says does not confute the Jewish position, nor does it suggest that there is another way of looking at such cases, such as is suggested by the Dominical saying in Lk. 13.2–5.[1] The saying is concerned only with the particular case in question at the moment: the purpose of this man's blindness is that God's works should be manifested in him.[2] This points forward to the healing miracle; for the one who performs "God's works"[3] is Jesus, whom the Father has entrusted with the doing of them (5.36). Thus the purpose of the blind man's suffering is the same as that of Lazarus' illness, namely, ἵνα δοξασθῇ ὁ υἱὸς τοῦ θεοῦ δι' αὐτῆς (11.4), which was also the purpose of the miracle at Cana: ἐφανέρωσεν τὴν δόξαν αὐτοῦ (2.11). Of course, Jesus' miracles are "works of God" only in so far as they are σημεῖα,[4] as indications or symbols of the real works, or of "the work", which he does on behalf of the Father. Thus the following story must be seen from the start in the light of this symbolism: he who gives the light of day to the blind man is the "light of the world".[5] This is stated immediately in v. 5, and it is further developed in the subsequent discourse.

The activity of the Revealer is limited,[6] as is stated by **vv. 4f.** V. 4 says of the Revealer that he must use his time to the full.[7] V. 5 is addressed

---

reference can hardly be to sins committed in a pre-existent state, even though the idea of the pre-existence of souls had found its way into syncretistic and Hellenistic Judaism (Wisd. 8.19f., further references in Br.; cp. Rud. Meyer, Hellenistisches in der rabb. Anthropologie 1937). Nor is it likely that a belief in the transmigration of souls is assumed here (J. Kroll, Die Lehren des Hermes Trismeg., Reg. p. 422). However, the question perhaps is intended to pose an impossible alternative in order to show up the absurdity of the dogma.

[1] Such as the principle formulated by Br.: "There is undeserved suffering, of which one cannot ask the reason but only the purpose."

[2] The elliptic clause ἀλλ' ἵνα κτλ. as in 1.8 etc. It is characteristic of the Evangelist (see p. 48 n. 3), whose editorial addition begins at this point and comprises vv. 4f. Thus the original continuation of Jesus' reply has been suppressed.

[3] The ἔργα τ. πέμψ. are the works which he who sends him, i.e. God, has given him to do, or alternatively has charged him with; cp. 10.32, and see pp. 194 n. 3, 222 n. 3. 265f.

[4] See pp. 113f, 125f, 218.

[5] On the concept φῶς τ. κόσμου see on 8.12. φῶς εἰμι τοῦ κόσμου 9.5 is not a proper ἐγώ-εἰμι statement, but is a modification of such a statement, designed to make the saying more plastic. This explains why the article has been omitted before φῶς (which Torrey thinks is a Semitism).

[6] Ἕως v. 4 = so long as; see Bl.-D. para. 455, 3 (similarly ὡς 12.35f., which is also read by some authorities in 9.4). Ὅταν in v. 5 has the same meaning (cp. Lk. 11.34).

[7] The text of v. 4 is disputed: א* WL Ꝏ 0124 sa read: ἡμᾶς δεῖ ... τοῦ πέμψ. ἡμᾶς; א ᵃACN ΓΔΘ and the Latin and Syriac translations read: ἐμὲ δεῖ ... τοῦ πέμψ. με. On the other hand B D 0124 bo pal Κυρ. Nonnus first ἡμᾶς then με. Thus the reading best attested is first ἡμᾶς then με, in other words the text of B D, etc. Nevertheless this text cannot be original, even though B. Weiss, Br. Lagr. Bl., and Barr. adhere to it. Ho., Htm.,

to the world, to whom he ministers, in the sense of the exhortation which is given more clearly in 12.35f., and so with an allusion to the warning about the "too late" (7.33; 8.21). And since this exhortation and warning, which is developed in the following discourse, is immediately intelligible, the reference to the limited time available to the Revealer (time which he must use to the full, v. 4), in this context can hardly say any more than that the Sabbath itself cannot limit Jesus' activity—this, of course, with an eye to v. 14. Thus v. 4 is an approximate parallel to 5.17.[1]

The healing of the blind man is described at first (v. 6) in a way similar to Mk. 8.23.[2] The detailed description of Jesus' preparations for the healing are very likely intended to show clearly that his action constituted a breach of the Sabbath laws; cp. vv. 14f.[3] The healing must

---

and Tischendorff want to read ἡμᾶς in both places; Bd., Hirsch favour ἐμέ, and this must be the original reading. ἐμέ was altered to ἡμᾶς in order to give the statement the character of a universally valid principle (i.e. for Christians), since it was thought offensive that the night should put an end to Jesus' activity, seeing he is, according to v. 5, the light of the world. The first correction led in some manuscripts to the second.—See following note, and cp. too A.v. Harnack, SA Berlin 1923, 107, who by reference to 3.11 wants to take the "we" as an emphasised "I", since in a certain sense all God's activity is Jesus' activity.

[1] There is no denying the artificiality of the relation of v. 4 to the context. It is surprising enough that the time limit on the revelation should be the occasion for a warning not only to the world, but to the Revealer to use the time aright; but it is even more surprising that he, who according to v. 5 is the light of the world, and whose departure from the world brings night to it, should according to v. 4, be dependent on day and night.—The difficulties arise because the Evangelist (as in 11.9f.) has used a part of the discourse on the light, taken from the revelation-discourses (which is the basis of vv. 39ff.), and inserted it at this point in order to bring out from the very start the symbolic character of the narrative. V. 5 following on v. 4 gives the impression that originally v. 4 spoke not of the work of the Revealer, but of man's ἐργάζεσθαι, which is tied to day-light. This was meant in the same metaphorical sense as περιπατεῖν in 11.9f.: just as man's possibility of working is tied to day-light, so his possibility of being saved is tied to the presence of the Revealer who, so long as he is in the world, is the "light of the world". Thus in the source v. 4 read simply:

δεῖ ἐργάζεσθαι ἕως ἡμέρα ἐστίν.
ἔρχεται νὺξ ὅτε οὐδεὶς δύναται ἐργάζεσθαι.

In order to preserve the continuity of the narrative the Evangelist has applied the statement to Jesus' activity, and has therefore added ἐμέ at the beginning and τὰ ἔργα τ. πέμψ. με after ἐργάζεσθαι. He probably also altered the original order of the verses; it is likely that v. 5 preceded v. 4 in the source. Possibly vv. 5, 4. were followed in the source by 11.9f.; see on 11.9f.

[2] For χαμαί = χαμᾶζε, and for πηλός = dough, see the references in Br. According to Bl.D. para. 473, 1 and p. 306 (on para. 248, 1) the αὐτοῦ, which has been separated from τ. ὀφθαλμ. and placed in front of it, corresponds to a dative.—On the use of spittle in healing and magic see Klostermann (Hdb. zum NT) and Str.-B. on Mk. 7.33; Gesch. der syn. Tr. 237, 1. = Hist. of the Syn. Trad. 221, n. 1.

[3] This explanation would, of course, not have been necessary in the original form of the story.—Kneading (of dough) was, according to Shab. 7, 2, one of the 39 forms of work forbidden on the Sabbath (Str.-B. I 615f.). On forbidden healing on the Sabbath, with particular reference to healings of eye-diseases, see Str.B. on 9.16.

still be completed by washing in the pool of Siloam (v. 7),[1] which restores the blind man's sight.[2] The interpretation of the name,[3] which has been added by the Evangelist if not indeed the editor, raises the symbolism of the narrative to the level of allegory. Jesus is the ἀπεσταλμένος (3.17, 34; 5.36 etc.); as the blind man receives the light of day through the water of Siloam, so faith receives the light of the revelation from Jesus, the "emissary".[4]

2) *The Discussion of the Miracle:* 9.8–38[5]

9.8–12: *The confusion of the crowd.* No account is given of Jesus' movements (unlike 5.13b), but instead we are told immediately of the excitement which is caused by the healing. In this the typical motive of "witnesses" is employed,[6] but here it is not used to prove the truth of the story by way of conclusion, but forms a prelude to the main narrative. The dilemma of the authorities is reflected in the crowd's confusion. Vv. 8f. recount the astonished questions of the people.[7] The healed man must remove all doubts that he is the same person as the man who was previously blind (v. 9), and must describe how the healing occurred (vv. 10f.).[8] Unlike the healed man in 5.12f., he does at least know the

---

[1] One may not ask how the blind man found his way.—On νίπτειν εἰς cp. the Greek λούειν εἰς and similar expressions, see Br. and Bl.-D. para. 205.—On the form of name Σιλωάμ (LXX Is. 8.6 for הַשִּׁלֹחַ) see Br. and Schl. ad loc.; Bl.-D. para. 56, 3; Dalman. Jesus-Jeschua 13.—On the the position of the pool see Str.-B. ad loc.; Dalman, O. and W. 327f.; R. Eisler, Ἰησ. βασ. II 518–525.—Was miraculous power attributed to the water of Siloah at the time of the story, as it was later? Cp. J. Jeremias, Golgotha 22, 6; Str.-B. gives evidence only of its power of ritual purification.—There is a certain analogy here to the sending of the leprous Naaman to the Jordan in II Kings 5.10.

[2] Βλέπειν, which is used throughout, differs from ὁρᾶν in that it specifically denotes the physical act of seeing.

[3] The explanation interprets the name, which is originally a substantive (emissio sc. aquae), as a passive participle. Cp. Eisler, Ἰησ. βασ. II 82. 1; 356, 1.

[4] It is possible that the Evangelist, with regard to the Jews' unbelief, had Is. 8.6 in mind: "Because this people have scorned the water of Siloah ...'. Allegorical interpretations of Siloah occur in Rabbinic Judaism, see Str.-B. ad loc.—Omodeo, Mistica 80, who uses the methods of the old exegesis, thinks that the healing also symbolises baptism.

[5] On the reflection of the historical situation of the community in the discussion, see p. 239f.

[6] Gesch. der syn. Tr. 241 = Hist. of the Syn. Trad. 225; Wendland, Die urchristl. Literaturformen 238f. (304f.).

[7] It is in accordance with the economy of this kind of narrative style that the parents are not included in the list of neighbours and other friends. They are kept back till vv. 18–23, where they have their part to play (see p. 329 n. 3). The fact that it is only now mentioned that the blind man was also a beggar (as in Mk. 10.46: προσαίτης, which is a late word, see Br.) is probably to be explained by the narrator's tacit assumption that all blind men were beggars.—On οἱ θεωροῦντες ... ὅτι πρ. ἦν see Bl.-D. para. 330: both ἦν and θεωρ. have the force of a pluperfect. Burney (78) thinks that ὅτι is a mistranslation of דְּ = ὅτε; this is questioned by Colwell 100f.

[8] By comparison with vv. 6f. the account is somewhat shortened; for the unnecessary

name of the one who has helped him, but has no idea where he might be found (v. 12). As conceived by the Evangelist, all this points to the astonishing and unpredictable nature of the event of revelation.

9.13–17: *First examination of the healed man.* The healed man is taken to the Pharisees;[1] they were the authorities to whom one had to turn on such occasions (v. 13). The reader knows that this is precisely the wrong course of action, for the unexpected and new should not be subjected to the old, manageable standards. Now we learn (after the event, as in 5.9) that the healing took place on the Sabbath (v. 14), and what was a source of amazement now becomes a source of offence. This state of affairs is briefly described in v. 15,[2] and in v. 16 we are told of the authorities' dilemma: the miracle seems to show that Jesus' actions are divinely accredited,[3] but the breach of the Sabbath laws[4] runs counter to this assumption, since it shows that Jesus is a sinner.[5] So again there is σχίσμα among them.[6] The healed man, when asked[7], confesses that he believes Jesus to be a prophet (v. 17). Jesus' miraculous power has made on him the same impression as did Jesus' miraculous knowledge on the Samaritan woman (4.19); yet as in the case of the woman, so here, this confession is only the first step. Certainly, such a step is important enough; but before this is stressed (vv. 30–33) and developed (vv. 35–38), we have a further account of the authorities' reaction to the

---

reflection on this made by earlier exegetes see Br.—The meaning of ἀνα = "again" in ἀνέβλεψα is no longer present; see Br. Wörterb. and cp. ἀνέζησεν Rom. 7.9.

[1] See p. 306 n. 5.—The anticipation of the object (τόν ποτε τυφλόν) by αὐτόν is in accordance both with Semitic (Burney 86) and with Greek usage (Colwell 50f.).

[2] πάλιν simply refers back to v. 10.

[3] On miracles as a proof of someone's authority see p. 134 n. 4 and Str.-B. ad loc.—One might ask whether the formulation οὐκ ἔστιν οὗτος παρὰ θεοῦ ὁ ἄνθρωπος has been inserted by the Evangelist in place of the phrase which originally occurred in the source, cp. 6.46; 7.29; 17.7; and p. 134. But this is uncertain. Br. compares I Macc. 2.15, 17: οἱ παρὰ τοῦ βασιλέως.

[4] The formula τηρεῖν τὸ σαββ. corresponds to שָׁמַר אֶת־הַשַּׁבָּת (Schl.) but is also possible in Greek, see p. 301 n. 5.

[5] The stress in ἄνθρ. ἁμαρτ. is not on ἄνθρ. but on ἁμαρτ., as is shown by v. 24; cp. Lk. 24.7, and the reference to sinners as ἄνδρες ἁμαρτωλοί in Ecclus. 15.7, 12; 27.30. Lk. 5.8 is not comparable.

[6] Cp. 7.43; 10.19. The Evangelist has clearly inserted this motif into the source; he is also responsible for v. 16b (ἄλλοι κτλ.: the ἄλλοι play no further part in the story) and also the conclusion of v. 17: ὁ δὲ κτλ. (see p. 336 n. 2). V. 17 originally followed on immediately after v. 16a, and was not intended as a serious question but as a shout of horror: "How can you say of him, that he has opened your eyes!" In the context the Evangelist probably altered also the beginning of v. 18. In all probability the source simply had: καὶ οὐκ ἐπίστευσαν περὶ αὐτοῦ κτλ.

[7] As a result of the Evangelist's rewriting of vv. 16f. (see previous note) the question in v. 17 now comes to mean: "What do you say to the fact that he ...", see Bl.-D. para. 456, 2. Burney's view (76) that ὅτι is a mistranslation of דְּ = ὅς is challenged by Colwell 101–102.

situation. Here the Evangelist seeks to portray the struggle of darkness against the light, and to show the sacrifice which is implied in the decision of faith.

9.18–23: *The examination of the parents.* The authorities[1]—the ἄλλοι of v. 16 remain unheard—now hit on the idea of questioning the fact of the miracle,[2] as being the easiest way of putting an end to the whole business (vv. 18f.). Thus the formal correctness with which they act does not protect them from actual misuse of the law. Now they examine the healed man's parents,[3] with the result, however, that the offending fact remains as real as ever, as does their dilemma. This dilemma of the authorities is brought out by the double οὐκ οἴδαμεν of the parents, which mercilessly leaves the authorities with the responsibility for their own judgement, and by the equally merciless αὐτὸν ἐρωτήσατε κτλ. (vv. 20f.).[4] The Evangelist adds vv. 22f., in order to explain that the parents' caution is a result of their fear of being cast out of the synagogue.[5]

9.24–34: *Second examination of the healed man.* Again the authorities have the healed man brought before them. Outwardly therefore they act correctly, and take considerable trouble over the matter.[6] But in reality they have already made up their minds: "We know that this man is a sinner." They would like to throw the responsibility on to

---

[1] The change from Φαρ. to Ἰουδαῖοι is to be attributed to the Evangelist's editing of the passage (see n. 334 n. 6) and is no indication of the secondary character of vv. 18–23 (see p. 329 n. 3).

[2] ἦν in v. 18 is pluperfect, as in v. 24, see p. 333 n. 7.

[3] Ἕως ὅτου v. 18 = "until" as in I Sam. 30.4: I Macc. 14.10; Lk. 13.8, etc., Bl.-D. para. 455, 3.—Αὐτοῦ after γονεῖς, which would be unnecessary in Greek, is an Aramaism according to Burney (88); but cp. Colwell 49f., who cites examples in popular Greek.

[4] Ἡλικίαν ἔχειν = to be old enough, to be of age, is common, see Br.; corresponding expressions are to be found in Rabbinic literature, see Str.-B.—Αὐτός is stressed, Bl.-D. para. 283, 4.

[5] Ἀποσυνάγωγος occurs only here in the NT, and in 12.42; 16.2. According to Schl. it corresponds to the Rabbinic מְנוּדֶּה; such a person is to be distinguished from the man who is completely separated from the community (מְשׁוּפָּד); see Str.-B. IV 293–333; Schürer II 507.543f.; Schwartz, Aporien 1908, 146f.—Vv. 22f. have clearly been added to the source at a time when the confession of Jesus as the Messiah (which as yet does not at all come into consideration in the context) meant automatic exclusion from the Synagogue. The Evangelist's style is apparent: on ταῦτα εἶπαν ... ὅτι, see ταῦτα λέγω ἵνα, 5.34, ταῦτα λελάληκα ἵνα 14.25; 15.11; 16.1, 4, 33; 17.13 and cp. I Jn. 2.1, 26; 5.13 and expressions like ταῦτα (τοῦτο) εἶπεν, etc., 6.59; 7.9, 39; 8.20, 30, etc. On the ἤδη-clause, cp. 7.14; 15.3; on ἵνα ἐάν 11.57 (which is also a material parallel); I Jn. 2.28; on διὰ τοῦτο κτλ. 6.65; 12.27; 13.11; 19.11; I Jn. 3.1; 4.5; similarly 5.16, 18; 8.47; 10.17; 12.18, 39.

[6] V. 22 makes it probable that the length of the examination reflects the intimidating examinations which Christians had to undergo before Jews and heathens (Baldensperger, Rev. H. Ph. rel. 2 (1922), 17f.). In the source the length of the proceedings is meant only to illustrate the παράδοξον of the event; and this is true of the Evangelist's version as well, inasmuch as for him the παράδοξον *is* the revelation event.

the healed man; he should give God the glory and confess the truth,[1] i.e. agree with them (v. 24). However he does not allow himself to be taken in by their bluff, but remains true to what he knows (v. 25).[2] The authorities' dilemma is shown in their repeated questions about what really happened (v. 26), as if—should the healed man for instance, contradict himself—they could still find something which would count decisively against Jesus; and it is shown even more clearly by the ironic reply of the healed man (v. 27). By pretending that he believes them really to be in earnest, he treats the insincerity of the inquiry with the greatest possible irony. In the face of this attack they are unable to maintain the appearance of objectivity any longer; they abuse him (v. 28),[3] and chase him out (v. 34). The Evangelist, who added vv. 22f., understands this to mean that they cast him out of the synagogue.[4] By doing this they take the view that, as disciples of Moses, they do not need to concern themselves with any other sort of discipleship. They know that God has given proof of Moses' authority,[5] but they do not know whether he has given any such proof for Jesus (v. 29). Their statement, "As for this man, we do not know whence he comes," confirms Jesus' saying that his origin is hidden from them (8.14; 7.28). The possession of their tradition, on which they base their security, only blinds them to the revelation which confronts them. Just as in 5.38ff. their appeal to Moses was turned into an accusation against them, so it is with

[1] Δὸς δόξαν τ. θεῷ is a formula which was used to urge someone to (grateful) acceptance (Ps. 67.35; Rev. 14.7; cp. Lk. 17.18, etc.), to obedience (Jer. 13.16; II Esr. 10.11; cp. Rom. 4.20; Rev. 16.9) and particularly to urge him to confess the truth (Josh. 7.19); it is used in this latter way here and in Rabbinic usage, see Str.-B. and cp. Dalman, Jesus-Jeschua 193f.; see also F. Horst ZAW 1929, 45ff.

[2] There is a certain contradiction between εἰ ἁμαρτ. ἐστιν κτλ. and the confession in v. 17, and this is to be attributed to the Evangelist (see p. 334 n. 6); however it is not serious, for the statement in v. 24 is simply a refusal to accept the judgment of the authorities.—Ἓν οἶδα (which is good Greek) is considered by Burney (112) for no reason whatsoever to be a mistranslation for τοῦτο (חָדָא has been incorrectly read as הָדָא). On the pluperfect ὤν, see Bl.-D. para. 339, 3.

[3] Ἐκείνου v. 28 is spoken scornfully (see Bl.-D. para. 291, 1). The Evangelist probably understood it as an involuntary recognition of the ἐκεῖνος in the other sense of the word (see p. 48 n. 3). "Disciple of (Moses)" is a common Jewish phrase which was taken over by Christianity (Str.-B.), but it is also quite permissible in Greek (Br. Wörterb.)

[4] V. 29 certainly comes from the Evangelist, with its characteristic τοῦτον οὐκ οἴδαμεν πόθεν ἐστίν, cp. 8.14; 7.27f.; also 2.9 (see p. 118 n. 5); 3.8; 19.9. In that case we must also ascribe v. 30 to the Evangelist (on ἐν τούτῳ cp. 4.37); but it is difficult to decide how much of what follows must also be ascribed to him, and moreover it is relatively unimportant. Sp. is probably right when he suggests that v. 28 was followed immediately in the source by καὶ ἐξέβαλον αὐτὸν ἔξω v. 34, and v. 33 certainly sounds as if it were written by the Evangelist (see p. 334 n. 3).—Ἐκβάλλειν, which in the source was used in the sense of Mk. 1.43, means for the Evangelist, "exclusion from the congregation of the synagogue" (cp. III Jn. 10).

[5] God spoke to Moses in Num. 12.2, 8, etc.; cp. Jos. ant. 8, 104: τοὺς δέκα λόγους τοὺς ὑπὸ τοῦ θεοῦ Μωϋσεῖ λαληθέντας.—On the variants in Pap. Egerton see Barr.

the words of the healed man; their conduct is exposed as monstrous.[1] For precisely their knowledge of God, which they claim to enjoy as disciples of Moses, should lead them to accept this proof of Jesus' authority. How can they refuse him recognition in view of the undoubted miracle which he has performed (v. 30)? The knowledge they enjoy—and the healed man by joining himself with them in the οἴδαμεν, shows that he too is a disciple of Moses, and indeed a genuine disciple!—is decisive here: they know that God will not hear a sinner, but only a righteous man[2] (v. 31). And this knowledge, taken together with the unheard-of cure,[3] provides the basis for an unbiased judgement (v.32). The conclusion is drawn and stated in negative terms in v. 33: the miracle proves that Jesus' authority is παρὰ θεοῦ (cp. v. 16).[4] The Jews show their own wickedness by refusing to let themselves be drawn into this line of argument, as they must if they are disciples of Moses, and by refusing to be instructed by the healed man (v. 34).[5] Even here they preserve the outward appearance of legality, inasmuch as the fact of his having been born blind is proof for them of his sinfulness. He was born in complete[6] sinfulness.[7] They do not see that in this they contradict themselves. Now it suits them to accept the fact of his blindness, which a short while before they had doubted (v. 18).

---

[1] Γάρ v. 30, as in 7.41, suggests an answer in the negative, or else it disguises the question: οὐ γὰρ ἐν τούτῳ ...; Bl.-D. para. 452, 2.

[2] The Jews must have learnt this from Is. 1.15; Ps. 66.16ff.; 109.7; Prov. 15.29 etc.; corresponding Rabbinic statements in Str.-B. on 9.16, 31.—The examples in Wetst. and Br. show that the principle was known in the Greek and Hellenistic world. Of course this takes it for granted that the miracle is in every case given by God; indeed in Jewish miracle stories on the whole the miracle is portrayed as the answer to prayer.—The combination in v. 31 of the Greek θεοσεβής (its only occurrence in the NT; the subst. only in I Tim. 2.6) and the Jewish "who does his will" is most unusual. ποιεῖν τὸ θέλ. αὐτ. here does not, of course, have the specific sense which it has in 7.17; it is basically the same as the conduct which is enjoined in Mic. 6.8. The formula occurs frequently in Judaism (Str.-B. I 467) and in the NT (Mk. 3.35; Mt. 7.21; 21.31; Eph. 6.6; Heb. 10.36; 13.21; I Jn. 2.17; cp. Rom. 2.18, etc.).

[3] 'Ακουσθῆναι = "become well known", as in Mk. 2.1; Act 11.22; ἐξ αἰῶνσς is the usual expression in Greek instead of ἀπ' αἰῶνος (Gen. 6.4; Is. 64.4; Lk. 1.70; Acts 3.21; 15.18).

[4] "Αν is omitted in the apodosis as in 8.39; 15.24; 19.11; Bl.-D. para. 360, 1.

[5] According to E. L. Allen (JBL 74 [1955], 90f.) the healed man represents the group of Jewish Christians who recognise Jesus as prophet and Messiah, and who are therefore excluded from the synagogue (cp. the ambiguous ἐξέβαλον v. 34, which can mean that they were excluded both from the place in which the action took place and also from the synagogue). Their confession, however, must be raised to a higher level; see on p. 107 n. 2.

[6] "Ολος = as a whole, i.e. completely, as in 13.10.

[7] Cp. Ps. 50.7: ἰδοὺ γὰρ ἐν ἀνομίαις συνελήμφθην, καὶ ἐν ἁμαρτίαις ἐκίσσησέν με ἡ μήτηρ μου. Ps. 57.4: ἀπηλλοτριώθησαν οἱ ἁμαρτωλοὶ ἀπὸ μήτρας, ἐπλανήθησαν ἀπὸ γαστρός. This corresponds to the Rabbinic characterisation of the heathen (Str.-B. ad loc.) or even of individual sinners (Str.-B. 528 on 9.2).

[illegible]: *The healed man's confession of the Son of Man.*[1] As in 5.14, Jesus now finds the healed man[2] and puts to him the decisive question, "Do you believe in the Son of Man?" (v. 35).[3] The phrasing of the question assumes that the man understands the title "Son of Man", and that he knows that it refers not to a figure who is to be expected in some future age, but to one who is present and who encounters men in this age.[4] "Belief" in the Son of Man cannot refer to the expectation of the Son of Man who will come on the clouds of heaven, but to the recognition of a present figure, as is shown by the healed man's immediate asking who the Son of Man is that he may believe in him (v. 36).[5] Yet even then it goes without saying that the title is taken in its messianic, eschatological sense.[6] The indirectness of the dialogue—due to the fact that Jesus does not ask straight out, "Do you believe in me?"— is designed to show the difference between the healed man's previous recognition of Jesus and the confession which is now required of him.[7] The healed man has recognised Jesus as a prophet (v. 17), as authorised by God (v. 33), and has thus come as far as he can within the Jewish sphere. But as yet he is unaware that his helper is the "Son of Man", the *eschatological* bringer of salvation. He does not know that, if he wants to see Jesus as he really is, he must leave the old sphere completely behind him. Any man who is basically honest, and on whom Jesus has made an impression, can come as far as he has come. But the decisive step only comes when the question is put explicitly, when a man is confronted by the self-revelation in the

---

[1] In view of the parallel structure of the two stories on which chs. 5 and 9 are respectively based, we must assume that the meeting between Jesus and the healed man in 9.35ff. was related in the source. The form of the account as we now have it must, however, largely be attributed to the Evangelist, whose style is apparent in v. 37. However it is not possible to distinguish between the source and the Evangelist's contribution.

[2] It is clearly assumed that the healed man recognises Jesus when he meets him. Naturally we may not ask how this is possible when he was unable to see him before the healing.

[3] Doubtless we should read (εἰς τ. υἱὸν) τ. ἀνθρώπου with B ℵ D syrˢ, and not τ. θεοῦ with ℜ pl latt.—It does not seem possible to me to take the sentence as a statement instead of as a question (Schl.).

[4] Thus the narrative assumes an understanding of the title "Son of Man", which was reached only in the Christian community; cp. Mt. 11.19, par. Lk. 19.10; Mk. 2.10, etc.

[5] Καὶ τίς = "who then?" cp. 14.22, and see Bl.-D. para. 442, 8, and H. Almquist, Plutarch u. das NT 74. Rabbinic questions beginning with "and" in Schl.—On the ἵνα-clause see Bl.-D. para. 483; according to Burney (76.85) ἵνα is a mistranslation of the Aramaic relative pronoun; it ought really to read εἰς ὃν πιστεύσω. This is challenged by Colwell 96ff.

[6] On the "Son of Man" see pp. 107, 143ff., 150ff.

[7] This is how the Evangelist meant it to be understood. In the source the phrase "to believe in the Son of Man" may have been used, because it was a naive way of referring to Christian faith; cp. Lk. 18.8; also Mt. 11.19 par.

word. Yet what the question asks is not unmotivated, and what the word asserts is not unintelligible: "You have seen him. He it is who speaks with you!" (v. 37).[1] The immediate cause of the confession is neither a theophany, nor a straightforward demand that he should believe, compliance with which would be no more than an arbitrary act of will. But whereas man's experience would remain obscure to him without the intervention of the spoken word, so too the word itself is only intelligible because it reveals to man the meaning of his own experience. This is why the healed man can confess, "Lord, I believe!"[2] and worship the Revealer[3] (v. 38).

3) *Controversy:* 9.39–41

Like 5.16–18, the paragraph 9.39–41 adds to the main narrative an account of a short controversy, and so leads into the following discourse. Again as in ch. 5, the dialogue centres round a saying (v. 39) taken from the discourse on which the following passage is based. The discourse is taken from the collection of revelation discourses. In this case the saying helps to bring out the symbolic meaning of the miracle story—Jesus, the "Light of the world"—more strongly than in ch. 5. The Evangelist is no more interested in the precise details of the scene than he was in ch. 5. Jesus issues his challenge, and the Pharisees, who are assumed to be standing near,[4] understand it, just as the "Jews" do in 5.18:

V. 39:

εἰς κρίμα ἐγὼ εἰς τὸν κόσμον τοῦτον ἦλθον,
ἵνα οἱ μὴ βλέποντες βλέπωσιν
καὶ οἱ βλέποντες τυφλοὶ γένωνται.[5]

---

[1] Ἑώρακας refers to the present moment; the perfect indicates that this sight has become a permanent possession (Schl.)—The use of καί-καί is characteristic for the Evangelist, cp. 7.28; 12.28. The second καί does not mean "and inspite of", as in 6.36; 15.24 (see p. 48 n. 2), but introduces a climax, "and precisely he who ...", On ἐκεῖνος see p. 79 n. 3; it is particularly striking here, since it refers to the speaker himself, Bl.D. para. 291,4.

[2] The form of address, κύριε, in the context means more than simply "master", and should be taken in the sense suggested by προσεκύνησεν (see following note).

[3] On προσκυνεῖν, see p. 189 n. 3. The word here denotes not the homage and reverence accorded to a man (I Sam. 20.41; Ruth 2.10), nor even that given to the miracle worker (Mk. 5.6; Mt. 8.2; 9.18), but that paid to the "Son of Man" as a divine figure, in the way that προσκ. in 4.20ff. 12.20 denotes reverence paid to God. Cp. Bousset, Kyrios 249; J. Horst, Proskynein 292f.; Horst says, perhaps rightly, that the healed man now fulfills the δὸς δόξαν τ. θεῷ (v. 24) in the true sense of the words.

[4] 'Οι μετ' αὐτοῦ ὄντες v. 40 means, of course, "who were (as it happened) standing near him" (cp. 11.31; 12.17; 18.18), and not "who stood by him" (Hirsch).

[5] The three lines have been taken from the source, in which, as is shown by 12.46ff., the coming light is described as judgement. Becker 84 also agrees that they come from the source, although he attributes τοῦτον to the Evangelist. It must remain uncertain whether the first line was originally the second half of a couplet (its first line may have been: ἐγώ

… in the coming of the Revealer into this world[1] is described … judgement.[2] And according to this saying the judgement consists in a radical reversal of the human condition: the blind will receive sight, and the seeing will become blind. From the start it is clear that the concepts "seeing" and "blind" are related to the concepts of "light" and "darkness", which in 1.5ff; 3.19ff. denoted the salvation given by God and man's shutting himself off from God. There the concepts "light" and "darkness" were not used metaphorically, but in their most proper sense, inasmuch as they referred to the salvation which man receives or rejects, that is to the gift or the loss of a definitive understanding of himself.[3] The same is true also of the concepts "seeing" and "blind". Yet of course it is possible simply to play with concepts, and the use of them may at any time become simply metaphorical.[4] Thus even in v. 39, following as it does 9.1–38, one will find traces of this metaphorical use, which reflect its proper use in a remarkable way. It is also clear from the start, as v. 41 makes very obvious, that the βλέποντες are spoken of with peculiar irony; they are the men who *imagine* they can see. This is why here, as in 3.19 the κρίμα[5] is judgement insofar as it effects a division, even though this at first seems not to be

---

εἰμι τὸ φῶς τοῦ κόσμου, which like ἐγώ εἰμι ὁ ἄρτος τῆς ζωῆς 6.35, 48, 51 may have been frequently repeated in the discourse, cp. 10.11, 14; 15.1, 5); see p. 345 n. 5.

[1] This is the first time in the Gospel that ὁ κόσμος οὗτος occurs, which is used also in I Cor. 3.19; 5.10; 7.31; Eph. 2.2 as a substitute for עוֹלָם הַזֶּה (elsewhere οὗτος ὁ αἰών is used). In John it occurs relatively infrequently (8.23; 9.39; 11.9; 12.25, 31; 13.1; 16.11; 18.36; I Jn. 4.17) in comparison with the absolute κόσμος. Ign. with one exception (Mg. 5, 2) always says simply ὁ κόσμος (8 times); but on the other hand he uses ὁ αἰὼν οὗτος, which never occurs in John; see Schlier, Relg. Unters. 129.—Has τοῦτον been added by the Evangelist?—Cp. Faulhaber 28.

[2] See 3.17–21, also 5.22–24, 27, 30.

[3] See pp. 40f.

[4] As in 8.12; 12.35f.; 11.9f.; cp. ch. 10.—The metaphorical use of "sight" and "blindness" is widespread, as it is of "light" and "darkness". Cp. Is 6.9; 42.16; 56.10; Mt. 15.14 (on this Wetst.) 23.16, 24; P. Oxy. I 1; V 840, 31 (Kl. Texte 8, 16; 31, 5). Further Aesch. Ag. 1623 (οὐχ ὁρᾷς ὁρῶν τάδε;); Plat. Phaed. 99e; Lucian vit. auct. 18 (τυφλὸς γὰρ εἶ τῆς ψυχῆς τὸν ὀφθαλμόν.). This usage is particularly developed in Gnosticism and mysticism, cp. C. Herm. 1, 27; 7; 10, 8f. 15; 11, 21; for the Mand. literature ZNTW 24 (1925), 110f., 123; cp. esp. Jn.-B. 175, 24f.:

I put it before his eyes, but he would not see,
I showed him, but he would not see with his eye."

179, 18ff.: "If a man put out his eyes with his own hand,
who can be his doctor?"

See also pp. 157 n. 5, 158 n. 1, and Bornkamm, Mythos und Legende 14.—This usage is found frequently in Philo, cp. ebr. 155–161; fug. inv. 122f.; migr. Abr. 38–42; rer div. haer. 77–80; leg. all. III 108–113; Cher. 58f.; somn. I 164; II 160-163, 192; decal. 67f.; spec. leg. I 54.

[5] Κρίμα (which in John occurs only here) was originally distinguished from κρίσις, the act of judging, as its result; however the distinction sometimes is lost.—Εἰς κρίμα without the article, see Bl.-D. para. 255.

the case, since the division between the blind and the seeing appears to have been made already before the coming of the light. But in reality it is not made apparent till the coming of the light, indeed it is only then that it is decided who is blind and who has sight.[1] The Pharisees against their will must bear witness that they are blind, although they do not know it (**v. 40**), and this is confirmed by Jesus (**v. 41**).[2]

Thus the "blind" and the "seeing", for whom Jesus' coming means the κρίμα, do not refer to any particular definable groups which were present before his coming. Rather *everyone* must face the question to which of the two groups he wants to belong. In fact till now they were *all* blind; for v. 41 shows that the "seeing" were only those who imagined they could see, while the "blind" were those who knew they were blind.[3] Moreover blindness is synonymous with being in darkness, which before the coming of the Revealer was the only possibility open to man (cp. 12. 46). But all men were blind only in a *temporary* sense; through the coming of the light both seeing and blindness receive a new and *definitive* meaning. This is what judgement means; the "blind" receive "sight". These are the men who "believe" in the "light", and whose seeing is no longer an attempt to find their way in the world, in the delusion that they are able to see, but the condition of illumination through the revelation. "Blindness" is no longer simply a wandering in the dark, which can always become aware that it is lost, and so have the possibility of receiving sight; for now it has forfeited this possibility. He who does not believe is judged (3.18) and judgement is carried out on him precisely in his holding on to the delusion that he can see. Of the blind who persist in their blindness it is said: "your sin *remains*".[4] This is the paradox of the revelation, that in order to bring grace it must also give

---

[1] See p. 159.—Ho.'s explanation relates it too closely to the preceding story. "In the first line not-seeing or blindness is used in a physical sense, while in the second line it is used in a spiritual sense. On the other hand seeing is understood spiritually in the first line and physically in the second." In fact in every case seeing and blindness are understood "spiritually".—On the ideas expressed here cp., apart from the Mandaean reference given on p. 340 n. 4, Ginza 180, 22f. "Oh! they that say: we belong to life and life is with us, while life is not in them!"; further Plat. symp. 204a: αὐτὸ γὰρ τοῦτό ἐστι χαλεπὸν ἀμαθία, τὸ μὴ ὄντα καλὸν κἀγαθὸν μηδὲ φρόνιμον δοκεῖν αὐτῷ εἶναι ἱκανόν· οὔκουν ἐπιθυμεῖ ὁ μὴ οἰόμενος ἐνδεὴς εἶναι οὗ ἂν μή οἴηται ἐπιδεῖσθαι.. Above all Mt. 11.25, where the νήπιοι correspond to the μὴ βλέποντες and the σοφοὶ καὶ συνετοί to the βλέποντες of Jn. 9.39. See also for an Indian parallel, P. Deussen, Allgem. Gesch. der Phil. I 2 (1899), 71:

> "Ever more involved in the depths of ignorance,
> Imagining themselves to be wise and learned,
> Thus they run aimlessly to and fro like fools,
> Like blind men, led themselves by a blind man."

[2] Becker 84 thinks that v. 41 belongs to the source.

[3] Εἰ τυφλοὶ ἦτε v. 41 means, "If you would recognize your blindness".

[4] Cp. 3.36; 12.46 and see p. 166f.. Cp. Faulhaber 44f.

offence, and so can turn to judgement.[1] In order to be grace it must uncover sin; he who resists this binds himself to his sin, and so through the revelation sin for the first time becomes definitive.[2]

b) The Light of the World: 8.12; 12.44–50; 8.21–29; 12.34–36

1) *The Call of the Revealer:* 8.12; 12.44–50

8.12:

πάλιν οὖν αὐτοῖς ἐλάλησεν ὁ Ἰησοῦς λέγων·[3]
ἐγώ εἰμι τὸ φῶς τοῦ κόσμου.
ὁ ἀκολουθῶν μοι οὐ μὴ περιπατήσῃ ἐν τῇ σκοτίᾳ,
ἀλλ' ἕξει τὸ φῶς τῆς ζωῆς.[4]

By calling himself the "light of the world" Jesus describes himself as the Revealer. He speaks words of promise and invitation. Here we can hear an echo of the ἐρχέσθω of 7.37. He is the light, not because he gives us the brightness by which we can light up those things in the world which we need and which interest us, but because he gave us the brightness in which existence itself is illumined and comes to itself, comes to life. The φῶς τοῦ κόσμου gives the φῶς τῆς ζωῆς.[5] The revelation

---

[1] See p. 154.

[2] It is therefore important in the discussion of the problem of "natural theology" to remember that not all men outside faith stand in the same perverted relationship to God, but that there is a difference between those who have not yet heard the word of revelation and those who have rejected it.

[3] On the sequence 9.41; 8.12, see p. 313. It makes no difference whether it was the Evangelist or the editor who added the introductory sentence.

[4] The discourse probably started with the single ἐγώ-εἰμι saying, as in 6, 35, which was then followed by the couplets. According to Becker 71, 77 the last line (ἀλλὰ κτλ.) has been added to the source by the Evangelist, like the ἀλλά-clauses in 3.36; 5.24.

[5] The genitives which are combined with τὸ φῶς are of different types. τὸ φῶςτοῦ κόσμου (objective genitive) means "light for the world" (cp. 1.4 τ. φῶς τῶν ἀνθρ. and Luc. Alex. 18: εἰμὶ Γλύκων ... φάος ἀνθρώποισι); not so in 11.9 (subjective genitive): τὸ φῶς τ. ζωῆς can either mean (genitive of source) "light, such as the ζωή (=life-giving force, see p. 39 n. 3) gives", which would fit in best with 1.4, ἡ ζωὴ ἦν τ. φῶς τῶν ἀνθρ., or (exepegetic genitive), "light which is life (vitality, see p. 152 n. 2)." As in 1.4 φῶς is not used metaphorically (see p. 40), nor is there any attempt to draw comparisons, no more than there was in 6.35; 10.11;15.1. For it is a question of the proper light (1.9). Thus Rabbinic statements which call God, the law, Israel or individual teachers a "light" or "lamp" (Dalman, W. J. 144; Str.-B. I 237f. II 357; Odeberg 286) are in no way parallel. Rather the use here is based on Gnostic usage which presupposes a metaphysical dualism of light and darkness, wherein light is both the life-force of the divine world and the revelation whose coming into the world brings about the division of light and darkness (see p. 43, 157 n. 5). Admittedly, the formula "I am the light" is not attested here (Odeberg 288), but not only is the messenger referred to again and again as the giver of light, but he is also called the "light", "the shining one", etc. (see p. 43 n. 3: ZNTW 24 (1925), 110f.; Br. ad loc., Odeberg 287), and he says of himself: "the messenger of light am I" (Ginza 58, 17, 23). On the "light of life", cp. esp. Ginza 178, 29ff.; there (179, 23ff.) Mandā d'Haijē (=γνῶσις τῆς ζωῆς, which is the messenger's title)

speaks to men who are not merely concerned with the individual problems of the world and their lives, but who are concerned with themselves as a whole, with their own authenticity. It is this question which pursues man. He must have light, as is shown by the objection of those who live by the idle belief that they can see (9.40): and therefore life is a way which can run its course either in light or in darkness,[1] a way which leads either to life or to death (vv. 21, 24).

The ἐγώ εἰμι[2] announces that in Jesus we are confronted with the light of the revelation. The ἐγώ is stressed not by contrast with other givers of light who promise revelation,[3] but by contrast with human security, which believes that it already possesses the light. It is not a question of setting on the right path an anxious inquiry, which looks falteringly for the light, but rather of arousing interest in the inquiry at all.[4] Thus the ἐγώ εἰμι characterises the unexpected in-breaking of the revelation into the world, the paradox that this in-breaking takes place in the person of Jesus. Therefore with regard to the statement that he is the light of the *world*, the decisive feature is not the universalism but the dualism; for without the revelation the world is darkness.[5]

Since the Revealer is the light, the faithful acceptance of the revelation—and here the use of light becomes metaphorical—can be referred

---

says, "I am come to stay with you, and to establish you in the light of life ... and you will be true men in my sight in the light of life." Further 182, 28ff.: "M.d.H. revealed himself to all the children of men, and redeems them from darkness to light, from gloom to the light of life." In Ginza 391, 12 the redeemed man who found the Kušta (= ἀλήθεια) speaks, "Then my eyes became full of light." The dualistic use of "light" and "darkness" is also found in the Qumran texts; see K. G. Kuhn, ZThK 47 (1950), 197ff.; 49 (1952), 308f. "Light of life" occurs in DSD 3, 7 (Brownlee: "the life-giving light"). The "truth of the world" DSD 4, 19 (Bardtke: "the truth which is destined for the earth") is analogous to φῶς τοῦ κόσμου.—Cp. G. P. Wetter, Beiträge zur Religionswiss. I 2 (1914), 171ff.—Har. Riesenfeld (Jésus Transfiguré 278f.), who wants to take 8.12 in the context of ch. 7, finds, as do others, allusions to the light-ritual in the feast of Tabernacles. Strathm. and Dupont (92f.) are sceptical about this and believe that the reference is to sayings of Isaiah (as 9.1; 42.6, etc.). Wik. rightly challenges both views.

[1] As in 12.35 περιπατεῖν is here used figuratively, or better metaphorically (cp. its proper use in the comparison 11.9f.), and refers to man's attitude or direction of life as a whole (in this sense Greek more usually has πορεύεσθαι, Soph. Oed. tyr. 884; Plat. Phaedo 82d). This use should, however, be distinguished from its employment in moral exhortations (I Th. 2.12; Rom. 13.13, etc.). The latter denotes the practical conduct of life as determined by man's search for norms (thus περιπ. κατά, Rom. 8. 4; 14.15, etc., or its qualification by an adverb, e.g. ἀξίως, I Th. 2.12; εὐσχημόνως Rom. 13.13, etc.), whereas the Johannine περιπ. is determined by the question of the sphere in which life moves (thus περιπατ. ἐν, which should be distinguished from the same construction in II Cor. 4.2; Col. 3.7, etc.). Hence the Johannine περιπ. embraces both the practical conduct of one's life and (what is of primary importance) faith itself.—F.-M. Braun (RB 62 [1955], 18) thinks it possible that v. 12 is based on the doctrine of the two ways.

[2] On ἐγώ εἰμι, see p. 225 n. 3. As in 6.35, etc. ἐγώ is predicate, τ. φῶς τ.κ. subject.

[3] There is no attack in John on other revealers (Mithras or other gods of light).

[4] See p. 81.

[5] See p. 54f.

will walk

to as *"following after"* him.[1] This refers only to faith, as did the eating of the bread of life and the drinking of the water of life. This interpretation is confirmed by the fact that ἀκολουθεῖν is immediately replaced by πιστεύειν (12.44). Yet because *he* is the light, faith can be called following; to have the "light of life" means to have *him*. And when he says ἐγώ εἰμι ὁ ἄρτος τῆς ζωῆς he could equally well say, ἐγώ εἰμι τὸ φῶς τῆς ζωῆς. He *gives* the light and at the same time he *is* the light. He gives it in that he is it, and he is it in that he gives it. The interrelation of these two ideas is of the utmost importance for the concept of revelation. Revelation is not transcendent in the sense that man is confronted by something which is quite beyond his understanding, and which has no intelligible bearing on his own life, for in faith man has the light; i.e. the revelation is an event which determines his existence. Yet the revelation is not like a possession which one has at one's disposal, nor is it like knowledge which one has acquired, nor like a quality which one has made one's own, for then it would be possible to forget the Revealer while concentrating on what has been revealed. The revelation never becomes some*thing* that has been revealed. The light which the believer *has* is always the light that Jesus *is*. Only so can the believer really make the light his own. For the folly of the blind who think they can see, consists precisely in the fact that they think they have an assured possession, and therefore they fall short of life and never come into their own in the true sense of the word.

The following sayings of the discourse[2] make clear the responsibility of the hearer when confronted by the word of the Revealer. They fall into three sections, of which the first (12.44f.), and the third (vv. 49f.) state that it is God who is encountered in the Revealer. The second section (vv. 46–48) expresses the idea founded on this, that the revelation is judgement.

12.44f.:

ὁ πιστεύων εἰς ἐμέ
οὐ πιστεύει εἰς ἐμὲ ἀλλὰ εἰς τὸν πέμψαντά με,

---

[1] Ἀκολουθεῖν is used metaphorically in this sense also in 10.4f., 27, whereas in 12.26; 13.36f.; 21.19f., 22 it refers to discipleship (see p. 99 n. 5), in the sense in which it is lived out by accepting Jesus' fate.

[2] On the sequence of 12.44–50 after 8.12, see p. 313. This order corresponds entirely to the style of the revelation-discourses: ἐγώ εἰμι ... ὁ πιστεύων, cp. 6.35, 48/47; 11.25 (corresponding in its figurative expressions to 15.1ff.); otherwise, wihout the preceding ἐγώ εἰμι, ὁ πιστεύων ... would, as it were, hang in mid-air.—Ed. Norden (Agnostos Theos 1913, 298f.) rightly felt that 8.12 was the introduction to a ῥῆσις. Nevertheless his view that the Evangelist distributed the motifs of this ῥῆσις among the different discourses in ch. 8 is confuted by the analysis given on pp. 312ff. For the same reason it is also impossible that Rom. 2.19 should refer to Jn. 8.12), and that Rom. 2.20 should allude to Jn. 8.31ff.

καὶ ὁ θεωρῶν ἐμέ
θεωρεῖ τὸν πέμψαντά με.[1]

The content of the two sentences, whose form is that of synonymous parallelism, is the same. For himself Jesus is nothing; he is the Revealer who makes God visible.[2] As in his actions and words God's words and actions are played out, so also in him God is really visible and accessible.[3] But this, of course, also implies that *only* in him is God visible and accessible. Thus man's relationship to him is decisive for his fate. This is first developed in positive terms in **v. 46**: "I have come as light into the world, that whoever believes in me may not remain in darkness." The sentence is only a variation on the theme of 8.12; the ἵνα . . . μὴ μείνῃ again reminds us that the world without the revelation is darkness, and that to reject the revelation is to persist in sin.[4] But the sentence here is used only as a foil for the decisive thought of the following verses,[5]

vv. 47f.:

καὶ ἐάν τίς μου ἀκούσῃ τῶν ῥημάτων καὶ μὴ φυλάξῃ,
ἐγὼ οὐ κρίνω αὐτόν.
[οὐ γὰρ ἦλθον ἵνα κρίνω τὸν κόσμον, ἀλλ' ἵνα σώσω τὸν κόσμον.]
ὁ ἀθετῶν ἐμὲ καὶ μὴ λαμβάνων τὰ ῥήματά μου
ἔχει τὸν κρίνοντα αὐτόν.
[ὁ λόγος ὃν ἐλάλησα, ἐκεῖνος κρίνει αὐτὸν [ἐν τῇ ἐσχάτῃ ἡμέρᾳ[6]]]

---

[1] The introductory formula 'I. δὲ' ἔκραξεν (see p. 75 n 1) καὶ εἶπεν has, of course, been added by the editor.—It is legitimate to ask whether the text of the source has been edited by the Evangelist (the scansion of the verses is uneven); perhaps the first couplet in the source simply read: ὁ πιστεύων εἰς ἐμέ, πιστεύει εἰς τὸν πέμψαντά με; οὐ ... ἀλλά certainly could have been added by the Evangelist, see p. 48 n. 3.

[2] On the synonymous use of πιστεύειν and θεωρεῖν, see p. 69 n. 4.—The first sentence is similar in form to a Jewish-Christian proverbial saying ("gnome", see on 13.20), but its actual meaning is more far-reaching. A "gnome" says that the superior instance in law is represented by the inferior instance, so that respect paid to the latter (or refused to it) is regarded as if it were paid to the former. This idea of representation can at the most be used figuratively in the revelation-discourses; for the Revealer does not *represent* God in a legal sense, but rather God is encountered in him, and in him alone.

[3] See pp. 248ff. and see on 14.8–11.

[4] See p. 341.

[5] V. 46 was probably composed by the Evangelist (the unqualified φῶς is surprising), and he has probably inserted it in place of another verse in the source, namely the verse he used in 9.39 which describes the coming of the φῶς as judgement (see p. 339 n. 5, this would give a better explanation for the ἐγὼ οὐ κρίνω in v. 47.

[6] It is quite obvious that the text of the source has been expanded by the Evangelist's own exegetical comments. The οὐ γάρ-clause in v. 47 is one of his typical explanatory comments and corresponds particularly closely to 3.17; see pp. 153 n. 1, 154 n. 1. Similarly the last sentence of v. 48 is his gloss, as can be seen from its prose style and the ἐκεῖνος, which picks up the subject again, see p. 79 n. 3. Finally the ἐν τ. ἐσχ. ἡμ. is a secondary addition, inserted by the ecclesiastical editor, see p. 219.

Thus the promise which Jesus makes brings man at the same time face to face with a decision. The revelation must be judgement if it is also to be grace, even though it is not its purpose to be judgement. Whereas 9.39 established the fact that it is judgement, now the other side of the matter is emphasised. Man himself bears responsibility for the judgement. If he rejects the word of revelation[1] he brings judgement on himself—a point made in two sentences of synonymous parallelism.[2] The Evangelist by his additions has stressed and clarified this idea. As in 3.17, he emphasises that Jesus came not to judge the world but to save it. He comments on ἔχει τὸν κρίνοντα αὐτόν (which corresponds to ἤδη κέκριται 3.18), that it is Jesus' word which will judge him.[3] If man brings down judgement on himself by rejecting the word, then in a certain sense the word is his judge.

The reason for this—and this brings us back to vv. 44f.—is that it is God whom we meet in Jesus.

Vv. 49f.:

ὅτι ἐγὼ ἐξ ἐμαυτοῦ οὐκ ἐλάλησα,
ἀλλὰ [ὁ πέμψας με πατὴρ αὐτός μοι ἐντολὴν δέδωκεν
τί εἴπω καὶ τί λαλήσω. Καὶ οἶδα ὅτι ἡ ἐντολὴ αὐτοῦ
ζωὴ αἰώνιός ἐστιν. ἃ οὖν ἐγὼ λαλῶ,]
καθὼς εἴρηκέν μοι ὁ πατήρ, οὕτως λαλῶ.[4]

Jesus' word of promise turns to judgement, because Jesus speaks not on his own authority but as he has been commissioned by the Father. The sentence, which the source clearly expressed in the same simple antithesis as elsewhere,[5] has been expanded by the Evangelist. For he expounds the idea of Jesus' unity with the Father, as elsewhere, in terms

---

[1] On ἀκούειν see pp. 259, 316, on φυλάττειν see p. 301 n. 5, cp. φυλ. ῥῆσιν Inschr. SA Berlin 1935, 719. 'Αθετεῖν, which occurs nowhere else in John, need not necessarily come from Lk. 10.16 (Br.). On λαμβάνειν τ.ῥημ. see pp. 76 n. 5, 146 n. 1.

[2] Cp. Ginza 183, 11f. on the blasphemers: "They will be struck by their own blows, so that my blow need not strike them." See also Ginza 60, 30f.

[3] As understood by the Evangelist, κρίνει v. 48 should be read as a present tense; for only then does the clause correspond to ἤδη κέκριται 3.18. The editor, of course, took it as κρινεῖ.

[4] The sentence in the source has been glossed by the Evangelist. This can be seen from the typical marks of the Evangelist's style, the αὐτός which picks up the subject again (as do elsewhere ἐκεῖνος and οὗτος, see p. 79 n. 1, cp. esp. 5.37, and for the picking up of a subject by αὐτός 5.36); further καὶ οἶδα ὅτι cp. 5.32; I Jn. 3.5, 15, and see Festg. Ad. Jül. 146f. Moreover the idea that Jesus obeys the ἐντολή of the Father is characteristic for the Evangelist (10.18; 14.31; 15.10). Of course, he is only giving particular emphasis to the idea of obedience, which is already present in the source, and which forms an essential part of the myth; see on 8.29. 'A οὖν ἐγὼ λαλῶ is used to bring the discourse back to the text of the source.

[5] 7.16f.; 8.28; 14.10, cp. 5.19, 30; 6.38. For a discussion of the idea itself see pp. 248ff.

of obedience:[1] in what he says Jesus only fulfils the Father's command. He fulfils it because this commandment—that is to say, his fulfilment of this commandment—or better his *mission* means eternal life for the world.[2] Thus the argument has come full circle, in that at the end the positive purpose of Jesus' mission is once more emphasized.

2) *Threats and Warnings:* 8.21–29; 12.34–36a

In his usual way the Evangelist interrupts the flow of the discourse by a discussion between Jesus and the Jews (8.21–29; 12.34–36).[3] The occasion for this is a saying of Jesus, which is again misunderstood by the Jews (**v. 21**): "I go away, and you will seek me and die in your sin; where I am going, you cannot come."[4] It is the same prophecy of doom which Jesus had already uttered in 7.34, ominously pointing to the fact that soon it will be "too late", and expanded here by καὶ ἐν τῇ ἁμαρτίᾳ ὑμῶν ἀποθανεῖσθε[5] an addition which is formally disruptive but which nevertheless gets to heart of the matter.

At first sight it might seem that there is no good reason why the Evangelist should put these words into Jesus' mouth immediately after 12.44–50. The reason becomes clear when one sees that the saying contains the "too-late" theme which in the source formed the conclusion of the discourse on light (12.35f.). This theme, which had already been announced at the beginning (9.4f.), is now worked up by the Evangelist into a scene in its own right. In preparing the way for 12.35f. he uses as an introduction in v. 21 the saying which he has already employed in 7.34.

---

[1] See n. 346 n. 4.

[2] Hirsch (II 99) thinks that καὶ οἶδα to ἐστιν is a secondary gloss, since he maintains that ἐντολή in this sentence (v. 50) has a different meaning from that which it had in the previous one (v.49). In his view the meaning there is, "My Father has commanded me"; the editor misunderstood this, thinking it meant, "He has given me the commandment which I must pass on to others.": i.e. God gave Jesus a new law, in the same way that he once gave Moses the Decalogue; the new law brings eternal life to the men who fulfil it.—Yet their seems to be no compelling reason for accepting this interpretation, which in fact is far from being an obvious explanation of the verses. Moreover the καὶ-οἶδα clause is very typical of the Evangelist, see n. 346 n. 4.

[3] On the link between 8.21–29; 12.34, 34–36 and 12.44–50, see p. 313.—As in 7.35 it is now assumed that his hearers are the "Jews", while the Pharisees disappear behind or among them (8.22; 10.19); ὄχλος (12.34) can be used interchangeably with οἱ Ἰουδαῖοι, see pp. 86, 295.

[4] In v. 21 the sentence of the source quoted in 7.34 (see p. 307) has been expanded by καὶ ἐν τῇ ἁμ. κτλ.—Becker also (79) ascribes v. 21 to the source, with the exception of και ἐν τ. ἁμ. ἀπο.

[5] The expression is typically OT, which also indicates that it has been added by the Evangelist; cp. Deut. 24.16; Ezek. 3.19; 18.24, 26; Prov. 24.9. It is possible that ἐν is instrumental (Bl.-D. para. 219,2), so that a more accurate translation would read, "of your sin" (Br.).

As in 7.35f. the Jews inevitably misunderstand Jesus' saying (v. 22), thinking stupidly that he intends to take his own life.[1] And as there they must unwittingly become prophets. He will indeed lay down his life (10.17f.)—but not in the way they think; for they themselves will kill him (v. 28).

Jesus ignores the question and goes on to describe the division between himself and them, a division which is explained by οὐ δύνασθε in v. 21.

v. 23:

ὑμεῖς ἐκ τῶν κάτω ἐστέ,
ἐγὼ ἐκ τῶν ἄνω εἰμί.
ὑμεῖς ἐκ τούτου τοῦ κόσμου ἐστέ,
ἐγὼ οὐκ εἰμὶ ἐκ τοῦ κόσμου τούτου.[2]

He and they belong to two different worlds, the godly and ungodly.[3] It is for this reason—as is said with reference back to v. 21[4]—that they will die in their sins (v. 24). Admittedly, the division between what is above and what is below need not be absolute. For the Revealer who comes down from above[5] enables man to ascend into the heights. The division is only made final by unbelief: "For unless you believe that I am he, you will die in your sins." The content of faith is indicated simply by ἐγώ εἰμι; it sounds, and is intended to sound, mysterious, for it raises the question, σὺ τίς εἶ; That is to say, they have failed to understand who he is. But who is he? What predicate are we to supply for the ἐγώ εἰμι?[6] In the immediately preceding sayings there is no title describing his mission which we might supply here without further ado;

[1] The misunderstanding is less well motivated than in 7.35f., but it would be wrong to seek for a motive in the situation. The intention is on the one hand to show the Jews' lack of understanding, and on the other hand to record their saying as an unconscious prophecy. On the condemnation of suicide in Judaism see Br. ad loc.; Str.-B. I 1027f.

[2] It is hardly possible to determine whether the couplet comes from the source, where it might have been the continuation of the saying quoted in v. 21 and suppressed in 7.34, or whether it was composed by the Evangelist by analogy with other similar antitheses contained in the revelation-discourses. The fact that the concept οὗτος ὁ κόσμος occurs would seem to indicate that it has been composed by the Evangelist, see p. 340 n. 1. Becker (77) ascribes it to the source, with the exception of both occurrences of τούτου, which he thinks have been added by the Evangelist to τ. κόσμου.—B. Weiss' view, that in the first couplet ἐκ denotes origin and in the second membership, invokes a distinction which is inappropriate here, for in John origin is synonymous with membership; see pp. 135 n. 4, 138 n. 1, 162 n. 3.

[3] On the contrast between above and below, see p. 161 n. 3. The concepts are neutral.

[4] Such references to preceding verses are characteristic of the Evangelist, see 6.36, 65; 8.24; 13.33; 14.28; 15.20; 16.15.

[5] See p. 298 n. 1.

[6] The question σὺ τίς εἶ (cp. 1.19) shows that ἐγώ here is thought of not as predicate but as subject (see p. 225 n. 3).

for ἐγώ εἰμι τὸ φῶς τοῦ κόσμου in 8.12 is too far away.[1] Manifestly we are not intended to supply any title. The meaning is rather that he is everything which he has claimed to be.[2] Thus all the other ἐγώ-εἰμι sayings are, as it were, reduced to this unqualified ἐγώ εἰμι[3]. Jesus' answer, however, to the question, "Who are you?", shows immediately that everything that he has claimed of himself is gathered up in the title "Son of Man".

The menacing ἐὰν γὰρ μὴ πιστεύσητε assumes that the Jews could know who he is, that it is their unbelief which is to blame. And so they receive an equally mysterious reply to their question (**v. 28**): "When you have lifted up the Son of Man,[4] then you will know that I am he." Jesus, then, refuses to give them a direct answer; if they do not know it now, they will know it when it is too late! They will realise the meaning of the "I am" when they "have lifted up the Son of Man"; for then they will realise that he is the Son of Man. τότε γνώσεσθε ὅτι ἐγώ εἰμι is manifestly ambiguous. It clearly refers back to the unqualified ἐγώ εἰμι in v. 24, while at the same time one must add to the main clause the subordinate clause, "that I am the Son of Man." Thus everything that he is, can be referred to by the mysterious title "Son of Man."[5] It is mysterious, not in so far as it is an eschatological title; for this was how his hearers understood it, as is shown by their question in 12.34; for them the Son of Man is the Messiah, the bringer of salvation. But it is mysterious in that they do not see that the eschaton which they await in the future is already present, that this man Jesus is the Son of Man.

Yet the mystery is still richer and more awe-inspiring. They also

---

[1] The question σὺ τίς εἶ shows that we may not supply ὅτι ἐκ τῶν ἄνω εἰμί from v. 23.

[2] So too Strathm., cp. Schl.: "The very absence of attributes gives a vivid description of what happens in faith. What faith affirms is Jesus; he it is to whom the believer binds himself, and not to this or that achievement or gift."—It may be that this bold form of expression was suggested to the Evangelist by God's saying in Is. 43.10: ἵνα γνῶτε καὶ πιστεύσητε καὶ συνῆτε ὅτι εγώ εἰμι—namely everything which God has affirmed of himself in Is. 43; cp. 41.4; 46.4; 48.12; Deut. 32.39. Cp. Kundsin, Char. u. Ursprung. 218.

[3] The ἐγώ εἰμι in 8.24, 28 is of a completely different character from the ἐγώ εἰμι in 8.58; the only other comparable occurrence of ἐγώ εἰμι is 13.19. But it is no more possible here, than it was in 8.58 (see p. 327 n. 5), to resolve ἐγώ εἰμι into "I am the 'I am'", and to take the statement as Jesus' assertion of his identity with God. For if the ἐγώ εἰμι was intended as a paraphrase of the divine name the Jews could not ask, "Who are you?" but would have to take offence at what to their ears would be a gross blasphemy. But it is clear that in this section Jesus is not so much an offence as a mystery to the Jews; the saying does not arouse anger but questions. Dodd (168.248, 350) and Barr. want to take ἐγώ εἰμι as אֲנִי הוּא (see p. 327 n. 5).

[4] Dodd (376–378) rightly asks why we have ὅταν ὑψώσητε and not ὅταν ὑψωθῇ. He suggests that the reason for this is the Evangelist's desire to make the play on the double meaning of ὑψοῦν: 1. lift up = to glorify; 2. lift up = to set on the cross.

[5] On υἱὸς τ. ἀνθρ. see pp. 105 n. 3, 107, 143ff. 149ff.

know from the tradition that the Son of Man not only brings salvation but is the eschatological judge as well. Yet they do not suspect that by "lifting him up" they themselves make him their judge. The double-meaning of "lifting up" is obvious. They lift up Jesus by crucifying him; but it is precisely through his crucifixion that he is lifted up to his heavenly glory as the Son of Man.[1] At the very moment when they think that they are passing judgement on him, he becomes their judge.

Thus the end will also bring *knowledge* for them. Yet the knowledge which they will then gain is not the same as the knowledge which they should enjoy now, and which faith already begins to share,[2] even though full clarity will be reached only later.[3] For those who refuse to believe in him now will see him not as the Revealer, but as the judge.[4] Then, as those who seek in vain (v. 21), they will realise that it is too late, and their knowledge will, in some form,[5] be the knowledge of despair. As in 7.33f. this prophecy of doom is, of course, not limited to Jesus' contemporaries, so that we would then have to look for a chronological date for the τότε (e.g. the destruction of Jerusalem). Rather it applies to all those who refuse to believe in the Revealer, whenever and wherever the word is heard; to all those who through their unbelief identify themselves with the Jews who set Jesus upon the Cross. The Cross was the Jews' last and definitive answer to Jesus' word of revelation, and whenever the world gives its final answer in the words of unbelief it "lifts up" the Revealer and makes him its judge.

The verses which come between the question and the answer are problematical in every respect, as is shown by the exegetes' difficulties and by the conjectures which have been made.[6] The only explanation I can find for

---

[1] On ὑψωθῆναι, see p. 152 n. 4. It is not necessary to postulate that this ambiguous formulation was suggested to the Evangelist by the fact that in Syrian and Palestinian Aramaic אִזְדְּקַף can mean both "to be lifted up" and "to be crucified"; see G. Kittel, ZNTW 35 (1936), 282ff. (This includes a critique of Hirsch's views, who draws conclusions about the origin of the Fourth Gospel from the fact that this usage was restricted to Northern Syria.) Fr. Schulthess, ZNTW 21 (1922), 220 draw attention to the Aram. אֲרִים, which can mean both "remove" and "lift up". Black shares Kittel's view.—For Dodd see on p. 349.

[2] 6.69.

[3] Cp. 2.22 and esp. 12.16, in which the τότε of 8.28 also occurs again.

[4] Odeberg's (295) interpretation is quite impossible, "When you have lifted up the Son of Man in your spiritual vision ..." According to him the saying is a prophecy of salvation like 7.17. Lagr. and others take it as a prophecy of the conversion of the Jews after the destruction of the temple. Hosk. as a prophecy of their conversion as a result of the Christian witness.

[5] See p. 308.

[6] For ὅ τι (or ὅτι) v. 25 Torrey suggests ἔτι, Holwerda οὐκ ἔχω ὅτι—Wellh. thinks that περὶ ὑμῶν v. 26 has been altered by an editor, whereas originally it read περὶ ἐμαυτοῦ.

verses **26 and 27** is that they are a fragment which has been inserted by the editor in its present place, for want of any better, because of the occurrence of ταῦτα λαλῶ in vv. 26 and 28. Its original place may have been in the context of 8.13–20. The statement that Jesus has much to say about the hearers and much to judge, seems to mean that he *could* do so but that he intends not to; he could, but the Father ...! Yet when Jesus says what he has heard from the Father, is this not a πολλὰ περὶ ὑμῶν λαλεῖν καὶ κρινεῖν?[1] The clause introduced by ἀλλά would make correct sense only if preceded by the statement that Jesus does not speak *on his own authority* (cp. 7.16; 12.49f.; 14.10; also 6.38; 7.28), for this would explain the stress on the fact that the Father is ἀληθής (cp. 7.28).[2] It hardly seems possible to venture any suggestion about the original text here.[3]

Further, the observation that the Jews failed to see that Jesus was speaking of the Father may well be appropriate in 5.37f.; 8.19, and even makes sense after v. 26. But why should it be included here, where the question at issue is who *he*, *Jesus*, is? Admittedly it is possible to show the connection between knowledge of Jesus' person and of the person of the Father, but this is not done in the text. And whereas in vv. 26f. it is assumed that it is possible (falsely) to identify the πέμψας με with someone other than the Father, in vv. 28f. the identity of the two is presupposed as automatic. We must therefore abandon the attempt to understand vv. 26f. in their present context.

The question then is whether **v. 25b** belongs to vv. 26f., which would mean that it, too, originally had no place in the context here, or whether one can take the sentence τὴν ἀρχὴν ὅ τι (or ὅτι) καὶ λαλῶ ὑμῖν as a preliminary answer to the question in v. 25a, preparing the way for the answer in v. 28.

(Τὴν) ἀρχήν, with or without the article, means "first", and can have a temporal sense like ἐν ἀρχῇ; it is then contrasted implicitly or explicitly with something occurring later,[4] but can never mean "from the beginning" (=ἐξ ἀρχῆς[5]). Very frequently however (τ). ἀρχήν is used not in a temporal

---

According to Merx the "original form" must have meant, "Who then are you, that you can speak like this? Answer: I told you long ago!"

[1] Br. seeks a way out of the difficulty. "Nevertheless Jesus continues to speak, because God in his truthfulness remains true to his promise and because therefore his messenger cannot make his preaching dependent on outward success or failure." Yet which promise does he refer to? For the word of promise spoken by the messenger (e.g. 8.12; 7.37) is *as such* also the word of judgement!

[2] I do not see how Schl. can infer from the ἀλλά-clause "This gives Jesus the right to remain silent." Rather the opposite seems true, that he is duty bound to speak.

[3] For example, πολλὰ ἔχω . . . κρίνειν [καὶ ἐγὼ ἐξ ἐμαυτοῦ οὐ λαλῶ] ἀλλ' . . ., or: . . . ἀλλ' <εἰ ἐμοὶ μὴ πιστεύετε> ὁ πέμψας με . . .

[4] It is often contrasted with νῦν, e.g. Thuc. II 74, 3: ὅτι οὔτε τὴν ἀρχὴν ἀδίκως . . . ἐπὶ γῆν τήνδε ἤλθομεν, . . . οὔτε νῦν . . . ἀδικήσομεν; similarly Anaxagor. Fr. 6 (Diels 3. ed. I 402, 10f.); Isocr. Nicocl. 28, p. 32. Without νῦν, but in the same sense, Androc. 3. 20; Gen. 41.21. In the sense of "the first time" as opposed to the second time, Gen. 43.18, 20; Dan. 8.1 Θ (LXX: τὴν πρώτην!); 9.21 LXX (Θ: ἐν τῇ ἀρχῇ).

[5] Accordingly this excludes the view often (Belser, Odeberg, while Lagr. thinks it possible) held about Jn. 8.25, that it means, "From the beginning I am, what I tell you." For that would require ἐξ ἀρχῆς. The same applies to the suggested translation, "From the beginning, whatever I may say to you, I have much to say about you and to judge."

but in a logical sense; "first" = "firstly", "from the start", and this use occurs particularly in negated statements or alternatively in sentences with negative force.[1]

If one tries to take τ. ἀρχ. (v. 25b) in a temporal sense it is difficult to see what it is contrasted with. If it is contrasted with the present situation one will have to translate (supplying ἐγώ εἰμι from the preceding question), "I am what I told you at the beginning." Yet the present tense of λαλῶ alone makes this impossible;[2] and further the ἐγώ εἰμι would not only have to be stated expressly, but would have to be qualified by (τὰ) νῦν. Nor can one translate, "Already at the beginning I was what I tell you now",[3] for—quite apart from other considerations—it is by no means a matter of course to supply ἤμην, and more importantly, there would have to be a νῦν before λαλῶ. On the other hand if one takes τ. ἀρχ. to refer to the present, the corresponding contrast must lie in the future;[4] it would be expressed in ὅταν ... τότε (v. 28). But it is hard to see how γνώσεσθε could correspond to ὅ τι καὶ λαλῶ ὑμῖν; one would have to assume that the text was corrupt.[5]

Thus most modern exegetes, following the early exegetes,[6] take it in a logical sense to mean "at all", just as early exegesis rendered it by ὅλως. The sentence is then taken as a question with a negative implication: "Do you ask why I am speaking to you at all?"[7] But that is not what they asked![8]

---

[1] Herod. 1, 193 (οὐδὲ πειρᾶται ἀρχὴν φέρειν = it does not even attempt ...); 3, 39; 4, 25 (τοῦτο δὲ οὐκ ἐνδέκομαι τὴν ἀρχήν = I do not believe that from the start.); Soph. Ant. 92 (ἀρχὴν δὲ θηρᾶν οὐ πρέπει τἀμήχανα not from the start, not at all); Phil. 1239; El. 439ff.; Plat. Gorg. 478c; Philol. Fr. 3 (Diels 3. ed. I 310, 5f.); further material in Br.—Without the negative Herod. 1, 9; Philo Abr. 116; decal. 89; cp. esp. Ps. Clem. Hom. VI 11, p. 77, 1f. Lag: διὸ τὸν λόγον ἐγκόψας ἔφη μοι· εἰ μὴ παρακολουθεῖς οἷς λέγω, τί καὶ τὴν ἀρχὴν διαλέγομαι.

[2] The question whether this and similar attempts at a translation do not in fact require λέγω instead of λαλῶ need not be considered here, since in John λαλεῖν can be used for λέγειν, cp. 12.50.—One is, of course, free to read either ὅτι or ὅ τι.

[3] Barr. wants to take it to mean, "I am from the beginning what I tell you." Black's explanation, which he attacks, does not appear in the second edition of Black's book.

[4] This seems to be the way it is taken by syr^s: "The first thing that I have to say to you (is) that I have much to say about you and to judge" (Merx). But what is the second thing? For it certainly does not occur in the ἀλλά-clause. Moreover this interpretation ignores the καί in front of λαλῶ.—Hirsch translates: "Since I am speaking to you [but ὅτι καὶ λαλῶ ὑμῖν cannot possibly mean this], I have, to begin with, much to say about you and to judge." But again the ἀλλά-clause does not add what he will go on to say. There is a further reason why this clause seems out of context here, namely that in the preceding clause περὶ ὑμῖν should be stressed (this is all the more noticeable if, with Hirsch, we omit εἰς τ. κόσμον in v. 26).

[5] The sense must then have been something like, "At the beginning, no matter how much I may talk to you, you will not believe; but there will come a time ..."

[6] See Br. and Lagr., also Strathm. and Wik.

[7] According to Bl.-D. para. 300, 2, this translation accords with Classical usage. One could also take it to mean, "You accuse me of speaking ..." But it is hardly possible to supply, "You accuse me". Moreover both these translation assume that the question: σὺ τίς εἶ; is not a genuine question at all, but merely a scornful rejection of Jesus, "Who then are you, that you should want to speak to us!" But after the intentionally mysterious

At best one could translate: "Why on earth am I still speaking to you at all?"[1] and this could indeed be seen as an introduction to v. 28. Then the argument would run as follows: "Who are you?". "There is no point in discussing that with you. But when you have lifted up the Son of Man, then you will know..."[2] Taken in this way, v. 25b would confirm the view that vv. 26f. should be left out here. But: *non liquet.*

The knowledge which will dawn on the unbelievers when it is too late was described by the τότε γνώσεσθε ὅτι ἐγώ εἰμι as the knowledge of Jesus as the *judge*. As such it is also the recognition, which again comes too late, of Jesus' divine *authorisation*; and so the sentence continues, "and that I do nothing on my own authority, but speak as the Father taught me." The combination of these two ideas corresponds to the argument in 12.44–50, where it is said that, because Jesus speaks God's word as the Revealer, the revelation is judgement. The Evangelist repeats this argument here, because he wishes to bring the discussion back to the text of the source, with its concluding discussion of the "too-late" theme, which he has prepared for by the scene in 8.21–28. **Vv. 28b–29** is the direct continuation of the part of the source used in 12.49f., to which the Evangelist has added his own gloss:

καὶ ἀπ' ἐμαυτοῦ ποιῶ οὐδέν,
ἀλλὰ [καθὼς ἐδίδαξέν με ὁ πατήρ, ταῦτα λαλῶ καὶ]
ὁ πέμψας με μετ' ἐμοῦ ἐστιν.
οὐκ ἀφῆκέν με μόνον,
ὅτι ἐγὼ τὰ ἀρεστὰ αὐτῷ ποιῶ πάντοτε.[3]

ἐγώ εἰμι in v. 24, and in view of the answer in v. 28, one can take the σὺ τίς εἶ only as a serious question.

[8] See previous note.

[1] Admittedly in that case τ. ἀρχ. really ought to come before λαλῶ (Wellh.). But we may surely take it that it has been placed where it is now for emphasis; it is taken up again, in a fashion, by the καὶ in front of λαλῶ. This is how Strathm. and Wik. understand it.

[2] The attempts to take the sentence as a statement, while understanding τ. ἀρχ. as "at all", are unsatisfactory. "Firstly and above all it is clear that I am speaking to you," (Schl. thinks this possible) fails because the καί is ignored, and because it is not really possible to supply "is clear". "From the start I am what I tell you" (which Bd. and Schl. think possible)—but here too the καί is ignored.

[3] One can see why Delafosse wishes to omit the clause ὅταν ὑψώσητε ... ἐγώ εἰμι in v. 28 as a gloss, for then vv. 26–29 apparently form a coherent whole. But the originality of the clause, which he omits, is demonstrated by its reference to v. 24, whereas vv. 26–27 break the continuity of the passage (see p. 350f.). The realisation that vv. 28b, 29 refer back to 12.49f. confirms the analysis. Hence for this reason, if for no other, Hirsch is mistaken in leaving v. 28 in its present position, but following it immediately by 12.33–36 and putting v. 29 after 12.32. The assumption that the editor "has allowed the two groups of statements in 8.29 and 12.33–36a to change places" (II 75) imputes a far too artificial method to the editor. The editor did not create disorder, but attempted to put a disordered text into some sort of order.—Becker (79) reconstructs the text of vv. 28b, 29 as we have done above, except that he brackets the καί at the beginning and adds ὁ πατήρ after οὐκ ἀφῆκέν με μόνον, following 𝔎 al.

In the language of the myth, the unity of the messenger[1] and the one who sends him delineates the idea of revelation.[2] The Evangelist by his gloss stresses that the unity is realised in Jesus' speaking what the Father has taught him.[3] By this means he leads the discussion back to the preceding section of the source, which had been interrupted by vv. 21ff. This explains why he was able to add at once the last saying in the source (12.35f.), which, by way of conclusion to the whole passage, brings a word of warning. But once again he interrupts the discourse with an objection raised by the ὄχλος,[4] which is listening to Jesus. This serves to bring out both the urgency of the moment and the world's blindness to the decisive event of the present.

The objection (**12.34**)[5] picks up Jesus' saying (v. 28) that they will lift up the Son of Man: "We have heard from the Law that the Messiah remains for ever! How can you say that the Son of Man must be lifted up?[6] What kind of a Son of Man is that?" The direct identification of the Son of Man with the Messiah shows that the question is prompted by their understanding of the Son of Man as the eschatological bringer

---

[1] On ποιῶ οὐδέν cp. 5.19, 30; on μετ' ἐμοῦ and οὐκ ἀφ ... μόνον cp. 16.32; 8.16. Cp. further 10.30.

[2] See p. 251. Further ZNTW 24 (1925), 108; Schlier, Relg. Unters. 39–42.—The idea is expressed frequently in Mandaean literature, e.g. Joh.–B. 39, 15f.: "But I have a support, in that I know that I do not stand alone"; 40, 1f.; "Thou art of our sowing and so we will not leave thee alone. Thou shalt not say; I stand here alone." Giṇza 146, 9f.: "Thy speech is our speech, be united to us and not cut off." Cp. Ign. Mg. 7, 1: ὥσπερ οὖν ὁ κύριος ἄνευ τοῦ πατρὸς οὐδὲν ἐποίησεν, ἡνωμένος ὤν κτλ. For further material see on 10.30—On τὰ ἀρεστὰ ... ποιῶ see ZNTW 24 (1925), 113f.; Schlier, Relg. Unters. 42; cp. esp. Ign. Mg. 8, 2: ('Ιησ. Χρ.) ὃς κατὰ πάντα εὐηρέστησεν τῷ πέμψαντι αὐτόν; further Ginza 147, 29ff. (For the fact that ἀρεστός is frequently used in relation to God, see Br.).

[3] See p. 249 n. 1 and cf. 7.16.

[4] The fact that the ὄχλος, which has not previously been mentioned in this context, suddenly crops up as Jesus' audience is typical of the lack of clarity of the portrayal (see p. 339), and cannot be put forward as an objection to the analysis. The ὄχλος had to be given as the subject of the question, because the question was intended to give expressions to the primitive stand-point of popular eschatological hopes.

[5] 12.33 should not, as Hirsch suggests, be placed here, but should be left in its place immediately after 12.32. For this note must follow on immediately after the saying on which it comments (cp. 7.39); if it were placed here it would be divided from it by vv. 28b, 29.

[6] Even though Jesus has not said δεῖ ὑψωθῆναι *expressis verbis* in 8.28, this cannot be considered an objection to the new order of the verses. For he has spoken of the lifting up of the Son of Man. If one leaves 12.34–36 in its traditional place we are faced with a much greater difficulty, namely, that Jesus has not previously spoken of the Son of Man at all (see p. 313). It is easy to see why the Evangelist chose the phrase δεῖ ὑψωθῆναι; the ὄχλος unwittingly mouths the statement of faith.—According to Torrey (JBL 51 [1932], 320ff.) there is a misunderstanding here because of the double meaning of the Aram. word אִסְתַּלַּק which lies behind ὑψωθῆναι, which in Aram. can mean "to be lifted up into the heights" and "to depart". He thinks that the ὄχλος takes Jesus' saying 12.32 to mean, "When I have departed from the land." Against this it must be objected that 12.34 comes after 8.29, and that it was composed by the Evangelist, who wrote Greek.

of salvation.[1] Yet their error does not lie in this, but in the fact that in their imagination they pull down the eschatological event into the dimensions of this-worldly events and fail to understand that it is an event which denies the world. The ὄχλος stands for the desires and imaginings of Jewish apocalyptic,[2] according to which the bringer of salvation will come down from heaven to usher in the age of salvation on earth, an age which has no end.[3] Here as elsewhere[4] the Evangelist is concerned to attack this apocalyptic conception of salvation. The salvation which God's Revealer brings is not a state of affairs which will one day exist in the world, and which man will have at his disposal, freed from care because the bringer of salvation "remains for ever." The revelation is much more a denial and a questioning of the world; the acceptance of its gift therefore demands that man abandon all human desires and imaginations, all human striving for possession and mastery, even the desire to master the future, just as it demands that he abandon his traditional notions of life and death.[5] And so the Revealer does not come "to remain for ever", but he comes soon to depart again. He "must be lifted up", as the Evangelist says in the terminology of the Gnostic myth,[6]—not of course in order to replace Jewish mythology by Gnostic mythology, but because Gnostic mythology enables him to express his fundamental idea, that the Revealer by his coming does not become a phenomenon of this world, but that he remains a stranger who takes his leave again. This will be brought out clearly in the Farewell Discourses. It is only in his departure that the meaning of his coming is revealed. The encounter with the Revealer turns the present moment into the

---

[1] In later Jewish eschatology the traditional figure of the Messiah (the Davidic king of the age of salvation) often gave way to the Son of Man (whose origin is in the myth), that is, in so far as the two figures were not actually combined; see Bousset, Rel. d. Jdts. 259ff.; Moore II 331ff.—On μένειν εἰς τ. αἰῶνα, see p. 222 n. 7, and Schl. on 8.34.

[2] The ὄχλος appeals to the νόμος, i.e. to the OT (cp. 10.34). It is hard to say whether the Evangelist had particular references in mind. According to Jer. 24.6; Ezek. 37.25; Joel 3.20 Israel will dwell in the land for ever. According to I Kings 8.25; 9.5 the throne of David will never be empty. According to Ezek. 37.25 David will be Israel's ruler for ever (cp. Is. 9.6; Ps. 72.5; 110.4 in a Messianic interpretation). According to Dan 7.13f. the kingdom of the Son of Man is an everlasting kingdom. On the everlastingness of the Messianic age in Jewish hopes, see Orac. Sib. III 49f., 766; Ps. Sal. 17.4; Eth. En. 62, 14; Rabbinic references in Merx 328. Cp. Tryphon in Justin, Dial. 32, 1.—Μένειν in 12.34 means "remain" in a general sense, and not in the special sense of "to remain alive", as in 21.22 and elsewhere.

[3] The fact that in more developed apocalyptic systems the Messianic age does come to an end and is followed by a new aeon (Bousset, Rel. des Jdts. 286ff.; Str.-B. IV 799ff.) and that therefore the age of the Messiah is limited (admittedly not by his "lifting up"! see Str.-B. III 824ff.) has no bearing on the popular hopes which are represented by the ὄχλος.

[4] See pp. 128f. 154ff. 166, 189f. 213f.

[5] See pp. 257f.

[6] See p. 150 n. 1. ZNTW 25 (1925), 126f.

eschatological moment. If this moment could be prolonged, it would no longer belong to eschatological time but to worldly time. It is this which gives the moment of encounter its importance and responsibility, which makes it the moment of decision concerning life and death.[1]

Jesus appears not to take up the question of the ὄχλος; he simply warns them to make use of the present moment. **vv. 35f.**

[ἔτι μικρὸν χρόνον τὸ φῶς ἐν ὑμῖν ἐστιν.]
περιπατεῖτε ὡς τὸ φῶς ἔχετε,
    ἵνα μὴ σκοτία ὑμᾶς καταλάβῃ.
καὶ ὁ περιπατῶν ἐν τῇ σκοτίᾳ
    οὐκ οἶδεν ποῦ ὑπάγει.
ὡς τὸ φῶς ἔχετε,
    πιστεύετε εἰς τὸ φῶς,
        ἵνα υἱοὶ φωτὸς γένησθε.[2]

What is important, in contrast to the Jewish hope—and consequently to all imaginary visions of a future salvation—is not looking away from the present moment and becoming lost in a mythical future, in which the dreams of a romantic fantasy are to be realised and put at man's disposal; rather the important thing is to be open to the present moment, which is invaded unexpectedly by the word of the Revealer. It is—and is again and again—only a fleeting moment: "The light is with you for only a little longer!" Here again is the warning that soon it will be too late, as in 7.33f.; 8.21. And so too we hear the warning in which reality and image are curiously intermingled: "Walk while you have the light, lest the darkness overtake you.[3] He who walks in the darkness does not know where he goes." It seems to be a comparison, pure and simple, in which τὸ φῶς and σκοτία have their primary sense of day-light and the darkness of night.[4] But even though the sentence καὶ ὁ περιπατῶν κτλ. is a perfectly typical figurative maxim, the first sentence is given a metaphorical sense by its imperative form and

---

[1] Cp. Faulhaber 43f.

[2] These are clearly the concluding verses of the discourse on the light in the source. The first sentence, which makes the link with v. 34, presumably comes from the Evangelist. The longer last lines are in accordance with the style of the discourses (see p. 76 n. 4.—The textual variants are of no importance.

[3] On περιπατεῖν see p. 343 n. 1. Ὡς like ἕως 9.4 (occurring as a variant also in 12.35f.) = so long as, as in Lk. 12.58; Gal. 6.10; see Bl.-D. para. 455, 3. καταλαμβάνειν (used here differently from 1.5) = overtake, surprise, and in Greek is also frequently used alike of night and darkness and of death, see Br. and Liddell and Scott.

[4] The fact that the sentence is intended to be understood in the first place as a comparison is shown by the use of σκοτία without the article (understandably some MSS add the article).—On the figurative use of light and darkness see p. 41; see also p. 341 n. 1, cp. Job 12.25; and esp. Prov. 4.18f. Rabbinic references in Str.-B. ad loc.

consequently, the meaning of τὸ φῶς oscillates with peculiar ambiguity between "day-light" and "true" light. In consequence the maxim is also infected with the same ambiguity. If one listens closely one realises that it contains an allusion to the Gnostic's knowledge of his origin and destiny.[1] So the final warning can be added, without any explicit statement that here the image finds its application: "While you have the light, believe in the light!"

Finally, in the last line a note of promise is struck: "that you may become sons of light." The believer, then, need no longer fear the onset of night; for him the mystery of the ἔτι μικρὸν χρόνον has been resolved.[2] And so the eschatological promise—as understood by the Jewish, primitive Christian tradition and by the Gnostic tradition[3]—takes on a new meaning. For the believer already enjoys in the present what apocalyptic speculation had expected from a future transformation of the cosmos.

c) Conclusion: 12.36b; 10.19–21[4]

When he has said this, Jesus "hides" himself again (12.36b; cp. 8.59) and leaves his audience[5] to themselves. There is a close parallel here with 9.16. There the examination of the healed man by the Pharisees led, as here, to a σχίσμα,[6] and further, the discussion in 10.20f. corresponds exactly to 9.16. The only difference is that here the claims made by Jesus in his discourse have caused even greater offence. The opposing party no longer condemns him as ἄνθρωπος ἁμαρτωλός, but

---

[1] See p. 143 n. 1. The comparison is, of course, by no means far fetched; cp. Plato, Phaedo 82d, where he says of the man governed by his ἐπιθυμίαι: ὡς οὐκ εἰδόσιν, ὅπῃ ἔρχονται.

[2] In Semitic usage the concept of the son (or child) with the genitive of a thing refers to membership of and determination by the thing referred to; Str.-B. I 476ff.; Schl. on 17.12.

[3] In Jewish and Gnostic belief *light* is the essence of the divine world and consequently also of the eschatological salvation (see pp. 42 nn. 3, 4). Those who are resurrected will be transformed into φῶς or δόξα, cp. I Cor. 15.42ff.; Phil. 3.21, etc.; Bousset, Rel. d. Jdts. 277; Str.-B. I 752 on Mt. 17.2; Volz, Eschatologie 396ff. For Gnosticism cp. Ginza 391, 12; 396, 19.37; 562.20ff.; Od. Sal 11.11; 15.2; 21.3; 25.7.—The formula "sons of light" also occurs in Lk. 16.8, and in I Th. 5.5; Eph. 5.8 it denotes eschatological existence; in Ign. Philad. 2, 1 it is expanded to τέκνα φωτὸς ἀληθείας. In Mandaean literature the beings which inhabit the world of light are called "sons of light" (Odeberg 335). It is also used to refer to the members of the Ess. community of the Qumran texts. Cp. DSD 1, 9; 2, 16; 3, 24f. and DSW (=1QM): "The book of the struggle of the sons of light against the sons of darkness." See also K. G. Kuhn. ZThK 47 (1950), 312.

[4] On the link with 10.19–21, see p. 312.

[5] See p. 347 n. 3.

[6] πάλιν refers back to 9.16, as is shown by v. 21.

accuses him: δαιμόνιον ἔχει καὶ μαίνεται; he is possessed and mad.[1] The other party judges like the ἄλλοι in 9.16, and believes the healings of the blind man to be a proof of Jesus' authority. Thus the κρίμα for which the "light" has come, is reflected in the σχίσμα.

D. 10.1-39: The Good Shepherd

The discourse on the Good Shepherd and the discussions which go with it have their introduction in 10.22ff.[2] and their conclusion in 10.31–39. We must first ask how far the introduction extends, and where we are to fit in the misplaced section 10.1–18. The introduction certainly comprises vv. 22–25; but we should probably also include v. 26, where the οὐ πιστεύετε of v. 25 is taken up again. By means of the metaphorical use of πρόβατα v. 26 leads directly into the discourse on the Good Shepherd.[3] On the other hand vv. 27–30 form a closely knit unit, and are clearly the conclusion of the discourse. The last saying in v. 30 provokes the Jews to anger (v. 31).[4] Now of course it is not possible simply to insert 10.1–18 between vv. 26 and 27. V. 1 does not lead easily on from v. 26, and v. 27 follows on v. 18 even less easily. Above all, however, 10.1–18 is not an ordered whole, but is comprised of separate units. And whereas they are all held together by the image of the shepherd and the sheep, they are not closely related to each other; in fact some of the individual units themselves hang together only very loosely.

10.1–5, which is explicitly rounded off in v. 6, contains (according to v. 6) a παροιμία, whose point is the contrast between the shepherd and the thief and the robber, a contrast which is brought out by the fact that the shepherd goes into the fold through the gate, while the thief chooses another way. The gate which is spoken of here is the gate which leads to the sheep, and inasmuch as the παροιμία is about Jesus' person, it represents him as the one whom the sheep follow as their rightful and familiar shepherd. Admittedly the equation between Jesus and the shepherd is not made in so many words; for the section as a whole is a typical parable, and gives a finished picture.

10.7–10 forms a new section with its own introduction. At first it seems as if this is the beginning of a new παροιμία, which discusses Jesus by means of the image of the door. In fact, however, this is only true of v. 7 and v. 9, whereas v. 8 and v. 10 again deal with the contrast between the shepherd and

[1] Δαιμόνιον ἔχει as in 8.48, 52; see p. 299 n. 5. On the charge of μαίνεσθαι cp. Wisd. 5.4; Acts 26.24f.; (I Cor. 14.23); Plat. Phaedr 249d: ἐξιστάμενος δὲ τῶν ἀνθρωπίνων σπουδασμάτων καὶ πρὸς τῷ θείῳ γιγνόμενος νουθετεῖται μὲν ὑπὸ τῶν πολλῶν ὡς παρακινῶν, ἐνθουσιάζων δὲ λέληθε τοὺς πολλούς. Dio Chrys. or. 12, 8, p. 199, 12.

[2] On the misplacement of the sections 10.1–18 and 10.22ff., see p. 312.

[3] Cp. the way in which the theme of the discourse on the bread of life is introduced by a metaphorical expression in 6.27, and similarly the theme of the discourse on the light in 9.39–41.

[4] It does not seem possible to me to insert 10.1–18 after v. 29, as is frequently done by English scholars; see Howard 264.

the thief and robber.[1] Thus while vv. 8 and 10 seem to continue the thought of vv. 1–5, vv. 7 and 9 run counter to it, for here the door is not thought of as the way through which the shepherd goes into the sheep, but as the door through which the sheep are led out to pasture and led back again into the fold; and in so far as this section refers to Jesus, the image alters from verse to verse. Vv. 7–10 give the impression of being an explanatory gloss on the παροιμία, commenting on the details of vv. 1–5.[2] There is therefore no ground for objecting to the sequence of vv. 7–10 on vv. 1–6. Furthermore, it seems wholly appropriate that the interpretation should be separated from the παροιμία itself by a new introduction, since v. 6 had stressed the unintelligibility of the παροιμία. One can ask only if the interpretation, with its confusion of the various images, is itself uniform. What seems probable is that the interpretation has made use of the original continuation of vv. 1–5 in vv. 8 and 10, whereas vv. 7 and 9 are the Evangelist's glosses. In any case the whole section is based on a source text, to which the Evangelist has added a descriptive framework, together with his own comments. There is no reason to doubt that the discourse on the Good Shepherd also comes from the book of revelation-discourses.

V. 11 makes a fresh beginning, and in vv. 11–13 Jesus appears as the Good Shepherd, whose nature is described by the contrast with the hireling. The thief and robber play as little part here as the door. Like vv. 1–5, the section is a parable pure and simple—apart, that is, from the introductory sentence ἐγώ εἰμι κτλ. Manifestly, then, this is the original beginning of the discourse on the Good Shepherd, as may be seen by analogy with the other revelation discourses. At the same time it also provides the best link with vv. 22–26. The discourse on the Good Shepherd is the answer to the question in v. 24, εἰ σὺ εἶ ὁ Χριστὸς κτλ., and at the same time it is a refusal to give an answer, because Jesus speaks ἐν παροιμίᾳ and not, as asked, παρρησίᾳ. The meaning of ἐγώ εἰμι ὁ ποιμὴν ὁ καλός is brought out by describing the notion of ποιμήν by means of a parable in vv. 11–13. Since this is also what vv. 1–5 do, the obvious thing seems to be to place vv. 1–5 (–10) after vv. 11–13, so that we now have the original beginning and the original continuation.

V. 14 again makes a fresh start by repeating the ἐγώ εἰμι .Vv. 14–18 are not a unity in themselves. The ἐγώ εἰμι is not followed by a parable of any

[1] The reading of v. 7 in sa, "I am the shepherd of the sheep", must be taken as a conjecture, which attempts to cover up the disparity between vv. 7 and 8, and consequently between vv. 7f. and vv. 1–5. And yet such unity as may be produced in this way is destroyed by v. 9. Wellh. who wants to read ποιμήν in v. 7 instead of θύρα, has therefore to omit v. 9 as a gloss. Sp. believes that vv. (6) 7–10 are a secondary addition, because the verses give an allegorical interpretation of the parable of the shepherd in vv. 1–5; but even if this latter statement is right, the assertion that vv. (6) 7–10 are a secondary addition is only correct inasmuch as vv. 1–5 come from the Evangelist's source, while vv. 6–10 are his own composition; see below. Wendt wants to distinguish vv. 1–9, the parable of the door, from vv. 10ff., the parable of the shepherd; but Jesus is compared with the door only in vv. 7 and 9. —For a discussion of other explanations, see J. Jeremias, ThWB III 178, 26ff.

[2] Ἐγώ εἰμι ἡ θύρα (τ. προβ.), unlike the other ἐγώ εἰμι sayings, is not the Revealer's introduction of himself, but an explanatory statement like ὁ σπείρων ... ἐστὶν ὁ υἱὸς τ. ἀνθρ. Mt. 13.37, etc.

kind. The relation between Jesus and his own is described in vv. 14f. in non-figurative language, although the term which is used to describe this relationship, γινώσκειν, reminds one of the description in the parable in vv. 1–5. The shepherd calls the sheep by name, and the sheep know his voice. On the other hand the last clause of v. 15 contains another motif, that of τιθέναι τὴν ψυχήν, which is characteristic of the shepherd, and which comes from the comparison in vv. 11–13. This motif is developed in the equally non-figurative verses, 17f.; but in v. 16 we have a completely new motif, the vision of the one fold and the one shepherd. Moreover v. 16 uses metaphorical language, for which the images (αὐλή, ἄγειν, ἀκούειν τῆς φωνῆς) are again taken from the parable vv. 1–5. Clearly vv. 14–18 should be taken with vv. 7–10 as explanatory glosses on the preceding two-part parable, vv. 1–5, 11–13; and again one asks whether all these glosses come from the *same* pen. Clearly, part of this complex, vv. 14–18, comes from the source, namely the beginning, ἐγώ εἰμι to κἀγὼ γινώσκω τὸν πατέρα (vv. 14, 15a). The style alone is proof of this; as is also the fact that the new beginning with the repeated ἐγώ εἰμι, is in accordance with the style of the book of revelation-discourses.[1] This view is finally confirmed by the fact that vv. 14, 15 and vv. 27–30 form a closely-knit unit, and were clearly a continuous section in the source.

Thus we are brought to two conclusions: 1) The original *order* of the whole complex (which was composed by the Evangelist on the basis of his source) is as follows: 10.22–26, 11–13, 1–10, 14–18, 27–39. 2) The source on which the complex is based comprised 10.11–13, 1–5, 8, 10, 14–15a, 27–30. We have not taken into account here that it is possible that these sections of the source may contain explanatory comments of the Evangelist's. We will have to go into this question when we proceed with the exegesis; we shall then also have to see whether the editor limited himself to the task of restoring the order of the confused text, or whether he himself also added to the Evangelist's comments.[2]

a) Introduction: 10.22–26

Verses 22 and 23 indicate the time and place of the scene; it is the feast of the Dedication of the Temple,[3] and Jesus is in Solomon's

---

[1] See p. 339 n. 5.

[2] Joh. Schneider, Coniect. Neotest. XI 1947 (Festschr. f. A. Fridrichsen) 220–225 gives a different analysis. According to him the discourse originally consisted of vv. 1–18 (in the order in which they have been handed down) and vv. 27–30; between which the Evangelist has inserted vv. 19–26, which however originally came at the end of ch. 9.—L. Cerfaux (loc. cit. 16–19) allows the traditional order of the text to stand and attempts to show that the discourse is constructed after the same pattern as that used in OT, Jewish and synoptic parable-discourses. The first part, vv. 1–5, gives a "parabole-allégorie", and this is followed in the second part, vv. 7–16, by the "application-explication". Cerfaux does not discuss vv. 17ff. here.—J. Jeremias (ThWB III 179, 4ff.) suspects that vv. 7–10 are an allegorical interpretation of vv. 1f., and that it comes from another pen than vv. 1–5.

[3] Τὰ ἐγκαίνια (for חֲנֻכָּה) was the feast of the reconsecration of the Temple after its desecration by the Syrians. The reconsecration was carried out by Judas Maccabaeus on

porch.[1] The reason we are told that it is winter[2] can hardly be simply to provide an explanation for Jesus' choice of locality, but to indicate that the end is near. The seasons of the year reflect the progress of the revelation.[3] V. 24 also shows that Jesus' ministry is approaching its end. The following speech is the last great revelation-discourse of Jesus to the people. Admittedly it is now hardly directed to the people in the way that his earlier speeches had been; it no longer contains the appeals and invitations and warnings of those speeches. Jesus is already in a sense separated from his audience, and speaks of himself and his own as it were from afar. Indeed, the place in which the scene is set is itself an indication of this, for according to Acts 5.12 (3.11) Solomon's porch was one of the meeting places of the early Christian community.[4] Thus the time and the place serve to point to the importance of the following scene.

Similarly the demand of the "Jews" (**v. 24**) shows that this is a crucial moment in Jesus' history. The uncertainty has lasted long enough,[5] and there must be an end to it! The final question is put to Jesus, and he must give a decisive answer, whether or not he is the Messiah. Had he not said so clearly enough in his discourses? Not clearly enough to satisfy the "Jews"; for them, who now demand an answer παρρησίᾳ,[6] all Jesus' previous self-revelations had been παροιμίαι. He is the concealed Revealer, because he cannot give them any proof of

---

the 25th Kislev 165 B.C., cp: I Macc 4, 36–59; II Macc. 1.9, 18; 10.1–8; Jos. ant. XII 316–325; Schürer I 208f.; Str.-B. ad loc.; Moore II 49.—For a discussion of the view that the Feast of the Dedication fell on the winter solstice, see Ed. Norden, Die Geburt des Kindes 1924, 26f.

[1] Solomon's porch, which according to Jos. ant. XX 220.; bell. V 185 survived from the temple constructed by Solomon, lay on the east side of the temple; cp. Jos. ant. XV 396–401; bell. V 190–192. 411–416; Str.-B. on Acts 3.11 (II 625f); Dalman, O. u. W. 310f.; Jerusalem und sein Gelände 1930, 116ff.

[2] Kislev falls in the months of November and December; see Schürer I 745ff.

[3] See p. 174, on 3.30; and cp. Hosk.—According to Hirsch the feast of the Dedication of the Temple was chosen here by way of contrast, because it was the Jewish feast most foreign to Christianity. "Jewry made the final break with Jesus at a feast which was concerned with the renewal of the temple cult and thereby ... they dedicated the temple to destruction." Huber makes the fantastic suggestion (Begriff der Offenb. 9) that there is a connection between the discourse on the Good Shepherd and Ps. 29 (ψαλμὸς ᾠδῆς τοῦ ἐγκαινισμοῦ τοῦ οἴκου τοῦ Δαυείδ).—There seems to be no play on the light symbolism, which might have been suggested by the name sometimes given to the feast, τὰ φῶτα (Jos. ant. XII 325).

[4] See Kundsin, Topol. Überl. 38f.

[5] Αἴρειν τ. ψυχήν = to put in a state of great expectancy, keep in suspense; see Wetst., esp. Jos. ant. III 48: οἱ δ' ἦσαν ἐπὶ τὸν κίνδυνον τὰς ψυχὰς ἠρμένοι; Ps. 24.1; 85.4 are different. Hosk. wants to take αἴρ. τ. ψ. v. 24 in the same sense as in v. 18: How long dost thou continue to take away our life?—namely, by the threat of the collapse of Judaism. —This is scarcely credible.

[6] On παρρησία, see p. 291 n. 3. Here παρρ. as contrasted to παροιμία means, as in 16.25, 29, openness; cp. Mk. 8.32.

his authority in the way they require. For the justice of his claim is apparent only to those who make the decision of faith, and his gift is visible only to those who are aware of their own emptiness. Therefore it is for the circle of the believers only that his speech is no longer a παροιμία (16.23–25, 29). The symbolism of the scene reaches its height in this apparently meaningless εἰπὸν ὑμῖν παρρησίᾳ. They demand an answer which would relieve them of the decision, an answer such as Jesus has till now at most only been able to give to the Samaritan woman (4.26) and the healed blind man (9.37). Yet he has never[1] and can never say it in the way *they* wish him to say it. He cannot reveal himself by "direct", only by "indirect" communication;[2] for him to speak παρρησίᾳ is solely an eschatological possibility (16.25).

So Jesus cannot now simply reply by an ἐγώ-εἰμι statement; for him to do so would be for him to acknowledge their conception of the Messiah and of the world. He can answer their question only indirectly (**v. 25**): "I told you, and you do not believe."[3] He has long ago told them what he can and must tell them. They have not understood, because they do not believe. Just as they have seen without "seeing" (6.36), so they have heard without "hearing". For how has he told them? "The works which I do in my Father's name, they bear witness to me." His work of revelation, which he carries out on behalf of the Father,[4] is his witness,[5] and that is not an unambiguous speech, nor "direct communication", but one which demands a decision from the hearer.

Thus v. 25 says: Everything was in vain! And why? The explanation is given by **v. 26**, which expresses the peculiarly Johannine concept of predestination.[6] The fact that the "Jews" are not among those whom God "draws" (6. 44), that they have their origin in the depth, in "this world" (8.23), is here couched in metaphorical language: "But you do

---

[1] Goguel's view (Introduct. au NT II 1924, 427f.; Rev. H. Ph. rel. V 1925, 519) that v. 24 goes back to source, because the question about the previous self-revelations is meaningless, seems to me to be quite wrong.

[2] Cp. Kierkegaard, Training in Christianity, 134f., esp. 135: "The statement can be quite direct; but the fact that he is involved in it, that he (as a sign of the contradiction) says it, makes it an indirect communication." Cp. also Temple 138f.171 and Hosk. ad loc.

[3] ἐπιστεύσατε B pc must be a correction. On καί=but, see p. 48 n. 2.

[4] On ἐν. τ. ὀν., see p. 270 n. 2.

[5] The witness of the works, as in 5.36; see p. 265f.—Hirsch (II 84f.) wants to omit vv. 25b, 26a (τὰ ἔργα to οὐ πιστεύετε) as an editorial addition, because they disrupt the unity of the discourse by anticipating the ἔργα-motif (vv. 32ff.) and obscure the connection with the parable of the shepherd. The latter is surely not the case, nor is there any reason to object to the fact that the discourse is, as it were, framed by the ἔργα motif. For not only the idea of the μαρτυρεῖν of the ἔργα, but also the style is characteristic of the Evangelist, particularly the way the subject is picked up again by the demonstrative, see p. 79 n. 1.

[6] See pp. 230f, 233f., 317.

not believe, because you do not belong to my sheep."[1] This anticipates the motif of the following discourse and thus leads into it.[2]

The *discourse* is a παροιμία (v.6), and as such it is the paradoxical answer to v. 24—paradoxical, because of the character of the revelation. It is also paradoxical in that it deals with the relationship of Jesus to his own, and of his own to him. It thus indicates that knowledge of the Revealer can be realised only within the circle of his own; and so indirectly it explains the οὐ πιστεύετε. At the same time by dealing with this theme, by moving, that is, within a sphere to which its hearers are strangers, the discourse makes clear what is the only possible way in which the Revealer can reveal himself. He cannot enter the sphere of unbelief and unbelief can be attacked only by being confronted with the sphere of faith. Just because of its paradoxical character, therefore, the discourse, in spite of appearances, contains an invitation.

Finally it is important to notice that the discourse on the Good Shepherd is the last of the revelation-discourses to be addressed to the people.[3] By setting forth the relation of the Revealer to his own, it makes its final appeal to the world—while saying substantially nothing different from the other discourses—and shows to the world the highest possibility of faith. It is therefore at the same time the transition to the second part of the Gospel, where the discourses deal expressly with this reciprocal relationship; they no longer talk *about* this relationship but rather talk *from the stand-point of* the relationship. The very fact that the discourse on the Good Shepherd talks *about* the relationship distinguishes it from the Farewell discourses. In the παροιμία of the shepherd the faithful are referred to in the 3rd person; in the παροιμία of the vine (ch. 15) we read: You and I!

b) *The Good Shepherd:* 10.11–13, 1–10, 14–18, 27–30[4]

1) *The Good Shepherd and the Hireling:* 10.11–13

Jesus starts with the ἐγώ εἰμι of the revelation discourse;[5] the first sentence is not part of the parable, so that there is no need to paraphrase,

---

[1] On εἶναι ἐκ, see p. 138 n. 1.—ℜD pm it add καθὼς εἶπον ὑμῖν. This can only be a gloss, which belongs to the following verse and refers back to vv. 3f. or to v. 14. The glossator must have noticed that the passages, which really belong together, have been separated in the present text.

[2] See p. 358 n. 3.

[3] Of course Jesus also addresses the people in 12.20–33; 8.30–40; 6.60–65; but this discourse is not a typical revelation-discourse.

[4] This is based on a section of the revelation-discourses, as is suggested by the ἐγώ εἰμι statement, and confirmed by the explanatory additions in vv. 6, 7–10, 15b–18, see p. 359f. Since the discourse has the form of a parable, the structure of the verse is very loose.

[5] See p. 225 n 3.

"I am to be compared with a good shepherd." For here, as in the statements about the bread of life and the light of the world (6.35; 8.12), we have a title and not a comparison. He *is* the good shepherd. Just as all the waters of the earth point to the one living water, and as all bread on the earth points to the one bread of life, and as all day-light points to the light of the world, just as every earthly vine is contrasted with the "true" vine, so too every shepherd in the world is contrasted with the "good" shepherd. Shepherding in the world is only an image and pointer to the true, proper shepherding which is shown in the rule of the Revealer. It is in this sense that Jesus is the *good* shepherd. Of course the Evangelist might have put ἀληθινός instead of καλός.[1] Yet καλός brings out the Revealer's significance in a particular way; for καλός refers not only to his absoluteness and decisiveness, but also to his "being for . . ." This in itself already indicates that the title presupposes or demands a self-understanding of man, which takes cognisance of man's being as "being which is dependent on . . .". Man who is driven on in his quest by this knowledge—whether implicit or explicit—is confronted by the word of the Revealer, ἐγώ εἰμι: I am he, for whom you seek; I am the good shepherd.

The *image of the shepherd* has been used in many forms and ways in history.[2] In Oriental[3] and Greek antiquity[4] the comparison between the *ruler* and the shepherd, and between his people and the herd, was wide-spread and ancient. It is so common in the OT that the comparison is not normally

[1] In the Revealer's conception of himself καλός is used in an absolute sense (cp. the chorale "Tut mir auf die schöne Pforte" "Open to me the beautiful gate"). The reason for the choice of καλός instead of ἀληθινός (1.9; 6.32; 15.1) is because it is common, and more appropriate as a description of shepherds (Str.-B. ad loc.; Fiebig, Angelos I 1925, 58; Ginza 181, 18ff.). Καλός is rarely predicated of God; see Peterson, Εἷς Θεός 31f.—In the LXX καλός is used to translate יָפֶה and טוֹב; here of course it is used in the sense of ἀγαθός, as is said explicitly in act. Thom. 25.39, p. 141, 3; 157, 13; Exc. ex Theod. 73, 3 ποιμ. ἀγαθ., so too Philo agric. 49. Cp. Schweizer 132.

[2] See Wilh. Jost, ΠΟΙΜΗΝ 1939; A. Parrot, Le "bon pasteur", Mélanges Syriens offerts a M. A. Dussaud I (1939), 171–182.

[3] For Babylonia and Assyria see M. Jastrow, Die Religion der Bab. und Ass. I, 1902.69; Br. Meissner, Bab. und Ass. I, 1920, 48f.; A. Jeremias, Das AT im Lichte des alten Orients, 4. ed. 652f.; L. Dürr, Ursprung und Ausbau der israelit.-jüd. Heilandserwartung 1925, 117ff.; H. Gressmann, Messias 210f.—For Egypt: Dürr, op. cit. 120f.—In Parseeism Yima, the king of the first age, is the "good shepherd"; Chantepie de la Saussaye, Lehrbuch der Religionsgesch. 4. ed. II, 1925, 213; Bertholet, Religionsgesch. Lesebuch 2. ed. 1 (1926), 28.

[4] In the Greek world this way of referring to rulers and kings was common, as from the time of Homer (ποιμὴν λαῶν); see Liddell and Scott; νέμειν is used both of shepherds and kings. In Plato Rep. 343 a. b Thrasymachos upholds the view that it is absurd to think τοὺς ποιμένας ἢ τοὺς βουκόλους τὸ τῶν προβάτων ἢ τὸ τῶν βοῶν σκοπεῖν, and similarly the ἄρχοντες, like the ποιμένες, are only concerned with their own gain. On the other hand Socrates argues; 345 c, d: ...τῇ δὲ ποιμενικῇ (sc. τέχνῃ) οὐ δήπου ἄλλου τοῦ μέλει ἤ, ἐφ'

given at length, but is reduced to allusions and metaphors. As Moses was once the shepherd of the sheep of God (Is. 63.11; cp. Ps. 77.21), so God has taken David from his flock—

> "to be the shepherd of Jacob his people, of Israel his inheritance.
> With upright heart he tended them, and guided them with skilful hand". (Ps. 78.70–72)

God must find a man to lead the people, lest it become "like sheep who have no shepherd" (Num. 27.17). If faithless Israel repents, God will give her shepherds after his own heart, who will feed her with knowledge and understanding (Jer. 3.15). Instead of the bad shepherds who neglect and scatter the sheep, God will provide better ones (Jer. 23.1–4; cp. 2.8; 12.10). The Messianic son of David will one day guard the united flock as its only shepherd (Ez. 34.23; 37.24; cp. Mi. 5.3).

Similarly in Ps. Sal. 17.45 it is said of the Messiah:

> ποιμαίνων τὸ ποιμνίον Κυρίου ἐν πίστει καὶ δικαιοσύνῃ,
> καὶ οὐκ ἀφήσει ἀσθενῆσαι ἐν αὐτοῖς ἐν τῇ νομῇ αὐτῶν.

In Judaism the prophets, like Moses and David, are also called good shepherds, and the evil leaders of the people are called bad shepherds, as they are in the OT.[1] Correspondingly Israel can be referred to as a flock.[2]

Since in the ancient Orient[3] and in the OT, *God* is thought of as king, he is correspondingly referred to *as the shepherd:* "For he is our God, and we are his people, the sheep of his pasture" (Ps. 95.7; 79.13; 100.3; cp. Gen. 49.24). He is invoked as "shepherd of Israel" (Ps. 80.2) and the Psalmist cannot understand his anger against the sheep whom he tends (Ps. 74.1). Once "he led his people forth like sheep and guided them in the wilderness like a flock" (Ps. 78.52; cp. 77.21; Is. 63.14); and in the age of salvation he will again lead her to pastures and streams (Is. 49.9f.). The image of the victorious ruler is combined with that of the shepherd who cares for his sheep (Is. 40.10f.), and both his care[4] and his gathering in of the scattered flocks is described in Jer. 31.10; cp. Mi. 2.12; 4.6f.[5] The image is embroidered with great allegories in Ez. 34; Zach. 11.4–17, and above all in the allegorical

---

ᾧ τέτακται, ὅπως τούτῳ τὸ βέλτιστον ἐκποριεῖ. Cp. Polit. 267dff. (Comparison of the king as the νομεὺς καὶ τροφὸς ἀγέλης with the cow-herds); Xenoph., Cyrop. VIII 2, 14; Epict. Diss, III 22, 35. For further discussion, including the application of the image of the shepherd to philosophers, see E. Lohmeyer, Christuskult und Kaiserkult 1919, 48f.

[1] Str.-B. II 536f.; P. Fiebig, Angelos I (1925), 57f.; Odeberg 314ff. J. Jeremias, ThWB IV 857, 19. Cp. II Esd 5.18 (Phaltiel to Esra): "Do not abandon us, like the shepherd who leaves his sheep to the wicked wolves."; Asc. Jes. 3, 24.—Odeberg (318) points out that in Rabbinic literature the Messiah is never referred to as the shepherd.

[2] Odeberg 316f.

[3] Dürr, op. cit. 121f.; Gressmann op. cit. 211f.; W. Eichrodt, Theologie des AT I, 1933, 119; Joh. Hempel, Gott u. Mensch im AT 2. ed. 1936, 181f.

[4] The shepherd's care is usually represented as the care he takes to provide the sheep with good pasture (Is. 49.9; Ezek. 34.14) and water (Is. 49.10; Ps. 23.2).

[5] The picture of the scattered flock also occurs in I Kings 22.17; the picture of the lost sheep in Is. 53.6; the search for the lost sheep in Ezek. 34.4, 16.

portrayal of world-history in Eth. En. 85–90, in which the image has completely lost its original vividness.[1] On the other hand, the image of God as shepherd can be related to the individual, to the righteous man. Jacob calls God his shepherd (Gen. 48.15), and the righteous man in Ps. 23 praises the care of God, his shepherd.[2]

The image of the shepherd in the NT is very largely dependent on the OT. The judgement on the people who are like sheep without a shepherd (Mk. 6.34; Mt. 9.36), refers back to Num. 27.17; in this the idea that Jesus is the true shepherd is in some sense present. Equally Jesus is thought of as the shepherd in Mk. 14.27, where following Zach. 13.7 it is said: πατάξω τὸν ποιμένα καὶ τὰ πρόβατα διασκορπισθήσονται.[3] Yet here the flock is no longer the people, but the disciples; in Lk. 12.32 they are called a small flock, but the figure of the shepherd plays no part.[4] In his Messianic role Jesus is referred to as the Shepherd in I Pet. 2.25 (where there is an allusion to Is. 53.6), and Heb. 13.20 and I Pet. 5.4 show that even at that stage it had become a traditional way of referring to him.[5] Yet in this use its meaning has been weakened. There is no longer any mention of his tending the flock,[6] and in Rev. 12.5; 19.15 the saying in Ps. 2.9 (in the LXX version) is used to describe the Shepherd-Messiah, not in relation to his community, but to his enemies. Equally, of course, it soon became traditional to describe the community as a flock,[7] and to think of the leaders of the community as its shepherds.[8]

---

[1] Here the Messiah appears not as a shepherd, but as a white bullock.

[2] Philo's use of the image of the shepherd does not belong to this tradition, even though he does occasionally quote Ps. 23.1, when he wishes to describe God (agric. 50) or the Logos (mut. nom. 115) as the shepherd. God's flock is the κόσμος (agric. 51); usually, however, Philo uses the image in such a way that it is the αἰσθήσεις which are the flock (sacr. Abr. et C. 105; quod det. pot. ins. sol. 25; post. C. 98; agric. 34) or the seven τοῦ ἀλόγο δυνάμεις (mut. nom. 110; cp. post. C. 66; agric. 30), and the νοῦς which is the shepherd (sacr. Ab. et C. 105; agric. 30.34.48.66), or the λογισμός (sacr. Ab. et C. 105; agric. 29; mut. nom. 111), or the ὀρθὸς λόγος (post. C. 68; agric. 51), or the θεῖος λόγος (mut. nom. 114.116). In this Philo follows the tradition of the Cynics and the stoics; see J. Quasten in "Heilige Überlieferung" (presented to J. Herwegen) 1938, 51ff. Ποιμαίνειν (=to protect) is already to be found in Aesch. Eum. 91, where it is used of Hermes.

[3] In Barn. 5.12, Zech. 13.7 is quoted in a rather different sense; here Jesus is seen as the shepherd of the people.

[4] The parable of the lost sheep is a pure comparison (Lk. 15.4–7; Mt. 18.12–14), for Jesus' ministry is compared with the work of a shepherd, while Jesus himself does not appear in the traditional role of "the" shepherd. Nor has the division of the sheep and the goats (Mt. 25.32ff.) anything to do with the traditional conception of the shepherd.

[5] Cp. Mart. Pol. 19, 2: Jesus as the ποιμὴν τῆς κατὰ τὴν οἰκουμένην καθολικῆς ἐκκλησίας. Cp. also III Esd 2.34.

[6] Rev. 7.17 is the only occasion where the motif is used (following Ezek. 34.23, etc.) to describe heavenly blessedness. But the one who grazes is not the shepherd but the ἀρνίον!

[7] Acts 20.28; I Pet. 5.2f.; I Clem. 16.1; 44.3; 54.2; 57.2; Ign. Philad. 2, 1. Jn. 21, 15–17 also shows how common was the idea of the Church as the flock of Jesus. The representation of the different sinners as a flock of sheep is a mere allegory, as is the designation of the ἄγγελος τρυφῆς καὶ ἀπάτης and the ἄγγελος τῆς τιμωρίας as shepherds, Herm. sim. VI.

[8] See previous note; cp. further the ποιμένες, who are bracketed with the διδάσκαλοι in Eph. 5.11. In Herm. sim. IX 31, 4–6 also the leaders of the community are called shepherds;

In some respects *the picture of the shepherd given in Jn. 10* corresponds to the OT tradition. The shepherd leads the flock (v. 4), and guides them to the pasture (v. 9); he protects them from the wolves (vv. 11–13), and in this distinguishes himself from the bad shepherd.[1] There is, however, a decisive difference in Jn. 10, namely that the shepherd is not thought of as the Messianic ruler; there are no traces whatsoever of the kingly figure. Equally his flock is not the people of Israel, but his "own", and there is no analogy of any kind to the saying in Mt. 9.36. On the other hand Jn. 10 contains motifs which do not occur in the OT, viz. the motifs of the fold, and of the contrast between the shepherd and the thief and robber. This, however, would be of little importance, were it not that they are closely connected with another important difference. For there is no mention in the OT of an idea which forms an essential part of the Johannine picture of the shepherd, namely the reciprocal relationship (referred to by γινώσκειν) between the shepherd and the sheep,[2] which is described in terms of the shepherd's calling and the sheep hearing his voice. By comparison with these differences the points of agreement with the OT tradition, restricted as they are to the general characteristics of the shepherd, seem to be of small importance. The differences, however, show that the Johannine shepherd is either an original conception, or else that it stands in another tradition.[3]

It seems that the latter is the case. In itself it is probable that the image of the shepherd was taken from the Gnostic tradition, like the images in the rest of the revelation-discourses. We can see the tradition of the image of the shepherd most clearly in the *Mandaean literature,* in which the messenger is on several occasions compared to the shepherd. In the highly disparate collection of moral injunctions which are contained in the second half of the Right Ginza V 2 (p. 180.5ff.), and which make much use of traditional Gnostic images,[4] we find the exhortation: "Have confidence in Mandā

---

they are distinguished from the lord of the sheep. In act. Petri et Andr. 4, p. 119, 10 Peter is addressed as πατὴρ καὶ ποιμήν.—In the Zadokite fragment the leader of the community is referred to (13, 9) as the shepherd of the flock.—On the founders and thiasarchs of Greek societies as "shepherds", see E. Maass, Orpheus 1895, 181.

[1] The figure of the hireling corresponds approximately to the bad shepherds of the OT tradition. Yet the latter are thought of as being positively bad, whereas John is only concerned with the fact that the hireling will not risk his life in danger. The fact that Rabbinic law lays down strict limits for the obligations of paid shepherds (μισθωτοί cp. Str.-B. ad loc., Bornhäuser 58f.) adds nothing to our understanding of the comparison. The image of the hireling as such cannot be traced back to any particular tradition, for it could occur in any of the traditions (see below p. 371 n. 2); Jn. 10 is the only known case where it occurs as part of the symbolism of the shepherd. Cp. Plut. de recta rat. aud. 1, p. 37e, where the μισθωτός is contrasted with the θεῖος ἡγεμών, the λόγος.

[2] The difference is brought out characteristically in Ezek. 34.30: "And then (when God has brought the flock to safety) they shall know that I, Jahweh, their God, am with them."

[3] Barrett (JTS 48 (1947), 163f. and in his commentary) does not take sufficient notice of the decisive differences.

[4] Cp. the terminology of the light symbolism, which runs through the whole tradition (the "light of life" 181, 6; 182, 13.15) the "voice of life" (180, 5), the "call" (181, 11; 182, 27), Mandā d'Haijē as the "vine" (181, 27). Cp. also 182, 28ff. (see above p. 342 n. 5); 180, 22f. (see above p. 341 n. 1); 183, 11f. (see above p. 346 n. 2).

d'Haijē. Like a good shepherd who watches (his sheep), he will keep far from you all spirit of apostasy. Like a good shepherd who leads his sheep to their fold, he will set you down and plant you down before him." The two long passages on the shepherd in Joh-B. (p. 42.19ff.) show that the injunctions employ traditional material; this is confirmed by the fact that the images of the wolves and the lions, which occur in this context, crop up again as metaphors in the injunctions (183.1f.). The first passage in Joh-B. (44.27ff.) is a revelation discourse, in which the figure of the shepherd is used figuratively: "I am a shepherd, who loves his sheep." Two later additions turn the image into an allegory;[1] the original comparison describes the shepherd's concern to provide pasture and safety: "I carry the sheep thence, and give them water to drink out of my cupped hand ... I bring them to the good fold, and they graze near me." (45.3ff.). "No wolf jumps into our fold, and they need have no fear of the fierce lion. ... No thief penetrates into the fold, and they need not worry about an iron knife"[2] (45.11ff.). An injunction has been appended in 48.1ff., in which the image has been allegorised, and which in its present form is probably of a later date, while retaining the old tradition[3] in the language and style. The very fact that the shepherd has become a boatman here, rescuing the sheep in his boat from the flood, shows how old and well-established the figurative language was. The call of the "shepherd"[4] rings out: "My little sheep, my little sheep, come! Follow my call! ... Everyone who has heard my call and taken heed of my voice and turned his gaze on me I will seize with both hands ... Everyone who did not hear my call, sank."

In its present form the second passage (51.5ff.) is of a later date, as is shown by its attack on other religions (including Christianity). Yet the motif which determines the structure of the passage and the figurative language are old. The commissioning and sending out of the messenger from the heavenly world[5] are here portrayed as the charging of a shepherd: "Come, serve me as a loving shepherd, and watch over thousands and ten thousands for me." In the exposition image and metaphor mingle together. The figures of the lion, the wolf and the thief occur again. The conclusion relates briefly how the messenger accepts the commission, watches over the thousand sheep, pursues those who are lost, and protects the number with which he was charged.

Everything indicates that the image of the shepherd is an integral part of early Mandaean figurative language. Here we discover again traits which

---

[1] The additions are 45.5–11 and 46, 5–47.14; they differ from the old parable both stylistically and linguistically; see Ed. Schweizer, EGO EIMI 1939, 64ff.

[2] The knife is carried by the thief to slaughter the sheep, cp. Jn. 10.10.

[3] The water floods mentioned here do not have their literary origin in the flooding of the Babylonian area, the later homeland of the Mandaeans, as do those mentioned in the insertion in 46.5–47.14. It is the mythical flood of the sea of Suf, from which the Redeemer, who comes in the "shining ship" (48.10), rescues his own.—On the sea of Suf see Jonas, Gnosis I 322, 4.

[4] He calls after he has climbed up to the "highest point"; cp. Od. Sal. 33.3: the virgin of grace "went up to a high peak and her voice rang out".

[5] On this motif see ZNTW 24 (1925), 105f., also 108.

are important for the Johannine discourse on the Good Shepherd, not only the shepherd's care for pasture and water, the fold, the protection from the wolf and the thief, but notably the most important, namely that the shepherd is not a regal figure, but the Redeemer sent from the heavenly world. It is not a people that he gathers together, but his own, who are lost and in danger in the world. The terms in which his relationship to them is described are noteworthy. He "loves" the sheep and carries them "on his shoulders" (Joh-B. 44.27f.), he calls them (48.2ff.), and they are rescued when they hear his voice (48.11ff.). There is admittedly no explicit mention of their mutual knowledge of each other; but neither does this expression occur in Jn. 10 in the comparison proper, but only in its interpretation (vv. 14f. 27) and, for the rest, the motif of knowledge is characteristic of Mandaean and indeed of Gnostic literature as a whole. The coming of the Revealer on his mission "to those who know him and understand him", and who go to meet him, is described in Joh-B. 218.1ff.; 200.18. Cp. Mand. Lit. 205:

> "The coming of Hibil-Uthra is like the coming of Šitil, when he goes to the house of his friends.
> When the disciples heard the voice of Anoš, of the great Uthra,
> They honoured and praised the great life beyond measure."[1]

The only element which does not occur in the Mandaean shepherd-texts is the contrasted picture of the hireling, and consequently the fact that the shepherd risks his life for the sheep.

The fact that the image of the shepherd became wide-spread in Gnostic and Gnosticising circles is attested by the apocryphal Acts of the Apostles, even though here we must reckon also with the influence of Jn. 10.[2] It is surely, then, not without significance that in Hermetic Gnosticism the god to whom the role of the Revealer was specifically attributed was the god who, from of old, had been cast in the role of the shepherd, namely Hermes. Admittedly this is not the only reason why be became the Revealer, for he was also the messenger of the gods and the guide of souls. The fact that nevertheless the figure of the shepherd and the Revealer are closely connected is shown

---

[1] Further references in ZNTW 24 (1925), 117f., also 118f. See also Bornkamm, Myth. und Leg. 43f.; E. Käsemann, Leib und Leib Christi 1933, 74ff. (on the gathering motif).

[2] The image of the shepherd occurs among other Gnostic motifs in act. Thom. 25 and 39. In 25 Christ is addressed p. 140, 9ff.: φύλαξον δὲ αὐτοὺς καὶ ἀπὸ τῶν λύκων, φέρων αὐτοὺς ἐν τοῖς σοῖς λειμῶσι. πότισον δὲ αὐτοὺς ἀπο τῆς ἀμβροσιώδους σου πηγῆς . . . κύριος ὢν καὶ ἀληθῶς ποιμὴν ἀγαθός. Similarly in 39, p. 157, 13ff.; cp. 59, p. 177, 2f.; 67, p. 184, 18ff. The motif of the gathering in of the lost sheep 57, p. 174, 8f. The prayer in 156 has a Gnostic ring; here p. 265, 5ff.: καὶ ἀνῆλθες μετὰ πολλῆς δόξης, καὶ συναγαγὼν πάντας τοὺς εἰς σὲ καταφεύγοντας παρεσκεύασας ὁδόν, καὶ ἐπὶ τῶν ἰχνῶν σου πάντες ὥδευσαν οὓς ἐλυτρώσω· καὶ εἰσαγωγὼν εἰς τὴν ἑαυτοῦ ποίμνην τοῖς σοῖς ἐγκατέμειξας προβάτοις . . . συνάγαγε αὐτὰς εἰς τὴν σὴν μάνδραν (fold); the following passage also uses Gnostic terminology.—The value of the evidence provided by Mart. Andr. 9, p. 52, 4; 14, p. 55, 18; Mart. Matth. 3, p. 220, 4 is uncertain; but even if the references to Christ as the ποιμήν should all be secondary, they still afford proof of the popularity of this designation in the circles which handed down this literature.

by the name Ποιμάνδρης, which is given to the Revealer in C. Herm. 1, and also by the shepherd's costume of the revealing angel, Herm. vis. 5.[1]

In other respects the syncretism of the traditions at that time makes it difficult to decide how far earlier mythological tradition was responsible for the forming of the Gnostic image of the shepherd.[2] It would be necessary to see what evidence could be found for the influence of other traditions, perhaps even Gnostic tradition, apart from the New Testament, on early Christian representations of Christ as the Good Shepherd.[3]

This "being for . . ." is described in the comparison of **vv. 11–13** in terms of the highest possible form which being for others can assume, and this is done by means of a comparison between the good shepherd and the hireling.[4] The Revealer is the "good shepherd" because—like a good shepherd—he stakes his life for the sheep,[5] whereas the hireling

---

[1] Reitzenstein, Poimandres 1904, 11f.32ff.; M. Dibelius, ext. note on Herm. vis. V 7 in the supplementary volume to the Hdb. zum NT; also on sim. IX 1, 4.

[2] The Egyptian Anubis also appears as a shepherd; similarly the Phrygian Attis (see Br. ext. note on Jn. 10.21 and the literature cited there). There is a mythological tradition in the Abercios inscription (H. Hepding, Attis, 1903, 84) in which Abercios describes himself as:

μαθητὴς ποιμένος ἁγνοῦ,
ὃς βόσκει προβάτων ἀγέλας ὄρεσιν πεδίοις τε,
ὀφθαλμοὺς ὃς ἔχει μεγάλους πάντη καθορῶντας.

[3] I would not like to risk an opinion on whether this is so in the account in the Praetextat Catacomb (Wilpert, Plate 51), where the shepherd protects the flock of sheep from hostile beasts. But it does seem to me to be the case with the picture of the shepherd on the tomb of Beratius Nicatoras (in Asia Minor). The shepherd is carrying a sheep on his shoulders; on the left and right of him are a dragon and a lion. There is also a portrayal of the heavenly journey of the soul; cp. J. Quasten, Mitteil. des Deutschen Archäolog. Inst., Röm. Abt. 35 (1938), 50ff. The dragon and the lion are typical of Mandaean texts. The good shepherd also appears among the Gnostic Christian scenes on the "Tomb of Aurelius" in a version which still awaits a final interpretation (Atti della Pontif. Accad. Rom. di Archeol., Ser. III Memorie, Vol. I. Part. II, 1924, Plate 12). For a discussion of the allegorical treatment of lambs in early Christian sculpture see F. Gerke, ZNTW 33 (1934), 160–196. On the portrayal of Christ as the shepherd see Joh. Kollwitz, RAC III 5f.11f.

[4] What we have is a parable and not an allegory. The article in front of ποιμήν and μισθωτός corresponds to the style of parables (Mk. 4.3: ὁ σπείρων, Lk. 12.39: ὁ οἰκοδεσπότης etc.), and figurative sayings (4.36; Mk. 2.19; Mt. 24.28, etc.). Thus it would be wrong to think that the μισθωτός refers to a particular person, for example the Jewish authorities, although it is true that their relation to the Jewish people corresponds to the relation of the μισθ. to the flock. But this is equally true of all false authorities. Above all we must not attempt to allegorise the wolf. Schwartz thinks that it represents the Romans, but of course Jesus does not rescue his flock from the Romans at all! Nor does it refer to the devil (Schl., Odeberg); the parable is intended only to illustrate by way of contrast the radical sense in which Jesus' being is being for his "own". H. J. Schoeps (Theol. u. Gesch. des Judenchristentum 92, 4) thinks there is an "anti-Mosaic tendency" in vv. 10–12.

[5] Τιθέναι τ. ψυχήν here (and perhaps also in 13.37f.; 15.13) means to stake one's life, to risk it, to be prepared to lay it down, as in the LXX Judg. 12.3; I Sam. 19.5; 28.21. On the other hand in vv. 17f. it means to lay down one's life, like δοῦναι τ. ψυχήν elsewhere, and like the Latin vitam ponere (Wetst.). This cannot be the meaning in v. 11; for whereas it is characteristic of a shepherd to risk his life for his sheep it is not characteristic for him

in the crucial situation, which is the test of true shepherding, leaves the flock in the lurch and abandons it to the wolf.[1] The comparison shows what a true shepherd is to a flock, without actually stating it explicitly. Indirectly the explanation of the hireling's behaviour (οὗ οὐκ ἔστιν τὰ πρόβατα ἴδια) makes it clear that true being for others must be grounded in a mutual relationship. The sheep belong to the true shepherd; they are not merely dependent on him as they might be dependent on a μισθωτός, but they are also of value to him; they mean something to him, as he does to them.[2] But this also implies that he has a claim on them. The security which man finds in the Revealer is not the sort of security which can be bought and bargained for; it can be attained only by giving oneself to him as his own. In general man is quite prepared to secure God's help for his own security. But does he really want God as his God, the God who is for him—or does he only want him as a μισθωτός? Is he seriously concerned that God should be for him, or is he merely serving an idol?

2) *The Good Shepherd and the Thief and Robber:* 10.1–6

Before the comparison can be given its application, it is developed further by contrasting the nature of a shepherd with the κλέπτης and λῃστής. **Vv. 1–3** describe the difference between the shepherd and the thief and robber.[3] The shepherd goes to the sheep by the lawful way into

thieves + robbers

---

to sacrifice it for them. The Rabbinic נָתַן נַפְשׁוֹ עַל (or מָסַר) can have both meanings, as is shown by the examples in Schl. on Mt. 20.28 and Str.-B. ad loc. and on Acts 15. 26; cp. also Fiebig, Angelos I (1925), 58f.; E. Fascher, Deutsche Theologie 1941, 41–44. ℵ* D read δίδωσιν instead of τίθησιν (cp. v. 15), which is surely the result of the influence of traditional formulae (I Macc. 2.50; Mk. 10.45 par.; also Gal. 1.4; Tit. 2.14 etc.). Vv. 17f. show that τιθ. is original, as do 13.37f.; 15.13; I Jn. 3.16.

[1] On (ὁ) οὐκ ὢν ποιμ. see Bl.D. para. 430, 1; Raderm. 212; Moulton, Proleg. 231f.; οὐκ with the participle occurs only here in John.—Μέλει μοι περί τινος also 12.6; Mk. 12.14, etc., also Classical; Bl.-D. para. 176, 3.—The last sentence (v. 13) is clearly an explanatory gloss added by the Evangelist; the poor link with the preceding verse has led to the insertion of ὁ δὲ μισθ., φεύγει in many manuscripts.

[2] This comes out very clearly in the description of Themistios I, p. 10f. Dind. where the ποιμήν is also contrasted with the μισθωτός: ποιμνίον ἐκεῖνο εὔκολον τοῖς λύκοις, ὅτῳ ὁ ποιμὴν ἀπεχθάνοιτο . . . κακὸς βουκόλος . . . αὐτὸς δὲ ἔσται μισθωτὸς ἀντὶ βουκόλου . . . ὁ δὲ ἀγαθὸς νομεὺς πολλὰ μὲν ὀνίναται ἐκ τοῦ ἔργου, πλείω δὲ ἔχει ἀντωφελεῖν, θηρία τε ἀπερύκων καὶ πόας ὑγιεινῆς προορώμενος· καὶ μὲν δὴ ἀντιφιλοῦσι μάλιστα βόες μὲν ἀγαπῶντα βουκόλον κτλ. Philo post. Caini 98 and agric. 26ff. contrasts the κτηνοτρόφος and the ποιμήν as images of the λογισμός, according as they manage the αἰσθήσεις badly or well; similarly mut. nom. 110ff. Cp. also Plat. Rep. I p. 341c–346e.—On shepherding in general see Tovia Ashkenazi, Tribus seminomades de la Palestine du Nord 1939, 162–165.

[3] Like vv. 11–13, vv. 1–5 are a genuine parable which may not be allegorised (so rightly Lagr.). Thus the figure of the thief and robber cannot refer to one particular figure. It is equally applicable to anyone who unlawfully claims to have control over the flock, i.e. to every corrupter of the faithful or of those who are called to faith, to everyone who

the fold,[1] which is opened for him as a matter of course by the door-keeper,[2] whereas the door is shut on the thief, who therefore has to climb in over the wall.[3] This account describes nothing less than the shepherd's right of ownership over the sheep; and consequently at the same time it describes his relationship to them, which is based on his right of ownership. For him the way to them is not closed. But their relationship to him is also hinted at in this account; for on the basis of vv. 3 and 4 we may surely add that the sheep are accustomed to the way he comes to them, whereas they would be frightened by the thief climbing over the wall. However, this is not intended to provide a criterion by which the sheep can recognise the shepherd. As if they needed any criterion! As if the flock of sheep were a society of doubters and critics! On the contrary, the comparison is intended to show that the sheep recognise the shepherd with instinctive certainty,[4] and therefore we are

---

might be a temptation to them—always, that is, in a particular concrete historical situation. Thus Odeberg's suggestion that it refers to the Devil is wrong, however much it is true that the Devil works in every man who corrupts the faithful. In the Evangelist's situation it might equally well refer to the Jewish authorities (which is the usual interpretation) and to the false teachers of I John; also to the Pseudo-Messiahs (Wellh.) and the Pseudo-Saviours of the Hellenistic world. It cannot, however, refer to the Herodians (Schwartz), to whom Zn. adds the Hasmonaeans, the Sadducees and all Messianic claimants, while expressly excluding the spiritual authorities! Wellh. believes that it cannot refer to the Jewish authorities "because it is not the case that the flock does not follow them". But he does not see that the flock is not the Jewish people but the ἴδιοι.—Cp. Carpenter 388, 2. John A. T. Robinson (ZNW 46 [1955], 233–240) thinks that vv. 1–5 is a combination of two parables: 1. vv. 1–3a (whose theme is the θυρωρός as in Mk. 13.34; cp. Lk. 12.36, 39); 2. vv. 3b–5 (whose theme is the shepherd and the sheep). According to him vv. 1–3a come from an "authentic and early tradition of the teaching of Jesus". I do not find this convincing.

[1] Αὐλή refers to a courtyard round a house, which can be used as a sheep-fold, see Br.—It would, of course, be wrong to attempt an interpretation of the αὐλή (Odeberg: the heavenly world, even the "seventh court" of heaven). V. 16 gives a secondary interpretation.

[2] The θυρωρός must not be given a specific interpretation. It is neither Moses (Chrsys.), nor the Baptist (Godet, Zn.), nor even the Father (Calvin, Bengel, Schl., Odeberg), nor Jesus himself (Aug.). Exegetes who have taken it to refer to God seem to have been misled by vv. 7 and 9 into interpreting the θύρα in v. I as Jesus. Then the ποιμήν must refer to the disciples, who have been charged by Jesus with the leadership of the community (this interpretation is not followed by Odeberg, for whom Jesus is both the shepherd and the door). Yet everything in vv. 1–5 is concentrated on the contrast between the shepherd and the thief and robber. The θύρα has no special importance of its own, and the statement about the θυρωρός has merely been added to give greater vividness (so rightly B. Weiss, Ho., Bd.). Moreover it is impossible that ποιμήν in vv. 3–5, particularly if we have regard to vv. 14f., 27, should refer to anyone other than Jesus.

[3] Ἀλλαχόθεν (=ἄλλοθεν) occurs only here in the NT; it is a colloquial word, see Br.—Ἀναβαίνων shows that the court is enclosed by a wall. There are occasional references to the fact that the fold is closed when the flock is inside, Str.-B. on v. 1.

[4] Zn.'s tortured allegorisation of the passage carries itself ad absurdum. According to him the three characteristics of a true shepherd are fulfilled in Jesus. 1. he comes lawfully, inasmuch as he has submitted to baptism, and carries out his ministry in the legitimate places of worship, the synagogue and the temple. 2. He has gained entry there—"neither in the synagogue nor in the temple did the officers dare to forbid him to teach". 3. In general his teaching was not strange to the ears of the people (here he refers to 8.30f.; 7.31, 47f.,

told: "*And the sheep hear his voice.*"[1] They have long known him, and so immediately recognise him. The familiarity of their relationship is illustrated further in **v. 4.**[2] The shepherd leads the sheep out into the pasture; he goes before them, and they follow him because they know his voice.[3]

The application of the comparison is immediately clear. His "own" recognise the Revealer with the same unfailing certainty with which the sheep recognise their shepherd. Obviously the fact that the shepherd comes regularly, daily to his flock to take them out into the pasture, has no direct significance for the application of the comparison. For when the Evangelist speaks of Jesus' "coming",[4] he means his coming into the world, the coming of the Revealer, of the σρὰξ γενόμενος, once and for all. The comparison clearly takes account of this when it describes how the sheep follow the call of the shepherd (vv. 3f.; cp. v.27), and the interpretation of the comparison confirms this when it says ἐγὼ ἦλθον, ἵνα ζωὴν ἔχωσιν (v.10) or, κἀγὼ δίδωμι αὐτοῖς ζωὴν αἰώνιον (v. 28)—expressions which are always used to describe the purpose of the one decisive "coming". The fact that the Revealer, when he comes, is already known to his own, means no more nor less than the statements elsewhere that whoever comes to him is drawn by the Father (6.44), is given him by the Father (6.37), or has had it given to him by the Father (6.65). Those who hear his voice are those "who are of the

---

12a). "Although the crowd's attitude to him was changeable and although from time to time voices were raised against him, he did develop with individual members of his people a firm and deep personal relationship"!!

[1] This in the sense of οἴδασι τ. φωνὴν αὐτοῦ v. 5 (cp. 18.37), even though one cannot translate, "they harken *to* his voice". For since φωνεῖ is not said till the following verse, we must imagine the scene as follows. The sheep hear the voice of the shepherd greeting the door-keeper, while he is still outside the fold, and they rejoice at his coming. He then comes to them, calls them by name (this illustrative touch is also found in other similar descriptions, cp. Theocr. 2, 101; 4, 46; Longus, Past. IV 26, 4; 38, 4; see Br.) and leads them out.—If ἴδια in τὰ ἴδ. προβ. is stressed and is not merely a substitute for αὐτοῦ (Bl.-D. para. 286), then it means "the sheep who belong to him"—but there is no intended contrast with the sheep belonging to another owner, who are also in the αὐλή (Sp.). Φωνεῖ (he calls) which ℜ Θ pm change to καλεῖ (he names), is hardly proof of an Aram. source, as suggested by de Zwaan (JBL 57, 1948, 161). —On κατ' ὄνομα = each individually, see H. Almquist, Plutarch u. das NT 74.

[2] Ἐκβάλλειν is used here in a weakened sense as in 5.7, etc. Cp. BGU 597, 4: ἵνα βάλῃ τὸν μόσχον πρὸ τῶν προβάτων. The image of the shepherd leading his flock also comes in Num. 27.17 (Joshua); Ps. 80.2 (God). Was it the normal custom for shepherds to walk in front of their flock? Schweizer op. cit. 147, n. 37 thinks not, but this is how it is portrayed in the picture of the shepherd in Apollon. Rhod., Argaun. I 575–578.

[3] **V. 5** is clearly the Evangelist's own explanatory addition. The reflections on the ἀλλότριος (for whom one must not, of course, give a specific interpretation) obtrude on the dominant contrast between the ποιμήν and the κλέπτης καὶ λῃστής. Originally v. 4 must have been followed by vv. 8 and 10.

[4] See p. 298 n. 1.

truth" (18.37); similarly he cannot be understood by those who are "from below", who are children of the Devil (8.23, 42–47). This is why in v. 26 it was said: ἀλλ' ὑμεῖς οὐ πιστεύετε, ὅτι οὐκ ἐστὲ ἐκ τῶν προβάωτν τῶν ἐμῶν.[1]

It is therefore quite wrong to think that it is the Christian community, the Church, which corresponds to the flock of sheep in the comparison.[2] For the flock corresponds to all those who are "of the truth", even though they are scattered in the world and do not yet belong to the community. They do not become his flock only when they have been gathered together in the community—for then one would have to speak of a pre-existent Church, to which all those belong who are revealed as his own when they are confronted by the word. The Gnostic undercurrent in this conception is unmistakable; for according to Gnostic teaching those who are called by the Redeemer—the pre-existent souls, the particles of light scattered in the world—were originally one body, the body of the archetypal man, the heavenly figure of light, who long ago was overthrown and rent in pieces by the demonic powers of darkness. The work of the Redeemer is to gather together the scattered sparks of light and to bring them back to their original unity.[3] In John the mythological elements in this idea have been jettisoned; he no longer speaks of the fall of the archetypal man, or of the pre-existence of souls. What he does retain, however, is the idea that man's true being is more than his temporal historical existence, and that therefore man has from the very beginning a relationship (however hidden) to the Revealer, even before he has been confronted by him. Of course, since the myth has been rejected, this relationship is not something given in man's nature, something free from all ambiguity, of which man only needs to be "reminded". Man himself must make the decision for it. For if the call of the Revealer goes out to all men, then everyone has the

---

[1] Lütgert (Joh. Christ. 85f.) is right here: "The emphasis of the discourse is on the fact that there is a relationship between the shepherd and the flock which lies beyond their conscious communication and historical relationship with each other." The fact that Jesus is recognised as the true shepherd "has nothing to do with the activity of the 'historical' Jesus, for the effects of that activity are precisely what has to be explained; rather it is based on the fellowship of the flock, which reaches out over the historical relationships and is grounded in Jesus' unity with God."

[2] Thus, e.g. Schl. and Carpenter (388, 2). Above all the flock cannot possibly be the Jewish people (Ho., Zn., Wellh.); this interpretation has been suggested by the secondary v. 16.

[3] ZNTW 24 (1925), 118f.; Schlier. Relg. Unters. 97ff.; and Christus und die Kirche im Eph. 37ff.; Käsemann, Leib und Leib Christi 65ff.; Jonas, Gnosis I 104ff.—See below p. 384 n. 2.—Cp. esp. the hymn in Clem. Al. Paed. III 12 (101, 3), p. 291, 17ff. St. and act. Jo. 100, p. 201, 1ff.; if the expression γένος προσχωροῦν ἐπ' ἐμὲ φωνῇ τῇ ἐμῇ πειθόμενον here, in fact, comes from Jn. 10, then the interpretation given in the chapter is very much in character; cp. on this Schlier, Christus und die Kirche 44.

possibility of discovering his true being in belonging to the Revealer—but also, of losing it.[1]

If therefore the "flock" of which Jesus is the shepherd is not an historical entity, but a pre-temporal community, then of course the meaning of the comparison is also applicable to the historical Church. For this, too, is the "flock", which must constantly realise itself by following the voice of the "shepherd." For even if in the first place the comparison only speaks of the one decisive coming of Jesus, he is nevertheless—as is shown by the Farewell discourses—again and again the one who comes. Even when he comes in the Spirit, it is still true that his own know him, while the world knows him not (14.17).

The comparison reaches its conclusion in v. 4 (5). In the source it was then followed by its application; the Evangelist has added several touches to this,[2] and made a clear break between it and the comparison in v. 6. V. 6 tells of the hearers' inability to understand[3] this "riddle".[4] In so doing it not only explains v. 26 and prepares the way for vv. 31ff., but also throws light on the purpose of the discourse by means of the contrasting picture of the uncomprehending audience. It is only his own who can understand the Revealer.

3) *The Interpretation:* 10.7–10, 14–18, 27–30

i. *The exclusiveness and the absoluteness of the Revelation*: 10.7–10

At first (vv. 7–10) the interpretation on the whole stays close to the contrast between the shepherd and the thief and robber, which was sketched out in vv. 1–4. It then goes on to deal with the relationship of the shepherd to the sheep. Admittedly in the first section we also find an exposition of the door.[5] The only explanation for this confusion seems to be that the Evangelist has expanded the text of the source with his own glosses (vv. 7, 9). For as vv. 14–15a, 27–30 show (which certainly come from the source), the comparison was also followed in the source by an interpretation which took up the images as metaphors. Thus vv.8 and 10 must also have been part of the source, and indeed they fit in very well after v.4.[6]

---

[1] See pp. 135f. 159, 231f.

[2] See pp. 317f, and see below.

[3] The OT and Jewish expression οὐκ ἔγνωσαν τίνα ἦν (see Schl.) is typical of the Evangelist's style.

[4] Παροιμία (which occurs again in the NT only in 16.25, 29; I Pet. 2.22) like παραβολή means both proverb and riddle; see Br. ad loc. and Wörterb. Aristoph. Thesm. 528; II Pet. 2.22 show that the proverb can also be a figurative saying.

[5] See p. 358.

[6] Otherwise one would have to assume that vv. 8 and 10 come from the Evangelist and vv. 7 and 9 from the editor. Yet v. 7 and v. 9 at least show no signs of the editor's special interests, such as are betrayed by 6.51b–58; 5.28f.; 10.16.

V. 8 stresses, in language which is completely metaphorical, *the exclusiveness and the absoluteness of the revelation:* "All who came before me are thieves and robbers". At the same time it also stresses the inner, as it were, instinctive security of faith: "but the sheep did not heed them". In this saying the Revealer sets himself apart from all other pretended revealers of past ages as the sole Revealer.[1] It is a purely secondary question to ask which particular historical figures might be referred to here as those who came before Jesus. The saying is of fundamental significance and refers to all pretended revealers, all pretended saviours who have ever called men to them, who have ever been followed by men. Thus there is no allusion here to rival revealers of the Evangelist's time (although of course the saying judges them also), nor to the religious authorities of that time.[2] The present moment is considered as the eschatological moment, in which the light shines in the darkness, that till then had been spread over the whole world. Thereby, of course, judgement is also passed on the religions of the age, in so far as they appeal to supposed revealers of earlier ages. If the source comes from Gnostic circles,[3] then Moses and the prophets of the OT will also have been included among the number of the Pseudo-Revealers.[4] Naturally this was not the way in which it was taken by the Evangelist. Yet he can take the saying over in its categorical form, because in his view Moses and the other authorities of the OT are nothing other than witnesses to Jesus, and so cannot possibly be considered as possible

---

[1] There is of course no difference in the meaning of and the claims made for ἔρχεσθαι when it is predicated of those who came before Jesus and when it is predicated of Jesus himself (v. 10). Thus one may not explain it here by reference to the Semitic pleonasm "to come to do something" (Schl.). What we are concerned with here is the "coming" of the Revealer (see p. 298 n. 1). The phrase corresponds to the Gnostic idea of the Revealer's supremacy over all his predecessors; cp. Baruch's saying to the twelve year-old Jesus, in the Gnostic Book of Baruch: πάντες οἱ πρὸ σοῦ προφῆται ὑπεσύρησαν Hipp. V 26, 29, p. 131, 23 W. Br. rightly draws attention to the Mandaean view, that the original revelation has been corrupted by the heralds and remains corrupted until the heavenly messenger appears. On the other hand the contrast between the φαῦλοι κατάσκοποι who are sent out by men and the κύριος κατάσκοπος, which is to be found in Antisthenes (Wetter, Sohn Gottes 165, 3) is not really parallel.—Odeberg is right here.

[2] It is not possible to take this to refer to the Pharisees or the Jewish authorities (Schl., Strathm. and many others). For "coming" in the sense in which it is alone intended here (see previous note), cannot be predicated of the Pharisees and their like. Nor is such an interpretation demanded by εἰσίν, for this has no chronological sense, i.e. it says nothing about the time when they came, but refers solely to the standing of the Pseudo-Revealers. —Barr. thinks it refers to false Messianic claimants and fraudulent saviours, as does Wik. —O. Cullmann (JBL 74 [1955]) thinks that the allusion is to figures like the "Teacher of Righteousness" in the Zadokite fragment and in the Habbakuk commentary (IQ Hp.)

[3] See p. 19.

[4] This is of course how Jn. 10.8 is understood by the Christian Gnostics and the Manichaeans, see Br.

rival revealers or bringers of salvation.[1] It is thus difficult to say whom he had particularly in mind as those who came before. If he did not just simply mean the heathen religions in general, he was probably thinking of the revealers and saviours of the Hellenistic Gnostic world, whose followers still existed in his day.[2] It is possible, however, that he was thinking of the Gnostic doctrine that the Revealer incorporated himself in different persons in different ages.[3] For his eschatology this is a false doctrine, since for him there is only this one turning point in the ages—the point at which Jesus the Revealer appeared. In fact, this present moment occurs again and again wherever the word of Jesus takes effect, so that those who "came before me" cannot be limited to particular figures in the past. All pretended revealers of all ages are swept away by the "coming" of Jesus which is experienced in faith.

V. 10 begins like a parable, but in fact the language is metaphorical. For in the second line instead of the expected ποιμήν we have ἐγώ. The verse speaks of the contrast between the true Revealer and false revealers with regard to their significance for men. The latter bring only destruction,[4] whereas, the former gives life and fulness.[5]

The Evangelist's glosses, although formally disruptive, match exactly the ideas of the source. **V. 9** expands the motif of v. 10 into a promise of salvation,[6] and **v. 7** uses the image of the door in a variation on the motif of the exclusiveness and absoluteness of the revelation.[7]

---

[1] So rightly Schweizer and Hosk. Cp. 5.39, 45ff.; 8.56; 12.41.—This same is, of course, true of the Baptist, who for the Evangelist is nothing but a witness to Jesus; cp. 1.6–9, etc.—One can easily see why some copyists failed to understand the meaning of the saying, and in order to save, as they thought, the OT authorities, either omitted πάντες (D) or πρὸ ἐμοῦ (א 𝔎 al syr[s] it pesch), which latter reading is accepted by Lagr. and Bl.

[2] It is absurd to think that this refers to "persons of princely rank", particularly the Herodians (Zn.). The only political saviours who might be referred to here are those who were religious saviours as well, i.e. the Pesudo-Messiahs. It could possibly refer also to the Roman emperors, but there is no reference to the emperor cult anywhere else in John.

[3] See pp. 26 n. 2, 59 n. 2.

[4] Test. Abr. 10, p. 88: οὗτοί εἰσιν κλέπται, οἱ βουλόμενοι φόνον ἐργάζσθαι καὶ κλέψαι καὶ θῦσαι καὶ ἀπολέσαι may be based on Jn. 10.8. Yet the mention of slaughter as one of the typical marks of a thief seems to be traditional; see p. 368 n. 2.

[5] Καὶ περισσὸν ἔχ. is omitted in D, simply because of the homoioteleuton. In fact it can be dispensed with without making any difference to the sense, for the concept of ζωή contains this idea as well. It has been expanded in the interests of rhetoric. Περισσὸν ἔχειν = to have more than enough, as in Xen. An. VII 6, 31 and elsewhere.

[6] On σωθήσεται see p. 154 n. 1. Εἰσελεύσεται καὶ ἐξελεύσεται is a typically OT way of describing (by a complementary expression) a permanent state of affairs (Deut. 28.6; I Sam. 29.6; Ps. 121.8 etc.; Rabbinic refs. in Schl.). The description does not really quite fit here (see next note), but it corresponds to the leading in and out of the sheep by the shep- herd in Num. 27.17. The pasture as in Is. 49.9; Ezek. 34.14; Ps. 23.2, etc.

[7] Black (193, 1) suspects (as did Torrey before him; see Barr.) that there is a misunderstanding of the Aram. text in v. 7. It ought to read "I am the shepherd of the sheep." But this cannot apply to v. 9. According to Jeremias vv. 7–10 are an allegorical interpretation

The first section of the parable, vv. 11–13, showed the "being" of the Revealer as a "being for his own", and thereby indicated that the Revealer's "being for . . ." corresponded to the "being in belonging" of his own; the second section, vv. 1–5, proceeds to expound this "being in belonging". Both these elements are brought out in the first section of the interpretation; for vv. 9 and 10 describe what the Revealer means to his own while vv. 7 and 8 make clear the absolute and exclusive claim which is made by this "being in belonging".

Basically this claim is contained in all the Revealer's discourses, but since it is here made explicit, we must define more exactly what the force of this claim is, as it is understood by the Evangelist. Jesus' ἐγώ εἰμι . . . always means that there is only *one* who can lead man to salvation, only *one* Revealer. There are not various possible answers to man's quest for salvation, but only one. A decision must be made. This is the basis of the *intolerance of the revelation.*

Tolerance, i.e. the recognition of every honest intention as of equal right, is demanded in that sphere of man's activity where the goal is left to man's intention and ability. Where we are concerned with the *ultimate* goal of all man's activities, where indeed the goal *itself* is uncertain, *itself* the object of man's search—and this is always the case outside the revelation—then there is nothing else left to man but to search honestly. Thus outside the revelation man is always a seeker, so that it is pointless for man to pass judgement on others; what is required is tolerance. All that man can ask of others is that they should recognise what he understands and the way he understands himself. He cannot demand that they should understand what he understands and share

of vv. 1f. which does not apply to vv. 1–5 (see on p. 360).—Formally vv. 7 and 9 are explanatory glosses on the θύρα of vv. 1f., in which the door is no longer thought of as the shepherd's entrance, but as the way through which the sheep go in and out of the fold (see p. 359). The ἐγώ-εἰμι statement **v. 7** is not the Revealer's self-introduction, but an interpretative gloss (see p. 359 n. 2). This explains the ὅτι, which does not occur in the self-introductory formulae, and which seems strange here and has been omitted by BL; this also explains τ. προβάτων, which is foreign to the style of the ἐγώ-εἰμι statements. In **v. 9** on the other hand we have a genuine ἐγώ-εἰμι statement, and it is probable that the reason why the Evangelist added his glosses was because the source (or tradition) contained this sentence, which he has expanded by καὶ εἰσελ. καὶ ἐξελ. (see previous note). Originally there was only mention of entering into the fold, and the image of the Revealer as the door had nothing at all to do with the parable of the Good Shepherd. The door is originally (like the way 14.6) the entrance to life (to the world of light). On the door to the world of light in the Gnostic tradition see ZNTW 24 (1925), 134f.; Br. ext. note on 10.21; Odeberg 319–326; J. Jeremias, ThWB III 179, n. 80; Schweizer, 143, n. 14; Kundsin, Char. und Urspr. 239f.—Cp. also Herm. sim. IX 12, 6 (on this M. Dibelius) and Ps. Clem. Rec. II 22.—On the doors of heaven in Jewish apocalyptic see Barr.—The Jewish parallels in Odeberg are questionable; the difference which he emphasises between the door of the underworld opened by the Revealer (as a way out) and the door of the world of light (the way in) is relative. Originally, both doors were identical, since for Gnosticism the world we live in is itself the underworld or hell; cp. e.g. Schlier, Christus und die Kirche im Eph. 18ff.

the same self-understanding, the same light which he believes he has found for himself.

Yet man's search ends when he is confronted with the revelation which opens up to every man the true understanding of himself. Here absolute recognition is demanded. Here there can be no tolerance. But of course it is the *revelation* which is intolerant; *men* can only be tolerant of each other. Indeed in so far as men are required to uphold the intolerant claim of the revelation, it is principally against themselves that it is directed. The intolerance of the "homo religiosus" and the dogmatician is not the intolerance of the revelation.

Admittedly there is an *analogon* in the human sphere to the intolerance of the revelation. Already in antiquity there is a form of intolerance in the sentences of death and banishment, which the Polis imposed in its attempt to defend itself against the perversion of the Nomos by the Sophists, who set up man—i.e. subjectivity—as the "measure of all things". This intolerance demands that man commit himself to the Polis; but it does not bind men's consciences by imposing a doctrine of an exclusive way of salvation. Accordingly the idea of "tolerance" in antiquity is not fundamental in character. *The modern idea of fundamental tolerance* arises only in reaction to Christian intolerance, to the claim that salvation is given to man only in the name of Jesus Christ. The first classical formulation of the opposition to this claim is contained in Symmachus' petition against the removal of the Ara Victoriae from the Senate House in Rome by the Emperor Gratian (382): "Quid interest, qua quisque prudentia verum requirat? uno itinere non potest perveniri ad tam grande secretum."[1] Yet inasmuch as the modern idea of tolerance has—in radical relativism—ultimately abandoned any idea of an objective *verum*, it has led once more to a form of *profane intolerance*, through the recognition that a relativistic acceptance of all claims—the "righteousness" of the "historical virtuoso"[2]—cripples any kind of commitment whatsoever.

In *this* sphere true tolerance can only be a recognition of the sincerity with which a man gives himself to a particular cause. Yet the believer does not commit himself to the revelation in order to champion its cause, but only in order to listen to it, to recognise its victory. His intolerance is not a denial of the sincerity and seriousness of the non-believer's commitment. For in this respect the non-believer may often be both a model and a reproach to him. As a man he must tolerate his fellow. His intolerance consists in refusing to make concessions in gaining

---

[1] Symm. Rel. III 10, p. 8, 1ff. Meyer.

[2] Nietzsche, Unzeitgemässe Betr. II (Vom Nutzen und Nachteil der Historie), p. 154f. (Kröner's pocket edition).

a hearing for the revelation, for the claim of that power which has made all human commitment obsolete and illusory. It consists in upholding the "truth" that all human commitment and endeavour, through which man seeks to find his true being, is bound to fail; that the revelation demands that man abandon his attempt to find himself by giving himself up to this or that cause, because God in his revelation has already given up himself for men; that Jesus has come to give life and fulness. It is this faith in the revelation which leads to the peculiar security of faith, whereas man's commitment is essentially insecure and his heroism but the reverse of his despair.

ii. *The security of faith:* 10.14–18, 27–30

The peculiar security of faith had already been indicated in the parable of vv. 1–5, which spoke of the sheep hearing and recognising the voice of their shepherd, and also in the metaphorical statement in the interpretation (v. 8), that those who belong to the Revealer do not heed the false prophets. The interpretation now moves on to deal with the key-word γινώσκειν (vv. 14f, 27), leaving aside for the most part the metaphors in the parable. The concept of knowledge is used to bring out the nature of the mutual relationship between the Revealer and his own. This description of the reciprocity of faith is used to characterise the security of faith, which finally emerges as the main theme in vv. 28–30.[1] At the same time the motif of the Revealer's "being for" his own, which was illustrated in the first part of the parable (vv. 11–13), is taken up again and presented in its fullest form.

The discourse makes a fresh start in **v. 14** with the repetition of ἐγώ εἰμι ὁ ποιμὴν ὁ καλός,[2] and this new beginning draws attention to the importance of the theme, "*I know my own and my own know me*".[3] Here for the first time the relationship between the Revealer and his own is described as a mutual γινώσκειν. The description is taken from the terminology of mysticism, and similar formulations occur also in Gnostic literature. They serve to describe the mutual determination of elements which have been combined together into a single whole.[4]

The verb γινώσκειν, which is used to describe this relationship,

[1] Vv. 14, 15a, 27–30 come from the source, see p. 360.

[2] See p. 339 n. 5.

[3] The ℜ text reads καὶ γινώσκομαι ὑπὸ τῶν ἐμῶν, which in fact makes no difference to the sense; the active voice is more in accord with the expressions in the parable; ὑπό with the genitive and the passive is only otherwise found in John in 14.21; III Jn. 12.

[4] ThWB I 693, 23ff. and 692, 11ff. in general; see Br. ad loc. and O. Weinreich AR 19 (1916–19), 165–169. Further act. Jo. 100, p, 201, 11f.—Such statements of reciprocity need not in themselves have a mystical sense. As such they only state that in the case of two mutually related people their being also is mutually determined, that the one is for the other and realises his being in this relationship. Hence such formulations also occur in erotic

does not of course denote a rational, theoretical knowledge, in which the thing known is separated from the knower as the objective percept is separated from the percipient; it denotes rather an inward realisation, in which the knower's whole existence is determined by that which he knows, namely God. It is a knowing in which God discloses himself to man, and in so doing transforms him into a divine being.[1] Because such γινώσκειν—whether it be man's knowledge directed towards God, or God's knowledge directed towards man—denotes a relationship in which the partners are by nature bound together, it is possible to speak of man's *knowledge* of God, and of his messenger as eternal life (17.3). Just as the unity between the Father and the Son (10.30) can be referred to as the Son's *being* in the Father and the Father in the Son (10.38; 14.11; 17.21), it can also be described by saying that the Son "knows" the Father (10.15; 17.25). Similarly εἶναι ἐν can also be used interchangeably with γινώσκειν (15.1ff.; 17.21). The fact that this γινώσκειν bears fruit as an existential disposition in the observance of the commandments (I Jn. 2.3, 5) and in ἀγάπη (13.34f.; 14.21ff.; 15.12, 17; I Jn. 4.7f.)[2] is not yet mentioned in ch. 10, but it will be developed in the Farewell Discourses. Such things are intelligible only to the circle of the faithful, and are consequently omitted in a discourse addressed to the "Jews".

However there is a further similarity between this final revelation discourse held before the people and the Farewell Discourses, in that the relationship between the Revealer and his own is described as a *reciprocal* relationship. For the fact that they not only "know" him, but that he "knows" them shows both that they are determined by him and that he is determined by them. And this is the highest statement that can be made about the Revealer. For it asserts what was already hinted at in the comparison in vv. 11–13, namely, that the being of the Revealer is nothing more nor less than a "being for" them.[3] In

---

literature, as in the well-known verse, "Ich bin dîn und du bist mîn" (I am thine and thou art mine). Dodd's treatment 187–200 of the mutual relationship between God and the Revealer is most apt and instructive.—J. Dupont, Gnosis, 1949 argues against the derivation of the formula from Hellenistic mysticism.—The Johannine formulations: 10.14f., 38; 14.10, 20; 17.21, 23 (6.56).

[1] ThWB I 695, 10ff.

[2] ThWB I 711, 19ff.

[3] Cp. Od. Sal. 8, 12ff.:

"Know my knowledge,
    Ye who are truly known of me;
Love me fiercely,
    Ye who are loved of me!
For I turn not my face from my own.
    Because I know them"

(The text here is given in Gressmann's translation [Neutest. Apokr. 2. ed. 1924, 444] which is not always reliable.)

mysticism this statement of the reciprocal relationship between God and mystic is used to describe a kind of unity between the two in which all differences between them disappear, but where it is used in conjunction with the idea of revelation it naturally takes on a different meaning. For although the believer's γινώσκειν means that his being is *grounded* in the Revealer's γινώσκειν, the Revealer's being, although it is "being for" them in an absolute sense, is in no way *grounded* in their γινώσκειν. Indeed it is precisely because it is a true "being for" them that it cannot be grounded in their conduct towards him; on the contrary it is grounded in God, who makes him the Revealer. Thus the mutual relationship is not a circular process, as it is in mysticism, in which the mystic raises himself to equality with God,[1] but a relationship which is established by God. And this relationship frees man from the circularity of the mystical relationship, in which in the end he can encounter only himself. The revelation unmasks the deception of the mystical relationship to God, in that it never loses its character as address and challenge—an address which comes to man from beyond his own world; it unmasks the mystic's striving for God as a striving to turn God's address into his own human word, which he can hear in the depths of his own soul.

This is exactly what is meant by **v. 15**: "because (on the grounds that) the Father knows me, and I know the Father";[2] i.e. the relationship of believers to him is grounded in his relationship to God. Not only does the Revealer's relationship to God exclude any mystical relationship with him, it also excludes any form of pietistic relationship. He does not yield himself up to man's tender emotions: for he is none other than the Revealer, in whom God addresses man.

By describing Jesus' relationship to God in the same terms of reciprocity, the interpretation implies that he is the Revealer, and that God is manifest in him. This on the one hand brings out the absoluteness of his "being for" God; i.e. he is nothing apart from what he is for God, and precisely because of this he makes the absolute claim to be the Revealer. On the other hand this also brings out God's absolute

---

[1] Cp. e.g. Angelus Silesius:

"I know that God cannot exist for a moment without me,
If I come to nought—he will render up his spirit in his torment."

Or;

"There is nothing but I and thou—and if we two did not exist
Then God would no longer be God, and the heavens would fall!

Such statements could be brought into line with the Johannine understanding of the believer's relationship with God only if they were taken as paradoxical statements of the security of faith.

[2] Καθώς, as often in John here introduces not merely a comparison but an explanation; cp. 13.15, 34; 15.9f., 12 etc., esp. 17.11, 21. These references show that it would be wrong to make a complete break between vv. 14 and 15 and then to translate v. 15, "As the Father knows me, so I too know the Father."

"being for" him—and because he is the Revealer, for men; i.e. God is not God apart from his revelation. And as in v. 14 the Revealer's knowledge, which establishes his relationship with his own, is prior to the knowledge of his "own", so too, in v. 15 God's knowledge of the Revealer, which establishes their relationship with each other, is prior to the Revealer's knowledge which is grounded in God. This is not a description of the life of the Godhead, as a mystic circle of intermingling waters; it is a description of God's act of revelation.[1] And because vv. 14f. is, as it were, a variation on the theme of 1.1f., it also prepares the way for v. 30: ἐγὼ καὶ ὁ πατὴρ ἕν ἐσμεν.

Admittedly the Evangelist has interrupted the flow of the discourse by inserting **vv. 15b–18**, which must be seen as his own comment on the text of his source.[2] He provided a lead in to his own comments by adding to vv. 14f, καὶ τὴν ψυχήν μου τίθημι ὑπὲρ τῶν προβάτων,[3] taking the motif from v. 11, with the difference however that here τιθέναι τὴν ψυχήν means "to lay down one's life", as is shown by vv. 17f.[4] The link with v. 15a is somewhat forced, as the sentence does not really follow on at all well from the statement about the reciprocal relationship. The actual content of the sentence, however, is quite justified here, as it asserts the Revealer's absolute "being for" his own which is also expressed in the reciprocity formula.

Nevertheless this idea is not taken up again till vv. 17f. Before this there is a further interruption in **v. 16**, which can only be explained as a secondary gloss inserted by the editor.[5] It has been prompted by a specifically ecclesiastical interest, as is shown by its prophecy of the mission and of the universal church. Even though the same idea is expressed in 11.52 and 17.20 by the Evangelist, it is easy to see that it would be missed in the discourse on the Good Shepherd[6] by the editors, and consequently inserted by them at this point. The fact that v. 16 is secondary is also suggested by the additional interpretation of the αὐλή in v. 1 in terms of the Jewish people.[7] It is not only in this that the

---

[1] See p. 35.

[2] It is easy to pick out the typical marks of the Evangelist's style. On διὰ τοῦτο ... ὅτι v. 17 see pp. 92 n. 2, 238 n. 2. On οὐδεὶς ... ἀλλ' ἐγώ see p. 48 n. 3. On the appended ταύτην τ. ἐντολ. κτλ cp. expressions like 6.27; 9.23 and cp. the sense of 12.49f.; 14.31. N.B. also the specifically Semitic expressions in v. 18, see below.

[3] On the reading δίδωμι (א*DW) see p. 370 n. 5.

[4] On τιθέναι τ. ψυχήν see p. 370 n. 5. On the difference in meaning in v. 11 and vv. 17f. see also v. Dobschütz, ZNTW 28, (1929), 162; admittedly he wants to retain the meaning in v. 11 for v. 15b; however this is impossible in view of the clear reference in v. 17 to v. 15b.

[5] So too Wellh., Hirsch, Schweizer (150) and others, whereas Sp. omits vv. 17, 18 (except for the concluding sentence).

[6] On the traditional comparison between the Church and Jesus' flock see p. 366 n. 7.

[7] It is the αὐλή and not the herd which is taken to refer to the Jewish people! Odeberg (330) thinks that v. 16 simply means that there are men whom Jesus numbers among his

fold

Revealer will find his own but in all the world. There was no need to state explicitly that these sheep would first have to be gathered together by the missionary work of the disciples. It goes without saying that he is active in their work,[1] so that he can say, "I must bring them also". In his messengers they will hear *his* voice, and he will be *their* shepherd as well. So there will be *one* flock under *one* shepherd, i.e. *one* church of which he is Lord.[2]

In vv. 17f. we have a closer explanation of the meaning of Jesus' surrender of his life (v. 15b), in which his "being for" his own is finally manifested. **V.17**, "For this reason the Father loves me, because I lay down my life, that I may take it again."[3] The sentence makes two assertions: 1) His sacrifice is part of his work, makes him the Revealer; for the Father's "love" for him denotes (as the Father's γινώσκειν in v.15) his relationship to the Father, and so claims for him the dignity of the Revealer.[4] That is to say, he is the Revealer in his "being for" his own, which is confirmed in his death. Of course we should not be betrayed by the mythological language into bringing the idea down to a trivial human level, thinking that Jesus had first to win the love of the Father (and consequently his own dignity) by his death. For the Father loved him πρὸ καταβολῆς κόσμου (17.24); and one might equally well say that he surrenders his life because the Father loves him. What is being said here is that in his sacrifice the Father's love for him is truly present, and that this sacrifice is therefore a revelation of the Father's love.

2) Jesus' surrender of his life is, humanly speaking, not final; he will take again the life which he has laid down.[5] Or to put it in the terms

---

sheep, who do not yet belong to the flock but must first be brought to it. However this view is contradicted both by ἐκ and ταύτης.

[1] Cp. 4.37f.

[2] It is possible that the prophecy in Ezek. 34.23; 37.24 has had some influence on the formulation here. There the people are promised the Davidic king as their one shepherd (Ezek. 34.23 LXX: καὶ ἀναστήσω ἐπ' αὐτοὺς ποιμένα ἕνα καὶ ποιμανεῖ αὐτούς 37.24: ... καὶ ποιμὴν εἷς ἔσται πάντων.). There is no good reason to assume that the idea of the myth of the gathering of the scattered particles of light lies behind this (see p. 374 n. 3), for then we would doubtless have συναγαγεῖν instead of ἀγαγεῖν (cp. Ign. Mg. 10, 3; Od. Sal. 10.5; act. Thom. 156 p. 265, 5.15; Mart. Andr. 14, p. 55, 2).—The Stoic idea of the unity of mankind should be distinguished both from the ecclesiastical and the mythological idea of unity. The Stoics also used the image of the herd to give expression to their idea (Stoic. vet. fr. I 61, 2ff. v. Arn.: ἵνα . . . εἷς δὲ βίος ᾖ καὶ κόσμος, ὥσπερ ἀγέλης συννόμου νόμῳ κοινῷ συντρεφομένης); see Br., who draws attention to the philosophical idea of the original and finally recurring unity of religion.

[3] This is the correct translation, for of course the ἵνα clause indicates neither the intention nor the purpose of the τίθημι τ. ψ. μ. On vv. 17f. see E. Fascher, Deutsche Theologie 1941, 37–66.

[4] On the Father's ἀγαπᾶν see p. 165 n. 1.

[5] It is possible that this τιθέναι and λαμβάνειν τ. ψυχήν is symbolised in the τιθ. and λαμβ. of the ἱμάτια in 13, 4.12; see Carpenter 405, 1; but Fascher, op. cit. 42 disagrees. —On λαμβ. τ. ψ. cp. ἀνέστησεν ἑαυτόν Ign. Sm, 2; on this Schlier, Relig. Unters. 69, 2.

of the Farewell Discourses, Jesus' death on the cross is his exaltation, for it is precisely in this sacrifice that he truly shows himself as the Revealer.

V. 18 also emphasises the revelatory character of his death. His death is not merely a fate which overtakes him (cp. 14.30), but it is a free act.[1] As the Revealer's act it is at the same time the act of his freedom[2] and of obedience, by which he fulfils the Father's command.[3] Precisely because he is nothing for himself, he has absolute freedom.[4] Considering the fundamental character which such a statement has in John, it would hardly be right to suggest that there is a naive, apologetic interest behind v. 18.[5] If the saying was meant to show Jesus' foreknowledge of his death, then we would expect future tenses in vv. 17f., as in the vaticinia in Mk. 9.31f.; 10.33f. and elsewhere. By contrast one may perhaps lay special emphasis on the present tenses in vv. 15b, 17f. For it is not simply here a question of the death on the cross; for this is only the necessary end of his surrender of his life (necessary, that is, by the very nature of this surrender), which had its beginning in the ὁ λόγος σὰρξ ἐγένετο of 1.14; in the same way, too, Jesus' δοξασθῆναι on the cross is at one with the δοξασθῆναι which takes place throughout his whole life.[6]

Vv. 27–30 link up with vv. 14, 15a,[7] disregarding, as it were, the note vv. 15b–18. In **vv. 27f.** we have two variations on the two corresponding statements in v. 14, each time in the reverse order; γινώσκουσί με τὰ ἐμά in v. 14 corresponds to τα πρόβατα . . . ἀκούουσιν in v. 27a and to ἀκολουθοῦσίν μοι in v. 27c; γινώσκω τὰ ἐμά of v. 14 is repeated in v. 27b and then restated in the statements in v. 28. And so in these repetitive variations the idea of the *security of faith,* which was indirectly contained in vv. 14f., emerges as the main theme.

The security of faith is, as it were, two-fold. On the one hand it is described as a subjective security by the statements that his own know the Revealer and follow him, as had been said in the parable (v. 3f.),

---

[1] The aor. ἦρεν (so ℵ*B against the other authorities) like ἐβλήθη and ἐξηράνθη 15.6 is gnomic; Bl.-D. para. 333, 1.—Αἴρειν τ. ψυχήν is a Semitic phrase, see Schl., ἐξουσίαν ἔχειν also corresponds to Semitic usage, see Schl. and also Fascher op. cit. 44f.

[2] On ἐξουσία = right, authority, see p. 57 n. 5.

[3] On the fulfilment of the ἐντολή cp. 14.31; 15.10 and see p. 346 n. 4. Fascher op. cit. 46 rightly points out that ἐντ. in the Pap. means not only "commission", "command" but also "authorisation", "power".

[4] According to Stoic doctrine man has the ἐξουσία over his life and consequently the right to commit suicide (Ad. Bonhoeffer, Epiktet und das NT 1911, 6ff.; E. Benz, Das Todesproblem in der stoischen Philosophie 1929, 54ff. 68ff.). There is no reference in Jn. 10.18 to ἐξουσία of this kind, which is grounded in mankind. See on 15.13 for the question how far a voluntary human self-sacrifice can provide an analogy for Jesus' sacrifice.

[5] Thus Ho., Htm., Br., Wrede, Charakter und Tendenz 51f. Cullmann suspects that there is a contrast here with the "Teacher of Righteousness", see p. 376 n. 2.

[6] See on 12.28f.; 13.31f.

[7] Vv. 14, 15a, 27–30 formed a continuous passage in the source, see p. 360.

and indeed at the beginning of the interpretation (v. 8). This is the security which faith enjoys, because it is a simple act of hearing and obeying; if it sought for reasons it would immediately lose its security. As the faith which hears it is *itself* the proof of its security; by accepting the witness it confirms the truth of God.[1] It is itself a proof of its security, but only because it is the faith which *hears*, i.e., because it finds its security in him in whom it believes, i.e., its security has in fact its ground outside itself, which is why it only finds security in hearing. This "objective" security is characterised by the statement, "and I know them", and further by the promises in v. 28. It is precisely because the security of the faithful is the security alone of those who hear, because this is the only way in which it can become a this-worldly experience and a fact in men's lives, that the security is unshakeable. The world has no longer any power over the believer, for his security lies beyond the world; "I give them eternal life and they shall never perish, and no one will snatch them out of my hand."[2]

Vv. 29f. expressly give grounds for the last statement of v. 28. This is parallel to those which were given in v. 15 for v. 14. The security which the believer finds in the Revealer is grounded in the latter's relationship to God, in his unity with God. Thus the believers' relationship to Jesus is as such their relationship to God; no one can snatch them away from Jesus, because no one can snatch them away from God.[3]

---

[1] Cp. 3.33 and see pp. 163, 232.

[2] Οὐ μὴ ἁρπάσῃ, which is read by ℵDL pc, while other authorities have οὐχ ἁρπάσει, has probably been assimiliated to the previous sentence.—The pathetic οὐ μή as in the promises 4.14; 6.35, 37; 8.12, 51; 11.26. On the promise οὐ μὴ ἀπόλ. cp. 3.16; 6.39; 17.12; 18.9. Ἁρπάζειν ἐκ τ. χειρός is used non-figuratively in II Sam. 23.21; figuratively in Plut. Ages. 34, p. 615d and elsewhere (see Wetst. and Br.). Cp. also Is. 43.13: ἐγὼ κύριος ὁ θεὸς ἔτι ἀπ' ἀρχῆς, καὶ οὐκ ἔστιν ὁ ἐκ τῶν χειρῶν μου ἐξαιρούμενος.

[3] In v. 29 B latt read ὃ ... μεῖζον; ℜ syrr, Basil., Chrys., Cyr. Al.: ὃς ... μείζων. There are also various combinations of these, (or copyist's errors) ὃ ... μείζων (ℵ LW) and ὃς ... μεῖζον (A). D supports the sense of the ℜ text: ὁ δεδωκώς μοι πατὴρ μείζων. Aug. takes the text of B (Tract. in Jo 48, 6) to be an explanation of Jesus' equipment for his calling given to him by the Father, i.e. of his nature as the Logos. R. Schütz omits vv. 26–28 as an interpolation, and links v. 29 with v. 25: Jesus' works bear witness to his unity with the Father which no man can take away from him (ZNTW 10 [1909], 324ff.; 18 [1917/18], 223; similarly Sp.). But it is absurd to think of Jesus' nature as the Logos, or of his unity with the Father as that which the Father has given him. For the Father has "given him all things", *because* he loves him (3.35; 5.20), i.e. *because* he is the Logos joined with him in unity. In the context what the Father has given him can only refer to his own, whom he will not allow to perish (6.37, 39; 17.6, 9. 12, 24; 18.9). Since however (in spite of Lagr.) it would not be possible to say of the latter that they were μεῖζον πάντων, the reading must be incorrect; it must have been caused by a copyist's oversight when the copyist was expecting an object after δέδωκεν. The only reading which makes any sense is ὃς ... μείζων: "the Father who has given them to me is greater than all things"; it goes without saying that αὐτά should be supplied as object after δέδωκεν v. 28; the only question is whether one should also supply it in the following sentence after ἁρπάζειν, or whether one should take

He and the Father are one.[1] This last statement, which had already been hinted at in v. 15, gives the most pointed expression to the idea of revelation which it has yet received; it goes further than the statements about the unity of the Father and the Son in 5.19f.; 8.16; 12.44f., and is comparable only with the θεὸς ἦν ὁ λόγος in 1.2: in Jesus and only in him does God encounter man.[2] The idea is stated in this abrupt form, that it may provoke the offence which belongs by nature to the revelation event, to God's attack on the world.

c) Conclusion: 10.31–39

For Jesus' hearers his challenging words are blasphemy. They have the same effect as his saying in 8.58. They want to stone him (**v. 31**).[3] The Evangelist is not interested in describing the scene in detail. Jesus calmly continues speaking and this, as in 8.13–20, leads to a dispute in which the "Jews" are caught out at their own game. The symbolical nature of the scene must be obvious; it represents the struggle of the revelation with the world. Or, more precisely, it affords an example of the ἐλέγχειν περὶ ἁμαρτίας as understood by 16.8f.

Jesus' first words, **v. 32**, help to clarify the situation.[4] His reproachful question is like the questions in 7.19, 23; 8.46. What is the real reason for the world's hatred? It is only that he does "(good) works" on behalf

---

the sentence, which is in the nature of an explanation, to mean: "No one can snatch anything out of the Father's hand."—Whereas Barr. defends the reading ὃς ... μεῖζον, Dodd, (433, 1), Wik., and Strathm. favour ὃς ... μείζων.—This view is confirmed by the parallels in Mand. Lit. 182f.: "Your Father has widespread power at his disposal which extends beyond every frontier.... The good man clothes his sons and wraps them round, lifts them up and shows them the nature of the great peace of life."—For the argument against Burney's (101f.) view, that there has been an error in translation here, see Goguel, Rev. H. Ph. rel. 3 (1923), 379; Colwell 103f. Black (62) thinks it likely that there has been an error in translation, because he doubts whether it is permissible to supply an object for δέδωκεν. R. G. Bury, JTS 41 (1941), 263 suspects that the text is corrupt here.

[1] Schl. is essentially right when he says that the passage is far from suggesting that the movement of Christian life passes from Jesus to the Father; yet in the context v. 30 is intended only to characterise the security of faith, which Schl. also emphasises.

[2] The statement in v. 30 should, of course, be understood in terms of the idea of revelation, and not taken as a cosmological theory such as is found in a Stoic statement: ἅπαντά τ' ἐστιν αἰθήρ, ὁ αὐτὸς ὢν καὶ πατὴρ καὶ υἱός (Chrysipp. in v. Arnim, Stoic. vet. fr. II 316, 20). True analogies can be found in the Gnostic mythology, which is influenced by the idea of revelation. Cp. pp. 151 n. 3, 281 n. 4, 354 n. 2.—Odeberg (331f.) thinks that ἐγώ here (like ἐγώ εἰμι 8.58, see p. 327 n. 5) is a rendering of the mysterious divine name אני, which in Rabbinic Judaism was used to refer to the divine Shekhina (his evidence for this is not convincing), and he paraphrases v. 30: "In me (J) the Shekhina is present, and now (in me) the Father and the Shekhina are united and Salvation is brought about." This is a totally unnecessary complication of what is a simple sentence. On the ideas here cp. further pp. 244f., 248f.

[3] Οὖν (D pc it) is probably original, as against πάλιν (or οὖν πάλιν) which is read by the other witnesses and which refers explicitly to 8.59.

[4] Ἀπεκρίθη as in 2.18, see p. 124 n.6.

of the Father.[1] The concept of "(good) works" summarises his whole activity as the Revealer. They are his miracles,[2] but only inasmuch as they are σημεῖα, only insofar as they form a unity with his ministry of the word.[3] Thus his words as well as his miracles are part of the (καλὰ) ἔργα, indeed it is really they alone which are the "(good) works". If his revealing activity is the ground of the world's hatred, then it is clear that the world is ignorant of its salvation, and that his activity for the world must become an attack upon it. The world's sin is revealed in the fact that it takes as a reproach what is in fact intended for its salvation. And it gives proof of its blindness by imagining that the attack on itself is an attack on God (**v. 33**). Again it is clear that the world has no knowledge of God;[4] for what it calls God is only the religious transfiguration of its own standards and judgements.[5] This again shows that it could know about God—for otherwise its conduct could not be called sin—but that this knowledge has been terribly perverted,[6] in that instead of shattering their peace, it only nurses them into a false security. Formally they are quite right; the penalty for blasphemy is stoning,[7] and it is blasphemy for a man to set himself up as God.[8] But when the "Jews" talk about God, we can see that they are in no sense prepared to hear God when he speaks to them. They cannot grasp that he confronts them in everyday life in a man like themselves. They only know *one* way of "making oneself God", and thus betray their own vanity, their striving for δόξα παρ' ἀλλήλων (5.44). Yet their unbelief is not merely a rejection and refusal of the revelation, but positive hostility and hatred, a positive onslaught on it. Indeed it could not be otherwise, if the good is

---

[1] On Jesus' ἔργα see pp. 222 n. 3, 265f., 331 n. 3; this is the only instance in John where they are called καλά, though this occurs frequently elsewhere: Mt. 5.16; I Pet. 2.12; I Tim. 5.10; 6.18, etc. Since the position of καλά varies in the tradition it is possible that it is a gloss. In any case it could perfectly well be left out, in view of the ἐκ τοῦ πατρός, as it is in v. 37.—'Εκ (τ. πατρός) cp. 3.27; 6.65 like παρά 1.14; 5.44; 6.45, etc.; it is synonymous with τὰ ἔργα τοῦ πατρός μου v. 37; it makes no difference whether one takes it to mean "works which the Father has granted him to do" (5.36), or "which he has charged him with" (4.34; 9.4); they are the works which he does "in the name of the Father" (v. 25). Δεικνύναι as in 2.18. Λιθάζετε conative present, Bl.-D. para. 319.—Cp. the similarly reproachful question asked by Mani, see Br. ad loc.

[2] Cp. the reproach in 7.23.

[3] See pp. 113f., 218, 232f., 265f., and cp. how in 5.20 the healing miracle is combined into a single whole with the μείζονα ἔργα, and how in chs. 9 and 11 the miracles demonstrate the Revealer's activity; cp. above all the parallelism between the ῥήματα and ἔργα 14.10. See further on vv. 37f.

[4] 5.37; 7.29; 8.19.

[5] See pp. 267, 309.

[6] See pp. 267ff., 276f., 309ff.

[7] See p. 328 n. 3. On βλασφ. see E. Bickermann. ev. de l'Hist. des Rel. 112 (1935) 175–177.

[8] See p. 244 n. 6, also Str.-B. and Schl. on 10.33.

understood not as a gift of God, but as the goal of man's efforts in which he realises himself. If the revelation fails to arouse faith then it must arouse hostility.

Vv. 34–36 give a *proof-text* in defence of Jesus. Jesus draws the Jews attention to their law[1] on which they have based their judgement on him (v. 33). In fact the Scriptures refute them, for they contain a saying in Ps. 82.6 in which God addresses men as gods.[2] If God can expressly refer to a man as God, then it follows—a minori ad maius[3]—that Jesus is all the more entitled to call himself God's Son.[4] For God has "consecrated him and sent him into the world".[5]

This kind of Scriptural argument is used in 7.23; 8.17f., but here it is not so closely related to the context. For ὅτι εἶπον· υἱὸς τοῦ θεοῦ εἰμι does not correspond exactly either to Jesus' saying in v. 30, or to the Jewish rebuke in v. 33. It is a way of arguing which is typical of early Christian proofs from Scripture,[6] and seems out of place in the Fourth Gospel. It seems likely, then, that it has been inserted here by the editor.[7] Otherwise one would have to see it as a parody on Jewish Scriptural theology, such as we have in 8.17f.[8] This sort of intellectual subtlety always picks out what suits its own case and can easily be defeated at its own game.

---

[1] 'ὑμῶν, which is omitted by ℵ p45 D it syr^s, may be an addition; cp. 8.17 and see p. 86 n. 3. On ἔστιν γεγραμμ. see p. 000. Νόμος like תורה can refer to the whole of Scripture; cp. 15.25; I Cor. 14.21; and see Str.-B. ad loc.; see Kümmel, ZNW 33 (1934), 111, n. 22.

[2] This is quoted without any regard for the original meaning and context of the verse. In the Psalm those addressed are divine beings (the gods of the nations). In Rabbinic exegesis the saying is sometimes taken to refer to the Israelites, and sometimes to the "serving angels", Str.-B.

[3] Cp. Str.-B. III 223–225; the type of argument used in Jn. 10. 35f. comes at the end of the list given there: "If (such and such is true), then is it not (completely) true that ... ?"

[4] On v. 35: ὁ λόγος τ. θ. does not refer to God's word in general, but to his saying in Ps. 82.6 (Ho., Lagr.). On the other hand ἡ γραφή refers not to the Scriptural reference but to the Scriptures as a whole. 'Ο λόγος ἐγένετο πρός is a typically OT and Jewish phrase (Gen. 15.1; Hos. 1.1 and Schl.). καὶ οὐ κτλ. is not an aside, but part of the conditional clause. On λυθῆναι see p. 244 n. 2. "The fact that λυθῆναι can be applied to the saying which describes God's gift, rather than to the commandment itself, is parallel to the use of νόμος to refer to the Psalter." (Schl.).—On v. 36: "Ον ὁ πατὴρ κτλ. has been placed in front of the main clause; see Bl.-D. para. 478. On the colloquial use of direct speech: βλασφημεῖς see Bl.-D. para. 470, 1.

[5] 'Ηγίασεν καὶ ἀπεστ. εἰς τ.κ. is a hendiadys. The setting apart from the profane sphere referred to by ἁγιάζειν is at the same time the preparation for his calling, his mission; see on 6.69; 17.17, 19 and cp. Jer. 1.5: ... ἡγίακά σε, προφήτην εἰς ἔθνη τέθεικά σε. Ecclus. 49.7 says of Jeremiah, ἡγιάσθη (נוצר) προφήτης. Joh.-B. 217, 17f.: It chose out a Mânà and sent him to us", cp. Ginza 70, 1ff.—Cp. R. Asting, Die Heiligkeit im NT 311; and see on 6.69.

[6] It is possible that the use of Ps. 82.6 was taken from an early Christian apologetic tradition which had already formed, for early Christianity was very soon obliged to defend its own assertion of Jesus' divinity against Jewish attacks (Str.-B. on v. 33); see Br. ad loc.

[7] So too Hirsch, who admittedly ascribes only vv. 34, 35 to the editor. This is not possible, for the argument a min. ad mai. vv. 34–36 is a single unit.

[8] See pp. 282f.

Jesus' reply **vv. 37f.** is closely related to the idea of revelation. "If I am not doing the works of my Father,[1] then do not believe me; but if I do them, even though you do not believe me, believe my works". But which are these works? This can hardly refer here to his miracles alone, as opposed to his other works. Admittedly it is possible for the miracles to develop man's initial receptivity to the revelation into true faith,[2] so that this charge could mean, "Hold fast to the fact that the miracles have given proof of my authority,[3] and learn to understand these miracles as σημεῖα."[4] Yet this sort of remark would be more in place in a discussion following the performance of a miracle than here. Moreover the miracles in ch. 5 and ch. 9 also caused offence, so that it would be hard to see why they should be appealed to here as proving his authority. Yet the main point is that the meaning of vv. 37f. must be the same as the meaning of 14.11, where the disciples are also pointed away from Jesus' person to his ἔργα. Yet as 14.10 shows, the works here are not the miracles but Jesus' ῥήματα, of which the miracles, as speaking σημεῖα, can only be a part.[5] Thus as in v. 32, the ἔργα in vv. 37f. must refer to Jesus' revealing activity as a whole.

But in what sense can Jesus point away from his own person to his work, when in fact his work consists of nothing but his constant assertion of the ἐγώ εἰμι, when his work is concerned wholly with his preaching, in which he speaks of his person as the Revealer? It is only possible to find an answer if one makes a clear distinction between the word which speaks only *about* a thing, and the word in which the thing *itself* is present, between the speculatively or dogmatically oriented word and the word which addresses man and penetrates into his existence. If Jesus' words were merely dogmatic statements about his person, they would not merit belief; they can be believed only when they are heard as a personal address and only so can they be called his works. This indeed is how the Evangelist always portrayed them; not as words which bring new dogmas, but as words which destroy dogma; as words which question man's natural understanding of himself, and which seek to transform his hidden and distorted knowedge of God and his desire for life into a true and authentic knowledge and life. This is the only sense which can be attached to vv. 37f. Man is not asked to believe in a set of dogmas on the authority of a preacher without credentials; what

---

[1] Τὰ ἔργα τ. πατρ. = the works which my Father has granted me, or charged me with; see p. 388 n. 1.

[2] Nicodemus in 3.2 is prompted by the miracles to come with his questions to Jesus; for the blind man the miracle is the way to faith; cp. p. 209.

[3] See p. 134 n. 4.

[4] See p. 388 n. 3.

[5] See p. 388 n. 3.

is demanded of man is a faith which experiences Jesus' words as they affect man himself.[1] The charge to man to believe his works can only mean that man must allow himself to be questioned by Jesus' words, must allow the security of his previous understanding of himself to be shattered, and must accept the revelation of his true existence. The knowledge that he and the Father are one (v. 30), or as it is stated now, "that the Father is in me and I in the Father",[2] stands not at the beginning but at the end of the way of faith. It cannot be blindly accepted as a dogmatic truth, but is the fruit of faith in the "works" of Jesus. When it is first heard it can only cause offence; but this causing offence is an integral part of the Revealer's "work".

The conclusion of the scene is recorded in the briefest of ways in **v. 39** as it was in 7.30, 44; 8.20, 59.[3] The reader must read between the lines to learn that Jesus' "hour" has not yet come (7.30; 8.20).

---

[1] As is rightly seen by Hirsch I 268f.—See p. 266.

[2] Ἵνα γνῶτε καὶ γινώσκητε distinguishes the act and the state of knowing; πιστεύσητε for γινώσκ. in ℵℜ is a clumsy correction. πεπιστεύκαμεν καὶ ἐγνώκαμεν 6.69 gives the sense much more closely. On γινώσκειν see p. 380f. On the reciprocity formula, which is used here to describe the unity between Father and Son, see pp. 380f.

[3] See p. 302 n. 3.

IV. 10.40-12.53; 8.30-40; 6.60-71; The Revealer's Secret Victory over the World

The fourth part of the first chief division comprises two sections, 10.40–11.54 and 11.55–12.33, together with fragments that probably belong here, 8.30–40; 6.60–71. The first section is grouped about the miracle of the raising of Lazarus, the second relates the last appearance of Jesus in Jerusalem. Together they represent the conclusion and the result of the public work of Jesus: his last act leads to the decision of the authorities to kill him, and his last words lead to the final division between faith and unbelief. In this way the whole forms the transition to the Passion Narrative, and to the scene of Jesus' departure from his own that precedes it.

If the farewell discourses teach us to understand the passion of Jesus as the completion of his work and as his glorification, the bridge passage is also illuminated by this truth. A characteristic irony fills the first section. It is present not alone in the words of the High Priest (11.50), who contrary to knowledge or intention prophesies the saving significance of the death of Jesus, but also in the entire passage: the authorities of this world sentence to death the one who raises the dead to life. The futility of the world's fight against the Revealer and its victory over him is thereby signified. Such irony also pervades the second section: the royal entry of Jesus is the way to the cross; but the hour of desperation is the hour of glorification, and the end of the one who is judged by the world is the judgment passed upon the world. Both sections make it plain that the decisive test for those who belong to Jesus is whether they understand this—in the first section through the question directed to Martha, πιστεύεις τοῦτο; (11.26), and in the second through the question directed to the disciples, μὴ καὶ ὑμεῖς θέλετε ὑπάγειν; (6.67).

While the two sections form the transition to chs. 13–20, they are in a way equally the conclusion of the first chief division of the Gospel, and to this extent they possess yet another peculiar significance. They correspond in their symbolic meaning to the two parts of the "overture" in ch. 2. The symbolism of the miracle of Lazarus lies not alone—by analogy with other miracle stories—in its representation of Jesus as the giver of life; rather it is peculiarly isolated by the frame in which it is set, and so, like 2.1–12, the narrative gains the character of an epiphany story. And while the condition of ch. 12 makes a complete characterisation of it difficult, this much is nevertheless clear, that the narrative of the Entry of Jesus into Jerusalem, around which the rest is grouped, symbolises the eschatological event wrought out in his passion: by it Jesus becomes Lord of the world, as 2.13–22 had prophesied; and as there, the Jews here also appear as the blinded instruments of the revelation event.

A. 10.40–11.54: Decision for Death

The first section 10.40–11.54 is framed by the two passages 10.40–42 and 11.54. The former serves the purpose of marking the break between what has preceded and what follows. It is as though a pause takes place before the decisive crisis sets in. Jesus has ended his provocative activity in Jerusalem, and he withdraws into a remote region. But 11.54 presents this "end" and "withdrawal" even more clearly and strongly: Jesus goes into solitude. Between the partial and the entire seclusion of Jesus is set his emergence into the open 11.1ff. In this way it is lifted out of the flow of events and becomes relatively isolated, although as an occurrence with decisive consequences for his destiny, it is firmly woven into the course of events. Accordingly the Lazarus story, by reason of the frame in which it is set, is turned into an epiphany-narrative, analogous to 2.1–12 (see above). And this analogy appears the more forcefully in that, as in 2.1–12, the emergence of the Revealer for his miracle-working action takes place at the hour of his choice, conformable to him, in sovereign disregard of what the world wants or expects.[1]

a) Introduction 10.40–42[2]

The public activity of Jesus has reached its end. The circle is completed (v. 40): Jesus goes back to the place from which he began,[3] to

---

[1] See p. 289 n. 1.

[2] The question may be raised whether in this editorial segment of the Evangelist's use has been made of the σημεῖα-source, in which an utterance like 10.41 may have stood. It is difficult to suppose that in 10.40–42 a recollection of the fact that Jesus kept himself hidden in his last days lingers on (Htm.); and certainly one ought not to claim here a historical tradition that is also reproduced in Mk. 10.1 (Bd.); Mk. 10.1 does not contain a historical tradition at all, but is an editorial fragment (Gesch. der synopt. Tr., p. 365 = Hist. of the Syn. Trad. p. 340). Goguel (Introd. II 429f.) would find here a fragment of the source uncovered in 7.1ff: Jesus waits in seclusion for favourable circumstances, and meanwhile remains in contact with his followers in Judea (the πολλοί of v. 41). It is preferable to suppose that here, as in 11.54–57, the fact comes to light that in these places "in the time of the Evangelist a Christian community existed with its own local, though meagre tradition" (Kindsin, Topol. Überl. 49f.; cp. 20f.; in ZNTW 22 (1923) 89f. he suggested that these passages reflect the flight of the disciples from Jerusalem after the stoning of Stephen).

[3] Πάλιν, omitted only from syr^{s} and e, harks back to 1.28.

the area east of Jordan, where the Baptist had baptized.[1] Here he stays for a while,[2] admittedly not in absolute withdrawal, for "many come to him" (**v. 41**).[3] Obviously he is to be pictured as still concluding his work; yet this activity is carried on in a remote area, and nothing is reported about it. This section is intended only to mark the break (see above). The situation, however, gives occasion for making the testimony of the Baptist, with which 1.19ff. began, to be confirmed out of the mouth of the people. The Baptist himself can no longer appear as a witness; his end is presupposed (5.33–35). Therefore those who once heard his testimony now have to confirm its accuracy, even as they declare the Baptist's inferiority over against Jesus, which in fact the Baptist himself had confessed.[4] That this is the cause for many coming to faith (**v. 42**) is here, as so often,[5] shown by the fact that the work of Jesus was by no means without result. Admittedly the comment, as elsewhere is schematic; the results remain obscure, and have no influence on developments. It is not at all clear whether the Evangelist desires that this faith, occasioned through the σημεῖα, be deemed as unsatisfactory.[6] It is also characteristic for the schematic character of the passage that no mention is made of the disciples accompanying Jesus, although their presence is presupposed in 11.1ff. The interest is wholly concentrated on the person of Jesus.

b) The Resurrection and the Life 11.1–44

The crisis is coming on; the ὥρα of the passion is drawing near. The outward occasion of the fateful crisis is the raising of Lazarus, and the Evangelist has brilliantly illuminated this significance of the event. The disciples have a foreboding that the way to their friend will be a way to death (11.7–16), and the word of Jesus spoken to them (v. 9) hints that the day of his activity is drawing to its close. The raising of Lazarus provides the impetus for the resolution of the Sanhedrin that Jesus must die (11.47–53), and the

---

[1] Πρῶτον either = "at first", "the first time" (as 12.16), and then the change of place for baptism would be in mind; or as τὸ πρότερον (so ℵ D Θ al) it simply = "earlier" (as presumably 19.39); see Bl.-D. §62.

[2] If with D 𝔖, 𝔎 pl ἔμεινεν is to be read, against B ἔμενεν, the aorist is complexive (Bl.-D. §332, 1).

[3] Since ἔλεγον ὅτι κτλ can hardly be directed to Jesus, but describes what was said about him, the stop is to be placed not before καὶ πολλοὶ ἦλθ. πρ. αὐτ. but after the phrase. What follows is then to be translated: "And people said . . ."

[4] 1.15, (27), 30; 3.27–30.—In the formulation 'I. μὲν σημ. ἐπ. οὐδέν the polemical intention is plain: the Baptist was viewed by his followers also as a miracle worker; see Bldsp. 89, 5; Reitzenstein Taufe 61, R. Meyer, Der Prophet aus Galiläa 1940, 40.115; also Gesch. d. syn. Trad. 22, 329.3 = History of the Syn. Trad. 23, 302.1; and see pp. 4f., 29.

[5] 2.33; 4.39; 7.31; 8.30; 11.45; 12.42.

[6] 2.23; see p. 131.

recollection of this miracle afterwards confirms yet again the decision for his death (12.17–19).

Just as in this way expression is given to the conviction that it is the outworking by Jesus of his vocation that brings him to the cross, so it is similarly evident beforehand that the meaning of the cross is the δοξασθῆναι of Jesus (11.4, see below); and as an unwitting prophet the High Priest must intimate how this δοξασθῆναι will be accomplished (11.51f.). The Evangelist deliberately selected this sign; as a raising from the dead it is not only the greatest of the miracles he recounts, but standing at the beginning of the passion of Jesus it makes him appear as the ἀνάστασις and the ζωή (v. 25).[1]

The report about the sign, which has no parallels in the Synoptics, will be taken from the σημεῖα-source.[2] Since the Evangelist does not, as in Chs. 6, 5 and 9, use the miracle story as a point of departure for the following address or discussion, he has considerably furbished it with shorter and longer additions, and so made it subserve his purpose.[3] By this means the person of Lazarus is thrust into the background, and the sisters have been made the chief persons.[4]

---

[1] B. W. Bacon's hypothesis (Hibbert Journ. 1917 Jan., after Windisch, ZNTW 20. (1921) 89) is bizarre: the raising of Lazarus occurs at the date given in 10.22, in the feast of the Dedication of the Temple; the Evangelist by his narrative wishes to christianise the Jewish Chanukka-feast that serves as a memorial to the heroes and martyrs of the Maccabaean time. Even more fantastic is Grill's exposition (II 162–192): Mary and Martha are originally the dawn and dusk of Indian mythology, Lazarus is the moon, and Jesus is Sabazios-Dionysus.

[2] Stylistically the narrative attaches itself to the other presumed sections of the σημεῖα-source. The language is without crude semitisms, yet it is semitising; cp. the frequent setting of the verb at the beginning, the asyndeta or primitive linking of sentences; further the ἴδε vv. 3.36 or ἔρχου καὶ ἴδε v. 34 (see p. 100 n. 2); the absolute ἀποστέλλειν v. 3 could be a semitism (cp. Rev. 1.1 and Schl. on Mt. 27.19); similarly ποιεῖν ἵνα v. 37 (cp. Ezek. 36.27; Eccles. 3.14; Rev. 3.9; 13.12, 15f. Col. 4.16; Bl.-D §392, 1e), the statement of time in v. 17 (see p. 241 n. 6) and φωνῇ μεγάλῃ v. 43 (Schl. ad loc. and on Mt. 27.46). See also H. Preisker, Wundermächte u. Wundermänner der hellenist.-röm. Kultur u. die Auferweckung des Lazarus in Joh. 11. (Wissensch. Ztschr. d. Univers. Halle 2 (1952), Gesch.-wiss. Reihe 6, 519–523).

[3] The tension between the miracle and the meaning that is symbolised through it is more perceptible here than in chs. 6 and 9; outwardly viewed Wellh.'s judgment is correct: "If that (namely the saying of Jesus in vv. 25f.) holds good, then the resurrection of Lazarus is completely superfluous. The saying, which is the point of vv. 21–27, robs the whole event of all meaning." Nevertheless that verdict is correct only if judgment is passed from the viewpoint of the miracle story which the Evangelist has taken from his source, but not from his own point of view. The Evangelist has more or less already adduced that consideration, and he brings to expression the two possibilities of attitude that can be taken to the σημεῖον through the differentiation made between Martha and Mary, see below.

[4] The analyses of Wendt, Spitta, Schwartz and Wellh. (see also P. Wendland, Die urchristl. Literaturformen 305f. or 239f.) have achieved no illuminating result, and it is questionable whether one can be reached. The linguistic investigation yields no satisfying criteria, even though it confirms this. Certainly it is plain that Jesus' sayings in vv. 9f. 25f. are derived not from the σημεῖα-source, but from the revelation-discourses. The style of the Evangelist, however, is not always sharply distinguished from that of the σημεῖα-source. All the same the sentence construction in vv. 28–32 does distinguish itself from the more primitive forms of the source; and on the other hand the semitisms mentioned in the preceding note are all to be found in the presumed text of the source. The sections characterised

The arrangement is simple. 11.1–16 is the introduction both with respect to the external progress of the event and regarding its significance. It falls into two sections: vv. 1–5 give a statement of the outward and inward situation, vv. 6–16 show by the dialogue between Jesus and his disciples the consequence that follows from the situation. 11.17–44 is the main part, and again it falls into two sections: vv. 17–27 and vv. 28–44, in both of which the possibility is presented of understanding Jesus as the ζωή. Vv. 28–44 consist of the segments given in the outward course of the narrative, vv. 28–32, 33–40, 41–44. Possibly a conclusion is lacking, and has been replaced by 11.45–53.

1) *Introduction:* 11.1–16

i. 11.1–5

Verses 1, 3, 5, state the external situation: in Bethany[1] a man lies ill,[2] and his name is Lazarus[3] (**v. 1**). In vv. 3 and 5 it comes to light

---

by the theological ideas of the Evangelist are certainly compositions of his, namely vv. 4, 7–10, 16, 20–32, 40–42; in these, as elsewhere, he employs sayings from the revelation-discourses. V. 13 is a comment of his, whereas v. 2 is derived from the ecclesiastical redactor, as the Kurios title betrays (see p. 176 n. 2. There remain over vv. 1, 3, 5–6, 11–12, 14–15, 17–19, 33–39, 43–44, in which one might be tempted to perceive the text of the source. Yet many obscurities show that these verses are not an original report; presumably an old narrative had already been edited when it was taken up into the σημεῖα-source, and the Evangelist has further worked over it. We are unable to clear up all the difficulties; it is probable that originally the sisters, if named at all, were anonymous, and that their identification with Martha and Mary is secondary; see below for the details: n. 1 below, 397 nn. 1, 3, 4, 400 n. 6, 401 nn. 1, 3, 405 nn. 1, 4, 406 n. 3, 407 nn. 6, 7 and 9. Dodd (363) contests the legitimacy of a literary-critical analysis of ch. 11.

1 As to the situation of *Bethany* east of the Mount of Olives see Dalman, O. und W. 265f.; Str.-B. and Schl. on Mt. 21.17. For the reader the village is characterised as the home (see p. 000 n. 000) of the two sisters, who are already well known to him. The village was known from Lk. 10.38–42, and probably also from further legendary elaborations. Their κώμη, into which Jesus comes in his journey through Samaria to Jerusalem, is not named in Luke, and indeed in consequence of his outline of the journey, Luke could not have thought of Bethany. Such identification is commonly secondary (Gesch. der synopt. Tr. 68f., 257f. = Hist. of the Syn. Trad. 64f., 242f.). The statement cannot simply be an addition of the Evangelist, for it is neither declared nor obviously intended that Martha and Mary are the sisters of Lazarus (Schw., Wellh.). Admittedly this is presupposed in what follows, but the identification appears to be secondary, see below. V. 2 is a gloss of the ecclesiastical redactor (see p. 395 n. 4); its purpose is to identify the Mary who is here named with the woman who is known from Mark 14.3–9 par. (Lk. 7.37f.); the procedure corresponds to a tendency to link data given in the tradition to a world known to the reader. That story is found also in Jn. 12.1–8, but it is improbable that v. 2 alludes to it; rather with Bl.-D. §339 we should interpret: "M. was (more exactly 'is') the one who, as you know, anointed . . . .".

2 On ἦν δέ τις see on 5.5. On Λαζ. ἀπὸ βηθ. cp. Jos. bell. 2, 585: ἀνὴρ ἀπὸ Γισχάλων and see p. 103 n. 3.

3 Λάζαρος (as Lk. 16.20; Jos. bell. 5, 567)=לְעָזָר, an abbreviation of אֶלְעָזָר (=he whom God helps), Str.-B. on Lk. 16.20. To make mention of one on whom Jesus performs a miracle by his proper name is unusual in the old tradition (Mk. 10.46; Lk. 8.41); see Gesch. der synopt. Tr. 256f.=Hist. of the Syn. Trad. 241f. It is an oft repeated supposition that the name Lazarus is derived from Lk. 16.19–31 (so that the story should show that the Jews do not believe, even when Lazarus rises from the dead).

that he is a friend of Jesus. His sisters Mary and Martha[1] send to Jesus the message (v. 3), "See, the one whom you love is ill."[2] Of course this message is an indirect request that Jesus should come and heal the sick man. The motivation for the request is supplied to the reader in **v. 5.**[3] In between, in **v. 4,**[4] stands a saying of Jesus relating to the meaning of this sickness, and it is presupposed that it is addressed to the disciples who surround him: the illness will not lead to death,[5] its purpose is the glorifying of God. Naturally in the first instance that means—like the analogous expression 9.3b[6]—that it will be the occasion for Jesus to perform a miracle. Correspondingly the explanatory ἵνα δοξασθῇ κτλ is meant to affirm that this deed will also glorify Jesus who, in that he seeks the δόξα of the Father (7.18), at the same time acquires his own δόξα (8.54), for the δόξα of the Father and the Son form a unity.[7] But doubtless there is more at issue here than simply a δοξασθῆναι through a miraculous act. Back of this prior meaning there lies the other: the miraculous action of Jesus will bring him to the cross; that is, however,

---

[1] Such at least is to be affirmed from the text that now lies before us. If the sisters originally were unnamed then αἱ ἀδ. αὐτοῦ would be expected. Was it originally simply stated: ἀπέστειλαν οὖν πρὸς αὐτὸν λέγοντες (one sent to him)?—On the names מַרְיָם or מִרְיָם and מָרְתָא see Str.-B. I 36; II 184. On the family relationships of Lazarus see J. N. Sanders, NTSt I (1954/55), 29–41—in my view an artificial construction.

[2] For φιλεῖν, that reappears in v. 36, a change is made in v. 5 and ἀγαπᾶν appears without any difference of meaning (see p. 253 n. 2); the verbs do not have a specific Johannine meaning here, but denote the human relationship; see M. Dibelius, Festg. für Ad. Deissmann 181. M. Paeslack, Zur Bedeutungsgesch. der Wörter φιλεῖν usw in der Septuaginta u. im NT (no date), 140 wishes to differentiate between φιλεῖν and ἀγαπᾶν; similarly V. Warnach, Agape 1951, 155.1; 357. Further see the literature cited in W. Bauer's (=Arndt and Gingrich) lexicon under φιλεῖν. According to R. Eisler (Rätsel 373ff.) v. 3 indicates that in the source there must have been a preceeding narrative that explained ὃν φιλεῖς. Eisler identifies Lazarus on the one hand with the "Rich Young Man" whom Jesus, according to Mk. 10.21, "loved", and on the other hand (as Kreyenbühl before him) with the "Beloved disciple" of John, and through further combinations he deduces as a source a "Gospel of Lazarus".

[3] According to v. 3 we should expect that Lazarus would be named as the only, or at least the first object of the love of Jesus. The impression is conveyed that τὴν M. καὶ τ. ἀδ. αὐτῆς καί is a secondary insertion.

[4] In the source v. 5 immediately followed on v. 3. V. 4 (as 9.3–5) is derived from the Evangelist; he anticipates the ὡς οὖν ἤκουσεν of the source (v. 6) by ἀκούσας δέ, in order to link on to the ἀσθενεῖ of v. 3 his sentence about the meaning of the ἀσθένεια. V. 4 shows his characteristic style: on οὐκ . . . ἀλλά and on the exposition of the concept δόξα τ. θ. through the ἵνα-sentence, see p. 48 n. 3; for πρὸς θαν. cp. I Jn. 5.16f., for ὑπὲρ τῆς δόξης cp. III Jn. 7 ὑπὲρ τ. ὀνόματος, for δι' αὐτῆς at the end of the sentence cp. 1.7; 3.17; I Jn. 4.9.

[5] It is difficult to believe that a double meaning is intended, so that the disciples had to interpret: "not for death", while Jesus meant: "not to remain in death" (Br). That would not be a Johannine double meaning at all (see p. 135 n. 1). Rather the sentence is intended for the reader: death is not the end and meaning of the illness.

[6] See p. 331.

[7] See on 12.28; 13.31f.

it will lead to his ultimate glorification. The position of the story makes that clear (see p. 394), and from now on the mention of Jesus' δοξασθῆναι has this meaning in view: 12.16, 23, 28; 13.31ff; 17.1, 4f.

ii. 11.6-16

If vv. 1–5 have described the situation in its outward and inward aspects, the dialogue of Jesus with his disciples makes plain the importance of the decision entailed in Jesus' resolve to help his friend. In the presentation there is a certain tension between this characteristic motif of the Evangelist's: Jesus' departure leads to death, and the other one, which comes from the source: Jesus delays (in a manner at first incomprehensible) the fulfilment of the request. The same motif is here present as that which we meet in 2.3f.; 7.6ff.: the work of Jesus has its own hour. The motif has a definite place in a miracle story, but the Evangelist gladly adopts it, because it demonstrates the freedom of the Revealer from worldly points of view;[1] and it has a particular significance in this context, where the choice of the right hour for the miracle is at the same time the first step to the δοξασθῆναι of the passion.

The second motif is dominant in **v. 6**, admittedly in such a manner that the meaning continues to be hidden: the delay of Jesus seems to be without reason, and only in v. 15 does it receive an explanation. Not till the third day[2] does Jesus decide to set out for Judea[3] with his disciples (v. 7).[4] With that the first motif is touched on: the disciples know what εἰς τὴν Ἰουδαίαν πάλιν means; they remember the Jews' intention to stone him (10.31),[5] and they give a warning to Jesus about the way that will lead to death (**v. 8**). The answer of Jesus (**vv. 9f.**) expresses pictorially the same thought as 9.4:

---

[1] See pp. 117, 121, 292f..

[2] Was there for the Evangelist a symbolic significance in the fact that Jesus chose the third day?

[3] Ἐις τ. Ἰουδ., instead of the expected εἰς τὴν βηθανίαν, links the section with 10.40, and is intended to provoke the objection in v. 8. Naturally it is derived from the Evangelist; in the source v. 11 followed immediately on v. 6: [ἔπειτα from v. 7] μετὰ τοῦτο λέγει αὐτοῖς. (So rightly Faure, ZNTW 21 (1922), 114, 1, who however is mistaken in the belief that the verses derived from the Evangelist had formed an original connection with 10.40–42. Admittedly this connection does exist, but it is due to the editorial work of the Evangelist).—As vv. 11–15 show, the source presupposed that the disciples formed the entourage of Jesus, as in 9.2. But as in ch. 9 the disciples afterwards (from v. 17 on) disappear; they have no significance for the miracle, nor have they for the intention of the Evangelist.

[4] On the pleonast. ἔπειτα μετὰ τοῦτο see Bl.-D. §484.—"Αγωμεν as vv. 15f.; 14.31; Mk. 1.38; Epikt. Diss. III 22, 55 etc.

[5] For νῦν = only recently, even yet, Br. refers to Jos. ant. 11, 24; c. Ap. 1, 46. It is common in Greek, cp. Plato resp. 341c. etc.

[οὐχὶ δώδεκα ὧραί εἰσιν τῆς ἡμέρας;]
ἐάν τις περιπατῇ ἐν τῇ ἡμέρᾳ, οὐ προσκόπτει,
[ὅτι τὸ φῶς τοῦ κόσμου τούτου βλέπει·]
ἐὰν δέ τις περιπατῇ ἐν τῇ νυκτί, προσκόπτει,
[ὅτι τὸ φῶς οὐκ ἔστιν ἐν αὐτῷ.[1]]

The idea is formulated as a general statement: the day comprises twelve hours,[2] i.e. it is limited—bounded by the night that will set in (cp. 9.4). The two ἐάν-clauses contain in the form of a simple description the exhortation to make full use of the day (cp. 9.4). In the context it is self-evident that this saying (as 9.4) must first be related to Jesus himself, and give the reason for his decision: he must use to the full the short time that still remains to him on earth.[3]

With the ταῦτα εἶπεν of **v. 11** the veil, as it were, falls again on the mysterious background of the story; ignoring vv. 8–10, Jesus speaks of his intention to make the journey to Lazarus.[4] And indeed he speaks in an ambiguous manner, with the result that the παράδοξον of the raising of the dead appears all the greater: he intends to "wake up"[5] Lazarus, who has "fallen asleep". The disciples misunderstand the statement in a quite gross manner[6] (**v. 12**), as the Evangelist's addition

---

[1] Without doubt the saying is derived from the Discourse on Light in the revelation-discourses; the Evangelist has scattered parts of this Discourse in various sections: 9.4f. 39; 8.12; 12.44–50, 35f., see pp. 332, 342f., 345, 356f. Cp. Kundsin, Char. u. Urspr. 226, and esp. Becker 91, 114–116. Presumably in the source 11.9f. and 9.4f. were closely related, and perhaps one may venture to reconstruct the original connection in this way: 9.5, 4 (see p. 332 n. 1); 11.9, 10; 12.35, 36. This would have been the second part of the Discourse on Light; the first comprised 8.12; 12.44–50 (9.39 would originally have stood in place of v. 46, see p. 345 n. 5). In 11.9f. the Evangelist has glossed the text by the substantiating ὅτι-clauses (cp. his procedure in 12.47–50; see pp. 345 n. 5); in the first of these the τοῦ κόσμου τούτου (see p. 342 n. 5) is unmotivated; the second has the artificial meaning "for he has no light in himself" (Mt. 6.23 and Lk. 11.35 are not in mind; rather cp. Philo spec. leg. 192 concerning the prophet: ἔχοντι νοητὸν ἥλιον ἐν αὑτῷ); the correction of ἐν αὐτῷ by ἐν αὐτῇ D is quite understandable. I also regard the introductory question οὐχί κτλ. as coming from the Evangelist's pen; it is in characteristic Semitic style for the introduction of a parabolic saying, cp. Mt. 10.29 par.; Lk. 14.28, 31; 15.8; Gesch der synopt. Tr. 195f.—Hist. of the Syn. Tr. 180f.

[2] On the division of hours of the Jewish day, Str.-B. ad loc.

[3] As in 9.4 no consideration is given of the fact that so far as Jesus is the light, there is no night impending for him. This shows that the saying (as 9.4, see p. 332 n. 1) originally did not apply to him at all, but was an exhortation to the hearers. Ho. and Br. (after Apollinaris Cat. 315, 20) are wrong in interpreting: Jesus wishes to still the disciples' anxiety; before his hour has come the Jews cannot do him any harm.

[4] On the original connection between vv. 11 and 6f., see p. 398 n. 3.

[5] Ἐξυπνίζω (also LXX) is a Hellenistic word; classical Greek has ἀφυπνίζω see Br.

[6] This is no "Johannine" misunderstanding (see p. 135 n. 1) for it has nothing to do with the confusion of the heavenly and earthly. Rather a primitive artificial device of the source lies behind this (cp. Mk. 5.39). As to the counsel of the disciples that sleep is healthy, cp. the parallels in Wetst. and Str.-B. The double meaning of κοιμᾶσθαι is very old, see on this Lidzb. On κοίμησις (only here in the NT) see the Th.WB.

in **v. 13** explains.[1] Jesus, however, makes his meaning clear (**v. 14**) by openly saying[2] that Lazarus has died. The explanation of κεκοίμηται also clarifies the meaning of ἐξυπνίσω αὐτόν, and it now becomes comprehensible (**v. 15**) why Jesus was glad for his disciples' sakes that he had not gone earlier;[3] they must witness the miracle of the raising of the dead and lay hold of faith.[4] The ἄγωμεν,[5] taken up once more from v. 7, evokes the response of Thomas (**v. 16**), and that makes the first motif sound out again: the way they are taking is to lead to death. Thomas' statement, which incidentally is directed not to Jesus but to his companions, is not a warning but signifies a resignation to the fate that threatens alike the disciples and Jesus.[6] For the first time the truth emerges that the disciples must accept for themselves the destiny that lies ahead of Jesus; the farewell discourses are to develop this theme, and the resigned submission is to give place to a firm resolution. For the present it is but a blind devotion that is at stake, as appears from the fact that it is Thomas[7] who utters the statement—he who in 14.5 shows himself to be blind and who, according to 20.24ff., must "see" in order to be able to believe.

2) *The Resurrection and the Life:* 11.17–44

i. *Jesus and Martha* 11.17–27

Vv. 17–19 describe the external situation, which is the presupposition for that which follows. When Jesus comes to Bethany the deceased man has already lain four days[8] in the grave (**v. 17**)[1]. The distance from

---

[1] Cp. the expositions on 2.21; 7.39; 12.16, 33.

[2] On παρρησία see p. 291 n. 1.

[3] Ὅτι depends not on πιστ. but on χαίρω. The interpolated ἵνα-clause, explaining the δι' ὑμᾶς, is possibly derived from the Evangelist. See Schweizer 95, n. 102.

[4] Ἵνα πιστ. is spoken as if 2.11 had not preceded it. There is no interest in the development of the disciples; the presentation is schematic, see p. 195 n. 2. The supposition that the faith of the disciples had been shaken through Lazarus' death in the absence of Jesus (Schl.) imports an interest foreign to the Evangelist.

[5] So from the point of view of the text, as it lies before us. In fact the Evangelist has anticipated in v. 7 the ἄγωμεν of the source.

[6] That μετ' αὐτοῦ relates to Lazarus is a bizarre idea of Zahn's. Naturally v. 16 along with vv. 7–10 are due to the Evangelist; in the source v. 17 followed on v. 15, as also ensues from the αὐτόν of v. 17, which refers back to v. 15, and has no relation to v. 16.

[7] Θωμᾶς is a Greek name (Bl.-D § 53, 2d). and was used as an equivalent for the Semitic תְּאוֹמָא (= twin), see 14.5; 20.24; 21.2.

[8] On τέσσ. ἤδη ἡμ. ἔχοντα see p. 241 n. 6. The four days in the grave indicate that the death took place four days earlier, since according to Oriental custom a dead person is buried on the day of his dying (cp. Acts 5.6, 10). The fourth day therefore was chosen because the Jews believed that the soul continues to remain in the neighbourhood of the corpse for three days, so that on the fourth day all hope of a revival has disappeared; see Schl. ad loc., Str.-B. and Br. on v. 39; Bousset, Rel. des Judent. 297, 1; Dalman, Jesus-

Jerusalem to Bethany[2] is expressly declared (**v. 18**) in order to provide the motive for the presence of the Jews (**v. 19**). The latter, in conformity with custom,[3] have come in order to console the sisters; so far as the narrative is concerned, their presence is necessary because they are needed as witnesses of the miracle.

With **v. 20** the decisive scene commences: on receiving the news that Jesus is coming, Martha runs towards him and meets him outside, before he reaches the village (so it is to be inferred from v. 30), while Mary remains in the house.[4] In the outburst of Martha **vv. 21f.**, expression is given to faith in Jesus' supernatural power. The first sentence—hardly thought of as a reproach, but rather as a painful regret—reveals the trust in the healer that Martha, no less than others, brings to him. It acts as a foil for the second sentence, wherein what is new and proper to faith in Jesus comes to view: Martha knows that God will grant him any request. Of course, her statement is an indirect request to raise her brother; but it is significant that it is formulated not as a request but as a confession, of which νῦν οἶδα as clearly stands in contrast to the νῦν ἐγνώκαμεν of 8.52, as it is in agreement with the νῦν

Jeschua 170, 197f.; E. Böklen, Die Verwandtschaft der Jüd.-christ. mit der pars. Eschat. 1902, 28f.; Lehmann-Hass, Textbuch zur Religionsgesch.[2] 1922, 162f.—How the four days are reckoned, e.g. whether the two days of v. 6 are included or not (see Br.), is irrelevant.

[1] V. 17 sounds as though Jesus has come directly to the grave, which would be in contradiction to vv. 34, 38. But v. 17 does not contain a clear statement of place; see n. 3.

[2] 'Ην is assimilated to the time of the narrative, as v. 6; 18.1; 19.41; that Jerusalem is no longer standing at the time of the narrator (Merx) is therefore not to be concluded. An accusative for the question "How far?" is replaced, as often by ἀπό; see Bl.D. §161, 1; Raderm. 122; Br. and Schl. ad loc. The statement of distance (15 stadia = 3 kilometers, Str.-B.) is inexact, according to Dalman, O. und W. 13, 266.

[3] The variant in the 𝔎 text: πρὸς τὰς περὶ M. κ. M. need not have a different meaning from πρὸς τὴν M. κ. M., see Br.—Concerning the custom of "consoling the mourners", see Str. B. IV 1, 592–607. It is remarkable that in v. 33 the Jews are not described as consolers but as the weeping. Wellh. is of the opinion that v. 33 has in view the procession of mourners at the grave or immediately afterwards on the way from the grave; from that he concludes that the purpose of v. 17 is to say that Jesus went at once to the grave (see n. 1 above). He further deduces that vv. 18f. are secondary. The original report therefore related that when Jesus came to the grave he met the mourners, who had just buried Lazarus. Consequently τεσσ. ἤδη ἡμ. ἔχοντα v. 17 must also be judged as secondary, and with that v. 39 is shown to be a similar addition. This construction may well be right; it also eliminates the figures of Martha and Mary from the original form of the narrative (see p. 395 n. 4). Nevertheless this original form will hardly have come from the Evangelist (Wellh.), but will already have been edited in the σημεῖα-source; for the enhancement of the greatness of the miracle, by the statement that Lazarus was already dead for three days, certainly corresponds to the tendency of the tradition of miracles, but not to that of the Evangelist, for whom the miracle becomes a symbol. And obviously by the naming of Martha and Mary his source offered him the possibility for composing vv. 20–32.

[4] The differentiation between the sisters is deliberate; the precise point of the story is bound up with it. The Evangelist could have received his impetus from Lk. 10.38–40 for this, but it is impossible to equate the the characters of the sisters in John with the way they appear in Luke.

οἴδαμεν of 16.30.[1] The saying therefore has transcended its situation, and becomes an expression of faith in the ability of Jesus to help, indeed in Jesus as the Revealer to whom God gives everything (3.35 etc.). But it is also significant that her faith in his power is faith in the power of his prayer; this is further elucidated in vv. 41ff. The Revealer, accordingly, is removed from the sphere of the θεῖος ἄνθρωπος, as the old miracle story sees him; it is recognised that everything he possesses he has from God.

Nevertheless the dialogue that follows shows that fundamentally it is simply a picture of faith that is drawn here, not the delineation of an individual (Martha) mighty through faith. Jesus grants Martha's request with the ambiguous ἀναστήσεται ὁ ἀδελφός σου (**v. 23**), and she is not satisfied with it, because she relates it to the ἀνάστασις ἐν τῇ ἐσχάτῃ ἡμέρᾳ (**v. 24**).[2] The Johannine technique of misunderstanding is plain, but its execution is unclear, because of the way the Evangelist has bound himself to the miracle story. For basically the primitive concept of ἀνάστασις is not corrected by the fact that instead of declaring the eschatological ἀνάστασις of popular thought, Jesus by his miraculous power brings about an immediate ἀναστῆναι of Lazarus, but as vv. 25f., show, by the fact that the idea of the eschatological ἀνάστασις is so transformed that the future resurrection of Martha's belief becomes irrelevant in face of the present resurrection that faith grasps. The raising of Lazarus is only a symbol of this.

Vv. 25f.

ἐγώ εἰμι ἡ ἀνάστασις καὶ ἡ ζωή.
ὁ πιστεύων εἰς ἐμὲ κἂν ἀποθάνῃ ζήσεται,
καὶ πᾶς ὁ ζῶν καὶ πιστεύων εἰς ἐμὲ οὐ μὴ
ἀποθάνῃ εἰς τὸν αἰῶνα.[3]

Jesus speaks as the Revealer.[4] He is the Resurrection[5] and the Life, since for those who believe in him, i.e. who acknowledge him as the

---

[1] See H. Riesenfeld, Nuntius nr. 6 (1952), 41–44, on καὶ νῦν of v. 22 in the sense "but nevertheless".

[2] On the Jewish resurrection hope see Schl. ad loc., and Th.WB I 270, 10ff; II 858, 4ff.

[3] Doubtless the saying is derived from the revelation-discourses. I venture the suggestion that we are here dealing with a fragment of the discourse used in 5.19ff. It is open to question how far the Evangelist had edited its formulation—whether perhaps καὶ πιστεύων εἰς ἐμέ in v. 26 has been added by him; see p. 403 n. 6. Cp. the analysis in Becker 90f.

[4] On ἐγώ εἰμι see p. 225 n. 3.

[5] 'Ανάστασις should not be interpreted in an active sense (any more than ζωή) as "the raising from the dead" (Schl.). The meaning of the ἐγώ εἰμι would be misunderstood in this way; for it does not characterise the nature or the action of the ἐγώ, but his gift or his significance. Odeberg stresses (334) that the corresponding term to ἀνάστασις is the Aramaic

Revealer of God, life and death as men know and call them are no longer realities. If the Revealer is described as the ζωή (cp. 14.6) and as the ἀνάστασις, the reason for that is not simply that the dialogue is directed against the primitive conception of resurrection and would affirm that whatever is significant in that idea finds its answer in Jesus; it also brings to expression that the ζωή is an eschatological phenomenon; i.e. that it is accessible only in the ἀνάστασις.

"I am the life" is not a description of the metaphysical nature of Jesus; it speaks of his gift for the man who comes to faith and thereby "rises."[1] That he is the ζωή in his significance for faith is exactly what is meant by the linking together of ἀνάστασις and ζωή.[2]

The self-predication is unfolded in a couplet. The two lines say the same thing,[3] positively and negatively; by a paradoxical mode of expression[4] they remove the concepts of death and life into another sphere, for which human death and human life are only images and hints: the believer may suffer the earthly death, but he has "life" in a higher, in an ultimate sense.[5] And for the man who tarries[6] in the earthly life and is a believer, there is no death in an ultimate sense; death for him has become unreal. Life and death in the human sense—the highest good and the deepest terror—have become unreal for him; in so far as he sees the Revealer with eyes of faith, he stands before God himself. *"Nam mors animae abalienatio est a Deo."*[7]

---

equivalent קימתא, a word that is also technical in the Mandaean sources, not the Rabbinic תחיית המתים (vivificatio mortuorum). The reason adduced for this, that in the context the latter has no meaning, is certainly unsatisfactory.

[1] Thus there is more here than the assertion: "He who one day will raise the dead is now standing before you" (R. Hermann, Von der Antike zum Christentum, Festgabe für V. Schultze 1931, 32). Rightly Wik. and Dupont 213.

[2] It can only be a mistake that in 𝔓45 a 1 syr^s Cypr. καὶ ἡ ζωή is lacking. In act. Jo. 98, p. 200, 8s among other characteristically Gnostic titles, Jesus is also accorded the titles ζωή and ἀνάστασις; a hint is provided thereby of the origin of these titles in the Gnostic tradition, even if Jn. 11.25f. has influenced the act. Jo.

[3] It is wrong, with Calvin, Bd., Schl., among others to find a different meaning in the two lines, the first teaching the resurrection and the second the indestructibility of the resurrection life. That presupposes an unsatisfactory interpretation of πᾶς ὁ ζῶν v. 26, see n. 6 below. Dodd also finds a different meaning in the two verses: the first promises the believer eternal life as something future after death, the second as something in the present.

[4] It is significant that it does not say ἡ ἀληθινὴ ζωή (which in fact would be excellent), as Ign. Eph. 7.2 and elsewhere; see ThWB II 840, 4ff.; 861, 6ff.; 865. n. 268.

[5] See pp. 257f.

[6] Since ὁ ζῶν in the second line corresponds to the κἂν ἀποθάνῃ in the first, like the latter it must be taken from the point of view of human thinking, and so be understood of the earthly life. Hermann op. cit p. 32 is therefore wrong: "He who has gained the life that is promised to faith *and yet*(!) *remains a believer*". This interpretation, and that represented by Calvin and others (see n. 3 above), could at most be that of the source if καὶ πιστ. εἰς ἐμέ were an addition of the Evangelist (see p. 402 n. 3). But the Evangelist would then have corrected the source in a highly significant manner.

[7] Calvin ad loc.

Martha?

The question πιστεύεις τοῦτο[1] therefore asks whether a man is ready to let life and death as he knows them be unreal. In general one is glad to hear that the destruction of life that ensues on death is itself null and void, but only if—whether in relief or anxiously—he may hold fast to life, which he knows to be the highest of all goods. But faith lets this go also. That means: it does not claim to know of what kind the ζωή is that is promised. If the promised gift bears the same name as the good that men regard as the highest good, and if it be called ζωή, then admittedly what man calls "life" is a hint of that "life"; it is a hint—but only in the sense that what he *ought* to be in this life *in actuality*, indeed, what he would *really wish* to be, even though it is perpetually veiled, is real in that ζωή. The promised ζωή therefore cannot be described concretely, nor can it be defined in its content; it is not the "spiritual" life in the idealistic sense,[2] nor a phenomenon of the consciousness, the life of the soul, the mystic *unio*.[3] Any representation of the "what" and "how" of the promised ζωή could only speak of human possibilities, and the highest of these would not be better than the most primitive in comparison with the promised ζωή, which as eschatological reality—as ἀνάστασις καὶ ζωή—stands beyond human possibilities. Readiness for *that* means the ready acceptance of earthly death, i.e. the giving up of man as he now knows himself and now wants to be. For the world, therefore, the ζωή appears under the mask of death.[4]

The answer of Martha (**v. 27**) shows the genuine attitude of faith, in that she avoids the statement about the ζωή, drops the "I," and speaks only of "Thou"—of him who confronts her as the Revealer of God, and whom she acknowledges as such in faith.[5] She cannot see the promised ζωή; but she can recognise that in Jesus the eschatological invasion of God into the world has come to pass. The names which her confession attributes to him are eschatological titles; and of these the third one is the most significant here, because ὁ εἰς τὸν κόσμον ἐρχόμενος most plainly affirms the inbreaking of the beyond into this life.[6]

---

[1] Only here and in 1 Jn. 4.16 in the Johannine writings does πιστεύειν take an acc. obj.; see Huby, Rech. sc. rel. 21 (1931), pp. 406f.

[2] On the Greek interpretation of authentic life see Th.WB II 836, 3ff.; 838, 36ff. Philo stands in this tradition; for example in the reinterpretation of the well known saying of Heraclitus he comes close to the paradox of Jn. 11.25f., see ThWB II 861.15ff.

[3] See p. 258 n. 3.

[4] So also in Paul, 2 Cor. 4.7ff.; see Th.WB. III 20.35ff.

[5] It is incomprehensible how many exegetes can say that Martha did not rightly understand Jesus. Dibelius (Fest. für Deissmann 185) is right in affirming that v. 27 is the christological confession of the Church.

[6] On the Messianic title ὁ ἐρχόμενος see Klostermann on Mt. 11.3 (Hdb. zum NT), cp. further 3.19; 6.14 and see p. 298 n. 1. The title is lacking in the confession 1.50;

ii. *The Raising of Lazarus* 11.28–44

11.28–32. Vv. 28–32 on the one hand describe the outward event which is the presupposition of that which follows, on the other hand they direct attention to the dominant theme of the entire section. The broad argument in 11.28–44 shows that the raising of Lazarus is not only a symbol for the saying in vv. 25f. (it could have been much more briefly recounted if that were so). Rather 11.28–44 provide an antitype to 11.17–27: a description is given of the primitive faith of those who need the external miracle in order to recognise Jesus as the Revealer.

Passing over everything that is not really necessary,[1] it is related that Martha makes[2] her sister go to Jesus (**vv. 28f.**). That she does it secretly[3] cannot be due to the Jews in their enmity lying in wait for Jesus; on the contrary they appear largely as a neutral ὄχλος (v. 42), on whom the act of Jesus has varying results (vv. 45f.). In the economy of the description λάθρᾳ can only have the meaning of differentiating between Mary and the ὄχλος of the Jews, and to direct the reader's attention above all to Mary. For the event itself λάθρᾳ is, of course, without effect, for the presence of the Jews is necessary for the following scene (vv. 33ff.). That the first scene takes place before the κώμη (**v. 30**) similarly serves that differentiation.[4] Mary goes to Jesus—naturally in silent hope, or at least in expectation; the Jews, on the contrary, good-natured but hopeless, think only about the road to the grave (**v. 31**).[5] For them it is a mere accident that they met Jesus.

secretly village

The decisive verse is **v. 32**, in which Mary utters the same words as Martha had also spoken, while Martha's second statement (v. 22) is lacking in Mary's mouth. The former, accordingly, represents the first step of faith, from which her sister advanced. As with Martha, we ought not to say that Mary speaks in a complaining or reproachful fashion. If her words do not express an undefined hope for a miracle, they do at

---

4.42; 6.69, and above all in 20.31, which otherwise is in agreement with 11.27. I Jn. 2.23; 4.15; 5.5 contain only υἱὸς τοῦ θεοῦ.

[1] It is neither reported that Martha took her leave of Jesus, nor that he gave her a charge for her sister (φωνεῖ σε v. 28). It is also not related that Martha again returns to Jesus, although v. 39 presupposes that she is present, because the Evangelist is here interested only in Mary. These inexactitudes (see also on v. 30) are insufficient to demand critical excisions; vv. 28–32 (like vv. 20–27) are entirely compositions of the Evangelist; the Semitic language (cp. Schl.) is characteristic of him.

[2] On ἐφώνησεν . . . εἰποῦσα (instead of λέγουσα) see Bl.-D. §420.2.

[3] On λάθρα or λάθρᾳ see Bl.-D. §26.

[4] Why Jesus in the meantime has not gone further should therefore not be asked. Admittedly the original narrative may have reported differently; see p. 401 n. 3.

[5] Ταχέως v. 31 is no different from ταχύ v. 29, see Bl.-D. §102, 2.—Δόξαντες κτλ is explicable from the custom of weeping at a grave; cp. Wisd. 19.3. Instead of ἵνα κλαύσῃ (on this see Raderm. 154f.) Bl.-D. 390, 4 wish to read with syr[s] Chrys: κλαῦσαι.

any rate frame the expectation that Jesus has some consolation for her. Her haste to come to him shows that.[1] She has not, however, attained to Martha's certainty.[2]

11.33–40.—The miracle of the raising is prepared for in vv. 33–40.[3] The wailing of Mary and of the Jews provokes the height of agitation in Jesus (v. 33). In this context it cannot be otherwise interpreted than his wrath over the lack of faith, expressed in the wailing that is raised about the death of Lazarus[4] in his presence—the presence of the Revealer. For this motif, the faithlessness of the people concerned despite his presence, dominates also vv. 36f. and 39. The absurdity of this lack of faith is laid bare, and in the setting of the miracle story it represents doubt in the power of Jesus to raise the dead. Yet this is really a symbolic picture of the faithlessness that does not understand that the Revealer is the Resurrection and the Life, in whose presence earthly death is void (vv. 25f.).

---

[1] In this sense there is a certain parallel in the passage already cited by Wetst., Cic. in Verr. V 49, 129: mihi obviam venit et ita me suam salutem appellans . . . filii nomen implorans mihi ad pedes misera iacuit, quasi ego eius excitare ab inferis filium possem.

[2] In reverse to this Hirsch sees Martha (whose answer in v. 27 he ignores) as the "type of the common ecclesiastical Christianity with a Judaistic admixture", while in the adoring and silent Mary "the Christian attitude to suffering and death is depicted" (I 290f.).

[3] At v. 33 the Evangelist takes up again the source he had left at v. 20. In this (the already edited σημεῖα-source, see p. 395 n. 4) v. 33 followed on v. 19, and v. 33 began: 'I, οὖν ὡς εἶδεν αὐτὰς κλαιούσας κτλ. How far the Evangelist edited vv. 30–40 cannot be said with certainty. V. 33 is wholly derived from the σημεῖα-source (see the following note) and similarly v. 34. Vv. 35–37 closely hang together and refer back to ch. 9; such a reference would not be unthinkable in the σημεῖα-source; yet the verses have the effect of an interpolation, after which (in v. 38) the connection with v. 34 is taken up again through πάλιν ἐμβρ, ἐν ἑαυτ. Thus vv. 35–37 are derived from the Evangelist, who wishes to strengthen the chief motif (see above in the text). V. 40 naturally comes from the Evangelist, while v. 38 (to πάλιν . . . ἑαυτ.) belongs to the source.

[4] Br. asks whether there is a polemic here against the wailing for the dead that is characteristic of the Jews, analogous to the polemic of the Mandaeans and Manichees. In truth there is a certain analogy, but the polemic is to be interpreted in the sense of the Evangelist. In the source however the ἐνεβριμ. κτλ had a quite different meaning: the spiritual ("pneumatic") arousal of the θεῖος ἄνθρωπος was described; cp. 13.21 and C. Bonner Harv. Theol. Rev. 20 (1927), 171–180: ἐμβριμᾶσθαι and ταράσσειν are, like στενάζειν (cp. Mk. 2.34; Rom. 8.26 etc.) used as voces mysticae (cp. also the μανία and the ταραχθῆναι of the recipient of revelation C. Herm. 13.4, 6). Otherwise ἐμβριμ. (with dat. or absolutely) is used in the sense of "let fly at (a person), be angry". And if here also, in the Evangelist's meaning, the strong emotion of wrath is signified, that does not fit the ἐτάραξεν ἑαυτ., which can only designate the spirit-inspired ("pneumatic") excitement. The strong emotion therefore is intended as self-produced, but certainly not in opposition to the Stoic ideal of ataraxy, as ancient and modern exegetes think; see Br.—τῷ πνεύμ. with ἐνεβριμ. is fully synonymous with ἐν ἑαυτῷ v. 38; it is a semitism, cp. Mk. 8.12. On the early exegesis see Br.; on Calvin and Godet: M. Dominicé L'humanité de Jésus d'après Calvin 1933, 208f. Attempts to explain the remarkable ἐνεβρ. τ. πνεύμ. και ἐτάρ. ἑαυτόν as translation semitisms may be seen in de Zwaan, JBL 57 (1938), 162f. and Black 174–177. Cod. D weakens the sense in reading: ἐταράχθη τῷ πνεύματι ὡς ἐμβριμούμενος.

Jesus now allows himself to be led to the grave (**v. 34**).[1] The statement that he wept (**v. 35**)—where the weeping must be understood as a sign of agitation in the sense of v. 33—has hardly any other purpose than to provoke[2] the utterance of the Jews (**vv. 36f.**),[3] and so to set in a yet brighter light the motif of the faithlessness in the presence of the Revealer.[4] Jesus—again in that anger over the faithless—comes to the grave,[5] which is blocked up by a stone (**v. 38**). His command to remove the stone provokes the objection of Martha (**v. 39**)[6]; again it brings to consciousness that motif,[7] and Jesus thrusts it aside with the reminder of his earlier word to Martha (**v. 40**). He had promised her the resurrection of her brother (v. 23), even if in the light of vv. 25f. this can only be a symbol for the real experience of faith.[8]

11.41–44.—Thus prepared, the narrative of the miracle now follows,[9] the character of which is made plain from the beginning—in the Evangelist's sense—by **vv. 41f.** Jesus directs his gaze to heaven for prayer,[10] but he utters no request; he gives thanks for the hearing

---

[1] The reflection of the early exegetes (see Br.), how the omniscient can ask questions, is foolish. The narrative is naive, like Gen. 3.9; 18.9, where accounts are given of God's questions to man.

[2] On the reflections of the early exegesis, see Br.

[3] For the interchange between ἔλεγον and εἶπαν see Bl.-D §329.

[4] V. 36 relates to vv. 3 and 5, v. 37 to the healing narrative of ch. 9. Vv. 35–37 presumably are derived from the Evangelist, see p. 406 n. 3.

[5] The σπήλαιον shows that a grave is in mind in the style of the Jewish rock graves, as they are described in the Mishna; see Str.-B. I 1049–51 on Mt. 27.60.

[6] The description of Martha as ἀδελφὴ τ. τετ. (struck out in syr[s]. θ al) certainly does not show that she is here considered as the only sister of Lazarus (Wellh.); but it is likely that, since few details about the sisters can have been given in the source, vv. 20–32 go back to the Evangelist (see p. 395 n. 4); their statement does not at all suit the upshot of the dialogue in vv. 20–27. On τεταρταῖος (only here in the NT. see Br.) see p. 400 n. 8. With ἤδη ὄζει the narrator manifestly does not take thought on the fact that according to v. 44 the deceased was embalmed.

[7] In the source, from which the Evangelist certainly took v. 39 (see p. 401 n. 3), the motive was different: the παράδοξον of the miracle must be heightened; cp. Theod. Mops. (in Mr.) and Wendland, Literaturformen 240 or 306.

[8] The formulation of v. 40 is not the same as v. 23; this surely can only be to stress that God's δόξα is manifest in the miracle; cp. v. 4.

[9] As v. 40, so vv. 41f. come from the Evangelist; that is seen by their theological content, their terminology (ἵνα πιστ. . . . ἀπέστειλας cp. 6.29; 17.3, 8, 21 and elsewhere) and their style (on the characteristic ἀλλὰ . . . ἵνα cp. 1.8, 31; 3.17; 9.3; 11.52; 12.9, 47; 14.31; 17.15 and esp. 13.18; 15.25; see also p. 48 n. 3). To the source only ἦραν οὖν τὸν λίθον v. 41 belongs; v. 43 joined on to that, and from it only (καὶ) ταῦτα εἰπών is to be taken out, and to it perhaps the subj. Ἰησοῦς (οὖν) should be added.

[10] Cp. 17.1. In Ps. 123.1 the worshipper directs his eyes to God in heaven (Ps. 121.1 to the mountains). In Judaism the raising of the eyes in prayer is seldom mentioned, but occasionally it is presupposed, as Mk. 6.41 parr., Lk. 18.13 show; on this Str.-B II. 246; G. Harder, Paulus und das Gebet 1936, 7, 5. According to Philo Vit. Mos. I 190 the διάνοια of the pious has learned ἄνω βλέπειν τε καὶ ὁρᾶν. See Hom. Il. 15, 232; 24, 307; Cicero Somn. Scip. 1. On the address in prayer πάτερ see Str.-B I 392; Schl. on Mt. 11.25; Moore II 208; Schrenk ThWB IV 980f., 984f., 1003f. Hosk discusses the question in detail and is right.

already granted (v. 41). It thus appears that the Son of God does not need to make a request in prayer; and precisely this appears to be stressed in v. 42: since the Son is constantly sure of the Father's hearing, he never needs to make request; if he prayed on this occasion it was only for the sake of the people present, "that they might grasp faith" that God sent him. To what extent can they do that when they see him pray? Since they would see the miracle in any case, even if he had not prayed, the meaning must be that they can rightly understand his miracle only if they understand it as a gift of God to him; that is, if they grasp that he is no magician, no θεῖος ἀνήρ, who works by his own power and seeks his own δόξα (7.18; 8.50), but the one whom God sent, and who does nothing of himself, but does only that which the Father has given him to do.[1]

Jesus' prayer therefore is the demonstration of that which he has constantly said about himself, that he is nothing of himself. But does it not thereby become a spectacle, a farce? It is obvious that Jesus' words in vv. 41f. are not heard by the bystanders; they only see his attitude of prayer, and in this situation they must understand his prayer as one of request. Are they deceived? No, for it is the request of one who stands in perfect unity with the Father.[2] That he stands before God as one who asks is shown by the fact that the Father's attitude to him is described as ἀκούειν (ἤκουσάς μου); if he knows that the Father constantly hears him (πάντοτέ μου ἀκούεις), it is implied by that he, the Son, never steps out of the attitude of the asker, but continually holds fast to it. For this reason he does not need to be quickened out of a prayerless attitude to make petition by reason of a particular act; rather when, in a particular situation, he recalls to consciousness his relation to God, as that of one who makes request, his request must immediately change to thanks. For he who knows himself to be perpetually in the attitude of a petitioner before God cannot do other than recognise himself as a man to whom God perpetually gives gifts. But correspondingly he cannot know himself as one perpetually heard if he does not know himself as one perpetually asking. The character of his communion with God is clearly delineated by this: he does not need to make prayer requests like others, who have to rouse themselves out of their attitude of prayerlessness and therefore godlessness; for he continually stands before God as the asker and therefore as the receiver.[3] In him that

---

[1] See p. 401f. on v. 22; further p. 249 n. 1.

[2] Lütgert, Joh. Christol. 90ff. understands Jn. 11.41f. correctly; only the analysis ought to be sharper. Cp. J. M. Nielen, Gebet. u. Gottesdienst im NT 1937, 18f., and Hosk. ad loc.

[3] Is. 65.24 (καὶ ἔσται πρὶν κεκράξαι αὐτοὺς ἐγὼ ὑπακούσομαι αὐτῶν κτλ.) is no parallel, for there it is not the one who prays, but God who is described.

which is promised to his followers as eschatological possibility is realised.[1] The demonstration of his prayer therefore consists simply in this, that he *shows* himself as the one who he *is*; and at the same time, doubtless, he gives the possibility of misunderstanding, of appearing as another.[2] But it is in this continual provocation of misunderstanding that he ever moves.

Now at last Jesus speaks the word[3] that effects the miracle, and he calls Lazarus out of the grave (**v. 43**)[4]. The coming forth of one who is still wrapped up in bands (**v. 44**)[5] is itself a minor miracle.[6] The final statement of Jesus has the significance of demonstrating the return to ordinary life[7] of the one who has been raised. The effect of the miracle is not described, and in particular no further mention is made of the sisters. The Evangelist has passed over whatever related to this in the source, or has utilised it in v. 45. He has in fact, set the story in a larger context, as is seen in the next section.

c) The decision of the Sanhedrin that Jesus must die: 11.45-54[8]

As in 7.43; 9.16; 10.19, the effect of the miracle is divisive (**vv. 45f.**)[9] Nevertheless the author's concern here is not to describe the σχίσμα,

---

[1] Cp. 14.13; 15.7, 16; 16.23f.; 1 Jn. 3.21f.; 5.14f. In *this* sense it is correct that the attitude of Jesus in vv. 41f. is "not human"; it is correct in so far as eschatological existence is no longer (merely) human. For this reason, however, it is untrue that his praying has become an "appearance" (Wrede, Charakter und Tendenz 46f.) or "only an accommodation to human forms" (Htm.). Rather it is the praying that springs from a relation to God that provides both a norm for judging every human relationship and the eschatological goal.

[2] This demonstration is imitated in the dying prayer of Thomas, act. Thom. 167, p. 282, 3f.; ταῦτα δὲ λέγω οὐκ ἐνδοιάζων, ἀλλ' ὅπως ἀκούσωσιν οὓς ἀκοῦσαι χρή.

[3] The saying is characterised as inspired through φωνῇ μεγ. ἐκραύγ.; see p. 75 n. 1 and Ign. Philad. 7.1: ἐκραύγασα . . . μεγάλῃ φωνῇ, θεοῦ φωνῇ.

[4] Vv. 43f. are derived from the source, see p. 407 n. 9.

[5] On κειρία = bands and σουδ. (a loan word from the Latin) = handkerchief, see Br. ad loc. and lexicon; and for κειρ, see also Raderm. 12; ὄψις here (other than in 7.24) means face, as in Rev. 1.16 and often. On the original significance of binding up the dead (securing against their coming back), see L. Radermacher, Philologus 65 (1906), 147f.; J. Scheftelowitz, Das Schlingen- und Netzmotiv im Glauben und Brauch der Völker 1912, 27; Fr. Pfister, Wochenschrift für klass. Philol. 1914, 918f. According to Str.-B bands for winding round the hands and feet appear not to be mentioned in Rabbinic literature, but the handkerchief is.

[6] It is so understood in early exegesis, see Br.

[7] See Gesch. der synopt. Tr. 240 = Hist. of the Syn. Tr. 224f.

[8] J. Finegan (Die Überlieferung der Leidens- und Auferstehungsgeschichte Jesu 1934, 40f.) rightly considers vv. 45–54 as a Johannine composition that has no source behind it. The style of the Evangelist is plain: as to ὅτι see vv. 47f.; 7.35; 8.22; for ὤν v. 49; 1.18; 7.50; 10.33; 12.17; 18.26: for τοῦτο δὲ . . . εἶπεν vv. 51f. see p. 212 n. 4; for οὐκ . . . ἀλλά v. 51 and 52f. see p. 48 n. 3; for ἀλλ' ἵνα vv. 52f. see p. 407 n. 9. Eisler's supposition is fantastic, Ἰησ. βασ. II 232.1, that the source for this section is the "Logia" of Matthew. But neither can I share Goguel's belief in an early tradition that he considers to have been

but to show how the unbelieving[1] Jews denounce[2] Jesus to the authorities, and so occasion the development of the action. It is precisely unbelief that unwittingly and unintentionally must precipitate the δοξασθῆναι of Jesus, as v. 51 will make yet more clear.

The high priests and Pharisees[3] call a session of the Sanhedrin,[4] and they are at a loss[5] in face of the undeniable miracles of Jesus (**v. 47**).[6] If he is allowed to carry on, the Romans will step in and blot out the existence of the nation.[7] This consideration (**v. 48**) shows that the authorities are aware that to believe on Jesus means to acknowledge his messianic claim; but it also shows that the authorities are no more capable of grasping the meaning of this claim than the people were who wanted to make Jesus king (6.15; cp. 12.12f.). They are dominated by the idea which they urge before Pilate in 19.12, for they do not the understand that the βασιλεία of Jesus is not ἐκ τοῦ κόσμου τούτου.[8]

This blindness reaches its peak in the proposal of the chairman Caiaphas,[9] the high priest of that year (**vv. 49f.**).[10] The words of rebuke

---

worked over here (Introd. II 430ff.; Jesus 464), any more than Dodd's view, that vv. 47–53 are a piece of tradition.

[9] On v. 45: the nom. οἱ ἐλθόντες instead of the gen. is bad; on ἐπίστ. κτλ see p. 130 n. 3.

[1] So syr[s] rightly characterises τινές.

[2] For the Pharisees as authorities, see p. 86 n. 6; 306 n. 5.

[3] Ἀρχιερ. and φαρ. together, as 7.32,45; see p. 306 n. 5.

[4] On the Sanhedrin as the highest Jewish authority and its membership, see Klostermann on Mk. 8.31 (Hdb. zum NT); Schürer II 237–267; Str.-B. I 997–1001. The plural ἀρχιερεῖς is frequent and includes the officiating high priest, his predecessors in office and the members of the high-priestly families.

[5] τί ποιοῦμεν is obviously a deliberative question; the indic. pres. instead of the subj. or the indic. fut. is only seldom met (Bl.-D §366; Raderm. 155; various witnesses correspondingly correct).

[6] Ὅτι is elliptical, as in 7.35 (?); 8.22: "we so ask because . . . ."

[7] τόπος can mean either the city of Jerusalem (syr., Chrys. t. VIII 386e) or, more probably, the temple; cp. Acts 6.13f., 7.7; 2 Macc. 3.12, 18, 30; 3 Macc. 1.9; 2.14; rabb. lit. in Schl. ad loc. The Jewish people here, as not infrequently (Br.), is called ἔθνος instead of λαός as in v. 50. The gen. ἡμῶν represents the sympathet. dat., Bl.-D. §284.1.

[8] In the Slav. Jos. (Kl. Text 11[2], p. 22) the viewpoint represented in Jn. II.48 is combined with that given in 18.36.

[9] On εἷς τις = a certain, see Bl.-D. §301, 1. Καϊάφας (קַיָּפָא) was in office 18–36 A.D. (Schürer II 271). He is named as High Priest in the trial of Jesus in Mt. 26.3, 57, but not in Mk. and Lk.; he appears elsewhere in Lk. 3.2, Acts 4.6, and in Jn. 18.13f., 24, 28.

[10] τοῦ ἐνιαυτ. ἐκ. is hardly a temporal gen. with the meaning "in, within" (Bl.-D. §186, 2; cp. A. Bischoff, ZNTW 9 (1908) 166f. against Zn.); obviously it means "(High Priest) of that year", and so it presupposes that the person of the High Priest changed annually, as was the case with pagan high-priestly officials in Syria and Asia Minor (see Br.). The Evangelist therefore, as his understanding of the Pharisees also shows (see p. 306 n. 5) is mistakenly oriented about Jewish legal relationships, for the Jewish High Priest was chosen for life. Even if account be taken of the fact that in that period the High Priests were often in office for a shorter time, owing to frequent deposition through the Romans (Schürer II 268ff.), the mode of statement is not satisfactory, since Caiaphas, in distinction from his

with which his proposition is introduced sets the blindness crassly in the light: it is precisely the cleverness and deliberation that find acceptance in this world and always knows a way out that here lead to destruction. An issue that cannot be comprised under political categories is judged as if it were a political question. Political sagacity requires that the lesser evil be preferred to the greater, and it demands that the fundamental principle be put into effect that the individual be sacrificed in the interest of the nation.[1] Of a truth this statement is to be validated in a very different sense from that which Caiaphas intended (**vv. 51f.**); and so in the light of a tragic irony the latter appears as a prophet against his knowledge and intention.[2] There will indeed be a fulfilment of what he said, for Jesus is to die for his people, and also for the children of God who are scattered in all the world.[3] That which political astuteness

---

predecessors, officiated for a particularly lengthy time. Eisler, Ἰησ. βασ. I 127, 2; II 776 attempts to justify John's statement historically. According to de Zwaan ἐνιαυτοῦ is a poor translation instead of ἔτους. The meaning is: "who in that significant year was High Priest"; so also Barr.

[1] Συμφέρει with ἵνα instead of inf. as in 16.7; Mt. 5.29f.; 18.6; see Bl.-D §393, 1; Schl. on Mt. 5.29; on the evasion of the comparative see Raderm. 69. ὑπέρ here means "in place of"; so also v. 52, though in this case it carries at the same time the implication "in favour of". For the maxim of Caiaphas see 2 Sam. 20.20–22; Jon. 1.12–15; Jos. bell 11, 103ff. The principle is explicitly formulated in the passages in the commentaries of Merx, Schl. and Str.-B ad loc., see further Dalman, Jesus-Jeschua 157. For the same principle in Greek and Latin literature, see Windisch on 2 Cor. 5.14 (Meyer's Komm.), and as a proverb see Türkische Märchen (Märchen der Weltliteratur) 199.

[2] Cp. 7.35; 8.22. That it belongs to a prophet's calling not to speak ἀφ' ἑαυτοῦ see p. 187f. The Greek world also is acquainted with the view that a man under certain circumstances does not speak or act ἀφ' ἑαυτοῦ, but is inspired by a god to word or deed (see the examples in Br., in which however the moment of tragic irony is lacking; on these see P. Friedländer, Die Antike I [1925], 17, 305). But the Greek idea would not have further motivated here the unconscious prophecy; had it been so the irony would have lain in the planning of the individual as being at the mercy of the dark power of fate (cp. Plut. de fato 7, p. 572c). On the other hand the Evangelist bases the prophecy on the fact that Caiaphas was the High Priest; i.e. it was due to the inspiration attaching to his *office*. Accordingly the Jewish examples for unconscious prophecy (Str.-B.) are also unsatisfactory parallels. It is hardly likely that the main idea prompting the Evangelist was that the High Priest once gave oracles through Urim and Thummim (Ex. 28.30; Lev. 8.8; Num. 27.21; Jos. ant. 6, 115; according to 3,218 it no longer applies to the present); for John Hyrcanus it appears that προφητεία is not given with the office but is something special, in addition to it (Jos. bell. 1, 68f.); the examples in Schlatter prove nothing for the connection between office and prophetic inspiration. E. Bammel (ThLZ 79 (1954), 351–356) does show that in Rabbinic thought the tradition of the prophetic character of the high-priestly office was a living one. That appears also to be attested through the Hab.-Commentary (1 QpH) 10.9; see K. Elliger, Studien Z. Habakuk-Kommentar vom Toten Meer 1953, 209. It is probable that the Hellenistic view is at the root of the concept in John, expressed by Philo in Spec. leg. IV 192: . . . ἐπειδὴ καὶ ὁ πρὸς ἀλήθειαν ἱερεὺς εὐθύς ἐστι προφήτης, οὐ γένει μᾶλλον ἢ ἀρετῇ παρεληλυθὼς ἐπὶ τὴν τοῦ ὄντος θεραπείαν, προφήτῃ δ' οὐδὲν ἄγνωστον. On priest-prophets in Hellenistic Egypt see E. Fascher, προφήτης 1927, 76–93; F. Cumont, Die orientalische Rel. im. Röm. Heidentum[3] 1931, 81, 87; Br., excursus on 1.21; but cp. also Lohmeyer, Urchristentum 1 163f.

[3] Noack 135f. wishes to interpret the ὅτι in v. 51 not as recitative but as as causal. Fridrichsen is much too ingenious in reading out of v. 52 that Israel should be the

will lead the worldly authority to do is going to have to serve not their own will but the accomplishment of God's will, as Jesus had already declared in 10.17f.[1]

The decision that Jesus must die, which was long ago purposed (5.18; 7.1; 8.40, 59; 10.31), is now at last taken (**v. 53**). But it is not possible to carry it out immediately, for in the meantime Jesus has gone into retreat,[2] and he stays with his disciples in Ephraim (**v. 54**).[3] V. 57 shows how the authorities set about pursuing their end.

B. 11.55–12.33; 8.30–40; 6.60–71: The Way to the Cross[4]

a) The Entry into Jerusalem: 11.55–12.19

11.55–12.19 form a connected composition, consisting of various fragments. 11.55–57 is a neutral description, creating a pause between the events. But since the intermission is filled with questioning and allusion to the threat that lies ahead, awakening thereby a sense of tension, the fragment at the same time serves as an introduction to what follows. The story of the anointing 12.1–8 brings Jesus into the neighbourhood of Jerusalem. It assists the connection of the action, since Jesus' presence in Bethany is the occasion for the ὄχλος streaming in, and so it inevitably hastens the catastrophe (vv. 9–11). At the same time, however, it has the effect on the reader of a retarding pause, and yet in such a manner as to create a foreboding of what is coming (v. 7).—The entry 12.12–19, with its contrast between the jubilation of the people (vv. 12–18) and the mood of the authorities (v. 19), forms the high point of the narrative. Through its being placed between vv. 10f. and 19, with their foreboding of evil, it is set in the light in which it should be seen:

---

instrument of salvation for the whole world (B. Sundkler, A. Fridrichsen, Arbeiten und Mitteilungen aus dem neutest. Seminar zu Uppsala VI 1937, 40f.).

[1] Συνάγειν εἰς ἕν is a Greek expression; see Br. On the content see p. 384 n. 2; esp. Od. Sol. 10.5f., on which see Burney 169; Did. 9.4, on which see Knopf (Hdb. zum NT, Ergänzungsbd.).

[2] On παρρησίᾳ see p. 291 n. 1. Montgomery regards ἐν τ. Ἰουδαίοις as a mistranslation for ἐν τ. Ἰουδαίᾳ; see Colwell 115f.

[3] Εἰς Ἐφρ. λεγ. πόλιν: the use of λεγ. (cp. 19.17) as in papyri; see Colwell 41. Ephraim is of uncertain identification, see Br.; according to Dalman, O.u.W. 231ff. the village now called et-taijibe is meant, about seven kilometers northeast of Bethel. Chrys. t. VIII 390c reads Ἐφρατά; D reads ἀπῆλθεν εἰς τὴν χώραν Σαμφουρεῖν (= Sepphoris) ἐγγὺς τῆς ἐρήμου εἰς Ἐφραὶμ λεγομένην πόλιν. Cp. also Kundsin 49f. According to Wellh. the flight of Jesus 11.54 is a doublet of 10.40; the statement 10.40 stands in its right place, factually however 11.54 is to be preferred, since it reports an actual journey; the statement is a fragment of the foundational document, to which however 11.55–57 as little belongs as 11.45–53. This criticism (with its consequences) is prompted by the prepossession about a foundational document in the Gospel. In fact 11.54 is as schematic as 10.40. On the legal situation presupposed, see E. Bickermann, Rev. de l'Hist. des Rel. 112 (1935), 213f.: after the decision of the Sanhedrin Jesus flees; thereupon the προγραφή is decreed (v. 57).

[4] On the character of the entire section see pp. 392f.

it is exactly the messianic entry that leads Jesus to his death; and it reveals a misunderstanding, in so far as the people that joyfully surround Jesus as their king falsely understand the messianic claim (as 6.15). And yet this is completely right: the Revealer continually has to call forth misunderstanding in order to achieve his work. And therefore this way that leads to death is exactly the way that leads to perfection; and so Jesus really does enter Jerusalem as the eschatological King, though in another sense than is apparent.

The section is composed with great artistry, but in reality it has used familiar traditions. Doubtless 11.55–57 are the Evangelist's own composition (see below); in 12.1–8 he appears to recount the story of the anointing on the basis of a written source, which he edited and enlarged with vv. 9–11 (see below). He seems also to have used a written source in 12.12–19 and enriched it with additions (see below). Whereas in the Synoptics the anointing follows the entry into Jerusalem, the order is reversed in John. Possibly this is due to the Evangelist finding the two stories in this order in his source, but he himself may have seen a deeper meaning in it: the story of the anointing is a prophecy of the passion which has its real beginning with the entry into Jerusalem.[1]

1) *Introduction:* 11.55–57[2]

The verses describe the situation awaiting Jesus when he comes to Jerusalem. **V. 55** makes the chronological statement that the passover feast is impending;[3] the pilgrims are streaming to Jerusalem, and that early enough to undertake the necessary Levitical purifications.[4] The city therefore is full of pilgrims to the feast, and their reflections (**v. 56**) describe the situation from its inward aspect. As at the feast of Tabernacles (7.11–13), so now also the crowd is occupied with the question, "Will Jesus come?" People incline to the opinion: "Certainly not! For everybody knows— so **v. 57** in this context is to be understood[5]—that

---

[1] Somewhat differently Htm: the dying Jesus (for such the story of the anointing indicates him) must be presented before the triumphant Jesus (which the entry shows him to be).

[2] The introduction is an editorial composition of the Evangelist's. For ἦν δὲ ἐγγύς with a following announcement of a feast, see 2.13; 6.4; 7.2. The statement of time follows καὶ . . . as in 2.13; 5.1; 10.22; pc. 3.22. Ἐζήτουν οὖν καὶ ἔλεγον corresponds to 7.11; τί ὑμῖν δοκεῖ; reflects the habit of Semitic colloquial speech (Schl. ad loc and on Mt. 17.25). On δεδώκεισαν δὲ . . . ἵνα ἐάν τις . . . cp. 9.22 (see p. 335 n. 5).

[3] On τὸ πάσχα τῶν Ἰουδ. see pp. 86 n. 2.

[4] Cp. Ex. 19.10f.; Num. 9.10; 2 Chron. 30.17f.; Str.-B . ad loc., cp. also 18.28. Ἁγνίζειν for cultic lustrations as in LXX (Br.) and Acts 21.24, 26; 24.18; often in Josephus (Schl.). Cp. E. Williger, Hagios 1922, 62f.

[5] From the danger that threatens Jesus the multitude concludes that he will not come. Whether their considerations are also supported by the observation that "Jesus does not show himself among those who obtain cleansing for themselves" (Schl.) is irrelevant.

the authorities[1] have given command for his arrest."[2] The anticipation therefore is aroused for what is to follow.

2) *The Anointing in Bethany:* 12.1–8[3]

Vv. 1f. announce the situation: the incident takes place six days[4] before the Passover,[5] in Bethany at a banquet.[6] It is not said who the host is.[7] It is simply reported that Mary anoints the feet of Jesus and wipes them with her hair (**v. 3**). The depth of her devotion is made plain in a naive fashion by emphasising the amount and the expense of the ointment;[8] and her humility is indicated by the fact that she does

---

[1] Their designation as in 11.47. For the situation see p. 412 n. 3. On the relation of the anointing stories Jn. 12.1–8 and Lk. 7.36–50 see J. H. Sanders. NtSt 1. (1954/55), 29–41.

[2] Ὅπως is not elsewhere used in Jn and it is infrequent in the New Testament generally; here it serves to avoid a double ἵνα; Bl-D §369, 4; Raderm. 203.

[3] The narrative, like its parallels Mk. 14. 3–9 = Mt. 26. 6–13, belongs to the biographical apophthegms (Gesch. der syn. Tr. 37 = Hist. of the Syn. Trad. 36f.). It is shown to be a secondary variant 1. by the mention of the persons by name (vv. 2f., 4), 2. by the elimination of the point of the story (see on vv. 6–8); 3. by the introduction of the motif of the support of the poor (see p. 415 n. 8). The Evangelist's source was neither Mk. nor Mt. (so also Goodenough 152ff.); for manifestly he was not the first to introduce Martha in v. 2 and to identify the anointing woman, who is still nameless in Mk. and Mt., with Mary, but he found this representation in his source. Otherwise it would be a matter for surprise that he ascribes the chief role to Mary and not, as in ch. 11, to Martha. Above all however he would doubtless have stated that the meal took place in the house of Lazarus, and the latter would have been characterised as the brother of Martha and Mary (or they as his sisters). It could be viewed as conspicuous that Martha and Mary are not introduced, but obviously acquaintance with them is presupposed as 11.1, and in fact the role of Martha corresponds to the narrative of Lk. 10.40. On the other hand ὅπου ἦν κτλ., which links on to ch. 11, is derived from the Evangelist, and similarly in v. 2 the sentence ὁ δὲ Λάζαρος κτλ. See also n. 5, 7 below, 415 n. 7.

[4] On πρὸ ἐξ ἡμ. τ. πάσχα, which has analogies in LXX, Josephus and other Hellenistic writers, as also in inscriptions and papyri, see Br. and Bl.-D §213; p. 397f.

[5] Possibly the source already contained this statement of time; for as Mk. and Mt. show, the story was early bound up with the Passion narrative. Whether the Evangelist had in mind a fixed reckoning of the days is doubtful. At all events the calculation cannot certainly be known, for we do not know whether the Passover day is to be reckoned as the 14th (cp. 18.28) or the 15th Nisan, or whether it should be included in the calculation or not. Accordingly the 8th to 10th Nisan are all possible.

[6] Δεῖπνον ποιεῖν as in Mk. 6.21; Lk. 14.12, 16; also LXX and papyri, see Br. (= Arndt and Gingrich) lexicon.

[7] According to Mk. 14.3 par. the meal takes place in the house of Simon "the Leper". It is hard to believe that the Evangelist struck out this statement. If it originally belonged to the tradition, it could have been eliminated when the persons of Martha and Mary were brought into the story. It should now be clearly understood that Jesus is a guest with the sisters, as in Lk. 10.38–42. According to Sanders (see on p. 397 n. 1) op. cit. 39, Simon is the father of Martha and Mary and Lazarus.

[8] Λίτρα only here and 19.39 in the New Testament (also in papyri and Jos. ant. 14, 106 and elsewhere; see Br. lexicon); it corresponds to the Roman pound (libra), which in time of the Caesars was 327.45 gr. (Br.), while Str.B., following Rabbinic statements, reckon it as 273 gr. The amount is extravagant, cp. Hug in Pauly-Wiss., Real. Enc. second series I.2, col. 1860. Μυρ. νάρδου πιστικῆς (= ointment of genuine nard, see Klostermann on Mk. 14.3 in the Hdb. zum NT) as Mk. 14.3; πολυτίμου as Mt. 26.7 ℵ A.D.Θ, while Mk. 14.3

not anoint the head of Jesus, but his feet.[1] The fragrance of the ointment fills the house—a feature intended both to describe the magnificence of the occasion,[2] and also to have a symbolic significance: the εὐωδία τῆς γνώσεως will at once fill the whole world.[3]

In any case the deeper significance that this act of homage has for Jesus is made plain by what follows. In this respect the original point of the narrative is all too briefly expressed, namely that this extravagant act of love,[4] even when contrasted with reasonable and purposeful beneficence, has its own special value. Naturally this idea is not entirely wanting. The reflection that the wasted money would have been better used in helping the poor (**v. 5**)[5]—in Mk spoken by τινές, in Mt. by the μαθηταί—is here put into the mouth of Judas (**v. 4**).[6] In so far as the Evangelist has subordinated the motif,[7] by characterising Judas (as in 6.71) as the future betrayer, and by stating that he did not honestly mean it but merely deplored that the money had eluded him (**v.6**),[8] he has to this extent destroyed the real point. And that is even more emphasised by the fact that the saying of Jesus referring to v. 5 is only dragged in at **v. 8**. If, as is likely, v. 8 is really a marginal gloss that

---

reads πολυτελοῦς. Perhaps πολυτιμ. first entered the text from Mt. as v. 8, see below. νάρδου omitted in D it.

[1] That she anoints the feet certainly has significance (see in the text); anointing the feet of a guest is also attested in Rabbinic literature (Str.-B.I 427f.; cp. also Aristoph. Vesp. 609). Meanwhile the statement could go back to the influence of Lk. 7.38, where it is related that the woman who came with ointment wetted the feet of Jesus with her overflowing tears and dried them with her hair. For the motive of the drying of the feet is explained only in the Lucan context. Is καὶ ἐξέμαξεν κτλ a secondary addition? The repetition of τ. πόδας could hint of that; cp. Schwartz (1908, 178).

[2] In the source this was certainly the only meaning.

[3] So repeatedly the older exegetes; see Br.—Ign. Eph. 17.1 (διὰ τοῦτο μύρον ἔλαβεν ἐπὶ τῆς κεφαλῆς αὐτοῦ ὁ κύριος, ἵνα πνέῃ τῇ ἐκκλησίᾳ ἀφθαρσίαν goes back to the Mk-Mt. Version. Cp. also 2. Cor. 2.14f.; Nestle, SNTW 4 (1903), 272; 7 (1906), 95f.; E. Lohmeyer Vom göttlichen Wohlgeruch, SAHeidelb. 10 (1919) Abh. 9.

[4] See Gesch. der syn. Tr. 37 = Hist. of the Syn. Trad. 36f. According to J. Jeremias, ZNTW 35 (1936), 75–82, the point of the story lies in the fact that in place of the alternative alms or luxury Jesus set alms or work of love; the Rabbinic distinction between alms and work of love is the presupposition for this.

[5] The formulation essentially corresponds to Mk. 14.5, especially the declaration as to the price, which is lacking in Mt. 26.9.

[6] It corresponds to the tendency of the tradition to name anonymous persons; cp. Gesch. der syn. Tr. 71f., 256f., 338 = Hist. of the Syn. Trad. 67f., 241f., 310.

[7] V. 6 is a composition of the Evangelist's. On οὐχ . . . ἀλλ' see p. 48 n. 3. Γλωσσόκομον = cash-box only here and 13.29 in the New Testament. On the Hellenistic word (also in LXX and Josephus) see Br. Lexicon; it also penetrated as a loan word into Rabbinic literature (Schl., Str.-B.). Βάλλειν εἰς γλ. is also attested.

[8] Κλέπτης shows that βαστάζειν must be understood in the frequently attested sense of pilfer, steal (Br.). It is then presupposed that the disciple group receives and distributes gifts for the poor, hence perhaps the custom reflected in Acts 4.37 or in later church use.

entered the text at a later date,[1] it becomes all the clearer that the narrative is actually concerned with the other point, also appended to the early story in Mk and Mt: the anointing of Jesus is an anticipation of the anointing of his dead body (**v. 7**).[2] If the story in John did conclude with this saying, it stands at the head of the narrative that follows as an impressive prophecy; it thus forms a contrast-parallel to the prophecy of Caiaphas. Like this enemy, the woman disciple did more than she realised.

3) *A Bridge Passage:* 12.9–11[3]

The purpose of vv. 9–11 comes to light in vv. 10f.: it is to sound out the persecution motif that runs right through the whole section (11.53, 57; 12.10f. 19). **V. 9** has the significance of providing a motivation; in its light it is comprehensible that the ὄχλος of v. 9 is opposed to that of v. 12, which is derived from the source (see below). By the ὄχλος mentioned in v. 9 is meant the πολλοὶ ἐκ τῶν 'Ιουδαίων of 11.19, as v. 17 shows; these are the people who stream to Bethany when they hear the news that Jesus is there again,[4] and they are driven by curiosity. It is this concourse of people that occasions the decision of the authorities (**vv. 10f.**), a decision which goes even beyond that of 11.53; Lazarus

---

[1] V. 8 is lacking in D b.r. syr^s; it corresponds (with transposition of the first words) precisely to Mt. 26.11.

[2] That is the clear meaning of Mk. 14.8; Mt. 26.12. In John the formulation is hardly comprehensible, yet it can have no other meaning. One can only translate: "Leave her! she must keep it for the day of my burial". (B. Weiss: "that she preserved it"; Bl.: "she should have saved it" are equally improbable). That is, Mary should keep the rest of the ointment for the burial. (Unlike Mk. 14.3 she does not break the vessel in pieces; see Schwartz). But then it is said that Jesus is already anointed with the ointment for the burial, or that the intention of this anointing finds its fulfilment at his burial. It is comprehensible that copyists have corrected the text; in the *Koine* and pm ἵνα is struck out and τετήρηκεν is written for τηρήσῃ. P. Schmiedel conjectures ποιήσῃ instead of τηρήσῃ, following Mt. 26.12. Torrey (343) assumes a mistranslation: after ἄφες αὐτήν the imperfect followed, intended as a question: "should she keep it for the day of my burial?" This would give a good sense, which could also be obtained through the conjecture ἵνα τί = why? So Kühne, Th.StKr 1926, 476f. De Zwaan also supposes a mistranslation here. Strathm. translates: "she has preserved it"; Wik.: "she should preserve it". Dodd (370) makes no decision. Barr. proposes the choice: "Let her remember, when my body is consigned to the grave without due care, that she has anointed it by anticipation"—or (since τηρεῖν = remember is very doubtful), "Let her observe the last rite *now*, with a view to the day of my burial".

[3] Vv. 9–11 are a composition of the Evangelist's. On (ἦλθον) οὐ (μόνον) . . . ἀλλ' ἵνα see p. 48 n. 3; specially on ἀλλ' ἵνα see p. 407 n. 9; ἐβουλεύσαντο . . . ἵνα as 11.53; the motivating ὅτι-sentence at the conclusion as 3.18; 5.38; 8.20; 10.13 and elsewhere. According to de Zwaan ὑπῆγον . . . καὶ ἐπίστ. v. 11 is a mistranslation for περισσοτέρως ἐπίστευον or ἐπερίσσευον πιστεύοντες (corresponding to 15.16), while according to Black (91) ὑπῆγον here as 15.16 is an Aramaism and is pleonastic.

[4] Thus the article before ὄχλος is understandable as anaphoric, i.e. harking back to 11.19 (Bd. would strike it out with B K pm). and the position of πολύς does not need to be understood as predicative after the analogy of πᾶς and ὅλος (Bl.-D.) (270, 1; Raderm. 112).

also has to die![1] The decision plays no further part in what follows, it merely serves to characterise the extravagance of the wrath of the adversaries; nevertheless it may well be intended to sound out the motif expounded in 15.18–16.4a: the disciple of Jesus has nothing better to expect than Jesus himself.[2]

4) *The Entry into Jerusalem:* 12.12–19

The Evangelist has clearly taken the basis of vv. 12–19 from a source. For the crowd called in by him in v. 9, and which one would expect should form the escort of Jesus, is not immediately mentioned; instead a new ὄχλος,[3] namely the band of pilgrims that have come to Jerusalem for the feast, bring Jesus with them. Only later (v. 18) is the Lazarus miracle adduced as the motive prompting those who went to meet him. And it comes to light in v. 17 that the Evangelist thinks of the ὄχλος of v. 9 as also accompanying Jesus. Accordingly it would seem that vv. 17ff. are derived from the Evangelist, and vv. 12ff. from the source.[4] It is questionable to whom vv. 14f. are to be ascribed. If these verses stood in the source, they were a secondary addition even there, for as its supplementary character betrays, it filled out the report after the pattern of the Synoptics. But it is not impossible that the Evangelist himself was responsible for this enlargement in order to express the thought of v. 16, for this verse is to be put to his account.[5]

The source cannot be one of the Synoptic Gospels; for it differs from the Synoptic report, in that in the latter the jubilant escort of Jesus is formed from adherents who are journeying with him to Jerusalem, whereas here on the contrary the multitude comes out from Jerusalem to meet him.[6]

In the mind of the Evangelist **vv. 12f.** connect up immediately with 11.55f. The pilgrims at the feast who are present in Jerusalem go out on the following day[7] with palm branches to meet Jesus,[8] and they

---

[1] On πολλοὶ . . . ἐπίστευον see 11.45 and p. 132 n. 3.

[2] So also Htm.

[3] Here also the article (lacking in 𝔓 ℵ D pm) is anaphoric, and indeed it is related to the following

[4] If vv. 12f. are derived from the same source as 12. 1–7, τῇ ἐπαύριον could also be derived from this. The editorial character of vv. 17f. results from the reference to ch. 11. Further on διὰ τοῦτο . . . ὅτι v. 18 see p. 238 n. 2.

[5] If we wanted to assume that vv. 14f. were derived from the ecclesiastical redaction as a filling out in accordance with the Synoptics, then v. 16 would also belong to the same redaction. That would have the consequence that 2.17, 22 must also be ascribed to this editorial activity (see p. 124 n. 2), and likewise—with even less hesitation—7.39b (see p. 303 n. 5).

[6] In this point the Synoptic report would deserve the advantage regarding the question of historicity. In any case it is wholly determined by the proof from prophecy, whereas in John the motive of prophecy is a later addition. Cp. Gesch. der syn. Tr. 281 = Hist. of the Syn. Trad. 281.

[7] Syr^{s} completes in acc. with Mk. 11.1 parr: "On the following day Jesus went out and came to the mount of Olives, and the multitude . . . ."

[8] The βάϊα τῶν φοινίκων correspond to the στιβάδες Mk. 11.8 and κλάδοι Mt. 21.8 (on βάϊα, which in themselves mean palm branches, see Br. lexicon). Palm branches are an adornment of the victory festival and the triumphant king (I Macc. 13.51; II Macc. 10.7;

welcome him as the messianic King.[1] The fear of the authorities (11.48) thus appears to be justified. As by an afterthought it is reported in **v. 14** that Jesus rode on a young ass;[2] εὑρών gives the impression that he found it accidentally.[3] The significance of this fact however is emphasised in **v. 15** through the citation from Zech. 9.9, which Mt. 21.5 had also inserted into the Marcan account.[4] It is stated in **v. 16**, in a way that is parallel to 2.17, 22, that it is not till after the glorification of Jesus that the disciples gained an insight into the fact that the entry of Jesus into Jerusalem fulfilled the Zechariah prophecy.[5]

Rev. 7.9; see Schl. and Str.-B.). According to Br. the articulated *the* palm branches perhaps alludes to a Christian cultic usage. In fact such could have had an influence on the account; for in Jerusalem there were no palm trees, from which the pilgrims would have had to cut the palm branches, so that Schl. and Eisler presume that palm leaves are meant which belonged to the festival foliage of the Tabernacle-booths and were kept in the houses; see Schl. ad loc; Eisler, Ἰησ. βασ. II 475; further Dalman, I. und W., 274; Arbeit und Sitte I 64, 434. As the palm branches, the phrase εἰς ὑπάντησιν (DGLal: συνάντ., AKUal: ἀπάντ.) surely shows that we are dealing with the entry of the Messianic King. For the expression belongs to the terminology with which the bringing of the king and of exalted persons is described; see E. Peterson, ZsystTh 1929, 682–702; Schl. on Mt. 8.34. Cp. W. R. Farmer, JThSt 1952, 62–66.

[1] The first part of the cry of welcome is derived, like Mk. 11.9, from Ps. 117. 25f. The LXX has rightly translated the הוֹשִׁיעָה נָּא of the Hebrew text as σῶσον δή. This cry (2 Sam. 14.4; 2 Kings 6.26 is directed to the king, in Ps. 20.10 to God for the king) has become a cry for salvation; cp. Mk. 11.9; Mt. 21.9; Did 10.6 and see Dalman W. J. 180–182; differently Eisler, II 472–75. In the psalm εὐλογημένος κτλ. was meant collectively and applied to those entering the temple; here it is understood individually and is related to the Messianic King as the ἐρχόμενος (see p. 404 n. 6). Ἐν ὀν. κυρίου is hardly to be linked with εὐλογ. (Heitmüller, Im Namen Jesu 86), rather it is to be linked with ὁ ἐρχ.; it means therefore "in the commission of" (see p. 270 n. 2). If in Mk. 11.10 the praise of the βασιλεία of David follows the cry of salvation taken from the psalm, so here praise is given to the βασιλεὺς τοῦ Ἰσρ., corresponding to the way ὁ ἐρχόμενος is enlarged by ὁ βασιλεὺς in Lk. 19.38.

[2] Ὀνάριον only here in the NT. Is the diminutive chosen because of the πῶλος in the citation?

[3] Admittedly it is difficult to conclude that the legend of Mk. 11.1ff par. was still unknown to the narrator (whether the Source or the Evangelist, see p. 417). For this will surely gradually have developed from the datum deduced from Zech. 9.9, that Jesus rode into the city on an ass. But vv. 14f. so decidedly have the character of an addendum, it must be presumed that the addendum has been anticipated in remembrance of the already well known story. (See also n. 4).

[4] Instead of χαῖρε σφόδρα Zech. 9.9, which Mt. 21.5 continues, we have here μὴ φοβοῦ, which could well be a reminiscence of Is. 41.10; 44.2 (Zeph. 3.16). In what follows the text of Zechariah is even more markedly abbreviated than in Mt, hence the wording diverges from that of the LXX.

[5] See p. 128 n. 2. Δοξασθῆναι 12.16 corresponds to ἐγερθῆναι 22.2 (see p. 304 n. 1). Ἐπ' αὐτῷ instead of the expected περὶ αὐτοῦ (so D 1241) does not mean that the Scripture rests upon him (Bd.), but it corresponds to the rabbinic בּוֹ (Schl. on Mt. 11.10); cp. Rev. 10.11—If the disciples are thought of as the subject of ἐποίησαν, the procuring of the ass, recounted in Mt. 11.1ff., is in view (see n. 2). But the subject can just as well be the ὄχλος or "people" (cp. 15.6; 20.2), and that would be good Greek usage (Colwell 59f.); ταῦτα ἐποίησαν then signifies the homage paid to Jesus.—According to Grill II 207–210 the narrative again rests on the Dionysus mythology: the foal of an ass is the Dionysiac animal for riding on, and at the same time is a symbol of the Hellenistic peoples.

Vv. 17–19 repeat the motif of vv. 9–11, and accordingly begin with an account of the acclamation of the people. Because of vv. 9 and 12 a distinction between two ὄχλοι is made in a decidedly clumsy fashion;[1] v. 17 relates to the ὄχλος of v. 9, which witnessed the miracle of Lazarus, and v. 18 to the ὄχλος of v. 12, whose enthusiastic reception is now subsequently read back also into that σημεῖον. The significance that this very miracle has for the death of Jesus, and so according to 11.4 for his δοξασθῆναι, is therefore expressly emphasised; and at the same time a hint is again provided, through the ἐμαρτύρει of v. 17, that the person of Jesus forms the subject of the trial between God and the world.[2] Even when the Evangelist follows the tradition he sees the story of Jesus as the κρίσις of the world.

The reflection of the Pharisees[3] shows how the decision that Jesus must die is confirmed in their minds: they have been right! If they do not act as they had decided, the danger will never be banished;[4] for the whole world is running after him![5] Without their knowing it, their utterance stands as a piece of self-justification in the setting of the great trial; and at the same time it is a further unconscious prophecy concerning the σωτὴρ τοῦ κόσμου like 7.35; 11.51f., the fulfilment of which is intimated in the next scene.

b) The Mystery of the Death of Jesus: 12.20–33; 8.30–40; 6.60–71

In 12.20–50 the text of the Gospel does not appear to be preserved in its original form. It ought to be clear that the retrospect on the public ministry of Jesus in 12.37–43 must originally have formed the conclusion of the whole first half of the Gospel. 12.44–50 is an isolated fragment that belongs to the discourse on the Light, beginning at 8.12;[6] and similarly 12.34–36, which is hardly an appropriate continuation of 12.20–33, originally will have belonged to the discourse on Light.[7] The question arises whether 12.33 was the

---

[1] Since D E* L al it sy make of the ὅτε in v. 17 a ὅτι, they identify the two ὄχλοι. The ὤν v. 17 expresses contemporaneity with the sentence introduced by ὅτε; Raderm. 227.

[2] On μαρτυρεῖν see p. 50 n. 5; on the picture of the trial pp. 85f. 296f. etc.

[3] No distinction is intended in the fact that those here named Φαρισαῖοι are called ἀρχιερεῖς in v. 10; in 11.47, 57 both are named together. Πρὸς ἑαυτ. = πρὸς ἀλλήλους Bl.-D §287.

[4] Οὐκ ὠφελεῖν οὐδέν as 6.63; cp. Mt. 27.24 and elsewhere; see Arndt and Gingrich lexicon.

[5] D L φ al lat sy add ὅλος to ὁ κόσμος. "The (whole) world" in the sense of "everybody" is a Semitic mode of speech (Schl.; Str.-B.); similarly (ἀπ)έρχεσθαι ὀπίσω for "follow"; cp. Mk. 1.20 with Mt. 4.22 and see Job 21.33; Lk. 14.27; Jude 7; cp. πορεύεσθαι ὀπίσω Deut. 13.5; Jer. 2.25; Lk. 21.8; 2 Pt. 2.10.

[6] See pp. 313, 344f.

[7] See pp. 313, 354f.

conclusion of the complex that preceded it and that 12.37–43 originally followed it. In itself that should not be regarded as impossible. Since however it earlier appeared that the supposedly connected fragments 8.30–40, 6.60–71 perhaps belonged to the situation of κρίσις implied in 12.23–33,[1] the further question suggests itself whether these fragments can be understood as a suitable continuation of 12.23–33. Without doubt that is the case. Moreover 6.60–71 would also be extraordinarily well placed as a conclusion of the whole and as a transition to the second part. If this judgment be held with reserve, and if we reckon with the possibility that a piece of the original text may be lost, we can venture to make an attempt to interpret the text in the combination outlined above.

1) *Access to Jesus:* 12.20–33

It is very difficult to attain to a confident judgment about 12.20–33. The puzzling features of the text, which admittedly are resolved in part through an insight into the Evangelist's technique in composition, have frequently led to critical sorties on the text here.[2] Certainly it seems to me that 12.23–33 are understandable as a unity. A text from the "revelation-discourses" lies at its base, and to it vv. 23, 27f. belong. The Evangelist has enlarged it in vv. 24–26 through material taken from the Synoptic tradition, which he has edited in a peculiar manner; further, he has in his own way interrupted the discourse of Jesus at vv. 29f. by a short dialogue, and added v. 33 as an interpretation.

How are we to decide about the introductory scene 12.20–22? In any event, to outward appearance it is a fragment lacking a continuation. The request of the Ἕλληνες which was mediated to Jesus in a circumstantial fashion through Philip and Andrew, asking that they might be taken to Jesus, remains without an answer. The Ἕλληνες immediately disappear from the scene, and it is difficult to suggest that we view this as analogous to the disappearing of Nicodemus in ch. 3, for Jesus discourses with him for quite a while. Now it is true that the discourse of Jesus in vv. 23–33 can be understood as an indirect answer to that request (see below); and therefore the possibility must be reckoned with that the Evangelist—whether he himself created this scene or whether he took it from a source—considered vv. 20–22 as an introduction to vv. 23–33, whose function was to prepare the way for an understanding of the discourse. Accordingly we shall so proceed in the interpretation that follows. Nevertheless we must realise that in so doing we are simply following the train of thought of the discourse; for the suspicion

---

[1] See pp. 286, 314.

[2] Wellh. sees in 12.20–36 sheer disordered fragments; Wendt regards vv. 28b–30 as an addition of the Evangelist to his source; Sp. would join v. 23 immediately on to v. 19, and strikes out vv. 26 and 30 (apart from other corrections), while Hirsch ascribes only v. 26 to the editor. See further Howard 258ff. and see below p. 425 n. 3. Ed. Meyer (I 334f.) thinks that vv. 28ff. were originally the continuation of the scene in vv. 20–22: "The narrative that lies at the base of this will have gone on to say that Jesus requests and receives for the Greek proselytes a confirmatory sign".

cannot be suppressed that between v. 22 and v. 23 a whole piece has fallen out. This is increased especially through the fact that in v. 29 the ὄχλος appears without warning. According to vv. 20–22 we have to assume that Jesus is surrounded only by his disciples; if it were to be imagined that he was in public, surrounded by the people, then it would be difficult to understand why the Ἕλληνες could not address him directly.

The text of the revelation discourse has parallels in a discourse of Mandaean texts, in which a description is given of the situation of the heavenly messenger in this earthly world, and in part of the situation of the soul that comes from the heavenly world.[1] The messenger and the soul are alike in origin and in being, and their mythical destiny is the same, so that the same thing can be said of both, and the texts often allow no clear judgment whether it is the messenger or the soul that is the subject of discourse. The texts in question describe the anxiety that overtakes the messenger (or the soul) in face of the persecutions of the demonic powers of the world;[2] these are suffered partly in view of his task to fulfil in the world the charge of the "Father",[3] partly in view of the hour in which his "measure is full" and he prepares himself to leave this world.[4] In his anxiety[5] he raises "his eyes upwards to the place of light".[6] His lament and his cry for help[7] receive an answer; a consoling voice sounds out from the height, and a helper is sent to him.[8]

---

[1] G. P. Wetter (Verherrlichung 57f.) hazarded the view that the scene in Jn. 12.20ff. imitated a Christian mystery, in which the role of the cult divinity was acted by the priests. This construction, improbable in itself, is now clearly refuted by the Mandaean parallels.

[2] See Lidzbarski, Mand. Lit. 208; cp. also H. Odeberg, Die mand. Religionsanschauung (Uppsala Univ. Årsskr. 1930, Teologi. 2), 8f.

[3] Especially John -B. 224, 6ff.; cp. Mand.Lit. 192f. (XXII); 202 (XXXIII); 208f. (XLII); related to the soul, Ginza 328, 9ff.; 477, 1ff. and in numerous parts of the second book of the Left Ginza.

[4] So especially in a succession of songs in the 3rd book of the Left Ginza, which begin: "My measure is full and I go forth" (numbers 15, 36, 44), or, "I am redeemed, my measure is full" (no. 22). Cp. also Ginza 183, 25ff; John B.59.2f. Somewhat differently the songs 18, 37, 45 in the 3rd book of the Left Ginza: "Although I was still young, my measure was full". Everywhere here it is the soul that speaks.

[5] Cp. e. g. Ginza 328, 26: "(I) became anxious and made my soul anxious"; 477, 19: "I went into anxiety, and fear came over me"; 503, 5: "I was terrified, anxiety came upon me"; further 184, 1f.

[6] Mand. Lit. 193.4; Ginza 546, 31; 564, 36.

[7] So continually in the pertinent songs in the 2nd book of the Left Ginza, in which the soul laments that it is sent into exile out of its heavenly home in this perishable earth in bodies wherein it is exposed to the persecution of the evil powers; further Ginza 328, 9ff.; 346.15ff.; John-B 59, 1ff.; 62, 10ff.; 68, 4ff.; 224.6ff.; Mand. Lit. 208 (XLII); 209 (XLIII); 223f. (LVI). Cp. also of songs of the Left Ginza named in n. 4 above, 533, 3ff.; 546, 23ff.; 564, 18ff.; 571, 31ff.; further 592, 14ff. Cp. also Jonas, Gnosis I 109–113.

[8] In the songs in the 2nd book of the Left Ginza a messenger or "helper" appears with words of promise and consolation ("To us shalt thou ascend", 457, 1 and the like); or it is said: "There came the call of the great helper" (477, 25). Correspondingly in the relevant songs in the 3rd book a Uthra, "helper", is sent, who brings the soul up; or the word of promise of this helper is simply reported (572, 19ff.). The sending of the "helper" similarly is referred to in Ginza 328, 31; 346, 24; 593, 10. Likewise the hearing of the

Naturally the text used by the Evangelist cannot be reconstructed with certainty, but the interpretative verses 29f. and 33 are clearly separable from it. With magnificent assurance the Evangelist for his own ends set in the forefront the saying in v. 23, which in the source,[1] along with v. 31, can only have followed the utterance of v. 28. The original motive for the introduction of the ταραχή, the lament and the cry, lies in v. 27. The Evangelist has probably transformed the lament through inserting the objection, ἀλλὰ διὰ τοῦτο κτλ.[2] In the source the requests πατὲρ σῶσον κτλ. and πατὲρ δόξασον κτλ. will have stood in parallelism and have had the same meaning; the Evangelist differentiates between them in consequence of his own view of the δοξασθῆναι of Jesus (see below). In v. 28 an answer follows the complaint, promising the granting of the request. The νῦν of the ταραχή (v. 27) is therefore replaced by the νῦν of the δοξασθῆναι (v. 23) or the ὑψωθῆναι (vv. 31f.). The exaltation of the Son of Man however is catastrophic for the cosmos; in the language of the myth, because the Redeemer takes out of the clutches of the demons of darkness the sparks of light, which once were caught by the darkness and by means of which the demons formed the world;[3] in demythologised language, because the messenger, in virtue of his exaltation, draws after him those who belong to him (v. 32[4]).

---

request Mand. Lit. 193, 5ff.; the sending of the messenger Mand. Lit. 202, 9ff.; 225, 1ff.; John-B. 60, 15ff.; 69, 3ff. A promise answers the request Mand. Lit. 208f. (XLII and XLIII). In John-B. 224, 10f. a staff is sent to the lamenting messenger "which bestowed on me speech and hearing".—Cp. Ginza 296, 37ff. and 316, 28ff., the promise to the messenger that when he is afraid, a helper will assist him; similarly 317, 1ff., that the heavenly "voice' will come to him. Cp. again Ginza 184, 4f.: "O man, who callest after life, and whom life answereth". That this has to do with the old traditional type is shown by Od. Sol 21.1–3:

"My arms I lifted up on high;
Even to the grace of the Lord:
Because He had cast off my bonds from me;
And my helper had lifted me up to his grace and his salvation.
And I put off darkness,
And clothed myself with light"

(translated by Harris and Mingana, Odes and Psalms of Solomon, II, 1920, 319f.). See also ZNTW 24 (1925), 123–126.

[1] There is no reason for doubting that the source contained the title "Son of Man" (= man); see pp. 149 n. 4, 105 n. 3, 107, 261.

[2] The query could also well be posed whether the question καὶ τί εἴπω; has been inserted by the Evangelist. But in the Mandaean texts questions are often bound up with the lament; cp. especially Ginza 572, 35f.: "Whom shall I call, and who will answer me, who will be a helper to me?"—One could rather hazard the suggestion that the objection proposed by the speaker to himself is not an *insertion* into the source but the *recasting* of its original wording, which could have run: διὰ τί ἦλθον εἰς τὴν ὥραν ταύτην; for questions of this kind are typical in the Mandaean texts; cp. Ginza 328.11ff.; John-B. 224, 6ff. ("O Lord, the Great! What have I sinned, that thou hast sent me into the depths? . . . "). So continually in the relevant songs of the 2nd book of the Left Ginza ("Who has made me dwell in the *tibil*?" "Who has thrown me into the sorrow of the world?" "Why . . . did they cast me into the physical garment?" etc.).

[3] See pp. 25, 64, 157 n. 5, 374.

[4] See on v. 32.

i. *The Request for Access:* 12.20–22

Some "Greeks", who also have come to Jerusalem to be at the feast, desire to become acquainted with Jesus,[1] though no motive for their request is mentioned. Doubtless they are so called proselytes;[2] if they are not described as such (as προσήλυτοι or σεβόμενοι) but are called Ἕλληνες, obviously this is because they should be viewed as representatives of the Greek world. The way they have to take is complicated; they turn to Philip;[3] he informs Andrew about it,[4] and they both then present the request to Jesus. In the words that follow, however, Jesus appears to ignore the request. What he says in vv. 23ff. is at least not a direct answer, and in fact no such answer is given further on; indeed not a word more is said about the Ἕλληνες in the subsequent discourse.

The meaning of this scene is immediately clear from its position after v. 19; the unconscious prophecy there expressed, ὁ κόσμος ὀπίσω αὐτοῦ ἀπῆλθεν, is illustrated through the request of the Ἕλληνες: the Greek world is asking after Jesus! Accordingly the fact that the Greeks must turn to the disciples in order to reach Jesus could also have a symbolic meaning: the access of the Greek world to Jesus is mediated through the apostles.[5]

If 12.20–23 can be interpreted as a unity,[6] yet another result emerges: the request of the Greeks to be led to the historical Jesus finds no fulfilment; it is a false request. Vv. 23–33 show that the Revealer,

---

[1] This meaning of ἰδεῖν is common in Greek, see also Lk. 9.9: 23.8; Acts 28.20; Rom. 1.11. Cp. Diog. Laert. VI 34: ξένων δέ ποτε θεάσασθαι θελόντων Δημοσθένην.

[2] In distinction from the Ἑλληνισταί (Acts 6.1) Ἕλληνες are those born Greeks (see 7.35); see Windisch ThWB II 506, 25ff. Since they come to Jerusalem for the feast they are proselytes, whatever their grade may have been; they belong therefore to the ἀλλόφυλοι, ὅσοι κατὰ θρησκείαν παρῆσαν Jos. bell. 9, 427. Cp. what is said of the προσήλυτοι and σεβόμενοι or φοβούμενοι τὸν θεόν Schürer III 174f.; Str.-B. ad loc and II 715–23.—Ἀναβαίνειν as 2.13; προσκυνεῖν of the cultic worship of God as Acts 24.11; see pp. 189 n. 3, 339 n. 3.

[3] On Philip see p. 102 n. 3. In 1.44 it was stated that Bethsaida was his native city. If this is now described as of Galilee, then possibly a geographical error has been committed see p. 103 n. 3), or it reflects the fact that the Jewish inhabitants of the East bank of the lake called themselves Galileans (Schl.). But perhaps we have to presume that a Galilean (other- wise unknown) Bethsaida must here be distinguished from the well known non-Galilean town of that name; so D. Buzy, Rech. sc. rel. 28 (1938), 570ff.Cp. K. Furrer, ZNTW 3 (1902), 264.

[4] On Andrew, who as in 1.44; 6.8 appears with Philip, see pp. 101 n. 1, 102 n. 3. Were these two disciples missionaries together to the heathen? They are the only two among the Twelve who bear Greek names.

[5] It is not impossible that a later Christian usage has served as a pattern for the conception of this scene, according to which a Gentile, who wanted to join the community, had to be recommended by two members of the Church. Wetter (Sohn Gottes 70, 1) alludes to scenes in the stories of the monks, in which visitors have to be announced through disciples.

[6] See pp. 419f.

in order to be perfected as Revealer, must take his departure from the earth, that precisely as the exalted Lord he may "draw all men to himself" (v. 32). The question at issue is not at all the attaining of a direct historical "contemporaneity;" the important thing rather is to gain a relationship to the exalted Lord. It is therefore understandable that the request of the Greeks should come just at this point, for the ὥρα of the δοξασθῆναι has arrived.

ii. *The Law of Access:* 12. 23–26

The hour has come (**v. 23**) to which allusion was earlier made (7.6, 8, 30; 8.20); it is the hour when the Messenger will return to the heavenly glory.[1] The paradox of this hour is plainly brought home: the hour of the δοξασθῆναι is at the same time the hour of the passion. That is the first meaning of the parabolic utterance **v. 24**, the unexpressed application of which can easily be filled out: as the seed of corn must "die" in order to produce fruit, so also the way to the δοξασθῆναι of Jesus can lead only through death. If this saying does not yet clearly express the peculiar paradox, that he who is "exalted" on the cross is *as such* the one exalted to the δόξα, nevertheless an essential moment of the δοξασθῆναι is made especially plain by it. For the way that this traditional picture[2] is applied here is differentiated from applications of it known elsewhere through the opposition μόνος μένει . . . πολὺν καρπὸν φέρει. What is plainly said in v. 32 (in mythological language) is here only hinted at: the δοξασθῆναι of Jesus is not a mythical event that concerns him alone, but an event of salvation history: to his δόξα belongs the gathering of his community. To this extent v. 24 can be understood as an indirect answer to the request of the Ἕλληνες: through his passion Jesus will become accessible for them as the exalted Lord.

At this point a dominical saying, well known from the Synoptic

---

[1] On ἡ ὥρα ἵνα as 13.1; 16.2, 32 instead of ὅτε 4.21 f. see Bl.-D. §382, 1: against Burney, who (like Odeberg 277f.) regards the expression as a semitism, see Colwell 99f.—Naturally ὥρα is not to be understood in a very narrow sense, so that the ὥρα of 12.23 is set up in opposition to that of 13.1; 17.1. Everywhere the same *now* is meant.

[2] The motive is broadened; in 1 Cor. 15.36f. it is applied to the death and resurrection of the individual, as also in the Rabbinic literature (Str.-B. ad loc. and on 1 Cor. 15.37) and 1 Clem. 24.4f. (further material on this in Knopf, Hdb. zum. NT). Elsewhere it is applied to the individual development of a human life, as also in the Rabbinic literature (Str.-B. ad loc.) and Epikt. IV 8, 36f.—Hippol. El. VI 16, 6 (ἐὰν δὲ μείνῃ δένδρον μόνον, καρπὸν μὴ ποιοῦν, (μὴ) ἐξεικονισμένον ἀφανίζεται) could have been influenced by Jn. 12.24 in its formulation, but in content it has nothing to do with it (rightly Bd.). Dodd 372, 1 alludes to the Hellenistic (Gnostic) concept of the soul or divine Anthropos as the seed, which derives from the upper world and must again return to it. There is little probability of contact with this idea here.

tradition, but here reproduced in a Johannine rendering,[1] is attached in **v. 25**: life[2] is of so peculiar a character, it so completely eludes any desire to have it at our own disposal, that it is lost precisely when we desire to hold it fast, and it is won exactly when we give it up. If the first impression of v. 25 leads us to assume that it applies to Jesus himself, and that it is intended to illustrate the saying of v. 24, namely that the way to his δοξασθῆναι leads through death, v. 26 nevertheless shows that in v. 25 we have rather an extension to the disciples of the validity of the law to which Jesus is subject.[3] **V. 26** itself is a Johannine variant of a Synoptic saying[4] about discipleship. In the Synoptic version it answers the question, "Who is my real disciple?" and the answer runs, "He who follows me."[5] The Evangelist however has given the saying a fresh meaning. For him it answers the question "Who will (after my departure) follow me (into the heavenly δόξα)?" and the answer runs, "He who is my servant."[6] For manifestly ἀκολουθείτω is

---

[1] That ἕνεκεν ἐμοῦ (καὶ τοῦ εὐαγγελίου) of Mt. 10.39; Mk. 8.35 parr. is lacking in John is certainly original; cp. Lk. 17.33. The Evangelist on his part has enlarged the saying through the interpretative addition ἐν τῷ κόσμῳ τούτῳ (see p. 340 n. 1) εἰς ζωὴν αἰώνιον (cp. 4.14, 36; 6.27). The paradox of the saying is thereby weakened; similarly through the exchange of verbs in the antithesis: φιλεῖν—ἀπολλύναι over against μισεῖν—φυλάττειν, whereas in the Synoptic setting (apart from Lk. 17.33) the same verbs remain: σώζειν (or εὑρεῖν)—ἀπολλύναι. The Evangelist could have chosen φυλ. (see p. 301 n. 5) on account of the addition εἰς ζ. αἰών. Cp. Dodd, NtSt 2 (1955/56), 78–81, who comes to very similar conclusions on v. 25.

[2] ψυχή here naturally means "life", as 10.11, 15, 17 etc.

[3] The undeniable tension that exists between vv. 24, 25 and 26 suggests the question whether v. 25 or v. 26 (or both) have been added by the ecclesiastical redactor from the Synoptic tradition. If v. 26 be struck out, v. 25 then contains an unambiguous relation to the destiny of Jesus. But then πολὺν κάρπον φέρει of v. 24 loses its force, and the relation to vv. 20–22—which admittedly cannot be affirmed with certainty—is completely lost in vv. 23ff. If, as is more natural, v. 25 be eliminated, these considerations fall away. But against the elimination of vv. 25 and 26 it must be said in the same way that their formulation is characteristically Johannine. In that case we should be content to find in vv. 24–26 an insertion of the Evangelist into his source, see p. 420.—If that be accepted, it is then clear that ἕνεκεν ἐμοῦ of the Mk-Mt text is also valid for John. V. 25 does not simply express the general truth of "die and become", but it speaks of the law which is valid for the disciples of Jesus; cp. Gogarten, M. Luthers Predigten 1927, 537.

[4] Mk. 8.34 parr. Mt. 10.38 = Lk. 14.27. The Evangelist has abbreviated the wording of the saying through leaving out mention of cross bearing (see below), and he has lengthened it through καὶ ὅπου κτλ. On ὅπου . . . ἐκεῖ cp. 14.3; 17.24.

[5] So most plainly Lk. 14.27, whereas in Mt. 10.38 the weaker ἄξιός μου εἶναι has taken the place of μαθητής μου εἶναι. The Marcan wording does not express the meaning so plainly, because here discipleship is denoted by ὀπίσω μου ἐλθεῖν and ἀκολουθεῖν, whereas in the Matthaean-Lukan version ἀκολουθεῖν (or ἔρχεσθαι) ὀπίσω μου denotes precisely the *condition* for discipleship, which in the Marcan wording is represented by ἀπαρνεῖσθαι ἑαυτόν. All the Synoptic versions continue to retain as an epexegesis of the demanded discipleship or self denial αἴρειν (or λαμβάνειν or βαστάζειν) τὸν σταυρὸν αὐτοῦ, which is lacking in John.

[6] If the wording of the saying that lay before the Evangelist already contained διάκονος instead of μαθητής (Lk), that probably is due to the influence of the Pauline and Deutero-Pauline usage (2 Cor. 3.6; 6.4; 1 Th. 3.2; Col. 1.23, 25; Eph. 3.7; 1 Tim. 4.6).

expounded through the Johannine καὶ ὅπου κτλ; it must therefore be an imperative of promise. Admittedly the promise that the servant will follow him, and that he will be where Jesus is, is peculiarly ambiguous. The meaning in the foreground conveys a promise to the servant to follow him into death.[1] But just as for Jesus himself the exaltation on the cross is at the same time his δοξασθῆναι, so also the promise of following him and being where he is means the promise of participating in his δόξα.[2] The promise is taken up again in the conclusion, where it unambiguously runs: "If any man follows me, the Father will honour him."[3] The promise of v. 26 therefore anticipates the promises of the Farewell Discourses, that those who belong to him will be with him (in his δόξα), and that the Father will love them.[4]

The train of thought in vv. 23–26 is quite compact,[5] and it ought not to be said that the point of view oscillates, directing attention now to the figure of Jesus (vv. 23f.) and now to the disciples. Rather a unity is maintained: Jesus as the Revealer does not permit attention to be drawn to himself, and the sayings about him are not mythology or speculation. His exaltation can be spoken of only in terms of its significance, i.e. as it is law and promise for those who wish to be his followers. One can treat of Jesus and of those who belong to him only together. The same holds good also for the teaching of the Gnostic myth on redemption. But exactly by reason of the fact that vv. 23–26 have as their premise the mythologically formulated statement about the connection between the Redeemer and those who belong to him (vv. 31f.), historical considerations replace the cosmic connection which the myth has in view. It is not the "nature" of those who belong to him but their "ministry" that establishes their unity with him.

If we can regard vv. 20–26 as having a compact connection,[6] then the answer to the question about access to Jesus (vv. 20–22) is given: Whoever asks after access to the historical Jesus is directed to the way that leads to the *exalted Lord.*[7] The exalted Jesus however is not directly

---

[1] On ἀκολουθεῖν see pp. 99 n. 5, 344 n.1.

[2] Because ἀκολουθείτω is promise, as also because it is ambiguous, the Evangelist has to leave out the motive of cross bearing, which the Synoptic versions contain and which probably originally belongs to the saying.

[3] The meaning of the promises, to follow him into the δόξα and to be with him—and, to be honoured by the Father, is naturally the same. On τιμήσει κτλ. cp. 4 Macc. 17.20 of the martyrs who stand before God's throne: καὶ οὗτοι οὖν ἁγιασθέντες διὰ θεὸν τετίμηνται. For the heavenly or eschatological τιμή see Rom. 2.7, 10; 1 Pt. 1.7; Heb. 2.7, 9.

[4] Cp. 17.24; 14.3 and 14.21; 16.27; 17.23–26.

[5] It is hardly likely therefore that the sequence of vv. 23–26 has been motivated through dependence on Mk. 8.31–35 (contra Htm): according to him vv. 23f. correspond to Mk. 8.31, and by reason of association vv. 25f. = Mk. 8.34f. are then added.

[6] See pp. 419f.

[7] See p. 424.

accessible, say in moments of ecstatic or mystic vision which suspend the historical existence of man. Rather the way to him is the way of "service," which leads to the acceptance of death as a man follows in his steps.

iii. *The Achievement of Access:* 12.27–33

V. 27 makes a fresh start, and in a certain way vv. 27–33 run parallel to vv. 23–26.[1] The ὥρα of the δοξασθῆναι, of which v. 23 had already spoken, is more exactly defined in vv. 27f.; and its significance, of which v. 24 had spoken allusively, is described in the language of the myth in vv. 31f.

V. 27 represents the situation of the messenger in the language of the myth: νῦν ἡ ψυχή μου τετάρακται, i.e. "I am afraid."[2] If in the Evangelist's view this can have little or nothing to do with a psychological description of one who, in truth, has no need at all of the divine promise for the conquest of his fear (v. 30), the more the objective meaning of the νῦν should become plain. The sayings that follow interpret it as the "now" of decision: What is the right word, the right prayer for this hour?[3] What is the right meaning of this ὥρα? The ὥρα is the hour of death; the hour in face of which human fear trembles, and from which human fear desires to be rescued: πάτερ, σῶσόν με ἐκ τῆς ὥρας ταύτης. Is such a desire the right answer for the question of this hour? No![4] Flight from this hour would destroy its significance.[5] Its meaning can only be that it does not have the man's interest in view but the service of God. The right word therefore can only run, πάτερ, δόξασόν σου τὸ ὄνομα (**v. 28**[6]). With that word, however, the myth is decisively corrected; for in the myth the requests σῶσόν με and

---

[1] On the question whether vv. 23, 27, 31f. belonged together in the source, see p. 422f.

[2] Ψυχή, in accordance with common usage (like καρδία, 14.1, 27), simply denotes "I"; cp. Mk. 14.34.—In distinction from 11.33 naturally it is neither the wrath nor the pneumatic excitement (see p. 406 n4.) which is described, but the anxiety of the Messenger, whom the demonic powers of the world are threatening, see p. 421 n.5. Parallels in content are found in 14.1, 27, in language Gen. 41.8; Ps. 30.10; 41.6f.; 54.5; Lam. 2.11.

[3] By the insertion of ἀλλὰ δὶα τοῦτο κτλ. (see p. 422f.) the Evangelist has made πάτερ, σῶσόν με κτλ. into a question.

[4] Ἀλλά = no, as in classic Greek after a self question, B.-D. § 448, 4. On ὥρα see p. 117 n.1.

[5] The unrelated διὰ τοῦτο must be paraphrased: "on this account, namely because of this hour", i.e. "in order to take on" what it brings. Admittedly it is grammatically simpler with Schw. and Sp. to understand it as a question: "But did I then come *for this purpose* (namely to ask σῶσόν με) in this hour?" On the other hand it is pedantic to demand a grammatical point of relation for διὰ τοῦτο.

[6] The ὄνομα of the Father denotes the Father himself, and for this reason, because the Father is glorified precisely when he is acknowledged or named *as* Father; cp. 17.6 and see p. 59 n.2.

δόξασον are synonymous: inasmuch as the messenger is set free from earthly existence, the Father who set him free is glorified at the same time. In John however the Father is glorified in that the Son takes on himself earthly existence in its utter depth.[1]

Inasmuch as Jesus in this hour appears like a man in his fear, it is evident that every man ought in such an hour to make such a decision. But naturally Jesus is not simply the prototype, in whom the behaviour demanded of man becomes visible in an exemplary manner (cp. 13.15); he is also and above all the Revealer, whose decision alone makes possible in such an hour the human decision for God (cp. 16.33). It is not the struggle of his soul that should become visible, but the decision that he actually made; not the hour of an individual βίος, but the hour that decided the destiny of the world (v. 31). And the significance of the δι' ὑμᾶς of v. 30 means that it holds good not only of the φωνή in v. 28, but also of the prayer in v. 27 to which the φωνή supplies an answer.

The meaning of the ὥρα certainly cannot be made manifest to one whose gaze is fixed on the individual and biographical element, or to one whose interest simply questions its significance for the history of the world or of the human spirit. For it is the divine φωνή[2] that alone makes the hour what it is: καὶ ἐδόξασα καὶ πάλιν δοξάσω; the request will be heard because it has already been heard.[3] The future δοξάζειν is a

---

[1] Since the Evangelist will have known the tradition attested in Mk. 14.32–42 parr. to which there is no parallel in his own passion narrative, vv. 27f. are to be looked on as the counterpart to this, composed by him (cp. H. Windisch, Joh. und die Synoptiker 94, 110; M. Dibelius, The Crozer Quarterly 12 (1933), 257f. or Botschaft u. Geschichte I 1953, 262). Σῶσόν με corresponds to the prayer Mk. 14.36, and the ἀλλ' οὐ κτλ, that follows on there is radicalised in δόξασον κτλ. Correspondingly ἦλθεν ἡ ὥρα of Mk. 14.41, which possibly still lingers on in v. 23, has been changed into the νῦν of v. 31, and by this means the visible, historical event becomes the invisible event of salvation history that is fulfilled in it.—If the Evangelist knew the Gospel of Mark it is possible that just as in vv. 25f., he had Mk. 8.34 in view, so now he intended to give a counterpart to Mk. 9.2–8. But it is also possible that he still knew the story of the Transfiguration Mk. 9. 2–8 in its original sense as a resurrection narrative (cp. Gesch. der syn. Tr. 278f. = History of the Syn. Trad. 259f.), and therefore understood the φωνή v. 8 as a counterpart to the voice from heaven Mk. 9.7.

[2] That the heavenly voice should answer the cry of the Messenger corresponds to the representation of the Mandaean Texts; see p. 421 n.8. In the light of the fact that the φωνή v. 29 is interpreted by the ὄχλος as thunder, cp. Ginza 533, 22f., after the soul's cry of lamentation: "Immediately there occurred a quaking in the world", namely because a Uthra is now sent as helper. Similarly Mand. Lit. 210, in the description of the ascent of the Messenger (or the soul), which signifies judgment for the world, it is stated: "There was a voice in heaven, a thunder in the house of the stars". In this context the Jewish idea of the בַּת קוֹל (Br. ad loc and Str.-B. I 125–134) is out of place, but on the contrary Mart. Pol 9.1 is so to be understood. Concerning voices from heaven which call up the dying, see also Frz. Bieler θεῖος ἀνήρ I 46. On φωνή generally see p. 259 n. 2.

[3] The καὶ . . . καί closely binds together the two utterances and corresponds to καθὼς (. . . . οὕτως), which is a favourite expression of the Evangelist elsewhere, cp. especially 17.2.

πάλιν δοξάζειν; it corresponds therefore to a δοξάζειν that has already preceded. But this is to be understood neither of the δόξα of Jesus in his "pre-existence" (if for no other reason than that it has to do with the δοξάζειν of the Father's ὄνομα, which is already glorified through the work of Jesus as the Revealer, 17.4), nor of individual events of the life of Jesus, but of his activity as a whole; therein indeed he sought the glory of the Father (7.18), through it the works of the Father became manifest (cp. 9.4. with 11.4), and looking back on it he could say, "I glorified Thee on the earth, in that I completed the work which thou didst give me to do" (17.4). The glory which God received through the work of the Son in truth consists in the fact that God became manifest (17.4, 6). Inasmuch as God made him the Revealer, God has glorified his own name; if he glorifies it further, that means that Jesus will continue to remain the Revealer, and indeed precisely through his death.[1]

Accordingly in the ὥρα (v. 23), and in the νῦν (vv. 27, 31) *past and future are bound to each other.* That the hour of death is the hour of glorifying God rests on the fact that the entire work of Jesus serves the revelation. But that his entire work can be revelation similarly rests on the fact that he also takes up his death into his service. But all that is included in its significance, i.e. in so far as it is God's revelation, the deed of the Father who glorified and will glorify, who wills that this life with its end be understood as *his* doing.[2]

Just as past and future are bound together, so therefore also *the δόξα of the Father and the δόξα of the Son are bound to each other*. For if the Father is glorified through the work of the Son, i.e. reveals himself, so at the same time the Son is glorified as the Revealer.[3] Grammatically ἐδόξασα and δοξάσω should be supplied with τὸ ὄνομά μου as object; in consequence of the omission of the object there arises a deliberate ambiguity: in so far as God causes his ὄνομα to be recognised, he causes at the same time the Revealer to be recognised. Therefore the ὥρα is indeed the hour when the Son is glorified (v. 23), just as the Father also sought the glory of the Son in the work that the Son achieved in the past (5.23; 8.50, 54). That which happened to the glory of God happened equally that the Son might be glorified (11.4); indeed, the Son must be glorified, that he may be able to bring about the glory of

---

[1] Correspondingly the statement also holds good that the κρίσις of the world is accomplished through the work of Jesus that has already taken place (3.19; 5.22, 24, 30) as through his present work, which determines the future of the "now" (v. 31) and of all future (16.8–11).

[2] See further on 17.1; see also pp. 198f.

[3] See further on 17.1.

the Father (17.1); he is in truth the Revealer: Father and Son are one (10.30).[1]

In so far as the ὥρα of Jesus is understood in the light of the δι' ὑμᾶς of v. 30, it is at the same time the hour of decision for the man to whom the Revealer directs his word. In the ταραχή of Jesus *his* ταραχή is represented at the same time (cp. 14.1, 27). Will he understand that the death of Jesus essentially belongs to the revelation of God? That all the teaching of Jesus about his being sent, in which all human standards and valuations are set in question and destroyed, receives its seal in the death of Jesus? That therefore his teaching cannot be appropriated as mere instruction, as general truth, as a philosophy of life, whether of pessimism or asceticism, but only as an action that has its goal in death and is completed in death as radical surrender to the glory of God? Will he understand that the revelation of Jesus is the glorification of God and thereby the judgment of the world?

In **v. 29** the Evangelist has again made clear, through his medium of the misunderstanding, how difficult such understanding is to man.[2] The ὄχλος[3] does not understand the divine voice which authenticates Jesus as the Revealer. Some hold that the voice from heaven is a peal of thunder,[4] an irrelevant happening in nature—they are the indifferent, who do not observe that what is here taking place concerns them. Others think that an angel spoke with Jesus;[5] they have a certain interest, but it is a false one: the interest of the uninvolved, perhaps mixed with sympathy or respect, but also without realising that they themselves are the ones addressed.[6] But this is precisely what they should know; for οὐ δι' ἐμὲ ἡ φωνὴ αὕτη γέγονεν ἀλλὰ δι' ὑμᾶς (**v. 30**). As the Revealer does not need to utter an express petition in prayer (11.42), so he does not need for himself a special divine word of consolation.

---

[1] See pp. 386f.

[2] Perhaps the source offered the Evangelist a foundation or stimulus for v. 29 also; cp. Ginza 577, 17ff., where the soul, to whom the "helpers" appear, says concerning the powers of the world: "They did not see the high Father, they did not see my helpers; they did not see my gentle guide, who drew me out of their midst and led me away . . . . He clothed me with his own splendour. . . . .".

[3] Its appearance is unmotivated and surprising, see p. 421.

[4] That on the contrary in the Old Testament (Ps. 29. 3–9; Job 37.4; 1 Sam.12.18) and elsewhere in the ancient world (Wetst., Br., Frz. Boll. Aus der Offenbarung Johannis 1914, 18f.) thunder can be interpreted as a heavenly voice, has nothing to do with this statement; cp. rather p. 428 n.2. The question may legitimately be raised whether the Evangelist has reformulated for his description a sentence in the source which spoke of the thunder in parallelism with the φωνή.

[5] For the idea that an angel speaks from heaven, see Gen. 21.17; 22.11; 1 Kings 13.18.

[6] A similar differentiation of judgment appears in the Rabbinic narrative, cited by Schl., concerning the rescue of a girl from drowning: was the rescue a natural event or was

The true meaning of the hour is described in **v. 31**: the judgment of this world now takes place.[1] The ruler of this world[2] will now be thrown out of the domain over which he formerly held sway.[3] The significance of the hour of decision is thus described in the cosmological terminology of the Gnostic myth.[4] If in the Evangelist's mind the myth has lost its mythological content and become historicised,[5] his language on the other hand serves to eliminate the traditional eschatology of primitive Christianity.[6] The turn of the ages results now;[7] naturally in such a way that the "now" of the passion stands in indissoluble unity with the work of Jesus in the past and with his future glorification; indeed it actually established this unity (v. 28). Since this "now" the "prince of the world" is judged (16.11); the destiny of man has become definitive, according as each grasps the meaning of this "now," according as he believes or not (1.36; 5.25). No future in this world's history can bring anything new, and all apocalyptic pictures of the future are empty dreams.[8]

The κρίσις consequently is also the separation. For if Jesus **v. 32**

---

it a miracle? On the other hand this related to the judgment of a situation which in itself was unambiguous.

[1] The Evangelist could have added each time τούτου to κόσμου, see p. 340 n.1; it is lacking however in 14.30; its omission in 12.31 D al can hardly be original; see also S. A. Fries, ZNTW 6 (1905), 129f.

[2] The ἄρχων τοῦ κόσμου (τούτου) naturally is not death but the devil. In the New Testament the expression is found only here and 14.30; 16.11. Synonymous are ὁ θεὸς τ. αἰῶνος τούτου 2 Cor. 4.4. (on which see Windisch in Meyer's Kommentar) and ὁ ἄρχων τ. αἰῶνος τούτου Ign. Eph. 17.1; 19.1; Mg. 1.3; Tr. 4.2; Rom. 7.1; Phld. 6.2. Cp. also the expressions which occur in 1 Cor. 2.6, 8; Eph. 2.2; 6.1 (on these see Lietzmann and Dibelius in the Hdb. zum NT). The conception of the devil as the ruler of the world entered Judaism from Iranian dualism (Bousset, Rel. des Judent. 331ff. 513ff.); the former took over κοσμοκράτωρ as a loan word (Str.-B. ad loc), and it is widely current in Gnostic and Gnosticising literature; see Br. ad loc. and Schlier, Rel. Unters. 129; Christus und die Kirche 6, 2; 11.1. The attempt of Fries op. cit., to prove that not the devil but Metatron is meant, on the ground that in Jewish literature שַׂר הָעוֹלָם (ἄρχων τ. κόσμου) never denotes the devil but only (God and) the Metatron, is impossible.

[3] Βληθήσεται ἔξω, which D has instead of ἐκβλ. ἔξω, is a meaningless variant; βληθ. κάτω of Θ it syr[s] and several Fathers will be a correction in accordance with Lk. 10.18; Rev. 12.7–12; 20.3.—That the ascent of the Messenger signifies the destruction of the world and of its (or their) ruler is the teaching of the Gnostic myth, see pp. 23, 157 n.5; ZNTW 24 (1925), 136; Br. ad loc.; Schlier, Relg. Unters. 14ff.—Mand. Lit. 222, "I will kill the evil one and cast him into the end of the world" deals, it is true, with the evil man; nevertheless the latter is an incorporation of the ruler of the world, just as the believer is of the Messenger.

[4] Cp. the employment of the Gnostic myth for the description of the saving work of Christ in 1 Cor. 2.6–8; Phil. 2. 6–11; Col. 2.15, and especially the Ascension of Isaiah.

[5] The placing of vv. 23–26 before vv. 27–33 serves this very purpose; see p. 426.

[6] See pp. 128f., 153ff., 166f., 189f., 195ff., 257f., 305f., 326.

[7] In correspondence with Gal. 4.4: 2 Cor. 5.17.

[8] According to Gourbillon (in Wik. 198) 3.14–21 is to be inserted between v. 31 and v. 32. Regarding Wik. see the remarks on pp. 313–4.

says—again in the language of the myth[1]—that as the exalted, i.e. the glorified Lord,[2] he will draw all men[3] to himself,[4] it is self-evident that he certainly offers this possibility to all men, but that this is realised only in those who belong to him, who as his servants will be with him (v. 26; 14.3; 17.24).

The promise is ambiguous. For how will he draw to himself those who belong to him? Doubtless by virtue of the fact that he has overcome death for them, and given them a share in the δόξα that he as the exalted Lord has with the Father beyond death (17.24). And within the myth this is the only meaning of the statement. But the ὑψωθῆναι of Jesus is at the same time, as the remark of the Evangelist in **v. 33** expressly says, his "exaltation" on the cross,[5] which in a paradoxical manner is also his δοξασθῆναι. If he as the exalted Lord draws after himself those who belong to him, he draws them also to the cross, i.e. the hate and the persecution from the world which he encountered. The farewell discourses will explicitly develop that theme.[6] But for those who belong to him this "being drawn" to him is at the same time a being exalted ἐκ τῆς γῆς. They will then, however much they are still ἐν τῷ κόσμῳ (17.11), no longer be ἐκ τοῦ κόσμου, in the sense of essentially belonging to the world (17.14, 16); they are no longer ἴδιον of the

[1] See ZNTW 24 (1925), 131f. In addition Ginza 429, 16ff; John-B. 81, 2f.; 84, 2ff.; 160, 22ff. ("I lead my friends . . . I will draw them on high with glorious banners to thrones"); Exc. ex Theod. 26; 58 (ἀναλαμβάνειν and ἀναφέρειν); Iren. I 13, 6 (ἀνασπᾶν); act. Andr. 5' p. 40, 17 (ἀνάγεσθαι); act. Jo. 100, p. 201, 4 (ἀναλαμβάνεσθαι). In Od. Sol. 31 it is described how the Redeemer on ascending to the Highest "presents" his sons (קרב, Frankenberg: προσφέρειν, is that the παραστῆσαι of 2 Cor. 4.14 and elsewhere?). The cross is described in act. Jo. 98, p. 200, 12 as ἀναλωγὴ βεβαία; cp. on this Schlier, Relg. Unters. 122 and generally 110ff. (concerning the μηχανή of Christ) and 136ff. (concerning the heavenly journey). In Act. Thom. 156 p. 265, 5f. (see p. 369 n.2); 169, p. 283, 7f. (esp. 17f.) the executed apostle appears to the believers in the role of the Redeemer and says: ἀνῆλθον γὰρ καὶ ἀπέλαβον τὸ ἐλπιδόμενον . . . καὶ μετ' οὐ πολὺ συναχθήσεσθε πρός με. To this corresponds συλλαμβάνεσθαι act. Jo. 100, p. 201, 3; cp. the idea that the Redeemer "gathers" his own, see pp. 374 n. 3; 384 n. 2; 412 n. 1.—The thought is spiritualised when in Ign. Eph. 9.2 πίστις is the ἀναγωγεύς; similarly C. Herm. 4.11b, where the view of the εἰκὼν τοῦ θεοῦ leads the way to the height; see Odeberg 100.—See also on 14.3.

[2] Ὑψωθῆναι and δοξασθῆναι are synonymous; see pp. 152 n.4, 307 n.4; ἐάν as in 14.3 almost = ὅταν; cp. 8.22. ἐκ τ. γῆς is frequently lacking in the Patristic tradition; see M. E. Boismard, RB 57 (1950), 391.

[3] Πάντα which ℵ*D latt read instead of πάντας can hardly be other than the acc. sing. masc., so that the variant has no significance for the sense. That would however also be the case if we had to understand πάντα as omnia (latt); Bl.-D §138, 1.

[4] On ἕλκω see p. 000; ἑλκύσω is Hellenistic for ἕλξω Bl.-D §101.

[5] Is the comment derived from the Evangelist (so Dodd 434) or from the editor (see p. 212 n. 1 on 18.9)? On the form of the comment see p. 212 n.4.—Σημαίνειν is a technical term for the allusive speech of the oracle (see Br.). The comment is "false" (Wendt, Sp.) in so far as ὑψωθῆναι in the source was interpreted unambiguously in the sense of the Myth; but the Evangelist actually corrects this.

[6] 15.18ff.; 16.1ff.; 17.14.

κόσμος (15.19), and therefore they stand, as he does, the other side of death (17.24).[1]

The promise of v. 32 therefore is spoken under the sign of the cross; like vv. 25f. it is bound to the law of discipleship unto the cross. Correspondingly it is in the hour of humiliation that the Revealer declares the promise; a man has to let himself be addressed by the Man of humiliation. Thus in a certain way the "drawing to himself" is at the same time a "thrusting from himself." It is precisely to humiliation that the divine φωνή gives the glory and dignity of the δόξα, and in so doing it gives it eternity. "Humiliation belongs to him just as essentially as exaltation. In case there was one who could love him only in his exaltation—such a man's vision is confused, he knows not Christ, neither loves him at all, but takes him in vain."[2]

2) *The Offence:* 8.30–40[3]

As often, so now also the words of Jesus find faith in many hearers (**v. 30**).[4] Whether such faith is genuine must show itself by its ability to stand the test and overcome the offence that the Revealer and his word signify for the world. To such a test however the "Jews who believed"[5] are immediately subjected through the next saying of Jesus (**vv. 31f.**); and it is significant that the offence which this saying offers arises precisely from the fact that it is a *promise*. Again it becomes plain that the world does not know at all what it *really* wants; when it meets the salvation after which it aspires, then that must become an offence to it. Its lostness becomes its sin, because men do not commit themselves unreservedly to the salvation that is offered to them; i.e. they are unwilling to give themselves up, and because of this they commit themselves to their lost condition. As they are blind men who think that they see, so they are slaves who consider themselves to be free.

ἐὰν ὑμεῖς μείνητε ἐν τῷ λόγῳ τῷ ἐμῷ,
ἀληθῶς μαθηταί μού ἐστε,
καὶ γνώσεσθε τὴν ἀλήθειαν,
καὶ ἡ ἀλήθεια ἐλευθερώσει ὑμᾶς.[6]

---

[1] See Faulhaber op. cit. 42f.

[2] Kierkegaard, Training in Christianity, ET by W. Lowrie, 1947, 153f.; cp. generally the entire discourse "From on high he will draw all men unto himself". On v. 32 see also Dodd 247.

[3] For the sequence of 8.30–40 after 12.20–33 see p. 420.

[4] See p. 130 n.3.

[5] For the interchangeability of πιστεύειν εἰς αὐτόν v. 30) and πιστ. αὐτῷ (v. 31) see p. 252 n.2; cp. also J. Huby, Rech. sc. rel. 21. (1931), 407f.

[6] The sentences, unlike some of those that follow (vv. 34f., 38), can hardly be derived from the revelation discourses. Already Merx (232) had noticed the Gnostic character of

It is not immediate assent but steadfastness of faith[1] that gives character to genuine discipleship.[2] And it is for such faith that the promise holds good. Elsewhere ζωὴ (αἰώνιος) is promised to faith,[3] but here the promise is a double one: knowledge of the truth, and freedom.

It is self evident that the ἀλήθεια here is not the "truth" generally, the disclosure of all that exists in the sense of the Greek quest after ἀλήθεια. It is not a rational knowledge that is promised to the believer, in virtue of which he could break through the appearance of things, traditional opinions and prejudices, and win an undisguised, comprehensive vision into existence, in order rightly to perceive each individual reality according to need and interest. Rather the question after ἀλήθεια is orientated on the question after the ζωή as the authentic being of the man who is concerned about his life, to whom this question is proposed because he is a creature.[4] God's ἀλήθεια thus is God's reality, which alone is reality because it is life and gives life, whereas the seeming reality which belongs to the world is ψεῦδος, because it is a reality contrived in opposition to God, and as such is futile and brings death.[5] The promise of knowledge of the ἀλήθεια therefore is actually identical with the promise of ζωή.

---

the promises. Of a truth in Gnosticism the earthly world is regarded as a prison, and bodily existence as the captivity of the souls (Jonas, Gnosis I 106; Schlier, Relg. Unters. 154; Bornkamm, Myth. und Leg. 113). The Messenger is the *Emancipator* (Schlier op. cit. 154f., and concerning the λύτρωσις, Christus und die Kirche 73, 2; further Bornkamm op. cit. 12, 19); he bursts the heavenly wall (Schlier, Chr. und die Kirche 18ff.). Cp. Od. Sol. 17.10ff.:

And nothing appeared closed to me;
Because I was the opening of everything.
And I went towards all the bondsmen to loose them;
That I might not leave any man bound and binding.

(Tr. by R. Harris and A. Mingana, op. cit. 290).

Further Od. Sol. 42.15ff., the request of the captives for freedom, and Od. Sol. 10. In addition to the passages cited in ZNTW 24 (1925), 135 see also Ign. Phld. 8.1: πιστεύω τῇ χάριτι 'Ι. Χριστοῦ, ὃς λύσει ἀφ' ἡμῶν πάντα δεσμόν. Act. Thom. 43, p. 161, 9. "When will the captives be redeemed?" ask the souls, Ginza 524, 28; and Ginza 547, 17, a voice calls out of the height: "The prisoners shall be freed"; see further Ginza 549, 6ff.; 558, 1ff.; 561, 20; 583, 11ff. and elsewhere.

[1] Μένειν ἐν as a designation of faithfulness (so 1 Tim. 2.15; 2 Tim. 3.14) is also customary in Greek; see Br. For the Johannine usage see pp. 266 n.4, 267 n.1, 321 n.1.

[2] 'Αληθῶς here = ὄντως (v. 36) in accordance with frequent linguistic usage. Μαθητής is here a description of the Christian as 13.35; 15.8 and in Ign. Mg. 9.1; on this see Schlier, Relg. Unters. 57. On the history of the word in primitive Christianity see Arndt and Gingrich, A. v. Harnack, Mission und Ausbreitung[3] I 381–384 (= Expansion of Christianity II 1–4).

[3] 3.15f. etc.

[4] See pp. 44, 47.

[5] As to the connection between ἀλήθεια and ζωή on the one hand, and of ψεῦδος and θάνατος on the other, see p. 321; Faulhaber 86. On the whole theme see ThWB s.v. 'Αλήθεια.

God's reality however is called ἀλήθεια in so far as it manifests in Jesus the fight against the ψεῦδος.[1] Correspondingly the knowledge of it is promised to faith in Jesus. That means first, that this *knowing* is not contemplating in the sense of the Greek θεωρεῖν, which grows out of distance and gives distance, but that it is the reception of the truth which grows out of obedient submission to the revelation, and therefore from the fact that a man wills to live in a spirit of self-surrender, not motived by the ψεῦδος in alleged independence, but as a creature.[2] That means at the same time therefore that faith will be a comprehending faith, providing that it opens itself to its object and that it is not the blind acceptance of a dogma. For life is for a man the illumination of existence in that authentic self-understanding that knows God as its Creator.[3] The consequence of πιστεύειν and γινώσκειν is not viewed in such a way that whoever accepts the dogma becomes the possessor of esoteric knowledge in mystagogical teaching. Nowhere—not even in the farewell discourses—does Jesus state such a view. Nor is it that a new world of thought opens itself to the believer through his sinking down and gazing inwardly; nowhere is there a hint of such ideas; faith always remains bound to the Word, and does not hover out or beyond in mystic vision. Rather the general way faith is characterised shows it as an attitude which surrenders the previous self-understanding of man, and that the γινώσκειν is nothing less than a factor in the structure of faith itself, namely faith in so far as it understands itself.[4] Consequently

---

[1] Christians therefore are called II Jn 1 οἱ ἐγνωκότες τὴν ἀλήθειαν. According to 1 Jn. 2.21 εἰδέναι τὴν ἀλήθειαν is characteristic of them. Rightly Wrede, Char.und Tendenz 1f.

[2] On γινώσκειν as "perceive" see p. 54f.

[3] See pp. 40–45, 258.

[4] In Jn πιστεύειν and γινώσκειν are not distinguished with respect to their object. That the Father sent Jesus is object of faith (11.42; 17.8, 21) as of knowledge (17.3); that he or his teaching comes from the Father is believed (16.27–30) as it is perceived (7.17). The ἀλήθεια is perceived (8.32), but similarly believed, since faith believes on him who is the ἀλήθεια (14.6). That Jesus is the Christ is believed (11.27; 20.31), but also at the same time it is perceived by faith (6.69). Accordingly πιστ. and γιν. can stand alongside each other in synonymous parallelism (17.8). Since πιστ. customarily denotes the first turning to Jesus, πιστ. can stand in the first place where both verbs are bound together (6.69; 8.31f.; cp. 10.38). Nevertheless that the reverse order is also possible (16.30; 1 Jn. 4.16) shows that πιστ. and γιν. cannot be distinguished simply as beginning and end stages, so that in Christianity there are "Pistics" and Gnostics. Γινώσκειν cannot be separated from πιστ., but πιστ., if it is to be genuine, must at the same time be a γιν.; i.e. perception is a structural element of faith. Whereas all human knowledge of the ἀλήθεια is always only one of faith, the relationship of Revealer to God is designated solely as γιν. and not also as πιστ. For man there is an end of faith only when his earthly existence is at an end and a θεωρεῖν is granted him, which is no longer directed to the δόξα veiled in the σάρξ of the Son, but which is directed to the δόξα directly (17.24).—In Od. Sol. 42.8f. knowing and believing stand in synonymous parallelism. It is different in Is. 50.10: ἵνα γνῶτε καὶ πιστεύσητε καὶ συνῆτε, where perception is the presupposition for believing and comprehending. For the whole subject cp. ThWB I 712, 41ff. and s.v. πίστις; further Faulhaber 33f.; Howard, Christianity according to St. John 151ff.

nothing essentially different is promised than what is in 7.17: as little as the object of faith is visible outside faith, so surely is faith itself a knowing, and indeed for this reason, because God's revelation in which faith believes is ἀλήθεια, divine reality, and as such it is life giving and a power that illuminates human existence. If to open oneself to it means to understand it as ἀλήθεια, its object also opens itself to faith.[1]

In a certain way therefore the promise to faith is only faith; faith has everything it needs; the knowledge of faith *is* eternal life (17.3). Nevertheless a further promise can be given, which affirms that the existence of the believer is determined through the knowledge of the ἀλήθεια: ἡ ἀλήθεια ἐλευθερώσει ὑμᾶς. It is not a question of a temporal consequence following upon knowledge of the truth and freedom in a rationalistic-positivistic sense, namely that from knowledge issue practical consequences for the development of the individual or for the fellowship. For just as knowledge of the ἀλήθεια is by no means to be identified with the knowledge of that which exists, neither does ἐλευθερία at all denote the growing human freedom of the spirit that comes from such knowledge, which gives form to the individual and cultural development, and rules over the affiliations that are given in nature, tradition and convention. Rather, so surely as faith gradually comes to itself in the believer (hence the future ἐλευθερώσει), so surely does it come to be only that which it is already: the believer *is* free as a man who knows the ἀλήθεια and so lives by it.

If however the ἐλευθερία is not freedom of the spirit in the rationalistic-positivistic sense, neither is it in the Stoic or Idealistic sense. For of course its realisation has to be interpreted also as a coming-to-itself, i.e. as a *becoming* free, which in turn is always based on the fact that the man who knows *is* free. Now in truth, in Stoicism and Idealism knowledge is based on the original freedom of man that belongs to him as λόγος or spirit. In knowledge this original condition of freedom is disclosed and carried through vis-a-vis all relations, so that to become free is nothing other than the accomplishment of original freedom in the self-knowledge of man.[2] Thereby the authentic self of man is reckoned to be his spirit, his inner nature, and at the same time it is presupposed that this inner nature stands at a man's disposal, so that he is free as he returns to it.[3]

In John ἐλευθερία cannot be described as the substance of the knowledge that reveals the being of man.[4] And it is only appearance that

---

[1] See pp. 162, 274–5.

[2] For the Stoic concept of freedom see Schlier ThWB II 488, 51ff.; H. Jonas, Augustin und das paulinische Freiheitsproblem 1930, 8ff. Several citations also in Br. ad loc.

[3] See especially Jonas op. cit.

[4] It could not e.g. be said in Jn. γνώσεσθε ὅτι ἐλεύθεροί ἐστε.

there exists in John the same connection as to the foundation of freedom, namely that becoming free takes place in the fulfilment of the freedom that is supposed to exist already. For naturally freedom is to be asserted, not however in the original being of man, but through God's revelation which meets man in the Word as the eschatological event. Since he makes this freedom his own in faith, his *being* free, in the sense of the freedom appropriated by him, is grounded in his *becoming* free, conceived in terms of the faith that lays hold of it. And in so far as faith can never cease, in so far therefore as this becoming free has to continue (as μένειν ἐν τῷ λόγῳ) and therefore has constantly to be achieved anew, a man experiences this condition of *being* free only as a perpetual *becoming* free. That however is based on the fact that his freedom is not the independence of his inwardness bestowed by nature and history, but freedom from the "world," which he falsely organises;[1] i.e. freedom from all that he was before, from his past, from himself.[2] Freedom as eschatological gift signifies for him the opening of the future, of himself as a future phenomenon, a new thing. But that will become fully clear only from the following discussion[3] on freedom.

The Jews understand v. 33 quite rightly, that such a promise contains a judgment upon them; They are bondmen. And they contest this judgment by referring to their being children of Abraham.[4] Their question[5] shows that they also rightly understand freedom as the freedom which the relationship to God gives to man. But they fail to recognise that freedom can only be eschatological gift; they hold that it is the characteristic of the Jew, who already has it as his possession in virtue of his being a child of Abraham.[6]

---

[1] See pp. 54f.

[2] See pp. 135f.

[3] In the discussion the Evangelist appears in vv. 34f. to have used the continuation of the saying from the revelatory discourses that is cited in vv. 31f. Possibly we could reconstruct as follows

πᾶς ὁ ποιῶν τὴν ἁμαρτίαν δοῦλός ἐστιν
[. . . . . ?]
ὁ [δὲ] δοῦλος [οὐ?] μένει ἐν τῇ οἰκίᾳ εἰς τὸν αἰῶνα,
ὁ [δὲ] υἱὸς [οὐ?] μένει εἰς τὸν αἰῶνα (see p. 440 n.2).

After the first line a member of the double verse has presumably been struck out. On the style πᾶς ὁ . . . see p. 319 n.4. The analysis in Becker 79f. is different.

[4] On the formulation σπέρμα 'Αβρ. see Rom. 9.7; 11.1; 2 Cor. 11.22; Gal. 3.16; Heb. 2.16 and Str.-B. ad loc. On the pride of the Jew in his descent from Abraham see Mt. 3.9 par. and on this Str.-B. I 116–121.

[5] On this πῶς of incomprehension see pp. 136 n.1, 230 n.1.

[6] That is the standpoint of Pharasaic Judaism. Whereas the Zealots based the struggle for political freedom on the principle that the Jew is subject to no man but to God only (Jos. bell 2.118; 7.323ff.), for the Rabbinic viewpoint the freedom of the Jew is independent of his political situation; it is based on his being a son of Abraham or son of God, and on his possession of the Thora; see Schl. ad loc.; Str.-B. 1.116f.; Odeberg 296f.; Arn. Meyer, Das Rätsel des Jacobusbriefes 1930, 154; Hosk. 339. R. Eisler asserts ('Ιησ. βασ. II 66, 5) that

The answer of Jesus in **v. 34**, introduced by the passionate ἀμὴν ἀμὴν λέγω ὑμῖν, alludes to their erroneous idea: "Everyone who does sin is a bondman."[1] The idea of freedom therefore is determined by the fact that the concept of bondage is defined as a ποιεῖν τὴν ἁμαρτίαν. Stoicism and Idealism could also well speak in this way;[2] they however would start out from the presupposition that "sin" rests only on the error of man as to what his authentic being is, as to the difference between that which is ἐφ' ἡμῖν and that which is οὐκ ἐφ' ἡμῖν, and so finally on the error as to the nature of freedom as of something originally proper to him. Admittedly therefore in the Stoic view no ἁμαρτάνων is an ἐλεύθερος, in so far as the ἁμαρτάνων places himself in the servitude of ἀλλότρια, of things that are ἔξω, that are οὐκ ἐφ' ἡμῖν and therefore οὐ πρὸς ἡμᾶς. Nevertheless he is never enslaved to the ἁμαρτάνειν, because his ἴδιον, his spirit is the realm which is independent of everything ἔξω and always remains ἐφ' ἡμῖν. He needs only to be illuminated in order to achieve the freedom that is proper to him.[3] The inquiry after freedom here always remains the inquiry after independence from that which I myself am not, and freedom is won through restriction to the self;[4] ἁμαρτάνειν, however much it leads to servitude to things, is never necessity.

The statement, however, that he who does sin is a bondman is intended to affirm that the sinner is enslaved exactly to sin, that he has lost himself, and is not able to withdraw to a safe area of inner freedom.

---

the statement of Jesus is a reinterpretation of the promises of freedom made by the Galilean Judas (Jos. bell. 7.343f.).—Accordingly the freedom affirmed by Jesus to the Jews is not the political (so de Wette among others), "whereby the Egyptian and Babylonian house of servitude appears to have been forgotten, and the appearance of freedom in the Roman empire too favourably adjudged" (Ho.); nor is it the social (Godet, B. Weiss: "Freedom of person was, with certain reservations, guaranteed to all descendants of Abraham").

[1] Τῆς ἁμαρτίας is an interpretative gloss, which admittedly is not false factually, but it destroys the point, since it depends on the definition of the concept of slave ("a slave is one who does sin, and thus is a slave of sin"). The gloss is lacking in D b syr[s] and Clem. Al.; it could in fact be a wholly secondary insertion. Black, Dodd (177, 2) and Wik. also regard it as probable that τ. ἁμαρτ. is a (correct) interpretative addition, while Becker (8) wishes to retain it in the text.—The saying could serve as a confirmation that the source was originally composed in Aramaic, for if translated back into Aramaic it contains a word play; see Black 128f.

[2] That the φαῦλος is a δοῦλος is a perpetually recurrent Stoic saying; see v. Arnim, Stoic. vet. fragm. I 54, 23ff.; III 86, 30f.; 155.17f.; 156, 14f.; Plut. Cat. min. 67, p. 692c; Epikt. diss. II 1, 23 (οὐδεὶς τοίνυν ἁμαρτάνων ἐλεύθερός ἐστιν); IV. 1, 3; further Br. ad loc.

E. 297

[3] Epict, iv. 1, 41ff. etc., especially II 26, 1: πᾶν ἁμάρτημα μάχην περιέχει. ἐπεὶ γὰρ ὁ ἁμαρτάνων οὐ θέλει ἁμαρτάνειν, ἀλλὰ κατορθῶσαι, δῆλον ὅτι ὃ μὲν θέλει οὐ ποιεῖ . . . 7: λογικῷ ἡγεμονικῷ δεῖξον μάχην καὶ ἀποστήσεται. I 17, 14: εἰ γὰρ ἀληθές ἐστι τὸ "πάντας ἄκοντας ἁμαρτάνειν" (Plat. Protag. 345d), σὺ δὲ καταμεμάθηκας τὴν ἀλήθειαν, ἀνάγκη σε ἤδη κατορθοῦν.

[4] See Jonas op. cit.

For the Revealer leads him to freedom indeed, not through demanding that he reflect on his originally free self, but through calling him to faith—to faith in him whom God sent to save the lost world. Just as his coming as eschatological event makes an end to the world, so the freedom which he promises is the eschatological gift; it is therefore freedom from the world, and that means at the same time freedom from the past, and so the freedom of man from himself. For the world is indeed *man himself*, who constitutes it;[1] and the past is *his* past, his "whence" from which he comes, and which determines him.[2]

Man can receive freedom from himself only as a present, as eschatological gift; he cannot acquire it himself. For everything that he undertakes of his own accord is determined from the first through that which he already is. Only he who could act under the motive of that which he is not would be free; but that means: freedom is only an eschatological possibility, given by God through the revelation. Its conception however presupposes the admission that one is a bondman, a slave to one's own past, to the world, to sin.

Of that the Jews are ignorant when they talk about freedom simply in virtue of their past, i.e. their descent from Abraham.[3] For certainly they would have been right in appealing to being Abraham's children if they had interpreted the significance of this as a promise for the future which yet lays obligations upon them. From their descent from Abraham they should have understood freedom as a divine gift; they misunderstand it, however, as a possession that belongs to them. To look into the past, into history, is right indeed if it is a look at God's deeds which commit to faithfulness, since they always direct a man away from himself to God's future. Whether the adherence of the Jews to their history is genuine faithfulness must prove itself by whether they recognise God's revelation in Jesus, which sets a question mark against them in their present way of life.[4] That they here deny that their faithfulness to history is not genuine the following will show.

---

[1] See pp. 54f.

[2] See pp. 135f.

[3] Since the Jews appeal to their descent from Abraham and not to their morals or their faithfulness to the law, the discussion does not advance into the circle of Jewish debates about the relationship of actual sins to the "evil impulse" and the possibility of ruling the "evil impulse", which Odeberg 297–300 adduces for comparison (cp. esp. Ecclus. 15.11–17). In general these discussions show that the Jewish outlook also knows an area of inner freedom; it is however the purely formally understood freedom of the will to obey or not to obey the commands of God; see Bousset, Rel. des Judent. 404ff.; Moore I 453ff. The Rabbinic statements cited by Str.-B. ad loc., have no fundamental character but simply amount to the truth, "He who gives the devil his little finger has his whole hand taken".

[4] See pp. 267-8, 273, 276f., 325f.

First however in vv. 35f. freedom is yet once more characterised as the eschatological freedom which man can receive only through Jesus. The Evangelist in v. 35 obviously uses for this purpose a further statement from the source, to which he has given a definite meaning through his addition in v. 36. **V. 35** appears to have been originally a parabolic saying: as a slave[1] has no certain place, no right of domicile, in distinction from the son of the house, so the sinner (as a "slave") has no certainty of the future, whereas the man who has been freed by the Revealer is certain of the future.[2] V. 36 however shows that the Evangelist desires that the υἱός in v. 35 be understood as Jesus,[3] and so he find the opposition between the one free man and the slaves of sin. By this means the picture, which he has destroyed in v. 35, he allows entirely to fall from view in v. 36, in order to enunciate the thought of v. 32 in a more precisely defined form in the light of vv. 33–34: Jesus promises freedom; he *alone* can bestow it, and *only that* is genuine freedom.[4]

That the reception of genuine freedom presupposes the abandonment of the false security is shown in vv. 37–40, since the discussion of vv. 33f. is continued. The Jews rightly appealed to the fact that they stand in relation to Abraham as his children (**v. 37**: οἶδα . . .); nevertheless they understood it only in an external fashion—and in truth that is *not* right (ἀλλά). For if their relation to Abraham was a genuine one, they would believe in Jesus; instead of that they wish to kill him.[5]

---

[1] In the parabolic saying the articles before δοῦλος, οἰκία and υἱός are the generic articles of the parabolic style, as in Mk. 4.3 etc.

[2] It is of course possible not to interpret v. 35 as a parabolic saying, namely if one felt it permissible to understand the concepts as technically used metaphors. The μένειν εἰς τ. αἰῶνα gives rise to the possibility for such a consideration, for it seems to fall out of the picture. Naturally it could not be meant in the sense of 6.27; 12.34 (see p. 222 n.7 and Schl. on 8.34). Rather μένειν in connection with οἰκία would have the meaning of "dwell", "lodge" (see p. 100 n.1). Then οἰκία, in accordance with current Gnostic terminological use, would be a metaphor for "world", just as "dwell" would be a metaphor for the earthly life in the world (Jonas, Gnosis I 100ff.). Then however one would have to assume that the Evangelist changed the statement of the source into its opposite; the original meaning would have been: "The slave must dwell in the house for ever, the Son not", since the Son will leave the world and return to the heavenly homeland. That is not impossible. In any case the οἰκία must not be equated with the "Father's house" of 14.2; for without any closer definition the mere οἰκία cannot have this meaning; moreover in the "Father's house" the δοῦλος has no place at all, not even a transitory one.

[3] So also Zn., Br., Schl., Bd. That this is the needful interpretation is shown by the οὖν linking up v.36 with v. 35. Also the Evangelist can hardly have understood μένει εἰς τ. αἰῶνα other than in 6.27.—Since we are dealing with the subsequent interpretation of an earlier saying, we can afford to tolerate the harshness which lies in the opposition of the general ὁ δοῦλος and the individual ὁ υἱός. It is difficult simply to strike out v. 36 as an editorial addition, as Wellh., Sp., and Hirsch wish to do.

[4] "Only he" corresponds to the tone which ὁ υἱός carries in the context, "only that" corresponds to the ὄντως in the sequence after v. 33.

[5] Ζητεῖτέ με ἀποκτεῖναι has an equally fundamental character as the murderous will, with which the Jews are reproached in 8.44 (see p. 321); to this corresponds the general

Their behaviour, which flows from the supposed certainty of their possession, makes it transparently clear that they are unfaithful to their history, in so far as it is the history that has been guided by God. This divinely directed history, at the beginning of which stands Abraham, would only really be *their* history if they grasped the meaning of the figure of Abraham, which points to the future, the eschatological future.[1] Since they fail to understand it and make of the status of Abraham's children a secure possession, they change their history into pure past. Their history, properly understood, had the meaning of releasing them from their specific past and of directing them to the God-given future; to give to them therefore a future and life, so that the "whence" out of which they live at any given time, is God's future; instead of that their history has been distorted to mere past and has become a power that robs them of the future, i.e. that robs them of life; their "whence" is that of death; their father is, as v. 38 will suggest, the devil. And so their murderous purpose is but the behaviour that corresponds to their self-understanding.[2]

As in 5.38 the faithlessness of the Jews to their history was characterised by the reproach that they are not faithful to the word of God,[3] so here their murderous intention is traced back to the fact that the word of Jesus finds no place in them.[4] His word is indeed God's word, as **v. 38** asserts in mythological language:[5]

> ἃ ἐγὼ ἑώρακα παρὰ τῷ πατρὶ λαλῶ·
> καὶ ὑμεῖς οὖν ἃ ἠκούσατε παρὰ τοῦ πατρὸς ποιεῖτε.[6]

Because his word has its origin in God, they do not understand him; for their origin, which determines all their action, is a different one—

---

motivation ὅτι ὁ λόγος κτλ., which is plainly distinguished from the special motivation in 7.19ff. The reproach therefore does not demand for 8.30–40 the postulate of an insertion into a context wherein the subject was expressly a murderous intent of the Jews. Moreover this is sufficiently illustrated by 11.45–53; 12.10f., 19.

[1] See pp. 326f.

[2] See p. 321.

[3] See pp. 266f.

[4] Χωρεῖν when spoken of the λόγος signifies in Greek the wandering, the spreading itself abroad of the word (see Wetst.); accordingly we may interpret: "My word does not reach to you, finds no place with you". Frequently this is interpreted in connection with v. 31: "It makes no advance with you".

[5] V. 38 could again be a citation from the revelatory discourses. On the mythological terminology, see pp. 145 n.5; 249 n.1 and especially 250f.

[6] The text is uncertain, nevertheless the variants are insignificant in content. Both times ὅ instead of ἅ in 𝔎; inversion of ἃ ἐγώ in 𝔎D; ἑωράκατε instead of ἠκούσατε in ℵ* 𝔎D (a pedantic correction; see p. 69 n. 4): παρὰ τῷ πατρί in the second clause instead of παρὰ τοῦ πατρός in 𝔎D. Only a few variants of D could be held as original: the insertion of μου or ὑμῶν after πατρί or πατρός, and the insertion of ταῦτα before λαλῶ and ποιεῖτε. Becker (80) regards the οὖν as an addition to the source. It is lacking in W al lat syr[sin], possibly correctly.

and in truth it is the devil (so the antithesis implies). They who regard themselves as Abraham's children in reality are the devil's children;[1] they actually want to kill the man who speaks God's word to them.

The Jews who in v. 33 had appealed to their status as Abraham's children in order to prove their freedom, realise that Jesus has denied their relation to Abraham,[2] and they assert defiantly and blindly: ὁ πατὴρ ἡμῶν 'Αβραάμ ἐστιν (**v. 39**). Jesus contradicts them, both by repeating his earlier statement (v. 37): they cannot be Abraham's children, because they are wanting to kill him, and by a declaration that precedes this, and that makes clear the conclusiveness of the statement:[3] "*If you were Abraham's children you would do Abraham's works!*"[4] The correctness of their assertion should have proved itself by their action; for the behaviour of a man is determined by his "whence", his origin.[5] But their action contradicts them, for they are not doing the works of Abraham,[6] but on the contrary they are wanting to kill him (**v. 40**). In v. 38 their murderous intention was traced back to the fact that they do not understand the word of Jesus because it is God's word; so now the same fact serves to make plain the preposterous nature of their murderous will. Instead of "because" the term "although" is now used: The Jews are wanting to kill Jesus although he is a man who has said the truth to them.[7] But since ἀλήθεια is characterised as that which he has heard from God, and since play is again made with the double meaning of the word—"to say the truth" in the

---

[1] See pp. 316f.

[2] Obviously there is no misunderstanding of the Jews in the sense that they insisted, in opposition to Jesus, on their natural descent from Abraham; they rightly understood, and they affirm along with their uncontested natural relationship their spiritual or salvific membership in Abraham (rightly Odeberg 302). There exists therefore no contradiction at all between vv. 37 and 39 (Wellh., Schw.), as if v. 39 denied that the Jews were children of Abraham while v. 37 had recognised it.

[3] A consistent argument is present here. Assertion: The Jews are not children of Abraham. Proof: 1. to be children of Abraham shows itself in "works of Abraham", 2. the Jews want to kill Jesus, 3. that is no work of Abraham. Conclusion: the Jews therefore are not children of Abraham.—The inference is not expressed; it is self evident in the context.

[4] For the thought it is irrelevant whether we read with B ποιεῖτε, and then understand the sentence as an imperative: "If you are Abraham's children, then do also the works of Abraham!" But ποιεῖτε will be a correction, due to the fact that the unreal (i.e. contrary to fact) ἐποιεῖτε (ℵD pm, and in addition ἄν is read C K L pm) did not appear to suit ἐστε of the protasis (instead of this ἦτε is read in C ℜ pl); see Bl.-D §260, 1 and Br. ad loc.

[5] See pp. 138 n.1, 317f. The general notion that the filial status has to be preserved by following in the same spiritual way is naturally often expressed elsewhere; see Br. as loc.

[6] The concept "works of Abraham" is Rabbinic (Str.-B.). Among such works are reckoned "a benevolent eye, a modest mind and a humble spirit". But Jn. 8.39 scarcely has special works in view; rather ἐπίστευσεν could be reminiscent of Gen. 15.6.

[7] The concept ἄνθρωπος is not stressed; ἄνθρωπος is simply equivalent to τις, as 4.29; see Bl.-D. §301, 2.

general moralistic sense, and "to reveal the reality of God"[1]—the "although" also gains the meaning of "because": they are wanting to kill him exactly because he is the Revealer. Corresponding to that, the concluding statement, "*Abraham did not do that*", not only has the meaning, "It was far from Abraham to do a deed of that kind, to kill a man who speaks the truth." Far beyond that, the statement alludes to Abraham's attitude to the revelation: Abraham was not like them, closed against the coming Revealer.

If the murderous will of the Jews is proof that they are not Abraham's children, and therefore also that they are not free, manifestly this murderous will is a particularly clear sign of their lack of freedom. In very truth! By the fact that they wish to get rid of him, their hidden fear betrays itself—it is the "dread of the good."[2] For it is exactly the "good" that demands from man the inner freedom for self-surrender. This hidden fear however describes the good as evil, and persecutes it. In this perversion bondage finds its clearest and most terrible expression; in its view the promise of freedom is itself the offence.

3) *The Separation:* 6.60–71[3]

That the revelation is an offence, a scandal, had been demonstrated from the beginning through the misunderstandings and the demands made of Jesus for his authorisation; in 8.30–40 the offence had been made an explicit theme, and 6.60–71 shows that this offence leads to a final separation, even to a separation within the circle of the disciples itself. It becomes apparent who is a genuine disciple and who has attained only to a provisional, unauthentic faith. The offence was given exactly to the Jews who "had become believing" in him (8.31); they represent unauthentic discipleship. Genuine discipleship that "remains in his word" is represented by the Twelve. They are here named as such for the first time in John, and—apart from 20.24—for the only

---

[1] See p. 322. For the first meaning cp. Ps. 14.2, in the characteristic of the pious man: λαλῶν ἀλήθειαν ἐν καρδίᾳ αὐτοῦ.

[2] Kierkegaard, Concept of Dread, ET by W. Lowrie, 1946, 105ff., 123ff.

[3] Concerning the subsuming of 6.60–71 under this place, see pp. 285ff., 420. Hirsch would strike out the whole section as an addition of the editor; against this see Evang. Theologie 4 (1937), 125f. The section is a composition of the Evangelist's with the aid of synoptic tradition (see in the text). It is typical that Jesus addresses himself to idle talk that was not directed to him (see p. 297); the question, with which he begins, is similar to that in 16.19. On the comment of v. 64 see p. 212 n.4 cp. especially 13.11; for the citation of himself v. 65, see p. 348 n.4. On the explanatory, διὰ τοῦτο v. 65, see p. 92 n. 2, cp. esp. 13.11; on ἔλεγεν δέ v. 71, see p. 126 n. 2. Semitisms characteristic of the Evangelist are: the repeated αὐτοῦ after μαθητής, vv. 60, 61, 66; the setting of the predicate forward, vv. 68, 70; εἰδέναι ἐν ἑαυτῷ, v. 61; ἀπελθεῖν εἰς τ. ὀπίσω and περιπατεῖν μετά v.66 ; also the formulation of v. 64a (Schl.).

time. Doubtless elsewhere they are presupposed as the constant companions of Jesus,[1] but no account is given of their choice; the Evangelist assumes an acquaintance with the Synoptic tradition.[2] One story about the disciples however that derives from this tradition he has used here for his composition and has peculiarly transformed it, namely the story of Peter's confession of Jesus as Messiah. As this forms the decisive point in the Markan Gospel and introduces a new period of instruction of the disciples, so in a quite analogous manner, only much more radically, John has made Peter's confession the turning point. From now on the activity of Jesus is wholly limited to the circle of his followers.

The words of Jesus seem to many of the "disciples" to be a "hard speech,"[3] "who can listen to it?"[4] (**v. 60**). That the offence is taken actually by the disciples makes the character of the "scandal" perfectly plain: it is necessary for those very people who do not adopt an unfriendly and hostile attitude to Jesus, but seek a relationship to him, to endure the test. Many falter and "grumble" like the Jews (**v. 61**).[5] Jesus knows that,[6] for he sees through men (2.25). In the Evangelist's view however this knowledge represents only that it belongs to the nature of the revelation to arouse offence; he who has grasped that knows straight off that men will grumble when they hear the offensive word.

To that apprehension the question of Jesus corresponds: "What are you taking offence for?"—a question that is neither astonished nor reproachful, but one that simply remarks the facts:[7] "So it comes about

---

[1] See pp. 115 n.5.

[2] In a certain sense however 6.60–71 is the Johannine substitute for the Synoptic account of the call of the Twelve.

[3] That is, an address which demands too much insight and good will. Σκληρός as characteristic of the λόγος is also in Greek (see Wetst. and Br.); cp. esp. Eur. tr, 1036N: πότερα θέλεις σοι μαλθακὰ ψευδῆ λέγω ἢ σκληρ' ἀληθῆ; φράζε. σὴ γὰρ ἡ κρίσις. So also in LXX Gen. 21.11; 42.7; Deut 1.17; likewise Jude 15, after En. 1.9. There is a corresponding phenomenon also in Rabbinic literature, see Schl. On the ἐντολαί Herm. mand. XXII 3, 4; 4, 4.—The revelatory word is similarly characterised in C. Herm 13, 2–6 (αἴνιγμά μοι λέγεις . . . ἀδύνατά μοι λέγεις καὶ βεβιασμένα).

[4] 'Αυτοῦ refers to the λόγος, not to Jesus. 'Ακούειν in the context means "listen to", and then δύνασθαι passes over into the meaning of "be willing" (see Br., who alludes to Epikt. II 24, 11). In the mind of the Evangelist the statement will be ambiguous, inasmuch as it ought at the same time to be interpreted: "who is able to hear it?"—namely in the sense of genuine hearing, see p. 259.

[5] Cp. 6.41 and p. 229 n.4.

[6] Εἰδέναι ἐν ἑαυτῷ is not Greek and corresponds to a Jewish manner of speech (see Schl.), which is variously repeated in the New Testament; cp. Mk. 2.8; 5.30; Mt. 16.7.

[7] On account of the logical relationship to the following sentence τοῦτο ὑμᾶς σκανδ. is to be understood as a question; it corresponds to a conditional clause ("if this indeed, what then . . .?").

then, that the language of the Revealer is an offence to you!"[1] "How will it then be,"[2] he continues (**v. 62**), "if you see the Son of Man ascending where he was before?"[3] Clearly we have to understand: "Then the offence really will be great!" If one was inclined to object that the ἀναβαίνειν of Jesus could not be a σκάνδαλον, but rather would remove the offence of the σκληρὸς λόγος, then there would be a failure to understand that this ἀναβαίνειν is not at all achieved as a glorious demonstration before the world of the δόξα of Jesus; it is indeed no other than the ὑψωθῆναι and δοξασθῆναι that takes place on the cross. What the disciples will "see" of that is simply what is described in chs. 13–19; and in so far as there is anything to see in the outward sense, the unbelievers will also see it. Indeed it is these latter who themselves will "raise high" the Son of Man (8.28); and when they recognise then that "it is he," it will be too late, and in their despair they will recognise him as the judge.[4] What in 8.28 is a threat is in 6.62, in conformity with the context, a question: will they overcome the σκάνδαλον of the cross, or will it mean for them the judgment?[5]

The question does not have the character of unambiguous refusal, but it does contain nevertheless that moment of repulsion that is essentially bound up with the "drawing to himself."[6] Indirectly it is the question of decision, as later it is posed directly in v. 67. The hearer of the word of Jesus ought to be clear as to its implications: if he takes offence even now at the word of Jesus, he certainly will take offence at the cross.

Not that the cross will bring a second and new offence; it simply makes it ultimately plain what the *one* offence is: it is that a mere man, whose life ends in death, solemnly lays the claim that he is the Revealer of God! And this declaration, which demands of man the abandonment of all his securities, is clearly seen at the cross to be a demand for the surrender of life itself, a demand to follow right to the cross.[7]

---

[1] On σκανδαλίζειν = "to bring to a fall", in a transferred sense, see Arndt and Gingrich lexicon; it appears in Jn also at 16.1; the substantive 1 Jn. 2.10.

[2] On aposiopesis see Bl.-D. §482.

[3] 'Αναβαίνειν corresponds to the καταβαίνειν mentioned in 6.33, 38, 50f. But the discourse of 6.27–59 is by no means a presupposition for the understanding of v. 62. The concept continually meets us in varied terminology, see p. 307 n.3. That v. 62 does not hark back to the verses mentioned is evident from the fact that the catchword ἄρτος τ. ζωῆς does not occur in vv. 60ff.; also from the fact that the Son of Man is not spoken of in the discourse vv. 27–59, apart from the editorial fragments v. 27b (see p. 225 n.1) and v. 53 (see p. 235). Concerning vv. 62f. see also Ed. Schweizer, EvTheol 12 (1952/53), 356f.

[4] See pp. 348f.

[5] See pp. 149f. on 3.12.

[6] See p. 432.

[7] See pp. 425f, 432.

How does the offence arise? It arises when one's gaze is directed to the σάρξ. Then certainly the claim of Jesus must be incomprehensible; for in truth the judgment holds good (v. 63):

τὸ πνεῦμα ἐστιν τὸ ζωοποιοῦν,
ἡ σὰρξ οὐκ ὠφελεῖ οὐδέν.[1]

The hearers naturally also know that,[2] and the statement could almost be introduced like 4.35: οὐχ ὑμεῖς λέγετε ὅτι, and it would then have to continue as there, ἰδοὺ λέγω ὑμῖν. Or it could be said of this statement as in 4.37: ἐν γὰρ τούτῳ ὁ λόγος ἀληθινὸς ὅτι. For it is right *hic et nunc* to draw the consequence of that which everybody knows to be general truth: "*The words which I have spoken to you are spirit, and they are life!*"[3] But these ῥήματα[4] are precisely the σκάνδαλον! In that case therefore the statement, τὸ πνεῦμα κτλ. is not an alleviation that helps to remove the offence, as if it invited to a spiritualising reinterpretation,[5] but the statement is a call to decision. Only faith that comes to decision sees what is σάρξ and what is πνεῦμα; it is not to be found through faithless reflection, which measures by available criteria. The πνεῦμα is God's miraculous power, and that is not established by any reckoning.

The σάρξ therefore is ambiguous! If attention is not to be directed to the σάρξ but to the words of Jesus, nevertheless in a certain sense it must be directed exactly to the σάρξ: for ὁ λόγος σὰρξ ἐγένετο![6] The

---

[1] The sentence sounds like a citation; whether it is derived from the revelation discourses is doubtful, since the antithesis does not manifest their characteristic style; cp. perhaps 1 Cor. 15.50 and see the following note. Becker (68) does not view v. 63 as belonging to the source; that the verse however is a citation is also presumed by K. G. Kuhn, EvTheol 12 (1952/53), 276, n. 31.

[2] The Old Testament also knows that the "Spirit" (of God) makes alive, see Gen. 2.7; 6.3, 17; 7.15, 22; Ps. 104.29f.; Job 34.14f.; Ezk. 37.5f. (πνεῦμα ζωῆς . . . καὶ δώσω πνεῦμά μου εἰς ὑμᾶς καὶ ζήσεσθε), 9f. The allusion by Young to Is. 40.6 is not illuminating. See further 2 Macc. 14.26; 2 Cor. 3.6; Rabbinic material in Schl. ad loc. In dependence on Stoic teaching Phil. opif. m. 30: ζωτικώτατον τὸ πνεῦμα; see also C. Herm. 9, 9.—On the concept of πνεῦμα see p. 139 n.1.

[3] Are the words πνεῦμά ἐστιν καὶ an editorial addition, with the intention of making the reference to the preceding sentence needless? In v. 68 anything corresponding to this is lacking.

[4] In v. 63 to hold that ῥήματα is a false rendering of דְּבָרִים (or מִלִּין) = "things (about which I spoke)" (Burney 108f.) is an arbitrary fancy. Dodd (342, 3) also understands ῥήματα as words, but he explains the contradiction with 6.53–57 by saying that it comprehends the sacrament, of which these verses speak, as *verbum visibile*. The idea that words are life, or the concept "words of life" (v. 68), is found in Jewish thought (Schl. on vv. 63 and 68) as also in Mandaean (Br. on v. 68); cp. also Od. Sol. 12; Act. Thom. 124, p. 234: τοῦτο δὲ ζῶντες λόγοι μηδέποτε παρερχόμενοι. In the Turfanfr. M1 the hymn book is described as "full of living words".

[5] Πνεῦμα here as little signifies the spiritual sense of the γράμμα as it does in 2 Cor. 3.6.

[6] On this Hosk. 83 and passim is very good.

offence indeed *ought* to arise, and **faith** is the hearing that overcomes it, inasmuch as attention fixed on the σάρξ perceives the δόξα; if it sees the σάρξ only as σάρξ, then it does not overcome it. Jesus' ῥήματα are σάρξ in so far as they come to the hearer as the claim of a man who "makes himself equal to God" (5.18). The hearer overcomes the offence, but not by finding in the words a "spiritual" content, eternal truths and timeless ideas, but through believing that God meets him in the claim of this man. That Jesus' words are "spirit and life" is a promise, not an illuminating truth.

Thus vv. 60–63 make the offence of Jesus and his word plain to the last degree, in order to let the demand of faith appear in its absurdity. Vv. 64–71 show that such a demand has the consequence of causing separation: faith and unbelief divide off. So long as the decision question was not urgent they were indistinguishable, but Jesus knows that the separation will take place (**v. 64a**): "*But there are many of you who do not believe*;" they have (so we must interpret) to this point not apprehended, but thought that they were believers. But who can be sure of his faith? "*Therefore I told you: no man can come to me unless it is given to him from the Father*" (**v. 65**).[1] Faith is exercised in the abandonment of one's own certainty; a man therefore can never achieve it as a work of his own purposeful action, but he experiences it only as something effected by God.[2] In the hour of decision it is shown whether faith was one's own work or the gift of God.

The Evangelist, after his manner,[3] expressly emphasised in a note the knowledge of Jesus (**v. 64b**), and in an anticipation of that which was to follow he drew attention at the same time to Jesus' foreknowledge of the extremest possibility of unbelief, that of the betrayal.[4]

Since it has become clear that the teaching of Jesus is σκληρὸς λόγος

---

[1] For the citation of oneself see p. 348n.4; it is difficult to view v. 65 as specially harking back to v. 44 (as Noack 114f. thinks), see p. 285 n.4. Either the reference does not go back to a specific utterance, but recalls the repeatedly expressed "deterministic" thought in general (6.44; 8.43f.; cp. also 3.27); or it should be referred to a definite utterance, and then this is not contained in the text of the Evangelist as we have it. Διδόναι (see p. 172 n.5) with the sense it has here is used again only in 3.27; 19.11. Διὰ τοῦτο is not explained through the following (= because), see p. 238 n.2, but it relates to that which precedes; ὅτι is recitative as in 9.23 etc. (see p. 335 n.5).

[2] See pp. 230f.

[3] See p. 212 n.4; cp. esp. 13.11.

[4] That Jesus knew beforehand of the betrayal is an important motif of early Christian apologetic; see 13.11, 18f., 21–30; Mk. 14.18–21 parr. If the foreknowledge is described as ἐξ ἀρχῆς, it is undoubtedly the beginning of the discipleship or the moment of choice (v. 70) that is meant (cp. 15.27; 16.4; 1 Jn. 2.7 etc.), not the knowledge of the pre-existent Lord from the primeval beginning (cp. 1.1f.; 1 Jn. 1.1; 2.13f.); the primeval knowledge of the Metatron (Odeberg 46) therefore is no parallel.

the hour of decision has now arrived; many disciples now[1] fall away from him and forsake him (v. 66).[2] This factor is itself yet another renewal of the offence, a temptation: around Jesus it is becoming lonely; when the majority withdraw from him, who will be willing to continue with him? And so Jesus puts (v. 67) the decisive question to the Twelve: "*Do you not also wish to go away?*" But just in this critical situation *the genuine confession of faith* is quickened, and in the name of the Twelve Peter gives it expression (v. 68). It is strictly formulated with respect to the situation and to the words of Jesus that had preceded: "*Lord, to whom should we wish to go away? You have words of eternal life!*" The character of genuine confession is thereby shown in so far as it 1. grows out of the *situation*, and therefore is not general assent to a teaching but an act of decision, and in so far as it 2. is the *answer* to the question posed by the revelation, and is not the result of speculation.[3]

Nevertheless at the same time the confession is raised beyond the limits of the situation, because it articulates in the statement the *knowledge*[4] that grows out of faith: "*You are the Holy one of God*" (v. 69); because it is not simply an expression of inner experience, but it clearly formulates where faith stands; and because the believer does not speak of himself but of him on whom he believes. But also in this formulation the character of the confession as answer is preserved: the σὺ εἶ corresponds to the ἐγώ εἰμι, which, whether expressed or unexpressed,

---

[1] It comes to the same thing whether ἐκ τούτου is interpreted as "consequently" (so 19.12) or as "from now on". At all events it is not a gradual development that is in mind, but an apostasy that is now taking place.

[2] The sentence receives its pathos through the double expression which is almost equal to a parall. membr.—'Απέρχεσθαι εἰς τὰ ὀπίσω not as 18.6 "to turn back" but "to go away", in the sense of "to fall away, apostatise", like Is. 1.4 נָסוֹג אָחוֹר (conjecture for Mass. נָזֹרוּ אָחוֹר); 50.5; cp. ὑπάγειν ὀπίσω Mk. 8.33 par. Elsewhere (ἐπι) στρέφειν εἰς τὰ ὀπίσω = "to turn oneself about" 20.14; Mk. 13.16 (on which see Schl. on Mt. 24.18). Περιπατεῖν μετά is a characteristically Semitic designation for fellowship; it makes no difference whether περιπ. is meant in a literal or transferred sense; see Schl. ad loc. and cp. Rev. 3.4.

[3] This character of the confession plainly comes to the fore through comparison with the Synoptic passages, wherein the same tradition has gained a more primitive form (Mk. 8.27–29 parr.). The motives of the Johannine setting are definitely prefigured there: the confession is the answer to Jesus' question; it is set off against that which the "people" say about Jesus. But these motives first plainly emerge in John, because the confession grows out of a defined situation and overcomes the offence.

[4] On πεπιστ. καὶ ἔγνωκ. see p. 435 n.4. This formulation also favours the view that 6.60–71 should be linked on to 8.30–40; the sequence πιστεύειν-γινώσκειν, which according to 8.31f. characterises the man who "remains" with the word of Jesus, is realised precisely in the Twelve, for whom Peter speaks, as men who have not "gone away" but remained with him.

sounds through all the sayings of Jesus.[1] But at the same time the *newness* which is proper to every authentic confession is consciously given expression, since the saying of Peter attributes to Jesus a title which has played no role in his own sayings.[2] Peter confesses Jesus neither as the Messiah, nor Son of Man, neither as the "Son," nor as "him whom God sent," nor even as the σωτήρ, but as the "Holy One of God."[3] Thus none of the customary messianic or saviour or redeemer titles from the Jewish or Hellenistic-Gnostic tradition is chosen, but a designation which has no recognisable tradition at all as a messianic title.[4] This description expresses first of all that Jesus stands over against the world simply as the one who comes from the other world and belongs to God,[5] and indeed that he is the sole one to do so: he is *the* Holy one

---

[1] Here also the distinction from Mk. 8.29 is clear, where σὺ εἶ is indeed found, but not in that correspondence.

[2] In many, especially later, witnesses the confession is refashioned in accordance with 11.27 or Mk. 8.29 or Mt. 16.16. On the original form of the text, attested by ℵ D, there can be no doubt.

[3] Therein also the distance from Mk. 8.29; Lk. 9.20 is shown. Only Mt. 16.16 goes a step further in the direction of Jn.

[4] Jesus is described as ὁ ἅγιος also in 1 Jn. 2.30 (3.3 as ἁγνός); Rev. 3.7 as ὁ ἅγιος, ὁ ἀληθινός. But in neither instance are we confronted with a title; the meaning is not, "He who is the Holy One", but "he who is holy". Acts 3.14 calls Jesus ὁ ἅγιος καὶ δίκαιος, as Mk. 6.20 does the Baptist; and in the prayer to God of Acts 4.27, 30 he is named as ὁ ἅγιος παῖς σου. As a Messianic title ὁ ἅγιος τοῦ θεοῦ occurs only in Mk. 1.24 = Lk. 4.34. Whether the title has an earlier history it is hardly possible to say. J. Naish, Expositor 8, ser. 22 (1922), 66 considers he can give evidence to show that ἅγιος is a technical designation for one consecrated in the mystery cults, and that Jesus is delineated "as the supreme and representative initiate". The Gospel gives no clue for ascribing this view to the Evangelist.

[5] Ἅγιος denotes the divine sphere over against the world, and therefore also that which is marked out as apart from the profane world and belongs to God; see p. 389 n. 5. (On the original meaning of the concept of holiness see G.v.d. Leeuw, Phänomenologie der Religion 23ff.). The idea of splendour (δόξα) and power can be linked with the idea of the holy, as also the thought of the morally pure. Nevertheless these two things do not constitute the concept of holiness.—Naturally "holy" is an attribute of beings who belong to the divine sphere, like angels (Tob. 11.14; 12.15; Eth.En. 1.9; Mk. 8.38; Rev. 14.10 etc., see Bousset, Rel. des Judent. 321, 2) and the πνεῦμα. The sphere of the *cultic*, as demarked out from the world, is holy (Ps. 106.16 LXX: Aaron as ὁ ἅγιος τοῦ κυρίου); so the Temple (Acts 6.13 etc.) and Jerusalem (Is. 48.2; Mt. 4.5 etc.); so also the chosen people (Num. 16.3 etc.). Cultically consecrated persons (Jdc. 13.7; 16.17) or persons chosen by God, like prophets (Sap. 11.1; Lk. 1.70; Acts 3.21; 2 Pt. 3.2) and apostles (Eph. 3.5) are holy, and in this sense Jesus is the ἅγιος παῖς of God (see previous note). The cultic meaning can at the same time be an *eschatological* one. Therefore they who participate in the blessed end time are holy (Is. 4.3; Dan. 7.18, 22), and the community of the end time is called holy (En. 38.4; 47.4; 62.8 etc., see Str.-B. II 691), and therefore the Christians in their eschatological consciousness call themselves ἅγιοι (Rom. 1.7; 8.27, etc.). It is *God* however who is holy simpliciter (Is. 6.2; Lev. 11.44; 19.2; Jn. 17.11; 1 Pt. 1.15f.; Rev. 4.8; 6.10), He is "the Holy One" (Bousset, Rel. des Judent. 312, 4; Str.-B. III 762f.; Moore II 101f.). On the whole subject see A. Fridrichsen, Hagios-Qados 1916; Ed. Willinger, Hagios 1922; R. Asting, Die Heiligkeit im Urchristentum 1930 (in addition Norsk teol. Tidsskrift 1931, 21–43); Procksch and Kuhn, ThWB I 87–116; W. Staerk, Soter I 1933, 109f.

of God. Thus the title expresses Jesus' special relation to God, corresponding to the phrase ὃν ὁ πατὴρ ἡγίασεν 10.36. And as in that passage it continues, καὶ ἀπέστειλεν εἰς τὸν κόσμον,[1] so here also the title ὁ ἅγιος τ.θ. not only expresses the negative thought that Jesus does not belong to the world; since the confession is the result of experiencing that Jesus has ῥήματα ζωῆς αἰωνίου, an intimation is at the same time given as to what he is *for* the world: he represents God in the world as the Revealer who bestows life. But as these ῥήματα are also the σκληρὸς λόγος, this holiness of his includes his judicial office. The Holy One whom God has consecrated (10.36) is at the same time he who is equipped with δόξα,[2] because his δόξα consists in the fact that he is the Revealer who has the ἐξουσία of κρίνειν and of ζωοποιεῖν (5.21, 27).

Finally however in this context, following on 12. 20–33 and anticipating 17.19, it must be said that the title ὁ ἅγιος τοῦ θεοῦ also denotes Jesus as the one who has consecrated himself as a sacrifice for the world; vv. 70f. especially have reference to the story of the Passion. Not alone the question of Jesus in v. 62, but the confession of Peter also stands in the light of the mystery of the death of Jesus.

Peter made his confession in the name of the Twelve.[3] If according to vv. 67–69 these are the true disciples because in their victory over the σκάνδαλον they decided for Jesus, so according to **v. 70** they are the Twelve whom he has "chosen."[4] These two factors are not mutually exclusive, on the contrary they subsist with each other.[5] Inasmuch as the believer makes a decision for Jesus, he knows that he does not exist out of his own resources but from his; and as 15.16 says, he ought not to interpret his decision as if he has chosen Jesus, but that Jesus has chosen him. This situation is peculiarly illuminated in **vv. 70f.**, in which the Evangelist again depends on the tradition of the community.[6] The intention of these verses is to show that even for those who emerged out of the circle of the unbelievers and penetrated into the circle of the

---

[1] See p. 389 n. 5.

[2] M. Dibelius, Festg. für Ad. Deissmann 1927, 182, 2.

[3] He speaks in the first person plural, and that this is a genuine plural is shown by the αὐτοῖς of v. 70.

[4] Cp. 13.18; 15.16, 19. Naturally ἐκλέγεσθαι is to be understood as in Lk. 6.13; Acts. 1.2, and not in accordance with the dominical saying of the Diatessaron (Ephr. ed. Aucher-Moesinger 50): elegi vos antequam terra fieret (cp. Eph. 1.4).

[5] See p. 231f.

[6] Cp. Mk. 14.17–21 parr., which is freshly cast in Jn. 13.21–30.—Ἔλεγεν v. 71 = "he meant thereby" (as 8.27) is good Greek; see Colwell 57f. As in the Synoptics the betrayer is called Ἰούδας; the Synoptics never use the father's name (Σίμωνος without article, see Bl-D. §162, 2); rather they describe him as Ἰσκαριώτης (see Lohmeyer on Mk. 14.10 in Meyer's Kommentar, Klostermann on Mk. 3.19 in the Hdb. zum NT), which here is used as the father's surname (ℵD al read ἀπὸ Καρυώτου, which in D stands also in 12.4; 13.2, 26; 14.22).

μαθηταί, who also overcame the offence that diminished this circle down to the Twelve, no certainty is given. If, as is repeated with deliberate emphasis at the conclusion, it is none other than "one of the Twelve" who becomes the betrayer, who then can be certain? Who will build on his own decision, or make of the consciousness of his election a sure possession? Indeed the higher a man has advanced, the greater will be his fall. It is then the breach of faith which betrays Jesus; he who is capable of that is a devil.[1] Therefore whoever belongs to the company who are represented by the circle of the δώδεκα[2] and did not stumble at the σκάνδαλον of the σκληρὸς λόγος, ought to know how great is his responsibility, and how much is at stake for him. Accordingly this conclusion powerfully expresses the greatness and the daring of the confession.

---

[1] Διάβολος is not to be understood as an appelative = "slanderer", but as always in Jn, as "devil" (8.44; 13.2; 1 Jn. 3.8,10). If Jn knew the Synoptics it would have to be admitted that he consciously changed the conclusion of the scene in Mk. 8. 27–33, in that in place of the saying of Jesus that rebuked Peter as a Satan (Mk. 8.33; Mt. 16.23) he set the description of Judas as a devil.

[2] It is the circle of the community, which in the farewell discourses also is represented by the Twelve.

Conclusion: 12. 37-43

12. 37–41 gives a retrospect on the public activity of Jesus that has now concluded, and it establishes that its total result is: οὐκ ἐπίστευον εἰς αὐτόν (**v. 37**). The astonishing thing is that the ministry of Jesus is described here by means of the expression σημεῖα ποιεῖν, although his σημεῖα were subordinated to the discourses, and his real work was achieved in the revelatory word. Now for the onlooker who remained unaffected by the word, the σημεῖα might well be the characteristic element of his work (7.31; 10.41), just as in the eyes of the authorities they are the deceptive feature (11.47). It should be remarked that there will have been an external ground for this characteristic finding a place in the retrospect: vv. 37f. could, like 20.30f.,[1] be taken over from the σημεῖα-source, in which this way of formulating was regarded as helpful.[2] But the fact that the Evangelist was able to adopt it shows how for him the concepts σημεῖα and ῥήματα (λόγοι) flow together: the σημεῖα are deeds that speak, and their meaning is developed in the discourses; moreover the ῥήματα are not human words but words of revelation, full of divine and miraculous power—they are indeed miraculous works.[3] Hence the Evangelist also, when looking back, could characterise the work of Jesus as a σημεῖα ποιεῖν.

The result—the unbelief—is explained in both citations **vv. 38–40** as a necessity ordained of God; in it is fulfilled simply that which the prophet Isaiah had predicted.[4] If the citation of Is. 53.1 (v. 38) has an

---

[1] See p. 113.

[2] That is confirmed by the fact that the two citations vv. 38 and 40 can hardly have been written by *one* hand (Faure, ZNTW 21 [1922] 103ff.). In v. 38 Is. 53.1 is cited from the LXX verbatim, whereas the citation from Is. 6.10 in v. 40 does not use the LXX (syr[s] pesh assimilate to the LXX). That the introductory formulae of the citations are different cannot of course serve as a criterion for the separation of sources; for the Evangelist also uses the formula ἵνα πληρωθῇ (13.18; 15.25; 17.12). It is plain however on the one hand that vv. 39f., with its διὰ τοῦτο . . . ὅτι is derived from the Evangelist (see p. 238 n. 2), and on the other hand that v. 41 refers not to v. 38 but to v. 40 (against Faure; cp. F. Smend, ZNTW 24 [1925] 150). If vv. 39ff. go back to the Evangelist (the same applies also to vv. 42f.), then vv. 37f. must have been taken by him from his source. Dodd (379f.), who does not undertake any critical separation, considers (surely rightly) that both citations belonged to the testimony material of primitive Christianity.

[3] See p. 114f., 217f. and cp. 6.63.

[4] In the note of **v. 41** the Evangelist justifies the interpretation of Is. 6.10 in relation to the work of Jesus. The beholding of the glory of Jesus by the prophet must mean the Temple vision of Is. 6 (so clearly ℵD pm lat sy, which read ὅτε instead of ὅτι [according to

apologetic intention in the source, as the early Christian proof from Scripture often did have,[1] its connection with Is. 6.10, which was added by the Evangelist,[2] gains for it a new significance. For in the Evangelist's mind the idea of determination ought to illuminate the character of the revelation: the revelation brings to light the authentic being of man.[3] Looking at Jewish unbelief, which is not an accidental factor, the question should rise up in a frightening manner before the reader as to what he belongs to, "whence" he comes, and what determines his existence. The thought that one's actual behaviour in an individual instance is determined by the deepest ground of being does not destroy responsibility, but for the first time really awakens it; it brings to consciousness the importance of the concrete action. Man cannot look on his authentic being as something given in nature, rather he discovers it in his decisions. In the thought of the Evangelist the recollection of the prophecy has the sharpest appeal.

This purpose of awakening the will is discernible also in the last of

---

Burney 78 ὅτι is a mistranslation; Colwell 100f. and Black 60 deny it] and probably also W: ἐπεί). According to 1.18 indeed the prophet cannot have seen God himself (Büchsel judges otherwise, Joh. und der hellenistische Synkr. 78, while according to Delafosse 12.41 comes from the ecclesiastical editor, who corrects 1.18). Correspondingly in v. 40 the subject of ἰάσομαι is Jesus. That the pre-existent Logos stands as the subject of the Old Testament theophany has its analogies; cp. Philo somn. I 229f.; Justin apol. I 62.63; cp. also 1 Cor. 10.1. It ought not to be replied to this interpretation of εἶδεν τὴν δόξαν αὐτοῦ that the prophetic view of the future must rather be meant, for to the Evangelist both fall together: that which Isaiah beheld in the Temple at that time was the future δόξα of Jesus which would be given him through his work; cp. p. 326 n. 3. So also Dupont (269–273), who however prefers to think of the future Jesus. According to the Targum on Is. 6.9 Isaiah saw the divine shekina. Young (215–221) shows that in Judaism numerous speculations attached to the vision of Isaiah.

[1] Is. 53.1 is also cited in Rom. 10.16 in the apologetic argument. In v. 38 ἀκοή means "preaching", as in Rom. 10.16f.; Gal. 3.2, not, as Schl. thinks, "what we (namely Jesus; cp. 3.11) have heard". The βραχίων does not denote something else alongside that, but characterises the preaching as a divine act. On the introductory formula see Str.-B. I 74 on Mt. 1.22.

[2] See p. 452 n.2. Since the imperatives of the Hebrew text are changed into past indicatives, God (not the devil, Cyril of Alex.) appears as the one who effects the obduracy, and Jesus becomes the subject of ἰάσομαι. Whether the Evangelist has taken his text from a translation that lay before him, or whether he made it himself, can hardly be determined; according to Barrett (JThSt 47 [1948], 167, 2) the text goes back to the Targum, while according to Goodwin (JBL 73 [1954], 70f.) it is cited after the LXX. The precedence given to the blinding corresponds to the meaning which this picture has for him; see on ch. 9, esp. p. 340 n. 4. It is noteable that he has not used the stimulus given in ἰάσομαι to employ the picture of the Revealer as physician, although the image is traditional in the Gnostic circle of ideas and quickly passed over into Christian literature; cp. Br. ad loc and on Ign. Eph. 7.2 in the supplementary volume to the Hdb. zum NT; A v. Harnack, Mission und Ausbreitung[4] I 129ff. = Expansion of Christianity I 126ff.; Reitzenstein, Taufe 207; Bornkamm, Mythos und Legende 12.

[3] See pp. 155f., 158f., 317. Br. is right in maintaining that οὐκ ἠδύναντο may not, with Chrys., be equated with οὐκ ἤθελον, namely in the sense of a weakening of meaning. For the Evangelist however the two thoughts are bound up with each other.

the sayings added by him (**vv. 42f.**); it shows the difficulty of the decision for faith in those who indeed believe,[1] but who dare not stand up for it. They are afraid of being expelled by the Pharisees[2] from the synagogue.[3] There are even many of these among the "ruling class",[4] but thus they especially come from the ὄχλος.[5] As however 3.22; 8.30ff. had already made known, their faith is not a genuine faith; for the honour that men bestow is of greater account to them than that which comes from God,[6] and according to 5.44 that is the decisive hindrance to faith. At all events these irresolute people are different from the radically unbelieving; we recall that Nicodemus interceded for Jesus in the Council (7.50), and took part in his burial (19.39), similarly as Joseph of Arimathea, whose discipleship was a secret one through fear of the Jews (19.38). Obviously such secret disciples still have the possibility of their faith becoming genuine.

How then will the man who surveys this result decide? The conclusion makes it plain to him that the issue at stake is to put the δόξα τοῦ θεοῦ before the δόξα τῶν ἀνθρώπων. Will he summon up courage to dare it?

[1] Ὅμως μέντοι only here in the N.T.; ὅμως occurs nowhere else in John (in the N.T. only elsewhere in 1 Cor. 14.7; Gal. 3.15); μέντοι is a favourite expression with Jn (4.27; 7.13; 12.42; 20.5; 21.4), otherwise only in 2 Tim. 2.19; Jas. 2.8; Jud. 8; see Bl.-D §450, 1f.

[2] These are thought of as authorities; see pp. 86 n.6, 306 n.5.

[3] See p. 335 n.5.

[4] On the ἄρχοντες see p. 133 n. 4. Examples are Nicodemus (3.1; 7.50; 19.39) and Joseph of Arimathia (19.38).

[5] See p. 130 n.3.

[6] Ἤπερ only here in the NT.; ℵ L λ 565 pm read ὑπέρ; see Bl.-D §185, 3.

CHAPTERS 13-20
THE REVELATION OF THE ΔΌΞΑ BEFORE THE COMMUNITY

Chapters 13-20
The Revelation of the ΔΌΞΑ Before the Community[1]

I. 13.1-17.26: The Revealer's Farewell

The subject-matter of the new section of the Gospel becomes clear from its opening scene: it deals with the relation of Jesus to his disciples, with his ἀγάπη to his ἴδιοι. His mission, seen as a whole, is itself the divine ἀγάπη (3.16) as it becomes operative in the world. The first part (chs. 3–12) had shown this ἀγάπη in its struggle to win over the world to itself; it had shown how ἀγάπη necessarily implies σκάνδαλον for the κόσμος, and how the latter allows the σκάνδαλον to become its own condemnation. The second part shows the ἀγάπη revealing itself to the community of "his own", firstly by direct means, in the farewell scenes of the night before the passion, and then indirectly in the passion itself, and in the Easter event.

The synoptic Gospels also have a section describing the period in which Jesus is alone with his disciples after the end of his public activity and before the event of the passion (Mk. 13.1–14.42, and par.s). There too the disciples are taught about the future (Mk. 13.1–37); there is a meal by night, and with it the prophecy of the disciples' fate (Mk. 14.17–31); and like John, they include a prayer of Jesus (Mk. 14.32–42). But in the synoptics the account is broken down into separate scenes, which are spread over the space of several days; Jesus does not always move in the same closed circle of disciples, and the meal in Bethany precedes the last supper with the disciples (Mk. 14. 3–9). There is also the detailed description of the preparations for the last supper (Mk. 14.12–16) which disrupts the unity of the narrative; and lastly, the account of the Sanhedrin's resolve to bring Jesus to execution and of Judas' betrayal (Mk. 14.1f., 10f.) has also found its way into the description.

In John, on the other hand, everything that immediately precedes the passion, and leads up to it, is compressed into the conversations and discourses of a single night. There is no further change of scene and only the

[1] For the division into these two sections see p. 48, 111f. (esp. 111 n. 2).

closed circle of disciples surrounds Jesus. Thus we have a visible illustration of the inner unity that holds together all that is said and everything that happens in the Johannine Gospel. *The Revealer's farewell to his own* is the one theme of chs. 13–17; and in the treatment of this theme the idea of revelation is finally clarified. What actually happens from then on is made subservient to it, and it dominates all that Jesus says. The result is that all the synoptic motifs,—the teaching about the future, the prophecy of the disciples' fate, the prayer of Jesus,—all these are characteristically recast; moreover (and this is the strangest part of the Johannine presentation), the climax to the synoptic account of the last meal—the institution of the Lord's Supper—can be completely left out.

Thus in comparison with the synoptic account, the writer succeeds in achieving a tremendous concentration on the last night, and the result is a much more definite break with all that had gone before. The colourful pictures of the first part have disappeared; the noise of the cosmos has died away; the stillness of the night prevails. But above all, although Jesus is the same, in as much as he is the Revealer, it is as if he were another man. He is no longer now the one who stands in the struggle, but the one who speaks to his own, i.e. to his own community. In the Synoptics Jesus teaches the disciples at every stage of his ministry; sometimes the teaching is combined with that of the crowd, and sometimes it runs alongside it;[1] but in John, it is transferred in its entirety to the last night.[2] The result is the radical division of the Gospel into two, illustrating a fundamental Johannine idea: the work of Jesus is the κρίσις which brings about the division between light and darkness. Of course, it would be an over-simplification to say that chs. 3–12 portray the sphere of darkness, and chs. 13–17 the sphere of light. While it is true that the struggle of light and darkness is portrayed in the first section, the darkness, the κόσμος, remains the background to the teaching of the disciples in the second part, and as such it is not to be forgotten. The community is in the world and must work in the world (17.15, 18); it exists on earth only in express opposition to the world; and to it as the people who have "come to the light" (3.21) the saying applies: τὸ φῶς ἐν τῇ σκοτίᾳ φαίνει (1.5). Thus it is of symbolic significance that the scene takes place at night.

When, however, the disciples are mentioned here, they are never explicitly called the twelve. 13.21–30 does of course suggest the familiar circle of disciples, namely the Twelve; and Peter, Thomas, Philip, Judas, and Judas Iscariot, each of whom plays a part in the narrative, certainly belong to it. But in 13.23 there appears a disciple, "whom Jesus loved," and who is not to be sought among those whom we already know. Certainly any explicit mention

---

[1] That is, in the secret teaching on the destiny of the Messiah, beginning in Mk. 8.27 and par. s, after being anticipated e.g. in Mk. 4.10–13, and par. s, 7.17–23 and par. s.

[2] When the apocryphal tradition transfers this kind of teaching of the disciples to the 40 days after the resurrection, it is to a certain extent in harmony with the Johannine version, acc. to which Jesus is really speaking as the δοξασθείς. But it is just on this point that it spoils John's account, because acc. to him the δοξασθείς cannot be directly approached (see below).

of the δώδεκα appears to be consciously avoided. The circle of disciples gathered round Jesus represent the ἴδιοι generally,[1] and only once is there any reflection on the difference between their various generations (17.20). It is *the community* in which Jesus stands at the moment, which he addresses, and for which he prays; the community, the founding of which is described symbolically in 13.1–20, and the law of whose life—already hinted at in 13.12–20—is developed in 13.34f.; 15.1–17.

The question whether the present order of the text of chs. 13–17 is the correct one is prompted by the observation that 14.25–31 is obviously the conclusion of the farewell discourses: 1. The addition of the phrase παρ' ὑμῖν μένων in 14.25 to the words ταῦτα λελάληκα ὑμῖν, in contrast to 15.11; 16.1, 4, 25, 33 where they also occur, shows that here they give a final summary of Jesus' teaching.[2] 2. Vv. 26–28 bring together in brief compass all the motifs that have been dealt with before. 3. The words εἰρήνην ἀφίημι ὑμῖν in v. 27 is the parting wish of Jesus. 4. Vv. 30f. lead on to the event of the passion: ἔρχεται κτλ., in v. 30 looks forward to 18.1ff., and the last words ἐγείρεσθε κτλ., round off the factual account of the scene; the only fitting continuation is 18.1ff.[3] Thus chs. 15–17 are left in mid-air; the suggestion that the discourses they contain and Jesus' farewell prayer were spoken en route has no foundation in the text and is absurd.

The conclusion is unavoidable that chs. 15–17 are either a secondary insertion, or they are not in their right place. The first[4] alternative is impossible because they are fully Johannine in both content[5] and form. Like the discourses in chs. 13 and 14 they exhibit the Evangelist's characteristic method of composition, which is to use the revelation-discourses as his basis (as he does throughout the Gospel). And it would not be reasonable to suppose that an independent editor, writing in the form and spirit of the Gospel—and he would have to be such and not just an opportunist interpolator—would put the section in this impossible position, rather than insert it e.g. between 14.24 and 25. There remains, therefore, only the second conclusion, which has frequently been drawn: chs. 15–17 are not in their right place. The order as we have it is partly due to accident, and partly to puzzled attempts to arrange the disordered material as well as possible.[6]

---

[1] The ἴδιοι are referred to in 13.1; the designation μαθηταί, the one that occurs most frequently, is clearly used in 13.35; 15.8 in its broad sense (cp. 8.31). See p. 434 n.2. Dodd, 398, 399 also explains it in this sense.

[2] Πολλά in v. 30, which does not occur in syr^s, is a bad addition, which has admittedly penetrated to all mss. Its purpose is to get over the difficulty that there are still further discourses to come.

[3] What M. Dibelius says in The Crozer Quarterly 12 (1935) 262 seems impossible to me. In 14.30f. he would find an old tradition, lacking any significance in its present context (ἔρχεται γὰρ ὁ τοῦ κόσμου ἄρχων. ἐγείρεσθε, ἄγωμεν ἐντεῦθεν), but which the Evangelist has taken along with him.

[4] Thus Wellh. Ed. Meyer, (Urspr. I 313), Br, while P. Corssen ZNTW 8 (1907) 125–142) tries to avoid this conclusion by eliminating ἐγείρεσθε ἄγωμεν ἐντεῦθεν in 14.31 as an insertion from the synoptic Gospels (a solution he applies elsewhere as well).

[5] This is rightly stressed by Corssen (see previous note).

[6] One can of course ask why the redactor did not insert chs. 15–17 in front of 14.25.

The attempt to re-discover the original order must be made, however uncertain our conclusion may be. Where, in what has gone before, does ch. 15 fit in best? Amongst the various suggestions,[1] the most obvious is to append it to 13.35; 15.1–17 is precisely a commentary on the command of love in 13.34f. Moreover 13.36ff. follows excellently on 16.33; this would result in the restoration of the traditional order of the prophecies of the disciples' flight and of Peter's denial (so Mk., Mt.).[2]

But the matter is not yet finished, with the insertion of chs. 15–16 after 13.35; for what happens to ch. 17? It cannot be placed after 14.31; for this can only be followed logically by 18.1, beyond which there is of course no room for ch. 17. It is also impossible to find a home for it within the discourses;[3] its place can only be at the beginning.[4] It could be maintained that it originally preceded the whole section ch. 13–17. The caesura between chs. 3–12 and the history of the passion and Easter would be excellently marked by this prayer. After the changing scenes in chs. 3–12, and particularly after the conclusion in 12.37–43, ch. 17 would mark an interval before the new action begins. Nevertheless it is difficult to imagine that the prayer

---

However, it is easier to regard the present order as the result of a redaction made necessary, for good or ill, by the fragmented condition of the narrative, than to regard it as the result of an independent editing such as the first hypothesis presupposes. Acc. to Str. (271f.) 13.31–14.31 and 15.1–16.33 are two different drafts made by the Evangelist, who left behind him an unfinished work. Very improbable, because the two sections cannot be regarded as different versions of the same theme. Similarly, acc. to Strathm. and Barr. Chs. 15–17 give a version parallel to ch. 13; Wik. leaves the choice open between this possibility and a change of order (he also brings in the views of other Catholic exegetes).

[1] Bacon wants to attach ch. 15 to 13.20 and gives us the following order: 13.1–20; 15.1–16.33; 13.21–14.31 (leaving out 13.36–38 as an interpolation); 17.1–26.—Spitta cuts out 13.12–20, 36–38 from the "basic document" and suggests: 13.21–31a; 15.1–17.26; 14.1–31, at the same time omitting smaller additions within the different sections. Similarly Moffat (see Howard 264) and Bernard; except that they make 13.31b–14.31 follow on 16.33 and leave ch. 17 at the end. —Warberton Lewis suggests (see Howard 264): 13.1–32; 15.1–16.33; 13.33–38; 14.1–31; 17.1–26. Wendt arranges as follows: 13.31–35; 15.1–16.33; 13.36–14.31; 17.1–26. So too MacGregor, except that he sees 13.36–38 as a later addition. In spite of all these considerations, G. Stettinger, Textfolge de joh. Abschiedsreden 1918, with special ref. to the discussion with Spitta, wants to defend the received order as the original one.

[2] An apparent difficulty arises from the fact that Peter's question in 13.36 seems to refer to Jesus' saying in 13.33. But this is an illusion; in fact, Peter's question is not possible before 16.5. For this reason, one must conclude that v. 33 gave the redactor his reason for putting 13.36ff in its present position. The only difficulty in my opinion, in placing chs.15 and 16 before ch. 14 is the fact that in 14.16 the Paraclete, who had already been spoken of in 15.26; 16.7ff., 12ff., appears to be introduced afresh. But this is resolved when one sees that the Evangelist has used a section of the source in 14.16. Furthermore, the impossibility of making the statement 16.5 after 13.36; 14.5ff. confirms the change of order. And 16.16ff. must clearly be the first treatment of the theme of the μικρόν, because it is expressed here as a problem, whereas in 14.19 it no longer needs any discussion.

[3] So Sp., see note 1.

[4] The objection can scarcely be raised that 17.8 presupposes the disciples' confession of faith in 16.30. For ch. 17 is the Revealer's prayer for the community which he leaves behind him on earth. 17.8 refers to the faith of this community, and does not look back to one particular event.

(ch. 17) had no setting,[1] and one hesitates to posit an account of its setting, which has since been lost by accident or in the process of a redaction. In fact, however, the contents of the prayer (Jesus' δοξασθῆναι and the preservation of the community) point to the setting of the discourses, in which Jesus, returning home to his δόξα, takes leave of his own. In this case the proper place is after 13.30. This is confirmed by the excellent way in which the words of Jesus in 13.31: νῦν ἐδοξάσθη κτλ. follow on from the prayer; the petition δόξασόν σου τὸν υἱόν (17.1) has been heard—the one who is praying knows this; and this is why, when Jesus speaks to his own in the discourses that follow, he can speak to them as the one who is essentially the δοξασθείς already. Indeed, one can regard the discourses precisely as a commentary on the ideas expressed in the prayer. Further confirmation is found in our now being able to understand why there is no account of the actual last supper in John: ch. 17 takes its place (see below).

From 13.31a: ὅτε οὖν ἐξῆλθεν one could therefore move straight on to 17.1: Ἰησοῦς ἐπάρας τ. ὀφθ ... εἶπεν. However, I would suggest that the prayer did have a special introduction, and that this is contained in 13.1. The redactor has certainly been at work in 13.1–3; for the corrections in the MSS and the exegetes' dispute show at once that the present text is impossible. For the analysis of the passage see below; I suggest the introduction to ch. 17 originally read: ὅτε οὖν ἐξῆλθεν, εἰδὼς ὁ Ἰησοῦς ὅτι ἦλθεν αὐτοῦ ἡ ὥρα ἵνα μεταβῇ ἐκ τοῦ κόσμου τούτου πρὸς τὸν πατέρα, ἀγαπήσας τοὺς ἰδίους τοὺς ἐν τῷ κόσμῳ εἰς τέλος, ἐγείρεται ἐκ τοῦ δείπνου κα ἐπάρας τοὺς ὀφθαλμοὺς αὐτοῦ εἰς τὸν οὐρανὸν εἶπεν. In any case it is clear that εἰδώς κτλ of 13.1 is extremely appropriate as an introduction to the prayer of ch. 17; the prayer is indeed said in the ὥρα of the μεταβῆναι, and is the demonstration of his ἀγαπᾶν.

The structure of the whole complex—on the basis of the new order—is very simple. 13.1–30 records Jesus' last meal with his disciples; 17.1–26 gives us the farewell prayer; 13.31–35; 15–16.33; 13.36–14.41 contain the farewell discourses and conversations.

A. 13.1–30: The Last Supper

a) The Founding of the Community and its Law: 13.1–20

The section 13.1–20 is clearly divided into two parts, vv. 1–20 and vv. 21–30. They form two closely connected scenes, the footwashing and the prophecy of the betrayal, bound together through the setting of the supper. The introduction to the first scene has been expanded by the redaction (see below); only the details of time in vv. 1 and 2, along with the whole of v. 3, are original. The narrative proper divides into 1) vv. 4–11, the footwashing, with

[1] Is a monologue conceivable at all in the earliest and immediately subsequent literature of Christianity? For without any setting, as far as its form is concerned, this is what the prayer would be.

the dialogue between Peter and Jesus, and 2) vv. 12–20 a discourse of Jesus which interprets the footwashing and ends with some dominical sayings. In actual fact, however, vv. 4–11 have already given an interpretation of the footwashing, even if it is not immediately apparent as such, and the second explanation runs contrary to the first. According to the first, the footwashing is a symbolic action by Jesus, portraying the service that Jesus has done for his disciples, the meaning of which they would only later understand. According to the second, the action is an example of service for the disciples to follow. That the two do not form an original whole follows from the statement in v. 7 that the disciple will comprehend the significance of the footwashing only at a later stage. It would be a grotesque misunderstanding of the Johannine style to maintain that the words γνώσῃ δὲ μετὰ ταῦτα find their fulfilment a few moments later in vv. 12–17.

It ought to be clear that the first explanation is the specifically Johannine one, and marks of the Johannine style bear this out (see below). The explanation embraces vv. 6–10, which, like v. 3, are the work of the Evangelist.[1] He has used a source which gave an account of the footwashing as the basis for his narrative, and has attached an explanation (vv. 12–20) to the act (vv. 4f.). The source passage belongs to the category of apophthegms, in which an action or descriptive framework forms the background to a dominical saying;[2] and here we are dealing with an apophthegm formed at a relatively late stage, because it is Jesus' own action that gives rise to his saying.[3] The fact that the Evangelist uses this apophthegm and gives it a new interpretation, does not mean that he wants to exclude the old one, but to establish it afresh. It is the task of the exegesis to demonstrate the inner unity of the two interpretations.[4]

In the textual analysis, we have not yet dealt with the fact that both interpretations have been enlarged by appendices and notes of a redactional character; and the question to which stage of the tradition they belong remains. Now the additions, vv. 10b, 11 and 18, 19 clearly belong together; and their associations with 6.64, 70 and with 14.29; 16.4, together with their

---

[1] Similarly Wellh.; Von Dobschütz ZNTW 28 (1929) 166 omits vv. 6–11 as a "sacramental addition" to the narrative of the footwashing, which is "attuned in its entirety to the ethical level of exhortation". Sp. too, divides vv. 1–11 from vv. 12–20, but omits vv. 12–20 from the "basic document". E. Lohmeyer (ZNW 38 1939, 74–94) sees a uniform piece of the tradition in 13.1–20, which the Evangelist has enlarged with some additions.

[2] Gesch. der synopt. Trad. 8 = Hist. of the Syn. Trad. 11. Acc. to W. L. Knox (HTrR 43 1950, 161–163) the Evangelist is using a piece of the tradition into which he has inserted v. 7 and vv. 10f.

[3] Clearly the dominical saying in Lk. 22.27, or a variant of it, lies at the basis of the formation of this section; see Gesch. der synopt. Trad. 49 = Hist. of Syn. Trad., 47f.

[4] The source document is written in a Semitic type of Greek. In the narrative, the verb is normally brought forward to the beginning of the sentence. The following points are characteristic: ἤρξατο in v. 5, the superfluous αὐτοῦ in v. 12, the question (v. 12) (see Schl.), the conclusion *a mai. ad min.* in v. 14, perhaps also ποιεῖν with the Dat. in v. 12. The sentences belonging to the Evangelist show a Semitic colouring (as elsewhere), in addition to his own special stylistic characteristics: e.g. the bringing forward of the verb, ἔχειν μέρος μετά in v. 8.

stylistic characteristics (see below) show that they are not to be ascribed to a secondary redaction but to that of the Evangelist himself. In addition v. 16 and v. 20 have been appended to the second interpretation.[1] Since both verses are variants of synoptic dominical sayings, and since neither is formulated in a way characteristic of John, they cannot have been inserted by the Evangelist himself; we are led to the same conclusion by the fact that the Evangelist's own addition, vv. 18f separates these two logia, which in fact belong together. It only remains to ask whether they have been inserted by the ecclesiastical redactor, as a supplement from the synoptic tradition, or whether they had already attached themselves to the apophthegm of the footwashing in the source the Evangelist had before him. The latter, a frequent occurrence in the tradition,[2] is probably the case; otherwise it is hard to understand why the redactor did not insert the two verses next to each other.

1) *Exposition:* 13.1–3

The temporal phrase in v. 1 πρὸ δὲ τῆς ἑορτῆς τοῦ πάσχα cannot refer to the whole sentence, but only to εἰδώς[3]; because to date ἀγαπήσας ... εἰς τὸ τέλος ἠγάπησεν would be absurd. Now the sentence, "Since Jesus, before the feast of the passover, knew that his hour had come", would make sense in itself; but it makes no sense when it is stated as the reason for ἀγαπήσας ... ἠγάπησεν. And it would make just as little sense simply to take εἰδώς temporally, because this again would come back in the end to a dating of εἰς τέλος ἠγάπησεν. The best one could do, would be to take πρὸ δὲ τ. ἑορτ. τ. π. as a chronological statement referring to the section as a whole, and prefaced to it, without any grammatical connexion.[4] Then εἰδώς ... ἠγάπησεν αὐτούς would be a sentence complete in itself. But this would be strange.[5] Moreover the εἰδώς of v. 1 clashes with that of v.3, both in form and content. Thus one is forced to the conclusion that εἰδώς ... εἰς τέλος ἠγ. αὐτ. is an insertion into an existing text. But since this insertion cannot be explained as an arbitrary redactional gloss,[6] the sentence is probably a piece of the disordered text, for which the redactor has found a home in the wrong place; the supposition lies to hand that it is the original introduction to ch. 17.[7] In which case, of course, one must draw the conclusion that ἠγάπησεν αὐτοὺς is not original; for to take εἰδώς κτλ as following on ὅτε οὖν ἐξῆλθεν of 13.31a[8] again involves linking the words εἰς τέλος ἠγ. to one

---

[1] With regard to v. 15 and v. 17 see below, pp. 476 n.3, 475 n.3.

[2] Gesch. der Synop. Trad. 64f. = Hist. of the Syn. Trad. 61f.

[3] Thus syr^s and the old expositors, see Zn.

[4] Thus Htm., Hirsch.

[5] Τῇ ἐπαύριον would be a partial analogy (6.22). See p. 216 n.6.

[6] What motive could have made a redactor anticipate εἰδώς in v. 3 by using the same word in v. 12?

[7] See p. 461. Moreover, however awkwardly the Red. has dealt with the form of the passage, he has proceeded correctly as regards its subject matter, by placing ἠγάπησεν at the beginning of the whole virtually as its theme.

[8] See p. 461.

particular point in time, and this is meaningless. I therefore suggest that εἰς τέλος originally belonged to ἀγαπήσας τ. ἰδ. τ. ἐν τ. κ., and that instead of ἠγάπησεν there was originally ἐγείρεται ἐκ τοῦ δείπνου (or perhaps ἀνέστη). This the redactor could not use, because it anticipated v. 4; he changed it in the simplest possible way, admittedly without being able at the same time to produce a consistent text.

Out of v. 1, therefore, only the chronological reference πρὸ δὲ τ. ἑορτ. τ. π. is to be retained as original; and this should be taken together with the words in v. 2 καὶ δείπνου γινομένου, which define the occasion more specifically. Both statements are made with reference to ἐγείρεται in v. 4. But two more clauses have pushed their way in: a new gen. abs. in v. 2, and a subordinate participle in v. 3, which is to be taken causally: εἰδώς κτλ. It is hard to believe that this overloading is original. Since v. 3 is Johannine in both form and content, the gen. abs. of v. 2 is probably to be excluded as a redactional gloss;[1] its purpose—which is quite unnecessary—is to prepare us for vv. 11, 18f, 21–30.[2]

In **v. 1** Jesus' last supper with his disciples is put in the period πρὸ τῆς ἑόρτης τοῦ πάσχα.[3] As is shown by what follows, the day

---

[1] There is no need at all to read in to the formulation of 13.27–29 a reference to v. 2, thereby proving, by means of vv. 21–30, that v. 2 is an original part of the text; see below. If we are to take every possibility into account, we can of course also ask whether εἰδώς κτλ. in v. 3 is not a redactional insertion, and whether this verse, and not v. 1, was not the original introduction to ch. 17. But even if v. 3 were not in itself unsuitable for this purpose, it would remain true that it does not have the motif of ἀγαπᾶν as v. 1 does; moreover the formal difficulties force one to regard v. 1 as an insertion, while v. 3 fits its position well, once v. 2 has been eliminated. Hirsch, who retains v. 1, omits v. 3 as a red. addition (as he does v.2).

[2] The text of v. 2 is uncertain: τοῦ διαβόλου κτλ. .B ℵ L read: εἰς τ. καρδίαν ἵνα παραδοῖ (or παραδῷ) αὐτὸν Ἰούδας Σίμωνος Ἰσκαριώτης; against this D ℜ pl lat read: εἰς τ. καρδίαν Ἰούδα Σίμωνος Ἰσκαριώτου (D: ἀπὸ Καρυώτου as in 6.70 etc.). Syr[s] (and some codd. it) agrees with what the second reading states: "And Satan had entered the heart of J., the son of S., the Scar., that he should betray him". Against B etc. is not only the fact that it would be peculiar to say: "The devil had put it into his (own) heart", but above all, that the sense would then require βεβλημένου (for βάλλεσθαι εἰς νοῦν = to put into one's head, see Wetst. and Br.); and in spite of Orig. and Lagr., one cannot translate B's text: "Now that the devil had already put it into his (i.e. Judas') heart, that J. ...". The view that Schl. considers and then rejects, that the devil had put it into Jesus' heart, is absurd. The original text can only be that of D etc. (on the syr. text, see Merx). B.'s text will be a correction made in the attempt to avoid the contradiction with v. 27. Cp. Herm. mand. V 2.2, the ἐνέργεια of the ὀξυχολία: παρεμβάλλει ἑαυτὴν εἰς τὴν καρδίαν τοῦ ἀνθρώπου ἐκείνου. Cp. too Hom. Od. 15, 172f.; ὡς ἐνὶ θυμῷ ἀθάνατοι βάλλουσι, and Pind. Ol., 13, 16 (ἐν καρδίαις βάλλειν).

[3] This expression which occurs also in Lk. 2.41, is not the one used in Judaism, where it is either simply "The Passover" or "the feast of unleavened loaves" (Lk. 22.1) or "the unleavened loaves" (Mk. 14.12 and par. s). The Passover lamb was slaughtered on the afternoon of the 14th Nisan, and consumed on that evening. There followed the feast of unleavened loaves from the 15th to the 21st Nisan. A less exact use of language could call the whole 7 day feast the Passover, or conversely, the feast of the unleavened loaves; see Str.-B. I 985. 987f. on Matt. 26.2, 17; see further p. 123 n.2. Merx, following syr[s], wants to read: "before the unleavened", which is an obvious correction of the Greek-Christian linguistic expression.

immediately before the Passover feast is intended, that is to say, the 13th Nisan.[1] **V. 2** states more exactly the time and place of the event: καὶ δείπνου γινομένου.[2] The meal in question is an ordinary one; as is shown by v. 30, it is in fact the customary main meal in the evening, and not the Passover meal, as in the synoptic account; for it is the 13th Nisan, and there is no mention at all of a Passover meal.[3] So much for the outward facts relating to the setting; **v. 3** turns our attention to the inward ones: εἰδὼς (ὁ Ἰησοῦς) ὅτι κτλ![4] These words give a particular significance to the event that follows, and this is immediately developed, at least by implication, in the dialogue vv. 6ff. Εἰδώς will be used again three times, following its occurrence here at the beginning of the actual history of the passion: once, at its end, when "everything is . . finished" (19.28); and twice between these two instances, in the introduction to the "highpriestly" prayer (ch. 17),[5] and again, where Jesus hands himself over to the world to suffer at its hands (18.4). The purpose of this repetition is to characterise everything that happens here as revelation-event: Jesus acts as the one who "knows," as the perfected "Gnostic,"[6] whose action and suffering do not have their origin or goal in the causal continuity of temporal events, but in whom God

---

[1] In themselves, the words πρὸ τ. ἑορτ. τ. π. need only designate the proximity of the Passover feast (thus Joach. Jeremias, Die Abendsmahlworte Jesu 1935, 36–38, 2nd ed. 1949 44–46; while unable to deny the contradition with the synoptic chronology in 18.28, he seeks to overcome it in 13.1). But its proximity had already been mentioned in 11.55 and stated more exactly in 12.1. But above all, 13.1 is tied down to the 13th Nisan, by the fact that 18.28 takes place on the following day; and this is definitely the 14th Nisan. The dating of the last supper on the 13th and the death of Jesus on the 14th Nisan contradicts the synoptic chronology, acc. to which the days concerned are the 14th and 15th Nisan. The fruitless attempts to harmonise the Johannine and Synoptic chronology can be left on one side: (Zn: a forced interpretation of John in line with the synoptics; Str.-B: in John the dating is acc. to the official Sadduceean reckoning and in the synoptics acc. to the popular Pharisaic method; but cp. Dalman: Jesus–Jeschua 80ff.). Nor is the historical question, which of the two datings is correct (perhaps the Johannine), of any importance for the interpretation of John; see also on 13.30.

[2] γενομένου (𝔎D pl lat) instead of γινομένου (B ℵ*L W) is either simply a mistake or a senseless correction; for the meal is not yet over, but continues after v. 21. Δ. γινομένου does not necessarily mark the beginning of the meal; if it did, ἐγείρεται in v. 4 would imply a pause (see p. 466 n.5). But γίνεσθαι need not mean the commencement of the meal, but simply its taking place (thus γίνεσθαι is used with ἀγορά, σύνοδοι, τὰ Ὀλύμπια, δεῖπνον etc., see the lexicon). The meaning is simply: "On the occasion of a meal"; see Windisch, Joh. und die Synoptiker, p. 71.

[3] It is worth remarking that footwashing has no place in the Passover ritual, see Dalman, Jesus–Jesch., p. 108.

[4] That the verse comes from the Evangelist's hand is proved both by the Gnostic terminology, which he continually uses to express the idea of revelation, and by the importance of the verse for the composition (see above). The indispensable ὁ Ἰησοῦς has been sacrificed in the process of editing, since this has encroached on vv. 1 and 2.

[5] 13.1 is to be taken as the introduction to ch. 17, see p. 461.

[6] See p. 143 n.1, note 1, 279f.

himself is active, that God with whom as the "Father" he is at one. Again the language of Gnosticism is used to express the idea of the revelation: Jesus knows that "the Father has given all things into his hands,"[1] that he "came forth from God,"[2] and "goes unto God"[3] again. Just as the whole event of the passion is to be understood as revelation event, so in particular is the following account of the footwashing, that is, as a mystery for the world's sight and judgment.

2) *The Footwashing, and its First Interpretation:* 13.4–11

In **vv. 4f.** the action is described in detail,[4] so that the reader at once realises the absurdity of the event—an absurdity that Peter gives expression to in the very next verses (6–8), and which is afterwards acknowledged by Jesus himself (v. 12–14). Jesus, the master, (v. 13) stands up[5] in order to do for the disciples what would normally be done by a slave.[6] Peter's protest in **v. 6**[7] calls attention to the puzzling nature of the event.[8] To a certain extent, it stands on the same level as

---

[1] See p. 165 n.1, 251, 253 n.3.

[2] See p. 138 n.1, 298 n.1.

[3] See p. 272 n.5. Cp. E. Pfeiffer, Virgils Bukolika 1930, 102f.

[4] Λέντιον (linen-cloth) is a Latin loan-word that has penetrated the Greek and Judaic languages; see Br. and Str.-B; βάλλειν = to pour into, is normal usage (e.g. Epict, Diss. IV 13, 12; Jdc. 6.19); νιπτήρ (basin) is not attested elsewhere, but ποδανιπτήρ is: Herod, II 172. The use of ἄρχεσθαι (Dalman, W.J. 21f) to denote the beginning of the action, so characteristic of the Synoptics, only occurs here in John; the Semitism indicates use of the source: see p. 462 n.4. It is doubtful that the laying aside of the ἱμάτια (the outer garment) means symbolically the laying down of his life; still more doubtful that the λέντιον prefigures the cloth in which Jesus' body was wrapped (Loisy); there is indeed no explicit mention of it in 19.40.

[5] The words ἐκ τ. δείπνου could make one think that the meal had already begun (see p. 465 n.2). However it may have been inserted into the source by the Evangelist or Red., on the grounds that the phrase δείπνου γινομένου in v. 2 lay too far back following the insertion of (v. 2 and) v. 3, and that a reminder was needed as to the setting. But the absurdity of the footwashing lies in its being carried out by the Master, not in the strange choice of time and place. This plays no part in Peter's question, or in the two interpretations that follow the action. The word ἐγείρεται itself does not necessarily presuppose that Jesus and the disciples had already sat down at the table (see Dalman, W. J. 18 f and Schl. ad loc). That they had in fact done so is shown by πάλιν in v. 12, and ἐγείρεται only serves to stress the astonishing nature of the act; and yet see p. 474 n.2.

[6] On footwashing as one of the duties of a slave, see Str.-B., Br., and Schl. ad loc. W. L. Knox (HThR) 43, 1950 161–163) recalls the Hellenistic saying that one should not go ἀνίπτοις ποσίν to a λόγος.

[7] There is as little indication that Peter comes last in order (Orig.) as there is that he comes first (the Catholic exegesis since Aug., Loisy also). The question of the order is of no interest to the narrator. Peter, as so often in the old tradition, is representative and spokesman; see G. der Syn. Trad. 336 = Hist. of the Syn. Trad. 308.

[8] ℜ D pl read ἐκεῖνος after λέγει αὐτῷ in v. 6, which makes the style even more Johannine. Νίπτεις is praes. de con. (cp. 10.32; Bl.–D § 319). Σύ is stressed, as is rightly drawn out by Chrys.'s paraphrase—414e = Cat. 337, 1, albeit with a false nuance: ταῖς χερσὶ ταύταις, ἐν αἷς ὀφθαλμοὺς ἀνέῳξας καὶ λεπροὺς ἐκάθηρας καὶ νεκροὺς ἀνέστησας, τοὺς ἐμοῦ νίπτεις πόδας;

the Jews' protestations and questions in the earlier narrative, and as those of the disciples in what follows. Peter's judgment is κατὰ τὴν σάρκα (8.15), κατ' ὄψιν (7.24). The "healthy human mind" is not capable of grasping what is apparently absurd.[1] And yet, in his answer in v. 7—solemnly introduced by ἀπεκρ. καὶ εἶπεν—Jesus is not just rebuking him for his ignorance; he is also at the same time exonerating him and promising that although he cannot yet know what is happening to him through this act of service, he will understand it afterwards.[2] Μετὰ ταῦτα: it is obvious that this does not mean "a few moments later," as if the second interpretation in vv. 12f. were to give Peter "gnosis." Rather, μετὰ ταῦτα refers to the decisive turning-point that is now imminent, to the death and resurrection of Jesus.[3] For then the Spirit would bestow knowledge, and lead into all truth (14.26; 16.13); then Jesus would no longer speak in riddles, but in plain language (16.25);[4] then the disciples would be able to judge what Jesus had done for them in his act of service.

It is significant that it is the *knowledge* of what is now happening that is referred to the future. One cannot say that the footwashing portrays an event that will take place in the future. For v. 10 reads: "You are all clean"; i.e. through the footwashing, Peter has already received what he has to have; it is just that he does not yet know it, and he will realise it only after the passion and Easter. This is in harmony with the fundamental conviction of this Gospel, that the coming and the going of Jesus are a unity. Of course, his coming and his action would be nothing without his "glorification" through the passion. But this is not added to it as something new, for from the beginning it has already been contained in his coming;[5] his death is only the demonstration of

---

[1] There can of course be no question of explaining Peter's protest in terms of a psychology of the individual; it does have a certain analogy (even if not an exact one: Lohmeyer) with Matt. 3.14.

[2] The fact that ἄρτι does not occur in syr^s or in certain lat. mss. is immaterial, because what it stands for is implied in the words μετὰ ταῦτα that follow. On οὐκ οἶδας = "You cannot know", see A. Fridrichsen, Coniect. Neotest. VII (1944), 6. The personal pronouns are unstressed in Jesus' answer, as is often the case in John, see Colwell 51–55.

[3] This is also shown by the passages that speak of the understanding which is given through the resurrection, in contrast to the earlier lack of understanding (2.22; 12.16), e.g. 16.12f. (οὐ ... ἄρτι ... ὅταν δέ), 22 (νῦν μὲν ... δέ); 13.19, 36 (νῦν ... ὕστερον); 14.29. Wellh.'s question as to whether v. 7 refers to a later ecclesiastical institution is absurd. Nor of course can μετὰ ταῦτα mean specifically: "After you have denied me, and yet remained my disciple" (Schl.)—although without doubt all the λύπη and ταραχή of the disciples is included in what is said to lie ahead of them.

[4] This is the Johannine version of the Gnostic–Christian idea that only the Resurrected Lord can give the full revelation; see Act. Io. 96 p. 198, 20ff: τίς εἰμι ἐγὼ γνῶ (γνώσῃ?) ὅταν ἀπέλθω. ὁ νῦν ὁρῶμαι τοῦτο οὐκ εἰμί· ὄψει ὅταν σὺ ἔλθῃς.

[5] See p. 429.

what has always happened in and since his incarnation.[1] His death is not exceptional because it happens to *him*, but because of the special experience or knowledge which the believer gains in the light of the cross. The cross shows him the whole truth of ὁ λόγος σάρξ ἐγένετο, it leads him to the λύπη and ταραχή (as chs. 16 and 14 show) from which the χαρά and εἰρήνη grow. Thus in the statement: γνώσῃ δὲ μετὰ ταῦτα Peter is not referred to outer events, which are to instruct him; he is referred to his own existence. The possibility which he already has as a believer discloses itself to him, by being appropriated when faith is put to the test.

What then, is the meaning of the footwashing? One thing is immediately clear from Peter's opposition: he does not understand that Jesus humbles himself to serve his own. And just how much this goes against the instinct of the natural man is shown by his repeated and increasingly vehement resistance, **v. 8.**[2] We are not, of course, to interpret this psychologically,[3] but as a matter of fact: the natural man simply does not want this kind of service. Why not? The service in question is not just any personal act of kindness—for why should this not be acceptable to the natural man?—but it is service performed by the incarnate Son of God. And even if man can reject it out of pride, Peter's words do not just express this kind of pride,[4] but rather the basic way men think, the refusal to see the act of salvation in what is lowly, or God in the form of a slave.

Jesus answers that only the man who accepts this service[5] has fellowship with him, remains united with him, that is, as he is on his way to the δόξα.[6] But it is this that is all-important for the disciple and

---

[1] Cp. 14.31: ἀλλ' ἵνα γνῷ ὁ κόσμος κτλ.

[2] On "Simon", which syr[s] reads instead of Peter, see Merx ad loc. and on Matt., 160–171; but N.B. also A. Dell, ZNTW 15 (1914, 14–21). Instead of νίψῃς D reads ντψεις, which after οὐ μή is equivalent to the subj.; Bl.-D § 365, 2. On εἰς τ. αἰῶνα see p. 186 n. 4. οὐ μὴ … εἰς τ. αἰῶνα is characteristic of John, see 4.14; 8.51; 10.28; 11.26.

[3] Nor may one suppose that the repeated refusal is a sign of politeness; for in that case the second refusal would have to be half acceptance, as the rabbinic rule prescribes, Berach. 34a (Str.-B.I 122 on Mt. 3.14).

[4] Wrongly, B. Weiss (similarly Ho.): "Instead of submitting in true modesty, as he should have done, Peter now refuses categorically and with a passionate determination …; by this he shows that the modesty that inspires his refusal is not free of natural self-will, or from the pride that does not want to accept any act of loving service".

[5] That it simply says σε instead of τοὺς πόδας σου, is only a shortened form of speech. But it does show that the footwashing is not being contrasted with total immersion; if this were so, then the shortened form would be impossible; see on v. 10.

[6] The phrase ἔχειν μέρος μετά τινος (only here in John) is due to the O. T. Judaic expression: (or עִם) הָיָה חֵלֶק לְ. The meaning was originally: to have a share with a person in something (Dt. 10.9; 14.27, 29; Schl. on Mt. 24.51); it is then used more or less generally to denote the sharing of a destiny (II Sam. 20.1; Is. 57.6; Ps. 49.18; Mt. 24.51; Rev. 20.6; 21.8; Ign. Pol. 6.1; Schl. op. cit.), not however the personal sharing of life and way of

that gives his discipleship ultimate significance, namely that he is to be where Jesus is (12.26; 17.24). But if that is the case, then everything depends on his accepting this service.

Peter has now learned (v. 9) that this is important; but he has not yet understood in what way. For now his refusal turns into its very opposite: he demands more than he has already received. Thus he does not understand that Jesus' gift is something unique and complete in itself, that allows of no distribution in larger or smaller amounts, nor affords any lesser or greater degree of assurance. The Revealer withdraws himself from the man who wants more, in that he shows the foolish man that he already has what he needs (v. 10): as one who has washed himself is completely clean, and needs no further washing,[1] so too the man who has received Jesus' service needs no further assurance that he is on the way to the δόξα.[2]

---

thinking; thus it is to be distinguished from κοινωνίαν ἔχειν μετά (I John 1.3, 6f.) and from εἶναι ἐν (ch. 15) (against H. Seelemann, Der Begriff κοινωνία in NT 1933, 95f.).

[1] Χρείαν ἔχειν is Johannine; mostly with ἵνα, see p. 130 n. 3. ὅλος as in 9.34.

[2] The meaning of this verse, the text of which is uncertain, is disputed. Εἰ μὴ τοὺς πόδας (which D supplements still further by: οὐ χρ. ἔχει τὴν κεφαλὴν νιψ. εἰ μὴ τ. ποδ.) does not occur in ℵ c v codd., Orig., Tert., and is perhaps missing from other lat. fathers too (see Zn. and Lagr.). If one includes these words, v. 10 speaks of two washings, the first complete one, total immersion, and the one that follows, partial, in which only the feet are washed. The first would be the decisive one; the second, although still necessary, only of secondary importance. This is contrary to the solemnity of vv. 8f., acc. to which it is the footwashing that appears to be absolutely decisive. And what would be intended by the two washings? Acc. to the explanation most frequently adopted, λούεσθαι refers to baptism as the "general cleansing" and the footwashing to the Lord's supper, which forgives unavoidable new sins. (The saying would then be a polemic, directed against further baptisms or washings, therefore against Jewish cleansing-rites, or rather against Jewish-Gnostic baptist sects). But to suppose that the footwashing represents the Lord's Supper is grotesque, especially when it actually takes place on the occasion of a meal. H. v. Campenhausen (ZNTW 33 1934 259–271) regards the footwashing as a protrayal of baptism (as also A. Schweitzer, Die Mystik des Apostels Paulus 350 (E.T. The Mysticism of Paul the Apostle, 1931, 360); P. Fiebig, Angelos 3 (1930), 121–128; O. Cullmannn, Urchristent. u. Gottesd. 68–72; the latter at the same time asserts that there is a reference to the Lord's Supper); contrasted with this is the cleanliness achieved through the λούεσθαι, describing cleansing through the word of Jesus (acc. to 15.3). The representation of baptism as footwashing is due to the ancient Church baptismal rite, whereby the catechumen only stands in water up to his ankles. On this view, v. 10 is directed against the advocates of the earliest rite (that of John's disciples), acc. to which the catachumen was entirely immersed. Thus the saying means: whoever has been made clean by Jesus' word, has no need of further washings, except baptism, and for this it is sufficient to wash the feet. But can there be two antitheses in v. 10? That is to say: 1. whoever becomes clean through my word only needs baptism and no further washing; and 2. in baptism only the feet need to be washed; there is no need of total immersion. Only the first antithesis seems possible to me: whoever is cleansed by the word, only needs baptism (portrayed as footwashing). (The point of the saying would then be the same as on the other view.)

But the fact that both these interpretations distinguish between two essential cleansings argues against them both. It is said of the λελουμένος that he is *completely* clean (καθαρὸς ὅλος), and yet if, after the λούεσθαι, there is still need of a footwashing, then he cannot be completely clean. We are forced, in my opinion, to conclude that εἰ μὴ τοὺς

except the feet

Whoever has received Jesus' act of service is united with him to share his destiny, and is thus assured of the way to the δόξα; Jesus' service has cleansed him. The words, "And you are clean," are valid for everyone who belongs to the community of the disciples. While the service Jesus performs is symbolised by the footwashing, its essential nature is not expressly defined; and yet basically it is self-evident, as 15.3 expresses it: "Already you are clean, because of the word I have spoken to you." Thus the *word* has cleansed them.[1] His service is accomplished in the word which he speaks, and which by speaking it, he himself is. For his word is not a doctrine that could be separated from his person, a complex of ideas with general validity. Rather, he is himself encountered as the word, in all the separate things he says; because he

---

πόδας is a bad addition (so too Lagr.; Hosk., F. M. Braun RB 1935 22–33; E. Lohmeyer op. cit. 81ff.; Fridrichsen op. cit. 95,11; Barr., uncertain: Wik. and Strathm.). It is the result of explaining λούεσθαι in terms of baptism (an explanation made possible by the use of language attested in I Cor. 6.11; Eph. 5.26; Tit. 3.5; Acts 22.16; Heb. 10.22), while at the same time refusing to see the footwashing as a portrayal of baptism. Account had to be taken of the former as well as of the latter, however one answered the question as to the meaning of the footwashing. It is improbable that it was regarded as an archetype accounting for an ecclesiastical sacrament of footwashing, i.e. that the narrative assumed the character of an aetiological cult-legent (G. Bertram, Die Leidensgeschichte und der Christuskult 1922, 41; Kundsin, Topol, Überl. 56), because there is no evidence for such a sacrament before Augustine (Joh. Zellinger: Bad und Bäder in der altchristlichen Kirche 1928). Footwashing is admittedly mentioned more frequently in the lives of the monks (G. P. Wetter, Der Sohn Gottes 60, 3).

If the text is read without εἰ μὴ τ. πόδ. we are clearly left with a parabolic saying: "Just as the man who has had a bath needs no further washing, but is completely clean, so. ..." (λούεσθαι = to take a bath, and νίπτεσθαι = to wash oneself, or to be washed, come to mean the same in certain circumstances [as in P. Oxy. 840, 32–34; Kl. Texte 31, 5] but do mean different things in themselves, e.g. in Philo somn. I 148). Indeed the sentence could refer to a proverb (perhaps also to Jewish discussions about ritual washings). Its application can only be: "So too the man who has received fellowship with me through the footwashing, needs no further cleansing". It is clear that in the answer to v. 9 the λελουμένος of v. 10 is the man who has received the footwashing, which is shown to be equivalent to a thorough washing, making one completely clean (see p. 468 n. 5). The λελ., who is not satisfied with what he has received is reprimanded in v. 10; it is Peter, who has received the footwashing, and wanted still more.

But this has not in itself decided the question as to the meaning of the footwashing; it could be a sacramental washing, but in that case only baptism. However this question cannot be decided on the basis of v. 10, but only on the basis of the context as a whole; see above, in the text.

P. Fiebig also takes λελούμ. to refer to the footwashing, but he retains εἰ μὴ τ. πόδ. by understanding ὁ λελ. 1. as a present, and 2. as a Semitic casus pendens: "It is true of the one who is now being washed by me, that he only needs to have his feet washed". This doesn't seem possible to me. R. Eisler's interpretation (ZNTW 14 1913 268–271), which regards the footwashing as a portrayal of the mystical fellowship with Jesus on the grounds that it is a wedding custom, is a curiosity. There is evidence that it was such in both the Gentile (Servius Aen. IV 167) and Jewish worlds (but only late). In John, on this view, Jesus the heavenly bridegroom carries out the footwashing on his mystical bride, the church. But there is no trace of wedding mysticism in John.

[1] So also A. Fridrichsen ZNW 38 (1939), 94–96, and E. Lohmeyer op. cit. 83 f.

is the Revealer, the presence of God—in the form of the flesh, with death as his destiny—becomes event in him. Thus to accept his service means to believe; it means readiness to accept the disintegration of all the standards which the world uses to judge what is great and divine. Whoever can do this is free from the world, and thus "pure." The purity which is mediated through the word, as the service which Jesus performs, can be nothing other than the freedom which is promised (8.32) for "abiding in his word," for fidelity in belief.[1] Whoever accepts his act of service, i.e. whoever believes his word, needs no other means of salvation.

It remains only to raise the following question: if Jesus' service is depicted specifically in the footwashing, does this mean that the believer receives it in the actuality of a particular event, in which, as in the footwashing, the cleansing is symbolically portrayed, i.e. in baptism?[2] This question becomes more pressing in view of the probability that the polemic in v. 10 is not only directed against all attempts to secure a guarantee of salvation by means other than faith, but more particularly against the introduction of special means of purification, namely washings or baptisms.[3] If that is the case, there are only two possibilities; either v. 10 is directed against supplementing Christian baptism by further washings (or by its repetition); and in this case the footwashing portrays baptism as the natural Christian practice, as the act by which each man receives and appropriates Jesus' service. Or on the contrary, the service Jesus performs, through the word and

[1] See pp. 436–440. Καθαρός only here and in 15.3 in John, both times in a metaphorical sense; in I Jn. 1.7, 9 καθαρίζειν is due to cultic linguistic usage (the subj. in I Jn. 1.7 is τὸ αἷμα Ἰησοῦ), but is also metaphorical. The interpretation of purity as freedom from the world does not contradict the view that sees it as freedom from ἁμαρτία and ἀδικία (I Jn. 1.7, 9), cp. 8.34; and yet I Jn. 1.7, 9 has a narrower sense than Jn. 8.32; 13.10, in so far as we are concerned there with the Christians' purity from the guilt of sin, in the context of the polemic against the Gnostic idea of the sinlessness of the Gnostic.

[2] The "cleansing" which acc. to Tit. 2.14; Heb. 1.3; II Pt. 1.9 is accomplished by Jesus, and more specifically by his blood in I Jn. 1.7; Heb. 9.14 (cp. Herm. sim. V 6.2), is mediated acc. to Eph. 5.26; Heb. 10. 22 by baptism.

[3] It must be borne in mind that the dividing line between pure Christian communities and syncretistic ones can scarcely be drawn in the earliest era of Christendom (cp. W. Bauer Rechtgläubigkeit und Ketzerei im ältesten Christendum 1934, where unfortunately the Jewish-Christian baptismal sects are not dealt with); one must furthermore bear in mind that John specifically attacks the Baptist-Sect (see pp. 16f. 48, 108, 168f.), and that the Gnosticism with which he does battle is itself organised in baptist sects. Concerning the baptismal movement see W. Brandt, Die jüdischen Baptismen 1910; Elchasai 1912; G. Hölscher, Gesch. der israelitischen und jüdischen Rel. 1922, 207ff., 237ff.; Urgemeinde und Spät-jüdentum (Avh. ut. av Det Norske Videnskaps Akademi i Oslo II Hist.-Filos. Kl. 1928, Nr. 4); espec. Jos. Thomas, Le Mouvement baptiste en Palestine et Syrie 1935.—Jn. 13.10 is explained in terms of the polemic against baptismal rites by B. Brandt, Die jüdischen Bapt. 121f.; Hölscher, Urgem. und Spatj. 12 (cp. 19); both see in Heb. 6.1f. the evidence for a Christendom that practised a variety of washings (βαπτισμοί). Cp. Schl. on v. 9: "John resists a baptismal practice which, like that of the Essenes, Hemerobaptists, or of Banus, necessitated the continual repetition of the washings."

as the word, is considered to be fundamentally opposed to every form of sacramental purification, baptism included.[1]

If it is strange to conceive of an early Christian movement in which baptism was rejected, this cannot be excluded a priori; one could explain it as arising out of opposition to the movements that had ascribed an excessive value to baptism and baptismal washings. In point of fact, John's attitude to the sacraments is problematical. He makes no mention at all of the Lord's Supper;[2] in his account of the last meal Jesus' prayer takes its place.[3] He deals with re-birth, without referring to baptism.[4] The disciples are considered to be καθαροί, without any account being given of their baptism; they are pure through Jesus' word (15.3). On the other hand, John tells us without hesitation that Jesus baptised, just as the Baptist did (3.22; 4.1); furthermore, the combination of μαθητὰς ποιεῖν and βαπτίζειν in 4.1 seems to show that entry into the circle of disciples was bound up with the reception of baptism. But 3.22 and 4.1 are far from being stressed, and the sacraments play no part in Jesus' proclamation. One can therefore explain the facts only by concluding that, while the Evangelist came to terms with ecclesiastical practice in regard to baptism and the Lord's Supper, it remained suspect to him, because of its misuse, and that this is why he has made no mention of it.[5] The truth is that the sacraments are superfluous for him: the disciples are "clean" through the word (15.3), just as they are "holy" through the word, according to the prayer that takes the place of the Lord's Supper (17.17). If the Evangelist did come to terms with the sacraments, he can only have understood them in the sense that in them the word is made present in a special way. Similarly, he does not ascribe a special significance, alongside the incarnation and work of Jesus, to his death and resurrection as the events on which the sacraments are founded, but rather sees the whole as a unity.[6] In conclusion, it would be difficult to maintain that the footwashing represents

---

[1] Thus Kreyenbühl II 102–119; Reitzenstein Taufe 160, 1. One cannot eliminate this possibility by, for instance, arguing that in that case the Johannine Gospel would not have been accepted by the Church. It was possible to incorporate the sacraments into it both by interpretation and interpolation. Indeed, the latter is what has happened in 3.5; 6.51b–58.

[2] 6.51b–58 is an ecclesiastical interpolation; see pp. 218f., 234-7.

[3] See p. 461, and on ch. 17; see too pp. 485f. Cp. M. Dibelius, ThBl 21 (1912), 10f, or Botschaft und Geschichte II 1956, 174f., re Heb.'s anti-cultic bearing.

[4] (ἐξ) ὕδατος in 3.5 is an ecclesiastical interpolation; see p. 138 n. 3.

[5] The view that the Evangelist kept silent about the sacraments because of the *disciplina arcanorum* seems to me to be without foundation (Joachim Jeremias, Die Abendmahlsworte Jesu 1935, 48f.). There is no trace of it even in Justin; it may be that its beginnings reach further back than the fourth century, when it was first properly developed, but in any case it is only from the end of the 2nd century that it seems "quietly to make itself known" (G. Anrich, RGG 2nd. ed. I 532; further, G. Anrich Das Antike Mysterienwesen in seinem Einfluss auf das Christentum 1894, 126ff.; N. Bonwetsch RE 3rd. ed. II 53f.).

[6] See p. 467–8. Only 19.34 seems to show the sacraments as grounded in the death of Jesus; and this also appears to be the meaning of I Jn. 5.7f. However, both these cases could be attributed to the ecclesiastical redaction. It is worth remarking that the attitude of I John to the sacraments is just as problematical as that of the Gospel; see on I Jn. 2.20, 27. Otherwise, O. Cullmann, Urchristent. und Gottesd. 1944, 39–77; W. Michaelis, Die Sakramente im Joh-Evg. 1946.

baptism; it portrays, rather, Jesus' service, which he performs through the word, and as the word, on behalf of his own.[1]

Peter wanted more than he had already received, but the words "And you are clean" refer him back to what he already has.[2] The plural ὑμεῖς shows that Peter had spoken as the disciples' representative,[3] and if we take the farewell discourses as a whole, it is clear that the disciples represent the Christian community as such. The words καθαροί ἐστε and γνώσῃ δὲ μετὰ ταῦτα hold good for all those who in faith make Jesus' service their own (v. 7). They can never know in any final or conclusive way what it means that they are the cleansed people; there is always the need to re-discover the meaning of their purity afresh. For them, of course, Jesus' passion and Easter are not historical occurrences about to happen in the immediate future. But then the decisive thing to which Jesus referred Peter was not the events as such, but his experience of them. In the same way, through the μετὰ ταῦτα, the believer is continually referred forward to those moments of his life, in which the proclamation of the Crucified leads him into λύπη and ταραχή; and it is only in this λύπη and ταραχή, when his faith is being tested, that he is able to grasp what that faith means. For the radical realisation of the meaning of Jesus' service comes with the appropriation of that service in the fulfilment of existence within history, not in dogmatic knowledge, or a "Christian view of the world."

In **v. 11**[4] the Evangelist has inserted the comment that amongst the disciples there is one who is unclean: the betrayer. And as in 6.64, 70 he has put the prediction in a place where it stands out, and he repeats it in v. 18. In neither case is it primarily the apologetic motif that is at work; the intention is rather to destroy any false security of belief.[5] The disciple can understand the affirmation of his purity correctly only when he knows there is one who is unclean among the disciples. Even to belong to the circle of disciples whose feet have been washed by Jesus[6] is no guarantee.[7]

---

[1] Cp. A. Fridrichsen op. cit. 96: "... whether John himself thought of baptism in this connection must remain very questionable". Neither does Barr. see the footwashing as portrayal of baptism. So too, acc. to Lohmeyer op. cit. 82ff. there is no portrayal of a cultic cleansing, but it is a sacramental act, i.e. the "institution into a priestly apostolate".

[2] See p. 468.

[3] See p. 458.

[4] The Evangelist's style can be recognised : on ᾔδει γάρ see 2.25 (4.44); 6.6, 64; on διὰ τοῦτο see 6.65 and p. 92 n. 2. Thus the verse is not a redactional gloss, but a comment by the Evangelist himself (see p. 462f.); the comment really begins in v. 10b: καὶ ὑμεῖς κτλ.

[5] See pp. 450f.

[6] The idea that Judas' feet were not washed, which was the view of the old expositors, has been wrongly read into the text; the narrative in 13.20–31 presupposes that no exceptions have been made: until then the traitor cannot be recognised by any outward sign.

[7] It could be said that the juxtaposition of καθαροί ἐστε and ἀλλ' οὐχὶ πάντες

3) *The Second Interpretation:* 13.12–20

Vv. 6–11 have fully developed only one aspect of the paradox presented by the picture of the Master washing his disciples' feet: the disciple is to accept such service. The other side comes into its own in vv. 12–20: the disciple, for his part, is to render this kind of service to his fellow disciple.[1] **V. 12** introduces the new scene[2] by picking up vv. 4f.[3] and using the same detailed narrative style as was used there. The way is then prepared for the content of the teaching by the rhetorical question: γινώσκετε τί πεποίηκα ὑμῖν;[4] And it becomes immediately clear from the use of ὑμῖν that Jesus' exemplary action is not just an illustration, floating as it were in empty space; on the contrary, the disciples have actually experienced it performed on themselves.

V. 13 stresses firstly the paradoxical nature of what has taken place: it is actually[5] their teacher and lord,[6] who has washed the disciples' feet. If he, so **v. 14** continues a maiore ad minus,[7] has done this for them, they are bound to perform the same service for each other.

---

corresponds to the juxtaposition of indicative and imperative in Paul (Rom.6.1ff.; I Cor. 5.7 etc.).

[1] A source forms the basis of vv. 12–20 (as of vv. 4f.) see p. 461f.

[2] Is the word πάλιν, well attested but missing in some cases (see v. Soden), an ancient addition? In which case it would be absolutely clear that the footwashing did not interrupt the meal, see p. 466 n. 5.

[3] "Οτε οὖν, which picks up the thread from v. 4, following the interruption, could come from the Evangelist (see p. 217 n. 5); the source read something like: εἶτα ἔλαβεν τ. ἱμ. κτλ.

[4] The question is asked as if vv 6–11 had not already gone before; as a rhetorical question it clashes with οὐκ οἶδας ἄρτι in v. 7. On the form of the question cp. Sifre Num, 115 (in Schl.'s translation): γινώσκετε τί πεποίηκα ἀντοῖς; Actually, ποιεῖν with the Dat., in the sense of doing something (good or bad) to someone, is not good Greek (Bl.-D. § 157, 1); in the LXX it more often stands for עָשָׂה לְ (e.g. I Sam. 5.8; Is. 5.4; Hos. 10.3). But it does occur in Greek literature, e.g. Antiphon fr. 58 (Diels-Kranz II 364, 5); Epict. Diss. I 9, 21; IV 6, 23 and see Liddell-Scott.

[5] Καλῶς = "correctly" as in 4.17; 8.48; see p. 299 n. 3.

[6] Ὑμεῖς (unstressed!) can scarcely mean "you hail me", as if ὁ διδ. and ὁ κύρ. were vocatives (which would be the correct grammatical interpretation: cp. Bl.-D. § 147, 3 and cp. 20.28), but rather "you name me" (which, to be correct, would have to be καλεῖτε), because the point lies in the contrast between φωνεῖσθαι and εἶναι; thus ὁ διδ. and ὁ κύρ. have the status of proper names introduced into the text in the Nomin. (Bl.-D. § 143 and cp. I Sam. 9.9).—ὁ διδ. and ὁ κύρ. define each other; thus κύριος is not a cultic term (see p. 176 n. 2); nor is it simply a polite form of address (as in 6.68; 11.3, 12 etc.): διδ. is the equivalent for the Jewish term רַבִּי for a teacher, and κύρ. is the equivalent of מָרִי. Both are ways of addressing respected persons, esp. Rabbis (Dalman W. J. 267f.), and are also used together elsewhere (Str.-B. ad loc). Thus διδ. (3.2, 10; 11.28) and ῥαββί (1,38, 49 etc.) are interchangeable in John, and in 1.38 ῥ. is explained as διδ. The absence of any repetition of the personal suffixes in the Greek version is normal usage (cp. Mk. 4.38; 9.17 etc.); syr[s] brings them back again. Cp. Bousset Kurios 82, and on the development of the use of διδ. see Harnack, Mission und Ausbreitung 3rd ed. 383, 2; Schlier, Relig. Unters. 56f.

[7] The typical Jewish conclusion קַל וָחוֹמֶר (Str.-B. III 223–226) is characteristic of

V. 15 repeats the imperative of v. 14 as a general statement: Jesus' action is an example binding on his disciples,[1]—whereby of course the footwashing is intended as a symbolic act, representative of loving service in general.[2] Thus we have here an anticipation of the exposition (in 13.34; 15.12) of the command of love as the last testament of the departing Revealer; in the same way the whole section 13.1–20 acts as a prelude to the discourses that follow.[3]

As in v. 12, ὑμῖν, which is again attached to ἐποίησα, is fundamental for the interpretation of the passage. Jesus' exemplary action is not to be regarded as an ideal illustration, or as a pattern or model of a universal moral truth, such as history (Historie) or rhetoric could depict;[4] it has been experienced by the disciple as service. Only the man whom Jesus has served can see him as the ὑπόδειγμα. Whatever may have been its meaning in the source, the Evangelist takes καθώς in an explanatory sense, as in 13.24; 15.12: they are committed by reason of what they have received.[5] Thus Jesus' work is not something lying open to view as an objective achievement, or as a factor to be taken into account in world history; and this is true, whether we are looking at it as part of our cultural heritage, or whether we are looking at the historical figure of Jesus as such. If we look at what he did simply in order to find "what it all adds up to" we will fail to see him; it is not as if the proclamation had the task of depicting his personality, or e.g. of showing what has become of Peter. He is only to be seen in that *which on each occasion he is for me*. Thus the imperative only holds good for the sphere in which Jesus' service has been received—only the man who is loved can himself love; and its fulfilment is not by performing a work analogous to his, but by readiness for the same existing for the other. The imperative does not demand an action in return, to be rendered to Jesus—14.15–24 will explain how the disciples' love cannot have him as its

---

the received source. D's πόσῳ μᾶλλον brings out the nature of the conclusion even more clearly.

[1] Ὑπόδειγμα, which the Atticists reject in favour of παράδειγμα, is the example, model, or pattern, which is shown to the onlooker either in deed or word; see ThWB II 32, 38ff.—For ἵνα following ὑπόδ. διδόναι, in the same sense as following expressions of ought, of being bound to, see Bl.-D. § 393. Schl. quotes rabbinic par. s to the ἵνα-clause.

[2] Thus vv. 14f. mean the same as Lk. 22.27; see p. 462 n. 3.

[3] V. 15 could be the work of the Evangelist, stressing the sense of v. 14; on the explicatory ἵνα-clause see p. 48 n. 3, and cp. esp 13.34; on καθώς cp. 13.34; I Jn. 2.6; 4.17 (also 2.27; 3.3, 7, 23). Cp. Kundsin, Character 207.

[4] Apart from Xen. mem. IV 3, 18 (Socrates as model) in Br. cp. Epict. Diss. IV 8, 31 (of the ideal κυνικός): ἰδοὺ ἐγὼ ὑμῖν παράδειγμα ὑπὸ θεοῦ ἀπέσταλμαι μήτε κτῆσιν ἔχων μήτε οἶκον μήτε γυναῖκα μήτε τέκνα, ἀλλὰ μηδ' ὑπόστρωμα, μηδὲ χιτῶνα μηδὲ σκεῦος, καὶ ἴδετε, πῶς ὑγιαίνω.

[5] See p. 382 n. 2.

immediate goal—but rather the turning to one's fellow. Jesus is not the ὑπόδειγμα for an Imitatio; but by receiving his service a new opportunity of existence together is disclosed to the disciple; and his readiness to grasp this opportunity will show whether he has rightly received the service. While there is no question of the disciple's being directed to perform a *work*, he is being led into an *action* that is grounded in the action of Jesus, and which for this reason can never assume the character of a work. 13.34f. and 15.1–17 will develop this further; and in the course of this development the peculiarity inherent in the command of love will emerge: viz. that it is a command binding on the circle of those in discipleship, on the community. Admittedly in the source it would be hard to take the ἀλλήλων of v. 14 as referring to the limited circle of those in discipleship;[1] but the Evangelist does understand it in this sense.[2]

In the original version of the source, v. 17 may have formed the conclusion of the section.[3] Here the exhortation becomes a promise, in the form of a beatitude:[4] Blessed is he who acts in accordance with what he has heard and known![5]

[1] A limitation to one's fellow disciple is as little in view here as in e.g. Mk. 9.50, or in Mt. 5.23f.; Lk. 17.3f.

[2] One may not limit the love-service demanded of the disciples in vv. 12–20 to their forgiveness of each other (Zn. Schl.), as if this followed from the connexion of vv. 12–20 with vv. 6–11. For the footwashing in vv. 6–11 does not just portray the forgiveness of sins through Jesus, but his service in its entirety. Moreover, 13.1–20 is the prelude to 13.34f.; 15.1–17, where there is no mention of the need to forgive one another.

[3] V. 17 could of course also belong to the logia in vv. 16 and 20 that had already been inserted in the source. These have been linked together by the key-word πέμπειν (see Gesch. der Synop. Trad 160f., 351f = Hist of Syn. Trad. 149f., 325f); in that case the insertion of v. 17 would perhaps provide a basis as regards subject-matter for the promise of v. 20: "Blessed are you, if you render a service of love to each other. For it is accounted as rendered to me". But it is also possible that v. 20 was attached to v. 16 in order to guard against a misunderstanding, or rather to provide a counter-weight: certainly the apostle is less than he who sent him (v. 16), but that does not mean that he may be treated with less respect (v. 20).—One can scarcely regard v. 17 as one of the Evangelist's insertions (οἴδατε could recall the frequent use of the word in I John, see 2.20f.; 3.5, 15, and the whole saying I Jn. 2.29); he would surely have placed it at the end of the section.

[4] Μακάριοι does not refer to "the blessing which true discipleship brings with it" (B. Weiss), but to the salvation which is given to the true disciple. Macarisms in the 2nd person, seldom in Greek, are characteristic of the Semitic use of language; see ZNTW 19 (1919/20), 170; Ed. Norden, Agnostos Theos 1913, 100, 1; H. L. Dirichlet, De veterum macarismis (Religionsgesch. Vers. und Vorarb. XIV 4) 1914.

[5] ταῦτα refers to what has been said in v. 16, or vv. 12–16; εἰ = if therefore, as a result of what has been said; ἐάν = if in the future; Bl.-D. § 372, la; Raderm. 175f.—The exhortation as *proverbialis sententia* (Calvin) is common; cp. Lk. 11.28; Mt. 7.21, 24–27; Jas. 1.22, 25; Rom. 2.13; II Clem. 3.1–5. Jewish parallels in M. Dibelius on Jas. I.22, p.109 (Meyer's Comm.); Str.—B.1. 467, 469f.; III 84ff.; Greek parallels in Br. ad loc, esp. Hes. Op. 826f.; τάων εὐδαίμων τε καὶ ὄλβιος, ὃς τάδε πάντα εἰδὼς ἐργάζηται ἀναίτιος ἀθανάτοισιν; esp. often in Epict. Cp. Calvin on v. 17: Neque enim vera cognitio dici meretur, nisi quae fideles eousque adducit, ut se capiti suo conforment. Vana potius imaginatio est, dum Christum et quae Christi sunt extra nos conspicimus.

Even in the source the apophthegm had been augmented by appended logia, which were intended to strengthen and particularise the imperative in vv. 14f.[1] **V. 16** is a variant of the dominical saying which occurs in Mt. 10.24 and Lk. 6.40 (in a curtailed version).[2] The form of the saying is typical of a *mashal*, in this case of a parabolic saying.[3] The reminder that the servant is not greater than his lord, that the messenger[4] is not greater than he who sent him, strengthens the argument about "all the more . . . ." in vv. 13f.[5] **V. 20** gives weight to the exhortation[6] by adding the promise that any loving service rendered to a messenger of Jesus is really rendered to Jesus himself, and thus also to God. For this purpose a dominical saying is used, which occurs in the synoptic Gospels in the variants Mt. 10.40 and Lk. 10.16.[7] Between v. 17 and v. 20 the Evangelist has inserted another comment of the same kind as v. 11.[8] **V. 18** makes a further reference to the betrayer,[9] and again the intention is to warn the disciple against any false

---

[1] See p. 462f.

[2] Originally a secular proverb? See Gesch. der synopt. Trad. 103, 107 = Hist. of Syn. Trad. 99, 103. John is not quoting the Matthaean version, for he would have had no reason for changing διδάσκαλος—μαθητής to ἀπόστολος—πέμψας, because the former would have suited the context better. V. 20, which was connected with v. 16 in the source, also shows that ἀπόστ.—πέμψ. in v. 16 is original. The variants are easy to explain. Rabbinical parallels in Str.-B. ad loc and I 577f. on Mat. 10.25. Correctly Dodd, NtSt 2 (1955/56) 75–77: v. 16 is due to oral tradition; cp. Noack 96. Against this, H. F. D. Sparks (JTS 1952, 58–61) seeks to prove the dependence upon Matt, and this argument is rejected by P. G. Smith (ibid. 1953) 31–35.

[3] See Gesch. der synopt. Trad. 181 = Hist. of Syn. Trad. 168. 15.15 shows that we are concerned with a parabolic saying, and that the disciples are not really thought of as Jesus' slaves. Κύριος, like δοῦλος, is to be understood parabolically, and has no cultic significance; see foll. note.

[4] 'Απόστολος, within the sphere of the parabolic saying, means "Messenger", not "apostle" (see prev. note), see K. H. Rengstorf, ThWB I 421, 40ff. 'Απόστ. only here in John. See Joh. Munck Studia Theol III (1950), 103.

[5] The idea of vv. 12–15, that it is the service which is *experienced* that is binding, is not brought out in v. 16, a fact which also points to v. 16 being secondary in this context.

[6] V. 20 must be interpreted in this way, at least in its present context, even if the relation of v. 20 to v. 16 may have meant something different in the source, see p. 476 n. 3. One must therefore put up with the difficulty that in v. 16 the (servant and) messenger is charged with the exhortation, while in v. 20 the exhortation to loving service is made with the messenger as the one to be served.

[7] With regard to the relation of the synoptic variants to each other and to Mt. 10.41f.; Mk. 9.37, 41f., see Gesch. der synopt. Trad. 152f. = Hist. of Syn. Trad. 142. The Rabbinic literature affords parallels in its frequent use of the principle: "The one who is sent by a man, is as the man himself," Str.-B. I 590; II 167, 466, 558; ThWB I 415, 3ff. As with v. 16, Dodd (op. cit. 81–85) supposes the source in v. 20 to be oral tradition.

[8] Οὐ περὶ πάντων ὑμῶν λέγω corresponds to ἀλλ' οὐχὶ πάντες in v. 11; it does not of course follow on well from the μακάριοι of v. 17. Some mss. try to improve the text by inserting γάρ after οἶδα.

[9] 'Εγὼ (unstressed!) οἶδα τίνας ἐξελεξάμην is similar to 6.70. Instead of τίνας ℜD pm read οὓς which is more correct grammatically. Orig. XXXII 14, 152 (p. 447, 16 Pr.) paraphrases: τίς ἐστιν ἕκαστος ὧν ἐξελεξάμην, Zahn: τίνες εἰσὶν οὓς. ... Both are right; but Zn. is wrong to put ἐγὼ οἶδα τίν. ἐξελ. and also ἵνα ... πληρωθῇ in parenthesis, in his desire

assurance and thus to strengthen the exhortation to ποιεῖν (v. 17). Here the prophecy is made in the form of a quotation from Ps. 40.10.[1] And in this context, the words are not used primarily to stress the fact that the dreadful event had been foreseen or pre-determined by God, but to state the incredible fact that the betrayer eats at the same table as Jesus,[2] and belongs to the circle of his friends. But the apologetic motif does come into its own in **v. 19**: the dreadful nature of such an event should not shake the disciple's faith in the Revealer;[3] Jesus had foretold it.[4] This apologetic motif is, of course, to be modified on the lines of the Evangelist's thought: he does not refer to Jesus' prior knowledge in order to overcome the difficulty caused by a single fact, which is what Judas' betrayal is. On the contrary, just as the allusion to the betrayer is intended to shake the disciple's assurance and to draw attention to a possibility he always has to face, so too the difficulty that the Evangelist is concerned with is the ever present one, that there are disloyal disciples. It is this, fundamentally, that Jesus knows beforehand: it is a matter of fact, which springs from the nature of revelation, that is to say, from its relation to the world. We are not of course told here as clearly as we are later (16.1, 4, 32f.; 14.29) that Jesus' foreknowledge is of this kind.

Thus two interpretations of the footwashing have been combined. The significance of this combination becomes clear when one realizes that both sections deal with the community created by Jesus' service, expounding it as the fellowship of the disciples with him and amongst themselves. The explicit theme of the first section is the fellowship with Jesus; this is shown to be grounded in an event that contradicts the

---

to read ἀλλ' ὁ τρώγων ... ἐπῆρεν ... as corresponding to οὐ περὶ πάντ. ὑμ. λέγω. On the contrary, the elliptical ἀλλ' ἵνα ("but the scripture had to be fulfilled") is characteristic of the Evangelist, see p. 48 n. 3.

[1] On γραφή see p. 128 n. 3. Here the actual verse of scripture is intended. On ἵνα πληρ. see p. 452 n. 2. The quotation is not taken from the LXX, which translates הִגְדִּיל by ἐμεγάλυνεν (John's version being ἐπῆρεν) and deviates in other ways too (see foll. note). Μετ' ἐμοῦ, which is inserted by ℵ ℜD, could well be supplementation following Mk. 14.18 or Lk. 22.21.

[2] The table fellowship is described by ὁ τρώγων μου τὸν ἄρτον (LXX: ὁ ἐσθίων ἄρτους μου), just as in Mk. 14.18 by ὁ ἐσθίων μετ' ἐμοῦ; cp. Mk. 14.20 and par. s: ὁ ἐμβαπτόμενος μετ' ἐμοῦ εἰς τὸ τρύβλιον and Lk. 22.21: ἡ χεὶρ τοῦ παραδιδόντος με μετ' ἐμοῦ ἐπὶ τῆς τραπέζης. The fact that John reads τὸν ἄρτον instead of the LXX's ἄρτους is no proof that he was thinking of the Lord's supper, because the Heb. also has the singular.

[3] The parallel ἵνα-clauses: 13.19; 14.29; 16.1, 4, 33 all have the same meaning. While in 14.29 it is simply ἵνα πιστεύσητε, in 13.19 ἵνα πιστεύητε is supplemented by ὅτι ἐγώ εἰμι, which like 8.24, 28 has no predicate to define it. "The Revealer" is to be supplied, as in 8.24; see p. 348f. Is the wording (πρὸ τοῦ γένεσθαι) due to the recollection of Is. 46.10?

[4] Because of v. 10 and 6.70 ἀπ' ἄρτι cannot mean "from now on"; it simply marks the contrast to ὅταν γένηται and means "now", or "now already", as in 14.7; νῦν in 14.29 means the same.

natural reason, namely in the service rendered by Jesus, the binding power of which will prove itself in the historical existence of the disciple, if he is prepared to base his life on this event and on it alone. The second section adds that this fellowship of the disciples with Jesus at the same time opens up a fellowship amongst themselves, and that for the former to exist, the latter must be made a reality through the disciples' action. The structure of the discourse on the vine 15.1–17 has a corresponding duality: μείνατε ἐν ἐμοί in 15.1–8 corresponds to 13.6–11; and μείνατε ἐν τῇ ἀγάπῃ 15.9–17 corresponds to 13.12–20. Thus 13.1–20 describes the founding of the community and the law of its being.

b) *The Prophecy of the Betrayal:* 13.21–30

There can be no talk of the community, without reckoning with the possibility that one of its number is unworthy. But in the circle of those who have received Jesus' service, unworthiness is synonymous with betrayal. The consciousness of belonging to the body of disciples must not seduce any of them into the illusion of security. The Evangelist had emphasised this immediately after the emergence of the body of disciples as a limited circle (6.66–71), and he has twice drawn attention to the fact in the previous scene which dealt with the founding of the community (vv. 11, 18). He now uses a special scene,[1] that of the prophecy of the betrayal (13.21–30), in order to express the idea in tangible form.

The scene 13.21–30 stems from the tradition the Evangelist received: that he used one of the synoptic accounts[2] does not admit of proof, and is improbable. It cannot be decided with complete certainty whether he used a written source at all, because his own stylistic characteristics are evident throughout. Vv. 27–29 are often held to be an insertion (whether inserted by the Evangelist into his source, or by the redactor into the Evangelist's text), on the grounds that these verses break the continuity between v. 26 and v.30. But in fact only vv. 28f. do so, because v. 30 follows on well from v. 27; λαβὼν τὸ ψωμίον v. 30 does not contradict μετὰ τὸ ψωμίον v. 27, but picks it up again.[3] Vv. 28f. however supply one of the Evangelist's characteristic comments;[4] and the only question is whether it is a comment on his own

[1] This explains why 13.21–30 follows on 13.1–20. Acc. to Loisy, 13.1–20 portrays the law of love, and 13.21–30 the persecutions and troubles the disciples will have to face. But in 13.21–30 the evil does not come from outside but from the community itself.

[2] Mk. 14.18–21; Mt. 26.21–25; Lk. 22.21–23; see Gesch. der synopt. Trad. 284f. = Hist. of Syn. Trad. 264f.

[3] This is not affected by the possibility that v. 27b is an insertion of the Evangelist's into a source document, see below.

[4] See p. 212 n. 4. On τινὲς γὰρ ἐδόκουν cp. 11.13, 31; 16.2 (20.15). The misunderstanding is also typically Johannine (see p. 127 n.1. The disciples do not understand a single word

narrative, or on that of a source. Verses 27 and 30 on either side both have ἐκεῖνος (see page 48 n. 3) of which the Evangelist is so fond; but this could be attributed to his stylistic editing of a source-text,[1] and does not necessarily argue against his having used a source.[2] And the word σατανᾶς of v. 27 may be considered a point in favour of his having done so, because the Evangelist always uses διάβολος;[3] but the strongest argument is as follows: the way the narrative in vv. 23f. is set out clearly implies that Peter and the other disciples received the answer to their question as to who the traitor was from the disciple on Jesus' breast. What Peter does is clearly secret; but it is not stated, and would be unreasonable to suppose, that the question the disciple puts to Jesus and Jesus' answer to it are also secret. If that were really intended it would at least have to be stated that Peter's attempt had failed to achieve its object. But vv. 28f. presuppose that no-one heard the answer. Thus vv. 28f. must in actual fact be considered an insertion by the Evangelist into his source. But it is just as clear that he has edited the source elsewhere as well. Without doubt, the insertion of the saying of Jesus in v. 21 comes from him (see below); and he is also responsible for describing the disciple who "reclined on Jesus' bosom",—whose closer identity is left unspecified in the source—as the one ὃν ἠγάπα ὁ Ἰησοῦς v. 23.[4] In v. 27 the sentence λέγει οὖν κτλ. is to be attributed to him, because it gives such forceful expression to the idea of Jesus' conscious action in his passion; and the phrase ἦν δὲ νύξ with its symbolic significance (v. 30) will have been inserted by him. In addition there are isolated idiomatic expressions such as ἐκεῖνος vv. 27, 30 (see below) or οὕτως v. 25 (admittedly not attested with complete certainty) that may come from him. The source gave an account, similar to that of the synoptics, of the prophecy Jesus made during a meal, that one of his disciples would betray him. The identification of the traitor with Judas, which does not occur in the Markan or Lucan version, had already been brought into the account by Mt., who simply makes Judas ask: μήτι ἐγώ εἰμι ῥαββί; to which Jesus replies: σὺ εἶπας. The Johannine source shows much greater skill, in that it takes the words ὁ ἐμβαπτόμενος μετ' ἐμοῦ εἰς τὸ τρύβλιον (Mk. 14.20), which originally meant simply a "table-companion", like the phrase ὁ τρώγων μου τὸν ἄρτον in v. 18, and weaves them into an action that

wrongly (see p. 135 n. 1); they take ποιεῖν (v. 27) to refer to action in space and time, whereas it is in fact the action of a supra-temporal power that is at work in Judas. Certainly it is demonic action, and not divine; but this too has its place in the revelation event that God has ordained. 7.35f.; 8.32 are comparable.

[1] Τότε in v. 27 (which is not textually certain) could also have been inserted by the Evangelist, who uses it in 8.28; 12.16. But in 7.10; 11.6, 14 it could have been provided by the resp. sources.

[2] Εὐθύς is perhaps a sign that v. 30 comes from a source; it does not occur elsewhere in John, except in 19.34, which may be an interpolation.

[3] Perhaps also ἦν ἀνακείμενος in v. 23, the only real case of a periphr. conjugation in John. The expression is certainly an indication that the meal which is spoken of in vv. 21–30, in contrast to vv. 2–20, is the Passover meal; for on this occasion reclining at table was obligatory, see below p. 481 n. 5.

[4] W. Soltau, ThStKr 1915, 375 and Hirsch (II 102) could be right here, although not in their conclusion that the addition goes back to the redactor.

identifies the traitor. It is also characteristic of the source, that it attributes the betrayal to Satanic inspiration. But it is precisely this characteristic that made the account in the source especially appropriate for the Evangelist: for he is not concerned in the first place, as the old account was, with the identification of the traitor, but with the nature of his act.

The beginning of the new scene is clearly marked in **v. 21**,[1] and the reader is forcefully made aware of the significance of what is to follow by the way Jesus' saying is introduced: ἐταράχθη τῷ πνεύματι καὶ ἐμαρτύρησεν καὶ εἶπεν. Jesus is speaking as a prophet.[2] He is to be betrayed—by one of the disciples, from the circle gathered round him![3] His statement makes them perplexed **v. 22**; who could be meant?[4] But nobody dares ask outright, and Peter,—who is of course acting on behalf of the other disciples again—tries to discover the answer through the mediation of the beloved disciple, whose place is nearest to Jesus[5] (**v. 23**).[6] This disciple,—a mysterious figure: there has been no mention of him before, and one never discovers who he actually is,[7]—has the

---

[1] The transitional expression ταῦτα εἰπών as in 7.9; 9.6; 11.28, 43; 18.1; cp. 11.11.

[2] On ἐταρ. τ. πνεύμ. see p. 406 n. 4; on ἐμαρτ. see p. 50 n. 5. It is not Jesus' emotional crisis, but his speaking in the spirit, that is described; cp. G. Bertram, Die Leidensgeschichte Jesu und der Christuskult 1922, 36.

[3] The words are in exact agreement with Mk. 14.18, except that ἀμήν is repeated here, and the phrase ὁ ἐσθίων μετ' ἐμοῦ does not occur (so too in Mt. 26.21).

[4] Here the account departs from that of Mk/Mt., acc. to which the disciples become uncertain about themselves and ask: μήτι ἐγώ; Here, as in Lk. 22.23, each seeks the traitor amongst the others.

[5] The Greek-Roman custom of reclining at table is presupposed here (see Br.); it had become widespread in Palestinian Judaism at the time of the NT; see G. Hölscher, Sanhedrin und Makkot (Ausgew. Mischnatraktate 6) 1910, 53, 7; Dalman, O. und W. 297 f.; Str.-B. IV 618 and cp. esp. Plin. Ep. IV 22, 4: Cenabat Nerva cum paucis; Veiento proximus atque etiam in sinu recumbebat. On reclining at table during the Passover meal see J. Jeremias, Die Abendmahlsworte Jesu 2nd. ed. 1949, 22–26. On the order of precedence at the meal see Dalman Jesus-Jeschua 106f., and cp. DSD 6. 8–13, and on this, K. G. Kuhn Ev. Theol. 1950/51, 511, note 21, who maintains that the meal described in John 13 is in accordance with the rules of DSD.—On the periphr. conjugation, ἦν ἀνακ. see p. 93 n. 2. The context makes it clear, as do the other occurrences of the formula, 19.26; 21.7, 20, that ὃν ἠγάπα ὁ 'I. denotes preferential love; cp. 20.2. Hosk. sees symbolical significance in the allusion to 1.18 afforded by this description of the disciple; so too Barr.

[6] Νεύει shows that Peter is acting secretly; thus λέγει αὐτῷ is thought of as a whisper. V. 25 makes it clear that the words εἰπὲ τίς ἐστιν mean he is to ask Jesus who is intended. The ambiguous phrase is corrected in AD syr[s] and elsewhere: νεύει οὖν τούτῳ Σ. Π. πυθέσθαι (or πυνθάνεσθαι Bl.-D § 328) τίς ἂν εἴη.

[7] Jos. Martin, Symposion (Studien zur Gesch. und Kultur des Altert. XVII 1/2) 1931, 316 finds here the *topos* of the "love-pair", developed in the Symposia literature under Plato's influence: "Jesus and John are firmly anchored in the last supper, by the well established topos of the two who love each other". Improbable; as is the author's phantasy that the Evangelist, under the influence of the Symposia literature, has "created a complete literary symposium"; see below p. 483 n. 3.

courage to ask Jesus (**v. 25**),[1] and receives the answer (**v. 26**) that it is the one to whom Jesus passes the next morsel.[2] He gives it to Judas,[3] who is thereby identified as the traitor.[4] But the narrative does not dwell on this, but so to speak branches off, by drawing our attention to the act of betrayal as such. This is described in two ways (**v. 27**): firstly, by the statement that after the sop Satan took possession of Judas,[5] and then by Jesus' command: "What you do, do quickly."[6] Both of these have the effect of taking the act out of the sphere of human, psychologically-motivated action. It is not a man who is acting here, but Satan himself, the antagonist of God and the Revealer. And yet at the same time we are shown the ultimate nothingness of this antagonist, whose illusory being is only the rebellion of the nothing.[7] In so far as his action intervenes in the history of the Revealer, it is disposed according to the will of the latter. Jesus gives him so to speak his cue, by giving Judas the sop[8] and telling him to do what he has to do without delay. The Evangelist's comment in **vv. 28f.** on the disciples' lack of understanding has the effect of emphasising the incomprehensibility of the incident even more strongly.[9]

The traitor is now excluded from the circle of the disciples: after he has received the sop, he goes out (**v. 30**). No account is given of what he does now: the narrator has no historical interest in story-telling. The first time Judas will appear again is 18.2, 5, where he is needed for the action. The scene closes by stating when the incident took place: ἦν δὲ νύξ. Its nocturnal setting may well have been part of the narrative of Jesus' last supper in the tradition, as I Cor. 11.23 leads one to suppose;

---

[1] οὕτως means "accordingly", not "without ado" (cp. 4.6 p. 177 n. 4, and 11.48). It is missing in ℵ D λ al. Instead of ἀναπεσών ℵ* ℜ D pm read ἐπιπεσών. ℌ D al insert οὖν after it.

[2] Ψωμίον before John only in Pap., see Br.

[3] Judas is referred to as in 6.71, see p. 450 n. 6.

[4] See pp. 480f.

[5] The idea of possession by demonic spirits, which is the presupposition behind this expression, is widespread in both Jewish and Gentile worlds, see Str.-B. ad loc; Schl. on Mt. 12.45; Bousset. Rel. des Judent. 336–339; Br. ad loc; Cumont, Die orientalischen Rel. im römischen Heidentum 3rd. ed. 1931, 139–141. 286–290; Bousset. AR 18 (1915), 134ff. Τότε (it does not occur in ℵ D al lat syr[s] Orig) does not necessarily imply a contrast (cp. Lk. 22.3 or indeed v. 2), but rather draws attention to the significance of the moment: "This was the moment in which. ...!"

[6] Ὃ ποιεῖς is conative present, cp. v. 6; τάχιον as in Heb. 13.23 and elsewhere = quickly; see Bl.-D. § 244, 1; Raderm. 70; Br. ad loc. The sentence means therefore: "What you intend to (must) do, do immediately". Cp. Epict. Diss. IV 9.18: ποίει ἃ ποιεῖς.

[7] See p. 321.

[8] "It is a kind of satanic sacrament, which Judas takes to himself": W. Wrede, Vorträge und Studien 1907, 136; cp. the whole passage 136f.

[9] See p. 479 n. 4 and Wrede, Messiasgeh. 184. The idea that Judas was in charge of the money, also in 12.6 (see p. 415 n. 8). The supposition that Judas should buy provisions for the festival presupposes that it had not yet started; see p. 465 n. 1.

but in any case it has a deeper meaning for the Evangelist:[1] it is to point out that the night which puts an end to Jesus' earthly work has now come.[2] The fact that the night is now the background to the prayer that follows and to the farewell discourses portrays once again in symbolical fashion the truth of 1.5: τὸ φῶς ἐν τῇ σκοτίᾳ φαίνει.[3]

The figure of the beloved disciple is encountered here for the first time; he appears again with the same characterisation (ὅν ἠγάπα or ἐφίλει ὁ 'I.) in 19.26 at the cross beside the mother of Jesus, and in 20.2–10 in the Easter history, beside Peter. He also appears beside Peter in 21.20–23 and is described in 21.24 as μαρτυρῶν περὶ τούτων καὶ ὁ (v. 1: ὁ καὶ) γράψας ταῦτα. He is usually presumed to be the ἄλλος μαθητής, who as the γνωστὸς τῷ ἀρχιερεῖ makes it possible for Peter to enter the αὐλή of the High Priest; and finally he is identified with the witness at the cross in 19.35, on the strength of 21.24, and on the grounds that apart from the beloved disciple mentioned in 19.26 no-one else stayed to the end at the foot of the cross.[4]

18.15f. must be excluded immediately from these passages; for there is no indication that the ἄλλος μαθητής is the beloved disciple; nor is the fact that he appears beside Peter any proof that this is so. Furthermore 19.35 and ch. 21 are to be taken by themselves, the first as a redactional gloss, and the second as a redactional appendix. Here, the term beloved disciple stands for a particular historical figure, clearly an authoritative one for the circle which edits the Gospel and one whose authority is placed side by side with that of Peter. It is also clear that the redactor regards the beloved disciple as the author of the Gospel, and holds him to be an eyewitness. The attempts to identify this figure are without number; as a rule he is regarded as the "Presbyter" John, mentioned by Papias, who must have played a part in the post-apostolic era in the church of Asia Minor[5]—whereby it remains an open question, whether one agrees with the view of the redactor that this Presbyter was the author of the Gospel and an eyewitness.[6]

---

[1] Cp. the symbolism in the description of the time of year in 10.22 (see p. 361). Wik., Dodd (402) and Strathm. also confirm the symbolism of v. 30.

[2] 9.4; 11.10; 12.35; cp. also Lk. 22.53.

[3] Cp. Howard 189: "Yet the Paschal moon was shining at the full. He (John) was thinking of the dark night of the soul." Martin maintains that ἦν δὲ νύξ is a typical remark "for the ending of a symposium, or for the description of its duration" (see p. 481 n. 7); he also draws attention to the "dialogue technical purpose" of Judas' departure, and compares it to the departure of Alexidemos in Plutarch's Symposium. The latter of course goes out before the meal because he is annoyed at not receiving a place of honour.

[4] One has no right to identify him with one of the two disciples who were called first (1.35ff); see p. 101 n. 3.

[5] Papias in Eus. h.e. III 39, 3–8.

[6] From among the extensive literature see Br., extended note on 13.23; A. Jülicher, Einleitung in das NT 390–423; esp. W. Heitmüller ZNTW 15 (1914) 189–209. More recently Omodeo, Mistica 169–192; Hirsch II 130–190. Just as once J. Kreyenbühl and R. Eisler, so now F. D. Filson (JBL 68 1949, 83–88) and J. N. Sanders (NtSt 1 1954/55, 29–41) want to identify the beloved disciple with Lazarus.

If the redactor is right, the Evangelist is portraying himself in the figure of the beloved disciple, and at the same time asserting that he is an eyewitness. The latter is in any case out of the question; for while there is no doubt that the Evangelist includes himself in the circle of those who utter the ἐθεασάμεθα of 1.14,[1] it is equally certain that he cannot have been an eyewitness in the sense of one who gives first-hand testimony:[2] and it is incredible that he should have nevertheless wanted to assert this about himself. One could sooner understand his wanting to portray himself as the author of the Gospel in the guise of the beloved disciple, and doing so without at the same time claiming to belong to the historical circle of the twelve. For it cannot be maintained that the beloved disciple, as the Evangelist uses the term, is a particular historical figure. If he were, there would be no accounting for the fact that the Evangelist does not speak of him by name, as he does the other disciples, but refers to him in that mysterious way. The beloved disciple rather is an ideal figure.[3]

The more detailed interpretation of the relevant passages must start with 19.26f., the scene in which Jesus hands his mother over to the beloved disciple, as her "son". If this scene has symbolic significance, which can scarcely be doubted, it can only be that the mother, professing loyalty to the crucified, and remaining at the cross to the end, stands for Jewish Christendom.[4] And the beloved disciple therefore represents Gentile Christendom,—not of course with regard to its ethnic character, but in so far as it is the authentic Christendom which has achieved its own true self-understanding.[5] The self-awareness of this Christendom, emancipated from the ties of Judaism, shows itself in the two scenes 13.21–30 and 20.2–10, where the beloved disciple appears beside Peter, the representative of Jewish Christendom. It is he and not Peter who reclines in Jesus' bosom, and can mediate Jesus' thought. And the relation between Jewish and Gentile Christendom is

---

[1] See p. 69f.; I Jn. 1.1 is also to be understood in this sense.

[2] It is unnecessary to go over the well-known reasons for this conclusion cp. the lit. mentioned in n.6 on p. 486. It is sufficient to point to the Evangelist's way of dealing with the tradition, which emerges from the whole interpretation of the Gospel.

[3] M. Dibelius (Festg. für Ad. Deissmann 179f.): The beloved disciple is for the Evangelist the "type of discipleship in his sense", the "archetype of a discipleship which makes bearers of revelation out of hearers of revelation". Acc. to Loisy he is the type of the perfected Gnostic, the type of Jesus' spiritual witnesses. Cp. Omodeo, Mistica 65: the beloved disciple is "la figura esoterico-misterica che deve giustificare nella sua pienezza la rivelazione e l'interpretatione nuova della vita di Gesù".

[4] The Evangelist could not let the beloved disciple be found next to Peter at the cross, as he can elsewhere, because he could not let Peter appear there in contradiction to the tradition.

[5] Thus Pauline Christendom also comes under the category of Gentile Christendom; and if one has to posit an actual historical figure who represented this free Christendom for the Evangelist, Bacon's view that Paul is intended is the best as regards his subject matter. It is of course impossible, because the Johannine theology and terminology, while being theologically akin to the Pauline, bears no historical relation to it, and John develops his argument against Judaism in a completely different way from Paul (see e.g. the article πίστις in ThWB). Like Paul, the Evangelist is himself a "Gentile Christian" in this sense, even if he may have been a Jew by birth, as his language makes very probable.

portrayed in characteristic fashion in 20.2–10, where each in his own way, by using the term in two senses, can claim to be "in front of" the other. We can now understand why the beloved disciple receives no name, and why he cannot be identified with any of the historical disciples. He is an intruder into their circle, and yet he belongs to them. Does the Evangelist want to use this figure to portray himself? In a certain sense, yes; in so far as he bears in himself the self-awareness and consciousness of superiority of free Gentile Christendom. But it is not his person, but what he stands for that is represented by the beloved disciple.

In the Johannine presentation of the last supper, the meal itself only serves as an introduction to Jesus' symbolic action, and to his sayings—in particular to the prophecy of the betrayal. The meal itself has no part to play, and this being so, it follows that there is no account of the institution of the Lord's Supper. This appears to give grounds for the verdict: "It shows the greatest disregard that John has allowed himself vis-à-vis his readers, concerned as they are for the synoptic tradition, that he abstains from making any reference at all to the Lord's Supper".[1] What is one to make of this disregard on John's part? There is no substance in the apologetic argument that John is only supplementing the synoptic writers, and that he can thus pass over the account of the Lord's Supper, because of his readers' familiarity with it. Are not his readers also familiar with the stories of the prophecy of the betrayal, and of Peter's denial?[2] The Johannine presentation is complete in itself, and at no point in it could there be a place for the Lord's Supper, which, if it is considered part of the farewell meal at all, can only be its climax.[3] Equally impossible is the argument that the Evangelist keeps silent about the Lord's Supper on the grounds of Disciplina Arcani.[4]

But is this really a case of disregard on John's part? Does the Evangelist really refrain from making any reference to the Last Supper? Far from it! The conclusion that John did not recognise any institution of the Eucharist by Jesus at the last meal,[5] certainly goes too far. But it is true to say that he

---

[1] Windisch, Joh. und die Synoptiker 72; pp. 70–79 contain a thorough discussion of the problem.

[2] Windisch, rightly, op. cit. against the supplementation theory. It results in the curious dispute about where one should imagine the Lord's Supper is inserted in the Johannine account. For the Protestant discussion see B. Weiss 394f., and for the Catholic Tillmann 246.

[3] It would of course be logically possible to suppose that part of the text has been lost, but this in fact is ruled out, because Jesus' prayer takes the place of the Lord's Supper, see above in the text.

[4] See p. 472 n. 5.

[5] Windisch op. cit. 74. He mentions in passing the possibility that the Johannine criticism wishes to say: the Eucharist was not instituted at the last supper, but at the miraculous feeding. Alb. Schweitzer (Die Mystik des Apostles Paulus 354f. E. T. The Mysticism of Paul the Apostle, 365f.), uses John to correct the synoptic account: Jesus cannot possibly have given out bread and wine as his body and blood at the last supper, because the spirit that gives the power of immortality to the elements of the meal only became operative after Jesus' death and resurrection. Similarly M. Goguel, Trois Études 1931, 19f., and Loisy (Congr. d'Hist. du Christ. I 79): the Christ who is present on earth cannot distribute himself as food. Differently, E. Lohmeyer (ThR NF 9 1937, 300–304;

brings in the "highpriestly" prayer of Jesus in the place of the Lord's Supper, and that he does so with unmistakeable reference to the sacrament of the Eucharist. His treatment is the same as in ch. 6, the discourse on the bread of life; he showed there that the attainment of life was the fruit of faith in Jesus (as the word of revelation), and not dependent on the sacrament, to which the primitive view had attached it. In the same way here, he lets Jesus' prayer take the place of the sacrament. The ideas that are characteristic of the Lord's Supper, viz. that the community is grounded in the sacrificial death of Jesus for his own, and united in a mysterious fellowship with him (by partaking in the body and blood) and that this community is the "new covenant",—these ideas are taken up and transformed in the prayer, and then in the discourse closely connected with it. The fellowship of his own with him and with each other, that is the holy community, is established in the death of Jesus as the ὥρα of his δοξασθῆναι, established, that is, by him who has "sanctified" himself for them (ὑπὲρ αὐτῶν! 17.19). And this community is united with him both by its knowledge and faith, and by love, and it is this that unites its members amongst themselves; but love is the content of the καινὴ ἐντολή, which corresponds to the καινὴ διαθήκη.[1] Thus the Evangelist would not have attacked the ecclesiastical sacrament; he accepts it, as he does the sacrament of baptism.[2] But as a sacramental action it is irrelevant to him, and could even be said to be suspect; and his presentation gives what can only be considered its authentic meaning.[3]

B. (13.1) 17.1–26: The Farewell Prayer

a) The Introduction: 13.1[4]

With the words ὅτε οὖν ἐξῆλθεν (13.31) the outward circumstances of the scene so to speak sink from view, and we are left simply with the farewell itself. And here the λύπη and ταραχή of those to whom the

JBL 56, 3 1937, 249–252); John follows the Galilean tradition, acc. to which the Lord's Supper does not have its origin in a special institution at the last meal of Jesus, but in the custom practised regularly by Jesus at his meals.

[1] That καινὴ ἐντολή corresponds to καινὴ διαθήκη has been rightly seen by Windisch op. cit. 73. But the discourse on the vine has not been motivated by the drinking of wine at the Eucharist, see below.

[2] See p. 472. H. Clavier, Rev. H. Ph. rel. 31 (1951), 286–289, is of the same opinion as regards John's attitude to the sacraments.

[3] It is possible that the Evangelist was not only thinking of the words of institution, known to us from I Cor. 11, 24f., Mk. 14.22–24 and par. s, but also of liturgical prayers attached to the celebration. A. Greiff (Das älteste Pascharituale der Kirche, Did. 1–10 und das Johannesevg. 1929, draws attention to the following points of contact between John 17 and Did. 10: the mode of address "Holy Father", Did. 10.2—Jn. 17.11; the thanksgiving for the holy name: 10.2—17.6, 26; preservation from evil: 10.5—17.11, 15; the sanctification of his own: 10.5—17.11; the consummation in love: 10.5—17.22.

[4] The interpretation follows the order of the text as reconstructed on p. 460f.

Revealer is bidding farewell are uppermost; but we are not made directly aware of the grief that is filling the disciples by what they say themselves, but only indirectly by the words of the departing Revealer, which are spoken into this situation. For it is not the kind of farewell scene in which both sides are equally moved; rather, the one who is taking his leave is fully in charge. And right at the outset, the phrases εἰδὼς . . . and ἀγαπήσας . . . make this clear: he is in command.

Jesus is the perfected Gnostic, who knows his origin and his goal,[1] whose coming into the world and going forth from it do not present him with a puzzling, incomprehensible fate. He knows, too, the hour of his going forth,[2] and he knows that it has now come.[3] Thus what happens now is not a chance or tragic event, nor does it have its origin in human plans or decisions, nor can it be understood in terms of them. Jesus does not choose the right hour to go to his death, as a hero might.[4] In the fate he undergoes, the event of revelation is carried through to its completion.

In 12.23 this ὥρα had been described as the hour of his δοξασθῆναι. Here—and the difference is purely one of form—it is described as the hour of his μεταβῆναι ἐκ τοῦ κόσμου τούτου.[5] For it is introduced here to show its significance for the disciples. For them, it is primarily The Hour, because he is going; they have still to learn that this μεταβῆναι is at the same time a δοξασθῆναι. But the reader is immediately made aware that his μεταβῆναι is not only the end, but at the same time the consummation of his work: ἀγαπήσας εἰς τέλος; he showed them his love right to the end, which means at the same time, right to its completion.[6] This is not of course a biographical comment designed to show the extent of Jesus' heroism—that he remained true to his own, "right up

---

[1] See pp. 143 n. 1, 279f., 465f. Εἰδώς does not of course have any apologetic sense, as Ammonius Cord. Cat. 331 (in Br.) maintains.

[2] On ὥρα ἵνα see p. 424 n. 1. On ὥρα in general, see p. 117 n. 1.

[3] See p. 424; with regard to the actual contemporaneity of 12.23; 13.31 and 17.1 see p. 424 n. 1. It can scarcely be right that a third epoch begins with 13.1, the first beginning in ch. 2 (see v. 4!) and the second in ch. 7 (see 7.6, 8) with the statement that the hour had not yet come; for ch. 2 does not imply the beginning of an epoch, and ch. 7 is no more a decisive turning-point than 4.43 or 10.40. Nor is it at all clear that 13.1 is modelled on Lk. 9.51 (Goguel, Introd. 225, 2), or on Lk. 22.14 (Loisy).

[4] Contrast e.g. Oedipus in Sophocles Oed. Col.

[5] Μεταβῆναι ἐκ τ. κόσμου does not simply mean "die", as in the Rabbinic passages quoted in Str.-B. and Schl., in which, characteristically, it is not said "from *this* world". It is the terminology of the Gnostic myth, and is to be understood in its correlation with his "coming" (see p. 298 n. 1); see p. 307 n. 3. On ἐκ τ. κ. τούτου see p. 340 n. 1.

[6] Here at least εἰς τέλος does not mean "at the end", "finally", as in Lk. 18.5; nor does it mean as in Ps. 9.19 etc. "for always", but "up to the end", "to the last", as in Mk. 13.13 etc.(cp. ἄχρι τέλους Rev. 2.26). But as frequently happens (e.g. I Thess. 2.16; Ps. Sal. 1.1) this can come to mean "right to the uppermost", "to the culmination" (see Br.); acc. to Bl.-D. § 207.3, "by far the commonest meaning" is "completely", "totally".

to his last breath"; the intention is to show that even the end itself is nothing other than an act of love, nay more, that it is the necessary end, in which the work of love he had begun finds its consummation.

Here for the first time ἀγαπᾶν is used explicitly to describe Jesus' work as Revealer in its entirety,[1] just as in 3.16 that work had been attributed to the Father's love for the world; and here also for the first time, the ἴδιοι are explicitly designated the object of this ἀγαπᾶν. In chs. 3–12 Jesus' work was portrayed as a battle with the world, and as κρίσις, and the κρίσις became clear chiefly as condemnation. And yet in the last great discourse in the presence of the people, ch. 10, the interpretation of his activity as an ἀγαπᾶν directed to the ἴδιοι had become discernible in the imagery there used; and at the end of his public activity, the final division had taken place, on the basis of which a limited circle of disciples forms itself round Jesus (6.60–71).[2] But it is only looking back at the end of his ministry that we can see the whole of it clearly: it was never really anything other than an ἀγαπᾶν τοὺς ἰδίους. In the prayer and the farewell discourses this ἀγαπᾶν is set before us in its fullness, in that everything that was παροιμία until now, is to be made clear in παρρησία (16.29); there is now only the occasional hint of the motif of judgment (13.33), in the reminder that that "too late" (7.33f.; 8.21f.; 12.35f.) is now becoming reality.

It is not necessary after ch. 10 to enlarge on the question who the ἴδιοι are.[3] They are his own (10.14) whom the Father has given him (10.29). And although *they* are the object of his love, whereas in 3.16 it was the κόσμος that was the object of the Father's love, this distinction between the two involves no contradiction, but is quite appropriate. Of course the love of the Son, like that of the Father, is directed towards the whole world, to win everyone to itself; but this love becomes a reality only where men open themselves to it. And the subject of this section is the circle of those who have so opened themselves.[4] In the actual situation as it was, this circle was represented by the twelve

[1] The interchange of ἀγαπᾶν and φιλεῖν in 11.3, 5, 36 is of no fundamental significance; see M. Dibelius, Festg. für Ad. Deissmann 181.

[2] See p. 443ff.

[3] The interpretation of Merx is quite unbelievable; on the strength of syr^s he wants to read τὰ ἴδια, which refers back to 1.11: Jesus now leaves his own possession, the world, after he had loved it to the uttermost and created a means of redemption for it. But under τὰ ἴδια of 1.11 is understood mankind as such, which the Logos can claim as his own possession as the Creator (see p. 56), while the ἴδιοι of 13.1 are his own in the sense of ch. 10.

[4] M. Dibelius is right (Festg. für Ad. Deissmann 173–179) when he says that ἀγαπᾶν does not describe the "ethical" attitude of love, but its self-communication. It would however be clearer to say that the meaning of the word is not orientated on the subject but on the action itself. 'Αγ. and ζωὴν διδόναι are of the same kind; the Revealer "gives" life to the *world* (6.33), and yet he only "gives" it to *his own*, who actually receive it (10.28)

(eleven); but the use of the term ἴδιοι here, and not μαθηταί, is significant; it shows that they are the representatives of all those who believe,[1] and it also shows that they are being viewed in terms of their essential relation to the Revealer, which is grounded not in the temporal but in the eternal.[2]

But the description of the ἴδιοι as ἐν τῷ κόσμῳ[3] brings out the full significance of the situation for the first time: they stand over against Jesus, as he leaves the world, as those who are remaining in it. He leaves them behind in the world;[4] and so it comes about that the very people whom no-one can snatch out of his hand are peculiarly separated from him. And yet it is to be precisely through this farewell, which creates the distance between them, that his ἀγαπᾶν is first brought to its fulfilment.

Thus we arrive at the theme of the prayer and farewell discourses that follow, a theme that had already been touched on in 12.20–33. It is the problem of the Revealer's farewell, the problem of the distance between him and the believers, the question of their relation to him, once the direct personal relationship has come to an end. The theme therefore is *the indirectness of the revelation.*[5]

But 13.1 serves specifically to introduce the prayer of ch. 17, and shows it to be both a farewell prayer and an act of ἀγαπᾶν. It is a petition for the realisation of the Revealer's δόξα (vv. 1–5), and also an intercession for the community (vv. 6–26), and both parts show it to be a prayer of love.[6]

A text from the "revelation discourses" forms the basis of the prayer, as it does the basis of the discourses to come. A number of additions by the Evangelist, in which he commentates on the text and expands it, can be easily identified; other points remain uncertain.[7] The prayer is an example of a type we are familiar with from Gnostic literature, spoken by the Messenger on his departure from the world.[8]

---

[1] See p. 458f., 473.

[2] See pp. 373–4, 459 n. 1.

[3] Schl.'s parallels from Rabbinic literature are wrong. In all the expressions πάντα τὰ ἔθνη τὰ ἐν τῷ κόσμῳ, πᾶς μαμωνᾶς ὁ ἐν τῷ κόσμῳ etc., ἐν τῷ κόσμῳ only serves to strengthen the concept πᾶς. But in Jn. 13.1 the farewell-setting gives it a special antithetical meaning.

[4] The motif is stressed throughout: 17.11f.; 15.18f.; 16.28ff.; 14.1ff.

[5] Rightly, Schl., Der Glaube im NT 4th. ed., 185f.: "By only giving us Jesus' word to the disciples in the form of farewell discourses, John has made very clear where the most important question of faith lies for him, i.e. in the fact that the community is separated from Jesus and has to believe in one whom it does not actually know or see".

[6] Since David Chytraeus (1531–1600), who described the prayer as *praecatio summi sacerdotis*, it has normally been called the "high-priestly prayer".

[7] In any case the prayer is not simply a "literary product" of the Evangelist (Br.).

[8] ZNTW 24 (1925) 130f.; in addition also Joh. B. 236–239; C. Herm. 1, 29–32, and

b) The Petition for Glorification: 17.1–5

The prayer itself is introduced by the words (v. 1): ἐπάρας τοὺς ὀφθαλμοὺς αὐτοῦ εἰς τὸν οὐρανόν;[1] Jesus adopts the ceremonial posture for prayer. This is the last time the Revealer appears in a purely human posture; for after the words νῦν ἐδοξάσθη in 13.31, which express the granting of the prayer, everything human is laid aside from him; in the discourses that follow he speaks as the δοξασθείς, and it is also as the δοξασθείς, that he moves through the event of the passion.

πάτερ, ἐλήλυθεν ἡ ὥρα.[2]
δόξασόν σου τὸν υἱόν,
ἵνα ὁ υἱὸς δοξάσῃ σέ.

The simple πάτερ, with which Jesus addresses God, accords with the terminology used throughout the Gospel to describe the relationship between God and the Revealer. But it is also the believers' normal way of addressing God, and outwardly no difference can be seen.[3] Like the posture of prayer, the mode of address portrays the paradox that the Revealer holds himself within the limits of what is human, in order to achieve the culmination of his work as Revealer.

The decisive hour has come.[4] To fulfil its purpose, it must become the hour of glorification (12.23); this is the first petition of the prayer, and is in fact its whole contents. Thus it becomes the eschatological hour, which marks the turning-point of the ages.[5] The petition δοξασόν contains a prime motivation: ἵνα . . . δοξάσῃ σε, which at once makes it

---

the Manichaean text T II D 173a² (Reitzenst, J.E.R. 37). Further, add. note on John 17 in Br.; Bornkamm, Myth. und Leg. 39, 1. See also Dodd 420–423. For separate points see below.—The character of the farewell prayer is misunderstood by T. Arvedson, Das Mysterium Christi, 1937, 132, when he regards it as analogous to thanksgiving prayers which accompany the enthronement of a king or of the ruler of the world.

[1] See p. 407 n.10. The variant ἐπῆρε ... καὶ εἶπεν (𝔎) is of no interest.

[2] The first line has been put in front of what follows, which (in the source) runs in parall. membr.; cp. 6.35 (p. 226).

[3] Otherwise in 20.17.

[4] With regard to the relation of 12.23; 13.31; 17.1 to each other see p. 424 n. 1. Here, and in what follows, the prayer and farewell discourses have served as the model for Hölderlin's Empedocles. Cp. Hölderlin, Sämtliche Werke, ed. by Hellingrath III 162, 3f.: "Nearer and nearer draws my hour".

[5] Δόξα is the attribute of the eschatological revelation of the Messiah and of the time of salvation, cp. Mk. 8.38; 13.26; Mt. 19.28; 25.31; Rom. 8.18; I Thess. 2.12 etc. But the glorification of the messenger also belongs to the eschatological turning-point of the ages in the Gnostic myth; see p. 431. Magnificent robes are conferred on the ascending redeemer (or on the individual soul that has been made equal to him): Mand. Lit. 226, 5; Ginza 524, 8; 562, 20f.; he is clothed in light (Od. Sal. 21.3; cp. 10.1ff.; 25.7f.) and appears as a shining star (Schlier, Relig. Unters. 28ff.). Cp. also the end of the Hymn to the Redeemer, Act. Thom. 112f. p. 223, 9ff. The prayer for glorification: Mand. Lit. 208, see p. 499 n. 9; see further p. 491 n. 2.

clear that the *Father's* δόξα is one with that of the Son: the one does not exist without the other.[1] The final aim is the Father's δόξα, which that of the Son has to serve; but similarly the Father's δόξα can only be realised when the Son receives δόξα.

But in what does the Son's glorification consist? In so far as the interpretation is centred in the first place on the myth, in the language of which the statements are made, Jesus' δοξασθῆναι is accomplished in his leaving the earth and returning to the heavenly mode of existence, the essence of which is δόξα.[2] But even in the myth this δόξα is not only the substance and appearance of the heavenly existence, but also the divine power in action.[3] Thus Jesus' δοξασθῆναι also means that he is equipped with power, that he becomes fully effectual. Finally however, δόξα is "honour," and δοξάζειν can mean "to honour,"[4] so that Jesus' δοξασθῆναι means at the same time the recognition and honour accorded him, which he had previously been denied.[5]

What however does Jesus' exaltation into the heavenly mode of existence mean in the context of the Gospel? What is the significance of his work, and of his honour? His work consists,—such is the interpretation given in v. 2—in his being able to give eternal life to his own; thus he who is δοξασθείς is at work in his community. And he is at work there as the Revealer; for, according to v. 3, the life which he bestows is nothing other than the knowledge of God and of himself as the Revealer. He is therefore at work where he is recognised and honoured as the Revealer, and this means his δόξα is at the same time the honour due to him. Thus by his δόξα he is portrayed as the active bearer of the revelation, who is recognised for what he is, and as such he is simultaneously the heavenly one;[6] for this is the reason why his

---

[1] See p. 429.

[2] Δόξα as the essence of the heavenly world; vv. 5, 24; Lk. 24.26 etc. The interchange of δοξασθῆναι with ὑψωθῆναι in 3.14 etc. shows that the former is in the first place his ascent into the heavenly world, see p. 152 n. 4; see also p. 307 n. 3. On the δόξα of the ascending Revealer see Schlier Relig. Unters. 14, 17, 22f., and cp. I Tim. 3.16: ἀνελήμφθη ἐν δόξῃ; Act. Thom. 156 p. 265, 5: ἀνῆλθες μετὰ πολλῆς δόξης.

[3] See p. 67 n. 2.

[4] See p. 268 n. 6, 301 n. 2. Cp. I Sam. 2.30: τοὺς δοξάζοντάς με δοξάσω, καὶ ὁ ἐξουθενῶν με ἀτιμωθήσεται and the formal parallels often quoted with ref. to Jn. 17.1, 5 in Pap. Graec. Mag. VII 502ff: κυρία Ἶσις ... δόξασόν με, ὡς ἐδόξασα τὸ ὄνομα τοῦ υἱοῦ σου Ὧρος. The meaning of δοξάζειν could be said to oscillate here between "honour" and "equip with (miraculous) power". Cp. further in the Isis Inscription of Kyme Z 40: οὐθεὶς δοξάζεται ἄνευ τῆς ἐμῆς γνώμης (W. Peek, Der Isis Hymnus von Andros 1930, 124). For δοξάζειν = to praise, at the end of miracle stories, see E. G. Gulin Die Freude im NT I 1932, 100, 1. On the δόξα-acclamation (perhaps of Syrian origin) see E. Peterson, ΕΙΣ ΘΕΟΣ 1926, 224ff., 324f.

[5] 8.49f., 54; see pp. 298f.

[6] Cp. I Tim. 3.16: alongside ἀνελήμφθη ἐν δόξῃ stands ἐπιστεύθη ἐν κόσμῳ.

and the Father's δόξα belong inseparably together.[1] When he reveals the Father he honours him and makes his power effectual, he glorifies him. And when the Father is glorified, the Son receives δόξα as the bearer of revelation, as the only way to the Father. The two cannot be separated from each other, when the idea of revelation is properly grasped. There can be no δόξα pertaining to the Messenger that does not also involve the δόξα of the Father, and vice versa.

This means however: Jesus' δόξα is not something already existent, a metaphysical quality which could be seen apart from revelation and faith, such as could be acknowledged theoretically in a christological dogma; no, it is brought about in his work as Revealer and in men's response to that work *within history*. His δόξα consists in the fact that history has received the possibility of faith (and unbelief), and thus of life (and death) through his work. Nor does his work come to an end with the end of his earthly life, but begins precisely then, in its real sense. He has not brought doctrines or ideas, which independent of him have since become the common heritage of history, and behind which he has himself disappeared. He is "glorified," i.e he has become the eschatological event, beyond which history cannot go, itself the end for the whole of history. In the acknowledgement or repudiation of him is afforded for all time the decision as to whether history is life or death.

The ὥρα of separation is the hour of δοξασθῆναι. But if that is the case, when Jesus at this point asks: δόξασόν σου τὸν υἱόν and when he according to v. 5, is now to receive back the δόξα, which he once had in his pre-existence,—does that not mean that he had no δόξα during his earthly ministry? But did he not have it then? Did not the believers see the fullness of his δόξα (1.14)? Must he not have had it already, if, as in v. 4, he glorified the Father on earth, and was thereby himself glorified? This too is what the voice from heaven had declared in 12.28: ἐδόξασα! And in **v. 2** this very fact is brought in to support the petition: καθὼς ἔδωκας αὐτῷ ἐξουσίαν πάσης σαρκός;[2] for this means the same as καθὼς ἐδοξάσας αὐτόν.[3] The Father who loved the Son had given everything

---

[1] See 5.23 (p. 256); 12.28 (p. 427f.). Cp. also Od. Sal. 10.4: "I was strong and powerful and took the world captive. That was (done) by me to the honour of the Highest, of God my Father."

[2] Καθώς explains the whole statement δόξασον κτλ., and not just the ἵνα-clause. On the explanatory καθώς see p. 382 n. 2.—The sentence (like all of vv. 2f.) is a prosaic comment, and has been inserted into the source by the Evangelist. Πᾶσα σάρξ (כָּל־בָּשָׂר) = all mankind, will be one of his characteristics (only here in John).

[3] The insertion of πάσ. σαρκ. shows that ἐξουσία (fullness of power) is not here the power of the spiritual man (see p. 57 n. 5), but is a Messianic term (see 5.27 and pp. 260f.). It is the royal power which belongs to God (cp. Num. 16.22; Jer. 32.37; I Clem. 59.3; Herm. Mand. IV 1, 11) and which he transmits to the Messiah; cp. the passages in the Psalms which are interpreted as Messianic prophecies: Ps. 2.8; 8.7 (G. Stählin ZNTW 33

into his hand (3.35 and 13.3); he had given him the ἐξουσία to exercise judgment (5.19ff.); his coming into the world was itself the eschatological event (3.19; 9.39). Therefore: the petition δόξασον, so far from contradicting the view that Jesus' earthly life was a ministry in δόξα, is itself supported by the very fact that it was so. What is requested has already been given to him, and it is for this reason that it is requested. But in what sense? Is the δόξα, which he had, to be bestowed on him for the future too? Mythologically speaking, yes! And this is what was said in 12.28: ἐδόξασα: καὶ πάλιν δοξάσω.

However it is not in fact a case of the renewal of the old δόξα, or indeed of changing the old, lesser δόξα for a future, higher one.[1] The old δόξα was indeed that of the μονογενής, in its complete fullness: and could the future possibly involve more than was said in 3.35: 5.19ff.? But what the δόξα was, it was only sub specie of the present ὥρα; indeed it will only really become that now. In other words: The evangelist has depicted the work of Jesus in such a way that it can only, and should only, be understood in the light of the end: as eschatological event. In the ὥρα of separation *past and future are bound together*, so that the latter gives meaning to the former.[2]

As a historical event Jesus' life is very soon to become something in the past; but viewed as such it does not reveal his δόξα. This past possesses eternal and decisive present actuality by being bound to the future through this ὥρα. One cannot hold on to the past, nor can one linger in it. Jesus thwarts any such attempt by separating himself from his own, so that they are in the world without him. Whoever wants to linger by the figure of the "historical Jesus," reconstructed by means of historical recollection, must soon become aware that he is without him. The revelation as the κρίσις of all history is not a chapter embodied in the history of the world, but stands over against it as a constant future; the Revealer as δοξασθείς is the lord and judge who possesses ἐξουσία πάσης σαρκός.

But to put it the other way round, the δοξασθείς is at the same time and always the σὰρξ γενόμενος. His is both the exaltation and the humiliation, and the humiliation is not obliterated through the return into the heavenly δόξα (v. 5). Whatever is said of the exalted Lord is true of the humiliated man as well.[3] This is why the coming of Jesus is the judgment: it is precisely the historical figure of Jesus, precisely his human history

---

[1934], 232) and Rev. (2.26) 12.10; Mt. 28.18. On the Father's διδόναι see p. 165 n. 1) Ἔδ. describes the act of handing over, whereas δεδ., that follows, states that what was given has become a present possession. But the distinction is not important, cp. 3.35 etc.

[1] Thus e.g. Grill I 316–318; Pribnow 112.

[2] See p. 428f.

[3] In e.g. 3.14f. the exaltation and in 3.16 the abasement are named as the means of procuring ζωή; see p. 151ff.; see further p. 432.

that has become the eschatological event by means of the ὥρα of δοξασθῆναι. Furthermore the revelation does not consist in e.g. inward illumination or in mystical visions,[1] but it is always and only present in the proclamation of the σὰρξ γενόμενος. And it is not special endowments of might, or "miracles"[2] that are to demonstrate his power in the future, but the fact that the word of the σὰρξ γενόμενος judges, and brings the dead to life (5.24f.).

The final clause that follows expounds the ἐξουσία which the Revealer possesses, and which reaches out over "all flesh," by showing the purpose it is to fulfil: ἵνα πᾶν ὃ δέδωκας αὐτῷ δώσῃ αὐτοῖς ζωὴν αἰώνιον.[3] While our attention is drawn to the positive effects of the revelation here,[4] in harmony with the setting, the negative, judgmental effect also emerges indirectly through the contrast between πᾶσα σάρξ and πᾶν ὃ δέδ. αὐτῷ.[5] Jesus' ἐξουσία, of course, also reaches out over those whom the Father has not "given" him; for they also meet their fate through the revelation, whether they know it or not: judgment is passed on them.

A further addition[6] expounds the concept ζωὴ αἰώνιος as *the knowledge of God and of his Messenger* (**v. 3**). The sentence anticipates the idea of vv. 6f. (source), and in this context it has the purpose of making clear wherein the δόξα of God and of the Son consists, that is to say, in the fact the God is revealed through his Son. This is why both God and his Messenger,[7] not merely God alone, must be said to be the object

---

[1] However much faith in the revelation may receive expression in such visions.

[2] However many miracles may be given to the believers.

[3] In the mss. δώσῃ (ℵ^c AC) or δώσει (BEH pm) αὐτοῖς alternate with δώσω αὐτῷ (ℵ* pc) or ἔχῃ (D omitting αὐτ.). On the fut. instead of the subj., see Bl.-D § 369, 2; Raderm. 178. The sentence shows the Evangelist's style; on the neutral (πᾶν) ὃ δέδωκας see v. 24; 6.37, 39 (see p. 233 n. 2); as regards placing the obj. in front, see 6.39 (see p. 233 n. 4; on καθὼς ... ἵνα see v. 21; 13.34.

[4] On the description of it as the gift of ζωὴ αἰώνιος see pp. 39 n. 3, 152 n. 2. On διδόναι see p. 57 n. 5; cp. esp. 10.28; I Jn. 5.11.

[5] On the "determinist" sense of the expression see p. 231f., 233.

[6] A definition characteristic of the Evangelist, see 3.19 and p. 153 n. 1. Temple: v. 3 "is a comment inserted by the Evangelist". Dupont (176): v. 3 is "une profession de foi, énoncée sous une forme doxologique". The phrase Ἰησοῦς Χριστός only here and in 1.17 in John (more frequent in I and II John), see p. 17. Some mss. have the indicat. γινώσκουσιν, see Raderm. 173.

[7] The phrase ὃν ἀπεστ. serves to portray Jesus as the Revealer (see p. 50 n. 2). The reason why the Evangelist chooses the solemn Ἰησ. Χρ. is that it is the formulation used by the community in its profession of faith; cp. e.g. I Jn. 4.2; Rom. 1.4; I Tim. 6.13; II Tim. 2.8. In this way the profession of faith is presented as the result of Jesus' work. This is why God too receives the traditional attributes μόνος and ἀληθινός; on μόνος see p. 271 n. 3; on ἀληθ. see p. 53 n. 1; often as an attribute of God, see ThWB I 250, 14ff.; Schl. ad loc. Both attributes combined in Athenaeus VI 62 p. 253 (3rd Cent. B.C., in Br.); I Clem. 43.6; Martyr. Justini 4, 9; cp. Philo spec. leg. I 332: τὸν ἕνα καὶ ἀληθινὸν θεόν. The attributes are liturgical, and do not imply any distinction between Father and Son (thus Orig., see Br.); cp. the linking of God and Jesus Christ in statements like I Tim. 6.13; II Tim. 4.1; Mt. 28. 19; see H. Lietzmann, ZNTW 22 (1923), 269–271; Gesch. der Alten Kirche II 1936,

of γινώσκειν; because the Father is only known as the one who has sent the Son, and because there can be no knowledge of the one without the other.[1] That knowing means acknowledging is clear;[2] this is why it can be said that ζωὴ αἰώνιος is nothing other than this knowledge; in it man finds his way back to his Creator, and thus has life;[3] in it he is completely determined by the one who is known, by God;[4] in it he has freedom from sin and death.[5]

In **vv. 4f.** the petition commences afresh, although the motive for it precedes the petition itself:

> ἐγώ σε ἐδόξασα ἐπὶ τῆς γῆς
>   τὸ ἔργον τελειώσας ὃ δέδωκάς μοι (ἵνα ποιήσω).
> καὶ νῦν δόξασόν με, πάτερ, παρὰ σεαυτῷ
>   τῇ δόξῃ ᾗ εἶχον (πρὸ τοῦ τον κόσμον εἶναι) παρὰ σοί.[6]

In v. 2 the grounds for the petition had been that the Father had already given the Son ἐξουσία, whereas here they are that the Son has already glorified the Father on earth.[7] They are both the same; the Father is glorified in the completion of the work with which the Son had been charged,[8]—but the work which the Father had "given"[9] the

---

104. Young (223f.) understands the revelation of the ἀληθινὸς θεός and of his ὄνομα as eschat. revelation, following Is. 52.5; 55.13; 62.2; 65.15.

[1] Of course it does not follow from the juxtaposition that God and Jesus Christ stand alongside each other as two separate objects of knowledge. Rather, the one is recognised together with the other, in acc. with the idea of revelation in John; cp. 14.9. Nor can one take τὸν ... θεόν as a predicative object, ref. both to σέ and to 'I. Χρ. (Bousset, Kyrios 246; A. v. Gall ΒΑΣΙΛΕΙΑ ΘΕΟΥ 1926, 459); see on I Jn. 5.20.

[2] See pp. 435f.; On this point see Faulhaber 56f.

[3] 1.4, see p. 44. Contrast Plut. de Is. et Os. lf. (see below p. 509 n. 3).

[4] See p. 380f.

[5] 8.32 see pp. 433ff.

[6] The text of vv. 4f. is from the source, and follows on from v. 1. The Evangelist may have expanded it by ἵνα ποιήσω and πρ. τ. τ. κ. εἶναι. On the variants in the Patristic tradition see M.-E. Boismard RB 57 (1950), 394f.—See also Dupont 268.

[7] The proof that ἐπὶ τ. γ. belongs to ἐδόξασα and not to what follows is to be found in the construction of the verse, and in the way in which ἐπὶ τ γ. and παρὰ σεαυτῷ correspond to each other antithetically. Ὃ δέδωκας and ᾗ εἶχον correspond in the same way. Ἐπὶ τῆς γῆς means the same as ἐν τῷ κόσμῳ; see p. 162 n. 3.

[8] On τ. ἔργ. τελ. see p. 194 n. 3. ℜ and Θ read ἐτελείωσα instead of τελειώσας. The assurance that the messenger has fulfilled his commission is also found in similar places in the Gnostic myth. Joh.-B. 224, 17f.: "Thereupon I fulfilled in order the works which my father had set me. I pressed down the darkness, and raised up the light to a high degree. Without a mistake I ascended. ..." Mand. Lit. 190; Od. Sal. 10.4f.; 17.8ff.; C. Herm 1.29. (Transferred to the individual souls, Ginza 471, 25f.; Manich. Turfan Fr. T. II D 173a², ZNTW 24 1925, 114). In detail, Act. Thom. 144–148, e.g. p. 252, 8f.: ἰδοὺ τοιγαροῦν ἐπλήρωσά σου τὸ ἔργον καὶ τὸ πρόσταγμα ἐτελείωσα, similarly p. 255, 1ff.: on that, see ZNTW 24 1925, 114f., and esp. 131, 2. Also Act. Thom. 113, p. 224, 13f.—The question whether the formal language of oriental royal inscriptions survives in such expressions (Arvedson op. cit. 133) can remain undecided.

[9] On ἔργον see p. 194 n. 3, 222 n. 3, 265f., 362, 387f. Instead of δέδωκας there is the

Son is the κρίνειν and ζωοποιεῖν; that is to say it is the realisation of the ἐξουσία.[1] What the Revealer has to do and what he may do, his duty and his rights are one and the same. His most compelling obligation is the freest act of his will; his ἔργον stands beyond the category of achievement.[2]

Just as the reference to the past in v. 2 served as motivation for the petition in v. 1, so here the petition (καὶ νῦν κτλ.) is put as a conclusion drawn from the evidence of the past; and δόξασον is now defined more closely: τῇ δόξῃ ᾗ εἶχον . . . παρὰ σοί.[3] The language is mythological: the Son's desire is to be raised again out of his earthly existence into the heavenly glory, which once he had in his pre-existence:—It accords fully with the thought-form of the Gnostic myth. But what are its implications for the concept of revelation in the Gospel? Jesus' δοξασθῆναι consists in two things: first in his earthly life becoming the eschatological event—the event that makes an end of the whole of history, by being the κρίσις for all history; and secondly, it consists in the world's recovering the character of creation by means of the same eschatological event.

What this δόξα is which the pre-existent Logos had, follows from 1.1–4: the Logos was the revelation of God; he was God as the self-revealer.[4] Of course the σὰρξ γενόμενος was also nothing other than that. But in the Incarnate, the revelation is judgmental power over against the cosmos, which has made itself independent of God. In the pre-existent Logos the revelation was creative power,[5] which would have been "light" for men, had they understood themselves as creatures.[6] But the purpose of the revelation in its judgmental aspect can only be to free the world from the independence it has assumed, and to make the believers "children of light" (12.36) who know themselves to be creatures.[7] To say that the Incarnate is to return to the heavenly δόξα which he once had, is to say that the revelation as judgmental power is to achieve its purpose by making it again possible to understand the

---

variant ἔδωκας as in vv. 6, 8, 11, 22, 24.

[1] 5.20f., 36; see p. 265f.

[2] See p. 384.

[3] On the wording see Ign. Magn. 6, 1: ὃς πρὸ αἰώνων παρὰ πατρὶ ἦν; Act. Io. 100 p. 201, 12: γίνωσκε γάρ με ὅλον παρὰ τῷ πατρὶ καὶ τὸν πατέρα παρ' ἐμοί. See further ZNTW 24 1925 104f.; Schlier. Relig. Unters. 33f.

[4] See p. 35.

[5] Πρὸ τοῦ τόν κόσμον εἶναι is not of course intended to define the δόξα simply as existing temporally before the creation, but as existing *beyond* the created world; it has the same judgmental sense as ἐν ἀρχῇ in 1.1, see p. 35.

[6] See p. 44.

[7] See pp. 44f.

world as creation. Men had ignored the word of God in creation; the purpose of Jesus' work is to make it perceptible again; to give sight back to the blind eyes, so they can see the "light of men," which for them is life (1.4). The revelation as the eschatological event means judgment for the world, but it also means the discovery of the world as creation.[1]

c) The Intercession for the Community: 17.6–26

The explicit request for glorification is contained in vv. 1–5. The real intercession starts with v. 9. Vv. 6–8 look back on the Revealer's work, which now lies in the past, describing it more fully than did the allusion to it in vv. 2 and 4; these verses can also be regarded as providing a further reason for the petition δόξασον. But the emphasis in vv. 6–8 lies in the description of the believers, so the verses are better taken as providing an introductory motivation for the intercession. The intercession itself asks for the preservation and sanctification of the community (in vv. 9–19), in the course of which we hear for the first time of the theme of the community's oneness (v. 11), for which Jesus then prays in vv. 20–23. The petition that the community be perfected forms the conclusion in vv. 24–26.

1) *The Founding of the Community:* 17.6–8

ἐφανέρωσά σου τὸ ὄνομα τοῖς ἀνθρώποις.
οὓς ἔδωκάς μοι ἐκ τοῦ κόσμου.
σοὶ ἦσαν κἀμοὶ αὐτοὺς ἔδωκας,
καὶ τὸν λόγον σου τετήρηκαν.

In **v. 6** the Revealer's work is described in the language of the myth: he has declared the name of God,[2] i.e. he has made it known to those whom God has given him out of the world, who were God's

---

[1] See p. 45. The wording of v. 5 differs from that in the Hymn to Christ in Phil. 2.6–11, in that there the ascended Christ receives an honour that exceeds that of his equality with God in his pre-existence, namely that of the κύριος. In fact though, there is no difference, because the decisive element in the κύριος-honour is the *acknowledgment* of the Son of God, which the Johannine Jesus, too, only receives after the ascension.

[2] Φανεροῦν as in 2.11; 7.4; 9.3; the same as γνωρίζειν in v. 26; 15.15. On the revelation of the divine ὄνομα cp. from the Naassene Hymn, Hippol. El. V 10, 2 p. 103, 18ff. W: σφραγῖδας ἔχων καταβήσομαι . . . μυστήρια πάντα δ' ἀνοίξω, μορφὰς δὲ θεῶν ἐπιδείξω. [καὶ]τὰ κεκρυμμένα τῆς ἁγίου ὁδοῦ, γνῶσιν καλέσας, παραδώσω. The Revealer brings mysteries: Ginza 296, 9ff.; 316, 20; 319, 3f.; 392, 29; Mand. Lit 193, 1ff. For the Act. Thom. see Bornkamm, Myth. und Leg. 13. Further Pap. Graec. Mag. II 127f.; XII 92ff: .... ἐδωρήσω τὴν τοῦ μεγίστου ὀν‹όματός› σου γνῶσιν. On the significance of the knowledge of the divine name in Gnosticism see W. Heitmüller, Im Namen Jesu 217. See further Od. Sal. 8.21f.; 15.6–8; 22.6; 23.22; 39.7f.; 41.15; 42.20. Thus, Ps. 21.23 is not comparable: διηγήσομαι τὸ ὄνομά σου τοῖς ἀδελφοῖς μου.

possession from the beginning,[1] and who now faithfully preserve the revelation they have received.[2] For the Evangelist—and for the source too—the imparting of the name of God is not the transmitting of a secret, power-laden word, such as in the mysteries, or in the soul's heavenward journey, or in magic, takes effect by being spoken; rather it is the disclosure of God himself,[3] the disclosure of the ἀλήθεια.[4] In the work that Jesus does, God himself is at work, in him God himself is encountered.[5] And it makes no difference whether one says that Jesus reveals the name of God, or that he reveals his own δόξα.[6] But the believers are they whom God has given him (they cannot regard their faith as their own work),[7] and who have been taken out of the world; by their faith they testify that their origin does not lie in the world, but that from the very beginning[8] they were God's possession.[9] As those who preserve God's word, mediated through the Revealer, they form the community for which he prays.[10]

The Evangelist now develops his account of the knowledge that has been given to the community. **V. 7** states that the believers have

---

[1] On the Father "giving" the Son the believers, see p. 165 n. 1); see further p. 386 n. 3. In Gnostic terms these are the spiritual ones, the φύσει σωζόμενοι (see pp. 64 n. 2, 135 n. 4, 374f.). Cp. esp. Ginza 296, 3ff. (the messenger's commission): "Choose and bring chosen ones out of the world ... choose and bring the souls, who are honourable and worthy of the place of light. Impart to them instruction. ..." On παρὰ σοῦ see p. 232 n. 4.

[2] For the Evangelist, the meaning of τηρεῖν (on the form of the perfect, see Br. and Bl.-D. § 83.1) is the same as in the expression τηρεῖν τὸν λόγον (see p. 301 n. 5, Nonnus always has φυλάττειν for τηρεῖν in Jn. 17). In the terminology of the Gnostic myth τηρεῖν is both the loyal observance and the preservation from profanation. Cp. Hippol. El. 27, 2, p. 133, 2 W: τηρῆσαι τὰ μυστήρια ταῦτα καὶ ἐξειπεῖν μηδενὶ μηδὲ ἀνακάμψαι ἀπὸ τοῦ ἀγαθοῦ ἐπὶ τὴν κτίσιν. Pap. Graec. Mag. XII 93f. (continuation of the quotation in note 1): καὶ τηρήσω ἁγνῶς μηδενὶ μεταδιδοὺς εἰ μὴ τοῖς σοῖς συνμύσταις εἰς τὰς σὰς ἱερὰς τελετάς. On τηρεῖν τὸ βάπτισμα or τὴν σφραγῖδα see F. J. Dölger, Sphragis 1911, 130ff.

[3] Cp. 12.28 (see p. 427 n. 6); so too vv. 11f., 26. The ὄνομα which Jesus revealed has been "given" him by God, acc. to v. 11; it is nothing other than the "words", which God has "given" him, acc. to v. 8; and just as he "revealed" the ὄνομα, so he has "given" the ῥήματα (v. 8) or the λόγος of God (v. 14) to his own.

[4] See pp. 434ff.

[5] See p. 190f. and cp. 14.9.

[6] Cp. 2.11, see p. 119. By what he does, Jesus reveals God's works (9.3), or God's and his own δόξα (11.4).

[7] See pp. 231, 317.

[8] See p. 159; similarly with regard to the unbelievers p. 317.

[9] Σοί is the plural of the adj. pronoun, and not the dat. of σύ. As a formal parallel, Br. compares Epict. Diss. IV 10, 16 (the dying philosopher speaks to God): σὰ γὰρ ἦν πάντα, σύ μοι αὐτὰ δέδωκας.

[10] As a parallel to the whole section see Od. Sal. 17.12ff, where the redeemer looks back and says: "And I imparted my knowledge without grudging
And my prayer was in my love; and I sowed
My fruits in hearts, and transformed them into myself;
And they received my blessing and lived;
And they were gathered to me, and were saved."
Cp. further C. Herm 1.29: ... καὶ ἔσπειρα αὐτοῖς τοὺς τῆς σοφίας λόγους κτλ.

come to know Jesus truly as the Revealer:[1] they have recognised what God has given him to be in fact the gift of God.[2] And they have done so at this moment;[3] it is in the face of the Passion that the realisation of faith is brought about; in the face of death, which normally tears up the bonds between man and man, they find their true relationship to him for the first time. **V. 8** adds: the believers only come to such knowledge because Jesus has given them the words which the Father gave him,[4] and because they accepted these words, i.e. they believed.[5] In this way the Evangelist is developing both the statement in v. 6, "Thy word they have preserved"—they were the Father's words which Jesus handed on to them, and also the phrase πάντα ὅσα δέδωκάς μοι in v. 7; the words which he handed on to them are themselves God's gift to Jesus. From this kind of faith grew the true knowledge,[6] καὶ ἔγνωσαν ἀληθῶς . . . , which in turn is the means whereby faith comes to itself,[7] καὶ ἐπίστευσαν. For what is known and what is believed are in fact the same; ὅτι παρὰ σοῦ ἐξῆλθον and ὅτι σύ με ἀπέστειλας mean the same thing.[8] And the meaning is this: to understand Jesus as the Revealer and so to come to know God (v. 3). This therefore is the Christian Community: a fellowship, which does not belong to the world, but is taken out of the world; one that owes its origin to God, and is established by the Revealer's word, recognised as such in the light of the Passion, i.e. in the light of rejection by the world; a fellowship, that is to say, which is established only by the faith that recognises God in Jesus.

2) *The Petition for the Preservation and Sanctification of the Community:* 17.9–19

It is for the community thus portrayed that the departing Revealer prays: ἐγὼ περὶ αὐτῶν ἐρωτῶ **v. 9.**[9] And this is not really a second

---

[1] On the form of the perfect ἔγνωκαν see Br. and Bl.-D. § 83.1.

[2] Cp. 3.35; see p. 165 n. 1.

[3] Νῦν is clearly stressed as in v. 13; 13.31; 16.5.

[4] Cp. 12.49f. etc.

[5] On λαμβάνειν see pp. 56 n. 3, 76 n. 5. The change of tense (τετήρ. and ἔγνωκαν in vv. 6f., ἔλαβον and ἔγνωσαν in v. 8) is due to the fact that vv. 6f. describe the believers' essential nature, while v. 8 tells us how it came to be so. Variants are without significance.

[6] Ἀληθῶς is intended to denote the authenticity of the γινώσκειν, not, as in 7.26, where it means "actually", to state the fact of γιν.

[7] See pp. 435f.

[8] Similarly in 16.30, the content of πιστεύειν is ὅτι ἀπὸ θεοῦ ἐξῆλθες. On Jesus' ἐξέρχεσθαι see p. 298, and on his being sent p. 50 n. 2.

[9] Similarly in Mand. Lit. 190f. (cp. 194), the intercession follows on the redeemer's review of his completed work: "I planted plants of life,
Genuine, believing men.
I command my builder,
Direct your eyes to my plants ..."

petition, in addition to the prayer δόξασόν σου τὸν υἱόν, because he has his δόξα by being active in the community and acknowledged by it.[1] But before the intercession unfolds it is expressly stated that it refers only to the community, not the unbelieving world.[2] Of course, God's love which is effective in the Son reaches out over the whole world (3.16); and in so far as the prayer for the community also means praying that the world may be won over through it (vv. 21, 23), to this extent the world is included in the intercession. But when Jesus says: τήρησον κτλ. (v. 11ff.), he can of course only be speaking in regard to those who believe: for the unbelievers, the glorified Lord is the judge.[3]

ἐγὼ περὶ αὐτῶν ἐρωτῶ [. . .], ὅτι σοί εἰσιν·
καὶ τὰ ἐμὰ πάντα σά ἐστιν καὶ τὰ σὰ ἐμά.[4]

The departing Revealer pleads for his own—and here too reasons are introduced for the petition—, because they belong to God,[5] whose possession they remain, even when he has given them to the Son.[6] For there is no difference between what the Father possesses and what the Son possesses (**v. 10**); they are indeed both one (10.30).[7] But if that is the case, what is the point of the intercession? The reason why the community belongs to God is not to be found in its cosmic or substantial φύσις—here the crucial idea of the myth is abandoned—, but in God's eschatological revelation in history, and in the community's decision in favour of this revelation. The community belongs to God, only in so far as it belongs to Jesus; i.e. it has its origin in eternity only in so far as it holds fast to its origin in the eschatological event that is accomplished in Jesus.[8] To say that it belongs to Jesus is significant only in that it thereby belongs to God (τὰ ἐμὰ πάντα σά ἐστιν); that it belongs to God becomes a fact only in that it belongs to Jesus (τὰ σὰ ἐμά).

Cp. also Mand. Lit. 208:

"The brightness of life rests on me,
It rests on my disciples,
Whom the Seven in this world persecute."

[1] See p. 491.

[2] V. 9b οὐ περὶ κτλ. is certainly by the Evangelist; on the style see p. 48 n. 3. That there is a reference here to Jer. 7.16; 11.14; 14.11 (σὺ μὴ προσεύχου περὶ τοῦ λαοῦ τούτου) is improbable; there is no corresponding contrast there.

[3] See pp. 154f., 339f., and cp. 16.8–11.

[4] This is a possible reconstruction of the wording of the source; but, as regards vv. 10f., it remains completely uncertain; see note 2. One could also regard καὶ τὰ ἐμὰ κτλ. as the Evangelist's interpretation and read καὶ δεδόξασμαι ἐν αὐτοῖς as the second section of the couplet.

[5] "Ὅτι does not substantiate δέδωκάς μοι, but ἐρωτῶ.

[6] Cp. the same idea in mythological language in Od. Sal. 31.4: "He (the Redeemer) brought him (the highest) the sons who had been reclaimed by him".

[7] See pp. 386f. and cp. 16.15.

[8] Cp. Faulhaber 57.

Because the appropriation of God's revelation takes place in *the decision faith makes for Jesus*, the community stands in the uncertainty of all historical existence, to which no direct relationship with God is given. But because it is *the revelation of God* that it appropriates to itself in its faith in Jesus, it stands in the complete certainty of the knowledge that Jesus is there before God on its behalf; he prays to the Father for it.

καὶ δεδόξασμαι ἐν αὐτοῖς,
καὶ οὐκέτι εἰμὶ ἐν τῷ κόσμῳ·
καὶ αὐτοὶ ἐν τῷ κόσμῳ εἰσίν,
κἀγὼ πρὸς σὲ ἔρχομαι.[1]

The reason given here for the petition makes the position of the community even clearer. Certainly it belongs to Jesus because of a historical decision; but this decision is for the eschatological event, and not for any particular possibility history contains, for ethical, political, or cultural action and values. Certainly Jesus has his δόξα[2] in the community, but not as one of the great figures of history, who remain present in the actions they performed and the effects these have had. "It is in the disciples that one can see what Jesus is."[3] But what is he? As the Revealer of God he is the Judge of the world, through whom the world is called in question; and he has his δόξα in the community inasmuch as it too means judgement for the world, and that through it the world is called in question.[4] And the very fact that constitutes the merit of the community, viz. that he is glorified in it, necessarily means dismay for its members, ταραχή and λύπη: that although they are in this world, they are not from it. This is implied in the statement that he who is glorified in the community is no longer in the world (**v. 11**). His δόξα cannot be seen at the present time like the glory of a Messiah.[5] There is no way of pointing to it in the world, except paradoxically, in that the community which is a stranger to the world is also an offence to it. Thus the community cannot prove itself to the world. Nor can its members comfort themselves in the things they possess, in the fact that

[1] Without doubt the source lies behind this section; but its form cannot be established with certainty, see p. 500 n. 4.

[2] Instead of δεδόξασμαι D reads ἐδόξασάς με, which is a correction that does not however alter the meaning (see 12.28 and p. 428f.). Nor is there in fact any difference in ἐγώ σε ἐδόξασα (v.4), in virtue of the integral connexion between the δόξα of the Father and the Son. But in the context of vv. 10f., the emphasis is laid on the δόξα which Jesus has, and continues to have, in the community; hence the perf., while in v. 4, as in 12.28, it had to be an aorist.

[3] Schl. ad loc.

[4] This is developed in 16.8–11.

[5] This view has already been expressed in 12.34, see pp. 355f.

they believe, in their dogma, their cult, their organisation. All this is significant only as a sign that they have been called out of the world, not as the enjoyment of what they have inherited. The Revealer is not present for the community in its worldly affairs: "I am no longer in the world." And yet *they* are in the world![1] That is their situation and their task: they are an association of people in this world who yet have to lead their existence in an unworldly manner. And it all depends on their understanding the words correctly "and I am going to Thee": i.e. that they must be without him, i.e. without any kind of worldly security, and that this is where they find their assurance, and that they are *glad* that he is going to the Father (14.28).

Now at last the meaning of the intercession becomes clear.

πάτερ ἅγιε, τήρησον αὐτούς
ἐν τῷ ὀνόματί σου ᾧ δέδωκάς μοι,
[ἵνα ὦσιν ἓν καθὼς ἡμεῖς].

From what has gone before it is at once clear that the prayer for their protection is the prayer that the community which stands in the world be protected from falling back into the world's hands, that it be kept pure in its unworldly existence.[2] Vv. 15f. repeat the prayer, and show that the request for protection is the same as the prayer for holiness. Holiness means in fact being stripped of the world.[3] And the mode of address "holy Father" is in harmony with this.[4] Just as τήρησον corresponds to ἁγίασον in v. 17,[5] so ἐν τῷ ὀνόματί σου corresponds to ἐν τῇ ἀληθείᾳ. And just as the ἀλήθεια of God is manifest reality in Jesus,[6] so is the ὄνομα of God. It is the name that God has "given"

---

[1] Cp. the messenger's prayer to the Father in Joh.-B. 236, 20ff.: "Woe is me for my disciples, who are thrown into darkness ...". And cp. esp. the messenger's anxiety for the purity of the believers: 237, 16ff.

[2] On τηρεῖν see p. 301 n. 5. As here, also I Thess. 5.23 (Rev. 3.10); so too φυλάττειν II Thess. 3.3; Jude 24. Cp. the prayer in Λόγος τέλειος: θέλησον ἡμᾶς διατηρηθῆναι ἐν τῇ σῇ γνώσει Pap. Graec. Mag. I 607f. or Scott Hermetica I 376; Reitzenst. H.M.R. 287. In magic: Pap. Graec. Mag. XII 260ff.: ἄσπιλον ἀπὸ παντὸς κινδύνου τηρηθῆναι, φοροῦντί μοι ταύτην δύναμιν.

[3] See pp. 389 n. 5, 449 n. 5.

[4] "Holy Father" also in Od. Sal. 31.5; as mode of address in prayer Did. 10.2; Act. Petri cum Sim. 27, p. 74, 4. God is frequently described as "holy" in the OT and in Judaism, see Bousset, Rel. des Judent. 312; Str.-B. III 762f.; A. Fridrichsen Hagios = Qadoš 22ff., 61ff. Seldom in the Greek, but often in the Hellenistic world, due to Semitic influence, see Cumont, Die oriental. Rel. im röm. Heidentum 3rd. ed. 266; Fridrichsen op. cit. 51f.; Ed. Williger Hagios 1922, 81ff.; Br. dictionary. God is addressed as ἅγ. in Hellenistic Judaism, see Fridrichsen op. cit. 63; cp. ἅγιος ὁ θεός and ἅγιος εἶ in the hymn C. Herm. 1.31.

[5] R. Asting, Die Heiligkeit im Urchristentum 1930, 307 wants to make what is an artificial distinction between τηρεῖν and ἁγιάζειν; but cp. the equivalence of τηρεῖν ἐκ in v. 15 with ἁγιάζειν ἀπό in Herm. vis. III 9, 1.

[6] See pp. 74 n. 2, 190f., 433f.

Jesus,[1] that he reveals him (v. 6), i.e. it is nothing other than the ῥήματα, which God has "given" him for him to utter (v. 8). By this ὄνομα God is to protect the community in the world; i.e. the revelation which Jesus has brought is to be active in the community as the power that does away with the world.[2]

If it is true that the existence of the community depends on its maintaining its purity, i.e. on its receiving and preserving its raison d'être and nature not from the world but from beyond it, then unity is an essential part of that nature. Accordingly the prayer for the oneness of the community is joined to the prayer for the preservation of purity; here it is only briefly mentioned, but later it will be more fully developed (vv. 20–23).[3] The paradigm and basis[4] for the community's oneness lies in the oneness of the Revealer with the Father; the deeper significance

---

[1] D²N 69 al lat read οὓς (δέδ. μοι) which is obviously a correction (assimilation to v. 6). The only possible variants are ᾧ (ℵ BCLW Θ pm) and ὅ (DU pc), between which it is hard to decide on textual evidence. Acc. to Burney 102f. ὅ was original and was a wrong translation of דְּ, which should have been rendered by οὕς. J. Huby too (Rech. sc. rel. 27 1937, 408ff.) defends ὅ (in the sense of οὕς) as the original, and points to vv. 2, 24; 6.37, 39. But ὅ δέδ. μοι can hardly be taken in that way, coming immediately after αὐτούς; it can only refer to ὄνομα, so that ὅ and ᾧ are synonymous. Huby holds the statement that God has given Jesus his name to be impossible, because the words "to reveal him" cannot be expanded; but something further must be said to correspond to τὰ ῥήματα ἃ δέδ. μοι in v. 8, and to expand it in this way is very likely, following v. 6.

[2] It is easiest to take ἐν instrumentally; but it could also be understood as an ἐν of place, because it is in fact the same, whether the protection takes place through the power or in the sphere of the ὄνομα; in the latter case as well, the name would be understood as the protecting power. The idea of the name of God being a means of power is frequent both in OT and in Judaism; see O. Grether, Name und Wort Gottes im AT 44ff.; W. Heitmüller, Im Namen Jesu 132ff. In the Hellenistic linguistic usage ὄνομα actually becomes synonymous with δύναμις; cp. the attributes which can be given to ὄνομα, Br. dictionary, s.v. 3a, and on this Pap. Graec. Mag. XIII 183f., 501ff., 555f., esp. also XIII 796ff.: τὸ γὰρ ὄνομά σου ἔχω ἓν φυλακτήριον ἐν καρδίᾳ τῇ ἐμῇ κτλ.; cp. Did. 10.2; see below. (Similarly, ὄνομα and πνεῦμα can come to mean the same, see Reitzenst. Poimandres 17.6; F. Preisigke, Vom göttlichen Fluidum 1920, 33f., and cp. I Cor. 6.11). The Gnostic aeons can be called both ὀνόματα and δυνάμεις, see K. Müller, Nachr. der Ges. der Wissensch. zu Göttingen, Phil.-Hist. Kl. 1920, 180–182. The formula τηρεῖν ἐν τ. ὀν. certainly goes back to the belief in the "power" of the spoken name, but John no longer holds this view; thus it must not be taken to mean that the protection is brought about by the community naming or using the name of God (Heitmüller, Im Namen Jesu 84), or that it is designated a cultic association through the naming of the name of Jesus (Bousset, Kyrios 225). For John God's ὄνομα is nothing other than the revelation by which Jesus makes God knowable, as is shown by the parallels with ἀλήθεια in v. 17, with ῥήματα in v. 8 and with λόγος in v. 14, see p. 498 n. 3. Parallel, or corresponding to it, is the formula διατηρεῖν ἐν τῇ σῇ γνώσει (p. 502 n. 2); cp. Did. 10.2 εὐχαριστοῦμέν σοι, πάτηρ ἅγιε, ὑπὲρ τοῦ ἁγίου ὀνόματός σου, οὗ κατεσκήνωσας ἐν ταῖς καρδίαις ἡμῶν, καὶ ὑπὲρ τῆς γνώσεως . . .

[3] The ἵνα-clause in v. 11, which anticipates this motif, has been inserted by the Evangelist.

[4] On καθώς in the sense of supplying a reason, see p. 382 n. 2.

of such a grounding will become clear in vv. 20–23. At this stage further reasons are given in support of the petition for protection.

> ὅτε ἤμην μετ᾿ αὐτῶν
> ἐγὼ ἐτήρουν αὐτοὺς [ἐν τῷ ὀνόματί σου][1] καὶ ἐφύλαξα,
> καὶ οὐδεὶς ἐξ αὐτῶν ἀπώλετο
> εἰ μὴ υἱὸς τῆς ἀπωλείας
> [ἵνα ἡ γραφὴ πληρωθῇ].[2]

Once more the petition's motivation (**v. 12**) forces its way in, by the description (as in 11a) of what is happening to the community: the Revealer is leaving it behind him, alone in the world. Its insecurity seems to stand in contrast to the assurance that his actual presence once gave it. Once he protected and guarded his own,[3] so that none of them was lost, except the one who was so destined.[4] Thus one can understand the desire that arises in the following generations of Christians to have belonged to the first generation of eye-witnesses. But what are the facts about the security which the first generation is supposed to have enjoyed, in contrast to those who came after? Was no one in fact lost? And if we try to find comfort in the fact that only the one for whom it was decreed was actually lost, who knew then whether he himself was not so destined? And who from the later generations knows that he would not have been the one to be lost? One can only look back on that security as something which was once given; one cannot build on it as something present, as that desire wrongly tries to do. No! The contemporaries of Jesus had no advantage over their successors; and this is what the intercession is about: it is a prayer that no essential distinction grow out of the difference in the external historical situation of the successive generations; and this very petition shows that there is no such distinction: the same protection in which Jesus' disciples lived in his lifetime will also fall to the lot of those born afterwards; whoever belongs

---

[1] ℵ* syr[s] may be right in omitting ᾧ (or οὕς) δέδωκάς μοι; it is a pedantic supplementation out of v. 11.

[2] The words ἐν τ. ὀν. σου, which make the line unnecessarily long, will be the work of the Evangelist, as without any doubt the phrase ἵνα ... πληρ. On the other hand εἰ μὴ κτλ. may have been in the source already, where of course the article would have been intended in a general sense: if a member of the community is lost, then he never was a true member (cp. I Jn. 2.19). The Evangelist took the art. to refer to an individual, and related it to Judas; hence the addition of ἵνα κτλ., echoing 13.18. And yet he may have regarded the case of Judas as typical; so Hosk. with ref. to I Jn. 2.19. For the statement that no-one destined for salvation is ever lost, see 10.28f. and p. 386 n. 2.

[3] Thus, it is also the task of the Mandaean messenger to "guard" the believers, Ginza 335, 9f.; 353, 1ff.

[4] On the expression υἱὸς τῆς ἀπ. see 12.36 (p. 357 n. 2); the gen. is one of belonging (cp. esp. Is. 57.4; II Sam. 12.5; Jub. 10.3; Mt. 23.15). In II Thess. 2.3 this is the title of Antichrist; in Act. Pil. II 4 (22), 3 p. 327 Tischend., it is said of Satan.

to the real disciples, will not be lost. For what was the essence of the τηρεῖν and φυλάττειν Jesus carried out at that time? What else was it but his revealing God's name to his own (v. 6), his imparting to them the words that the Father had given him (v. 8)? But all that would fall to the lot of later generations too.

Indeed, even more than that! It is only his going forth from the world that makes the meaning of his earthly life fully clear, only then is the revelation completed: νῦν δὲ πρὸς σὲ ἔρχομαι (**v. 13**).[1] Now is the hour of separation, and the words spoken in that hour[2] disclose the significance of the separation, and bring the disciples' existence for the first time to its completion as eschatological existence. For this is what it means to say that *the joy*, which Jesus has, is to be given them in completeness, in fullness. Χαρά, like εἰρήνη, which takes its place in 14.27; 16.33,[3] is a word used to describe the eschatological, other-worldly salvation.[4] Such joy is the Revealer's possession, because he is

---

[1] The sentence could be the first half of a couplet which followed immediately upon the text of v. 12 in the source. The Evangelist has substituted his own wording (καὶ ταῦτα λαλῶ κτλ.) for the second half; it could originally have expressed the same thought as v. 11: καὶ αὐτοὶ ἐν τῷ κόσμῳ εἰσίν, which would fit in well with the conjectured continuation in v. 14. V. 13 is held to be the Evangelist's work because ταῦτα λαλῶ goes together with the formula ταῦτα λελάληκα (see p. 335 n. 5), which goes back to him in all cases. Furthermore the expression χαρὰ πεπληρωμένη is characteristic of him, see 15.11; 16.24; I Jn. 1.4, II Jn. 12.

[2] In view of the contradiction involved here with what has gone before ἐν τῷ κόσμῳ must mean: now, while I am still in the world, at the moment of departure. Clearly ταῦτα λαλῶ refers not only to the prayer but also to the following farewell discourses, cp. 15.11.

[3] Εἰρήνη and χαρά used together to portray the eschatological salvation also in Is. 55.12; Rom. 14.17 (15.13); Gal. 5.22; Jub. 23.29; Eth. Enoch 5.7, 9; Od. Sal. 31.3; Act. Thom. 148, p. 258, 1. In Philo too εἰρήνη and χαρά belong together as the consequence of ἀρετή Leg. all. I 45; III 81; Cher. 86. For this reason alone Gulin's interpretation (op. cit. 63f) is too narrow: he thinks that the joy referred to is that found in the way of suffering which leads on to glory.

[4] *Joy* is a characteristic both of the cultic ceremony, and of the time of salvation (largely conceived on analogy with the cultic ceremony, or anticipated in it). It occurs both in the Egyptian portrayals of the future (Ad. Erman, Die Literatur der Ägypter 1923, 147, 156f. or Altorientalische Texte zum AT, ed. H. Gressmann 2nd. ed. 55.48), in the prophecies of the OT (e.g. Is. 9.2; 35.10; 55.12; 65.18; Zeph. 3.14; Zech. 9.9; 10.7; Ps. 126.3ff.), in those of Judaism (Bar. 5.1; Syr. Bar. 30.2; 73.1f.; Eth. Enoch 5.7, 9; 25.6; Sibyll. III 619, 785f.; for the Rabbinic instances, see foll. note), and also in the prophecies of pagan Hellenism (Verg. Ecl. IV 50ff.). So too in the NT (Mt. 25.21, 23; Lk. 1.14; 2.10; I Thess.2.19f.; I Pet. 1.8; 4.13; Rev. 21.4 etc.); and yet here, this joy is thought of as already present, without thereby losing its eschatological character (Rom. 15.13; II Cor. 1.24; 8.2; Gal. 5.22 and elsewhere); it finds expression in cultic exaltation (Acts 2.46; 11.28D; Mart. Pol. 18.3). Cultic joy is also characteristic of the mysteries; the ceremonial summons on the third day (εὕρεσις) of the Roman Isis festival is: εὑρήκαμεν, συνχαίρομεν (Athenag. 22, p. 140, 20f. Geffcken); in the Attis festival the 25th. March is celebrated after the two days of mourning as τὰ Ἱλάρια (H. Hepding Attis 1903, 167f.); Pap. Graec. Mag. IV 624ff. describes the joy of the congregation of God (Dieterich, Mithraslit. 10, 19ff.); cp. also Apul. Met. XI 24 p. 286, 8ff. Helm. and esp. the final prayer of the Λόγος τέλειος (Pap. Graec. Mag. III 599f.; Scott Hermetica I 374/6; Reitzenst. H.M.R. 286): χαίρομεν, ὅτι

leaving the temporal world, indeed he is even now no longer in the world (v. 11). To say that this joy is to be shared by the disciples πεπληρωμένη, is to say, as in 15.11, that the joy they have already received through him will be brought to its culmination; the significance of turning to him in faith is found in the believer's life becoming complete as eschatological existence.[1] The joy is also shown to be

---

σεαυτὸν ἡμῖν ἔδειξας, χαίρομεν, ὅτι ἐν πλάσμασιν ἡμᾶς ὄντας ἀπεθέωσας τῇ σεαυτοῦ γνώσει. Here the cultic piety of the mysteries has been elevated to a form of mysticism, and the "joy" has an eschatological other-worldly character, and this is also true of Gnosticism. Acc. to. C. Herm. 13.8 χαρά enters the soul as the second δύναμις (after γνῶσις) in the rebirth: παραγενομένης ταύτης ... ἡ λύπη φεύξεται. And in 13.18 the re-born Gnostic gives thanks: γνῶσις ἁγία, φωτισθεὶς ἀπὸ σοῦ διὰ σοῦ τὸ νοητὸν φῶς (ὑμνῶ). ὑμνῶν δὲ χαίρω ἐν χαρᾷ νοῦ. Cp. also the text from the "Doctrine of Cleopatra" in Reitzenst. H.M.R. 314. For the Mandaeans "joy" is a characteristic of the world of light (Br. on 15.11 and E. G. Gulin Die Freude im NT II 1936, 37, 1) and the eschatological day is "the great day of joy" (Mand. Lit. 134); joy has been brought to the believers by the revealer (Mand. Lit. 196):

"You came from the house of life,
You came, what did you bring us?
I brought to you, that you do not die,
That your souls be not imprisoned.
For the day of death I brought you life,
For the dreary day, joy."

In the Od. Sal. joy and life belong together (31.6f.; 41.3); the redeemer proclaims joy (31.3) and the believers receive it from him (31.6; 32.1), so that they rejoice day and night (41.7; 28.2; 40.4); the Lord is their joy (7.1f.; 15.1); they rejoice in the Lord (41.3); they are filled with holy joy as the fruit which they bring to the Lord (8.1f.; 23.1). So too, joy is characteristic of the Gnosticising Christendom of the Act. Thom. (c. 14, p. 120, 8; c. 142, p. 249, 2.6.14; c. 146, p. 255, 11; c. 148, p. 258, 1). In Philo, the motif of eschatological-mystical joy, which comes from this tradition, is combined with the Stoic doctrine of joy; the former is evident when he describes the pure joy as something other-worldly, which belongs to God alone (Abr. 201–207; spec. leg. II 54f.), and which is given to man only in the mystical union with God (H. Lewy, Sobria ebrietas 1929, 34–37). Cp. the triad of gifts that fall to him who is perfected: πίστις, χαρά and ὅρασις θεοῦ (praem. et poen. 24–51). On the whole subject see ThWB I 19, 25ff. 40ff.; II 771, 23ff.; 722, 2; 773, 12ff., and s.v. χαρά; Ed. Norden, Die Geburt des Kindes 1924, 57f.; Gulin II 36ff.

[1] E. G. Gulin. Die Freude im NT II 1936, 67–71 maintains that here as elsewhere in John χαρά is to be understood "metonymically", i.e. that it means the object of joy; he wants to take πληροῦσθαι, on analogy with 7.8; 12.38 etc., to mean "to be fulfilled", "to come about". The meaning of v. 13 is then: since Jesus gives them "his joy", the object of their joy actually comes about, i.e. their joyful expectations are fulfilled. Now it is certainly right that the πληροῦσθαι of the χαρά cannot mean that their state of joy has reached its climax. But neither can πληροῦσθαι mean here "to be fulfilled", as it can with γραφή or καιρός; for the concept χαρά does not contain within it the notion of determinability. Πληροῦσθαι means rather (cp. also on τελειοῦν in v. 23): to be brought to the eschatological consummation. In Rabbinic circles "complete joy" describes the eschatological joy that is to begin with the Messiah (Pes. Kah. 21, 147a, in Schl., Spr. und H. 51, and on Mt. 9.15), joy which in contrast to all earthly joy is total (Pes. Kah. 29, 1896 in Schl. Spr. and H. 51f. and on Jn. 3.29; this and further examples in Str.-B. on 3.29. On the other hand, in Str.-B. on 16.24 the "perfect joy" is joy in the law). Now in John of course the point is not the contrast between earthly and Messianic joy, but the culmination of the joy which the disciples already have, as disciples (otherwise it would have to be: τὴν ἐμ. χαρὰν τὴν πεπλ.). But the dependence on this kind of language is clear; the culmination is thought of eschatologically, as in 15.11; 16.24; I Jn. 1.4; II Jn. 12; see on v. 23.

eschatological by saying that no-one can take it away (16.22); it is therefore, like the εἰρήνη which he bestows (14.27), of a different kind from the joy which the world can give and receive. It is *his* joy which they are to share; i.e. they are not to receive the same *kind* of joy as his, but the very joy that he *has* is to be theirs; and this is so because their joy is grounded in his when the significance of his coming and going is borne home upon them, namely that it is the eschatological event. They are not to wait for a dramatic cosmic event in the future, but even now they are to be men who have "crossed over from death to life," although they are still in the world. If one asks what the joy is about,[1] it is clear that nothing can be pointed to in answer; their joy is simply the knowledge that they are separated from the world and belong to him.

The paradox of this eschatological joy is expressed in **v. 14**:

ἐγὼ δέδωκα αὐτοῖς τὸν λόγον σου,
καὶ ὁ κόσμος ἐμίσησεν αὐτούς.[2]

This sentence makes plain the tension in which the disciples stand: they have received the word of God through Jesus, and yet[3] they have been abandoned to the hatred of the world.[4] That this "and yet" is in fact a "therefore" is explained by the Evangelist: like Jesus himself, they no longer belong to the world, nor is their origin in the world.[5] The world loves whatever belongs to it (15.19), and whatever separates itself from it is the object of its persecution and hatred. But the fact that the world's hatred is due to the community's becoming (through the word) the eschatological dimension in which the world is annulled, means that this very hatred is the criterion for the community as to whether it does in fact no longer belong to the world, as Jesus does not belong to it.

Precisely this is the community's task: to exist in the world as the eschatological community (**v. 15**): Jesus does not ask that God should take his own out of the world, but that he should protect them from

---

[1] Cp. the list of the various causes of joy in Philo, leg. all. III 86f.; quod. det. pot. ins sol. 136f.; spec. leg. II 185; praem. poen, 32, 50.

[2] V. 14a is the continuation of the source's text (see p. 505 n. 1); v. 14b may be the work of the Evangelist (like v. 15), with the source's continuation (v 16) serving as model. The last clause (καθὼς κτλ.) is missing in D pc it syr^s due to homoiotel.

[3] On καὶ in this sense see p. 48 n. 2.

[4] 'Εμίσησεν describes as an already accomplished fact what would actually only be imminent if the setting of the prayer were to be taken as historically true (see v. 18). The fiction of historicity is employed in 15.18–16.4, where the disciples are addressed, and there the future tense is used. In the same way the messenger, Joh.-B. 238, 20ff. shows his Father the believers' suffering in the world: "For they are thrown into distress. They have to bear anger and deceitful persecution ..."; cp. 237, 2ff.

[5] On εἶναι ἐκ in this sense see p. 138 n. 1. On the subject-matter see p. 432.

the evil.[1] These words are directed against two things. First, against the primitive Christian expectation of the imminence of the end, and the longing for the glorious Parousia, which will make the community an ecclesia triumphans; no, the church's essential nature involves being the eschatological community in which the world is annulled *within* the world.[2] Secondly, the words are directed against the temptation that continually threatens the community, viz. of falling back into the world's hands; the community must not allow itself to be misled through the world's hatred into being disloyal to its essential nature; it must not allow itself to become engrossed in its place in world-history, or regard itself as a factor of cultural importance, or find itself in a "synthesis" with the world and make peace with the world. It must retain its unworldly character, it must remain "protected from the evil," i.e. from the "world;"[3] otherwise it would lose its essential nature (**v. 16**):

> ἐκ τοῦ κόσμου οὐκ εἰσίν,
> καθὼς ἐγὼ οὐκ εἰμὶ ἐκ τοῦ κόσμου.[4]

The statement is repeated once more: as the origin and essential nature of the Revealer, to whom the community owes its existence, does not lie in the world, neither does that of the community itself. The reminder that this is so serves as a fresh motivation of the prayer for protection, which is now repeated in a new form (**v. 17**):

> ἁγίασον αὐτοὺς ἐν τῇ ἀληθείᾳ·
> ὁ λόγος ὁ σὸς ἀλήθειά ἐστιν.[5]

---

[1] V. 15 is the work of the Evangelist; on οὐκ ... ἀλλά see p. 48 n. 3; on ἀλλ' ἵνα p. 407 n. 9. Αἴρειν ἐκ τ. κόσμου is a rabbinic formula, see Schl.; so too τηρεῖν ἐκ corresponds to the rabbinic use of language (also in Rev. 3.10), see Schl.

[2] In Ginza 463, 1ff. the believer is exhorted: "Endure to the end, and live in the world, until your lot is full". Similarly 464, 16ff.: "Thus endure to the end, and live in the house of misery, ... look at us and keep yourself clean". F. M. Braun (RB 62 1955 20) rightly stresses the difference from the (Essene) Qumran community, which separated itself from the rest of the Jewish community.

[3] On the designation of the world as evil see pp. 54f. It makes no difference actually whether ἐκ τοῦ πον. is taken as a masc. or as a neuter. In the light of I Jn. 2.13f.; 5.18 one is inclined to take it as a masc. (cp. Mt. 6.13; 13.19, 38; Eph. 6.16 and esp. II Thess. 3.3: φυλάξει ἀπὸ τοῦ πονηροῦ). But I Jn. 5.18f. shows that the mythological idea is only a linguistic form, as also in I Jn. 3.12. If it is understood as a neuter, Did. 10.5 affords a parallel: τοῦ ῥύσασθαι αὐτὴν (sc. τὴν ἐκκλησίαν) ἀπὸ παντὸς πονηροῦ.

[4] A sentence from the source which the Evangelist has already used in v. 14 (see p. 507 n. 2); καθώς did not originally have any substantiating sense here, and the Evangelist could scarcely have taken it in that way either. V. 17 also comes from the source; the second half is characteristically different from the Evangelist's definitions; he would have written something like: αὕτη δέ ἐστιν ἡ ἀλ., ὁ λόγος σου, ὃν ἐλάλησα.

[5] 𝔎 pm: ἐν τ. ἀλ. σου, which is a correction; B pc: ἡ ἀλήθεια, which is in fact right; but as a dimension sui generis ἀλ. does not need the article, see Bl.-D § 253.

Marked off from the world, the community is to live in the world as holy community.[1] But it can only enjoy this state of separation from the world in virtue of the revelation[2] on which it is founded, which is nothing other than the word of God transmitted to it through Jesus.[3] Thus its holiness is not due to its own quality, nor can it manufacture its differentiation from the world by itself, by its rite, its institution, or its particular way of life; all this can only be a sign of its difference from the world, not a means of attaining it.[4] Its holiness is therefore nothing permanent, like an inherited possession: holiness is only possible for the community by the continual realisation of its world-annulling way of life, i.e. by continual reference to the word that calls it out of the world, and to the truth that sets it free from the world.

Thus the community's holiness is not just something negative, but involves a positive task as well (**v. 18**): as the Father sent the Son into the world, so the Son sends his disciples.[5] As the sending of the Son is

---

[1] On the prayer for protection, and on the concept of holiness see p. 502. On ἁγιάζειν = to take out of the sphere of the profane and place in the sphere of the divine, see I Cor. 6.11; Pap. Graec. Mag. IV 522 (Dieterich Mithraslit. 4.22f.): ἁγίοις ἁγιασθεὶς ἁγιάσμασι ἅγιος. The ἐκκλησία as ἁγιασθεῖσα Did. 10.5. Br. dictionary; examples in LXX, in Williger Hagios 100, 4; cp. esp. Ecclus. 45.4 where ἡγίασεν, (namely God, with Moses as object) is parallel to ἐξελέξατο αὐτὸν ἐκ πάσης σαρκός, and cp. the Jewish formula: "May he be praised who has sanctified us through his laws" (Schl. ad loc. and on v. 19; Str.-B. ad loc.); see further p. 502 n. 5. As regards subject-matter cp. Mand. Lit. 128: "He separated off the friends of his Kusta (=ἀλήθεια)-Name from the darkness to the light, from the evil to the good, from death to life, and set them up in the paths of the Kusta and of faith". Cp. above all, Act. Thom. 156, p. 266, 3: ἁγίασον αὐτούς ἐν μιαρᾷ χώρᾳ (this will be the correct reading); the request corresponds exactly with the Johannine one: the believers, who are in the world, are to be raised up from it. (The continuation, p. 266, 4ff. translates the request into Pauline terminology). I Clem. 60.2 has a more limited meaning: καθάρισον ἡμᾶς τὸν καθαρισμὸν τῆς σῆς ἀληθείας, where the ref. is specifically to the forgiveness of sins.

[2] 'Ἐν is doubtless instrumental; see pp. 502f. (esp. 503 n. 2). Like ὄνομα, ἀλ. can also be conceived as δύναμις, see ZNTW 27 (1928), 152 157f.

[3] On ἀλήθεια, and on its relation to λόγος, ῥήματα, ὄνομα see pp. 498 n. 3; 502f.; see also Asting, Heiligkeit im Urchristentum 313f. Cp. Mand. Lit. 165: "You are established and set firm, my chosen ones, by the discourse of truth that is come to you ..." (further in Asting). Thus the meaning of ἀλ. is not the same as in the formal parallel in Ps. 118.142 (English Ps. 119) ὁ λόγος σου ἀλήθεια (אֱמֶת) = "Thy word stands firm"; so too in R.Exod. 38, 1 (in Schl.). Dodd rightly 175. In Plut. de Is. et Os. 1f., p. 351e the holiness mediated by the cult is contrasted with that attained by the ὄρεξις τῆς ἀληθείας. But here ἀλ. is not the revealed reality of God, but the correct knowledge of what is; for the εὔδαιμον of αἰώνιος ζωή is: τὸ τῇ γνώσει μὴ ἀπολιπεῖν τὰ γινόμενα (not to lag behind reality in one's knowledge of it), or γινώσκειν τὰ ὄντα καὶ φρονεῖν.

[4] In Judaism on the other hand holiness is assured by fulfilling the commandments: Tanch. שלח 31, 74 (Schl. on v. 19): ἐφ' ὅσον ποιεῖτε τὰς ἐντολάς, ὑμεῖς ἐστε ἡγιασμένοι· ἀπεκλίνατε ἀπὸ τοῦ νόμου, γεγόνατε βεβεβηλωμένοι (Schl.'s version). In Ign. Eph. 2, 2 (ἵνα . . . κατὰ πάντα ἦτε ἡγιασμένοι) the community preserves its holiness by unanimous obedience to the bishop and presbytery.

[5] V. 18 can hardly come from the source, the text of which is perhaps at an end with v. 17; and yet see p. 512 n. 4. The sending out of the elect into the world by the Redeemer

not only his destiny but his task, so also is the sending of the community through the Son.[1] The community has a task analogous to his, and rooted in it.[2] Thus the world is as little a static quantity as the community is. In so far as it does not believe, it is of course judged; but what was true of the person and word of Jesus is also true of the continuing existence and word of the community in the midst of the world: both call the world in question, and demand a decision. The community takes over Jesus' assault on the world, his ἐλέγχειν and κρίνειν (as 16.8–11 puts it)—the assault which is at the same time the paradoxical form of his courtship of the world (3.16), and which continually opens up for the world the possibility of faith (vv. 21, 23). But it does not take over this assault or the duty to win the world solely by embarking on missionary enterprises; it does so simply by its existence.

The community can only undertake its task if it remains what it is: separated off from the world, with its existence grounded purely in the revelation of God in Jesus. And so the prayer turns back to the idea of the holiness of the community, and in **v. 19** it provides us with an interpretation of the old account of the Lord's Supper and its ὑπὲρ ὑμῶν:[3] καὶ ὑπὲρ αὐτῶν ἐγὼ ἁγιάζω ἐμαυτόν.[4] Jesus, the ἅγιος τοῦ θεοῦ (6.69), proves his holiness by sacrificing himself for his own.[5] His holiness

---

has no parallel in the myth. The only idea that could perhaps be considered such is that of the "dark house" of the world being illumined by the soul that sojourns in it (Ginza 514, 18f.; 515, 20ff.; 109, 6ff.).

[1] 'Απέστειλα, Aorist, like ἐμίσησεν, v. 14; see p. 507 n. 4. That the disciples' commission is a sending into a destiny of suffering (Gulin op. cit. 57) is correct; but ἀποστέλλειν is primarily the commission for a task.

[2] On the substantiating καθώς see p. 382 n. 2.

[3] I Cor. 11.24, cp. ὑπέρ in Mk. 14.24 and in all the expressions which speak of the death of Christ as a sacrifice for the community, see p. 235 n. 1; see further 10.15; 11.50f.

[4] 'Εγώ, which is missing from ℵ A W pc, is uncertain; in any case it is not especially stressed.

[5] 'Αγιάζω, put here in the farewell prayer at the beginning of the Passion, and used together with ὑπὲρ αὐτῶν, means "to make holy", in the sense of "to consecrate for the sacrifice"; cp. too, Chrys., who explains: τί ἐστιν· ἁγιάζω ἐμαυτόν; προσφέρω θυσίαν (in Br., with the continuation). Outside the Bible the word is infrequent see Br. dictionary and see p. 509 n. 1. In the LXX ἁγιάζω frequently renders קִדֵּשׁ = to consecrate, to dedicate to God or the sphere of the cult (Fridrichsen, Hagios-Qadoš 8). Consecration for the sacrifice is intended in Ex. 13.2; Deut. 15.19, and in Ex. 28.41, the priest's consecration. Jn. 17.19 can scarcely be alluding to this too (although in Philo the Logos is considered both Priest and High Priest, leg. all. III 82; de somn. I 215; II 183); if it were, Jesus would be being depicted as both priest and sacrifice (as in Heb. 9.11–14; thus B. Weiss, Ol. Moe ThLZ 72 1947, 338); and it is of course correct that Jesus' self-sacrifice takes the place of the priestly sacrifice. But Jesus' giving up his life is not thought of as a priestly act in 10.18, or in 15.13 either. Cp. too IV Macc. 17.20: the martyrs as ἁγιασθέντες. On the other hand, the "sanctifying of the self" of the pious Jew, which consists in fulfilling the laws, (Schl. and Str.-B. ad loc) is no parallel; it only has the negative sense of separation, and does not contain the element of ὑπέρ. Since there is no disputing the allusion to the words of the Lord's Supper, Asting's interpretation (Heiligkeit 314f.) must be wrong: "I am going back

like his sonship and his δόξα, are not attributes he has for himself, but are the same as his own special being in virtue of which he is God's son, that is to say, his being for the world, or for his own;[1] so too his holiness is nothing other than the fulfilment of this his being for the world, his being for his own. Since the essential nature of the world does not consist in a cosmic-substance which is different from God, but in its being judged over against God, in its revolt against God,[2] it is also true that his holiness is no static difference in substance from the world, but is something Jesus achieves only by completing the stand he has made for God and against the world. But this completion means sacrifice. In the sacrifice he is, in the manner of God, so *against* the world that he is at the same time *for* it;—for his own, in so far his significance for the world is realised in them. Thus the significance of his sacrifice is found in this: ἵνα ὦσιν καὶ αὐτοὶ ἡγιασμένοι ἐν ἀληθείᾳ= that his own, too, be truly sanctified.[3] That does not, of course, mean that they are to be a sacramental fellowship flooded through with heavenly powers—it is precisely the account of the institution of the sacramental meal that the Evangelist has replaced by Jesus' prayer;[4] it means that they should be taken out of the world, as that which is evil (v. 15); and, just as according to 15.3 they are clean by reason of his word, so they are to be taken away from the world through the ἀλήθεια, through the disclosure of God that takes place in Jesus' word (vv. 16f.); and, finally, it means that they are to remain "protected" through the "name of God" (v. 11). It could, of course, also have been said: "that they also sanctify themselves for each other."[5] And without doubt the sending of the community into the world (v. 18) also involves the challenge of being prepared for sacrifice as it follows in the steps of Jesus. But only the other side is expressly stated: the purpose of Jesus' sacrifice is fulfilled in the existence of a fellowship of his own that is grounded in him and raised out of the world.[6]

---

into the heavenly sphere on their behalf". M. Dibelius (Festg. für Deissmann 182, 2) rightly says that the starting-point for understanding ἁγ. is the notion of being sent (see pp. 449f.); but he is wrong to exclude the idea of sacrifice for this reason; for John both are a unity; for him the Passion already begins with the incarnation.

[1] See 4.34 (p. 194); 5.19 (p. 249); 12.44f. (p. 344); 10.14f. (pp. 381f.).

[2] See pp. 54f., 321.

[3] Since ἐν ἀλ. has no article here, in contrast to v. 16, it must be taken adverbially = ἀληθῶς (as also in I Jn. 3.18; II Jn. 1 and III Jn. 1 are ambiguous), even if to take it in the sense of ἐν τῇ ἀλ. is right in the context (thus 4.23f.; II Jn. 3f.; III Jn. 3f.; the article can be omitted: see Bl.-D. § 258). The ref. then is to the true holiness, in contrast to all cultic holiness (4.23f.; see pp. 191f.), not in contrast to the holiness the disciples used to have (Asting, Heiligkeit 315).

[4] See pp. 484f. also p. 472. Acc. to Hoskins the Evangelist is interpreting Mk. 14.22–25.

[5] Cp. the continuation of 13.12–20 on 13.6–11.

[6] Gulin op. cit. 57 wants to take it as meaning: that they be consecrated (for sacrifice). But the words ἐν ἀλ., and the parallelism of ἁγιάζειν and τηρεῖν, make this view improbable.

3) *The Petition for the Oneness of the Community:* 17.20–23

The theme that had been briefly touched on in v. 11 now becomes the subject of the petition in its own right: the unity of the community. And at this point (**v. 20**)[1] we are told explicitly that Jesus' intercession does not just relate to the historical situation, in which the Evangelist makes him speak it, but is made for all believers, now and in the future.[2] This is of course also true of the previous petitions; but one can easily understand why it is expressly stated here for the first time: the prayer for the community's unity consciously embraces its extension through time. Thus petition is made for all believers, without reference to space and time: ἵνα πάντες ἓν ὦσιν (**v. 21**).[3] But what is the real meaning of the unity here requested? The petition cannot be for the gathering together of those who, although scattered throughout the world, belong to the Revealer in virtue of an original kinship with him.[4] For Jesus is praying for those who are already gathered together, for the believers. And by combining the prayer for unity with that for protection in v. 11, the Evangelist has shown that he sees Jesus as praying for the inner oneness of the community, for its essential unity. This is not of course thought of as unity of organisation.[5] The words περὶ τῶν πιστευόντων διὰ τοῦ λόγου αὐτῶν εἰς ἐμέ (v. 20)[6] state indirectly that it is a unity in the tradition of the word and of faith; and the Gospel itself and I John (cp. esp. 1.3) are actual examples of how the word is passed on.

One might perhaps ask why there is no mention here of the unity of love, as in I John it is developed as the consequence of faith. But express treatment of the theme ἀγάπη is withheld, and there is only a

---

[1] V. 20 is clearly the Evangelist's work; on οὐ μόνον, ἀλλὰ καί see p. 238 n. 2.

[2] Cp. Act. Petri c. Sim. 9 p. 96, 3f.: ὑμεῖς οὖν, ἀγαπητοί μου, καὶ οἱ νῦν ἀκούοντες καὶ οἱ μέλλοντες ἀκούειν. Cp. also the exhortation in Mand. Ginza 26. 1ff., which is addressed to "all Nasoreans who now are, and who will yet be born," Cp, also Lit. 140: "Now we pray to thee (the believer to Manda dHaije) ... for ourselves, for our friends, for the friends of our friends, the friends of the great race of life, and the whole body of the Nasoreans of life, which is poured into, and disseminated on the Tibil (on earth) ...".

[3] For patristic variants see Boismard RB 57 (1950), 396f.

[4] This would be to think in the terms of the myth (see pp. 369 n. 1, 2; 374f. 384 n. 2) and cp. esp. Act. Io. 95, p. 198, 9: ἑνωθῆναι θέλω καὶ ἑνῶσαι θέλω. In fact there could be a textual source at the basis of the petitions in vv. 20–23, in which the request had this sense. But it has been so severely edited by the Evangelist that it can hardly be reconstructed.

[5] In Ign. the idea has come to be expressed in this way; cp. Eph. 5.1: ... ὑμᾶς μακαρίζω τοὺς ἐνκεκραμένους οὕτως (those united with the bishop), ὡς ἡ ἐκκλησία 'I. Χριστῷ καὶ ὡς 'I. Χριστὸς τῷ πατρί, ἵνα πάντα ἐν ἑνότητι σύμφωνα ᾖ. Mg. 1.2: Ign. wishes the communities ἕνωσις σαρκὸς καὶ πνεύματος 'I Χριστοῦ . . . πίστεώς τε καὶ ἀγάπης, . . . τὸ δὲ κυριώτερον 'Ιησοῦ καὶ πατρός. Cp. also Ign. Eph. 2.2.

[6] Τῶν πιστευόντων is a descriptive participle, without temporal ref., as in Rom. 1.16 and elsewhere. Διὰ τ. λόγ. αὐτ. does not, of course, only refer to the preaching of the first generation, but to Christian preaching in general. Schl. rightly points to the difference between διὰ τοῦ λ. here, and διὰ τὸν λ. in 4.39, 41.

hint of it in the clause καθὼς σύ, πατήρ, ἐν ἐμοὶ κἀγὼ ἐν σοί, which is added to the words ἵνα πάντες ἓν ὦσιν, to tell us what kind of unity it is and wherein it is grounded. The unity of his own is to be *of the same kind as* that between the Father and Son;[1] i.e., therefore, just as the Son's being is a being for the Father, and vice-versa, so the being of the individual believers must be a being for each other—in the bond of ἀγάπη,[2] (cp. esp. 13.34 and 15.12). And just as the Father is encountered in the Son, because the Son is nothing by himself individually, so within the community no one ought to see, or cherish, or criticise the individual character of his fellow believer, but ought to look on him only as a member of the community.[3] It is not personal sympathies, or common aims that constitute the unity, but the word that is alive in them all and that gives the community its foundation; and each member represents the demand and gift of the word over against his fellow believer, in that he is for him.[4]

But such unity has the unity of Father and Son as its basis. Jesus is the Revealer by reason of this unity of Father and Son; and the oneness of the community is to be based on this fact. That means it is not founded on natural or purely historical data, nor can it be manufactured by organisation, institutions or dogma; these can at best only bear witness to the real unity, as on the other hand they can also give a false impression of unity. And even if the proclamation of the word in the world requires institutions and dogmas, these cannot guarantee the unity of true proclamation. On the other hand the actual disunion of the Church, which is, in passing, precisely the result of its institutions and dogmas, does not necessarily frustrate the unity of the proclamation. The word can resound authentically, wherever the tradition is maintained.

Because the authenticity of the proclamation cannot be controlled by institutions or dogmas, and because the faith that answers the word is invisible, it is also true that the authentic unity of the community is invisible—even if it should testify to itself (according to 13.35) in the ἀλλήλους

---

[1] On the unity of Father and Son, and on its exposition by means of the formula of reciprocity, see pp. 383f. In 17.21 the unity is described as a mutual being in each other, as in 10.38; 14.10; cp. the "Bee" of Solomon of Bosra c. 37 (Reitzenst. J. E. M. 100); see also Wetter, Verherrlichung 77ff.

[2] Just as the Father loves the Son, vv. 23f., 26; see p. 165 n. 1.

[3] Cp. Ign. Mg. 6.2: μηδεὶς κατὰ σάρκα βλεπέτω τὸν πλησίον, ἀλλ' ἐν 'Ι. Χριστῷ ἀλλήλους διὰ παντὸς ἀγαπᾶτε.

[4] Thus Ho.'s exposition is wrong: for him the unity "is to be thought of primarily as a unity of motives and goals of spiritual aspiration, determined by the unity of the image of God in the consciousness of every individual. ..." This is clearly an idealist conception. B. Weiss is no better; while protesting against Ho., he takes the unity as "a unity of life mediated by the mystical fellowship of life with Christ and God". Br. rightly sees that it is the specific unity of the church that is intended.

ἀγαπᾶν. It is invisible because it is not a worldly phenomenon at all; this is the meaning of the second ἵνα-clause, which picks up the first ἵνα καὶ αὐτοὶ ἐν ἡμῖν ὦσιν.[1] Thus ἓν εἶναι means the same as ἐν ἡμῖν εἶναι; the community is united, in that it no longer belongs to the world but is totally orientated[2] on the revelation-event that takes place in Jesus and is an eschatological phenomenon. But this is why the invisibility of the unity is not the invisibility of an idea, but of the eschatological event, which is comprehensible only to faith and which takes place again and again in history. Christendom is not a dimension within world-history, so that the "essential nature" that constitutes its unity could be established only by a survey of history, and which therefore would actually be hidden from those living within that history. Rather, this unity takes place again and again in proclamation and faith.[3]

The purpose or result of such unity[4] is: ἵνα ὁ κόσμος πιστεύῃ ὅτι σύ με ἀπέστειλας. If there is such an eschatological community in the cosmos, in history, then there is always the possibility of faith for the world. The community is of course always a cause of irritation for the world, and can always inflame its anger (v. 14). But this means that the possibility of deciding for the Revealer is also always given to it, and this was and always will be the means of overcoming the offence. Admittedly there is also the possibility of a decision against him, and thus the possibility of the knowledge that implies despair.[5] But the prayer does not dwell on that, but rather on the possibility of faith.[6] And that is why the prayer for the community is at the same time an intercession for the world, in which (as v. 18 has already said) the community has been set its task.[7]

Vv. 22f. provide fresh motivation for the prayer for the unity of

---

[1] The two ἵνα-clauses dependent on ἐρωτῶ (v. 20), (the third ἵνα-clause is no longer dependent on it), run contrary to one another as regards their form, but are actually parallel in meaning. Perhaps one of the two belonged to the source. Ἓν, which is inserted into the second clause before ὦσιν in ℵ 𝔎 pl lat, is of course a correction, to bring it into line with the first clause, even if it is not incorrect as regards content.

[2] On εἶναι ἐν see p. 321 n.1.

[3] See pp. 307f.

[4] The third ἵνα is not, like the first two, dependent on ἐρωτῶ (v. 20), but states the purpose or result of the ἕν (or ἐν ἡμῖν) εἶναι. But even if the faith of the world is thought of as *resulting from* the community's oneness, yet this result does not appear in the context of the prayer as the ultimate goal of that unity.

[5] Cp. 8.28 and see p. 349.

[6] The fact that it is ἵνα ... πιστεύῃ, and not e.g. ἵνα γινώσκῃ, makes it certain that we must interpret in this way, and not following 8.28; furthermore the words ἵνα γιν. in v. 23 must clearly also be taken in the light of ἵνα πιστ. It makes no difference whether πιστεύῃ (ℵ* B C W) or πιστεύσῃ (𝔎 D Θ) is read.

[7] See p. 509f. and cp. Faulhaber 58f. Dodd (406) stresses that John, in contrast to the popular eschatol. expectation, sees a revelation for the world in the fact that the divine love in Christ is alive in the community's unity of love.

the community; once again, knowledge on the part of the world is stated to be its ultimate goal (v. 23b), but in addition to that the unity is described as the purpose and fulfilment of Jesus' work of revelation.[1] This idea is expressed twice, to stress its importance: he has given to his own the δόξα which the Father had bestowed on him in order that they should be one, as he and the Father are one (v. 22); he is in them, and the Father in him, so that they may be perfect in unity (v. 23a).[2] The meaning of both sentences is the same; they state that Jesus' work finds its fulfilment in the existence of a unified community. His work is described first by saying that *he has given his own the* δόξα *bestowed on him by the Father.* Here again the language of the myth[3] is used to describe his work as Revealer; for what else does the sentence mean than that he revealed to them the name of God (v. 6), which God has given him (v. 11)? Or that he imparted to them the words of God which he had received from God (v. 8)? He has bestowed his δόξα on them, in that he is acknowledged among them as the Revealer and by this means is himself glorified (v. 10). Thus on the one hand the faith of the community can be called its δόξα, a gift bestowed on it by him, and it too can be said to be glorified in the same way as he; and on the other hand his δόξα consists in his being the Revealer and being believed to be such;[4] because both these things are true, it can also be said of the *community* that it receives a share in his work of revelation. Thus v. 18

---

[1] The sentences ἵνα ὦσιν κτλ. in vv. 22 and 23 are clearly parallel final clauses, and correspond to the first two ἵνα-clauses of v. 21. The second ἵνα-clause in v. 23 (ἵνα γινώσκῃ) is not parallel to them; it corresponds to the third ἵνα-clause of v. 21. The plethora of clauses in vv. 21–23 is without doubt due to the fact that the Evangelist has worked over a source. Yet there is no cause for supposing redactional glosses, and then cutting them out, as Hirsch (II 117f.) does. It is incorrect to say that vv. 20f. speak of the later Gentile Christians, while αὐτοῖς in v. 22 refers to the disciples who actually heard the prayer; no, just as vv. 20f. refer not only to the disciples who were present, but also to future disciples, so too the believers of every age are included in the αὐτοῖς of v. 22. The historical setting, in which the Evangelist has put the prayer, should not be forced, nor is δέδωκα in v. 22 to be limited pedantically to the actual historical occasion.

[2] Since the two ἵνα-clauses are parallel (see previous note), the sentences κἀγὼ τ. δόξαν κτλ. (v. 22) and ἐγὼ ἐν αὐτ. κτλ. (v. 23) must also be taken as parallel to each other.

[3] The idea that the messenger "glorifies" the believers, i.e. equips them with the brilliance or light which he himself possesses, is common in the Mandaean writings; see Schlier, Relig. Unters. 66. Cp. esp. Mand. Lit. 193: "He revealed hidden mysteries and laid his splendour on his friends". Mand Lit 128:

"Be my splendour, and I will be your splendour;
Be my light, and I will be your light".

Ign. Eph. 2.2: πρέπον οὖν ἐστὶν κατὰ πάντα τρόπον δοξάζειν Ἰ. Χριστὸν τὸν δοξάσαντα ὑμᾶς. Thus R. Otto's suggestion (Reich Gottes und Menschensohn 1934, 274, E.T. Kingdom of God and Son of Man, 1938, 383), that v. 22 is the Johannine version of the promise in Lk. 22.29, has little probability. The idea comes from the Gnostic myth, and the form it takes has been given to it by the Evangelist, whose style is clearly recognisable; on the anticipated object, see v. 2 and p. 233 n.4.

[4] See p. 491.

had already affirmed that he is sending his own into the world as the Father had sent him; and v. 21 had already represented the community's task for the world as the ultimate goal, and this will be immediately repeated in v. 23b. In fact one can say: that he has given them his δόξα means that after his departure they are to represent him in the world; it means that the "history" of Jesus will not become an episode in the past, but will remain continually present in the world as the eschatological event in the eschatological community.[1]

But the parallel sentence: "I am in them, and Thou art in me" (v. 23) says the same thing. For he is not "in them" in the sense of being an image in their historical recollection, such as awakens sentimental or pious veneration, or challenges to enthusiastic imitation, but precisely as the Revealer, as the one in whom God is. And the following discourses will show that this his being is made real in them in the witness they bear to him through the word which proclaims him.

This fact, viz. that he is present in the community as the Revealer, is to find its crowning glory in the oneness of the community: "In order that they may be one as we are one" (v. 22),[2] "that they may be perfected into unity" (v. 23a).[3] Would one not expect the reverse, namely

---

[1] Corresponding to the analogy that exists in the myth between the redeemer and the redeemed, there is an analogy between Jesus and his own in John. As he is sent into the world, so he sends them (17.18); as he is in the world, and yet not from the world, so too are they (17.14, 16; 15.19); as the world hates him, so too it hates his own (17.14; 15.18ff.). Just as his work was a μαρτυρεῖν, so too is theirs (15.27); they bring the same works to fruition as he (14.12); the world's fate is determined by its attitude to them (I Jn. 4.5f.; 5.1), as it is by its attitude to him (8.42; 18.37); just as he has overcome the world (16.33), so will their faith (I Jn. 5.4); see also pp. 509f.

[2] The καθὼς-clause that defines this unity provides us here with the simpler description of it as: καθὼς ἡμεῖς ἕν (sc. ἐσμέν), in place of the reciprocal formula of v. 21; cp. v. 11; 10.30.

[3] Here (not as in 4.34 etc., see p. 194 n.3) τελειοῦν has an eschatological sense, like πληροῦν in v. 13 (see p. 506 n.1). In the Mandaean writings "perfection" frequently occurs as an eschatological predicate. The abode of blessedness is the "house of perfection" (Ginza, frequently, see the index in Lidzb.). The "wicked Abathur" certainly made things, but never produced anything "perfect" (Ginza 205, 28ff.). The pious wait for "the light to be perfectly established"; the believers are called "the perfected" (index to Ginza). See further on I Jn. 2.5. Cp. C. Herm 4.4: ὅσοι μὲν οὖν συνῆκαν τοῦ κηρύγματος καὶ ἐβαπτίσαντο τοῦ νοός, οὗτοι μετέσχον τῆς γνώσεως καὶ τέλειοι ἐγένοντο ἄνθρωποι, τὸν νοῦν δεξάμενοι. Further Did. 10.5: μνήσθητι, κύριε, τῆς ἐκκλησίας σου τοῦ ῥύσασθαι αὐτὴν ἀπὸ παντὸς πονηροῦ καὶ τελειῶσαι αὐτὴν ἐν τῇ ἀγάπῃ σου. Act. Thom. 54, p. 171, 10f.: Jesus hands over a virgin to Thomas with the instruction: σὺ ταύτην παράλαβε ἵνα τελειωθῇ καὶ μετὰ ταῦτα εἰς τὸν αὐτῆς χῶρον συναχθῇ. How far this is the terminology of the mysteries (see Reitzenst., H.M.R. 338f. and Br. dictionary on τέλειος 2b), and how far the language of dualism, which distinguishes between the mundane and the divine as the imperfect and the perfected, will often be hard to say, because the subject-matter of both is related. The linguistic practice, acc. to which τελειωθῆναι refers to the perfection of dying blessedly, is also related (I Clem. 50.3; Mart. Andr. 11. p. 64.4; Mart. Matth. 31, p. 261, 23 etc.), but here the temporal element plays a part at the same time: to reach the end of one's course.

that the unity of the community is the condition on which it can represent him in the world as the true eschatological community in which he is present? How can the community's oneness be described as the objective to be attained by his presence in it? That would be impossible if the unity were thought of as a mundane phenomenon, as a unity that can be realised and organised in institutions and dogmas.[1] That kind of unity is incomprehensible as an end in itself; it can only be a means to an end. But neither is the conception of unity, that we find here, one of human-brotherly concord;[2] for it is unthinkable that that could be the final goal of Jesus' revelatory work or the raison d'être of the eschatological community, however certain we may be that the concord of the ἀλλήλους ἀγαπᾶν is to be a mark of the community (13.35). It is rather the case that if we can isolate unity from the being of the community (as a community of faith) and describe it as its raison d'être, then it can be regarded as an essential characteristic of the community only in so far as it is eschatological. Without doubt,—and we could already have drawn the conclusion from v. 21[3]—the community's oneness expresses the fact that it is the eschatological community, in which the world is annulled, and in which the differences of human individuality, that are typical of any human association and in fact help to make it up, are simply excluded. This unity stands for the radical other-worldly orientation of the community, that binds all individual believers and every empirical association of faith into a supra-worldly unity, across and beyond all differences of a natural, human kind. Accordingly, the kind of unity it is, and the ground of that unity, are described by means of the clause καθὼς ἡμεῖς ἕν (v. 22, cp. v. 21), and v. 23 can say: they are to be *perfected* into unity.[4] This unity is always called in question in the history of the community; there is always the danger that it will be forgotten or even denied. And whether the community remains true to its character, i.e. whether it remains the eschatological community in which the world is annulled, the community grounded in and preserved by the eschatological event and by nothing else, depends on the knowledge of this unity. Only thus does it possess the δόξα bestowed upon it by Jesus; only thus is he glorified in it.

Finally this knowledge is needed if the community is to fulfil its task of representing the Revealer in the world, and of giving the world the possibility of deciding for him (v. 23b). This decision, called

---

[1] See pp. 512, 513f.

[2] Nonnus describes the disciples' unity by mean of ὁμόφρονες (XVII 34) and ὁμόζυγες (XVII 64.68).

[3] See p. 512f.

[4] See p. 516 n.3.

πιστεύειν in v. 21, is now said to be γινώσκειν,[1] without any difference of meaning. The content of this γιν. is the same as in v. 21: ὅτι σύ με ἀπέστειλας, i.e. the knowledge of Jesus as the Revealer. But here there is an addition: καὶ (ὅτι) ἠγάπησας αὐτοὺς καθὼς ἐμὲ ἠγάπησας.[2] That is to say, the knowledge is nothing other than knowledge of the fact that the community represents the Revealer, and that in it as the eschatological community God's revelation is present in the world.

4) *The Petition for the Perfecting of the Believers:* 17.24–26

Up till now the prayer has been that the community which the Revealer is leaving behind in the world should remain true to its essential nature as the eschatological community, and thus fulfil its purpose in the world; now it reaches out beyond this. The new invocation, πατήρ, and the stressed θελῶ, which now takes the place of ἐρωτῶ (vv. 9, 15, 20), draw attention to the new direction the prayer is to take;[3] and the repetition of the invocation gives it a special importance. Jesus requests of God that those who belong to him should be with him to see his glory (**v. 24**).[4] What is the meaning of this petition? There can be no question of interpreting it in the sense of the primitive Jewish-Christian apocalyptic eschatology, which was rejected in 3.18f.; 5.24f.; 11.25f. Can the prayer have anything at all to do with a future vision of Jesus' δόξα, beyond the temporal, earthly existence of the believer? Does not the believer already see the Revealer's glory in this temporal, earthly existence (1.14), which has taken on eschatological significance for him?[5] Is not Jesus glorified precisely in his community (v. 10)? And is not the community to be in him and he in it (vv. 21, 23), so that his own, even when they are in the world, are with him, and see his glory? Was he not resolved against requesting that

---

[1] See p. 514 n.6, and on the relation of πιστεύειν to γινώσκειν in general see p. 435 n.4.

[2] Instead of ἠγάπησας D φ al a b r syr read ἠγάπησα, an assimilation in form to 15.9 and in content to the preceding words, ἐγὼ ἐν αὐτ. καί συ ἐν ἐμοί, such as interrupts the continuity.

[3] Θέλω can hardly be taken in the sense of a last will and testament (Godet); for the prayer is not concerned with an inheritance that Jesus is leaving behind him. Nor may one weaken the term to mean "I would like"; the expression is very bold: Jesus has nothing on earth in his own right, and only fulfils the Father's will (see 4.34 and p. 249 n.1), and yet here he, so to speak, makes a demand upon God. It is an expression of the assurance of faith that he is there for his own as the glorified one.

[4] V. 24 exhibits the Evangelist's style. The subj. of the ὅπου clause (ἐκεῖνοι) is anticipated in the absolute ὃ δέδωκας. cp. v. 2; 6.39 and see p. 233 n.4. On ὅ δέδωκας see Black 61f., who decides against the supposition of a wrong translation. On θέλω ἵνα see Schl. and Bl.-D. § 392, 1.

[5] One could almost put the question in this form too: have not the disciples, acc. to 1.14, already seen Jesus' δόξα during his time on earth? But 1.14 is not a historical observation, but the confession of the believers as a whole (see pp. 69f.). Even Jesus' contemporaries could only make the confession in the subsequent knowledge of what had remained hidden from them during his earthly life.

God take them out of the world (v. 15), and was not the whole intercession concerned with the annulment of the world by the community while it was within the world?

But the attempt to interpret v. 24 in this way would fail to do justice to the paradoxical nature of the statements which speak of the present vision of the δόξα, and of the annulment of the world already achieved by the community. The community does not now enjoy an existence that is already complete and independent in its own right, but exists by believing, i.e. by continually overcoming both the present, mundare existence, and the offence afforded by the fact that the δόξα can only be seen in the σάρξ γενόμενος. The community lives, and the believer lives, from the future; and his faith has meaning so long as this future is not an illusionary dream or a *futurum aeternum.* The petition is for the realisation of the future. By asking that his own should be with him, where he is, Jesus' prayer clearly looks back to the statements that he is leaving the world, that he is already no longer in the world in which his own still find themselves (vv. 11.13). Thus the petition can only be a request that the separation from him be a temporary one, that they should be united with him again after their worldly existence.[1] "To be with him, where he is" is something other than his being "in them," of which v. 23 spoke; and the vision of the δόξα, to which v. 24 refers, is different from that of 1.14. It is the δόξα that is freed from the veil of the σάρξ, the δόξα which he is himself entering, and into which his "servant," according to 12.26, will follow him: he will come again, according to 14.3, and gather his own to himself. Thus the vision intended is that of which I John 3.2 says: ὀψόμεθα αὐτὸν καθώς ἐστιν.[2]

---

[1] The language is that of the myth; cp. the messenger's petition to the Father in Joh.-B. 236, 26ff.: "If it is thy wish ... let the measure of my disciples be made full, and so may my disciples rise to the place of light". Further, Joh.-B. 161, 3f.: "I and my friends of the Kusta (=ἀλήθεια) will find our place in the Skina (= dwelling) of life". Act. Thom. 35, p. 152, 16ff.: καὶ ὄψη αὐτὸν καὶ σὺν αὐτῷ ἔση εἰς τὸν αἰῶνα, καὶ ἐν τῇ ἀναπαύσει αὐτοῦ ἀναπαήσῃ καὶ ἔσῃ ἐν τῇ χαρᾷ αὐτοῦ. Re-interpreted in terms of mystical experience: Od. Sal. 3.2, 5f.:

> "And his members are with him.
> And on them do I hang, and he loves me:
> I love the beloved,
> and I am loved by Him.
> Where His rest is,
> there also am I
> And I shall be no stranger".

In Lohmeyer, Σὺν Χριστῷ (Festg. für Deissmann 218–257), apart from 235f., there are no real parallels.

[2] Despite Hosk.'s protest, Wellh. is right, in that there is no thought here of the union of the church with Jesus at his parousia; the thought is rather that his own should in each case come to the vision of the δόξα through death.

But nothing positive can be said about it in explanation; for what is said in I John 3.2 is just as relevant here; οὔπω ἐφανερώθη τί ἐσόμεθα. And so the δόξα is only defined by means of the mythological sentence: "which Thou hast given me, because Thou hast loved me before the foundation of the world,"—which says in fact exactly the same as that καθώς ἐστιν.[1] The only thing that is clear is that an existence for the believers with the Revealer beyond death is requested, and thus promised. Death has become insignificant for them (11.25f.); but not in the sense that they can ignore it because their earthly life is now complete and meaningful in itself; but because their life is not enclosed within the limits of temporal-historical existence. Nor can the revelation be understood as an immanent process of world history, which begins with the coming of Jesus, seen as the emergence of a new idea in the history of thought. The reality of the revelation does not lie in the inward superiority of light over darkness, enabling the believer to stand outside the battle, safe in the knowledge of the eternal values and in inward union with them. On the contrary, meaning is given to the temporal event in that it is determined by powers which are not immanent in it but which have their reality beyond the reality it has, yet without being eternal in the sense of idealist thought. The temporal event is never complete or meaningful in itself, and therein lies its importance: what happens can fail to turn out as it should, and history is not a symphony in which everything is woven harmoniously into a whole; no, in history judgment is carried through. But this holds out a promise at the same time: what happens, can achieve its purpose. History runs its course before the judgment-seat of God. Thus it is also true of the believer that his participation in life is not exhausted in his historical existence within time, even though nothing positive can be said about the "then" beyond death. The Evangelist avoids all speculation about any heavenly journey of the soul, and refrains from any description of conditions of another world, such as form part of Gnostic mythology.[2] But the fact that he has seen that "the view beyond has been barred" from us, does not make him fall back on the opinion that human life can find its completeness in this world; he knows the double possibility: that it falls to pieces in condemnation, or that it is eternal in faith.

Because this eternity is bound up with faith, Jesus refers to the

---

[1] On the Father's love of the Son see p. 165 n.1. On πρὸ καταβ. κόσμου see v. 5 and p. 31 nn. 2, 3. The formula is also used in Mt. (13.35) 25.34; Lk. 11.50; Eph. 1.4 and elsewhere in the NT. It does not occur in the LXX, or in Philo or Jos., but is found in Ass. Mos. 1.14; Od. Sal. 41.15. The Rabbinic phrase would be: ἀπ' ἀρχῆς κτίσεως κόσμου, s ee Schl. on Mt. 13.35. Textual variants in v. 24 are without significance.

[2] John clearly avoids the Gnostic term ἀνάπαυσις (see p. 519 n.1). On the impossibility of seeing the future ζωή see also pp. 402f.

knowledge they have in faith as the motivation for his prayer for his own (v. 25). The invocation πατὴρ δίκαιε points at once to the inner connexion between present and future: in the gift of the future the present faith finds its fulfilment; in this way it accords with the fact that God is just.[1]

The question what faith means is answered by speaking of it as the knowledge of God, which according to v. 3 is αἰώνιος ζωή, and by contrasting this knowledge with the world's failure to know: καὶ ὁ κόσμος σε οὐκ ἔγνω. The close connexion of this sentence, by means of καί, with the preceding words is a reminder of the world's guilt: although the Father loved the Son before the foundation of the world, i.e. although the world has its origin in the love of God, so that the possibility of revelation has always been there from the beginning,[2] the world has not known God. The believers' knowledge is contrasted with this; and yet the antithesis is not, simply: οὗτοι δέ σε ἔγνωσαν, but: ἐγὼ δέ σε ἔγνων καὶ οὗτοι ἔγνωσαν ὅτι σύ με ἀπέστειλας. All knowledge of faith is grounded in knowledge of God,[3] and therefore is faith in him as the Revealer (cp. v. 3). Once more it is stressed (v. 26) that the work he performs is the knowledge they receive: καὶ ἐγνώρισα αὐτοῖς τὸ ὄνομά σου;[4] and lest this work appear as something complete in itself, or the revelation as a body of doctrines, it is further stated: καὶ γνωρίσω.[5] The future γνωρίσω is only possible on the basis of the past ἐγνώρισα; and the past ἐγνώρισα only becomes significant when it is continued by a future γνωρίσω. But with this knowledge the love of God is bestowed on his own: ἵνα ἡ ἀγάπη ἣν ἠγάπησάς με ἐν αὐτοῖς ᾖ. God's eternal love, of which the Son himself is the recipient and which existed πρὸ καταβολῆς κόσμου, is to become the believers' own, i.e. is to become the determining power of their life.[6] In what does it consist? If it is true that love is the being *for*—in the radical sense in which this is at the same time a being *from* . . . , then God's eternal love, directed to the Son, consists in his being the creator. God's being from . . . is his being as Creator, in which he establishes his being for . . . .[7] He is not a being who exists

---

[1] Δίκαιος is a frequent attribute of God in the OT and in Judaism, see e.g. Ps. 118.137; 140.5; 144.17; Deut. 32.4; Song of Sol. 2.36; 10.6; Jos. ant. XI 55; bell. VII 323. In the NT, in Rev. 16.5; I Jn. 1.9; Rom. 3.26.—I Clem. 27.1; 60.1 shows that the designation has passed over into liturgical usage. Also used as a pagan attribute of God in Hellenism, see Br. dictionary.

[2] See pp. 39f. One can hardly take the first καί as corresponding to the second, as if ἐγὼ δέ σε ἔγν. were a parenthesis (Lagr.).

[3] See p. 381.

[4] On the meaning of this phrase, worded almost as in v. 6, see pp. 497f.

[5] It makes no difference whether one takes the double καί as simply linking the sentences, or as corresponding in the sense: "not only ... but also".

[6] On εἶναι ἐν see p. 321 n.1.

[7] See Fr. Rückert, Die Weisheit des Brahmanen I 15; II 12.

for himself; indeed, he is never without the Logos, through whom he is the self-revealing Creator.[1]

If then this eternal love is to be handed on by the Revealer to the believers, this means that in the revelation the creation as such is restored, that the world is brought back to its original relationship with God as his creation.[2] God the Creator is present to the believers through their possession of the Revealer: κἀγὼ ἐν αὐτοῖς.[3] Thus the ultimate goal of the faith that knows is that the revelation always remain present, i.e. that the existence of the believer be determined by the revelation through which the world becomes creation again.

But this is not, as might be thought, a description of the vision of the δόξα in its other-worldly fulfilment;[4] vv. 25f. serve rather as motivation of the prayer in v. 24. But by grounding the prayer in the idea that the Revealer's work finds its goal in the determination of a believing existence by the eternal love of God, transmitted through the Revealer, the Evangelist is maintaining the inner unity of believing existence in this world with its fulfilment in the world to come. For clearly nothing further can be given beyond the gift of the love of God, and any further questioning about the future has not only become meaningless but would also be a case of unbelief.

If it is true that Jesus is in the community in that the revelation is alive in it, then he is also in it in this prayer. Who is in fact praying? Not the "historical Jesus," but historically speaking, the community.[5] But he is himself speaking in the community as the δοξασθείς.

C. 13.31–16.33: Farewell Discourses and Conversations

The footwashing and the two interpretations of it had dealt with the theme of the farewell in the manner of an overture, and two things had become clear about the believers' fellowship with the Revealer: first, that it is rooted in the service he performed, and secondly that it manifests itself within the historical life of believers. Jesus' prayer had shown that the significance of the farewell lay in its being the hour of his δοξασθῆναι, and had made known both the danger and the promise inherent in the situation in

---

[1] See p. 35.

[2] See pp. 496f.

[3] The co-ordination of the two parts of the ἵνα-clause corresponds to that in v.3; see p. 494f.

[4] It is not concerned with the εἶναι μετ' ἐμοῦ of v. 24, but with the εἶναι ἐν αὐτοῖς of v. 23 again.

[5] Cp. the analogy of the community prayer in Did. 10, see p. 486 n.3. One is not entitled to call the farewell prayer a "mystagogical instruction" (Arvedson op. cit. 133); the discourses that follow are much more of that character. Rather, in ch. 17, the community is calling to mind the last will and testament of Jesus. Cp. Hosk. 495.

which the community was placed, now that the Revealer had left it on its own. At this stage the isolation of the community in the world becomes the dominant theme; it is the theme of *the indirectness of the revelation.*[1]

The structure of the section is simple.[2] It starts by repeating once more the ground covered in 17.1–8: the significance of the hour of farewell lies in its being the hour of the δοξασθῆναι of both Jesus and God (13.31f.); this is followed by a brief description of what the farewell involves, of the separation with its accompanying distress (13.33). 13.34f. tells us that the way of overcoming this distress is to be found in the command of love, expounded as Jesus' last will and testament; and 15.1–17 develops this fact and shows how the distress is overcome. Thus 13.31–35 and 15.1–17 deal with the theme of the farewell and of Jesus' testament and 15.18–16.11 are concerned with the community's position in the world. This is followed by 16.12–33: the believers' future as the eschatological situation. Finally 13.36–14.31 forms the conclusion; it deals with the believers' fellowship with the Son and the Father.

a) Farewell and Testament: 13.31–35; 15.1–17

1) *Introduction:* 13.31–35

13.31: νῦν ἐδοξάσθη ὁ υἱὸς τοῦ ἀνθρώπου,
καὶ ὁ θεὸς ἐδοξάσθη ἐν αὐτῷ.
32: εἰ ὁ θεὸς ἐδοξάσθη ἐν αὐτῷ,[3]
καὶ ὁ θεὸς δοξάσει αὐτὸν ἐν αὐτῷ,
[καὶ εὐθὺς δοξάσει αὐτόν].[4]

Νῦν is the moment when Jesus has spoken the prayer; the request δόξασον (17.1) is fulfilled: ἐδοξάσθη ὁ υἱὸς τ. ἀνθρ. It is that νῦν, in which past and future are bound together,[5] stressed particularly at this point by the paradoxical juxtaposition of ἐδοξάσθη (v. 31) and δοξάσει (v. 32). The subject is that δόξα which is at the same time the Son's and the Father's:[6] καὶ ὁ θεὸς ἐδοξάσθη ἐν αὐτῷ.[7] What has already happened *sub specie aeterni* unfolds itself in the temporal future; and because

---

[1] See p. 489. Joh. Monck, Discours d'adieu dans le NT et dans la littérature biblique (Aux sources de la Tradition Chrétienne 1950, 154–170), only deals briefly with the Johannine farewell discourses.

[2] On the order of the text, see pp. 459f.

[3] The fact that this phrase does not occur in ℌ D al it syr^s is due to homoiotel.; on the way in which the second part of the preceding couplet is picked up in the verse that follows, see pp. 15f.; Schweizer 45.

[4] Vv. 31f. come from the "revelation discourses"; the last phrase, which is excessive, has been inserted by the Evangelist to relate the whole to the situation of the Passion. It is possible that in v. 31 the source only read ὁ υἱός, and that the Evangelist has inserted τοῦ ἀνθρ.; on υἱὸς ἀνθρ. see p. 105 n.3.

[5] See pp. 429., 492f.

[6] See p. 429, 491.

[7] ἐν is to be taken in both cases instrumentally. To take it as an ἐν of place would

this is so, the word δοξάσει (as if this future were at a distance from the νῦν) can be picked up again in καὶ εὐθὺς δοξάσει αὐτόν, which is a reference to the immediately imminent passion. It draws our attention again to that paradox inherent in the concept of δόξα, viz. that the δόξα becomes apparent precisely in the cross;[1] and it also indicates a rejection of the naive primitive Christian eschatology, for there the revelation of Jesus' δόξα was expected only at his coming Parousia (Mk. 8.38).

If the future expressed by δοξάσει is already contained in νῦν ἐδοξάσθη *sub specie aeterni*, and there is no "in between" which divides the revelation of the δοξασθείς in the future from that of the σὰρξ γενόμενος in the past, there is nevertheless such an "in between" *sub specie hominis:* τεκνία,[2] ἔτι μικρὸν μεθ' ὑμῶν εἰμι (**v. 33**). The period of his personal presence has come to its end: ζητήσετέ με, καὶ . . . ὅπου ἐγὼ ὑπάγω ὑμεῖς οὐ δύνασθε ἐλθεῖν.[3] His own will miss him; they will not realise the full significance of that νῦν immediately. Their faith has to stand the test.

The Evangelist brings this out very clearly by making Jesus emphasise that what is here said to the disciples is the same as what was said to the Jews (7.33f.; 8.21). Thus, to some extent the believers are in the same position as the men of the κόσμος. Of course the situation does not contain for them, as it does for the latter, that element of the "too late"; but both look back in the same way on a "no longer", and the beginnings of despair are there for the disciples too. They have to learn that the Revealer has not come to be at their disposal through their faith. What now lies in the past does not guarantee the future, but is called into question by it. Jesus, in whom they believed, disappears from them, and they are left with no security.

Then how can their relationship with him be retained in the face of this isolation? With this question the theme of the section has been reached, and in **v. 34** it receives its first answer:[4] ἐντολὴν καινὴν δίδωμι

---

come to mean the same thing, viz. the δόξα of the one is represented by that of the other On this idea cp. Od. Sal. 17.1:

"I was crowned by my God:
He is my living crown."

[1] See p. 397f.

[2] The mode of address τεκνία, only here in the Gospel, occurs more frequently in the first letter. It is the way the teacher addresses his pupils (see Str.-B. ad loc.), and is always to be attributed to the author. It suggests, as does the designation of the disciples as μαθηταί in v. 35, that the Evangelist desires to present a counterpart to the Rabbinic portrayal of the future, acc. to which the Messiah will one day expound the Torah anew (Str.-B. IV 1–3). On analogous farewell scenes in the βίος of philosophers, see L. Bieler Θεῖος ἀνήρ I 1935, 45.

[3] V. 33 is of course the Evangelist's work, like vv. 34f. On the speaker quoting himself, or on references back, see p. 348 n.4. Cp. also the preceding note.

[4] The second and third answers will be given in the exposition of the μικρόν of the "time between" in 16.16–24 and 14.18–20.

ὑμῖν.[1] The future is subjected to an imperative![2] Their anxiety was centred on their own actual existence, but now they are directed towards an existence that has the character of an "ought." The illusion that they possess him in such a way that he is at their disposal is confronted by another kind of possession: one which consists in fulfilling a command. Their despairing gaze into the past that is no more is redirected to the future, which comes and lays its obligation upon them. An unreal future, which would only be a persistence in the past, is made into the real future which demands faith. And in so far as the content of the ἐντολή is ἵνα ἀγαπᾶτε ἀλλήλους, the care for oneself is changed into a care for one's neighbour. But since it is precisely this becoming free from the past and from oneself that is subjected to the imperative, the future that is grasped as command coincides with the future that is promised for loyalty of faith; for it was freedom from the past and from oneself that was promised to the believer.[3] Thus the imperative is itself a gift, and this it can be because it receives its significance and its possibility of realisation from the past, experienced as the love of the Revealer: καθὼς ἠγάπησα ὑμᾶς. For καθώς expresses the integral connexion between the ἀλλήλους ἀγαπᾶν and Jesus' love which they have experienced; it does not describe the degree or intensity of the ἀγαπᾶν (Loisy), nor does it depict the way that Jesus took as the way of service; rather it describes the basis of the ἀγαπᾶν.[4] And that is why the ἵνα-clause is repeated with the stressed καὶ ὑμεῖς: it thereby becomes clear that precisely this ἀλλήλ. ἀγ. is the fulfilment of the purpose of Jesus' love.[5]

It is therefore not the case that Jesus is setting up an ethical principle at his departure, to take the place of his presence; a principle to which human life in general should be subjected, and which was observable in the historical figure of Jesus. For in that case the problem of the farewell, the problem of the disciples' relation to the Revealer who has disappeared from them, would not have been solved; this relation would have been dissolved, there would be no further need of the

---

[1] Vv. 34f. come from the Evangelist. In v. 34, apart from the characteristic καθώς (p. 382 n.2), and the twofold ἵνα-clause, this is shown by the fact that he has also inserted the ἀγαπή motif in the source-text that lies at the basis of ch. 15. V. 35 is one of his descriptive definitions, cp. 16.30; I Jn. 2.3, 5; 3.16, 19, 24; 4.9, 13; 5.2, all followed by a ὅτι-clause; without one in I Jn. 3.10; 4.2; with a following ἵνα: 15.8; I Jn. 4.17. In all these cases ἐν τούτῳ = ἐκ or διὰ τούτου (so also in Greek use, see Br. ad loc.); it is otherwise in 4.37; 9.30.

[2] If the word ἄρτι of the preceding sentence is drawn into the one following, as in syr^{s} (acc. to Merx), the movement of thought becomes clear: "But for now, for the period of separation, I give you a new command".

[3] See pp. 436f.

[4] See p. 382 n.2, and cp. F. K. Schumann, Um Kirche und Lehre 1936, 184ff.

[5] The second ἵνα-clause is not parallel to the first, dependent on ἐντολὴν δίδωμι, but states the purpose of the καθώς-clause.

Revealer, and the future would lie in one's own hand to be grasped. But then the past too would have lost its meaning; it would have become a matter of indifference for the future, even if it still had educational importance. But the bonds of the past are not loosed by depriving it of all significance vis-à-vis the future. Rather the future looses from the past in the sense that it destroys any attempt to possess the past and control it, and thus makes its true fruition possible. The past was for the sake of the future; and the resolute turning to the future on the basis of the past remains in a proper way in the past:[1] free from it, in so far as it is *my* past, and bound to it, in so far as *God* has been at work in it.

The significance of the *past* lies in the fact that the encounter with Jesus was experienced as his service which made the believer free; thus the significance of the *future* can only be that in it this freedom is brought to fruition. And this takes place in the fulfilment of the command of love. Because this command and its fulfilment are grounded in the Revealer's love which has actually been experienced, the believer always remains bound to the Revealer's service, and is never centred on himself. And to put it the other way round, the faith which has accepted that service can only continue to come to fruition in the attitude of service, i.e. of love. Only if they are themselves loving do they who belong to him remain in the experience of his love; in the same way they can, and do love, only on the basis of this experience. Thus the believers' past and future are bound to each other like the former and the future δόξα of the Revealer himself: the future receives its meaning from the past, and the past becomes significant in the future. But that means that in the future, despite their separation from him, they remain united to him. In their action, his act is present.

And this is so, precisely because the command is ἀλλήλους ἀγαπᾶν. There is no such thing as a love of which Jesus is the direct recipient (cp. 14.15–24); if it thought that there were, such love would not have understood him to be the Revealer, i.e. the one in whom God is encountered; there is no love of which God is the direct recipient (I John 4.20); Jesus' love is not a personal emotion, but is the service that liberates; and the response to it is not a mystical or pietistic intimacy with Christ, but the ἀλλήλους ἀγαπᾶν.

This also explains in what sense this ἐντολή is called καινή. That is to say, not as a newly discovered principle or cultural ideal proclaimed by Jesus in the world. The command of love is not "new" in virtue of its relative newness in the history of ideas. It is not "new" in this sense

[1] See pp. 439f.

either in regard to the O.T.[1] or to the pagan ancient world; in both the claims of a life of service wherein each serves the other—whatever its motivation may have been—had long been understood.[2] The recognition of this claim has, after all, been inherent from the beginning in the possibilities of human intercourse.[3] And even if one could say that the command of love was new at any one point in history, it would very soon become old, and it can in fact be described as such when one looks back into the past, as in I John 2.7. But Jesus' command of love is "new," even when it has been long-known, because it is the law of the eschatological community, for which the attribute "new" denotes not an historical characteristic but its essential nature.[4] The command of love, which is grounded in the love of the Revealer received by the disciples, is "new" in so far as it is a phenomenon of the new world which Jesus has brought into being; and indeed I John 2.8 describes this newness as that of the eschatological event.

V. 35 states that the new world becomes reality in the community: reciprocal love within the community is the criterion of the discipleship of Jesus for those outside. The fact that the command of love is fulfilled there demonstrates the strangeness of the community within the world, and results in the world calling those who love, the disciples of Jesus. Not just because theirs is a community in which love is both an injunction and an actual practice.[5] Much rather because love itself there takes on a form that is strange to the world. In the community the command

---

[1] Cp. Lev. 19.18. The eulogy at the sabbatical morning prayer of the priests in the temple goes: "Whoever lives in this house, let him plant among you brotherhood and love, peace and friendship" (Str.-B. ad loc.). Acc. to Jos. bell. 2.119, the Essenes are preeminent among the Jews as φιλάλληλοι. For the Mandaeans see Ginza 20, 12ff.; 38, 8ff. (Love and bear with one another); Joh.-B. 55(Love and teach each other).

[2] It is regarded particularly as a political imperative in the ancient πόλις, and as such is one of the main concerns of Platonic and Aristotelian philosophy. In Stoicism the imperative is extended to the whole of mankind and is grounded in the concept of humanity. In late Stoicism φιλάνθρωπος, κοινωνικός, εὐεργετικός etc. belong to the ideal man, and the attitude of selfless, serving love is apparent in Marcus Aurelius in an impressive way. On the φιλία of the Pythagoreans, see on v.35. See also H. Haas, Idee und Ideal der Feindesliebe in der ausserchristl. Welt 1927.

[3] Cp. Bultmann, Glauben und Verstehen vol. I, 1933, 241f.

[4] On καινός as an eschatological predicate see TWB III 451, 15ff. It is used both in the Jewish and Jewish-Christian eschatology, and also in the Gnostic. Acc. to Ign. Eph. 19.2 the Redeemer's descent is announced by a star, the καινότης of which arouses astonishment; on this, see Schlier, Relig. Unters. 28ff., and esp. Exc. ex Theod. 74:... ἀνέτειλεν ξένος ἀστὴρ καὶ καινός, καταλύων τὴν παλαιὰν ἀστροθεσίαν καινῷ φωτί, οὐ κοσμικῷ λαμπόμενος, ὁ καινὰς ὁδοὺς καὶ σωτηρίους τρεπόμενος.

[5] Cp. Text. Apol. 39: vide, inquiunt, ut invicem se diligant; Min. Fel. Oct. 9, 2: amant mutuo paene antequam noverint. In itself this would be no definite criterion, for cp. Jambl. Vit. Pythag. 33, 230 p. 123, 24ff. Deubner: οὕτω θαυμαστὴν φιλίαν παρέδωκε (sc. ὁ Πυθαγόρας) τοῖς χρωμένοις, ὥστε ἔτι καὶ νῦν τοὺς πολλοὺς λέγειν ἐπὶ τῶν σφοδρότερον εὐνοούντων ἑαυτοῖς, ὅτι τῶν Πυθαγορείων εἰσί. See also L. Bieler op. cit. 125f.

of love is grounded in the love of God which is encountered in the Revealer, and this means that its fulfilment must bear the nature of world-annulment; by it all human love is peculiarly modified, in a way that both limits and broadens it. God is the "middle term"[1] in all loving, and all loving becomes the proclamation of Jesus[2]—which means that it can always become an offence too, not just in the individual case, but especially because the association formed by this kind of love cuts across the associations of the world in a special way. The ways in which the world can react to this love, and the fact that the community fulfils its commission to the world therein (17.21, 23), are not the subject of explicit reflection here; but the subject is brought to our attention inasmuch as 13.31–35; 15.1–17 is followed by 15.18–16.11, a section which deals with the place of the community in the world.

Although the associates of Jesus are described as his μαθηταί,[3] it is clear that this predicate "disciple," or "pupil," is not intended as a historical description, but as a definition of their essential nature. The association with Jesus, therefore, is not realised by possessing articles of knowledge or dogmas, nor in institutions or experiences of individual piety, but in "pupil-hood," in obedience to the command of love. But μαθητὴς εἶναι defines not only the obedience, but also the honour: as "disciples," his own are free; the command is at the same time the gift.[4]

This also explains why the command of love seems to undergo a limitation through the ἀλλήλους. It is no general love of mankind, or love of one's neighbour or enemy that is demanded, but love within the circle of disciples. Naturally this does not mean that the all-embracing love of one's neighbour is to be invalidated; but here it is a question of the very existence of the circle of disciples. How does the departing Revealer remain present for his own? By the vitality of the gift of his love in their love of each other, and by their representation within the world of the new world, which became reality through him.[5]

Thus the ἀγαπᾶν, as the criterion of eschatological existence, is limited not because it has to do with a group that is orientated on the *world*, but because it has to do with the *eschatological* community, and this means that the world always has the possibility of being included within the circle of the ἀγαπᾶν.[6] It excludes itself only when it rejects the

---

[1] Kierkegaard, Leben und Walten der Liebe, German, Jena 1924, 113ff. (E.T. Works of Love, 1962, 112f.).

[2] Cp. Ign. Eph. 4.1: ἐν τῇ ὁμονοίᾳ ὑμῶν καὶ συμφώνῳ ἀγάπῃ Ἰ. Χριστὸς ᾄδεται.

[3] Ἐμοί is adjectival, as in 15.8. On μαθητ. see p. 434 n.2.

[4] See p. 524f. and cp. 8.31f.

[5] Cp. Faulhaber 38f.; Schumann, Um Kirche und Lehre 196, 13. Otherwise, C. R. Bowen, Journ. of Religion 13 (1933) 39–49.

[6] Cp. Schlatter, Der Glaube im NT 4th. ed. 492f.; Howard, Christianity 170.

faith to which it is continually challenged by the community's existence, whether the challenge be by the word it proclaims, seeking to win the world over (16.7ff.), or by the offence it presents to the world—also a means of winning it over. But the community itself fulfils its commission to the world (17.21, 23) only if its ἀγαπᾶν remains the response to the love of Jesus, and so long as it does not exchange it for an ἔργον of the world, or for efficacy within world-history. It is not the effect it has on world history that legitimates the Christian faith, but its strangeness within the world; and the strangeness is the bearing of those whose love for each other is grounded in the divine love.

2) *The True Vine:* 15.1–17

The discourse that runs from 15.1 to 15.17,[1] without any interruption for dialogue, is a commentary on 13.34f., in the sense that it goes more deeply into the grounds of the command of love, already briefly defined by καθὼς ἠγάπησα ὑμᾶς. The exposition of the command of love as the essential element in constancy of faith makes it clear that faith and love form a unity; i.e. that the faith, of which it can be said, καθὼς ἠγάπησα ὑμᾶς, is authentic only when it leads to ἀγαπᾶν ἀλλήλους. Thus the first part of the discourse, vv. 1–8, is an exhortation to constancy of faith in the language of μείνατε ἐν ἐμοί, and the second part (vv. 9–17), which defines ἐν ἐμοὶ more closely as ἐν τῇ ἀγάπῃ τῇ ἐμῇ, places the command of love on this foundation. In this way 15.1–17 is also a commentary on 13.1–20; for the two parts here correspond to the two interpretations of the footwashing.[2]

i. μείνατε ἐν ἐμοὶ 15.1–8:

V. 1: ἐγώ εἰμι ἡ ἄμπελος ἡ ἀληθινή,
καὶ ὁ πατήρ μου ὁ γεωργός ἐστιν.

With the words ἐγώ εἰμι the Revealer presents himself again as the object of the world's desire and longing; if one asks about the "true vine", then the answer is given: "The true vine am I".[3] There is no comparison here,[4] or allegory.[5] Rather, Jesus as the true, authentic

---

[1] Again a piece of the "revelation-discourses" lies at the basis of the discourse; the Evangelist has commented on it and expanded it with his own additions.

[2] See p. 478.

[3] Another example of the recognition formula: ἐγώ is predicate, and ἡ ἀμπ. ἡ ἀλ. is subject; see p. 225 n.3.

[4] The absence of any particle of comparison, the definite article, and the term ἀληθ. all show that this is no comparison or parable, such as might have been suggested by the sight of a vine climbing up the side of the house, or of the golden vine over the Temple gate (Zahn, Temple; other psychological reflections of the same kind in Stettinger, Textfolge 44). But naturally the title ἄμπελος, like ποιμήν in ch. 10, presents the opportunity of appending metaphorical and comparative discourse. See also Schweizer 114ff.

[5] Placing ἐγώ εἰμι at the beginning is at once contrary to the form of an allegory;

S

"vine" is contrasted with whatever also claims to be the "vine".[1] To understand the discourse aright, we must realise that it does not draw attention to the vine with regard to its fruit, or to the wine that it bestows,[2] but simply to the tree itself with its shoots, and that the shoots are perfused with vital power from it; from the tree they receive their power to grow and to bear fruit, and they wither away if they are cut off from it: *the vine is the tree of life*. Just as one can speak of ὕδωρ ζῶν and of ἄρτος and φῶς τῆς ζωῆς, so one can speak of ἡ ἄμπελος τῆς ζωῆς.[3] But there is a difference here from the sayings about the water and the bread of life: the Revealer is not contrasted with the mundane means of life, as the bestower of that life which had been hoped for in vain from those means; the contrast is rather between the life which can be seen in nature in the vine, and the Revealer as the *source* of the true life. That he is the true vine means that no natural life is the true life, that life, such as man seeks and longs for, can be had only in association with Jesus.

Just as the myth has dreams of a water of life and of a bread of life,[4] so it has of a tree of life.[5] But what is dream there is reality here:

---

if it were the clarificatory formula of an allegory, it would have to come at the end; see also Schweizer 120f.

[1] The language is characteristic of dualism. Jer. 2.21, with a viewpoint limited to one temporal world, speaks of the pure vine as "genuine" (אֱמֶת, LXX ἀληθινή), in contrast to the vine that has degenerated, using the terms parabolically, or metaphorically.

[2] Loisy is therefore wrong when he says that the description of Jesus as the vine shows que le discours est dans un rapport aussi étroit avec l'eucharistie, que le contenue des chapitres XIII et XIV. On various Syriac versions, which appear to have read ἀμπελών (vineyard etc.) instead of ἄμπελος, see Merx and Zahn ad loc., and esp. Schweizer 158, note 106.

[3] Thus Nonnus also says: ἐγὼ ... ζωῆς ἄμπ. εἰμι. Cp. the juxtaposition of φῶς ἀλ. (1.9; I Jn. 2.8) and φῶς τ. ζωῆς (8.12); and of ἄρτος ἀλ. (6.32) and ἄρτος τ. ζ. (6,35, 48). Od. Sal. 1.2ff.:

"They wove for me a crown of truth
And it caused thy branches to bud in me.
For it is not like a withered crown which buddeth not ...
But thou *livest* upon my head. ..."

[4] See pp. 183f., 223.

[5] Schweizer 39–41 has shown that the vine in John 15 does not have its origin in the OT-Jewish tradition, but in the myth of the tree of life; he gives examples from the plethora of Mandaean parallels. (In the Mandaean literature, too, the tree of life is a vine; elsewhere it is variously portrayed, acc. to period and culture, e.g. as an olive-tree, pine or ash; see also ZNTW 24 (1925) 116f.) On the tree of life see also W. Mannhardt, Der Baumkult der Germanen 1875: Aug. Wünsche, Die Sage vom Lebensbaum und Lebenswasser 1905; Uno Helmberg, Der Baum des Lebens (Annales Acad. scient. fennicae Ser. B 16, 3) 1922; Ad. Jacoby, Zeitschr. fur Missionskunde und Religionswissenschaft 43 (1928), 78–85; W. Boette, Handwörterbuch des Deutschen Aberglaubens 5 (1932/33), 460; Hildeg. Urner-Astholz Basler Nachrichten 1952, 28 Sept. On the conception of the archetypal man or redeemer, as the tree of the world see E. Käsemann, Leib und Leib Christi 1933, 69ff.; also Schlier Relig. Unters. 48ff. In the Christian tradition the tree of life lives on in combination with

ἐγώ εἰμι. Ἀληθινή therefore means first, in the formal sense, "genuine", "real", in contrast to the "imagined", "unreal";[1] but because the passage deals with the search for life, it also means "divine", in that there is only "real" life in God, and in contrast to that, all natural, mundane life is only an appearance or lie.[2] On the one side is the κόσμος, with everything that it offers as means of life, making it all look like vital energy, and thus deceiving man's longing for life. Certainly this longing for life is to be fulfilled, but from another side; i.e. at the cost of recognising and giving up all the deceptive possibilities of the κόσμος as appearance, and instead of them choosing the one divine possibility disclosed in the revelation: "The true vine am I".

The discourse raises the question of decision only indirectly, because it is delivered to the circle of those who have already decided. Hence the motif of promise also gives place to that of exhortation; and it is an exhortation to abide. It is grounded in the words ἐγώ εἰμι; for they imply that he alone is the source of life for all men, including the believers. Before the exhortation is given, the phrase καὶ ὁ πατήρ μου ὁ γεωργός ἐστιν[3] declares that Jesus' existence for his own is grounded in

---

the cross (often represented as a vine); cp. F. Piper, Evang. Kalender, Jahrb. für 1863, 17–94; F. X. Kraus, Real.-Enz. der christl. Altert. II 983ff.; Wünsche op. cit. 23ff.; H. Bergner, Monatschr. für Kirchl. Kunst 3 (1898), 333f.; L. v. Sybel ZNTW 19 (1919/20) 85–91; 20 (1921) 93f.; R. Bauerreiss, Arbor Vitae 1938; Eth. Stauffer, Die Theol. des NT 4th. ed. 1948, 113. This combination is met with as early as Ign. Trall. 11.2; on this see Schlier Relig. Unters. 108, 1; also Käsemann op. cit. 70f.

[1] On ἀληθινός see p. 53 n.1. If the text is a translation from the Aramaic or Syriac, then it is possible that it is only by translating דְּקוּשְׁתָּא by ἀληθινός that it comes to have this meaning, whereas in the source the vine of the Kusta always meant the vine of the divine world of "truth"; see Schweizer 60, note 122.

[2] A partial analogy can be found in the Platonic manner of speech, acc. to which the "true" being only belongs to the world of ideas, in contrast to the phenomena of the world of becoming and decaying (ThWB I 240, 10ff.). Yet of course the reality of the life mediated by the Revealer is not that of the idea (Büchsel, Begr. der Wahrh. 40f.). A true analogy is afforded by the use of language we find in Hellenism (ThWB I 240, 27ff.; 250, 41ff.). Cp. too Act. Thom. 36 p. 153, 23ff.: ἀλλὰ λέγομεν περὶ τὸν ἄνω κόσμον, . . . περὶ τῆς ἀμβροσιώδους τροφῆς καὶ τοῦ ποτοῦ τῆς ἀμπέλου τῆς ἀληθινῆς. In Act. Thom. 61 p. 178, 8ff. σωματικός and ἐπίγειος are contrasted with ἀληθινός and παράμονος; see further 12 p. 118, 7f.; 14 p. 120, 12; 88 p. 203, 14f.; 124 p. 233, 25f.

[3] It could be accidental that God is called γεωργός and not ἀμπελουργός (Lk. 13.7; Philo, plant. 1, distinguishes the two), because γεωργός sometimes means vinedresser elsewhere (Mk. 12.1ff.; Porphyr. abst. 3, 10; cp. Phil. somn. II 163). On the other hand it seems that God was frequently compared to a γεωργός (C. Herm. 14.10; on which see J. Koll, Herm. Trism. 32), so that γεωργός became a metaphor for, or even a title of, God (Pap. Graec. Mag. I 26; on this see A. Dieterich Abraxas 1891, 123f.; Reitzenst. Poim. 143). Philo, who talks of God's γεωργία (plant. 139), calls him φυτουργός, plant. 2.73.94; conf. ling. 61.196; so too Act. Thom. 10 p. 114, 13. Ignatius speaks in the same way in Trall. 11.1, and in Phld. 3.1 of the φυτεία πατρός, and of its opposite in Act. Phil. 119 p. 84, 12: γεωργία τοῦ ἐχθροῦ (cp. Ign. Eph. 10.3: τ. διαβόλου βοτάνη; cp. Trall. 6.1). In the Mandaean lit., "Planter" is a frequent description of both God and the Revealer;

his existence from God,[1] which is an indirect way of saying that as the Revealer he makes it possible for his own to approach the Father.

But the purpose of drawing our attention to the relationship with God that Christ mediates is not the same as in 10.14–18, 27–30, where that relationship was described as the ground of faith's assurance; here the analysis draws out its judgmental significance:

V. 2: πᾶν κλῆμα ἐν ἐμοὶ μὴ φέρον καρπόν,
αἴρει αὐτό.[2]
καὶ πᾶν τὸ καρπὸν φέρον,
καθαίρει αὐτὸ ἵνα καρπὸν πλείονα φέρῃ.[3]

These judgmental statements are put in front of μείνατε (v. 4) and prepare us for understanding the word μένειν.[4] The relationship with God means the destruction of human security—for the believer as well. It does not provide enjoyment of peace of mind, or a state of contemplation, but demands movement, growth; its law is καρπὸν φέρειν.[5] The nature of the fruit-bearing is not expressly stated; it is every demonstration of vitality of faith,[6] to which, according to vv. 9–17, reciprocal

correspondingly, the Revealer or the soul (souls) is seen as the plant; see Schlier, Relig. Unters. 48ff. and esp. the messenger's discourse in Ginza 301.10ff.:

"I am a tender vine ...
And the great (life: i.e. God) was my planter".

The Revealer as God's planting and as the tree of life (see p. 530 n.5) coincide. The Gnostic myth also seems to be at the basis of the expositions in Philo, plant. 4ff., where the κόσμος is conceived as a tree planted by God; see Heinemann following Leisegang, Philos Werke IV 1923, 148ff.

[1] Cp. 10.14f., 29f.; see pp. 380f., 385f.

[2] Bl.-D. § 466, 3 would read ἀρεῖ with lat., and corresponding to it καθαριεῖ (D).

[3] V. 2 could come from the source, for which participles with "every one who", often used antithetically, are characteristic (as they are of the Mandaean discourses): cp. 3.20; 4.13; 6.45; 8.34; 11.26; 18.37; I Jn. 2.29; 3.4, 6, 9f. etc. (copied by the Evangelist in 3.15f.; 6.37, 40; 17.2); cp. Schweizer 45n. 244, where Mand. parallels are cited; see below p. 537 n.1. Becker (109) regards v. 2 as an addition to the source.

[4] The discourse oscillates between literal and pictorial language. For even if Jesus is not *compared* with a vine, the picture of one certainly comes before the mind of the reader, so that he takes the concepts κλῆμα, καρπὸν φέρειν etc. as metaphors. Κλῆμα only here in the NT, but frequently in LXX; also frequent in Greek usage (see Br.). The object is placed in front, in the nom. absol., as it often is; cp. Bl.-D. § 466. On the treatment of the vine in the ancient world see Wetstein.

[5] Cp. R. Browning (see p. 70 n.2), (Browning's Poetical Works, 2nd series, London 1891, pp. 251f.):

"Therefore I say, to test man, the proofs shift,
Nor may he grasp that fact like other fact,
And straightway in his life acknowledge it,
As, say, the indubitable bliss of fire."
"Well, was truth safe for ever then? Not so. ..."

[6] Καρπὸν φέρειν signifies the evidence for vitality of faith (not however specifically missionary work: Schl.) and does not mean success or reward (Rom. 1.13; 6.21f.; Phil. 1.22). Similarly Mt. 3.8 (and par. s) and elsewhere. The metaphor of bearing fruit is

love above all belongs. The description of the life of faith as a growing, vital activity is the prime concern here. The first sentence says: the shoot that bears no fruit is cut off;[1] its connexion with the Revealer is done away with, i.e. it is cut off from life and abandoned to death (v. 6).[2] The second statement develops the idea. Nobody can rest content in the knowledge of having borne fruit; no-one can rely on what he has achieved. The imperative καρπὸν φέρειν does not demand a limited, demonstrable achievement; πλειόνα καρπὸν φέρειν is binding: "enough is never enough!" The idea finds expression in metaphorical language: God, as the vine-dresser, "purifies" the fruit-bearing tendril, that it may bear more fruit.[3] There is no reflection on the way in which God is to carry out the purification; the idea is simply: God takes care that the believer can never give himself over to rest; he continually demands something new from him, and continually gives him new strength.[4]

V. 3 seems to contradict the notion of existence in faith as a

---

infrequent in the Mandaean writings; but see Ginza 275, 33f.: "You are like the bad vine that bears no fruit"; Joh.-B. 204: "The vine that bears fruit ascends; that which bears nothing is cut off". Normally "fruit" or "fruits" is a metaphor here for the divinity or heavenly world (cp. Od. Sal. 10.2; 11.23). On the other hand in the Od. Sal. the picture is still full of life, cp. 11.1f.:

"My heart was cloven,
And its flower appeared;
And grace sprang up in it:
And it brought forth fruit to the Lord."

Further 11.12; 38.17. The Redeemer sows his fruits in the hearts of believers (17.13), they produce fruit through him (14.17), and bear their fruits (8.2; 11.1); their lips bear witness to the fruits (12.2; 16.2). Cp. also Act. Thom. 61 p. 178, 10.

[1] In the Mandaean literature, "to be cut off" is a frequent expression, used to denote separation from the world of life and light. The evil are to be "cut off", and the pious not; see previous note and Ginza 60.28; 87.37; 320.16ff.; 324.22; 328.8 etc. (Schweizer 161, note 119). Sometimes the phrase is: "cut off from the place of light", but often the word is used absolutely. Used in connexion with the picture of the vine, cp. Lit. 252f.: "and thy pure shoots are to thrive excellently ... they are to be united with thee, and not be cut off".

[2] This is not of course a reference to exclusion from the organised church. This is the opinion of Hirsch, who sees it as a sign of an ecclesiastical redaction, which he thinks he can reconstruct to a great extent in ch. 15.

[3] Καθαίρειν and ἀποτέμνειν both belong to the cultivation of the vine acc. to Philo agric. 10; somn. II 62.

[4] The purity is to be understood in terms of the vine imagery; it is the preparation for bearing fruit. There is no ref. here to moral or cultic purity; thus C. Herm. 13.15 is different; there the man who is freed from the τιμωροί (the powers of darkness) by the γνῶσις and filled with the divine δυνάμεις, is addressed as follows: καλῶς σπεύδεις λῦσαι τὸ σκῆνος (namely the σῶμα)· κεκαθαρμένος γάρ, or in the allegorical re-interpretation in terms of the mysteries, Philo somn. I 226: ἐπειδὴ γὰρ ἐκάθηρεν ἡμᾶς ὁ ἱερὸς λόγος τοῖς εἰς ἁγιστείαν εὐτρεπισθεῖσι περιρραντηρίοις (differently, Bousset, Kyrios 170, 2). Nor of course does καθαίρειν stand for the church's disciplinary action, however much it may be able to undertake the task of καθ. in certain circumstances. Loisy, rightly against this view: the καθ. takes place à travers les épreuves de la vie, par l'action de l'esprit et la pratique de la charité. Temple thinks onesidedly simply of the learning that comes through suffering.

continually directed movement, by giving us the comforting assurance: ἤδη ὑμεῖς καθαροί ἐστε. But the possibility of misunderstanding this is eliminated by saying: διὰ τὸν λόγον ὃν λελάληκα ὑμῖν.[1] The believer is not referred to himself or to the point he has already reached, to his "conversion" or his achievement. The reason for his purity lies outside himself; not of course, in ecclesiastical institutions or means of salvation, but in the Revealer's word and in that alone.[2] The community is pure and will always be pure, because, in the word, it possesses the power that is continually moving, life-creating.[3] But the word of comfort in v. 3 must stand beside the warning of v. 2, in order that no misunderstanding arises, such as would suppose that the relationship to God, the belonging to Jesus, were a goal to be reached—a goal which the believer ever more closely approaches through continuous movement. Rather the fact of belonging to him is itself the basis that creates the movement;[4] but only where the latter takes place is the former really present. No-one can set himself in motion, but he is to allow himself to be set in motion. The certainty of salvation is given to the believer: "you are already clean"; but in such a way that his attention is directed to the "Word". If, anxious about his faith, he were to look at himself, to see whether he were living in the movement demanded of him, precisely in that kind of reflection he would be standing still. If he is in true motion, then he has no time for reflection. Whoever remains in motion by looking at the word, has certainty.

V. 4: μείνατε ἐν ἐμοί,
κἀγὼ ἐν ὑμῖν.[5]

V. 2 and v. 3 had described the nature of the believer's association with the Revealer in the indicative mood; and yet the imperative was already implicit in it: "Bear fruit!" Now the discourse adopts the imperative mood: "Abide in me!"[6] The circumstances of the farewell

---

[1] V. 3 is certainly the Evangelist's work.

[2] See p. 533 n.4. Διά = "on account of", "by virtue of"; here comes very close to the instrumental διά with the gen.

[3] The perfect λελάλ., summing up the whole of Jesus' work, shows that the λόγος is not a single utterance, but the word of Jesus as a whole, as in 5.24; 8.31; 12.48 etc. Of course this λόγος includes the forgiveness of sins, but does not refer specifically to it (Zahn). See pp. 470f.

[4] Cp. Faulhaber 52: what is demanded is "a conscious acknowledgment that everyone, before and always and even without his own decision for him, is loved by Jesus".

[5] Thus far, v. 4 may come from the source; the explanatory καθώς-clause may be the factually relevant interpretation of the Evangelist, at the same time preparing us for the sentence in v. 5 that comes from the source. See also Becker 109. On the consecutive καί (in κἀγώ) = "then", see Bl.-D. § 442, 2.

[6] 'Εν denotes the union in which the "one who abides" allows himself to be determined by him in whom he "abides" (as in μείνατε ἐν ἐμοί) or, vice versa, in which he determines him (as in κἀγὼ ἐν ὑμῖν); see p. 321 n.1 and following note. In so far as the picture

form the background to this discourse; and in this setting the demand for *loyalty* makes itself heard, for this is what μείνατε implies.[1] But the meaning of loyalty varies, depending on who or what is its object. It is not a question here of loyal steadfastness to a cause, in the sense of standing up for something; for one cannot throw one's weight behind the validity of the revelation, nor could that result in a reciprocal relationship, such as is the case here. Moreover it is not a question of a relationship of loyalty between persons; the imagery of the relationship of the tendril to the vine shows us at once that the believer's relationship to the Revealer is not one of personal loyalty, in which what is given and what is demanded are always equally shared by both sides, even if the gift from one side had founded the relationship. Rather it is the relationship of faith; but faith is the unconditional decision to base oneself on the act of God, at the cost of giving up one's own ability. Μένειν is persistence in the life of faith; it is loyal steadfastness to the cause only in the sense of always allowing oneself to be encompassed, of allowing oneself to receive.[2] The loyalty that is demanded is not primarily a continued being *for*, but a being *from*; it is

---

of the vine is still in the hearer's mind, the ἐν in the first half means "on"; it must at the same time be taken as "in", in that it corresponds to κἀγὼ ἐν ὑμῖν.

[1] Μένειν ἐν is used in John, 1. of men, and denotes the abiding in that which a man has or is, the loyalty, which holds fast for the future what has been given in the past and grasped in the present (see p. 267 n.1.) Thus the believer "abides" in the Revealer, 15.4–7; I Jn. 2.6, 27f.; 3.6 (so also Ign. Eph. 10.3), or in God, as in I Jn. 4.13, 15f.; or, it can be said, he "abides" in the word (8.31), in ἀγάπη (15.9f.; I Jn. 4.16 (so also Od. Sal. 8.22); or in the light, I Jn. 2.10; the sinner, on the other hand, "abides" in death (I Jn. 3.14). Differently only in I Jn. 2.24, where the "abiding" in the Son and the Father is not a demand of loyalty, but a promise. 2. When spoken of the Revealer or of God, μένειν ἐν denotes the eternal validity of the divine act of salvation for the believer. Thus the Revealer "abides" in the believers, as in 15.4f.; I Jn. 3.24, or God "abides" in them (I Jn. 4.12f., 15f. (cp. 14.17 said of the πνεῦμα: παρ' ὑμῖν μένει καὶ ἐν ὑμῖν ἔσται). So too, it can be said that in the believers there "abides" the χρῖσμα (I Jn. 2.27), God's σπέρμα (I Jn. 3.9), the ζωὴ αἰώνιος (I Jn. 3.15), the ἀγάπη τ. θεοῦ (I Jn. 3.17; cp. Od. Sal. 14.6). Used of God's relation to Jesus, 14.10. The language used about the word "abiding" in the believer is different; for here (apart from I Jn. 2.14), the stress is not on the word as the blessing of salvation, but as command, and its "abiding" in the believer denotes his loyalty (5.38), as in 15.7; I Jn. 2.24. Thus in view of the difference between 1. and 2., where μένειν ἐν is used reciprocally in a sentence, as in 15.4f.; I Jn. 2.24; 3.24; 4.13, 15f., there is an element of paradox present. For the reciprocal relationship between believer and Redeemer cp. Od. Sal. 8.10ff.:

> "Keep my secret
> Ye who are kept by it;
> Keep my faith,
> Ye who are kept by it;
> And understand my knowledge,
> Ye who know me in truth.
> Love me with affection,
> Ye who love" (Cp. 28.3f.).

[2] Thus μένειν is not identical with the ὑπομονή that is demanded elsewhere in the NT, although the μένειν of faith certainly includes ὑπομονή.

not the holding of a position, but an allowing oneself to be held, corresponding to the relationship of the κλῆμα to the ἄμπελος. In this sense the relationship can be a reciprocal one; indeed it *must* be.[1]

How then do the two imperatives, "abide" and "bear fruit" (v. 2) relate to each other? The καθώς-clause, which is purely a comparison,[2] makes the abiding appear as the condition of fruitbearing, whereas according to v. 2 the fruitbearing is the condition for abiding in the vine. But it is in accordance with the reciprocity of the relationship that both can and must be said.[3] There is no abiding in him (no being held), without bearing fruit; nor is there any bearing fruit, without abiding in him (without allowing oneself to be held). What is demanded has already been given, i.e. the possibility of the future, which however has still to be grasped by the believer. This is why even the farewell is no reason for dismay; it makes quite clear that the significance of the past lies in the disclosure of the future.

It is therefore no more true that the reciprocal μένειν ἐν describes a mystical relationship of believers to Jesus,[4] than it is that the "abiding" in him is orthodoxy or ecclesiastical conservatism.[5] For the Revealer is not the mediator of a doctrine that can be received once for all; his word is not a dogma, nor a view of the world, but the free word of revelation that makes alive and that establishes anew one's whole existence. Μένειν means holding on loyally to the decision once taken, and one can hold on to it only by continually going through it again. So too the words κἀγὼ ἐν ὑμῖν do not say that Jesus continues to be present in the Christian church and culture in the sense of being present within the history of the world and the history of ideas; they speak of the promise that he will always remain the ground and origin of the possibility of life.

With v. 5 the discourse makes a new start:[6]

---

[1] See p. 535 n.1.

[2] The fact that it corresponds to οὕτως makes this clear; καθώς is different therefore from that in 13.34 etc.

[3] The apparent contradiction is no reason for making any literary-critical divisions, but is itself the point to be made.

[4] See pp. 381f. Differently Bousset, Kyrios 177ff. Because he fails to see that in John, Jesus has the character of Revealer, he finds it remarkable that John almost confines himself to a mysticism of Jesus, scarcely knowing one of God. Goodenough (167) actually tries to find Stoic pantheism in John 15.

[5] So too in Mand. Lit. 217, closely related as regards form: "Abide strong and steadfast in me, you who know me ... my friends ... do not change the discourse of my mouth. ..."

[6] The repetition of ἐγώ εἰμι is in accordance with the style of the revelation-discourse, see 6.35, 47, 51; 10.11, 14; see also p. 339 n.5. On Becker's only slightly deviating reconstruction of the source in vv. 5–7, see Becker 109.

ἐγώ εἰμι ἡ ἄμπελος,
ὑμεῖς τὰ κλήματα.
ὁ μένων ἐν ἐμοὶ κἀγὼ ἐν αὐτῷ.
οὗτος φέρει καρπὸν πολύν.

The idea of v. 4 is now formulated as a promise, but taken in the context of the whole, this admittedly is subordinated to the exhortation as the addition stresses again: ὅτι χωρὶς ἐμοῦ οὐ δύνασθε ποιεῖν οὐδέν.[1] Of course man can achieve all kinds of technical and moral success χωρὶς αὐτοῦ. But we are not concerned here "with the natural and worldly life and being, but with the fruits of the Gospel" (Luther). And in the face of that, everything else is an οὐδέν,—not in the sense of any kind of pessimism or quietism, but on the basis of the knowledge of man's real life: of a knowledge that contains within it the greatest power for action, because it does not need to think about achievement, and is thus freed from deadening anxiety; the knowledge that alone can give meaning to all worldly activity. Thus the words χωρὶς ἐμοῦ . . . οὐδέν correspond to χωρὶς αὐτοῦ ἐγένετο οὐδὲ ἕν: man is a created being, and owes his existence to the word of God.[2] He is not his own master, nor can he make any new beginning for himself. In faith man is brought back into the lost relationship of creation, in that he understands the words: χωρὶς αὐτοῦ οὐδέν. apart from me, nothing

V. 6: ἐὰν μή τις μένῃ ἐν ἐμοί,
ἐβλήθη ἔξω ὡς τὸ κλῆμα καὶ ἐξηράνθη.[3]

---

[1] The ὅτι-clause does not fit into the rhythm, and is an addition of the Evangelist's to his source-text. Ὁ μένων corresponds to the participles in 6.35, 47; 8.12; 11.25; 12.44, or to those with πᾶς (see p. 532 n.3). The continuation of the ἐγώ εἰμι clause with participles accords with the style of the revelation-discourse (Prov. 1.33; Ecclus. 24.21f.; Od. Sal. 33.12); a minatory participle often follows one of promise antithetically (cp. the construction of Prov. 2; also Prov. 8. 35f; prophetic discourse in Orig. c. Cels. VII 9 p. 161, 12ff. Koetsch.; Kerygma Petri in Clem. Al. Strom. VI 48, 2 p. 486, 9ff. St; Ps. Clem. Hom. 7 p. 15, 16ff. Lag. Very frequent in the Mand. literature, see p. 532 n.3 and Kundsin, Charakter 257f.). It goes without saying that a relative clause can take the place of a participle (4.14; I Jn. 2.5; Orig. c. Cels, as above; C. Herm. 4.4f., where the pattern is turned into a narrative), as can an ἐάν-clause (v. 6; 6.51; 7.17, 37; 8.31, 51; 12.47; I Jn. 1.6ff.; 4.12; Ps. Clem. Hom. 7 as above; Sib. 1, 130). These promises and threats can of course follow an ἐστίν-clause (I Jn. 1.5ff.; Ker. Petri, as above; after "Thou art", Od. Sal. 8.12f.) or an imperative, which calls for conversion (Ps. Clem. Hom. as above; Sib. 1,30; C. Herm. 4.4f.). Κἀγὼ ἐν ὑμῖν (which unlike v. 4 is a postscript here) develops the participle μένων incorrectly; καὶ ἐν ᾧ ἐγὼ μένω (Bl.-D. § 468, 3) would be more correct.

[2] On the tradition of χωρὶς αὐτοῦ οὐδέν, see on 1.3 p. 37 n.5; further K. Deichgräber, Rhein. Mus. 87 (1938), 6; Br. quotes Ael. Arist. Or. 37, 10: Ἀθηνᾶς ἡγουμένης οὐδὲν πώποτε ἀνθρώποις ἡμαρτήθη οὐδ' αὖ πράξουσί ποτε χρηστὸν ἄνευ τῆς Ἀθηνᾶς. The quotations in Str.-B. and Schl. only illustrate the linguistic expression, not the idea.

[3] Thus far the source, which the Evangelist has expanded by καὶ συνάγουσιν κτλ. (καὶ ἐξηρ. or ὡς τὸ κλῆμα could be his work too), under the influence of imagery such as Mal. 3.19 (4.1); Ezek. 15.4; Mt. 3.10, 12; 7.19; 13.30, 40. Lohmeyer (Urchristentum I 29)

Alongside the promise stands the threat:[1] whoever is not loyal, will be destroyed. This destruction consists in being separated from the trunk that transmits the life. Βληθῆναι ἔξω does not imply ecclesiastical excommunication, nor does the burning refer to the fires of hell.[2] The destruction is already a reality for the man who only belongs to the community outwardly, but is in fact οὐκ ἐξ ἡμῶν (I John 2.19). Just as μένειν and καρπὸν φέρειν are not two things that follow each other, nor are μὴ μένειν and ἔξω βληθῆναι.

After the threat comes a further promise (v. 7):[3] and it is the promise of the prayer that will be granted,[4] made to those who "abide" in the Revealer, i.e. who remain loyal to him; to those in whom "his words abide", i.e. for whom his words retain their authoritative validity.[5] In v. 4 Jesus promised them that he would abide in them, and that they therefore would bear much fruit. How does this promise relate *to the promise that their prayer will be heard?*[6] The prayer referred to is clearly a possibility that goes beyond the καρπὸν φέρειν. In prayer the believer, so to speak, steps out of the movement of his life, inasmuch as the prayer is not an action that satisfies the claim of the moment—which for the believer is the demand of love. But as he prays the believer also steps out of the context of his life, in that he is certain of the prayer's being granted, and he no longer has need to fear the future about which he prays, as of something that threatens to destroy him. He can be certain that the prayer will be heard, whatever he prays for; for what else could be the content of his petition, whatever form it may

---

maintains that John has here preserved motifs from the Baptist's discourse, taken from the Sayings-source [i.e. Q, Tr.]. The aorists ἐβλ. and ἐξηρ. could be taken gnomically (Bl.-D. § 333, 2), or as the expression of an inevitable result (Bl.-D. §333, 2; Raderm. 152.155; on this see examples in Br.), certainly not in the sense that the divine verdict has preceded the human conduct (Schl.). The variants μείνῃ (𝔎 pl) and αὐτό (𝔓 D pm, pedantic correction) are insignificant.

[1] See p. 537 n.1; the ἐάν-clause takes the place of a participle, see above.

[2] The discourse keeps to the picture; i.e. not as in Mk. 9.43, 47; Mt. 25.41 etc.

[3] V. 7 is the work of the Evangelist; to talk of the abiding of the word in the hearer is characteristic of him (see p. 266 n.4); the ἐάν-clause with its two halves does not fit into the rhythm. The idea is appropriate to the context, but has nothing to do with its imagery; the Evangelist also inserts it in v. 16; 14.13; 16.23f., 26; cp. I Jn. 3.21f.; 5.14f.

[4] John only uses ὃ ἐάν (B ὃ ἄν) here and in I Jn. 3.22; 5.15; III Jn. 5; elsewhere it is frequent, see Bl.-D. § 107, 371. The variant αἰτήσεσθε ℵ 𝔎 al is without significance.

[5] The μένειν of the ῥήματα in the believer (see p. 535 n.1) means the same as τὰς ἐντολὰς or τὸν λόγον τηρεῖν (vv. 10, 20). It does not add anything further to the believers' μένειν ἐν ἐμοί, but highlights the element of obedience that is contained in the idea of loyalty of faith.

[6] As v. 16 shows, the prayer that is certain of being heard is not identical with bearing fruit but is its result (just as, acc. to v. 5, Jesus' μένειν in those who are steadfast in faith results in their bearing fruit); but there is a sense in which it can also be included in the fruit-bearing, see on v. 8. The Mandaean Revealer also promises that prayer will be heard; see Mand. Lit. 66. 140; Ginza 260.6f.; 268.1ff.; 389.27ff.

take, than the Revealer's μένειν in him, and his μένειν in the Revealer?[1] The granting of such a prayer, which raises him out of the context of his human life in the world, is itself the documentation of his eschatological existence.[2]

Clearly in so far as prayer is a single occurrence that takes place within the context of the newly constituted life of the believer, it can be included within the καρπὸν φέρειν, and thus v. 8[3] can set everything that has been said till now under the final goal, and state that the Father's glorification[4] takes place in the believers' bearing fruit and in their being Jesus' disciples.[5] But the glorification of the Father is at the same time that of the Son, and therefore the last words of the passage bring us back to the beginning (13.13f.), and give a surprising answer to the pressing question raised by the farewell: his δοξασθῆναι, which seems to separate him from his own, in fact unites him with them; for through their faith he is glorified. But the final words of the passage return to the beginning in another way: for beside the phrase ἵνα καρπὸν πολὺν φέρητε, instead of καὶ ἐγὼ δοξασθῶ ἐν ὑμῖν (cp. 17.10) stand the words καὶ γένησθε ἐμοὶ μαθηταί. Thus the connexion with 13.35 is secured: the disciples' union with the separated Revealer is achieved in their discipleship; and after vv. 4–6, the radical meaning of μαθητὴς εἶναι has become clear as a reciprocal μένειν ἐν. Accordingly by the same means we arrive at the transition to the second part of the discourse; for as 13.35 had defined discipleship as the ἀλλήλους ἀγαπᾶν grounded in the love of Jesus, so now the phrase μένειν ἐν ἐμοί is interpreted as a μένειν ἐν τῇ ἀγάπῃ, and so the command of love is brought back to its origin.

ii. μείνατε ἐν τῇ ἀγάπῃ 15.9–17

Vv. 9–17 run parallel to vv. 1–8. V. 1 had begun with a reference to the Father, from whom Jesus derives his being for his own, and v. 29 does the same; there the imperative μείνατε proceeds from the existence of Jesus for

---

[1] This kind of prayer is acc. to I Jn. 5.14 an αἰτεῖσθαι κατὰ τὸ θέλημα αὐτοῦ, and this accords with its condition being the μένειν of the ῥήματα.

[2] See p. 408f.

[3] V. 8 comes from the Evangelist, for whom ἐν τούτῳ ... ἵνα is characteristic (see p. 525 n.1). Ἵνα explains ἐν τούτῳ (Bl.-D. § 394) which does not refer back to the preceding verse; if it did, the hearing of the prayer would be the glorification of the Father (not an impossible idea: see 14.13), and the purpose of the glorification would then be καρπ. φέρειν, and that is nonsensical.

[4] The aorist ἐδοξάσθη is either gnomically atemporal, or an expression of the certainty of what is to come, see p. 537 n.3.

[5] Even if γενήσεσθε (ℵ A E etc.) is a preferable reading to γένησθε (BDL al), καὶ γεν. is not a separate sentence, but belongs within the ἵνα-clause. On the use together of subjunctive, aorist, and future, see Mt. 5.25; Phil. 2.10f.; Eph. 6.3; Bl.-D. § 369, 3; Raderm. 178. Ἐμοί is adjectival, as in 13.35; L is wrong in reading μοι, as is D* with μου. γίνεσθαι means "to become" or "to be" in the sense of "to prove oneself", as in Mt. 5.45; I Cor. 14.20 etc., see Br.

his own (v. 4, which followed immediately upon v. 2 in the source), and the same is true in v. 9b. The phrase ἤδη ὑμεῖς καθαροί ἐστε in v. 3, which contains the indicative that necessarily accompanies the imperative, is paralleled in v. 14 by ὑμεῖς φίλοι μού ἐστε; and the motif χωρὶς ἐμοῦ οὐδέν in v. 4 is similarly paralleled by the words οὐχ ὑμεῖς ... ἀλλ' ἐγώ in v. 16; thereby the destiny of the man who is chosen is seen in terms of καρπὸν φέρειν, like that of the disciple in vv. 2ff. And finally, just as in v. 7 the highest point possible in the disciple's existence is seen to be the prayer that is assured of being heard, so too in v. 16b. Vv. 9–16 vary the theme of vv. 1–8, in the sense that μένειν ἐν ἐμοί is now expounded as μένειν ἐν τῇ ἀγάπῃ τῇ ἐμῇ, and the picture of the vine has disappeared in the process, apart from the metaphor καρπὸν φέρειν.[1]

V. 9: καθὼς ἠγάπησέν με ὁ πατήρ,
κἀγὼ ὑμᾶς ἠγάπησα.[2]
μείνατε ἐν τῇ ἀγάπῃ τῇ ἐμῇ,
(καθὼς ἐγὼ μένω αὐτοῦ ἐν τῇ ἀγάπῃ).[3]

The climax of the statement lies in the imperative μείνατε: the preceding sentence tells us the grounds on which it is based. It is grounded in the revelation-event, i.e. in Jesus' service, and this in turn is grounded in the love of God, of which Jesus is the recipient.[4] As always, this love is not personal affection, but the being of the disciple for his neighbour, that completely determines his own existence.[5] To abide in love, which is what is demanded of the disciple, means continuing in the love he has received, in the state of being loved; it means—and this has already been stated in v. 4—that his existence is to be based completely on the Revealer's service,[6] as the footwashing had already made clear symbolically.[7]

---

[1] In vv. 9f. the Evangelist is still clearly following the source, which spoke of ἀγάπη in the sense of the myth, as the love of God received by the Son and mediated through him. That this love forms the basis of the command of love, is the Evangelist's conception, and 13.34f. is his work. His style is unmistakeable in vv. 11–13, and can also be seen in vv. 14–17; and yet v. 14 and v. 16 (apart from the last ἵνα-clause) could have been taken from the source.

[2] The position of ὑμ. ἠγ., which varies in the MSS, is without significance.

[3] The second half of the second couplet in the source is to be taken from v. 10. The Evangelist has interpreted μείνατε as the τηρεῖν of the ἐντολαί, so as to be able to bring in the command of love. Acc. to Becker (110) vv. 9f. belong to the source.

[4] Cp. v. 1 and see p. 531f. Καθὼς has its substantiating sense, as in 13.34 (see p. 382 n.2), at least for the Evangelist; in the source it may have only been comparative, as in 12.50; 14.31; and v. 10. Κἀγώ κτλ. is of course a concluding clause, as in 17.18; 20.21.

[5] See pp. 164f., esp. 165 n.1, and see too Calvin, ad loc.

[6] See p. 536. Cp. Od. Sal. 8.23:
"Abide in the love of the Lord,
Ye beloved ones in the Beloved:
Ye who are kept, in Him that liveth:
Ye who are saved in Him that was saved."

[7] See pp. 468f.

To continue in the love they have received, however, is not to enjoy the peace of mind that comes from a self-sufficient assurance of salvation, nor is it indulgence in devotions or ecstasy. It is only real in that movement that consists in bearing fruit; it takes place in keeping the commandments (**v. 10**). As in v. 2 the condition of μένειν was the καρπὸν φέρειν, so here it is the τηρεῖν of the ἐντολαί;[1] thus vv. 9ff. expound v. 2. But before we are told more exactly what τηρ. τ. ἐντ. actually involves, the grounds for the command are stated once again, in terms of καθὼς ἐγὼ κτλ.[2] The believers' relationship to the Revealer is analogous to the relationship of the latter to the Father: it is indeed grounded in it. And this relationship is not a metaphysical communion of substance, nor is it a mystical relationship of love; what makes him the Revealer is the being of the Father for him, and his being for the Father is fulfilled in his obedient work as the Revealer.[3] So too the believers' obedience is to correspond to the service which they have received from him. And only then have they really received this service, when they "keep his commandments," which in fact is only one commandment,[4] the commandment of love (v. 12); i.e. when his being for them becomes the authoritative law of their life.[5]

If the τηρεῖν of the ἐντολαί basically draws the disciple's attention to what he already is in reality, the intention of the exhortation to τηρεῖν is not to make him *anxious* about himself; rather it is to make him *joyful*, and **v. 11** says explicitly that this is the purpose of the Revealer's teaching:[6] ἵνα ἡ χαρὰ ἡ ἐμὴ ἐν ὑμῖν ᾖ. His joy is to become *theirs*: i.e. in their association with him, the eschatological existence, which belongs to him of right, is given to them—as his prayer had already requested for them (17.13).[7] And the words (ἵνα) καὶ ἡ χαρὰ

---

[1] On τηρεῖν τ. ἐντ. see p. 301 n.5.

[2] Instead of ἐγώ, ℵ D lat read κἀγώ. And μου does not occur in B. Neither is of importance.

[3] See pp. 346 n.4; 382f. The perfect τετήρηκα, in the farewell situation, stands in contrast to the present τηρῶ in 8.55. Cp. 10.18; 12.50; 14.31.

[4] Just as the Father's ἐντολαί to Jesus (15.10) are in fact *one* ἐντολή (12.49f.), so Jesus can speak both of his ἐντολαί (15.10; 14.15, 21), and of his ἐντολή (13.34; 15.12). Cp. the interchange of sing. and plur. in I Jn. 2.3f. etc. and 2.7f.; esp. the interchange within I Jn. 3.22f. In the same way, corresponding to τηρεῖν τὸν λόγον (8.51f.; 14.23; 15.20; 17.6), is the phrase τοὺς λόγους τηρεῖν (14.24) or τὰ ῥήματα φυλάσσειν (12.47). Cp. in general the interchange of λόγος (8.31, 43; 12.48; 17.14 etc.) with ῥήματα (3.34; 6.63; 17.8 etc.). On ἐντολή in the NT see Goguel L'Eglise primitive 508f.

[5] See p. 526, and Faulhaber 54.

[6] V. 11 is the Evangelist's work. On ταῦτα λελ. ἵνα see p. 335 n.5 ταῦτα refers to what has gone before, as always in this manner of speech, and ἵνα is final, i.e. it states the purpose of λαλεῖν as in 5.34; 16.1, 4, 33; 17.13; I Jn. 2.1; 5.13.

[7] See on 17.13 pp. 505ff., and Gulin II 38. 59f. Cp. Od. Sal. 8.1f.:

"Let your love be multiplied from the heart, even unto the lips,
to bring forth as fruit to the Lord holy joy." (Bultmann's tr.).

ὑμῶν πληρωθῇ make the same point that was made there, that everything which they had previously had from him was only preparatory, a beginning, that still had to come to fruition—and this precisely through his farewell from them. What is already reality in him, is to become reality in them; this is the meaning of his exhortation to μένειν, to τηρεῖν of the ἐντολαί.

V. 12[1] now states the contents of the ἐντολαί, which appear in the last analysis as *one* ἐντολή;[2] it is the ἀλλήλους ἀγαπᾶν, i.e. that ἐντολή, which Jesus had already brought them at the beginning of the discourse (13.34) as his last will and testament; and again, as there, the ground of the command is given in the καθὼς κτλ. The radical nature of the command of love as the unconditional being for one's neighbour is brought out in **v. 13** by stating the highest possibility love can reach: the giving up of one's life[3] for one's friends.[4] This highest possibility is however to be characteristic of the ἀλλήλους ἀγαπᾶν demanded of the disciple; for he is to love καθὼς ἠγάπησα ὑμᾶς, i.e. his love is to have its ground and its norm in the love received from Jesus.[5] There is no express statement that Jesus' love consists in his giving up his life; but in the context it is obvious,[6] and it is indicated by the fact that in what follows Jesus addresses his disciples as his φίλοι. If v. 13 is read in the light of v. 12, it describes quite generally, and as a principle, the highest possibility of the love Jesus demands; but it is illumined subsequently by the words of v. 14, in which Jesus calls the disciples his friends, and must therefore be understood at the same time as a description of καθὼς ἠγάπησα ὑμᾶς.[7]

---

[1] Verses 12f. come from the Evangelist. V. 12 itself is a definition typical of his work (p. 48 n.3), and closely related to it is the form of v. 13, to which III Jn. 4 is an exact parallel; in both cases the ἤ before the ἵνα is missing, see Bl.-D. § 394.

[2] See p. 541 n.4.

[3] Τιθέναι τ. ψυχ. can hardly just mean: to stake one's life (see p. 370 n.5), although this comes to mean the same, taking the context as a whole. The absence of τις in ℵ* D*, which is allowed in Bl.-D. § 394, can only be a correction.

[4] That to lay down one's life for one's *enemies* (Rom. 5.6ff.) would be a still greater act of love, is left on one side in this context, which is only concerned with depicting the ἀλλήλ. ἀγ. of those who are bound together as friends. In this context, the meaning of v. 13 is as follows: no-one shows his friends greater love than the man who lays down his life for them. Just as the pre- and non-Christian world is acquainted with the command of love (see p. 526f.), so it is too with its highest possibility: death forthe sake of others (e.g. Tyrt. 6.1ff.; Diehl, Anthol. Lyr. Gr. I 9f.). The only thing that is specifically Christian is the grounding of the command, and, in line with this, its realisation (see pp. 527f.).

[5] Gulin 58f. rightly says that there is also here a veiled summons to the discipleship that involves suffering.

[6] The words ὑπὲρ αὐτῶν in 17.19 show it to be a presupposition of the prayer. It is stated expressly in I Jn. 3.16.

[7] Thus v. 13 contains within itself a double meaning (but no ambiguity in the sense of 2.19 etc., see p. 127 n.1); the first one holds good in connection with the preceding context, and the second in connection with what comes after. Yet v. 13 does not have an "independent significance", nor is it foreign to the context of the whole (Dibelius, Festg. für Deissmann 168ff., or Botschaft und Geschichte I 1953, 204–220). But it is certainly

V. 13 then already tells us indirectly that the disciples are Jesus' friends; and this is presupposed in **v. 14**, where it says: ὑμεῖς φίλοι μού ἐστε, ἐὰν κτλ. It is not a question of their still having to *become* his friends by fulfilling his commands; they *are* his friends already, as v. 15 states; the phrase ἐὰν κτλ. specifies the condition whereby what they already are can be fully realised in them. Thus ἐὰν is used in the same way as in v. 10, and the idea corresponds to v. 2, just as the phrase ὑμεῖς φίλοι μού ἐστε corresponds to ἤδη ὑμεῖς καθαροί ἐστε in v. 3. The only new element is that the believers' union with the Revealer, which is the basis of their life, and which in v. 2 was described in terms of the connexion of the shoot to the vine and in v. 10 as the abiding in his love, is depicted here in terms of *friendship*.[1] With the help of this concept, vv. 15f. develop in greater detail what the union with the Revealer means for the disciples; and then against this background the commandment of v. 12 is taken up again by way of conclusion in v. 17.

The φίλος concept serves to clarify the meaning of the union with Jesus, in so far as he is contrasted with the δοῦλος (**v. 15**). The "friend" therefore is the man who is free, and his freedom is understood as in 8.31–36, that is to say, as the eschatological gift resulting from the revelation.[2] In 8.32 this gift was seen in terms of knowledge of the "truth," and the same is the case here; it is attributed to the fact that Jesus has made known to his disciples everything that he has heard in the Father's presence, i.e. that he has brought them the "truth," that he has revealed the Father.[3] Just as in 8.34 it was the slave of sin who was contrasted with the free man, so here it is the δοῦλος, "who does not know what his master does"; i.e. who does not understand the master, who lives in darkness, and thus in continual anxiety. The two together form a whole, just as one can also say the reverse, that the

---

possible that it picks up a current maxim (or hints at one), which spoke of love in general human terms.

[1] The reason why the concept φίλοι is brought in, where one might expect ἀγαπητοί, could be that the former was used in v. 13 to describe love's highest possibility (on the basis of a maxim? see previous note). But it is more probable that the wording of v. 13 has been chosen because the ideas of vv. 14f. were already present in the Evangelist's mind. In that case it will have been the source that has suggested the wording, as v. 14 may well come from there (see p. 540 n.1), see below p. 544 n.7. One cannot believe that the use of the title φίλος is due to polemic against the primitive Christian and Pauline view of Christ as the κύριος, and the believers as his δοῦλοι (Bousset, Kyrios 155).

[2] On freedom see pp. 436ff.

[3] On οὐκ οἶδεν see on p. 467 n.2. On truth see pp. 434ff. On πάντα ἃ ἤκουσα κτλ. see pp. 251; 253 n.4. On ἐγνώρισα see 17.26 (p. 521); there the obj. is the Father's ὄνομα, which in fact means the same as πάντα ἅ ἤκουσα; cp. 17.6, 26 with 17.8,14. Πάντα does not contradict 16.12, thereby coming under suspicion of being a gloss (Br.); for v. 15 is spoken *sub specie* of the work Jesus accomplished, the completion of which through the Spirit is not thought of as the filling in of gaps; see on 16.12.

"friend" is freed, and being free knows God and lives in the light.[1] The disciples are no longer δοῦλοι,[2] thanks to the Revealer's γνωρίζειν, but free men and friends.[3]

V. 16 οὐχ ὑμεῖς με ἐξελέξασθε,
ἀλλ' ἐγὼ ἐξελαξάμην ὑμᾶς·
καὶ ἔθηκα ὑμᾶς ἵνα ὑμεῖς ὑπάγητε
καὶ καρπὸν φέρητε
καὶ ὁ καρπὸς ὑμῶν μένῃ.[4]

At this point, however, the relation of friendship that exists between the Revealer and the disciples is defined in a way that differentiates it from any such relationship in the Greek or modern sense. The latter is a reciprocal relationship, in which each partner stands fundamentally on the same footing as the other, and in which each seeks the friendship of the other;[5] but while the friendship between Jesus and his own is certainly reciprocal, there is no equality in it. If they are Jesus' friends, this is not because they had sought his friendship, nor does Jesus call himself their friend, but only them his friends. "*You have not chosen me, but I have chosen you.*" The use of the word ἐκλέγεσθαι points to the fact that, incapable as they are of doing anything without him, they could not even seek his friendship on the basis of their own importance; for what is it, out of which they have been chosen?[6] It is the κόσμος, in which man is a captive, and out of which only the revelation can free him and make him capable of becoming a φίλος.[7]

---

[1] It means the same to say that the revelation leads into the παρρησία, cp. I Jn. 3.21; 5.14.

[2] Οὐκέτι refers to the fact that as disciples they no longer belong to the world; it does not refer back to a previous stage of their discipleship, e.g. to 13.16; there, as in 15.20, we are simply concerned with a parabolic saying.

[3] The contrast between φίλοι (of God) and δοῦλοι also occurs in Philo: migr. Abr. 45; sobr. 55; see Br. and E. Peterson, Zeitschr. für Kirchengesch. NF 5 (1913) 179. See also Paeslack op. cit. (see on p. 397 n.2), 94-96, 142, and Warnach, Agape 410f. The attributes φιλοκαῖσαρ, φιλοσέβαστος etc. are no analogy, as Deissmann, Licht vom Osten 4th. ed. maintains (324). Further, see n.7.

[4] Apart from the last ἵνα-clause, v. 16 could have been taken from the source. If it formed the end of the discourse there, the extra half couplet is in place, see pp. 76 n.4; 166 n.2; 271 n.1; 356 n.2. Admittedly the Evangelist could have edited the text, and inserted καὶ ἔθηκα ὑμ. or ὑπάγητε καί. Becker (110f.) assigns vv. 14–16, with some cuts, to the source.

[5] See pp. 535f.

[6] 'Εκλέγεσθαι (as in 6.70; 13.18) does not imply any contrast with those who have not been chosen, but rather draws attention to the κόσμος, see v. 19. In Ginza 179, 25ff. the messenger says: "I have separated you from the peoples and generations, I will establish you for the truth in love. ..." In Mand. Lit. 75 he is addressed with the words: "Thou hast chosen us out, and raised us from the world of hatred, of jealousy and discord. ..."

[7] It is possible that the notion of election can be found in the concept φίλος itself. In the Greek world, the φίλος of the Gods is originally the man who has been sanctified

This means, however, that the reciprocity of the relationship created by his choosing them is of a different sort from that of a purely human friendship. Their relationship to him cannot be a direct response to his amicable love, which would mean that he could be called their friend.[1] They can respond to his friendship only indirectly; how, is stated in the words that follow: "*And I have appointed you, that you go forth and bear fruit, and that your fruit abide.*"[2] Thus their response to his love consists in the demonstration of the vitality of their faith, and the metaphor of bearing fruit is picked up again to make the point. The context itself suggests that the "bearing of fruit" takes place in the ἀλλήλους ἀγαπᾶν; and yet it would be wrong to limit it to that; the

---

or consecrated by a god (e.g. the herald), therefore in some sense he is one who has been chosen out. Cp. Fr. Pfister (Pauly-Wissowa, Realenc. der klass. Altertumswissensch. XI 2127f.), who asks whether φίλος belongs to the pronominal root σφ; the basic meaning would then be: "belonging to, peculiar to oneself, one's own". On the further usage of φίλος θεοῦ (or θεῷ) see Peterson op. cit. 161ff. (see p. 544 n.3). The concept is thought of from a moral standpoint in the Socratic-Platonic and Stoic schools: the σώφρων or the σόφος is the friend of God (disputed by Aristotle and Epicurus). "Friend of God" is a title of distinction elsewhere in the history of religion: cp. Fr. Pfister, Blätter zur bayr. Volkskunde 11 (1927), 37; G.v.d. Leeuw, Phänomenologie der Rel. 453ff. Oriental usage in Peterson op. cit.; on φίλος as a title of honour for court officials, see Deissmann, Bibelst. 195f.; L.v.O. 324. The element of election is clear in the OT designation of Abraham as the friend of God (Ex. 33.11; Is. 41.8; II Chron. 22.7; cp. Daniel 3). Abraham retains this title in Judaism (Peterson op. cit.; Dibelius in Meyer's commentary on Jas. 2.23; Knopf in the supplement to the Hdb. z. NT, on I Clem. 10.1), and from there Christendom and Islam take it over. Judaism broadens the use of the term to include Moses, other men of piety, and Israel (Wis. 7.27; Str.-B. II 564f.; Schl. on v. 15); so too Philo calls Abraham and Moses the friends of God, and extends the term to the prophets. He understands the title in the Greek sense, just as for him, in the last analysis, every σόφος is the friend of God (Peterson op. cit.). Christendom did not immediately take over the expanded use of the term. Apart from Jn. 15.14f. the Christians only appear as friends of Jesus in Lk. 12.4; on the other hand they are called friends among themselves (Acts 27.3; III Jn. 15). The title is also found in this sense in pagan θίασοι (Peterson op. cit., G. P. Wetter, Der Sohn Gottes 63, 2); it did not establish itself in Christendom (Harnack, Mission und Ausbr. 3rd. ed. I 405f.), but it was a favourite in Gnostic circles. Among the Mandaeans the pious were very often denoted the friends of the Revealer (also of [the name] of the Kusta); and here the "friends" are those to whom the Revealer "comes" (Mand. Lit. 108.139.205), and to whom he brings the revelation or teaching (Mand. Lit. 79.193; Joh.-B. 92, 3; 167, 23ff.; 221, 17; Ginza 333, 27ff., quoted with ref. to 3.35, p. 165). Similarly among the Manichaeans (Peterson op. cit.). Among the Christian Alexandrians the title "friend of God' plays an important role in regard to martyrs and ascetics, but above all in the mystical sense, which later again gives it importance in mediaeval mysticism.

[1] This inversion, that God is the friend of the virtuous man, is found in Greek usage; so too, characteristically modified, in mysticism and pietism, see Peterson op. cit.

[2] On τιθέναι = "to institute to", "to appoint to", cp. I Cor. 12.18, 28; II Tim. 1.11; Acts 20.28; also in this sense in Greek usage (with double acc.), see Br. Cp. also the Rabbinic העמיד תלמידים (to make disciples), Str.-B. II 341 on Jn. 4.1. That this τιθ. refers back to that in v. 13 (Hosk.) would be too ingenious. Ὑπάγειν does not mean "going out" (on missionary journeys: Lk. 10.3), but is a pleonasm often found in both Greek and Semitic usage; see Colwell 32 and Black 91.—Lagr. regards the sentence as the disciples' commission to be apostles, and finds in it la clef de tout ce discours.

attitude demanded of the disciples in 15.18–16.4a vis-à-vis the world is also part of "bearing fruit."[1] The exhortation conceals a promise: "*and that your fruit abide*," i.e. the promise is none other than that the believer's new life shall last for eternity.[2]

But the promise does not end there:[3] it also includes, as in v. 7, the promise of the gift to the disciples of the prayer that they can be sure will be granted. Can anything further be promised, beyond eternity of life? In the last analysis, no; but the assurance of being heard, so important for the Evangelist,[4] is the sign for the believer that he stands in the eternity of life.[5] He stands in life, in so far as he stands in faith in the Redeemer; thus the access of prayer to God also remains mediated by the Redeemer. The believer prays "in the name" of Jesus; that is—and here v. 16 goes beyond v. 7[6]—he prays in the confession of faith in Jesus, as it were on his authority.[7] And so χωρὶς ἐμοῦ οὐδέν embraces prayer as well.

V. 17 is a summary statement[8] that marks the end of the section vv. 9–17 and also concludes the whole discourse; and the repetition of the ἀλλήλ. ἀγ. from 13.34f.; 15.12, stressing that this is Jesus' own command, serves to complete the circle.

The two themes μένειν ἐν ἐμοί (vv. 1–8) and μένειν ἐν τῇ ἀγάπῃ τῇ ἐμῇ (vv. 9–17) together form a whole. Μένειν ἐν ἐμοί is the demand for loyalty of faith from the believer; it includes within it, by implication, the commandment ἀγαπᾶν ἀλλήλους, in so far as it is also a summons to καρπὸν φέρειν. The demand μένειν ἐν τῇ ἀγάπῃ comprises in the first place the commandment of love, and yet it is inseparable from the summons to faith. The discourse as a whole, therefore, like both its parts, deals with *faith and love as a unity*. The reason for the emphasis placed on this unity, and for the interweaving of the summons to faith

---

[1] Cp. I Jn. 3.23 where πιστεύειν and ἀγαπ. ἀλλ. are summarised as the content of the ἐντολή.

[2] Μένειν refers here to the continuation of what is present in the future, as in 6.27; 12.34; I Jn. 2.17. Of course the words εἰς ζωὴν αἰών. could well have been added in 15.16, as in 6.27; see p. 222 n.7, and on that Herm. vis. II 3, 2.

[3] Again a new ἵνα-clause is appended, not co-ordinated with the first, but subordinated to it, as in 13.34; 17.21, 23, 24; it is an addition to the source by the Evangelist. The reading αἰτῆτε (B L Φ) instead of αἰτήσητε makes no difference as to meaning.

[4] See p. 538 n.3.

[5] See p. 538. Prayer also appears in Epict. diss. II 27, 29 as a characteristic of friendship with God: εἰς τὸν οὐρανὸν ἀναβλέπειν ὡς φίλον θεοῦ. So too, in Philo, its sign is παρρησία (Peterson op. cit. 170, 2.178).

[6] So also 14.13; 16.24, 26.

[7] See p. 270 n.2.

[8] Ταῦτα ἐντ. … ἵνα appears to be parallel to ταῦτα λελάληκα ἵνα (see pp. 335 n.5; 541 n.6). And yet ταῦτα cannot refer here to what has gone before, but is explained by the following ἵνα (as in vv. 12 and 13); the object of ἐντέλλ. can only be ἀγαπᾶν. V. 17 therefore picks up v. 12 again in conclusion (Htm., Lagr.).

and the summons to love in this way, is that life as we experience it seems to indicate a temporal succession in the order of faith and love, against which the real unity of the two must be maintained. The hearing of the word and the doing of it, the decision of faith for the word that has been heard and the decision of love for the brother's claim, these we experience in a relation of temporal succession. But what is their real relation to each other? It would be a misunderstanding to hold that it is really a succession, to regard the word as an introduction to action, and the action as the application of what has been heard.

According to John 15 faith and love are, in fact, a unity. Faith is not authentic unless it is steadfast; i.e. unless it is the kind of faith that enables a man to decide beforehand the way all future action is to go. The fact that the Word assures faith of the love of God manifest in Jesus, and that this love is only received when it becomes the means whereby a man is himself freed to love, means that the Word is only properly heard when the believer loves *in that he is a believer.*[1] Thus to hear in faith is to anticipate the future, because it is actually later in the temporal sequence that the brother makes his claim on the believer's love. In his decision of faith the believer anticipates the concrete decisions called for by the claims of his brother in everyday life. To summarise, therefore, faith is at once the resolute decision for the word that has been heard, and the resoluteness that embraces all possible future decisions. Thus faith cannot be perceived as an isolated phenomenon, either by the believer himself, or by anybody else who looks on from outside. It is real only in the resoluteness that sustains the whole of life; and because that resoluteness is grounded in the believer's decision for the Word, his faith is sure of itself only in the sense that it holds before him the reason for his decision, i.e. it keeps him looking at the Word.[2] Μένειν ἐν ἐμοί is therefore μένειν ἐν τῇ ἀγάπῃ τῇ ἐμῇ. That is the last will and testament of the departing Revealer, in virtue of which believers remain united with him.

b) The Community in the World: 15.18–16.11

15.18–16.11 are clearly a unity in themselves. The theme is the community in the world, and it is dealt with in two sections: 1. The world's hatred, 15.8–16.4a; 2. The judgement of the world 16.4b–11. At the base of it lies a piece of the "revelation-discourses", which had three sections: 1. The parallelism of the community's fate with that of the Revealer: just as he encountered the world's hatred, so will they (15.18–20); 2. The world's sin: its hatred of the Revealer is hatred of the Father (15.21–25); 3. The

---

[1] Cp. F. K. Schumann, Um Kirche und Lehre 1936, 208.
[2] See pp. 526f., 534f.

demonstration of the world's sin: the Paraclete will convict it of sin (15.26–16.11). The Evangelist has altered this arrangement by interpreting the first part of the third section, which referred the μαρτυρεῖν to the Paraclete's indictment, of the community's preaching, and by using it to link the prophecy of the world's hatred with that of the community's preaching. He does not pick up again the motif of the source's third section until 16.8 (following an extended introduction: 16.4b–8), after he has dealt more factually with the motif of the world's hatred (treated in a general way in 15.18–21 or –25) and related it to the historical circumstances of the community (16.1–4a). This results in 15.18–16.4a forming a complete section in itself, with the theme of the world's hatred of the community. The source's second motif, which attributes this hatred to hatred against the Father, is subordinated to this theme, and we are also told the reason for the world's hatred of the community: it is the community's preaching. The text of the source, which the Evangelist has frequently expanded with his own comments, cannot always be recognised with complete certainty, but is clearly visible in outline.[1]

1) *The World's Hatred:* 15.18–16.4a

i. *Revealer and Community share the same Destiny*: 15.18–20

V. 18: εἰ ὁ κόσμος ὑμᾶς μισεῖ,
γινώσκετε ὅτι ἐμὲ πρῶτον ὑμῶν μεμίσηκεν.[2]

V. 19: εἰ ἐκ τοῦ κόσμου ἦτε,
ὁ κόσμος ἂν τὸ ἴδιον ἐφίλει . . .[3]

V. 20: εἰ ἐμὲ ἐδίωξαν
καὶ ὑμᾶς διώξουσιν.
εἰ τὸν λόγον μου ἐτήρησαν,
καὶ τὸν ὑμέτερον τηρήσουσιν.

The Evangelist adds his own comment in v. 19b in order to relate this section to what has gone before: the world's hatred is its reaction to the election of the φίλοι (v. 16), which raises them up from the world.[4] If the φίλοι experience this hatred, it should not astonish them;[5]

---

[1] This textual analysis will be substantiated in what follows.

[2] Γινώσκετε ὅτι could be one the Evangelist's additions; cp. 5.32; 12.50 (see pp. 263 n.2; 346 n.4). He is fond of this kind of expression; cp. I Jn. 2.29 (Festg. Ad. Jül. 142) and the frequent οἴδαμεν ὅτι in I John (ebenda 146).

[3] Vv. 19b, 20a are additions of the Evangelist's; on ὅτι ... διὰ τοῦτο see 8.47 and p. 92 n.2 ; on references back see p. 348 n.4; μνημον. as in 16.4. One may well ask whether the similarity of subject-matter that exists between v. 20bc (εἰ ἐμὲ κτλ) and Mt. 10.25 has led to the introduction of v. 20a, which is a variant of Mt. 10.24; this would not of course imply that John was dependent on Matt; cp. Noack 96–98. Becker (111) assigns vv. 18f., with some exceptions, to the source, but not v. 20.

[4] See p. 544 n.6 and also p. 527.

[5] This is the sense of v. 18, more clearly formulated in I Jn. 3.13: μὴ θαυμάζετε ... εἰ μισεῖ ὑμᾶς ὁ κόσμος.

for, as they must remind themselves,[1] it is the result of the fact that they belong to Jesus and therefore must themselves experience what he went through before them (v. 18b).[2] This reference to his destiny is not of course intended for the sake of *solamen miseris socios habuisse malorum*, but to teach them that their essential union with him involves their sharing an identical destiny. Thus the φίλοι are told that they must regard their destiny as unavoidable: just as he is the object of the world's hatred, because he no longer belongs to it (8.23) but rather stands over against it, so the same is true of them: the world will hate them because they no longer belong to it (17.14).

This is stated indirectly in v. 19a, and the Evangelist expresses it outright in his comment in v. 19b. The reference to the earlier saying of Jesus must also serve to confirm it (v. 20a).[3] This maxim does not itself express the idea that identity of destiny results from such an essential union, but in this context it must be understood like that. V. 20bc re-phrases the basic conception: just as persecution overtook the Revealer, so it will the φίλοι; and to the extent that he found faith,[4] they too will find it—but that means, they too will encounter the world's unbelief. Διώκειν does not so much intensify the concept of μισεῖν, but rather gives it a special direction; for the world's hatred could just as well manifest itself in enticement or seduction (cp. 6.15; 7.3). This hatred is not just a psychic phenomenon, but the world's fundamental attitude to the revelation, an attitude that operates in every modus of its life. But persecution is clearly, so to speak, the normal modus of the hatred, in which it can be observed without any disguise. Essentially however this hatred—and this is why at the end unbelief is mentioned—is rejection of the revelation.

To be told that their essential union with the Revealer involves sharing his destiny is both a comfort to the φίλοι, a confirmation that they really are φίλοι, and also a warning as to what it means, to be a "friend" of Jesus: a warning of what they must be prepared for.[5]

---

[1] Whether γινώσκετε is indicat., or, more probably, imperative, is of no importance.

[2] Πρῶτον = πρότερον Bl.-D. § 62. Ὑμῶν, which does not occur in ℵ D a b al, is regarded by Zn. as an early addition, but retained by Merx on the grounds of the uniform Syriac tradition.

[3] The ref. is without doubt to 13.16. Acc. to Syr[s] only μνημ. ὅτι εἶπον ὑμῖν should be read, and Merx regards this as right, because τ. λογ. is a refined use of Greek. D reads τοὺς λόγους οὕς, ℵ 579 τὸν λόγον ὅν.

[4] Μου is not itself stressed, but it becomes important through the contrast with ὑμέτ., see Bl.-D. § 284, 1. On τ. λόγον τηρεῖν see p. 301 n.5.

[5] Ign. Rom. 3.3: οὐ πεισμονῆς τὸ ἔργον, ἀλλὰ μεγέθους ἐστὶν ὁ Χριστιανισμός, ὅταν μισεῖται ὑπὸ κόσμου. The Mandaean writings also contain frequent talk of the persecutions which the pious have to endure in the world, e.g. Ginza 296, 18f. (the "great life" speaks to Anōš, the messenger): "Instruct the Nasoreans, Mandaeans and elected ones whom Thou hast chosen from the world, who are persecuted in the name of the life in the

ii. *The Sin of the World:* 15.21–25

V. 21, with which the Evangelist moves on to the next section of the source, summarises the basic conception of the previous passage: "All that[1] they will do to you, on account of my name"—i.e. "because you confess me, are my friends,"[2] and then it goes on to add the comment: "because they do not know him who sent me." The comment adds no new subject-matter to the words διὰ τὸ ὄνομά μου; for his ὄνομα is nothing other than the challenge he presents as the Revealer whom God has sent. To acknowledge the Father would be to acknowledge him also, his name; to persecute his friends on account of his ὄνομα is not to know the Father.[3] Thus the world's reaction is defined as unbelief, and unbelief—in which a man blockades himself against the Father—is at once shown to be sin. This brings us to the transition to what follows; for at this point it will be made explicit that the world's behaviour is sin.

V. 22: εἰ μὴ ἦλθον καὶ ἐλάλησα αὐτοῖς,
ἁμαρτίαν οὐκ εἴχοσαν.
νῦν δὲ πρόφασιν οὐκ ἔχουσιν
περὶ τῆς ἁμαρτίας αὐτῶν.[4]

V. 24: εἰ τὰ ἔργα μὴ ἐποίησα ἐν αὐτοῖς
[ἃ οὐδεὶς ἄλλος ἐποίησεν][5]

Tibil (the earthly world)". Further Ginza 383, 18ff., 404, 30ff.; Mand. Lit. 160, 208; Joh.-B. 64, 11ff. etc. The messenger laments because of the persecution of his own Joh.-B. 236, 20ff.; 237, 2ff.; the soul laments Ginza 474, 9ff.; Mand. Lit. 132, 213 and prays because of the persecutions Mand. Lit. 108f. The soul is comforted Ginza 127, 8ff.; 260, 2ff.; 268, 4ff., or exhorted to withstand the persecutions Ginza 22, 25ff.; Mand. Lit. 195. Of course such analogies could be the result of the analogous historical situation of the communities. But there is also a kinship in subject-matter that goes beyond that, in that both here and there persecution and the world's enmity are regarded as resulting from the opposition between God (or the Revealer) and the world. Similarly, in the Mandaean writings too, the messenger is himself the one "whom all the worlds persecuted" (Mand. Lit. 193, see p. 421; see also Jonas, Gnosis I 109ff.). So too the Od. Sal. contain the persecution-motif: 5.4; 23.20; 28.8ff.; 42.5, 7; in the Act. Thom. it finds expression in the legend (see Bornkamm Myth. und Leg.). For ridicule of the revelation by the world, cp. C. Herm 1, 29; 9, 4b; Ascl. I 12a; III 21 (Scott p. 308, 15f.; 334, 14), and in the Hermet. Fragm. in Scott 432, 20ff.

[1] Ταῦτα πάντα (πάντα om D 579 pc) embraces both the μισεῖν and διώκειν of vv. 18–20.

[2] Cp. Mk. 13.13 and par. s; Polyc. Phl. 8, 2 and esp. I Pet. 4. 16.

[3] Cp. the accusations in 5.37; 7.28; 8.19, 54f.

[4] V. 23 breaks the rhythm, both formally and conceptually. It could be part of the source, but if so, it must have occupied a different place, perhaps after v. 24; in which case, the Evangelist, who brought it forward, must have cut out the other half of the verse that went with it. The verse could however be the Evangelist's own work, in line with such verses as 5.23b; 12.44; 14.9b; I Jn. 2.23. Acc. to Becker (111f.) v. 22 belongs to the source, but not vv. 23–25.

[5] This phrase may have been added by the Evangelist.

ἁμαρτίαν οὐκ εἴχοσαν.
νῦν δὲ καὶ ἑωράκασιν καὶ μεμισήκασιν
καὶ ἐμὲ καὶ τὸν πατέρα μου.

What the world does is sin, because it turns itself against Jesus, who has shown himself to be the Revealer by his words and his actions.[1] If there were no revelation, then there would no be sin either, in the decisive sense of the term.[2] But as it is, there is no longer any excuse.[3] The verdict: "They are sinners," is expressed in v. 22 by the words πρόφασιν οὐκ ἔχουσιν, and in v. 24 by ἑωράκασιν καὶ μεμισήκασιν;[4] and through the declaration that to hate Jesus is also to hate the Father, it is made clear that this kind of hatred, where there is the possibility of sight, is itself sin. The Evangelist has inserted **v. 23** to prepare us for this understanding of v. 24. For what else would sin be, if not hatred directed against God? But the unbelief that rejects Jesus is precisely this; for God is present in him.[5] Sin therefore is not primarily immoral behaviour; it does not consist in any particular action, but is unbelief, and it will be defined as such explicitly in 16.8.

The Evangelist by way of comment in **v. 25**,[6] adds the observation that this kind of hatred fulfils the prophecy he quotes.[7] Manifestly the emphasis that the prophecy lays on the groundlessness[8] of this hatred provides the Evangelist with confirmation of the guilt that attaches to it.

iii. *The Disciples' Task in the Face of the World's Hatred:* 15.26–16.4a

In the source, the train of thought culminated in the demonstration of the world's sin,[9] and the allusion to the coming Paraclete served

---

[1] On the ἔργα of Jesus see pp. 265f.; 331 n.3; 362; 387ff. Jesus' words and his actions are a unity, only split up into synon. parallels for rhetorical reasons; thus at the end it is sufficient simply to say ἑωρ., to which syr[s] pedantically adds "my works" (which is of course formally correct); but the seeing of the works includes the hearing of the words. On unbelieving seeing see pp. 232f.

[2] See pp. 157ff., 166, 341. On εἴχοσαν instead of εἶχον see Bl.-D. § 84, 2; ἄν is left out as in 8.39; 19.11; see Raderm. 159.

[3] Πρόφασις = excuse, see Br. dictionary and Schl. ad loc.

[4] On καὶ ... καί = "although ... yet" see 6.36.

[5] Cp. 8.19; 10.30; 12.44; 14.9 etc.

[6] Zn. artificially wants to take ἀλλά (omitted by syr[s]) as a contrast to ἑωρ. in v. 24. It is of course the unexpressed thought that connects the two verses that explains it: "such a reaction is indeed inconceivable, but ...".

[7] On the introductory formula see pp. 124 n.3; 452 n.2; ἵνα is elliptical, as in 13.18; on ἐν τ. νόμῳ αὐτῶν cp. 8.17; 10.34 and see p. 86 n.3. In Ps. 34.19; 68.5 the worshipper's enemies are described as οἱ μισοῦντές με δωρεάν; cp. also Ps. 118.161: ἄρχοντες κατεδίωξάν με δωρεάν, and Ps. Sal. 7.1: οἳ ἐμίσησαν ἡμᾶς δωρεάν.

[8] Δωρεάν does not = *gratis* (Mt. 10.8; Rom. 3.24) or *frustra* (Gal. 2.21), but *immerito* (חִנָּם; Targ. סָנְאַי מַגָּן = "those who hate me without a cause" Str.-B.).

[9] See pp. 547f.

this purpose too; but the Evangelist now turns back to his main theme, the world's hatred of the disciples, and at this point he deals specifically with their task for the world.

α. The Disciples' Task: 15.26–27

Vv. 18–20 contained a general, undefined prophecy of the hatred which the disciples would encounter; before this prophecy is expounded in greater detail in 16.1–4a, it is explained in 15.26f. why the disciples are to encounter it. The reason given in vv. 18–20 was their essential union with the Revealer; and in v. 26 they are told that this union of life shows itself in the task of witnessing to him. But characteristically, it is not simply said, "You will be (or ought to be) my witnesses," but in the first place: "The Paraclete, the Spirit, will be my witness."[1]

After Jesus' departure, the situation on earth will remain unchanged inasmuch as the offence which Jesus' work offered the world will not disappear. The witness, which till now he had borne to himself, will be taken over by the Paraclete, the Helper, whom he will send from the Father. This (**v. 26**) is the first mention of the *sending of the Paraclete*, and the subject will be dealt with again in 16.5–11, 12–15; 14.15–17, 25f.[2] If the Paraclete originally was a mythological figure,[3] the Evangelist leaves no room for doubt that by this term he understands the Spirit given to

---

[1] H. Windisch (Festg. Ad. Jül. 110–137) maintains that all five sayings on the Paraclete in the farewell discourses are secondary, i.e. that they were originally independent sayings belonging together, which the Evangelist has worked into his text (Howard agrees with him, Christianity 74). With ref. to 15.26 he regards it as quite clear that the saying is an interpolation. This fails to recognise two things: 1. the continuity of the source, in which the Paraclete had to be introduced as witness to the world's sin (16.8–11) at this point, following 15.21–25, and 2. the Evangelist's train of thought, which puts the detailed prophecy of persecution (16.1–4a) after the more general one (15.18–20), but only after finding the ground for the world's hatred in the disciples' witness.

[2] The fact that the Paraclete appears as an already familiar figure in 15.26, while seeming to be introduced for the first time in 14.26, could throw doubt on the new order suggested for the farewell discourses. But 15.26 only presupposes a general familiarity with this figure in the Evangelist's circle (cp. the figure of the Son of Man in Mt. 25.31). More important, however, one cannot draw any conclusions as to the order of the discourses from the way the Paraclete passages are worded, because the Evangelist took the passages from his source, which (in 14.16 as well) gave him the wording (see p. 460 n.2). On the other hand the conclusion that 15.26 was the first occasion the Paraclete was met with in the original order of the farewell discourses seems to follow from the Evangelist's explanatory addition: the source only read:

ὅταν ἔλθῃ ὁ παράκλητος,
    ὁ«ς» παρὰ τοῦ πατρὸς ἐκπορεύεται,
μαρτυρήσει περὶ ἐμοῦ
    «και» ἐλέγξει τὸν κόσμον περὶ ἁμαρτίας
(16.8; see below p. 561 n.3).

Acc. to Becker, the source of v. 26 contained only the phrases: ὅταν ἔλθῃ ὁ παράκλητος, μαρτυρήσει περὶ ἐμοῦ. On the Paraclete-passages in the source see Becker 102.

[3] See additional note.

the community, which early Christendom was conscious of having received as the gift of the exalted Lord (or of God). In 14.26 (20.22) he uses the common early Christian description τὸ πν. τὸ ἅγιον, but here as in 14.17; 16.13. he says τὸ πν. τῆς ἀληθείας.[1] The ἀλήθεια is for him the self-revelatory divine reality,[2] and the function of the Spirit consists in bestowing revelation by continuing Jesus' revelatory work, as is stated by the words μαρτυρήσει περὶ ἐμοῦ (cp. 14.26). Jesus will send this Spirit from the Father, and from the Father he will come forth.[3] This two-fold designation makes the reference to the idea of revelation certain; even after Jesus' departure, God's revelation will be mediated through him: *he* it is, who sends the Spirit (sic, without additional description: 16.7), who bears witness to *him*; but he does so in his unity with the Father, who has made him Revealer; he sends the Spirit from the *Father*; the Spirit proceeds from the *Father*, just as it is said in 14.16 that the Father sends the Spirit at the Son's request, or in 14.26 that he sends him "in the name" of the Son. All these expressions say the same thing.[4]

The word μαρτυρήσει indicates[5] that the Spirit is the power of the proclamation in the community, and this is made fully clear by the

[1] Τὸ πνεῦμα τ. ἀλ. also occurs in Test. Jud. 20, with its opposite πν. τῆς πλάνης (this also occurs in I Jn. 4.6), but in a narrower sense. There the underlying idea is the animistic one, whereby man's good and bad potentialities are attributed to πνεύματα. The same kind of language is used in Herm. Mand. III 4. It is clearly the terminology of a syncretistic Judaism which the Evangelist is using. The πν. ἁγ. as Ruhā da Kuštā appears in the sacral formula of the Marcosians, Iren. I 21, 3. In the Mandaean writings the R. d. K. has been made the evil principle. We also find the doctrine of the two spirits in DSD 3.18ff., where the first (the good one) is called the "spirit of truth" or the "spirit of light"; see also Kuhn ZThK 49 (1952) 305, and Ev. Theol. 12 (1952/53), 278–281; Albright, The Background etc. (see on p. 17) 168.

[2] See pp. 74 n.2, 190f., 321; 434ff.

[3] 'Εκπορ. is an atemporal present, cp. 3.31 and elsewhere. Both conceptions of the sending of the Spirit occur elsewhere. That the exalted Lord sends him is stated both in 16.7, I Jn. 3.24; 4.13 and in Mk. 1.8; Lk. 24.49; Acts 2.33. Corresponding to this, πν. is the πν. of the κύριος in II Cor. 3.17f.; Gal. 4.6; Phil. 1.19; Acts 5.9; I Pet. 1.11 (cp. Rom. 8.2). It can as well be termed πν. θεοῦ: Rom. 8.11, 14; I Cor. 2.10ff.; I Pet. 4.14; I Jn. 4.2f. etc., and πν. θεοῦ and πν. Χριστοῦ can be interchanged, as in Rom. 8.9. Thus God can be described as the bestower of the πν. too: II Cor. 1.22; Gal. 3.5; Acts 2.17; Heb. 2.4 etc., while other expressions remain undefined, as in Rom. 5.5; Gal. 3.2 etc. Tit. 3.6 has the following combination: God has poured out the πν., διὰ 'I. Χρ.

[4] The "didactic-apologetic, perhaps also polemical significance" of the relative clauses in v. 26 is limited to this point (Windisch op. cit. 118). There is no speculative interest in relations within the Trinity. Ho. rightly speaks (ad loc.) of the "variability of the ideas, which is not to be exploited for the purpose of substantiating immanent, divine relations of subsistence".

[5] On μαρτυρεῖν see pp. 50 n.5; 144f., 160ff.; 262ff.; 278ff. The Evangelist is of course thinking of the community's proclamation of the word, whereby μαρτ. retains its forensic significance, because acc. to 16.4b–11, this proclamation has its place within the great lawsuit between God and the world (see pp. 84f., 297 and elsewhere). But v. 26 has nothing to do with Mk. 13.11 (and par. s) which refers to the special situation of the disciple accused

juxtaposition of the disciples' witness and that of the Spirit: καὶ ὑμεῖς δὲ μαρτυρεῖτε (v. 27).[1] For the witness borne by the disciples is not something secondary, running alongside the witness of the Spirit. How else could e.g. the Paraclete's ἐλέγχειν, as it is portrayed in 16.8–11, be accomplished than in the community's proclamation?[2] But when, as in Acts 5.32 (15.28), the Spirit's witness and the witness of the community are spoken of as two factors distinct from one another, this shows first that the working of the Spirit is not unhistorical or magical, but rather requires the disciples' independent action, and secondly that the disciples cannot accomplish on their own what they are in fact able to do. They may not rely on the Spirit, as if they had no responsibility or need for decision; but they may and should trust the Spirit. Thus the peculiar duality, which exists in the work of Jesus himself, repeats itself in the Church's preaching: *he* bears witness, and the *Father* bears witness (8.18). But the community's preaching is to be none other than witness to Jesus; for the word μαρτυρεῖτε is of course to be supplemented by the περὶ ἐμοῦ of the μαρτυρήσει. Its place has been taken by ὅτι ἀπ' ἀρχῆς μετ' ἐμοῦ ἐστε.[3] Their preaching is therefore to be a "repetition" of his preaching, or a "calling to mind," as is said in 14.26. It is very remarkable, however, that the term ἐστέ is used and not ἦτε.[4] Thus their being with him ἀπ' ἀρχῆς has not come to an end with his farewell, but continues further; and this is the only basis on which their witness is possible. Their witness is not, therefore, a historical account of that which was, but—however much it is based on that which was—it is "repetition," "a calling to mind," in the light of their present relationship with him.[5] In that case it is perfectly clear that their witness and that of the Spirit are identical.[6] The Gospel is itself evidence of the kind of witness this is, and of how that which was is taken up again:

---

before an earthly court (against Sasse ZNTW 24 [1925] 271; Howard 228f.; Windisch op. cit. 118). Naturally witness through work (cp. 14.12) is included, as in the case of Jesus himself.

[1] Καὶ δὲ as in 6.51 (see p. 234 n.4); I Jn. 1.3. Μαρτ. can scarcely be an imperative (Zn.) even though it does describe the disciples' task. The present tense tells the disciples the role they will take; "You are (ordained to be) witnesses".

[2] Thus Weizsäcker, rightly: Apostol. Zeitalter, 3rd. ed. 519; Wrede Messiasgeheimnis 189f., and Hosk.

[3] 'Απ' ἀρχῆς as in I Jn. 2.7, 24; 3.11; II Jn. 5f., from the beginning in time; so too ἐξ ἀρχῆς in 16.4; 6.64.

[4] Zn. misses the sense by taking it as a perfect: "You have been".

[5] Thus the disciples' μαρτυρεῖν does not consist in "their relating simply and straightforwardly the history they have experienced" (Torm, ZNTW 30 [1931] 133; similarly, R. Asting, Die Verkündigung des Wortes 1939, 685); see H. v. Campenhausen, Die Idee des Martyriums 40, 1.

[6] See on 16.13; 14.26. To say that the disciples' own witness is no longer thought of as inspired, i.e. that the Spirit stands alongside them, independent of them, seems to me to be a fundamental mistake; as it does to say that this strongly suggests that under the term

Since much that at the first, in deed and word,
Lay simply and sufficiently exposed,
Had grown
Of new significance and fresh result;
What first were guessed as points, I now knew stars.[1]

β. *The World's Hatred:* 16.1–4a

In 15.18–20 the only reason that had become apparent for the world's hatred of the disciples was that they had been raised up out of the world as friends of Jesus; and now, after the disciples have been depicted as witnesses of Jesus, the groundlessness of this hatred is made absolutely clear. For as witnesses, they are, like Jesus himself, acting *for* the world,—and this is why they encounter the world's hatred. For the world will interpret this work of theirs as an attack on itself, and will respond to it with hatred and persecution.

The Evangelist uses the words ταῦτα λελάληκα ὑμῖν ἵνα[2] (**v. 1**) to show the direction in which the prophecy and admonition of 15.18–27 are pointing: the disciples have to withstand the test in the actual historical situation; will they remain loyal, or will they fall away? Will they withstand the attempt to make them stumble?[3]

The historical circumstances are first indicated by the words ἀποσυναγώγους ποιήσουσιν ὑμᾶς (**v. 2**). The period we are concerned with is that in which the Christian community is forced to free itself from association with the synagogues,[4] and thus to abandon the protection of a *religio licita*. It is the period which stretches approximately from Paul to Justin, and one cannot pinpoint it any more exactly than that.[5]

Paraclete one should think of "an independent person, such as a prophet, in whom the Spirit is manifested" (Windisch op. cit. 118). Nor is it the case that the Spirit "supplements" the historical tradition; if that were so, his witness would have to come after that of the disciples.

[1] R. Browning (see p. 70 n.2), Oxford Book of Christian Verse p. 422.

[2] See pp. 335 n.5; 541 n.6.

[3] On σκανδ. see p. 445 n.1. It can mean specifically, to entice to apostasy by persecution; Mk. 4.17 (and par. s); Mt. 24.10; Mk. 14.27, 29 (and par. s); Mart. Petri 3 p. 82, 22.

[4] Cp. 9.22; 12.42 and see p. 335 n.5.

[5] Of course the problems raised by the relation of Christians and Christian communities to the association of synagogues differed depending on whether they were Jewish or Gentile Christian, and also they varied considerably in different parts of the oikoumene. Paul regards the ἐκκλησία as the true Israel (Gal. 6.16; cp. Phil. 3.3), and not as any new religious association. It is not clear how far he tried to keep the Christian communities within the association of synagogues. II Cor. 11.24f. shows that he did not break off all connections as a matter of course. However that may be, his communities are no longer within the synagogical association; nor does it seem that they broke away only when compelled to do so. As regards Palestine, Mk. 13.9 (and par. s); Lk. 6.22 attest that the Christian communities first of all established themselves within the synagogue, and only

Certainly we are not dealing with the first period; for ἀλλ' ἔρχεται ὥρα[1] clearly contrasts that which is already familiar and no longer a matter of astonishment with something new and astounding: it will come to martyrdom! In so far as the execution of a Christian is seen as an act of service offered to God,[2] it is probably Jews who are being thought of as its instigators;[3] this would refer us to the post-Pauline period, in which Jewry no longer contented itself with corporal punishment (II Cor. 11.24) and excommunication from the synagogue, but regarded the independent existence of Christian communities as competition and tried to render it harmless by bringing them before the courts of the pagan authorities.[4]

The disciples of Jesus are not to take offence at this kind of fate; for they know—as **v. 3** states, with almost word for word repetition of 15.21[5]—the grounds for the world's enmity. The sentence is a parenthesis, and is followed by **v. 4a**, which picks up the idea of v. 1 with the words ἀλλὰ ταῦτα λελ. ὑμ.,[6] thus bringing the whole section to an end. In place of the negative ἵνα μὴ σκανδ., we now have the positive ἵνα . . . μνημονεύητε αὐτῶν, indicating that the disciples' existence is orientated on that "calling to mind," just as it belongs to the task of the Paraclete to call to mind (14.26).[7]

---

attained their independence as the result of excommunication. Acts bears this out to some extent for the Hellenistic world, and the same conclusion can be drawn for Asia Minor from Rev. 2.9.

[1] 'Αλλά = "nay more", as in II Cor. 1.9; 7.11; Bl.-D. § 448, 6. Syr[s] read καί, which Merx accepts, along with the future ἐλεύσεται. On ὥρα ἵνα see p. 424 n.1; on ὥρα as a pre-determined point of time see p. 117 n.1.

[2] With regard to the strictly incorrect combination λατρείαν προσφέρειν (λατρ. is the act of service), Br. compares the expressions δεήσεις and εὐχὴν προσφ. in Heb. 5.7; Jos. Bell. 3, 353.

[3] Cp. NuR 21 (191a): "... that everyone, who spills the blood of the godless, is like one who offers a sacrifice" (Str.-B. ad loc.).

[4] Cp. Acts 17.5ff.; 18.12ff.; Mart. Pol. 13.1; Justin Dial, 95, 4; 110, 4; 131, 2; 133, 6. The Evangelist is thinking of this kind of systematic opposition to the Christians, not of particular occurrences, in which Jews took it upon themselves to kill Christians (Stephen: Acts 8.1ff.; James, Euseb. h. e. II 23, 17f.), or made the attempt to do so (II Cor. 11.25; Acts 14.19), although that kind of thing kept recurring, as in the rebellion of Bar-Kochba. Cp. Justin Dial. 16.4: οὐ γὰρ ἐξουσίαν ἔχετε αὐτόχειρες γενέσθαι ἡμῶν διὰ τοὺς νῦν ἐπικρατοῦντας. ὁσάκις δὲ ἂν ἐδυνήθητε, καὶ τοῦτο ἐπράξατε.

[5] Merx regards the absence of v. 3 from syr[s] as indicating its original omission.

[6] 'Αλλὰ does not occur in D* syr[s] (see Bl.-D. § 448, 3). The first αὐτῶν is missing from ℵ D syr[s], the second from D syr[s]. Both are accidental or arbitrary omissions. It makes no difference whether one refers the first αὐτῶν to the words immediately before, or to the Jews (if it is their ὥρα, 2.4; 7.6 would be comparable); Schl. prefers the latter and cuts out the second αὐτ.

[7] The mode of expression is an involved one. But that should not mislead one to regard the explicatory ὅτι as a mistranslation for ἅ (Burney 75f.), or to stress the unstressed ἐγώ—omitted by syr[s]—, or to eliminate it as "stupid" (Merx); it is pleonastic, as in v. 7 and frequently elsewhere; see Burney 79–82.

The question arises as to the motive for introducing this prophecy, the historical relevance of which is stressed by the ἵνα-clauses in v. 1 and v. 4. Clearly it is not so much apologetic, in the primitive sense that the fact of persecution need not be a cause of offence because Jesus has already foreseen and foretold it; this would mean the offence was to be overcome by the knowledge that he had foreseen and foretold that persecution was going to occur *as a matter of fact*.[1] The intention rather is to make them understand the necessity of the event within the *very nature of things*, and this is the force of the parenthesis in v. 3.[2] The reminder of the words that Jesus had spoken discloses to the disciple the necessity of suffering, and gives him the strength to overcome it.

2) *The Judgment of the World:* 16.4b–11

i. *The Disciples' Situation:* 16.4b–7

The Evangelist returns to the words of his source, which he had left on one side in 15.26, concerning the μαρτυρία of the Paraclete.[3] In the context he gives it, this μαρτυρία is the crowning of the whole section because it gives significance to the task set the disciples, a task which leads to persecution and death, and provides a justification for it: in the work of the Paraclete, i.e. in the activity of the disciples, is achieved both the victory of the revelation over the world and the judgment of the world. The Evangelist, however, not only puts this promise against the dark background of the persecutions (16.1–4a); he actually intensifies the darkness by describing the disciples' situation as one of isolation and sadness (vv. 4b–7).

The point of vv. 4b–7 lies in vv. 6b and 7, which prepare the ground for the promise of the Paraclete in vv. 8–11. **V. 4b** is a somewhat forced transitional expression, which brings us, by means of the contrast ἐξ ἀρχῆς—νῦν δέ, into the situation of the farewell.[4] While one might expect, after vv. 1–4a: "Now, however, because I am departing, I must tell you," the words νῦν δὲ ὑπάγω πρὸς τὸν πέμψαντά με (**v. 5**) do not lead on to that kind of statement,[5] but introduce instead an account of the disciples' situation.

---

[1] Cp. Just. Apol. 33, 2: ἃ γὰρ ἦν ἄπιστα καὶ ἀδύνατα νομιζόμενα παρὰ τοῖς ἀνθρώποις γενήσεσθαι, ταῦτα ὁ θεὸς προεμήνυσε διὰ τοῦ προφητικοῦ πνεύματος μέλλειν γίνεσθαι, ἵν' ὅταν γένηται μὴ ἀπιστηθῇ, ἀλλ' ἐκ τοῦ προειρῆσθαι πιστευθῇ.

[2] See p. 478 on 13.19.

[3] See p. 552 n.2.

[4] On ἐξ ἀρχῆς see p. 554 n.3. Instead of ὅτι Burney (78) would prefer to read ὅτε; see p. 424 n.1.

[5] Thus the sentence ταῦτα ... ἤμην is not aimed at explaining why the prophecy of the disciples' suffering occurs for the first time at this stage in the Gospel—in contrast to

It is the νῦν of his farewell, which for him is the hour of exaltation.[1] But the disciples are not thinking about that; they are not looking at *him*, but at *themselves*: οὐδεὶς ἐξ ὑμῶν ἐρωτᾷ με κτλ. (**v. 6**). They are not asking[2] where he is going to—the answer would be: to the Father, and that would solve their difficulty—but they are in λύπη because they are about to be left in their distress.[3] Their λύπη cannot however be soothed away artificially; they can only master it by coming to understand the necessity of their being left alone: ἀλλ' ἐγὼ τὴν ἀλήθειαν λέγω ὑμῖν, συμφέρει ὑμῖν ἵνα ἐγὼ ἀπέλθω (**v. 7**).[4] The disciples' λύπη is due to a misunderstanding; his going away, as 14.28 will confirm, should be a reason for joy. Why? ἐὰν γὰρ μὴ ἀπέλθω, ὁ παράκλητος οὐ μὴ ἔλθῃ πρὸς ὑμᾶς· ἐὰν δὲ πορευθῶ, πέμψω αὐτὸν πρὸς ὑμᾶς.[5]

In mythological language we are told that the revelation, which took place in Jesus' work, only retains its significance as the real, absolute revelation, when it retains the element of futurity. 15.26 has already said that the Paraclete is the Spirit in whose working Jesus' revelation is continued, and this will be made still clearer in 14.26. The way this work is carried out will be described almost at once, in vv. 8–11. But first, in v. 7, the presupposition for its continuation must be made clear: the historical Jesus must depart, so that his significance, the significance of being the Revealer, can be grasped purely by itself. He is only the Revealer, if he *remains* such. But he remains it only by sending the Spirit; and he can only send the Spirit when he has himself gone. In content the statement means the same as the others, that Jesus must be exalted or glorified in order to be the one who he really is.

It is clear that the Evangelist does not want to depict this unique historical occasion of the farewell psychologically, but rather he desires

---

Matt. where it comes as soon as ch. 10 (Loisy); its purpose is to be found in the fact that "it serves as a connecting link with the idea of departure, and of the coming of the Paraclete which depends upon it" (Br.). Becker (97f.) assigns v. 5a to the source.

[1] It is the νῦν of 17.13; 12.31; 13.31; cp. the ὥρα of 12.23; 13.1; 17.1.

[2] That what is meant is: "You do not ask, because each of you knows now where I am going to" (as B. Weiss maintains), is an unreasonable correction of the meaning of the text; it is the result of the attempt to get over the contradiction with 13.36; 14.5 (where, on the present order of the text, the disciples have in fact asked). Zn. attempts to overcome the difficulty by explaining that Thomas's question in 14.5 is "not a sympathetic questioning about Jesus' destiny." Dodd (412, 2) tries a different way. Barrett thinks he can overcome it by stressing the fact that the tense used in 16.5 is the present ἐρωτᾷ and not ἠρώτησε.

[3] Ταῦτα λελάλ., which picks up v. 1 and v. 4a, refers to the prophecy of the persecutions; but in the light of v. 7, on which the discourse is orientated, and having regard to the farewell discourses as a whole, we must take it to mean: "You are filled with sadness, because you have to withstand all this without me, abandoned by me".

[4] ἐγὼ is unstressed both times; see Burney 79–82. Τὴν ἀλ. λέγω has the formal meaning: it is true, what I say; i.e. = ἀμὴν ἀμὴν λέγω ὑμῖν. On συμφέρει ἵνα see p. 411 n.1. On the first ἀπέλθω, instead of the present, see Radermacher 178.

[5] Instead of οὐ μὴ ἔλθῃ, ℵ ℜ D pl read: οὐκ ἐλεύσεται.

to point out the fundamental relationship of the disciple to the Revealer.[1] It is not a human or personal relationship, such as one can cultivate with another man; it was not that in the case of the first disciples, nor is it so for later generations. For the former he becomes the Revealer in the full sense of the term only by departing from them, and by setting their gaze free from his human presence; so also he cannot become the Revealer for the latter by being presented to them as a historical phenomenon, or as a human personality, by means of historical recollection. This is why the former, as "disciples at first hand," have no advantage over the latter, the "disciples at second hand," when it comes to their relationship to him in faith as the Revealer.[2] For both, he stands the same distance away.

The revelation is always only indirect; but because it occurs within the sphere of human history, it gives rise to the misunderstanding that it is direct. In order to destroy this misunderstanding the Revealer must take his leave; he must leave his own in their λύπη, in temptation, for it is in this λύπη that the disciple is freed from the things that are directly given (which are always slipping away into the past) and turned towards that which is only indirectly attainable and always in the future.[3] Of course, historically speaking, the disciples of later generations,

---

[1] If this is not understood, Carpenter's verdict becomes understandable: he concludes that the question why the Spirit could not already have been at work during Jesus' lifetime, does not admit of an answer. Above all, one is not entitled to raise the question of the relation of the Paraclete to the Spirit of God in the OT; the Spirit, which is foretold by the Johannine Jesus, is nothing other than the power of proclamation, grounded in Jesus, and at work in the community.

[2] Kierkegaard. Phil. Fragm., tr. David Swenson, Oxford Univ. Press 1936: "There is no disciple at second hand. The first and the last are essentially on the same plane ..." "This immediate contemporaneity is merely an occasion, which can scarcely be expressed more emphatically than in the proposition that the disciple, if he understood himself, must wish that the immediate contemporaneity should cease, by God's leaving the earth". "The immediate contemporaneity is so far from being an advantage that the contemporary must precisely desire its cessation, lest he be tempted to devote himself to seeing and hearing with his bodily eyes and ears, which is all a waste of effort and a grievous, aye a dangerous toil".

[3] Taken in this sense, Loisy is right: "L'esprit est comme enfermé dans la chair du Christ sur la terre; il gagnera, pour ainsi dire, par la glorification de Jésus, la pleine liberté de son action". Corssen (ZNTW 8 [1907] 130) is ambiguous: "So much more important for the Evangelist was the inner religious experience than the historical fact taken by itself" —for religious experience does not mediate any direct revelation either. Ed. Meyer (III 646, 3) finds an analogy with "the Persian doctrine that Ahuramazda had denied the Zoroastrian immortality, because it would have meant that resurrection and redemption were not then possible". Hardly! And there is absolutely no question of our being concerned here with "the moral estimation of Jesus' death, which sees it as the imminent crowning of his life's work, as the highest proof of his obedience to God and of his victory over the world" (Ad. Bonhöffer, Epiktet und das NT 1911, 326). Hölderlin is far closer to understanding it aright: "He must, at the right time, away, He, through whom the Spirit has spoken" (Empedocles II 4, v. Hellingrath III p. 154, 19f.). Cp. also R. M. Rilke, Die

who have not enjoyed the company of the earthly Jesus, will not experience the λύπη of his farewell in the same way. But the danger of misunderstanding the revelation by regarding it as direct is just the same for them. For what was misleading for the first disciples was the illusion of a false certainty which thought that it possessed the revelation in what was directly given, in immediate experiences and gifts, and which therefore was bound to hope that it would never have an end. But the fact that everything that is given and experienced in time is essentially transient is brought home to the disciple by the circumstance that the Giver himself goes away. Otherwise he would be misunderstood about his gift. He can only be the Revealer as the one who is always breaking the given in pieces, always destroying every certainty, always breaking in from the beyond and calling into the future. Only thus is the believer, as he turns to the gift, protected from turning back to himself and lingering by himself, instead of allowing himself to be torn away from himself, in accordance with the intention of the gift, and to be directed again and again into what is still to come. The intention of the revelation is to set the believer free;[1] the certainty which it gives is not the continuation of the present—of something that has in fact already gone by—but the eternity of the future.[2] This is why it is also true of the disciple of a later generation that he can never retain in his grasp that in which the revelation first encountered him, whether it was an experience within his own soul, or Christian knowledge, or culture. For him, too, Jesus is the one who is always taking his leave; and if he does not know the λύπη of being left, neither will he experience the χαρά of union.

But this is what is meant by saying that the revelation is the word, and indeed the word in its being spoken: that is, the word which does not mediate a subject-matter to be appropriated once and for all, but which is always spoken into the world's situation, and which thereby calls the hearer out of the world. Only in the word was Jesus the Revealer, and only in the word will he continue to be it; for the Paraclete, who is to take his place, is the word. The word is very far from being a closed doctrine, or complex of statements, nor on the other hand is it the historical account of Jesus' life. It is the living word; that

---

Sonette an Orpheus I 5: (English translation: Sonnets to Orpheus; tr., with introduction and notes by J. B. Leishman: the Hogarth Press.)

Could you but feel his passing's needfulness!
Though he himself may dread the hour of drawing nigher.
Already, when his words pass earthliness,
He passes with them far beyond your gaze.

[1] See pp. 436ff.

[2] See p. 536.

is, paradoxically, the word which is spoken by the community itself; for the Paraclete is the Spirit that is at work in the community. And to ensure that we do not think of this word as the human spirit aroused to self-awareness in the believers,[1] it is made quite clear that the Paraclete is the Spirit who is to be sent by Jesus[2] to continue his work. The point is made expressly in vv. 13f. and 14.26; at this stage it is the other side of the matter that comes into view: the continuing newness and futurity of the word arises from its being spoken at any time out of the actual situation. Not in the sense of its being the meaning to be found in each situation or the consequences to be drawn from it, as if it were at any given time the interpretation of the meaning of history.

For the word is at the same time spoken into a situation; i.e. it is spoken as the word of revelation *against it*. If therefore the community has any understanding of the word of revelation that brings it into being, it can and must know that it has always to interpret the word afresh and to speak it into its own present as the word that is always the same—that word that is the same because it is always new. If the community is capable of that, then it has the revelation and shows itself to be the authentic community that lives from the future. And in doing this, it has overcome its forsakenness and λύπη. Moreover—and at this point we arrive back at the context—this is the source of its comfort in time of persecution; for it is this that gives it the victory over the world.

ii. *The Judgment of the World:* 16.8–11

V. 8: καὶ [ἐλθὼν ἐκεῖνος] ἐλέγξει τὸν κόσμον περὶ ἁμαρτίας
[καὶ περὶ δικαιοσύνης καὶ περὶ κρίσεως].[3]

The function of the Paraclete is ἐλέγχειν:[4] he will uncover the world's guilt. The image that comes before the eyes is that of a lawsuit

---

[1] Hegel finds in the Johannine sayings about the Paraclete the proof for his historio-philosophical interpretation of Christianity as the absolute religion, in which the spirit comes to itself in human self-awareness, is in its own presence, and thus in the truth. Cp. Otto Kühler, Sinn, Bedeutung und Auslegung der Heiligen Schrift in Hegels Philosophie 1934. 18ff.

[2] See pp. 552f.

[3] On the text see p. 552 n. 2. 'Ελθὼν ἐκεῖνος picks up the source's ὅταν ἔλθῃ (15.26); καὶ π. δικ. καὶ π. κρ. will be an addition of the Evangelist's; so too the explanation that follows, vv. 9–11. Acc. to Becker (103) vv. 5b–11 come from the Evangelist.

[4] On the role of the Spirit as plaintiff, see Test. Jud. 20; Wis. 1.7–9 is not comparable, because John is concerned with a cosmic drama, not with the conviction of sinful individuals. This too is the reason why no analogy is afforded by Philo's statements about the ἐλέγχειν of the συνείδησις (quod det. pot. ins. 146) or about the Logos interpreted as conscience (deus imm. 135; fug. et inv. 188), ideas which rest on Stoic tradition (H. Leisegang, Der Heilige Geist I 1919, 80f.). It is precisely *not* with the judgment of conscience that John is concerned. Wrong too, H. Weinel, Die Wirkungen des Geistes u. der Geister 1899, 189.

of cosmic dimensions, taking place before the court of God.[1] The world is accused, and the Paraclete is the prosecutor.[2] But the mythical side of the picture has completely faded away, for the lawsuit is not to take place at the end of time, but immediately after Jesus' departure, within history. Nor is it to take place in the inward workings of men's consciences,[3] but in simple historical facts which speak with complete clarity—though of course, they speak only for ears that believe. For these facts are not the historical effects of Jesus' life, in so far as these can be seen as phenomena of world-history, but the existence of Jesus' disciples, in so far as his word is alive within them.[4] Just as the judgment of the world took place in his coming, because it was the coming of light (3.20), so it continues to take place in the continuing proclamation of his word by the community. It is not Christian polemic or apologetic as such that is thought of here.[5] For this presupposes that there is a common basis for discussion and persuasion, and that one can point to criteria by which the world can recognise that it is in the wrong. But the lawsuit is played out on a higher level; the world itself does not begin to realise that the existence and preaching of the Christian community is its own conviction; it cannot perceive the Paraclete (14.17); it cannot grasp the basis for the judgment—for how should it, for instance, regard the sentence ὑπάγω πρὸς τὸν πάτερα of v. 10? Only faith understands the truth of Luther's hymn: "For why? His doom is writ."

The judgment consists in the world's sinful nature being exposed by the revelation that continues to take place in the community. This is brought out by relating the ἐλέγχειν of the Paraclete to the three dimensions ἁμαρτία, δικαιοσύνη, and κρίσις. The absence of the article proves that it is the three *ideas* that are called in question, and not three

---

[1] See p. 553 n. 5, etc. This idea is a Gnostic motif, elaborated radically in Ginza 436, 28ff.: Adam brings before the "great life" the "legal case with ref. to the world", i.e. he makes accusation about the creation, which has resulted in the souls being abandoned to the domination and persecution of the lower powers. Acc. to Ginza 256, 28ff. the Uthras have been sent down into the world to conduct the case against it, to pronounce the souls pure, and to bring them into the heavenly world; see Jonas Gnosis I 136f. The sections in DeuteroIsaiah in which Jahweh disputes with the nations are a partial analogy (41.1ff., 1ff.; 43.9ff.). But here Jahweh is defending himself and calling Israel to bear witness on his behalf. Basically, Israel is the forum there, before which Jahweh justifies himself (cp. 43.14ff.; 44.6ff.; 46.1ff.); see p. 564 n. 2. Cp. Baudissin, Kyrios III 1929, 395.

[2] In the source this imagery begins in 15.26 where μαρτυρήσει means (for the source) "he will make accusation".

[3] We are not therefore to think of a sequence of events similar to that recorded in I Cor. 14.24.

[4] Nor is there any ref. here to the sequence of events described in Mk. 13.9ff. (and par. s). And yet the Evangelist will be conscious of having disclosed the real meaning of the promise of the Spirit in Mk. 13.11 (and par. s).

[5] Thus Htm., Bd., and others.

cases of sin, righteousness and judgment. It would therefore be wrong to supplement the three substantives with three subjective genitives.[1] It is remarkable that the question is not the direct one: on whose side is the ἁμαρτία, and whose the δικαιοσύνη? Who is it who is judged? But rather: what do ἁμ., δικ. and κρ. mean? The judgment that takes place in the revelation consists in disclosing the true meaning of the standards and values current in the world.[2] But this means at the same time disclosing who is the sinner, who the victor, and who it is that is judged.

V. 9: περὶ ἁμαρτίας μέν, ὅτι οὐ πιστεύουσιν εἰς ἐμέ.[3] The meaning of sin is expounded in the sense of 15.21–25; it is unbelief vis-à-vis the Revealer. The world reacts to Jesus by clinging on to itself, by μένειν ἐν τῇ σκοτίᾳ (12.46; cp. 9.41; 3.36), and precisely this is sin. Sin therefore is not any single ghastly action, even if that action be the crucifixion of Jesus; sin is not moral failure as such, but unbelief and the bearing that springs from it, i.e. the world's conduct determined by unbelief and taken as a whole. From now on that is "sin." That does not mean that the reference is to the historical fact of the Jews' unbelief at that time; on the contrary, this unbelief has, from then on, been the world's reaction to the word that is proclaimed to it, the word which is continually bringing it into the presence of the revelation, where a decision has to be made.[4] It is not therefore that the world has at one time failed to recognise a great man, but that it has rejected the revelation, and continues to do so. The world understands sin as revolt against its own standards and ideals, the things which give it security. But to shut oneself off from the revelation that calls all worldly security in question and opens up another security—that is real sin, in contrast to which all that used to be sinful was only temporary and passing.[5]

V. 10. περὶ δικαιοσύνης δέ, ὅτι πρὸς τὸν πατέρα ὑπάγω καὶ οὐκέτι θεωρεῖτέ με. The meaning of δικαιοσύνη is made clear by Jesus' going to

---

[1] Thus Hosk., rightly. That one cannot supplement ἁμ. with τοῦ κόσμου, δικ. with μοῦ, and κρ. with τοῦ κόσμου is at once clear, because to do so would "result in an intolerable tautology" in the last part of v. 11. Rightly too, Br. and Temple.

[2] Zn.'s view is absurd: the Paraclete will prove that there are such things as sin, righteousness and judgment ("three ethical truths not recognised by the world")! The world knows that much itself; what it does not know is how to apply these concepts; i.e. it does not know that, in using standards such as these, it is condemning itself.

[3] Of course in vv. 9–11 ὅτι has in each case the purpose of expounding, not substantiating what has been said.

[4] The meaning is clear, even if one cannot with certainty appeal to the present tense πιστεύουσιν for confirmation; it may be that this is not an expression of continuous present actuality, but a true present, like ὑπάγω in v. 10. In that case, however, the present unbelief would be conceived as representative of the continuing unbelief of the world. In any case θεωρεῖτε in v. 10 is not limited to the actual moment, and the perf. κέκρ. in v. 11 also describes the continuing reality of the verdict pronounced at this moment.

[5] See pp. 159, 166, 341, 550; wrongly, therefore, Hosk., who says: unbelief is the *origin* of sin.

the Father. How? In so far as the terminology is that of the lawsuit, δικ. means "innocence"; not, however in the moral sense of uprightness,[1] but in the forensic sense of being in the right, of winning one's case.[2] As the lawsuit here is between God and the world, it is equally clear that it is a question of δικ. in the sense of righteousness adjudged by *God*,[3] of victory in the eschatological sense. What this kind of δικαιοσύνη means is made clear by Jesus' departure to the Father; i.e.

---

[1] In this sense Jesus is called δίκαιος: Acts 3.14; 7.52; 22.14; I Pet. 3.18 (cp. II Cor. 5.21); I Jn. 2.1, 29; 3.7; in acc. with this is ποιεῖν τὴν δικαιοσύνην in I Jn. 2.29; 3.7, 10; otherwise δικαιοσύνη does not occur in John at all, apart from here.

[2] See E. Hatch, Harv. Theol. Rev. 14 (1921), 103ff., on the forensic meaning of δικ. In the Book of the Covenant the צַדִּיק is the one who is right in court, and הִצְדִּיק means "to let a man gain his case" (Ex. 23.7; cp. Deut. 25.1; II Sam. 15.4 etc.; for the later usage see Str.-B. III 134). In the oriental use of language, the connexion between *righteousness* and *victory* is clear (cp. Baudissin, Kyrios III 134). Yahweh's צִדְקוֹת, for which the people praise him, are his victories (Jud. 5.11), the "mighty acts" which he has done to the advantage of the nation (I Sam. 12.7). Of the time of the judgment it is said:

וַיִּגְבַּה יְהוָה צְבָאוֹת בַּמִּשְׁפָּט וְהָאֵל הַקָּדוֹשׁ נִקְדַּשׁ בִּצְדָקָה

(Is. 5.16; LXX: καὶ ὑψωθήσεται κύριος σαβαὼθ ἐν κρίματι, καὶ ὁ θεὸς ὁ ἅγιος δοξασθήσεται ἐν δικαιοσύνῃ. The "mantle of righteousness" (מְעִיל צְדָקָה: LXX χιτὼν εὐφροσύνης) with which God has wrapped Zion (Is. 61.10) is the eschatological glorification; both there and elsewhere the eschatological decision is conceived as a lawsuit: Is. 41.1, 21; 43.9; 44.7; Jer. 25.31; Joel 4.1f., 12 (in the negative sense Is. 1.18; 3.13; Hos. 4.1; Mic. 6.1f.). In the Mandaean writing זכא means "to be not guilty, to be victorious" (Lidzb. Joh.-B. 1f.); the higher beings, which are called "innocent", are designated ἀνίκητοι (Lidzb. ZDMG 61 [1907] 696, 6). The substantive זאכותא means "guiltlessness", and "the state of victory"; see ZNTW 24 (1925), 128f.; Peterson Εἷς Θεός 159f.; T. Arvedson, Das Mysterium Christi 1937, 39f. Above all, it is characteristic that the victory of the messenger (or of the soul) goes together with his ascending from the earth into the world of light. It is said of the three messengers Hibil, Sitil, and Anōš (Mand. Lit. 13, cp. 144): "They ... carried out a lawsuit, and were the victors, ... they are victorious and not defeated. They came from a pure place, and are going to a pure place". Ginza 257, 5f. (the "first" speaks to the three Uthras): "You will go out victorious, when your works are complete". Ginza 444, 25f. (to the soul) "Rise up, conduct your legal action, and be victorious"; cp. Ginza 521, 5f.; Mand. Lit. 230. So too, in the Od. Sal. "to be justified" is identical with the crowning of the victor, and with his ascending: 17.1ff.; 25.10ff.; 29.4f.; 31.5. The same kind of language is used in I Tim. 3.16 (ἐδικαιώθη ἐν πνεύματι ... ἀνελήμφθη ἐν δόξῃ); Ign. Phld. 8, 2; Rom. 5.1 (see Schlier, Relig. Unters. 171). The difficulty Windisch makes of δικ. in John 16.9 (Festg. Ad. Jül. 120, 2) is therefore quite unjustified. Carpenter is right (394f.), but he refers vv. 8–11 onesidedly to the apologetics and polemics of the time. Dalman, Jesus-Jeschua 194, with ref. to Lk. 7.29, 35, takes δικ. rightly in its formal-juridical sense, meaning the justification of the divine activity, but he does not take account of the eschatological character of this event. Moreover νικᾶν in Greek can also mean the victory in the lawsuit; see e.g. Aristoph. Equ. 95; Av. 445.447. 1101; Peterson op. cit. 159; Br. dictionary. On "victory" and "life" see Er. Peterson Εἷς Θεός 314.

[3] Δικ. also has this meaning in the Pauline expression δικαιοσύνη θεοῦ; and yet the δικ. θεοῦ is not identical with the δικ. of Jn. 16.9f.; it is not applied to Christ, but to the believer, and the concept is used within a specifically Pauline antithesis, which is absent from John.

it is, as v. 33 puts it, the overcoming of the world, the annulling of the world. And the significance of this annulment of the world becomes clearer, in so far as it is the justification of the man whom the world deals with as a sinner (9.24), and the victory of the one who was put to death on the cross; it is therefore the complete freedom from the verdict and power of the world. And this eschatological freedom is also depicted by the words: καὶ οὐκέτι θεωρεῖτέ με: he has become invisible to the world, and unassailable by it; he no longer belongs to it. This, therefore, is δικαιοσύνη, and the disciples are to look at this, if they want to know what victory is. They have a share in this victory by their faith (I John 5.4f.; 2.13f.; 4.4). What seemed to them a reason for λύπη is in fact a reason for joy: the fact that they no longer see him.[1] For the world, this victory is just as much a κρυπτόν (7.4) as is the real nature of ἁμαρτία; as the world sees things, to suffer the wreckage of death means condemnation by God;[2] the world can only see victory in what is visible. But the significance of the victory lies precisely in the overcoming of the visible by the invisible; this is why the world does not know that it is condemned, or that it is conquered. But this is what the Paraclete will show.

V. 11: περὶ δὲ κρίσεως, ὅτι ὁ ἄρχων τοῦ κόσμου τούτου κέκριται. The concept of κρίσις that is in question here is, of course, that of the *divine*, eschatological judgment. The world speaks of this judgment as a cosmic event in the near or more distant future, whether it be in the sense of a naive apocalyptic eschatology, or in terms of a conviction that one can read off the judgment of the world by means of an historio-philosophical interpretation of world-history. In each case the world thinks it possesses the criteria for this judgment in its concepts of ἁμαρτία and δικαιοσύνη. But as it deceived itself over the meaning of ἁμ. and δικ., so too it fails to see that the κρίσις is already ensuing, that the prince of this world is already judged;[3] i.e. it fails to see that it is itself already judged—condemned for holding on to itself, to its own standards and ideals, to what can be seen.

Thus the revelation states definitively what ἁμαρτία, δικαιοσύνη and κρίσις mean; i.e. what they mean after and in the light of the fact that

---

[1] It could also be said: ὅτι οὐκέτι θεωροῦσίν με. But θεωρεῖτε emphasises the paradox of the victory more strongly, in that the words are spoken from the standpoint of the disciples: they are to know that the very fact that they no longer see him is his victory; cp. 20.29.

[2] Cp. Od. Sal. 42.10 (13): "I was not rejected, though I was reckoned to be so,
I did not perish, though they devised (it) against me."
31.8 (7): "And they made me a debtor, when I rose up,
I, who had been no debtor."
Cp. 17.3; 25.5f.; 28.9f.

[3] See on 12.31 (p. 431).

the revelation of God took place in Jesus. But is nothing of this visible in the world? While the Paraclete enables only the believers to see the significance of what happened, his ἐλέγχειν does nevertheless encounter the world, in so far as it is carried out in the community's proclamation. This word and the claim it lays on men is heard in the world, and after hearing it, the world can never be the same again. There is no longer any such thing as an unprejudiced Judaism or an impartial Gentile world within the circumference of the word of proclamation. Man has no atemporal being, which is not qualified by history, nor is there any human existence—this is the purpose of the sending of the Paraclete—which is not decisively qualified by this particular history. The world struggles against this idea, that a contingent historical event should be the eschatological event, the means of grace or of judgment for the world. This is a σκάνδαλον for it; for it claims the right to subject everything that happens within it to its own standards, and to judge it by them.

The κόσμος possesses all three concepts, ἁμ., δικ. and κρ., and because it possesses them it has—as with its knowledge of light, of the water of life, and of the bread of life—a preliminary understanding of the revelation; i.e. it can equally well open itself to the word of proclamation as it can close itself against it. This is why it can be sinful, because it knows: man can gain himself (δικαιοσύνη), or he can lose himself (κρίσις), and which he does is his own responsibility; he can be guilty (ἁμαρτία). His destiny is decided in relation to the word.

The section 15.18–16.11 is a coherent discourse, like 13.31–35, 15.1–17; there is no interruption for dialogue, nor do the disciples say anything in conclusion. This shows quite clearly that there is no psychological interest in depicting an actual historical farewell-scene, but that the scene is only the symbolical representation of the situation in which the believers always live their lives, a situation which they have to overcome by continually calling the revelation to mind.

Additional Note: The Paraclete

It is clear that the Evangelist has taken the figure of the Paraclete from his source and interpreted it, in the context of the Christian tradition, as the ἅγιον πνεῦμα.[1] The original significance of the figure is shown to us by the functions ascribed to it in the source: 1) the Paraclete is sent by the Father (14.16), or he proceeds from the Father (15.26); 2) he is not visible to the world, but only to the believers (14.17); 3) he teaches, and leads into, the truth (14.26; 16.13); 4) he does not speak on his own account (16.13); 5) he bears

[1] See Br. on 14.9; Windisch op. cit. 122f.; Gulin 49.

witness to Jesus against the world, and convicts the world of sin (15.26; 16.8). In all this he is described as the Revealer, like Jesus himself; for Jesus is also (1) sent by God (5.30; 8.16 etc.) and has gone forth from God (8.42; 13.3 etc., see p. 298 n. 1); (2) as Revealer is visible only to the believers, and not to the world (1.10,12; 8.14,19; 17.8 etc.); (3) teaches, and leads into the truth (7.16f.; 8.32,40ff. etc.); (4) does not speak on his own account (7.16f.; 12.49f.; etc. see p. 249 n. 1); (5) bears witness to himself (8.14), and convicts the world of sin (3.20; 7.7 etc.). *The Paraclete therefore is a parallel figure to Jesus himself*; and this conclusion is confirmed by the fact that the title is suitable for both (14.16: . . . καὶ ἄλλον παρακλ. δώσει ὑμῖν).[1]

It is clear from 14.16 that the source taught that there were two sendings of two Paracletes, Jesus and his successor, the one following the other. Neither the Christian tradition, nor his own purposes could possibly have led the Evangelist to this duplication of the figure of the Revealer. He could take over the figure of the Paraclete who is to succeed Jesus only if he found there an appropriate form for expressing his conception of the ἅγιον πνεῦμα. And the figure itself must have originated in a body of opinion, according to which the revelation was not exclusively concentrated on *one* historical bearer, but shared amongst various messengers following upon each other, or repeated in them. This view is, however, widespread in pagan, Jewish, and Christian Gnosticism; it is found in the Pseudo-Clementines, in the Mandaean Literature and elsewhere, and it has been systematically developed in Manichaeism.[2]

---

[1] W. Michaelis (Coniect. Neotest. XI 1947, 147–162) tries to avoid this conclusion by taking ἄλλον (14.16) pleonastically: "There will be another one too, and as Paraclete (or, 'that is to say, the Paraclete')". Even if that is correct, there would still be two messengers, two parallel figures; but I Jn. 2.1 confirms that the Evangelist applies the title "Paraclete" to Jesus. That verse does not come from his source, nor has παράκλ. the importance there which it has in John 14–16. But the fact that Jesus is given here the otherwise unusual title παράκλ. leads one to suppose that the tradition or his source suggested it to him—at the same time allowing for modification in meaning in terms of the *interpretatio Christiana*.

[2] Bousset, Hauptpr. 171ff.; Bultmann, Eucharistion 18f.; Reitzenstein, Das Mand. Buch des Herrn der Grösse (SA Heidelb. 1919, 12) 49ff.; Histor. Zeitschr. 126 (1922), 10; ZNTW 26 (1927), 53; Is. Scheftelowitz, Die Entstehung der manich. Rel. und das Erlösungsmysterium 1922, 40, 8.82; W. Staerk, ZNTW 35 (1936) 232ff.; Die Erlösererwartung in den östl. Religionen 1938, 40ff. 91ff.; E. Percy, Untersuchungen über den Ursprung der joh. Theologie 1939, 159ff.; 297, note 43. G. Bornkamm (in the Festsch. for Rudolph Bultmann 1949; 12–35) wishes to explain the parallelism of the two Paraclete figures in terms of the idea of the Forerunner and Perfecter: just as the Baptist is the forerunner of Jesus, so Jesus is of the Spirit. The fact, also stressed by Michaelis (see previous note), that John only knows two "messengers", and not more, as Gnosticism does, cannot stand as a refutation of the explanation in terms of the Gnostic tradition. The mythological idea of a plurality of "messengers" could certainly be transformed and given new and independent expression (even in the Evangelist's source). So of course could the Forerunner-idea be transformed by the Evangelist; but could the transformation go so far as to make Jesus the forerunner—and in fact by so doing, subordinate him? In spite of the parallelism between Jesus and the Paraclete, who comes after him (demonstrated in detail by Bornkamm), and in spite of the Messianic character of the figure of the Paraclete (which Bornkamm draws attention to by ref. s to apocalyptic), there can be no doubt that the sending of Jesus is not only preparatory, but also decisive; thus the Paraclete, who follows him, can be said to be sent by him, or at his request (15.26; 16.7; 14.16, 26), and is depicted as the one who is to

But the actual *title* παράκλητος could also very well come from Gnosticism, in the sense of "supporter", "helper". Παράκλ. was originally taken as a passive, and is often rendered by the Latins by *advocatus*;[1] but later it assumes an active meaning, sometimes being taken as if it were παρακαλῶν,[2] sometimes by the practice of regarding it as synonymous with the active συνήγορος.[3] Even if παράκλ. did not become a technical term for the counsel in a court of law (as was the case with the latin *advocatus*),[4] the concept is hall-marked by the juridical sphere: παράκλ. means the one who speaks before the judges in favour of the accused; it means the intercessor and helper.[5]

Where man's situation before God is conceived as responsibility before the judge, παράκλ. is named the intercessor before God, the Mediator. It is frequent in this sense in Judaism, which has taken the word into its own vocabulary.[6] Alike angels and men, and also sacrifice, prayers, penitence and good works can all be described as Paracletes, which step in on man's side before God. Thus according to Philo *praem. poen.* 166f. sinners acquire God's καταλλαγή by means of three παράκλητοι: the goodness of God himself, the intercession of the pious fathers, and their own improvement; and according to spec. leg. I 237 the παράκλ. of the man who is asking forgiveness is κατὰ ψυχὴν ἔλεγχος (twinge of conscience, remorse). The high priest, however, according to vit. Mos. II 134, takes as his παράκλ. before God, God's son, the κόσμος, when he prays for the χωρηγία ἀφθονωτάτων ἀγαθῶν.[7] Here the juridical sense has almost disappeared; and it does completely

---

glorify Jesus and take of what he has (16.14); he is to bear witness to Jesus (15.26) and to call to mind Jesus' words (14.26). It is quite clear that the Paraclete is subordinated to both the Father and Jesus, who belong together (16.14f.). Acc. to Bornkamm, "the forerunner-perfecter-motif has been taken over by a Christology which recognises a dual manner of existence in the Redeemer: he comes as the one who suffers, and dies—and, in a new form, as Judge and Perfecter". But has not Jesus already come as Judge (3.19; 5.27; 9.39; 12.31)? Bornkamm does not overlook these objections. But when at the end he very rightly says: "Thus the Spirit-Paraclete is basically none other than the exalted Christ, the Christ who teaches and leads his community by the word, and who becomes manifest to the world too, in its existence and proclamation" (see above p. 553f., 561), he transforms the motif of the forerunner in such a way that nothing is left of it. Further clarification of the question is to be expected in a work about the forerunner-motif, which Phil. Vielhauer is preparing.

[1] See Zn., Br., on 14.16.

[2] The first definite evidence for this is in Christian authors, e.g. Orig. de. or. 10, 2 (see Br.); Oecumen. p. 191: παράκλητον τὸν ὑπὲρ ἡμῶν φησι τὸν πατέρα παρακαλοῦντα.

[3] Linked together in Clem. A. Quis div. salv. 25, 7.

[4] Instead of which, συνήγορος (oppos.: κατήγορος).

[5] Demosth. Or. 19, 1; Lykurg. Fr. 102; Phil. Jos. 239; in Flacc. 13.22f. 151; Did. 5, 2 = Barn. 20, 2: πλουσίων παράκλητοι (opp.: πενήτων ἄνομοι κριταί).

[6] Str.-B. II 560–62; Schl. ad loc. On the idea of the intercessor before God in the OT and Judaism see Nils Johannson, Parakletoi 1940.

[7] Philo uses παραιτητής in the same sense: mut. nom. 129 (the pious as intercessors for the sins of others); vit. Mos. II 166 (Moses as intercessor for the nation, alongside μεσίτης and διαλλακτής); spec. leg. I 244 (the high-priest for the nation's sins). Similarly, in Test. Levi 5.6 the angel that intercedes for Israel before God is called ὁ παραιτούμενος; so too Test. Dan. 6.2, and in addition: μεσίτης θεοῦ καὶ ἀνθρώπων.

wherever παράκλ. has the general meaning of intercessor, mediator.[1] Thus according to op. mundi 165 the αἰσθήσεις bring their gifts to the λογισμός, and take with them the πειθώ as παράκλ., so that the λογισμός should not reject them.[2]

This much, therefore appears fundamental to the structure of the concept παράκλ.: the παράκλ. is a speaker (or worker) *on someone's behalf, before somebody else*; hence the kinship with μεσίτης and διαλλακτής.[3] And yet even this duality of reference seems to be abandoned sometimes, under the influence of παρακαλεῖν = to comfort; for otherwise there is no reason why Aqu. and Thdtn. both render מְנַחֲמִים in Job 16.2 by παράκλητοι (LXX: παρακλήτορες, Symm. παρηγοροῦντες).[4]

Because the intercessor and mediator is in effect a helper, παράκλ. can sometimes simply be translated "helper", all the more because παρακαλεῖν can have the sense: "to ask for help".[5]

In Christian circles, apart from its secular use,[6] we find both meanings for παράκλ., intercessor (*deprecator*) and comforter (*consolator*). Orig. in de princ. II 7, 4 (p. 151, 12ff. Koetsch) expressly distinguishes the two meanings; the first is valid of Christ (I John 2.1f.), the second of the Spirit (John 14.26f.). It is correct that παράκλ. in I John 2.1 has the sense of *deprecator*, and this is the first time it occurs in Christian literature,[7] becoming more frequent later;[8] so too the conception of παράκλ. as *consolator* is frequently found apart from Orig.[9]

But neither meaning fits the παράκλ. of John 14–16. In so far as Jesus himself is a παράκλ. according to 14.16, he cannot thereby be described as "intercessor"; for John does not portray him as such. Not even the prayer in ch. 17 portrays him as the one who steps in before God the Judge, interceding for the sins of his own. Nor can the word παράκλ. describe Jesus as "comforter"; for he is not portrayed as a comforter,[10] nor is "comforting"

---

[1] Thus in Diog. Laert. IV 30 Bion rejects a babbler, who annoys him with his begging, with the words: τὸ ἱκανόν σοι ποιήσω . . . ἐὰν παρακλήτους πέμψῃς καὶ αὐτὸς μὴ ἔλθῃς.

[2] Cp. also Phil., op. mundi 23.

[3] P. 568 n. 7.

[4] Admittedly, Bd. assumes that this translation has been influenced by an early interpretation of the Johannine παράκλ. as the Comforter.

[5] Thucid. I 118: αὐτὸς (the Delphic God) ἔφη ξυλλήψεσθαι καὶ παρακαλούμενος καὶ ἄκλητος. Epict. diss. III 21, 12: τοὺς θεοὺς παρακαλεῖν βοηθούς. Plut. Alex. 33: παρεκάλει τοὺς θεούς. With ref. to Wis. 7.22; 8.3f.; 9.1f., 4, 9, one would be tempted to translate παράκλ. in Philo op. mundi 23 also simply as "helper": οὐδενὶ δὲ παρακλήτῳ— τίς γὰρ ἦν ἕτερος — μόνῳ δὲ αὐτῷ χρησάμενος ὁ θεὸς ἔγνω δεῖν εὐεργετεῖν . . . τὴν ἄνευ δωρεᾶς θείας φύσιν οὐδενὸς ἀγαθοῦ δυναμένην ἐπιλαχεῖν ἐξ ἑαυτῆς but here too "intercessor" is what is intended.

[6] Did. 5, 2, see p. 568 n. 5.

[7] The idea of Christ as the heavenly intercessor does occur elsewhere (Rom. 8.34; Heb. 7.25; 9.24; I Clem. 36.1; with ref. to the Spirit in Rom. 8.27), but not with the title παράκλ.

[8] See Zn., Br. on 14.16; Bd. on 15.26.

[9] See Zn., Br., Lagr. on 14.16, Bd. on 15.26.

[10] Παρακαλεῖν does not occur at all in John. Therefore no allusion is to be made here to the Jewish Messianic title "Menachem" = Comforter (Bousset, Relig. des Judent. 227;

one of the functions that belong to the Spirit. It is equally true that the Spirit is not an "intercessor" for the disciples before God; this cannot be the reason for his possessing the title παράκλ.[1] The Spirit, like Jesus himself, is Revealer; and when he as such becomes the world's accuser, he is appearing as the direct opposite of intercessor. Thus the idea of the Holy Spirit as the intercessor which occasionally occurs in rabbinic literature—and of which, without the title παράκλ., Rom. 8.27 is an example—cannot explain the figure of the Paraclete in John, especially in view of the fact that in Judaism the title פְּרַקְלִיט is not used to describe this role of the Spirit, but only סְנֵיגוֹר.[2] But there is no point in going back to Jewish ideas to discover the origin of the figure of the Paraclete, because the interpretation of this figure as Spirit is secondary.

Its origin can only be explained if one can point to a body of opinion in which the figure of the Revealer (or the Revealer himself) bore a title which could be translated by παράκλ. This is however the case in the Gnosticism which is attested by the Mandaean writings and the Odes of Solomon.[3] In the Mandaean literature there is frequent mention of helpers, and helping beings. In Ginza 328, 27ff. the soul complains that it has no helper on earth; a "higher helper" is sent it;[4] so too Ginza 346, 21ff.; 572, 36ff. where a helper comes to it in Manda dHaije, who is elsewhere frequently described in the same way.[5] In Lit. 134 the son of the first great life is praised for coming,

---

Str.-B. I 66; H. Gressmann, Messias 460f.). Barrett (apart from his commentary, in JTS 1950, 1–15) rightly sees that παράκλ. cannot mean "intercessor" in John. But he wants to regard the two meanings of παρακαλεῖν, "to comfort" and "to exhort", as combined in John, while J. G. Davies (JTS 1953, 35–38) decides in favour of the meaning "Comforter".

[1] In the lawsuit against the world that takes place before the throne of God, he could only be considered Christ's intercessor. But the meaning of the title παράκλ. is not to be sought there, but rather in the task which he—like Jesus himself—has to carry out for the disciples.

[2] It is only *one* place: LvR 6 (109a); to this can be added Midr. HL 8, 9f. (132b), where the "heavenly voice" (בַּת קוֹל) is described as סְנֵיגוֹר. Both in Str.-B. II 562. S. Mowinckel, questionably, adds Test. Jud. 20 to this. In ZNTW 32 (1933) 97–130, he tries to prove that Judaism knew of the idea of the spirit (to which older ideas of an intercessory angel were transferred) as both intercessor and accuser (the two notions together forming a unity in the concept of "witness"). But this would help to explain the Johannine Paraclete only to the extent of explaining how the Evangelist could identify the figure of the Paraclete, which had come to him from elsewhere, with the Spirit, and how he could add the title παράκλ. to Jesus in I Jn. 2.1. But Judaism affords no explanation either of the functions of the Paraclete in Jn. 14–16, or of the title itself. He is very far from being an intercessor here, and in so far as he is accuser he could not be called παράκλητος, but only κατήγορος or μάρτυς. The fact that in Jewish linguistic usage פְּרַקְלִיטָא and קַטֵּיגוֹרְיָא are opposites (examples in Mowinckel 102; Str.-B. II 560f.; W. Lueken, Michael 1898, 22f.), makes it clear that the accuser's function cannot be included in the title παράκλ. (as it can in μάρτυς).

[3] Br. and Windisch op. cit. also point to the Mandaean figure of the helper.

[4] In the hymns of the second book of the left Ginza the soul's lament is regularly followed by the coming of the helper; see p. 421 n. 8.

[5] Cp. Lit. 52,107, 139, 212; Ginza 284, 28; 285, 8; cp. Lit. 132. Other mythological figures are also considered helpers, see Ginza 320, 1; 322, 12f.; Joh.-B. 60, 15f.; 69, 3f.

preparing the way, and being a helper, guide and leader, for the souls. The believer affirms in Lit. 212:

> "Yes, I have come to love my Lord Manda dHaije, (and hope)
> That in him, there will come to be a helper for me,
> A helper and a sustainer,
> From the place of darkness to the place of light."

The messenger calls to them, Lit. 195:

> "Endure the world's persecutions,
> With genuine, believing hearts.
> Revere me in uprightness,
> That I may present myself and be to you a helper,
> A helper and a sustainer . . ."

The figure of the helper has, however, also become an independent mythological being, carrying the title Jawar = Helper, as its proper name.[1] It often takes the place of Manda dHaije,[2] or stands beside him;[3] more often one finds the combination Jawar Manda dHaije; so too it takes the place of Hibil,[4] or is combined with it.[5] It is said of Jawar, e.g., that he establishes dwellings for the righteous,[6] that he institutes baptism;[7] he is the Revealer, who has held gentle and sincere discourses;[8] he receives from the divinity the title "our word", "word of life";[9] because of his name the believers separate themselves;[10] for his sake they are persecuted.[11]

In the Od. Sal. the figure of the helper has been de-mythologised. The Lord is praised as "helper" in 7.3 for revealing himself in flesh;[12] similarly in 8.6; 21.2 (cp. 5), while in 25.2 God is called the helper.

One difficulty, greatly stressed by Michaelis (Coniect. Neotest. XI 1947, 147–162), lies in the fact that the function of the "helper" is not always described by the same term in the Mandaean writings; a variety of words is used, in a variety of ways. But this fact does not seem decisive to me, nor do the doubts raised by G. Bornkamm (see on p. 467 n. 2). Becker (98–102) refers to the Mand. figure of the helper, but says cautiously: "We do not maintain

---

[1] Frequently also Jawar-Ziwa.

[2] For instance, when Jawar-Ziwa is depicted as the "victorious", who "has secured the victory" (Ginza 141, 36; 177, 8; 204, 6f.; 238, 16), phrases otherwise used to describe Manda dHaije (e.g. Lit. 156, 165, 187). Or when there is talk of holding fast to the discourse of Jawar-Ziwa (Ginza 268, 37), and in general, where Jawar appears as messenger and revealer; see also note 8.

[3] Joh.-B. 238, 25; Lit. 55, 149f., 247.

[4] Thus, in the first section of the 5th book of the right Ginza.

[5] See Lidzbarski, Ginza, Index 599.

[6] Lit. 204, 243; Ginza 302, 30ff.; Joh.-B. 208, 6ff.

[7] Lit. 21, 149, 270f.

[8] Lit. 71f., 74, 85f., 256.

[9] Ginza 289, 10f.; in Ginza 291, 31f. he is called: "The word, the beloved first creation, in whom the life had pleasure. ..." In Ginza 295, 15f. Anoš says: "I am a word, a son of words, I who have come hither in the name of Jawar".

[10] Joh.-B. 204, 30.

[11] Ginza 310, 14; Joh.-B. 237, 4.

[12] Cp. also Od. Sal. 22.6, 10; 25.2.

that we have proved parallels to John 14.16, but only that we have outlined a body of opinion analogous to that which has produced the mythologoumenon of the ἄλλος παράκλητος."

The most probable explanation therefore may be taken to be that the figure of the παράκλητος, which the Evangelist found in his source, is this Gnostic figure of the "helper".

c) The Believers' Future as the Eschatological Situation: 16.12–33

The situation of the farewell and the problem it poses form the presupposition for the conversations in 16.12–33. The question is whether the future, which the hour of farewell is bringing in, will obliterate that which has been, or whether it will bring it to its true fruition. It depends on whether the disciples understand that the eschatological happening (Geschehen) which broke in upon the world with Jesus will remain an event (Ereignis) in *their* existence; it depends on whether they will see their situation as the eschatological situation. Ch. 17 had focused our attention on the disciples as the eschatological community; 13.31–35; 15.1–17 had laid down the "new", that is to say eschatological, command of love; 15.18–16.11 had shown that as the eschatological community they would encounter the world's hatred, and that the eschatological judgment of the world is carried through in their existence. At this point, the question is put to them: do they really want to exist as the eschatological community? What resolve, what commitment is demanded of them? In contrast to the preceding discourses, Jesus' words are now continually interrupted by dialogue. This provides the structure for what is to be said, and also adds a peculiar sense of excitement. To overcome the λύπη demands a definite assurance, which must be won in the struggle.

The theme is dealt with in three sections: 1) 16.12–15, the promise of the continuation of the revelation in the future; 2) 16.16–24, the future as the situation of χαρά; 3) 16.25–33, the condition for comprehending the eschatological existence. In the first and second sections the words of Jesus are based on the source containing the revelation-discourses, while in the third section this seems to have been used only in one verse (v. 28).

1) *The Continuation of the Revelation in the Future:* 16.12–15

V. 12: ἔτι πολλὰ ἔχω ὑμῖν λέγειν,
ἀλλ' οὐ δύνασθε βαστάζειν ἄρτι.[1]

[1] It is doubtful whether v. 12 comes from the source; the wording calls to mind concluding expressions in general use: cp. II Jn. 12; III Jn. 13; Dion. Hal. IX 30, 4: ἔχων ἔτι πλείω λέγειν παύσομαι. On the other hand it also recalls the statement in the mysteries that there are ἄρρητα μυστήρια, which only the τέλειοι or πνευματικοί are capable of understanding; see Br. In any case a prophecy of the Paraclete, taken from the source, lies at the basis of what follows, and this can be isolated from the Evangelist's interpretations, and it may well be that v. 12 was its introduction. Becker too (103) ascribes v. 12 to the source.

The discourse starts again and the first words show that the subject is not, as it was before, the *content* of the future—the task and destiny of the disciples—but *the future as such*. The intention behind the prophecy of the continuance of the revelation, contained in vv. 13–15, is to bring about a state of *readiness for the future*, and v. 12 prepares the way for this. The future will be richer than can be stated beforehand. Jesus still has much to say, but the disciples are not yet able to bear it.[1] The language that is used arises out of the situation of departure, but the words should not be understood psychologically; rather they indicate the essential nature of the case. Readiness for the future is not only demanded by that particular hour, but it describes the very *existence* of the disciple. The believer has not been taken away from the world (17.15); he has a future in it, and must withstand whatever it brings and demands. What he has to go through, however, cannot be anticipated in words, which he could not even put together; the believer can only measure the significance and claims of what he has to undergo when he actually meets it. He anticipates the future in faith, not in foreknowledge. And thus the apparent contradiction between v. 12 and 15.15 is comprehensible: Jesus cannot state all that the future will bring, and yet he has said it all,[2] everything, that is, that makes the believer free and ready for it. One cannot simply take cognizance of his word and then preserve it within a body of knowledge; it shows the believer its significance and its power each time he is face to face with the future. The power of Jesus' word, becoming effectual each time afresh, will always illumine the future; this is the meaning of the next prophecy.

V. 13: ὅταν δὲ ἔλθῃ (ὁ παράκλητος),[3]
ὁδηγήσει ὑμᾶς εἰς τὴν ἀλήθειαν πᾶσαν.[4]

---

[1] Βαστάζειν is used figuratively, as in Rev. 2.2f. (cp. Acts 15.10; Mt. 11.30), but this is also Greek usage (see Br.); it corresponds to סבל in Rabbinic lit. (Schl., Str.-B.). Ἄρτι = "now already", as in v. 31; 13.7.

[2] See p. 543 n. 3. Wrede (Messiasgeh. 192) points out "a clear contradiction" in John: "Jesus points to a future revelation, to a higher communication, than that which the disciples are receiving at that time, and yet he tells them everything in his lifetime". He rightly regards this contradiction as intentional (on the part of the Evangelist); the statements, "Jesus has already said everything that he is still concealing", and, "He has as yet said nothing in such a way that it could be understood", belong together.

[3] This was clearly what the source read: the Evangelist inserted ἐκεῖνος (see p. 48 n. 3), interpreting the Paraclete as the πνεῦμα τ. ἀλ. at the same time (see pp. 552f.). Becker reconstructs the source in the same way (103).

[4] D reads ἐκεῖνος ὑμᾶς ὁδηγήσει; e m vg. Eus. Cyr. Hier.: διηγήσεται ὑμῖν τὴν ἀλ. π., which is an obvious correction. If ἐν τῇ ἀλ. π. (ℵ D L W Θ al, instead of εἰς τὴν ἀλ. π.) is original, then in this context the meaning can only be: "into all truth"; ἐν instead of εἰς would be in line with its frequent use with verbs of motion (Bl.-D. § 218). In the LXX ὁδηγεῖν ἐν denotes leading within an area, or in the direction afforded by a path (Ps. 5.9; 26.11 etc.; in the same sense, the Dat. is used by itself: Ps. 85.11); to denote the goal ἐπὶ is used (Ps. 24.5).

If the Spirit is at work in the word that is proclaimed in the community,[1] then this word gives faith the power to step out into the darkness of the future, because the future is always illumined afresh by the word.[2] Faith will see the "truth" in each case, i.e. it will always be certain of the God who is manifest in the word, precisely because it understands the present in the light of this word.[3] The promise is no different from that in 8.31f.[4]

If it is true that the Spirit is, so to speak, to take Jesus' place, and if the Spirit's leadership is to bring the believer for the first time to the fullness of truth, then this is because Jesus and his word only come to their true fruition by this means. In this sense the following sentence gives the grounds (γάρ!) for the promise:

οὐ γὰρ λαλήσει ἀφ' ἑαυτοῦ,
ἀλλ' ὅσα ἀκούει λαλήσει.[5]

---

[1] See pp. 552ff.; 560f.

[2] "Always ... afresh" is expressed by the word πᾶσαν (put at the end, as in 5.22; 10.4). The OT provides formal parallels to ὁδηγεῖν εἰς τ. ἀλ. such as Ps. 24.5: ὁδήγησόν με ἐπὶ τὴν ἀλήθειάν σου and Ps. 85.11: ὁδήγησόν με . . . τῇ ὁδῷ σου, καὶ πορεύσομαι ἐν τῇ ἀληθείᾳ σου, as well as others which speak of walking in the truth (Ps. 26.3; I Reg. 2.4; Is. 38.3 etc.). But in the OT the "truth" (אֱמֶת) is not, as it is in John, the truth which is believed and known, but is either the law, the norm of behaviour, or a man's integrity or loyalty. Thus even the passages Wis. 9.11; 10.10, 17, which speak of the ὁδηγεῖν or of the ὁδός of Wisdom are no true parallels. And those which speak of the spirit as guide are only analogous in form (Is. 63.14; Ps. 143.10); so too Philo gig. 55, while the ref. in vit. Mos. II 265 is to the spirit of prophetic inspiration, which shows to the νοῦς the ἀλ. (i.e., not God's reality, but what is right in each situation). True parallels, in so far as it is a matter of being led to the divine reality, are C. Herm. 7, 2: ζητήσατε χειραγωγὸν τὸν ὁδηγήσαντα ὑμᾶς ἐπὶ τὰς τῆς γνώσεως θύρας . . . 9, 10: ὁ δὲ νοῦς . . . ὑπὸ τοῦ λόγου μέχρι τινὸς ὁδηγηθεὶς φθάναι μέχρι τῆς ἀληθείας. 10, 21: εἰς δὲ τὴν εὐσεβῆ ψυχὴν ὁ νοῦς ἐμβὰς ὁδηγεῖ αὐτὴν ἐπὶ τὸ τῆς γνώσεως φῶς; cp. 12.12; 4, 11. Wik. and Dodd (174) also interpret the passage correctly. The latter (223) also refers to the parallels in Philo and C. Herm. DSD 4, 2ff. refers to the "ways" along which the "spirit of truth" and the "spirit of darkness" guide mankind.

[3] The notion that the Spirit protects the believers from self-deception and spurious piety is of course correct, but foreign to this context. A true parallel is to be found in Od. Sal. 7.21 (24).

"For ignorance has been destroyed,
Because the knowledge of the Lord hath arrived."

[4] Cp. Hölderlin, Empedocles II 4 (v. Hellingr. III pp. 156, 18ff), where the revelation is not of course continued in the word of proclamation, but in the word of nature:

"What I have said,
While remaining here, is little,
Yet perhaps the ray of light will take it
Down through the twilight clouds
To the still source, which may bless you,
And you may think of me".

[5] 'Ακούσει (B D W), instead of ἀκούει (א L), is an assimilation to the other futures; ἀκούσῃ in ℜ pm does not need to be taken into account. Ἄν is frequently added. Becker regards v. 13b as a gloss of the Evangelist's.

The statement affirms that the word that is at work in the community really is the word of revelation and not human discourse; i.e. it is like the word that Jesus spoke, which did not come from himself.[1] It is irrelevant from whom the Spirit hears the word, whether from Jesus or from God; for, as v. 15a reminds us, they are one and the same. This means that the Spirit's word is not something new, to be contrasted with what Jesus said, but that the Spirit only states the latter afresh. The Spirit will not bring new illumination, or disclose new mysteries; on the contrary, in the proclamation effected by him, the word that Jesus spoke continues to be efficacious.[2]

Before vv. 14f. make this explicit, the addition: καὶ τὰ ἐρχόμενα ἀναγγελεῖ ὑμῖν tells us the essential significance of the word in this context: it illuminates the future. If the sentence is not an addition of the ecclesiastical redactor,[3] but comes from the Evangelist himself, he has certainly modelled it on the common Christian idea of the πνεῦμα τῆς προφητείας (Rev. 19.10), at the same time giving a bold interpretation of that idea. For it is quite clear in the context, that there is no thought of apocalyptic prophecy; there would indeed be no reason why Jesus could not have made such prophecies himself, nor why the disciples could not bear them "now." Rather the meaning is this: the future will not be unveiled in a knowledge imparted before it happens, but it will be illuminated again and again by the word that is at work in the community.[4]

V. 14: [ἐκεῖνος ἐμὲ δοξάσει, ὅτι]
ἐκ τοῦ ἐμοῦ λήμψεται
καὶ ἀναγγελεῖ ὑμῖν.[5]

---

[1] See p. 249 n. 1.

[2] To suppose that the Spirit will initiate into the great mysteries, while Jesus only brought the small ones (Windisch op. cit. 120) is wrong (see also below p. 576 n. 2). It is also wholly wrong to find here the "tendency to downgrade" the Spirit's proclamation. That the Spirit can only state the word of Jesus afresh is the proof of the authenticity of the word which is proclaimed in the community. Rightly, Hosk., who stresses that this implies the rejection of private inspiration.

[3] This conclusion does not seem inevitable to me. Only if it is correct, is there any ref. to the Book of Revelation. (Sasse op. cit. 274; Windisch op. cit. 131, 1). In John, apart from vv. 13f., ἀναγγέλλειν occurs only in 4.25; 16.23 v. 1.; also I Jn. 1.5, with ref. to Christian preaching (so also Acts 20.20, 27; I Pet. 1.12); ἀγγελία, used of the proclamation, in I Jn. 1.5; 3.11 as v. 1. alongside ἐπαγγελία; ἀπαγγέλλειν in 16.25; I Jn. 1.2f., with ref. to the proclamation (so also Acts 26.20; Mt. 11.18 (= Is. 42.1); Heb. 2.12 [= Ps. 21.23]). P. Joüon (Rech. sc. rel. 28 (1938), 234f.) thinks that ἀναγγ. always has the special sense of reporting something that has been heard. Young finds the language of Isaiah in the use of ἀναγγέλλειν (= reveal).

[4] See Faulhaber 53; Str. 295. Differently, Temple: the ἐρχόμενα are the Passion, Resurrection and Ascension, which the Spirit will expound, when they have taken place. Acc. to Hosk. the ἐρχ. are the new epochs of the church, in the sense of 4.23.

[5] I have some reservations about this reconstruction of the source's word-order.

This is an express statement that the Spirit's word does not displace or surpass the word of Jesus, as if it were something new. Rather it is the word of Jesus that will be alive in the community's proclamation; the Spirit will "call it to mind" (14.26). And herein is to be found the completion of Jesus' glorification.[1] The word of Jesus is not a collection of doctrines that is in need of supplementation, nor is it a developing principle that will only be unfolded in the history of ideas; as the Spirit's proclamation it always remains the word spoken into the world from beyond. On the other hand the Spirit is not the "inner light" that brings new knowledge on its own authority; it is the ever new power of Jesus' word; it retains the old in the continual newness that arises from the speaking of the word in the present.[2]

In a note (**v. 15**) the Evangelist[3] comments on what has been said in v. 14 by reminding us of the unity of Father and Son (10.30; 17.10): that the Spirit continues the proclamation of the word of *Jesus* means that it is the word of God, i.e. revelation.

2) *The Future as the Situation of the Eschatological* χαρά: 16.16–24

Vv. 12–15 had spoken of the future, and had done so in such a way as to present all that had been experienced up to then as something preliminary. The present is the critical time, the moment of λύπη; it is this that has to be overcome, in order to find true unity of past and future. The question, which had arisen as early as 13.33, is reframed and asked again here. There it was said: ἔτι μικρὸν μεθ' ὑμῶν εἰμι, and

---

[1] See p. 491.

[2] Loisy has rightly seen that the Paraclete's revelation is not a complete doctrine, limited to the text of the NT, or to ecclesiastical tradition: it is identical with Jesus' preaching, being its "*illustration et développement*", without at the same time being limited or fixed in size. This is correct, so long as *développement* is not understood in the sense of the development of the history of ideas. It is also correct to see this as the Evangelist's justification of his own work (thus e.g. Windisch: Joh. und die Synopt. 147), only not in the sense of the κόσμος, as if a new stage in the development of the history of dogma should be justified. Wrede (Messiasgeh. 186–203) has seen the main point, in his refutation of Weizsäcker's view that the Evangelist is appealing to the Spirit as the source of new revelation, in contrast to the older apostolic doctrine. This would entail entirely new subject-matter, which is not the case; Jesus has already said all that the believer must know. Wrede is also right in pointing out that the Johannine view of the Paraclete is analogous to the Markan Messianic secret; for the teaching given by the Paraclete is not set over against an earlier stage of revelation (for this teaching is the same as that given by Jesus), but the disciples' lack of understanding. The only mistake Wrede makes is to regard this lack of understanding as a weakness that can be overcome, instead of seeing that it constitutes the essential preliminary for believing knowledge, which will only become true understanding through the test it has to undergo again and again in the future.

[3] Cp. 13.11; the comment in v. 15 is inserted into the text, as in 6.65. On the ref. to what was said earlier, see p. 348 n. 4; on διὰ τοῦτο, ... ὅτι, see p. 92, n, 2. Λήμψεται, which in many cases is read instead of λαμβάνει, is an assimilation to v. 14.

the law of their communal life was given to the disciples for the time of their isolation as Jesus' testament to them; moreover the situation they were in and the task they had in the world were pointed out to them. Now they are told: in reality that μικρόν is not followed by a time of isolation; this is only a transitional stage, a second μικρόν. Everything that was said in 13.34f.; 15.1–16.11 about the commandment and the community's task, subordinated as it was to the promise of the coming Paraclete, now appears in a new light: μικρὸν καὶ ὄψεσθέ με.

V. 16: μικρὸν καὶ οὐκέτι θεωρεῖτέ με,
καὶ πάλιν μικρὸν καὶ ὄψεσθέ με.[1]

There is a double μικρὸν[2] then to be expounded! 1. the short interval till Jesus' departure, and 2. the short interval till they see him again. But while that can be stated quite simply, it is far from easy to understand it, and the difficulty is emphasized by the disciples' discussion in **vv. 17–19**, in which they quote the words of Jesus. The question is raised from their midst[3] as to what the words mean; and of a truth, the fact that the discovery of their meaning depends upon understanding the farewell, the departure of Jesus, is shown by the words καὶ ὅτι ὑπάγω πρὸς τὸν πάτερα in v. 17, which the question, with the help of v. 10, adds to the words of Jesus, repeated from v. 16.[4] The disciples are as far from understanding what Jesus has said about his departure as the Jews had been earlier (7.36).[5] They do not turn to him directly; it is as if he had already left them. But in the perplexity which affords them no answer, they are met by the word of Jesus.[6] He begins by pinpointing their question,[7] in order to go on with greater emphasis—ἀμὴν ἀμὴν λέγω ὑμῖν:

---

[1] V. 16 comes from the source; the original continuation was v. 20; vv. 21–22a may also belong to the source, certainly v. 22b (πάλιν δὲ ὄψομαι κτλ.) and v. 23a (up to οὐκ ἐρ. οὐδέν) do; perhaps also the ἵνα-clause in v. 24. Ὅτι (ἐγὼ) ὑπάγω πρὸς τὸν πάτερα, which is added to v. 16 in 𝔎 pl, the Syrian versions and the later Latin mss., is a gloss on v. 17, unless καὶ ὅτι ὑπάγω κτλ. should be cut out there, too, against the attestation of the mss. Certainly v.10 provides sufficient motivation for the wording of v.17, and v.19 does not repeat the ὑπάγω. Becker (103) assigns v. 15a (πάντα ... ἐμά ἐστιν) to the source, as well as v. 16.

[2] Μικρὸν καὶ is a Semitic form (Greek would be κατὰ μικρόν) = עוֹד מְעַט; cp. Ex. 17.4; Hos. 1.4; Is. 10.25; Jer. 51 (28), 33; ἔτι is normally added, as in 13.33; 14.19.

[3] Ἐκ τῶν μαθ. sc. τινές, as in 7.40; see Bl.-D. § 164.2; Raderm. 125; hardly a Semitism, see Colwell 86. The speakers clearly represent the disciples as a whole, cp. v. 29, where the οἱ μαθ. are speaking.

[4] Unless the repetition is a gloss, see note 1.

[5] Τί ἐστιν τοῦτο ὃ λέγει ἡμῖν is a Rabbinic phrase, see Schl. On οὐκ οἴδαμεν κτλ. (v. 18), Schl. quotes Mech. on Ex. 22.3: ὅρκος ὅτι οὐκ οἶδα τί λαλεῖς.

[6] The motif of omniscience (see 1.48; 2.24 etc., esp. 6.61) serves to point out his superiority over the bewildered disciples.

[7] On ζητεῖν see p. 171 n. 3.

V. 20: κλαύσετε καὶ θρηνήσετε ὑμεῖς,
ὁ δὲ κόσμος χαρήσεται.
ὑμεῖς λυπηθήσεσθε,
ἀλλ' ἡ λύπη ὑμῶν εἰς χαρὰν γενήσεται.[1]

In 13.33 the situation of the *first* μικρόν was depicted as that of fruitless searching; here it is one of lamentation,[2] of λύπη. The fact that the χαρά of the κόσμος corresponds to it gives it its special significance; it is not personal sadness at the loss of a loved one, at the decease of a great man. It is rather the situation of loneliness in the κόσμος, the situation in which men find themselves when they are called out of the κόσμος by Jesus (17.16; 15.19) and yet are at the same time still in it, given over to its hatred (15.18–16.4a). The κόσμος rejoices at the departure of Jesus, because his appearance called it in question in its security; it hates the community because the latter's existence means the continuation of the offence. The community, however, in belonging to Jesus, must take upon itself loneliness within the κόσμος and must accept its hatred, precisely because it belongs to Jesus and no longer to the world (15.19). This implies λύπη, θλῖψις (v. 33), ταραχή (14.1). For its situation is not transparently clear; it has to find itself within that situation.[3]

And of a truth, this it must do at once, quicker than it thought: μικρὸν καὶ οὐκέτι θεωρεῖτέ με. We are not concerned here with a psychological analysis; the first μικρόν must be seen to be an essential part of the matter we are dealing with (as must the second). In the historical situation, which serves to illustrate the matter itself, μικρόν means the short period before the passion. But it has a deeper significance than that: first, in the light of the definitive separation to come, all the past seems a μικρόν, however long or short it may in fact have been. But more important still, μικρόν means basically the time of the encounter with the revelation, which is followed by that Too-late;[4] that is to say, it means the time of faith's answer, the time of tarrying with eyes on the gift, the time of experience, of making the freedom one's own, the time of thoughtful consideration, of conscious understanding. All that is only a μικρόν, and can only be so. There is no tarrying in the experience, if what is experienced is not to fall into pieces. The Revealer at each point encounters experience within history in the actual Word that

---

[1] Becker also assigns v. 20 to the source, regarding vv. 17–19 as the work of the Evangelist.

[2] Κλαίειν and θρηνεῖν are also combined in Jer. 22.10, to describe the lamentation for the dead; κλαίειν is also used for this in 11.31, θρήνειν in II Reg. 1.17.

[3] See ThWB IV 323, 15ff.

[4] See pp. 307f.

is spoken, as the σὰρξ γενόμενος (e.g. in John's gospel itself). If faith responds to him, it still does not have him at its disposal.[1] The Revealer disappears again, because he does not intend to be eternally present as the σὰρξ γενόμενος, but as the δοξασθείς. The tarrying with the word that has been apprehended, either in experience or in thought, is never more than a μικρόν; that is true of each stage of faith and of knowledge that is reached. Jesus goes forth—he goes into his δόξα. To believe in the glorified one is not to stand on the same level as he, in direct contact with him, as if he were at faith's disposal. The disciples cannot immediately come to the place where he is (13.33). There always remains that peculiar distance between the believer and the Revealer; the believer always has to stand the test of looking into the apparently empty and dark future and of waiting. And yet it is also true of that waiting: καὶ πάλιν μικρόν. The λύπη of isolation is to become χαρά.[2]

It is not however as if the promise simply meant that χαρά will follow λύπη after an interval of time; on the contrary χαρά has its origin in λύπη. Λύπη is an essential part of Christian existence, if the meaning of the revelation is to become clear. This is what **v. 21**[3] is saying, by means of the illustration of the woman in travail: she suffers her λύπη, her θλῖψις, for the sake of her χαρά:[4] her χαρά springs from her

---

[1] Cp. R. M. Rilke (The Book of Hours: tr. A. L. Peck: Hogarth Press 1961, p. 113):

And if at night by someone's grasp you're pressed,
so that you're forced to come into his prayer:
You are the guest
that still will onward fare.

And yet Christian isolation has to be distinguished from that of mysticism, in so far as the latter means the rupture of a direct relationship with God. Pribnow (16, 11) compares the pain involved in the rupture of the cultic-mystical experience (Epict. diss. IV 1, 106; Apul. met. 11, 24 p. 286. 15ff. Helm.).

[2] Γίνεσθαι εἰς is a Semitism, see Mk. 12.10 (=Ps. 117.22); Rev. 8.11; 16.19 etc., Bl.-D. § 145, 1. For a true parallel, cp. Act. Thom. 142 p. 249, 5ff.

[3] The variants (D it syr ἡμέρα instead of ὥρα; D 579 c λύπης instead of θλίψεως) are of no importance.

[4] The imagery of the birthpangs of the woman in travail is used frequently and variously: Is. 21.3; 26.17; 37.3; 66.7–9; Jer. 30.6; Hos. 13.13; Mic. 4.9f.; also in the Book of the Psalms in the Qumran literature: (1 QH) Pl 37, 7f.; 39, 31; see JBL 74 (1955), 189; 75 (1956), 31. It also occurs in the Greek world: Hom. Il. 11, 269 (for the joy following the birth, cp. Hymn. Hom. 1, 125f.: χαῖρε δὲ Λητώ, οὕνεκα τοξοφόρον καὶ καρτερὸν υἱὸν ἔτικτεν). With ref. to Israel's "redemption": R. to Hl. 2, 14 (Schl. ad loc.); on the "pains" of the final age which precedes the appearance of the salvation, see Bousset, Relig. des Judent. 250f.; Volz, Eschatologie 147; Moore II 361; Str.-B. I 950. It is not likely that the Evangelist (or his source) is alluding to this idea (Ho., Htm., Stählin, ZNTW 33 (1934), 241ff.; Gulin II 35f.), because he makes no use of the characteristic word ὠδῖνες (Mk. 13.8 and par. s), which would be natural here. In any case there would have to have been a radical transformation of the idea, because the subject is not the pains of the world, which is bringing something new to birth, but the pains of the individual believers (Br.). Loisy's allegorising is absurd: the woman in travail is the woman mentioned in Rev. 12, i.e. the believing synagogue, the mother of Christ, and also believing mankind, the mother

λύπη.[1] The λύπη, which now envelops the disciples, is to be understood like that (v. 22):

> καὶ ὑμεῖς οὖν νῦν μὲν λύπην ἔχετε,[2]
> πάλιν δὲ ὄψομαι ὑμᾶς,
> καὶ χαρήσεται ὑμῶν ἡ καρδία,
> καὶ τὴν χαρὰν ὑμῶν οὐδεὶς αἴρει ἀφ' ὑμῶν.[3]

If the disciples' λύπη is grounded in their loneliness, so too is their χαρά, because it springs from their turning away from the κόσμος; their loneliness also has the positive significance of freedom (8.32), and of this the disciples will become fully aware: they will "see Jesus again," i.e. in turning away from the world, they will experience their fellowship with him, and "their heart will rejoice;"[4] this joy of theirs is out of the world's reach.

That ὄψομαι ὑμᾶς does not mean the Parousia in the sense of Jewish or primitive-Christian apocalyptic[5] follows at once from the fact that the χαρά of reunion must correspond to the λύπη of separation. Just as the latter depicts the situation of the believer within the κόσμος, so must the former. Accordingly, only the judgment of the world as described in vv. 8–11, and not the cosmic drama of apocalyptic thought can correspond to the believer's χαρά. If this were not the case, what would be the sense of the second μικρόν? If the idea were that the μικρόν lasts until the Parousia in the apocalyptic sense, then the union portrayed in 13.34f.; 15.1–17 (the "friendship" of Jesus, which according to 15.11 is the very means of fulfilling the disciples' χαρά) would have to take place in the stage of λύπη, and so too would the disciples' work as depicted in 15.18–16.11! Furthermore, ὄψομαι ὑμᾶς cannot be different from ἔρχομαι πρὸς ὑμᾶς in 14.18, which, according to 14.19, is not visible to the κόσμος; therefore it cannot be the apocalyptic drama that is intended. Again, the disciples' inability to understand would have no sense

---

of the chosen; the birth is the resurrection of Jesus, and, however, also his Parousia. Dodd (395f.) accepts the view that the idea of the "birthpangs" of the final age is present here, and understands the πάλιν μικρόν of v. 17 in the light of this idea: the resurrection, which is to follow Jesus' death immediately, is the fulfilment of the eschatological hope.

[1] Rightly, B. Weiss. Ho., Br.: the parable "preaches more than just the ancient wise saying that conquered troubles are forgotten", on which Br. quotes Soph. in Stob. Anth. III 29, 37; cp. Soph. Ai. 264.

[2] Ἕξετε (A D (L) W al it) is an alternative reading to ἔχετε (P 22 B ℵ* 𝔎 pm).

[3] Instead of αἴρει B D* lat read ἀρεῖ, which is a pedantic correction. Becker (104) ascribes v. 22 to the source, also however v. 21 apart from its ending: διὰ τ. χαράν κτλ.

[4] The heart as the subject of joy, as in Is. 66.14; Jer. 15.16 etc.; the heart is also the subj. of joy in Rabbinic (see Schl.) and Greek usage (e.g. Eur. El. 401f.); from the world of the mysteries, cp. Act. Thom. 146 p. 255, 2.

[5] Characteristically, it is not said: ὀφθήσομαι ὑμῖν, cp. Heb. 9.28. E. Lohmeyer, Galiläa und Jerusalem 1936, 11f., admittedly finds in these words the set phraseology used to describe the Parousia.

if it were a matter of the mythological ideas of Ascension and Parousia; if Jesus' words had referred to his glorious second coming, the disciples would have understood him at once.[1] Precisely this motif of the disciples' lack of understanding shows that the going and coming again of Jesus do not have their old mythological sense, but are to be re-interpreted. It is indeed possible that the μικρόν is an answer to the questions which worried the community as the result of the delay in the expected parousia.

It is more feasible to refer ὄψομαι ὑμᾶς *to the Easter experiences*,[2] and there is no doubt that the Evangelist is thinking of these. But he sees their significance in the experience depicted in vv. 20–22,[3] which is not limited to the Easter-experiences, and this means that the latter lose their special importance. Like the parousia, the Easter event is translated into the experience of the believer, an experience that is always possible and always necessary. And by combining the terminology of Easter and the Parousia, the Evangelist shows that for him they mean the same thing. Within the sphere of the Easter terminology, phrases are used which speak of their seeing each other again (16.16–20, 22; 14.19), of the knowledge that the Jesus who died, lives (14.19), of his appearance before the disciples, but not before the world (14.21–23). To the idea of the Parousia belong the corresponding expressions of ὑπάγειν (16.5,10,17; 14.4f., 28) and ἔρχεσθαι (14.3,18,23,28), the talk of "that day" (16.23,26; 14.20) and of the "coming of the hour" (16.25). Indeed Pentecost belongs to Easter and the Parousia too, in so far as the sending of the Paraclete as the Spirit is the Pentecostal event, which thus coincides with Easter and the Parousia because in the Paraclete Jesus himself comes to his own.[4]

Thus the Evangelist has used the primitive Christian ideas and hopes to describe the stages through which the life of the believer has to pass, and on which it can also come to grief. The Revealer encounters man first of all in the word that is spoken to him, the word that requires an answer from him. If, in his answer, he turns to the Revealer for the first time, and this turning records itself in experience and knowledge,

---

[1] Thus Loisy, rightly; see also Faulhaber 91 (note 6). I regard G. Stählin's attempt to interpret the Johannine predictions of the second coming in terms of the traditional expectation of the parousia as unsuccessful (ZNTW 33 (1934) 241ff.). K. Kundsin (op. cit. 210ff.) has rightly seen that we are concerned here with the experiences of individuals; but that the ref. is to the experience of martyrs, to whom Jesus comes in order to take them home, is not at any rate true of 16.16–24. For the promise is valid for the whole community, of which the disciples are the representatives. And how should one conceive of the situation whereby the martyr, whom Jesus has brought home, is to pray in Jesus' name, and be certain that his prayer will be heard (vv. 23, 26)? The situation presupposed is the same as in 17.15, and the problem of the farewell discourses is precisely the disciples' fellowship with Jesus while they are separated from him, remaining in the world.

[2] Thus B. Weiss, Ho., Br. Here too the point can be made that the voice is not ὀφθήσομαι; cp. I Cor. 15.5ff.; Lk. 24.34.

[3] So too 14.18–20; see ad loc. See also Goguel, Trois Études 1931, 22f., 28.

[4] Thus Htm., correctly, while Bl. acknowledges at least the identification of Easter and Pentecost.

this is nevertheless only something preliminary, a μικρόν, in which the eternal appears as present reality. But the believer remains in time, in which the present passes away as something preliminary, and the believer—for whom the world has become strange—stands so to speak in emptiness. If he turns his gaze back to what is past, he is in λύπη: it has gone by! But this very emptiness is also only a μικρόν, a temporary thing, something "between," an essential stage if he is to understand the significance of his faith correctly. He does not have faith as a timeless possession, but only as a gift that has always to be grasped afresh. How long this "between" is, as a measurable period of time, is neither here nor there; it can be reduced to a moment, as is shown by 14.19, where the two μικρόν of 16.16 are drawn together into one. In fact, however, every Now that the believer experiences is hall-marked by the fact that in it the first decision taken for Jesus has to be maintained. Faith of course is based on the past, in so far as the eschatological word called it into being in the past; and the Paraclete, who is to show it the ἀλήθεια in the future, is only to call to mind what has already been heard by it. But the believer is based on the past only in that he was called to the eschatological existence then, an existence that is continually directed towards the future.[1] He remains loyal to the word he has heard when he remains always ready to hear it afresh, when he does not tarry in *his own* past but in the word's actually being spoken; for the speaking of the word, as the eschatological event, is a mode of being that anticipates every act of faith. The believer always has to catch up with this anticipatory existence, which is peculiar to the word; in catching up with it, he is however always at the end of time; his existence stands under the ὄψομαι ὑμᾶς.

The promise καὶ τὴν χαρὰν ὑμῶν οὐδεὶς αἴρει ἀφ' ὑμῶν is not contradicted by the fact that the believer can only attain the Christian χαρά by going through the λύπη. He can of course give up his χαρά, but nobody can take it away from him, because it does not have its origin in him but in the revelation, and because it is not a phenomenon of the world and it therefore always stands before him as a new possibility. This statement contains an implied contrast to the joy of the κόσμος (v. 20). Its pride in possessing and achieving is realised as χαρά precisely over against the Christian community, with which it compares itself, and whose "unfamiliarity with the things of the world" and "aloofness from life" are the occasion of ridicule and contempt on the part of the κόσμος. It can see the community's λύπη, its loneliness and its helplessness, but it cannot see its transformation into χαρά (cp. 14.17,19),

---

[1] See Faulhaber 54f.

because it does not understand its essential nature.[1] The community, however, sees that behind the χαρά of the κόσμος lies anxiety, which any moment could take the joy away.[2]

The nature of the joy of faith is described in **vv. 23f.**;[3] first: καὶ ἐν ἐκείνῃ τῇ ἡμέρᾳ ἐμὲ οὐκ ἐρωτήσετε οὐδέν. The words ἐν. ἐκ. τ. ἡμ.[4] tell us at once that it is the eschatological joy. In what does it consist? It is not described as a psychic condition of rapture, but is defined as the situation in which the believers no longer need to ask anything.[5] They will no longer stand there as those who cannot understand (vv. 17f.: 14.5, 8, 22), and the question, which till then was appropriate to their situation, will die away in silence. Jesus, as vv. 25–30 make clear, will no longer be a riddle to them. That, however, is *the eschatological situation*: to have no more questions! In faith, existence has received its unequivocal explanation, because it is no longer explained in terms of the world, and is therefore no longer a puzzle. But this is to say that the believers live in *joy*; because it is the nature of joy that all questioning grows silent, and nothing needs explaining. That is why the lilies and the birds, which have no "care" i.e. no questions, are the "teachers of joy."[6] We are not told the cause or object of the joy;[7] eschatological joy has no object that can be stated.[8] It rejoices at absolutely nothing—from the point of view of the κόσμος, whose joy is always occasioned by something particular, and is thus always dependent on conditions obtaining at a particular time. The κόσμος can only be more or less joyful,

---

[1] Cp. Hölderlin, Empedocl. II 4 (Helling. III 138, 20ff.):

Dost thou not understand? Now, it is only right
That even the all-knowing one should sometime wonder!
Thy work is finished, and thy deceits
Cannot touch my joy. Dost thou understand that too?

[2] Cp. the two kinds of grief in II Cor. 7.10.

[3] The first sentence from v. 23 may be from the source; v. 24b belongs to it as the second half of the couplet: ἵνα κτλ. The form of words ἐν ἐκ. τ. ἡμ. may stem from the Evangelist, who wanted to relate the statement to the eschatology of the community. On the other hand, Becker (104) ascribes v. 23b to the source, although with reservations.

[4] On ἐν ἐκ. τ. ἡμ. as a description of the eschatological age, see Zech. 12.3f, 6, 8f.; Mt. 7.22; Lk. 10.12; 17.31 etc. Cp. the analogous transference of "Day" in Od. Sal. 41.4.

[5] Ἐρωτᾶν means of course "ask a question", as in vv. 5, 19, 30; for the disciples are depicted as those who do not understand, who up till now only ask questions (cp. also 13.37; 14.5, 22). It would therefore be wrong to take ἐρωτᾶν in the sense of the αἰτεῖν that follows, meaning "to request", and therefore to find the point of the statement in the contrast between ἐμὲ—τὸν πατέρα (B. Weiss, Bd.). The change of verb would then be incomprehensible; moreover ἀμ. ἀμ. λέγω ὑμῖν does not introduce a contrast, but a new idea. Rightly, Hosk., Wik., Barr.

[6] Kierkegaard, Christl. Reden, German 1929, 332ff., E. T. Christian Discourses, 1939, 351ff.

[7] In contrast to this, cp. the portrayals of the eschatological glory in apocalyptic; see p. 507 n. 1, and in general see on 17.13, pp. 505ff.

[8] See p. 507, and for χαρά in general, pp. 505ff.

not unconditionally joyful; joy cannot be the definition of its existence, because it is never without questions, and can at best only forget them.[1] The believers' existence on the contrary is joy which no-one can take away, because it is not dependent on a cause which can be surrendered to the world and is thus without care or questions. The believers stand beyond the κόσμος, and rejoice that He "sees them again." In seeing him, they understand themselves, and thus at the same time everything which the world can bring against them. Their existence has become transparent to them; they have become "sons of light" (12.36); the anxiety of blindness has been taken away from them, and the future is no longer threatening; they live in an eternal "today"; their day is the eschatological ἡμέρα.[2] Thus the work of the Revealer is brought to completion, and the world has become creation again.[3]

The eschatological joy is delineated further by saying with great emphasis (ἀμ. ἀμ. λέγω ὑμῖν) that it is the situation of the *prayer that is assured of being heard*, which 15.7,16 had already described as faith's highest possibility.[4] The fact that such a possibility is based on the revelation event is expressed in a strange way, by saying that not only the disciples' asking but also the Father's giving takes place (as in 15.16)

---

[1] The Greek believes that for mortal man there is no such thing as pure joy; see ThWB IV 315, 1ff. Cp. Hölderlin, Empedocles II 4 (Hellingrath III 157, 4f.) "There comes and goes joy, but it never belongs to mortal man". Acc. to Schiller, joy is the "divine spark", the "daughter of Elysium", i.e. joy is of eschatological character. That a secret worry always accompanies human joy is expressed in the Greek anxiety about the over-abundance of happiness, which calls down the envy of the gods; or cp. also the verses of Mörike: "Do not overwhelm me with joy, or with sorrow . . ."

[2] Cp. Kierkegaard op. cit. That true joy demands the eternity of today, of the Now, is shown both by the word of "Faust": "To this moment I could say: Tarry, thou art so beautiful!", and by Nietzsche, when he says: "All desire longs for eternity . . . " But the unbearable thought that the joy will disappear can drive a man to request that he be taken away at the height of his joy: "Now am I blessed! Pierce my heart!" (C. F. Meyer). Cp. the request that Hölderlin's Empedocles makes of the gods (II 4, Hellingr. III 1511 26ff.):

"As soon as I can no longer enjoy my holy happiness
In the strength of youth, without staggering,
. . .
Then to warn me, to send quickly into my heart
An unexpected fate . . . ."

Behind the peculiar retributive theory of Herm. sim. VI 4 there lies strangely concealed the knowledge that torment extends the Now, while the time of joy is like a timeless moment: the torment of one hour of punishment inflicted on the τρυφῶντες corresponds to thirty hours of lust.

[3] See pp. 44f.

[4] See pp. 540, 546. Kundsin (see p. 581 n. 1) wants to identify the prayer that is certain to be answered with the prayer of the martyr: he who prays in the name of Jesus prays as the companion of Jesus in his suffering. But how, in that case, are we to think of the Father's granting the prayer, which also takes place in the name of Jesus? And in any case the prayer mentioned in 15.7, 16 is not connected with martyrdom, but with the union of love with Jesus. See p. 581 n. 1.

ἐν τῷ ὀνόματί μου, i.e. by invocation of Jesus.[1] But the one corresponds to the other: the prayer invokes Jesus, and is legitimated by acknowledging him; and God fulfils the prayer, in that by so doing he acknowledges Jesus, i.e. he acknowledges his own work of revelation. Until the coming of Jesus, this had not happened; the prayer is the prayer of the eschatological situation.[2] For the words ἐν τ. ὀν. μου of course do not refer to a formula of petition hitherto unused, but depict the relationship that obtains between the man who prays and the Revealer.

The two characteristics of χαρά, viz. the lack of need to ask questions and the assurance that prayer will be heard, form an inner unity, and this is very clearly expressed in I John 3.21; 5.14 by describing prayer in terms of παρρησία. The lack of need to ask questions, the freedom from anxiety and care is at the same time freedom, openness before God, before whom men need no longer hide themselves. Thus the Evangelist is able to give a new meaning to the exhortation that has come down to him in the tradition, αἰτεῖτε καὶ λήμψεσθε:[3] it enables him to draw attention expressly to the eschatological situation; and in this sense he can complete the exhortation to prayer with the words: ἵνα ἡ χαρὰ ὑμῶν ᾖ πεπληρωμένη.[4]

Vv. 12–15 promise the *coming of the Paraclete*, while vv. 16–24 promise the *second coming* of Jesus himself. How are the two related to each other? The same juxtaposition occurs in 14.15–17 and 14.18–20; also, in the reverse order, in 14.21–24 and 14.25–26. The attempt to eliminate the Paraclete sayings for textual-critical reasons as "foreign elements" in an earlier text is attractive, but cannot be maintained.[5] It is only right in so far as the promise of the Paraclete and the promise of Jesus' coming again go back to two different motifs in the tradition. The view that they compete with, or contradict, each other in John's gospel can be held only when they are not interpreted in the Evangelist's sense. He not only re-interprets the traditional motif of the expectation of the Parousia by combining it with the Easter motif,[6] but also gives a new interpretation to the promise of the Spirit by identifying the Spirit with the mythical figure of the Paraclete.[7] Each of these motifs, handed down from tradition, has been stripped of its original mythological character, and the true intention of the old mythology thereby brought out

[1] The bringing forward of ἐν τ. ὀν. μου so that it goes with αἰτ. τὸν πατ. in P[22] ℵ D pl is certainly a correction; cp. 14.26, where the Father sends the Spirit ἐν τ. ὀν. μου.

[2] Cp. Luther on Rom. 8.27 (II 207, 19ff. Ficker): how is one to understand the words ἕως ἄρτι κτλ., seeing that Jesus had already taught them to pray the Our Father? Sed petiverunt in nomine suo, non in nomine Christi, sc. inferiora, quam Christus est, non in spiritu sancto, sed secundum carnem.

[3] Mt. 7.7 and par. s; cp. Jas. 1.5; Herm. mand. IX 2.4. Καί is consecutive, see Burney 95f.

[4] See pp. 506, 541f.

[5] See p. 552 n. 1.

[6] See pp. 581f.

[7] See pp. 552f.

in its purity in the Evangelist's meaning; if that is so, then just as Easter and the Parousia are interpreted as one and the same event, so too Pentecost cannot mean a second event alongside them, but must coincide with the appearance of the one who has risen and who will come again. In which case 16.12–15 and 16.16–24 say the same thing; the only difference is that vv. 12–15 contain an initial promise of the continuation of the revelation in the future, while vv. 16–24 expound this in full as the promise of the eschatological existence.

3) *The Condition for comprehending the Eschatological Existence:* 16.25–33

16.12–24 re-interpreted the old naïve eschatology by expounding existence in faith in Jesus, made possible for the first time by his departure, as itself the eschatological existence. In this everything for which the community had hoped from the future cosmic events, and for which they thought they had a guarantee and an anticipation in the experiences of Easter and the gift of the Spirit,[1] is actually already fulfilled. The believer's existence is disclosed as the eschaton, and this disclosure is made in the form of a prophecy. Once again the Evangelist safeguards the prophecy from misunderstanding: not only are its contents to be understood anew, but also the prophetic utterance as such is not to be taken as a simple foretelling of future events which are to occur, without the believer himself participating in or being responsible for the realisation of what is promised. The believer's existence is disclosed as itself the possibility given by the revelation; its realisation takes place in the new venture of faith itself. There is no reference at all to a new condition of the world which is still to come in the future. What is to come is real only for faith and in faith (faith as believing existence), and therefore it must always be won against the opposition of the world. The prophecy is not a direct one, such as could be accepted simply by holding it to be true; it is given ἐν παροιμίαις, and will only be understood in its fulfilment.[2]

This is stated in the first sentence in **v. 25**: ταῦτα ἐν παροιμίαις λελάληκα ὑμῖν. These words do not explain the purpose of what has been said up to now,[3] but mark an ending; then and now are contrasted

---

[1] 'Απαρχή (Rom. 8.23); ἀρραβών (II Cor. 1.22; 5.5; Eph. 1.14); cp. Heb. 6.4f.

[2] Vv. 25–33 are probably almost entirely the work of the Evangelist. On ταῦτα λαλ. see p. 335 n. 5. Characteristic of his work are the following: the introduction of the contrast παρρησίᾳ, by means of the involved repetition of (οὐκέτι) ἐν παροιμίαις; the prayer-motif (v. 26: cp. vv. 23f; 15.7, 16; 14.13) and the formulation that goes with it: οὐ λέγω ὅτι (on the bringing forward of the negatived opposite, see p. 48 n. 3; cp. also 15.15); lastly, the dialogue (vv. 29–32). The only probable quotation from the source is v. 28, which will be the beginning of the text used in 14.1ff.

[3] A ἵνα-clause, such as occurs in 15.11 etc., is missing; see p. 541 n. 6.

with each other, as they were in 14.25. All that had been said previously[1] was enigmatic talk[2]—true, but incomprehensible, as the disciples' inability to understand had just demonstrated (v. 17) and as would be shown again (v. 29; 13.36f.; 14.4f., 8,22). Now it is quite right to observe: "For us, a certain effort is required to find anything enigmatic in such words as these; on the whole they are transparent to us at first glance";[3] it is also correct that one cannot distinguish between enigmatic and overt sayings in the discourses of Jesus in John, but rather that all discourses are both overt and "enigmatic."[4] The reason however is this: it is possible to understand the words of Jesus only in the reality of believing existence. Before that they are incomprehensible—not in the sense of being difficult to grasp intellectually, but because intellectual comprehension is not enough. It is precisely this that the disciples must realise, namely that the commitment of one's whole existence is required to understand these words. They will be comprehensible in the new (i.e. eschatological) existence: ἔρχεται ὥρα ὅτε κτλ.:[5] only then will Jesus speak to them παρρησίᾳ.[6]

Not that he will say anything new; not even that the meaning of what has already been said will gradually become comprehensible to the mind; for Jesus had never imparted theoretical knowledge. Rather, what was once said will become clear in the eschatological existence, for which it was spoken from the beginning. All that can be said as simple communication had been said long ago; and with the words περὶ τοῦ πατρὸς ἀπαγγελῶ ὑμῖν we are not embarking on any new theme; for that the Father loves him, that he has given him ἐξουσία, that he has sent him etc., has been said frequently,[7] nor can anything else be said of the Father than how he works in his Son.[8] Nor will the Spirit teach them anything new, the Spirit who ἐκ τοῦ ἐμοῦ λήμψεται (v. 14) and

---

[1] Ταῦτα ought not to be limited to vv. 23f. (B. Weiss), because its opposite is the future παρρησία-discourse. The old situation is contrasted as a whole with the completely new one (Htm; Wrede, Messiasgeh. 196).

[2] On παροιμία see p. 375 n. 4.

[3] Wrede, Messiasgeh. 286. Wr. may also be right in saying that the ἐν παροιμίαις motif comes from the tradition and is a development of the Synoptic λαλεῖν ἐν παραβολαῖς. Loisy, wrongly: Jesus has applied ce langage figuré pour s'accommoder à la faiblesse de ses auditeurs.

[4] Wrede op. cit. 197f.

[5] Ὥρα is not used here in the general sense of the predetermined hour (see p. 117 n. 1), but is the eschatological hour in the narrower sense, as in 4.21; 5.25; I Jn. 2.18; Rev. 14.7, 15; Mk. 13.32 etc.

[6] On παρρησία see pp. 291 n. 1; 361 n. 6.

[7] 3.35; 5.20, 26f., 36 etc.

[8] On ἀπαγγέλλειν see p. 575 n. 3. Loisy has rightly seen that there is no ref. to any particular theological speculation: Jésus n'a jamais parlé du Père que par rapport à sa propre mission. What he proclaims of himself, he proclaims of the Father, and vice versa. He and the Father are one (10.30).

ὑπομνήσει ὑμᾶς πάντα ἃ εἶπον ὑμῖν ἐγώ (14.26).[1] In the last analysis the truth of the matter had already become clear in 10.24f., when Jesus in reply to the plea of the Jews εἰπὸν ἡμῖν παρρησίᾳ said, εἶπον ὑμῖν καὶ οὐ πιστεύετε. Only for the eye of faith does the veil of παροιμία fall away.[2] *Faith* can see that the Father's love reaches out also to the believers, and not just to the Son; and *to that extent* Jesus is to make known something new περὶ τοῦ πατρός.[3] That is what the following sentences say.

For why is the eschatological situation (the words ἐν ἐκείνῃ τῇ ἡμέρᾳ draw attention to its eschatological nature)[4] again described in **vv. 26f.** as that of prayer in the name of Jesus? Not only because the believers' παρρησία, which manifests itself in prayer (I John 3.21; 5.14), corresponds to the παρρησία of Jesus' discourse. For the assurance that prayer would be heard was already given in vv. 23f. What is new here, in contrast to vv. 23f.; 15.7,16, is the emphatic statement that Jesus does not need to ask the Father to answer the prayers.[5] Of course this does not mean that the believer is to stand in a direct relationship to God and no longer requires the mediation of Jesus. The direct relationship to God is explicitly denied in 14.8f., and prayer is made by invocation of Jesus.[6] Rather the words οὐ λέγω κτλ. are intended to point out the full significance of this newly disclosed possibility of prayer: the disciples have, as it were, stepped alongside Jesus, or even taken his place: αὐτὸς γὰρ ὁ πατὴρ φιλεῖ ὑμᾶς. As the Father loves the Son (3.35; 5.20), so he loves the believers too,[7] and indeed, as was said in 17.23, 26, with the same love with which he loved *him*. Thus the words οὐ λέγω κτλ.

---

[1] See pp. 554, 575f.

[2] See p. 361f..

[3] Cp. Hosk. on v. 25: the distinction between the original teaching of Jesus and the teaching of the Church is justified and explained.

[4] See p. 583 n. 4. The comparison with e.g. C. Herm. 13 brings out the essential point. There too, what the Revealer says is in the first place an enigma (αἴνιγμα); what has been said must be speculatively developed. The way this happens is that the mystagogue's communication is only capable of "reminding" the mystic, but it reminds him of that which he must draw up from his own being. For it is also true there, that authentic knowledge is not the accepting of a doctrine, but experience, not however historical experience, but the mystical vision. But there, the doctrine must be kept secret, ἵνα μὴ ὦμεν διάβολοι τοῦ παντὸς εἰς τοὺς πολλούς, while Jesus' words are παροιμίαι in spite of their outward παρρησία.

[5] The newness does not consist in the disciples' having been informed (by means of the words ἐν τ. ὀν. μου that have been brought forward): this is not prayer about matters of personal concern, "which finds its way easily to the Father's heart, but (it consists rather in) requests which they bring before God in his commission, asking for power and success for the the work of their calling" (B. Weiss). Against this view Loisy, rightly: Les disciples peuvent-ils donc avoir un intérêt personel en dehors de l'oeuvre du Christ, et de faire des prières, qui ne se rapportent pas à celle ci?

[6] As in v. 24; 15.16; 14.13; see p. 270 n. 2. Cp. also I Jn. 2.1.

[7] There is no difference between φιλεῖν and ἀγαπᾶν, see pp. 253 n. 2, 397 n. 2.

imply that the disciples represent him in the world and thereby participate in his honour, the honour of being loved by the Father;[1] and the sign that this is so is their prayer. It is, so to speak, the prayer of Jesus himself;[2] but only in that it is a prayer "in his name." And that their position in the world, and God's relationship to them, do not mean a dissolution of their relationship to Jesus is stated expressly, in the reason given for what has been said: ὅτι ὑμεῖς ἐμὲ πεφιλήκατε καὶ πεπιστεύκατε κτλ. They are what they are only in virtue of their relationship to him, i.e. only because they believe in him as the Revealer of God, as the clause ὅτι ἐγὼ παρὰ τοῦ θεοῦ ἐξῆλθον puts it.[3]

V. 28[4] once more draws attention to the grounding of their existence in his purpose of revelation, in a sentence that gives a summary description of his work,[5] and also acts as a link to what follows:

ἐξῆλθον ἐκ τοῦ πατρὸς καὶ ἐλήλυθα εἰς τὸν κόσμον·
πάλιν ἀφίημι τὸν κόσμον καὶ πορεύομαι πρὸς τὸν πατέρα.[6]

The sentence is put there without any connection, almost as a doctrinal statement, and it serves to point out the background against which the discourses and conversations are to be seen. The founding of the community is not an event belonging to the history of this world, nor is it the historical achievement of a great man, but it is revelation event, sent into the world by God. It does not enter time in the sense of becoming immanent in time as a factor within the historical development of the world: the Revealer leaves the world again.[7] And in the context the emphasis is placed on this: the community has to realise that it only possesses the revelation in that peculiar indirectness. The work of the Revealer will be effectual for it only in the eschatological

[1] The views are mistaken that regard the sentence as guarding against the danger that faith's bond with Jesus might lead to unbelief vis-à-vis the Father (Schl.), or against the danger that the granting of his intercession would lead to a diminution of their trust in God (Bl.).

[2] Loisy, Bd.

[3] Instead of θεοῦ (ℵ* A Θ 33 al) B C*D L read πατρός, which conforms with v. 28. On the subject-matter see p. 298 n. 1. Thus Philo migr. Abr. 174f. is no parallel: ἕως μὲν γὰρ οὐ τετελείωται (ἡ ψυχή), ἡγεμόνι τῆς ὁδοῦ χρῆται λόγῳ θείῳ . . . (Ex. 23.20f.). ἐπειδὰν δὲ πρὸς ἄκραν ἐπιστήμην ἀφίκηται, συντόνως ἐπιδραμὼν ἰσοταχήσει τῷ πρόσθεν ἡγουμένῳ τῆς ὁδοῦ. ἀμφότεροι γὰρ οὕτως ὀπαδοὶ γενήσονται τοῦ πανηγεμόνος θεοῦ. See below p. 605 n. 6.

[4] V. 28 may come from the source, see p. 586 n. 3. Becker (105) thinks so too.

[5] On the terminology see p. 307 n. 3. The coming and the going of Jesus summarise his work as a unity, see p. 82 n. 6 etc.

[6] Instead of ἐκ τοῦ πατρ. (B C L pc), ℵ 𝔎 pl read παρὰ τ. πατρ., which was done to conform with v. 27. The fact that ἐξῆλθον . . . πατρός is missing from D W b syr^{s}- is a mistake.

[7] Πάλιν in its original Greek sense = "correspondingly (looking back to something), in a contrasting correspondence", as in I Jn. 2.8; I Cor. 12.21; II Cor, 10.7 etc.; see Br.

existence (*Existenz*) which faith grasps hold of, and not in existence (*Dasein*) within the world. And that that means: solely in continual mastery of worldly existence, is made clear by the following dialogue.

For when the disciples say in v. 29 that Jesus is now speaking ἐν παρρησίᾳ, there is a sense in which they are right. In one sense Jesus does speak differently in the farewell discourses[1] from the way he had spoken before; and it is exactly the prophecies of the future in vv. 12–28 that put all that had been said up to now in a new light, by describing what had been said as only preparatory. On the other hand, since vv. 12–28 do not complete the preparatory teaching with a definitive statement, but promise definitive knowledge for the future, the disciples are not right—or are right only in so far as their answer anticipates the future. To that extent their answer is appropriate; it is the expression of the daring of faith when it grasps the future as the present on the strength of the word of proclamation. In their reply therefore they express once more the Yes of faith, as they did before (explicitly in 6.69).[2] And it is no coincidence that both in 6.69 and here their faith is described as knowledge and faith: νῦν οἴδαμεν . . . ἐν τούτῳ πιστεύομεν, implying of a truth that the knowledge that discloses itself to faith is the ground for faith.[3]

The disciples have realised this truth: ὅτι οἶδας πάντα καὶ οὐ χρείαν ἔχεις ἵνα τίς σε ἐρωτᾷ.[4] This is a confession of his omniscience; and yet the words, "Thou knowest everything," are not developed, as one might expect, by "and hast no need to ask anyone,"[5] but by "Thou hast no need that anyone ask thee"; i.e. thou knowest already what anyone could ask thee,[6] as had just been demonstrated in v. 19. The

---

[1] Νῦν cannot be taken simply to refer to the previous verses, 25–28, nor just to v. 28; it stands for the farewell situation in general, as in 17.5, 7; 13.31.

[2] Wrede (Messiasgeh. 191) is right in saying that v. 29 cannot mean: at this moment occurs a transformation of the disciples' knowledge. But one cannot say that v. 29 is a "subordinate motif in the presentation". It is these verses that are to make plain the peculiar nature of faith: just as in the first encounter, Jesus' word can only be a παροιμία, so too the Yes to this word can only be a preliminary faith; and yet just as the encountering word is ἀλήθεια, so the preliminary faith is already knowledge, such as anticipates the future.

[3] 'Εν τούτῳ = "therefore", Bl.-D. § 219, 2 (ἐν as in Mt. 6.7;Ac ts 7.29 etc.). The fact that the knowledge to which faith leads becomes itself the grounds of faith, is inherent in the structure of faith; the more faith comes to itself and the more transparent it is to itself, the more certain it becomes as faith; see p. 435 n. 4.

[4] Χρείαν ἔχειν ἵνα as in 2.25; I Jn. 2.27; Bl.-D. § 393, 5.

[5] That is how syr[s] corrects: "that thou shouldest ask anyone". To have no need to ask anyone is a characteristic of omniscience, cp. Ginza 425, 39ff.: "Thou knowest, and it is manifest to thee, my Father; the secret things are revealed before thee. Thou needest no teaching, nor to ask anything". Cp. also Is. 41.28.

[6] Cp. Jos. ant. 11, 230: Jonathan calls on God as witness: τὸν . . . καὶ πρὶν ἑρμηνεῦσαί με τοῖς λόγοις τὴν διάνοιαν ἤδη μου ταύτην εἰδότα. There is scarcely an allusion to Is. 45. 11.

omniscience of the Revealer therefore is not understood as an abstract attribute, but as his knowledge which communicates itself to his own.[1] Οἶδας πάντα means basically: "Thou art the Revealer," and it is the assent to Jesus' statement in v. 27.[2] The answer to every question which can worry the believer has been contained in the revelation from the beginning. The believers know that nothing unforeseen can come upon them, and their questions can die away into silence. Their confession is therefore, so to speak, their answer to Jesus' promise in v. 23: "On that day you will ask me nothing more." Their knowledge anticipates the eschatological ἡμέρα, and demonstrates that faith is eschatological existence. And yet it does not say, καὶ ὅτι οὐ χρείαν ἔχομεν ἵνα σε ἐρωτῶμεν,[3] for the disciples' statement is a confession which speaks not of them, but of him whom they confess.[4]

The faith that confesses stands within the temporal sphere (*Dasein*), in which the future is realised in the temporal course of events. Faith dares to grasp the future beforehand, in its confession; but has it not said too much? This is what Jesus' reply in **v. 31** is questioning: ἄρτι πιστεύετε;[5] the crux is to understand the "Now."[6] Does the believer know that in his confession in the present he is taking the future upon himself? Or does he imagine that there can be a definitive Now for him, a definitive confession, which would not always need to be made afresh? It will not have gone unnoticed that the disciples' confession in v. 30 has picked up only the ἐξῆλθον and not the πορεύομαι of Jesus' own statement in v. 28. The questions of Peter (13.36) and of Thomas (14.5) show that faith's difficulty lies in explaining the apparent forsakenness and in accepting the loneliness in which the believer, who wants to exist eschatologically, is placed within the world. What Jesus now says (**v. 32**) refers to this difficulty: ἰδοὺ ἔρχεται ὥρα κτλ.[7] His words are in the first

---

[1] Οὐ χρείαν ἔχεις κτλ. is, as Dibelius (Festg. für Ad. Deissmann 171, 1) rightly says, a conceptual parallel to ἐν παρρησίᾳ λαλεῖς.

[2] On Jesus' knowledge, as that of the perfected Gnostic, see pp. 143 n. 1; 487, etc. The disciples' confession is thus fundamentally different from the statement of Nicodemus in 3.2.

[3] Cp. Mech. to Ex. 15.2, acc. to Schl.: as God revealed himself at the sea, οὐ χρείαν ἔσχεν οὐδεὶς ἐξ αὐτῶν ἐρωτᾶν τίς ἐστιν ὁ βασιλεύς.

[4] See p. 449.

[5] The question has a judgmental sense, as in 13.38. Even if the sentence is taken as a statement, the sense is no different.

[6] The fact that ἄρτι (v. 31) picks up the νῦν of v. 30, brings out the problematical nature of the Now. Νῦν means "now" = "now at last", looking back at the past (cp. Herm. mand. XII 6, 4: κύριε, νῦν ἐδυναμώθην); ἄρτι means "now already", looking to the future (cp. v. 12; 13.7, 33, 37; ἀπ' ἄρτι: 13.19; 14.7; cp. Men. Epitr. 298: λέγ' ὃ λέγεις· ἄρτι γὰρ νοῶ). On this, see H. J. Ebeling, Das Messiasgeheimnis u. die Botschaft des Marcusevangelisten 1939 161f.

[7] Ἕκαστος with a plural verb is good Greek, see Bl.-D. § 305; εἰς τὰ ἴδια = "to one's own place", or "home", cp. 19.27; Acts 21.6. Cp. I Macc. 6.54: ἐσκορπίσθησαν ἕκαστος

place a prophecy of the disciples' flight, which was about to take place.[1] But the hour of this event is solemnly introduced as the ὥρα which is coming and has already come, a formula used earlier of the ὥρα of the true worship of God (4.23), and of the ὥρα of the awakening of the dead (5.25); thus this hour also is to be considered the hour of the eschatological event.[2] For man, therefore, the eschatological hour is first of all an hour of dismay; before he can appreciate its χαρά he has to experience its λύπη. The historical situation of the disciples at the time of the death of Jesus represents the situation which repeats itself constantly in the life of the believers. Again and again the world seems to conquer, and again and again the disciple wavers and seeks refuge in his native haunts, in the world, leaving Jesus alone. Not that he could or should defend him, by loyally following him! In fact he is not abandoning the Revealer to the world, but by imagining him to be so abandoned and by despairing of him he is rather abandoning himself. The Revealer in reality is not alone: καὶ[3] οὐκ εἰμὶ μόνος, ὅτι ὁ πατὴρ μετ' ἐμοῦ ἐστιν. Indeed, in him the Father is at work, the Father with whom he is one,[4] and therefore, as v. 33 will state explicitly, in his apparent defeat he is in fact the conqueror.

The statement that the coming hour has the appearance of horror for human eyes was made precisely with the eager confession of faith in mind: ταῦτα λελάληκα ὑμῖν ἵνα ἐν ἐμοὶ εἰρήνην ἔχητε (**v. 33**). The fall that is about to take place[5] has been mentioned in order to strengthen the believer's faith. For he would be given over to despair if he had to regard the confession he made at one moment as definitive, in the sense

---

εἰς τὸν τόπον αὐτοῦ. Gospel of Peter 59 (Kl. Text 3, 8): ἡμεῖς δὲ οἱ δώδεκα μαθηταὶ κυρίου ἐκλαίομεν καὶ ἐλυπούμεθα, καὶ ἕκαστος λυπούμενος διὰ τὸ συμβὰν ἀπηλλάγη εἰς τὸν οἶκον αὐτοῦ.

[1] The Evangelist is employing the tradition which used Zech. 13.7 to express the prophecy of the disciples' flight (Mk. 14.27; Mt. 26.31), just as in v. 32b and v. 33 he gives his own rendering of the prophecy of the resurrection (Mk. 14.28 and par.s). It is possible that σκορπ . . . ἴδια is a supplement of the redactor, following the Synoptics (Corssen, ZNTW 8 [1907] 139f.), for the phrase contradicts the statement in ch. 20 that the disciples stayed in Jerusalem. In any case ἵνα ἐμὲ μόνον ἀφῆτε (which is not contradicted by 18.8 or 19.26f.) would be quite enough, and by being a mere hint could itself have given rise to the supplementation. Cp. also Dibelius (Festg. für Deissmann 171f.), who refers to the Johannine introduction and ending to the passage, and only errs in saying that vv. 29–32 are a digression. Strathm. wants to take εἰς τὰ ἴδια in an undefined sense: "each to his own nook"; H. v. Campenhausen (SA Heidelb. 1952, 4, 52) agrees. Differently, Wik. and Barr.

[2] N Θ insert the νῦν of 4.23; 5.25 after καί.

[3] On καί = "and yet", see p. 48 n. 2.

[4] Cp. 8.16, 29; 10.30. Did the Evangelist want to imply a tacit rejection of the tradition of the cry of God-forsakenness from the cross (Mk. 15.34 and par.s)? The Stoic idea is no parallel: οὐδείς ἐστιν ἄνθρωπος ὀρφανός, ἀλλὰ πάντων ἀεὶ καὶ διηνεκῶς ὁ πατήρ ἐστιν ὁ κηδόμενος (Epict. diss. III 24, 15 in Br.)

[5] Ταῦτα λελ. (see pp. 335 n. 5; 541 n. 6) can only refer here to the immediately preceding.

that it could never be made again if he once denied it. He must learn that his "I believe" is to be accompanied by an "help thou my unbelief" (Mk. 9.24); that his way also leads through the depths, and that after falling he may find the way back to himself, by learning to understand the meaning of ἐν ἐμοί.[1] The certainty of his faith does not rest on the believer himself, but on the Revealer in whom he believes. And precisely this uncertainty, which the believer meets with again and again, teaches him to direct his gaze away from himself to the Revealer, so that it is indeed possible to speak of *felix culpa*. That which in the earthly existence can only be realised in time is already reality in the Revealer, and in spite of all weakness will be enjoyed by the faith that is directed to him, namely, εἰρήνη. This is the eschatological salvation, which was described in vv. 22, 24[2] as χαρά. When the believers look towards the Revealer, they stand in the salvation, in the peace which lies beyond the battle; they have the εἰρήνη in their faith.[3]

The price of attaining this peace is of course the readiness to withstand the world's enmity: ἐν τῷ κόσμῳ θλῖψιν ἔχετε.[4] But faith can go to meet it with confidence. Jesus as one who, so to speak, no longer tarries on the earth, as manifest divinity,[5] cheers his own with the words: ἀλλὰ θαρσεῖτε; and this is the reason why: his victory over the world, already portrayed in picture form in 12.12–19,[6] is certain: ἐγὼ νενίκηκα τὸν κόσμον.[7] The world has already lost its case; it is condemned.[8]

---

[1] Ἐν ἐμοί is valid of the whole statement, not just of εἰρ. On ἐν ἐμοί cp. 15.4 and see pp. 321 n. 1; 381.

[2] On the relatedness of χαρά and εἰρήνη see p. 505 n. 3. Εἰρήνη, used as an eschatological attribute, always means "salvation", corresponding to the Hebrew שָׁלוֹם (e.g. Is. 54.13; 57.19; Jer. 36 (29).11; Ezek. 37.26; Ps. 84.9; Rom. 2.10; 8.6; 14.17; see ThWB II 404, 15ff.; 407, 36ff.; for Judaism, see also G. Kittel, Saat auf Hoffnung 57 [1920] 109–124). Just as שלום can mean the "peace" that is included within the salvation, so too, very definitely, can εἰρήνη, in virtue of Greek linguistic usage. It is in each case subject to the context; but the distinction no longer holds good when "peace" is intended eschatologically, as in v. 33 and 14.27 (opp. ταραχή). The Mandaean writings also know of the eschatological "peace of life" (Mand. Lit. 17. 104. 107. 183), and for the Od. Sal., too, "peace" is an eschatological attribute (8.6f.; 9.6; 10.2; 11.3; 35.1). Manichaean examples in Br. on 14.27.

[3] Cp. the parallelism of the ἵνα-clauses in v. 33; 13.19; 14.29.

[4] Instead of ἔχετε D φ pc lat syr[s] read ἕξετε.—Θλῖψις only here in John (except for v. 21); often used elsewhere for the community's affliction, see Rev. 1.9; 2.9f.; Acts 14.22 etc. Becker (105) would ascribe v. 33b (ἐν τ. κόσμῳ κτλ.) to the source.

[5] Θάρσει, as the shout of encouragement by the manifest divinity (Mk. 6.50 and par.s; Rev. 23.11), is the same as μὴ φοβοῦ (L. Köhler, Schweizer Theol. Ztschr. 1919, 1ff.; J. Hempel, Gott und Mensch im AT, 2nd. ed. 1936, 8). The intention is normally to overcome man's terror at the appearance of the divinity (e.g. Dio Chrys. or. 36, 40 p. 15, 18 de Budé). In a paradoxical way that is also the case here: the terror caused by the Revealer is not due to his visible glory, but to his apparent defeat.

[6] See p. 412f.

[7] Jesus' victory is "not simply an event in the past (which does not exist within the eschatological view of time), but is the symbolical archetype *and* and the real surety of all

[For n. 8 see overleaf.]

Just as the joy, which Jesus has, is to become the disciples' possession (17.13; 15.11), so his victory is their victory. Thus εἰρήνη is not peace of mind, or the Stoic ἀταραξία,[1] but the possibility of existing as a believer, a possibility which is to be continually grasped afresh;[2] thus it can also be correspondingly said that the victory which has conquered the world is faith (I John 5.4). The εἰρήνη only becomes real in the actualisation of the believing existence, and this existence is eschatological, in that it continually overcomes the world and understands itself in terms of the future it has already grasped hold of. But this kind of existence has become a possibility through the victory of the Revealer, on whom faith fixes its gaze.[3]

Εἰρήνη has therefore become a description of the eschatological situation, and thus we arrive at the theme of the fourth section, 13.36–14.31, in which the winning of εἰρήνη out of the ταραχή of the farewell is treated in a similar way to the gaining of χαρά out of the λύπη in 16.12–23. To some extent the two sections run parallel; in both the promise of εἰρήνη forms the conclusion. 14.29f. corresponds to the prophecy of the offence in 16.31, 32a, and . . . ἵνα ὅταν γένηται πιστεύσητε corresponds to the question: ἄρτι πιστεύετε. The words ἔρχεται γὰρ ὁ τοῦ κόσμου ἄρχων in 14.30 correspond to κἀμὲ μόνον ἀφῆτε 16.32, just as καὶ ἐν ἐμοὶ οὐκ ἔχει οὐδέν corresponds to καὶ οὐκ εἰμὶ μόνος. In both 16.12–15, 16–24 and 14.15–17, 18–20 the promise of the Paraclete and that of the second coming of Jesus follow one another. Moreover the two sections are formally the same, in that the discourse is

---

redemption; it is the essential reality for the believer, because in suffering and emancipation is the prior-completion and therefore pre-determination of one's own destiny" (thus H. Jonas, Gnosis I 303, on the Manichaean redemption-drama).

[8] Cp. vv. 8–11; 12.31, and on the imagery of the lawsuit, see pp. 553 n. 5; 562. How far the idea of the victory won in martial battle is combined with the victory in the lawsuit (see p. 564 n. 2) in the concept νικᾶν, it is hard to say. In Rev., where νικᾶν is an eschatological term as here, the first of these ideas is dominant (3.21; 5.5; 6.2; 17.14, cp. the promises for the νικῶν in 2.7, 11 etc.). Apart from I Chron. 29.11 (LXX for נֵצַח) the Old Testament does not know of "to conquer" as an eschatological term. The idea of the victorious God occurs frequently elsewhere, and the idea of the divine victory seems to have been widely used in Hellenism, particularly as the result of Iranian mythology. It plays a part in acclamations and prayers, and especially in magic (νίκη used with χαρίς, δύναμις, δόξα etc.) It also occurs in Gnosticism; cp. Od. Sal. 9.11:

> All those who have conquered shall be written in His (the Lord's) book.
> For your scribe is your own victory.
> And She (Victory) sees you before her,
> And wills that you shall be saved". Cp. 18.6f.; 29.9.

Abundantly attested in the Mandaean writing (see p. 564 n. 2). Cp. E. Peterson Εἷς Θεός, esp. 152ff., 312ff.; O. Weinreich, Neue Urkunden zur Sarapis-Religion 1919, 21. 33ff.

[1] Epict. diss. III 12, 9ff. (Br.) is not therefore a true parallel.

[2] Just as, following Paul, one can speak of an *aliena iustitia*, so following John, one could speak of *an aliena pax*.

[3] Cp. I Jn. 2.13f.; 4.4, and esp. 5.4f.

interrupted by the disciples' questions, and here the disciples are mentioned individually: Peter (13.36f.), Thomas (14.5), Philip (14.8) and Judas (14.22).

d) The Fellowship with the Son and the Father: 13.36–14.31

The farewell discourses could be brought to an end with 16.33, and it is no cause for wonder that the Redactor found their conclusion at this point. However 14.25 (27)–31 is just as much a conclusion, and the question of the relation of the one to the other remains to be answered. It is clear that 14.31 is the real conclusion, because it leads on to the treatment of the story of the passion.[1] But apart from that, it now becomes apparent that 13.36–14.31 must follow ch. 16. For 13.36 introduces the question of the "discipleship", the significance of which is evident only at this point. The disciples' situation in the world had been analysed in 13.31–35, 15.1–16.33 from different points of view, and against the background of the farewell: the disciples remain in the world, united with the Revealer who has gone from them; as his friends they receive from him the power to live; they continue his work, and meet with his fate; they represent him, and take part in his victory *in the world.* Is their union with him limited to their existence in the world? Will their participation in his victory be restricted to their overcoming the world while remaining in it?—It is the same as in ch. 17: there, the petition (17.15) not to take the disciples out of the world, but rather to protect them from evil in the world, is followed by the petition to give them a share in his other-worldly glory (17.24); so too here, 13.31–35, 15.1–16.33 are followed by the promise of "discipleship", demonstrating (after the promise has been made in 13.36–14.4) the inner unity of the promised future in the world beyond with the present eschatological existence.

1) *The Promise of Discipleship:* 13.36–14.4[2]

In a conversation, the construction of which reminds us of 16.29–33,[3] the question of "discipleship" (*Nachfolge*) is raised, and is answered

---

[1] See p. 459.

[2] The dialogue 13.36–38 is clearly the Evangelist's composition, while 14.1–4 largely stems from the "revelation-discourses". In 13.36–38 the same piece of Gospel tradition has been used as occurs in Mk. 14.29–31 (and par.s), just as 16.32f. was the counterpart of Mk. 14.27f. (see p. 592 n. 1). This order confirms the reconstruction of the text (see p. 460). If the Evangelist follows the tradition attested by Mk. and Matt., this does not mean that he used one of these Gospels. The wording of v. 38 recalls Lk. 22.33f. But the idea that John is following Lk. in the order: prophecy of the betrayal (Lk. 22.21–23), prophecy of the denial (Lk. 22.31–34), as Br. maintains, is an illusion, if the reconstruction of the text is correct. Corssen (see p. 592 n. 1) wants to strike out vv. 36–38 as an interpolation of the redactor, on the grounds that the verses break the continuity between 13.31–35 and 14.1ff.

[3] Cp. the parallelism: 16.30 (confession of the disciples), 31 (critical question by Jesus), 32 (shaming prophecy), 33 (comfort) and 13.37 (confession by Peter), 38 (critical question and shaming prophecy by Jesus); 14.1ff. (comfort). There is also correspondence between ἄρτι in 16.31 and νῦν in 13.36 (or οὐ . . . ἄρτι: 13.37); ὕστερον, which is expressly stated in 13.36, is implied in 16.33.

at first negatively: it does not lie within the disciple's own free choice to follow Jesus; he has to wait (13.36–38). What Jesus says next (14.1–4) adds the positive side: he will come and bring the disciples to himself.

The intention behind the question Peter asks (v. 36), ποῦ ὑπάγεις; is, as Jesus' answer shows, to follow him wherever he may go.[1] What actual possibilities Peter was thinking of is irrelevant; like the question in v. 37, his is simply the expression of that misunderstanding which imagines Jesus' ὑπάγειν and the disciples' ἀκολουθεῖν as happenings or possibilities taking place within the sphere of the world; and to that extent the question is as foolish as the deliberations of the Jews in 7.35, 8.32; and at first it is answered negatively: ὅπου ἐγὼ ὑπάγω οὐ δύνασαί μοι νῦν ἀκολουθῆσαι.[2] But behind Peter's question lies the disciple's readiness to follow Jesus, and thus he receives the *promise*: ἀκολουθήσεις δὲ ὕστερον, admittedly a promise that in the first place only tells him to wait. And this is what Peter cannot understand (v. 37). The next question he puts: διὰ τί κτλ. shows that he does not know that Jesus' ὑπάγειν is an eschatological event. As a result he holds the ἀκολουθεῖν to be a human possibility, even if to grasp it may involve the commitment of life itself: τὴν ψυχήν μου ὑπὲρ σοῦ θήσω.[3] If Jesus' answer in v. 38[4] only meant: "You are not strong enough for such a commitment"; if, that is to say, the οὐ δύνασαι were only due to Peter's character, while a stronger man could have summoned up the strength for ἀκολουθεῖν, or if the statement is only: "At the moment you are too weak; you must first become stronger," then the dialogue would have no fundamental significance, nor would the false presupposition that lies behind Peter's words be put right. But the purpose of the text is clearly to make this correction.

For the same reason therefore the meaning cannot be: "You will not suffer martyrdom now, but only later." For in that case too, Peter's

---

[1] On the relation of v. 36 to v. 33 see p. 460 n. 2. The apparent contradiction between 13.36 and 16.28 is the same as that between 13.36 and 7.33, which Peter must also have heard; it should also be noticed that the disciples only repeat ἐξέρχεσθαι in 16.30, and not πορεύεσθαι (from 16.28). The contradiction repeats itself in Thomas's question, which is also impossible psychologically.

[2] Ἐγὼ is attested only in ℵ D φ pm, but it accords with Johannine style. On the other hand, one has no confidence in συνακολ. of D* or in the σύ before the νῦν in D²e.

[3] Τιθέναι τ. ψυχήν is better understood as "to commit one's life to" rather than as "to give up one's life"; see 370 n. 5; 542 n. 3; but cp. Lk. 22.33: εἰς θάνατον πορεύεσθαι, Mk. 14.31: συναποθανεῖν σοι.

[4] The "twice", inserted by syr^s to φωνήσῃ, is, in spite of Merx, secondary and comes from Mk. 14.30. That John corrected Mk. 14.30 (Huber 27, 2) cannot be proved, because it cannot be proved that John "must have known" Mk. On the "cock-crow" as the normal way of marking the division between night and day, see Str.-B. I 993; Klostermann on Mk. 14.30.

conception of (ὑπάγειν and) ἀκολουθεῖν would not be corrected; on the contrary it would be presupposed that Peter and Jesus were agreed about the meaning of ἀκ., and that the only thing Peter could not grasp was why he could not at this moment follow Jesus to death.[1] But his first question: ποῦ ὑπάγεις; shows clearly that his understanding of ἀκ. hangs on that of ὑπάγειν, and is therefore wrong; and moreover 14.4f. shows that everything depends upon understanding ὑπάγειν.

What is true of Jesus' ὑπάγειν is also true of the ἀκολουθεῖν: neither is a human undertaking, or comprehensible as an occurrence within mundane, human dimensions. Just as the former is both departure from the world and also victory over the world, so too is the ἀκολουθεῖν a following (*Nachfolge*) into the δόξα of the exalted one; it is that ἀκ., which was promised in 12.26 to Jesus' servant, who will then be where Jesus is (cp. 17.24).[2] Certainly this kind of following involves the readiness to accept Jesus' destiny, and thus the readiness to die (12.25); just because it means world-annulment, it is a following unto death—whatever form death may take for each disciple. Thus the following of Jesus has become a possibility in this double sense—as world-annulment and as following into the δόξα—only because of Jesus' victory over the world; it is therefore possible solely through faith in the Revealer, in whose ὑπάγειν the victory over the world is accomplished.

It is this that Peter fails to understand, and that has to be repeated again and again both to him and to the other disciples (16.7; 14.28). The most glaring expression of Peter's lack of understanding is found

---

[1] This at once contradicts the wording of v. 37, the sense of which is: "I am ready to follow you, *even if* it should cost me my life!" Jesus' answer would then have to be understood like this: "You will follow me, but only later, and then by martyrdom". But Peter had declared himself ready for martyrdom; in Jesus' answer the stress can only be on ὕστερον; it cannot be a prophecy of martyrdom, but sets out to teach that the believer's existence depends on the ὑπάγειν of Jesus that *precedes* it; cp. 16.7; 14.28. But 21.18f. has had the effect of making it almost self-evident that Jesus is prophesying martyrdom for Peter. Against this, Bd. rightly: "The promise is not confined to martyrs". In the NT ἀκολουθεῖν has not yet become a technical expression for following unto death (H. v. Campenhausen, Die Idee des Martyriums 59). It describes discipleship first of all in terms of being a pupil, i.e. the carrying out of life acc. to the teaching and laws of the master (see p. 99 n. 5); the meaning can be broadened by the fact that the taking on of the master's destiny also belongs to the position of a pupil (see p. 344 n. 1 and cp. Mk. 8.34 and pars.; Rev. 14.4). Jn. 12.26 alludes to this sense (see p. 425f.); and yet, as in 13.36f., the primary meaning is: a following into the δόξα, into which the Revealer has gone before (see following note); it is the *Gnostic* idea of discipleship; see E. Käsemann, Das Wandernde Gottesvolk 1938, 114ff. Moreover, Peter must be regarded as the disciples' representative; his question contains just as little individual concern for himself as do the disciples' questions in 14.5, 8, 22. Thus what Jesus says in v. 36 (as in 14.1ff.) is valid for all; and Peter's denial (v. 38) is only a representative event.

[2] Ἵνα ὅπου εἰμὶ ἐγὼ κτλ. in 14.3 corresponds to ὅπου εἰμὶ ἐγὼ κτλ. in 12.26 (cp. 17.24). This means that the ἀκολ. of 13.36f. must be understood in the light of 12.26 (see previous note), and that 13.36–14.4 is a continuous and homogeneous whole.

in his words, ὑπὲρ σοῦ: he does not know that *he* cannot enter the field "for" the Revealer, but only the Revealer for him (cp. 17.24)! It is therefore clear that the following of Jesus is not an act of heroism. Whoever should think that—this is the meaning of the prophecy of the denial—will come to grief; the world will very quickly become lord over him, as it was really lord over Peter already, in his thinking that the following of Jesus was a heroic deed.

Of course in v. 36 ὕστερον implies that Peter must first become mature; but the concern is not with the development of strength of character, but with the attainment of the decisive knowledge of faith. Ὕστερον is to be understood as equally fundamental as μετὰ ταῦτα in 13.7:[1] Jesus must first have gone and have conquered the world; or: in the light of Jesus' death, by going through his own ταραχή and by becoming aware of his own powerlessness, Peter must first become convinced of Jesus' victory[2] before he can follow him. His ἀκ. will then consist, as will be stated in 14.1–4, in Jesus fetching him; what is required of him, on his side, is not an act of heroism, but expectant preparedness.[3]

Just as in 16.33 so here, a promise that encourages the believer follows the prophecy that puts him to shame.[4] It is a promise made to all the disciples, and therefore a sign that in vv. 36–38 the figure of Peter is to be regarded as representative, as are the questions of the other disciples.[5] Jesus is speaking in the language of the myth.[6]

14.1: μὴ ταρασσέσθω ὑμῶν ἡ καρδία·
πιστεύετε εἰς τὸν θεόν; καὶ εἰς ἐμὲ πιστεύετε.
2: ἐν τῇ οἰκίᾳ τοῦ πατρός μου μοναὶ πολλαί εἰσιν [. . .],
(καὶ) πορεύομαι ἑτοιμάσαι τόπον ὑμῖν.
3: καὶ ἐὰν πορευθῶ καὶ ἑτοιμάσω τόπον ὑμῖν,
πάλιν ἔρχομαι καὶ παραλήμψομαι ὑμᾶς πρὸς ἐμαυτόν,
4: ἵνα ὅπου εἰμὶ ἐγὼ καὶ ὑμεῖς ἦτε.
καὶ ὅπου ἐγὼ ὑπάγω οἴδατε τὴν ὁδόν.

---

[1] See p. 466.

[2] See p. 467f.

[3] In so far as discipleship is to manifest itself as martyrdom in the actual course of history, vv. 36–38 make *the significance of martyrdom* clear. It is not the heroic surrender of one's life that makes death the death of a martyr, but rather the faith that death is a sharing in the destiny of Jesus, and thus a sharing in his victory over the world. Martyrdom is therefore primarily possible as the documentation of the believer's eschatological existence, and as such is significant as a special form of "witness", of proclamation. What makes it martyrdom is nothing other than the *understanding* of death which the martyr has in common with *all* believers, for whom Jesus is just as much the ὁδός (14.6), as he is for the martyr. See esp. v. Campenhausen, Die Idee des Martyriums.

[4] D a c make the transition easier by adding καὶ εἶπεν τοῖς μαθηταῖς αὐτοῦ.

[5] See p. 597 n. 1.

[6] 14.1–4 mainly stems from the source of the "revelation-discourses". Their originally

The words μὴ ταρασσέσθω ὑμῶν ἡ καρδία (v. 1 and v. 27) form a framework around the conversations that follow. The εἰρήνη promised in 16.33 must be attained in battle with the world, because it is of another kind from that which the world knows (v. 27). Through their faith in the Revealer the disciples find themselves in opposition to the world, and because he leaves them alone, they are in ταραχή.[1] But just as λύπη does not have to be overcome because it is a πάθος but because it is a transitional stage, and just as it has the positive significance of being the origin of χαρά (16.21), so neither is ταραχή to be repulsed as a πάθος, in place of which there should come the ἀρετή of ἀταραξία. The command

---

mythological character is illustrated particularly well by the Mandaean parallels. In Ginza 259, 33ff., Manda dHaije says: "I will go to assign a place to Hibil in the new abode, and then I will come quickly to you. Do not be afraid of the sword of the planets, and let there be no fear or anxiety among you. Afterwards, certainly, I come to you. The eye of life is directed to you. I covered you with the garment of life, which it had lent you. Truly, I am with you. Every time that you seek me, you will find me; every time that you call me, I will answer you. I am not far from you." In Ginza 261, 15ff. Manda dHaija speaks to Anoš: "Do not be afraid or anxious, and do not say: they have left me behind in this world of evil. For I am coming to you soon" (cp. 264, 4f.). Similarly in Ginza 268, 4ff., he says: "Behold, I am going to the house of life now, then I will come and will free you from the evils and sins of this world. . . . I will lead you up on the way on which Hibil the righteous and Sitil and Manda dHaije are ascending, away from this world of evils". Cp. Mand. Lit. 226:

Continue steadfast in thy assurance,
    Until thy lot is complete.
When thy lot is complete,
    I myself will come to thee.
I will bring thee robes of brilliance
. . .
I will free thee from the evils,
    rescue thee from the sinners.
I will let thee live in thy Škina,
    in a pure place I will rescue thee".

Similarly in the prayer to Manda dHaije in Mand. Lit. 138: "Thou art he who builds up, and brings out from the midst of nations . . . everyone who is called, desired and invited. To everyone whose lot is full, thou art a helper, guide and leader to the great place of light and to the brilliant dwelling"; see also ZNTW 24 (1925), 137f. Cp. further, the words of Simon, Mart. Petri et Pauli 53, p. 164, 10f.: παραυτίκα ἀπελθόντος μου εἰς τὸν οὐρανόν, πέμψω τοὺς ἀγγέλους μου πρὸς σὲ καὶ ποιήσω σε ἐλθεῖν πρὸς μέ (cp. 74 p. 209, 15f.). The singer's certainty in Od. Sal. 3.5ff. (see p. 519 n. 1) corresponds to this; see also Lohmeyer, Festg. für Deissmann 235f. Becker (106) also reconstructs the text as it is given above, in vv. 1–3. But he regards v. 4 as the work of the Evangelist, a transitional sentence leading on to the question by Thomas, which has been inserted. On the patristic LA: πολλαὶ μοναὶ παρὰ τῷ πατρί, see Boismard, RB 57 (1950), 389f.

[1] The ταραχθῆναι of the καρδία accords both with Semitic linguistic usage (Ps. 54.5; 142.4; Lam. 2.11) and with Greek (ταράσσειν καρδίαν Eur. Bacch. 1321; ταράσσομαι φρένας Soph. Ant. 1095 (cp. 1105: καρδίας δ' ἐξίσταμαι); ταρ. φρένα Eur. Hipp. 969); cp. the ideal of ἀταραξία. The anxiety of the soul which is alone in the world is also a motif of the myth, see p. 421 n. 5. The demonic powers of evil try to terrify the soul; they say: "He will be disloyal, his heart is becoming anxious" (Ginza 394, 1). Act. Andr. 17 p. 44, 29f. could be an imitation of Jn 14.1: τὸ δὲ περὶ ἐμὲ μέλλον συμβαίνειν μὴ ὄντως ταρασσέτω ὑμᾶς κτλ.

to overcome the ταραχή does not have its basis in the ideal of the man at harmony with himself, nor does the ταραχή arise from human weakness, but from the collision of the world with the revelation. Moreover it is this that gives the ταραχή its positive significance: in it the disciple experiences the break with the world. Would the disciples come to realise the fruitfulness of their loneliness, if it did not fill them first with dismay? The ταραχθῆναι is thus in one sense appropriate for the disciple; it is always contained in his faith as that which has been overcome.

The way to overcoming it however is pointed out in the words: πιστεύετε κτλ. "Do you believe in God? Then believe also in me;[1] for you can only believe in God through me!" Thus, paradoxically, faith in God is described as the epistemological ground (*Erkenntnisgrund*) for faith in Jesus, whereas elsewhere, namely vis-à-vis the Jews (5.38; 8.46f.), faith in Jesus was regarded as the epistemological ground for faith in God. But the paradox puts the believer to the test; it places him before the either-or: because faith in God can only be mediated by Jesus, the believer must realise that to give up faith in Jesus would also be to give up faith in God.[2] To be placed in front of this either-or, however, is the strongest possible exhortation to faith.

The promise (**vv. 2f.**)[3] that follows the exhortation is in its entirety made in mythological language: Jesus, who now takes his farewell, goes into the heavenly home, into "the Father's house";[4] there, there

---

[1] "The chiastic word-order lays the stress on the contrast between εἰς τὸν θεόν and εἰς ἐμέ" (Zn). It may seem the most natural to take both the sentences connected by καί as co-ordinated imperatives (as do the old Latin mss., Theod., Cyr. Al., and B. Weiss, Ho., Htm., Br., Bd., Bl., Hirsch., Hosk., Strathm., Barr.). But sentences like v. 9; 8.19; 12.44 suggest that the relation of the two sentences is rather one of subordination; thus Orig.: ἐπεὶ πιστεύετε εἰς τ. θ., καὶ εἰς ἐμὲ πιστεύετε. Similarly Zn. (who does however regard both πιστ. as imperatives), Lagr. (who only takes the second as an imperat.) and Wik. Even if one regards both πιστ. as indicatives, the sentence remains an indirect exhortation.

[2] There is no reason for taking πιστεύειν here, in contrast to its normal use in John, as meaning "to trust" (Ho., Br.). Schlatter's explanation (Der Glaube im NT 4th ed. 189) misses the point: "Because Jesus, as a dying man, seems incapable of being the goal of faith, we are expressly referred to the one who remains the basis for an unshakable trust". But John does not know of the kind of faith in God which could give strength to faith in Jesus, i.e. which could also exist without the latter.

[3] On the language of vv. 2f.: τόπον ἑτοιμάζειν also in I Par. 15.1 and Rev. 12.6; Rabbinic examples in Schl., but it is also good Greek (e.g. ἑτοιμάζειν δῶμα: Eur. Alc. 364). On ἐάν, which as in 12.32 almost = ὅταν, see Br. Ἔρχομαι has a future sense (Bl.-D. §323, 1; Colwell 61–64); παραλήμψ. expresses the further result. On παραλ. cp. Cant. 8.2: παραλήμψομαί σε, εἰσάξω σε εἰς οἶκον μητρός μου. Consolatory form of words, used in letters, in Deissmann, L.v.O. 144: δόξα . . . τῷ . . . θεῷ . . . τὴν ψυχὴν ἥνικα συμφέρει παραλαμβάνοντι.

[4] Cp. in the Mandaean writings the "house of life" or the "house of perfection"; see the indices in Lidzb. on the Mand. Lit. and on Ginza. Cp. Philo somn. I 256: the soul, which has become lord over πάθος and κενὴ δόξα, will sing hymns to God; it is said of it:

are "many dwellings,"[1] in which he can prepare places for the disciples, so that he can come again and bring them to him.[2] The Evangelist has interrupted the text of the source with the comment: εἰ δὲ μή, εἶπον ἂν ὑμῖν ὅτι,[3] which is not absolutely clear; its purpose must be to stress the certainty of what has been said.[4] So much is in any case clear: the abandonment of the disciples is only temporary; Jesus will come and bring them to him.

οὕτως γὰρ δυνήσῃ καὶ εἰς τὸν πατρῷον οἶκον ἐπανελθεῖν, τὴν ἐπὶ τῆς ξένης μακρὰν καὶ ἀνήνυτον ζάλην ἐκφυγοῦσα.

[1] Μονή = dwelling (cp. μένειν in 1.38f.), see Br. dictionary. Jewish apocalyptic knows of the heavenly dwellings of the righteous (Eth. Enoch 39, 4; 41, 2; Slavonic Enoch 61, 2; Volz, Eschat. 405f.). The Gnostic Mark speaks of the ὑπερθεν δώματα Iren. I 14, 3 or Hipp. El. 44, 1 p. 176, 18; in the hymn Act. Ioa. 95, p. 198, 9f. it is said: οἶκον οὐκ ἔχω καὶ οἴκους ἔχω . . . , τόπον οὐκ ἔχω καὶ τόπους ἔχω. In Act. Thom. 27, p. 142, 17f., Wisdom is summoned: ἐλθὲ ἡ μήτηρ τῶν ἑπτὰ οἴκων, ἵνα ἡ ἀνάπαυσίς σου εἰς τὸν ὄγδοον οἶκον γένηται. Above all, the bright, shining dwelling and the heavenly Škinas play a great part in the Mandaean writings, see the indices to the Mand. Lit. and to Ginza, esp. Škina; see further p. 598 n. 6; ZNTW 24 [1925] 132f. Manichaean examples in Br. Related to the idea of the heavenly dwellings for the believers is that of the heavenly building into which the believers are built; see Schlier, Relig. Unters. 120f.; Christus und die Kirche 49, 2. The harmony exhibited by the sentences in vv. 2f. with the Gnostic mythology is itself the refutation of O. Schaefer's attempt (ZNTW 32 [1933] 210ff.) to understand the Father's οἰκία as the universe (which in spite of 8.35 would be quite unJohannine), in which there is more than one dwelling, i.e. there is not only this earth, but also heaven, so that Jesus' departure from the earth does not mean that he vanishes into nothing. Similarly, R. Eisler, Ἰησ. βασ. II 246: God's house or palace is the wide world, in which the "restless wanderer" . . . finds "many places of rest".

[2] See pp. 598 n. 6; 432 n. 1; 519 n. 1. This idea is completely different from the mythology of Jewish-Christian eschatology; the promise refers to the ascent into the world of light of the individual soul after death; see below, note 8. Temple takes the μοναί as "places of rest", i.e. as stations of spiritual progress. These are in the "Father's house", because the man who is on the way to heaven is really already in heaven.

[3] Ὅτι does not occur in ℜ al it, but is firmly enough attested. Acc. to Hosk. the promise alludes to Mk. 14.12–16; hardly credible!

[4] To take ὅτι causally (B. Weiss, Lagr., Tillm., Bl., Wik., and Barr.) inevitably results in a triviality: either 1. one must relate ὅτι to εἶπον ("Otherwise I would have told you, because I am going there, and must therefore know"), or 2. one must regard εἰ δὲ μή ... ὑμῖν as a parenthesis, and take ὅτι as the reason given for the statement μοναὶ πολλαί εἰσιν (which comes to mean the same). It is better to take ὅτι as explicative (as Orig. does) and either interpret: 3. "Otherwise I would have told you that I am going ...", i.e. "the dwellings are already prepared, and I do not need to say that I am going to make a place for you"; thus Zn.; opposed by Lagr.: precisely, and only, if the dwellings are ready, does it make sense to go and book a place. But above all: acc. to v. 3 Jesus is in fact going in order to prepare a place (Wellh. gets over this by eliminating ἐὰν πορ. ... τόπον ὑμῖν in v. 3; against this solution Omodeo, Mistica 57, 1). Or 4. one can take the sentence as a question (Ho., Htm., Br., Bd., Hirsch, Strathm.; so also Noack (148), who suggests that a μή has been omitted before εἶπον, through haplography): "Would I not otherwise have said that I am going ...?" Of course Jesus has not yet said that directly, but he has indirectly, in 12.26, 32; 17.24; and the fact that the ἵνα-clause in v. 3 recalls the wording of 12.26; 17.24, makes this the most probable interpretation. Torry (341) suggests a mistake in translation: εἰ δὲ μή is due to wrongly regarding וָלֵא (fitting) as וְלָא, so that we should really read: συμφέρει, λέγω ὑμῖν, ὅτι πορεύομαι, or perhaps better: ἀμὴν ἀμ. λέγω ὑμῖν·

The words παραλήμψομαι ὑμᾶς πρὸς ἐμ. take this promise further than ὄψεσθε μέ in 16.16 and ὄψομαι ὑμᾶς in 16.22. The transitoriness which this παραλ. brings to an end cannot be that second μικρόν of 16.16. The promise of the "heavenly dwellings" and of "being where he is" is something different from the promise of the χαρά, into which the believers' λύπη is to be changed. It is that they will see the other-worldly δόξα of the Revealer, no longer veiled by σάρξ, in an existence beyond death, such as was hinted at in 12.26 and requested in 17.24.[1] This accords with the fact that we are not dealing here in the first place with the believers' situation in the world but with the question about the ὁδός. In this sense the argument in the farewell discourses corresponds to the development of thought in the prayer of ch. 17, which dealt with the believers' situation in the world in vv. 9–23, and then with the eternity of their existence beyond death in vv. 24–26. But the inner unity of the believers' existence in the world and in the other-worldly future was made very plain there,[2] and the same is true here. The question about the ὁδός is very quickly deflected into a question about the present fellowship with the Revealer, so that the anxiety in which the believer is placed is not anxiety about the promised other-worldly future, but about the believing existence in the world. This is why the promise of an other-worldly future after death does not contradict the idea that the resurrection is already experienced in faith now (5.24f.; 11.25f.). On the other hand this kind of faith is accompanied by the certainty of the nothingness of impending bodily death—but only on the condition that it does not become an object of anxiety. It is precisely in the ταραχή of isolation that the believer can hear the

συμφέρει ... (cp. 16.7). But the rhythm of the sentences argues against this; and if it is one of the Evangelist's additions we are dealing with, then there is no question of a mistake in translation. Corssen's attempt (ZNTW 8 [1907] 134f.) is impossible: he wants to take εἰ δὲ μή as a contrast not to ἐν τ. οἰκ. κτλ. but to πιστεύετε: "If you could not believe correctly (i.e. that I and the Father are one), then I would say that ...".

[1] The eschatology that lies at the basis of this promise is not that of the Jewish-Christian hope (thus Dodd 404), but is the individualistic eschatology of the Gnostic myth, the connexion of which to the cosmological eschatology (see pp. 64; 157 n. 5; 431 n. 3) is left completely on one side here. The Revealer's ἔρχεσθαι, promised in v. 3, is not therefore the parousia of Jewish-Christian eschatology (B. Weiss, Zn., Schl., Bd.). Wellh.'s postulation of interpolation (see p. 601 n. 4) rests on the presupposition that this is what is referred to. But the presupposition is shared by Sp. and Loisy; the latter with the modification that in the Evangelist's thinking the Parousia is blended with the spiritual *unio* which precedes it (similarly Ho., Htm., Bl.). Kundsin (see p. 581 n. 1) rightly sees that it is concerned with Jesus' coming in the hour of death; but that it deals specifically with the martyr's death, is not possible in view of the generality of the promise, and is totally excluded by vv. 4–9. The distinction Zn. makes, is also impossible; he maintains that vv. 2–3a "are valid for those disciples, who in the discipleship of Jesus ... are to enter glory through their death", while v. 3b "is valid for the body of disciples as a whole, which is to continue on earth, until the Lord comes again".

[2] See pp. 521f.

promise that he has a home, that in the Father's house there are "many dwellings," and thus also a place for him.[1] But he is only entitled to hear the promise in the isolation which is peculiar to faith.

Jesus' words in **v. 4** state that the promise is valid solely for the faith which sees in his ὑπάγειν the victorious departure to the Father, but they also make it clear that faith knows the way to follow him: καὶ ὅπου ἐγὼ ὑπάγω οἴδατε τὴν ὁδόν. This saying contains a two-fold significance: 1. in close connexion with v. 3: about that place, where you will be with me, you cannot be in any doubt, for you know whither I am going. But it does not only say ὅπου ὑπάγω οἴδατε, but also at the same time (οἴδατε) τὴν ὁδόν. Thus 2: you also know the way there.[2] And the latter now becomes the real theme. But knowledge of the ὁδός goes hand in hand with knowledge of his departure, i.e. in the last analysis with knowledge of him as the Revealer, and this means that the question as to the ὁδός is answered by talking about *him*.

2) *The Unity of Way and Goal:* 14.5–14

The wording of v. 4 was provocative; the believer was addressed on a subject he ought to have known about, and yet did not. It has the effect of drawing his attention to what has been given him, and thus of inciting him to ask a question about it. It is Thomas[3] who does so (**v. 5**)[4] —foolishly, like the Jews (7.35f.; 8.22), because he should have known long ago whither Jesus is going. His question is typical of the mythological standpoint, which can only conceive of the goal and the way as things within the world.[5] And yet to this extent the question has been

[1] There is no question of the promise of the "many dwellings" referring to the different grades of blessedness, as the Presbyters of Iren. V. 36, 2 maintain (whether this quotes an independent dominical saying or John is questionable, acc. to v. Loewenich 126, 1). Speculations about the different χῶραι in which the ascending ψυχαί find their place, each acc. to its τιμή, after the separation from the body, are to be found in the Hermetical passages in Scott, Hermetica I 506ff.; on this, see Kroll. Trism. 267ff. The "many dwellings" simply describe the fullness, the richness of the world of light; cp. Od. Sal. 3.6: "And I shall be no stranger, for with the Lord Most High and Merciful there is no grudging (חסמא = φθόνος)"; ἀφθονία is superabundance as well as liberality. Cp. Vergil Aen. 6, 673: nulli certa domus, namely a beyond, the wide spaces of which are at the disposal of all blessed ones.

[2] The two-fold meaning becomes even plainer in the text read by 𝔎 F pl lat sy: καὶ ὅπου ἐγὼ ὑπάγω οἴδατε καὶ τὴν ὁδὸν οἴδατε. But this is a clarificatory correction, which spoils the rhythm.

[3] See p. 400f. D adds: ὁ λεγόμενος Δίδυμος.

[4] Before πῶς, ℵ 𝔎 pl lat read a καί. ℵ 𝔎 pl continue: (πῶς) δυνάμεθα εἰδέναι τὴν ὁδόν. Clearly a correction.

[5] Cp. the reflections of Šum-Kušta in Joh.-B. 59, 2ff.: "My lot is full. I will now go, but do not know who will lead me (so as to ask him) how long my way is ... and no-one is there to fetch me." Again the mythological basis of the words that are used is clear. The knowledge of the *way*, along which the soul which is separating itself from the body has to go to enter the world of light, and the knowledge of the *leader* who knows the way.

put correctly: it makes clear that the disciple's knowledge of his own way depends on knowledge of Jesus' ὑπάγειν.

Jesus' answer in v. 6 corrects the mythological thinking:

> ἐγώ εἰμι ἡ ὁδὸς καὶ ἡ ἀλήθεια καὶ ἡ ζωή·
> οὐδεὶς ἔρχεται πρὸς τὸν πατέρα εἰ μὴ δι' ἐμοῦ.[1]

---

can be described as a corner-stone of Gnosticism (W. Anz, Zur Frage nach dem Ursprung des Gnostizismus 1897; Jonas, Gnosis I 205ff.). The redeemer brings as γνῶσις information about the κεκρυμμένα τῆς ἁγίας ὁδοῦ (Hipp. El. V. 10, 2, see p. 497 n. 2). The Peratai speak (Hipp. El. V 16, 1, p. 111, 9ff. W): μόνοι . . . ἡμεῖς οἱ τὴν ἀνάγκην τῆς γενέσεως ἐγνωκότες καὶ τὰς ὁδούς, δι' ὧν εἰσελήλυθεν ὁ Ἄνθρωπος εἰς τὸν κόσμον, ἀκριβῶς δεδιδαγμένοι διελθεῖν καὶ περᾶσαι τὴν φθορὰν μόνοι δυνάμεθα. Cp. V 26, 23, pp. 130, 17f.; ἀναβὰς γὰρ πρὸς τὸν ἀγαθὸν ὁ πατὴρ ὁδὸν ἔδειξε τοῖς ἀναβαίνειν θέλουσιν. Exc. ex Theod. 38: ἵνα . . . τῷ σπέρματι δίοδον εἰς πλήρωμα παράσχῃ. 74: ὁ κύριος ἀνθρώπων ὁδηγὸς ὁ κατελθὼν εἰς γῆν. In Iren. I 13, 6; 21, 5 (=Epiph. 36, 3, 2–5) and Orig. c. C. VI 31 Gnostic formulae are recorded which prepare the way into the world of light for the soul. The prayers in Act. Thom. 148, 167 (p. 257, 10ff.; 281, 6ff.) request that the soul go on its way to the goal unharmed; cp. esp. p. 281, 8f.: ὁδήγησόν με σήμερον ἐρχόμενον πρὸς σέ. Acc. to Od. Sal. 39, 9ff., the Redeemer has prepared the way (cp. Od. Sal. 7.3; 13f.; 11.3; 22.7, 11; 24.13; 33.7ff.; 41.11). Examples from the Mandaean literature are more than abundant. Cp. Mand. Lit. 38: "Thou hast shown us the way, along which thou hast come out of the house of life. Along it we want to make the journey of true, believing men, so that our spirit and our soul abide in the Škina of life ...". 134f.: "Thou camest, hast opened the door, made level the way, trodden out the path.... Thou wast a helper, guide and leader to the great race of life. Thou hast ... brought it out to the great place of light, and to the shining dwelling." Further, 77, 97f., 101, 132f.; Joh.-B. 198, 20f.: "I have levelled a way from darkness to the bright dwelling"; 199, 3f.; 239, 14; Ginza 95, 15; 247, 16ff.; 271, 26f.; 395, 3ff. (the Kušta as the "way of the perfect, the path that ascends to the place of light"); 429, 17ff.; 439, 14ff.; 487, 8ff.; 523, 23ff.; 550, 16ff. etc., see below p. 606 n. 3. Cp. the Manichaean hymn in Reitzenst. J.E.M. 23f. The same terminology is found in Hermetic Gnosticism; cp. C. Herm. 7, 2; 9, 10; 10, 21 (see p. 474 n. 2), cp. 4, 11; 10, 21 and the teaching on the πρὸς ἀλήθειαν ὁδός in the fragments in Scott, Hermetica 390–392. Acc. to C. Herm. 1, 26, 29 the Gnostic will on his part be a καθοδηγός for the others. On Zosimos see Reitzenst. H.M.R. 301. It would be worth researching into the question how far the Platonic symbolism of the way lies at the basis of this kind of mythology (P. Friedländer, Platon I 74ff.). Cp. ZNTW 24 (1925), 133f.; Reitzenst. H.M.R. 295ff.; J. Kroll, Herm. Trism. 380ff.; Schlier, Relig. Unters. 137ff.; Bornkamm, Mythos und Leg. 12; E. Käsemann, Das Wandernde Gottesvolk 1938, 52ff. E. Percy wrongly disputes the weight of the Gnostic analogies (Untersuchungen 225f.).

In contrast to this, the parabolic linguistic usage of the OT (e.g. Ps. 143.10; Is. 63.14) is as little relevant as e.g. Epict. diss. I 4, 29 (praise of Chrysippus): ὢ μεγάλης εὐτυχίας, ὢ μεγαλου εὐεργέτου τοῦ δεικνύοντος τὴν ὁδόν; or Wis. 10.10, 17 (at most there could be an echo of the myth in 9.11, which speaks of the ὁδηγεῖν of σοφία). On the other hand Philo does show the influence of the Gnostic manner of speech; for him the θεῖος λόγος is the ἡγεμὼν τῆς ὁδοῦ of the soul (migr. Abr. 174f., see p. 589 n. 3), and he interprets the βασιλικὴ ὁδός of Num. 20.17 as the way of Gnosis and the vision of God, see J. Pascher, Η ΒΑΣΙΛΙΚΗ ΟΔΟΣ 1931.

The idea of the "way" belongs together with that of the "door"; on the latter see p. 377 n. 7; Ed. Schweizer, EGO EIMI 143, 14; Kundsin, Charakter 239f. The motif of the heavenly wall, in which the redeemer makes a breach, also has place within the circle of these motifs, see Schlier, Christus und die Kirche 18ff.; Käsemann, Das Wandernde Gottesvolk 101f., 145ff.

[1] Becker too ascribes v. 6 to the source.

By describing himself as the way Jesus makes two things clear: 1. his case is different from that of the disciples; he does not need a "way" for himself, as the disciples do, rather he is the way for them; 2. the way and the goal are not to be separated as they are in mythological thinking.[1] In the myth the redemption has become embodied in a cosmic event, and therefore—contrary to the intention of the myth—it is conceived as an intra-mundane event, as a divine history, which takes place apart from the existence of man, who is referred to it as the guarantee of his future.[2] According to John the redemption is an event which takes place in human existence through the encounter with the Revealer, with the result that the believer's present is already based on his future; his existence is eschatological existence; his way is at the same time his goal.

'Εγώ εἰμι ἡ ὁδός: this is pure expression of the idea of revelation. The Revealer is the access to God[3] which man is looking for,[4] and what is more—as is implied in the phrase ἐγώ εἰμι and is stated explicitly in the words οὐδεὶς κτλ.—the only access. Not, however, in the sense that he mediated the access[5] and then became superfluous;[6] i.e. not in the sense of a mystagogue, who brings doctrines and celebrations that are the means to the vision of God. On the contrary, he is the way in

[1] An analogy to this is found in Gnosticism, when the revealer is sometimes described not only as the one who brings Gnosis, but as the Gnosis himself; see Schlier, Relig. Unters. 60f., and cp. the Mandaean revealer who is called Manda dHaije = γνῶσις τῆς ζωῆς; see Reitzenst. H.M.R. 394f. and cp. Ign. Eph. 17, 2: διὰ τί δὲ οὐ πάντες φρόνιμοι γινόμεθα λαβόντες θεοῦ γνῶσιν, ὅ ἐστιν 'Ι. Χριστός; In such cases it is not always possible to decide whether the phrase used is rhetorical, or whether the view of faith (or of mystical experience) is moving out beyond the mythological idea. That v. 6 abandons the myth, is shown by vv. 7–9. G. Wingren, Studia Theol. III (1951), 122 expresses himself against my interpretation.

[2] See pp. 64f.

[3] One is not entitled to isolate the sentence from its context within the Gospel as a whole, as Kundsin does (op. cit. 212, see p. 581 n. 1), and interpret it in terms of the Passion-situation only, so that the "way" is the martyrdom endured in union with Jesus.

[4] The context makes it clear that ἐγώ is not subject, but predicate, i.e. that this is a case of the recognition-formula (see p. 225, n. 3).

[5] Rightly Dupont (213f.), who stresses that we are not concerned here with a description of Jesus' own being, but with an account of his significance for us. Similarly Dodd 178.

[6] Thus Philo's λόγος, see p. 589 n. 3. So too in Plotinus, of the ἐπιστήμη (Enn. VI 9, 4 p. 513, 2ff. Volkm.): "Thus it is not possible either to speak or write of it (the ἕν), just as it is said: but we speak and write only of being led to it, of awakening from the ideas to the vision ὥσπερ ὁδὸν δεικνύντες τῷ τι θεάσασθαι βουλομένῳ. For the teaching only reaches to the way, to the awakening, after that the vision must itself bring to fruition whoever wants to see" (translation by Harder). Similarly Jambl. de myst. 9, 6, p. 280, 16ff. Parthey, of the οἰκεῖος δαίμων of man: μέχρι τοσούτου κυβερνᾷ τοὺς ἀνθρώπους, ἕως ἂν διὰ τῆς ἱερατικῆς θεουργίας θεὸν ἔφορον ἐπιστήσωμεν καὶ ἡγεμόνα τῆς ψυχῆς· τότε γὰρ ὑποχωρεῖ τῷ κρείττονι ἢ παραδίδωσι τὴν ἐπιστασίαν, ἢ ὑποτάττεται, ὡς συντελεῖν εἰς αὐτόν, ἢ ἄλλον τινὰ τρόπον ὑπηρετεῖ αὐτῷ ὡς ἐπάρχοντι.

such a manner as to be at the same time the goal; for he is also ἡ ἀλήθεια καὶ ἡ ζωή: the ἀλήθεια as the *revealed* reality of God,[1] and the ζωή as the *divine* reality which bestows life on the believer in that it bestows self-understanding in God.[2] All three concepts are bound to each other by the word ἐγώ:[3] just as Jesus is the way, in that he is the goal, so he is also the goal, in that he is the way. He cannot be forgotten in the enjoyment of the goal, for the believer cannot have the ἀλήθεια and the ζωή as acquisitions at his own disposal: Jesus remains for him the way. Of course that is not to say that ἀλήθεια and ζωή are a goal that is always to be striven for and that is an infinite distance away; on the contrary, in going along the way the goal is reached. Not however in the sense of Stoicism or idealism, where the goal is ideally present in the infinite way; for the way is not the πρὸς τὸ μὴ ἁμαρτάνειν τετάσθαι διηνεκῶς (Epict. diss. IV, 12, 19), nor is it a "perpetual striving to make the effort"; rather it is the state of existence that is subjected to the actual word of Jesus within history, for there God is present.[4] But the believer finds God only in *him*, i.e. God is not directly accessible; faith is not mystical experience, but rather historical existence that is subject to the revelation.

That means that there is no "short cut" to the correct understanding of ἀλήθεια and ζωή. The discovery of this ἀλήθεια is not something established once and for all, at men's disposal, such as could be communicated in "condensed form" like a truth of science; on the contrary everyone has to take the way to it for himself, for only on the way does this truth disclose itself. Similarly Jesus *is* the truth; he does not simply *state* it. One does not come to him to ask about truth; one comes to him as the truth. This truth does not exist as a doctrine, which could

---

[1] See pp. 74 n.2; 190f.; 321; 434ff.; 509 n.3. Becaus in Hellenistic linguistic usage ἀλήθεια can mean the divine reality, it can also be said in magic: ἐγώ ειμι ἡ ἀλήθεια (Pap. Graec. Mag. V 148).

[2] See pp. 38ff., 184f., 257ff., 321, 402f.

[3] The combination of the concepts ὁδός, ἀλήθεια and ζωή is typically Gnostic, for it must be remembered that for ἀλ. the corresponding word γνῶσις (which John avoids) can be used. Cp. Mand. Lit. 77: "Thou hast brought us out of death. Thou hast shown us the way of life, and hast made us walk the path of truth and faith." In Ginza 271, 26ff. the Kušta is addressed: "Thou art the way of the perfect, the path which ascends to the place of light. Thou art the life from eternity. . . . Thou art . . . the truth without error." Acc. to Od. Sal. 38 the truth is the one who leads to the life; Od. Sal. 11.3; 33.8 speaks of the way of truth (in contrast to the ways of φθορά and ἀπώλεια); cp. 15.4ff. On the combination of ἀλ. and ζωή see ThWB I 241, 14ff.; cp. C. Herm. 13, 9: τῇ δὲ ἀληθείᾳ καὶ τὸ ἀγαθὸν ἐπεγένετο ἅμα ζωῇ καὶ φωτί; the combination of ζωή and γνῶσις occurs in the concluding prayer of the Λόγος τέλειος (Scott, Hermetica I 376; Pap. Graec. Mag. III 602). On John Lightfoot's suggestion that ἀλ. and ζωή be taken as adjectival attributes ("the true and living way"; cp. Heb. 10.20), see Howard, Christianity 182f.

[4] Otherwise Phil., somn. I 66: ὁ δὴ ξεναγηθεὶς ὑπὸ σοφίας εἰς τὸν πρότερον ἀφικνεῖται τόπον, εὑράμενος τῆς ἀρεσκείας κεφαλὴν καὶ τέλος τὸν θεῖον λόγον, ἐν ᾧ γενόμενος οὐ φθάνει πρὸς τὸν κατὰ τὸ εἶναι θεὸν ἐλθεῖν, ἀλλ᾽ αὐτὸν ὁρᾷ μακρόθεν κτλ.

be understood, preserved, and handed on, so that the teacher is discharged and surpassed. Rather the position a man takes vis-à-vis the Revealer decides not whether he *knows* the truth, but whether he *is* "of the truth," that is to say, whether his existence is determined by the truth, whether the truth is the ground on which his existence is based. And as in Christianity everyone has to start for himself from the beginning,[1] so too there is no such thing as a history of Christianity within world-history, in the sense of a history of ideas or problems, in which one progresses from stage to stage, from solution to solution; each generation has the same original relation to the revelation.[2]

If however that is the answer to the question Thomas raised, as to the way that leads to the goal which is beyond historical existence, then this much is clear: the questioner is referred back to his own historical existence. His questioning cannot reach out beyond it and demand further guarantees. He can only hear the promise within that existence: πάλιν ἔρχομαι καὶ παραλήμψομαι ὑμᾶς πρὸς ἐμαυτόν. And his attention is brought back to himself in such a way as to make him understand that he is grounded solely on God's revelation, from which he lives; his attention is not drawn to any power or achievement of his own, nor to any divine element within him. Only faith is certain of the future.

The paradox that the way and the goal are the same is brought to our notice once more in vv. 7–11, again introduced by a provocative word from Jesus, which is followed by a foolish request from Philip. **V. 7:** εἰ ἐγνώκατέ με, καὶ τὸν πατέρα μου γνώσεσθε.[3] Jesus is the Revealer, in that in him the Father is present;[4] if the disciples have known *him*,

---

[1] Contrast the education in Goethe's "pedagogical province", where it is rather the case that "wise men privately allow the boy to find what is fit for him; that they *shorten* the detours, through which a man can all too readily fall from his vocation".

[2] Kierkegaard, Einübung im Christentum, German 2nd ed. Jena 1924 20ff., 179ff., E. T. Training in Christianity, 1941, 26ff., 197ff.

[3] This is the reading of ℵ D pc; against this B C* 565 al read: εἰ ἐγνώκειτέ με, καὶ τ. πατ. μ. ἂν ᾔδειτε, while syr^s has: "If you have not recognised me, will you also recognise my Father?", which has clearly arisen out of ℵ D. Both readings go well with what has gone before, but only that of ℵ D accords with what follows; for acc. to B C v. 7a denies what v. 7b affirms, while acc. to ℵ D v. 7a states the condition for the possibility of the affirmation in v. 7b. The original text (ℵ D) has clearly been corrected in different ways in B C and syr^s, in order to provide motivation for what seems in the light of v. 7b an impossible request by Philip (8.19 clearly having an influence on B C). But in this way the point of vv. 7–9 is lost, the point being that the disciple already has the possibility, to which he is still blind. Rightly Barr., while Dodd (164, 2) remains doubtful. On the identity of γινώσκειν and εἰδέναι see p. 283 n.1. V. 7a probably comes from the source, in which it belonged together with v. 9a. The Evangelist has abandoned the parallelism for the sake of the dialogue. Acc. to the source, one should read: ὁ γινώσκων (γνοὺς) ἐμὲ καὶ τὸν πατ. μ. γινώσκει (ἔγνωκεν) καὶ ὁ ἑωρακὼς ἐμὲ ἑώρακεν τὸν πατέρα. Becker (106) does not see a piece of the source in vv. 7f.

[4] See pp. 250f., 345. On the époptic johannique see H. Clavier Rev. H. Ph. rel. 31 (1951), 289–291.

then they will also know the *Father*. They *will* do so? In fact they *have* already, as v. 9 states: ὁ ἑωρακὼς ἐμὲ ἑώρακεν τὸν πατέρα. But the possibility inherent in the encounter must be made a reality, it must be grasped explicitly; the eschatological existence has to be realised within history. Believing existence (*Sein*) is historical existence (*Existieren*) within time; the possibility that has always been there remains a continual future before the believer, and therefore one can say γνώσεσθε just as well as ἑωράκατε. This is precisely the point of the dialogue: to show that the believer who is discouraged, and who cannot see his own possibility, only needs to discover what he already has; and on the other hand also to show what this entails, namely that believing existence is no permanent, settled state of affairs, but rather the grasping hold of the possibility that has been given.

That this possibility is already within the disciples' grasp, is the force of the provocative words: ἀπ' ἄρτι γινώσκετε αὐτὸν καὶ ἑωράκατε. This is already the situation![1] But here Philip[2] is blind, and therefore he asks: κύριε, δεῖξον ἡμῖν τὸν πατέρα, καὶ ἀρκεῖ ἡμῖν (**v. 8**). 'Αρκεῖ ἡμ.[3] does of course show that he has correctly understood the intention behind Jesus' words, which direct the questioner of v. 5 to his present situation; Philip does not want to reach out beyond the present, if only he can see God in it. His foolishness however is to demand a direct vision of God over and above the revelation.[4] Jesus' answer shows him the folly of this, by re-directing his attention to the indirect vision of God in the Revealer (**v. 9**). The implication behind the reproachful question: τοσοῦτον χρόνον κτλ.[5] is that all fellowship with Jesus loses its significance unless he is recognised as the one whose sole intention is to reveal God,

---

[1] As in 13.19 ἀπ' ἄρτι means "now already"; see pp. 478 n.4; 591 n.6. Hirsch wants to reject ἀπ' ἄρτι, on the grounds that after it Philip's reply is impossible!

[2] On Philip see p. 102 n.3.

[3] Ἄρκει with the dat. (good Greek) corresponds to the Rabbinic דַּי (Schl.).

[4] Philip demands to see God τοῖς τοῦ σώματος ὀφθαλμοῖς (Chrys. hom. 74, 1 t. VIII 435a). "If one has rightly understood the misunderstandings in the Fourth Gospel, then one can be in no doubt that Philip means a completely crude "showing", such as is fitting for every perceptible object" (Wrede, Messiasgeh. 190). And yet the Evangelist may well have more than just one kind of "vision of God" before his mind, as the object of his polemic: e.g. theophanies (thus Chrys. op. cit.: ἴσως περὶ τῶν προφητῶν ἀκούων ὅτι εἶδον τὸν θεόν, so also Ephraem in Merx 373), or epoptia of the mysteries (cp. e.g. G. Anrich, Das antike Mysterien-wesen 1894, 30f., 33f.; Dieterich, Mithraslit. 2nd ed. 86f.), or mystical experiences (e.g. Od. Sal. 21; 25; C. Herm. 4, 11), or experiences of philosophical meditation (in Anrich op. cit., examples from Plato, Philo and Plotinus). But the eschatological vision of God, such as Gnosticism promises, may also be intended; cp. Act. Thom. 113 p. 224, 11ff. and esp. 61 p. 178, 4ff.: ἔπιδε ἐφ' ἡμᾶς . . . ἵνα τὸν σὸν πατέρα θεασώμεθα καὶ κορεσθῶμεν τῆς αὐτοῦ τροφῆς τῆς θεϊκῆς. In addition, cp. the Manichaean hymn in Reitzenst. J.E.M. 23: "... I will bring thee ... to the place (of Paradise) ... and will show thee the Father, the ruler (for) ever."

[5] XD pc read, unclassically, τοσούτῳ χρόνῳ, cp. Bl.-D. § 201.

and not to be anything for himself; but it also implies that the possibility of seeing God is inherent in the fellowship with Jesus: ὁ ἑωρακὼς ἐμὲ ἑώρακεν τὸν πατέρα.[1] What need is there for anything further (πῶς σὺ λέγεις κτλ.)? The only vital thing now is that the disciple understand the question posed by his situation, a question demanding a decision from him.

This question is posed by Jesus' words in **v. 10**: οὐ πιστεύεις ὅτι ἐγὼ ἐν τῷ πατρὶ καὶ ὁ πατὴρ ἐν ἐμοί ἐστιν;[2] The faith at issue is the faith that man really encounters God in his encounter with Jesus, that Jesus and the Father are one. The formula of reciprocity is again used to describe this unity,[3] but what follows makes it clear that it must be understood in terms of the idea of revelation. In Jesus' word, the work of the Father is brought to fruition; on his own, and for himself, Jesus is nothing: he is simply and without exception the revelation of the Father, and the words ὁ δὲ πατὴρ (ὁ) ἐν ἐμοὶ μένων give added emphasis to the fact.[4]

The reference to Jesus' unity with the Father, which is apparent in what he says, enables what was put as a question in v. 10 to be repeated now as an imperative (**v. 11**): πιστεύετέ μοι κτλ. And just as the Jews were told in 10.38, so the disciples are here: εἰ δὲ μή, διὰ τὰ ἔργα αὐτὰ πιστεύετε.[5] In the light of v. 10, these ἔργα can only be Jesus' revelatory works in the word he speaks. And, as in 10.38, faith in this work is distinguished from faith that is directed only to what has been said. The man, for whom Jesus has not already become authoritative, so that he could believe his word without question, should look at what his word effects: i.e. he should look at himself. Jesus' word does not communicate mysteries or dogmas, but discloses a man's reality. If he

[1] See p. 607 n.3. It is worth noting that the concept εἰκών does not occur here either; see p. 82.

[2] The ὅτι-clause will come from the source (as the main sentence?), where it followed the sentences quoted in vv. 6f. and v. 9. How far v. 10 belongs to the source remains doubtful. Becker (106) regards the sentence ὁ ἑωρακώς κτλ. in v. 9 as a section of the source which followed that which is retained in v. 6. The continuation would then be v. 10b: τὰ ῥήματα κτλ.

[3] Cp. v. 20; 10.38; 17.21; see pp. 381f.; 513 n.1.

[4] The variant readings are unimportant: instead of λέγω there occur λαλῶ (א ℜ pl lat) and λελάληκα (D pc); before μένων, א ℜ D pl read the article, perhaps rightly. The dropping of αὐτοῦ after τὰ ἔργα (Tert. al) or its replacement by αὐτός is a bad correction. On ἀπ' ἐμ. οὐ λαλῶ see pp. 145 n.5; 249 n.1 (see generally pp. 249ff.). On μένειν ἐν see pp. 267 n.1; 321 n.1; 535 n.1; on the ἔργα of God see p. 331 n.3.

[5] The changing of αὐτά to αὐτοῦ (B) makes sense and is in fact correct, in so far as the ἔργα are the Father's, acc. to v. 10; but the correction spoils the emphasis of the sentence. (Schl., Glaube im NT 4th ed. 195, 1, refers to Polyb. I 35, 4: δι' αὐτῶν τῶν ἔργων λαβεῖν τὴν πίστιν and to VII 13, 2: δι' αὐτῶν τῶν πραγμάτων.) The insertion of μοι after the second πιστεύετε (B ℜ pl) is also understandable. In syr[s], vv. 10b, 11 are missing, but probably only by mistake.

tries to understand himself by subjecting his existence to this word, then he will experience the work of the Father on him.[1] The nature of the experience is stated in **v. 12**: the Father's work will continue to come to fruition in those who believe in Jesus: ὁ πιστεύων εἰς ἐμὲ τὰ ἔργα ἃ ἐγὼ ποιῶ κἀκεῖνος ποιήσει.[2] This promise accords both with the commission that the disciples received to continue witnessing to him (15.27), and to the promise that they would share his destiny, in virtue of their essential unity with him (15.18ff.).[3] It also corresponds to the promise of the Paraclete, who is to continue what Jesus had done, and whose work is carried through in the community's proclamation of the word (15.26f.; 16.4b ff.). The disciples are to regard the taking up of their task—and this is the point here—as the Father's work. What further need have they then to ask: δεῖξον ἡμῖν τὸν πατέρα? Indeed, the Father's work, which began with what Jesus did, is to prove its power more and more in what they do: καὶ μείζονα τούτων ποιήσει.

This promise does not mean that the disciples' activity is to embrace a larger geographical area than that of Jesus, or to have greater success; still less, that they are to do greater miracles than he.[4] For if their work is to be of the same sort as his, then it can be as little measured by human standards as his. And just as the success of what he did was visible only to faith, so the same will be true of the success they have. But the ὅτι-clause: ὅτι ἐγὼ πρὸς τὸν πατέρα πορεύομαι states expressly why their work will be greater than his. It will be greater in so far as his is seen within temporal boundaries, and is brought to an end by his departure. In that sense it is "incomplete," and has not yet fulfilled its intention. As eschatological event, however, it cannot be limited to one time or place within history; it can only be seen to be such after his departure, when it is taken up again in the Easter and Whitsun preaching of the community, and thus protected from the misunderstanding that it is simply a historical phenomenon. Jesus' word is word of revelation in its continual newness on every occasion when it is present. Only when it is effective in this way in the community does Jesus' work come to its fruition. Thus there is no question here of supplementing or surpassing

[1] See pp. 265f.; 390f. On the relation of ῥήματα and ἔργα see also p. 145 n.5.

[2] It is doubtful whether, or how far, v. 12 comes from the source. On the κἀκεῖνος which picks up ὁ πιστεύων see p. 79 n.3. It is possible that the last sentence (ἐγὼ πρός τ. πατ. πορ.) was the introduction to v. 14 in the source (see p. 612 n.1), or to the prophecy of the Paraclete in vv. 16f.

[3] See p. 516 n.1.

[4] Cp. e.g. the words of the messenger about the "men of tested righteousness", in Ginza 319, 3f.: "I brought them secret discourses, so that they show their miraculous powers to the ill-disposed", and in general cp. 319, 1ff.; 296, 9ff. Most of the exegetes refer to missionary successes and miracles; see esp. Heitmüller, Im Namen Jesu 79f. So also Strathm. and Barr.; rightly, against this view, Wik.

Jesus' work in any quantitive way. For every part within the revelation is at one and the same time the whole; but that is only true *sub specie* of the future event, which is "greater" than the past in the sense that in it the significance of what is past is preserved and thus fulfilled for the first time. Thus Jesus' coming into the world is itself the judgment (3.19; 9.39), and yet the hour of his departure is the judgment (12.31) and the hour of his victory (16.33). Again, the lawsuit is only decided in the work of the Paraclete, who convicts the world (16.8–11). And the ἔργα, which 16.8–11 had described as the working of the Paraclete in the community, for whose sake Jesus had to depart (16.7)—these are the μείζονα ἔργα, which are possible on the basis of his departure.

To speak of the disciples' μείζονα ἔργα is of course to speak paradoxically; for they are in fact the works of him without whom the disciples can do nothing (15.5). And the juxtaposition of that promise with the promise that their prayer will be heard, which makes what they do appear as something given (v. 13), reminds us at once that all the disciples' work is rooted in his work, and is in fact his work. Whatever they ask for, appealing to him in asking it,[1] will be given to them—a promise already made them in 15.16; 16.23f., 26;[2] but it does not say here, as it did there, that the prayer is directed to the Father, and that the Father will hear it. Instead the prayer is directed—remarkably—to Jesus himself,[3] and it is he, who will hear it.[4] Actually this is no different from what was said in 16.23, i.e. that the Father will hear the request in the name of Jesus.[5] But the wording, whereby the Father is so to speak by-passed, has the effect in this context of guarding the promise of the μείζονα ἔργα from the misunderstanding that the disciples stand alongside of Jesus, independent of him, on the grounds of their own relationship to God. God remains for them mediated by Jesus, and the point is made emphatically by stating that it is he who will hear their prayer. But this means that what will happen will be no different from what occurred in his work as Revealer, through which he glorified God on earth (17.4). If he hears their prayer, then he does so ἵνα δοξασθῇ

---

[1] See p. 270 n.2.

[2] Only in 15.7 is there no exact definition of the prayer.

[3] After αἰτήσητε (B αἰτῆτε), all witnesses omit a με, which is strongly attested in v. 14. It must however be supplied, in order to accord with τοῦτο ποιήσω. See following note.

[4] Wellh. and Sp., who regard v. 14 as a redactional gloss, change ποιήσω (a correction that has penetrated into the text from v. 14) into ποιήσει. One can be misled into doing this, if one fails to take the sentence ὅτι ἐγὼ ... πορεύομαι as strictly substantiating what had gone before, while at the same time closely connecting this ὅτι-clause with ὅ τι ἂν κτλ. If one were to do that, then it would clearly be most natural not to supply με to αἰτήσητε but αὐτὸν (see previous note). But the ἵνα-clause that follows presupposes ποιήσω; after ποιήσει one would expect e.g.: ἵνα ὁ υἱὸς δοξασθῇ διὰ τοῦ πατρός (or ἐν τῷ πατρί).

[5] See pp. 584f.

ὁ πατὴρ ἐν τῷ υἱῷ. Thus Jesus' own request in 17.1 will have been answered: as the δοξασθείς he hears the disciples' prayer, but he does so, in order to glorify the Father. And to say that this takes place in his hearing the disciples' prayer is to say once more that his work as Revealer is carried on in the work the disciples do. This knowledge will give their prayer its assurance, and from that will grow the strength to do the μείζονα ἔργα. In order to give them this assurance the promise is repeated once more in **v. 14** and emphasised by the words: ἐγὼ ποιήσω.[1]

3) *The Love-relationship to the Son and to the Father:* 14.15–24

In place of the key-word πιστεύειν, which occurred at the outset in v. 1 and them dominated vv. 10–14, the word ἀγαπᾶν now appears, and it holds vv. 15–24 together. The love which is directed to the Revealer had been mentioned only fleetingly up to now (8.42; 16.27); at this point it becomes the explicit theme. This love in fact can be nothing other than faith.[2] But the reason why it is dealt with specifically becomes clear from vv. 15, 21, 23f.[3] The intention of the ἐάν-clauses in vv. 15, 23 ("If you love me, then . . .") is not to state that when love for Jesus is present in the disciples, then the result must be the τηρεῖν of the ἐντολαί;[4] the intention rather is to define the nature of the love, as the definition-sentence in v. 21 makes plain: the ἀγαπᾶν is simply the τηρεῖν

---

[1] The fact that after αἰτ. ℜ D pm omit με, could be due to assimilation to v. 13, as could τοῦτο instead of ἐγώ in BAL al lat. That the whole of v. 14 is missing from some witnesses (X 565 al b syr[sc]) is due to oversight. One could of course ask whether v. 14 is a redactional gloss. But there is no clear motive for its insertion, because the theme it expresses is already uppermost in v. 13; and had the redactor wanted to replace a ποιήσει in v. 13 by ποιήσω (see p. 611 n.4), then it is incomprehensible why he put it alongside the other, instead of correcting the text of v. 13. According to Zahn, admittedly, v. 14 would have special significance alongside v. 13: the prayer referred to in v. 13 is that directed to the Father, while that in v. 14 is directed to Jesus: "In case, however, they not only make their requests in his name to the Father, but also to him himself...." But ἐάν τι in v. 14 cannot be different from ὅ τι ἂν in v. 13 (cp. 15.7: ὃ ἐὰν, 15.16: ὅ τι ἂν, 16.23: ἄν τι). It is however possible that v. 14 comes from the source (see p. 610 n.2). For in the Mandaean writings, too, the departing messenger gives his own the promise that their prayer will be heard, see p. 538 n.6; e.g. Mand. Lit. 140: "You will call, and soon I will answer. You will pray with your hand, and I will not reject it with my hand". Cp. also Mart. Petri et Pauli 50 p. 162, 1ff. (Simon to Nero): . . . ἵνα ἐν τῷ πορεύεσθαί με εἰς τὸν οὐρανὸν πρὸς τὸν πατέρα μου γενήσομαι σοι εὐϊλατος.

[2] See p. 316 n.5. In 16.27 φιλεῖν and πιστεύειν are used together.

[3] The realisation that a new theme is dealt with in vv. 15–24 invalidates Windisch's exposition of the association which he says led to the appending of the sayings on the Paraclete (vv. 15–17) to the words on prayer in vv. 13f. (Festg. Ad. Jül. 114).

[4] Thus I Clem. 49.1: ὁ ἔχων ἀγάπην ἐν Χριστῷ ποιησάτω τὰ τοῦ Χριστοῦ παραγγέλματα.

τὰς ἐντολάς. The question therefore which activates the section vv. 15–24 is this: what is this love, which is directed to Jesus? And this question, too, has to be understood in the context of the "farewell situation." Can the disciples still love him, when he has gone? Can the next generation love him, without having had a personal relationship to him? Can it, for instance, take him to itself with the love of the mystic? The clear presupposition of vv. 15, 21, 23f. is that the believer must love Jesus, indeed that he wants to do so, and this presupposition implies that love is a personal relationship; that is to say, a false conception of the relationship to the Revealer, to the divinity, is presupposed here, one that is characteristic of man: man desires to "love" the divinity, i.e. to achieve a personal, direct, relationship to it.[1] And precisely God's appearing "in flesh" seems to foster this misunderstanding, and to establish a relationship of faith which is a direct personal one, even if—in an unauthentic acknowledgement of his "departure," of his belonging to the other world—this is understood as a mystical love-relationship. Over against this, a new understanding of love is unfolded: the ἀγαπᾶν that is directed to the Revealer, can only be a τηρεῖν of his ἐντολαί, of his λόγος.

But as well as the imperative of the τηρεῖν, the disciple who asks about the possibility of ἀγαπᾶν also receives a *promise*, and that in a three-fold ascending order: the Paraclete will come (vv. 15–17), Jesus himself will come again (vv. 18–21), Jesus and God himself will come (vv. 22–24). In a different way, therefore, the longing that lies behind that misunderstanding will be satisfied. The disciple who is left alone by the Revealer and referred to the τηρεῖν of the ἐντολαί will not remain alone. The union for which he longs will be given him—precisely when he is not anxiously concerned about it.

But this promise corrects a false conception as well, for it is the promise of the Spirit, of the Parousia, of the eschatological presence of God—a promise which was always exposed to the misunderstanding of being regarded as a promise of the fulfilment of the human longing for the direct actuality of the divine. Just as in ch. 16 both hope and promise are wrested from the ban of the mythological thought-forms, so here the old Jewish-Christian eschatology is re-interpreted.[2] What is hoped for, and what is promised, is not one day to become a direct actuality, but it will in fact be present as the believing existence is carried through.

It would appear that the theme of 13.36–14.4—the following of Jesus beyond death—has been finally forgotten here. But by means of

---

[1] Expression is given to this longing in Hölderlin's Empedocles, in the figure of Pausanias, whom the poet contrasts with the departing Empedocles (III 157, 8ff. v. Hellingr.)

[2] See pp. 580f.; 585.

v. 23 the ending is peculiarly linked to the beginning. If 14.2 directed the believer's gaze to the heavenly μονή in the presence of God, of which he may be certain, in 14.23 he is, so to speak, made to look in the other direction: God will make his μονή in the believer.

A piece of the "revelation-discourses" lies at the basis of the composition; in the source v. 16 probably followed the last sentence of v. 12 or v. 14.[1] Vv. 16–19 come from the source, interrupted only by comments of the Evangelist; v. 20 is clearly the work of the Evangelist, as is the dialogue vv. 21–24.

this point relevant to 21:15ff.

i. *The Promise of the Paraclete:* 14.15–17

V. 15: the answer to the question how a relationship of love can be established with the departed Revealer is this: it consists in the disciple fulfilling his commands.[2] The parallelism of τηρεῖν τὰς ἐντολάς[3] with τὸν λόγον μου τηρεῖν (v. 23),[4] and the fact that the latter simply means "believe,"[5] show that the intention of the answer is to refer the man who asks about a love relationship to Jesus back to the faith relationship. Whoever seeks a direct relationship to the Revealer is reminded that there can only be an indirect one. One cannot associate with him as with another man; it is not possible to become one with him in mystical fervour. To love him means to be obedient to his demands, and this obedience is faith.[6] It is of course natural, following 13.34; 15.12, 17, to think of the command of love, and this is certainly included in the summons to faith, just as 15.9–17 make it equally certain that faith as an abiding in love cannot be a reality without the ἀλλήλους ἀγαπᾶν. However, this side of the matter is not stressed in this context.[7] It is faith that is demanded, demanded of course in the fulness of its significance as existential living.

---

[1] See pp. 610 n.2; 612 n.1.

[2] The future τηρήσετε (B L al), which corresponds to the double ποιήσει in v. 12 and to ποιήσω in vv. 13, 14, and also to the futures in vv. 16, 18, 20, 21, 23, is certainly original. Τηρήσητε (א 33 pc) is a copyist's error, τηρήσατε (Ꝟ D syr^{sc}) a correction.

[3] See p 301 n.5.

[4] Cp. how in I Jn. 2.4f. τηρεῖν τ. ἐντ. and τ. λόγον are interchangeable.

[5] See pp. 301 n.5; 324 n.4. The term which belonged originally to ethical exhortation, is used of the obedience of faith, just as are the φυλάττειν of the ῥήματα (12.47), and the ποιεῖν of the θέλημα of God (7.17). It is therefore wrong to find here the sign of the legalisation of the growing Catholic Church (Ho., Br., Weinel, Bibl. Theol. des NT 4th. ed. 1928, 583). In so far as one can speak of this tendency at the time of John, this passage is precisely its corrective.

[6] So too the love directed to the Revealer (8.42; 16.27) is faith.

[7] It is in accord with this that there is no mention here of the ἐντολή (which is what the command of love is described as in 13.34; 15.12), but of the ἐντολαί in the plural.

V. 16: κἀγὼ ἐρωτήσω τὸν πατέρα,
καὶ ἄλλον παράκλητον δώσει ὑμῖν
[ἵνα ᾖ μεθ' ὑμῶν εἰς τὸν αἰῶνα].[1]

The coming of a Paraclete is promised to faith, a Paraclete whom the Evangelist in v. 17a, (as in v. 26; 15.26; 16.13) interprets as the Spirit; but that means: the promise is the promise of the continuation of the revelation, as in 16.12–15.[2] There is no need for the disciples to be without that which they had always received from Jesus, after he has gone from them; the Spirit will be for them what Jesus had been: a παράκλητος, a helper.[3] But it will be *his* help that they will then experience for the Father will send the Spirit at *his* request. The *Father* will send him, just as Jesus was once sent by the Father; i.e. as the revelation was once present in Jesus whom the Father had sent, so too in the future it will still be the revelation of the Father through the Son.[4] Therefore the fact that the believer who asks about the possibility of a love-relationship is referred to the relationship of faith need not disappoint him. For faith is no διάθεσις τῆς ψυχῆς; it is not the bearing of the man who is orientated on and shut in upon himself, but is the answer to the Revealer's never-ceasing question; it is the bond which binds the believer to the Revealer.

There is, however, no question of the Spirit at work in the community being a magical power, which proves its presence by violent physical or psychical experience; it is not a force, that as it were overpowers the community, which simply has to wait for it without doing anything itself. No, the Spirit is the power of the proclamation of the word in the community.[5] Thus there is a peculiar paradox inherent in the promise; the word of revelation, which the community is always encountering, is the very word which the community itself utters. It is responsible for the proclamation, and only when it grasps this responsibility does it experience the power of the word as the word of revelation. The grasping of this responsibility is that τηρεῖν τὰς ἐντολάς, that faith (v. 15) for which the promise holds good. And faith has its basis in the

---

[1] The variety of word-order in the ἵνα-clause in the various mss. is without significance; so too the changing of ᾖ into μένῃ (following v. 17) in 𝔎 D pl. Burney (76) maintains that ἵνα is a wrong translation of ד (= ὅς); against this, Colwell 96–99. Black (58f.) also regards ἵνα as a wrong translation for ὅς; A. W. Argyle JTS 1954, 210, and E. Ullendorf NtSt 2 (1955/56), 50f. both disagree.

[2] See pp. 572ff.

[3] See pp. 566ff. In the source the sentence was clearly the first introduction of the Paraclete; see pp. 460 n.2; 552 n.2. Acc. to Becker (107) v. 15 belongs to the source, as does v. 16 with the exception of the last clause (ἵνα κτλ). Temple wants to take ἄλλον as meaning "besides", analogously to Lk. 23.32.

[4] On the different expressions used to describe the sending of the Paraclete, see p. 553.

[5] See pp. 553f., 561, 572ff.

appearance of Jesus, which broke through the circle of intra-mundane events in order to create a new history—a history of the efficacy of the Spirit, of the proclamation of the word.

A new history—this is what is implied in the words ἵνα ᾖ μεθ' ὑμῶν εἰς τὸν αἰῶνα.[1] Jesus' life and work have come to an end as an event in world-history; the revelation which he brought will never come to an end. But in accordance with its origin, this new history will not have the character of world-history. The Spirit is depicted in **v. 17** in such a way as to make this clear:

> ὅ(ν) ὁ κόσμος οὐ δύναται λαβεῖν
> [ὅτι οὐ θεωρεῖ αὐτὸ οὐδὲ γινώσκει],
> ὑμεῖς (δὲ) γινώσκετε αὐτό(ν)
> [ὅτι παρ' ὑμῖν μένει καὶ ἐν ὑμῖν ἔσται].[2]

The statement that the world cannot "receive"[3] this Spirit[4] does not mean that the unbeliever cannot become a believer, but rather describes the essential contrast between the community and the world.[5] The world *qua world* cannot receive the Spirit; to do so it would have to give up its essential nature, that which makes it the world.[6] In the antithesis it is stated you "know" him—not in the sense that a previous knowing is the presupposition for the receiving, but because "knowing" and "receiving" describe the same process. So too the clause ὅτι οὐ θεωρεῖ κτλ.[7] does not give the reason why, but is really a description,

---

[1] The ἵνα-clause may well be an insertion by the Evangelist into the text of the source. On εἰς τ. αἰῶνα, see p. 186 n.4. If there really is, in this sentence, an allusion to a promise such as Mt. 28.20, this fact makes the Evangelist's intention even clearer: he wants to interpret Jesus' continuing presence as that which is given in the Spirit.

[2] After γινώσκει ℜ pm insert αὐτό, D L al αὐτόν; B D* al it syr^{cp} read ἐστίν instead of ἔσται; g vg take μενει as a future; see p. 617 n.1. The sentence comes from the source, in which the neuters were masculines, referring to the παράκλ. (v. 16). The ὅτι-clauses are comments by the Evangelist. So too Becker, 107.

[3] Λαμβάνειν, as in 20.22 of the receiving of the Spirit (see p. 76 n.5; δέχεσθαι would be better Greek; cp. I Cor. 2.14), accords with normal Christian terminology, e.g. in Rom. 8.15; I Cor. 2.12; Acts 8.15ff. etc.; corresponding to this is the use of διδόναι, in I Jn. 3.24; 4.13; Rom. 5.5; II Cor. 1.22; Acts 8.18 etc.

[4] The Evangelist says τὸ πν. τῆς ἀληθείας, as in 15.26; 16.13; see p. 553.

[5] It is therefore wrong to suppose that the intention of the statement is to explain why the Paraclete lends his services to a small part only of mankind (Windisch, Festg. Ad. Jül. 115).

[6] The world's "being able to" is at the same time "its wanting to", so that the definition of the σαρκικοί as μηδεμίαν ἔχοντες ἐπιθυμίαν θείου πνεύματος in Iren. V, 8, 2 is quite correct. I Cor. 2.10f. describes the same essential contrast.

[7] In this sentence θεωρεῖ and γινώσκει are not to be distinguished, just as in the antithesis we have only: ὑμεῖς γινώσκετε. Zn. and Bd. want to explain the omission of θεωρεῖτε (καί) by saying that while the disciples have a knowledge of the Spirit, they do not have a "seeing", because the supersensual Spirit cannot be seen (contrast Merx, who wants to follow r b, and read θεωρ. καὶ γιν.). This pedantic treatment fails to understand the Johannine concept θεωρεῖν. In 14.19 and 17.24 it is used precisely with ref. to the

just as the words ὑμεῖς γινώσκετε are substantiated on the other side by the clause παρ' ὑμῖν μένει κτλ.[1] This is why Bengel can say: *est quasi epanodos. Mundus non accipit quia non novit: vos nostis quia habetis. Itaque "nosse" et "habere" ita sunt coniuncta, ut non nosse sit causa non habendi, et habere sit causa noscendi.* In truth the Spirit is not something which one can first get to know and then have, or first have and then get to know. Possessing and getting to know coincide, because the Spirit is the *how* of believing existence; whoever allows his existence to be disclosed by the revelation exists in its light.

The world is as little able to recognise the community for what it is as it was able to recognise the Revealer, because it does not know what constitutes the community, viz. the power of the revelation that is at work in it. Recollection of this fact can give the community its peace and its pride in face of the world's hostility (15.18–16.4a); but it must also act as a warning: the community has its power only in its faith in the invisible, not in the visible, not in what can be proved or controlled. The Paraclete is not the "Christian Spirit," at work in world-history as a factor in the history of ideas, and such as could be detected by the historian in institutions or persons, in cultural advance or social achievement, etc. The Spirit is visible to faith and to faith alone.

ii. *The Promise of Jesus' Coming Again:* 14.18–21

At this point the promise of Jesus' return appears alongside the promise of the Paraclete, and this confirms the view that the latter is nothing other than the promise of the continuation of the revelation. Both these promises presuppose the same background, that of the farewell and the question it raises; both are made on the same condition: τηρεῖν τὰς ἐντολάς; and both have the same meaning. The prophecy of the Paraclete picks up the early Christian idea of Pentecost, and similarly that of Jesus' coming again takes up the primitive expectation of the Parousia;[2] precisely in the coming of the Spirit, Jesus comes

---

supersensual, and in 6.40 and 12.45 with ref. to the perceptible, exactly in so far as this is not viewed with regard to its sensual perceptibility. Of course, in addition to this, it can be used to denote sensual perception (6.19; 9.8 etc.), and is so used specifically in paradoxical contrast to the non-sensual θεωρ. (14.19; 16.10, 16ff.).

[1] The Latin tradition understands μενει as μενεῖ; on the other hand, instead of ἔσται there is some support for ἐστίν. The present μένει accords well with the present tenses in the first ὅτι-clause, and as its continuation ἔσται is certainly more correct; for μένει and ἔσται mean the same. On μένειν see p. 535 n.1. The fact that here we do not have as elsewhere ἐν, but παρά, accords with the mythological use of language (which is corrected by the phrase ἐν ὑμ. ἔσται): the παράκλ. stays "by the side of" those who need help; cp. v. 25.

[2] See pp. 580f., 585. Acc. to Windisch (Festg. Ad. Jül. 111), the idea that Jesus will come to his own *in the Spirit* is a "combination that arose subsequently, due simply to the fact that the promise of the coming again in vv. 18f. and vv. 23f. is embedded in the

himself; precisely in the community's Spirit-inspired proclamation of the word he himself is at work as Revealer.

V. 18: οὐκ ἀφήσω ὑμᾶς ὀρφανούς,
ἔρχομαι πρὸς ὑμᾶς.

The first line refers again to the λύπη of the farewell-situation;[1] our attention however is no longer allowed to dwell on it, but is drawn to the future: ἔρχομαι πρὸς ὑμᾶς.[2] The reference is not to the coming of the Redeemer as the soul's guide at the death of the pious, of which vv. 1–3 spoke; for there is no mention of any καὶ παραλήμψομαι ὑμας here.[3] Nor is there any reference to the glorious coming of the judge of the world on the clouds of heaven.[4] Rather it is the coming already promised in 16. 16–24, which the disciples will experience in the immediate future:

V. 19: ἔτι μικρὸν καὶ ὁ κόσμος με οὐκέτι θεωρεῖ,
ὑμεῖς δὲ θεωρεῖτέ με
[ὅτι ἐγὼ ζῶ καὶ ὑμεῖς ζήσετε].[5]

Just as there is no longer any need after 16.16–24 to speak at length of the λύπη, so neither is there any further reference to the two-fold μικρόν (16.16). Our attention is directed straight from the *now* of the

---

present text between two prophecies of the Paraclete". It is correct that the prophecies of Jesus' coming again and of the coming of the Spirit go back to two different motifs within the tradition; but why could not the Evangelist himself be responsible for combining the two in this way?

[1] The teacher's abandonment of his pupils is sometimes portrayed in Rabbinic literature by means of the image of the orphan (Str.-B. ad loc.). From Greek literature, cp. Plato Phaed. 116a, of Socrates' pupils: ἀτεχνῶς ἡγούμενοι ὥσπερ πατρὸς στερηθέντες διάξειν ὀρφανοὶ τὸν ἔπειτα βίον. In the language of the myth see Luc. de morte Peregr. 6: ἀλλὰ νῦν ἐξ ἀνθρώπων εἰς θεοὺς τὸ ἄγαλμα τοῦτο οἰχήσεται . . . ὀρφανοὺς ἡμᾶς καταλιπόν. It is of course simply a picture; Jesus is not thought of as the father of the believers, in the sense of the Rabbinic Abba (Dalman W. J. 278f.); nor are we to think of the language used in the mysteries (Reitzenst. HMR 40f.), or of the fact that in Philo the Logos is sometimes described as πατήρ (quod deus s. imm. 134; conf. ling. 43), or that in the Mandaean writings Manda dHaije can also be called the father of the believers (Joh.-B. 204, 20).

[2] Ἔρχομαι is to be interpreted in the light of the Gnostic myth, see p. 598 n.6. In John it refers simultaneously to the primitive Christian expectation of the Parousia. That the Evangelist wants to recall this hope is shown esp. by the use again of the phrase ἐν ἐκείνῃ τῇ ἡμέρᾳ in v. 20 (see 16.23, 26). In a similar way the mythological expectation of the παρουσία of the Revealer (the νοῦς) is re-interpreted in C. Herm. 1, 22 (see below p. 623 n.4). The motif is developed fictionally in Act. Thom. 88 p. 204, 4f., where the apostle who represents the Revealer comforts the Mygdonia: κἂν ἐγὼ πορευθῶ, οὐ καταλείψω σε μόνην, ἀλλὰ Ἰησοῦς διὰ τὴν εὐσπλαγχνίαν αὐτοῦ μετὰ σοῦ.

[3] It seems probable to me that it *was* in the source, and that the Evangelist dropped it, because he wanted to give the promise a new meaning.

[4] Zn. wants to take ἐρχ. in v. 18 in the sense of the primitive Christian Parousia, on the grounds that the coming of the Paraclete would be unnecessary if the disciples were to see Jesus again almost at once. But in the Paraclete, Jesus comes himself!

[5] Instead of ζήσετε, ℵ 𝔎 D pl read ζήσεσθε; see Bl.-D. § 77.

farewell to the *then* of the re-union. The interval of λύπη between *now* and *then* has, so to speak, disappeared, and the μηκέτι θεωρεῖν is now only stated of the κόσμος, and no longer of the disciples.[1] That the subject here is not the Parousia in the primitive-Christian sense is shown at once by the phrase ὁ κόσμος με οὐκέτι θεωρεῖ; it is rather the same as the promise of the Paraclete, whom the world cannot see either (v. 17). That is to say we are concerned with the *Easter experience*; the words ὅτι ἐγὼ ζῶ καὶ ὑμεῖς ζήσετε[2] make this clear, and it is confirmed by Judas's question in v. 22. The early Christian Easter-message is that the one who was given over to death is alive, and bound up with that, that the life of the believers is grounded in his resurrection life.[3] The translation therefore must be as follows: "For as (because) I live, you too will live."[4] The special feature of this promise in John and in particular in this passage, is that the experience of Easter is seen as the fulfilment of the *Promise of the Parousia* as it was in 16. 20–22; the result is two-fold: first, the promise of the Parousia is stripped of its mythological character, and secondly, the Easter experience is affirmed as the continuing possibility of the Christian life.[5] Indeed, by making Jesus say ζῶ and not ζήσω, the Evangelist strips the Easter event of its outwardly miraculous character; he is already speaking as the resurrected one, as the δοξασθείς (13.31).

---

[1] In order to find a prophecy of the Parousia in the primitive sense of the term in v. 19, Zn. has to deny that ἔτι μικρόν goes with ὑμεῖς δὲ κτλ!

[2] The ὅτι-clause may have been inserted by the Evangelist, because he wants to refer the promise to the Easter-faith. So too Becker (107), who also ascribes v. 18 and v. 19 to the source. Like the ὅτι-clauses of v. 17, the one here substantiates what has gone before. Zn. denies this, so as not to have to refer the promise to Easter, and wants to take it as an independent sentence, in which ὅτι ἐγὼ ζῶ gives the grounds for καὶ ὑμεῖς ζήσετε ("Because *I* live, *you* too will live"). But the argument he uses, viz. that the future vitality of the disciples cannot be the grounds for their seeing the resurrected one, cannot be maintained. For in fact the only possibility of seeing the resurrected one is that the disciple "lives"; for if he were dead, he would belong to the κόσμος, which cannot see the resurrected one. Thus without doubt, the ὅτι-clause (in which the words καὶ ὑμ. ζήσ. are also dependent upon the ὅτι) gives the grounds for the θεωρεῖτε. But it is right, that the "living" is not a given state, upon which the "seeing" can or must follow; on the contrary, the one is given along with the other, so that either can be said to be the ground of the other, just as is the case with λαμβάνειν and γινώσκειν in v. 17 (see pp. 616f.). This argument also holds good against Corssen (ZNTW 8—1907—129), who appeals to 9.8; 5.42 in order to take ὅτι explicatively, because "living" cannot be the ground, but only the result of "seeing". Dupont (209) wants to do the same.

[3] He who has been raised is the ἀρχηγὸς τῆς ζωῆς (Acts 3.15), who has brought ζωή and ἀφθαρσία to light (II Tim. 1.10); he is the one through whose ζωή we are saved (Rom. 5.10), whose ζωή is ours (Col. 3.3f.); cp. Lk. 24.5, 23; Acts 1.3; 25.19; Rom. 6.10; 14.9; II Cor. 13.4; Heb. 7.8, 25; Rev. 1.18; 2.8 etc. See ThWB II 866, 5ff.

[4] In the correspondence of the two halves, ἐγὼ and ὑμεῖς are stressed; thus as regards meaning, the two co-ordinated clauses are in a relation of subordination, the second to the first.

[5] See p. 581.

The reason why the Evangelist has not introduced the future experiences of Easter (vv. 18f.) and Pentecost (vv. 15–17) in their chronological order is that he wants the Easter experience to be regarded as the fulfilment of the hope of the Parousia.[1] And so he introduces his description of the content of this experience (**v. 20**) as he did in 16.23, 26, with the formula that traditionally introduces the eschatological hope: ἐν ἐκείνῃ τῇ ἡμέρᾳ. The content of the experience however is this: γνώσεσθε ὑμεῖς ὅτι ἐγὼ ἐν τῷ πατρί μου καὶ ὑμεῖς ἐν ἐμοὶ κἀγὼ ἐν ὑμῖν.[2] The first part of the ὅτι-clause (ὅτι ἐγὼ ἐν τῷ πατρί) simply describes the knowledge of the unity of Father and Son, i.e. the knowledge that Jesus is the Revealer.[3] But has not that always been their faith, on the basis of which they are his disciples (6.68)? Certainly, but vv. 8–10 had shown how uncertain this faith still was. It is to this faith that γνώσεσθε promises certainty. In this sure knowledge faith comes to itself;[4] and as such it is at the same time self-knowledge, based on knowledge of the Revealer. This is stated by the second part of the ὅτι-clause: knowledge of the Revealer is knowledge of one's own existence in him.[5] The description of the Revealer as the light and the life had made it clear from the outset that authentic existence and true self-knowledge are a unity.[6] With this kind of faith-knowledge, however, the original creature-relationship which had been lost has been won back.[7] After what he has already said the Evangelist has no need to develop here the riches of the eschatological existence that has become transparent to itself in the revelation; in knowing the Revealer, the believer knows the ἀλήθεια which makes him free (8.32); he has joy and confidence in prayer (16.16–24). And that this kind of existence becomes reality in the actual historical living out of one's life, in the ἀλλήλους ἀγαπᾶν, and in the realisation of the task of μαρτυρεῖν, has already become clear from 15.1–17; 15. 18–16.11, and it will be described in I John as the τηρεῖν τὰς ἐντολάς (3.24), as the ὁμολογεῖν (4.15) and as the μένειν ἐν τῇ ἀγάπῃ (4.16).

Because this is so, because eschatological existence must become

---

[1] Rightly Ho., Hrm., Br.

[2] In the phrase γνώσ. ὑμ., ὑμεῖς is of course, as often, unstressed, while in the ὅτι-clause ἐγώ and ὑμ. are again stressed, so that the sense is: "that as I am in the Father, so also you...."

[3] The fact that the formula of reciprocity is not used here to describe the unity of Father and Son (as it is in vv. 10f.; 10.38; 17.21; see pp. 381f.; 513 n.1) but only the unity between the believers and Jesus, is without importance; in 17.21 it is the other way round. Schl. rightly stresses the fact that the plural ὑμεῖς makes plain the unmystical nature of the sentence. "The mystic always thinks unavoidably of the individual".

[4] See p. 435 n.4.

[5] The believers' relationship to the Revealer is described by means of the reciprocity-formula, as in 10.14; 15.5 (6.56).

[6] See pp. 43ff., 53.

[7] See pp. 44f., 496f., 521, 537, 584.

reality as historical existence, that which is its fruit can also be termed its condition. The believer must affirm, he must himself *want* to be, what he already *is* in the Revealer. And so, in **v. 21** the promise can be attached to the condition,[1] and we arrive back at the point of departure, at the question of a love-relationship with the Revealer: ὁ ἔχων τὰς ἐντολάς μου καὶ τηρῶν αὐτάς, ἐκεῖνός ἐστιν ὁ ἀγαπῶν με;[2] i.e. the longing for a relationship of love is fulfilled in the relationship of faith. But in place of the promise of the Paraclete (vv. 16f.), and of the ἔρχομαι πρὸς ὑμᾶς (vv. 18f.) there now appears a promise which describes this fulfilment in a way that allows of no misunderstanding: the disciple who was searching for love will in fact experience love in his faith! But it is significant that it does not say immediately: κἀγὼ ἀγαπήσω αὐτὸν but first of all: ὁ δὲ ἀγαπῶν με ἀγαπηθήσεται ὑπὸ τοῦ πατρός μου, thereby averting the disciple's precipitate longing for a love-relationship with Jesus. That does not of course mean that the Father's love is something different from the Son's—for the Father and the Son are one—still less that a relationship of love is to be established between the disciples and two divine persons! It is rather to make it absolutely clear that the love of the Son is not encountered in the form of personal love on the human level. He is the Revealer, who is recognised aright when he is not sought for his own sake—e.g. in love such as exists between friends, or in inwardly devout or mystical love; he is the Revealer when God is sought in him. The truth of the matter, as was already promised in 16.27 and hinted at in 17.23, is this: *the believer encounters the love of God.*

But God's love is encountered in the *Revealer*, and so the statement continues: κἀγὼ ἀγαπήσω αὐτὸν καὶ ἐμφανίσω αὐτῷ ἐμαυτόν. Here ἐμφανίσω, like θεωρεῖτέ με in v. 19, describes the Easter experience,[3] which means, as the Evangelist sees it, that it also describes the eschatological coming of Jesus. Accordingly the promise that the believer's longing for love will find fulfilment is no different in content from the promise contained in vv. 15–20. But it is stated that in this, his longings really do find fulfilment. The implications of the statement are two-fold:

---

[1] Bl. thinks that in v. 21 the promise that had previously been given to the circle of disciples becomes a promise directed to the individual, while on the other hand Bd. says that what was said in vv. 15–20 for the first circle of disciples is expanded in v. 21 to refer to all later believers. In fact the disciples always represent the believers of every age.

[2] A typical definition-sentence of the Evangelist's; see pp. 48 n.3; 153 n.1. The relation of ἔχειν to τηρεῖν corresponds to that of ἀκούειν to φυλάττειν (12.47) or to πιστεύειν (5.24). Ἔχειν ἐντολάς is a Rabbinic expression (Schl.).

[3] Ἐμφανίζειν is not a technical expression in primitive Christian linguistic usage; v. 22 shows that it here refers to the Easter appearances; cp. Acts 10.40: ἐμφανῆ γενέσθαι, used of the resurrected one (the same expression is used of God in Rom. 10.20, following Is. 65.1). Moses pleads with God in Ex. 33.13, 18: ἐμφάνισόν μοι σεαυτόν. Used of the σοφία ἐμφαν. in Wis. 1.2, of ghosts (Wis. 17.4), of God (Jos. ant. I 223), of gods (Diog. Laert., Prooem. 7), of the ἐκκλησία (Herm. vis. III 1, 2; 10, 2).

it implies first that his longing contains within it a misunderstanding from which it has to be purified; and secondly that there is a true longing that stirs him, and that this does find fulfilment. And in so far as his longing is concerned with the ultimate fulfilment of life, this also means that in all his longing man does not know what he *really* wants; it means that the revelation presents him with the possibility of coming to his own authenticity, i.e. presents him with the question whether he really wants to be himself. What he *really* wants, and what he must want as a creature who has his life through the Logos—and what expresses itself even in his longing for love, is this: not to exist from his own resources or for his own sake. This finds fulfilment when in faith in God's revelation he is given to himself; there he experiences the love of God and of the Revealer.

iii. *The Promise of the Coming of Jesus and of God:* 14.22–24

The foolish question of Judas in v. 22 serves to make even clearer what the promise means, namely that the relationship to Jesus is a relationship to God, and that therefore the faith relationship to Jesus transposes the believer into the eschatological existence. The question is similar to the challenge made by Jesus' brothers in 7.4, and expresses once more the world's understanding of revelation as an intra-mundane demonstrable event.[1] And in truth, if this is what the revelation is, then there would be no reason why the risen and returning Lord should appear only to the disciples. But since Easter and the Parousia are one and the same, the question[2] has a double significance.[3] 1. Why does the resurrected Jesus only show himself to the disciples? This is the question raised by unbelief.[4] 2. How can the eschatological hope find

[1] This Judas, differentiated from Iscariot, is the one mentioned in Lk. 6.16; Acts 1.13, and said to be the son of James. He is otherwise unknown; for there are no grounds for equating him with the brother of James (Jude 1), or with Thaddaeus (Mk. 3.19) or Lebbaeus (Matt. 10.3). Syr[s] reads instead, Thomas, and syr[c] Judas Thomas, which may be due to the tradition of the Act. Thom., which identify the Lord's brother Judas and Thomas.

[2] (καὶ) τί γέγονεν ὅτι (καὶ is omitted by B Dal lat syr; instead of γέγ. D syr read ἐστίν) means simply "wherefore?", see Bl.-D. 299, 4; Raderm. 739; see also p. 338 n.5, and Black 104.

[3] The eschatological ἔρχεσθαι in v. 23 shows that the question is not confined to the Easter appearances, to which ἐμφαν. refers, but also includes the Parousia.

[4] This question, to which an answer is given as early as Acts 10.40f., is raised by Celsus, or his Ἰουδαῖος, and Origen answers it in c. C. II 63–73. Cp. 63 p. 184, 30ff., Koetsch: ἐχρῆν, εἴπερ ὄντως θείαν δύναμιν ἐκφῆναι ἤθελεν ὁ Ἰησοῦς, αὐτοῖς τοῖς ἐπηρεάσασι καὶ τῷ καταδικάσαντι καὶ ὅλως πᾶσιν ὀφθῆναι; 67 p. 189, 10ff.: ... οὐδ' ἐπὶ τοῦτ' ἐπέμφθη τὴν ἀρχήν, ἵνα λάθῃ. 70 p. 192, 8ff. Origen replies partly by putting forward the idea that the divine manifestation of the resurrected Lord would not have been bearable for all eyes (64–66 pp. 186, 29f.; 187, 18f.; 188, 29ff.), and by saying that the resurrected Lord only showed himself μετά τινος κρίσεως ἑκάστῳ μετρούσης τὰ δέοντα (66 p. 188, 19f.; cp. 67 p. 189, 7f.), and partly his answer is the correct one: ἐπέμφθη γὰρ οὐ μόνον ἵνα γνωσθῇ, ἀλλ'

its fulfilment in the Easter experience, awaiting as it does the manifestation of Jesus as Lord over the whole κόσμος? This is clearly a question which arose from the community itself.[1]

Jesus does not give a direct answer (**v. 23**). His words, almost bypassing what Judas had asked, answer the all-important question as to the possibility of a love-relationship, a question which is based on the same misunderstanding that prompted Judas to ask his question: the longing for the direct present actuality of the Revealer. Again, the questioner is referred to the relationship of faith by the words ἐάν τις ἀγαπᾷ με, τὸν λόγον μου τηρήσει,[2] and the promise attached to it: καὶ ὁ πατήρ μου ἀγαπήσει αὐτόν. This makes it clear, as in v. 21, that the longing for love is fulfilled when the relationship of faith becomes a reality. But instead of καὶ ἐμφανίσω αὐτῷ ἐμαυτόν we now have: καὶ πρὸς αὐτὸν ἐλευσόμεθα καὶ μονὴν παρ' αὐτῷ ποιησόμεθα.[3] This adds nothing new to the subject-matter; the change in the terms used (as compared with v. 21) only shows again that Easter and Pentecost are the same event.[4] And the fact that it is not only Jesus' coming that is foretold, but also

---

ἵνα καὶ λάθῃ (67, p. 189, 12f.); Jesus' call rang out clear and loud during his life-time (73) and the idea that sinners would not have to be punished was an absurd notion on the part of Celsus (71). Macarius Magnes asks the same kind of question as Celsus, in Apocr. II 14 p. 23 Blondel, namely, why the resurrected Lord did not appear to Pilate, Herod or the High-Priest, but only to doubtful women καὶ ἄλλοις ὀλίγοις οὐ σφόδρα ἐπισήμοις ... εἰ γὰρ ἦν ἐμφανίσας ἀνδράσιν ἐπισήμοις, δι' αὐτῶν πάντες ἂν ἐπίστευον. See also W. Nestle, Zeitschr. f. Religions—u. Geisteswiss. 4 (1952), 3.

[1] Cp. e.g. Phil. 2.11; above all, Ign. Eph. 19, 2f., and on that, Schlier Relig. Unters. 5ff.

[2] See pp. 613f. Acc. to Becker v. 23 (from ἐάν τις onwards) belongs to the source.

[3] D e syr[c] read ἐλεύσομαι and ποιήσομαι. Clearly an attempt to make this verse the same as v. 3, which means taking πρὸς αὐτόν and παρ' αὐτῷ as referring to the πατήρ. Ποιήσομεν (Ꝃ pm) is an unimportant variant. On the patristic LA καὶ ἐγὼ καὶ ὁ πατὴρ ἐλευσόμεθα, see Boismard RB 57 (1950), 392f.

[4] Ἐλευσόμεθα is doubtless meant to recall the eschatological ἔρχεσθαι (see J. Schneider, ThWB II 663, 54ff.; 666, 18ff.). But there is also an allusion to the Gnostic hope of the coming of the Redeemer (see p. 598 n.6), as the words μονὴν ποιεῖσθαι make abundantly clear.

Cp. Mand. Lit. 198:

"(Behold) the house of my acquaintances, who know of me,
that among them I dwell,
In the heart of my friends,
in the mind of my disciples."

Ginza 389, 23ff.:

"I come, to examine the hearts....
To see in whose heart I dwell,
In whose mind I find rest."

Ginza 461, 15ff. (to the soul "comes" her "helper" and says):

"Thou shalt dwell with me,
and in thy heart will we find a place."

In Ginza 271, 29f., the Kušta is praised:

"Thou art the life from eternity,
thou who wentest in, and found a place in (every) steadfast heart."

the coming of God, again stresses the point that Jesus is nothing for himself; it makes clear that the man who wants and can have fellowship with Jesus, must and can be certain of the presence of the majesty of God himself. And the words μονὴν . . . ποιήσομεθα, added to ἐλευσόμεθα draw out the element of finality in this relationship.[1] Jesus and the Father will *abide* with the believer, and he has no need to ask anything further; the ἀρκεῖ ὑμῖν (v. 8) will be fulfilled.

If v. 23 gives a definitive answer to the question of v. 15, it also shows us the unity of the whole section. The question as to the vision of God (vv. 5–11) has been answered, and the question about following Jesus (13.36–14.4), which had been answered in the first place by reference to the heavenly μοναί into which Jesus will bring his own, has now ceased to be a matter of anxiety; the anxiety has been directed to God's μονή in the believer.

If so much is promised for the believer's *future*, this must not make us forget that what was promised in vv. 7–11 should and can already become present reality. There is therefore no question at all of the promise referring to any miraculous event, to something which has still to "happen." The whole compass of the miraculous in the Revelation event is stated in the one sentence: ὁ λόγος σὰρξ ἐγένετο—a sentence which includes the Passion and Easter within it. For if, at the actual moment which forms the background to the promise in 14.23, these events are still to come, yet they are only the demonstration of that which occurred directly with the incarnation *sub specie dei*, even if it is true that without the Passion and Easter nothing would have occurred;[2] for even ὁ λόγος σὰρξ ἐγένετο is no miracle, but states that in the historical Jesus God is present. The believer is not discharged from his historical being; believing existence consists in just this: in making what has already happened one's own.[3] In one sense Easter always lies in front

---

Further, see Ginza 244, 37f.; 327, 30ff. (of the soul?); 464, 24; Joh.-B. 204, 13f.; Od. Sal. 32.1f.:

> "To the blessed joy comes from their heart,
> the light from him, who dwells in them."

C. Herm. I 22: παραγίνομαι ἐγὼ ὁ νοῦς τοῖς ὁσίοις καὶ ἀγαθοῖς . . . καὶ ἡ παρουσία μου γίνεται «αὐτοῖς» βοήθεια, καὶ εὐθὺς πάντα γνωρίζονται καὶ τὸν πατέρα ἱλάσκονται ἀγαπητικῶς καὶ εὐχαριστοῦσιν εὐλογοῦντες καὶ ὑμνοῦντες τεταμένοι πρὸς αὐτὸν τῇ στοργῇ. Ign. Eph. 15,3: πάντα οὖν ποιῶμεν ὡς αὐτοῦ ἐν ἡμῖν κατοικοῦντος, on which see Schlier, Relig. Unters. 143.

[1] Μονή = dwelling, as in v. 2; μονὴν ποιεῖσθαι = "To make one's dwelling", or "to abide", Thuc. I 131; Jos. ant. VIII 350; XIII 41; BGU 742. If the language comes from the Gnostic myth, the reader will nevertheless think of the OT hope of God's coming to dwell amongst his people: Ez. 37. 26f.; Zech. 2.24 (LXX 2.10: τέρπου καὶ εὐφραίνου, θύγατηρ Σειών, διότι ἐγὼ ἔρχομαι καὶ κατασκηνώσω ἐν μέσῳ σου).

[2] See pp. 428f., 467f.

[3] The paradox is the same as that in Paul: we are justified, and yet the justification still lies in front of us.

of the believer; and even if he no longer needs to be worried or anxious as to whether God will come and go again, but knows that God will "abide" with him, yet he still has to remind himself that he must never look back and allow his gaze to rest on himself as one who is perfect; nothing has been "finished with."

In this way too Judas's question in v. 22 is answered. Formally, the antithesis in vv. 23f. provides an indirect answer: ἐάν τις ἀγαπᾷ με . . . ὁ μὴ ἀγαπῶν με. Faith is the condition for seeing him who has been exalted; thus because the κόσμος does not believe, it will not see him. But the words καὶ ὁ λόγος κτλ. added to **v. 24** are not simply a comment, impressing on us again the authority of what Jesus says;[1] they make it clear that the unbelief which is denied the vision of the exalted one is not a merely negative attitude but disobedience, the rejection of oneself over against the revelation, a rejection which has already been judged. The λόγος of Jesus is itself the judge (12.48). The eschatological event is therefore also carried through on the κόσμος, even if the latter is blind to the fact. But this state of blindness is itself the judgment it suffers (9.39). This means, in so far as Jesus already has and still does reveal himself to the whole κόσμος, that the presupposition behind the question in v. 22 is false. For the possibility that Jesus "reveal" himself to the κόσμος is always given it in the ὁ λόγος σὰρξ ἐγένετο. And he does indeed reveal himself to the unbelieving κόσμος, namely in the sense that it is judged and ends in despair.[2] Faith knows this, because it overcomes the difficulty involved in the fact that the revelation does not demonstrate its authenticity by an intra-mundane proof, but rather leaves it open for the κόσμος to regard it as an illusion.

4) *Conclusion:* 14.25–31

Vv. 25–31 finally conclude the farewell discourses; they summarise the principle motifs of promise and exhortation, and lead on from the discourses to the Passion Event. The words ταῦτα λελάληκα ὑμῖν (**v. 25**) embrace all that has been said before.[3] The phrase παρ' ὑμῖν μένων, added here in contrast to 15.11; 16.1, 4, 25, 36, looks back on the whole of the now completed earthly existence of Jesus, and makes clear that the hour of separation has now come. If we bear 16.11 in mind, ταῦτα λελ. comes to mean: "Only so much could I say to you."[4] Just as in 16.25

[1] On the wording, see p. 249 n.1; cp. esp. 7.17; 8.28; 12.49f. It is ὁ λόγος ὃν ἀκ. *sub specie dei*, in contrast to the preceding τοὺς λόγους μου, which is spoken from man's point of view, for the λόγος always encounters man in separate λόγοι.

[2] See pp. 308, 350.

[3] See pp. 335 n.5; 541 n.6.

[4] Cp. Hölderlin, Empedocles: "What I have said,
The while I tarry here, is little"
(v. Hellingrath III 156, 18f.).

there was no ἵνα-clause to record the purpose of the λαλεῖν, neither is there here; instead a line is drawn between the past and the future; the past is shown to be only preparatory. But the fact that it is incomplete and has been broken off is no reason for despairing of it, or for concluding that it was worth nothing. For the future is under the promise of **v. 26**: ὁ δὲ παράκλητος κτλ. The use of the current Christian terminology to describe the Paraclete (ἅγιον πνεῦμα)[1] shows again that he is the power given to the community, the power in which the eschatological event continues to be carried through; and ὃ πέμψει κτλ.[2] is a reminder that it is the revelatory work of Jesus that is being continued: the Father will send the Spirit "in the name of" the Son, just as he will listen to the disciples' requests "in the name of" Jesus (according to 16.23).[3] And the ideas of earlier prophecies are picked up again to describe the Paraclete's work:

> [ἐκεῖνος] ὑμᾶς διδάξει πάντα
> καὶ ὑπομνήσει ὑμᾶς πάντα ἃ εἶπον ὑμῖν ἐγώ.[4]

Διδάξει has the same comforting sense as did the promise in 16.13a: the revelation has not come to an end with Jesus' farewell, but will be bestowed anew in every future.[5] Ὑπομνήσει corresponds to the assurance given in 16.13b–15: the future revelation will take up Jesus' own work again;[6] it will be "recollection" of this—not of course in the sense of a historical reconstruction, but as the act whereby the eschatological event that broke in in him is realised in the present.[7] The community's μαρτυρία is not a historical report, but is the witness in which Jesus'

---

[1] See p. 553.

[2] See p. 553.

[3] See pp. 584f.

[4] The sentence may have been taken from the source, but ἐκεῖνος naturally is due to the Evangelist. Ἃ ἂν εἴπω, read by D al, destroys the sense. ἐγώ should perhaps be omitted, with ℵ 𝔎 D pl. Becker (108) also ascribes the sentence to the source. He puts ὁ δὲ παράκλητος at the beginning, instead of ἐκεῖνος, and also omits ἐγώ at the end.

[5] In I Jn. 2.27 διδάσκειν is regarded as a function of the χρῖσμα; by this means it is shown that the Spirit does not speak in new revelations, loosed from the ties of history, but in the continuity of the office of proclamation.

[6] See pp. 575ff., and O. Cullmann (Aux sources de la Trad. Chrét. 59), who refers to A. Dahl, Anamnesis. Mémoire et commemoration dans le christianisme primitif (Studia Theol. 1947), 94. There is of course no differentiation made here between two functions of the Spirit (B. Weiss, Zn.); διδ. and ὑπομ. are one and the same (*contra* R. Eisler, Rätsel 396f.).

[7] This fact distinguishes the promise from the one formally related to it, in C. Herm. 13, 15: ὁ Ποιμάνδρης, ὁ τῆς αὐθεντίας νοῦς, πλέον μοι τῶν ἐγγεγραμμένων οὐ παρέδωκεν, εἰδὼς ὅτι ἀπ' ἐμαυτοῦ δυνήσομαι πάντα νοεῖν καὶ ἀκούειν ὧν βούλομαι καὶ ὁρᾶν τὰ πάντα. Cp. also C. Herm. 13, 2. Here the mystic has become independent of the revelation.

own witness is renewed; like his word, it places the hearer again and again in front of the *now* of the eschatological decision.[1]

Just as vv. 25f. summarise the promise contained in 16.12–15, so **v. 27** takes up the ideas of 15.18–16.7 again, and in particular those of 16.16–24:

> εἰρήνην ἀφίημι ὑμῖν,
> εἰρήνην τὴν ἐμὴν δίδωμι ὑμῖν.
> οὐ καθὼς ὁ κόσμος δίδωσιν,
> ἐγὼ δίδωμι ὑμῖν.
> μὴ ταρασσέσθω ὑμῶν ἡ καρδία
> μηδὲ δειλιάτω.[2]

Εἰρήνην ἀφίημι is, so to speak, the Revealer's parting word of farewell. But it is more than just the good wishes that are normally expressed at a parting; Jesus leaves the εἰρήνη behind him, virtually as a parting gift;[3] he "gives" the εἰρήνη to those who remain.[4] And while there is certainly an allusion to the customary words of farewell,[5] this εἰρήνη is not happiness (*Heil*) in the sense of continuing prosperity, such as is normally intended, but it is that εἰρήνη which took the place of χαρά in 16.33: the eschatological salvation (*Heil*),[6] which is specially marked out as such by defining it as εἰρήνην τὴν ἐμήν—just as it is *his* χαρά, which his own are to share, according to 17.13; 15.11.[7] It is the εἰρήνη of the one who has left the κόσμος behind him; just as *he* no longer belongs to this world (17.14)—this is what the farewell gift is saying—so neither do *his own*. If this εἰρήνη is also "salvation" (*Heil*) in the comprehensive sense of the Semitic שָׁלוֹם, the element of "peace" contained therein is brought out and given special importance by the

[1] See pp. 554, 257. Rightly, Hosk.

[2] V. 27 may come from the source; Becker (109) thinks it does.

[3] Ἀφίημι means "to leave behind", as in v. 18; 4.28 and elsewhere; it is not a legal term, describing the testator's estate; see **ThWB** I 507, 46ff.

[4] In Rabbinic linguistic usage, "to give the peace" can describe the uttering of the greeting, but it can also mean the establishing of the peace (Schl. ad loc., who does not however quote any example of its usage in the first person). Parallel to ἀφίημι, δίδωμι can only mean: "I bestow", cp. Hag. 2.9 (where God is speaking): ἐν τῷ τόπῳ τούτῳ δώσω εἰρήνην; Is. 26.12: κύριε ὁ θεὸς ἡμῶν, εἰρήνην δὸς ἡμῖν; II Thess. 3.16.

[5] One thinks of the Semitic words of farewell: πορεύου εἰς εἰρήνην in I Reg. 1.17 (לְכִי לְשָׁלוֹם); 20.42; 29.7; Mk. 5.34; Acts 16.36; cp. I Cor. 16.11; Jas. 2.16 etc., with variations in the final greetings at the end of letters: III Jn. 15, I Pet. 5.14; cp. Gal. 6.16; Eph. 6.23; II Thess. 3.16. The fact that a magical efficaciousness can be ascribed to salutations (Mt. 10.12f.; Lk. 10.5f.; see Merx on Mt. 5.47, II 1, 116f.; Lyder Brun, Segen und Fluch im Urchristentum 1932, 34) need not be considered with ref. to John.

[6] See p. 505 n.3 on εἰρήνη and χαρά in their eschatological sense.

[7] See pp. 507, 541f.

situation to which the words μὴ ταρασσέσθω ὑμῶν ἡ καρδία refer.[1] And certainly this peace is also peace of the heart,[2] but it is more than that: it is *his* peace which he gives the believers as the possibility of their existence, a possibility already there, before they have found themselves within it; it is *his* peace, in which they must discover themselves in order to come to that "complete inward composure."[3]

The eschatological nature of the εἰρήνη is made still clearer by the words: οὐ καθὼς ὁ κόσμος κτλ. In the κόσμος, and according to its standards, their situation is one of λύπη and θλῖψις (16.20–22, 23). Their εἰρήνη is as far from being visible to the κόσμος as their χαρά. But this should not mislead the community to strive after the peace of the κόσμος;[4] its peace is no real peace, but at best the peace of death.[5] Thus the promise becomes an imperative: μὴ ταρασσέσθω κτλ.,[6] an exhortation we are already familiar with, from the beginning of the discourse (v. 1), and one that corresponds to θαρσεῖτε in 16.33. The disciples' peace is inherent in the possibility of freedom from the κόσμος; but they have to grasp this possibility.[7]

V. 28 repeats once more that they can do this with confidence; they have heard his promise, that while he is indeed to go from them, he will also come again. Whether the ἔρχομαι is that of v. 3, which finally frees the disciple from life within the bounds of the κόσμος, or whether it is that of v. 18, which is realised in the experiences of earthly life within history, what is significant is that the saying does not end in the comforting tones of the promise, but in a warning which takes up again the thought contained in 16.7. Only the man who has grasped

---

[1] See p. 593 n.2.

[2] "The complete inward composure"; cp. B. Weiss, Ho., Zn.: "The satisfied and satisfying disposition of the soul." This is Philonic; see note 4. Even further from the truth is the view that Jesus wants to say: "They are not to lose heart through the terrlfying experience they are to undergo" (Zn.).

[3] See pp. 593f.

[4] Philo too knows that only God can bestow εἰρήνη; cp. Vit. Mos. I 304: δωρησάμενος ὁ θεὸς Φινεεῖ τὸ μέγιστον ἀγαθόν, εἰρήνην, ὃ μηδεὶς ἱκανὸς ἀνθρώπων παρασχεῖν. But for him, such εἰρήνη is composure of the soul, and it is present in its fulness only in God; in somn. II 250–254 he explains the name Jerusalem as ὅρασις εἰρήνης; such a city of peace could not exist on earth, ἀλλ' ἐν ψυχῇ ἀπολέμῳ καὶ ὀξυδορκούσῃ (τέλος) προτεθειμένῃ τὸν [δὲ] θεωρητικὸν καὶ εἰρηναῖον βίον, in a soul, to which στάσις and ταραχή are strange. Indeed, it can be said finally, ὅτι θεὸς μόνος ἡ ἀψευδεστάτη καὶ πρὸς ἀλήθειάν ἐστιν εἰρήνη, ἡ δὲ γενητὴ καὶ φθαρτὴ οὐσία πᾶσα συνεχὴς πόλεμος; cp. ebr. 97ff.; leg. all. III 80f.: the λόγος as ἡγεμὼν εἰρήνης.—God as the θεὸς or κύριος τῆς εἰρήνης, in Rom. 15.33; 16.20; II Cor. 13.11; Phil. 4.9; II Thess. 3.16; Heb. 13.20. The εἰρ. θεοῦ in Phil. 4.7, τοῦ Χριστοῦ in Col. 3.15, τοῦ εὐαγγελίου in Eph. 6.15.

[5] See Faulhaber 55.

[6] On ταρ. see p. 599 n.1; δειλιᾶν (to be in despair), only here in NT.

[7] Kundsin (see p. 581 n.11) appreciates the seriousness of the promise of peace, but he would explain it in terms of the peace that is attained through martyrdom (op. cit. 212).

the meaning of Jesus' departure will experience his coming: εἰ ἠγαπᾶτέ με κτλ.[1] They think they love him, and their love struggles with the thought of being abandoned by him. But that is not the love that is appropriate to him; it misunderstands his being and his work; it brings his appearing down to the level of human, worldly existence, and expects an intra-mundane bestowal of happiness from him. The love that he demands is the faith which sees in him the Revealer,[2] faith as the living out of the eschatological existence in which the world has been annulled. They should rejoice that Jesus is going from them, i.e. they must realise that what he ought to be for them, he is as the glorified one;[3] in their search for a relationship with him, he remains an eschatological figure, not someone within history. This is the meaning of what is at first sight a strange way of substantiating what has been said: ὅτι ὁ πατὴρ μείζων μού ἐστιν.[4] Of course, whoever understands Jesus aright, sees in him the Father (v. 9); he is one with the Father (10.30), and the Father has handed everything over to him (3.35; 5.21, 27; 17.2). But whoever wants to contain him within the sphere of human relationships does not see him in this light. Such a man has, so to speak, forgotten God above him, and must be reminded that God is greater than the Revealer, that he is nothing for himself, but only does the will of the Father (4.34; 5.30; 6.38; 7.16f.; 8.28; 12.49f.), and that only so, does he reveal the Father. Thus the explanatory clause ὅτι ὁ πατὴρ κτλ. corresponds to συμφέρει ὑμῖν in 16.7, with its reference to the coming Paraclete; i.e. the reason for the disciples' joy is to be this, that Jesus shows himself to be the one in whom God's eschatological work takes place, the one who breaks up every moment of the present that tries to cling to itself, the one who destroys every composure that would like to guarantee itself against the future; they are to rejoice because Jesus.

---

[1] Ἀγαπᾶτε, read by D* H L φ al, is clearly a correction; 𝔎 al insert ὅτι before πορεύομαι.

[2] See pp. 613f.

[3] The myth, too, knows this idea; cp. Ign. Rom. 3.3: οὐδὲν φαινόμενον καλόν. ὁ γὰρ θεὸς ἡμῶν Ἰ. Χριστὸς ἐν πατρὶ ὢν μᾶλλον φαίνεται. Exc. ex. Theod. 18, 2: σκιὰ γὰρ τῆς δόξης τοῦ σωτῆρος τῆς παρὰ τῷ πατρὶ ἡ παρουσία ἡ ἐνταῦθα, see Schlier, Relig. Unters. 76f.

[4] Merx wants to follow syr[sc] and read: ὅς μείζων μού ἐστιν, on the grounds that this does away with the (seemingly) artificial explanatory clause. This indeed implies that "along with his exaltation to the God enthroned in heaven, ... there must also be a glorification for him" (Zn.); but this glorification is not conceived as something, which Jesus has *for himself*, so that his departure is "something gratifying to him" (B. Weiss), an "exaltation of life" (Ho.), and the joy of the disciples a comradely "sharing in his joy". Jesus' glorification is rather his perfection as Revealer (see pp. 491ff.), and the disciples' joy—in accordance with the συμφέρει ὑμῖν of 16.7—is due to the fact that as the glorified one, he is the Revealer *for them*. There is therefore no need to refer to Schiller's Maria Stuart V 4 (Ho.), nor to Plato Phaed. 63b (Br.), but, on the other hand, one should certainly compare the ending of Hölderlin's Empedocles (III 163ff., v. Hellingr.).

as the one who is coming, is always standing before his own, and as the δοξασθείς is drawing them into his eschatological existence.[1]

After this summary and exhortation, **v. 29** leads on to the historical situation. As in 13.19; 16.4, 32f., the disciples are exhorted to be prepared for what is coming: it is foreseen, and therefore should not dismay the believer when it actually occurs.[2] Here too the historical situation has an archetypal significance. In the last analysis Jesus is not foretelling an historical event, but rather the separation of the Revealer from his own, a separation which is essential for the revelation event, and which every believer will ever and again experience in different forms.[3]

We finally arrive at the historical situation in **v. 30**: οὐκέτι λαλήσω μεθ' ὑμῶν.[4] What has to be said has already been said—which means, over and above its significance in that situation, that the revelation is complete and definitive in the historical Jesus; if the Spirit is to continue his work, then he is to do so only in the sense of "calling to mind" (v. 26) what Jesus had said. As far as observation is concerned, Jesus' work comes to its end by the world becoming lord over him: ἔρχεται γὰρ ὁ τοῦ κόσμου ἄρχων. The persecutors are already approaching (18.3); but Jesus is not referring to them, but to the power that is behind them.[5] For it is an eschatological event (*Geschehen*) that takes place in the intra-mundane event (*Ereignis*); it is the battle between God and the demonic power. Fundamentally its outcome has already been decided: καὶ ἐν ἐμοὶ οὐκ ἔχει οὐδέν:[6] the κόσμος has no right to Jesus, and cannot

---

[1] See pp. 492f., 558ff.

[2] See pp. 478 n.3; 557; 591f. Ἵνα πιστεύσητε contains within it the ἵνα μνημονεύητε of 16.4, and as regards meaning, is equal to ἵνα ... εἰρήνην ἔχητε of 16.33. On the absolute πιστ. see p. 51 n.3. Vv. 29f. correspond to 16.31, see p. 594.

[3] See pp. 558f.

[4] Πολλά, which does not occur in syr[s], is certainly an early interpolation, "a bad stop-gap" (Merx), which was to get over the difficulty caused by the fact that in the present order of the text, there are still discourses to follow; one cannot think of any reason for dropping it from the text.

[5] On ἄρχων τοῦ κόσμου see p. 431 n.2. Cp. how in 13.27 Judas was depicted as Satan's tool; see p. 482. The sentence is the Johannine transformation of the old tradition; see Mk. 14.41f.: ἦλθεν ἡ ὥρα ... ἰδοὺ ὁ παραδιδούς με ἤγγικεν; see below, p. 631 n.6.

[6] On the καί see p. 48 n.2. The interpretation of the sentence was obviously an uncertainty to the copyists. The variants εὑρήσει οὐδέν (Ꞩ al f) and οὐκ ἔχει οὐδὲν εὑρεῖν (D a) clearly mean: Satan cannot find anything sinful in Jesus (cp. 8.46); Ho., Zn., Br., Bd., Bl., expound accordingly, but this is a moralistic conception (see R. Hermann, ZsystTh 7 (1930), 747). The expression καὶ ἐν ἐμοὶ οὐκ ἔχει οὐδὲν goes back to the Semitic ואין לו עלי or ואין לו אצלי כלום = "he has no right to me, no claim on me" (Str.-B., Schl.). But ἔχειν in the sense of "to have a right (or claim)" is also good Greek, see ThWB II 816, 13ff. and cp. BGU 180, 4: ἔχειν χρόνον ἀναπαύσεως = "to have the right, to be unburdened for an interval of time" (Preisigke, Wörterb.). One can also take ἔχειν in the sense of "to have the power" (cp. Philostr. Vit. Apoll. VI 5 p. 209, 28f. Kayser: Θαμοῦν ἤλεγξαν οἱ Γυμνοὶ καὶ ἔσχον = "and won the upper hand"); one would then have to take

therefore find anything against him. Indeed *his* action must bring about what is to happen. This divine teleology is expressed in the saying of **v. 31**: ἀλλ' ἵνα γνῷ ὁ κόσμος κτλ.:[1] in his death Jesus proves that he is the Revealer. For his "loving the Father" i.e. "fulfilling the Father's commission"[2] is accomplished through his whole life being an attack on the κόσμος (7.7)—albeit for the sake of the κόσμος (3.16). His death therefore is not the heroic holding fast to his task even in failure, nor is it the culmination of his faith in martyrdom—he is neither a believer nor a martyr—but his death is itself his task, already included within ὁ λόγος σὰρξ ἐγένετο;[3] this is why his death is his victory over the world;[4] for the death sentence which it pronounces on him has been anticipated by him as a death sentence upon the world. As an outward event his death is simply the demonstration of the fact that he has already conquered the world. But this demonstration is itself the last question put to the world, the last possibility it has of losing confidence in itself, and of "recognising" that he is the Revealer.

The words ἐγείρεσθε, ἄγωμεν ἐντεῦθεν mark the end of the scene started in 13.2, and lead on to ch. 18.[5] Thus we arrive at the traditional Passion narrative.[6]

ἐν ἐμοί in the sense of I Cor. 14.11: "In my case (as far as concerns me) he is powerless". Rather differently, J. Jeremias, ZNTW 35 (1936), 76: "against me he is powerless" (accepting the supposition of a Semitism).

[1] On the elliptical ἀλλ' ἵνα (as in 13.18) see p. 48 n.3. It is unreasonable to try to find the apodosis to it in the ἐγείρεσθε that follows.

[2] This is the only place where ἀγαπᾶν is used to describe the relationship of Jesus to the Father, elsewhere it is the love of the Father to the Son (see p. 165 n.1); but this is not surprising, in view of the interchangeability of the relationship. The Son's love is identical with his obedience (cp. 14.15, 21), as it is depicted here and in 4.34; 5.30; 6.38; 12.49f.; καί in v. 31 is therefore epexegetical. (It makes no difference whether one reads ἐντολὴν ἔδωκεν (as in 12.49) with B L al, or ἐνετείλατο with ℵ A Θ.)

[3] See p. 468.

[4] Hölderlin has imitated this in Empedocles (III 160, 19ff. v. Hellingr.):

> "Yet am I not vanquished by mortal men,
> And go in my own power fearlessly down
> The self-chosen path; this is my happiness,
> This my right."

[5] It is inconceivable that II Sam. 15.14 (ἀνάστητε καὶ φύγωμεν) has influenced this sentence (Finegan, Überl. der Leidenund Auferstehungsgesch. Jesu 43, 3). Torrey (341f.) wants to overcome the difficulty of the present order of the text by positing an error in translation: the words ἐγ., ἀγ. ἐντ. correspond to קוּמוּ נֵאזֵל מִכָּה which is a misreading of אֱקוּם וְאֵזֵל מִכָּה ("I will rise and go forth from here"). The sentence forms the transition to ch. 15: "I must leave you and go forth from here; notwithstanding, abide in me!" Corssen omits the sentence, see p. 459 n.4. de Zwaan, similarly to Torrey, wants to take "go forth from here" as an Aramaic euphemism for "die". Dodd (406, 1) takes ἄγωμεν in its military sense, in which it does not mean setting out, but advancing (against the enemy); see also Dodd 408f.

[6] Cp. Mk. 14.42: ἐγείρεσθε ἄγωμεν (see p. 630 n.5).

II. 18.1-20. 29: The Passion and Easter

Fundamentally, after the declaration in 13.31, νῦν ἐδοξάσθη ὁ υἱὸς τοῦ ἀνθρώπου, it was as the Exalted and Glorified Lord that Jesus had addressed his followers. His work on earth was therefore completed. And yet he does not utter the τετέλεσται until he is on the cross, 19.30. For the ὥρα of his δοξασθῆναι (12.33; 17.1), of his μεταβῆναι ἐκ τοῦ κόσμου (13.1), embraces the Passion event as a whole; and in the νῦν of 13.31 the entire action that follows is anticipated. Admittedly it is not anticipated in the sense of the historian, whose contemplation of the past gathers the individual occurrences into a great, unitary, decisive event; rather that which happens in the event of the Passion is anticipated in the resolution of Jesus, who in his obedience takes upon himself that which the Father has commanded (14.31), and who loves his own εἰς τέλος (13.1). Basically this decision was already anticipated in the ὁ λόγος σὰρξ ἐγένετο, 1.14.[1] But if this decision were to be understood in its full significance, everything that it comprises had to become visible, i.e. the Passion had to be recounted; and while the Evangelist does this he does not simply follow the dictates of the traditional form of the kerygma or Gospel.

Undoubtedly his *passion narrative* does follow the tradition; but it is now seen in a new light. For the Passion can no longer be told as a horrible and inexplicable happening that has to be referred back to an incomprehensible divine δεῖ,[2] the understanding of which is a problem for the Church. Rather the Passion grows out of the work of Jesus as the necessary consequence of the struggle of the light against the darkness; it is the victorious conclusion of this struggle. If the divine δεῖ was indeed spoken once, right at the beginning of the story (3.14), the Johannine sayings of Jesus that refer to his end are nevertheless distinguished in a characteristic manner from the Synoptic predictions of suffering.[3] They are not secret instructions given to the disciples, but they stand in organic connection with his public teaching. And in this respect Jesus in the Farewell Discourses simply tells his own that which he had always told them,[4] namely that the period of his work is bounded by the hour of his departure,[5] that he is to go away,[6] and that his departure will be a catastrophe—not for him but for the world.[7] That the

[1] See p. 631.
[2] Cp. Mk. 8.31; Mt. 26.54; Lk. 17.25; 22.37; 24.7 etc.
[3] Mk. 8.31; 9.31; 10.33f. parr.
[4] Cp. the explicit reference to earlier statement in 13.33.
[5] 7.6, 8, 33; 8.21; 9.4f.; 11.9f.; 12.35f.
[6] See p. 307 n.3.
[7] 7.34; 8.21, 28; 12.31.

Jews will kill him has been repeatedly announced,[1] and Jesus himself reproaches them for it;[2] but never does he prophesy his ἀποκτανθῆναι,[3] rather he speaks of his δοξασθῆναι,[4] his ὑψωθῆναι,[5] that the Jews themselves are to bring about.[6] Precisely because his decision has taken up the Passion as the crown of his work, it is his glorification. Fundamentally therefore he does not appear in the Passion story as the sufferer, but as the one who takes the initiative, and it is symptomatic that in 14.31 it is stated, οὕτως ποιῶ, and not, say, οὕτως δεῖ γενέσθαι.[7] He is the one who actually takes the initiative in his trial (18.1–11); in the examination before the High Priest (18.12–23), as also before Pilate (18.28–19.16); on the cross he makes known his last wish (19.26); he, as it were, gives the sign that the drama has reached its end (19.28), and he dies in the consciousness of having completed his work (19.30). Whereas in the eyes of the world his opponents have achieved a conquest, in the light of a devastating irony they appear as the conquered. On the one hand they meticulously observe the requirements of their law of purity in the very act of handing over Jesus to the judge; on the other hand, they can only reach the goal of their hatred through unreality and lying denunciation. Thereby they themselves make a mockery of the hope of their own people, as the heathen judge attests to them through the inscription on the cross (19.19–22). If to outward seeming they are the superior, even when the abused and thorn-crowned man is presented to them as their king (19.14), they have no idea that that is what he really is, and that in this event all human greatness and human pride are broken. For a man with eyes to see, the Passion is the demonstration of the obedience of Jesus, and therefore the proof of his δόξα.[8]

If then the Passion is but the crown and conclusion to all that has gone before, it is nevertheless true that a new motif in the Revealer's conquest of the world comes into view. For now a phenomenon appears on the scene that to this point has played no role, viz. *the Roman State.* The world brings its case against the Revealer to the forum of the state.[9] It becomes plain that the struggle between light and darkness cannot simply be played out in private, nor in the discussions that take place in fraternities and official religion. The world has been shaken to its foundations by Jesus' attack, so it seeks help from the power set over it to maintain order, and in this way the state too is drawn into the eschatological event. It cannot simply ignore the revelation. And in so far as it is compelled to adopt an attitude, Jesus shows himself here also as the Lord, and reveals his δόξα.[10]

---

[1] 5.18; 7.1, 25, 30, 44; 8.20, 59; 10.31, 39; 11.53.
[2] 7.19f.; 8.37, 40; 10.32.
[3] Cp. Mk. 8.31; 9.31; 10.33f. parr.
[4] 11.4; 12.23; see pp. 397f., 523.
[5] 3.14; 12.32.
[6] 8.28.
[7] Cp. perchance Mt. 26.54.
[8] See 14.30f. and p. 630f.
[9] See pp. 563ff. etc.
[10] That could be the meaning of the Pilate episode. It is not apologetically motivated.

If therefore the cross is understood as the crowning conclusion of the event that commenced with the ὁ λόγος σὰρξ ἐγένετο, and if as an isolated act it does not have a specific saving significance,[1] it is equally true that the significance of the resurrection as an event—even maybe a cosmic event—does not lie in its effecting something new that the word of Jesus had not already accomplished. Rather it is the demonstration of his victory over the world that had already been wrested from it (16.33). The νῦν, in which the turn of the ages took place, had already been spoken, 12.31. Indeed, the unity of the incarnation and resurrection had been set forth at the beginning, when the coming of the light into the world was described as the judgment (3.19). And if in the general Christian and Pauline view the life-creating power of Jesus was not released until his resurrection,[2] the Johannine Jesus, like the Father, has life in himself from the first (5.26); he *is* the resurrection and the life (11.25; 14.6); and as he earlier raised Lazarus from the dead by virtue of his power, so he promises life to the man who believes in his word (5.24f.; 11.25f.), without any mention being made of his resurrection. Similarly his coming as the "Son of Man" is not put off to a future appearing; he was already the "Son of Man" in his work on earth.[3] Consequently his teaching does not include the synoptic predictions of his ἀναστῆναι or ἐγερθῆναι,[4] rather he speaks of his ὑπάγειν, ἀναβαίνειν etc.[5] Moreover the Farewell Discourses had shown that Easter, Pentecost and the Parousia are not cosmic and mythical events, but that in their true meaning they are all the one decisive event: the return in the experience of faith of the Jesus who had departed from the earth.[6]

What then can be the meaning of the Easter happenings that the Evangelist, in dependence on the Tradition, still reports? They can only be σημεῖα, as the miracles of Jesus were.[7] Hence the Evangelist is able to comprehend them (20.20) under the σημεῖα of which his book tells; and they can claim only the relative significance that attaches to the miracles.[8] Just as 4.48 declared that faith ought not really to require miracles, and as was illustrated through the confrontation with Martha and Mary, 11.17ff., so the last Easter

---

(Htm., Br.), as if allusion should be made to the innocence and political harmlessness of the Christians and their unprejudiced attitude to the Roman state.

[1] Σταυρός or σταυρωθῆναι as a particular saving event is never the subject of discussion; cp. by contrast 1 Cor. 1.17ff.; 2 Cor. 13.4; Gal. 3.1; 5.11; 6.12, 14; Phil. 2.8; 3.18 etc. Especially in the words of Jesus these terms are never met with in Jn (unlike Mt. 20.19; 26.2); they are also lacking in the Johannine Epistles. From the first σταυρωθῆναι is interpreted as ὑψωθῆναι 3.14; 8.28; 12.32; see p. 152 n.4.

[2] Cp. Acts 3.15; 5.30f.; 1 Pt. 1.3, 21; 3.21; 1 Cor. 15; Rom. 6.1ff.; 8.11; Phil. 3.10; 2 Cor. 4.14.

[3] 1.51; 3.14; 5.27; 6.62; 8.28; 9.35; 12.23, 34; see pp. 105 n.3; 149 n.4; 260f.

[4] This terminology is lacking also in the Johannine Epistles. In Jn ἀναστῆναι is only in the editorial gloss 20.9; ἐγερθῆναι only 2.22 (for which 12.16 has δοξασθῆναι) and in the editorial postscript 21.14.

[5] See p. 307 n.3. Cp. also G. Bertram, Festg. für Ad. Deissmann 1927, 211ff.

[6] 16.16–24; see pp. 581, 584.

[7] Cp. S. V. McCasland, The Resurrection of Jesus 1932, 142f.

[8] See pp. 113f., 208f., 218, 232f., 452.

story (20.24–29) concludes with a saying that peculiarly relativises the previously recounted stories: "Blessed are they who do not see and yet believe!"

In the Passion and Easter narrative the Evangelist follows the tradition, and when looked at from without his adherence to it is particularly close.[1] That he follows a written source is assured on the grounds that 1. he produces sections and individual statements which he does not utilise in accordance with his theology, like the denial of Peter, the casting of lots for the cloak of Jesus, the indications of place 19.13;[2] 2. his additions are often separable from an earlier writing that lies at their base.[3] It is also plain that his sources are not the Synoptic Gospels, nor even one of them. Admittedly there is no compelling proof that he used here a single writing that contains a coherent account. But this alone is probable, for the Passion of Jesus had called forth a complete representation of events, earlier than the other themes of the story of Jesus,[4] and there could hardly have been a Passion narrative without a following Easter story. The unified linguistic and stylistic character also speaks in favour of the unity of the source that was used. The language is a vulgar, lightly semitising Greek; its characteristics are briefly sketched here, while the literary critical analysis will be made known in the exposition of the individual sections.[5]

The *sentence-construction* is very simple; only in 19.17f., 31, 33f. do any complicated junctures occur. Conj. participles subordinated to the verb: εἰδώς (18.4: 19.28); ἰδών (19.26); εἰπών (18.1, 38); 20 (14), 20, (22); ἀκούσας (19.13); others in 19.2, 17, 29, 30, 33, 39; 20. (5, 6, 15, 16), 20; qualifying the subject: 18.10; (19.5, 38; 20.6); qualifying the object (19.26; 20.6f.); 20.12, (14). (Participle with article as apposition (19.39); 20 (8), 24; participle as completing the verb [18.32]; 19. (6.12)).—Especially remarkable is the avoidance of subordination: 18.10, 12, 16, 29, (31, 33); 19.39, 40; 20.1 (f.) (five finite verbs); in 19.2f. the participle stands with five verbs!—The genitive absolute is found only in 18.22; 20.1; 19.26 (twice). Infinitive constructions: (18.31) after ἔξεστιν, [18.32] after μέλλειν, (19.7) after ὀφείλειν, (19.10) after ἐξουσίαν ἔχειν, (19.12) after ζητεῖν. Relative sentences: simple relative 18.1, [9], (13); 19.17, (22, 26), 41; (20.7); ὅπου 18.1, 20; 19.18, (20), 41; 20.12, 19; καθώς 19.40; (20.21).—Temporal sentences: ὡς 19.33; ὡς οὖν (18.6); 20.11; ὅτε (19.23); 20.24; ὅτε οὖν 19. (6, 8), 30.—Causal clauses: ὅτι 18.2, 18; 19. (7, 20), 42; 20.13, (29); γάρ (18.13); 19. (6), 31, 36; 20. [9], (17); ἐπεί 19.31.—Final sentences: ἵνα 18. (37), 39; 19. (4), 16, 28, 31, [35], 36, 38; ἵνα μή (18.28,

---

[1] Dibelius, Formgesch. 179f. = From Tradition to Gospel, 179f.

[2] Dibelius, Formgesch. 204, 4 = From Tradition to Gospel, 204.1. Cp. also Dibelius, Die altest. Motive in der Leidensgeschichte des Petrus- und des Joh-Evg., ZATW. Beih. 33 (Festschr. for Baudissin), 125–150; M. Goguel, Les Sources du Récit Johannique de la Passion 1910.

[3] The analysis can only partly be supported through linguistic criteria, since the Evangelist's stylistic peculiarities are not marked in the narrative.

[4] Gesch. der synopt. Trad. 297f. = Hist. of the Syn. Trad. 275f.; Dibelius, Formgesch. 178ff. = From Trad. to Gospel, 178ff.

[5] The verses presumed to be derived from the Evangelist are set in round brackets, additions of the editor in square brackets.

36); 19.31; elliptical ἵνα [18.9, 32] 19.24. Further, the paratactic final clause: 18.39 (Bl.-D. § 366.3; Raderm. 222).—Consecutive clauses: ὥστε is lacking; οὐκοῦν (18.37).—Conditional sentences: ἐάν (19.12); 20.25; εἰ 18.(8), 23, (30, 36); (19.11); (20.15).—Dependent statements: ὅτι 18. (8), [9], (14, 37); 19. (4, 10, 21, 28), [35]; 20. [9], (14), 15, 18).—Indirect questions: 19.24; 20. 13, (15).

The *connections of sentences*[1] are very primitive. Asyndeton occurs very frequently; often it is found when the new sentence begins with a verb of saying: 18.17, 20, 23, 25, 26, (30, 31 (v. 1), 34, 35, 36, 37, 38); 19. (6, 7, 11), 15 (twice), (22); 20.13, (15, 16, 17), 28, (29).—οὖν is very frequent; often it stands after the verb that introduces the sentence, 18.11, 16, 17, (24), 25, 28, 29, (31) (twice?), (37), 39; 19. (5, 10), 15, 16, (v. 1.), (21), 24, 32, 39, 40; 20. (2, 3, 6, 10), 20, (21), 25; after the subject introducing the sentence, 18.4, 10; 19. (26), 29 (v. 1), or the object, 19.29; between the article and the subject or name at the beginning of the sentence, 18. (3), 12, 19; 19.13, (20), 23, 31—πάλιν οὖν 18. (7), 27, (33, (v. 1.)); οὖν πάλιν 18. (33), 40; (20. 10, 21).—ὅτε οὖν, see below under temporal clauses; τότε οὖν 19. 1, 16; (20.8).—More seldom δέ after the verb introducing the sentence, 18. 15, 18, (31 (v. 1)), 39; 19.19, (20.4); frequently ἦν δέ κτλ, 18.10, (13), 25, 28, 40: 19. (14), 19, 23, 41; after the subject introducing the sentence 20.11, 24; similarly in an intermediate position after the article, 18. 15, 16; (19.9.12); δὲ καί after the verb standing at the beginning of the sentence, 18. 2, 5; 19. 19, (39); νῦν δέ (18.36); μὲν ... δέ. 19. (24) f., 32 f.; οὐ μέντοι (20.5)—Other beginnings of sentences: εἶτα (19.27); 20.27; μετὰ τοῦτο 19.28; μετὰ δὲ ταῦτα 19.38; ἐκ τούτου (19.12): διὰ τοῦτο (19.11).

As to *semitisms*, one should not adduce under this heading the fact that the verb most commonly precedes the subject and often stands at the beginning of the sentence;[2] the same applies to superfluous forms of αὐτός, 18.1b, 19, 21; 20.26, for they occur too seldom; and εἷς instead of τις, 18.22, is not necessarily a semitism (Bl-D. § 247.2; Raderm. 76). But the following may well be semitisms: εἶπεν σημαίνων (18.32), ἐκραύγασαν λέγοντες 19.6, [12], as ἀπεκρίθησαν καὶ εἶπαν [18.30], or in the singular 20.28 (Bl.-D. § 420). Further ἦλθον (οὖν) καὶ ἦραν 19.38 (see Schlatter ad. loc.), τρέχει καὶ ἔρχεται (20.2) (Schl.), πορεύου ... καὶ εἰπέ (20.17) (Schl. on Mt. 28.7), possibly also the consecutive καί (20.15), but hardly the τί κλαίεις (Schl.). Other semitisms could also be: κακὸν ποιεῖν (18.30) ἐντεῦθεν καὶ ἐντεῦθεν 19.18; ἀπ' ἐκείνης τῆς ὥρας (19.27) (Schl. on Mt. 9.22); τῇ μιᾷ τῶν σαββάτων 20.1; ἕνα ... καὶ ἕνα 20.12 (Schl. on Mt. 24.40). Also ὃ γέγραφα γέγραφα (19.22)? (Schl. and Str.-B.); ἔστη εἰς τὸ μέσον 20.19? (Schl. but cp. Xen. Cyrop. iv. 1.1: στὰς εἰς τὸ μέσον); φέρε τὸν δάκτυλον σου ὧδε 20.27? Naturally εἰρήνη ὑμῖν 20.19, (21), is Semitic, probably also the ἀφιέναι and κρατεῖν τὰς ἁμαρτίας 20.23, although in these cases we are dealing with technical terminology.

---

[1] In this respect the textual tradition is repeatedly uncertain.
[2] Wellh. 133; Colwell 21ff.

A. 18.1–19.41: The Passion

a) The Arrest of Jesus: 18.1–11

The pericope corresponds to Mk. 14. 26, 32–52 parr. As in the latter passage, it is here related that after the last meal and the conversations with the disciples that then took place Jesus goes off to the Mount of Olives, and an armed troop appears, led by Judas. Apart from variations in detail (see below), the difference between the Johannine and the Synoptic account consists in the Evangelist's omission of the narrative about the disciples sleeping and Jesus' struggling in prayer (Mk. 14. 32–42). This has been replaced by 12.27f. (p. 428 n.1), and no more than an allusion to it remains. John was unable to retain this story, for in his account Jesus already acts as the δοξασθείς (13.31). The same viewpoint is seen in John's very important statement, which goes beyond the Synoptic narratives: the police fall to the ground at his ἐγώ εἰμι (v. 6); and whereas Jesus puts himself at their disposal, he ensures that nothing happens to the disciples (vv. 8f.). So the first scene reveals that the Passion does not come upon him as his fate, rather *he* is the one who acts, and *he* controls the situation.

Further, the purpose of the Evangelist is shown in the statement that the Roman militia takes part in the arrest. Even if it be historically correct that Jesus was arrested and condemned by the Romans and not by the Jews,[1] John's representation hardly rests on a superior knowledge, for on the whole it is not historical. It is even questionable whether Roman soldiers and Jewish temple police would have worked together (though El. Bickermann thinks otherwise, Rev. de l'Hist. des Rel. [1935] 217f.); in any case it is unbelievable that the chiliarch led the prisoner to the Sanhedrin (v. 12) instead of to the Antonia. And would he also afterwards have escorted him to Caiaphas on the instruction of Annas (v. 24)? The Evangelist, however, has a special interest in view. Whereas he gives no account at all of the hearing before the Sanhedrin, leading to the condemnation of Jesus, he supplies a very detailed report of the trial by Pilate, which is only briefly described by the Synoptics; his interest lies in the encounter of Jesus with the Roman state, consequently he highlights this even at the arrest.[2]

That the Evangelist himself has fashioned the narrative is clear; but it is equally clear that he depends upon the tradition, and in fact he has obviously used a *written source.* Vv. 10f. could well have originated from it, for it is

[1] Cp. Schürer II 261; H. Lietzmann, SA. Berlin 1931, XIV 310–322; ZNTW 30 (1931), 211–215; 31 (1932) 78–84; M. Dibelius, ditto 30 (1931), 193–210; Fr. Büchsel, same volume 202–210; 33 (1934) 84–87; M. Goguel, ditto 31 (1932), 289–301; H. J. Ebeling, ditto 35 (1936), 290–295; P. Fiebig, ThStkr 104 (1932) 213–228; A. Oepke, ditto 105 (1933), 392f.—Cp. also M. Goguel, Vie de Jésus 453f.; Introd. II 450f.; El. Bickermann op. cit. (see above) 169–241; J. Jeremias, ZNW 43 (1950/51), 145–150; T. W. Manson, ibid. 44 (1952/53), 255f.; G. D. Kilpatrick, The Trial of Jesus 1952.

[2] The claim that the Romans were not to arrest Jesus, but only wanted to be present for safety precautions in case of a resistance (Schl., Lagr.), founders on v. 12. Moreover in v. 18 the soldiers have disappeared in a remarkable fashion.

difficult to ascribe to the Evangelist the legendary accretion that Mk. 14.47 has suffered here. Also vv. 4f. (up to εἰδὼς ... ἐπ' αὐτόν) will have been taken from the source; for otherwise it is incomprehensible why Judas—who, although already known, is yet again characterised as ὁ παραδιδοὺς αὐτόν—is expressly stated in v. 5 to be standing by, whereas in v. 3 he was named as the leader of the troop.[1] In the source the statement of v. 5 would have prepared the way for the intervention of Judas, and so the scene of the kiss of Judas (Mk. 14.45), which here would have had the meaning of confirming the ἐγώ εἰμι of Jesus. The Evangelist has broken it off and replaced it by v. 6, and in v. 7 he takes up again the motif of v. 5 in order to be able to join v. 8 on to it. What is derived from the source in vv. 1f. it is difficult now to tell.[2]

V. 1 links on to 14.31 and makes a transition to the new scene.[3] Jesus leaves the city,[4] and with his disciples crosses the Kidron,[5] whose ravine divides the Mount of Olives from Jerusalem.[6] He comes with them into a garden,[7] which (**v. 2**) Judas knows to be a place where Jesus and the disciples frequently stayed.[8] This observation prepares for the following scene.[9]

The action starts with **v. 3**. Without any account being given of what else took place between Jesus and the disciples in the garden,[10] it is

---

[1] We cannot conversely ascribe v. 3 to the source, for it would be incomprehensible why the Evangelist on his own initiative should have inserted the comment in v. 5.

[2] It is difficult to show that in v. 1 the σύν, which elsewhere in Jn meets us only in 12.2 (21.3), should stand, while v. 2 has μετά, which is constantly used elsewhere. That the subject Κεδρών is used attributively can be reckoned as Johannine, see Raderm. 108.

[3] Ταῦτα εἰπῶν as v. 38; 7.9; 9.6; 11.28, 43; 13,31; 20.14, 20, 22 (21.19).

[4] Ἐξῆλθεν, which corresponds to Mk. 14.26; Mt. 26.30, includes the departure from the house and the city. On the topography see G. Dalman, Jerusalem und sein Gelände 1930, 262.

[5] The correct and probably also original variant is τοῦ κεδρών (A W pc lat syr[s]). Κεδρών (קִדְרוֹן = murky, black) is used in the LXX indeclinably, like Χεβρών, Ἀμμών etc. (1 Kings 2.37; 2 Kings 23.6, 12; see Bl.-D. § 56, 2), while Josephus declines it (Ant. 1.17; τὸν χειμάρρουν Κεδρῶνα and elsewhere, see Br.). The variant τοῦ Κέδρου (א* D a brsa) is manifestly intended as a declined form of the proper name, whereas τῶν Κέδρων (K pl) derives the name from κέδρος = cedar (so also in LXX 2 Sam. 15.23; 1 Kings 15.13). The brook is called χειμάρρους as in LXX and Josephus, i.e. ὁ ἐν τῷ χειμῶνι ῥέων πόταμος (Suidas). Concerning the Kidron see Dalman, O. und W. 338f.

[6] Jos. bell. 5, 70. It is hardly likely that the reader should think on the fact that David once had fled across the Kidron (2 Sam. 15.23ff.).

[7] As in Lk the name Gethsemane is lacking (Mk. 14.32; Mt. 26.36); moreover it is not explicitly stated that the garden lies on the Mount of Olives (Mk. 14.26 parr.).

[8] On ᾔδει δὲ καί cp. v. 5; 2.2; 3.23; 11.57; 19.19, 39 (21.25). Lk 21.37; 22.39 declares that in his last days in Jerusalem Jesus used to stay on the Mount of Olives.

[9] It is too heavy a burden for the statement to bear to suppose, with Br., that v. 2 was intended to stress that Jesus went to the well known place because he wanted to be found, and that by this means the opponents' mockery is countered, "How can he flee who desires to be reckoned as God's Son!" (The Jew in Orig. c.C. II 9 pp. 135ff. K.).

[10] See pp. 637f.

immediately reported that under the guidance of Judas[1] a troop of Roman soldiers[2] and a number of servants of the Jewish Sanhedrin come,[3] equipped with lanterns, torches[4] and weapons. They come, as the reader knows, to arrest Jesus; and at the same time, as the reader equally knows, there comes the ἄρχων τοῦ κόσμου (14.31)—who nevertheless can achieve nothing against Jesus. It is precisely this that **v. 4** expresses through the εἰδώς, which takes up again the motif from 13.1, 3.[5] In the superior knowledge of the Gnostic, Jesus as it were challenges those who had come to arrest him.[6] Through his ἐγώ εἰμι (**v. 5**) he places himself at their disposal.[7] The reader, who has in mind the earlier ἐγώ εἰμι, doubtless hears more in that than the context actually says; the Redeemer is speaking—and so he comprehends the miraculous effect that the saying has (**v. 6**): the myrmidons of the law shrink back and fall to the ground,[8] as a man sinks down before the epiphany of Deity.[9]

---

[1] Λαβών naturally does not signify that Judas commands the troop, but only that he shows the way.

[2] Σπεῖρα = cohors (600 men) or = manipulus (220 men); see Arndt & Gingrich lexicon; it is commanded by a χιλίαρχος (v. 12). On the participation of the Romans see p. 637.

[3] ℵ D L a read ἐκ τῶν φαρ., B simply τῶν φαρ.; τῶν is lacking in C ℜ pl. On the ἀρχιερ. καὶ φαρ. as authorities see p. 306 n.5. The ὑπηρέται are the Levitical Temple police, see Joach Jeremias, Jerusalem zur Zeit Jesu II B 1937, 72f.

[4] Φανός (also as a loan word in Rabbinic lit., see Str.-B.) = torch, light, and contrary to the opposition of the Atticists is also used in the sense of λυχνοῦχος = lantern (Arndt & Gingrich); so here, alongside λαμπάς, which is the usual word for torch. Dion. Hal. Ant. XI 40, 2 attests that lanterns and torches belonged to the equipment in a Roman camp (ἐξέτρεχον . . . ἅπαντες. . . φανοὺς ἔχοντες καὶ λαμπάδας). "With lanterns and torches" sounds Semitic (see Str.-B.); cp. however Thuc. VI 58: μετὰ γὰρ ἀσπίδος καὶ δόρατος εἰώθεισαν τὰς πομπὰς πέμπειν.—It need occasion no surprise that in a night expedition lanterns and torches should be taken, despite the full moon. However the Evangelist does not think about the full moon, see p. 483 n.3.

[5] See p. 465. Naturally εἰδώς . . . ἐπ' αὐτόν is inserted by the Evangelist into the source.

[6] Ἔρχεσθαι ἐπί of the fulfilment of a curse Mt. 23.35; Deut. 28.15, 45; of terrors that fall upon men Ps. 54.5 v. 1; of (coming) events Jos. Ant. IV 128; Dion. Hal. Ant. XI 40, 6 (with dat. Xen. Hist. Gr. VI 5, 43: κίνδυνος); Rabbinic evidence in Schl. on Jn. 14.28 and Mt. 23.35.—The like applies elsewhere to ἐπέρχεσθαι Lk. 21.26; Jas. 5.1; 1 Clem. 51.10; Herm. vis. III 9, 5; IV 1, 1; sim. VII 4.

[7] We have here the profane formula of recognition; see p. 225 n.3. The answer (as v. 7) designates Jesus by his customary name in the world Ναζωραῖος (in Jn only 18.5, 7; 19.19). So also Mt. 2.23; 26.71; Lk. 18.37; 24.19 and frequently in Acts; along with this is Ναζαρηνός Mk. 1.24; 10.47; 14.67; 16.6; Lk. 4.34 (there are variants almost in every case). On the original meaning see the literature cited by Arndt & Gingrich. Jn will have understood "of Nazareth", see 1.46f.—As a parallel to the narrative cp. Eurip. Bacch 434ff.: Dionysus allows himself to be taken without resistance (πρᾷος), though admittedly γελῶν.

[8] Χαμαί = χάμαζε as 9.6. The asseveration of Zn and Lagr. is comical, that "self-evidently it was not the entire company, numbered by the hundred", which fell to the ground, but only "the leaders standing at the head". It is nevertheless, as 7.30, 44; 8.20, 59; 10.39 a miraculous occurrence; see pp. 302 n.3.

[9] Cp. Dan. 10.9; Rev. 1.17. The psychological effect of the personality of Jesus is as little in mind as in 7.46f.; see p. 310 n.1; G. Bertram, Die Leidensgeschichte Jesu und der Christuskult 1922, 53.

The comment interposed about Judas standing by is unmotivated and can only be derived from the source;[1] though the Evangelist does not mention it, he certainly wishes to make it clear that Judas belongs to the side of the ἄρχων τοῦ κόσμου.[2]

As though nothing had happened, Jesus repeats his question (v. 7), and after making himself known again through the ἐγώ εἰμι as the one whom they were seeking (v. 8), he gives the order—for one cannot describe in any other way the sentence that is spoken, without any appearance of a request—to let his disciples go free. It is clearly presupposed that that takes place, although it is not recounted, and in fact one has to imagine that the prophecy σκορπισθῆτε (16.32) now has its fulfilment. Jesus himself, as it were, has thus occasioned the disciples' flight.[3]

A note (v. 9) adds that by this means a saying of Jesus should find its fulfilment;[4] obviously 6.39 (cp. 17.12) is meant. But how can the statement that Jesus does not let any of his own be lost, i.e. does not let any be deprived of the ζωὴ αἰώνιος be fulfilled by his saving them from the danger that threatens their outward life—something that 15.18–16.4a intimates can apply only for a limited period of time?[5] The outward deliverance can hardly be a symbolic picture of the eternal one; in the context of the Gospel it could at most be understood as implying that before the death and resurrection of Jesus the disciples would not have been a match for temptation; if they had been arrested and condemned with Jesus they would have apostatised, and so lost the life eternal. But dare one read so much between the lines? V. 9 therefore must be adjudged as a gloss of the redactor;[6] the same applies to v. 32, which shows itself to be redactional through its relationship with 21.19. The consequence of this must admittedly then be drawn: 12.33 should be interpreted not as a comment of the Evangelist, but as a comment of the redaction (see p. 432 n.5).

---

[1] See p. 638.

[2] Bertram (op. cit. 52f.) sees in the comment a correction of the Synoptic tradition: "Although they had one who could have pointed out Jesus to them, the Lord himself had to reveal himself to them".

[3] Whether on the ground of apologetic tendency (see the critical remark of the Jew in Orig. c. C II 9.12.18.45; see Br.) is doubtful. Nevertheless in this manner it also needs to be shown that Jesus is the one who is at work in every happening, that the Passion manifests his δόξα.

[4] On ἵνα πληρωθῇ see p. 452 n.2. Only here and in v. 32 is it used of a saying of Jesus and not of one from the Scripture. Οὓς δέδωκάς μοι, to which ἐξ αὐτῶν looks back, corresponds to an absolute nominative (see v. 11 and p. 233 n.4). A Semitism (Burney 84f.) need not be involved here; see Colwell 46, who alludes to Xen. Cyrop. VI 4, 9.

[5] As early as Chrys. t. VIII 490d, Catene 377, 11 the situation was evident (see Br.).

[6] So also Wellh., Sp.; the editor had well hit off the style of the Evangelist. Dodd defends the originality of v. 9.

The scene could now come to its conclusion; but in **vv. 10ff.**—doubtless in dependence on his source[1]—the Evangelist cites the motif, well known from the Synoptic Gospels, of the disciple who defends himself with a sword and cuts off an ear of the High Priest's δοῦλος.[2] In Mark and Luke this event has no consequences, but Mt. 26.52 reports that Jesus rebuked the disciple for his deed. The tradition that John follows does likewise,[3] though it combines with it the motif of Mk. 14.36, the drinking of the cup.[4] The Evangelist has taken up the tradition for the sake of this saying; as the entry to the Passion it corresponds to the last saying of the Farewell Discourses.[5]

b) Jesus before the High Priest and the Denial of Peter: 18.12–27

As in the Synoptics, the scene of the arrest is followed by that of the examination before the Sanhedrin; the pericope thus corresponds to Mk. 14.53–72 parr., though it exhibits remarkable differences from it. As in the Synoptics Jesus is brought before the High Priest and tried by him, and it is in this context that the report of Peter's denial is given. As in Mark and Matthew the scene takes place at night, whereas in Luke the denial certainly occurs in the night, but the examination does not take place till the next morning (22.66). In John it is not expressly stated that the trial takes place before the assembled Sanhedrin, nevertheless it may be allowed as self-evident. There is, however, a difference with respect to *the person of the High Priest.* According to Mt. 26.27 (cp. 26.3) this is Caiaphas (Mark and Luke do not give his name). For John also Caiaphas is viewed as High Priest; nevertheless the examination described does not take place before

---

[1] See p. 637f.

[2] The novelistic and legendary character of the development, as compared with the Marcan account, is seen here as in Lk. 22.50. As in Lk it is the right ear that is struck off (see Gesch. der synopt. Trad. 340 = Hist. of the Syn. Trad. 311f.); the statement that Jesus healed the ear again (Lk. 22.51) is lacking (op. cit. 306 = Hist. 282f.). Against this the report names the disciple as Peter, and the slave as Malchus (op. cit. 306, 338 = Hist. 283, 310). That the term δοῦλος is used, not ὑπηρέτης, is certainly not due to the idea that this δοῦλος is distinguished from the ὑπηρέται (vv. 3, 12) as the sole personal attendant of Caiaphas, a valet or the like (Zn.); it rests simply on the source or the tradition. (In general δοῦλοι and ὑπηρέται are to be distinguished; see v. 18 and J. Jeremias, Jerusalem z.Z. Jesu II. B 73). On ἦν δὲ ὄνομα see p. 48 n.3. The name Μάλχος (מלך) is attested by Josephus and by Mandaean and Palmyrene inscriptions (see Br., Zn., Str.-B.). Was Malchus an Arab, and therefore a slave? See Jeremias op. cit. II A 26, 63; B 219.

[3] In the formulation also βάλε τὴν μαχ. εἰς τ. θήκην reminds us of Mt. 26.52; on this cp. Jer. 29 (47).6; 1 Chron. 21.27. θήκη = scabbard was also taken over by the Jews as a loan word; see Schl.

[4] This metaphor, also common in the O.T. (Dalman W. J. 19), does not appear elsewhere in Jn.

[5] The question οὐ μὴ πίω (subj.) αὐτό signifies a strong affirmation, Bl-D. §365, 4; Raderm. 169f.

him, but before his father-in-law Annas (v. 13), and he too appears to be regarded as High Priest (vv. 19, 22). Afterwards he sends Jesus bound to Caiaphas (v. 24). What happened before Caiaphas is not reported; one has to presume that an examination likewise took place before him. Whether this second examination corresponds to the second sitting of the Sanhedrin on the following morning, which Mk. 15.1, Mt. 27.1 mention,[1] cannot be determined; for this is not thought of as an examination, but as a session for the purpose of making a decision, at which Jesus manifestly is not present.

The *abuse of Jesus*, which in Mk. 14.65 = Mt. 26.67f. follows the trial, but in Lk. 22.63–65 precedes it, has no real parallel in John. On the contrary he relates that, during the hearing, a slave struck Jesus because of his unseemly answer to the High Priest (vv. 22f.).

While John agrees with the Synoptics in combining the narrative of *Peter's denial* with the examination, he does not agree with them in the manner in which he does this. As in Mark and Matthew, the story of the denial is also divided into two parts, while in Luke it is recounted as a continuous narrative.[2] But whereas in Mk. 14.45 = Mt. 26.58 the first scene only gives a statement of the situation, and the threefold denial is then described after the trial, Mk. 14.66–72 = Mt. 26.69–75 (the first denial in the αὐλή, the two following in the προαύλιον), John sets the first denial in the first scene, v. 17 and the two others then follow at the conclusion, vv. 25–27.

The *chief difference* however consists in the fact that while in John, as in the Synoptics, the examination counts as a court session, only *one* question of the High Priest is reported, and that is quite general περὶ τῶν μαθητῶν αὐτοῦ καὶ περὶ τῆς διδαχῆς αὐτοῦ (v. 19).[3] No witnesses appear, and no definite accusations are lodged; the saying of Jesus about the temple (Mk. 14.58 = Mt. 26.61) plays no role. In particular the question of the High Priest about the messianic claim of Jesus and Jesus' answer to it are lacking (see Mk. 14.61f. = Mt., 26.63f., and cp. Lk. 22.66–70). Consequently there is not a word about the result of the session, or of the death sentence (Mk. 14.63f. = Mt. 26.65f., cp. Lk. 22.71).

It is plain that John has not utilised the Synoptics, but a source, in which the same tradition was differently formed; his account cannot be understood as an independent editing of the Synoptics (or of one of them), since his departures cannot be traced back to the theological motifs that are

---

[1] Unless it is simply intended there that the night session was not concluded till the morning through the passing of the resolution. In Lk at all events there is no question of a second trial; he knows only the one that takes place on the following day.

[2] That is however probably a secondary piece of editorial work by Lk; so J. Finegan, Die Überlieferung der Leidens- und Auferstehungsgeschichte Jesu 1934, 23 against Gesch. der synopt. Trad. 290 = Hist. of the Syn. Trad. 269.

[3] According to Bickermann, op. cit. 219ff., the distinction rests on the fact that according to Jn's representation the judgment of the Sanhedrin stood fast; Jesus is already "proscribed", and the only needful action was to deliver him to the Roman authority. Accordingly he is already fettered at the trial (in Mk. not until 15.1). The leading of Jesus before the High Priest had to be recounted for the sake of Peter's denial.

characteristic of him.[1] The use of a source of his own is confirmed by the fact that one can perceive a redactional insertion of the Evangelist's that has brought a lack of clarity into the narrative. Jesus is led before Annas (vv. 12f.), and he is described as the father-in-law of Caiaphas, while Caiaphas on his part is said to be ἀρχιερεὺς τοῦ ἐνιαυτοῦ ἐκείνου. Then, however, Annas suddenly becomes the High Priest; for v. 19 says that the ἀρχιερεὺς examines Jesus. But that can only be Annas, since Jesus is not sent from him to Caiaphas till later (v. 24). Therefore vv. 13f. (from πρῶτον on) are an insertion into the source,[2] and indeed an insertion of the Evangelist's, for in his eyes Caiaphas is reckoned as High Priest. He had introduced him as such in 11.49, and he alludes to that passage in v. 14. For the source Annas was the High Priest.[3] It follows then that the whole of v. 24 also is derived from the Evangelist. But further difficulties are thereby raised: 1. What meaning could the examination before Annas have at all, if he was not the official High Priest? 2. Why is the examination before Caiaphas referred to only by an allusion in v. 24, if this was the official hearing? 3. The remarkable change of scenes that takes place between v. 24 and vv. 25–27 thereby disappears; for vv. 25–27, as vv. 15–18, must be set in the court of Annas![4]

In face of this, the attempt to bring clarity into the account by transposing the verses is less illuminating. Admittedly this has been done already in syr^s, inasmuch as the latter places v. 24 after v. 13, and in this way it makes the examination of vv. 19–23 take place before Caiaphas. It also places vv. 16–18 after v. 23, so that the story of the denial is not divided.[5] But against the idea that this was the original order it must be objected: 1. the bringing of Jesus before Annas now appears as completely without purpose and content;

---

[1] Cp. M. Dibelius, Formsgesch,^{2} 204, 4, 217 = From Trad. to Gospel, 204, 1, 215f.

[2] It is impermissible to plead that Annas, the predecessor of Caiaphas, still bore the title of High Priest (Bd.), for the report clearly is talking about *the* High Priest, who is in office.

[3] This statement is an error, in so far as Annas, according to Jos. Ant. 18, 35, was deposed through the Procurator Valerius Gratus (A.D. 15), whereas according to Ant. 18, 35 Caiaphas was called to office through the same procurator perhaps three years later, and according to Ant. 18.95 he continued in office into the time of Vitellius. Admittedly we know too little of the events of the years 18–36 to be able to judge whether Annas exercised high priestly fuctions, even though not recognised by the Romans as High Priest. At all events it is conceivable that his prestige and his influence, even after his deposition, were so great that the community tradition could make him responsible for an event like the condemnation of Jesus. For that clues do exist. Apart from Mt. 26.3, 57 Caiaphas appears elsewhere in the N.T. only at: 1. Lk. 3.2, where καὶ Καιαφᾶ alongside ἐπὶ ἀρχιερέως Ἄννα is extremely strange and is probably interpolated (Loisy, Wellh. 81, 1; G. Hölscher, SB Heidelb. 1939/40, 3 [1940], 22); 2. Acts 4.5, where Καιαφᾶς coming after Ἄννας ὁ ἀρχ. similarly could be an interpolation (Wellh., Krit. Analyse der Apostelgesch. [Abh. der Gött. Ges. der Wissensch. 1914] 8 and Hölscher op. cit.), and in any case Annas is reckoned as High Priest. The same applies to Acts 5.17, if the conjecture accepted by Wellh. (ibid. 10) and Hölscher (op. cit. 23) is correct, that instead of Ἀναστὰς δὲ ὁ ἀρχ. we read Ἄννας δὲ κτλ.

[4] That Annas and Caiaphas had lived in two different houses yet possessed a common court is an artificial bit of intelligence. Anything of this sort would have had to be expressly reported.

[5] The succession of verses in syr^s is thus: 12, 13, 24, 14, 15, 19–23, 16–18, 25–27.

2. vv. 15 and 16, which clearly belong together, are now torn asunder.[1] Moreover it is not at all necessary to the clarity of the account that the story of the denial be related in an undivided manner.[2]

Shorter redactional interpolations of the Evangelist's lie in vv. 12 and 20. In v. 12 he has added the cohort with the chiliarch (see p. 637), and in v. 20 he has extended the source through his additions (see below).

The evangelist has probably edited his source in yet another respect. It is very unlikely that in the source the trial was limited to the meagre statement in vv. 19–21 (–23). Rather it will have contained an account, as the Synoptics, of (false) accusations, of the question about the Messiah and its affirmation, and of the condemnation. The Evangelist has broken it off and replaced it, so to speak, with v. 24. But why? For him no further importance could be attached to a discussion of Jesus with the Jewish authorities, since he had set this discussion back already in the time of the ministry of Jesus.[3] He had also cited the temple saying earlier on in 2.19. After all that had gone before, he could not throw up the question about the messiahship again; and an answer like Mk. 14.62, in which the old apocalyptic eschatology found expression, was absolutely impossible in the mouth of the Johannine Jesus.[4] For the Evangelist the interest in the trial of Jesus is wholly transferred to the encounter with the Roman state. The answer that Jesus gives to the High Priest in vv. 20f. cuts short any further discussion with Judaism: it needs no further question, not another word! Jesus long ago had said everything about which anyone could ask him.

The Roman soldiers[5] and the Jewish police lead Jesus bound[6] to Annas[7] (**v. 12**). In what follows Annas is treated as the High Priest,[8]

---

[1] The suggestion of W. R. Church (JBL 49 [1930], 275–383) seeks to avoid the latter; he puts the verses in the following order: 12, 13, 24, 14, 19–23, 15–18, 25b–27. But then the first offence still remains, and therefore it is very improbable that ἠκολούθει δὲ . . . Σίμ. Πέτρ. v. 15 was placed after v. 23, and not at the beginning. Lagr. leaves vv. 16–18 in their place, but he transfers v. 24 after v. 13. To this end he urges that in v. 24 the δέ, which ℵ, several miniscules, syr^{s} and several other witnesses offer instead of οὖν, is evidence that v. 24 belongs after v. 13, where only δέ is in place; since v. 24 has wrongly taken a position after v. 23, the δέ was corrected into οὖν. Moffat sets vv. 19–24 between vv. 14 and 15. Cyril of Alex. and miniscule 225 also bring v. 24 after v. 13 or 13a. As to other attempts at correction, see Church op. cit.

[2] Wellh. Sp., Delafosse also consider vv. 13f. and 24 to be editorial insertions; Sp. further regards vv. 16–18, 25–27 as interpolations, after the Synoptic gospels; similarly Schw. I 249ff. vv. 18, 25–27.

[3] H. Windisch, Joh. und die Synopt. 82 rightly: "The 'trial' had already taken place in several acts 5.19ff.; 10.22ff. . . . the conclusion was already settled in due form before the arrest, 11.47ff."

[4] So rightly Goguel, Vie de Jésus 491.

[5] In distinction from v. 3 the commander is here named; he is described as χιλίαρχος, and so as a tribunus militum, who leads a cohort; see Br. ad loc, and Arndt & Gringrich lexicon.

[6] In the Synoptics this is not expressly said; see p. 642 n.3.

[7] Πρῶτον is not intended to be a correction of the Synoptic report (Zn.), but anticipates v. 24; it is derived from the Evangelist, see p. 641f.

[8] See p. 641f.

but through a gloss of the Evangelist (**v. 13**) he is at once characterised as the father-in-law of the High Priest Caiaphas;[1] the latter, as **v. 14** remarks, is already known to the reader from 11.49f.[2]

Before an account is given of the proceedings before Annas, it is stated that Peter and another disciple have followed their arrested Master (**v. 15**). The other man is not identified, it is only said that he was an acquaintance[3] of the High Priest—and by this an explanation is given of how he was able to follow Jesus right into the court of the High Priest.[4] He further managed to persuade the woman who kept the door[5] to let Peter in (**v. 16**).[6] When she believes that she recognises Peter as one of the disciples, the first denial ensues (**v. 17**).[7] That has no

---

[1] On Καιαφᾶς and ἀρχιερ. τ. ἐνιαυτ. ἐκ. see p. 410 nn.9, 10. As to Annas see Schürer II 270; Str.-B. and Schl. ad loc.

[2] Συμφέρει here not with ἵνα (see p. 411 n.1) but with acc. and inf., see Bl.-D. §409, 3.—Instead of ἀποθανεῖν ℜ pm read ἀπολέσθαι.

[3] Γνωστός = acquainted, on friendly terms with, in distinction from συγγενής (v. 26) = related.

[4] Who the ἄλλος μαθητής is cannot be divined (Zn.: James the son of Zebedee!). There is no basis for identifying him with the "Beloved Disciple" (as C ℜ pl. do by the addition of the article), and in particular his appearance with Peter is no reason for it; for the two figures do not appear here, as in 20.3–10 and 21.1–23, as rivals or as contrasted types (Dibelius, Formgesch. 217, 3 = From Trad. to Gospel, 216, 1), and nothing more is reported about the "other disciple" than that he effects an entrance for Peter. Obviously it is not meant that he belongs to the Twelve. Dibelius presumes that he is a historical figure, Formsgesch. 217f. = From Trad. to Gospel 216f., and he even identifies him with the Beloved Disciple. But does he not owe his existence solely to the necessity of providing a reason for Peter's being able to enter into the αὐλή of the High Priest?

[5] It is very remarkable that a woman keeps watch at the door of the High Priest—and that at night! Reflections on this are given by Schl. and Lagr. Back of this is the fact that, according to the tradition, it was a παιδίσκη who occasioned the first denial (Mk. 14.66f. parr.). According to Black (192f) it is due to a misunderstanding of the Aramaic text.

[6] Whether the subj. of εἰσήγαγεν is the μαθητής or the θυρωρός is irrelevant. The narrative is very circumstantial. Why does the other disciple first go inside and then outside again, instead of taking Peter with him at the same time? According to Sp. v. 16 is an editorial verse, designed in order to insert the story of the denial, which originally was foreign to the context. One would agree with this if one could comprehend what significance the ἄλλος μαθ. had had in the source. (Did he perchance serve as an authority for the report? In that case he would originally have stood alone, and Peter's name already been inserted by way of correction! v. 15). In any case this editorial work would have been prior to the Evangelist and affected only his source. One could also suppose that v. 16 (from ἐξῆλθεν) was a gloss of the Evangelist. Then the scene would have to be imagined in this way, that the αὐλή was not, as in Mk. 14.54 parr., the court in which the servants stayed, but the hall in which the trial took place, while Peter stood outside, where vv. 17f. was played out. The Evangelist had misunderstood this, and naturally he had to bring Peter inside when he interpreted the αὐλή as the servant quarters. Concerning the palace of the High Priest see Dalman, O. und W. 347f.; αὐλή is often used for palace (even if not for the High Priest's) in Jos., see Schl. on Mt. 26.3.

[7] καὶ σύ = "you also" does not need to mean: like the ἄλλος μαθ., but it can simply mean: like so many; cp. Mk. 14.67 parr. That the denial occurs even as Peter enters, rests on the plausible consideration that each person is examined on entering. In comparison to the Synoptic account however the narrative is undoubtedly secondary, as the form of the θυρωρός shows; see n. 5.

immediate consequences, and Peter is able to mix with the servants who are warming themselves by a coal fire (**v. 18**)—the soldiers are not mentioned any more![1]

With **v. 19** the report broken off at vv. 13f., is taken up again. When the High Priest questions Jesus περὶ τῶν μαθητῶν αὐτοῦ καὶ περὶ τῆς διδαχῆς αὐτοῦ, manifestly a regular examination is intended, and it has to be imagined that the Sanhedrin is assembled. The examination begins with the attempt to gain a general understanding of the purposes of Jesus;[2] but in consequence of his reply nothing comes of it. He declines to answer the question[3] and alludes to the publicity of his work (**v. 20**).[4] His demand that those who heard him speak be questioned as witnesses (**v. 21**) affirms in truth: "You have known for a very long time what you are questioning about, or at least you could have known it!" From the outset, therefore, the reply of Jesus makes the examination appear as a farce.[5] If that also applies to the intention of the source employed by the Evangelist,[6] in his own mind something more should be gleaned from it. Clearly he himself is responsible for the statement: ἐγὼ παρρησίᾳ λελάληκα τῷ κόσμῳ and καὶ ἐν κρυπτῷ ἐλάλησα οὐδέν.[7] In them the thought of 7.4; 10.24 is expressed yet again: any desire that Jesus should make his claim credible by demonstrative publicity or unambiguous plain speech, so that the hearer is relieved of the necessity of decision, rests on unbelief. He has spoken publicly and openly, and it is only for unbelief that his word has been spoken ἐν κρυπτῷ.[8] In the present situation the statement of Jesus no longer signifies an indirect appeal for decision or for faith; rather it affirms, "You have already decided!" It is too late for discussion; the confrontation with Judaism is at an end.[9] In so far, however, as Judaism represents the "world"—and that this is the case is shown by the λελάληκα τῷ κόσμῳ (rather than ὑμῖν or the like)—it says: In the moment

[1] Ἀνθρακιά: a heap of (burning) coals; in the NT only here and 21.9.

[2] If Jesus is questioned concerning his disciples and concerning his teaching, it is difficult to think that two different points are stated. The answer of Jesus ignores the question about the disciples; it is included in that concerning his teaching.

[3] The two occurrences of ἐγώ are unstressed.

[4] In the gospel 6.27ff. is an example of the synagogue teaching, 5.14ff.; 7.14ff. 37ff.; 10.22 examples of teaching in the Temple. The παρρησία is expressly confirmed by the hearers in 7.26.

[5] The ἀρχιερεῖς show themselves 19.7 well instructed about the claim of Jesus.

[6] The motive is the same as Mk. 14.48 parr.

[7] Παρρησίᾳ in contrast to ἐν κρυπτῷ naturally means "publicly", see p. 291 n.1. There could be a reminiscence of Is. 45.19; 48.16, were God says: οὐκ ἐν κρυφῇ λελάληκα οὐδὲ ἐν τόπῳ γῆς σκοτεινῷ, or οὐκ ἀπ' ἀρχῆς ἐν κρυφῇ ἐλάλησα κτλ.

[8] See pp. 290f., 361f.

[9] Jesus' answer therefore has a different meaning from the related words of Socrates, who in Plat. Apol. 19d appeals to his many hearers and 33b contests that he ever taught secretly (ἰδίᾳ) anything different from what he had publicly.

when the world imagines that it can drag Jesus before its forum and make him answerable to it, then the verdict "Too late" must be pronounced. In this way Jesus refuses to give an account of himself to it. But does he not later give an account of himself to Pilate? Yes, and by this consideration the reader already has his attention drawn to perceive that Pilate by no means represents the world in the same way as the Jews and their ruler!

The peculiar variation of maltreatment[1] has been taken by the Evangelist from the source (**vv. 22f.**). A servant of the High Priest regards Jesus' answer as improper,[2] and he strikes him.[3] Jesus repulses him, and his words[4] make plain the absurdity of the blow; for how could the man prove to Jesus his wrong! The words are extraordinarily reminiscent of 8.46;[5] and inasmuch as this concluding picture of the servant uncouthly beating Jesus is set alongside the High Priest conducting his examination, it is evident how the world lowers itself when through its representatives it demands that Jesus appear before its tribunal that it may carry through an ἐλέγχειν περὶ ἁμαρτίας. For basically the ὑπηρέτης acted no differently from the ἀρχιερεύς; neither is capable of perceiving the ἐλέγχειν and μαρτυρεῖν that Jesus accomplishes (3.20; 7.7).

That, however, is the conclusion. The Evangelist has omitted[6] any further report that was in the source, and he gives no account of the proceedings before Caiaphas, to which he alludes in **v. 24**; and since the hearing before Annas came to no result, neither does he give any account of a decision of the Sanhedrin; nevertheless it is likely that we have to assume that a similar decision is reached as that in Mk. 14.64. The conclusion of the story of the denial now follows.[7] **V. 25** links on, after the interruption, to v. 18. Now it is the servants[8] who believe that they can recognise in Peter a disciple of Jesus. When he contests it,

---

[1] See p. 641.

[2] Cp. the prescript of the Book of the Covenant Ex. 22.28: ἄρχοντας τοῦ λαοῦ σου οὐ κακῶς ἐρεῖς. On the ταπεινότης which is seemly for one accused before the Sanhedrin, cp. Jos. Ant. 14, 172.

[3] Ῥάπισμα (cp. Mk. 14.65) originally = a stroke with a rod, later also a slap on the face; see Br. There is a Rabbinic tale of a high handed intervention by a court attendant during a trial in Str.-B. II 513.

[4] Κακῶς λέγειν = to speak in an unseemly fashion, to blaspheme, Ex. 22.28; 1 Macc. 7.42; also Greek. e.g. Aristoph. Av. 503.; cp. also esp. Eur. Hippol. 298f. On μαρτυρεῖν see p. 50 n.5,; it is here synonymous with ἐλέγχειν; cp. 3.20; 7.7 Δέρειν as Lk. 22.63.

[5] See pp. 322f.

[6] See p. 642.

[7] The Evangelist does not seem to reflect on whether vv.25–27 take place during the trial vv. 19–23 or during v. 24.

[8] Similarly as at the third denial in Mk. 14.70; Mt. 26.73, whereas the second denial in Mk. is occasioned by the same maid as the first, in Mt. it is through another maid, in Lk. through a male servant.

somebody renews the assertion who saw Peter in the garden at the arrest, and who is described as a relative of the slave whosc ear Peter cut off (v. 26).[1] Again Peter denies it—then the cockcrow sounds out (v. 27).[2] The prophecy of Jesus (13.38) is thus fulfilled. The Evangelist does not say so expressly, nor does he add any word at all, neither as to how Peter felt,[3] nor concerning his further behaviour. He has simply related the story of the denial in accordance with the tradition, and indeed he had to relate it because of 13.38. In itself it has no particular significance for him;[4] so far as he is concerned its meaning lies in its connection with the thought of 13.36–38.

c) *Jesus before Pilate:* 18.28–19.16a

18.28–19.16a is an organic unity. It comprises 1. the handing over of Jesus to Pilate 18.28–32; 2. the first hearing and its result 18.33–38; 3. the question: Jesus or Barrabas 18.39–40; 4. the flogging, mocking and display of Jesus 19.1–7; 5. the second hearing and its result 19.8–12a; 6. the condemnation of Jesus 19.12b–16a. The structure is determined by the change of the two scenes: "The Jews, because of the impending feast, outside before the praetorium, Jesus within, and Pilate hovering in the most literal sense between the agitation and hate of the world and the calm 'testimony of the truth'".[5] In this way the six scenes become organised into two groups: 18.18–19.7 and 19.8–16a, and each of them ends with Jesus being led out: ἰδοὺ ὁ ἄνθρωπος 19.5 and ἰδοὺ ὁ βασιλεὺς ὑμῶν 19.14, and the cry that follows σταύρωσον. In both groups the emphasis falls on the scene between Pilate and Jesus, and from it an extraordinary lustre each time shines out; by that splendour the Satanic powers, who are active in both concluding scenes, are unmasked and to each of the scenes a deeper content is given, inasmuch as in this light the one who is mocked is seen to be the mightier.

The account offers a remarkable interweaving of tradition and specifically Johannine narration. Since the Evangelist has employed and edited a source for both 18.1–11 and 18.12–27, the same is to be assumed for 18.28–19.16. The sections used in 18.1–27 doubtless were parts of a connected Passion story, which also lies at the base of 18.28–19.16a and beyond. One must conceive the account in the source as corresponding to the Synoptic Passion

---

[1] Schl. considers συγγενής signifies compatriot, because slaves were no Jews. But were the ὑπηρέται then slaves, and not rather men of the Levitical Temple police? See Jeremias, Jerusalem z.Z. Jesu II B 72f. The statement is peculiar for Jn's report; according to Mt. 26.73 Peter's pronunciation betrays him. Moreover according to Lk. 22.59 the third denial takes place perhaps an hour later.

[2] On the cockcrow see Gesch der Synopt. Trad. 290, 2 = Hist. of the Syn. Trad. 269, 2; Dibelius, Formgesch. 218.—From Trad. to Gospel 216; Jeremias op. cit. I 53f.

[3] Cp. Mk. 14.72 parr.: ἔκλαιεν or ἔκλαυσεν πικρῶς.

[4] Dibelius, Formgesch. 217 = Trad. to Gospel 215f.

[5] E. Lohmeyer, ThR, NF.9. (1937), 197.

story, for the Passion was recounted relatively early as a connected whole.[1] Several difficulties can be explained by this interweaving of source and editing, even if the separation of the elements cannot be carried through everywhere with the same assurance.

First of all it is plain that 18.33–37 and 19.7–11 are specifically Johannine compositions. They are interrupted by 18.39–19.6. But it would be a mistake to regard 18.39–19.6 as a subsequent completion of the narrative drawn from the Synoptics,[2] especially since the account is strongly distinguished from that of the Synoptics; rather it is the source itself that lies at the root of 18.39–19.6. Then has the Evangelist simply inserted 18.33–37 and 19.7–11 into this, so that after the abstraction of these sections the text of the source is thereby laid bare? No, rather a suppressed piece of the source's text has obviously been replaced by 18.33–37. That is indicated by ἐκραύγασαν οὖν πάλιν in 18.40; an account must have been given earlier of the κραυγάζειν of the Jews. In addition, the flogging and mocking of Jesus by the soldiers has its right place after the court procedure, where Mark and Matthew also put it.[3] Moreover the ridicule of the soldiers has a motive only if the title βασιλεύς had played a role in the prosecution and condemnation; that also must have been recounted in the source. 19.1–3 will have formed its conclusion. Everything that follows, i.e. 19.4–16a, is accordingly the composition of the Evangelist—at least in the form in which it now lies before us;[4] for without doubt motifs from the suppressed portion of the source have been used in 19.4–16a. Naturally the τότε οὖν παρέδωκεν κτλ 19.16a[5] will be one such; in the source it must have followed 18.40, in correspondence with the Synoptic report, in which Pilate's offer, accompanied by an appeal to the custom at the feast, is the last attempt to set Jesus free (Mk. 15.6–15 parr.). Further the narrative of 19.13–15 will have been in part derived from the source, as also the statement of place in 19.13 and the demand for crucifixion in 19.15—[6] only in the source that will have preceded 18.39. Moreover 19.6–16a shows the peculiarity of the Evangelist not only in the dialogue vv. 9–11, but also in the motif of vv. 12–15, i.e. in the appeal of the Jews to Caesar. The motif that Pilate is influenced by the threat of denunciation (v. 12), and that the Jews through their hatred sacrifice their messianism in alleged faithfulness to Caesar (v. 15c) is foreign to the Synoptic report; yet by contrast it forms an excellent contrapuntal motif to 18.33–37.

---

[1] Gesch. der synopt. Trad. 297f. = Hist. of the Syn. Trad. 275f.; Dibelius, Formgesch. 21f., 178ff. = From Trad. to Gospel, 22f., 178ff.; R. H. Lightfoot, History and Interpretation in the Gospels 1934, 126ff.

[2] So Schw., Wellh., Delafosse.

[3] Mk. 15.15b, 16ff.; Mt. 27.26b, 27ff. (the scene is lacking in Lk); cp. Jos. bell. 2, 308.

[4] A confirmation of this is the οἱ Ἰουδαῖοι of 19.12, 14, so characteristic of the Evangelist; cp. 18.31, 38 and see below. In the passion account of the Synoptics the subj. οἱ Ἰουδαῖοι never appears, only naturally ὁ βασιλεὺς τῶν Ἰουδ.

[5] More exactly stated: the sentence of the source must have consisted of 19.16a and 19.1; cp. Mk. 15.15b.

[6] Naturally it can very well be the case that the formulation of the demand for the crucifixion in 19.6 corresponds more exactly to the source; here it is not the Ἰουδαῖοι whom

But 18.28–32 also is not derived from the source as a whole. Apart from v. 32, which is a gloss of the ecclesiastical redactor, ἀπὸ καιαφᾶ in v. 28 is naturally inserted by the Evangelist.[1] Further if λάβετε αὐτὸν ὑμεῖς κτλ in 19.6 is due to the Evangelist, it could also go back to him in 18.31;[2] but with v. 31 we must also attribute v. 30 to him. Doubtless the source reported an accusation, such as is presupposed in Mk. 15.2 and is related in Lk. 23.2, namely that Jesus claimed to be βασιλεύς; the Evangelist took the motive for 18.33–37 from that account. The entire section 18.30–37 is thus derived from the Evangelist. V. 38b is taken from the source: ἐγὼ οὐδεμίαν ... αἰτίαν (cp. Lk. 23.4, 14); whether the same applies to v. 38a (... ἐξῆλθεν ...) depends on whether the source already contained the change of scenes, of which the Synoptic report is ignorant. Very probably this motif, that carries the structure of the entire narrative, comes from the Evangelist; in any event 18.33 and 19.4, 9 go back to him, and probably also 18.38a.[2] In that case it is also likely that the comment in v. 28b, αὐτοὶ κτλ, that motivates the change of scenes, is derived from the Evangelist, and therefore the statement of time also in 19.14.

Attention has been called to the parallelism in the narratives that tell of Jesus being brought out, 19.4f. and 19.13f., in order to explain 18.39–19.6 as a secondary insertion.[3] But we are not dealing with rival doublets here; rather a deliberate parallelism lies before us which the Evangelist has created. The scene in 19.4f.—coming after 19.2f.!—is naturally subordinated to the ἰδὲ ὁ βασιλεὺς ὑμῶν 19.14; but the Evangelist saves it up for the conclusion, in order to depict in 19.15 the abysmal humiliation of the Jews through the answer that they give.

Probably the source has also provided 18.28a (apart from ἀπὸ τοῦ Και.), 29, 38b, 39–40;[4] 19.1–3, and motifs in 19.13, 15, 16a. But the Evangelist is responsible for ἀπὸ τοῦ Και. 18.28, as also 18.28b, 30–38a; 19.4–16 (with use of the source-motifs referred to). A source narrative analogous to the Synoptic account therefore lies at the base of John's report; the Evangelist has cleverly set it forth and organised it through the repeated change of scenes. By means of the dialogue with Pilate he placed in the centre of the

---

we meet but the ἀρχιερεῖς and ὑπηρέται whom we would expect for the source. Similarly the formulation of Pilate's question 19.15: τὸν βασιλέα ὑμῶν σταυρώσω can be derived from the source; it has its parallel in the mocking θέλετε ἀπολύσω ὑμῖν τὸν βασιλέα τῶν 'Ιουδ. Mk.15.9.

[1] That again is confirmed through the οἱ 'Ιουδ.; see p. 649 n.4.

[2] Once more the 'Ιουδ. serves to confirm this. It is an ineptitude when Jesus is said 19.9 to be in the praetorium, without any explanation having been given in 19.5 that he was again brought into it. But I do not believe that this situation provides an occasion for critical analyses. Similarly the obvious fact is not stated that Pilate, according to 18.40, again entered the inner area of the praetorium, as is presupposed in the ἐξῆλθεν of 19.4. Still more careless is the narrative in 19.12, where it has to be explained that Pilate again comes before the praetorium and announces the result of the trial through his ἐγὼ οὐχ εὑρίσκω ἐν αὐτῷ αἰτίαν or the like.

[3] Wellh., Sp., also Hirsch, who ascribes 18.39f.; 19.4–6 to the editor, and inserts 19.1–3 into 19.13.

[4] It is perhaps a sign that 18.38b is derived from the source that only here in Jn (apart from 2 Jn. 12; 3. Jn. 10) βούλομαι is to be met; elsewhere it is always θέλω.

picture the traditional motif that Jesus was accused as an alleged βασιλεύς; in this way he has made plain the paradox of the royal claim of Jesus, and at the same time shown how the Jews by their accusation pass judgment upon themselves. The way is therefore prepared for 19.16b–22, where it is shown that in the crucifixion of Jesus the condemnation of Judaism is fulfilled.

1) *Jesus is handed over to Pilate:* 18.28–32

Jesus is led[1] from Caiaphas to the Praetorium, i.e. to the official residence of the procurator in Jerusalem.[2] It was early in the morning[3] (**v. 28**). If the ἦν δὲ νύξ of 13.30 is pondered, one could well suppose that the mention of the time could have a deeper meaning here also: the day of the victory of Jesus over the world is breaking.[4] The Jews refrain from entering the Praetorium so as not to defile themselves[5] and thereby be excluded from eating the Passover meal.[6] For the Evangelist without

---

[1] The Roman escort is not mentioned; the Evangelist naturally presupposes it. The source has the ἀρχιερεῖς in view and the ὑπηρέται named in vv. 3, 12, 18.

[2] For πραιτώριον as official residence of the governor see Arndt & Gingrich, and Dibelius, excursus on Phil. 1.13 in Hdb. zum NT. The procurator of Judaea customarily resided in Caesarea. It is contested as to where he lived in Jerusalem when he stayed there (at festival seasons). According to the usual view he stayed in Herod's palace (as to its position on the north west corner of the upper city see Dalman O. und W. 355ff.); so Schürer I 458; Kreyenbühl, ZNTW 3 (1902), 15ff., Dalman op. cit.; Wandel. ThStkr. Sonderheft 1922, 158f. In opposition to this C. Sachsse, ZNTW 19 (1919/20), 34ff. supports again the Antonia castle, lying at the north west corner of the outer court before the Temple.

[3] It is hardly likely that we have before us the technical use, according to which πρωΐ signifies the fourth watch of the night (Mk. 13.35) in accordance with Roman enumeration, and so the time 3–6 a.m.

G.504

[4] Schlier in R. Bultmann, H. Schlier, Christus des Gesetzes Ende, 1940, 29.

[5] Gentile houses were held to be unclean; see Schürer II 92; Bousset, Rel des. Judent. 93f.; Str.-B. II 838f.

[6] It is therefore the day of the 14th Nizan, on the evening of which the Passover meal is eaten (cp. 19.14, 37 and see p. 465 n.1). According to Str.-B. and Torrey the expression φαγεῖν τὸ πάσχα can also signify the participation in the festival sacrifice of the 15th Nizan (חֲגִיגָה), and in Torrey's view perhaps even the entire celebration of the festival week (Str.-B. II 837; Torrey, JBL 50 [1931], 239f.). But that is contested by Zeitlin, JBL 51 (1932), 270, with good reasons; and if Jn. 18.28 ought to be understood in this manner, the interpretation would have had to be ensured through the context, which is by no means the case; cp. Joachim Jeremias, Die Abendmahlsworte Jesu 1935, 8. = Eucharistic Words of Jesus, 20. At all events according to the representation of the Evangelist, the real Passover meal had not yet taken place. And indeed, if it were wished to assume that v. 28b came from the source, in face of the fact that τὸ πάσχα φαγεῖν Mk. 14.12, 14 parr.; Lk. 22.15 (as 2 Chron. 30.18; 2 Esr. 6.21) signifies "to eat the Passover lamb", there would yet be no grounds for interpreting the phrase in v. 28 in any other way, unless one wanted to read the Synoptic chronology into Jn (Zn., Torrey). If syr[s] in v. 28 reads "the unleavened (bread)" instead of "the Passover", perhaps it is of the opinion that the Passover lamb is already consumed; nevertheless this substitute can also be purely mechanical, since syr[s] everywhere in Jn puts "the unleavened (bread)" for τὸ πάσχα. Accordingly v. 28 is to be understood of the eating of the lamb, so Str.-B. II 837ff.; Dalman, Jesus-Jesch. 80ff.; B. Weiss, Ho., Htm., Br., Bd., Bl., Lagr.

doubt a bitter irony lies in that fact: while the Jews are leading to death the one whom God has sent, they meticulously hold fast to their ceremonial prescriptions.[1] In the context however the comment is intended to provide the basis for the structure of the report that follows, and so for the repeated change of scenes.[2] Whether Jesus was immediately led into the Praetorium[3] is irrelevant.

Now therefore the world's prosecution of Jesus gains publicity: he is brought before the forum of the state. Pilate, the procurator,[4] comes out and enquires after the accusation which the Jews have to bring against Jesus, whom he calls, as one still unknown to him, "this man" (**v. 29**). The Jewish authorities give no real answer to this, but in a brusque manner describe Jesus in quite general terms as an evildoer (**v. 30**).[5] Therein the embarrassment of the world is expressed. It has made its decision against the revelation and wants to be rid of the man who disturbs its peace. It cannot do it of itself; it cannot silence his word through its own word. And since the means at its disposal are ineffective against his superiority, it appeals for help to the authority of the state; the world acknowledges that the state is set over it, but misuses it for its own purposes, exactly as it misuses for its purposes its religious law.[6] That its nature is lying and murder[7] is plain. And since it pushes on to the state the responsibility of discovering the crime of the accused, it confesses in its embarrassment (characterised through the brusque form) that it cannot bring anything against Jesus that can bear the light of day. What it really wants it does not dare immediately to say, but it betrays itself at once.

Pilate dismisses the unreal accusation, and assigns the responsibility[8] to the Jews (**v. 31**). Inasmuch as they allude to the fact that they

---

[1] Bd.; cp. the way the Jewish legal procedure is subjected to irony in ch. 9.

[2] Under no circumstances therefore is the sentence of v. 28b to be viewed as a "casual remark" (Zn.), an "incidental comment" (Joach. Jeremias). Does the Evangelist, by his not letting the discussions between Pilate and Jesus take place outside, wish to make clear that the Synoptics or other reporters have not made known what to him is the most important thing? So Goguel, Introd. II 220; Bickermann op. cit. 222f.

[3] Schl. would conclude this from αὐτοί (= only they).

[4] That Pilate is not expressly introduced is no difficulty (Wellh.); Mk. 15.1 also does not introduce him. Pilate is known to all Christian readers, cp. I Tim. 6.13. As to the person of Pilate, who governed Judea 26–36 (37?) A.D., see Schürer I 487ff.; J. Jeremias, Jerusalem, z.Z. Jesu II B, 55, 8; G. Hölscher, SB. Heidelb. 1939/40, 3 (1940), 24f.

[5] According to Raderm. 66 κακὸν ποιῶν is "unusual" for κακῶς ποιῶν. Bl.-D. §353, 1 would read with 𝔎 pl. κακοποιός (א* κακὸν ποιήσας, C* pc κακοποιῶν). κακὸν ποιεῖν is perhaps a Semitism.

[6] See pp. 266f., 273, 310f.

[7] See pp. 320f.

[8] The words of Pilate have this meaning. Certainly in the Evangelist's mind play is also made through them on the impotence of the world; but that Pilate wanted to mock the Jews is hardly correct. It would not be suitable for this moment of the proceedings; it is

do not have the right to carry out a death sentence, they show what they want: the death of Jesus. That is what the world wants: with the help of the state to silence the revelation by force. Will Pilate yield? Will the power of the state allow itself to be misused?

V.32 is a comment of the ecclesiastical redactor, which harks back to 12.33.[1] It affirms that the illegality of the Jews is grounded in the divine teleology: according to his own word Jesus had to suffer death through the cross; therefore he could not be executed by the Jews, but only by the Romans.

2) *The First Examination and its Result:* 18.33–38

In order to examine Jesus without witnesses Pilate goes into the Praetorium[2] and has Jesus brought before him.[3] His question (**v. 33**), whether Jesus is the king of the Jews, is not motivated in the account (taken from the source) that has thus far preceded.[4] The Evangelist begins here with his own free composition; the catch-phrase—the question about the kingship of Jesus—had been given to him in the tradition (Mk. 15.2 parr.), and presumably in the text of the source which he replaces by vv. 33–37.[5] The significance of the question is determined by the fact that Pilate, i.e. the state, understands the concept of king only in the political sense. Pilate therefore proceeds now in an objective manner in so far as he, despite the mistrust of the accuser voiced in v. 31, investigates conscientiously whether there was occasion for proceedings by the state. Does Jesus claim a political status which the representative of the public authority could not recognise? The answer of Jesus (**v. 34**) makes him realise that there was no occasion at all for him to interpose against Jesus;[6] and Pilate must admit (**v. 35**) that he had let himself be pressed by the Jews into the position of the judge.

After this has been established Jesus can answer the question of Pilate, which the latter had repeated in a general manner by his τί

---

otherwise with 19.6. On the question as to the historical possibility, see p. 637 n.1. The αὐτόν after κρίνατε is lacking in ℵ* W 565 al c.

[1] See p. 640 on v. 9. Dodd (433ff.) wishes to understand v. 32 as especially characteristic for the Evangelist.

[2] Πάλιν does not say "for the second time", but Pilate goes "again" inside, since he had come out v. 29.

[3] 'Εφώνησεν naturally has this meaning. There is therefore no offence here (Wellh., Sp.); for this purpose it is wholly irrelevant whether Jesus is already within or not; see above on v. 28.

[4] On the form of the question cp. Epikt. diss. III 22, 91: σὺ εἶ ὁ Διογένης; (Br). But σύ is hardly emphasised; the stress lies, in correspondence with the investigation, on βασ. τ. 'Ιουδ.

[5] See p. 649.

[6] ('Αφ') ἑαυτοῦ = σεαυτοῦ (𝔓N); Hellenistic, see Bl.-D. §64, 1; Raderm. 73, 77.

ἐποίησας (v. 36). Indirectly the answer is Yes; but Jesus does not speak directly about himself, rather he speaks about his βασιλεία:[1] it is not "of this world," i.e. it does not have its origin in this world, and therefore it is not of this world's kind;[2] it is—in the Johannine sense—an eschatological phenomenon.[3] The proof for this is simple: if the kingdom of Jesus were like the ruling power of this world, and if therefore it had a political character, Jesus would have troops at his disposal, which would not abandon him without resistance to the hand of Pilate.[4]

The reader knows that if the βασιλεία of Jesus is not "of this world," and is not "from here,"[5] it is ἄνωθεν, and therefore superior to all worldly dominion (cp. 3.31). He knows also the peculiar claim which this βασιλεία makes on man. But at first only the negative aspect is stated; and the further question of Pilate, "*So you are nevertheless a king?*" (v. 37) leads to the positive aspect. Pilate questions further, because Jesus indeed has indirectly affirmed that he is a king; and now Jesus affirms it directly: Yes, he is a king![6] But of what sort is his kingdom? Some kind of claim to sovereignty must be his, otherwise his statement would have lost all meaning! "*For this reason I have been*

---

[1] See p. 135 n.2. On the style of the answer (the second clause takes up again the second half of the first) see E. Schweizer, Ego Eimi 45, 97.

[2] On εἶναι ἐκ see p. 135 n.4. On ὁ κόσμος οὗτος see p. 340 n.1. It does not mean: ἐν τ. κόσμῳ, as Acta Pil. B c. 3 p. 294 Tischend. read; concerning this and concerning Augustine's repudiation of it, see Schlier, Christus des Gesetzes Ende 34f.

[3] According to Hegesippus the relatives of Jesus defend themselves before Domitian along the lines of the naive Jewish-Christian eschatology, Eus. H. E. III 20, 4: ἐρωτηθέντας δὲ περὶ τοῦ Χριστοῦ καὶ τῆς βασιλείας αὐτοῦ ὁποία τις εἴη καὶ ποῖ καὶ πότε φανησομένη, λόγον δοῦναι ὡς οὐ κοσμικὴ μὲν οὐδ' ἐπίγειος, οὐράνιος δὲ καὶ ἀγγελικὴ τυγχάνοι, ἐπὶ συντελείᾳ τοῦ αἰῶνος γενησομένη, ὁπηνίκα ἐλθὼν ἐν δόξῃ κρινεῖ ζῶντας καὶ νεκροὺς καὶ ἀποδώσει ἑκάστῳ κατὰ τὰ ἐπιτηδεύματα αὐτοῦ. O Michel, Das Zeugnis des NT von der Gemeinde 1941, 68, n. 55 wishes to understand v. 36 in the light of Dan. 7.14; very questionable. Dodd (229f.) alludes to Philo's spiritualising interpretation of the kingship as a parallel to Jn. 18.36f.

[4] The position of ἄν oscillates; it is also lacking in several witnesses, see Bl.-D §360, 2. It makes no difference whether one translates, "they would fight" or "they would have fought" (Bl.-D 360, 3). On the ἵνα clause see Bl.-D §361. Discussion on how far Jesus can describe his disciples as ὑπηρέται settle themselves when it is realised that this is not the case at all. The meaning is simply: if I were a worldly king I would have ὑπηρέται who would fight for me. On ἀμύνεσθαι = fight, see Br. ad loc. and lexicon (Arndt & Gingrich).

[5] 'Εντεῦθεν appears here as equivalent to ἐκ τοῦ κόσμου τούτου. "The opposition between 'here' and 'there' is parallel with the opposition between 'above' and 'below'; the former however is more seldom than the latter" (Schl.).

[6] Σὺ λέγεις = "Yes", as Mk. 15.2 parr. The Rabbinic example given by Schl. and Str.-B. I 990 on Mt. 26.25, and the comparison of Mt. 26.64 with Mk. 14.62, show that the σύ does not need to be stressed, as if the sense were: "*You* say that", and the responsibility for the assertion were pushed on to the questioner (contrary to Bl.-D §441 3). Apart from v. 36, where the question is indeed factually affirmed, the continuation shows that in Jn. 18.37 σὺ λέγεις = "Yes", for the continuation becomes senseless if one attempts to understand it otherwise. It is self evident that the ὅτι is recitative and not causal. After εἰμι ℵ al complete with an ἐγώ.

born, and for this I have come into the world, that I should bear witness for the truth."[1]

That this concerns a claim which goes forth to the world from beyond it is signified by γεγέννημαι καὶ . . . ἐλήλυθα εἰς τὸν κόσμον, whereby γεγέννημαι to a certain extent is orientated to the viewpoint of Pilate, for whom Jesus is first and foremost a man and nothing more: he, this man, has come for this reason . . . . But because in this man one is confronted with a claim other than human, the mythological ἐλήλυθα εἰς τὸν κόσμον is paradoxically bound up with γεγ.: the origin—and therefore the being—of this man is not from this world, but he has "come"[2] into this world. And in truth he has come in order to "bear witness" for the "truth," i.e. in order to make God's reality[3] effective over against the world[4] in the great trial between God and the world.[5] He indeed has come into the world for judgment (9.39; 3.19), and his witness is at the same time an accusation against the world (7.7). It is in this "witness" that he lays his claim to sovereignty;[6] he himself is the ἀλήθεια to which he bears testimony (14.6), and he testifies on behalf of himself (8.14, 18). He is the judge, who decides over life and death (5.19ff.). So he stands now also before Pilate, who according to the world's standard is *his* judge. "Everyone who is of the truth hears my voice."[7]

With this saying a peculiar turn takes place: the question about the *law* becomes a question about *faith*. For without doubt Pilate himself is put on the spot through this statement; he is asked whether he is willing to listen to the voice of the Revealer, and he must show whether he "is of the truth." In this case he would know what the βασιλεία of Jesus is all about; he would recognise him as the βασιλεύς. The same possibility exists therefore for the state also, or more exactly, for the person who represents the state. That would mean, however, that the possibility was given for action in the service of the state to be

---

[1] Naturally it is not the ἐγώ, occurring at once, that is stressed, but the doubly occurring εἰς τοῦτο. Is the sentence derived from the revelatory discourses?

[2] On ἔρχεσθαι εἰς τὸν κόσμον see p. 298 n.1. Naturally this is not to be linked up with the expression that occurs in 1.9. (See p. 52 n.2).

[3] See pp. 74 n.2; 321; 434ff.

[4] See pp. 50 n.5; 144; 160ff.; 262ff.; 278ff.

[5] See pp. 85f., 296, etc.

[6] The Stoic expression, the βασιλεία of the wise, which Philo also knows (Br. ad loc.; J. Weiss on 1 Cor. 4.8 in Meyer's Kommentar) is therefore no parallel; similarly the usage of mysticism, (E. Underhill, Mysticism, 1918, 286).

[7] Εἶναι ἐκ τ. ἀληθ. (see pp. 135 n.4; 138 n.1) is synonymous with εἶναι ἐκ τοῦ θεοῦ, ἐκ τῶν ἄνω see p. 162 n.3; On ἀκούειν of the φωνή see 5.25 and p. 259 n.2; 8.47 is especially parallel. Concerning εἶναι ἐκ τ. ἀληθ. see also Dodd 176. The expression "sons of thy truth" (בני אמתכה or בני אמתך) occurs in the Qumran book of psalms (1 QH) P1.41, 29f.; 45.11.

performed in public for the revelation, i.e. in recognition of it, since that service is in fact carried out by people.

There seems however to be yet a third possibility, besides refusal and recognition, and Pilate clearly wishes to adopt it with his counter question: "What is truth?",[1] i.e. he takes the point of view that the state is not interested in the question about the ἀλήθεια—about the reality of God, or as perhaps it ought to be expressed in Pilate's way of thinking—about reality in the radical sense.[2] He remains on the outside. For the person who represents this standpoint that means that he shuts the door on the claim of the revelation, and in so doing he shows that he is not of the truth—he is of the lie.

But the situation of Pilate is different from that of the Jews who represent the world, whose father is the devil, and who therefore are bent on murder and lying (8.44). As the representative of the state Pilate does not belong to them, as is immediately shown (v. 38): he declares to the Jews that he can establish no misdeed of Jesus that could serve as a cause for his condemnation. In fact therefore this possibility arises: the state is able to adopt the point of view that the question about ἀλήθεια has nothing to do with it. As v. 36 established, the state as state is not affected by the claim of Jesus to sovereignty, and this claim can appear to it as fantastic and vain. Of course the consequence must then be that Pilate lets Jesus go free,[3] and that the state freely permits the proclamation of the word. As the state it cannot indeed do

---

[1] The question is rhetorical; it expects no answer but breaks off the conversation; Pilate goes outside. If an answer were expected, and if silence on the part of Jesus were the refusal of such, then this silence would have had to be expressly mentioned, as in 19.9.

[2] The question should not be psychologically interpreted (Zn: "Mockingly rejected"; W. Schmid-O. Stählin, Gesch. d. griech. Lit. III 1, 148: a "cynical question"); Dibelius rightly objects to its interpretation as a question of philosophical scepticism, Rev. H. Ph. rel. 1933, 42; for Jn such scepticism is not open to discussion. The question rather has to be understood in the light of the subject discussed in vv. 33–37; it is thus the expression of the neutrality of the State, which as such is not interested in the question that moves man as to the determining reality of his life. O. Spengler (Untergang des Abendlandes II 1922, 262f. = The Decline of the West II 216f.) misses the meaning when he interprets the encounter between Pilate and Jesus as the opposition of the world of "facts" and the world of "truths". For if the world of Pilate is rightly understood as the world of "facts"—and so in Spengler's sense as that also of reality—the world of Jesus nevertheless is not rightly understood as that of "truths" in Spengler's sense, namely the ideal world. Rather one reality emerges and confronts the other, and of course the reality of the "facts" is held to be only seeming reality. Cp. Hans von Soden, Was ist die Wahrheit? (Marb. Akad. Reden 46) 1927, 5f., 9f.) That Pilate's question is a *refusal* of the truth, and therefore that here "the tolerant and neutral political power . . . by virtue of the truth which Jesus attested, had to expose its spiritual foundation and give expression to its hidden denial of the truth" (Schlier op. cit. 38) seems to me to be incorrect. The truth is not rejected by the State as such, but by its representative.

[3] Cp. the continuation of the citation on p. 654 n.3 (Eus. H. E. III 20, 5): ἐφ' οἷς μηδὲν αὐτῶν κατεγνωκότα τὸν Δομετιανόν, ἀλλὰ καὶ ὡς εὐτελῶν καταφρονήσαντα, ἐλευθέρους μὲν αὐτοὺς ἀνεῖναι, καταπαῦσαι δὲ διὰ προστάγματος τὸν κατὰ τῆς ἐκκλησίας διωγμόν.

more, even when its representatives recognise the claim of the revelation. For if it wanted to force the world by exercise of powers belonging to the state to recognise the βασιλεία of Jesus, then certainly it would have misunderstood and denied it, and made it into a worldly βασιλεία.

Pilate rejected the possibility of recognition and chose the possibility of neutrality. Will he hold fast to it? Can he? For so much is clear: if the claim of Jesus does not concern the state as such, if his βασιλεία does not enter into rivalry with political organisations of this world, his claim nevertheless does not permit the world to rest in peace, for it concerns every man, and so it stirs up the sphere within which the state establishes its order. For the βασιλεία is not an isolated sphere of pure inwardness over against the world, it is not a private area for the cultivation of religious needs, which could not come into conflict with the world. The word of Jesus unmasks the world as a world of sin, and it challenges it. In order to defend itself against the word it flees to the state, and demands that the latter put itself at its disposal. But then the state is torn out of its neutrality precisely in so far as its firm hold on to neutrality signifies a decision against the world. And now the question arises: will it have the strength for that, if its representative refuses to recognise the claim of the revelation? For its power in fact rests on the strength of its representative.

3) *Jesus or Barrabas?* 18.39–40

That Pilate does not have the strength to maintain the standpoint which he had taken is shown immediately. In dependence on his source, which runs parallel to the Synoptic tradition,[1] the Evangelist relates that Pilate resorts to the custom of releasing a prisoner to the Jews at the Passover feast[2] and proposes that he should set Jesus free (**v. 39**).[3] When he mockingly calls him the "king of the Jews," manifestly that is to recognise the unreality of his kingship. His hope, however, that the Jews will accept his proposition and that he will then be quit of the affair is disappointed; the Jews ask[4] that instead of this man Barrabas be set free (**v. 40**). Since Barrabas is characterised as a ληστής,[5] the irony of the situation is plain: the lie of the Jews is revealed; they who have

---

[1] Mk. 15. 6–15a parr.

[2] The custom is not historically attested; see Br. ad loc.; Gesch. der synopt. Trad, 293, 3 = Hist. of the Syn. Trad. 272, 2; Klostermann on Mk. 15.6 (Hdb. z. NT); Lohmeyer on Mk. 15.6ff. (Meyer's Kommentar).

[3] On βούλεσθε . . . ἀπολύσω see Bl. D. §366, 3; Raderm 222.

[4] On the unmotived πάλιν see p. 649. Windisch (Joh. und die Synopt. 84) would relate it to vv. 29–32. G K 33 al it correct it to πάντες, ℜ pm vg read πάλιν πάντες.

[5] According to Mk. 15.7; Lk. 23.19 Barrabas was a political criminal, just as Jos. is accustomed to call messianic revolutionaries (the Zealots)λησταί; see ThWB IV 263, 20ff.

denounced Jesus as an alleged political criminal ask for the release of a real political evil-doer. And Pilate is caught; if he does not remain strong he must comply. Of course the Evangelist is not interested in whether Pilate really does let Barrabas go free,[1] but he only shows how Pilate is led further down the slippery slope.

For in making his proposal he committed himself to that slippery slope. He did not draw the only possible consequence of his declaration in v. 38; he did not dare to make a decision, which in fact had to be a decision against the world; rather he attempted to push the decision on to the Jews. He was afraid of the world, and before it he gave up the authority of the state. By this token he was to choose a fourth possibility, to put the power of the state at the disposal of the world.

4) *The Flogging, Mocking and Presentation of Jesus:* 19.1–7

Yet once more Pilate makes the attempt to save himself from the necessity of a decision against the world by trying to change the minds of the Jews. If in 18.39 he went further than he could be responsible for as representative of the state, so now with a vengeance, inasmuch as he gives up Jesus, of whose innocence he is convinced, to flogging and to insult. His intention is to act in a politically clever manner; he yields part way to the desire of the world, in the hope that thereby it will be satisfied.

Following his source the Evangelist relates that Pilate had Jesus whipped (**v. 1**).[2] whereupon the soldiers then subjected him to their crude ridicule, in that they made sport of his kingship and maltreated him (**vv. 2f.**).[3] That happens with the consent of Pilate, or at least he makes it serve his purpose (**v. 4**). Going out to the Jews,[4] he announces

---

[1] So Mk. 15.15. parr.

[2] According to Mk. 15.15 Jesus is flogged immediately before the crucifixion, as corresponded to Roman custom (see Klostermann on Mk. 15.15, and see p. 649). As to the right of Pilate to have Jesus whipped before the judgment ("de plano"), see Bickermann op. cit. 225. According to Lk. 23.16, 22 Pilate had the intention of chastising Jesus and then letting him go free.

[3] Crowning with thorns and clothing with the red mantle is recorded in reverse order Mk. 15.17, Mt. 27.28f.; πλέξαντες κτλ. is almost word for word as Mt, while πορφυροῦν reminds us of Mk; the κάλαμος is lacking in Mt; the mocking obeisance as in Mk and Mt (καὶ ἤρχοντο πρὸς ἀυτόν is lacking in 𝔎 pm). As to the possible soldiers' custom that lies at the back of the mockery scene, see Gesch. der synopt. Trad. 294, 1 = Hist. of the Syn. Trad. 272, 3; Klostermann and Lohmeyer on Mk. 15.16–20. The crown of thorns is perhaps a caricature of the halo of Hellenistic rulers; so H. St. J. Hart, JThSt. 1952, 66–75. The red mantle is typical for the victor as the white (Lk. 23.11) for the king; see H. Almquist, Plutarch u. das NT, 76.

[4] It is presupposed that in the meantime (since 18.40) he had again entered the Praetorium.

to them the presentation of Jesus.[1] The form of this beaten and mocked man should demonstrate to the Jews *ad oculos* that there was no evil to be found in Jesus. Clearly the purpose in this is to make the person of Jesus appear to the Jews as ridiculous and harmless, so that they should drop their accusation.[2] Hence Jesus has to step forth (v. 5) as the caricature of a king,[3] and Pilate presents him with the words: ἰδοὺ ὁ ἄνθρωπος,[4] That is the man! Look at the pitiful figure! But to the mind of the Evangelist the entire paradox of the claim of Jesus is in this way fashioned into a tremendous picture. In very truth, such a man it is who asserts that he is the king of truth! The declaration ὁ λόγος σὰρξ ἐγένετο has become visible in its extremest consequence.[5]

Pilate's expedient does not have the intended result; instead of the anticipated laughter the cry rings out, "Crucify! Crucify!" (v. 6).[6] If the authority of the state yielded once to the world, and thereby showed its weakness, the world will now go all the further in its demands. Pilate admittedly now does make an attempt to be strong, and to bring the matter to an end. His λάβετε αὐτόν κτλ.[7] cannot have the same meaning as 18.31; for since it was there established that the Jews do not have the *ius gladii*, this can signify only the refusal of the Jewish desire: I do not give my consent to crucify Jesus;[8] if you want his crucifixion, then you must undertake it yourselves! That is, Pilate refuses the demand of the Jews with wrathful irony.[9] But since he has let himself be drawn at all into a discussion, it is too late; the Jews remain obdurate; they have two more trump cards to play.

---

[1] Verses 1–3 are closely bound up with vv. 4–6 through v. 4, and one ought not to make two scenes out of them in order to find seven scenes in 18.28–19.16 (E. Lohmeyer, ZNTW 27 [1928], 18f.; to the contrary W. Bauer ThR, NF.1 [1919], 143f.).

[2] There is not a hint that Pilate wishes to awake the sympathy of the Jews, and it is little credible; rightly Schl.: "A Christ who defencelessly suffers the violent scorn of the soldiers' antisemitism is harmless, and therefore innocent"; so also Zn., Lagr. Nevertheless it is highly improbable that Pilate wanted to appeal to the φιλανθρωπία of the Jews (contrary to Schl.). According to Hosk. Pilate only continues the soldiers' mockery. There is no occasion to assume a difference here between the source and the Evangelist.

[3] Φορεῖν of the wearing of a garment as Mt. 11.8; Jas. 2.3, of the wearing of crowns and wreaths Ecclus. 11.5; 20.4, corresponds to Greek usage.

[4] Ἰδού as ἰδέ v. 14; see p. 95 n.2. A linguistic parallel is offered by Is. 40.9, but it is not credible that the Evangelist wanted to make play on it. Dodd (437) thinks that in ὁ ἄνθρωπος an echo of ὁ υἱὸς τ. ἀνθρώπου should be heard, and that therefore a deep irony is contained in it.

[5] See p. 62.

[6] Σταύρωσον as Mk. 15.13f. (for the doubling cp. Lk. 23.21 and see Bl.-D §493, 1; Raderm. 70). The subject of the cry is not the ὄχλος as in the Synoptics, but the ἀρχιερεῖς (plural, as 7.32 etc., see p. 306 n.5) and their ὑπηρέται, as corresponds to the source.

[7] The correspondence of the two clauses shows that ὑμεῖς and ἐγώ are emphasised.

[8] Also the crucifixion as a punishment inflicted by the Jewish authorities does not come into question. That the λάβετε κτλ. is not seriously meant is seen in the fact that the Jews do not take it seriously, and do not welcome the idea.

[9] Rightly Lagr.; Schlier (op. cit. 42) appears to me to interpret falsely here.

They justify their request[1] by appeal to their law that prescribes the sentence of death for a blasphemer against God.[2] Jesus has violated this law with his assertion that he was God's Son (v. 7).[3] Naturally in so speaking they are not wanting to take Pilate's word (v. 6) seriously and on their side carry out the death sentence (in accordance with Lev. 24.16 it had to be by stoning); rather with these words, which incidentally betray the real ground of their hatred, they wish to force Pilate to pronounce sentence of judgment in that they adduce a reason for their demand that must be plausible to him.[4] In point of fact their words have the opposite effect at first, and vv. 8–12 introduce a retarding motif. Why? Without doubt because the Evangelist desires to heighten the enormity of the condemnation of Jesus; he shows how the judge's anxiety before the world engulfs even the anxiety before the numinous that Pilate meets in Jesus, and how anxiety before the world tears asunder not alone the requirements of the law but also those of religion.

But one further point calls for consideration. The subject of the conversation of Jesus with Pilate—parallel to that of 18.33–37—is the relation of the power of the state and that of God. It should become clear that the authority of the state as established by God stands over against the world, that it does not belong to the world, and therefore it can and ought to act independently of the world, and that the carrying out of the state's activity stands before the either-or: God or the world? The responsible representative of the state can as well be open for God as for the world. So far as the state is concerned openness for God would simply mean straightforward objectivity in the knowledge of its responsibility for the right. Pilate has chosen the standpoint of neutrality in respect to the claim of Jesus, and from the state's point of view he could do so, inasmuch as a recognition of the revelation cannot be demanded from the state as such.[5] His neutrality would have been in the right if it had represented nothing more than the impersonal objectivity of his office. It has already been seen that this objectivity would mean decision against the world; and now it is indicated that precisely this objectivity demands openness for God. An unchristian

---

[1] It is impermissible to interpret that they enter into a state of embarrassment, and that now at last they have to admit why they want Jesus' death; for the continuation does not correspond to that. If it were meant, then Pilate would have had to say: λάβετε αὐτόν and to make it clear that he was uninterested in the affair.

[2] See p. 328 n.3.

[3] Cp. 5.18; 10.33 and see p. 244 n.6. It is clear that υἱὸς θεοῦ is not meant in the specifically messianic sense (= king), but as always with Jn in a metaphysical sense; see p. 93 n.1.

[4] One could perhaps interpret their words here from the historical consideration that in accordance with Roman principle, the governor should indulge the religious wishes of the populace.

[5] See p. 657.

state is possible on principle, but not an atheistic state. The question, "Will Pilate have strength for decision against the world, if he refuses recognition to the Revealer?"[1] finds repetition therefore in the form, "Will Pilate be open for the claim of God given through his office, if he personally refuses the claim of Jesus?"

5) *The Second Examination and its Result:* 19.8–12a

The words of the Jews have a different effect on Pilate than was expected (**v. 8**). If earlier on he was afraid of the Jews—i.e. of the world, now he really does experience anxiety,[2] for he hears that Jesus claims to be a son of God, and therefore (since he can understand it only in this way) a superhuman being who awakens numinous fear, and on whom to lay violent hands[3] as a θεομάχος would be crazy. After all, who can know in what form the deity may meet him?[4] So for Pilate Jesus becomes sinister. He goes with him into the Praetorium,[5] and he asks him openly, πόθεν εἶ σύ; Naturally the question has the meaning, Have you sprung from man or from a god? Are you a man or a divine being?[6]

Jesus can as little give a direct answer to that as he could to the question of the Jews, 10.24. Indeed Pilate could do no other than misunderstand him. The knowledge as to who he is can emerge only through the offence, it cannot be imparted through mere statement.[7] So Jesus remains silent.[8]

---

[1] See p. 657.

[2] Μᾶλλον has this meaning; admittedly there was no express mention of the φοβεῖσθαι of Pilate earlier; but his compliant behaviour manifested it sufficiently.

[3] See ThWB IV 534, 23ff. and the literature there mentioned.

[4] G. P. Wetter, Der Sohn Gottes 90f., rightly compares two scenes from Philostr. Vit. Apoll. There in IV 44 Apollonius is accused before the tribunal in Rome. "After a miracle has taken place the governor Tigellinus takes him aside, because he is afraid that he is dealing with a demon. And now he asks him who he is. Apollonius immediately names his father and his home town. He denies that he is a μάντις, that he is 'something great', and yet God is with him. The chapter concludes impressively with these words: ἔδοξε τῷ Τιγελλίνῳ ταῦτα δαίμονιά τ' εἶναι καὶ πρόσω ἀνθρώπου, καὶ ὥσπερ θεομαχεῖν φυλαττόμενος, χώρει, ἔφη, οἷ βούλει; σὺ γὰρ κρείττων ἢ ὑπ' ἐμοῦ ἄρχεσθαι. The scene in I 21 is similarly delineated: here also the governor asks who he is; he answers by explaining that the whole world belongs to him. The former then becomes angry and threatens Ap. but he answers calmly. The governor is now astounded and asks: "By the gods, who are you?" Ap. then gives the answer. And now the governor remembers him, and that he is a θεῖος ἄνθρωπος.

[5] Jesus is again inside, without it having been explained that he has been taken within; see p. 650 n.2.

[6] It is on the lips of Gentiles that the theme of the πόθεν occurs, which in some form or another is called forth ever and again by the appearance and claim of Jesus; pictorially it is already in 2.9; then 7.27f.; 8.14; 9.29f.

[7] See p. 361f. "So he must remain in the ambiguity of him, whose glory is manifest only to the believer" (Schlier op. cit. 45).

[8] It is the Johannine adaptation of the traditional motif of silence (Mk. 15.4f.;

Pilate attempts to make him speak (**v. 10**) by drawing attention to the fact that his life is in his hands.[1] But the reply of Jesus shows his superiority over any consideration as to what may become of him through Pilate's judgment, and his answer bids Pilate rather to ponder his own situation and its responsibility: "You would have had no power over me if it had not been given to you from above" (**v. 11**).[2] Pilate had directed Jesus to the power that he possessed as an official of the state. The reply of Jesus corrects this conception: the power and authorisation by virtue of which Jesus is now given into Pilate's hand does not proceed from the official position he enjoyed—or in so far as it actually does so, it has a deeper reason. Pilate would be unable to play his role as representative of the state "if it were not given him from above,"[3] i.e. the fact that Jesus has been given into his hands has been determined by God.[4] Pilate is the instrument through which the decree of God is put into effect. The decision of Pilate will in fact lead Jesus, in obedience to the ἐντολή of the Father (10.18; 14.31), to drink the cup which the Father gave him.

Because that is so the consequence follows: "Therefore he who delivered me to you has greater sin."[5] That Jesus is standing before Pilate as an accused man does not depend on Pilate's initiative. The initiative lies on the side of the Jews, who delivered Jesus to him in their hatred.[6]

Mt. 27.14). A certain analogy to this is recorded in Jos. bell. 6, 305; Jesus the son of Ananias, who before the fall of Jerusalem filled the city with his cries of woe, is tried by the procurator Albinos and asked, τίς εἴη καὶ πόθεν, but he answers with not a word. A more remote analogy is the (by all means only preliminary) silence of Aeschylus in the dispute with Aristoph. Ran. 832, 1020. On the legend of the silence of Socrates before the court, see Wilh. Schmid, Geschichte der griech. Literatur III 1 (1940), 243, 5.

[1] It is to be observed that ἐξουσία means not simply being able, or having the power to do something, but legitimated power, authority, right; see p. 57 n.5. The position of the word varies in the mss. Cp. Jos. bell. II 117: after the deposition of Archelaus, Pomponius is named as procurator: μέχρι τοῦ κτείνειν λαβὼν παρὰ Καίσαρος ἐξουσίαν.

[2] Instead of εἶχες (without ἄν, see Bl.-D. §360, 1; Raderm. 159) h 565 al read ἔχεις.

[3] On ἄνωθεν see p. 161 n.2.

[4] Cp. 3.27; 6.65. The statement does not mean, as was said here in the first edition, that the ἐξουσία to which Pilate makes appeal, the authority of the State, is given by God. Then it would have to read δεδομένη. Rightly Zn., Lagr. Hosk. and cp. especially v. Campenhausen, ThLZ 73 (1948), 387–391.

[5] Wendt I 153f., II 62 takes offence at the relationship of v. 11b. to v. 11a and regards 11.b. as a gloss; he maintains that in it v. 11a is falsely understood, so that the ἐξουσία which Pilate has over Jesus was given to him by the Jews, and thus ἄνωθεν was understood in a temporal sense (see p. 135 n.1). Wellh. also takes offence unnecessarily at v. 11b, and Delafosse thinks that in order to bring about a connection between v. 11a and 11b. ἄνωθεν must be understood: from the devil! Bd., following Wetstein, would interpret: "Therefore Caiaphas has greater sin (not: than he, but:) than he would have if he had received responsibility alone; but he has also made use of the God-given authority which is yours".

[6] The παραδιδούς is naturally neither Judas nor Caiaphas, but it is the Jews generally (see 18.30); the (general) singular is occasioned by the quasi proverbial formulation. I

But is Pilate thereby absolved from guilt? On the contrary when he, through anxiety over his position (**v. 12**), pronounces the death sentence on Jesus, he also "has sin." The fact that he acts as the instrument of God in no way excuses him, even as conversely the Jews also, although they act on their own initiative, are the unwitting instruments not alone of the devil but also of God, and they too are compelled to subserve the divine decree; for the same thing applies to them also, that they cannot do anything that is not "given from above" (cp. 3.27). Nevertheless Pilate is confronted with the question whether he will act objectively, as he was under obligation to do precisely in the light of the ἐξουσία, as he understood it, i.e. in the sense of the authority of the state, or whether he will betray the power of the state by putting it at the disposal of the world for its own ends. That he forthwith decides in favour of the second alternative constitutes his sin, less though it be in comparison with that of the Jews.

Pilate had shown through his question about the πόθεν that he knows what ἄνωθεν signifies; he understands the answer of Jesus, in so far as he sees that he stands under a destiny. His anxiety grows as he is confronted with the enigmatic figure of Jesus and the aura of the uncanny that surrounds him; accordingly he would like to set Jesus free (**v. 12a**).[1] But, as ἐζήτει already indicates, his position is compromised. Fear of the world and fear of the mysterious come into conflict. Who will come off victor?

6) *The Condemnation of Jesus:* 19.12b–16a

When the Jews perceive Pilate's intention,[2] they play their last trump and threaten him with denunciation before Caesar (**v. 12b**).[3] That turns the scale; the fear of the world gains the victory. Admittedly,

---

cannot really agree with v. Campenh. (see p. 662 n.4) that for Jn the State, represented by Pilate, as such belongs to the "world". The struggle between Pilate and the Jews on the contrary shows that the State has its own sphere and possibility of freedom over against the world. To this there is a correspondence in the way Jesus refuses information before the representation of the κόσμος (18.20f.; see p. 646), whereas he gives answer to Pilate. If Pilate condemns Jesus, he does so in defiance of his own conviction (18.38, see p. 656f.), and if he finally yields to the threatening of the Jews, he does not do it, as v. Campenh. thinks, out of political but out of egoistical interests: he does not want to lose his position.

[1] 'Εκ τούτου not "from now on" (which would contradict 18.38; 19.6) but "therefore".

[2] Concerning the carelessness of the narrative, see p. 650 n.2.

[3] Whether φίλος τοῦ Καίσαρος has reference to the official title (Br. ad loc. and Deissmann, L.v.0. 324 = Light from the Ancient East 383, 3) can remain doubtful; E. Bammel, with reasons worth weighing, champions the view that it has, ThLZ 77 (1952), 205–210. 'Αντιλέγειν means not only "contradict", but also "resist" (Tit. 2.9; Rom. 10.21 after Is. 65.2), which is good Greek, see Br. ad. loc. In the mss. ἐκραύγασαν and (less good) ἐκραύγαζον become interchanged.

Pilate makes yet one more attempt, or rather repeats the earlier one.[1] He has Jesus brought outside and take his place on the judgment seat (**v. 13**),[2] from which the sentence officially had to be pronounced.[3] Because of the significance of this moment the name of the place[4] and (**v. 14**) the time are precisely recorded.[5] The statement as to the time will also have a symbolic significance: the feast that celebrates Israel's historical deliverance by the act of God is now beginning, and through

---

[1] Instead of τῶν λόγων τούτων K N read τὸν λόγον τοῦτον.

[2] Ἐκάθισεν without doubt is meant intransitively, as 12.14 (so also Mt. 25. 31; Acts 12.21; 25.6, 17; Jos. bell. 2. 172: ὁ Πιλᾶτος καθίσας ἐπὶ βήματος ἐν τῷ μεγάλῳ σταδίῳ, cp. ant. 20, 130). The transitive interpretation is maintained by e.g. Loisy; Corssen, ZNTW 15 (1914), 339–340, partly out of historical considerations (the judge sits on the βῆμα only at the conclusion of the trial), and partly for contextual reasons (that Jesus is set on the βῆμα as king and judge corresponds to the cry ἴδε ὁ βασ. ὑμῶν). But then an αὐτόν would be indispensable. One should not raise questions about the historical possibilities; cp. on this M. Dibelius, ZATW, Beih. 33, 130f. Moreover καθίζειν ἐπὶ βήματος = "to sit on the judgment seat" is more established linguistic usage; see Br. and E. Dinkler, Marb. Jahr. f. Kunstwiss. XIII. Admittedly according to Justin apol. I 35, 6; Gospel of Pt 3.7 Jesus is set on the βῆμα or the καθέδρα (both = ἐκάθισαν αὐτόν); the subject there however is the Jews, and the action belongs to the scene of the mockery; see W. Bauer, Das Leben Jesu im Zeitalter der nt. Apokr. 208; Finegan, Die Überlieferung der Leidens- und Auferstehungsgeschichte Jesu 55.

[3] See Schürer I 429, 8; Bickermann op. cit. 223f.: the previous transactions (called ἀγράφως) had only the character of acquiring information; now for the first time Pilate acts as judge.

[4] Λιθόστρωτος = plastered; as substantive, the floor covered with sheets of marble, or a mosaic floor; see Wetst., Br. ad loc. and lexicon (Arndt & Gingrich). On Ἑβραϊστί see p. 240 n.6. The meaning of Γαββαθᾶ (not a translation of Λιθόστρωτος!) is uncertain. According to Dalman (Jesus-Jesch. 13; O.u.W. 355) it is גַּבַּחְתָּא (bald part of the forehead) or גַּבְּתָא (elevation). Str.-B. accept the latter, while Zn. and Wellh. (Joh 68) suggest גבתא (key). Concerning the locality of the place, see Dalman, O.u.W. 357. See now on the basis of recent excavations L. H. Vincent, RB 1933, 83–113; 1952, 513–530. But also P. Bénoit ibid. 531–550. Further W. F. Albright, Archaeol. of Palestine 247, and The Background etc. (see at p. 5) 158f.

[5] Παρασκευή presumably reproduces the aram. עֲרוּבְתָא. This, originally signifying the evening (sunset), became the usual term for the day before a feast day (the rest day), above all the day before the sabbath. So it could simply mean Friday, and manifestly it has this sense in vv. 31 and 42, even if it is not used in this sense in Hellenistic Judaism (Zeitlin, JBL 51 [1932] 268f.). If πάσχα can signify the entire seven days feast (so Torrey, JBL 50 [1930], 233; to the contrary Zeitlin, op. cit. 269f.), παρασκ. τοῦ πάσχα could mean "the Friday of the passover week". Meanwhile Jn. 19.13 can only have the meaning "the day before the passover feast" (so Str.-B. III 834ff.; Dalman, Jesus-Jesch. 82; Schl. ad loc; Zeitlin op. cit. 268f.); see p. 651 n.6. Hence the statement, contradicting Mk. 15.25 (crucifixion in the 3rd hour—9.00 a.m.; several mss. in Jn correct to this), that it was the 6th hour (= 12.00 noon), is suggestive: for the symbolism thus becomes possible, that Jesus dies at the time when the Passover lambs are slain; see below p. 677. J. Bonsirven (Bibl. 33 (1952), 511–515) shows that there was a tradition in Rabbinism in consequence of which the eating of the unleavened bread was commanded to take place in the 6th hour. He concludes from this that Jn represented Jesus not only as the Passover lamb, but also as the true unleavened bread. Dibelius (ZATW, Beih. 33, 131ff.) considers that the statement of time (which the tradition already offered the Evangelist) goes back to Am. 8.9. According to de Zwaan the number sign ד (= 3) has been wrongly read as ו (= 6).

the nation's sin the man in whom God is effecting the eschatological deliverance of the world is being condemned to death.

Since the decision must be given, Pilate now renews his endeavour; he commands that Jesus, who has been made by the soldiers a ridiculous figure, be brought out once more: ἴδε ὁ βασιλεὺς ὑμῶν. How can this dismal figure be taken seriously as an ἀντιλέγων τῷ Καίσαρι! But the instinct of hate sees more sharply. Of course, the assertion of the ἀντιλέγειν τῷ Καίσαρι is only a lie; but the world perceives the royal claim of Jesus plainly, even if in a perverted manner. Therefore it can only stick to its demand: "Away with him![1] To the cross with him!" **(v. 15)**. And one final effort of Pilate must also go by the board. His question, "Shall I crucify your king?" appeals to the Jews' sense of honour; for is it not an insult to them, if the Romans crucify Jesus on the ground that he wishes to be the king of the Jews? In such a case not only the person of Jesus is involved but, if the punishment should apply to the claim to the title, then the shame of the punishment applies to the Jewish people also. The correctness of this is seen immediately afterwards, in the objection of the Jews to the inscription on the cross with which Pilate takes revenge on the Jews.

This last attempt also proves useless. The answer of the ἀρχιερεῖς—and so of the nation's representatives—"We have no king apart from Caesar," surrenders the messianic claim of the people, and in that moment the Jewish people surrender themselves. The eschatological hope of the people comes to expression in the expectation of a messianic king; and in so far as the Jews represent the world, their behaviour means that the world, in its hate against the revelation, puts itself in the position of surrendering its hope; in its inmost being that hope moves it, even as a world at enmity with God, in its possibly unavowed but yet indestructible knowledge as to its own inadequacy, transitoriness, incompletion. The world makes itself an *Inferno* when it smothers this knowledge and consciously cuts off its hope. Therefore its last word, contrary to its desire, demonstrates that Jesus is the victor. Its unbelief towards him is the judgment on itself.

Against the power of the lie no attempt at conviction or persuasion avails. Pilate falls victim to the Jews, since he declined to exercise the authority of the state in an unbiased manner. He who personally shut his own heart to the claim of Jesus has not the strength to give heed to the claim of God that is established in his office. He hands over Jesus to the Jews for crucifixion **(v. 16a)**.[2] The flogging that preceded

---

[1] On the doubling of the ἆρον, see p. 659 n.6. On ἆρον Lk. 23.18; Acts 21.36; 22.22; P. Oxy. 119 (in Br.).

[2] Naturally it is not meant that Pilate hands over to the Jews the carrying out of the crucifixion; for as the appearance of the στρατιῶται vv. 23ff. and already the fact that two

crucifixion is not reported; it had already been recounted in v. 1.[1]

d) *Crucifixion, Death and Burial of Jesus:* 19.166–42

The Evangelist continues to follow his source. His insertions are separable from it. The source gives a similar report as the Synoptics, agreeing in many particulars and characteristically deviating in others (see below). Vv. 20–22 could be derived from the Evangelist; for here the motif of vv. 12b, 15c is apparent. Moreover the beginning of v. 23 shows that vv. 20–22 are an interruption: because of the interpolated ὅτε ἐσταύρωσαν τὸν'Ι. the Evangelist has to restore the connection with v. 19.

With v. 23 the source is taken up again and goes as far as v. 25. That the tradition early spoke of the women as witnesses of the crucifixion is seen in Mk. 15.40f. Certainly it is probable that the Evangelist has brought this notice forward; in the source, as in Mark, it will have stood at the conclusion, but he has set it here in order to make a connection for vv. 26f., which are his own composition. In that case the conclusion of v. 24: οἱ μὲν οὖν στρατιῶται ταῦτα ἐποίησαν is also his writing. In the source vv. 28–30 then followed; nevertheless of the two motivations given in v. 28 for the λέγει διψῶ, the first is derived from the Evangelist (εἰδὼς ... ὅτι ἤδη πάντα τετέλεσται), while the second (ἵνα τελειωθῇ ἡ γραφή) was offered by the source.[2] The τετέλεσται of v. 30 will then also have come from the Evangelist, and by it he replaced a saying from the source.[3]

The two sections vv. 31–37 and 38–42 stand in a certain opposition to one another; in vv. 31–37 the removal of Jesus from the cross is performed by the soldiers,[4] whereas according to v. 38 it is Joseph of Arimathea who takes Jesus from the cross. It is hardly likely that one of these two sections has been inserted into the source by the Evangelist; rather the two will already have lain combined in it.[5] For no specifically Johannine ideas are to be discerned in the one or the other section; on the contrary the chief motif of

---

other criminals are crucified with Jesus (v. 18) show, παρέδωκεν κτλ. is so meant that he declares the judgment that was desired by the Jews (perhaps differently in Lk. 23.25). This is completely proved by the inscription (v. 19) and by the request of the Jews v. 31. The report speaks with the same conciseness as Mk. 15.15, only that in Jn αὐτοῖς is added to the mere παρέδ. in order to make the situation plain.

[1] See p. 649.

[2] Wellh. also perceives the collision of εἰδώς and ἵνα.

[3] Whether it be a saying like Mk. 15.34 or Lk. 23.46, or a wordless cry like Mk. 15.37.

[4] Certainly it is not expressly said, but it is presupposed. Also Wellh. and Delafosse regard the juxtaposition of the two sections as not original. Delafosse holds that vv. 31–37 are interpolated. According to Wellh. rather vv. 38–42 are inserted, whereby the editor abbreviates the first account, but possibly used some sections, namely vv. 40–42 and in v. 38 ἦλθον καὶ ἦραν (so according to ℵ N pc it sa). Sp. strikes out vv. 35–40.

[5] The synoptic passion narrative has also grown together out of individual items, or its original frame has been extended through the insertion of individual items; see Gesch. der synopt Trad. 297ff. = Hist of the Syn. Trad. 275ff.

vv. 31–37, the fulfilment of the Scripture, corresponds rather to the tradition of the community,[1] and vv. 38–42 have the character of an edifying and legendary composition. In vv. 31–37 we see the work of the ecclesiastical redactor from whom vv. 34b, 35 are derived (see below). In vv. 38–42 the Evangelist has inserted the reference to Nicodemus (see below).

The source-narrative that lies at the base of the Evangelist's agrees with the Synoptic account of *the crucifixion* in stating that Jesus was crucified with two criminals on Golgotha (Mk. 15.22, 27), that an inscription described Jesus as the King of the Jews (Mk. 15.26), that the soldiers divided his clothes (Mk. 15.24), that in his thirst he was given vinegar to drink (Mk. 15.36), that he expired with a cry (Mk. 15.37), and that finally women were witnesses of the crucifixion (Mk. 15.40). The differences are as follows: not Simon of Cyrene (Mk. 15.21), but Jesus himself carries the cross; no mention is made of drinking wine before the crucifixion (Mk. 15.23), and no indication of time is given, while that supplied by Mark (15.25: the third hour) cannot be assumed, owing to v. 14 (see p. 664 n.5); the division of clothes is differently reported; nothing is mentioned of the mocking by the passers-by and those crucified with him (Mk. 15.29–32), nor is the darkness mentioned, nor the first cry of Jesus and its derisive interpretation (Mk. 15.33–36). Finally the τέρας of the torn Temple curtain is not described, nor the confession of the centurion (Mk. 15.39). The only point of agreement in the naming of the women relates to the person of Mary Magdalene. John has nothing corresponding to that which Matthew and Luke supply in addition to Mark (especially Mt. 27.51b–53; Lk. 23.27–31). Conversely John's source goes beyond the Synoptics in telling of the casting lots for the unsewn coat of Jesus (vv. 23f.) and the cry διψῶ (v. 28); features additional to these (vv. 20–22, 26f.) are due to the Evangelist.

In the *narrative of the burial* the source diverged more markedly from the Synoptics. The latter know nothing of the report about the taking down of Jesus from the cross occasioned by the request of the Jews (vv. 31–37). The agreement consists only in the feature that Joseph of Arimathea asks Pilate for the body of Jesus and buries him (Mk. 15.42–46); the astonishment that Jesus had died so speedily, and the part played by the centurion (Mk. 15.44f., possibly secondary in Mark) have no correspondence. Conversely the Synoptics do not report that the grave was situated in a garden, near the place of crucifixion (v. 41). It is not said in John that it was shut by means of a stone (Mk. 15.46), but this is presupposed in 20.1. In vv. 39b, 40 it is stated that Jesus was buried in the regular manner, hence it cannot later be said, as in Mk. 16.1, that on the Easter morning the women come to anoint the body of Jesus. For this reason no mention is made in John of the women looking on at the burial (Mk. 15.47 parr.), and the account of the burial in no way prepares for the Easter story.[2] Going beyond Mark, but in agreement with

---

[1] At most οἱ Ἰουδαῖοι should be allowed to the Evangelist (differently e.g. Mt. 27.62; 28.11).

[2] Of course in the Synoptics the linking of the accounts of the burial and Easter through the mention of the women is most probably a secondary element. Nevertheless in

Mt. 27.60; Lk. 23.53, v. 41 reports that the grave was a new one and as yet untouched; on the other hand it is not stated, as in Mt. 27.60, that it was Joseph's own grave. The information about the part played by Nicodemus at the burial does not go back to the source but to the Evangelist.

1) *The Crucifixion and the Inscription on the Cross:* 19.16b–22

Jesus is now led (by the soldiers)[1] out of the city[2] for crucifixion, which naturally takes place outside the city (**v. 16a**), and he has to carry his own cross (**v. 17**).[3] The place of the crucifixion[4] is called "Place of a Skull," or in the vernacular[5] Golgotha.[6]

Mk. 15.46 also the interment appears to have been meant as complete; see Finegan, Die Überlieferung der Leidens- und Auferstehungsgeschichte 78–80.

[1] See p. 665 n.2. The variants παραλαβόντες δέ M 700 al and οἱ δὲ παραλαβόντες φ or οἱ δὲ λαβόντες ℵ would correspond to the παρέδωκεν v. 16a, and so make the Jews appear as executors of the punishment. The correct text παρέλαβον οὖν ℌ marks a pause according to Johannine usage.

[2] Ἐξῆλθεν: naturally out of the city.

[3] That the condemned man carried a cross was the case according to Plut. de sera num. vind. 9, p. 554a; Artemidor oneir. II 56, p. 153, 20ff. Hercher, Brauch (Pauly-Wissowa IV 1731). Of course, according to Mk. 15.21 parr., Simon of Cyrene carries the cross of Jesus. The ancient Church and modern harmonisers assert that the two alternated (see Br. ad loc. and Klostermann on Mk. 15.21). The contradiction is probably to be explained on the assumption that a different tradition lies behind Jn's account, for the statement is quite unstressed (an αὐτός is lacking, and ἑαυτῷ, which according to Raderm. 129 means "alone", has no such strong emphasis). According to Black ἑαυτῷ (ethic dat.) is an Aramaism. Cp. also Lietzmann. S. A. Berl. 1934, 15, p. 8. It is also improbable that the Evangelist wishes to represent symbolically the call to discipleship, for which Mk. 8.34 parr. employs the picture of carrying the cross. For in the Johannine parallel 12.25 (see pp. 425f.) the picture is lacking, and it is not met with elsewhere in Jn. A typological reflection on Gen. 22.6, which the Church Fathers find here (see Br.) certainly lies far removed; but also a stress on the voluntary nature of the acceptance of suffering (Br.) will not be intended. The idea that a polemic is being directed against the Gnostic heresy (Pfleiderer, Urchristentum[2] II 384; Schwartz II 141f., Str. 318), according to which Simon was crucified in the place of Jesus, who exchanged his form with him (Iren. I 24, 4) is far from the horizon here.

[4] On the manner of carrying out a crucifixion see Klostermann on Mk. 15.23.

[5] On Ἑβραϊστί see p. 240 n.6.

[6] So in agreement with the Synoptics; only that Mk. and Mt. at first give the Aramaic names in reverse order, while Lk gives only the Greek translation.—Bl.-D. §132, 2 hold that the text has been badly disfigured, and wish to read after L X vg: εἰς τὸν λεγόμενον κρανίου τόπον Ἑβρ. δὲ Γολγ. Against this Joach. Jeremias (Golgotha 1, 1) defends as correct the text most commonly handed down (with B ℵ al ὅ instead of ὅς with ℜ pm); he regards κρανίου as a gen. of apposition (as 15.22; Mt. 27.33) and translates: "He came to the place, which is named the skull, which in Hebrew is called Golgotha". The translation of the Heb גֻּלְגֹּלֶת Jud. 9.53; 2 Kings 9.35) or the current Aramaic word גֻּלְגָּלְתָּא is correct (concerning other derivations see Jeremias op. cit.; Wandel, ThStkr 1922, Sonderheft, 134ff.). Probably the name comes from the skull-like form of the hill; the interpretation of Jerome as locus decollatorum cannot be right, since beheading was not a Jewish punishment. Legend gave currency to the fable that Adam's skull was buried there (K. Holl, Ges. Aufl. III 36ff.). As to the presumed situation of the place, see C. Sachsse, ZNTW 19 (1919/20), 29ff.; Dalman, O.u.W. 364ff.; Jerusalem und sein Gelände 72; Jeremias op.cit. or Angelos I (1925), 141ff.; Wandel op. cit.

With Jesus two other men were crucified, on his right and on his left (**v. 19**).[1] Pilate orders a tablet[2] to be affixed to the cross, on which is written the accusation that led to his condemnation, "Jesus the Nazarene, the King of the Jews" (**v. 19**).[3] The Synoptics give the same report;[4] the Evangelist, however, elaborates this motif further (vv. 20–22). In the context of his representation this inscription is not only a means of Pilate's revenge on the Jews who had forced him to condemn Jesus, and to whom he directs this insult, but through this inscription it is demonstrated that the condemnation of Jesus is at the same time the judgment of Judaism, which had surrendered the very hope that gave its existence its meaning—and so the judgment of the world, that for the sake of its security in the present gives up its future.[5] The judgment however does not consist merely in that Judaism lost its king, and the world loses its future. For then a certain tragedy would lie over the event; on the contrary it contains rather a deep irony. For as the Crucified, Jesus is really the king; the kingly rule, awaited in hope, is not as such destroyed, but established in a new sense; the cross is the exaltation and the glorification of Jesus. Pilate therefore, contrary to knowledge and intention, has become a prophet, like Caiaphas, 11.50f. (see p. 411 n.2). His inscription, betraying the price paid by his accusers,[6] is undoubtedly to be understood as a prophecy, as is indicated by its being written in three languages (**v. 20**):[7] the cross is an event that concerns the entire world; the βασιλεὺς τῶν 'Ιουδαίων is the σωτὴρ τοῦ κόσμου (4.42).

The Jews realise that they themselves are implicated in this inscription

---

[1] So also the Synoptics; Mk and Mt describe them as λῃσταί, Lk as κακοῦργοι. Since Jn adduces no such characteristic, he hardly saw therein an especial humiliation of Jesus, or the fulfilment of the prophecy of Is. 53.12 (cp. Lk 22.37). The fact that the middle place is the position of honour that befits the "king" (Schl.) would be thought of in the spirit of the soldiers who had made sport of Jesus, but does the report have this in view?

[2] Τίτλος is a Latinism (titulus); see Arndt & Gingrich, Bl.-D §5, 1b.

[3] According to Roman custom a board was carried before the condemned man or hanged about his neck, on which the (name and) crime of the condemned was stated. Suetonius Calig. 32; Cassius Dio 54, 8 (both given by Klostermann on Mk. 15.26); Eus. H.E. 1.5, 44. Public announcement of the judgment was also a Jewish custom, see Str.-B. on Mt. 27.37.

[4] The text of the inscription varies among the Synoptics. All give ὁ βασ. τῶν 'Ιουδ., Mt. also the name 'Ιησοῦς. Only Jn has ὁ Ναζ. (see p. 639 n.7). On the question of historicity see Gesch. der synopt. Trad. 293 = Hist. of the Syn. Trad. 272. T. F. Regard, Revue Archéologique, V. ser., tome 28 (1928), 95–105, endeavours to prove that Jn reproduces the Latin text of the inscription, while Mt. gives the "Hebrew" and Lk the Greek.

[5] See p. 665.

[6] The statement that many Jews read the inscription signifies it is made public what accusation was brought against Jesus. Doubtless τῆς πόλεως depends not on ὁ τόπος but on ἐγγύς.

[7] Concerning multi-lingual inscriptions see Br. and Schl. ad loc.

(**v. 21**), and the ἀρχιερεῖς ask Pilate to change the text.[1] He stands however by what he has written (**v. 22**).[2] Inasmuch as the world has made a claim on the state for its own ends, it has at the same time conceded its authority; this now becomes effective against itself.

2) *The Distribution of the Clothes of Jesus:* 19.23–24

V. 23 links directly on to v. 18, ignoring vv. 19–22.[3] The soldiers who guard the cross[4]—there are four of them, as appears from the following action[5]—divide among themselves the clothes of the crucified Jesus (not a word is spoken about those of the men crucified with him!), as may correspond with Roman custom.[6] In any case the account is given because the Church sees in it the fulfilment of the Scripture passage, Ps. 22.19, regarded as a prophecy.[7] The Synoptics give a similar report, although they recount the dividing by lots as a unitary act, and only with allusion to the passage in the Psalms, whereas here it is explicity cited, and from the two sentences of the verse, standing in synonymous parallelism, two actions have been spun out:[8] the pieces of the upper garment are divided by the four soldiers; the under-garment,[9] which is woven from one piece,[10] is assigned by means of the

---

[1] Μὴ γράφε instead of μὴ γράψῃς, because Pilate has already written, see Br., who paraphrases: "write no longer", or: "it should not from henceforth stand written". R. Eisler Ἰησ. βασ. II 530ff. regards the account as historical, and wishes to conclude from the Slavonic Josephus that the Jewish authorities caused a contrary inscription to be brought into the forecourt of the Temple.

[2] The first perfect is, according to Bl.-D §342, 4, more aoristic; for the second Br. compares Epikt. diss. II 15, 5: κέκρικα = "I have once for all decided". On the whole expression cp. Gen. 43.14: ἐγὼ μὲν γὰρ καθὰ ἠτέκνωμαι, ἠτέκνωμαι. Schl. and Str.-B. compare Rabbinic expressions such as (translated into Greek) ὁ πεπόιηκεν, πεποίηται, or νῦν ὃ γέγονεν, γέγονεν. Conversely Plato Symp. 189b: καί μοι ἔστω ἄρρητα τὰ εἰρημένα.

[3] The circumstantial resumption became necessary because the Evangelist inserted vv. 20–22 into the source; see p. 666.

[4] Cp. Petron. 111: miles qui cruces asservabat, ne quis ad sepulturam corpus detraheret.

[5] Four τετράδια are mentioned in Acts 12.4.

[6] Λαγχάνειν normally means to obtain something that is divided out (through the lot), but also to cast lots in order to solve something (see Arndt & Gingrich). Ps. 22.19 Symm.: ἐλάγχανον for יַפִּילוּ גוֹרָל (LXX ἔλαβον κλῆρον). On περί see Bl.-D §229, 2.

[7] Just as the Passion narrative quite early on was worked up on the basis of proof from prophecy (see Gesch. der synopt. Trad. 303f. = Hist. of the Syn. Trad. 280f.), and as Ps. 22 played a role in this, so the episode Jn. 19.23f. will have its origin in the messianic understanding of Ps. 22.19; see F. K. Feigel, Der Einfluss des Weissagungsbeweises 1910, 70ff. In Rabbinic literature also Ps. 22 was interpreted of the Messiah (along with other interpretations); see Str.-B. The citation is word for word after the LXX. On the double expression of the reflexive idea in the citation see Bl.-D. §310, 2.

[8] Entirely analogous to the way in which in Mt. 21.2ff., on the basis of Zech. 9.9, it was deduced that two beasts were used by Jesus entering the city.

[9] Ἱμάτιον is the outer garment (wrap, mantle), χιτών the undergarment worn next

lots. The Evangelist does not have a primary concern for proof from Scripture, although occasionally he does give it room;[1] he had reproduced the report from the source. One could ask whether the episode has a particular meaning for him, but there is nothing to indicate such.[2]

3) *Mary and the Beloved Disciple at the Cross:* 19.25–27

After the episode of the division of the clothes is ended (v. 24), the Evangelist reproduces the account of the women at the cross, which in the source presumably stood at the end of the narrative.[3] It serves as a transition to the episode in vv. 26f., which without doubt is the Evangelist's own composition. To make possible what is related in vv. 26f., the women have to stand immediately by the cross (v. 25),[4] and for that reason the Evangelist has perhaps altered an ἀπὸ μακρόθεν of the source, such as is found in the Synoptics (Mk. 15.40).

---

to the body. As to the clothing of Jesus see Col. Repond, Biblica 3 (1922), 3-14.

[10] Ἄραφος = unstitched, without seam; δι' ὅλου as P. Oxy. 53.10, "where the subject is a tree that is withered δι' ὅλου" (Br.). On woven garments see Str.-B.; Dalman, Arbeit und Sitte in Palästina V (1937), 126ff.

[1] See p. 452 n.2.

[2] According to Jos. ant. 3, 161 the χιτών of the High Priest (which naturally was not the undergarment but the outer coat) is woven from one piece and without seam. Philo interprets (fug. et inv. 110–112) the High Priest of the Logos and his garment of the homogeneous structure of the universe (cp. spec. leg. I 84–96; vit. Mos. II 117–135). In the background here stands the speculation about the primal man (see Reitzenstein, Taufe 132ff.; E. Käsemann, Leib und Leib Christi 76f., 89f.; J. Pascher, Ἡ βασιλικὴ ὁδός 1931, 61ff.; P. Saintypes, Essais de folklore biblique 1923, 405ff).. In Judaism this speculation was transferred also to Adam (see B. Murmelstein, Wiener Ztschr, für die Kunde des Morgenlandes 36 [1929], 57f.; W. Staerk, Erlösererwartung 14ff.). According to to Rabbinic tradition Adam received an unstitched coat from God; likewise then after him Moses (and the High Priest). It is not attested in the Rabbinic Literature that this motif, on the basis of the Adam-Moses-Redeemer typology, was applied to the Redeemer, but it is possible that this happened when the tradition was taken over into Christian theology. At all events the Adam-Moses-Redeemer typology was taken over (see E. Käsemann, Das wandernde Gottesvolk 128ff.; Staerk op. cit. 22ff.), and the interpretation of the coat of Jesus by Clement of Alex. Paed. II 113, p. 225, 4ff. could have been determined by the (admittedly transformed) cosmological speculation. Nevertheless this seems not to have been at the root of Jn's narrative, neither in the source, in which the unsewn coat is simply derived from Ps. 22.19, nor in the Evangelist's view, for whom Jesus as the Λόγος does not have cosmic significance as the Λόγος of Philo has. Moreover it would be difficult to understand what the disposal of the coat by lot should mean! That the coat should symbolise the unity of the Church (Cypr, de cathol. eccl. unitate 7, and more recent exegetes) is improbable on the same grounds and inherently. Nestle (ZNTW 3 [1902], 160 and 11 [1910], 241) thinks that the unsewn coat corresponds to the coat of Joseph, considered as the type of Jesus; against this G. Klein, ZNTW 5 (1904), 148. It does not seem to me at all possible that the High Priest's coat is in mind. The disposal by lot could of course symbolise in a derisive manner the finish of the Jewish high priesthood; but this cannot be represented as the χιτών of Jesus!

[3] See p. 666.

[4] Παρά with dat. of thing (not persons) only here in the NT. See Bl.-D. §238.

No answer can be given to the question whether the enumeration of the four women[1] is cited from the source, or whether the Evangelist has replaced one of the four names in the tradition by the Mother of Jesus. According to the Synoptics the Mother of Jesus does not appear at the cross, for in them she does not belong at all to the group of Jesus' followers: Mk. 3.31–35 parr. rather suggest the contrary conclusion. According to Acts 1.14, certainly, she belongs to the first community, along with the brothers of Jesus, although no mention is made of her relationship to the "Beloved Disciple."

Along with her three women are found at the cross. Mk. 15.40 and Mt. 27.56[2] also tell of the three, but the only agreement with John is in the naming of Mary of Magdala.[3] The sister of Jesus' mother, whose name is not given, is otherwise unknown. Similarly Mary τοῦ Κλωπᾶ[4] is not otherwise known. To identify these two women with those mentioned in Mark or in Matthew in company with Mary Magdalene, or with the women mentioned in Lk. 24.10 as with her at the empty tomb, is arbitrary.[5] Clearly the names of the women have frequently oscillated in the tradition. On the other hand the Evangelist is not interested in them as witnesses of the crucifixion; his interest centres on only one of them, the mother of Jesus.

With her the "beloved disciple," mentioned for the first time in this context, now appears (**v. 26**). Jesus looks on them both from the cross and directs them to each other: "Woman, see there, your son!",[6]

---

[1] At all events v. 25 could be understood to mean that *four* women are standing at the cross; for it is difficult to maintain that the double statement of name is intended to be in apposition to ἡ μήτηρ αὐτοῦ καὶ ἡ ἀδελφή . . . so that only two women are in view. For in that case the mother of Jesus would have to be reckoned as the daughter of Clopas (for she cannot be his wife or mother), and in the later tradition at least she is commonly regarded as the daughter of Joachim (W. Bauer, Das Leben Jesu im Zeitalter der neutest. Apokr. 8f.). Further it is improbable that the sisters were both called Mary. This consideration also tells against interpreting the first name as in apposition to ἡ ἀδελφὴ τ. μητρὸς αὐτοῦ and finding three women named.

[2] Lk. 23.49 speaks only in general terms of acquaintances and women, who looked on from a distance.

[3] She is also named in Lk. 8.2 as one of the women companions of Jesus, and appears in Mk. 16.1; Mt. 28.1; Lk. 24.10 as one of the women at the grave of Jesus.

[4] Τοῦ Κλωπᾶ can equally signify the father or the son or the husband; Bl.-D §162, 1, 3, 4; Ed. Meyer I 185, 1. The name Κλωπᾶς appears to be Semitic (Arndt & Gingrich) and is then to be distinguished from Κλεοπᾶς (abbreviated form for Κλεόπατρος). There is no reason for identifying this Κλωπᾶς with the one named in Lk. 24.18, who is otherwise unknown. Hegesippus names (Eus. H. E. III 11; 32.6; IV 22, 4) a Κλωπᾶς as brother of Joseph. The identification of Κλωπᾶς with the Alphaios named in Mk. 3.18 parr., the father of James, is quite arbitrary and rests on the motive of equating the Μαρία τοῦ Κλωπᾶ with the Μαρ. τοῦ Ἰακώβου τοῦ μικροῦ of Mk. 15.40.

[5] Thus the identification of the aunt of Jesus with Salome (Mk. 15.40), the mother of the sons of Zebedee (Mt. 27.56), Johanna (Lk. 24.10), or Susanna (Lk. 8.3), and the identification of Μαρία τοῦ κλ. with the other Mary named in Mk. 15.40; Mt. 27.61.

[6] On γύναι see p. 116 n.5; on ἴδε (in the mss. changing with ἰδού) see p. 95 n.2.

"See there, your mother!".[1] They both understand Jesus (v. 27), and the beloved disciple immediately takes the mother of Jesus home with him.[2] Doubtless this scene, which in face of the Synoptic tradition can make no claim to historicity, has a symbolic meaning. The mother of Jesus, who tarries by the cross, represents Jewish Christianity that overcomes the offence of the cross. The beloved disciple represents Gentile Christianity,[3] which is charged to honour the former as its mother from whom it has come,[4] even as Jewish Christianity is charged to recognise itself as "at home" within Gentile Christianity, i.e. included in the membership of the one great fellowship of the Church. And these directions sound out from the cross; i.e. they are the commands of the "exalted" Jesus. Their meaning is the same as his words in the prayer, 17.20f., the request for the first disciples and for those who come to faith through their word: ἵνα πάντες ἓν ὦσιν.

4) *The Death of Jesus:* 19.28–30

The Evangelist does not give any account of the mocking of the Crucified, about which the Synoptics report; perhaps he omits what his source may have said on this matter. In any case for him, after Jesus had in a fashion made known his last will in vv. 26f., the drama has come to its end. Jesus hangs on the cross not as a sufferer, but as the hidden "king"; he knows[5] that "by this time everything has come to its end—to its completion."[6] He gives as it were a sign of this, since "in

[1] Already Wetst. alluded to Lucian Toxaris 22 (the testament of the Corinthian Eudamidas): ἀπολείπω Ἀρεταίῳ μὲν τὴν μητέρα μου τρέφειν καὶ γηροκομεῖν, Χαριξένῳ δὲ τὴν θυγατέρα μου ἐκδοῦναι μετὰ προικός.

[2] On τὰ ἴδια see p. 56n.1. Wellh. deduces from the εὐθύς that the disciple must be an inhabitant of Jerusalem; probably he is the John mentioned in Acts. 12.12, whose mother also was named Mary; her house served as a place for the disciples to gather, and in the tradition she became the mother of Jesus and correspondingly her son became her adopted son; possibly he was considered to be the anonymous young man of Mk. 14.51 and then exalted to be the beloved disciple. But it could be that the Beloved Disciple was not a historical figure at all, see p. 483.

[3] See pp. 483f.. According to Ed. Meyer, SA Berlin 1924, 157–162, the beloved disciple is a figure invented by the Evangelist for the purpose of serving as an authorised witness for the Gospel, through which the old tradition is superseded. This motive does not in the least explain the scene at the cross.

[4] That the Mother of Jesus represents the Church (Hirsch) is an impossible assertion; the Church on the contrary is the Mother of believers and the Bride of Christ! So rightly Büchsel, Theol. Blätter 15 (1936), 147. Loisy also gives an interpretation of the Mother and the Disciple as above. Dodd (428, 2) rejects any symbolising of the scene.

[5] Ἐιδώς, inserted by the Evangelist (see p. 666), is the same as 13.1, 8; 18f., see p. 465. According to Hosk. Jesus inclines his head to his Mother and to the Disciple and "handed over the Spirit", namely to the believers, who stand under the cross. Dodd also (223, 428) entertains the possibility that παρέδωκεν τὸ πνεῦμα should be understood in the sense that Jesus bequeaths the Holy Spirit to the world.

[6] Τετέλεσται has the same double meaning as εἰς τέλος 13.1, which has now found its realisation in him (see p. 487). Manifestly it looks back to utterances like 4.34; 5.36 (see

order that the Scripture might be fulfilled,"[1] he says, "*I thirst*" (**v. 28**). In the Evangelist's view the fact of the Scripture fulfilment, which the source already observed, is also the sign that what is here taking place is being achieved in accordance with the divine plan. The immediately succeeding happening is also ruled by the motif of the Scripture fulfilment: the thirsty Jesus is given vinegar to drink—presumably by the soldiers (**v. 29**).[2]

So now everything has happened that had to happen; the work of

---

p. 194 n.3) and corresponds to that which was spoken sub specie of fulfilment ἐγώ σε ἐδόξασα . . . τὸ ἔργον τελειώσας κτλ. 17.4 (see p. 495 n.8 and cp. Act. Thom. 145, 146, 167, pp.252, 8f.; 255, 3; 282, 1. Τετέλεσται therefore does not simply mean, "It is at an end", still less, "It is endured", but rather, "It is brought to an end", namely the work that has been commissioned (see pp. 222 n.3; 495 n.8). It is necessary to understand πάντα, in accordance with 3.35; 5.20; 13.3; 15.15; 17.7; for all that the Father has "given", "shown" etc. to the Son is nothing less than his work which he accomplishes. Correct though it be that with the accomplishment of the work of Jesus the eschatological event is completed, πάντα τετέλεσται nevertheless cannot mean: the messianic end of all things has now set in (G. Stählin, ZNTW 33 (1934), 233). Accordingly Lk. 18.31 is no analogy: καὶ τελεσθήσεται πάντα τὰ γεγραμμένα (cp. Lk. 22.37). Rather Rev. 10.7 should be compared: ἐτελέσθη τὸ μυστήριον τοῦ θεοῦ; Ign Sm. 7.2: ἐν ᾧ (sc. τ. εὐαγγελίῳ) τὸ πάθος ἡμῶν δεδήλωται καὶ ἡ ἀνάστασις τετελείωται. In addition cp. Hom. Od. 22, 479 after the murder of the freeman: τετέλεστο δὲ ἔργον. By contrast peractum est, Seneca Herc. Oet. 1340, 1457, 1472, to which Fr. Pfister ARW 34 (1937), 53 alludes, has the meaning: "It is endured".

[1] Instead of the usual πληροῦν, here τελειοῦν is used for the fulfilling of Scripture. This is repeatedly understood (Ho., Br.) as if it were intended to signify the conclusive fulfilment of the entire content of the Scriptures. Nevertheless it seems, as in 13.18, that the fulfilment of a particular passage of Scripture is meant. Τελειωθῆναι is said Mart. Pol. 16.2 of the ῥήματα of Polycarp, who is characterised as διδάσκαλος ἀποστολικὸς καὶ προφητικός (cp. Jos. ant. 15, 4: τοῦ θεοῦ τοὺς λόγους αὐτοῦ [the prophecy of Pollion or Samaias] τελειώσαντος); τελεσθῆναι of the λόγοι τοῦ θεοῦ Rev. 17.17. (cp. 10.7, see previous footnote), of the Scripture Lk. 18.31:, 22.37 (see previous note); cp. also Lk. 12.50. (In the passages named in the previous note from Act. Thom. πληροῦν and τελειοῦν stand in synonymous parallelism, though naturally not of the fulfilment of Scripture). The Scripture passage that is meant is obviously Ps. 68.22: καὶ εἰς τὴν δίψαν μου ἐπότισάν με ὄξος. Ps. 22.16 hardly comes into question with it: ἐξηράνθη ὡσεὶ ὄστρακον ἡ ἰσχύς μου, καὶ ἡ γλῶσσά μου κεκόλληται τῷ λάρυγγί μου.

[2] This event is also reported in Mk. 15.36 parr. On ἔκειτο see 2.6. Since the motif of the fulfilment of Scripture determines the narrative, the question should not be raised whether the drink of vinegar is intended to be a refreshment (Dalman, Jesus-Jesch. 187f., cp. Arbeit und Sitte IV [1935], 403), or a mockery (Evg. Pt. 5.16). It is hardly likely that we are to understand that Jesus, who himself offers the water of life that stills all thirst (4.10ff.), here reaches the deepest point of fleshly existence (Dalman op. cit. 188f.). It is also very doubtful that a further allusion to the significance of the event is contained in the fact that the sponge filled with vinegar is stuck on a hyssop reed (so Mk. and Mt instead of the simple κάλαμος). Purifying power was ascribed to hyssop (Lev. 14.6ff.; Num. 19.6; Ps. 50.9; Heb. 9.19; Barn. 8.1, 6), and the blood of the Passover lamb had to be sprinkled on the lintel and posts of the door by means of a bunch of hyssop (Ex. 12.22). But it is scarcely believable that Jesus should be designated as the Passover lamb through the statement that a sponge with vinegar was stuck on a hyssop stem. The old conjecture of Joach. Camerarius is attractive; instead of ὑσσώπῳ he wishes to read ὕσσῳ (on a lance), as the miniscule 476 does in fact read; so Dalman op. cit. 187, cp. Arbeit und Sitte I (1928), 544, Lagr., Bd. Hyssop indeed is not particularly suitable for the purpose, see Str.-B.

Jesus is completed; he has carried out that which his Father had commanded him (10.18; 15.10; 14.31). After he had received the drink of vinegar he says, "*It is accomplished!*" (v. 30); he bows his head and dies.[1] The ἐγώ σε ἐδόξασα ἐπὶ τῆς γῆς, τὸ ἔργον τετελειώσας ὃ δέδωκάς μοι ἵνα ποιήσω (17.4), which in the prayer had been uttered *sub specie* of the completion of the work, has now become historical reality.[2] And in truth everything has now been finished, for in the eyes of the world the whole thing has been wrecked.

5) *The Taking down from the Cross:* 19.31–37

The following story, which has no parallel in the Synoptics, will be of a relatively late origin.[3] The Jews ask Pilate that the bones of the

---

[1] It is true that in Jn the Crucified does not really appear as one who suffers but as one who acts, yet it would be too ingenious to find in κλίνας τ. κεφ. the independence of the action: e.g. Jesus reclined the head not because of weakness but in order to sleep (Mt. 8.20 = Lk. 9.58), or with Ammon. Corder. Cat. 442 (Br.) to draw attention to the fact that first he reclines the head and then he dies, whereas normally the reverse happens. Quite certainly there is no thought of a temporal relation between κλίνας and παρέδ. According to Dalman op. cit. 196 Jewish parallels to the reclining of the head in death are lacking. Παρέδωκεν τ. πνεῦμα means just the same as ἀφῆκεν τ. πν. Mt. 27.50 and ἐξέπνευσεν Mk. 15.37; cp. πνεῦμα ἀφιέναι Eur. Hec. 571, ψυχὴν ἀφιέναι Eur. Or. 1171. It cannot be that the Rabbinic expression is in mind, "to devote his soul for something" (Schl.) since ὑπέρ is lacking (Dalman op. cit. 196f.). Παρέδωκεν τ. πν. just as little corresponds to εἰς χεῖράς σου παρατίθεμαι τὸ πνεῦμά μου Ps. 30.6, which Lk. 23.46 makes the dying Jesus say, since there is nothing corresponding to εἰς χεῖρας. Also to wish παρέδωκεν to emphasise the voluntariness of the death, in the sense of 10. 18 (Bd.), would be over subtle.

[2] It is possible that the formulation τετέλεσται (on its meaning see p. 673 n.6) is derived from the Gnostic tradition, and the word could be thought of as the concluding formula of a mystery. Dodd (437) rightly refers to C. Herm. 13.21, where in the mystery of the rebirth the initiate says to the mystagogue: σοῦ γὰρ βουλομένου πάντα τελεῖται. At the conclusion of the rebirth mystery in the Hades vision of Zosimos (Reitzenstein, Poimandres 8ff.; H.M.R. 312f.) it is said: ἡ τέχνη πεπλήρωται. Of course the thought is not contained in τετέλεσται that Jesus (understood as the mystery divinity) himself has come to the τελείωσις, or has become τελειωθείς (so Heb. 5.9; see on this Windisch in the Hdb. z. NT and, especially E. Käsemann, Das wandernde Gottesvolk 82–90; see also p. 516 n.3); for it is not written τετέλεσμαι or τετελείωμαι. But in the Gnostic myth one's own perfection and the perfection of one's work form a unity; and the apostle who Act. Andr. 9 p. 42, 2f. sighs ἵνα τέλειος γένωμαι, declares, inasmuch as he represents the Redeemer who has annulled the fall of the primal man through the way of suffering: καὶ τὸ ἐκείνου (of Adam) ἀτελὲς ἐγὼ τετέλεκα προσφυγὼν τῷ θεῷ (Act. Andr. 5 p. 40, 18f.). In the vision of Zosimos the mystagogue says in front of the altar, to which steps go up and down: πεπλήρωκα τὸ κατιέναι με . . . καὶ ἀνιέναι με . . . ἀποβαλλόμενος τὸ τοῦ σώματος παχύτητα τελοῦμαι.

One may also recall the formula that repeatedly occurs in various songs of the 3rd book of the Left Ginza: "My measure is full and I go hence" (532, 30; 546, 10ff.; 555, 10; 564, 9; 571, 25; 585, 27; cp. also 503, 36; 560, 1; Mand. Lit. 226). Here admittedly the soul speaks as it is separating out of the body; but in so far as there is a repetition in it of what happened to the Redeemer, the filling of the measure signifies at the same time the fulfilment of the work, the task; see p. 495 n.8.

[3] See pp. 666f.

executed men be broken and that the bodies be removed (**v. 31**).[1] The first request, as vv. 32f. show, was made that death might be hastened, for in view of the shortness of time death was not yet expected;[2] the second was made in order that the bodies should not hang on the cross during the Sabbath. The unexpressed reason for this is that the body of an executed man makes the land unclean; according to Deut. 21.22f., it should be taken down and buried before the onset of night.[3] The aversion of uncleanness on this occasion, however, has the special reason that it is "the day of preparation," and that the following day is not only a Sabbath, but that this[4] Sabbath is at the same time a "great" day.[5] In the light of the previous intimations of time, this cannot be otherwise understood than that this Sabbath coincides with the 15th Nisan.[6]

Pilate grants the wish of the Jews, and the soldiers smash the bones of the two men crucified with Jesus (**v. 32**),[7] but when they come to Jesus they discover that he has died already (**v. 33**). His bones therefore are not smashed, but for security one of the soldiers thrusts his lance into his side (**v. 34**).[8] A twofold prophecy thereby is fulfilled; first that

---

[1] Τὰ σώματα with singular predicate (μείνῃ), τὰ σκέλη with plural (κατεαγῶσιν and ἀρθῶσιν); in the latter case the individual acts are in view. On the displaced augment in κατεαγῶσιν see Raderm. 84. Σῶμα = corpse, very frequently, see Br.: αἴρειν does not mean "take down" (that would be καταίρειν, which however is unusual in this sense; instead of this καθαιρεῖν Josh 8.29; Mk. 15.46; Lk. 23.53; Acts 13.29); rather it means "pick up, fetch, carry away, remove", as v. 38; 20.15; Mk. 6.29; Mt. 14.12.

[2] The crucifragium was an independent punishment, but occasionally it also appears in connection with crucifixion, see Br.

[3] Cp. Jos. ant. 4, 202; bell. 4, 317.

[4] 'Εκείνου is to be preferred to ἐκείνη (read by B*H al).

[5] The Rabbinic tradition offers no example of this special argumentation, see Dalman, Jesus-Jesch, 168.

[6] See pp. 651 n.6; 664 n.5. If one thinks of 19.14 then παρασκευή will be understood in terms of the passover. But since the sabbath is mentioned at the same time, παρασκ. nevertheless (as v. 42) seems to be understood as "Friday". Certainly it is surprising that no mention is made of the passover, unlike 18.28; 19.14. That may well be due to the fact that this story is derived from a tradition according to which Jesus was crucified on the 15th Nizan, as in the Synoptics. According to the original report, then, the fact that the legs of Jesus were not broken did not represent him as the passover lamb; only the fulfilment of Scripture is shown in this circumstance,—or the situation was read out of Ps. 33.21 (see p. 677 n.1), exactly as the story of the χιτών was read out of Ps. 22.19 (see p. 670 n.7). According to the source the εγάλη ἡμέρα was the sabbath of the Passover week, which in this case fell together with the 16th Nizan; the day could be called "great", because on it (according to Pharisaic tradition) the omer offering (Lev. 23.1) was made; see Str.-B.

[7] Why the soldiers begin precisely with these should not be asked; the narrator recounts the most important thing last (see Gesch. der syn. Trad. 207—Hist. of the Syn. Trad. 191 concerning the law of "end stress").

[8] Quintilian, Declam. mai. VI 9 p. 119, 26 Lehnert: cruces succiduntur, precussos sepeliri carnifex non vetat. As to the deadly effect of the piercing of the heart, see Wetst. and Br.

which says, "No bones of his will be broken" (v. 36),[1] and the other which runs, "They will look on him whom they have pierced" (v. 37).[2] The double fulfilment plainly shows that God's plan of salvation is fulfilled in this event, that the crucified Jesus is the promised bringer of salvation.[3] If for the source the meaning of the event is exhausted in this idea,[4] for the Evangelist the first factor goes beyond this and affirms that Jesus is the true Passover lamb; according to Ex. 12.46 no bone of the lamb should be broken. In distinction from the Synoptics v. 14 implies that the crucifixion takes place at midday, while the Passover lambs are being slaughtered.[5] The end of the Jewish cultus, or the uselessness of its further observance, is thereby affirmed.

The ecclesiastical redaction has gained yet another and deeper meaning from the lance-thrust, in that it adds in v. 34b: καὶ ἐξῆλθεν εὐθὺς αἷμα καὶ ὕδωρ.[6] Doubtless a miracle is being recounted here,[7] and equally doubtless

---

[1] The introductory formula corresponds to 13.18; 15.25; 19.24, only that before ἵνα πληρωθῇ is set ἐγένετο γὰρ ταῦτα. This was necessary because two events (ταῦτα) are reported, for which the two Scripture passages are given. It is contested which passage of Scripture is meant in v. 36. In the Evangelist's intention we should think of Ex. 12.46, where it is said of the Passover lamb: καὶ ὀστοῦν οὐ συντρίψετε ἀπ' αὐτοῦ. But in the source Ps. 33.21 could be meant, where it is said (of the δίκαιοι): κύριος φυλάσσει πάντα τὰ ὀστᾶ αὐτῶν, ἓν ἐξ αὐτῶν οὐ συντριβήσεται. not only because of the passive συντριβήσεται, and because the Psalms especially have played a role in the working up of the passion story, but particularly because in vv. 31–37 no reference is made to the passover at all, which nevertheless would have been so natural; see also p. 676 n.6 and cp. Dibelius, ZATW, Beih. 33, 140. G. A. Barton, JBL 49 (1930), 13–19 finds in the circumstance that Jesus (like the Passover lamb) did not have the legs broken, the echo of ancient sacramental ideas.

[2] The introductory formula of the second citation does not occur precisely in this fashion anywhere else in the NT (though cp. Mt. 4.7; Rom. 15.10ff.; 1 Cor. 3.20; Heb. 1.5f.; 2.13; 4.5; 10.30) Quite similar is 2 Clem. 2.4, and exx. in the Rabbinic literature (Schl.). The reference is to Zech. 12.10. With ἐξεκέντησαν the text (apart from details) departs from the LXX, which on the basis of a faulty variant (רקדו instead of דקרו) reads κατωρχήσαντο. Thdn. and Aquila also have ἐξεκεντ. (Symm. ἐπεξεκ.), and other places in which Zech. 12.10 is cited as a messianic text and which make reference to it (Rev. 1.7; Justin Apol. I 52, 12 and elsewhere); Barn. 7.9 has κατακεντήσαντες (without this feature the verse meets us in Mt. 24.30). Perhaps an edited LXX text lay before the author; see Deissmann, Die Septuaginta-Papyri und andere altchristliche Texte (Aus der Heidelb. Pap. Sammlung I); O Michel, Paulus und seine Bibel 1929, 66f.; Rahlfs, ZNTW 20 (1921), 189f. Ἐις ὃν is presumably to be resolved as: εἰς τοῦτον ὅν, and not τοῦτον εἰς ὅν, since ἐκκεντεῖν is correctly construed with the accent; see Br.

[3] In the second citation it is difficult to feel that a definite subject of ὄψονται is reflected (only the fact of the piercing is of importance); it surely must have been the Jews (though it should certainly not be said, as Zn. thinks, that according to Zech. 12.10 they will be seized with penitent sorrow and wailing). In any case there is no thought of the sight of the Christ returning at the parousia, as in Rev. 1.7 and Justin; for these latter the ἐξεκέντ. does not refer to the lance thrust but to the crucifixion generally, or to the piercing of the hands and feet of Jesus; see also Delafosse 100ff. and Dibelius, ZATW, Beih. 33, 139f.

[4] See p. 676 n.6.

[5] See p. 664 n.5.

[6] That v. 34b (and 35) is a secondary addition is indicated at once by the consideration that in v. 37 the point of the citation is seen to be the lance thrust as such (this alone is

this miracle has a definite meaning. It can scarcely be other than that in the death of Jesus on the cross the sacraments of baptism and the Lord's Supper have their foundation.[1] Thus v. 34b goes back to the ecclesiastical redaction that in 3.5 inserted the reference to the water of baptism, and in 6.52b–58 the reference to the Lord's Supper;[2] the same applies to **v. 35**, that claims the testimony of an eye-witness for the miracle:[3] the eye-witness has attested the event, and his testimony is true.[4] The comment καὶ ἐκεῖνος οἶδεν ὅτι ἀληθῆ λέγει is mysterious, for who is the ἐκεῖνος? It cannot be the eye-witness himself, but must be another who is in a position to guarantee the truth of the testimony.[5] In that case, however, only Jesus himself can be meant.[6] But if we consider 21.24: οὗτος ἐστιν ὁ μαθητὴς ὁ μαρτυρῶν περὶ

---

prophesied in Zech. 12.10), whereas for the writer of v. 34b this is only the means by which the really important event is caused, the significance of which is emphasised by v. 35.

[7] Br. refers to Mart. Pauli 5 p. 115, 17, where milk spurts from the wound of the beheaded Paul, and to the old gloss on Mart. Pol. 16, according to which when the finishing blow is dealt a dove flies out of the body of Polycarp. Reflections as to the physical possibility (B. Weiss) are odd. Moreover the Rabbinic theory about the substance of the human body being blood and water (Str.-B.) affords no clue for the explanation. Naturally it cannot be concerned with polemic against Gnosticism; in that case the blood would have sufficed; see the following note.

[1] Br. quite rightly rejects the idea that there is a recollection here of the myth of Bel-Marduk, who is wounded in the New Year Festival. Patristic exegesis already interprets the water and blood of the sacraments. The interest in 1 Jn. 5.6 is quite different; over against Gnosticism Jesus is there characterised as he who δι' ὕδατος καὶ αἵματος ἐλθών. In this case water and blood are not the sacraments, but denote events that took place in the life of the Jesus who has "come in the flesh" (1 Jn. 4.2; 2 Jn. 7), namely his baptism and his death, and οὐκ ἐν ὕδατι μόνον, ἀλλ' ἐν τ. ὕδ. καὶ ἐν τ. αἵματι shows that this concept has nothing to do with Jn. 19.34; for here the paradoxical thing is not the blood but the water: not only blood, but also water! It is difficult to interpret in general terms, in the sense that the blood signifies the cleansing (1 Jn. 1.7), the water the quickening through the Spirit (7.37, 39). Ed. Schweizer (EvTh 12 [1952/53, 348–353], who is inclined to ascribe v. 34b also to the Evangelist, finds in vv. 34b, 35 allusion to the sacraments, which however the Evangelist interprets as witnesses for the reality of the death on the cross.

[2] See pp. 138 n.3; 218f.; 234f.; also 471f.

[3] There is no reason for holding (with Wellh.) that vv. 34, 35 and 37 in their entirety are interpolations. Merx. (p. 30) raises the question whether in v. 34 αἷμα καί is to be struck out in view of 7.37. That v. 35 is missing in some textual witness is doubtful proof that it is a secondary gloss.

[4] On ἀληθινός = true, see pp. 281 n.3; 298 n.2. Moreover elsewhere μαρτυρία is always qualified by ἀληθής.

[5] It is unsatisfactory to suggest a translation error here, because it concerns a comment of the ecclesiastical editor, who without doubt wrote Greek. Similarly the conjecture that ἐκεῖνος stands for ההוא גברא = ἐκεῖνος ὁ ἄνθρωπος (Torrey and Burrows in Colwell 56, and de Zwaan 169) affords no light at all. But also the insight that in vulgar Greek ἐκεῖνος stands for the personal pronoun (= he) and can take up again a previous αὐτός (Colwell 57), or that according to Rabbinic usage a speaker can refer to himself in the third person (Schl.) does not clarify the situation. It does not say καὶ ἐκ. ἀληθῆ λέγει, but ἐκ. οἶδεν ὅτι ἀλ. λέγει, and the subject of οἶδεν must be a different one from that of λέγει.

[6] One can hardly appeal to 3.28, 30; 7.11; 9.12, 28; 19.21 to prove that by the mere ἐκεῖνος Jesus is denoted, though this is true of 1 Jn. 2.6; 3.3, 5, 7, 16; 4.17; cp. also 2 Tim. 2.13. With regard to ἐκεῖνος, is one permitted to recall that according to Jambl. vit. Pyth. 255 (p. 137, 20 Deubner) the Pythagoreans describe their master with this term? Cp. also Eur. Bacch. 242f. Goguel (Introd. II 339ff.) thinks that ἐκεῖνος is intended as an

τούτων . . ., καὶ οἴδαμεν ὅτι ἀληθὴς αὐτοῦ ἡ μαρτυρία and 3 Jn. 12: καὶ ἡμεῖς δὲ μαρτυροῦμεν, καὶ οἶδας ὅτι ἡ μαρτυρία ἡμῶν ἀληθής ἐστιν the suggestion springs to mind that the text is corrupt,[1] and that originally it ran: καὶ ἐκεῖνον οἴδαμεν ὅτι, as Nonnos evidently read.

But who is meant by the ἑωρακώς? If v. 35 comes from the Evangelist, he would have appealed to a report passed on to him by the eye-witness to whom reference has been made,[2] and not set himself up as an eye-witness.[3] For if ὁ ἑωρακώς should signify, "I, who have seen it", the text would not have read μεμαρτύρηκεν but only μαρτυρεῖ (cp. 1 Jn. 1.2; 4.14; 3 Jn. 12). Nevertheless since the verse is derived from the redaction, it is possible for the eye-witness who "has attested" this and the author of the Gospel to be identical in its view, and without doubt that is the intention; for in its view the witness whose testimony is true is, according to 21.4, precisely ὁ γράψας ταῦτα, and the intention of awakening faith is the purpose of the Gospel, as 20.31 itself says.[4] Since, according to 21.20ff., the author of the Gospel is to be identified with the Beloved Disciple, in the view of the redaction he is also the ἑωρακώς of v. 35. That corresponds also to the narrative in v. 26.[5]

6) *The Burial:* 19.38–42

The burial of Jesus is reported similarly as in the Synoptics; here and there the Evangelist has edited his source.[6] As in Mk.15. 35–45, though admittedly at shorter length, it is related that Joseph of Arimathea[7] asks Pilate for permission to take the body of Jesus for burial[8] (**v. 38**). In Mark and Luke Joseph is described as a βουλευτής and is characterised as a pious Jew; here, as in Matthew, he is called a disciple of Jesus; admittedly he is one of the kind who hid their discipleship for fear of the Jews—a comment that could be due to the Evangelist, with 12.42 in mind. Pilate gives the desired permission, and the body is removed.[9] Moreover Nicodemus, who is known from 3.1ff.; 7.50ff.,

---

allusive designation of the editor of the Gospel, who added v. 35 as he did ch. 21, and was known to the first readers; this is very improbable. On οἶδεν cp. Barn. 9.9 (appeal to the knowledge of God).

[1] See Bl.-D. §291, 6 and the literature there mentioned.

[2] So Wendt I 222; II 104 and Bd.; both maintain that the ἑωρακώς is identical with ἐκεῖνος, but they distinguish him from the Evangelist.

[3] So Zn., commentary and Einl.[3] II 481f.

[4] It is of no consequence whether we make ἵνα κτλ. dependent on λέγει, or (viewing καὶ ἐκεῖνος . . . λέγει as parenthetical) on μεμαρτύρηκεν.

[5] On the discussion see especially Zn., Einl.[3] II 489f.

[6] See pp. 666f.

[7] Concerning Arimathia as a place see Klostermann on Mk. 15.43 and Dalman, O.u.W. 239.

[8] On αἴρειν = take, see p. 676 n.1. According to vv. 31–37 the taking of Jesus down from the cross is viewed as already completed. Cp. I Kings 13.29f.: καὶ ἦρεν ὁ προφήτης τὸ σῶμα τοῦ ἀνθρώπου τοῦ θεοῦ . . . τοῦ θάψαι αὐτόν. There is no reflection on the point that through their occupation with the body Joseph and Nicodemus make themselves incapable of celebrating the passover (Dalman, Jesus-Jesch. 86).

[9] ℵ N pc it sa read ἦλθον and ἦραν instead of the singular (syr[s] and D omit!); this

comes on the scene, and reference back to 3.1ff. is expressly made[1] (**v. 39**).[2] He brings a mixture of spices for the burial,[3] and of a truth in an immense quantity.[4]

The body of Jesus is now wrapped in linen bands,[5] in which the spices are strewn (**v. 40**); for the non-Jewish reader it is added that this corresponds to the Jewish mode of burial.[6] The burial had to take place speedily, as **v. 42** calls to mind, since it was Friday evening.[7] The pressure of time demands that the body be put in the nearest available grave that was at their disposal in the vicinity. Precisely that however is of divine ordering; for in this way Jesus receives his resting place in a new grave, in which no one had yet been laid[8] (**v. 41**); it is therefore not yet profaned, and so is suitable for the holiness of his body.[9] It lies in a garden, in the quarter where the crucifixion had taken place.[10] It is not stated that after Jesus was buried the grave was closed up by means of a stone, but that is self-evident, and it is presupposed in 20.1. The burial is described in v. 40 as concluded, not as provisional, and the narrative does not contain any premonition of the following Easter story.[11]

---

must surely be original, since the change into the plural would scarcely be comprehensible, especially as the singular is given in Mk. 15.46 parr. In fact v. 39a will be an addition of the Evangelist, who inserted the reference to Nicodemus (he is not mentioned in the Synoptics), for one would expect some mention of him after 3.1f. and especially 7.50. Since v. 39b betrays an interest foreign to the Evangelist, it comes from the source, which naturally had read φέροντες.

[1] Τὸ πρῶτον = τὸ πρότερον see p. 394 n.1.

[2] See p. 679 n.9; on φέρων Raderm. 210.

[3] Μίγμα only here in the NT (Bℵ* W ἕλιγμα = roll), elsewhere frequently attested (see Br.); σμύρνα = myrrh, a resin which was used along with incense and the like (Mt. 2.11; 1 Clem. 25.2) as an aromatic agent (see Br.); ἀλόη (only here in the NT) similarly an aromatic substance (see Br.). Hosk, thinks of 12.3; 2 Cor. 2.14–16; Eph. 5.2, in addition to which Ign. Eph. 17.1 should be added.

[4] The extravagant amount as 12.3; it expresses veneration. On λίτρα see p. 414 n.8.

[5] Ὀθόνιον as 20.5, 7; Lk. 24.12; frequent in papyri (see Br.).

[6] See p. 86 n.2. Br. raises the question whether this comment is intended to contrast with the Jewish custom another, possibly the Egyptian. On the Jewish custom see Str.-B. II 53 on Mk. 16.1.

[7] Παρασκευή = Friday as v. 31, see pp. 676 n.6; 664 n.5. The Source therefore is not thinking of the impending Passover, and agrees with the Synoptic statement (Mk. 15.42; Lk. 23.54; cp. Mt. 27.62).

[8] In the same sense Mt and Lk expand the Marcan text; see p. 667.

[9] Similarly Jesus (Mk. 11.2) rides on an animal that hitherto has been untouched. According to Num. 19.2 a sacrificial animal should not have borne any yoke; similarly Deut. 15.19; 21.3; Hom. Il. 6, 94; Horace Epod. 9, 22; cp. Georg. 4, 450 and Ovid Met. 3, 10f. According to 1 Sam. 6.7 only such cows could draw the holy tables of the covenant. And according to Deut 21.4 only an uncultivated place is permissible for cultic acts.

[10] This is not mentioned in the Synoptics. The grave in a κῆπος as 2 Kings 21.18, 26; 2 Esr. 13.16. On the situation of the grave see Dalman O.u.W 370ff.; Jerusalem und sein Gelände 74.

[11] See p. 667.

B. 20.1–29: Easter

a) The Easter Morning: 20.1–18

It is clear that in 20.1–18 two motifs vie with one another, or two pictures are bound to each other:[1] 1. the story of Mary Magdalene at the grave, 2. the story of Peter and the beloved disciple. The connection cannot be original. It is remarkable, for example, that in v. 11 Mary is standing at the grave, whereas according to v. 2 she had departed from it and no account is given of her return to it. Since, nevertheless, her return has to be presupposed, it is remarkable in the extreme that the experience of the two disciples, whom she must have met at least on their return from the grave, holds no significance for her. In vv. 11ff. she stands at the grave, as if the events recounted in vv. 3–10 had not happened. Further the commission which Mary receives from the Risen Christ, and then carries out (vv. 17f.), loses its point if two disciples (or at least one, see below on v. 8) have already come to a faith in the resurrection. Yet manifestly the message of Mary must be the first intimation about the empty grave, like the message which is committed to the women in Mk. 16.7; Mt. 28.7, and which according to Mt. 28.8 (cp. Lk. 24.9, 22f.) they also make known. Moreover when Mary looks into the grave she sees the angels, which the disciples did not see, and "which nevertheless must also have been there to see" (Wellh.). If vv. 3–8 are taken by themselves we are surely intended to understand that the sight of the empty grave leads the two disciples (or at least the one) to faith. In the combination with the story of Mary, however, it is not so understood; for according to this account the fact of the empty grave forms only an occasion for helpless questioning (vv. 2, 13, 15), so that it is puzzling why in such a setting this fact works so differently in v. 8. No hint is given that through looking into the empty grave Mary, like the disciples, should really have come to faith; rather the story of Mary is clearly related in the same manner and with the same idea as the Synoptic Easter narratives: the empty grave demands an interpretation through the mouth of an angel.

Obviously then the two stories are not an original unity; whereas the account of Mary is derived from the tradition to which the Synoptic stories about the grave also belong, the story about Peter and the beloved disciple doubtless goes back to the Evangelist.[2] The question arises however whether the second story can simply be lifted bodily from the context, regarded as an insertion from the text of the source. Taken as a whole vv. 3–10 certainly are derived from the Evangelist; and v. 2 is an editorial composition which he needed as a connection for vv. 3ff., and which he composed with the

[1] According to Wellh. and Schw. vv. 2–10 are interpolated, according to Hirsch vv. 2–11. Apart from minor glosses Sp. regards vv. 11b–13 as interpolated, Delafosse vv. 5b, 6, 8 (and 9)—both alike equally unilluminating. Lyder Brun, Die Auferstehung Christi in der urchristl. Überliefung 1925, 14f. finds in 20.1–18 the combination of two independent parallel compositions.

[2] So also Dibelius, ZATW, Beiheft 33, 136.

aid of the motif of v. 12.[1] But we must reckon with the possibility that in consequence of his editing he shortened the text of the source, and that in vv. 3ff. motifs are employed which belonged to the narrative about Mary, and that he rounded off the conclusion in accordance with his particular point of view.

It is actually possible that the description of what Peter sees in the grave in vv. 6f. originally belonged to the story of Mary; indeed that is very probable if this exact description originally "pursued the apologetic purpose of excluding the idea of a hasty robbing of the body by the disciples".[2] Yet this motif may be quite removed from the Evangelist; he could have taken over the description purely for the purpose of illustration.

In the narrative of Mary *the appearance of the angels* vv. 12f. is in uneasy juxtaposition with *the appearance of Jesus* vv. 14ff.; the question of Jesus v. 15 is a repetition of the question of the angels, v. 13, and the latter, together with Mary's answer, has no consequences. Hence in the narrative before us the coming of the angels on the scene, only to disappear immediately, is entirely superfluous, as a comparison with the episode of the angel in Mk. 16.5–7 will particularly make plain. For in the latter account the angel (or in Luke the two angels) reveal the fact of the resurrection and give a charge to make it known to the disciples, a charge which in John's Gospel is given by Jesus (v. 17). Nevertheless the episode of the angels is not an alien element, interpolated by a process of editing (whether by the Evangelist or by the final editor);[3] on the contrary the episode of the angels is original in the narrative of Mary; it corresponded to the type seen in Mk. 15.5–7.[4] (So Goguel rightly maintains, Trois Etudes 27. H. Grass (Ostergeschichten u. Ostergeschehen 1956, 58) points out that in Epist. Apost. the meeting with the angel has fallen out.) However, the original conclusion of the story of Mary has been broken off by the Evangelist, and in its place he has employed the commission motif vv. 14–18. The Evangelist had to strike out the conclusion, for like Lk. 24.11 (Mk. 16.10) it will have narrated the reception of the message by the disciples; on the one hand he did not want to be influenced by the effect of vv. 19–23, and on the other hand he could not represent the disciples as simply unbelieving, for according to vv. 3–10 that was impossible.[5] Vv. 14–18 reflect entirely the view of the Evangelist (see below).

The *source* therefore offered the Evangelist an Easter narrative of the type of the Synoptic tradition. It differed from the latter above all by the fact that it did not give an account about several women, but only of Mary

[1] So also Wellhausen.

[2] So Br., who refers to Mt. 27.64; 28.13–15; Evg. Pt. 8.20; Mart. Petr. et Pauli 21 p. 136, 22f.; Act. Petr. et Pauli 42 p. 197, 10f. Just Dial. 108, 2 etc. So also v. Campenhausen, SA Heidelb. 1952, 4, 29f.

[3] Vv. 12f. along with v. 14a are viewed as secondary insertions by Schw., Wellh. and Sp. (who already deletes v. 11b).

[4] So Goguel rightly maintains, Trois Études 27. H Grass (Ostergeschichten u. Ostergeschehen 1956, 58) points out that in Epist. Apost. the meeting with the angel has fallen out.

[5] See L. Brun, op. cit. 54.

Magdalene.[1] That shows that the Synoptic Gospels are not the source behind the Fourth Gospel;[2] and that is not at all surprising, since at this point the tradition was very variable.[3] Originally the story was an independent narrative, even if in the source it was linked with the foregoing Passion narrative;[4] that is obvious, since Mary comes on the scene without her companions of 19.25, and since the story of the burial 19.38–42 is complete in itself, and is not designed with a view to a continuation;[5] in particular the grave stone was not mentioned in v. 42.[6] It is possible that, as in Mk. 16.1, the coming of Mary originally was assigned a motive, and that in consequence of the combination with 19.38–42 (already in the source) that motivation was struck out.

Jesus was executed and buried on Friday; Mary Magdalene[7] comes to the grave on Sunday morning[8] (**v. 1**), as is reported of the women in Mk. 16.2 parr.; only here it is stated that it is still dark, while according to Mark the sun has risen. But unlike Mark's narrative no mention is made of the purpose of Mary's coming,[9] and therefore there is no reflection on who could roll the stone away from the door of the grave (Mk. 16.3); it is merely reported that she sees that the stone has been removed.[10] From that she draws the conclusion (**v. 2**) that the body has been carried away,[11] and—without looking into the

[1] According to Mk. 16.1 there are besides her "Mary of James" and Salome; according to Mt. 28.1 besides Mary Magdalene the "other Mary"; according to Lk. 24.10 along with her and "Mary of James", Johanna and "the others". Albertz, ThStKr 86 (1913), 483–516 wishes to prove that originally Jn related a story not about Mary Magdalene but about the Mother of Jesus. Grundmann ZNW 39 (1940), 116, agrees with him.

[2] It is hardly right to conclude from the plur. οἴδαμεν v. 2 (instead of which οἶδα stands in v. 13, see below p. 684 n.1) that the Source gave an account of several women (Schl.), especially since v. 2 is an editorial composition of the Evangelist. According to Wellh. and Sp. οἴδαμεν betrays the editor, who edited the Gospel in accord with the Synoptics. In the view of Hirsch (Auferstehungsgeschichten 11) Jn naturally knew the Synoptic accounts and "after his manner dramatically simplified and sharpened them".

[3] See n. 1 and pp. 671f.

[4] See p. 635.

[5] See pp. 666f.

[6] Similarly Mk. 16.1–8 is originally an independent piece of tradition, the combination of which with 15.42–47 is secondary; see Gesch. der syn. Trad. 308 = Hist. of the Syn. Trad. 284f.

[7] The mss. vary here and in the following between Μαρία and Μαριάμ.

[8] In the phrase ἡ μία τῶν σαββ. (אֶחָד בְּשַׁבָּת) τὰ σαββ. as often denotes the week (Str.-B. I 1052; Schl. on Mt. 28.1). The cardinal instead of ordinal number is a Semitism (despite Raderm. 71); see Bl.-D. §247, 1; Black 90.

[9] In Mk. and Lk the women wish to anoint the body (in Mt. they wish only to view the grave); did the narrative of Jn also originally run in this way? See above.

[10] As in Mk. 16.4; Lk. 24.2 this circumstance alone is reported, whereas in Mt. 28.2; Evg. Pt. 9.35ff. the event is described.

[11] The formulation τὸν κύριον is remarkable, for hitherto this title has not been accorded to Jesus in Jn. (see p. 176 n.2), and here also it is surprising, for Mary does not use it to describe him as the Risen Lord. It is probably to be explained on the supposition that the Evangelist chooses the term in adherence to the section of the source v. 13, where of course it says τὸν κύριόν μου. According to Black 91 ἦραν instead of the passive is an Aramaism.

grave?—she hastens, shocked and perplexed, to Peter and the beloved disciple[1] in order to bring this news to them. The two men immediately set out for the grave (**v. 3**), both running at top speed, but the beloved disciple out-distances Peter and reaches the grave first (**v. 4**).[2] He bends down and sees the linen bands lying,[3] but he does not step into the grave (**v. 5**).[4] Peter on the contrary, arriving afterwards, steps into the burial chamber and sees lying there the bands, as also the handkerchief that had covered Jesus' head, and everything in good order[5] (**vv. 6f.**). Only now does the beloved disciple also enter the burial place; he looks, and faith is kindled (**v. 8**).[6] Clearly, it is presupposed that Peter before him was likewise brought to faith through the sight of the empty grave; for if the writer had meant otherwise, and if the two disciples were set over against each other with respect to their πιστεῦσαι, it would have had to be expressly stated that Peter did not believe.[7] In this context the faith that is meant can only be faith in the resurrection of Jesus; it can be signified by the abs. πιστεύειν, because this means faith in Jesus in the full sense,[8] and so includes the resurrection faith.[9] As to the two disciples, it is then simply reported that they return home[10] (**v. 10**).

The emphatic ἦραν . . . οὐκ οἴδαμεν in v.2, corresponding to the formulations in vv. 13 and 15, in v. Campenhausen's view (op. cit. 29) is directed to the Jewish calumny that the disciples have stolen the body.

[1] Sp.'s idea that either ἄλλον or τὸν ὅν ἐφίλει ὁ 'Ιη. must be an addition is unjustified; the meaning is: "and to that other one who . . .", and after 13.23; 19.26 that is quite unambiguous.—Οἴδαμεν (v. 13 οἶδα, see p. 683 n.2) is not a genuine plural; it corresponds to a frequent Oriental mode of speech (see p. 134 n.3 and Dalman, Gramm. des jüd.-Paläst. Aram.² 265f.), and it also has Greek analogies (Colwell 111f.). Against Burney's belief that there is amistranslation here (112f.) see Torrey 329f.; Goguel, Rev. J. Ph. rel. 3 (1923), 379f.

[2] On the pleonastic προέδραμεν τάχιον see Bl.-D §484.

[3] Is βλέπει consciously distinguished from θεωρεῖ ("he looks on them") v. 6?

[4] The μνημεῖον is therefore a burial chamber, within which the real grave is found as a trough or as a bench (Dalman O.u.W. 387ff.). The fact that the angel sits gives reason to think of a bench.

[5] The order is perhaps intended to allay the thought of a robbery of the body; see p. 682 n.2. On σουδάριον see p. 409 n.5. On ἐντετυλ. (see Mt. 27.59; Lk. 23.53) cp Br. Pap. Gr. mag. VII 826: ἐντύλισσε τὰ φύλλα ἐν σουδαρίῳ καινῷ.

[6] The scribe of D in his expansion inserts οὐκ before ἐπίστευσεν (in the remaining d it is lacking). By this means the gloss v. 9, which is difficult to understand, is manifestly made comprehensible; nevertheless the insertion is unreasonable, for the story would lose its point if it dealt in a sceptical fashion with the rivalry of the two disciples. Cp. also A. Oepke, Zeitschr. d. Karl-Marx. Univers. III (1953/54), Sprachwiss. Reihe 11, 77ff.

[7] Goguel, Trois Études 26, differs, as also Hosk. and Barr.; Grass op. cit. 57 and Wik. are correct.

[8] See p. 51 n.3.

[9] That the faith of the two disciples demanded in v. 29 is faith without sight (so Htm., who moreover ascribes faith only to the beloved disciple) is very improbable in face of the statement εἶδεν καὶ ἐπίστευσεν. Naturally both believe without seeing the Risen One himself; nevertheless the empty grave does clearly count as proof for the resurrection.

[10] Πρὸς αὐτούς=home, see Br.; McCasland, The Resurrection of Jesus 49 would interpret: to Galilee.

V. 9 is a gloss of the ecclesiastical redaction.[1] The δεῖ αὐτὸν ἐκ νεκρῶν ἀναστ. sounds unJohannine, and reminds us of the Synoptic terminology or the language of the faith of the Community.[2] The gloss may well be intended to convey no more than the idea that till that point the two had not believed[3] since they did not yet understand the Scripture; now they became convinced through the sight of their eyes. The meaning can scarcely be: he believed also, without having understood the Scripture (Br.); for then instead of γάρ we should expect a δέ to be used.[4]

But what significance does the narrative of the two disciples have, coming to its conclusion at v. 10? The fact that these two were the first of all the disciples to come to faith in the resurrection of Jesus has no significance for what follows, and it is not presupposed, at least in vv. 19–23. The point cannot be in that direction; rather it must lie in the relation of the two disciples to one another, who race to the grave, and each in his way achieves precedence of the other. If Peter and the beloved disciple are the representatives of Jewish and Gentile Christianity,[5] the meaning manifestly then is this: the first community of believers arises out of Jewish Christianity, and the Gentile Christians attain to faith only after them. But that does not signify any precedence of the former over the latter; in fact both stand equally near the Risen Jesus, and indeed readiness for faith is even greater with the Gentiles than it is with the Jews: the beloved disciple ran faster than Peter to the grave!

The narrative returns again to Mary Magdalene. It is presupposed that she is back again,[6] and she stands at the grave, weeping (**v. 11**).[7] As she stoops down to look in the burial chamber she sees two angels dressed in white,[8] sitting at the head and the foot of the bench (**v. 12**). The question, "Why are you weeping?" gives her a chance to bewail her perplexity (**v. 13**).[9] But this dialogue is broken off through the

---

[1] So also Wellh., Schw.

[2] See pp. 632 n.3; 634 n.4.

[3] The ᾔδει read by ℵ*b c q ff² r is obviously a correction and assimilates to v. 8.

[4] Sp. eliminates v. 8b, and he can then retain v. 9 in the text as original: now v.9 declares why the two did *not* come to faith.

[5] See pp. 484f.

[6] See p. 681.

[7] Slight variants are without significance.

[8] Two angels as in Lk. 24.4 (on the number two see Gesch. der synopt. Trad 343ff. = Hist. of the Syn. Trad. 314ff.). As heavenly figures they are clothed in white, cp. Mk. 9.3 parr.; 16.5 parr.; Acts 1.10 etc. On the elliptical ἐν λευκοῖς (as Mt. 11.8) see Br.

[9] Here τὸν κύριόν μου is a formulation of the Source. It is difficult to say whether κύριος should have here the meaning of the (cultic) title; in any case in the thought of the Evangelist it is as little appropriate here as v. 2, see p. 683 n.11.

appearance of the Risen Jesus himself (**v. 14**), whom Mary, suddenly turning backwards, sees standing outside in front of the grave. She as little recognises him, however, as the Emmaus disciples recognise Jesus as he walks with them (Lk. 24.16).[1] Jesus addresses her, "Woman, why are you weeping? Whom are you seeking?" (**v. 15**).[2] But still the ban lies on her, and in her foolishness she thinks he is the gardener,[3] who possibly has removed the body to another place. Her foolishness is analogous to the foolish misunderstandings of 7.35; 8.22, just as οὐκ ᾔδει reminds the reader of 2.9,[4] and especially of the ignorance of Peter in 13.7 and of the disciples in 16.18. It is possible for Jesus to be present, and yet for a man not to recognise him until his word goes home to him. So also δοκοῦσα ὅτι has its parallels in 11.13; 13.29.

Now however Jesus calls Mary by her own name (**v. 16**), and the spell is ended:[5] she recognises him and says to him, "My Master!"[6] What it was that made her recognise him is not to be asked in this supernatural happening.[7] We can only ask what deeper meaning the narrative has; and there can hardly be any doubt: the shepherd knows his sheep and he "calls them by name" (10.3), and when they hear his voice they recognise him.[8] Perhaps we may also add: the naming of the name tells a man what he is; and to be known in such a way leads a man to the encounter with the Revealer.[9]

Mary's address to Jesus, which in a characteristic manner is distinguished from that of Thomas in v. 28, shows meanwhile that she

---

[1] As in Lk. 24.16 the eyes of the disciples "were held", so it is certainly to be understood here—and it is wrong to refer to the morning gloom (v. 1) as an explanation.

[2] On the address γύναι see p. 116 n.5.

[3] The address κύριε is naturally a mere courtesy form of address, since she does not recognise Jesus. On κηπουρός (only here in the NT; elsewhere frequent) see Br. According to v. Campenhausen op. cit. 3ff. the figure of the gardener comes from Jewish polemic, which among other things asserted that a gardener removed the body of Jesus.

[4] See p. 118 n.5.

[5] Στραφεῖσα should hardly be interpreted as at variance with ἐστράφη v. 14, so that the critical elimination of vv. 12–14a might get rid of the offence. For Mary must also have turned herself to Jesus at the words spoken in v. 15. Στραφεῖσα signifies the sudden and lively movement towards him, as μή μου ἅπτου v. 17 shows (this is specially prepared for in the insertion of ℵ³ Θ Ψ pc syr^s: καὶ προέδραμεν ἅψασθαι αὐτοῦ). Black supposes that στραφεῖσα depends on a misunderstanding of the Aramaic text, the reproduction of which in syr^s is correct: "she recognised him".

[6] Διδάσκαλος is not a perfectly suitable rendering of ῥαββουνί (my Lord). This term (also in Mk. 10.51) is a collateral form of ῥαββί (see p. 100 n.5) and occasionally is used as a mode of address to a notability; see Str.-B. II 25; Dalman, W. J. I 267, 279; Jesus-Jesch. 12; Black 21; Albright, Background etc. 158. According to Albright ῥαββουνεί is "a caritative of rabbi, standing for rabboni, 'my (dear [or] little) master'".

[7] Perhaps by the voice; but she had heard it already, v. 15, without recognising him by it.

[8] See pp. 372f.

[9] See p. 107.

does not yet fully know him, i.e. she does not grasp who he is as the Risen One. She still misunderstands him, insofar as she thinks that he has simply "come back" from the dead, and that he is again the man she knew as "Teacher"; that is to say, she thinks that the old relationship has been renewed, and in her joy she wants to embrace him—as a friend would do to a friend who has come back again. Jesus has to speak the word, "Do not touch me!" in order to restrain her.[1]

Admittedly he seems to be in a strange state of transition, as the following words indicate. Jesus has not *yet* ascended to the Father![2] If the wording were pressed, it would follow that when he had gone to the Father he would subsequently present himself to his followers for fellowship and for physical contact; and v. 27 could conceivably confirm this interpretation. But that can hardly be right. Of a surety, Jesus' ἀναβαίνειν is something definitive,[3] and his promised (πάλιν) ἔρχεσθαι 14.3, 18, 23 is not a return into an ordinary mode of life in this world, such as would permit familiar contact. The fellowship between the Risen Jesus and his followers in the future will be experienced only as fellowship with the Lord who has gone to the Father, and therefore it will not be in the forms of earthly associations. First and foremost οὔπω refers to Mary rather than to Jesus; she cannot yet enter into fellowship with him until she has recognised him as the Lord who is with the Father, and so removed from earthly conditions.[4]

If this be so the representation contains a peculiar critique of the Easter stories generally. The μή μου ἅπτου is directed not only against views that lie at the root of Mt. 28.9; Lk. 24.38–43, where the Lord

---

[1] The present imperative does not necessarily imply that she has already touched him, but it need only presuppose that she is trying to do it, and is in process of doing it; see Bl.-D §336, 3. There is no essential difference between ἅπτεσθαι of v. 17 and κρατεῖν of Mt. 28.9 (cp. Mk. 1.31 with Mt. 8.15). Admittedly this κρατεῖν does not mean "hold firmly", so that in correspondence with μή μου ἅπτου it must be understood: "Do not hold me fast!" (Tillm.), as if Jesus was in a hurry to move on. "Do not hold me up" (= delay me, Strathm.) does not really correspond to the verbal meaning of ἅπτ.; on the contrary "Let me loose" (Bd.) could be justified; nevertheless it would be better to render, "Do not cling to me" (Dodd, 443, 2). Barr. is uncertain. Torrey 324 considers that v. 17 is a wrong translation from the Aramaic; correctly it would have run "Do not touch me; (rather) before I ascend (literally: so long as I am not yet ascended) to the Father, go to my brothers". B. Violet (ZNTW 24 [1925], 78–80) thinks that μή μου ἅπτου does not form a clear contrast to πορεύου δέ, and he suggests that μή μου ἅπτου is wrongly translated; it should really read: μή μοι προσκολλῶ (προσκολληθῇς) or μή μοι ἀκολούθει (ἀκολουθήσῃς). F. Perles opposes this, ZNTW 25 (1926), 287. Bd. would conjecture πτόου for ἅπτου. Both Bd. and Michaelis also reckon with the possibility of mistranslation.

[2] Cp. οὔπω 2.4; 7.6 (both places understood in the sense of the Evangelist, see pp. 121, 292) and also 7.39b, if this clause is not to be eliminated as a gloss, see p. 303 n.5.

[3] See p. 307 n.3.

[4] H. Kraft, ThLZ 1951, 570, opposes my interpretation and he suggests instead that before Jesus has ascended, his body is still the sarx body of the dead, through contact with which Mary would become unclean. This is not exactly convincing!

permits physical contact, or even demands it;[1] it also illuminates the Easter narratives that the Evangelist himself reports. While he certainly has no need to contest the reality of the events narrated, it is plain that both in this one and in the story of Thomas he would have us understand that these events do not establish the genuine Easter faith. As Mary's words to Jesus show, the one whom she sees is by no means yet the Exalted Lord who promised his disciples that he would "come" and hold fellowship with them. The miracles of the substantial and mundane appearance of the Risen Lord, which in v. 30 are comprehended under the term, σημεῖα, have only the relative worth of σημεῖα generally, and their real significance is a symbolic one.[2] Consequently there is something peculiarly ambiguous and contradictory attaching to the Easter narratives. For in truth, if contact with physical hands is denied, how can seeing with physical eyes be permitted? Is not the latter also a worldly mode of perception? And on this basis can the Risen Jesus be thought other than an object of perception within the mundane sphere?[3]

The Risen Jesus gives no charge to Mary to tell the disciples that he has risen and will appear to them also;[4] rather she has to inform them: "*I am ascending to my Father and your Father, to my God and your God.*" Thus basically she has to tell them simply what Jesus himself had already told his followers.[5] The real Easter faith therefore is that which believes this; it consists in understanding the offence of the cross; it is not faith in a palpable demonstration of the Risen Lord within the mundane sphere.

The content of the Easter faith is intimated through the formulation πρὸς τὸν πατέρα μου κτλ. Hitherto Jesus had only said that he was going to the Father (14.12, 28; 16.10, 28), or to him who sent him (7.33; 16.5). If he now speaks in such terms as, "to my Father and to your Father," it is thereby implied that through his departure the Father of Jesus has become the Father of those who belong to him. For this reason he also says, "Go off to my brothers!"[6] Thus the

[1] Cp. L. Brun. op. cit. 19: Jn. 20.17 is a contradictory parallel to Mt. 28.9f.

[2] See pp. 113f., 212f., 218, 232f., 452.

[3] Both Dodd (441ff.) and Grass (61ff.) doubt or contest the idea that the Evangelist assumes a critical attitude to the Easter stories.

[4] In Mk. 16.7; Mt. 28.7 the women are directed by the angel to announce to the disciples that Jesus (has risen and) will appear to them in Galilee. In Lk, who like Jn reports only appearances in Jerusalem, they simply announce the fact of the resurrection which the angels have made known to them.

[5] 16.28; cp. 16.5, 10; 13.33; 14.4, 12, 28. L. Brun is quite right in maintaining that the greeting of the Lord through Mary is intended to be a "testimony that both awakens and strengthens faith"; but he is certainly mistaken in the view that it is not at the same time a test of faith for the disciples.

[6] Zn. wishes to delete μου with ℵ* D e Ir!

situation has come about that the love of God is directed to those who belong to Jesus just as it is directed to Jesus himself (16.27; 14.21, 23). Granted that it does not say simply, "to *our* Father," nevertheless it is not the difference in the divine sonship that is stressed—they are indeed his "brothers"—but the equivalence; of course there does exist a distinction, for the sonship of God that believers have is mediated through Jesus, so that we must understand: "to my Father, who (through me) is also yours." If it is further stated, "to my God and to your God," it is not a new thought that is thereby added, but the declaration gains a great pathos: the Father of Jesus is God! And through him God has become the Father of those who belong to Jesus![1]

It is completely comprehensible that no further description follows on this saying, whether it be of an answer from Mary or the cessation of the miraculous appearance. A simple terse statement is made (**v. 18**) that Mary carried out the commission laid upon her. She declares, "I have seen the Lord!"[2] and she makes known what he said to her.[3] No account is given of the impression that her message makes on the disciples—in contrast to Lk. 24.11, 22f.[4]

b) The Risen Jesus before the Disciples: 20.19–23

Just as the basic elements of 20.1–18 are taken from the Evangelist's source, it may be assumed from the outset that the same applies to 20.19–23. Easter stories telling of the appearance of the Risen Jesus to a single person, and others which report his appearing to the whole disciple group, were brought together quite early, as Mt. 28 shows.[5] Such will have been the case with the source of the Evangelist; and moreover it is probable that this

---

[1] In view of its specifically Johannine meaning it is hard to believe that we have here a "saying that had been handed on and firmly stamped" (Lohmeyer, ZNTW 26 [1927], 170, 1).

[2] Here for the first time in Jn. the κύριος-title has its genuine pathos. It is wholly suitable for the Risen One and meets us so in vv. 20, 25, 28: (21.7, 12); see pp. 683 n.11; 685 n.9. On the glosses 4.1, 6.23; 11.2 see pp. 176 n.2; 217 n.3; 395 n.4.

[3] Transition into indirect speech, as 13.29; see Bl.-D. § 470, 3. Burney wishes to approach it through the assumption of false translation (113); on the contrary Torrey 330; Colwell 113. Also various mss. correct in various ways.

[4] If the Source had reported anything of the kind, the Evangelist could not have used it; see pp. 683f.

[5] L. Brun speaks (op. cit. 33f.) of the juxtaposition of visions to the individual and to the whole (group) as the chief theme of the Easter account; see also Gesch. der synopt. Trad. 312 = Hist. of the Syn. Trad. 288. The chief motif of the individual vision is the proof of the resurrection of Jesus, that of the visions to the whole group the missionary commission (Gesch. der synopt. Trad. 312f. = Hist. of the Syn. Trad. 288f.); that is to be seen also in the Johannine narratives: the theme of 20.1–18 is (in the intention of the Source) the proof of the resurrection, that of 20.19–23 the commission, even if the proof motif (as elsewhere also) sounds through in v. 20.

source, like Mt. and Lk., set at its conclusion an account of the appearance of the Risen Lord to the whole band of disciples, when he handed over to them the charge of their calling, as in fact happens in Jn. 20.19–23.[1] Herein is a confirmation that the story in vv. 19–23 is complete in itself, and has no connection with what has gone before (apart from the editorial juncture in v. 19); this indeed was only to be expected if the passage was originally drafted by the Evangelist for this position. No recollection is made of the message of Mary (v. 18), nor of the fact that two disciples have already seen the empty grave (vv. 3–10). Similarly after vv. 22f. the reader is not prepared for a further Easter story, which in fact does then follow. Indeed, the story in vv. 19–23 is told in such a manner that no reader would ever assume that a disciple was missing; clearly vv. 19–23 are or were the story of an appearing of Jesus to all the disciples (apart from Judas Iscariot).[2] Finally it must be mentioned that vv. 19–23 are a variant of Lk. 24.36–49; Mt. 28.16–20,[3] and that both the miracle of the appearance of Jesus and his demonstrative self-presentation (vv. 19f.) are reported in the manner of popular legends;[4] similarly the commissioning of the disciples in vv. 23f. is remarkably differentiated from the manner in which the Evangelist had spoken of the charge given to the disciples in 15.18–16.11. Here it is not a matter of their μαρτυρεῖν, but in a terminology otherwise foreign to that of this Gospel, their task is described in terms of the ἀφιέναι and κρατεῖν of sins. Accordingly the story must have been taken from the source. The Evangelist of course has edited it, and above all vv. 21f. will have come from him. He adduces the story as a symbolic representation of the fulfilment of the promise in 14.18.

On the evening of the same day as that on which vv. 1–18 occurred, hence on the Sunday evening,[5] the disciples are gathered together—in Jerusalem, as doubtless we are intended to understand. Naturally Judas the traitor is not there, and also, as v. 24 afterwards reports, Thomas is absent (**v. 19**).[6] The disciples meet behind locked doors. The stated reason for this circumstance is their fear of the Jews, but essentially it is because by this means the coming of Jesus is shown to be a miracle,

---

[1] Concerning Mk. no judgment is possible, since the original conclusion has been broken off; see Gesch der synopt. Trad. 309 = Hist. of the Syn. Trad. 285f.

[2] Cp. M. Dibelius RGG² III 354. In the thought of the Evangelist of course v. 20 is significant with reference to the Thomas story, see below.

[3] Above all Jn. 20.19–23 is strikingly related to Lk. 24.36–49; this however does not allow the presumption that Jn. 20.19–29 has been "spun out" of Lk. 24.33, 36–40 (Hirsch, Auferstehungsgesch. 10).

[4] It is comprehensible that Wellh. Sp., Delafosse and Goguel regard v. 20 (or 20a) as an insertion.

[5] On τῇ μιᾷ τῶν σαββ. see p. 683 n.8. The Evangelist obviously has added τῇ ἡμέρᾳ ἐκείνῃ which serves the purpose of linkage. He certainly would not of his own accord have repeated τ. μιᾷ τ. σαββ; it stood therefore in the Source. Did οὔσης οὖν ὀψίας also stand in it? In any case Lk. 24.36ff. also takes place in the evening.

[6] See above. Moreover the Eleven are not expressly named, unlike Lk. 24.33; Mt. 28.16.

and thus from the first his form is characterised as divine.[1] Suddenly he appears in their midst,[2] and he greets them with the customary prayer for blessing.[3] That Jesus in the meantime had ascended to the Father, as he had said to Mary that he would (v. 17), and has now again returned to earth would be a false reflection—not only in the meaning of the source, but also in that of the Evangelist. Rather the sense is that he *has* ascended, and even *as such* he appears to the disciples; as such he is able to bestow the Spirit (v. 22), and as such he is afterwards addressed by Thomas as "my Lord and my God" (v. 28).

The fact that the Risen Jesus, as it were, authenticates himself and proves his identity with the man crucified two days earlier through showing his hands—which of course are understood as revealing the nail marks (cp. vv. 25ff.)—and his pierced side[4] (v. 20), is not only surprising with regard to the Gospel itself, but is also quite unmotivated within the narrative before us. In Lk. 24.39[5] the reason for this feature is the bewilderment and terror reported by the Evangelist. Something like Lk. 24.37f. will have stood in the source of John's Gospel also; our Evangelist has struck it out and retained v. 20 only, with its allusion to the Thomas narrative that follows. At the same time perhaps by this means he also emphasises that the Risen Lord and the Crucified are one. In any case for him the story has primarily a symbolic meaning; it sets forth the fulfilment of the promise ἔρχομαι πρὸς ὑμᾶς 14.18ff. The event is not the fulfilment itself, indeed the ἐκείνη ἡμέρα of 14.20 is not a historically determinable day, but the "eschatological" day, which breaks at any time for the believer whose faithfulness endures and overcomes the offence.[6] In harmony with this the εἰρήνη—and the

---

[1] In Lk. 24.36 only the sudden coming is recounted, not the fact that the doors had been shut. The latter is a purely literary motif; for there is nothing to suggest the thought that a search was being made for the guilty companions of Jesus (Goguel, ZNTW 31 [1932], 291).

[2] It is characteristic that there is no reflection at all on how he could arrive through a shut door. It is otherwise in Hom. Od. 6, 19f.: Athene hovers "like air that blows" by Nausikaa in the locked chamber; hymn. Hom. 3, 145ff.: Hermes comes through the keyhole like a mist. In analogous Hellenistic narratives there are reports of the miracle of the αὐτόματον of the opening door; O. Weinreich, Genethliakon W. Schmid 1929, 311–313.

[3] Εἰρ. ὑμῖν (sc. εἴη, Bl.-D. § 128, 5) is the Heb. greeting שָׁלוֹם לָכֶם (as vv. 21, 26); it is variously expressed in the greetings of the Pauline Letters. Several witnesses join Lk. 24.36 to the greeting.

[4] Whoever ascribes 19.34 to the editor (see p. 677 n.6) must naturally attribute to him καὶ τὴν πλευράν in 20.20. Certainly it could not have stood in the Source; but the Evangelist has introduced it in consequence of 19.34, probably in place of an original καὶ τοὺς πόδας, cp. Lk. 24.39.

[5] This interest is also reflected in Ign. Sm. 3, 2: καὶ ὅτε πρὸς τοὺς περὶ Πέτρον ἦλθεν, ἔφη αὐτοῖς· λάβετε, ψηλαφήσατέ με καὶ ἴδετε ὅτι οὐκ εἰμὶ δαιμόνιον ἀσώματον. See below p. 693 n.5.

[6] See pp. 617ff.

solemn repetition of the greeting hints that we have to understand εἰρήνη in the full sense of 14.27—which Jesus offers the disciples has in truth already been given to them in the hour of the departure (14.27). Easter is precisely the hour when their eyes are opened for that which they already possess; and vv. 19–23 are no more than the depiction of this event.

The meaning of this event is likewise illuminated by the statement ἐχάρησαν οὖν κτλ.,[1] a sentence which will already have stood in the source (cp. Lk. 24.41), but which in the Evangelist's mind illustrates the fulfilment of the promise, that from the λύπη of the departure the χαρά of meeting again should blossom anew (16.20 ff.). The blessing is repeated,[2] and to it the missionary charge is conjoined (v. 21); this is formulated in close dependence on the wording of the prayer in 17.18,[3] and of course it must be understood in the same sense.[4]

The fact that the narrative depicts the fulfilment of the promise in the farewell discourses is shown finally in that the Risen Jesus bestows the Spirit[5] on the disciples through his breath[6] (v. 22); Easter and Pentecost therefore fall together.[7] If in 16.8–11 the task of the Spirit

---

[1] 'Ιδόντες is not a complement to ἐχάρησαν but a genuine part. conj. (i.e. a participle as an independent adjunct) and = "When they saw him"; see Bl.-D. § 415.

[2] Probably a sign that at v. 21 the Evangelist's own writing begins.

[3] Doubtless the Evangelist's composition replaces a more original formulation of the Source, which should be thought of as perhaps analogous to Lk. 24.47 or Mt. 28.19f. The text of the Source is taken up again in v. 23.

[4] See pp. 509f.

[5] On λαμβάνειν see p. 616 n.3. Here it is completely clear that it is the Exalted Lord who appears and not merely one returned from beyond. Accordingly Windisch's doubt (Amicitae Corolla 311), whether 20.22f. could serve as the fulfilment of the Paraclete promise, is disposed of.

[6] In Gen. 2.7 God breathes in Adam the πνοὴ ζωῆς (ἐνεφύσησεν), cp. Wisd. 15.11; 4 Esr. 3.5; B. Berak. 60b (Schl. ad loc.); Pap. Gr. mag. XII 238; XIII 762. In Ezk. 37.5–10 the πνεῦμα (ζωῆς) is commanded: ἐμφύσησον εἰς τοὺς νεκροὺς τούτους, καὶ ζησάτωσαν. Here however it is the general idea of the vital life force that is in view. The exorcistic rite of breathing upon the baptisand is a different matter, see Br.; Fr. J. Dölger, Der Exorcism im altchristl. Taufritual (Stud. z. Gesch. und Kultur des Altert. III 1/2) 1909, 118ff.; H. Achelis, Canon. Hippol. (Texte und Unters. VI 4) 1891, 93. At the base of the rite lies a widespread custom: the transfer of beneficent "power" through breathing on a person, whether it be for the healing of the sick, for the conveying of power of office, otherwise for magical effects; cp. Leonh. Bauer, Volksleben im Lande der Bibel 1903; H. Gunkel, Das Märchen im AT 1917, 98; K. Sittl, Die Gebräuche der Griechen und Römer 1890, 345f.; E. Fehrle, Die kultische Keuscheit im Altertum 1910, 80ff. On breath as a vehicle of power see also G. van der Leeuw, Phänemenologie der Religion 257f.; Fr. Pfister, Kultus § 10, 2 (Pauly. Wissowa XI 2159, 18ff.); Fr. Preisigke, Die Gotteskraft in der frühchristl. Zeit 1922,229f.; H.Zimmern, Zum Streit um die Christusmythe 1910,55f. Concerning the breath of the deity, see W. Staerk, Die Erlösererwartung 312ff. According to Christian legend Adam receives the priesthood "because God blew in his face the Spirit of life" (Staerk op. cit. 13). In Sib. 9, 462 Mary's conception is achieved through the breathing in of χάρις: ὡς εἰπὼν ἔμπνευσε θεὸς χάριν. According to P. Goppelt, Typos 1939, 221f. Jn. 20.22 rests on the creation typology.

[7] See p. 585. It will have to be presumed that the promise of the future bestowal

was described as an ἐλέγχειν, so here correspondingly the bestowal of the Spirit is accompanied by the giving of authority to the disciples (v. 23).[1] Thus the judgment that took place in the coming of Jesus[2] (3.19; 5.27; 9.39) is further achieved in the activity of the disciples.[3] It is self-evident that it is not a special apostolic authority that is imparted here, but that the community as such is equipped with this authority; for as in chs. 13–16 the μαθηταί represent the community.

At this point the story ends. An interest in describing the disappearance of Jesus or the reaction of the disciples is not present.

c) Thomas the Doubter: 20.24–29

Strictly speaking the story of vv. 24–29 has no Synoptic parallels. Nevertheless its motif is not strange to the Synoptics. The doubt of certain disciples is reported also in Mt. 28.17;[4] Lk. 24.11, 21ff. (cp. especially v. 25), 37f., 41; also in Lk. 24.39–41 the physical demonstration of the Risen Lord is necessary to overcome the doubt of the disciples.[5] Accordingly we must not regard it as impossible that the source itself already contained this story. Admittedly it can only have been a secondary appendix, even for the source; for in vv. 19–23 the continuation in vv. 24–29 is not presupposed,[6] though certainly the

---

of the Spirit was given in the Source, as in Lk. 24.49; Acts 1.4f. On the attempt to reconcile Jn. 20.22 with Lk. 24.49; Acts 1.8 (or 2.1ff.) see Hosk. In contrast to this J. Koehler (Erfurcht vor dem Leben 75f.) finds here a polemic of Jn. against Acts.

[1] Ἄν = ἐάν as in 13.20; 16.33; nevertheless the mss. vary, see Br. and Bl.-D. § 107; on ἀφέωνται see Bl.-D. § 97, 3. V. 23 with its non-Johannine terminology again is clearly derived from the Source. Lk. 24.47 mentions ἄφεσις ἁμαρτίων as constituent of the kerygma; Mt. 28.19f. says nothing about it but contains something like an ordination (Wellh.). The office of forgiveness of sins is handed over to the community Mt. (16.19); 18.18; see the following note.

[2] The saying is a variant of Mt. 16.19; 18.18, but in place of the terms "bind" and "loose" we have ἀφιέναι and κρατεῖν. The former is usual for the forgiveness of sins, see ThWB I 506ff.; Str.-B. ad loc. κρατεῖν in this sense is singular and is to be understood as formed in contrast to ἀφιέναι (cp. Mk. 7.8), nevertheless the idea is O.T.—Jewish; cp. διατηρεῖν Ecclus. 28.1 and the Rabbinic נטר in Str.-B. In Ps. 130 however שמר (LXX διατηρεῖν) probably only signifies "to keep in memory". See O. Michel, Ev. Theol. 1950/51, 25; Dodd, NtSt 2 (1955/56), 85f. The latter shows that Jn. 20.23 cannot be dependent on Mt. 18.18 but has been derived from another branch of tradition.

[3] So at any rate it is to be interpreted in the sense conveyed by the Evangelist; this authority is especially linked with the giving of the Spirit. That it is limited to discipline within the community (L. Brun op. cit. 82) would be possible for the Source in view of the variants (see previous note), but in connection with the missionary command it is improbable.

[4] It could of course be a secondary addition.

[5] Similarly in the Gospel acc. to the Hebrews (the Nazarenes?) 8.8; Ign. Sm. 3.2 (see p. 691 n.5); lavishly drawn Epist. Apost. 9–12. According to the information of the Gos. acc. to Heb. a story appears to have been recounted especially about James similar to that about Thomas, see M. Dibelius, Der Brief des Jakobus (Meyer's Commentary) 11f. Cp. the analogies in the Apollonius story; see R. Reitzenstein, Hellenist. Wundererz. 1906. 48f.; L. Bieler, ΘΕΙΟΣ ΑΝΗΡ 1.48f.

[6] See p. 689f.

latter fragment does presuppose the former. That Thomas is characterised as εἷς τῶν δώδεκα could well tell in favour of vv. 24–29 originally standing in the source; not only because the δώδεκα are otherwise scarcely mentioned in this Gospel,[1] and in particular they are not mentioned at all elsewhere in chs. 13–20, but also because the reader already knows Thomas from 11.16; 14.5. Of course, for the Evangelist this story, which he keeps till the end, has a special significance; if he did take it from his source, naturally he edited it, since in vv. 25 and 27 he added the reference to the pierced πλευρά of Jesus, in accordance with 19.34a. Possibly the confession of Thomas in v. 28 may also be his own formulation, and in any case this is so of the last saying of Jesus in v. 29 (see below).

It is now reported (**v. 24**), as by way of supplement, that Thomas[2] was absent from the appearance of Jesus to the circle of the disciples. The others explain to him (**v. 25**) that they have seen the Lord; but he refuses to believe without being convinced by the evidence of his own eyes, and indeed without physical contact.[3] The event that follows tells how he is convinced in shame. Eight days later—thus again on a Sunday[4]—the disciples are once more gathered together in the house[5] (**v. 26**). Again the doors are locked, and again Jesus suddenly steps into the circle with his greeting—the prayer for blessing. This time he speaks only to Thomas, and Jesus asks that Thomas convince himself of the reality of the Risen Person before him, as he had in fact demanded (**v. 27**); and he tells Thomas to be no longer unbelieving but believing.[6] Thomas is so overpowered[7] that the confession springs to his lips, "*My Lord and my God!*" (**v. 28**). That confession is wholly appropriate to him who has risen; going far beyond the earlier confession, "My

---

[1] See pp. 115 n.5; 444.

[2] It is hardly likely that Thomas has been chosen for the role of the doubter because of his name (see p. 400 n.7), the meaning of which δίδυμος should be interpreted as "double" (cp. δίψυχος Jas. 1.8); against this see Lagr. R. Eisler (Ἰησ βασ II 418ff.) extracts from the name θωμᾶς = δίδυμος the hypothesis that the story is directed against the hostile objection that the disciples did not see the risen Jesus but his twin brother, who was the dead image of him; therefore Jesus has to appear to him also.

[3] τύπος in the sense of mark, print appears elsewhere also (see Br.); some mss. read τὸν τόπον, which could be conformed to the following τὸν τόπον (A Θ lat syr[s]; but of course B ℜ D pl have τύπον; ℵ* εἰς τὴν χεῖρα αὐτου). ℵ A B have the form τὴν χεῖραν, see Br.; Bl.-D. § 46, 1. The nailing of the hands was not mentioned in 19.17ff., any more than in the Synoptics; reflection on it could have been occasioned by Ps. 22.17: ὤρυξαν χεῖράς μου καὶ πόδας.

[4] So expressly syr[s]. Concerning the designation of Sunday see L. Brun op. cit. 23.

[5] Ἔσω (Hellenistic for εἴσω Bl.-D § 30, 3) here does not answer the question Whither? (Mk. 14.54 etc.), but Where? (Acts 5.23 etc.); Bl.-D. § 103. According to Zn. the scene is set in Galilee; Lagr. opposes this.

[6] On γίνου see p. 539 n.5. It means not "don't become", but "don't be", "don't show yourself as".

[7] Manifestly Thomas did not first undertake the contact, even if this is not to be deduced from v. 29, because there it only says ἑώρακας; see below.

Master" (v. 16),[1] it sees in Jesus God himself.[2] "He who has seen me has seen the Father," Jesus had said in 14.9 (cp. 12.45). Thomas has now seen Jesus in the way that Jesus wills to be seen and ought to be seen. By means of these words ὁ θεός μου, the last confession spoken in the Gospel makes it clear that Jesus, to whom it refers, is the Logos who has now returned to the place where he was before the Incarnation,[3] and who is glorified with the glory that he had with the Father before the world was (17.5); he is now recognised as the θεός that he was from the beginning (1.1).[4]

The answer of Jesus (v. 29) by all means confirms that in the statement of Thomas faith speaks; but at the same time the answer puts him to shame: "*Because you have seen me, have you believed?*[5] *Blessed are they who do not see and yet believe!*"[6] The confession then ought have been made earlier. When? Does the shameful element for Thomas lie in the fact that he did not have faith when the others informed him, "We have seen the Lord?" Does the story teach that faith in the Risen Lord is demanded on the basis of the utterance of the eye-witnesses?[7] Should no one desire that the same experiences be given to him as were

---

[1] ʽΟ κύριός μου in combination with ὁ θεός μου naturally can only be the cultic title. It makes no difference whether the words are understood as an address (the nominative form used as vocative, Bl.-D. § 147, 3) or as an exclamation of the confessor (sc. σὺ εἶ).

[2] In the LXX various combinations of κύριος and θεός are found; repeatedly in the address, in which יהוה אֱלֹהָי is reproduced with κύριε ὁ θεός μου; so Zech. 13.9, Ps. 29.3; 85.15 (where however the Heb. only has אֲדֹנָי); similarly Ps. 87.2. Or in the confession κύριός ἐστῖν ὁ θεός 1 Kings 18.39, or σὺ κύριος ὁ θεός μου Jer. 38.18; similarly 2 Sam. 7.28. The two are coordinated in the address only in Ps. 34.23; ὁ θεός μου καὶ ὁ κύριός μου (Heb. יהוה אלהי); cp. Ps. 43.5: σὺ εἶ ὁ βασιλεύς μου καὶ ὁ θεός μου. Similar combinations occur in Gentile literature; cp. the Address Epikt. diss. II 16, 13: κύριε ὁ θεός.—In dedications: τῷ θεῷ καὶ κυρίῳ Σοκνοπαίῳ. Ditt. Or. inscr. 655; deo domino Saturno (Inschr. aus Thala in Africa, Berl. phil. Wochenschr. 21 [1901], 475). In the Caesar cult: Suet. Domit. 13 of Domitian: Dominus et deus noster. Further exx. in Deissmann, L.v.O. 309f. = Light from the Ancient East 347ff. The combination also occurs in Christian writings as addressed to God, Rev. 4.11: ὁ κύριος καὶ ὁ θεὸς ἡμῶν. As a Christological confession act. Thom. 26 p. 142, 2: κύριος καὶ θεὸς πάντων ʼΙ Κρ.; as an address in prayer act. Thom. 10, 144, 167 p. 114, 5; 251, 1; 281, 6. Further exx. in Ad. Harnack, Dogmengeschichte [4] I 209, 1.

[3] Cp. 6.62; 16.28 etc.; see p. 307 n.3.

[4] Whether οὗτός ἐστιν ὁ ἀληθινὸς θεός 1 Jn. 5.20 refers to Jesus Christ is doubtful.

[5] It is evident that ἑώρακ. does not include "without touching me"; rather ὁρᾶν (as sensual perception) and πιστεύειν are radical opposites.

[6] It makes no difference whether πεπίστ. is considered to be a question or statement; in any case the two clauses ὅτι ... πεπίστευκας and μακάριοι κτλ stand in adversative relation. The formulation is doubtless derived from the Evangelist; on the form of the sentence cp. 1.50 (this sentence also must come from the Evangelist, as well as v. 51 see p. 98, and offers a parallel in content); 4.35; 6.61f.; 16.19, 31; generally the correction in the form of a question follows the laying down of an opinion or attitude of the one addressed. As to the form of the macarism see p. 476 n.4.

[7] So B. Weiss, Zn., Lagr., Menoud (Revue de Théol. et de Phil. 116 [1940], 20f.); Wendt I 28; only so is v. 29 the preparation for vv. 30f.

given to the first disciples, who are now for all time the trustworthy witnesses? Such questions arise, and yet it is strange that precisely this statement should find its illustration in Thomas, who himself was one of the first disciples. And above all, does not the reproach that falls on Thomas apply to all the other disciples as well? All of them indeed, like Mary Magdalene, believed only when they saw; and this applies also to the two mentioned in vv. 3–8, who indeed were convinced not through the appearing of the Risen Lord but through the sight of the empty grave.[1] Thomas demanded no other proof than Jesus had freely offered the others (v. 20). Then does the blessing extol those born later, because they have this precedence over the first disciples, in that they believe without seeing, and precisely on the basis of the disciples' word? That can hardly be possible.

Rather the doubt of Thomas is representative of the common attitude of men, who cannot believe without seeing miracles (4.48). As the miracle is a concession to the weakness of man,[2] so is the appearance of the Risen Jesus a concession to the weakness of the disciples. Fundamentally they ought not to need it! Fundamentally it ought not to be the sight of the Risen Lord that first moves the disciples to believe "the word that Jesus spoke" (2.22), for this word alone should have the power to convince them.[3]

Accordingly, as in the story of Mary, vv. 1f. 11–18, there is embedded in the narrative of Thomas also a peculiar critique concerning the value of the Easter stories; they can claim only a relative worth.[4] And if this critical saying of Jesus forms the conclusion of the Easter narratives, the hearer or reader is warned not to take them to be more than they can be: neither as narrations of events that he himself could wish or hope to experience, nor as a substitute for such experiences of his own, as if the experiences of others could, as it were, guarantee for him the reality of the resurrection of Jesus; rather they are to be viewed as proclaimed word, in which the recounted events have become symbolic pictures for the fellowship which the Lord, who has ascended to the Father, holds with his own[5].

---

[1] Cp. v. 8 καὶ εἶδεν καὶ ἐπίστευσεν.

[2] See pp. 133f., 207f., 233.

[3] Cp. E. Lohmeyer, Galiläa und Jerusalem 1936, 20.

[4] See pp. 687f. Rightly Temple 375, 391f.; a different view in Grass 71f., see also O. Cullmann (Aux sources etc. 52–61); O. Michel (EvTheol 1950/51, 18). According to Dodd (185f., 443) the story of Thomas shows that faith is the way to vision of the Exalted Lord.

[5] Cp. Goguel, Trois Etudes 23–28. The attitude that is demanded therefore is like that which comes to expression in 1 Pt. 1.8, and which is found in the same or similar way wherever the thought of God is genuinely considered. Tanch. לך לך 17a compares the Israelites with the proselytes: the former would not have submitted themselves to God on Sinai without the demonstration of the divine presence, whereas the latter does it without

This exhortation is the pertinent and impressive conclusion of the Easter stories. How could yet another farewell of the Risen Lord be narrated, such as is recounted in Lk. 24.51; Acts 1. 9–11? It is indeed the exalted Christ who appeared to the disciples; an ascension narrative therefore is not necessary.

20.30–31: The Conclusion of the Gospel

20.30f. is a clear conclusion to the Gospel, in which the selective character of the narrative is stressed and its purpose is declared.

It would be possible to relate far more of the "signs which Jesus did before the disciples" (**v. 30**);[1] therefore only a selection has been recounted! This observation is intended not only to excuse the author of the Gospel, but still more to make the reader conscious of the inexhaustible riches of the subject.[2] Naturally the declaration does not

---

having seen any event. According to Plato Theaet. 155e the ἀμύητοι are characterised: οἱ οὐδὲν ἄλλο οἰόμενοι εἶναι ἢ οὗ ἂν δύνωνται ἀπρὶξ τοῖν χεροῖν λαβέσθαι, πράξεις δὲ καὶ γενέσεις καὶ πᾶν τὸ ἀόρατον οὐκ ἀποδεχόμενοι ὡς ἐν οὐσίας μέρει. Cp. also C. Herm. 4, 9: τὰ μὲν γὰρ φαινόμενα τέρπει, τὰ δὲ ἀφανῆ δυσπιστίαν ποιεῖ· φανερώτερα δέ ἐστι τὰ κακά· τὸ δὲ ἀγαθὸν ἀφανὲς τοῖς φανεροῖς. If the story of Thomas had its origin in the discussion with the Jews about the resurrection (Baldensperger, Rev. H.Ph. rel. 1933, 129), it has lost its apologetic significance, at least in the Evangelist's editing of it.

[1] Allusions to other σημεῖα also in 2.33, 4.45; 12.37. Who are to be understood here under the term μαθηταί (ℌ ℜ D pm add αὐτοῦ): the narrower circle or a wider one?

[2] Such concluding expressions are traditional. Cp. Ecclus. 43, 27, after the enumeration of the miracles of God (παράδοξα καὶ θαυμάσια ἔργα): πολλὰ ἐροῦμεν καὶ οὐ μὴ ἀφικώμεθα . . . "Double as many—and we would not be at an end, and the conclusion of the discourse is: He is all". After the report about the struggles and the death of Judas Maccabaeus, it is said in 1 Macc. 9.22: καὶ τὰ περισσὰ τῶν λόγων Ἰούδα καὶ τῶν πολέμων καὶ τῶν ἀνδραγαθιῶν ὧν ἐποίησεν, καὶ τῆς μεγαλωσύνης αὐτοῦ οὐ κατεγράφη. πολλὰ γὰρ ἦν σφόδρα. Philo Vit. Mos. I 213, after the enumeration of the wonders of the creation: ἐκλίποι ἂν ὁ βίος τοῦ βουλομένου διηγεῖσθαι τὰ καθ' ἕκαστα, μᾶλλον δ' ἕν τι τῶν τοῦ κόσμου . . . μερῶν, κἂν μέλλοι πάντων ἀνθρώπων ἔσεσθαι μακροβιώτατος. Similar hyperbolic eulogies of the wisdom of the teachers are to be found among the Rabbis: "If all the heavens were pergament, and all the trees pens, and all the seas ink, that would not suffice", etc., see Str.-B. on 21.25; quite similarly in the Koran, Sur. 31, 26. Cp. Tschudi, Das Vilâjet-nâme des Hâdschim Sultan (Türk. Bibliotek 17) 1914, 107: "As it was in his (the author's) powers he wrote it down, and constantly he had the thought: It is necessary for those who love (God), who come after us.... The discourse will not be too long; i.e. these lofty wonders which I have recounted are (only) a drop from the sea, and a little bit of dust from the sun". Similarly in Greek Literature: cp. Luc. Demon. 67: ταῦτα ὀλίγα πάνυ ἐκ πολλῶν ἀπεμνημόνευσα, καὶ ἔστιν ἀπὸ τούτων τοῖς ἀναγινώσκουσι λογίζεσθαι ὁποῖος ἐκεῖνος ἀνὴρ ἐγένετο. Plut. Mor. 115e. 854f. Fr. Pfister, AR 34 (1937), 56, 1 refers to old Greek encomiums. In a similar manner it is said in introductory statements that the following can reproduce only a selection from the wealth of that which is available: Xen Hell. V 4, 1; Aelius Arist. II p. 361, 3ff. Keil, concerning the deeds of Serapis: ὧν ἱεραὶ θῆκαι βίβλων ἱερῶν ἀπείρους ἀριθμοὺς ἔχουσι. μεσταὶ δὲ ἀγοραί, φασί, καὶ λιμένες καὶ τὰ εὐρύχωρα τῶν πόλεων τῶν καθ' ἕκαστα ἐξηγουμένων. ἐμοι δ' ἐγχειροῦντι λέγειν ἀπέραντον ἡμερῶν πλῆθος ἐπιρρυὲν ἀτέλεστον ὁμοίως ἕξει τὸν κατάλογον

look back specially to the Easter stories, but like the similar statement of 12.37, it embraces the whole activity of Jesus, in which the Easter narratives are included. As with 12.37, it is at first surprising that the work of Jesus is described under the title σημεῖα, but it is comprehensible in view of the unity which, in the thought of the Evangelist, "signs" and words form.[1] As with 12.37, however, the formulation is obviously occasioned by the fact that the Evangelist is taking over the conclusion of the σημεῖα-source.[2] Precisely because in his presentation of the Gospel story he has on the one hand made plain the meaning of the σημεῖα as deeds that speak, and on the other hand represented the words of Jesus as divinely effected event, as ῥήματα ζωῆς (6.63, 68), he is able to use this conclusion of the source without fear of misunderstanding, and at the same time outwardly to conform his book to the form of Gospel literature as it had already become traditional.[3]

He announces the purpose of his book (**v. 31**) as he directly addresses the reader;[4] its purpose is to awaken the faith that Jesus is the Messiah, the Son of God.[5] So far as the Evangelist is concerned it is irrelevant whether the possible readers[6] are already "Christians," or are not yet such;[7] for to him the faith of "Christians" is not a conviction that is present once for all, but it must perpetually make sure of

---

κτλ. Further material in O. Weinreich, Antike Heilungswunder 1909, 199–201; here especially there are examples of exaggerated formulations, often with use of a citation from Homer (Il. 2, 489f.): "if I had ten tongues and ten mouths", or "innumerable as the waves of the sea, as the stars". In Christian literature also emphasis is frequently laid on the fact that Jesus did many more miracles than can be reported: see W. Bauer, Das Leben Jesu im Zeitater der neutestl. Apokryphen 364f.; in relation to martyrs see E. Lucius, Die Anfänge des Heiligenkults, 1904, 200, 1.

[1] See p. 452.

[2] In the Source 12.37f. and 20.30f. will have stood together; see Faure, ZNTW 21 (1922), 107ff. The expression ἐνώπιον τῶν μαθητῶν, which is not motivated by the Evangelist's presentation, favours the idea that the passage has been taken over from the Source, inasmuch as in the first part the disciples are not the real public, even if their presence is everywhere mentioned (apart from 4.46ff.; 5.1ff.). Moreover ἐνώπιον does not occur elsewhere in the Gospel (in this sense ἔμπροσθεν occurs in its place in 12.37), though certainly it does in 1 Jn. 3.22; 3 Jn. 6. Goguel (L'Église primitive 312) on ἐν τῷ ὀνόμ: "Il faut entender 'en invoquant ce nom' ou peut-être 'en le confessant' " (namely at baptism).

[3] Cp. Dibelius, Formsgesch. 37, 3 = From Trad. to Gospel, 40.3: the Evangelist has given his work a conclusion "which really would suit a book belonging to another category, viz. a collection of 'signs' of Jesus such as the synoptics describe. The author probably does this in order to let his book appear, like the Synoptics, as a Gospel".

[4] Unlike 19.35 the address here has good reason.

[5] On υἱὸς τ. θεοῦ see p. 93 n.1. The title in the sense of 1.34, 50; 3.18; 5.25; 10.36; 11.4, 27; (19.7); frequent in 1 Jn. esp. 4.15; 5.4, 13. No special stress lies on Ἰησοῦς, for the anti-Baptist tendency is hardly operative here.

[6] A precise circle of readers is obviously not in view.

[7] It is therefore without significance whether we read with B ℵ * θ πιστεύητε, or with the remaining witnesses πιστεύσητε.

itself anew, and therefore must continually hear the word anew. The meaning of faith, however, is to have life in his "name." It is possible that the Evangelist added this concluding sentence to the words of the source; in any case the phrase ζωὴν ἔχειν[1] is a favourite formulation of his for salvation,[2] and it corresponds to his view that the believer has salvation "in him,"[3] which is here expressed in the fuller phrase "in his name."[4] This emphasis that falls on the last word of the book also corresponds with the first mention of believers at the beginning of the book when they were described as πιστεύοντες εἰς τὸ ὄνομα αὐτοῦ (1.12).

---

[1] ℵ C* D L al add αἰώνιον.

[2] Ζωὴν ἔχειν 3.15f., 36; 5.24, 40; 6.40, 47; 10.10; corresponding to διδόναι 6.33, 10.28; 17.2. Joined to faith in the "Son", 3.16, 36; 6.40.

[3] 3.15; 16.33; cp. also εἶναι ἐν and μένειν ἐν, see pp. 321 n.1; 535 n.1.

[4] His ὄνομα i.e. he, see p. 59 n.2 and cp. esp. 1.12; 3.18; 1 Jn. 5.13.

Postscript: Ch. 21

Ch. 21 is a postscript; for with 20.30f. the Gospel reached its conclusion. The only question is from whom this postscript was derived. That the Evangelist himself added it, and put it after his first conclusion, then to append yet a second concluding statement (vv. 24f.), is extraordinarily improbable.[1] But there are other considerations that tell against the idea that ch. 21 comes from the Evangelist.

Language and style admittedly afford no sure proof.[2] The sentence construction is simple. Conjunctive participle occurs in vv. 7, 8, 12, 14, 19, 20, 21; supplementary participle, v. 19; subordinate to the object, vv. 9 (twice), 20, 25; with article as apposition vv. 2, 24 (twice). Gen. abs. vv. 4, 11. Infinitive constructions of the simplest kind after ὑπάγειν v. 3, after ἰσχύειν v. 6, after τολμᾶν v. 12, after θέλειν vv. 22f.; acc. and inf. after οἶμαι v. 25. Relative sentences: simple relative vv. 7, 20 (twice), in which twice occurs ὁ μαθητής, ὃν ἠγάπα ὁ Ἰη.; ὃς καί v. 20; ὅπου v. 18. Temporal sentences: ὡς οὖν v. 9; ὅτε v. 18; ὅτε οὖν v. 15; ὅταν v. 18; ἕως vv. 22f. Final and consecutive sentences are lacking. Causal sentence: ὅτι v. 17. Conditional sentences: ἐάν vv. 22f. Dependent statements: ὅτι vv. 4, 7, 12, 15f., 17, 23 (twice), 24.

Sentence connections (apart from μετὰ ταῦτα v. 1): asyndeta are frequent, often when the sentence begins with a verb of saying, so vv. 3 (twice), 5, 10 12, 15, 16 (three times), 17, 22. Οὖν: after the verb introducing the sentence vv. 5, 6, 7, 23; otherwise vv. 7, 21; ὡς οὖν and ὅτε οὖν see below. Somewhat more frequent δέ: vv. 1, 4, 6, 8, 18, 19, 21, 23. In addition μέντοι v. 4; γάρ vv. 7, 8; οὐκ . . . ἀλλά v. 23. *Semitisms* may well be seen in the pleonastic ἐξῆλθον v. 3, the consecutive καὶ εὑρήσετε after the imperative v. 6, and the expression ἐξῆλθεν ὁ λόγος v. 23.

As to the *vocabulary*, the fact that a series of terms are met only in ch. 21 is accidental and conditioned by the material.[3] It is striking however that the

---

[1] Lagr. endeavours to counter this argument through the view that 20.30f. stands in the wrong place; it belongs (he says) after 21.23, and has been displaced from there through vv. 24f. Cp. Menoud 29f. Similarly L. Vaganay, Revue biblique 1936, 1ff.; only that he places 20.30f. after 21.24 and holds that v. 25 only is secondary. While the view of a disorder of the text has nothing improbable in itself, it is nevertheless to be pondered that the present order of the Gospel goes back to a redaction, and it is hardly possible that this process of editing put 20.30f. on the wrong place. According to Hosk. 20.30f. concludes only the Easter narratives, not the entire Gospel; otherwise the latter lacks the missionary commission, which in fact is given in ch. 21.

[2] Concerning the stylistic agreement of ch. 21 with the rest of the Gospel, see especially Schl. and Goguel, Introd. II 287ff.

[3] There are: αἰγιαλός v.4, ἁλιεύειν v.3, ἀποβαίνειν v.9, ἀριστῆσαι v.12, ἀρνίον v.15, βόσκειν v.15, γηράσκειν v.18, γυμνός v.7, δίκτυον vv.6,8, ἐκτείνειν v.18, ἐπενδύτης v.7

following vocables are found only in ch. 21: ἀδελφοί as a designation of Christians, v. 23; ἐξετάζειν instead of ἐρωτᾶν v. 12; ἐπιστραφῆναι instead of στραφῆναι (1.38; 20.14, 16), ἰσχύειν instead of δύνασθαι v. 6 ("affected" according to Raderm. 37); τολμᾶν v. 12. Further it is surprising to find the disciples addressed as παιδία v. 5 (cp. however 1 Jn. 2.14, 18); causal ἀπό v. 6, and partitive ἀπό v. 10, instead of the usual ἐκ;[1] also ἐπί is used in v. 1 differently from elsewhere in the Gospel; similarly φανεροῦν v. 1. It is strange to read ἕως v. 22 instead of ἕως ὅτου (9.18) or ἕως οὗ (13.38); πλέον v. 15 instead of μᾶλλον (3.19; 12.43), οὐ μακράν v. 8 instead of ἐγγύς (often, e.g. 11.18); ὑπάγειν with inf. v. 3 (contrast 4.16; 9.7; 15.16). Also τί πρὸς σέ v. 22 is unusual (cp. 2.4).

It is not irrelevant to note the curious fact that the disciples are here assumed to be fishermen; whereas of course that agrees with the Synoptics, not a word of it has hitherto been said in this Gospel. Similarly it is only here that the sons of Zebedee appear (v. 2), hitherto they have not been named. Finally it is strange that at this point only, and not in 1.45, Nathaniel is described as hailing from Cana.

A still weightier consideration is that in ch. 21 the tradition of the appearances of the Risen Lord in Galilee emerges, and while this is attested by Mk. and Mt. it is completely ignored in ch. 20; in ch. 21 it comes without any preparation, without for example any mention being made of the journey of the disciples from Jerusalem to Galilee. But more! The story in 20.19–29 is related in such a manner that not only are no further appearances of the Risen Lord anticipated, but no more could be awaited. After the commissioning of the disciples in 20.22ff., it is more than surprising that the disciples, instead of bearing testimony, are found fishing in the Sea of Galilee, there to experience a new appearance which now has no real meaning at all; after the saying of Jesus in 20.29, a further visible manifestation of Jesus could hardly be recounted. Moreover it is apparent that the narrative of 21.1–14 was originally related as the first Easter story (see below); the editorial v. 14 shows that the story was set only subsequently in the place that it now occupies.

In addition the account in ch. 21 has a wholly different character from that which preceded it. The theme here is not the existence of disciple and community, not revelation and faith; rather quite special interests in persons come to the fore, and relationships in the history of the community. Certainly the problem of the relation of Jewish and Gentile Christianity emerges in 19.26f.; 20.3–10; but there it was faced as a fundamental issue, whereas here the topical question about the status of ecclesiastical authorities is echoed. In this passage the beloved disciple is not the representative of Gentile Christianity, but a definite historical person. It is also symptomatic that whereas allegory is foreign to the Gospel, it appears in v. 11, even if the precise

---

ζωννύναι v.18, οἶμαι v.25, πῆχυς v.8, πιάζειν vv.3,10, ποιμαίνειν v.16, προβάτιον v.16, προσφάγιον v.5, πρωΐα v.4, σύρειν v.8.

[1] Less striking is σύν v. 3 instead of the otherwise frequent μετά; for σύν anyway occurs also in 12.2; 18.1.

meaning of the number is not to be unravelled. Quite decisive, however, is the fact that in vv. 22f. the realistic eschatology is evident, against which the Gospel maintains a polemic, and which the ecclesiastical redactor has introduced by his interpolations.[1] It is precisely to this ecclesiastical redactor that ch. 21 goes back.

Finally the point is proved by v. 24. Inasmuch as the beloved disciple, of whom vv. 20–23 had spoken and who according to v. 23 had died, is described as author of the Gospel, it is perfectly plain that the Gospel as we have it was edited and provided with this supplementary chapter after his death. For the fiction that the author himself puts himself forward here as identical with the Beloved disciple, and at the same time wishes to attest his own death is quite unbelievable.[2]

Ch. 21 *is not a unity.* It is divided into the two sections vv. 1–14 and vv. 15–23, which cannot originally have belonged together. The analysis shows that vv. 1–14 were originally an independent Easter story, which reported an appearance of Jesus to a group of disciples at the Galilean Lake, and that it was due to an editor that the beloved disciple and Peter were assigned a particular role. Through this editing however the story has become a kind of introduction to vv. 15–23, where Peter and the beloved disciple are chief persons and where the other disciples, though still present, are completely ignored.

In vv. 1–14 the statement of v. 4 that the disciples did not recognise Jesus is immediately surprising. Is it comprehensible that without ado they carry out the command of a stranger (so v. 6)?[3] Of course one can urge that that need occasion no surprise in an Easter story: it must be understood that in this mysterious event a ban lies on the participants. Yet account must be taken here of the lack of clarity in the relation between vv. 4b and 12b; according to v. 12b the disciples know that they have to do with Jesus, without any prior statement being made (as is mentioned in connection with the beloved disciple, v. 7) that in the meantime they had recognised him. Probably v. 4b is to be ascribed to the Redactor as a preparation for the particular role of the beloved disciple in v. 7.

V. 7 in any case is an editorial addition. It interrupts the account of the miraculous catch of fish through the announcement of the Beloved Disciple (why was he not named in v. 2?!) that the Stranger is the "Lord", and through its describing how Peter thereupon sprang into the water—manifestly in order to reach Jesus as quickly as possible. According to v. 8 the rest of the disciples approach the shore in the ship, for they are not far out,[4] and they drag the full net in the water behind them. The information in v. 9, that when

[1] See pp. 223f., 261, 345 n.6.

[2] On the possibility of explaining vv. 23 and 24 (in whole or in part) as interpolations, see below, pp. 715f.

[3] Cp. Lk. 5.5, where Peter only hesitatingly obeys the corresponding command of Jesus, although Jesus does not there appear as an unknown person.

[4] Syr[s] corrects, in order to bring a better logic into the narrative, in that it draws this statement into v. 7: "(Peter) plunged into the sea and swam, and so came (to the beach), because they were not far from the land"—Merx holds this to be original.

they come to the shore they find a coal fire there, on which fish was roasting, and bread as well, is surprising after v. 5, in consequence of which the disciples obviously were sent out for a catch to procure provisions which were not at hand.[1] Should a miracle be reported that makes the fish caught by the disciples superfluous, and that shows human effort to be unnecessary in face of the omnipotence of the "Lord", who can miraculously provide what is lacking? But the catch of fish itself was a miracle, due to his omnipotence! Moreover in v. 10 Jesus again speaks from the standpoint of v. 5: the disciples must bring their catch! For what reason, if not to prepare a meal with the fish that had been caught? And in v. 11 Peter—manifestly at the command of Jesus—disembarks on to the shore and draws the net with the fish in it to land! But Peter was a long while before the ship, and therefore had swum to land before the other disciples! Of course it is not expressly said in v. 7 that he had arrived;[2] but that he who wanted to get in front of the others actually arrived after them would quite certainly have had to be stated expressly. Accordingly he was standing there for some time, and Jesus appears to take no notice of him! Vv. 9–11 can be understood in a natural way only in the sense that the disciples (along with Peter) drove the ship to land and sprang out,[3] and that Peter, at the command of Jesus, gets on the shore and hauls in the net.[4] The command δεῦτε ἀριστήσατε v. 12, coming after vv. 10f., must be interpreted as meaning that a breakfast of fish that had been caught should be prepared and eaten. According to v. 13 however that is not meant; rather Jesus distributed among the disciples the meal spoken of in v. 9.

This confusion can be understood only on the assumption that a written text has been enriched through editorial additions. Such are probably v. 4b, certainly v. 7, and vv. 9b and 13. Finally the statement as to the number of the fish that had been caught could go back to the redactor;[5] since it is not a round number, it doubtless has an allegorical meaning, and it is hardly credible that an early story contained such a feature. As to v. 14, see below. In v. 8 the text of the source cannot have remained intact, for there could have been talk of the ἄλλοι μαθηταί only if the behaviour of Peter had been explained in v. 7. Presumably the first clause of v. 8 is to be ascribed to the redactor; originally v. 6 was immediately followed by v. 8b (with δέ instead of γάρ). I suppose also that v. 11a originally ran: ἀνέβησαν (οὖν) οἱ μαθηταὶ καὶ εἵλκυσαν κτλ. The redactor again wished to ascribe to Peter a special role, and that hangs together with the allegorical meaning of v. 11b. The

---

[1] Sp. would transfer v. 9 after v. 11; but the difficulty is not thereby removed, not even when Sp. in v. 9 deletes καὶ ἄρτον and strikes out the whole of v. 13.

[2] Concerning syr^s see p. 702 n.4.

[3] ℵ* syr^s in v. 9 read ἀνέβησαν instead of ἀπέβησαν; that conflicts with ἀνέβη in v. 11 and cannot be original.

[4] 'Ανέβη v. 11 is to be understood of the embarking of Peter on the ship and is impossible; the net is not in the boat at all. ℵ and L admittedly do so interpret when they read ἐνέβη.

[5] Therewith naturally also καὶ τοσούτων ὄντων κτλ. Did by chance the Source read instead καὶ ἐσχίσθη τὸ δίκτυον? Cp. Lk. 5.6.

original conclusion of the story must have been ousted by v. 13. Somehow it must have explained the removal of the ban that, according to v. 12, lay upon the disciples. It will have spoken about a saying of Jesus either at or after the meal, and perhaps of an act of homage on the part of the disciples. It is especially natural to assume that Jesus handed over to the disciples their task with reference to the miraculous catch of fish that had just taken place, since he called them to be "fishers of men"; accordingly the miracle of the catch of fish will have had a symbolic significance.[1] It is possible that a miraculous disappearance of Jesus was then recounted, perhaps as in Lk. 24.31.

The additions of the redactor are not all of the same kind. Vv. 4b, 7–8a (and in v. 11), which contain the motif of Peter and the beloved disciple and prepare for vv. 15–23, belong to the redactor who composed ch. 21 as a whole and attached it to the Gospel. But vv. 9b, 13 in themselves have nothing to do with that narrative; they can only have the meaning of turning a real meal, at which Jesus finds himself with the disciples (as Lk. 24.30), into a miraculous cultic meal. It is hardly likely however that we have to distinguish two stages of the redaction, so that the editor of the whole had already found vv. 9b, 13 worked into the old Easter story. It is not difficult to presume that a variety of interests prompted the redactor.[2]

It has long been recognised that the story of the miraculous catch of fish which was contained in the source is a variant of Lk. 5.1–11.[3] The two

[1] Ed. Schwartz, ZNTW 15 (1914), 217 suggests that the original conclusion lies before us in vv. 15–17, and that it was dislodged through vv. 13f.; that is highly improbable, for after the miracle of the catch of fish Peter's ministry can hardly be fittingly represented by the picture of the shepherd, but only in a manner analogous to Lk. 5.10.

[2] Wellh. considers that in 21.1–14 two narratives are combined, namely a variant of Lk.5. 1–11 (see the following paragraph in our own text) and a variant of Mk. 6.45–5.2, i.e. a story of a miraculous catch of fish and a story of a miraculous feeding of the disciples; the latter described how the disciples by night went without Jesus over the lake and that early in the morning they find Jesus on the shore, where he has already prepared a meal for them; they do not know how he has arrived there, and they regard him as a ghost. But vv. 9 and 13 are insufficient to bear the weight of such a construction. Ed. Schwartz, ZNTW 15 (1914) 216f., broadens the basis for the story that allegedly was bound up with the story of the catch of fish; the former is said to consist of vv. 1–3, 4a, 9, 12, 13 and is an old Easter story: "The disciples who had fled to Galilee have returned to their earlier occupation and have gone out to fish. In the morning the Lord appears to them on the shore and he renews the table fellowship with them". But the breadth of the description in v. 3 and especially the ἐπίασαν οὐδέν is obviously the preparation for vv. 5f.! Goguel also (Introd. II 295ff.; HThR 25 [1932], 20ff.) accepts the idea of a combination of a story about a miraculous catch of fish with an Easter narrative. In like manner Htm. and Br. speak of the combination of two stories, while Brun (op. cit. 58) speaks only of the combination of two originally independent motifs. Grundmann is different again (ZNW 39 [1940], 113, 5), in that he finds an original Easter story by separating out vv. 1, 5f., 10f. as editorial. Grass (79–81) renounces a critical analysis; he sees in 21.1–14 an Easter narrative which is a variant of Lk. 5.1–11.

B. Davis

[3] Goguel, op. cit., shows that in Lk. the motif of Jesus giving instructions and the person of the sons of Zebedee are secondary. For purposes of comparison therefore these elements should be separated out. The stories about catching fish adduced by L. Bieler ΘΕΙΟΣ ΑΝΗΡ I 105ff. alongside Jn. 21 and Lk. 5 are no real analogies.

variants reveal the following differences. 1. In Lk. the summons to make the catch of fish is not motivated, as it is in Jn. 21, through the necessity to procure food, consequently no meal follows the catch of fish. In this respect Jn. 21 could give the impression of being original. Since however the narrative obviously had the meaning of illustrating the call to apostleship,[1] as is still the case in Lk., and probably was the case also in Jn's source (see above), the motivation of the catch of fish and the attached meal will be fictional decoration. 2. In Lk. the story is not, as in Jn., an Easter story, and in this respect Jn. 21 will have retained the original context.[2] Just as the stories of Peter's Confession and the Transfiguration, Mk. 8.27–30; 9.2–8, were originally Easter stories, which Mk. projected back into the "Life of Jesus",[3] so will the case have been with Lk. 5.1–11.[4]

The early Easter story, related in vv. 1–14, manifestly originally told of the first (and only?) appearance of the Risen Jesus to the disciples;[5] it does not presuppose that Jesus had already shown himself once to the disciples, and that they had been charged with their calling and equipped for it. The remarkable uncertainty in the relation of the disciples to Jesus attests the contrary.[6] Accordingly v. 14 is understood on the assumption that the redactor wished to combine the Matthaean-Markan tradition of a Galilean

---

[1] Like Mk. 1.16–20 the story presumably has arisen from the parabolic saying about catching men; see Gesch. der Synopt. Trad. 232, 26f. = Hist. of the Syn. Trad. 217f., 27f.

[2] Conversely Sp., Dibelius (Formsgesch. 110 = From Trad. to Gospel 113), Goguel. According to Sp. and Goguel Jn. 21.1–14 has been a miracle story, in the collection from which 2.1–11 and 4.46–54 are taken, and it was numbered as the third; such is attested by v. 14. But in that case the editor must not only have added ἐγερθεὶς ἐκ νεκρῶν, but ἐφανερώθη ... τοῖς μαθηταῖς must also have been his formulation, through which he had replaced the statement of the source. For if we are to judge in accordance with 2.11 and 4.54, the miracle must have been expressly described in the source as a σημεῖον; accordingly a sentence like ἐφανέρωσεν τὴν δόξαν αὐτοῦ ought to be expected. There remains only τρίτον as analogous to 2.11 and 4.54, and that is capable of being understood in a quite different way; see immediately in the text. Further if the editor was the first to make the story into an Easter narrative it is difficult to understand why he did not simply leave out the statement of v. 14.

[3] See Gesch. der synopt. Trad. 275ff., 278ff. = Hist. of the Syn. Trad. 257ff., 259ff.

[4] So also Bd. Certainly appeal ought not to be made to the saying of Peter in Lk. 5.8 to prove that Lk. 5.1–11 was originally an Easter story (see Harnack, Beitr. zur Einleitung in das NT I [1906], 158, 2; Hirsch Auferstehungsgeschichten 22f.), as if this was a "despairing confession of guilt". To the contrary, and rightly so, Dibelius, Formgesch. 110 = From Trad. to Gospel 113; Goguel, Introd. II 297, 2. It is probable that the Gospel of Peter closed with a wider variant of this Easter story, but on account of the mutilation of this conclusion it must be left out of consideration.

[5] That this story, or a variant of it, formed the original conclusion of Mk. (and of the Gospel of Peter) has a certain probability; see P. Rohrbach, Die Berichte über die Auferstehung Jesu 1898; A. von Harnack, Beiträge I 158, 2; B. H. Streeter, The Four Gospels 355f.; O. Cullmann, Petrus 1952, 62f., 202ff. Of the two motifs which the Easter narratives contain, in part separately and in part combined: 1. proof of the resurrection (so 20.24–29), 2. commission of the disciples (combined with 1 in 20.19–23; see also Gesch. der synopt. Trad. 312f. = Hist. of the Syn. Trad. 288f.), 21.1–14 contains at any rate the first. The motif of the commission is at most given indirectly through the command to catch fish, and was perhaps amplified in the suppressed conclusion (see pp. 703f). Lohmeyer (in my view quite unjustly) contests this, Gal. und Jerus. 18.

[6] V. 4b would attest it in the same way if it did not go back to the editor.

appearance of the Risen Lord with the Johannine representation.[1] Inasmuch as he now added this story after relating two appearances of the Risen Lord (20.19–23, 24–29),[2] he was compelled expressly to correct the tradition from which he took vv. 1–13 in this point, and to stress that what is here recounted is the third "revelation" of the Risen Jesus.[3]

The redactor, i.e. the author of ch. 21 as a whole, joined on to vv. 1–14 two conversations of Jesus with Peter, contained in vv. 15–23. A clear relationship to vv. 1–14 is not provided—e.g. by explaining that Jesus took Peter aside. The other disciples are simply ignored in vv. 15–23; only the beloved disciple, whose appearance in v. 7 actually goes back to the redactor, appears again in vv. 18–23.

The theme of the first conversation, vv. 15–17, is the entrusting of Peter with his task as leader of the community, that of the second, vv. 18–22 (explained by a note in v. 23), the relationship of Peter to the beloved disciple. The two sections have no inner connection with one another, but they give expression to a variety of interests. For the author the interest rests on the second, namely on the idea that the beloved disciple shares the same rank as Peter, to whom the Lord assigned the leadership of his community. In this context therefore vv. 15–17 have no independent significance; for the author is not interested in the office of Peter in itself, but in the transfer of his authority to the beloved disciple. Hence vv. 15–17 are simply the foil for vv. 18–23,[4] where it is taught that after Peter died as a martyr, the beloved disciple stepped into his place as an authoritative witness. It is clear therefore that vv. 15–17 are taken from the tradition, perhaps from a written source, whereas vv. 18–23 of course are the author's own composition.

A. 21.1–14: The Appearing of the Risen Lord by the Lake

V. 1 is a kind of superscription for the following story. The verse begins as if the Gospel had not concluded with 20.30f.; it leads on by means of a μετὰ ταῦτα like 3.22; 5.1; 6.1; 7.1, and it points back by means of a πάλιν to 20.1ff., 24ff.: a further "revelation" of the Risen Jesus is to be narrated.[5] The scene is the bank of the Galilean lake,[6]

---

[1] Cp. B. W. Bacon, JBL 50 (1931), 71.

[2] 20.1–18 naturally is not counted with the others, since it is not related in that passage that Jesus revealed himself to the *disciples*.

[3] So e.g. also Br., Bd.

[4] Similarly B. W. Bacon, JBL 50 (1931), 72: vv. 15–19 are a foil for vv. 20-25; the Beloved Disciple is set alongside Peter as the competent witness in the time when the heresies are springing up.

[5] Φανεροῦν here and v. 14 of the appearance of the Risen Lord, elsewhere in this sense only Mk. 16.12, 14. Elsewhere in Jn. φαν. is used of the revelation of him who walks

without any record being given of a journey of the disciples from Jerusalem to Galilee. **V. 2** provides a description of the situation: seven of the disciples find themselves on the lake. Of them the first three, Peter, Thomas and Nathaniel are known from the Gospel; as in 20.24, Thomas is characterised by his nickname; the fact that Nathaniel comes from Cana was not recorded in 1.45. Besides these there are two sons of Zebedee, who are not elsewhere mentioned by name in the Gospel, and two unnamed disciples. Why are the names of these last two not given? Do they belong at all to the circle of the Twelve?[1] No mention is made of the beloved disciple, whose presence is presupposed in v. 7; originally he had no place in the narrative,[2] but naturally the author must have identified him with one of the unnamed men. As to the inner frame of mind of the disciples, not a word is said.[3] From v. 3 it is to be concluded that the time is evening.

The action begins with **v. 3**: Peter declares his intention of going to catch fish, and the others join him. Any motivation, any retrospect on what has been experienced, is lacking here also. The fishing expedition—so it is further reported—on this night was unsuccessful.[4] Early in the morning—the disciples of course have come to land again—Jesus steps on the shore (**v. 4**). Where he comes from is not stated; his appearance is mysterious, as in Lk. 24.15, and the fact that the disciples do not recognise him is also a miraculous occurrence; their eyes are "held," like those of the Emmaus disciples, Lk. 24.16; undoubtedly in the context of the narrative that feature serves to prepare for v. 7.[5] The question of Jesus, whether they have fish for a meal (**v. 5**), they answer in the

---

in the flesh, 2.11; 7.4; cp. 9.3; 17.4 and see p. 497 n.2. As to the parousia see Col. 3.4; 1 Pt. 5.4; (1 Jn. 2.28; 3.2).

6 On the description see p. 211 n.3; ἐπὶ τῆς θαλ. = "by the lake", see Bl.-D. § 234, 3. On the attempts to locate the place, see Dalman, O.u.W. 147f.

1 According to J. Hausleiter, Zwei apostel. Zeugen für das Joh-Evg. 1904, the unnamed disciples are Philip and Andrew; similarly Bd. Lagr. raises the question whether οἱ τοῦ Ζεβ. is an old gloss which had the intention of naming the unnamed. It is unlikely that the two only serve the purpose of filling out the number seven, for otherwise their significance is not at all apparent. There is no reason to suspect that their names have been suppressed. The conclusion of the Gospel of Peter, which clearly gave a report of an appearance of the Risen Lord by the lake, names Peter, Andrew, Philip, Levi, who betake themselves to fishing; unfortunately the fragment breaks off at this point. According to Dibelius, Formgesch. 114, 1 the narrative goes back to a circle in which the Nathanael legends were current.

2 See p. 702.

3 Differently the Gospel of Pt. 14.59: the disciples return dejectedly from Jerusalem to their home country, take their nets and go to the lake. Hosk. is also so minded: "The scene is one of complete apostasy, and is the fulfilment of 16.32".

4 Πιάζειν of the catch of fish here and v. 10 as P. Lond. II p. 328, 76; otherwise of the capture of animals Cant. 2.15; Rev. 19.20.

5 See p. 702. Mk. 6.49 is not to be adduced for comparison (Lohmeyer, Galiläa und Jerusalem 18. 1), for the disciples do not regard Jesus as a φάντασμα.

negative.[1] He now tells them to throw out the net, and that on the right side of the boat;[2] they obey the command, and they catch so many fish that they cannot draw the net into the boat (**v. 6**).[3]

The beloved disciple recognises by the miracle—for so we are obviously intended to understand—that the stranger is the "Lord," and he informs Peter of that (**v. 7**). Whereas he draws no consequences from his knowledge, Peter, putting on his upper garment,[4] springs into the lake, and swims or wades—so we must fill out the narrative[5]—to the shore. No more however is said about him immediately;[6] rather it is related that the other disciples now arrive with the boat, and drag the net in the water after them (**v. 8**); the distance evidently was only slight.[7] As they come to land they see there a fire burning on which fish is roasting,[8] and bread in addition; a mysterious meal thus is already prepared (**v. 9**). Nevertheless Jesus commands that they should bring some of the fish they have caught (**v. 10**); thereupon Peter draws the net with the fish to land. (**v. 11**).[9] The miraculous nature of the catch is stressed through the statement as to the multitude of the fish and the fact that despite this number the net was not torn. The more unclear

---

[1] The question introduced by μή expects the answer "No"; as in 4.29 therefore it is formulated from the standpoint of those addressed; see Bl.-D. § 427, 2 and in addition p. 413; also Br. ad loc. On the address παιδία, see p. 701. Προσφάγιον means the accessories that are eaten with the bread (whether meat or vegetables); cp. P. Oxy. 498, 33, 39: ἄρτον ἕνα καὶ προσφάγιον. Further material in Br. It is equated by Moeris and Hesychius with ὄψον, which like ὀψάριον (see p. 212 n.6) can simply mean "fish", as here, vv. 10.13.

[2] The right side is the side of good fortune, cp. Lk. 1.11; Mt. 25.33; Mk. 16.5; Str.-B. I 980f.

[3] Ἀπό in a causal sense only here in Jn., otherwise frequent; see Br. and Bl.-D. § 210, 1.

[4] Ἐπενδύτης only here in the NT, often in LXX, is the outer garment; see Br. ad loc. and lexicon (Arndt & Gingrich); γυμνός does not need to be rendered "naked", but can signify "only in the undergarment". The fact that Peter clothes himself evidently has the meaning that he desires to appear before Jesus in a seemly manner.

[5] So syr^s, see p. 702 n.4.

[6] See p. 702.

[7] 200 cubits = 96–97 metres = 100 yards. On ἀπό see p. 401 n.2; on σύρειν Plut. de sollert. an 26 p. 977f. The clause, in supplying a reason, would naturally just as well or even better suit the behaviour of Peter (see p. 702 n.4); in its original connection with v. 6 (see pp. 702f.) it obviously gives the reason for the disciples being able to come to land with the heavy net without difficulties. The idea that the 200 cubits, in accordance with Philonic method, should symbolise the cleansing of the sinner in two steps (Carpenter 246) seems to me to be too finely drawn, particularly as the clause does not motivate the advance of Peter.

[8] Ἀνθρακιά as 18.18; ὀψάριον is obviously meant collectively, see n. 1; if it were meant to refer to a single fish in contrast to the multitude of fish that had been caught, an ἕν would be indispensable.

[9] It is improbable that this is intended to be a special miracle, for no (αὐτὸς) μόνος stands there.

the whole narrative,[1] confused as it is through the redaction, the more certain it is that the exact statements of v. 11 have an allegorical meaning. This can scarcely be other than that the multitude of fish represents the multitude of believers who are won through the apostolic preaching, even as it corresponds to the early picture of fishers of men. Why the multitude of believers is represented exactly through the number 153 does not allow of a satisfactory explanation; nevertheless it must have an allegorical meaning, since it is not a round number.[2] The fact that the net is not torn, despite the large number of the fish, will portray the indestructible unity of the Church;[3] this interest of the redactor comes to the surface also in the following section, vv. 15–23; and especially in the light of vv. 15–17, it will hardly be doubted that the intention is to portray Peter as the leader of the churchly fellowship, since it is he (and this representation presumably is due to the redactor)[4] who draws the net to the land.

Jesus now invites the disciples to a meal (**v. 12**); if the source had in view a meal of the fish that had been caught, v. 13 indicates that the redactor thought of the mysterious meal of v. 9. Yet before any description of the meal is given, attention is drawn to the timidity of the disciples who (by reason of the miracle of the haul of fish?)[5] have recognised him as the "Lord." No one dares to ask him: "Who are you?" Since they have indeed recognised him, the meaning of the question obviously must be, "Is it really you?" This is intended to describe the peculiar feeling that befalls the disciples in the presence of the Risen Jesus: it is he, and yet it is not he; it is not he, whom they

---

[1] See p. 702.

[2] The belief that the ancient zoologists reckoned the species of fish as 153, and thus that the fishes represented all the different kinds of men, is unprovable, despite Jerome on Ezk. 47.12, v. 595 Vallarsi; for then it would be but reasonable to look for the 153 not only among the fishes but also among men. It does not help towards an illuminating interpretation to learn that 153 is the triangular number of 17 (1+2+3 ...+17); for to maintain that this represents that the believers hold the ten commandments in the power of the sevenfold Spirit (Augustine Tract. 122 in Jo.) is certainly not a compelling idea. For 153 as a triangular number see also Rob. M. Grant, HThR 42 (1949), 273–275; Barr. On this basis it would lie nearer to hand to consider that the 17 nations enumerated in Acts 2.77ff. are meant (Bergh v. Eysinga, ZNTW 13 [1912], 296f.). The attempt to understand the number through gematria, like Rev. 13.18 (Merx. העלם הבא = ὁ αἰὼν ὁ μέλλων) also is unconvincing; see Br. and Merx ad loc; Goguel, Introd. II 292, 2. R. Eisler, Orpheus, The Fisher, 1921, 111f., does not agree with Augustine, but he also reckons that 153 is the sum of the number values of Σίμων = 76 and 'Ιχθύς = 77; he finds therein the meaning that Peter, by putting on the garment, put on Christ, and that through leaping into the lake he was baptised, and so became the mysterious 'Ιχθύς = 'Ιησοῦς Χριστός! According to Paul Vulliaud, Les textes fondamentaux de la kabbale 1930, 33, the number 153 is the number of the Passover lamb.

[3] An intentional contradiction to Lk. 5.6 is possible, but not certain; see p. 703 n.5.

[4] See p. 703.

[5] See p. 702.

hitherto have known, and yet it is he! A peculiar partition wall is erected between him and them.[1]

This partition is set aside, as Jesus now distributes bread and fish among the disciples to eat (v. 13). For even though he, as the Risen Lord, does not himself participate in the meal,[2] the sense can hardly be other than that table fellowship between the Risen Jesus and the disciples is now established. Then however this meal, which in fact consists not of the fish that had been caught but of the miraculously procured food (v. 9), is not a meal to satisfy physical needs, but has a mysterious, cultic character; it is a replica of the Lord's Supper. The author of ch. 21 had given the like interpretation of the bread of life bestowed by Jesus; this he did through his insertion of 6.51b–58,[3] and obviously he also understood the feeding of 6.1–15 as a replica of the eucharist.[4]

So ends the story, which in the form that lies before us offers such a remarkable confusion of motifs that one can hardly say wherein the real point lies. Into the old Easter story, which still permits us clearly to trace the mysterious nature of the event in v. 12, and which presumably interpreted the miracle of the haul of fish as a symbol for the call of the disciples, features are interwoven which betray a specifically

---

[1] The idea that the promise of 16.23 is fulfilled here (Schl.) founders on the (οὐδεὶς) ἐτόλμα.

[2] Joach. Jeremias, Die Abendmahlsworte Jesu 91 = Eucharistic Words 175f., thinks that the Risen Lord *eats* with the disciples. Communal eating is undoubtedly affirmed Acts 10.41 (possibly also 1.4: συναλιζόμενος). According to Lk. 24.30 Jesus distributes the bread, but disappears without eating with the disciples; according to Lk. 24.42f. Jesus does eat, but not the disciples; this latter passage is concerned with the demonstration of the real corporeality of the Risen Christ.

[3] See pp. 218f., 234ff.

[4] There is no εὐλογήσας or εὐχαριστήσας (cp. Mk. 14.22f.; Mt. 26.26f.; Lk. 22.19; 1 Cor. 11.24), though it is added by D f r syr[s]; its omission will be due to the fact that it is no longer the earthly Jesus who is here acting, but the Risen Lord (so also Ammonius Cat. in Cramer II p. 408). Of course the eating of fish will not, as such, have a eucharistic meaning. For the early Christian sources know no sacral eating of fish, and no interpretation in relation to Christ of a fish that has actually been eaten. Where there is talk of the eating of the fish-Christ, manifestly it is not fish that is eaten but bread and wine, interpreted as the fish-Christ. Moreover the fish is much more frequently linked with baptism (the water) than with the eucharist. (Information from H. von Soden.) The possibility that in v. 13 the fish is a mysterious designation for Christ is excluded by virtue of the fact that τὸ ὀψάριον is meant in a collective sense (see p. 708 n.8). The oldest certain witness for the fish-Christ symbolism is Tert. de bapt. 1; the age of the acrostic in Sib. VIII 217–250 is disputed. The oldest witnesses for Christ as the nourishing fish are the Aberkios inscription (before 216) and the Pectorios inscription (2nd–3rd century). The relevant texts are in Cabrol-Leclercq, Dict. d'archéol. chrét. VII 2, 2009ff.; moreover cp. Fr. J. Dölger's work Ichthys (since 1910). See also E. Lohmeyer, ThR, NF 9 (1937), 309f. Eisler op. cit. 238ff. not only finds in v. 13 the sacramental meal in which the fish-Christ is consumed, but he sees in this meal also the prefiguration of the eschatological meal, at which the fish Leviathan is given to eat, which will be roasted in the fire of the burning of the world (the ἀνθρακιά of v. 9)!

ecclesiastical interest: the cultic meal which the Risen Lord gives to his followers (vv. 9., 13), and the unity of the Church that is founded on Peter (v. 11). Above all the story serves the redactor as a preparation for vv. 15–23, and therein lies the reason for his insertion of vv. 4b, 7–8a. The original conclusion that v. 13 supplanted was unusable to the redactor, for the simple reason that he wanted to let vv. 15–23 follow on it. He merely makes the observation, in the comment of **v. 14**, that the appearance of the Risen Lord he had just related was the third, and in so doing he corrects the tradition from which he drew the story.[1]

B. 21.15–23: Peter and the Beloved Disciple

The second scene immediately joins on to v. 13 (it is separated from it only by the comment in v. 14), but admittedly it does so in such a way that Peter and the beloved disciple alone now come under consideration, while the presence of the other disciples at most is reflected in the question of Jesus (πλέον τούτων), and in the rest of the narrative they are then ignored. After the meal Jesus puts a question to Peter:[2] "Do you love me more than these?"[3] (**v. 15**). Peter's answer does not exactly correspond to the question; for he does not say that he loves Jesus more than the others, but he declines—obviously with modest reserve[4]—to pass a judgment on the others, and only affirms that he does love Jesus,[5] at the same time he respectfully ascribes to

---

[1] See p. 706.

[2] On the address Σίμων 'Ιωάννου see p. 101 n.6. Instead of 'Ιωάννου 𝔎 pl read 'Ιωνᾶ; the statement is lacking in ℵ*.

[3] Grammatically ἀγαπᾷς με πλέον τούτων can equally well mean, "Do you love me more than these love me?" or "Do you love me more than you love these?" Bd. prefers the latter, as also A. Fridrichsen (Svensk Exeg. Årsb. 5 [1940], 152ff.), but it cannot really come into question; for when it comes to the *object* of the love of a disciple, the Risen Lord stands beyond any rivalry.

[4] Should πλέον τούτων be viewed as a gloss, which is intended to bind this scene to the previous one? It is wanting in the repetitions of the question; it is lacking also in the first question in syr^s, the correctness of which Merx strongly advocates. It is hardly likely that we should find in the retreat from "Do you love me more?" to the mere, "Do you love me?" a fundamental consideration; the human manner of loving, in which there is a more or less, ceases in the presence of the Risen Lord; face to face with him there is only the either-or of loving and not loving, and before him no man can boast of loving *more*. It is unlikely that πλέον τούτων is a reflection of Peter's "self-overestimate" (Htm., Br., Bl.), for 13.37 does not portray any arrogance of Peter with respect to the other disciples; such an attitude rather lies in Mk. 14.29.

[5] The exchange of ἀγαπᾶν and φιλεῖν cannot be significant (p. 253 n.2), for in the third question Jesus also uses φιλεῖν instead of ἀγαπᾶν. V. Warnach, Agape 162, 1, judges otherwise.

Jesus, as to one omniscient, knowledge about it all.[1] In reply Jesus gives him the charge to feed his "lambs"; i.e. he entrusts to him the leadership of his community.[2] That this action is of solemn import is seen in the double repetition of the question, answer and commission (**vv. 16f.**).[3] The third occasion is particularly emphasised, in that Peter's distress over the further repetition of the question is underlined, and in his answer the appeal to Jesus' omniscience is strengthened.[4]

Vv. 15–17 are most commonly understood as the rehabilitation of Peter after his denial. That however is very questionable. It may be that the author, who presumably took the section from the tradition (i.e. from a source),[5] understood it in this way, since he attached it to the Gospel which relates the threefold denial of Peter. Nevertheless so far as he too is concerned, the real point cannot lie there; he looks on vv. 15–17 as a foil for vv. 18–23, and in any case if the section is taken by itself, it provides no hint of a relation to the account of the denial.[6] Surely the denial and the repentance of Peter ought to have found mention! And nothing like an absolution is expressed in the statement of Jesus.[7]

The story rather is a variant of Peter's commission to be the leader of the community, Mt. 16.17–19; cp. also Lk. 22.32.[8] If this fragment

---

[1] Cp. Ezk. 37.3, where the prophet answers God's question only with the words: σὺ ἐπίστῃ ταῦτα.

[2] On the picture of the shepherd, see pp. 363ff., esp. p. 366 n.7.

[3] The solemnity of the dialogue, which is already apparent in the mode of address, forbids an appeal to everyday speech for the formulation of question and answer, as Fridrichsen (Symb. Osl. 14 [1935], 47f.) would wish to make. The solemn threefold repetition reminds us of cultic or magical-juristic usage; cp. the threefold singing of cultic verses in Ed. Norden, Aus altröm. Priesterbüchern 1939, 240ff.; further Goethe, Faust I 1532, "You must say it three times".

[4] The occurrence in the commission of ἀρνία the first time, but προβάτια the second and third times (variants: v. 15 πρόβατα C* D it; v. 16 πρόβατα ℵ ℜ D pl, v. 17 similarly; syr^{s} according to Merx read in succession lambs, sheep, rams, but according to Burkitt ἀρνία, προβάτια, πρόβατα) is as truly without significance as the interchange of βόσκε vv. 15, 17 and ποίμαινε v. 16, or of ἀγαπᾶν and φιλεῖν (see p. 711 n.5). Howard is excellent, Christianity 138.

[5] See p. 709.

[6] Goguel, Introduction II 302 (cp. also HThR 25 [1932], 17f.) rightly refers to the fact that the early Christian tradition evidently did not feel that a rehabilitation of Peter was necessary; in any case nothing has been related about it. O. Cullmann thinks otherwise, Peter 204–206; he believes that he can establish a formal relationship between Mt. 16.17ff.; Lk. 22.31ff. and Jn.21.15ff., and he concludes that at the basis of Jn. 21.15ff. there lies a tradition according to which Jesus, on the evening before his crucifixion, in response to Peter's asseveration that he would follow him to the death, predicted his denial, but at the same time also his repentance and destiny to become the "Rock". In my view this is too articial a combination.

[7] So rightly Sp.

[8] And in so far as Jn. 20.22f. in the source dealt with the discipline of the community (see p. 693 n.3), this place also would belong to the variants.

of tradition was originally an Easter story, or had been derived from such,[1] the same is most naturally to be assumed for Jn. 21.15–17, and this is confirmed by the editorial arrangement;[2] it is noteworthy that the commission is not given to Peter in terms of mission, as in the later Easter stories Mt. 28.19; Lk. 24.47f.; Acts 1.7f., and as Jn. 20.21 also represents it; it is a commission for leadership of the community, as in Mt. 16.17–19. There can be no doubt that this version of the commission is the primary one; vv. 15–17 thus could well be derived from early tradition. The author uses this piece of tradition as a foil for vv. 18–23;[3] he does not have a special interest in the office of Peter; for him the authority of the office is important only because he claims it for the beloved disciple, for through Peter's death it has, as it were, become bereft of a holder. Any tendencies in the direction of ecclesiastical politics—for example the buttressing of the authority of the Roman community—is quite remote from vv. 15–17.[4]

Vv. 18f. stand apart from vv. 18–23, in that without so much as a glance at the beloved disciple, martyrdom is prophesied for Peter. No inner connection with vv. 15–17 is at hand.[5] **V. 18** is a prophecy by parable, at the base of which clearly lies a proverb:[6] "In youth a man is free to go where he will; in old age a man must let himself be taken where he does not will." That is to be a picture for Peter's destiny:[7] if

[1] See Gesch. der synopt. Trad. 277f., 287f. = Hist. of the Syn. Trad. 258f., 266f.

[2] When Sp. and Goguel think that the episode really belongs to the period of the Galilean ministry of Jesus, they are justified in their contention only to the extent that the source, from which the section presumably was taken, had already projected the old Easter story into the life of Jesus. Meanwhile nothing compels us to take this way here. Doubtless all stories which told of Jesus' commission of the disciples were originally Easter narratives, or it was the Risen Lord, the Exalted Lord who spoke in them.

[3] See p. 709.

[4] So far K. G. Goetz could be right, Petrus als Gründer und Oberhaupt der Kirche 1927, 14ff.; but it seems to me that he is in the wrong in contesting that Peter is here entrusted with the supreme leadership of the church.

[5] Certainly there does not seem to me to be sufficient reason to look on vv. 18, 19a as an odd fragment and to join v. 19b on to v. 17 (Goguel Introd. II 303f.). Moreover there is no inner connection subsisting between vv. 17 and 19bff. On the contrary the deliberate editorial connection between vv. 15–17 and vv. 18ff. ought to be plain.

[6] By this consideration the difficulty disappears, which was raised e.g. by Wellh., Schw. and Sp., that the temporal standpoint changes in the members of the antithesis, in that ὅτε ἦς νεώτερος addresses an old man, and ὅταν δὲ γηράσῃς a young man. In the proverb man as such is addressed, and naturally it began ὅταν ἦς νεώτερος. If the saying was to serve as a statement to Peter, then ὅταν ἦς had to be changed into ὅτε ἦς.

[7] The picture paints the helplessness of the old man who stretches out his hands to feel for a support or for someone to lead him (Bd., Wik.). 'Εκτενεῖς τ. χεῖράς σου therefore is neither to be related to crucifixion (for which of course ἔκτασις τῶν χειρῶν is characteristic, see Br. and esp. Bd.; also Barr.) which would necessarily involve a husteron-proton (Br.), nor does it relate to a criminal, who has to stretch out his hands in order to become fettered (Wellh. Hosk.). These two interpretations are wrong because ζωννύναι means "to gird", and not "to bind" in the sense of "fetter". The opinion of Delafosse also rests on

at one time he freely chose his way, he will be led unwillingly to his last journey—namely, as v. 19 explains, to martyrdom.[1] For if v. 19 expounds v. 18[2] as indicating the kind of death by which Peter will glorify God,[3] ποίῳ θανάτῳ shows that a natural death is not in mind. That is the only interpretation conformable with δοξάσει τὸν θεόν: it is precisely to the martyr that the possibility of glorifying God through death is given.[4]

After this prophecy the following ἀκολούθει μοι can be understood only as a call to follow into martyrdom; the author sees therein the fulfilment of the saying of Jesus in 13.36, which therefore he has misunderstood as a prophecy of martyrdom.[5] Admittedly he employs the ἀκολούθει in a double sense; in this scene that he has depicted, he clearly desires that the call of Jesus should at the same time be recognised as a demand made on Peter to follow Jesus on his way now. The scene therefore gains a symbolic meaning: as Peter is on the point of going after Jesus, he looks round and sees the beloved disciple (**v. 20**).[6] The scene of course is not really imaginable; for which way could the Risen

a denial of the postulate of a proverb: if Peter is blamed in v. 18 and praised in v. 19, then v. 19 must be a secondary gloss; v. 18 relates to Gal. 2.11ff., and the ἄλλος who takes Peter in tow is James!

[1] The proverb needs the explanation. There is no reason for deleting v. 19, and explaining v. 18 in the light of 15–17, as though to say: Once Peter acted according to his own will, and lived in a happy-go-lucky fashion; now he must enter into the service of Jesus and let himself be led by him (Schwartz, ZNTW 15 [1914], 217; so also, without deleting v. 19, Schl.). The picture of the helpless old man, who is delivered to the mercy of the leader, cannot possibly describe the dignity of the leader of the community! Moreover v. 19 is confirmed by v. 22, which says quite plainly enough that Peter, in distinction from the Beloved Disciple, will follow Jesus immediately into death.

[2] On σημαίνων see p. 432 n.5.

[3] Δοξάσει = ἤμελλεν δοξάζειν, see Bl.-D. § 349, 2 and cp. 18.32. On δοξάζειν, which could also be translated "glorify", see pp. 368 n.1; 428ff.; 490ff. J. Schneider, Doxa 1932, 119; E. G. Gulin, Die Freude im NT II 1936, 57, 2.

[4] Martyriological use of δοξάζειν also in 1 Pt. 4.16; Mart. Pol. 14.3; 19.2. From v. 18 naturally nothing is to be deduced on the special manner of the death. The opinion that nothing can be proved from vv. 18f. as to the historicity of the Roman martyrdom of Peter (K. Heussi, Neues zur Petrusfrage 1939, 24; Wiss. Zeitschr. Jena 1952/53, 68ff.) is right. Meanwhile it cannot be demonstrated that vv. 18f. have the purpose of promoting the legend. On the martyrdom of Peter, see O. Cullmann, Petrus 73–169 = Peter 71–157.

[5] See p. 597 n.1.

[6] It is noticeable that the beloved disciple is expressly characterised by reference to 13.23, whereas such a characteristic did not appear necessary to the author in v. 7. It is likely to be a secondary interpolation, an assumption made the more probable by ἀκολουθοῦντα; the latter is meaningless, since the point in vv. 20–22 is this, that Peter "follows", while the Beloved Disciple "remains". The interpolator did not wish the relative clause ὃς καὶ κτλ to limit the preceding ὁ Ἰησοῦς, and therefore he introduced the participle ἀκολουθοῦντα; by this means the transferred sense which ἀκολ. has in vv. 19 and 22 is excluded here. (No appeal should be made to the fact that ἀκολ. 14ff.[2], is lacking in v. 20 in א 014ff.[2], especially as in א the indispensable ὅς is also lacking. Wellh. deletes ἀκολ., Sp. also the relative clause.) The interpolator took up the connection again through τοῦτον οὖν ἰδὼν ὁ Πέτρος; through this an original καί is replaced.

Lord take on which Peter could accompany him! The scene therefore is given no external conclusion, but ends in v. 22 with the repetition of ἀκολούθει.

What meaning however does Peter's question have in **v. 21**: "Lord, how about this man?" What will happen to him?[1] It is impossible to determine in what sense the question is posed; but the answer of Jesus (**v. 22**). "If I will that he remain . . . what concern is that of yours?",[2] and the emphatic, "*You* (at any rate) follow me!" show how the question of Peter has to be understood: surely the beloved disciple also ought to "follow." It is the will of Jesus, however, that he should "remain"—i.e. remain in life[3]—and of a truth, till Jesus "comes."[4] It goes without saying that the ἔρχεσθαι of Jesus is neither the promise of 14.3, nor that of 14.18. It is not the first, for otherwise it would have to run: ἕως ἔρχομαι καὶ παραλήμψομαι αὐτόν; it is not the second, because ἔρχομαι here is not at all applicable as a statement of time. Rather v. 22 has in view the coming of Jesus in the sense of early Christian apocalyptic; only so is the "misunderstanding," and its correction in v. 23 to be explained. The theme of vv. 20–22 therefore is the difference in the destinies of Peter and the beloved disciple;[5] for the former martyrdom has been prophesied, for the latter it is promised that he will remain alive right up to the parousia.

Now **v. 23** of course affirms that the saying of Jesus was not a prophecy but only a hypothetical statement. It is clear that this is a subsequent correction which became necessary when the beloved disciple had died. The question suggests itself whether v. 23 is not a secondary interpolation; for if the author of vv. 20–22 had the (alleged) misunderstanding of v. 23 in mind, would he not have formulated the saying of Jesus in v. 22 equally unmistakably so as to convey his meaning? The consequence would further follow that v. 24 also, or at least καὶ (ὁ) γράψας ταῦτα, would have to be ascribed to the interpolator.[6] But that would mean that the Gospel had, so to say,

---

[1] On the ellipse see Bl.-D. § 127, 3; 299, 2.

[2] On the ellipse see again Bl.-D. § 127, 3; 299, 3; τί πρὸς σέ Epikt. Diss. III 18, 2; IV 1, 10 etc.; acc. to Bl.-D. § 373, 1 ἐάν in Jn. 21.22 is used in the sense of the classical "real" εἰ; in v.23 it is "safeguarded by the author ... against the interpretation 'if, as is, to be expected' which is the only possible one in Attic, and is also a conceivable one in Koine".

[3] For μένειν = to remain in life, cp. 1 Cor. 15.6; Phil. 1.25; the usage is normal, see Br

[4] Ἕως with present instead of future, see Bl.-D. § 383, 1.

[5] It is completely clear (and it is confirmed through v. 24) that in this contrast both figures are understood as definite historical persons and not as the embodiment of principles or groups—as if e.g. Peter should represent Jewish Christianity, or indeed Rome, and the Beloved Disciple Gentile Christianity or the Church of Asia Minor.

[6] So Goguel (Introd. II 321) is of the opinion that the editor of the Gospel added ch. 21, which already lay before him (not indeed as the work of the Evangelist himself, but in the tradition used by him), and he on his part enlarged it through v. 23 and vv. 24f.

been edited twice, first by the redactor who composed and affixed ch. 21 to the Gospel, and then definitively by the interpolator who added v. 23 and v. 24 (in whole or in part). This edition alone gained ascendancy in the Church, for the history of the text has no witness to the non-interpolated text. Accordingly one must have serious reservations with regard to this view, and in fact v. 23 does allow of being understood as deriving from the author of vv. 20–22. Historically, in any case, at the root of the prophecy in v. 22 and the saying which according to v. 23 was in circulation,[1] there lies the fact that a disciple of the Lord attained a surprisingly old age, so that the idea arose that he would remain alive till the parousia;[2] this opinion will early have gained the form of a dominical saying. The author of vv. 20–22 made use of this; he identified that disciple with the figure of the beloved disciple, known to him through the Gospel he had edited, and he transferred the prophecy to him. By this means he had gained a person who was acknowledged to be a witness from the earliest time as a guarantor for the worth of the Gospel, and indeed as its author. That by this time the man had already died (and this the author could not avoid noting in v. 23) was no real obstacle to his procedure; the only thing that mattered to him was to set the present Gospel under the authority of the oldest witness.

What interest does the author of ch. 21 have in the difference between the fate of the two disciples? It is hardly likely that vv. 20–22 are a defence against the belittling of the beloved disciple on the ground that he did not suffer a martyr's death. For Peter's question is not formulated in this sense, as the answer of Jesus shows. The answer presupposes rather that the "remaining" is in a certain sense an advantage; the beloved disciple *may* remain, according to the will of Jesus, whereas Peter must pass on earlier. Naturally there is as little intention of belittling Peter, who "glorified" God through his death. The really characteristic feature of the passage is that both men are represented as on the same level; the Lord decreed one thing for the one man and another for the other. Then, however, since the rank of Peter is not in doubt, and indeed was actually confirmed in vv. 15–17, the real point must lie in the fact that the same standing is claimed for the beloved

---

On the contrary one should hesitate before striking out v. 24, because if this is done it is not at all plain what interest the author of ch. 21 and especially of vv. 15–22 has in the beloved disciple. In fact it can only be to adduce him as a guarantor for the truth of the Gospel—precisely as v. 24 says.

[1] On ἀδελφοί as a technical designation of members of the Christian community see ThWB I 145, 8ff.; in Jn. only here, but repeatedly in I and III Jn.

[2] Sp.'s view, that on the contrary the legend arose on the basis of the saying in v. 22, but that this latter originally had the harmless meaning that the Beloved Disciple should remain by the boat and net till Jesus came and fetched him, is absurd. It could very well have contributed to the origin of the legend that a prophecy like Mk. 9.1 more and more adhered to the last survivors of the first generation; see Goguel, HThR 25 (1932) 17, n. 16; Grass 84f.

disciple. For "the beloved disciple," yes, but in fact, as v. 24 shows, for the Gospel which the author of ch. 21 edits. If in vv. 15–17 the author adduced that piece of tradition in which Peter's significance for the community is proclaimed, and if he then stated that Peter must suffer a martyr's death, whereas the beloved disciple "remains," it is thereby affirmed that the beloved disciple in a way takes Peter's place, and that the authority assigned to Peter has passed over to him; since the Beloved Disciple has in the meantime died, it means that it has passed over to this Gospel, in which his testimony sounds forth.[1] The purpose of vv. 15–23, and therefore in the last analysis of ch. 21 as a whole, is to substantiate the ecclesiastical authority of this Gospel.

Conclusion: 21.24–25

The author's interest in the figure of the Beloved Disciple, and therefore in the episode he has just related, emerges clearly in the conclusion, for the beloved disciple is now expressly stated to be the one whose authority stands behind the Gospel (**v. 24**).[2] He it is who "bears witness to these things,[3] and who wrote this";[4] i.e. he who bears his testimony in this passage is the author of the Gospel. For the truth of the testimony the author appeals to the consciousness of the community, καὶ οἴδαμεν κτλ.[5] For actually in this οἴδαμεν a definite circle speaks, namely the author and the group to which he belongs; but in his view it is not the voice of a limited circle that declares itself,

---

[1] Cp. Htm.: "Inasmuch as the greatly revered head of the Church, Peter, was officially recognised, the Gospel was made capable of recognition by the Church and commended to the whole Church". So also Bl. That this happens in the struggle against the heresies that are emerging (Bacon, JBL 25 [1932], 71ff.) is certainly right, as 1 Jn. shows, but no mention is made of it in Jn. 21. On the relation between Peter and the Beloved Disciple see O. Cullmann, Petrus 22ff., esp. 25f. (= Peter, 27ff., esp. 29f.).

[2] Concerning the improbability that v. 24 is a later interpolation see p. 715 n.6.

[3] It is obvious that the present ὁ μαρτυρῶν (B. ὁ καὶ μαρτ.) does not need to be viewed as affirming that the beloved disciple is still alive. According to v. 23 he has already died, but his testimony has not been silenced with his death, hence the present tense here. Naturally it could also mean ὁ μαρτυρήσας, corresponding to the μεμαρτύρηκεν of 19.35.

[4] It is clear that ὁ γράψας ταῦτα (so BD; in ℵ C ℜ pl. the ὁ is lacking; θ φ 33 pc read ὁ καί instead of καὶ ὁ) does not refer to the immediately preceding verses, which presuppose the death of the beloved disciple, and so neither does it generally relate to ch. 21. Quite evidently ταῦτα (as περὶ τούτων) looks back to the gospel; that is in any case proved by the retrospective character of vv. 24f. Dodd (JThSt 1953, 212f.) desires to relate the ταῦτα solely to the immediately preceding context, whether it be v. 22 only, or vv. 20 (or 15)—22, or ch. 21.

[5] So also 19.35? See p. 678.

which would be meaningless.[1] The idea rather is that the community knows that the testimony of the beloved disciple is always true; according to v. 23 the "brethren" know him as a witness of the first generation; accordingly the readers of the Gospel will receive as true the testimony that is borne in the Gospel.[2]

The author however feels a necessity of bringing the whole book, enlarged by the postscript, to a final conclusion, and this he does in **v. 25**[3] with an expression that imitates 20.30. It emphasises again, in a strongly hyperbolical manner, the inexhaustible fulness of the subject of the Gospel and therefore of the Christian message.[4] The whole world would not contain the books[5] that would be necessary if it were desired to record all the deeds of Jesus.[6]

---

[1] Goguel is right, Introd. II 309ff.: a definite circle cannot be meant. For either the readers know the circle which is editing the gospel, and then the appeal is superfluous; or they do not know it, and then it is meaningless. Cp. also οἴδαμεν 1 Jn. 3.2, 14; 5.15, 19f. The rhetorical οἶμαι v. 25 naturally has nothing to do with οἴδαμεν. Dodd (ibid) would understand οἴδαμεν as "one knows".

[2] Cp. III Jn. 12, where the author, in confirmation that his testimony about Demetrius is true, appeals to the fact that the people he is addressing know that his testimony is (always) true.

[3] V. 25 is lacking in ℵ *.

[4] See p. 697 n.2.

[5] B C* have the future inf. (which is very seldom in the NT. χωρήσειν; ℜ D pl read χωρῆσαι; see Bl.-D. § 350; Raderm. 99, 155.

[6] Καθ'ἕν = "one after the other", as Acts 21.19 and elsewhere; See Br.

List of Abbreviations (of Journals and Periodicals)

AO	Alter Orient
AR	Archiv für Religionswissenschaft
AThR	Anglican Theological Review
Bibl	Biblica
EvTheol	Evangelische Theologie
HThR	Harvard Theological Review
JBL	Journal of Biblical Literature
JThSt	Journal of Theological Studies
NRevTheol	Nouvelle Revue Théologique
NtSt	New Testament Studies
RAC	Reallexikon für Antike und Christentum
RB	Revue Biblique
Rech sc rel	Recherches de science religieuse
RevH.Phrel	Revue d'Histoire et de Philosophie religieuses
SA	Sitzungsberichte der . . . Akademie der Wissenschaften. (The location of the Akademie in question is given after SA (e.g. Berlin, Heidelberg). Only proceedings of the philosophical-historical category are cited.)
SymbOsl	Symbolae Osloenses
ThBl	Theologische Blätter
ThLZ	Theologische Literaturzeitung
ThR	Theologische Rundschau
ThStKr	Theologische Studien und Kritiken
ThWB	Theologisches Wörterbuch zum Neuen Testament (See Bibliography 3)
ThZ	Theologische Zeitschrift (Basel)
ZATW	Zeitschrift für alttestamentliche Wissenschaft
ZDMG	Zeitschrift der Deutschen Morgenländischen Gesellschaft
ZNTW	Zeitschrift für die neutestamentliche Wissenschaft
ZsystTh	Zeitschrift für systematische Theologie
ZThK	Zeitschrift für Theologie und Kirche
ZwZ	Zwischen den Zeiten

There is still no generally accepted style of reference for the *Dead Sea Scrolls* (Qumran-Texts). Recently the following abbreviations have been commonly used:

1QpH Pescher (Comment) on Habakuk

1QS Serekh ha-Yahad (Order of the Community; often cited as *Manual of Discipline* or as *Scroll of Law* or simply as *Sectarian Scrolls*.) Also marked as DSD, see below.

1QM Milhemet bne'Or (The War of the Sons of Light and the Sons of Darkness). Also cited as DSW.

1QH Hodayot (Thanksgiving Hymns). Also cited as DST.

I have employed these abbreviations with the exception of 1QS. Following the usual practice I refer to this text as DSD (taken from the American publication by W. H. Brownlee, 1951). I have not used any abbreviation for the *Damascus-Document* (also cited as CDC).

The *Corpus Hermeticum* (C. Herm.) is now often cited as Nock-Festugière, *Hermès Trismégiste* 1945–1954; but I did not think it necessary to change all the references.

List of Abbreviations* (of books cited)

Barr.	C. K. Barrett (1)
Bd.	J. H. Bernard (1)
Becker	H. Becker (2)
Bl.	F. Büchsel (1)
Black	M. Black (3)
Bl.-D.	F. Blaß [cited by paragraphs] (3)
Bldsp.	W. Baldensperger (2)
Bornhäuser	K. Bornhäuser (2)
Bousset, Rel. des Judent.	W. Bousset (Die Religion des Judentums im späthellenistischen Zeitalter) (3)
Bousset, Hauptpr.	W. Bousset (Hauptprobleme der Gnosis) (3)
Bousset, Kyrios	W. Bousset (Kyrios Christos) (3)
Br.	W. Bauer (1)
Bréhier	É. Bréhier (3)
Br. Wörterb.	W. Bauer (3)
Burney	C. F. Burney (2)
Burrows	M. Burrows (2)
Carpenter	J. E. Carpenter (2)
Colwell	E. C. Colwell (2)
Dalman, O. u. W.	G. Dalman (Orte und Wege Jesu) (3)
Dalman, W. J.	G. Dalman (Worte Jesu I) (3)
Deißmann, L. v. O.	G. Ad. Deißmann (Licht vom Osten) (3)
Delafosse	H. Delafosse (2)
Dibelius, Formgesch.	M. Dibelius (Die Formgeschichte des Evangeliums) (3)
Dillersberger	J. Dillersberger (2)
Dodd	C. H. Dodd, (The Interpretation of the Fourth Gospel) (2)
Dupont	J. Dupont (2)
Eucharisterion	*ΕΥΧΑΡΙΣΤΗΡΙΟΝ* (3)
Faulhaber	D. Faulhaber (2)
Festg. Ad. Jül.	Festgabe für Adolf Jülicher (3)
Gaugler	E. Gaugler (Das Christuszeugnis des Johannesevangeliums) (2)

* The numbers in brackets refer to the sections in the Bibliography.

Gesch. der. synopt. Tr.	R. Bultmann (Die Geschichte der synoptischen Tradition) (3)
Gl. u. Verst.	R. Bultmann (Glauben und Verstehen) (3)
Goguel, J.-B.	M. Goguel (Jean Baptiste) (3)
Goodenough	E. R. Goodenough (2)
Grant	F. C. Grant (3)
Grill I and II	J. Grill (2)
Gulin	E. G. Gulin (2)
Hdb. zum NT	Handbuch zum NT (3)
Hirsch I	E. Hirsch (Das vierte Evangelium) (1)
Hirsch II	E. Hirsch (Studien zum vierten Evangelium) (2)
Ho.	H. J. Holtzmann (1)
Hosk.	Ed. C. Hoskyns (1)
Howard	W. Fr. Howard (The Fourth Gospel in Recent Criticism and Interpretation) (2)
Htm.	W. Heitmüller (1)
Jonas, Gnosis	H. Jonas (Gnosis und spätantiker Geist I) (3)
Kroll, Herm. Tism.	J. Kroll (Die Lehren des Hermes Trismegistos) (3)
L.	A. Loisy (1)
Lagr.	M.-J. Lagrange (1)
v. Loewenich	W. vom Loewenich (2)
Masson	C. Masson (2)
Menoud	P.-H. Menoud (LÉvangile de Jean d'après les recherches récentes) (2)
Merx	A. Merx (1)
Meyer	Ed. Meyer (3)
Moore	G. F. Moore (3)
Moulton, Einl.	J. H. Moulton (Einleitung in die Sprache des Neuen Testamentes) (3)
Odeberg	H. Odeberg (2)
Omodeo, Mistica	A. Omodeo (La mistica Giovannea) (2)
Omodeo, Saggio	A. Omodeo (Saggio di Commentario al IV evangelio) (2)
Pascher, Königsweg	J. Pascher (Η ΒΑΣΙΛΙΚΗ ΟΔΟΣ. Der Königsweg zu Wiedergeburt und Vergottung bei Philon von Alexandreia) (3)
Percy	E. Percy (2)
Raderm.	L. Radermacher (3)
Reitzenst., H. M. R.	R. Reitzenstein (Die hellenistischen Mysterienreligionen') (3)
Reitzenst., J. E. M.	R. Reitzenstein (Das iranische Erlösungsmysterium) (3)

Reitzenst., or Schaeder, Studien	R. Reitzenstein and H. H. Schaeder (Studien zum antiken Synkretismus aus Iran und Griechenland) (3)
Reitzenst., Taufe	R. Reitzenstein (Die Vorgeschichte der christlichen Taufe) (3)
Schl.	A. Schlatter (1)
Schl., Spr. u. H.	A. Schlatter (Sprache und Heimat des vierten Evangelisten) (2)
Schlier, Relig. Unters.	H. Schlier (Religionsgeschichtliche Untersuchungen zu den Ignatiusbriefen) (3)
Schw.	E. Schwartz (2)
Sp.	F. Spitta (2)
Str.	R. H. Strachan (2)
Strathm.	H. Strathmann (1)
Str.-B.	H. L. Strack and P. Billerbeck (3)
Temple	W. Temple (2)
Thomas	J. Thomas (3)
ThWB	Theologisches Wörterbuch zum Neuen Testament (3)
Tillmann	F. Tillmann (1)
Torrey	C. C. Torrey (2)
B. Weiss	B. Weiss (1)
Wellh.	J. Wellhausen (2)
Wendt I	H. H. Wendt (Das Johannesevangelium) (2)
Wendt II	H. H. Wendt (Die Schichten im vierten Evangelium) (2)
Wik.	A. Wikenhauser (1)
Zn.	T. Zahn (1)

Bibliography*

1. COMMENTARIES†

C. K. Barrett—The Gospel according to St. John 1955.
W. Bauer—Das Johannesevangelium (Handbuch zum NT 6) 3 Aufl. 1933.
J. H. Bernard—A Critical and Exegetical Commentary on the Gospel according to St. John (International Critical Commentary), 2 vols. 1928.
F. Büchsel—Das Evangelium nach Johannes (Das Neue Testament Deutsch 4) 1934.
W. Heitmüller—Die Schriften des NTs, hrsg. J. Weiss, IV, 3 Aufl. 1918.
E. Hirsch—Das vierte Evangelium 1936.
H. J. Holtzmann—Evangelium des Joh. Hand-Commentar zum NT IV 1) 3 Aufl. by W. Bauer 1908.
E. C. Hoskyns—The Fourth Gospel. 2nd ed. 1947.
J. Jeremias—Das Evangelium nach Joh. 1931.
M.-J. Lagrange—Evangile selon St. Jean, 4th ed. 1927.
W. Lauck—Das Evangelium und die Briefe des hl. Johannes 1941.
A. Loisy—Le quatrième Evangile, 2nd ed. 1927.
G. H. C. MacGregor—The Gospel of John 1928.
A. Merx—Das Evangelium des Joh. (Die vier kanonischen Evangelien nach ihrem ältesten bekannten Texte II 2b) 1911.
O. Moe—Johannes-evangeliet 1938.
A. Schlatter—Der Evangelist Joh. 1930.
H. Strathmann—Das Evangelium nach Johannes (Das Neue Testament Deutsch 4) 2 Aufl. 1955.
F. Tillmann—Das Johannes-Evangelium (Die hl. Schrift des NTs 3), 4 Aufl. 1931.
B. Weiss—Das Johannes-Evangelium (Meyers Kommentar 2) 9 Aufl. 1902.
A. Wikenhauser—Das Evangelium nach Johannes (Das Neue Testament 4) 1948.
T. Zahn—Das Evangelium des Joh. (Kommentar zum NT 4), 5/6 Aufl. 1921

---

* It is impossible to give an exhaustive bibliography. For further works see the Elenchus Bibliographicus in Biblica 33 (1952), 82*–86*; 34 (1953), 86*–89*; 35 (1954), 90*–93*; 36 (1955), 84*–88*; 37 (1956), 82*–84*. The references are always to page numbers, except in the case of Blass-Debrunner, which is cited by paragraph.

† Abbreviations are given in parentheses where more than one work by the same author is cited.

2. BOOKS AND ESSAYS ON THE GOSPEL OF JOHN*

E. A. Abbot—Johannine Vocabulary 1905.—Johannine Grammar 1906.
B. Aebert—Die Eschatologie des Johannes 1937.
E. L. Allen—'The Jewish Christian Church in the Fourth Gospel', JBL 74 (1955), 88–92.
M. E. Andrews—'The Authorship and Significance of the Gospel of John', JBL 64 (1945), 183–192.
B. W. Bacon—The Fourth Gospel in Research and Debate 1910.—The Gospel of the Hellenists, ed. by Carl H. Kraeling 1933.
W. Baldensperger—Der Prolog des vierten Evangeliums 1898.
C. K. Barrett—'The Old Testament in the Fourth Gospel', JThSt 1947, 155–169.—'The Holy Spirit in the Fourth Gospel', JThSt 1950, 1–15.
H. Becker—Die Reden des Johannesevangeliums und der Still der gnostischen Offenbarungsrede 1956 (Becker).
J. Behm—'Der gegenwärtige Stand der Erforschung des Johannesevangeliums', ThLZ 73 (1948), 21–30.
G. Bert—Das Evangelium des Joh. 1922.
M. Blumenthal—'Die Eigenart des johann. Erzählungsstiles', ThStKr 1934/35, 104–212.
J. Boehmer—Das Johannesevangelium nach Aufbau und Grundgedanken 1928.
M. E. Boismard—Le Prologue de St. Jean 1953.
K. Bornhäuser—Das Johannesevangelium eine Missionsschrift für Israel 1928.
W. Bousset—Artikel 'Johannesevangelium' in Die Religion in Geschichte und Gegenwart III 1912, 608–636.
C. R. Bowen—'Love in the Fourth Gospel', Journ. of Religion 13 (1933), 39–59.
L. Bouyer—Le 4e Evangile. Introduction à L'Evangile de S. Jean 1955.
F.-M. Braun—'L'arrière-fond judaique du quatrième Évangile et la Communauté de l'Alliance', RB 62 (1965), 5–44.
E. C. Broome—'The Sources of the Fourth Gospel', JBL 63 (1944). 107–121.
G. W. Broomfield—John, Peter and the Fourth Gospel 1934.
F. Büchsel—Der Begriff der Wahrheit in dem Evangelium und den Briefen des Johannes 1911.—Johannes und der hellenistische Synkretismus 1928.
V. Burch—The Structure and Message of St. John's Gospel 1928.
C. F. Burney—The Aramaic Origin of the Fourth Gospel 1922.
M. Burrows—'The Johannine Prologue as Aramaic Verses', JBL 1924, 67–69.
J. E. Carpenter—The Johannine Writings 1927.

---

* Abbreviations are given in parentheses when more than one work by the same author is cited.—Cf. also the bibliographies by W. Bousset, ThR 12 (1909), 1ff.; 39ff.; Arn. Meyer, ThR 13 (1910), 15ff., 63ff.; 15 (1912), 239ff., 278ff., 295ff.; W. Bauer, ThR, N.F. 1 (1929), 135ff. Also the works cited above by Bacon and Howard.

H. Clavier—'Le problème du rite et du mythe dans le quatrième Evangile', RevH.Phrel 31 (1951), 275–292.—'Le Structure du quatrième Evangile', RevH.Phrel 35 (1955), 174–195.
C. Clemen—Die Entstehung des Johannesevangeliums 1912.
E. C. Colwell—The Greek of the Fourth Gospel 1931 (Colwell).—John Defends the Gospel 1936.
C. M. Connick—'The dramatic character of the Fourth Gospel', JBL 67 (1948), 159–169.
C. T. Craig—'Sacramental Interest in the Fourth Gospel', JBL 58 (1939), 31–41.
O. Cullmann—'Der johann. Gebrauch doppeldeutiger Ausdrücke', Th Z 4 (1948), 360–372.—Les sacrements dans l'évangile Johannique 1951.
H. Delafosse—Le quatrième Évangile (Christianisme 5), 1925.
M. Dibelius—Artikel 'Johannesevangelium' in Die Religion in Geschichte und Gegenwart III, 2. Aufl., 349–363.
J. Dillersberger—Das Wort vom Logos 1935.
C. H. Dodd—'The Background of the Fourth Gospel', Bull. of the John Rylands Libr. 1935.—The Interpretation of the Fourth Gospel 1953 (Dodd).—'Some Johannine 'Herrenworte' with Parallels in the Synoptic Gospels', NtSt 2 (1922/56), 75–86.
J. Dupont—Essais sur la Christologie de St. Jean 1951.
R. Eisler—Das Rätsel des Johannesevangeliums (Sonderdruck des Eranos-Jahrb. 1935) 1936.
D. Faulhaber—Das Johannesevangelium und die Kirche 1938.
H. Fischel—'Jewish Gnosticism in the Fourth Gospel', JBL 65 (1946), 157–174.
J. B. Frey—'Le Concept de 'Vie' dans l'Evangile de Saint Jean', Biblica I (1920), 37ff.,211ff.
P. Gardner-Smith—St. John and the Synoptic Gospels 1938.
E. Gaugler—Die Bedeutung der Kirche in den joh. Schriften (Diss. Bern) 1925.—'Das Christuszeugnis des Johannesevangeliums', in: Jesus Christus im Zeugnis der Hl. Schrift und der Kirche (2. Beiheft zur Evang. Theol.) 1936 (Gaugler).
E. R. Goodenough—'John a primitive Gospel', JBL LXIV, 2 (1945), 145–182. Cf. R. P. Casey, ibid. 535–542, and G.'s reply ibid. 543f.
C. Goodwin—'How did John treat his Sources?', JBL 73 (1954), 61–75.
Fr. C. Grant—'Was the Author of John Dependent upon the Gospel of Luke?' JBL 56 (1937), 285–307.
R. M. Grant—'The Origin of the Fourth Gospel', JBL 69 (1950), 305–322.
J. Grill—Untersuchungen über die Entstehung des vierten Evangeliums, 2 Bde. 1902, 1923 (Grill I and II).
E. G. Gulin—Die Freude im NT II. Das Johannesevangelium 1936.
R. Gyllenberg—'Die Anfänge der johanneischen Tradition', Neutest. Studien für R. Bultmann 1954, 144–147.
C. Hauret—Les Adieux du Seigneur 1952.
E. Hirsch—Studien zum vierten Evangelium 1936 (Hirsch II).—'Stilkritik u. Literaranalyse im vierten Evangelium', ZNW 34 (1950/51), 129–143.

R. F. Hoare–Original Order and Chapters of St. John's Gospel 1944.—The Gospel according to St. John. Arranged in its Conjectural Order and Translated into Current English 1949.
W. F. Howard—The Fourth Gospel in Recent Criticism and Interpretation 1931 (Howard).—Christianity according to St. John, 2. Aufl. 1947.
H. H. Huber—Der Begriff der Offenbarung im Joh.-Evg. 1934.
H. L. Jackson—The Problem of the Fourth Gospel 1918.
T. Jänicke—Die Herrlichkeit des Gottessohnes. Eine Einführung in das Johannesevangelium 1949.
J. Jocz—'Die Juden im Johannesevangelium', Judaica 9 (1953), 129–142.
N. Johansson—Parakletoi 1940.
J. Kreyenbühl—Das Evangelium der Wahrheit, 2 vols. 1900, 1905.
K. Kundsin—Topologische Überlieferungsstoffe im Joh.-Evg. 1925.—Charakter und Ursprung der joh. Reden (Acta Universitatis Latviensis, Ser. theol. I 4) 1939.—'Zur Diskussion über die Ego-Eimi-Sprüche des Johannesevangeliums', Charisteria Johanni Köpp octogenario oblata 1954, 95–107.
W. Larfeld—Die beiden Johannes von Ephesus 1914.
W. von Loewenich—Das Johannes-Verständnis im zweiten Jahrhundert 1932.
W. F. Lofthouse—The Disciple whom Jesus loved 1936.
W. Lütgert—Die Johanneische Christologie, 2 Aufl. 1916.
T. W. Manson—'The Life of Jesus: V', Bull. of the John Rylands Libr. Vol. 30, no. 2, 1947.
C. Masson—'Le Prologue du quatrième Evangile', Rev. de Theol. et de Phil., N.S. XXVIII no. 117 (1940), 297–311.
L. Mowry—'The Dead Sea Scrolls and the Background for the Gospel of John', The Biblical Archaeologist 1954, 78–94.
P.-H. Menoud—'L'Originalité de la Pensée Johannique', Rev. de Theol. et Phil. no. 116 (1940).—'L'Evangile de Jean d'après les recherches récentes', RevH. Phrel 29 (1941), 236–56; 30 (1942), 155–75; 31 (1943), 80–100; 32 (1944), 92ff. = Cahiers theol. de l'actualité protestante I, 1943.—L'Evangile de Jean d'après les recherches récentes 1947. (Menoud).
W. Michaelis—Die Sakramente im Johannesevangelium 1946.
J. A. Montgomery—The Origin of the Gospel according to St. John 1923.
D. H. Müller—Das Johannesevangelium im Lichte der Strophentheorie (SA Wien, phil.-hist. Kl. 161, Abh. 8) 1909.
F. Mussner—ΖΩΗ. Die Anschauung vom 'Leben' in vierten Evangelium 1952.
B. Noack—Zur johanneischen Tradition 1954.
H. P. V. Nunn—The Authorship of the Fourth Gospel 1952.
H. Odeberg—The Fourth Gospel 1929.
W. Oehler—Zum Missionscharakter des Johannesevangeliums 1941.
A. Omodeo—La mistica Giovannea 1930. (Omodeo, Mistica).—Saggio di Commentario al IV evangelio (I, 1–3, 21) 1932. (Omodeo, Saggio).
F. Overbeck—Das Johannesevangelium, ed. C. A. Bernoulli 1911.
E. Percy—Untersuchungen über den Ursprung der joh. Theologie 1939.

A. M. Perry—'Is John an Alexandrian Gospel?', JBL 63 (1944), 99–106.
H. Preisker—'Das Evangelium des Johannes als erster Teil eines apokalyptischen Doppelwerkes', ThBl 15 (1936), 185ff.
H. Pribnow—Die joh. Anschauung vom 'Leben' 1934.
W. H. Raney—The Relation of the Fourth Gospel to the Christian Cultus 1933.
E. B. Redlich—An Introduction to the Fourth Gospel 1939.
J. Réville—Le Quatrième Evangile, son origine et sa valeur historique[2] 1902.
E. Ruckstuhl—'Literarkritik am Johannesevangelium und eucharistische Rede', Divus Thomas 1945, 153–90, 301–33.—Die literarische Einheit des Johannesevangeliums 1951.
H. Sahlin—Zur Typologie des Johannesevangeliums. Uppsala Universitets Arsskrift 1945, 5.
J. N. Sanders—The Fourth Gospel in the Early Church. 1943.—'Those whom Jesus loved', NtSt 1 (1954–55), 22–41.
A. Schlatter—Sprache u. Heimat des vierten Evangelisten 1902.
H. Schlier—'Im Anfang war das Wort', Die Zeit der Kirche 1956, 274–87.
L. Schmid—Johannesevangelium und Religionsgeschichte 1933.
P. W. Schmiedel—Das vierte Evangelium gegenüber den drei ersten 1906.
J. Schneider—Die Christusschau des Johannesevangeliums 1935.
E. von Schrenck—Die joh. Anschauung vom Leben 1898.
E. Schwartz—'Aporien im vierten Evangelium', Nachr. der Gött. Ges. der Wiss. 1907, 342–72; 1908, 115–88, 487–560.
E. Schweizer—ΕΓΟ ΕΙΜΙ . . . Die religionsgeschichtliche Herkunft und theologische Bedeutung der joh. Bildreden 1939.
T. Sigge—Das Johannesevangelium und die Synoptiker 1935.
H. C. Snape—'The Fourth Gospel, Ephesus and Alexandria', HThR 47 (1954), 1–14.
W. Soltau—Das vierte Evangelium in seiner Entstehungsgeschichte, SB Heidelberg 1916.
F. Spitta—Das Johannesevangelium als Quelle der Geschichte Jesu 1910.
E. Stange—Die Eigenart der joh. Produktion 1915.
G. Stettinger—Textfolge der joh. Abschiedsreden 1918.
R. H. Strachan—The Fourth Gospel, Its Significance and Environment[3] (undated; 2nd ed. 1943).
W. Temple—Readings in St. John's Gospel 1945.
C. H. Torrey—'The Aramaic Origin of the Gospel of John', HThR 16 (1923), 305–44.
J. T. Ubbink—Het Evangelie van Johannes 1935.
B. Weiss—Das Johannesevangelium als einheitliches Werk 1912.
J. Wellhausen—Das Evangelium Johannis 1908.
H. H. Wendt—Das Johannesevangelium 1900. (Wendt I).—Die Schichten im vierten Evangelium 1911. (Wendt II).
G. P. Wetter—Die Verherrlichung im Johannesevangelium (Beitr. zur Religionswissenschaft II 1) 1915.—'Der Sohn Gottes'. Eine Untersuchung über Charakter und Tendenz des Johannes-Evangeliums 1916.
W. G. Wilson—'The Original Text of the Fourth Gospel', JThSt 1949, 59f.

H. Windisch—Johannes und die Synoptiker 1926.—'Die Absolutheit des Johannesevangeliums', ZsystTh 5 (1928), 3–54.—'Jesus und der Geist im Johannesevangelium', Amicitiae Corolla (Festschr. für Rendel Harris) 1933, 303–18.
P. Winter—'Μουογενὴς παρὰ πατρός', Zeitschr. f. Religions- u. Geistesgesch. 5 (1933), 335–65.
W. Wrede—Charakter und Tendenz des Johannesevangeliums, 2. Aufl. 1933.
C. J. Wright—The Mission and Message of Jesus 1938.
F. W. Young—'A Study of the Relation of Isaiah to the Fourth Gospel', ZNW 46 (1955), 215–33.
O. Zurhellen—Die Heimat des vierten Evangeliums 1909.
J. De Zwaan—'John wrote in Aramaic', JBL 57 (1938), 155–71.

3. BOOKS FREQUENTLY CITED*

W. Bauer—Griechisch-Deutsches Wörterbuch zum NT, 4 Aufl. 1952. E. T. A Greek English Lexicon of the NT 1957.
M. Black—An Aramaic Approach to the Gospels and Acts, 2 ed. 1954.
F. Blass—Grammatik des neutestamentlichen Griechisch, bearb. A. Debrunner, 6 Aufl. 1931. (Always referred to by paragraph numbers.) ET A Greek Grammar of the New Testament 1961.
G. Bornkamm—Mythos und Legende in den apokryphen Thomas-Akten 1933.
W. Bousset—Die Religion des Judentums im späthellenistischen Zeitalter (Handb. zum NT 21), 3 Aufl., hrsg. H. Gressmann 1926. (Bousset, Rel. des Judent.)—Hauptprobleme der Gnosis 1907. (Bousset, Hauptpr.)—Kyrios Christos, 2 Aufl. 1921. (Bousset, Kyrios).
E. Bréhier—Les Idées philosophiques et religieuses de Philon d'Alexandrie 1907.
R. Bultmann—Die Geschichte der synoptischen Tradition, 2 Aufl. 1931. E.T. History of the Synoptic Tradition 1965.—Glauben und Verstehen I, 2 Aufl. 1954. (Gl. u. Verst.).
O. Cullmann—Urchristentum u. Gottesdienst, 2 Aufl. 1950.
G. Dalman—Worte Jesu I, 2 Aufl. 1930. E.T. Words of Jesus (Dalman, W. J.)—Orte und Wege Jesu, 3 Aufl. 1924. (Dalman, O. u. W.).
G. A. Deissmann—Licht vom Osten, 3 Aufl. 1923. E.T. Light from the East 1965.
M. Dibelius—Die Formgeschichte des Evangeliums, 2 Aufl. 1933.
ΕΥΧΑΡΙΣΤΗΡΙΟΝ, Studien zur Religion und Literatur des ATs und NTs Herm. Gunkel . . . dargebracht, 2 Teil 1923.
Festgabe fur Adolf Jülicher 1927.
F. V. Filson—Origins of the Gospels 1938.
M. Goguel—Jean-Baptiste 1928.

* Abbreviations are given in parentheses where more than one work by the same author is cited.

F. C. Grant—The Growth of the Gospels 1933.

Handbuch zum NT hrsg. H. Lietzmann.

H. Jonas—Gnosis und spätantiker Geist I 1934.

J. Kroll—Die Lehren des Hermes Trismegistos 1914.

E. Lohmeyer—Das Urchristentum I 1932.

E. Meyer—Ursprung und Anfänge des Christentums, 3 vols. 1921.

G. F. Moore—Judaism in the First Centuries of the Christian Era, 3 vols. 1927, 1930.

J. H. Moulton—Einleitung in die Sprache des NTs 1911. E.T. A Grammar of NT Greek 1908, 1929.

——— and G. Milligan—The Vocabulary of the Greek Testament 1922.

J. Pascher—Η ΒΑΣΙΛΙΚΗ ΟΔΟΣ. Der Königsweg zu Wiedergeburt und Vergöttung bei Philon von Alexandreia 1931.

L. Radermacher—Neutestamentliche Grammatik (Handb. zum NT 1), 2 Aufl. 1925.

R. Reitzenstein—Die hellenistischen Mysterienreligionen, 3 Aufl. 1927. (Reitzenst., H.M.R.)—Das iranische Erlösungsmysterium 1921. Reitzenst., I.E.M.)—Die Vorgeschichte der christlichen Taufe 1929. (Reitzenst., Taufe).

——— and H. H. Schaeder—Studien zum antiken Synkretismus aus Iran und Griechenland 1926.

H. Schlier—Religionsgeschichtliche Untersuchungen zu den Ignatiusbriefen 1929. (Schlier, Relig. Unters.)—Christus und die Kirche im Epheserbrief 1930.

W. Staerk—Die Erlösererwartung in den östlichen Religionen (Soter II) 1938.

H. L. Strack & P. Billerbeck—Kommentar zum NT aus Talmud und Midrasch, 4 vols. 1922, 1924, 1926, 1928.

Theologisches Wörterbuch zum NT, hrsg. G. Kittel, 1933–. ET Theological Dictionary of the NT 1964–.

J. Thomas—Le Mouvement baptiste en Palestine et Syrie 1935.

P. Volz—Die Eschatologie der jüdischen Gemeinde im neutestamentlichen Zeitalter 1934.

I. Index of Greek Words

II. Literary and Historico-critical Questions

* The difference between Rabbinisms and Semitisms is of course often slight.

III. Theological Motifs

* See also Index I: ἀναβαίνειν, ἀφιέναι, γινώσκειν, δόξα, εἰδέναι, ἔρχεσθαι, καταβαίνειν, μαρτυρεῖν, μεταβαίνειν, μονογενής, νικᾶν, ὁδός, υἱός etc.

IV. Religio-historical Relations

Postscript to this Edition

by Hartwig Thyen

Since the publication of this commentary two new and important textual witnesses for the Fourth Gospel have been discovered and published. These are the papyri Bodmer II (P^{66}) and Bodmer XV (P^{75}) which are of fundamental significance for the whole textual history of the NT.

P^{66} contains the almost complete text of Jn 1–14.26. Only the two sheets which contained Jn 6.11a–35a are missing. As well as this, fragments of a further 46 sheets of the codex (parts of chapters 15, 16, 19, and 20.25–21.9) have been preserved. The excellent literary hand indicates a date around 200 for the text, indeed the papyrologist H. HUNGER ('Zur Datierung des Papyrus Bodmer II (P^{66})'), Anzeiger der österreichischen Akademie der Wissenschaften, phil.-hist. Klasse. No. 4, 1960, 12–333) dates the codex in the middle, or even the first half (!) of the second century.

In 1956 V. MARTIN published the text of Jn 1.1–14.26 as Papyrus Bodmer II in the Bibliotheca Bodmeriana. In 1958 there followed a supplement with the remaining fragmentary material. But it was only with the augmented and revised edition of this supplement (ed. J. W. B. BARNS 1962) that it was possible to check Martin's edition against the photographic reproductions of the whole codex. M.-É. BOISMARD reviewed the edition and prepared an extensive list of corrections on the basis of his comparison with the reproductions (RevBibl 70, 1963, 120–133; cp. also J. W. B. Barns, 'Papyrus Bodmer II. Some Corrections and Remarks', Muséon LXXV, 1962, 327–329).

The codex contains a considerable number of corrections in the hand of its writer. For our purposes we can pass over the corrected scribal errors, word misplacements, and variations in spelling. What is important however is the fact that on more than twenty occasions a 'Western' reading is deleted and replaced with an 'Egyptian' one. However on occasions it is also possible to observe the opposite process (cp. H. ZIMMERMANN, 'Papyrus Bodmer II und seine Bedeutung für die Textgeschichte des Johannesevangeliums', BZ, NF 2, 1958, 214–243). It is also interesting to note that a fragment of P^{66} was found in the Chester Beatty Library (cp. the photographic reproduction in the second edition of the supplement 135f.). It is therefore not inconceivable that the Chester Beatty and the Bodmer papyri should have come, not only from the same contemporary dealer, but also from the same ancient library (cp. K. ALAND, 'Neue ntl. Papyri II', NTS 10, 1963/4, 73f.).

P^{75} contains the text of Luke's Gospel and also of Jn 1.1–15.8 (102 of the original 144 pages are preserved in a fragmentary or complete form). The editors date the codex between 175 and 225 (V. MARTIN and R. KASSER, Papyrus Bodmer XIV–XV, Bibliotheca Bodmeriana 1961). P^{75} now provides a text which is very close to that of Vaticanus (B) but about 150 years older (cp. C. L. PORTER, 'Papyrus Bodmer XV (P^{75}) and the Text of Codex Vaticanus, JBL 81', 1962, 363–376, and also the complete collation of the texts for the Fourth Gospel by K. ALAND, NTS, 1964/5, 14–21).

There are occasions when P^{75} is the only Greek witness to agree with the Sahidic translation. Thus in Jn 10.7 it reads, as does the latter, instead of ἐγώ εἰμι ἡ θύρα τῶν προβάτων 'I am the shepherd (ὁ ποιμήν) of the sheep' (in Lk 16.19 P^{75} adds, like the Sahidic translation, the name of the rich man: ὀνόματι Νευής; this is possibly a scribal error for Νινευης).

All variations of substance in these two important papyri have since been incorporated by Kurt ALAND in the 25th edition of the Novum Testamentum Graecae (ed. NESTLE-ALAND, Stuttgart/New York 1963), so that the material is easily accessible to any reader of this commentary.

P^{66} establishes the editorial 'postscript' firmly as part of the text at this early date. Equally all the other glosses and interpolations of the 'ecclesiastical editor' are firmly established by these two papyri for this date. Apart from the passages which—as one might have expected—are missing (that is, the legendary gloss in 5.4 and the pericope of the woman caught in adultery 7.53–8.11; cp. the detailed discussion of this by U. BECKER, 'Jesus und die Ehebrecherin. Untersuchungen zur Text- und Überlieferungsgeschichte von Joh. 7.53–8.11', BZNW 28, 1963), the new witnesses present us with the 'canonical' Fourth Gospel. No text-critical evidence has been forthcoming for an editing of the text after its original composition. Thus it seems more than probable that the form in which we know the Gospel was the form in which it was always known *publicly* in the Church.

I now add a list of the most important literature on the two papyri—except where they have already been mentioned above—as well as a list of the most notable variants.

1. *Literature*

K. ALAND, ThLZ 82,1957,161–184; J. N. BIRDSALL, The Bodmer Papyrus of John, 1960; K. W. CLARK, 'The Text of the Gospel of John in Third Century Egypt', NovTest 5, 1962, 17–24; E. MASSAUX, 'Le PBodmer II (P^{66}) et la critique néotestamentaire', SacPag 1, 1959, 194–207; B. M. METZGER, JBL 78,1959, 13–20; also 'The Bodmer Papyrus of Luke and John', ExpTim 73,1962, 201–203; R. SCHNACKENBURG, 'Das Johannesevangelium. 1.Teil. Einleitung und Kommentar zu Kap. 1–4', Herders theol. Komm. z.NT IV/1, 1965,154–171. *Bibliography*: E. MALATESTA, 'St. John's Gospel 1920–1965', Analecta Biblica 32, Rome 1967, 18–21.

2. *Variants*

1.3: P^{66} οὐδέν; P^{75} οὐδε ἕν.

According to P^{75} the new section clearly begins with οὐδὲ ἕν; cp. on this point K. Aland 'Eine Untersuchung zu Joh 1,3.4', ZNW 59, 1968, 174–209.

1.13: P^{66} ἐγεννήθησαν; P^{75} ἐγενήθησαν. Both papyri then confirm the plural reading; cp. E. Haenchen, 'Probleme des johanneischen "Prologs"', ZThK 60, 1953,305–334, esp. 330f.

1.18: $P^{66.(75)}$ give weight to the reading μονογενής θεός.

1.19: $P^{66.75}$ om. πρὸς αὐτόν.

1.41: The reading πρῶτον is now given added weight to by $P^{66.75}$.

3.15: P^{66} ἐπ'αὐτῷ; P^{75} ἐν αὐτῷ.

3.31c: P^{75} om. ἐπάνω πάντων ἐστίν.

4.35: P^{75} om. ἔτι.

4.37: The whole verse is missing in P^{75}. But this is most probably only an error in copying due to the homoioteleuton ὁ θερίζων.

4.54: $P^{66.75}$ read like BC*G δέ after τοῦτο.

5.1: $P^{66.75}$ have no article before ἑορτή.

5.2: $P^{66.75}$ support the reading Βηθσαϊδα (or Βηδσαϊδα P^{66}), which is nevertheless probably secondary (see comm. above). P^{66} puts a point before and after the word 'pool' (·κολυμβήθρα·). This supports Bultmann's interpretation.

6.23: P^{75} confirms the reading εὐχαριστήσαντος τοῦ κυρίου (om.D).

6.36: με which Bultmann omits following A it syr^{sc}, is witnessed to by $P^{66.75.vid.}$

7.8: $P^{66.75}$ also read οὔπω instead of οὐκ. Yet one must still accept Bultmann's judgement that this is a case of toning down the categorical οὐκ (see comm. 288 n.3.).

7.37: P^{75} supports Vaticanus (B) by adding a πρὸς ἐμέ to ἐρχέσθω The writer of P^{66c} has subsequently corrected the πρός με into his text.

7.38: Bultmann's connection of ὁ πιστεύων εἰς ἐμέ with καὶ πινέτω which is the only way of giving sense to the passage, seems to be confirmed by the corrector (P^{66c}) of P^{66}.

7.52: P^{66}($P^{75\ vid.}$) confirms by placing an article in front of 'prophet' (ὁ προφήτης) the suspicion, which has often been entertained, that the 'prophet' refers to a specific eschatological figure (cp. 1.21,25; 6.14; 7.40 and see R. Schnackenburg, 'Die Erwartung des "Propheten" nach dem NT und den Qumran-Texten', in: Studia Evangelica, TU 73, 1959,622–639).

8.57: Whereas P^{66} supports the reading ἑώρακας, P^{75} reads ἑωρακέν σε which is however, with Bultmann, 'certainly a correction to conform with v.56'.

9.4: $P^{66.75}$ on both occasions have the plural: ἡμᾶς δεῖ κτλ. and τοῦ πέμψαντος ἡμᾶς.

9.27: P^{66} om. οὐκ.

9.38f.: P^{75} (et ℵ* Wb) om. ὁ δὲ . . . ὁ 'Ιησοῦς.

10.7: P^{75} reads ὁ ποιμήν instead of ἡ θύρα (see above p. 742).

10.8: P^{75} om. πρὸ ἐμοῦ.

10.29: $P^{66.75}$ confirms the reading which Bultmann takes to be the only meaningful one: ὃς . . . μείζων.

12.32: P^{66} reads like ℵ* (D) latt: πάντα.

12.41: The ὅτι is now given added weight by $P^{66.75}$.

12.47: P^{66c} gives added weight to the omission (though for dogmatic reasons?!) of μή before φυλάξῃ.

13.5: P^{66} reads the hapaxlegomenon in the NT ποδονιπτῆρα instead of νιπτῆρα.

13.10: P^{66} also has the addition εἰ μὴ τοὺς πόδας and indeed stresses it by the further addition of μόνον; cp. however M.-É. Boismard, 'Le lavement des pieds', RevBibl 71, 1964,5–24, and G. Richter; 'Die Fusswaschung im Johannesevangelium', Bibl. Unters, 1967, 37f. and 320.

13.32: P^{66} om. εἰ ὁ θεὸς ἐδοξάσθη ἐν αὐτῷ. This is probably a case of a copyist's error occasioned by the homoioteleuton.

14.2: The ὅτι is also omitted in P^{66}.

14.7: P^{66} confirms in both cases the text of ℵ D pc which Bultmann favours, viz. ἐι ἐγνώκατέ με, καὶ τὸν πατέρα μου γνώσεσθε.

18.15: P^{66} also has no article before ἄλλος μαθητής. The secondary article clearly is intended to identify 'the other disciple' with 'the beloved disciple'; see Bultmann, comm. 645 n.4, cp. Taber A. Kragerud, Der Lieblingsjünger im Johannes-Evangelium. Ein exegetischer Versuch, Oslo 1959,12 and 25f. Kragerud concludes from the superfluous and elaborate introduction of the 'other disciple' that it is a deliberate introduction of the 'beloved disciple'.